ROAD TRIP
USA

Cross-Country Adventures on
America's Two-Lane Highways

ROAD TRIP USA

Cross-Country Adventures on America's Two-Lane Highways

JAMIE JENSEN

CONTRIBUTING WRITERS:
Deke Castleman
Andrew Coe
Joe Cummings
Joyce Gregory
Tom Huhti
Marjorie Jensen
Dave Johnson
Doug Pappas
Jeffrey Perk
Kevin Roe
Kap Stann
Stuart Warren

MOON
PUBLICATIONS INC.

ROAD TRIP USA
CROSS-COUNTRY ADVENTURES
ON AMERICA'S TWO-LANE HIGHWAYS

Published by
Moon Publications, Inc.
P.O. Box 3040
Chico, California 95927-3040, USA

Printed by
Colorcraft, Ltd.

Please send all comments,
corrections, additions,
amendments, and critiques to:

ROAD TRIP USA
C/o MOON PUBLICATIONS, INC.
P.O. BOX 3040
CHICO, CA 95927-3040, USA
e-mail: travel@moon.com

1st edition—August 1996

Stephen Dunn's poem "The Sacred," from the volume *Between Angels* and the anthology *Drive, They Said,* is reprinted with kind permission of W. W. Norton & Co., Inc.

ISBN: 1-56691-036-6
ISSN: 1085-7036

Editor: Taran March
Associate Editors: Pauli Galin, Michael Greer, Kevin Jeys, Patricia Reilly,
        Lisa Stowell
Copy Editors: Elizabeth Kim, Nicole Revere, Asha Johnson
Production & Design: Dave Hurst, Rob Warner
Cartographers: Brian Bardwell, Chris Folks, Jason Sadler
Index: Deana Corbitt Shields

Cover Photo: US 66 Near Seligman, Arizona
        by Andreas Feininger, Life Magazine © Time Inc.

Distributed in the United States and Canada by Publishers Group West
Printed in Hong Kong

When you come to a fork in the road, take it.
—Yogi Berra

CONTENTS

page numbers in italics indicate route or destination maps

DID WE MISS SOMETHING?

Let us hear from you. We welcome comments from female travelers, handicapped travelers, traveling families, RVers, hikers, campers, and net surfers, also hotel and restaurant proprietors along the routes covered in this book. Check out our Web site at http://www.moon.com. Please address your comments to:

> Road Trip USA
> P.O. Box 3040
> Chico, CA 95927-3040, USA
> e-mail: jj@moon.com

ABBREVIATIONS

ATV—all-terrain vehicle
elev.—elevation
km—kilometer
kph—kilometers per hour
mph—miles per hour
Rte—Route
RV—recreational vehicle
U.P.—Upper Peninsula (Michigan)

ON THE ROAD

The journeys in this book are as wild and varied as the landscapes they traverse. All celebrate the notion that freedom and discovery await us on the open road. Poets and artists from Walt Whitman to Muddy Waters have long sung the praises of rolling down the highway, and no matter how times have changed we still believe there's nothing more essentially American than hitting the road and seeing the country.

America has always been a nation on the move. From colonial times onwards, each generation pushed relentlessly westward until the U.S. frontier finally closed around the beginning of the twentieth century. Taking advantage of the new internal combustion engine, and inspired by the slogan "See America First," Americans started exploring another frontier, the system of highways that developed between the Atlantic and Pacific coasts. The first transcontinental route, the Lincoln Highway from New York to San Francisco, was opened in 1915, and motor courts, diners, and other new businesses soon sprang up along the roadside to serve the passing trade.

The half-century from the 1920s until the arrival of the interstate highway system was the golden age of American motor travel, but this book is not especially motivated by nostalgia or longing for a lost "good old days." Almost all the things described in *Road Trip USA*—soda fountains and town squares, burl barns and minor-league baseball teams—are happily thriving in the modern world, and better yet, they are close at hand. The simple act of avoiding the soulless interstates, with their soggy franchises and identikit chains, opens up a parallel, and much friendlier, two-lane world. You'll chance upon monuments marking the actual sites of things you last thought about in high school history classes, or kitschy little souvenir stands flaunting giant dinosaurs outside their doors, and inside still selling the same postcards as they have since the Eisenhower years.

Throughout this book the contributing writers and I have tried to highlight the unique character of places along the routes, whether a town has raised a famous son or daughter or simply has a great diner serving up world-class French fries. I've treated travel as an end in itself, not just a means to get you to a certain somewhere. After traveling nearly 100,000 miles in search of the perfect stretch of two-lane blacktop, this is the book I wish I'd had with me all along. So get in your car, turn on the radio, roll down the windows—and drive.

—Jamie Jensen
Davis, CA

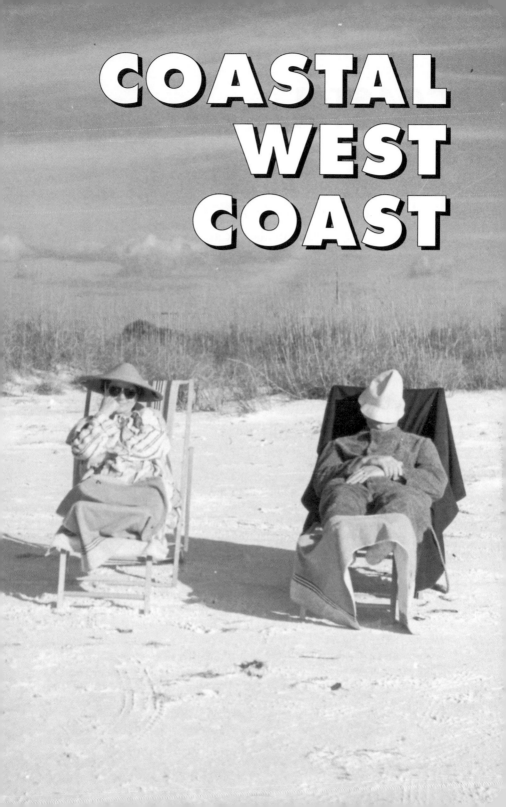

COASTAL WEST COAST

COASTAL WEST COAST

For some reason, when people elsewhere in the country refer to the West Coast, particularly California, they seem to think it's a land of kooks and crazies, an overbuilt suburban desert supporting only shopping malls, freeways, and body-obsessed airheads. All of which may be true in small pockets, but the amazing thing about the West Coast—from the dense green forests of western Washington, to the gorgeous beaches of Southern California—is that it is still mostly wild, open, and astoundingly beautiful country, where you can drive for miles and miles and have the scenery all to yourself.

Starting at the northwest tip of the United States at Olympic National Park, and remaining within sight of the Pacific Ocean almost all the way south to the Mexican border, this 1,500-mile, mostly two-lane route takes in everything from temperate rainforest to near-desert. Most of it is in the public domain, freely if not always easily accessible, and protected from development within national, state, and local parks, which provide habitat for such rare creatures as mountain lions, condors, and gray whales.

Heading south, after the rough-and-tumble logging and fishing communities of Washington state, you cross the mouth of the Columbia River and follow the comparatively peaceful and quiet Oregon coastline, where recreation has by and large replaced industry, and where dozens of quaint and not-so-quaint communities line the ever-changing shoreline. At the midway point you pass through the great redwood forests of Northern California, where the tallest and most majestic living things on earth line the "Avenue of the Giants," home also to some of the best (meaning gloriously kitsch) remnants of the golden age of car-borne tourism: drive-through trees, drive-on trees, houses carved out of trees, and much more. The phenomenally beautiful coastline of Northern California is rivaled only by the incredible coast of Big Sur farther south, beyond which stretch the beachfronts of

Southern California. The land of palm trees, beach boys, and surfer girls of popular lore really does exist, though only in the southernmost quarter of the state.

Along with the overwhelming scale of its natural beauty, the West Coast is remarkable for the abundance of well-preserved historic sites—most of which haven't been torn down, built on, or even built around—that stand as vivid evocations of life on what was once the most distant frontier of the New World. While rarely as old as places on the East Coast, or as impressive as those in Europe, West Coast sites are quite diverse and include the Spanish colonial missions of California, Russian and English fur-trading outposts, and the place where Lewis and Clark first sighted the Pacific after their long slog across the continent.

Last but certainly not least are the energizing cities—Seattle in the north, San Francisco in the middle, and Los Angeles and San Diego to the south—which serve as gateways to (or refuges from) the landscapes in between them. Add to these the dozens of small and not-so-small towns along the coast, with alternating blue-collar ports and upscale vacation retreats, and you have a great range of food, drink, and accommodation options. Local cafes, seafood grills, and bijou restaurants abound, as do places to stay—from youth hostels in old lighthouses to roadside motels (including the world's first, which still stands in lovely San Luis Obispo, California) to homespun B&B inns in old farmhouses.

ALONG THE WASHINGTON COAST

The coast of Washington is a virtual microcosm of the Pacific Northwest, containing everything from extensive wilderness areas to Native American fishing villages and heavily industrialized lumber towns. Starting at splendid **Port Townsend**, US-101 loops west around the rugged Olympic Peninsula, passing near the northwesternmost point of the continental United States while allowing access to the unforgettable natural attractions—sandy, driftwood-strewn beaches, primeval old-growth forests, and pristine mountain lakes and glaciated alpine peaks, to name just a few—of **Olympic National Park**. The roadside landscape varies from dense woods to clearcut tracts of recently harvested timber, with innumerable rivers and streams perhaps the most obvious signs of the immense amount of rainfall (up to 12 feet) the region receives every year. Scattered towns, from **Port Angeles** in the north to the twin cities of **Grays Harbor** on the coast, are staunchly blue-collar communities almost wholly dependent upon natural resources—not only trees, but also salmon, oysters, and other seafood. Though the tourism trade has been increasing steadily, visitor services are still few and far between, so plan ahead.

Though it's not on the coast, the Puget Sound port city of Seattle makes a good starting or finishing point to this coastal road trip. For details, see the Survival Guide to Seattle on pages 722-723.

Port Townsend
Few places in the world can match the concentration of natural beauty or the wealth of architecture found in tiny Port Townsend (pop. 7,001). One of the oldest

Fort Worden, on the north side of Port Townsend, is a retired military base that served as a location for the Richard Gere movie *An Officer and a Gentleman.* It now hosts an excellent series of annual music and arts festivals; contact the Centrum Foundation (360/385-3102) for schedules and more information.

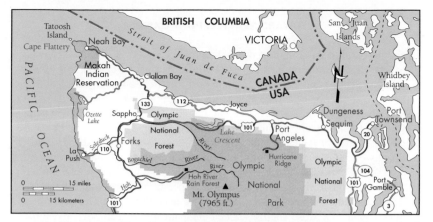

towns in Washington, Port Townsend was laid out in 1852 and reached a peak of activity in the 1880s. But after the railroads focused on Seattle and Puget Sound as their western terminus, the town sat quietly for most of the next century until the 1960s, when an influx of arts-oriented refugees took over the waterfront warehouses and clifftop mansions, converting them to galleries, restaurants, and comfy B&Bs while preserving the town's turn-of-the-century character.

Port Townsend is neatly divided into two halves: multistory brick warehouses and commercial buildings line Water Street and the wharves along the bay, while lovely old Victorian houses cover the bluffs above. It's basically a great place to wander, but there are a couple of sights worth seeing, particularly the landmark **City Hall** along the east end of Water Street at 210 Madison Street. Half of this eclectic gothic pile now houses a local historical **museum** (Mon.-Sat. 11 AM-4 PM, Sunday 1-4 PM; donations accepted), with three floors of odds and ends tracing Port Townsend history, including the old city jail where Jack London spent a night on his way to the Klondike goldfields in 1897. The City Hall is also a starting point for Joyce Webb's expertly guided **walking tours** (usually daily 10 AM and 2 PM; $5; 360/385-1967) of the waterfront district.

Not surprisingly, considering the extensive tourist trade, Port Townsend has a number of good restaurants. You'll find many of the best places at the east end of town near the corner of Water and Quincy Streets: for breakfast or lunch, try the **Salal Cafe** or **Bread and Roses**; for dinner, one of the best seafood places is the **Silverwater Cafe**, near the Quincy Street dock. The same historic building holds the amiable **Town Tavern** bar, and upstairs the **Waterstreet Hotel**, 635 Water Street (360/385-5467 or 800/735-9810), has rooms from $50 a night. The most comfortable accommodations in Port Townsend are the many Victorian B&Bs dotting the bluffs above the port area, including the ever-popular **Old Consulate Inn**, 313 Walk-

The natural cut of the Hood Canal on the east side of the Olympic Peninsula is one of the West Coast's prime oyster-growing estuaries, source of the gourmet Quilcenes, Hama Hamas, and other varieties available at roadside stands, shops, and restaurants throughout the region.

A brand-new Indian-owned **casino** looms above US-101 at the foot of once-placid Sequim Bay.

The Waterstreet Hotel

TOWARD SEATTLE: PORT GAMBLE

You have a number of options if traveling to or from Port Townsend. You can follow US-101 around the western Olympic Peninsula, or take a ferry via **Whidbey Island** and explore it and the even prettier **San Juan Islands** to the north. Last but not least, you can take a middle route across the Kitsap Peninsula, then ferry to Seattle; this last route has the great advantage of taking you through the lovely old logging town of **Port Gamble**, a slice of New England on the shores of Puget Sound. The entire town is a historic district, with dozens of immaculate Victorian buildings standing along maple tree-lined streets; it's also owned lock, stock, and barrel by Pope & Talbot Lumber, which built the town in the 1850s and still operates the large mill. After wandering past the saltbox houses, have a look inside the large **General Store**, which includes a barber shop, a seashell museum, and a small cafe; or visit the photo-filled historical **museum** (daily 10 AM-4 PM in summer only; $1) across the street.

---

er Street (360/385-6753), where a room with a view of Mount Olympus, and a hearty multicourse breakfast, will set you back about $100 a night. For less pricey lodging, there's a **campground** and an AYH/HI **hostel** (360/385-0655) in the old Army barracks at Fort Worden, on the coast two miles north of town.

Sequim and Dungeness

A half-hour southwest of Port Townsend via Hwy-20 and US-101, Sequim (pop. 3,616, pronounced "Skwim") sits in the rain shadow of the Olympic Mountains, and so tends to be much drier and sunnier than spots even a few miles west. Though it retains its rural feel, Sequim's historic farming-and-fishing economy is quickly switching over to tourism, with tracts of painfully ugly vacation and retirement homes filling up the rolling, waterfront landscape. It's ideal cycling country, for the moment at least.

Coming in from the east on US-101, the first thing you pass is the large, modern **John Wayne Marina**, built on land donated by the Duke himself, who spent a lot of time in Sequim cruising around on his converted U.S. Navy minesweeper, the *Wild Goose*. The US-101 frontage through town is lined by the usual franchised fast-food outlets, also unique **El Cazador**, a standard Mexican restaurant housed inside a minimally converted grain elevator. The restaurant fills the storage shed but does nothing with the tower—the rooms would be too small, despite the very high ceilings.

Just north of US-101 at 175 W. Cedar Street, the **Sequim-Dungeness Museum** (Wed.-Sun. noon-4 PM; donation) houses everything from 12,000-year-old mastodon bones discovered on a nearby farm, to exhibits of Native American cultures and pioneer farm implements.

The well-signed **Olympic Game Farm,** five miles northwest of Sequim, is a retirement home for former animal actors (like the bear that played TV's "Gentle Ben"). The farm is open for driving and walking tours (daily 9 AM-4 PM in summer; $5).

From the museum, a well-marked road winds north for 10 miles before reaching the waterfront again at Dungeness, where a seven-mile-long sand spit, the country's longest, protects a shellfish-rich wildlife refuge. All that remains of the abandoned fishing community that existed here through the 1890s is an old schoolhouse, though the excellent **Three Crabs Restaurant,** overlooking Dungeness Harbor, has been serving up plates of fish and local Dungeness crab for over 25 years. Stay at the nearby **Groveland Cottage,** a quaint B&B just a half-mile from the harbor at 4861 Sequim-Dungeness Way (360/683-3565), or at the popular waterfront **Juan de Fuca Cottages,** 182 Marine Drive (360/683-4433; book ahead), two miles to the west.

Port Angeles

A busy, industrial city at the center of the northern Olympic Peninsula, Port Angeles (pop. 17,710) is not a particularly attractive destination in itself, but it does make a handy base for visiting the nearby wilderness of Olympic National Park. Frequent **ferries,** one carrying cars and passengers ($25; 360/457-4491) and a faster one carrying passengers only ($10; 360/452-8088 or 800/633-1589), also shuttle across the water to pretty Victoria, British Columbia, leaving Port Angeles at the middle of the attractively landscaped waterfront, which is bound at both ends by huge lumber mills.

Gas stations and fast-food franchises line US-101 on the east side of Port Angeles, while local life centers on 1st Street, two blocks from the water. Here cafes such as **The Greenery** and **First Street Haven** offer good, inexpensive soup-and-salad style lunches and dinners. Places to stay vary from highway motels including the **Uptown,** 101 E. 2nd Street (360/457-9434), to the plush likes of the **Red Lion** (360/452-9215), on the water at the foot of Lincoln Street. For further information, contact the **North Olympic Peninsula Convention and Visitors' Bureau** (800/942-4042).

Hurricane Ridge

High above Port Angeles, Hurricane Ridge provides the most popular access to Olympic National Park. A paved road, open year-round during daylight hours, twists and turns up a steep seven percent grade to the mile-high summit, where, on a clear day, you can gape at the breathtaking 360-degree views of mountain, valley, and sea. A summer-only lodge at the crest provides food and drink, and a concession offers ski and snowshoe rentals on winter weekends. Trails lead down into the backcountry, where you're likely to spot marmots, deer, and bald eagles—and if you're lucky, maybe an elk or a mountain lion.

Information on road conditions and other aspects of visiting Olympic National Park is broadcast continuously on **530 AM.**

Most of the backcountry is wet, rugged, and devoid of trails; if you plan to camp overnight, be prepared and get a free **permit** from the Olympic Park **ranger station** (360/452-0330) in Port Angeles, two blocks south of US-101 on the road up to Hurricane Ridge.

Lake Crescent

One of the most idyllic spots in the entire Pacific Northwest, the fjordlike Lake Crescent lies right alongside two-lane US-101, just 20 miles west of Port Angeles. The lake is over eight miles long and some 625 feet deep; powerboats are banned, and the placid surface reflects the clouds and surrounding peaks,

Weather on the Olympic Peninsula varies widely from place to place. The peaks and coastal valleys of Olympic National Park receive as much as 200 inches of rainfall each year, while the town of Sequim, a mere 30 miles away, garners an average of just 17 inches annually.

OLYMPIC NATIONAL PARK

Olympic National Park, in the heart of the Olympic Peninsula, is a diversely beautiful corner of the country, combining features of Maine's rocky coast and the snowcapped peaks of the Rocky Mountains with the unique rainforests covering the park's Pacific coastal valleys. The rugged landscape, from rocky shores to impassably dense forests, resisted exploitation and development until the turn of the century, when local conservationists persuaded Teddy Roosevelt to declare most of the peninsula a nature preserve, a movement that eventually resulted in the establishment of Olympic National Park in 1939.

There are no roads and few trails across the peninsula, so you have to choose your points of entry depending upon what you want to see. The most popular part of the park is Hurricane Ridge, which rises high above Port Angeles and offers great views of the silvery peaks and the many glaciers that flank them. On the western slopes, the temperate rainforests of the usually wet and rainy river valleys hold some of the world's largest trees, all draped with the thick fabric of mosses, while the undeveloped coastline, added to the park in 1953, offers miles of sandy beaches and rocky headlands, littered only with driftwood logs and vibrant tidepools.

including 4,534-foot Storm King Mountain. A reconstructed paddle-wheel boat carries passengers on a scenic 75-minute **cruise** (four times daily; $15; 360/452-4520) around the lake; tickets are available from the Lake Crescent Lodge, where you can also rent **rowboats** ($5 an hour) and tour under your own steam. Also from the lodge, a popular mile-long hike follows a well-maintained nature trail up to the delicate cascade of 90-foot **Marymere Falls**, while along the north shore an abandoned railroad grade is open to hikers and mountain bikers.

Incomparably situated along US-101 on the southeast shore, **Lake Crescent Lodge** (360/928-3211) was originally built just in time for FDR's visit in 1937 and has been hosting visitors ever since. Fairly rustic rooms are available in the old lodge, which also has a cozy dining room; more modern accommodations are available in the adjacent cabins and motel, though the whole place is booked solid on summer weekends, so reserve as soon as you can. Room rates range $50-100 a night. Another nice place to stay is the **Log Cabin Resort** (360/928-3245), three miles north of US-101 on the northeast shore, with motel rooms for $40-100 and waterfront A-frame cabins.

> North of Lake Crescent, in the crossroads town of Joyce, the **Family Restaurant** serves the Northwest's biggest hamburgers: eight-inch diameter "Logger Burgers," piled high with cheese and onions atop a freshly baked bun. Great blackberry pie, too.

Cape Flattery and Neah Bay

From the village of **Sappho** on US-101, Hwy-133 leads north on a long and winding 40-mile detour to Cape Flattery, the northwesternmost tip of the continental United States. The route twists along the rocky and wooded shore of the Strait of Juan de Fuca, but reaching the actual cape itself is quite difficult. From the end of Hwy-133, a very rough unpaved road makes an 11-mile loop, from which parking areas give access to overgrown and usually muddy trails that, if you fight your way through the underbrush, bring you to the top of a 65-foot-high cliff overlooking the crashing surf and offshore **Tatoosh Island**.

> In the forested hills above US-101, **Sol Duc Hot Springs Resort** (360/327-3583) has cabins, campsites, a restaurant, and relaxing natural hot springs.

> The **Strait of Juan de Fuca**, the narrow inlet that links the open Pacific with Puget Sound and divides the U.S. from Canada, was named for the Greek sailor (real name: Apostolos Valerianus) who first mapped it while working for the Spanish Crown in 1610.

Hwy-133 is paved as far as the town of Neah Bay, a tiny and somewhat bedraggled community that's the center of the Makah Indian Reservation. Salmon fishing, both by Makah and by visitors, is about the only activity here, though the tribe does have the impressive and modern **Makah Museum** (daily 10 AM-5 PM in summer, closed Monday and Tuesday the rest of the year; $4), one of the best anthropological museums in the state. Most of the displays are of artifacts uncovered in 1970, when a mudslide revealed the pristine remains of a 500-year-old coastal village—the Pompeii of the Pacific Northwest. Other galleries display finely crafted baskets, a full-scale longhouse complete with recorded chants, and a whaling canoe from which fearless Makah harpooners would jump into the surf and sew up the jaws of dying whales, to keep them from drowning and sinking.

The fish-headed, human-legged statue overlooking the salmon port of Clallam Bay is known as The Fishman, for obvious reasons.

Forks

Bending southwest along the banks of the Soleduck River, US-101 passes through miles of green forests under usually rainy gray skies to reach Forks (pop. 2,862), the commercial center of the northern Olympic Peninsula. Named for its location astride the peninsula's three main rivers, Forks is a die-hard lumber town grappling with the inevitable change to more ecologically sustainable alternatives, mainly tourism. Visitors come to fish for steelhead during the late-summer runs, to beach-comb along the rugged coast, or to visit the remarkable rainforests of Olympic National Park to the southeast. The main attraction in Forks proper is the quirky **Timber Museum** (Tues.-Sat. 10 AM-5 PM; donations), on US-101 on the south edge of town, packed with handsaws, chainsaws, and other logging gear as well as antique cooking stoves and displays telling the town's characterful history. There's also a forest fire lookout tower perched outside the upper floor gallery.

With four gas stations, four motels, and a single stoplight, Forks is not a metropolis by any stretch of the imagination, but it does offer the best range of services between Port Angeles and Aberdeen. Eat at the **Rain Drop Cafe** or the **Pay 'n' Save Coffee Shop**, a block from each other on US-101 (next to the local library). Stay at the **Forks Motel** (360/374-6243) or the **Pacific Inn** (360/374-9400), which both charge about $45 a night; five blocks west of the stoplight, the **Miller Tree Inn** (360/374-6806) is Forks's only B&B. South of Forks along US-101, **Bogachiel State Park** has $8-a-night campsites (with showers) along the Bogachiel River.

For more complete information, contact the Forks **visitor center** (800/44-FORKS).

The temperate rainforests of the Olympic Peninsula receive an average of 140 inches (nearly 12 feet) of annual rainfall, most of it in winter, though regular downpours drench the region year-round.

If you're very lucky, you might spy one of the rare Roosevelt elk, for whose protection Olympic National Park was established; if you're unlucky, you might also come face to face with a mountain lion, which can be dangerous but generally avoids contact with humans.

Hoh River Rain Forest

If you have time to visit only one of the lush rainforest areas of Washington's northwest coast, head for the Hoh River Rain Forest, 12 miles south of Forks then 18 miles east along a well-signed and well-paved road. Not only is this the most easily accessible of these incredibly lush, old-growth areas, the Hoh River forest is also among the least disturbed, with a thick wet blanket of vibrant green ferns, mosses, and lichens covering every inch of the earth at the foot of massive hemlocks, cedars, and towering Sitka spruce. Displays inside the **visitor center** (daily 9 AM-4 PM, till 6:30 PM in summer; 360/374-6925) tell all about the forest's flora and fauna. There's also a wheelchair-accessible nature trail and a wide range of hiking trails, including the quickest access to the icy summit of 7,965-foot Mount Olympus, 22 miles away in the glacier-packed alpine highlands at the heart of the park.

The closest services to the Hoh River Rain Forest are in Forks, but budget travelers may want to take advantage of the $14-a-night bunks at the amiable **Rain Forest AYH Hostel** (360/374-2270), south along US-101 midway between the forest and the coast at Ruby Beach.

Kalaloch and the Pacific Beaches

Looping around the northern Olympic Peninsula, US-101 finally reaches the coast at Ruby Beach, and from there runs south through the wild coastal section of

Olympic National Park. While almost the entire coast south from Cape Flattery is protected with the national park, this is the only easily accessible stretch. Parking areas along the highway, numbered from "Beach 6" to "Beach 1" north to south, give access to 20 miles of generally deserted beach, backed by rocky bluffs and packed with tidepools and an incredible variety of flotsam and jetsam.

The old-growth forests of Olympic National Park provide prime habitat for the northern spotted owl, an endangered species whose preservation has sparked heated debate throughout the Pacific Northwest.

At the southern end of this short but sweet stretch of coastline, **Kalaloch Lodge** (360/962-2271) is a 1970s-style resort and campground, with a coffee shop and a nice restaurant overlooking a picturesque cove. There's also a gas station, a summer-only **ranger station** across US-101, and an oceanside **campground** just north. South of Kalaloch, US-101 turns inland along the northern border of the massive Quinault Indian Reservation, not reaching the Pacific again until the mouth of the Columbia River.

There are a number of small **Native American communities** on reservation lands along the coast, usually at the mouths of rivers. Most of these are fairly ramshackle collections of prefab houses and mobile homes; only La Push, 15 miles west of Forks on the Quileute reservation, has tourist services or facilities.

Lake Quinault

Spreading in a broad valley at the southwest corner of Olympic National Park, Lake Quinault offers lush rainforest groves within a short walk or drive of most creature comforts. The lake has served for decades as a popular resort destination—cabins, lodges, and stores dating from the 1920s line the southern shore, just outside the park boundary—and the old-growth forests here have survived intact, though the naked tracts of clearcut timber along US-101 north and south of the lake give a good sense of what the area might have looked like had Teddy Roosevelt and friends not stepped in to protect it around the turn of the 20th century.

The best first stop is the **ranger station** (360/956-2400) on the south shore, where you can pick up a map of the guided driving tour around the lake, including the location of the many record-size trees. More up-close and personal is the roughly four-mile-long **Quinault Loop Trail**, which winds on a paved path from the ranger station along crashing Cascade Creek up through an old-growth rainforest of alders and bigleaf maples, whose leaves grow upwards of 12 inches across. Midway along, the trail crosses a raised wooden boardwalk through a fecund cedar swamp, then drops down again along another creek before returning by way of the lakeshore.

The nicest place to stay, right next to the ranger station, is historic **Lake Quinault Lodge** (360/288-2571), with a rustic but spacious lobby opening onto lakefront lawns; room rates hover in the $100-a-night range. Besides offering comfortable and reasonably priced accommodations and very good food, the nearby **Rain Forest Village** (360/288-2535 or 800/562-0948), at the east end of the lake, also holds the alleged **World's Tallest Sitka Spruce**, a 191-foot giant.

From the Quinault Indian Reservation, **Hwy-109** runs along the Pacific Ocean through a series of fishing ports and beach resorts, rejoining US-101 at Hoquiam.

Grays Harbor: Hoquiam and Aberdeen

The Olympic Peninsula is cut off from the southern Washington coast by the spade-shaped bay of Grays Harbor, named for the early American sea captain and explorer, Robert Gray. Long the state's prime lumber port, Grays Harbor still processes huge piles of trees, but is seriously economically depressed and offers few spots worth searching out.

At the western end of Grays Harbor, the small and characterful town of Hoquiam (pop. 8,972) celebrates its lumber-based history with an annual Logger's Playday bash, complete with ax-throwing and tree-climbing competitions, the second weekend in September. The rest of the year, get a feel for the bygone days of the lumber industry at red-shingled **Hoquiam's Castle** (daily 11 AM-5 PM; $4), three blocks off US-101 at 515 Chenault Avenue, a 20-room mansion built in 1897 by a local lumber baron. The best place to eat in Hoquiam is the **Levee Street Restaurant**, right on the Hoquiam River at 709 Levee Street, serving excellent (though fairly expensive) fresh seafood as well as pastas. **River Haven**, at the foot of the bridge extending US-101 over the Hoquiam River, is more family-oriented and cheaper. Hoquiam also features one very nice B&B, the $65-a-night **Lytle House** (360/533-2320), next to Hoquiam's Castle at 509 Chenault Avenue; otherwise there are a half dozen motels.

East of Hoquiam at the head of Grays Harbor, Aberdeen (pop. 16,600), like its Scottish namesake, is even more heavily industrialized and thus even harder hit by the continuing downturn in the Northwest timber industry. Among the more high-profile of the state-sponsored efforts to move from timber to tourism is **Grays Harbor Historical Seaport** (daily 9 AM-5 PM; $3), a half-mile east of US-101 via Hwy-12, where Robert Gray's ship, the reconstructed *Columbia Rediviva*, is now on display.

The **Seventh Street Theater,** 313 7th Street in downtown Hoquiam, was the first movie theater in Washington, built in 1927.

Grunge rock hero and Nirvana lead singer **Kurt Cobain,** who killed himself at age 28, grew up in and around Aberdeen. A scholarship fund has been set up in his memory at Aberdeen High School.

From Aberdeen, **US-12** cuts inland to the east, passing through one of the most heavily logged areas in Washington before joining the I-5 freeway at the state capital of Olympia for the run north to Tacoma and Seattle.

Willapa Bay

One of the country's prime oystering grounds, Willapa Bay is sheltered from the Pacific by the Long Beach peninsula and fed by the Nasalle, Willapa, and North Fall Rivers. There are very few towns or even villages on this stretch of US-101, which winds past tidal marshes, cattle ranches, and extensively clearcut forests—which billboard after billboard proclaim to be "America's first industrial tree farm."

Raymond and South Bend

At the northeast corner of Willapa Bay, on the south bank of the Willapa River, stand two towns that jointly embody the resource-based history and economy of the Pacific Northwest. Raymond (pop. 2,901) has the lumber mills, while South Bend (pop. 1,551) calls itself the "Oyster Capital of the West"—a claim supported by the piles of oyster shells flanking the road outside packing houses like **Bendickson's Seafood**, on the north side of town. South Bend's other claim to fame is its landmark **Pacific County Courthouse**, which looms like a mini-Taj

If the weather's right for a picnic, fresh shellfish can be had at bargain prices—by the bite or by the half-gallon—from the area's many producers and wholesalers; look for their signs all along US-101.

Mahal on a hill just east of US-101. Step inside for a look at the 30-foot stained glass dome above the rotunda, and wander through the lushly landscaped park next door.

Long Beach Peninsula

On the western side of Willapa Bay, the Long Beach peninsula stretches for 30 miles of hard-packed sandy beaches along the roiling Pacific Ocean. Away from the few small towns, beaches and breakers abound along here, and you won't have any problem finding peace and solitude. The center of activity on the

Between Grays Harbor and Raymond, US-101 cuts away from the Pacific, while an alternative route, Hwy-105, loops to the west past miles of cranberry bogs through the salmon-fishing town of **Westport**.

Long Beach peninsula is the town of **Seaview**, two miles west of US-101, with a wanderable collection of crafts galleries and souvenir shops, and one of the coast's best B&Bs, the historic **Shelburne Inn** (360/642-2442), at Pacific Way (a.k.a. Hwy-103, the main road) and 45th Street. Rooms start at $70 a night. The inn also supports a friendly pub and a very good restaurant, **The Shoalwater**, rated by many as the best on the Washington coast.

North from Seaview, Hwy-103 runs the length of the thin, sandy peninsula, passing through historic fishing towns like **Long Beach** (where the "World's Largest Frying Pan" hangs on a rack along Main Street), **Oysterville**, and **Nahcotta**, both small but thriving tourist resorts. **The Ark** in Nahcotta, for example, is another of the state's most highly regarded restaurants.

Cape Disappointment

The high headland marking the place where the Columbia River finally merges into the Pacific Ocean, Cape Disappointment was named by the early explorer Capt. John Meares, who in 1788 incorrectly interpreted the treacherous sandbars offshore to mean that, despite reports to the contrary, there was no major river nor any mythical Northwest Passage here.

Besides the grand view of the raging ocean, the best reason to visit the cape is to tour the small but worthwhile **Lewis and Clark Interpretive Center** (daily 10 AM-5 PM; free), incongruously built atop a WW II-era artillery emplacement a short walk from the end of the road. On November 7, 1805, after five months and more than 4,000 miles, the explorers finally laid eyes on the Pacific from this point; they sat through nine days of continuous rain before fleeing south to Oregon (see pages 130-131 for more on Lewis and Clark). Displays inside the museum give the overall context for their journey of discovery, walking you through the different stages of their two-year roundtrip. The small "Cape D" **lighthouse** stands atop the 60-foot-high cliff, a half-mile walk from the museum.

The entire area around the cape is protected from development within **Fort Canby State Park**, and the nearest services—gas stations and a couple of cafes—are in nearby **Ilwaco**, a small rough-and-tumble fishing port two miles west of US-101.

A small state park, three miles west of the US-101 bridge across the Columbia River, marks the site where **Lewis and Clark** camped in December 1805 before heading south in search of better weather—which they never found.

Fort Columbia

Southeast of Cape Disappointment, toward the Oregon border, US-101 winds along the north bank of the Columbia River. Along with good views of the river's five-mile-wide mouth, the road passes by Fort Columbia, home to the region's one and only **youth hostel** (360/777-8755), which offers bunks in a converted hospital for $14 a night.

Cape Disappointment

ALONG THE OREGON COAST

Rarely losing sight of the Pacific Ocean during its 365-mile jaunt along the Oregon coast, US-101 winds past rockbound coast, ancient forests, and innumerable towns and villages. While the region also has its share of strip towns and places where the timber boom went bust, the beach loops, historic restorations, and more state parks per mile than any place in the country soften its few hard edges. Every 20 or so miles you'll pass through attractive if moderately touristy towns populated by at most a couple thousand people, but as a general rule it's the mileage between these hamlets that explains why most people visit—to take in one of the most dramatic meetings of rock and tide in the world.

Starting in the north along the Columbia River at historic **Astoria**, one of the oldest settlements in the western U.S., the route winds along the ocean past the very different beachfront hamlets of **Seaside** and **Cannon Beach** before edging slightly inland through the rich dairy lands of **Tillamook County**. Midway along, the popular vacation spots of **Lincoln City, Newport,** and **Florence** form the most developed corridor along the coast, but it's still easy to reach wild beauty, especially at the remarkable **Oregon Dunes** stretching to the south. The dunes end abruptly at the heavily industrial port of **Coos Bay**, beyond which the natural beauty returns with a string of state parks and the diverse coastal towns of **Bandon, Port Orford, Gold Beach,** and **Brookings**.

Astoria

The oldest American city west of the Missouri River, Astoria (pop. 10,069) is an upbeat mix of lovingly preserved past and busy contemporary commerce. Perched atop high hills at the southern lip of the Columbia River mouth, picturesque Astoria—a favorite backdrop for Hollywood movies—supports an active commercial fishing fleet and dozens of tugboats guiding tankers and container ships across the treacherous sandbars; as more than a few local bumper stickers proclaim, "We Ain't Quaint." Founded by and named after fur-trade magnate John Jacob Astor in 1811, Astoria protected the tenuous American claim to the Pacific coast until the opening of the Oregon Trail brought substantial settlement. By the turn of the century Astoria was still Oregon's second-largest city, but the downturn in both salmon fishing and logging since the end of WW II has caused an economic decline which, as always, town officials look to tourism to overcome.

By state law, there is no self-service gasoline in Oregon; all stations have attendants who pump the gas for you. There's no sales tax, either.

To find out about local issues and current events on the northern Oregon coast, pick up a copy of the excellent *Daily Astorian* newspaper (50 cents), or tune to commercial-free **KMUN 91.5 FM** for NPR news and diverse programming.

US-101 crosses across the Columbia River on the high-level Astoria Bridge, completed in 1966, which drops you at the west end of the downtown waterfront. To get a sense of the lay of the land, follow the signs along 16th Street up Coxcomb Hill to the **Astoria Column** (daily 8 AM-dusk; free) for a view of the Columbia meeting the ocean, the coastal plain south to Tillamook Head, and the snowcapped **Cascade Range** (including, on a clear day, Mount St. Helens) on the eastern horizon. A mosaic chronicling local history is wrapped like a ribbon around the column, tracing the many significant events in the town's past. A spiral staircase climbs to the top.

Back downtown, **Flavel House,** 441 8th Street (daily 10 AM-5 PM in summer; $4) is a red-roofed Queen Anne-style Victorian showplace restored as an elegantly furnished museum of Astoria's first millionaire, Columbia River pilot George Flavel. A half-mile east, near the foot of 17th Street on the north side of waterfront Marine Drive, the **Columbia River Maritime Museum** (daily 9:30 AM-5 PM; $4) displays a large and very impressive collection that tells the story of the lifeblood of this community: the Columbia River.

Fortify yourself at one of the many good seafood places along the water, ranging from the stylish but inexpensive **Columbian Cafe,** 1114 Marine Drive, to the more bare-bones **Cafe Uniontown** or the publike **Ship Inn,** the latter two under the bridge at Marine Drive and 2nd Street. Gourmets might want to visit adjacent **Josephson's Smokehouse,** 106 Marine Drive (503/325-2190), to sample the delicious array of smoked salmon, all prepared on the premises.

To absorb a full portion of Astoria's addictive ambience, stay the night at the bayview **Crest Motel,** 5366 Leif Erickson Drive (503/325-3141).

Fort Stevens, off US-101 on the way to Fort Clatsop, was "the only continental U.S. fortification bombed during WW II," sustaining a shelling from a Japanese submarine on June 21, 1942.

The tiny town of **Gearhart** was the home of influential chef and cookbook author James Beard, whose legacy lives on in the Pacific Way Bakery and Cafe, 601 Pacific Way (503/738-0245), which offers the coast's best croissants along with four-star lunches and dinners.

Fort Clatsop

In the conifer forests six miles south of Astoria and three miles east of US-101, Fort Clatsop (daily 9 AM-5 PM; $2) is a credible reconstruction of the site where Lewis and Clark camped during winter 1805-06. A range of exhibits in the visitor center, a full-scale replica of the 50- by 50-foot log fort, and summertime "living history" re-enactments help conjure the travails of that time. The expedition spent three miserable months here, mingling occasionally with the native Clatsop and Chinook tribes but mostly growing moldy in the incessant rain and damp while being bitten by fleas, sewing new moccasins, and making salt in preparation for the return journey back across the continent.

Seaside

Nothing else along the Oregon coast prepares you for the carnival ambience of downtown Seaside (pop. 5,359), Oregon's oldest seafront resort. Ben Holladay, who built the place in 1873, included a racetrack, zoo, and plush hotel to lure Portlanders to ride his rail line to the beach. Seaside is now the only beachfront amusement park on the West Coast north of Santa Cruz, Cali-

Seaside waterfront

fornia. Come during Spring Break, or any time during July or August, and join the hordes wandering from Broadway's Ferris wheel and video-game arcades to the concrete boardwalk (called "The Prom") along the beach.

Where Broadway meets the beach, a small traffic circle known locally as "The Turnaround" is marked by a placard proclaiming Seaside as "The End of the Lewis and Clark Trail." Eight blocks south of here between Beach Drive and The Prom is a replica of the Lewis and Clark **salt cairn**, where the explorers boiled seawater nonstop for seven weeks to produce enough salt to preserve meat for their return trip east. Farther south, you'll see **Tillamook Head** rising 1,200 feet off the beach; the view from the top was memorialized by William Clark as "the grandest and most pleasing prospect" he had ever beheld.

For food, enjoy Necanicum River views over breakfast at **Cafe Espresso**, 600 Broadway; brave the franchise-style facade of **Pig n' Pancake**, 323 Broadway, for waffles; or sample the clam chowder at **Dooger's**, 505 Broadway. **The Seaside Hostel**, 930 Holladay (503/738-7911), and **Gaston's B&B**, at the corner of 1st Avenue and The Prom (503/738-8320), are the best lodging values in town.

Ecola State Park

A mile south of the junction between US-101 and US-26 from Portland, turn toward the Pacific at the sign for Ecola State Park. The rainforested access road leads you to one of the most photographed views on the coast: looking south from Ecola Park, you can see Haystack Rock and Cannon Beach with Neahkahnie Mountain looming above them. Out to sea, the sight of **Tillamook Rock Lighthouse** to the northwest is also striking. Built in 1881 and in operation until 1957, the lighthouse

The word *ecola* means whale in the Chinookan tongue and was affixed to this region by the Lewis and Clark expedition, who found one of these leviathans washed up on a beach near here. This was the southernmost extent of their expedition on the Oregon coast.

is now used as a columbarium, storing the cremated remains of members of the Neptune Society.

Cannon Beach

Unlike most Oregon coast towns, Cannon Beach (pop. 1,221) is hidden from the highway, but it's one place you won't want to miss. Though it's little more than a stone's throw south of boisterous Seaside, Cannon Beach has long been known as an artist's colony, and while it has grown considerably in recent years thanks to its popularity as a weekend escape from Portland, it retains a rustic atmosphere.

In terms of traditional "tourist attractions" there's not a lot to do, but Cannon Beach is an unbeatable place in which to stop and unwind, or to take long walks along the seven-mile strand and then retreat indoors to the many good galleries, cafes, and restaurants. For breakfast, fill up on eggs Benedict at the **Lazy Susan Cafe** (closed Tuesday and Wednesday in winter), across from the Mariner Market at 126 N. Hemlock. Enjoy burgers and microbrews at **Bill's Tavern**, 188 N. Hemlock, or very good seafood dinners at the **Bistro**, 263 N. Hemlock, both of which feature live music most weekends. Reasonably priced rooms near the beach and town can be found at the **Starfish Motel**, 9645 S. Hemlock (503/436-0639); **McBee Motel**, 888 S. Hemlock (503/436-2569); and the smoke-free **Cannon Beach Hotel**, 1116 S. Hemlock (503/436-1392), a converted loggers' boardinghouse.

At the end of May, Cannon Beach hosts the largest and most enjoyable sand castle competition on the Oregon coast, with some 10,000 spectators and as many as 1,000 participants turning out with their buckets and spades.

For details on the annual events and other general information, contact the Cannon Beach **visitor bureau**, 201 E. 2nd Street (503/436-2623).

South of Cannon Beach, the Beach Loop, an extension of Hemlock, runs along a spectacular grouping of volcanic plugs, notably 235-foot-high **Haystack Rock**.

Manzanita and Neahkahnie Mountain

South of Cannon Beach at Oswald West State Park, a half-mile trail winds beneath the highway through an ancient forest to driftwood-laden Short Sands Beach and **Smuggler's Cove.**

If you pass through Bay City, pick up a copy of the contentious, Wal-Mart-hating *Bay City Slug*, an irascible local paper that will fill you in on local events and political battles.

South of Cannon Beach, US-101 rises 700 feet above the Pacific. Nowhere else along the Oregon coast does the roadbed sit so high above an ocean view. Soaring another thousand feet above you on the other side of this WPA-built road is Neahkahnie Mountain; of the dozen marked scenic overlooks and hiking trails in the next 20 miles, your itinerary should include Neahkahnie Wayside, which looks southward at the Nehalem Valley and the ocean between Manzanita and Cape Meares. South of the mountain, and thus spared much of the stormy coastal weather (annual rainfall averages 80 inches) is the upscale golfing resort Manzanita; you'll find two of the coast's best restaurants, the **Blue Sky Cafe** at 154 Laneda Avenue (503/368-5712), and **Jarboe's** (503/368-5113), across the street. Jarboe's is sumptuous and very expensive, by Oregon coast standards, at least, while the Blue Sky is more casual, though verging on haute cuisine.

South of Manzanita, **Nehalem Bay State Park** has a large campground with hundreds of sites (and hot showers). US-101 continues through a series of small towns before winding inland past the sloughs and dairy country along Tillamook Bay.

Tillamook

This town, where cows outnumber people by more than two to one, sprawls over lush grasslands at the southern end of Tillamook Bay. Its motto, "Cheese, trees, and ocean breeze," conjures a clear sense of the place. Tillamook, which translates from the Salish tongue as "land of many waters," is dominated by the **Tillamook Cheese Factory** at the north end of town, one of the busiest tourist draws in the state. Inside, a self-guided tour with informational placards traces Tillamook cheese making from the last century to the present, and a glassed-in observation area lets you watch the stuff being made.

Tillamook's other odd attraction is east of US-101 and south of town, where you'll see a pair of huge structures—300 feet wide, 1,100 feet long, and nearly 200 feet tall—with a sign referring to historic aircraft. This points the way toward the **Blimp Hangar Museum** (503/842-1130), wherein the story of WW II surveillance blimps built here is recounted. There are also displays about these craft as well as vintage airplanes, though most of the hangar space is rented out to private businesses.

A few miles south of Tillamook on US-101 is the access road for the highest waterfall in Oregon's Coast Range, 266-foot Munson Creek Falls.

Three Capes Loop

US-101 veers inland for 50 miles between Tillamook and Lincoln City, the next sizeable town south. If time and weather are on your side, head west along the coast via the well-signed, 35-mile-long Three Capes Loop. Running northwest from Tillamook, the loop reaches the mouth of the Tillamook Bay at **Cape Meares**, which has a restored 1890 lighthouse and an oddly contorted Sitka spruce known as the Octopus Tree.

Heading south through the coastal villages of Oceanside and Netarts, the loop proceeds through dairy country until it climbs onto the shoulder of **Cape Lookout**, where a small sign proclaiming "Wildlife Viewing Area" marks the beginning of a 2.5-mile trail that leads through an ancient forest to the tip of the cape, a hundred-plus feet above the water. Beside the coastal panorama, in winter and spring this is a prime place to view passing gray whales.

The Oregon coast's most famous promontory, **Cape Kiwanda**, sees some of the state's wildest surf battering the sandstone headland. Across from the cape is **Haystack Rock**, a 327-foot seastack a half-mile offshore. Along the beach south of the cape, surfers ride waves while dory fisherfolk skid their small craft along the sands every afternoon: a sight worth hanging around to see. The southernmost settlement on this scenic alternative to US-101 is neighboring **Pacific City**, where two fine restaurants, **Grateful Bread Bakery** and **The Riverhouse**, sit beachside on Brooten Road.

Lincoln City

The most overdeveloped section of the Oregon coast stretches for miles along US-101 through Lincoln City (pop. 5,892), seven miles of strip malls, outlet stores, motels, and fast-food franchises. With over a thousand oceanside rooms, Lincoln City does offer some of the coast's cheapest lodging, especially in the off-season when sign after sign advertises rooms for as low as $25 a night, but with so much scenic splendor elsewhere there's no other reason to stop.

Five miles northeast of Lincoln City, east of US-101 on Hwy-18, the **Otis Cafe** (503/994-2813) immortalizes American roadfood, offering excellent waffles and other breakfast treats along with epicurean lunches and berry pies for dessert. It's open for breakfast and lunch daily, plus dinner Thurs.-Sunday.

South of Lincoln City, 2.5 miles east of US-101, the **Drift Creek Covered Bridge** is the oldest of some 50 such structures in the state.

Seven miles south of Lincoln City a sign announces the **Salishan Lodge** (503/764-3600 or 800/452-2300), a beautifully landscaped rustic resort with good off-season value packages (three nights for $239), a five-star dining room, and a surprisingly affordable coffee shop, **The Sun Room**. Down the hill across US-101, **Siletz Bay** is a birdwatcher's paradise.

Depoe Bay was originally known as Depot Bay, named after a local Siletz Indian who worked at the local U.S. Army depot and called himself **Charlie Depot**.

Depoe Bay

Depoe Bay has an appeal, but so much of its natural beauty is obscured from the highway by gift shops or intruded upon by traffic that you've got to know where to look. In his book *Blue Highways,* William Least Heat Moon wrote, "Depoe Bay used to be a picturesque fishing village; now it was just picturesque." While it's true that most of the commercial fishing is long gone, you can still park your car along the highway and walk out on the bridge to watch sportfishing boats move through the narrow channel to what the *Guinness Book of World Records* rates as the world's smallest navigable harbor. South of the bridge is another record-setter, the Oregon coast's largest secondhand bookstore, the **Channel Bookstore**.

The **Sea Hag** restaurant, on US-101 in downtown Depoe Bay, is a time-tested seafood place, as is **Whale Cove Inn**, two miles south of town overlooking a picturesque inlet formerly used by bootleggers during Prohibition.

Cape Foulweather and the Devil's Punchbowl

Between Depoe Bay and Newport, the roadside scenery along US-101 and the parallel "old road," now signed as the Otter Crest Loop, is dominated by miles of broad beaches and sandstone bluffs, including the 453-foot headland of Cape Foulweather, named by Capt. James Cook and offering a 360-degree coastal panorama. Farther south, midway between Depoe Bay and Newport, the aptly named Devil's Punchbowl gives a ringside seat on a frothy confrontation between rock and tide. In the parking area you'll find a small lunch cafe, a branch of Newport's **Mo's**, graced by a chair where "The Boss" (singer Bruce Springsteen) sat on June 11, 1987.

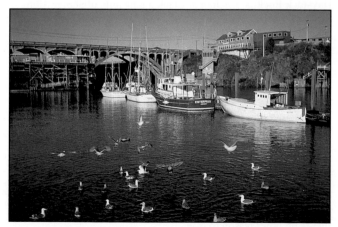

Depoe Bay

Newport

Another old fishing community turned tourist nexus, Newport (pop. 8,437) started in the 1860s on the strength of sweet-tasting Yaquina Bay oysters, which were in demand from San Francisco to New York City and are still available at local restaurants. Oysters, crabs, and clams, along with sea otters, sharks, and seabirds, are the stars of the show at the large and modern **Oregon Coast Aquarium** (daily 10 AM-6 PM in summer, till 4:30 PM rest of the year; $7.75), south of Newport across the Yaquina Bay Bridge. The aquarium includes an aquatic aviary where sea lions, tufted puffins, and other shorebirds cavort in a simulated rockbound coastal habitat.

On the north side of the US-101 bridge over Yaquina Bay, turn onto Hubert Street and head for the bayfront, where boatyards and fish-packing plants service a working harbor. Though it's still the state's second-largest fishing port, much of Newport's bay front has been consumed by souvenir shops, a wax museum, a *Ripley's Believe It or Not!* and other tourist traps. But you'll find the original **Mo's**, a locally famous seafood restaurant, at 622 Bay Boulevard; it and its annex across the street are the area's best dining values.

The coast and inland forests along the Siletz River near Newport were the primary location of the Ken Kesey novel (and Paul Newman film) *Sometimes a Great Notion.*

Dining options can be found at **Nye Beach**, a mélange of old-fashioned beach houses and destination resorts north of the harbor; just look for signs on the western side of US-101. **The Chowderbowl**, 728 N.W. Beach Drive (503/265-7477), features a salad bar/clam chowder special that's a favorite with coastal bikers and hikers. Around the corner, **Don Petrie's**, 613 N.W. 3rd Street (503/265-3663), serves excellent Italian food. Nye Beach is also home to the **Sylvia Beach Hotel**, 267 N.W. Cliff (503/265-5428), *the* place to stay in Newport. If you can't afford the theme rooms—about $75 a night, with decor evocative of different authors—there are dormitory bunk beds for $20 a night. Also on the west side of US-101 is the **Brown Squirrel Hostel**, a block from the beach on S.W. Brook Street (503/265-3729). You'll find many other cut-rate lodging options along US-101.

The very helpful **Newport Chamber of Commerce** (800/263-7844) has complete accommodations listings and other useful information.

Waldport

If you want to avoid lines and general tourist bustle, Waldport is a nice alternative to the resort towns surrounding it. Tourism is low-key here, and you can still sense the vestiges of the resource-based economy, byproduct of the town's proximity to rich timber stands and superlative fishing. Stop along US-101 at the **Alsea River Bridge Museum** (Wed.-Sun. 9 AM-4 PM; free) for interesting exhibits on coastal transportation and the local Alsea tribe, as well as a telescope trained on waterfowl and seals in the bay. At the south end of town, the local outlet of **At'sa Pizza** is highly recommended.

The Pacific coast around Newport marks the beginning of the cross-country **US-20** route, which runs east across the country to Boston and Cape Cod. Coverage of the route begins on page 404.

Portland is covered as a Survival Guide on pages 712-713.

Yachats

On the way into Yachats (pronounced "YA-hots"), beach loops

The old-growth forests of the **Drift Creek Wilderness** east of Waldport are prime nesting areas for the endangered northern spotted owl.

on either side of the Yachats River give a sense of why the area is called "the gem of the Oregon coast." The north bank's **Ocean Drive**—make a left immediately after crossing the bridge into town—has **The Yankee Clipper**, 125 Ocean Drive (503/547-4007), a sandwich shop with a window on the river meeting an angry sea. Back on US-101 at 4th Street, **New Morning Coffeehouse and Bookstore** has good espresso and a (sometimes) sunny outdoor deck-*cum*-sculpture garden, while **Leroy's Blue Whale** is a dependable, no-frills seafood restaurant.

The word "cottage" is a popular lodging label here, usually referring to a moderately-priced self-contained cabin or duplex with kitchen. On US-101 between Waldport and Yachats are a half-dozen different "cottage" complexes, each fronting the beach; **Cape Cod Cottages**, two-plus miles south of Waldport at 4150 US-101 (503/563-2106), is a good choice for location and comfort.

Cape Perpetua

For nearly 400 miles along the Oregon coast, US-101 abounds with state parks and viewpoints, but Cape Perpetua State Park deserves most of your attention. Stop first at the Siuslaw National Forest **visitor center** (503/547-3289), just east of US-101, for seacoast views, exhibits on forestry, and area history. From the visitor center, trails lead across the highway past wind-bent krummholz trees, piles of seashells and other artifacts left behind by native peoples, excellent tidepools, and two rock formations, "Spouting Horn" and the "Devil's Churn." During stormy seas both shoot huge spouts of foam into the air.

You can reach the top of 800-foot-high Cape Perpetua itself by following a two-mile-long road, marked by Cape Perpetua Viewpoint signs and leaving US-101 a few hundred yards north of the visitor center. Once atop the cape, walk the **Trail of the Whispering Spruce**, a half-mile loop around the rim of the promontory yielding, on a clear day, 150-mile views of the Oregon coast from a rustic, WPA-built stone observation point.

Heceta Head and the Sea Lion Caves

Halfway between Cape Perpetua and Florence, a small bridge just south of Washburne State Park marks the turnoff to Heceta Head Lighthouse, perhaps the most photographed beacon in the United States. Built in 1893, it was named for the Spanish mariner who is credited with being the first European to set foot in the region, but you'll have to be content with gazing at it across the cove from a small but rarely crowded beach.

Farther along US-101, 10 miles north of Florence, traffic slows to a stop at the gift shop that serves as the entrance to Sea Lion Caves (daily 9 AM-7 PM in summer, 9 AM-4 PM in winter; $6). You can ride an elevator down to America's largest sea cave and the only mainland rookery for the stellar sea lion. Fall and winter offer the best times to see (and smell!) these animals. Other times of year, they are visible for free from a viewpoint a hundreds yards up US-101.

Florence

If first and last impressions are enduring, Florence is truly blessed. As you enter the city from the north, US-101 climbs high above the ocean; from the south, travelers are greeted by the graceful **Siuslaw River Bridge**, perhaps the most impressive of a half-dozen WPA-built spans designed by Conde McCullough and decorated with his trademark Egyptian obelisks and art deco stylings. Unfortunately, the rest of town visible from US-101 is a bland highway sprawl of motels, gas stations, and franchised restaurants.

The best part of Florence, **Old Town**, is just upstream from the bridge along the north bank of the river. Here, among Bay Street's three blocks of interesting boutiques and galleries, you'll find a number of excellent seafood restaurants. Starting from a nicely landscaped waterfront park at the foot of Laurel Street, choose from the upscale **Bridgewater**, the 24-hour **Fisherman's Wharf**, a riverfront **Mo's**, and the **International C-Food Market**. Back on US-101, across from the A&W, the **Blue Hen** is a popular local cafe.

As far as places to stay, Old Town really lives up to its name at the antique-filled **Johnson House**, 216 Maple Street (503/997-8000), an affordable, century-old, Victorian B&B. Back on US-101 sit a half-dozen garden-variety motels with **The Money-Saver** (503/997-7131) closest to Old Town.

Giant rhododendrons and tumble-down shacks that rent out dune buggies and ATVs line US-101 between Florence and Coos Bay.

"Dune Country": Oregon's Sahara

For nearly 50 miles south of Florence, US-101 has an extensive panorama of oceanfront dunes. Though often obscured from view by forests, roadside signs indicate access roads to numerous dunescapes on both sides of the highway. Coming from the north, the first of these access points is **Honeyman State Park**, 10 miles south of Florence, where rhododendrons line a short trail leading to a 150-foot-high dune overlooking a miragelike lake. A longer trek, leaving from **Tahkenitch Lake** campground, gives a more in-depth look at the dunes' diverse flora and fauna, including swans and occasional black bears. Perhaps the best introduction is at **Umpqua Dunes**, nine miles south of the visitor center in Reedsport. From **Eel Creek Campground**, a 1.5-mile trail leads across small marshes and conifer groves en route to the sea, negotiating lunarlike dunes soaring 300-500 feet, some of the tallest in the world.

*To catch your daily dose of Rush Limbaugh and "modern country" hits, tune to **KWRO 630 AM**.*

Before setting out on any extended exploration, your first stop should be the **Oregon Dunes visitor center** (503/271-3611) at the junction of US-101 and Hwy-38 in **Reedsport**, along the Umpqua River midway between Florence and Coos Bay at the heart of the dunes. The helpful rangers can provide detailed information on hiking and camping throughout the park. Reedsport itself has a line of motels and burger joints—**Don's Old Fashioned** has legions of fans—and you'll find one more interesting option in the timber town of Gardiner, where the **Gardiner Guest House** (503/271-4005) offers comfortable B&B rooms in a restored Victorian home.

*While myrtle stands abound along Oregon's coast, the **House of Myrtlewood,** at 1125 S. 1st Street (800/255-5318) along US-101 on the southwest side of Coos Bay, is the most extensive, and the only one where you can watch objects being made.*

Coos Bay and Charleston

Even if you race right through, it's quite apparent that Coos Bay, once the world's largest lumber port, retains a core of heavy industry. Though many of the big mills have closed, you can still watch huge piles of wood chips, the harbor's number-one ex-

*Behind the Coos Bay visitors bureau stands a memorial statue of the region's favorite son, long-distance runner **Steve Prefontaine,** who electrified the athletic world before his sudden death at age 24 in 1974.*

port, being loaded onto factory ships in the harbor east of US-101. The chips are sent to Asia where they're turned into low-grade paper. You can also get a sense of Coos Bay's seagoing heritage by visiting the tiny, church-run **Seamen's Center**, a block west of US-101 at 171 N. Broadway, where every evening old salts mingle with foreign sailors and make model ships. Across the street, the handy Coos Bay **visitors bureau** (503/269-0215 or 800/824-8486) has maps and information on the entire "Bay Area" region.

Big breakfasts, eclectic but inexpensive lunches and dinners, great pies, and a good range of microbrewed beers are served at **The Blue Heron** across from the visitors bureau at 110 W. Commercial Street. There's no shortage of easy-to-find lodging, including **Motel 6** on US-101 at 1445 Bayshore (503/267-7171).

On the way to Shore Acres from Coos Bay is **Sunset Bay State Park,** Oregon's best swimming beach. Beyond Shore Acres is **Cape Arago State Park,** complete with tidepools and seals on offshore rocks.

The inland marshes around Bandon are prime cranberry-growing lands; the harvest is celebrated with a festival every September.

Charleston and Shore Acres

The historical antecedents for Coos Bay port development were laid a century ago by the Simpson lumber company, whose ships transported Oregon logs around the world. The ships returned with seeds that were planted in the Simpson estate's garden, 12 miles west of Coos Bay via the Cape Arago Highway, three miles beyond the busy commercial and sportfishing port of Charleston. Though the Simpson house burned to the ground in 1923, the 750-acre gardens are still a floral fantasia, now open to the public as Shore Acres State Park (daily 9 AM-dusk; $3 per car). Besides the formal gardens, there's an observation tower above wave-battered bluffs and a trail down to a delightful beach.

Bandon

There's no sharper contrast on the Oregon coast than the difference between industrial Coos Bay and earthy Bandon, 23 miles

holiday at Shore Acres

Bandon Lighthouse

to the south. Here, in the **Old Town** section along the banks of the Coquille River, are several blocks of galleries, crafts shops, and fine restaurants, marked by a gateway arch off US-101. Start a tour of Old Town at the corner of 1st and Baltimore, where Big Wheel Farm Supply houses the **Bandon Driftwood Museum** (daily 9 AM-5:30 PM; free). The combination of sculpted tree roots and fertilizer displays gives a good sense of Bandon's back-to-the-land, hippie ethos. A 10-minute walk down 1st Street takes you past a cannery to the old Coast Guard building, which now houses the **Coquille River Museum** ($1; 503/347-2164). Its exhibits on area history and local color are artfully done, but museum hours vary, so call ahead. South of town from 1st Street, a **Beach Loop** runs along a ridge overlooking a fantastic assemblage of coastal monoliths.

South of Bandon and 11 miles north of Port Orford, **Cape Blanco** is considered—by Oregonians, at least—the westernmost point of land in the contiguous United States. Named by early Spanish explorers for the white shells encrusting the 245-foot cliff face, the cape is also the site of Oregon's oldest (circa 1870) and highest lighthouse.

For fish and chips along the waterfront, the **Bandon Fish Market** is cheap and cheerful. **Andrea's Old Town Cafe**, 160 Baltimore Street, serves top-quality gourmet fare, as does the **Sea Star Bistro**, 375 2nd Street. The Sea Star is connected to the warm and woodsy **Sea Star Guesthouse** (503/347-9632), offering B&B rooms for $35-75, and AYH-approved hostel bunks for $14.

Port Orford and Humbug Mountain

Pastoral sheep ranches, cranberry bogs, berry fields, and Christmas tree farms dominate the 25-mile stretch south of Brandon, but as you pull into Port Orford (pop. 1,025), you'll notice a huge volcanic plug abutting the crescent-shaped shoreline. Known as **Battle Rock**, it's where early settlers fought off a party of hostile Indians; the rock is most impressive from the harbor below. Due to the southwest orientation, which subjects the harbor to turbulent winds and constant waves, fishing boats have to be lowered into the water by crane.

At the center of town, **The Wheelhouse** offers views of Battle Rock *and* breakfast specials, while the **Golden Owl Deli** along US-101 serves very good sandwiches. South of town on a hill above US-101, with views of the ocean, sits the fairly quiet **Seacrest Motel** (503/332-3040).

People who keep track of these things say that tiny **Port Orford** is the "Most Westerly Incorporated City in the Continental U.S.," as well as the rainiest place on the Oregon coast.

Six miles south of Port Orford you'll come to Humbug Mountain, whose 1,756-foot elevation flanks the west side of the highway. It's the coast's highest peak rising directly off the beach, and its steep contours and tree-covered slopes impart an eerily beautiful quality to the light on this section of US-101. The mountain's name was bestowed by prospectors who found that tales of gold deposits here were just "humbug."

South coast forests yield the increasingly rare Port Orford cedar, a fragrant, lightweight but strong wood valued at $10,000 a tree, thanks to a high demand for its use in Japanese home construction.

Prehistoric Gardens

West of the highway, midway between Port Orford and Gold Beach, you'll come across one of the Oregon coast's tackiest but most enduring and enjoyable tourist traps, the Prehistoric Gardens (daily 8 AM-dusk; $5.50). Standing out like a sore thumb on this otherwise unspoiled stretch of US-101, a collection of brightly colored, more or less life-sized dinosaur sculptures inhabits the evocatively lush green forest. Since 1953, when amateur paleontologist E.V. Nelson sculpted his first concrete T. Rex, two dozen more have been added to the forest menagerie.

Gold Beach

Gold Beach was named for the nuggets mined from area black sands during the mid-19th century, but despite its name this is one coastal town where the action is definitely *away* from the beach. The **Rogue River** defines the northern city limits and is the town's economic raison d'être. During salmon season, Gold Beach hotels and restaurants fill up with anglers, while **jetboat tours** of the wild river are also a draw. Along with many other operators hawking their services with billboards next to the highway, **Jerry's Jetboats** ($25; 247-4571 or 800/451-3645), by the bridge at the north end of town, takes passengers upstream to the isolated hamlet of **Agness**, where a homespun mountain lodge serves family-style fried chicken lunches and dinners (though the food is not included in the price of the jetboat ride).

Oregon myrtle, a lollipop-shaped laurel tree whose swirling blond grain spawned scores of roadside shops purveying clocks, bowls, and other souvenirs, can be seen overhanging the road around Humbug Mountain.

In town, good seafood can be had across the bridge at **The Rod n' Reel**; save room for the great pie here. Above-average, ocean-view rooms are available at **Ireland's Rustic Lodges**, on US-101 at 1120 S. Ellensburg Avenue (503/247-7718).

Samuel Boardman State Park

Between Gold Beach and Brookings, US-101's windy, hilly roadbed is studded with the cliffside ocean vistas, giant conifers, and boomerang-shaped offshore rock formations of Samuel Boardman State Park. The park covers most of the "Fabulous 50" miles between the two towns, and all of the above-mentioned features come together at **Natural Bridges Cove**, just north of the Thomas Creek Bridge, the highest bridge on the coast north of San Francisco's Golden Gate. Despite a sign, this turnout is easy to miss because, from the highway, it appears to be simply a parking lot fronting some trees; from the south end of the lot, however, a short trail through an old-growth forest leads to a viewpoint several hundred feet above three natural rock archways standing out from an azure cove.

South of the bridge, just north of suburban Brookings, one final piece of nature has been preserved at **Harris Beach State Park,** across US-101 from the Oregon Welcome Center. Here you can walk down to a driftwood-laden beach and look out at numerous bird-infested islands.

Brookings

The drive through Brookings's malled-over main drag offers only fleeting glimpses of the Pacific, and the town itself offers no real reason to stop. Still, if you're hungry, quality food at budget prices can be found right on US-101 at **Mama's Italian Restaurant,** 703 Chetco Avenue, where there really is a five-foot-tall Italian mama to heap your plate with pasta. Along with numerous highway motels, the **Historical Chetco Inn,** above the highway at 417 Fern Street, was designed by architectural luminary Bernard Maybeck but shows little of his flair; it recently stopped renting rooms, and is now a retirement home.

After the last 350-plus miles of scenic splendor, the final few miles along the coast south to California are somewhat anticlimactic, though just over the border is Redwood National Park, truly one of the West Coast's great places.

Mount Emily, just east of Brookings, was bombed by a submarine-launched Japanese seaplane in September 1942. Though the Japanese plans to ignite the entire coastline in a massive forest fire fizzled, the attack weakened a secession movement by southern Oregonians and Northern Californians to establish a new state, called Jefferson.

The warm mean annual temperature on the Oregon coast is conducive to beautiful flowers ranging from 20-foot high azaleas to acres of Easter lilies, of which Brookings produces 90% of the world's crop.

Northbound visitors may want to stop to pick up maps and brochures at the **Oregon Welcome Center** (daily 9 AM-5 PM, April-Oct. only), across US-101 from Harris Beach State Park.

ALONG THE CALIFORNIA COAST

Stretching along the Pacific Ocean for roughly a thousand miles from top to tail, the California coast includes virgin wilderness as well as the cutting edge of cosmopolitan culture, and covers the full spectrum in between. And for almost the entire way, coastal roads give quick and easy access to all the best parts, with panoramic views appearing so often you'll either run out of film, or simply give up trying to capture it all.

Starting in the north, the green forests of the Pacific Northwest continue well beyond the state border, forming a mountainous seaside landscape that lasts until the edge of metropolitan San Francisco. Along this stretch you'll find a number of old logging and fishing towns, varying from the burly blue-collar likes of Eureka and Crescent City to the upscale ambience of Mendocino, in and amongst endless acres of redwood forest.

The Smith River and Jedediah Smith redwood park were named in memory of the legendary mountain man, **Jedediah Strong Smith,** who in 1826 at the age of 27 led the first party of Americans overland to California.

At the approximate midpoint of the California coast sits San Francisco, deservedly ranked among the world's favorite cities. The hundred miles of coast stretching south from San Francisco hold numerous remnants of the Spanish and Mexican eras, exemplified by the town of Monterey and the beautiful mission at Carmel. Beyond here is another stretch of wild coastline, the rugged country of Big Sur.

Beyond the southern edge of Big Sur, opulent Hearst Castle marks the start of what most people consider Southern California, the rivers and trees of the north giving way to golden beaches, grassy bluffs, and considerably denser populations. A pair of very pleasant small cities, Midwestern-feeling San Luis Obispo and ritzy Santa Barbara, make excellent stops in themselves, smoothing the transition into the environs of Los Angeles, the unwieldy megalopolis that, seen from the I-5 freeway that links Los Angeles and San Diego, seems like one monstrous, 100-mile-long suburb. While it's true that the natural beauty that brought so many people to Southern California in the first place is increasingly endangered, some lovely, almost untouched places remain, hidden away but within easy access of the fast lane. We've pointed them out; enjoy them while they last.

Jedediah Smith Redwoods State Park

The northernmost of the great red-wood groves, Jedediah Smith Red-woods State Park covers nearly 10,000 acres of virgin forest along the banks of the Smith River. Stretching east of US-101, and most easily accessible from US-199, the park offers over 30 miles of usually uncrowded hiking trails through the pristine wilderness, and is considered by many to be the most perfect of all the redwood forests. One of the most enjoyable trails leads through **Stout Grove** past the park's tallest tree and a number of summertime swimming holes along the Smith River.

The park is jointly managed by the state and federal governments, which is why there are two **ranger stations** (707/464-9533 or 707/458-3134) across from each other along US-199 at the main entrance to the park, four miles east of US-101. There's also a good **campground** with hot showers.

Crescent City

The county seat and largest city in Del Norte County, Crescent City (pop. 4,380) is best treated as a base from which to explore the surrounding wilderness. The foggy weather that helps the redwoods thrive makes the city fairly depressing and gray, and what character it developed since its founding in 1853 has been further eroded by storms; a giant tidal wave, caused by the 1964 earthquake off Alaska, destroyed nearly the entire city.

Crescent City includes the usual motels (including a **Travelodge** and a **Best Western**) and restaurants, as well as one unique spot: the **Ship Ashore**, a gift shop, restaurant, and motel along US-101 on the north side of town, marked by a beached ship.

Crescent City does have the headquarters for **Redwood National Park;** a block east of US-101 at 1111 2nd Street (707/464-6101), this is the best source of information for southbound travelers.

Outside Crescent City, California's most violent, long-term criminals are kept behind bars in the state-of-the-art **Pelican Bay State Prison,** built in 1990.

Del Norte Coast Redwoods State Park

Spreading south from the Jedediah Smith redwoods, Del Norte Coast Redwoods State Park runs along the Pacific Ocean (and US-101) for about 10 miles, containing more than 6,000 acres of first- and second-growth redwoods as well as brilliant blooms of rhododendrons, azaleas, and spring wildflowers. Del Norte also protects miles of untouched coastline, the best stretch of which is accessible from the end of **Enderts Beach Road,** which cuts west from US-101 just north of the park entrance. From here, a 30-mile trail follows the coast to Prairie Creek.

The state park area is bounded on the south by an undeveloped section of Redwood National Park, within which the **Redwood AYH hostel** (707/482-8265), along US-101, 12 miles south of Crescent City and two miles north of the Trees of Mystery, is housed in a historic farmhouse and offers cozy dormitory accommodations and a few private rooms for about $12 a person.

Trees of Mystery and Klamath

Hard to miss along US-101, thanks to the massive statues of Paul Bunyan and Babe the Blue Ox looming over the highway, the Trees of Mystery (daily 8 AM–dusk; $6) are one of the coast's most virulent tourist draws. Along the "Tall Tales Trail," chainsaw-cut figures, backed by taped stories, stand in tableaux at the foot of towering redwoods; there's also a huge gift shop and a small free museum of Native American art and artifacts. Across the highway, **Motel Trees** (707/482-3152) has standard rooms from $40 and a coffee shop.

Along the banks of the mighty Klamath River, four miles south of the Trees of Mystery, the town of Klamath is a brief burst of highway sprawl, supported by anglers who flock here for the annual salmon runs. At the south end of town, drive through the **Tour-Thru Tree** ($2), then cross the Klamath River on a bridge graced by a pair of gilded cement grizzly bears.

All the land along the Klamath River is part of the extensive **Hoopa Valley Indian Reservation,** which stretches for over 30 miles upstream from the Pacific Ocean.

Prairie Creek Redwoods State Park

The largest of the trio of north coast redwood parks, Prairie Creek Redwoods State Park is best known for its large herd of endangered **Roosevelt elk,** which you can usually see grazing in the meadows along US-101 at the center of the park, next to the main **ranger station** (707/488-2171). A new freeway carries US-101 traffic around, rather than through, the Prairie Creek redwoods; to reach the best sights detour along the well-signed "Elk Prairie Parkway," which follows Prairie Creek through the heart of the park.

Another elk herd can be spotted among the coastal dunes at **Gold Bluffs Beach,** which stretches for 11 miles through untouched wilderness; there's a primitive **campground** and trails leading from US-101, or you can follow Davison Road northwest from US-101, three miles south of the ranger station. Apart from the elk, Prairie Creek offers the usual mix of old-growth redwood trees, which here more than in the other parks mingle with dense growths of Sitka spruce and Douglas firs to form a near rainforest of greenery.

Redwood National Park

Established in 1968, and later enlarged at a total cost of over $500 million, Redwood National Park protects some 100,000 acres of redwood forest, including the 30,000 acres previously preserved in the adjacent Smith, Del Norte, and Prairie Creek State Parks. To be honest, apart from the adjacent state parks, the trees preserved here aren't by any means the oldest, largest, or most beautiful; in fact, much of the federal parkland is second- or third-growth timber, clearcut as recently as the 1960s. Though redwoods are the fastest-growing softwoods on earth—growing three to five feet a year when young—the groves here are rather disappointing compared to those in nearby areas, and serve more as an environmental buffer zone than a tree-lover's pilgrimage site.

Though the Jedediah Smith, Del Norte Coast, and Prairie Creek redwoods are on state-owned land, they are managed jointly under the auspices of Redwood National Park.

That said, Redwood National Park does hold two special sights: the **Lady Bird Johnson Grove**, on a logging road a mile east of US-101, dedicated in 1968; and the **Tall Trees Grove**, which holds the world's tallest tree, the 368-foot Libbey Tree, reachable via an all-day hike and by summer-only shuttle buses (see below).

At the south end of the park, enjoy Teutonic breakfasts at the German-run **Rolf's Park Cafe**, attached to the fairly basic, $30-a-night **Prairie Creek Motel** (707/488-3841). The roadside strip town of **Orick** stretches south toward the coast, where the main Redwood National Park **visitor center** (707/488-3461) stands at the mouth of Redwood Creek; catch the Tall Trees Grove shuttle bus here.

Patrick's Point State Park

If your idea of heaven is sitting on a rocky headland listening to the roar of the Pacific while watching the sunset or looking for passing gray whales, you won't want to pass by Patrick's Point State Park. Three different 200-foot-high promontories at the middle of the park provide panoramic views, while the surrounding acres hold cedar and spruce forests—no redwoods— open pastures bright with wildflowers, great tidepools, a wide dark sand beach, and two **campgrounds** with hot showers. There's also preserved and restored remnants of a Yurok village; obtain further information and camping reservations from the **visitor center** (707/677-3570).

The groves of giant trees in Redwood National Park were used as a location for the *Star Wars* film *Return of the Jedi:* the characters cruised through the forest on airborne cycles.

Continuing south, US-101 becomes a four-lane freeway along the ocean to Arcata and Eureka.

Arcata's creative community comes alive every May for the world-famous **Kinetic Sculpture Race,** in which participants pedal, paddle, and otherwise move themselves and their handmade vehicles across land and sea to Ferndale, 38 miles away. For more information, call 707/725-3851.

Arcata

The most attractive and enjoyable town on the far north coast of California, Arcata (pop. 15,197) makes the best first (or last, depending upon your direction) overnight stop south of the Oregon border. The presence of Humboldt State University campus on the hills above US-101 accounts for the town's

The author **Bret Harte** was run out of Arcata by angry townspeople in 1860, after writing an editorial in the local paper criticizing a massacre of a local Wiyot tribe.

From Arcata, Hwy-299 continues east over the coast range through the beautiful Trinity Alps to **Weaverville,** well-preserved site of a mid-1850s gold rush. Hwy-299 links up with I-5 at Redding.

youthful, nonconformist energy, especially in the cafes, bookstores, and clubs that surround the lively **Town Plaza,** two blocks west of US-101 at 9th and G Streets, incongruously graced by palm trees and a statue of President McKinley.

You can admire the town's many Victorian cottages, hunt mushrooms, or hike in the redwoods; afterwards relax with a cup of tea or, better yet, a soak in a hot tub at homey **Cafe Mokka,** the world's only combo sauna and espresso bar at 5th and J Streets. Good cheap Mexican health food—try the tofu burritos—can be had from the popular **Casa de Que Pasa,** 854 9th Street a block from the plaza, while microbrewed beers flow from the taps of Arcata's amiable bars, many of which feature live music; try **Jambalaya** at 915 H Street, or the **Humboldt Brewery,** 856 10th Street.

For a place to stay, the centrally located **Hotel Arcata** (707/826-0217 or 800/344-1221), on the plaza at 708 9th Street, has rooms from $60, or you can take your pick of the usual motels along US-101.

Eureka

Now a fairly gritty and industrial port, Eureka's large natural bay was well known to fur trappers and traders long before it became a booming lumber and whaling port in the 1850s. Thanks to the lumber trade, Victorian Eureka grew prosperous, building elaborate homes including the oft-photographed but closed-to-the-public **Carson Mansion** on 2nd and M Streets, two blocks north of US-101.

Apart from this and a few other individual houses and commercial buildings, Eureka is not a particularly pretty town, but it does have a couple of good restaurants in what's left of its historic downtown quarter, including the

the Carson Mansion

publike **Cafe Waterfront** at 1st and F Streets, and the popular **Sea Grill**, a block from US-101 at 316 E Street. Another good place is the no-frills **Seafood Grotto** ("We Ketch 'em, Cook 'em, Serve 'em"), west of downtown along US-101 at 6th and Broadway. Accommodation options range from roadside motels—including a handy **Travelodge** on US-101 downtown—to upscale places like the **Carter House**, 301 L Street (707/444-8062 or 800/404-1390), a re-created Victorian manor with the state's best B&B breakfast.

For further information, contact the **Eureka Humboldt County Convention and Visitors' Bureau** at 1034 2nd Street (707/443-5097 or 800/338-7352).

One great place to stop in Eureka is the Romano Gabriel Wooden Sculpture Garden at 325 2nd Street. Just a stone's throw away from the Carson Mansion, but at the opposite end of the aesthetic spectrum, this brilliantly colorful folk art extravaganza of faces and flowers was created out of painted packing crates by a local gardener, who worked on it for over 30 years before his death in 1977.

Samoa

Even if you're just passing through, don't miss the chance to visit the busy mill town of Samoa, across the bay from Eureka but easily reachable via the Hwy-255 bridge. Follow the signs past the piles of logs and belching mill chimneys to the unique **Samoa Cookhouse** (707/442-1659), built at the turn of the century by the Louisiana Pacific lumber company, which still owns most of the peninsula. Inside the cookhouse, which is packed with logging memorabilia, take a seat at one of the 20-foot-long tables (redwood, of course, covered in checkered oilcloth) and dig into the family-style feast. There are no menus, just huge platters of food at ridiculously low prices— $5.95 for breakfast (from 6 AM, with great hash browns!) and $6.65 for lunch (served till 3 PM), $11.45 for a two-meat, four-course dinner (served 5-9 PM, till 10 PM in summer).

The area around Ferndale has been hit by numerous earthquakes, including a destructive tremor in April 1992 that registered 6.9 on the Richter Scale.

Ferndale

Well worth the 10-mile detour west of US-101, the historic town of Ferndale (pop. 1,331) is an odd fish along the woodsy Northern California coast, a century-old dairy town that would look more at home in middle America. The three-block-long, franchise-free Main Street includes a fully stocked general store and the Golden Gait/Gate Mercantile, and whitewashed farmhouses dot the pastoral valleys nearby. Ferndale's diverse history is well documented inside the **Ferndale Museum**, off Main Street at Shaw and 3rd Streets (hours vary; 707/786-4466).

The milk shakes and other diner fare at the **Fern Cafe**, 606 Main Street, have made it a popular place to eat, while *the* place to stay (or at least to see) in Ferndale is the lushly landscaped late-Victorian **Gingerbread Mansion**, 400 Berding Street (707/786-4000), with deluxe rooms from around $100 a night. Pick up free walking-tour maps and other visitor information at the **chamber of commerce** on Main Street (707/786-4477).

West of Ferndale, the narrow, winding Mattole Road loops around Cape Mendocino through the northern reaches of the so-called **"Lost Coast,"** a stretch of coastline justly famous for its isolated beauty.

Scotia

Back along US-101, on the banks of the Eel River midway between the coast and the Humboldt Redwoods, Scotia is the only true company town left in California. The Pacific Lumber Company (a.k.a. "PALCO") built it and still owns everything, from the two huge mills to the 10 blocks of white-painted houses, church, and schools that constitute this little community of about 1,000 people.

Stop first at the small **museum**, housed in the redwood-built Greek revival former bank at the center of town, to pick up passes for self-guided **tours** (Mon.-Fri. 7:30 AM-2 PM; free) of the world's largest redwood mill. Following a yellow painted line through the mill at your own pace, you can gawk at (and listen to—it's a noisy business) every stage of the milling process. First cut logs get de-barked by a powerful jet of water, then laser-guided band saws slice the logs into rough boards, which are turned into finished lumber. A raised catwalk runs through the center of the mill, and signs explain what's happening at each stage.

The one place to stay in town is the rustic **Scotia Inn** (707/764-5683), which has B&B rooms ($60-160 a night) and a very good restaurant; it's on Main Street, a block from the Scotia museum.

78 YEARS 1918-1996
SAVING THE REDWOODS

The protection of the mighty redwood forests of Northern California was made possible not by the state or federal governments but primarily by the efforts of the **Save the Redwoods League,** a private organization that has raised, since its founding in 1918, millions of dollars to buy or preserve over 160,000 acres of redwood forest. To support its efforts, write to 114 Sansome Street, Room 605, San Francisco, CA 94104, or call 415/362-2352.

Humboldt Redwoods State Park

Sheltering the biggest and best collection of giant redwoods anywhere in the world, Humboldt Redwoods State Park is an exceptionally breathtaking corner of an exceptionally beautiful region. Covering 50,000 acres along the Eel River, this is the true heart of redwood country, containing the largest and most pristine expanses of virgin forest as well as some of the largest, tallest, and most remarkable trees.

Even if you're just passing through, be sure to turn onto the amazing **Avenue of the Giants,** 31 miles of old highway frontage between Jordan Creek and Phillipsville running parallel to the faster and busier US-101 freeway through the park. At the north end of the park you'll find an impressive collection of trees in the well-marked **Founders Grove,** where a half-mile nature trail leads past the 362-foot-tall, 1,600-year-old **Dyerville Giant,** lauded as the world's tallest tree before it fell during the winter of 1991. West of Founder's Grove, across US-101, the 13,000 acre **Rockefeller Forest** is one of the largest old-growth forests in the world, and includes two of the park's champion trees, each over 360 feet tall and some 17 feet in diameter.

The best source of information on the park is the **visitor center** (707/946-2263) in **Weott,** which also has a pleasant **campground** ($14) with showers, right next door. You may have to drive a ways north (to Ferndale, Eureka, or Arcata) or south (to Garberville) from the park to find a good meal, though there are two nice places to stay at the southern end of the park: the **Country Inn** (707/943-3259) in Myers Flat has B&B rooms from $60, while the hamlet of Miranda holds the pleasant **Miranda Gardens Resort** (707/943-3011), with motel rooms and rustic cabins at $40-140 a night.

Most of the old towns along the Eel River were destroyed by a terrible flood in 1964, when the river rose as high as 35 feet above US-101.

The well-graded logging and fire roads through the Rockefeller Forest make excellent mountain bike routes.

REDWOOD COUNTRY ROADSIDE ATTRACTIONS

The stretch of US-101 through the redwood country of Humboldt County is lined by pristine groves of massive trees and provides boundless opportunities to come face-to-face with your own insignificance in nature's greater scheme of things. If you tire of this display of natural majesty, or simply want to keep it in context with the modern "civilized" world, you're in luck: every few miles, amongst the stately trees, you'll come upon shameless souvenir stands selling redwood burl furniture and chainsaw sculptures—including one featuring Biblical figures, called "Carving for Christ"—as well as tacky tourist traps like the "World of Bigfoot" or "Hobbittown USA," in Phillipsville. None of these is big or bold enough to detract from the main event—the big trees—but since they've been in operation since the earliest days of car-borne tourism, they're as much a part of the redwood experience as the trees themselves. Most charge only a couple of dollars' admission, so there's not a lot to lose.

While you're encouraged to stop at any and all of them—at least long enough to buy a postcard or two—some of the more tried-and-true attractions are the **Trees of Mystery**, marked by huge statues of Paul Bunyan and Babe the Blue Ox along US-101 in Klamath (see page 44); the **One-Log House** in Phillipsville, a mobile home carved from a single, 32-foot redwood log; and the **Shrine Drive-Thru Tree**, 13078 Avenue of the Giants (old US-101) in Myers Flat, which wagon-borne travelers drove through over a century ago. In the south, near the town of Leggett, are two more. **Confusion Hill** is one of those places where water runs uphill and the rules of physics seem not to apply. There's also a little railway train here that chugs uphill to a very nice grove of trees. **Chandelier Drive-Thru Tree**, south of Leggett off old US-101 on Drive-Thru Tree Road, allows you to drive your car through a 315-foot redwood tree.

Garberville and Redway

Since its recurring presence in the national media during the U.S. government's high-profile, late 1980s raids on local marijuana plantations, Garberville has returned to its previous sleepy self. The US-101 freeway bypasses the town, which stretches for a half-dozen blocks along Redwood Drive, the well-signed business loop off the highway.

Enjoy an early morning breakfast with the old-time locals at the **Eel River Cafe**, 801 Redwood Avenue, or enjoy an espresso and healthy food at the **Woodrose Cafe**, a block south at 911 Redwood Avenue. Garberville also has all the motels you could want, including the **Motel Garberville**, 948 Redwood Drive (707/923-2422).

Just west of Garberville on the old highway, Redway is a small and usually quiet enclave that's best known for organizing the annual **Reggae on the River** festival (707/923-3368), which attracts top performers and thousands of fans to French's Campground near Piercy every August. Redway is worth the short sidetrip during the rest of the year, if only for breakfast, lunch, or dinner at the **Mateel Cafe**, a health-conscious gourmet haunt along Redwood Avenue at the center of town.

Along US-101, four miles south of Garberville, one of the region's most characterful places is the **Benbow Inn** (707/923-2124), a circa 1926 mock Tudor hotel with fairly pricey rooms and a nice restaurant offering afternoon tea and scones on a sunny terrace overlooking Lake Benbow.

Leggett

No longer even a proverbial wide spot in the road since the US-101 freeway was diverted around it, Leggett marks the southern end of the Humboldt redwoods. One exceptional reason to stop here is the **Bell Glen** (707/925-6425), which spreads between the highway and the Eel River and offers a number of comfortable, romantic cottages (from $95) as well as clean but basic dorm beds ($15) in the **Eel River Redwoods Hostel**. A small but worthwhile restaurant on site specializes in local fish and seasonally varying entrees using fresh local produce.

At the south end of Leggett, a mile from the US-101/Hwy-1 junction along the old highway, stands one of the redwood region's most venerable and worthwhile roadside attractions, the "original" **Drive-Thru Tree** (daily 8 AM-dusk; $3). In addition to the famous tree, which had the hole cut through it in the 1930s, there's an above-average gift shop with a broad range of books, postcards, and schlocky souvenirs.

South of Leggett, US-101 runs inland, while scenic Hwy-1 cuts west over the coastal mountains to Mendocino, winding along the Pacific south to San Francisco.

Fort Bragg

From US-101 at Leggett, Hwy-1 twists over the rugged coastal mountains before hugging the coast through the

---

US-101 THROUGH THE WINE COUNTRY

If you don't have enough time to follow the gorgeous coastal route along Hwy-1, don't despair: the faster inland route is plenty pretty. US-101 runs through the heart of the wine country of Sonoma and Mendocino Counties, where vineyards and tasting rooms line the roadside, and extensive forests cover the surrounding hills and mountains. Amidst the scenery are a few diverse towns, ranging from the fairly industrial environs of **Ukiah**, midway along, to quiet communities like **Cloverdale**, **Geyserville**, and **Willitts**, where the "Skunk Train" runs over the coast to Fort Bragg.

If you only have time for one stop, make it **Hopland**, halfway between Leggett and San Francisco. As the name suggests, this is an old hop-growing district now home to the excellent Mendocino Brewing Company, makers of Red Tail Ale and other fine brews, which you can sample at the brewpub along US-101. Next door to the brewery, the **Cheesecake Lady** bakes excellent desserts and snacks; across the highway, the **Bluebird Cafe** serves up delectable and plentiful meals.

---

weatherbeaten logging and fishing communities of **Rockport** and **Westport**. The small and informal **Howard Creek Ranch** (707/964-6725) in Westport offers comfortable B&B rooms, an outdoor hot tub, and easy access to the driftwood-laden beach. Farther south, MacKerricher State Park protects seven miles of rocky coast and waterfront pine forest; the **campground**, as in all California state parks, is reservable through the private concessionaire DestiNet (800/444-PARK).

From Redway, a well-maintained road heads over the coast range to **Shelter Cove**, at the center of the wild "Lost Coast."

It takes more than an hour to cover the 44 miles between US-101 and the first real town, Fort Bragg (pop. 6,100), whose burly, blue-collar edge comes as something of a shock on the otherwise undeveloped, touristy Mendocino coast. Home to a large Georgia Pacific lumber mill and the region's largest commercial fishing fleet, Fort Bragg takes a mostly no-frills approach to the tourist trade, leaving the dainty B&B scene to its upscale neighbor, Mendocino. However, there are a few down-to-earth places to eat: very good, diner-style breakfasts are available at the oddly named **Egghead Omelettes of Oz**, 326 N. Main Street, while **The Wharf**, along the Noyo River at 780 N. Harbor Drive, serves good value seafood dinners. Fort Bragg's many motels, including the **Fort Bragg Motel**, 763 N. Main Street (707/964-4787), are the coast's only cheap accommodation options, after camping.

From Fort Bragg, the California & Western Railroad runs a number of historic steam- and diesel-powered **"Skunk Trains"** over the mountains to Willits and back. Half-day and full-day trips ($18-25; 707/964-6372) run year-round.

For more complete information on the Fort Bragg/Mendocino area, contact the **North Coast Chamber of Commerce**, 332 N. Main Street (707/961-6300 or 800/726-2780).

Mendocino

Mendocino

One of the prettiest towns on the California coast (as seen in TV shows like "Murder, She Wrote" and numerous movies), Mendocino (pop. 1,100) is an artists-and-writers community par excellence, and an upscale escape for wage-slaving visitors from San Francisco. Originally established as a logging port in the 1850s, Mendocino successfully preserved both its sandstone coastline—great for wintertime whale-watching—and its many New England-style clapboard houses, most of which have been converted into $100-a-night inns. The lovely **MacCallum House**, 45020 Albion Street (707/937-0289), includes a beautiful garden, good breakfasts, and a cozy nighttime bar and restaurant. Another fine place to stay is the circa 1858 **Mendocino Hotel**, on the downtown waterfront at 45080 Main Street (707/937-0511).

Along with its many fine art galleries and bookshops, Mendocino has one of California's best restaurants, **Cafe Beaujolais**, two blocks from the waterfront at 961 Ukiah Street (707/937-5614), which serves melt-in-your-mouth buttermilk waffles, delicious French toast, and an array of more unusual breakfasts; hearty soups, salads, sandwiches, and pizzas for lunch; and a prix fixe gourmet feast of California cuisine delicacies for dinner. Breakfast and lunch are served daily 8:30 AM-2:30 PM; dinner is served Thurs.-Sun. 6-9 PM.

Van Damme State Park

South of Mendocino at the mouth of the Little River, Van Damme State Park stretches for five miles along the coastal bluffs and beaches and includes some 1,800 acres of pine and redwood forest. The park's unique attribute is the oddly contorted **Pygmy Forest**, a natural bonsailike grove of miniature pines, cypress, and manzanita, with a wheelchair-accessible nature trail explaining the unique ecology; the trailhead is four miles east of Hwy-1. There's also a small and very popular campground, and a **visitor center** (707/937-0851) housed in a New Deal-era recreation hall.

One place worth keeping an eye out for is the tiny roadside community of **Elk,** 15 miles south of Mendocino along Hwy-1, which has a good cafe, a general store, and a trail leading down to the Pacific at Greenwood Cove.

Detour: Anderson Valley

From Hwy-1 south of Mendocino, Hwy-128 cuts diagonally across to US-101 through the lovely Anderson Valley, home to numerous fine wineries (including Husch, Navarro, and Kendall-Jackson) and the *Anderson Valley Advertiser,* one of California's most outspoken local newspapers. Anderson Valley also has its own regional dialect, called "Boontling," combining English, Scots-Irish, Spanish, and Native American words into a lighthearted lingo created, some say, simply to befuddle outsiders—to "shark the bright-lighters."

To find out more, stop in the valley's tiny main town, **Boonville**, at the bookshop alongside the Horn of Zeese coffee shop. Another place to check out is next door's Anderson Valley Brewing Company, a publike restaurant and saloon that's the birthplace of delicious Boont Amber, the state's finest microbrew.

At the north end of Gualala, across from the Chevron station, be sure to stop at **The Food Company** deli and sample some of the world's finest ginger cookies, baked fresh daily and truly delicious. The deli also offers a full range of picnic foods—salads, dips, breads, beers, wines—and did we mention the ginger cookies?

Gualala

The southernmost 40 miles of Mendocino coastline are almost totally undeveloped and virtually uninhabited, with green forests and coastal coves as far as the eye can see. Situated at the very southern edge of the county, the old logging port of Gualala (pop. 950) has remade itself in the image of Mendocino, with a range of B&Bs culminating in the Russian Orthodox domes of **St. Orres** (707/884-3303), a handcrafted inn and Francophile gourmet restaurant glowing with polished wood and stained glass, above Hwy-1 on the north side of town. You'll find less expensive lodging (rooms from $45 a night) and a locally popular restaurant right in town at the **Gualala Hotel** (707/884-3441).

Sea Ranch

Midway between Mendocino and the San Francisco Bay Area, the vacation home community of Sea Ranch was laid out in the mid-1960s by an enthusiastic group of then-young architects and planners, including Lawrence Halprin and the late Charles Moore, who hoped to show that development need not destroy or negatively impact the natural beauty of the California coast. Strict design guidelines, preserving over half the 5,000 acres as open space and requiring the use of muted natural wood cladding and other barnlike features, made it an aesthetic success, which you can appreciate for yourself at the **Sea Ranch Lodge** (707/785-2371). The lodge offers good meals and rooms for $100 a night.

The rest of Sea Ranch, however, is strictly private, which has raised the hackles of area activists, who after years of lawsuits finally forced through a few coastal access trails in the mid-1980s; these are marked by turnouts (parking $2) along Hwy-1.

Salt Point State Park

The many sheltered rocky coves of Salt Point State Park make it ideal for undersea divers, who come to hunt the abundant abalone. Along the five miles of jagged shoreline, pines and redwoods clutch the water's edge, covering some 6,000 acres on both sides of Hwy-1. Though parts of the park were badly burned in a 1994 fire, Salt Point is still a prime place for hiking or camping. For more information, or for a guide to the many remnants of the Pomo tribal village that stood here until the 1850s, contact the **visitor center** (707/847-3221).

One of the few positive effects of cutting down the native redwood forests that once covered the Northern California coast has been the emergence of giant-sized rhododendrons in their place. You'll find the most impressive display at the **Kruse Rhododendron Preserve,** high above Hwy-1 at the center of Salt Point State Park, where some 350 acres of azaleas and rhododendrons, some reaching 15 feet in height, burst forth in late spring, usually peaking around the first week of May.

In between Salt Point and Fort Ross, Beniamo Bufano's 72-foot *Peace* statue looms alongside Hwy-1 above craggy **Timber Cove.**

Fort Ross

If you're captivated by California's lively (if short-lived) history, one of the most evocative spots in the state is Fort Ross (daily 10 AM–4:30 PM; $5 per car; 707/847-3286), the well-restored remains of a Russian fur-trapping outpost built here in 1812. During a 30-year residency, the Russians farmed wheat and potatoes, traded with native tribes, and trapped local seals and sea otters for their furs, which commanded huge sums on the European market. The near destruction of the sea otter population by 1840 caused the company to shut down operations; later, the abandoned fort was badly damaged by the 1906 San Francisco earthquake. The state has completed a high-quality restoration and reconstruction project, using hand-hewn lumber and historically accurate building methods to replicate the original barracks and other buildings, including a luminous redwood chapel.

The **Russian River** breached its banks twice during the winter of 1994-95, exceeding its usual level by some 25 feet. The floods destroyed many businesses and houses, evident in the many abandoned buildings lining the Hwy-116 roadside.

Outside the fort's walls, a modern **visitor center** traces the site's natural, native, and Russian history, and offers information on the park's many fine hiking trails.

Jenner and the Russian River

South of Fort Ross, Hwy-1 climbs high above the rugged coastline, offering breathtaking vistas of the Pacific Ocean hundreds of feet below. Twelve miles south of Fort Ross, Hwy-1 reaches the resort community of Jenner (pop. 300), which stretches along the broad mouth of the Russian River.

From Jenner, Hwy-116 runs east along the river, passing through forests, vineyards, and popular summertime resort towns, the largest of which is **Guerneville,** 12 miles away, with a number of worthwhile cafes and an alternative-minded population. After 35-odd miles, Hwy-116 eventually links up with the US-101 freeway to and from San Francisco, providing a faster alternative to coastal Hwy-1.

Russian Orthodox chapel at Fort Ross

Sonoma Coast State Beaches

South of Jenner and the Russian River, Hwy-1 hugs the coast along 10 miles of rocky coves and sandy beaches, collectively protected as the Sonoma Coast State Beaches. Starting with Goat Rock at the southern lip of the Russian River mouth, a blufftop trail leads past intriguingly named and usually unpopulated pocket strands like Blind Beach, Schoolhouse Beach, Shell Beach, and Salmon Creek Beach.

Controversial **Bohemian Grove,** the world's most exclusive men's club, covers 2,500 acres of redwood forest just south of the Russian River outside the village of Monte Rio.

At the southernmost end, the park broadens to include the wildflower-covered granite promontory of **Bodega Head,** which juts into the Pacific and provides a great vantage point during the winter gray whale migrations.

While hiking along the Sonoma Coast, be careful: over 75 people have been drowned by sleeper waves, which rise unannounced and sweep people off the rocky shore.

Bodega Bay

Protected by the massive bulk of Bodega Head, the fishing harbor of Bodega Bay has grown into an upscale vacation destination, with Sea Ranch-style weekend homes lining the fairways of golf resorts and $120-a-night hotels overlooking the still busy commercial wharves. On the waterfront at 595 Hwy-1, the **Lucas Wharf Deli** dishes up fish and chips and clam chowder; more extensive and expensive meals are available at nearby restaurants.

South of Bodega Bay, Hwy-1 cuts inland around the marshy coastal estuaries, passing by the small town of **Bodega,** which Alfred Hitchcock used for many of the scariest scenes in his 1960 movie, *The Birds.*

Point Reyes

Between Bodega Bay and the Golden Gate Bridge, Hwy-1 slices through one of the country's most scenically and economically wealthy areas, **Marin County.** Though less than an hour from San Francisco, the northwestern reaches of the county are surprisingly rural, consisting of rolling dairylands and a few untouched small towns; Hwy-1 follows a slow and curving route along the usually uncrowded two-lane blacktop.

Tomales Bay marks the rift zone formed by the **San Andreas Fault,** which runs parallel to Hwy-1 and divides Point Reyes from the rest of Northern California.

After looping inland south of Bodega Bay, Hwy-1 reaches the shore again at oyster-rich Tomales Bay, around which it winds for 20 miles before reaching the town of **Point Reyes Station.** Here the unpretentious but excellent **Station House Cafe** at 3rd and Main Streets serves incredibly good breakfasts and delicious lunches that include great-tasting local oysters, on the half-shell or barbecued. West from town, the 74,000-acre Point Reyes National Seashore offers an entire guidebook's worth of hiking and cycling trails, broad beaches, dense forests, and more; stop at the Bear Valley **visitor center** (daily 9 AM-5 PM; free; 415/663-9020) for more information. Dozens of delightful inns and restaurants operate in and around Point Reyes; contact the West Marin Chamber of Commerce (415/663-9232) for complete listings. An AYH **hostel** (415/663-8811) is housed in an old farmhouse on the road to Drake's Bay.

Bolinas and Stinson Beach

Sitting at the southern end of the Point Reyes peninsula, Bolinas is a small town with a well-earned reputation for discouraging tourists; the signs leading you here from Hwy-1 are regularly torn down by locals bent on keeping the place—little more than a general store, a bakery, and a bar—for themselves.

In contrast, the broad strands of Stinson Beach, four miles south along Hwy-1, are the Bay Area's most popular summertime suntanning spots. A grocery store and deli, the Livewater Surf Shop (which rents boards and the essential wetsuits), and a couple of outdoor bar-and-grills along Hwy-1 form a short parade at the entrance to the beach; if you want to stay overnight, try the **Stinson Beach Motel**, 3416 Hwy-1 (415/868-1712).

If you have the chance to plan ahead, try to book a night at the **Steep Ravine Cabins**, just over a mile south of Stinson Beach on the ocean side of Hwy-1. Now part of Mount Tamalpais State Park, these 10 rustic redwood cabins are very basic roofs-over-the-head (bring sleeping bags and food; water faucets are just outside the door) in an absolutely beautiful coastal chasm. The cabins cost $30 a night, and reservations are handled by DestiNet (800/444-PARK).

Mount Tamalpais, Muir Woods, and Muir Beach

From the coast, a pair of roads, Panoramic Highway and the Shoreline Highway (Hwy-1), twist up and over the slopes of Mount Tamalpais (elev. 2,586), the signature peak of the San Francisco Bay Area. Known usually as "Mount Tam," the whole mountain has been protected in semi-natural state within a series of state and national parks, and its voluptuous slopes offer incredible views of the urbanized Bay Area and the untouched coastline; drive to within 100 yards of the top for a 360-degree panorama, or stop at the Pan Toll **ranger station** (415/388-2070) for a map of Mount Tam's hiking routes and fire roads.

A deep, dark valley between the coast and Mount Tamalpais holds the last surviving stand of Marin County redwoods, pre-served for future generations as the Muir Woods National Monument (daily 8 AM-dusk; free), and named in honor of turn-of-the-century naturalist John Muir. A paved, mile-long trail takes in the biggest trees, but since the park is often crowded with busloads of sightseeing hordes making the tour from San Francisco, you may want to explore the farther-flung areas, climbing up Mount Tamalpais or following Muir Creek two miles downstream to the crescent-shaped cove of Muir Beach, along Hwy-1.

Marin Headlands

If you can avoid the magnetic pull of the Golden Gate Bridge and San Francisco, take the very last turnoff from US-101

The all-terrain mountain bike, which now accounts for half of all bikes on (and off) the roads, was invented in the late 1970s by a group of daredevil Marin cyclists intent on cruising down the fire roads of Mount Tamalpais at the highest possible speed.

John Muir

At the junction of Hwy-1 and the US-101 freeway, a historic roadside restau-raunt has recently been resurrected as the **Buckeye Roadhouse,** 15 Shoreline Hwy. (415/331-2600), where you can feast on fine BBQ, great steaks and burgers, and delicious desserts in a lively, retro-Route 66 atmoshpere.

Every August since 1904, one of the country's wildest foot races, the Dipsea, has followed a rugged trail from the town of Mill Valley over Mount Tamalpais to Stinson Beach.

(northbound drivers take the second turnoff after crossing the bridge) and head west to the Marin Headlands, a former military base that's been turned back into coastal semi-wilderness. A tortuous road twists along the face of 300-foot cliffs, giving incredible views of the bridge and the city behind it, then continues west to Fort Cronkhite, where a **visitor center** (415/331-1450) has a reconstructed Miwok shelter and details on hiking and biking routes. Nearby barracks have been converted into an AYH **hostel** (415/331-2777), and on certain Sundays you can tour an intact but no longer functioning Nike missile silo.

For a memorable first or last look at San Francisco, from Pacifica follow the signs to **Sweeney Ridge,** the grass and wildflower-covered coastal summit from which, on November 4, 1769, the Portola expedition first laid European eyes on the great bay.

the opening of the Golden Gate Bridge

Across San Francisco

From the north, Hwy-1 enters San Francisco across the Golden Gate Bridge, where parking areas at both ends let you ditch the car and walk across the elegant mile-long span. Continuing south, Hwy-1 follows 19th Avenue across Golden Gate Park, reaching the coast again at the town of Pacifica.

San Francisco is covered in a Survival Guide on pages 718-719.

The San Mateo Coast

From the San Francisco city limits, Hwy-1 runs along the Pacific Ocean through the rural and almost totally undeveloped coastline of San Mateo County. The first eight miles or so are high-speed freeway, but after passing through the suburban communities of Daly City and Pacifica, the pace abruptly slows to a scenic cruise. The highway hugs the decomposing clifftops for the next few miles before reaching **Montara**, where the old but still functioning lighthouse has been partly converted into an AYH **youth hostel** (415/728-7177).

The first sizeable coastal town is **Half Moon Bay**, 25 miles south of San Francisco, but seemingly much more distant. A quiet farming community that's slowly but surely changing into a Silicon Valley suburb, Half Moon Bay still has an all-American Main Street, a block east of the Hwy-1 bypass, lined by hardware stores, cafes, bakeries, and the inevitable art galleries and B&Bs housed in 100-year-old farmhouses—like **Zaballa House**, at the north end of town at 324 Main Street (415/726-9123), which has comfortable, $75-a-night

Looking for the world's biggest waves? Head down to **Maverick's,** an offshore reef area a half-mile off Pillar Point, three miles north of Half Moon Bay. In winter, when conditions are right, 35-foot mega-waves draw expert surfers from all over the world. For a report, call Maverick's Surf Shop, 530 Main Street in Half Moon Bay (415/726-0469).

B&B rooms in the town's oldest building. The main event here is the annual **Pumpkin Festival,** held mid-October, which celebrates the coming of Halloween with a competition to determine the world's largest pumpkin—winning gourds weigh as much as a half-ton!

For further information, call the Half Moon Bay visitor center (415/726-5202).

Pescadero and Pigeon Point Lighthouse

The 50 miles of coastline between Half Moon Bay and Santa Cruz are one of the great surprises of the California coast: the virtually unspoiled miles offer rocky tidepools and driftwood-strewn beaches beneath sculpted bluffs topped by rolling green fields of Brussels sprouts, pumpkins, cabbages, and artichokes. The biggest town hereabouts, Pescadero (pop. 500), is a mile or so inland from Hwy-1, well worth the short detour for a chance to sample the fresh fish, great pies, and other home-cooked treats at **Duarte's Tavern,** 202 Stage Road, open daily for breakfast, lunch, and dinner at the center of the block-long downtown.

Pigeon Point Light Station

Ten miles south of Pescadero, the photogenic beacon of Pigeon Point Lighthouse has appeared in innumerable TV and print commercials; the graceful, 150-foot-tall brick tower is open for **tours** (Sunday 10 AM-3 PM; $2 donation), and the adjacent lighthouse quarters function as an AYH **hostel** (415/879-0633), with a hot tub perched above the crashing surf.

Año Nuevo State Reserve

Though the San Mateo coastline is quite beautiful, the waters are very cold—and home to a hungry population of **great white sharks,** which have been known to attack surfers as well as seals.

One of nature's more bizarre spectacles takes place annually at Año Nuevo State Reserve (8 AM-dusk daily; $5 per car), where each winter hundreds of humongous northern elephant seals come ashore to give birth and mate. The males reach up to 20 feet head-to-tail, can weigh as much as three tons, and have dangling proboscises that inspired their name. These blubbery creatures were hunted almost to extinction for their oil-rich flesh. In 1920, fewer than 100 were left in the world; their resurgence to a current population estimated at 80,000 has proved that protection does work.

Every December hordes of male elephant seals arrive at Año Nuevo, the seals' only onshore rookery, after spending the summer at sea, ready to do battle with each other for the right to procreate. It's an incredible show, the bulls bellowing, barking, and biting at each other to establish dominance; the "alpha male" mates with most of the females, and the rest must wait till next year. Pups conceived the previous year are born in January, and mating goes on through March. During the mating season, ranger-led **tours** ($4; 800/444-7275) are the only way to see the seals; these tours are very popular, so plan ahead and try to come midweek.

Big Basin Redwoods State Park

The oldest and largest of the California state parks, Big Basin Redwoods State Park protects some 16,000 acres of giant coastal redwoods. Established in 1902, the park has many miles of hiking and cycling trails, high up in the mountains. The heart of the park is most easily accessible from Santa Cruz, but a popular trail winds up from the coast to the crest, starting from Hwy-1 at Waddell Creek Beach, a popular haunt for sailboarders, who sometimes do flips and loops in the wind-whipped waves.

northern elephant seals

Midway between Año Nuevo and Santa Cruz, the **Davenport Cash Store,** on the east side of Hwy-1 in the village of Davenport, serves hearty breakfasts and lunches. Tiny Davenport is also the headquarters of the Odwalla fresh fruit juice company.

Santa Cruz

The popular beach resort and college town of Santa Cruz (pop. 51,500) sits at the north end of Monterey Bay, an hour's drive from San Francisco, at the foot of a 3,000-foot-high ridge of mountains. Best known for its Boardwalk amusement park, which holds the only surviving wooden roller coaster on the West Coast, and for the large University of California campus in the redwoods above, Santa Cruz takes its name from the ill-fated mission settlement begun here in 1777 but wiped out by an earthquake and tidal wave in 1840. Modern Santa Cruz was all but levelled by another earthquake in 1989, but has since recovered its stature as one of the most diverting stops on the California coast.

Natural Bridges State Park, two miles north of Santa Cruz via West Cliff Drive, has a natural wave-carved archway and, in winter, swarms of monarch butterflies.

The downtown area lies a mile inland, so from Hwy-1 follow the many signs pointing visitors toward the wharf and the beach, where plentiful parking is available. Walk, rent a bike, or drive along the coastal Cliff Drive to the world's first

the roller coaster at Santa Cruz

Surfing Museum (Wed.-Mon. noon-4 PM; donations), which is packed with giant old redwood boards and newer high-tech cutters, as well as odds and ends tracing the development of West Coast surfing. Housed in an old lighthouse, it overlooks one of the state's prime surfing spots, Steamer Lane, named for the steamships that once brought day-tripping San Franciscans to the wharf.

Santa Cruz Boardwalk

The bayfront Santa Cruz Boardwalk should really be your main stop; besides the dozens of thrill rides and midway games, it boasts the art deco Cocoanut Grove ballroom, where throughout the summer swing bands still play the sounds of the 1930s and 1940s, and two rides that are such classics of the genre they've been listed as National Historic Landmarks. The biggest thrill is the **Giant Dipper** roller coaster, a senior citizen compared to modern rides but still one of the Top 10 coasters in the country—the clattering, mile-long tracks make it seem far faster than the 40 mph maximum it reaches. Near the roller coaster is the beautiful Charles Looff **carousel**, one of only six left in the country, with 70 handcarved wooden horses doing the same circuit they've followed since 1911; grab for the brass rings while listening to music pumped out by the 342-pipe organ, imported from Germany and over 100 years old.

Santa Cruz has just about fully recovered from the 1989 Loma Prieta earthquake, which had its epicenter in the hills southeast of the city.

Along with these and many other vintage arcade attractions, the amusement park also features a log flume ride, a sky ride, a two-story miniature golf course installed inside the old bathhouse, plus a bowling alley and all the shooting galleries, laser tag, and virtual reality machines you could want. The Boardwalk, which has been paved but retains a great deal of charm and character, is open daily in summer, and weekends only during the rest of the year. Admission is free and individual rides vary in cost, with the Giant Dipper costing $3 a trip and all-day passes priced about $15. For more information, call 408/423-5590.

Santa Cruz Practicalities

A large part of the Santa Cruz economy depends upon visitors, and there are plenty of cafes, restaurants, and accommodations options to choose from. Eating and drinking places congregate west of Hwy-1 along Front Street and Pacific Avenue in downtown Santa Cruz, which has a number of engaging, somewhat countercultural book and record shops along with cafes like **Zoccoli's**, 1334 Pacific Avenue, which has great soups and sandwiches. Another place to consider is the **Santa Cruz Brewing Company**, an above-average brew-pub at 516 Front Street near the San Lorenzo River, which flows along the south edge of downtown. Vegetarians will enjoy the lively **Saturn Cafe**, open all day at 1230 Mission Street, along Hwy-1 on the north side of town.

Motels line US-1, and cheaper ones congregate around the waterfront area, with rates ranging $30-100 a night depending upon location and time of year; the one with the best sign, the Pacific View Court, stands atop Beach Hill, between the Boardwalk and downtown. Another characterful old place is the **Capitola Venetian Hotel** (408/476-6471), a 1920s mission-style complex on the beach at 1200 Wharf Road in Capitola, east of Santa Cruz along the ocean. Among the many nice B&Bs is the rustic **Babbling Brook**, 1025 Laurel Street (408/427-2437 or 800/866-1131).

For more complete listings or other information, contact the **Santa Cruz Visitors Council**, 701 Front Street (408/425-1234 or 800/833-3494).

The Mystery Spot

In the hills above Santa Cruz, east of Hwy-1 at 1953 Branciforte Drive, the Mystery Spot (daily 9:30 AM-5 PM; $4) is one of those fortunate few tourist traps that actually gets people to come back again. Like similar places along the Pacific coast, the Mystery Spot is a section of redwood forest where the usual laws of physics seem not to apply (trees grow in oddly contorted corkscrew shapes, and balls roll uphill). Among those who study vortexes and other odd geomantic places, the Mystery Spot is considered to be the real thing, but you don't have to take it seriously to enjoy yourself.

Watsonville, Castroville, and Moss Landing

Between Santa Cruz and Monterey, Hwy-1 loops inland through the farmlands fronting Monterey Bay. Part freeway, part winding two-lane, Hwy-1 races through, and to be honest there's not a lot worth stopping for: the beaches can be dreary, and the two main towns, Watsonville and Castroville, are little more than service centers for the local fruit and vegetable packers. Watsonville is still reeling from the 1989 earthquake, which destroyed half of the downtown area, though Castroville—where in 1947, then-unknown **Marilyn Monroe** reigned as "Miss Artichoke" during Castroville's Artichoke Festival, still celebrated each September—does have one odd sight: the "World's Largest Artichoke," a concrete statue outside a very large fruit stand at the center of town.

Back on the coast, midway along Monterey Bay, the port community of Moss Landing is a busy commercial fishery, with lots of trawlers and packing plants—not to mention pelicans aplenty. Moss Landing is also home to the research arm of the Monterey Bay Aquarium, to an obtrusively huge electicity generating plant, and to a handful of oyster bars and restaurants like **The Whole Enchilada** (right on Hwy-1 just south of the power plant), which has spicy seafood and a popular Sunday jazz brunch.

Much of the bayfront north of Monterey formerly belonged to the U.S. Marine Corps base at Fort Ord. Almost the entire parcel was turned over to the state of California to house the **California State University at Monterey Bay**, which opened its doors in 1995.

Detour: San Juan Bautista

Away from the coast, 15 miles inland from Monterey Bay via Hwy-129 or Hwy-156, stands one of California's most idyllic small towns, San Juan Bautista. It centers upon a grassy town square bordered by a well-preserved mission complex, complete with a large church and monastery standing since 1812. Two other sides of the square are lined by hotels, stables, and houses dating from the 1840s through 1860s, preserved in their entirety within a state historic park (daily 10 AM-4:30 PM; $2; 408/623-4881).

Completing the living history lesson, the east edge of the square is formed by one of the state's few preserved stretches of El Camino Real, the 200-year-old Spanish colonial trail that linked all the California missions with Mexico. Adding to the interest, the trail runs right along the rift zone of the San Andreas Fault, and a small seismograph registers tectonic activity. (Incidentally, San Juan Bautista was where the climactic final scenes of Hitchcock's *Vertigo* were filmed—though in the movie, they added a much more prominent bell tower with a seemingly endless staircase.)

The town's Main Street is a block from the mission, and is lined by a handful of antique shops, Mexican restaurants, and cafes like the **Mission Coffee Shop**, 300 3rd Street.

Coastal farms along the Monterey Bay grow nearly 85% of the nation's artichokes, which you can sample along with other produce at stands along Hwy-1.

Along Hwy-1 on the northwest edge of town, the elegant **Hotel Del Monte,** a grand resort that attracted the first wealthy tourists to Monterey beginning in 1880, is now surrounded by the large U.S. Navy Postgraduate School.

The internationally famous Monterey Jazz Festival is held every year at the end of summer. For performers, dates, and other information, phone 408/373-3366.

Monterey

The historic capital of California under the Spanish and Mexican regimes, Monterey (pop. 31,954), along with its peninsular neighbors Carmel and Pacific Grove, is one of the most satisfying stops in California. Dozens of significant historical sites have been well preserved, most of them concentrated within a mile-long walk called the "Path of History" that loops through the compact downtown area. Park in the lots at the foot of Alvarado Street, Monterey's main drag, and start your tour at **Fisherman's Wharf**, where bellowing sea lions wallow in the water, begging for popcorn from tourists. Next stop should be the adjacent **Custom House**, the oldest governmental building in the state, recently restored as the Monterey State Historic Park **visitor center** (10 AM-5 PM; 408/649-2836); here you can pick up maps or join walking tours of old town Monterey.

From the Custom House, which is now surrounded by the modern Doubletree Hotel complex, you can also follow the old railroad right-of-way west to **Cannery Row**, where abandoned fish canneries have been gussied up into upscale bars and restaurants—most of them capitalizing on ersatz Steinbeckian themes. The one real attraction here is the excellent **Monterey Bay Aquarium** (daily 10 AM-6 PM; $11.75; 800/756-3737), 886 Cannery Row, housed in a spacious modern building and loaded with state-of-the-art tanks filled with over 500 species of local sealife. The aquarium is rated by many as the best in the world; displays let visitors touch tidepool denizens, watch playful sea otters, or gaze into the gently swaying stalks of a three-story-tall kelp forest. In the auditorium, a video link to an offshore submarine shows live pictures of truly weird creatures living thousands of feet below the bay.

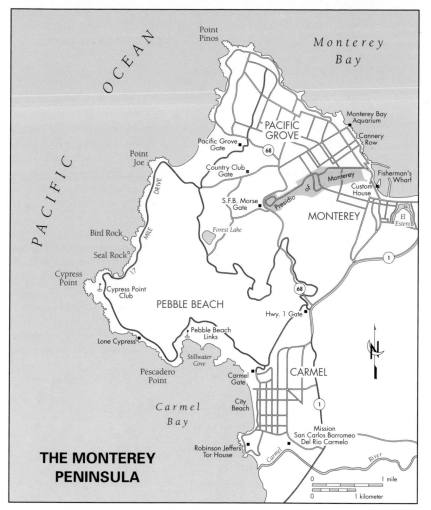

**THE MONTEREY
PENINSULA**

Because Monterey gets a considerable tourist trade, there's no shortage of restaurants, though good food at reasonable prices can be hard to find. One good bet is the **Old Monterey Cafe**, 472 Alvarado Street, serving large portions at breakfast and lunch. For seafood, catch an early-bird special (before 6 PM) at one of the dozen restaurants on the wharf—**Cafe Fina** does good pizzas as well. Top of the scale is flashy **Montrio**, 414 Calle Principal (408/648-8880), which serves San Francisco-style grilled chicken and fish in a converted fire station; reservations are essential, ever since *Esquire* magazine rated it "restaurant of the year" for 1995.

Places to stay vary widely, starting with a slew of budget motels like the **Motel 6** at 2124 Fremont Street (408/646-8585) in Seaside near old Fort Ord, now Cal-State University at Monterey Bay. Other moderate motels line Munras Street along the old highway frontage south toward Carmel, while downtown prices hover in the $120 range. One exception to downtown

One of Monterey's many intriguing historical sites is the whalebone pavement inlaid into the sidewalk in front of California's First Theater, near the waterfront at the foot of Pacific Street.

The writer John Steinbeck lived in and around the Monterey Peninsula for many years, and set many of his stories there. He was born and is buried in Salinas, east of Monterey on US-101. His last great book, *East of Eden,* told the story of his family's life as farmers in the Salinas Valley.

prices is the refurbished and centrally located **Monterey Hotel,** 406 Alvarado (408/375-3184 or 800/727-0960), which offers exceptionally good deals, from $50 a night for two people.

Pacific Grove

Perched at the tip of the Monterey Peninsula, Pacific Grove (pop. 16,117) is a quiet throwback to old-time tourism, dating from the late 1880s when the area was used for summertime Methodist revival meetings. The revivalists' tents and camps later grew into the West Coast headquarters of the populist chautauqua educational movement. The town still has a curiously Midwestern feel, from its many small churches to the rows of well-maintained Victorian cottages lining its quiet streets. Besides the many fine old buildings, the best reason to come here is the beautiful, fully accessible shoreline, which boasts some of the coast's best tidepools, sunset views, and endless opportunities for winter whalewatching.

Pacific Grove's main street, Lighthouse Avenue, runs through the 15-mph commercial district of galleries, movie theaters, and cafes—**Toastie's** is a comfy breakfast and lunch place at 702 Lighthouse Avenue. Nearby **Pepper's,** 170 Forest Avenue, serves very good, fresh Mexican food, while a range of fairly priced fish dishes are on the menu at **The Fishwife,** on Sunset Drive at the north end of the Seventeen Mile Drive. Places to stay are more reasonably priced than in Monterey or Carmel: the **Bide-a-Wee Motel,** 221 Asilomar Boulevard (408/372-2330), is a reliable, old-fashioned motor court two blocks from the ocean. Rustic **Asilomar Conference Center,** 800 Asilomar Boulevard (408/372-8016), has woodsy, Julia Morgan-designed cabins but is often filled with convention-goers. Of the many pricey B&Bs, the **Pacific Grove Inn,** 581 Pine Street (408/375-2825), offers the best value.

Until 1969, Pacific Grove's Methodist antecedents prevailed, and drinking alcoholic beverages was banned—as was reading Sunday newspapers—within the city limits.

One event that brought Pebble Beach to national attention was the annual golf tournament hosted by **Bing Crosby.** Originally an informal celebrity get-together, it grew into one of the main events of the professional circuit and is now the ATT-Pebble Beach Pro-Am, held each winter.

The Seventeen Mile Drive and Pebble Beach

Spanning the coast between Pacific Grove and Carmel, the Seventeen Mile Drive is one of the most famous toll roads in the nation. Opened in the 1880s, the route initially took guests at Monterey's posh Hotel Del Monte on a scenic carriage ride along the coast through the newly planted Del Monte Forest between Carmel and Pacific Grove. The formerly wild area underwent development beginning in the 1920s, first with golf courses like Pebble Beach and Cypress Point, and later with resort hotels and posh homes.

Enter the drive at any of the gates, where you'll pay the toll ($6.50 at time of writing) and be given a map and guide to the route, pointing out all the scenic highlights, especially the trussed-up old **Lone Cypress,** subject of so many Carmel postcards. It's definitely worth doing, if only to say you have; to be honest, the views from the drive are no more or less splendid than they are from the toll-free drives, like Ocean View Boulevard in Pacific Grove, Scenic Drive in Carmel, or Hwy-1 through Big Sur. You do, however, get to stop at the Lodge, where your toll will be deducted from the price of lunch or dinner. If you're in the mood to splurge on wanton luxury, you can also stay overnight at either of two extremely plush golf and tennis resorts: the modern, suburban-style country club of the **Inn at Spanish Bay**, which is also home to the Ansel Adams photography gallery; or the stately, old-money **Lodge at Pebble Beach**. Both resorts charge upwards of $300 a day.

Carmel

The exclusive enclave of Carmel-by-the-Sea (to give its complete name) began life in the early years of the 20th century as a small but lively bohemian colony inhabited by the literary likes of Sinclair Lewis, Mary Austin, and Upton Sinclair. However, with a few arts-and-craftsy exceptions, by the 1950s Carmel had turned into the archly conservative and contrivedly quaint community it is today—a place where Marie Antoinette would no doubt feel at home, dressing down as a peasant, albeit in Chaps by Ralph Lauren. Preserving its rural feel by banning street addresses (and skateboards, and home mail delivery), Carmel simultaneously loves and abhors the many thousands of tourists who descend on it every weekend to windowshop its many designer boutiques and galleries that fill the few blocks off Ocean Avenue, the main drag through town.

Though it's easy to be put off by the surface glitz, Carmel does have a lot going for it. The water is too cold and treacherous for swimming, but broad **City Beach** at the foot of Ocean Avenue gleams white against a truly azure cove. To the south, aptly named **Scenic Drive** winds along the rocky coast, past Robinson Jeffers's dramatic Tor House and a seafront Frank Lloyd Wright house (the latter now owned by rock star Sammy Hagar) to another broad beach at the usually unpopulated Carmel River State Park, a favorite spot for scuba divers exploring the deep undersea canyon.

Above the beach, just west of Hwy-1 a mile south of central Carmel, **Carmel Mission** (daily 9:30 AM-4:30 PM; donations) was the most important of all the California missions, serving as home, headquarters, and final resting place of Father Junipero Serra, the Franciscan priest who established Carmel and many of the 20 other California missions, and who is entombed under the chapel floor. The gardens—where on weekends wedding parties alight from limos to take family photos—are beautiful, as is the facade with its photogenic bell tower; this is the mission to visit if you visit only one.

Dozens of good and usually expensive restaurants thrive in Carmel, but one place to see, even if you don't eat there, is the tiny, mock-Tudoresque **Tuck Box Tea Room** on Dolores Street near 7th Avenue. Rebuilt after

Pacific Grove is the best known of about 20 places in California where millions of monarch butterflies spend the winter months. From October until March, the butterflies congregate on the "Butterfly Trees," a grove of pines on Ridge Road off Lighthouse Avenue, well posted from downtown.

In the hills above the Seventeen Mile Drive, the truly exclusive resort community of **Pebble Beach** includes some of the coast's most palatial homes; local realtors rarely advertise anything under a million dollars.

Lone Cypress

a recent fire but still dolls'-house cute, it servs up bacon-and-eggs breakfasts and dainty plates of shepherd's pie and Welsh rarebit for lunch; closed Monday and Tuesday. At the other end of the aesthetic spectrum is the **Hog's Breath Inn**, on San Carlos between 5th and 6th Avenues, owned by Clint Eastwood and specializing in "Dirty Harry" burgers and "Sudden Impact" sausages served to patrons seated on an outdoor patio. If you'd rather join locals than mingle with your fellow tourists, head to **Katy's Place**, on Mission Street between 5th and 6th, serving some of the world's best eggs Benedict.

Carmel boasts a single budget motel, the very pleasant **Carmel River Inn** (408/624-1575 or 800/882-8142) just west of Hwy-1 near the Carmel Mission. However, if you want to splurge on a bit of luxury, Carmel is a good place to do it. Besides the golf course resorts of nearby Pebble Beach, Carmel also has the commodious, 1920s-era, mission-style **Cypress Inn** at Lincoln and 7th (408/624-3871 or 800/443-7443), partly owned by dog-loving Doris Day (and featuring posters of her movies in the small bar off the lobby), with rooms from under $100. A relaxing spot away from downtown is the **Carmel Mission Ranch**, 26270 Dolores Street (408/624-6436 or 800/538-8221), within walking distance of the beach and mission and offering resort-level facilities at room rates that run $85-250 a night.

Point Lobos State Reserve

The sculpted headland south of Carmel Bay, now protected as Point Lobos State Reserve (daily 9 AM-5 PM, till 6:30 PM in summer; $6 per car), holds one of the few remaining groves of native Monterey cypress, gnarled and bent by the often stormy coastal weather. The name comes from the barking sea lions (*lobos del mar*) found here by early Spanish explorers; sea lions, otters, and—in winter—whales are often seen offshore or in the many picturesque coves.

The entrance to the reserve is along Hwy-1, three miles south of Carmel Mission, but in summer the park is so popular that visitors sometimes have to wait in line outside the gates. If possible, plan to come early or during the week.

Andrew Molera State Park

Spreading along the coast at the mouth of the Big Sur River, 21 miles south of Carmel, Andrew Molera State Park is a grassy former cattle ranch on the site of one of Big Sur's oldest homesteads. In the 1850s, immigrant John "Juan Bautista" Roger Cooper bought the land and built a cabin, which still stands along Hwy-1 near the park entrance. Well-blazed trails wind

---

Though most of Carmel's many art galleries seem directed at interior decorators, a few are worth searching out, including the **Photography West Gallery** on the southeast corner of Dolores and Ocean Streets, and the **Weston Gallery** on Sixth Avenue near Dolores Street, featuring the works of Edward Weston, Ansel Adams, and other Carmel-based photographers.

Carmel's leading light, **Clint Eastwood,** is ever-present: besides serving as mayor for many years, he owns the Hog's Breath Inn restaurant and the Mission Ranch resort. As a filmmaker, he used Carmel as the location for one of his most disturbing movies, the psychopathic 1970s film *Play Misty for Me.*

The photogenic **Bixby Creek Bridge,** 15 miles south of Carmel, was the largest concrete bridge in the world when built in 1932. The old coast road runs along the north bank of the creek, linking up with Hwy-1 at Andrew Molera State Park.

BIG SUR

Big Sur, the 90 miles of coastline south of Carmel from Point Sur Lighthouse all the way to Hearst Castle, is one of the most memorable stretches of coastline on the planet, with 5,000-foot-tall mountains rising straight up from the Pacific Ocean. Early Spanish missionaries dubbed it *El País Grande del Sur*, the "Big Country" to the south of Carmel, and the rugged land has resisted development or even much of a population—the current total of around 1,500 is roughly the same as it was in 1900, and for the 3,000 years before that.

Highway 1, the breathtaking drive through Big Sur, was finally cut across the very steep cliffs in 1937, requiring 20 years of convict labor and several fatalities. Named the state's first scenic route, so dedicated by Lady Bird Johnson in 1966, it's an incredible trip. Like the Grand Canyon and other larger-than-life natural wonders, Big Sur boggles the mind and, in an odd way, can be hard to handle; you have to content yourself with staring in awestruck appreciation, taking pictures, or maybe toasting the natural handiwork with a cold beer or glass of wine at one of the few but unforgettable cafes and restaurants along the way.

However beautiful the drive along Hwy-1, it's also narrow, twisting, packed with sluggish RVers on holiday weekends, and often closed by mudslides after torrential winter storms. (In 1983, the biggest storm in recent memory blocked the road for over a year.) There are also very few services, and most of the overnight accommodations are booked solidly during the peak summer season. Spring brings wildflowers, while fall gets the most reliably good weather. No matter when you come, even if you just drive through in an afternoon, be sure to stop whenever possible and get out of the car; scenic viewpoints line the roadside, and dozens of trails lead off into the wilds.

along both banks of the river down to the small beach, horses are available for hire, and there are quite a few nice places to camp (walk-in only, $3 per person).

The northern extent of Big Sur is marked by the volcanic hump of **Point Sur,** 19 miles south of Carmel, a symmetrical dome capped by a 100-year-old lighthouse.

Big Sur Village
South of Andrew Molera, Hwy-1 cuts inland toward the heart of Big Sur, the deep and densely forested valley carved by the Big Sur River. Consisting of little more than three gas stations, a couple of roadside markets, and a number of lodges and restaurants, the mile-long village of Big Sur (pop. 950) represents the only real settlement between Carmel and Hearst Castle.

At the north end of "town," the **Big Sur River Inn** (408/625-5255 or 800/548-3610) has moderately priced, rustic rooms in the lodge and in the motel across the highway; it's also a woodsy, warm, and unpretentious restaurant overlooking the river. Next door, on the river side of the highway, is a small complex that includes crafts galleries, a grocery store, and the homey **Big Sur Village Pub**, which features good beers, pizzas, and pub grub. Continuing south, the next mile of Hwy-1 holds Big Sur's three main family-oriented resorts, all offering rustic cabins and camp-

The best basic guide to Big Sur is an annual free newspaper, *El Sur Grande,* published by Monterey County and available at ranger stations and many other locations in and around Big Sur.

grounds along the river: **Riverside** (408/667-2414); **Ripplewood** (408/667-2242); and **Fernwood** (408/667-2422).

Pfeiffer–Big Sur State Park

Roughly a half-mile south of Big Sur village, Pfeiffer–Big Sur State Park is the region's main event, an 810-acre riverside forest that's one of the most pleasant (and popular) parks in the state. Besides offering a full range of visitor services—restaurant, lodge, campground, and grocery store (for details call 800/4BIG-SUR)—the park includes one of the Big Sur's best short hikes, a two-mile loop on the Valley View trail that takes in stately redwoods as well as oak and madrone groves, a 40-foot waterfall, and a grand vista down the Big Sur valley to the coast.

The park is also the main **ranger station** (408/667-2315) for the state parks in the Big Sur area. Just south of the park entrance, a U.S. Forest Service **ranger station** (408/667-2423) on the east side of Hwy-1 has information on hiking and camping opportunities in the mountains above Big Sur, including the Ventana Wilderness.

Pfeiffer Beach

South of Pfeiffer-Big Sur park, halfway up a long, steep incline, a small road turns west and leads down through dark and heavily overgrown Sycamore Canyon, eventually winding up at Big Sur's best beach, Pfeiffer Beach. From the lot at the end of the road, a short trail runs through a grove of trees before opening onto the broad white sands, loomed over by a pair of hulking offshore rocks. The water's way too cold for swimming, but the half-mile strand is one of the few places in Big Sur where you can enjoy extended beachcombing strolls. The beach's northern half attracts a clothing-optional crew, even on cool gray days.

The landmark red **farmhouse** along Hwy-1 at the entrance to Ventana was built in 1877 by pioneer rancher W.B. Post, whose descendants developed the Post Ranch Inn.

Ventana and the Post Ranch Inn

South of Sycamore Canyon, roughly three miles from the heart of Big Sur village, Hwy-1 passes between two of California's most deluxe small resorts. The larger of the two, Ventana (408/667-2331 or 800/628-6500), covers 1,000 acres of Big Sur foothill and offers saunas, swimming pools, and four-star accommodations in 1970s-style cedar-paneled rooms and cabins. Rates range $200-800 a night, and there's also a very fine restaurant with incredible views and reasonable prices, to which guests are ferried in a fleet of golf carts.

Completed in 1992 and directly across Hwy-1 from Ventana, the Post Ranch Inn (408/667-2200 or 800/527-2200) is at the forefront of eco-tourism, a low-impact but ultra-high-style luxury resort hanging high above the Big Sur coast. In order to preserve Big Sur's untarnished natural beauty, the Post Ranch Inn is designed to be virtually invisible from land or sea: the 24 accommodations—all featuring a king-sized bedroom and a jacuzzi bath with built-in massage table—blend in with the landscape, disguised either as playful treehouses raised up in the branches of the oaks and pines, or as underground cabins carved into the clifftop. Rates start at $300 a night, but if you want to have a look and plan for a future escape, tours of the resort are given Mon.-Fri. at 2 PM.

Nepenthe

One of the most popular and long-lived stopping points along the Big Sur coast, Nepenthe is a rustic bar and restaurant offering good food and great views from atop a rocky headland, a thousand feet above the Pacific. Named for the mythical drug that causes one to forget all sorrows, Nepenthe looks like something out of 1960s James Bond movie, built of huge boulders and walls of plate glass. The menu too is somewhat dated; burgers, steaks, and fried fish predominate.

*The hilltop where Nepenthe now stands was previously the site of a rustic cabin that **Orson Welles** bought for his wife **Rita Hayworth** in 1944.*

Sharing a parking lot, and taking advantage of similar views, the neighboring **Cafe Kevah** serves a veggie-friendly range of soups, salads, and quesadillas, plus good teas and coffees and microbrewed beers on a rooftop deck; you'll find a gift shop downstairs selling top-quality arts and crafts and knitwear by Kaffe Fassett, who grew up here and whose family owns the place.

Right along Hwy-1, at a sharp bend in the road just south of Nepenthe, the **Henry Miller Memorial Library** (irregular hours, usually daily 11 AM-5 PM in summer; 408/667-2574) carries an erratic but engaging collection of books by and about the author, who lived in Big Sur for many years in the 1950s.

A half-mile south of Nepenthe on the east side of the highway, one of the oldest and most atmospheric places to stay is **Deetjen's Big Sur Inn** (408/667-2377), a rambling and rustic redwood lodge built by a Norwegian immigrant in the 1930s and now offering comfortable rooms for $60-100 a night. Deetjen's also serves Big Sur's best breakfasts (8 AM-11 AM) and hearty dinners.

Julia Pfeiffer Burns State Park

If for some untenable reason you only have time to stop at one place along the Big Sur coast, Julia Pfeiffer Burns State Park (dawn-dusk daily) is as good a place as any. Spreading along both sides of Hwy-1, about 14 miles south of Big Sur village, the park includes one truly beautiful sight, a slender waterfall that drops crisply down into a nearly circular turquoise-blue cove. From the parking area east of the highway, a short trail leads under the road to an overlook, while other routes climb through redwood groves up to the chaparral-covered slopes of the Santa Lucia Mountains.

*Three miles south of Julia Pfeiffer Burns State Park, the new age **Esalen Institute** offers a variety of "Human Potential" workshops; they also have an incredible set of natural hot springs, right above the ocean and open to the public midnight-5 AM. For information or reservations, phone 408/667-3000.*

Lucia, Pacific Valley, and Gorda

The southern reaches of the Big Sur coast are drier and more rugged, offering bigger vistas but fewer stopping places than the northern half. The road winds along the cliffs, slowing down every 10 miles or so for each of three gas station/cafe/motel complexes, which pass for towns on the otherwise uninhabited coast. The first of these, 25 miles south of Big Sur village, is Lucia, which has a very good restaurant and lantern-lit cabins. High on a hill just south of Lucia, marked by a slender black cross, is the Benedictine **New Camaldoli Hermitage**, open to interested outsiders as a silent retreat. For details, phone 408/667-2456.

Continuing south, Hwy-1 runs through Pacific Valley, the hills above which are a popular hang-gliding spot, then passes by a number of small but pretty beaches and coves before reaching Gorda, the southernmost stop on the Big Sur coast. Beyond here, a series of small state parks lines the highway, but the next services are 25 miles farther south in San Simeon, at the entrance to Hearst Castle.

From Hwy-1 at Kirk Creek, five miles south of Lucia, the narrow **Nacimiento Road** makes an unforgettable climb over the coastal mountains past Mission San Antonio de Padua to the Salinas Valley, linking up with US-101 at King City.

In order to help prevent erosion and mudslides, the roadside along Hwy-1 in the southern half of Big Sur has been planted with odd-looking bunches of pampas grass, which help keep the hills from washing away.

San Simeon: Hearst Castle

At the south end of Big Sur, the mountains flatten out and turn inland, and the coastline becomes rolling, open range ranchland. High on a hill above Hwy-1 stands the coast's one totally unique attraction, Hearst Castle. Located 65 miles south of Big Sur village and 43 miles northwest of San Luis Obispo, Hearst Castle is the sort of place that you really have to see to believe, though simple numbers—144 rooms, including 36 bedrooms—do give a sense of its scale.

Even if Hearst's taste in interior design (or his megalomania, which by all accounts was understated by his fictional portrayal in Orson Welles's *Citizen Kane*) doesn't appeal, Hearst Castle cries out to be seen, if only as a revealing landmark to one of this century's most powerful and influential Americans. Hearst inherited the land, and most of his fortune, from his father George Hearst, a mining mogul, and began work on his castle following the death of his mother in 1919. With the help of the great California architect Julia Morgan, who designed the complex to look like a Mediterranean hill town with Hearst's house as the cathedral at its center, Hearst spent 25 years working on

William Randolph Hearst

his "castle," building, rebuilding, and filling room after room with furniture, all the while entertaining the great and powerful of the era, from Charlie Chaplin to Winston Churchill.

A small **museum** (daily 9 AM-5 PM; free) in the visitor center, next to where you board the trams that carry you up to the house, details Hearst's life and times. If you want to go on a **tour**, the Introductory Tour gives the best first-time overview, taking in the main house and the two swimming pools. Other tours specialize in different aspects of the house and gardens; each one costs $14 and takes around two hours. Advance reservations (800/444-7275) are all but essential, especially in summer.

Hearst Castle

Cambria

Without Hearst Castle, Cambria would be just another farming town, but being next to the state's number-two tourist attraction (after Disneyland) has turned Cambria into quite a busy little hive. Apart from a few hokey, tourist-trapping souvenir shops at the north end of town, it's a casual, walkable, and franchise-free community of arts and crafts galleries, boutiques, and good restaurants; from Hwy-1, Main Street makes a three-mile loop around to the east, running through the heart of town.

Hearty breakfasts are available at the **Redwood Cafe**, 2094 Main Street. Well-prepared multiethnic and vegetarian food is on the menu at **Robin's**, a half-block off Main Street at 4095 Burton Drive. Places to stay range from standard motels like the **Bluebird Motel**, 1880 Main Street (805/927-4634), to the rustic **Cambria Pines Lodge** (805/927-4200), on a hill above Hwy-1 at 2905 Burton Drive.

Morro Bay

Marked by the Gibraltar-like monolith of Morro Rock, which was noted by Juan Cabrillo in 1542 and now serves as a peregrine falcon preserve and nesting site, the busy commercial fishing harbor of Morro Bay (pop. 9,950) is lined by seafood restaurants like **The Galley**, 899 Embarcadero, a half-mile west of Hwy-1. A thin, six-mile-long strip of sand protects the bay from the Pacific Ocean, forming a seabird-rich lagoon that's included within Morro Bay State Park, a mile southeast of the harbor. Here you can rent **kayaks** ($6 an hour) from the stand next to the **Bayside Cafe** and cruise the estuary.

The rest of Morro Bay is pretty quiet; one unusual sight is the giant **outdoor chessboard** on the waterfront in City Park, along the Embarcadero at the foot of Morro Bay Boulevard. For details, or to reserve the waist-high playing pieces, call 805/772-6278.

San Luis Obispo

Located midway between San Francisco and Los Angeles at the junction of Hwy-1 and US-101, San Luis Obispo (pop. 43,000) makes a good stopping-off point, at least for lunch if not for a lengthier stay. Like most of the towns along this route, San Luis, as it's almost always called, revolves around an 18th-century mission, here named Mission **San Luis Obispo de Tolosa**, which is said to be the place where Franciscan missionaries first developed California's traditional red-tiled roofs. Standing at the heart of town, at Chorro and Monterey Streets, the mission overlooks one of the state's liveliest downtown districts, with dozens of shops and restaurants backing onto Mission Plaza, a two-block park on the banks of Mission Creek.

Besides the mission and the lively downtown commercial district that surrounds it, San Luis holds a singular roadside attraction, the **Madonna Inn**, which stands

For the musical accompaniment to driving along the Cambria coast, tune to "The Otter," **KOTR 94.9 FM,** which plays B-sides and album cuts from Van Morrison, Bonnie Raitt, and the like.

The **James Dean** memorial, 27 miles east of Paso Robles near the junction of Highways 46 and 41, is the site where the talented and rebellious actor crashed his silver Porsche and died on Sept. 30, 1955.

Five miles south of Cambria, **Harmony** (pop. 18) is a former dairy town turned arts-and-crafts colony, with a range of galleries and a small wedding chapel. The region's other flyspeck town, Cayucos, sits along the coast 10 miles further south.

Every Thursday evening, the main drag of San Luis Obispo, **Higuera Street,** is closed to cars and converted into a very lively farmer's market and block party—with stands selling fresh food and good live bands providing entertainment.

just west of US-101 at the foot of town. One of California's most noteworthy pop culture landmarks, the Madonna Inn is a remarkable example of what architecturally minded academic types like to call vernacular kitsch, decorated in a wild barrage of fantasy motifs: the bright pink honeymoon suites, known as "Just Heaven" and "Love Nest"; the "Safari Room" covered in fake zebra skins with a jungle-green shag carpet; the cavelike "Cave Man Room"; or over 100 others, of which no two are alike. *Roadside America* rated the Madonna Inn as "the best place to spend a vacation night in America," but if you can't stay the night, at least stop for a look at the gift shop, which sells postcards of the different rooms. Guys should head down to the men's room, where the urinal trough is flushed by a waterfall. Room rates run $80-150 a night; for reservations or more information, call 805/543-3000 or 800/543-9666.

Madonna Inn

Though the Madonna Inn has a huge, banquet-ready restaurant—done up in white lace and varying hues of pink—the best places to eat are located downtown, near the mission. For healthy food in a friendly, sunny space, try the **Rhythm Cafe** overlooking Mission Creek at 1040 Broad Street. For an outstanding Italian meal, head to **Buona Tavola**, 1037 Monterey Street. **Linnaea's Cafe**, 1110 Garden Street off Higuera, serves coffee and tea and sundry snack items all day and night; there's also the lively, multi-culti **Big Sky Cafe**, 1121 Broad Street, and the usual range of beer-and-burger bars you'd expect from a college town.

A pedestrian walkway in downtown San Luis Obispo, off Higuera Street between Garden and Broad Streets, has become known around the world as **Bubble Gum Alley**. Since the 1950s, local kids have written their names and allegiances on the brick walls, using chewing gum rather than the more contemporary spray paint.

Another San Luis landmark, the **world's first motel,** opened at 2223 Monterey Street in 1925. Originally called the Milestone Motel, the Spanish revival structure was later renamed the Motel Inn but went out of business long ago and now stands, forlorn but not forgotten, next to US-101 on the grounds of the Apple Farm restaurant and motel.

At the south end of Pismo Beach, **Nipomo Dunes State Preserve** holds endless acres of sand dunes and marshlands, as well as the buried remains of a movie set used in C.B. DeMille's *The Ten Commandments*.

Along with the Madonna Inn, San Luis has a number of good places to stay, with reasonable rates that drop considerably after the summertime peak season. Besides the national chains—**Embassy Suites**, **Howard Johnson's**, **Super 8**, two **Travelodges** and three **Best Westerns**—try the **Adobe Inn**, 1473 Monterey Street (805/549-0321), or **La Cuesta Motor Inn**, 2074 Monterey Street (805/543-2777 or 800/543-2777). For more information, contact the San Luis Obispo Chamber of Commerce (805/543-1323), or pick up a copy of the free weekly *New Times*.

Pismo Beach

South of San Luis Obispo, Hwy-1 and US-101 run along the ocean past Pismo Beach (pop. 7,800), a family-oriented beach resort where the main attraction is driving or dune-buggying along the sands. Pismo was once famous for its clams, now overharvested to the point of oblivion, but you may still see people pitchforking a few small ones out of the surf. The area has grown significantly in the past decade, thanks mainly to an influx of retired people housed in red-roofed townhouses, but Price Street, the old road frontage, offers a wide range of motels and fast-food restaurants—nothing very special, but handy.

Santa Maria and Guadalupe

South of Pismo Beach, the highways diverge. Hwy-1 cuts off west through the still agricultural areas around sleepy Guadalupe (pop. 5,479), where produce stands sell cabbages, broccoli, and leafy green vegetables fresh from the fields. The town itself feels miles away from modern California, with a four-block Main Street lined by Mexican cafes, bars, banks, and grocery stores.

Shopping malls and tract-house suburbs fill the inland valleys along US-101 through Santa Maria, a town best known for its thick cuts of barbecued beef, best sampled at the large and historic **Santa Maria Inn**, a half-mile west of US-101 at 801 S. Broadway.

Lompoc and La Purisima Mission State Historic Park

The rolling valleys around Lompoc produce most of America's commercial flower seeds, and consequently the fields along Hwy-1 blaze in brilliant colors throughout the summer months. Apart from colorful murals adorning downtown buildings, Lompoc is not up to much, despite the unusual nature of the area's two main nonagricultural employers: a minimum-security federal prison and the Vandenburg Air Force Base, site of numerous missile tests and the aborted West Coast space shuttle port.

With its long arcade reaching across the floor of a shallow, grassy valley, Mission La Purisima (daily 10 AM-5 PM; $5 per car) gives a strong first impression of what the missions may have looked like in their prime. Four miles northeast of Lompoc, between Hwy-1 and US-101 on Hwy-246, the mission here was originally built in 1812 but fell to ruin before being totally reconstructed as part of a WPA make-work scheme in the New Deal 1930s. During the restoration, workers used period techniques wherever possible, hewing logs with hand tools and stomping mud and straw with their bare feet to mix it for adobe bricks. Workers also built most of the mission-style furniture that fills the chapel and the other rooms in the complex. Also here: a functioning aqueduct, many miles of hiking trails, and a small museum.

Solvang

America's most famous mock-European tourist trap, the Danish-style town of Solvang was founded in 1911. Set up by a group of Danish immigrants as a cooperative agricultural community, Solvang found its calling catering to passing travelers,

In the 1930s, Nipomo was where **Dorothea Lange** took that famous photograph of a migrant mother huddling with her children in a farmworkers camp; it's also home to **Jacko's** popular steakhouse and cocktail bar, right off US-101 on Thompson Road, the old highway.

Between San Luis Obispo and Santa Barbara, US-101 turns inland from the coast around Point Conception, the traditional dividing line between central and Southern California. Nearly roadless and generally hard to reach, this untouched stretch of California coast is best seen from Amtrak's **Coast Starlight** train, which runs once daily in each direction (800/USA-RAIL for details). Whales, dolphins, and other wildlife, along with the launching pads of the aborted space shuttle port of Vandenburg Air Force Base, are just a few of the attractions of this lovely coastal cruise. To do it in a day, you have to return by Amtrak bus.

The town of Buellton, a block west of US-101 at the Solvang exit, holds one of California's classic roadside landmarks, **Andersen's Pea Soup Restaurant,** advertised up and down the coast.

EL CAMINO REAL AND THE CALIFORNIA MISSIONS

While the American colonies were busy rebelling against the English Crown, a handful of Spaniards and Mexicans were establishing outposts and blazing an overland route up the California coast, along the New World's most distant frontier. Beginning in 1769 with the founding of a fortress and a Franciscan mission at San Diego, and culminating in 1776 with the founding of another outpost at what is now San Francisco, a series of small but self-reliant religious colonies was established, each a day's travel apart and linked by El Camino Real, "The King's Highway," a route followed roughly by today's US-101.

Many of the colonies grew to become the state's largest cities; others were abandoned and all but disappeared. Some of the missions have been preserved, others restored in varying degrees of authenticity and apocryphal romance, and the route itself is in the process of being declared a national historic trail. Some of the best missions are listed below, north to south, followed by the dates of founding.

San Francisco Solano de Sonoma (1823). The only mission built under Mexican rule stands at the heart of this history-rich Wine Country town.

San Juan Bautista (1797). This lovely church forms the heart of an extensive historic park, in the town of the same name; see page 61.

San Carlos Borromeo (1770). Also known as Carmel Mission, this was the most important of the California missions; see page 65.

San Antonio de Padua (1771). This reconstructed church, still in use as a monastery, stands in an undeveloped valley, inland from Big Sur in the middle of Hunter-Leggett Army base.

San Miguel Arcangel (1797). The only mission not to have undergone extensive renovations and restorations—almost everything, notably the vibrantly colorful interior murals, is as it was.

San Luis Obispo de Tolosa (1772). It's the centerpiece of this small central coast city; see page 71.

La Purisima Concepcion (1787). A quiet coastal valley is home to this restored church; see page 73.

Santa Barbara (1782). Called the "Queen of the Missions," this lovely church stands in lush gardens above the upscale coastal resort city; see page 77.

San Gabriel Arcangel (1771). The most prosperous of the California missions, it now stands along a remnant of Route 66 east of Los Angeles.

CALIFORNIA MISSIONS (1769 - 1823)

San Francisco Solano de Sonoma (1823)

San Rafael (1817)

San Francisco de Asis (1776)

Santa Clara (1777)

San Jose (1797)

Santa Cruz (1791)

San Juan Bautista (1797)

San Carlos Borromeo (1770)

Soledad (1791)

San Antonio de Padua (1771)

San Miguel (1797)

San Luis Obispo de Tolosa (1772)

La Purisima Concepcion (1787)

Santa Ynez (1804)

Santa Barbara (1782)

San Buenaventura (1782)

San Fernando Rey (1797)

San Gabriel Arcangel (1771)

San Juan Capistrano (1776)

San Luis Rey (1798)

San Diego (1769)

UNITED STATES
MEXICO

El Camino Real

PACIFIC OCEAN

0   100 miles

0   100 kilometers

and the compact blocks of cobble-stoned streets and Olde Worlde architecture, highlighted by a few windmills and signs advertising the Hamlet Motel among many more suspicious claims to Danish-ness, now attract tourists by the busload. Many other U.S. towns (Leavenworth, Washington, and Helen, Georgia, to name two) have been inspired by Solvang's success, but to be honest there's nothing much to do here apart from walking, gawking, and shopping for souvenirs.

Just east of Solvang's windmills and gables, the brooding hulk of **Mission Santa Ynez** stands as a sober reminder of the region's Spanish colonial past. Built in 1804, it was once among the more prosperous of the California missions, but now is worth a visit mainly for the gift shop selling all manner of devotional ornaments.

Pop singer Michael Jackson's **Neverland Ranch** lies in the foothills of the Santa Ynez Valley, southeast of Solvang via the truly scenic Hwy-254, which loops inland south to Santa Barbara.

Local sybarites love to soak in the naturally hot waters of **Las Cruces hot spring,** tucked away up a canyon just south of the US-101/Hwy-1 junction.

Gaviota and Refugio State Beaches

Between Solvang and Santa Barbara, US-101 follows the coast past some of California's most beautiful beaches. Dropping through a steep-sided canyon, US-101 reaches the coast at Gaviota State Beach, where a small fishing pier and campground are overwhelmed by the massive train trestle that runs overhead. Continuing south, US-101 runs atop coastal bluffs past prime surfing beaches, usually marked by a few VWs pulled out along the west side of the highway. Midway along this stretch of coast, some 22 miles north of Santa Barbara, Refugio State Beach has groves of palm tress backing a clear white strand. There's

The ranch of former President **Ronald Reagan** spreads along the crest of the coastal hills above Refugio State Beach.

Santa Barbara is one of many great places along the coast to go on a whale-watching cruise, on the *Condor* or other boats. Trips take a half-day or full day, and some head out to the Channel Islands. Call for details or reservations (805/963-3564)

also a small, summer-only store, and a number of attractive campsites with hot showers.

Reservations for camping at Gaviota or Refugio, or at any California state beach, must be made through DestiNet (800/444-7275).

Santa Barbara

The geographical midpoint of California may well be somewhere near San Francisco, but the Southern California of popular imagination—golden beaches washed by waves and peopled by blond-haired surfer gods—has its start, and perhaps best expression, in Santa Barbara. Just over 100 miles north of Los Angeles, Santa Barbara has grown threefold in the last 50 years, but for the moment at least it manages to retain its sleepy seaside charm. Much of its character comes from the fact that, following a sizeable earthquake in 1929, the town fathers—caught up in the contemporary craze for anything Spanish revival—required that all buildings in the downtown area exude a mission-era feel, mandating red-tile roofs, adobe-colored stucco, and rounded arcades wherever practicable. The resulting architectural consistency gives Santa Barbara an un-American charm; it looks more like a Mediterranean village than the modern city that, beneath the surface, it really is.

For a good first look at the city head down to the water, where **Stearns Wharf** sticks out into the bay, bordered by palm tree-lined beaches populated by joggers, roller bladers, and volleyball players. From the wharf area, follow State Street away from the sands to the downtown district, where Santa Barbarans parade among the numerous cafes, bars, and boutiques. At the north end of downtown, the coast's best bookshop, Earthling Books, stands across from the excellent **Museum of Art**

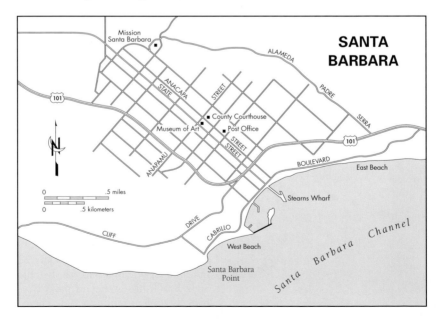

(Tues.-Sat. 11 AM-5 PM, Sunday noon-5 PM; $3), at 1130 State Street. A block east on Anacapa Street, the **County Courthouse** is one of the finest public buildings in the state, a handcrafted Spanish revival monument set in lush semitropical gardens, with an observation tower (daily 9 AM-5 PM; free) giving a fine view over the red-tiled cityscape.

Santa Barbara's reigning attraction, **Mission Santa Barbara** (daily 9 AM-5 PM; $2) stands atop a shallow hill a well-posted mile up from State Street, looking out over the city and shoreline below. Called the "Queen of the Missions" by the local tourist scribes, Mission Santa Barbara is undeniably lovely to look at, its rose-hued stone facade perfectly complemented by the roses and bougainvillea that frame the well-maintained gardens and lawns.

Santa Barbara has perhaps the coast's best variety of places to eat. Early risers can choose between the greasy spoon breakfasts (daily 6 AM-1 PM, Sunday from 7 AM) at **Esau's Coffee Shop**, 403 State Street, a block north of US-101, or the delicate pastries and strong coffees at **Tutti's Bakery**, across from the courthouse at 129 E. Anapamu Street. State Street holds most of the lunch and dinner places, ranging from the old-fashioned burgers and beers on tap in the dark wood dining room of **Joe's Cafe**, 536 State Street, to the healthy salads and sandwiches at the lively **World Cafe**, 1208 State Street near the art museum.

The city's accommodations, however, are among the central coast's most expensive, especially in summer when even the most basic motel can charge as much as $100 a night. Budget travelers have the option of the fairly new, $14-a-night **International Hostel**, 409 State Street (408/963-0154), while the nicest of many motels is the **Franciscan Inn**, 10 Bath Street (408/963-8845). At the top of the scale, the **Simpson House**, 121 E. Arrellaga Street (805/963-7067 or 800/676-1280), offers comfortable, centrally located B&B rooms for upwards of $90 a night. Money's-no-object visitors can enjoy the deluxe facilities of the **San Ysidro Ranch** (408/969-5046), in the hills above neighboring Montecito, where Jackie and JFK spent some of their honeymoon.

For further details on Santa Barbara, stop into the **Visitor Information Center** near Stearns Wharf at 1 Santa Barbara Street (408/966-9222 or 800/676-1266). For current events and nightlife listings, pick up a free copy of the weekly *SB Independent* newspaper at the excellent **Earthling Books**, 1137 State Street, which also operates a late-night cafe.

The Channel Islands National Park
South of Santa Barbara, US-101 widens into an eight-lane freeway along the coast. Looking out beyond the partially disguised offshore oil wells, on a clear day you can't miss the outlines of the Channel Islands, whose rocky shores are protected as a national park. Consisting of eight islands altogether, they sit from 12 to nearly 50 miles off the mainland, but only the smallest and closest, Anacapa Island, is easily accessible to the public; daily charters from Ventura Harbor are offered by **Island Packers** (805/642-1393).

The national budget chain Motel 6 got its start in Santa Barbara, where they now have five properties, including one near the beach at 443 Corona Del Mar (805/564-1392).

Former congressman (and wannabe U.S. senator) **Michael Huffington** lives in the wealthy enclave of Montecito, just south of Santa Barbara.

In the beach resort of **Summerland,** the Nugget Restaurant along the old highway at 2318 Lillie Avenue (805/969-6135) has a saxophone that President Clinton plays whenever he's vacationing here. The next exit to the south takes you to Santa Claus Lane, a seasonal shopping street with a giant-sized statue of St. Nick.

Ventura

Midway between Malibu and Santa Barbara, Ventura (pop. 95,000) is an oddly depressing place, its three-block Main Street lined by a couple of cafes and enough thrift shops (seven at last count) to clothe a destitute army. Apart from searching out vintage couture, about the only reason to stop would be to see the small and much-reconstructed **Mission San Buenaventura** (Mon.-Sat. 10 AM-5 PM, Sunday 10 AM-4 PM; $1), standing at the center of Ventura at 225 E. Main Street, just east of the US-101 freeway. A block from the mission at 113 E. Main Street, the **Albinger Archaeological Museum** (Tues.-Sun. 10 AM-4 PM; free) collects a wide range of artifacts—the oldest from 1500 B.C., the most recent from early American settlers—all excavated from a single site alongside the mission.

South of Ventura, US-101 heads inland through the San Fernando Valley to Hollywood and downtown Los Angeles, while Hwy-1 heads south through the 10 miles of stop-and-go sprawl that make up the farming community of **Oxnard** (pop. 149,457), then continues right along the coast through Malibu and West L.A.

Simi Valley

If you opt to follow US-101 rather than coastal Hwy-1 into Los Angeles, be sure to check out the somnolent suburb of Simi Valley, 20 miles east of Ventura. Home to the jury that acquitted the LAPD officers who beat Rodney King, it's also where the hilltop **Ronald Reagan Presidential Library** (daily 9 AM-5 PM; $4; 805/522-8444) fills 150,000 square feet of Spanish-style stucco; to get there, take US-101 to Hwy-23 North, exit at Olsen Road, and follow the signs.

The other Simi Valley sight to see is Bottle Village, a complex of small buildings built out of glass bottles in the 1940s and 1950s by the late Tressa Prisbey. Now in the process of being preserved as a park, it stands at 4595 Cochrane Street (805/583-1627).

Hwy-1: Malibu

Running right along the beach, the Pacific Coast Highway (Hwy-1) heads south from Oxnard past the rocky headland of Point Mugu, where the U.S. Navy operates a missile testing center and the Santa Monica Mountains drop into the Pacific Ocean. Most of the chaparral-covered granite mountains have been protected as parkland, with hiking, cycling, and riding trails offering grand views and a surprising amount of solitude. A series of state parks, including the lovely **Leo Carrillo State Beach**, mark your progress along the coastal road, but this stretch is basically natural wilderness—apart from the highway, of course.

South of Leo Carrillo, which marks the Los Angeles County line, houses begin popping up to block the oceanfront views. More elaborate multimillion-dollar homes dot the canyons above as well, forming the sprawling exurbia and movie star playground of Malibu, which stretches along Hwy-1 for the next 27 miles into Santa Monica and metropolitan L.A.

It's hard to get more than a glimpse of these palatial estates, but this is the address of choice for the movers and shakers of the entertainment world: if you can name them, they probably own property here. At the foot of the bluffs, below Pepperdine University campus (which was described by the late architect Charles Moore as "an overscaled motel set in obscenely vivid emerald lawns"), the legendary **Malibu Colony** stretches along the coast in high-security splendor. Most of the truly huge estates—Jack Nicholson's, or Barbra Streisand's, for example—are hidden away on square-mile ranches high up in the foothills.

Malibu's Leo Carrillo State Beach was named in memory of the philanthropist and movie star, best known for his role as the sidekick to the Cisco Kid.

The main route inland from the coast, Malibu Canyon Road, was the site of the key murder scene in James M. Cain's thriller The Postman Always Rings Twice.

The one place in Malibu that's fun (and legal) to explore is the area around the landmark **Malibu Pier**, which juts into the ocean at the heart of Malibu's short and rather scruffy commercial strip. North of the pier, which was used most famously in TV's *The Rockford Files,* **Surfrider Beach** stretches into Malibu Lagoon State Park. Located in the park is the historic **Adamson House**, 23200 Pacific Coast Highway (Wed.-Sat. 11 AM-2 PM; $2; 310/456-8432), a lovely old circa 1929 Spanish revival courtyard home, right on the beach and full of gorgeous tilework and other architectural features. Tours are given throughout the day, and fascinating exhibits portray Malibu history and the Rindge family who once owned the entire region.

From the Malibu area, the Pacific Coast Highway (Hwy-1) swoops along the shore, reaching the L.A. area at Santa Monica. Since Hwy-1 follows slow-moving Lincoln Boulevard and other surface streets across L.A., if you are in any sort of hurry take the Santa Monica Freeway (I-10) east to the San Diego Freeway (I-405), and follow that south as far as you're going. Coming from the south, do the opposite—or risk the time-consuming consequences.

Details on Los Angeles are given in the Survival Guide on pages 696-697.
L.A. is also the start of our Route 66 trek, beginning on page 628.

Huntington Beach

Winding south beyond the heavy industrial district that fringes the L.A./Long Beach harbor, Hwy-1 continues along the coast past a series of natural marshlands and small-craft marinas. The first real point of interest is the town of Huntington Beach (pop. 181,519), one of the largest communities in Orange County. Founded in 1909 by Henry Huntington as a stop along his legendary Pacific Electric "Redcar" interurban railway network, Huntington Beach is best known as the place where **surfing** was first introduced to the U.S. mainland. To attract Angelenos down to his new town, Huntington hired Hawaiians to demonstrate the sport, which at the time made use of huge solid wooden boards, 15 feet long and weighing around 150 pounds. Huntington Beach, especially around the pier, is still a very popular surfing spot—though contemporary surfers slice through the waves on high-tech foam-core boards, a third the size of the original Hawaiian longboards and weighing under 10 pounds. The history and culture of West Coast surfing, with examples of boards then and now, is recounted in the small but enthusiastic **International Surfing Museum,** 411 Olive Avenue (daily noon-5 PM) in the heart of the ramshackle beachfront business district.

Nearby, within a few blocks of the pier, is a handful of cafes, plus the handy **Colonial Inn Youth Hostel,** 421 8th Street (714/536-3315), with dorm beds for $13 and double rooms for $30.

Disneyland and the
Richard Nixon Presidential Library

Like a little bit of Middle America grafted onto the southern edge of Los Angeles, inland Orange County is a totally different world. In contrast to to L.A.'s fast-paced, edgily creative multiethnic stew, Orange County is suburban America writ large—mostly white, mostly well-off, and absolutely, totally bland. In short, a perfect place to build the ultimate escapist fantasy, the self-proclaimed "Happiest Place on Earth," Disneyland.

If you haven't been before, or not for a while at any rate, here are some useful tidbits of information: Disneyland is 20 miles south of downtown L.A., right off I-5 in the city of Anaheim—you can see the Matterhorn from the freeway. The park is open daily at least 10 AM-6 PM, including winter weekends; in summer, it remains open until midnight. Admission to the park, which includes all rides, costs $31 for one day, $55 for two days, and $75 for three days; kids under 12 save 20%, and parking costs $6. Disneyland

opened in 1945, when there was nothing around; now it's surrounded by motels, where it's well worth staying overnight so you can get an early start, go "home" for a while, and come back for the nightly fireworks show. For further park details, call Disneyland (714/999-4565); for lodging information, call the **Anaheim Convention and Visitors Bureau** (714/758-0222).

The phenomenon of Disneyland has been done to death by all sorts of social critics but the truth is, it can be great fun—provided you visit out of season, avoid the crowds, and really immerse yourself in the extroverted, mindless joy of it all. Most of the rides are great, each in different ways (I like "Pirates of the Caribbean" best), but there can be little forgiveness for "It's a Small World." Avoid it like the plague, or risk having the song ringing in your head for days afterward.

If you've already done the Disneyland thing, there is one other Orange County attraction you really shouldn't miss: the Richard Nixon Presidential Library (Mon.-Sat. 10 AM-5 PM, Sunday 11 AM-5 PM; $4.95; 714/993-3393), 18001 Yorba Linda Boulevard, 10 miles northeast of Disneyland off Hwy-91. The library is built on the very ground where the former president was born in 1914; it's also where he and his wife Pat are buried, side by side next to the restored craftsman-style bungalow where Nixon grew up. No matter what your feelings toward him, the spare-no-expense displays do a fascinating job of putting his long career into the distorted perspective you'd expect from the only president ever forced to resign from office. (If you've been to other presidential libraries, you may have noticed that not all are as well funded as this one. That's because the library was paid for by Nixon's friends and receives no federal money, no doubt how it gets away with presenting Watergate as a liberal plot to take over the country.) If you can take the show at face value, and not dwell on the many inaccuracies, highlights are many, such as the grainy pictures of the pumpkin patch where Alger Hiss supposedly concealed the microfilm that Nixon and Joe McCarthy used to put him in prison as a Communist spy, next to photos of Nixon and JFK as chummy freshman U.S. senators sharing sleeping compartments on a train. Particularly intriguing is the grand display of Christmas cards, exchanged by the Nixons with some very unlikely figures: Khrushchev and sundry Soviets, as well as every king, queen, and tinpot dictator you could name. The bestselling item in the gift shop? Postcards of Nixon greeting Elvis Presley, also available as placemats, china, and fridge magnets.

Visiting the Nixon Library also gives you a chance to test the nation's newest toll road. Inaugurated in late 1995 along the median strip of the Riverside Freeway (Hwy-91), a new lane was added for drivers willing to pay a variable toll (25 cents to $2.50, depending upon time of day), which is charged through the use of high-tech radio transponders affixed to the windshield.

Newport Beach

Back on the coast, if you want to get a sense of what wealthy Orange Countians do to enjoy themselves, spend some time along the clean white strands of Newport Beach. Located at the southern edge of Los Angeles's suburban sprawl, Newport started life as an amusement park and beach resort at the southern end of the L.A. streetcar lines. Up until the 1940s, thousands of Angelenos spent summer weekends at the **Balboa Pavilion**, at the southern tip of the slender Balboa peninsula, where a few remnants of the pre-video games amusements survive—a Ferris wheel, a merry-go-round, and those odd "Pokerino" games in which you win prizes by rolling rubber balls into a series of numbered holes.

To return to Hwy-1 from Balboa peninsula, you can either backtrack around the harbor or ride the **Balboa Ferry,** which shuttles you from the Pavilion across the huge harbor past an amazing array of sailboats, power cruisers, and waterfront homes.

Midway along the peninsula, well-posted near 23rd Street, Newport Pier is flanked by another holdout from the old days: the **dory fleet**, where every day small boats set off to catch rock cod and more exotic fish that, starting around noon, are sold straight from the boats at an outdoor market right on the sands.

A mile south of Balboa Pavilion, next to the breakwater at the very southern end of Balboa peninsula, **The Wedge** is one of the world's most popular and challenging bodysurfing spots, with well-formed waves often twice as high as anywhere else on the coast.

Crystal Cove State Park

Midway between Newport and Laguna Beaches, amidst the ever-encroaching Orange County sprawl, Crystal Cove State Park (daily dawn-dusk; $6 per car) protects one of Southern California's finest chunks of coastline. With three miles of sandy beaches and chaparral-covered bluff lined by well-marked walking trails, it's a fine place to enjoy the shoreline without the commercial trappings. Originally home to Native Americans, the land here was later part of Mission San Juan Capistrano and, until 1979 when the state bought it, the massive Irvine Ranch, which once covered most of Orange County.

The main parking area for Crystal Cove is at **Reef Point** near the south end of the park, where there are bathrooms and showers plus excellent tidepools, a fine beach, and a well-preserved collection of 1920s beach cottages. There is also a large section inland from Hwy-1, through the oakland glade of **El Moro Canyon**, which gives a vivid sense of Orange County's rapidly vanishing natural landscape.

Laguna Beach

Compared with the rest of Orange County, Laguna Beach (pop. 23,200) is a relaxed and enjoyable place. Bookstores, cafes, and galleries reflect the town's beginnings as an artists' colony, but while the beach and downtown area are still very attractive, the surrounding hills have been covered by some of the world's ugliest tracts of "executive homes," many of which burned in recent brush fires.

Right across Hwy-1 from the downtown shopping district, which is full of pleasant cafes and a wide range of art galleries, Laguna's main beach (called simply Main Beach) is still the town's main draw, with a boardwalk, some volleyball courts where the standard of play is very high, and a guarded swimming beach with well-maintained showers.

During the annual "Pageant of the Masters," Laguna Beach residents re-create scenes from classical and modern art by forming living tableaux, standing still as statues in front of painted backdrops. Held every summer, it's a popular event, so get tickets ($10-40; 714/494-1145) in advance.

Many other fine but usually less crowded and quieter beaches are reachable from Cliff Drive, which winds north of downtown Laguna past cove after untouched cove; follow the signs reading "Beach Access."

Adjacent to the beach, right on Hwy-1, is **Greeter's Corner Cafe**, locally famous thanks to the elderly gentleman, now deceased, who used to stand out front and wave at the passing traffic. The food is fine, and you can eat outside on the broad deck overlooking the beach. Another place worth searching out is the small **Taco Loco**, 640 S. Hwy-1 at the south end of the downtown strip, where the ultra-fresh Mexican food includes your choice of three or four different seafood tacos, from shark to swordfish, in daily-changing specials from about $1.50 each.

Places to stay include the centrally located, somewhat older **Hotel Laguna**, 425 S. Hwy-1 (714/494-1151), and the beachfront **Laguna Riviera Hotel and Spa**, 825 S. Hwy-1 (714/494-8421). On an oceanside bluff six miles south of Laguna Beach, the **Ritz Carlton Laguna Niguel** (714/240-2000 or 800/241-3333) is California's only Mobil five-star rated resort, with everything you could want from a hotel—all yours for $350 a day.

South of Laguna Beach, Hwy-1 follows the coast for a final few miles before joining up with the I-5 freeway for the 40-mile drive into San Diego.

Many visitors to the chapel at San Juan Capistrano are cancer patients saying prayers to **St. Pereguin,** the patron saint of medical miracles.

San Juan Capistrano

Of the 21 missions along the California coast, Mission San Juan Capistrano has been the most romanticized. When the movement to restore the missions and preserve California's Spanish colonial past was at its apogee in the 1930s, its main theme tune was "When the Swallows Return to Capistrano," popularizing the myth that these birds come back from the winter migration on St. Joseph's Day, March 19th; they do, along with several thousand tourists, but they are just as likely to reappear a week before or a week after—whenever the weather warms up.

The mission, which has lovely, bougainvillea-filled gardens, stands at the center of the small, eponymously named town, a short detour inland along I-5 from the coast. Besides the birds, the main attractions include the small **chapel**, the last surviving church where the beatified Father Serra said Mass, widely considered to be the oldest intact church and perhaps the oldest building of any kind in California; and the ruins of the massive **Stone Church**, a finely carved limestone structure that collapsed in an earthquake in 1812, just six years after its completion.

see the swallows

To get a sense of the huge scale of the Stone Church, a full-sized replica called the New Church has been constructed behind the mission, and now serves as the official mission church, open to visitors except during religious services. Across the street from the New Church, the Michael Graves-designed local library gives an intriguing postmodern take on the mission style.

San Clemente is also the site of "La Christianita," which in 1769 was the first baptism in Alta California. The event is remembered by a plaque in the civic center parking lot, a block east of I-5.

San Clemente

At the southern tip of coastal Orange County, San Clemente marks the midway point between San Diego and Los Angeles. A sleepy and unremarkable community, San Clemente is best known as the site of Casa Pacifica, the one-time Western White House of former president Richard Nixon, who lived here following his election in 1968 until after his impeachment in the

Between Los Angeles and San Diego, the I-5 freeway has replaced the notorious old **US-101** highway, a three-lane road whose center passing lane was so dangerous it earned the name "blood alley," the site of more fatalities per mile than any other stretch of road in the state.

mid-1970s. The white-walled, mission-style house at the south end of Avenida del Presidente (the western frontage road to the I-5 freeway) is more easily visible from the beach below, though the 25 acres of trees have grown up to obscure it in recent years.

Mission San Luis Rey

In the sun-bleached hills above the blue Pacific, four miles east of the ocean off the I-5 freeway along Hwy-76, Mission San Luis Rey (Mon.-Sat. 10 AM-4:30 PM, Sunday noon-4:30 PM; $3) was among the largest and most successful of the California missions. Its lands have been turned into Camp Pendleton, and most of the outbuildings have disappeared, but the stately church at the heart of the complex survives in fine condition, worth a look for the blue-tinted dome atop the bell tower and for the haunting carved stone skull that looks down from the cemetery gate.

*The northwest corner of San Diego County is taken up by the U.S. Marines Corps' massive **Camp Pendleton** training base, which fills 125,000 acres, running for 20 miles along the coast and 15 miles inland. There's also a prominent nuclear power plant right on the coast at **San Onofre.***

*A long but worthwhile detour inland from San Luis Rey brings you to the least visited but perhaps most evocative of all the California missions, **Mission San Antonio de Pala.** Located on the Pala Indian Reservation, 20 miles east of San Luis Rey along Hwy-76, then another 100 yards north along a well-marked side road, Mission San Antonio de Pala is the only California mission still serving its original role of preaching to the native people, and gives an unforgettable impression of California's mission era.*

*Some of the best views of the Southern California coastline can be had from the windows of Amtrak's **San Diegan** trains, which run right along the shore between San Clemente and Del Mar.*

Oceanside

At the southern edge of Camp Pendleton Marine Corps Base, Oceanside (pop. 130,000) is the largest city between Los Angeles and San Diego but offers little to attract the casual visitor—apart from guided tours of Camp Pendleton's amphibious-assault training exercises, and the state's longest fishing pier. The beaches aren't anything special, but if you're in the mood to shop for camouflage gear, watch the muscle cars cruise Hill Street, or drink beer with a gang of young recruits, this is the right place.

Carlsbad

Named for the European spa town of Karlsbad, in what's now Bohemia in the Czech Republic, Carlsbad (pop. 65,000) is best known as the home of **La Costa Resort and Spa** (619/438-9111), a 500-room complex of golf and tennis courts covering the hills on the inland side of I-5. **South Carlsbad State Park**, three miles south of town, is one of the nicest and most popular places to camp on the Southern California coast, its spacious campsites (with hot showers) standing atop a sandstone bluff above a broad beach. However, swimming can be dangerous, thanks to riptides.

If you don't want to camp, or pay the $6-a-day-parking fee, leave the car at the park entrance, which is well-marked on a surviving stretch of the old US-101 highway.

Del Mar and Torrey Pines

Though it comes to life every summer for the racing season at beautiful Del Mar Racetrack (built by Hollywood types like Bing Crosby, and seen in *The Grifters* and many other Hollywood movies), most of the time the town of Del Mar (pop. 4,860) is a sleepy little upscale suburb of San Diego, with big houses backing onto a fine, four-mile-long beach. The waves here are well suited to body-surfing, but the sands can be hard to reach in summer because of a lack of parking—weekdays it's less of a problem.

Besides hang-gliders, Torrey Pines is prime air space for remote-controlled **model gliders,** which float gracefully in the nearly constant onshore breeze. The primary launching spot is the small city park at the south end of Torrey Pines State Reserve.

South along the Camino Del Mar coast road from Del Mar, hang-gliders, tidepoolers, surfers, and beachcombers flock to the nearly 2,000 acres of bluffs and beaches protected in Torrey Pines State Reserve. Named for the long-needled pines that grow naturally only here, the reserve is crisscrossed by hiking trails leading down steep ravines between the bluffs and the sands.

Overlooking the Pacific from atop a bluff at the south end of the reserve, the **Salk Institute** is one of the world's most important centers for research in the life sciences. Founded by the late Jonas Salk, designed by Louis Kahn, and modeled in part on the gardens of the Alhambra in Granada, the institute is open for **tours** (Mon.-Fri. 10 AM, 11 AM, and noon; free; 619/453-4100).

Stretching inland and south from the Salk Institute is the spacious campus of **University of California at San Diego** (UCSD), beyond which spreads La Jolla and the greater San Diego area.

San Diego, which is also the beginning of our cross-country US-80 "Southern Pacific" route, is covered as a Survival Guide on pages 716-717.

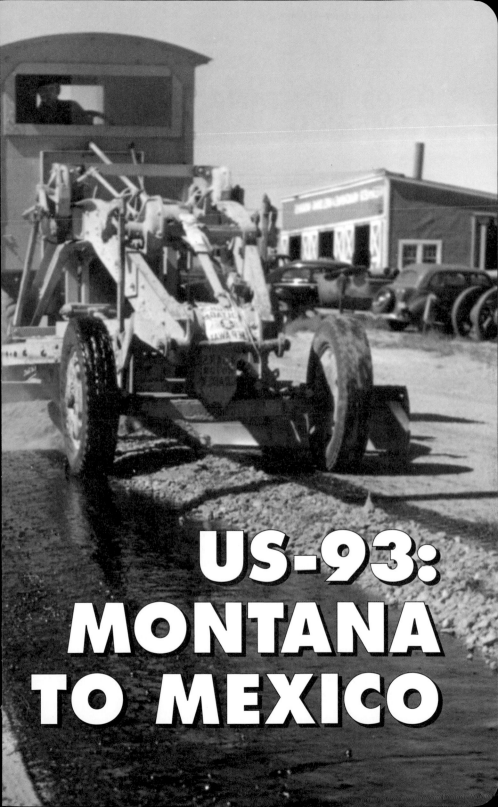

US-93:
MONTANA
TO MEXICO

US-93: MONTANA TO MEXICO

The western United States is often described as a land of contrasts, and no route through it gives a sharper sense of the region's extremes than US-93. Starting in the north at the foot of the Rocky Mountains, and winding up in the south at the Sonora Desert border town of Nogales, US-93 traverses some of the wildest and ruggedest lands the country has to offer: mighty mountains, raging rivers, and two very different deserts. Besides offering up-close looks at mile after mile of magnificent and almost completely untouched wilderness, US-93 also takes you right through the neon heart of what is surely the most extreme (and most extremely visual) example of our contemporary "civilization": Las Vegas.

The route divides into two completely different halves. The northern section, from the Canadian border south as far as Sun Valley, Idaho, is pure Rocky Mountain majesty. From the western flanks of Glacier National Park, US-93 runs along river valleys through diverse communities where skiing, hiking, and sightseeing have replaced mining and lumbering as the economic engines. South of Kalispell, the highway winds across the Flathead Indian Reservation along the western shores of Flathead Lake to Missoula, located at the heart of the bountiful country captured in *A River Runs Through It*. Western Montana's natural beauty reaches a peak in the Bitterroot Valley, which stretches south from Missoula all the way to the Idaho border. Besides scenery, the valley also abounds in history, holding many key sites pertaining to the explorers Lewis and Clark, the first whites to set foot in the region, and other sites related to the epic struggle of Chief Joseph and the Nez Perce tribe.

As you pass over the Bitterroots into Idaho along the Continental Divide, the scenery remains impressive as US-93 winds along the banks of the Salmon River, all the way to its source in the serrated Sawtooth Mountains, then drops down swifty into Sun Valley, the oldest and most upscale ski resort in the country.

South of Sun Valley, however, everything changes very suddenly. Roaring rivers and mountain forests give way to lava flows and deserted deserts, as US-93 races across the inhospitable landscape of the Snake River plain. This was the most difficult portion of the historic Oregon Trail, though the biggest difficulty facing today's travelers is the struggle to stay alert—there's very little to look for, apart from acres of potato farms reclaimed from the arid desert. The one real sight is the Snake River itself, which has carved itself into a deep gorge near Twin Falls.

Continuing south into Nevada, US-93 embarks on what is truly, if not officially, the "Loneliest Road in America," traveling across 500 miles of Great Basin desert. Though not for the faint-hearted (or those with unreliable cars!) it's an unforgettably beautiful journey; after hours (or days) of existential solitude, you drop down into the frenetic boomtown of Las Vegas.

Crossing Hoover Dam into Arizona, the route crosses old Route 66 west of the Grand Canyon, then races southeast across the lush Sonora Desert—known as the "world's greenest desert" because of its abundant flora and fauna—through Phoenix and Tucson to the Mexican border. This last stretch is among the most fascinating 100 miles of highway in the country, taking you past such intriguingly diverse and unique sights as the controversial Biosphere II scientific research center, the country's only intact Cold War-era missile silo, and a centuries-old missionary church, one of the most captivating pieces of architecture in the western U.S.

US-93 HIGHLIGHTS

ACROSS MONTANA

From the Canadian border, US-93 runs south and east along the Tobacco River valley, then cuts through the Flathead National Forest to the logging and ski resort towns of Whitefish and Kalispell. Continuing south along the shores of Flathead Lake, the route passes through the college town and cultural nexus of Missoula, south of which US-93 passes through some of the most beautiful terrain in the country, winding through broad valleys at the foot of the Bitterroot Mountains, past alpine lakes and snowcapped peaks all the way south to the Idaho border.

From the U.S./Canada border, which is open 24 hours every day, a scenic two-hour drive north will put you in **Banff and Jasper National Parks.** For more information on visiting, contact the "Discover British Columbia" tourist information and reservation center (800/663-6000).

For a truly unusual experience, spend the night in the former Forest Service **fire lookout** atop Webb Mountain, 20 miles southwest of Eureka. For details and rental rates, contact the U.S. Forest Service ranger station in Eureka (406/296-2536).

Whitefish also boasts Montana's one and only Frank Lloyd Wright building, an early 1950s bank and office complex on the east side of Central Avenue at 3rd Street called, directly enough, the **Frank Lloyd Wright Building.**

Eureka

Montana's northwest corner, where US-93 begins, is an isolated land of dense forests, broad rivers, and glaciated valleys. Besides providing natural habitat for herds of moose, elk, bison, and bighorn sheep, not to mention mountain lions, wolves, and grizzly bears, the thick groves of cedars, pines, and firs support the Northwest's other endangered species—the logger—whose angular clear-cuts and mono-crop tree plantations are also apparent as you pass through the region.

The international border between Canada and the U.S. is marked by a pair of Border Patrol huts and a couple of duty-free booze and cigarette stands, but little more; most of the traffic through here is lumber trucks, carrying logs to the large mill that dominates the U.S. side of the crossing.

The first sizeable town, 15 miles south of the border, is Eureka (pop. 1,200), a sleepy little place with a pair of gas stations, a couple of cafes, and a small "Historical Village" of pioneer buildings moved to a small park along US-2 at the south end of town. There's very little obvious visitor-oriented development in the area, though nearby is **Huckleberry Hannah's**, 3100 Sofie Lake Road (406/889-3381), a quiet and comfortable country B&B.

Whitefish

A major division point on the historic Great Northern railroad, whose tracks are still in use by Burlington Northern and Amtrak, Whitefish (pop. 4,300) was originally known as Stumptown because of the intensive logging operations centered here. Despite its proud industrial history, the blue-collar base has long since been eclipsed by tourism, and the city now calls itself the "Recreation Capital of Montana," with alpine lakes, fishing streams, hiking trails, and mountain scenery right on the doorstep.

The main attraction in Whitefish, for skiing in winter and hiking and mountain biking in summer, is **Big Mountain** (406/862-3511 or 800/858-5439), the 6,770-foot peak (with a 2,170-foot vertical drop) that looms over the northwest shore of Whitefish Lake. Besides giving access to the surrounding great outdoors, the town itself is a pleasant place to stop. A small **museum** (daily 10 AM-5 PM; free) and Great Northern gift shop inside the landmark train station, which is modelled upon the rustic lines of the Glacier National Park lodges and stands at the north end of Central Avenue, gives the historical overview of Whitefish; across the lobby the **chamber of commerce** (406/752-6166) has brochures, maps, and other information.

The best place to start the day is the **Out of the Blue Bakery**, 19 Central Avenue, which has great coffee and pastries and tabletops covered in Montana postcards. The **Buffalo Cafe**, 516 E. 3rd Street, is a popular breakfast and lunch spot, while Whitefish restaurants range from the amiable **Great Northern Bar and Grill**, 27 Central Avenue, to the more refined **Stumptown Station**, at 115 Central Avenue.

Besides the extensive resort accommodations available year-round at the Big Mountain resort, which range from $65 a night on up, you can choose from numerous motels (**Comfort Inn** and **Super 8** among them) along US-93 south of town. Two more accommodation options are east of US-93 on Whitefish Stage Road, a quiet alternative route between Whitefish and Kalispell: one is the attractive and comfortable **Turn in the River Inn**, 51 Penney Lane (406/257-0724 or 800/892-2474), along the Whitefish River; the other is the tidy **Whitefish Hostel**, 2155 Whitefish Stage Road (406/756-1908), with mountain bikes for rent and bunk beds for under $10 a night.

Kalispell

The nearest thing to an urban center in northwestern Montana, Kalispell (pop.

In the Whitefish/Kalispell area, tune to **KGZE 600 AM** for local news, talkshows, and classic pop hits of the 1950s, 1960s, and 1970s.

Kalispell marks the junction of US-93 and the trans-continental route **US-2**, which runs east through Glacier National Park (see pages 348-349) and west across Idaho and Washington to the Pacific Ocean.

12,000) spreads across the northern Flathead Valley at the junction of the Stillwater, Whitefish, and Flathead Rivers. Cut by two main thoroughfares, east-west US-2 and north-south US-93, at first glance it looks like yet another lumber mill-and-mining town, though there are signs of sophistication worth searching out, such as the engaging **Hockaday Center for the Arts** (Tues.-Fri. 10 AM-5 PM, Saturday 10 AM-3 PM; $1 donation), housed in the old Carnegie Library on 3rd Street, two blocks east of Main Street (US-93). Another few blocks east stands the impressive, perfectly preserved **Conrad Mansion**, built by pioneer trader and Kalispell founder Charles Conrad in 1895 and now open for guided tours (daily 10 AM-5:30 PM, mid-May to mid-Oct. only; $5).

Breakfasts don't get much better than those served at **Norm's News and Sodas Fountain**, 34 Main Street; around the corner on 1st Street, the **Alley Connection** is a good spot for lunch or dinner. Kalispell also has an above-average range of taverns, including the venerable **Moose's Saloon**, near the junction of US-2 and US-93 at 173 N. Main Street.

Besides numerous national motels (including a **Motel 6**, a **Super 8**, a **Red Lion** and a **Best Western**), Kalispell also has the **Kalispell Grand Hotel** (406/752-3616), a renovated downtown hotel and casino at 8 W. 1st Street, where doubles cost around $50 a night. There's also a friendly budget hostel on the way to Whitefish (see above). For more information, contact the **visitor center** (406/752-9091 or 800/543-3105).

Flathead Lake

One of the largest natural lakes west of the Mississippi River, deep-blue Flathead Lake is a magnet for outdoor recreation in western Montana. US-93 winds along the lake's hilly western shore, passing through a number of state parks and small resort communities that enjoy grand views of the Rocky Mountains to the east and the green foothills of the Flathead National Forest to the west.

The vacation village of **Lakeside**, on US-93 along the lake's northwest shore, has the best crop of motels; try the **Lake-Shore Motel** (406/844-3304), which has a boat dock and direct access to the lake.

Especially in July and August, **fruit stands** all around Flathead Lake specialize in fresh local produce like the delicious cherries grown in orchards on the lake's eastern shore. For carnivores, another place worth stopping is **M&S Meats and Sausages**, on US-93 a mile south of West Shore State Park, which has a huge array of housemade beef and buffalo jerky.

The Flathead Indian Reservation

The southern half of Flathead Lake is part of the Flathead Indian Reservation, home to a mixed population of Flathead Salish, Kootenai, and Caucasians, who make up around 80% of the reservation's population. The large reservation covers a 1.2 million-acre area, roughly 35 by 65 miles, hemmed in by the Mission and Cabinet Mountains, and it's mostly intact prairie and riverside wetlands, apart from a few small and not especially interesting towns.

The largest of these towns, **Polson**, at the bottom end of the lake where the Flathead River flows south, is a predominately white retirement community, with 24-hour gas stations, the area's only ATMs, a Safeway supermarket, and chain motels like **Days Inn** and **Super 8** as well as the pricey lake-front **Best Western KwaTaqNuk Resort,** 303 Hwy-93 East (406/883-3636 or 800/882-6363), owned and operated by the Salish-Chootney tribe.

Just two miles south of Polson along US-93, the bizarre but fascinating **Miracle of America Museum** (Mon.-Sat. 8 AM-5 PM, Sunday 2-6 PM; $2), which calls itself "Western Montana's Largest Museum," displays a mixed bag of kitchen appliances, toys, tractors, tanks, and framed newspaper clippings to give a unique view of America's industrial, military, and cultural history.

St. Ignatius and the National Bison Range

The wild Mission Mountains, rising to the east of the Flathead Reservation, were named for a Catholic mission established in the 1850s at St. Ignatius, a small town midway between Polson and Missoula. Like most reservation communities, it's a poor and fairly depressed place, worth a look for the imposing **St. Ignatius Mission** church (daily 9 AM-5 PM, longer hours in summer; donations), just east of US-93. Built by Flathead laborers in 1891, the church holds over 50 religious frescoes painted by Fr. Joseph Carignano, the mission cook.

While the town doesn't have a lot to offer visitors apart from the church, it does hold the tribally owned and operated **Flathead Indian Museum and Trading Post** (daily 9 AM-6 PM; 406/745-2951), a large gift shop, motel, and drive-through espresso stand along US-93 just south of town.

West of St. Ignatius, 18,500 acres of natural rolling prairie have been set aside since 1908 as the National Bison Range,

Chief Charlo

Elmo, at the north edge of the Flathead Reservation, hosts the annual **Standing Arrow PowWow** on the third weekend in July; **Arlee,** at the southern edge of the reservation, hosts the **4th of July PowWow.** These are two of the most popular Native American gatherings in Montana; for more information call the **Confederated Salish and Kootenai Tribal Council** (406/675-2700).

A RIVER RUNS THROUGH IT

In recent years Missoula has become something of literary center, thanks in part to the late Norman MacLean, whose novella *A River Runs Through It* rhapsodizes over the surrounding Rocky Mountain country and the larg-er-than-life lives lived there. The book, which was faithfully adapted into a film by Robert Redford, makes a great traveling companion, full of vivid description and insightful humor—Maclean writes that, growing up, he soon discovered that the world is "full of bastards, the number increasing rapidly the farther one gets from Missoula, Montana"—not to mention the fine art of fly-fishing as an essential metaphor for a life well lived.

where besides the 500 or so resident bison (a.k.a. buffalo) you might see deer, elk, pronghorns, and mountain goats. Allow around two hours to drive a complete circuit of the park; the entrance and visitor center are on the west side of the reserve, off Hwy-200 six miles west of the crossroads town of **Ravalli**. On US-93 in Ravalli, the **Bison Inn** has good food for breakfast, lunch, and dinner; the house specialty is buffalo burgers.

Missoula

Spreading along the banks of the Clark Fork of the Columbia River at the mouth of Hell Gate Canyon, Missoula (pop. 43,000) is an engaging mix of college-town sophistication and blue-collar grit. The two industries that built the city, railroads and lumber mills, have both diminished considerably since their turn-of-the-century heyday but still form the foundation of the local economy. The University of Montana campus has given Missoula a literate and left-leaning air not usually found in this neck of the woods.

Downtown Missoula stretches along the north bank of the river and contains a large number of elegant turn-of-the-century brick buildings housing a buoyant range of businesses, from department stores to bike shops. The three-story **Missoula County Courthouse**, at 200 W. Broadway, is well worth a look for its interior murals; the small **Missoula Museum of the Arts** (Mon.-Fri. noon-5 PM; donations), around the corner in the old Carnegie Library at 335 N. Pattee Street, houses traditional Western art as well as touring exhibitions.

Missoula's other social nexus, the **University of Montana** campus, spreads south of the river at the foot of dusty brown Mount Sentinel (the one marked with the large "M") and the Sapphire Mountains. It's a pleasant place to walk around—in summer at least, when cyclists and roller-bladers outnumber pedestrians on the many paths—keeping an eye out for posters advertising local events. The area west of the university is very quiet and residential, but holds one key Missoula stop: **Freddy's Feed and Read** at 1221 Helen Street, a combination health-food deli and bookstore that has been a local institution since the mid-1960s.

Missoula's number one attraction, the **Smokejumpers Aerial Fire Depot** (Mon.-Fri. 9 AM-4 PM, mid-June to mid-Sept.; donations), is seven miles west of town at the end of Broadway. Displays include dioramas, old photographs, and antique firefighting gear; hourly guided tours are led by the very people who jump out of airplanes to battle raging forest fires.

Thanks to the student population, Missoula has a wider than usual range of places to eat. Start the day at the **Mammyth Bakery**, 131 W. Main Street, which has great pastries. Lunch places include the **Stop-n-Go**, a good old-fashioned drive-in amidst the franchised fast-food outlets lining US-93 a half-mile south of downtown; and the more central **Goldsmith's**, near the university at 809 E. Front Street, serves an excellent Sunday brunch on their sunny terrace. For dinner, the urbane **Alley Cat Grill**, 125 W. Main, is one of Montana's finest restaurants. A few doors down, the landmark **Missoula Club**, 139 W. Main Street, is a perfectly preserved 1940s burgers-and-beer bar; for an even grittier Missoula scene, it's hard to beat the round-the-clock **Oxford Club**, where the brave try the eggs-and-brains, and everyone else drinks too much Bud.

There's no shortage of accommodations in Missoula, though it's always a good idea to book a room in advance. The nicest place to stay is **Goldsmith's**, a very comfortable B&B along the river at 809 E. Front Street (406/721-6732), but travelers on a tight budget will appreciate the **Birchwood Hostel**, 600 S. Orange Street (406/728-9799). A half-dozen motels line I-90 and US-93 (which follows Broadway west of Missoula, and Brooks Street south of town), including the clean and friendly **Brownie's Plus Motel**, 1540 W. Broadway (406/543-6614), and the usual national chains: **Best Western, Days Inn, Econo Lodge, Holiday Inn, Travelodge,** and a very nice **Red Lion**, located right along the river.

For more information on visiting Missoula and the surrounding country, contact the **visitor center**, across the river from the university at 825 E. Front Street (406/543-6623 or 800/526-3465), or the U.S. Forest Service **ranger station**, 340 N. Pattee Street (406/329-3511), which is headquarters for the entire region.

Missoula is also the national headquarters of the bicycling advocacy group **Adventure Cycling Association**, formerly known as Bikecentennial. They have a number of cycling and mountain-biking maps and guides to Missoula as well as the rest of the U.S. available at their office, 150 W. Pine Street (406/721-1776).

The Bitterroot Valley

South of Missoula toward the Idaho border, US-93 runs along the banks of the beautiful Bitterroot River through a broad valley bordered by parallel ridges of 8,000-foot peaks. Once you get past the undistinguished tract-house suburbs of Missoula that increasingly fill the valley's northern end, the US-93 roadside is lined by groves of cottonwood trees and occasional hamlets like **Florence**, where **Glen's Mountain View Cafe**, tucked away just west of the highway on the north side of town, is renowned throughout Montana for its incredibly good pies.

South of Florence, a well-marked alternative route, the **East Side Highway** (Hwy-203 and Hwy-269), runs parallel to US-93 a half-mile to the east, avoiding what traffic there is and passing rolling ranchlands, pioneer homesteads—some of which are among the oldest in the state—and occasional prefab trailers. The region is mostly open countryside, with a few small towns like **Stevensville**, Montana's oldest town. It was founded by Jesuits in 1841 around the still intact **St. Mary's Mission** (open Wed.-Sun. 10 AM-4 PM daily in summer; $2), at the end of 4th Street, two blocks west of Main.

If you're a fan of hot springs, or want to unwind after a day cross-country skiing, you won't want to miss the idyllic **Lolo Hot Springs Resort** (406/273-2290), in the mountains 26 miles southwest of Missoula via scenic Hwy-12. Moose wander through the wooded grounds, and the hot springs, where Lewis and Clark soaked themselves, have been extensively but attractively developed.

At the north end of the Bitterroot Valley, where Lolo Creek empties into the Bitterroot River, Lewis and Clark set up camp at what they called **Traveler's Rest** in September 1805 and again on their return in July 1806. A sign at the junction of US-93 and US-12 gives some of the story; the forest service has plans to build an interpretive center nearby.

Hamilton

The Bitterroot Valley's one sizeable town, Hamilton (pop. 2,700), stands at the southern end of the valley, where US-93 and the East Side Highway rejoin. Hamilton was laid out in the 1890s as a planned community by the multimillionaire "Copper King" **Marcus Daly**, whose 50-acre estate, **Riverside** (Tues.-Sun. 11 AM-4 PM; $5, grounds only $1) is an elegant 42-room Georgian mansion set in lushly landscaped gardens. Hamilton's other main draw is the large **Ravalli County Museum** (Mon.-Fri. 10 AM-4 PM; free), housed in a 100-year-old former courthouse on the corner of 3rd and Bedford, two blocks south of Main Street.

The best places to eat in Hamilton are the very popular **Coffee Cup Cafe**, on US-93 on the south side of town; the more upscale **Banque**, in an old bank at 225 W. Main Street; and the **Grubstake** (hours vary, call 406/363-3068), a steakhouse perched halfway up Downing Mountain with an unforgettable view. One of the best of many highway motels, the **Best Western Hamilton** is on US-93 at 409 S. 1st Street (406/363-2142).

Besides its convenience as a stopover, Hamilton is also the gateway to outdoor activities (hunting, fishing, and riding, mainly) in the Bitterroots; contact the **visitor center** (406/363-3131).

The Bitterroot Mountains

South of Hamilton, the serrated peaks and forested foothills of the Bitterroot Mountains close in along US-93 as the valley narrows sharply and woodlands (and campgrounds) replace farmlands along the roadside. Just 17 miles south of Hamilton, the pioneer village of **Darby** has a couple of cafes and a helpful **ranger station** (406/821-3913), the best source of information on hiking in the Bitterroots. South of Darby, US-93 cuts away from the Bitterroot River at the hamlet of Sula, beyond which the highway continues its slow climb up through seven miles of subalpine landscape to another of Montana's many pleasant resorts, **Lost Trail Hot Springs**, 8321 Hwy-93 South (406/821-3574 or 800/825-3574), open year-round with an attractive variety of moderately priced rooms and cabins, as well as a good on-site restaurant. Lost Trail is especially popular with cross-country skiers, who can traverse many miles of nearby trails, including the route followed by Chief Joseph and Nez Percé in 1877 while fleeing from the U.S. Cavalry.

From Lost Trail Hot Springs, US-93 climbs up to 6,995-foot **Lost Trail Pass**, which Lewis and Clark crossed in 1805 on their return from the impassable Snake River, and which now marks the border with Idaho. The pass also serves as a medium-sized downhill ski area.

The 150 miles of **mountain scenery** between Hamilton, Montana, and Sun Valley, Idaho, are perhaps the prettiest and least disturbed part of the Pacific Northwest.

The **Big Hole National Battlefield**, where 800 Nez Percé warriors, women, and children were attacked by the U.S. Army on August 9, 1877, lies east of the Continental Divide, 20 miles east of Lost Trail Pass via Hwy-43.

ACROSS IDAHO

In 1938, the WPA *Guide to Idaho* described the state's section of US-93 as "240 miles of beautiful mountains, ranging from soft flanks voluptously mounded to the lean and glittering majesty of toothed backbones." Though the official US-93 route was redirected around the mountains, not much else has changed since then: the old road is still in place, and still gives an un-matched tour of most of what Idaho has to offer.

Entering the state through an his-toric pass in the beautiful Bitterroot Mountains, the route drops down to follow the mighty Salmon River to its headwaters over 100 miles away near the frontier resort of Stanley, high up in the Sawtooth Mountains. South of the Sawtooths the route plunges into the plush resort community of Sun Valley, then races across the Snake River plain through Twin Falls to the Nevada border.

Salmon River

Beginning at the Montana border, atop Lost Trail Pass, US-93 winds steeply downhill through the 1.7-million-acre Salmon National Forest. Another 26 miles south of the pass, at the village of **North Fork**—where there's a combina-tion cafe/motel/general store/post office, and little else—US-93 crosses the Sal-mon River—often called the River of No Return because it is navigable only in a downstream direction. Running swiftly for nearly 300 miles west through the heart of the most exten-sive wilderness left in the lower 48

Across Idaho, towns and services are few and far between, and during the peak summer season it's a good idea to make arrangements for accommodations well in advance.

From North Fork, a paved road leads 20 miles west along the riverside to the tiny hamlet of **Shoup,** beyond which a number of rough roads lead to ghost towns and wilderness areas in the rugged mountains.

states, the Salmon River has carved one of the deepest gorges in North America, a full 1,000 feet deeper than the Grand Canyon.

Salmon

Surrounded by ranchlands in a broad valley between the Bitter-root and Yellowjacket Mountains, Salmon (pop. 2,941) is a picturesque place that has turned increasingly to tourism and outdoor recreation as its timber and ranching industries have faded. Also known as Salmon City, it makes a better base from which to explore the surrounding scenery than it does a destination in itself. Main Street, which US-93 follows through town, holds the small **Lemhi County Historical Museum** (Mon.-Sat. 1-5 PM; donations), 210 Main Street. The most popular place to eat is **Johnny B's Cafe**, open daily for breakfast, lunch, and dinner at 507 Main Street, while the quiet **Motel De Luxe**, at 112 S. Church Street (208/756-2231), offers inexpensive rooms a block off US-93. Rafting, hunting, and fishing guides are all over; the **visitor center**, next to City Hall at 200 Main Street (208/756-2100), has complete lists.

In 1805, explorers **Lewis and Clark** became the first Americans to cross the Continental Divide when they climbed over Lemhi Pass, 25 miles southeast of Salmon. Hoping to follow the Salmon River west to the Pacific, they discovered it was impassable and continued north over Lost Trail Pass, roughly along the route of US-93 as far as Traveler's Rest, near Missoula Montana.

Salmon River Gorge

South of Salmon, US-93 continues beside the Salmon River, climbing slowly through a landscape that alternates from open meadows to sheer canyons. Nearly 100 miles later the route arrives at the river's headwaters high up in the Sawtooth Mountains. There are few trees and no real towns along this stretch of US-93, and traffic still has to stop for the occasional cattle drive, but it's a very pretty drive, and you can stop almost anywhere for a quick walk or picnic along the river.

The appearance of the Salmon River canyon varies tremendously, reaching its deepest and most rugged at **Cronks Canyon**, also known as the Royal Gorge of Idaho, some 30 miles south of the town of Salmon. Cronks Canyon, whose multicolored walls look, according to the 1938 WPA *Guide to Idaho,* "as if a thousand broken rainbows had been drawn into the stone," also marks the approximate point where US-93 crosses the 45th Parallel—halfway between the North Pole and the Equator.

Challis and the Land of Yankee Fork State Park

The only town for 50 miles in any direction, Challis is an old mining camp that has grown into a miniature version of Salmon—albeit without the water or the tourists. Apart from boasting the all-time Idaho record for least rain in a year (seven inches), Challis is a very quiet market center for local cattle ranchers, with more bars—and barber shops—than you'd expect of a town this small.

On the south side of Challis, at the junction of US-93 and Hwy-75, the excellent and modern Land of Yankee Fork State Park **visitor center** (open daily 8 AM-6 PM in summer, Mon.-Sat. 9 AM-5 PM rest of year; 208/879-5244) has extensive displays of local mining history and maps to guide visitors to many evocative ghost towns and other relics sprinkling the surrounding hills. Gold was first discovered in the region in the 1870s, and nearby mines and mining camps boomed for the next 25 years, though by 1905 the last mine had closed. A few gold mines have reopened in recent years, though all of these are hidden away in isolated areas and protected behind high-security walls and fences; none is open to the public.

The Custer Motorway

If you're here in summer and have a few hours to spare, take the rough but very scenic alternative to Hwy-75, built by the Civilian Conservation Corps in the 1930s and called the Custer Motorway, which winds west from Challis into the Yankee Fork mining district, passing the remains of old stagecoach stations and stamp mills before reaching the ghost town of **Custer**. Undergoing restoration as the centerpiece of the Land of Yan-

Sammy Holman

kee Fork State Park, Custer now consists of a half-dozen mining shacks and log cabins, the Empire saloon, and the small but engaging **Custer Museum**, housed in the old one-room schoolhouse. Beyond Custer, a well maintained gravel road follows the Yankee Fork of the Salmon River south to Hwy-75, passing an abandoned gold dredge and other relics of mining operations, past and present, before rejoining the highway at Sunbeam, on the banks of the Salmon River.

Further details, and free maps of Custer and the Custer Motorway, are available from the Land of Yankee Fork State Park visitor center in Challis (see above).

At Challis, US-93 swings southeast toward Arco and the Craters of the Moon National Monument, which are covered under the US-20 route on page 420.

Sunbeam and Stanley

Though US-93 swings to the east, the original route, now Hwy-75, winds west into the mountains through the 2,000-foot deep canyon carved by the Salmon River. Besides passing through some of the state's most splendid scenery, Hwy-75 also runs past the small but pleasant year-round resort of Sunbeam (208/838-2211), which offers rustic log cabins ($40 a night, $200 a week), a nice campground, and a very good restaurant, serving up a range of reasonably priced, healthy gourmet food (and Idaho's best cup of coffee) on a sunny deck overlooking the confluence of the Yankee Fork and Salmon Rivers. Perhaps the greatest attraction in the area is the natural **hot springs**, forming rock pools of varying temperatures in the Salmon River a half-mile upstream from the resort.

Set in a broad basin at the eastern foot of the angular Sawtooth Mountains 58 miles west of Challis, Stanley is a tiny (pop. 71; elev. 6,260 feet) and isolated town that makes an excellent base for exploring the surrounding two-million-plus acres of alpine forest. In summertime, the population swells to around 500, including visitors, so although it's just 60 miles north of busy Sun Valley there's still plenty of room to move. Hikers and mountain-bikers, and cross-country skiers in winter, should have no trouble finding solitude in the 10,000-foot peaks; the **ranger** station (208/774-3681), four miles south of town on Hwy-75, can supply details of trails and campgrounds as well as rafting trips along the Middle Fork of the Salmon River.

If you're not camping, a good, locally owned accommodation is the **Creekside Lodge** (208/774-2213), off Hwy-21 at the center of town, which offers rooms with kitchenettes for $40-70 a night. If the lodge is full, the modern **Mountain Village Resort** (208/774-3661 or 800/843-5475) at the junction of Hwy-75 and Hwy-21 offers motel rooms, a decent restaurant, and a gas station.

Sawtooth National Recreation Area

Stanley and Sunbeam both stand along the northern border of the 750,000-acre Sawtooth National Recreation Area, which extends south for over 20 miles of untrammelled meadows, forests, and lakes, and includes the headwaters of many major Idaho rivers. It also holds one of the nicest places to stay in the Rockies: the historic **Redfish Lake Lodge** seven miles south of Stanley on Hwy-75 (May-Sept. only; 208/774-3536), on the east shore of Redfish Lake, which has rustic, log-walled rooms in the main lodge from around $50 a night, and spacious cabins for about twice that. The lodge also has a very good restaurant.

Redfish Lake takes its name from the millions of red-fleshed sockeye salmon found here by pioneers. These migratory fish travel nearly 2,000 miles round-trip, from their spawning grounds at Redfish Lake to the Pacific Ocean and back via the Columbia and Salmon Rivers. Their numbers are so depleted that the run is now on the verge of extinction.

South of Redfish Lake, Hwy-75 switchbacks steeply up to 8,752-foot **Galena Summit**, which gives a grand view over the surrounding Rockies, before dropping steeply down toward Sun Valley along the headwaters of the Wood River.

There are two main **visitor centers** for the Sawtooth NRA: a summer-only one near Redfish Lake, and the headquarters (208/726-7672) on the north side of Ketchum.

Sun Valley

The first, and still among the most famous, destination ski resorts in the U.S., Sun Valley was developed by Union Pacific railroad tycoon Averill Harriman in the 1930s. Harriman built a large mock-Tyrolean chalet, the **Sun Valley Lodge**, 1 Sun Valley Road (800/635-8261), and began to cultivate Sun Valley's exclusive reputation—reinforced by high prices for lift tickets rapidly approaching $50 a day—and five-star facilities, including golf courses, tennis courts, and gourmet restaurants. Though Colorado's Vail and other resorts now compete for the top-dollar trade, Sun Valley still attracts well-heeled clientele, if the many Lear jets and Gulfstreams parked at the local airport are any indication. (The airport is also served by Horizon Air, 800/547-9308.)

While the resort itself isn't huge, Sun Valley has come to stand for the larger area, including the towns of Ketchum and Hailey and much of the nearby wilderness. Somewhat surprisingly, compared with the rest of Idaho's mountain regions, the Sun Valley area is quite barren and treeless—ideal for skiing, perhaps, though not particularly beautiful. Besides skiers in winter, Sun Valley also draws golfers in summer and fall, not to mention anglers, who rate the Wood River as one of the nation's best.

For further information on visiting the Sun Valley area, especially regarding accommodations, contact the **Sun Valley Chamber of Commerce** (800/634-3347).

For details on hiking, camping, cross-country skiing, or mountain biking in the nearby forests, stop by the Sawtooth National Forest **ranger station** (208/622-5371), a mile east of Ketchum on Sun Valley Road.

Ketchum and Hailey

Though both places preexisted Sun Valley, the two old mining and sheep-ranching towns of Ketchum and Hailey have more or less lost themselves in the upmarket resort aura of their famous neighbor. Ketchum (pop. 2,500), the more touristy of the two, has wall-to-wall art galleries and T-shirt shops lining its traffic-jammed streets. It also supports dozens of very expensive resort hotels and restaurants that cater to Sun Valley's country club set, plus a handful of more interesting and affordable places along the 200 block of N. Main Street. Here you can choose from beer-and-burger bars like **X's Taphouse** and **Whiskey Jacques'**—the latter also serving good pizzas—or the Harley-friendly **Casino**, housed in one of Ketchum's oldest buildings. Also here, the cerebral **Main Street Bookcafe**, 201 N. Main, is a cafe-and-bookshop combo with a decidedly Bohemian bent. One exception to the anodyne ambience of Ketchum's accommodations is the **Bald Mountain Lodge**, a rustic former hot springs resort right in Ketchum at 151 S. Main Street (208/726-9963 or 800/892-7407); doubles start at $50 a night.

Ernest Hemingway

Hailey, 10 miles south of Ketchum and linked by a popular rail-trail bike path, is a more workaday town, founded originally in the 1880s as a supply center for local silver and lead mines. In contrast to the civic love affair Sun Valley has with the legacy of Ernest Hemingway, Hailey takes little notice of the fact that it was the birthplace (in 1885) of another noteworthy literary figure, **Ezra Pound**. His parents were here working for the government, but fled the snowy winters just two years later.

Shoshone

South of the Sun Valley area, Hwy-75 runs across 60 miles of south-central Idaho's rocky black lava flows. Halfway between Sun Valley and Twin Falls, the **Shoshone Ice Caves** (daily 8 AM-8 PM in summer only; $5) present a series of lava tubes developed into a low-key tourist trap. Just west of the highway, they're not particularly memorable, though their constant 50° temperatures do make a pleasant contrast to the often scorching summer heat.

The only town along this stretch of road, Shoshone (pop. 1,200) is a ranching and railroad center, and some of its build-

Ernest Hemingway is probably the most famous name associated with Sun Valley. Hemingway first came here in the 1930s, and worked on *For Whom the Bell Tolls* while staying at the Sun Valley Lodge. He returned in 1960, and a year later shot himself; he's now buried in a simple plot in the middle-rear section of Ketchum's small cemetery. Hemingway is also remembered by a small and surprisingly kitschy **memorial** along Trail Creek, a mile east of the resort.

Fifteen miles south of Hailey is the junction with US-20, where you can turn east to visit the tiny town of **Picabo**—after which the Idaho-based 1994 Olympic Silver Medal skier Picabo Street was named.

A large sign along Hwy-75, eight miles north of Shoshone, points the way across the lava fields to the Idaho Mammoth Cave Civil Defense Shelter.

ings have been constructed from local volcanic rock. Though it's a fairly timeworn place, Shoshone looks great at sunset, when its steel water tower glows and places like the **Frosty Isle Drive-In** on the north side of town, or the neon-signed **Manhattan Cafe** along the railroad tracks, all look especially appealing. Shoshone also marks the junction of Hwy-75 with US-93.

Many of Idaho's famous **potatoes** are grown in the "Magic Valley" area around Twin Falls; harvest season is late September.

Twin Falls

Named for a pair of 200-foot cascades in the Snake River, both of which have long been diverted for irrigation or to generate electricty, Twin Falls (pop. 27,750) is the heart of the extensive "Magic Valley" of highly productive irrigated croplands that cover half a million acres of south-central Idaho. Best known to people outside Idaho as the place where, in 1974, daredevil Evel Knievel tried and failed to ride a rocket-powered motorcycle across the Snake River canyon, Twin Falls is both a busy highway town—with a barrage of backlit and neon signs along US-93—and a quiet farming

---

EVEL KNIEVEL AND THE SNAKE RIVER CANYON

No one who lived through the 1970s could forget the name Evel Knievel, the ultimate thrillseeker who became rich and famous perfoming dangerous and virtually impossible feats on a motorcycle. Born in Butte, Montana, in 1939, Knievel dropped out of high school and worked a dozen different jobs before finding his true calling as a motorcycle daredevil. In 1965 he made his first jump, flying over a caged mountain lion and boxes of rattlesnakes at Moses Lake, Washington. Within a few years he hit the big time: leaping over the fountains at Caesar's Palace and jumping 50 cars at the L.A. Coliseum. Though he broke nearly every bone in his body as a result of his numerous crash landings, Knievel's feats were always bigger, better, and more dangerous than the last; as he liked to say, "Where there's little risk, there's little reward."

Banned by the government from attempting a leap over the Grand Canyon, Evel set his sights on the Snake River Canyon in southern Idaho, even leasing the land so no one could stop him, then building a massive ramp and working out the details of his custom-made, rocket-powered Harley Davidson X-2 Skycycle. On September 8, 1974, some 30,000 people turned out, along with many millions more watching on TV for Evel's big leap. Unfortunately, one of his parachutes deployed on take-off, and he floated gently down into the bottom of the gorge, safe and sound, and proud of having the guts to try—even if he didn't quite make it.

community, with little to offer travelers apart from a chance to fill the gas tank, eat, or get a night's sleep. Eat at the 24-hour **Depot Grill**, at 545 S. Shoshone Street along downtown's diagonal main drag; sleep at your choice of two **Best Westerns**, a **Comfort Inn**, an **Econo Lodge**, a **Super 8**, or any of a dozen others.

The one unique attraction of Twin Falls, the site of **Evel Knievel's** aborted motorcycle jump, is a mile north of town on US-93, south of the I-86 freeway. There's a large parking area and a visitor center at the south foot of the delicate Perrine Memorial Bridge, and it's well worth stopping for, not only to see the remains of his launch pad (a triangular pile of dirt, 500 yards east of the bridge) or the stone monument that calls him "Robert 'Evel' Knievel—Explorer, Motorcyclist, Daredevil." The views down into the 500-foot-deep gorge, the floor of which has been irrigated and filled with bright green golf courses, are also impressive, especially at sunset when the whole scene takes on an otherworldly glow.

Though the town can make a good jumping-off point for Sun Valley and the mountain wilderness farther north, there's not a lot to *do* in Twin Falls. The waterfalls for which the town is named are barely visible, since their flows have been diverted. **Shoshone Falls**, however, taller than Niagara, may still impress, especially in spring; check them out from the park at the end of Falls Avenue, seven miles east of US-93.

South of Twin Falls, there's a whole lot of nothing in the 47 miles before you reach the Nevada border at Jackpot. One place worth a stop is the summer-only Nat Soo Pah hot springs, halfway to Nevada about a mile south of Hollister, which has a giant spring-fed swimming pool and a tree-shaded picnic area and snack bar.

ACROSS NEVADA

US-93 runs south along the eastern edge of Nevada for 520 miles, 500 of which take you through an exceptional degree of desolation—endless straight and narrow valleys, two-car traffic jams, and towns few and far between. From the gambling oasis of Jackpot on the Idaho border to where the highway crosses into Arizona atop Hoover Dam, US-93 fully deserves its reputation as the Loneliest Road in America. Towns like Wells,
along I-80 in the northern half of the state, are big events; south of here it's 130 miles to the next watering hole, Ely, beyond which the old mining camp of Pioche and the desert hot springs resort of Caliente are the only wide spots in the road before you hit the staggering city of Las Vegas.

The other Loneliest Road in America, US-50, is covered on pages 516-578.

Jackpot
In every respect but one, Jackpot belongs more to Idaho than Nevada—a somewhat incongruous introduction to US-93 in the Silver State. Jackpot's visitors and work-

ers mostly come from Idaho, as do its power and water; even its clocks are set to Idaho time. The one little exception, however, is pure Nevada: border-town gambling. Jackpot was founded in 1956, mere months after Idaho banned slot machines, which didn't, to be sure, reduce the demand. In fact, Jackpot has thrived on the demand, as a pit stop in any of the town's casinos will attest. Jackpot is compact enough to give long-distance travelers just enough lights, action, and comfort to satisfy more immediate needs and then send them on their way again.

Cactus Pete's (702/755-2321) is the 10-story tower you can see for miles; along with the big casino, it has a great snack bar, a buffet, gourmet restaurant, showroom, lounge, and rooms for around $40 a night. **The Horseshu** (702/755-7777) across the street has a good coffee shop with typical Nevada meal deals, or stock up for the road at the supermarket next door. **Barton's 93 Club** (702/755-2341) has a motel annex and offers some of the cheapest rooms in Nevada—$20 weekdays, $25 weekends—if you can land one.

Wells

Some lone peaks, a stretch of badlands and buttes, and a couple of north-south-trending ranges usher US-93 down a long basin toward the little junction town of Wells (pop. 1,250). Just under 70 miles from Jackpot at the interchange of US-93 and the I-80 freeway, Wells was named by the Central Pacific Railroad, which chose the site for a depot and town to make use of the plentiful springs in the hills a few miles northeast. The old downtown— take a right on 6th Street and another right at the light—is the most intact abandoned "**railroad row**" on the entire mainline across northern Nevada.

Wells provides an explicit illustration of the West's transition from rail to road to superhighway: the newest action in town is at the east and west exit ramps of I-80; the "strip" between the exits is 6th Street (old US-40), the pre-interstate vintage 1950s and even 1960s, but derelict around the edges; commerce along the 125-year-old tracks is, of course, extinct.

Wells is situated at the northeastern base of the scenic **East Humboldt Range**. To get into the mountains, go under Wells's west exit ramp and follow the signs; the paved road climbs to 8,400 feet, passing one campground and terminating at another. For details, contact the U.S. Forest Service **ranger station** (702/752-3525) at the west end of town.

Continuing down US-93 affords a different view of the East Humboldts. Ten miles south of Wells you can take a right on Hwy-232, which makes a loop through luxuriant Clover Valley at the eastern base of the mountains, one of the most bucolic basins in Nevada. About six miles in from the highway is a right turn onto a rough dirt track. Look up to see **Hole-in-the-Mountain Peak**. Tallest peak in the East Humboldts (11,276 feet), the peak has a 30- by 25-foot natural window in the thin rock 300 feet below its summit, which gives you a spectacular little patch of blue (or silver, orange, or purple, depending on the time of day) right through the top of the range. Compelling.

Wendover

At the I-80 freeway, US-93 becomes the hypotenuse of an alternative route, which runs for 60 miles southeast to the Utah border at Wendover, then another 60 miles southwest to rejoin the mainline US-93 at Lages. Wendover, like Jackpot, is a thriving Nevada border town, with five major casinos and as many new golf-course-view subdivisions. Wendover's claims to fame include **Wendover Will**, the huge cowboy outside the Stateline casino who welcomes you to Nevada along the Utah state line; the **Bonneville Salt Flats** and speedway, where most of the world's land-speed records have been set over the past 80 years; and **Wendover Air Force Base**, where in 1945 the crew of the *Enola Gay* trained to drop an atomic bomb on Japan.

The Ruby Mountains and Elko

It's a long, solitary, 140 miles from Wells to Ely. US-93 shoots down Clover Valley to the southern edge of the East Humboldts where NV-229, a maintained gravel road, cuts off southwest toward the Ruby Mountains, also known as the Nevada Alps. This is one of Nevada's most scenic ranges: 100 miles long, with more than a dozen peaks over 9,000 feet.

The best access to the Ruby Mountains is through the engaging small city of Elko, 50 miles west of Wells via I-80. Besides maintaining its Basque culture, Elko hosts the very popular

Jackpot lies within the **Columbia Plateau** physiography of southern Idaho. This geographical anomaly is the only bit of land in Nevada that falls outside its two eminent deserts: the Great Basin, encompassing the top three-quarters of the state, and the Mojave, which covers the bottom quarter.

Wendover Will

Between Wells and Ely, US-93 bends away from the heart of the Ruby Mountains, running southeast through Steptoe Valley on a marathon drive down an elongated basin, hemmed in by the Schell Creek Range on the east and the Egan Range on the west. The only signs of civilization on this stretch are two **roadhouses:** one at **Lages** (78 miles south of Wells), the other at **Schellbourne** (40 miles north of Ely).

Cowboy Poetry Festival every January, a Cowboy Music Gathering the last week-end in June, and a 4th of July celebration. Take advantage of some of the fine restaurants like the **Star Hotel** (702/738-9925), near the railroad tracks at 246 Silver Street, which is worth the drive for the delicious lamb chops and other dishes.

For more information, contact the **Elko Convention and Visitors Bureau** (800/248-ELKO).

McGill

Tiny McGill, 128 miles south of I-80 and 12 miles north of Ely, is the classic Nevada company town, its workaday life revolving for the first 50 years of this century around a giant copper smelter. Mining company officials lived in the fancy houses around the "Circle" at the top of the hill just below the factory, while workers were housed according to their ethnic origins. The saloon and jail were conveniently built right next door to each other, and steam from the copper furnaces was piped to heat the town's houses. The company's been gone for more than 15 years, but the layout remains, along with acres of fenced-off brick factory buildings painted with fading signs encouraging workers to behave safely.

A few of McGill's buildings have been converted to current uses, but most are closed. US-93, which runs at the foot of town, attracts most of the businesses, including **Marie's Cafe**, the town's main place to eat, and the **McGill Club**, down the street in the old Cyprus Hall, considered one of the state's finest by many connoisseurs of local licensed establishments. (The jail, however, is now in Ely.)

The McGill smelter's last skyscraping smokestack was felled in September 1993. At 750 feet tall, it was until then the highest structure in Nevada.

Ely marks the junction of US-93 and US-50, the nation's longest transcontinental highway, which is described on pages 516-578.

Ely

Ely (pop. 4,750; pronounced "E-lee," as in Robert), is a sprawling crossroads community where US-6, US-50, and US-93 all intersect. For nearly 100 years Ely was a boomtown flush with the wealth from the massive Kennecott-owned Liberty Pit copper mines, Nevada's largest and longest-lived mining venture, which produced over a billion dollars' worth of ore while employing nearly 10,000 people at its peak during the 1950s.

Mountains of mine tailings tower over US-50 west of Ely, and five miles west of town there's a turn marked "Historical Mining Viewpoint" that leads south along a part-paved, part-dirt road for just over a mile to a viewing point high above the huge crater where hundreds of tons of ore were dug. The Magma mining company is currently leaching the metal out of the previously discarded ore, and has encircled the viewing area with historical photographs of the old mining operations, alongside chunks of rock—all of which are labeled to explain their geologic makeup.

After the mines closed down in 1982, the railway that had shuttled pay dirt from the mines to the smelter was abandoned—track, stock, and depot. The entire operation was turned into **Nevada Northern Railway Museum** (Wed.-Sun. 9 AM-4 PM May-Sept.; $3; 702/289-2085) in 1985, and now you can take a 90 minute, 14-

ELY

Fairgrounds

Nevada Northern
Railway Museum

White Pine
Public Museum

Ely

Hotel Nevada

East Ely

Copper Queen
Casino

0   1 mile
0   1 kilometer

mile loop tour of the rail yards aboard the Ghost Train, a 1910 Baldwin Steamer. The train leaves from the depot at the north end of E. 11th Street and uses a ton of coal and 1,000 gallons of water; trips are offered weekends only, and tickets cost around $15.

Apart from mining history (and motels, gas stations, and the only supermarket for 250 miles) there's not a whole lot to Ely. The heart of town is a neon-rich few blocks of Aultman Street (US-50) west of the US-93 junction, centering upon the landmark **Hotel Nevada**, 501 Aultman (702/289-6665), with its giant cowboy and neon-lit slot machines. Inside there are slot machines, pool tables, a cafe, and a bar with nightly live music. Rooms upstairs cost a bargain $30. Another place worth stopping at is the **Copper Queen Casino**, 701 Avenue I (702/289-4883), on the south side of Ely, where pricey motel rooms open directly onto a lobby shared by banks of slot machines and a small swimming pool; also nice is the quiet **Four Sevens Motel**, a block north of Aultman at 500 High Street (702/289-4747).

For food, the best of Ely's three coffee shop-style restaurants is **Evah's** across the street from the Copper Queen casino. There's also franchised fast food, including a newish McDonald's, or you can down a milk shake at the soda fountain inside **Economy Drug**, Aultman and 7th Streets.

Nevada's one and only national park, **Great Basin National Park,** stands along the slopes of Wheeler Peak, 30 miles east of US-93.

Connors Pass and Major's Place

Southeast of Ely US-93, spliced together with US-50 and US-6 into a single two-lane highway, continues for 25 miles before crossing the narrow waist of the Schell Creek at Connors Pass (7,722 feet elevation), one of only two fractions of US-93 in Nevada that climb above the tree line. (Unlike most of the rest of the country, tree line in Nevada has a lower, as well as an upper, limit: no trees grow here below roughly 4,000 feet.) As you ascend toward the pass, the air cools and freshens, the single-leaf piñon and Utah juniper appear and thicken, and, cresting the summit, the mighty Snake Range, including 13,061-foot Wheeler Peak, comes into view.

At Major's Place (no services), US-93 splits off from US-50 and US-6, the latter two heading east toward Utah, while US-93 cuts south, heading 80 long, solitary miles to the next contact with humans at Pioche. Once again, the highway rolls along taffy-pulled Spring and Lake valleys, ushered on its way by the Schell Creek, Fairview, Bristol, and Highland ranges on the west, and the Snake and Wilson Creek ranges on the east.

Note that there are **no** services—no gas, no food, no lodging or organized camping, not even a video rental store—for the 105 miles between Ely and Pioche.

Pioche

The only places that are more than a ghostly outline of civilization in the nearly 300 miles of Great Basin desert that US-93 crosses between Ely and Las Vegas are the wildly different towns of Caliente, Panaca, and Pioche. The oldest and most northerly of the three, Pioche (pop. 800; pronounced "pee-OACH"), is a one-time mining boomtown that had its heyday well over a century ago. Being so remote—back then exponentially more than now—during the 1870s Pioche descended to a level of anarchy that rivaled Bodie and Tombstone, and over 75 men were killed before anyone died of natural causes.

Corruption, too, was the order of the day, and you can tour Pioche's "Million Dollar" **Lincoln County Courthouse** on Lacour Street for a graphic example of it. Designed in 1871 at an estimated cost of $26,000, the courthouse wasn't completed until 1876, to the tune of $88,000. Then, unable to pay off the principal, the county commissioners kept refinancing the debt, while interest accrued, year after year; by the time it was paid off in 1937, the courthouse had cost a million bucks and been replaced by a more modern structure. Now restored, the old courthouse is open for self-guided **tours** (daily 10 AM-4 PM; donations; 702/962-5182) of the offices, the courtroom, and the old jail.

The eclectic **Lincoln County Museum** (daily 10 AM-4 PM; free), on Main Street at the center of town, is another good stop, as are nearby historic buildings such as the **Thompson Opera House** and the **Commercial Club.** The rusting remains of the **aerial tramway** that ran through Pioche, carrying ore to the stamp mills, can be explored—cables, cars, and all—from various points in town. Two state parks to the east (Echo Canyon and Spring Valley, 12 and 20 miles respectively) round out your Pioche-area sightseeing.

Pioche also has a motel, the **Motel Pioche** on Lecour Street (702/962-5551), as well as **Nancy's** restaurant and the **Silver Cafe,** a Chevron station, and a used-book store.

Panaca and Cathedral Gorge

Panaca, 11 miles south of Pioche and a mile east of US-93 on Hwy-319, was founded in 1864 by Mormon farmers in what was then a part of Utah, attracted to the valley by the plentiful water of Panaca Spring. The mining strikes at nearby Bullionville and Pioche disturbed their peace briefly, but Panaca—which has a single gas station-*cum*-minimart, plus a school and lots of houses—has a strong sense of tranquility and timelessness rarely felt in the rest of Nevada.

Just west of US-93, a mile north of Panaca, **Cathedral Gorge State Park** is a mini-Grand Canyon of eroded mud. A lake once covered this deep gully, and silt and clay were washed to the bottom by streams and creeks. The lake dried up, exposing the sediments, and erosion (which never sleeps) sculpted them into the fantastic procession of formations that you see today. The **campground** ($7 per site; 702/728-4467) here has shade trees, flush toilets, even showers.

Cathedral Gorge

Caliente

To Pioche's mining and Panaca's farming, Caliente (pop. 1,100), 15 miles south, adds railroading. This small town was built around the San Pedro, Los Angeles, and Salt Lake Railroad tracks in the early 1900s, a short while before Las Vegas itself was founded. The **Union Pacific Depot**, which was built in 1923 and still gets Amtrak service on the Las Vegas-to-Salt Lake City line, is the nerve center of Caliente, being restored to house government offices and an art and local history gallery.

The town supports two gas stations and a half-dozen motels, the best of which is the **Hot Springs** (702/726-3777), off US-93 on the north side of Caliente. Here your room comes with use of Roman baths, whose fire-hydrant faucets fill the five foot-square, four foot-deep tubs in three minutes flat with 115° water. Roadfood, however, is limited to three choices: the **Knotty Pine** coffee shop and casino; the **Branding Iron** cafe, across from the depot; and **Carl's Sandwich and Burger Shop**, next to the post office on US-93, which does a fine cheeseburger.

South from Caliente, US-93 bends due west for 43 miles. Newman Canyon just outside of town has high, sheer, smooth, volcanic-tuff walls similar to Rainbow Canyon's. You twist and climb out of the canyon to cross the Delmar Range at **Oak Springs Summit** (6,237 feet), where the juniper trees are a welcome change from the low desert scrub. Beyond is an even rarer sight, not only for this highway but for any highway: a little interface zone in which the junipers grow right next to Joshua trees. This is the first indication of the change from Great Basin desert, which lies to the north, to the front edge of the Mojave Desert, which spreads south and west. Pahroc Summit is next (just under 5,000 feet), then Six Mile Flat, and then **Hiko**, where Hwy-375 heads northwest to US-6 and Tonopah.

Panaca Spring, a fine local **swimming hole** with warm, sweet water, is found just outside town: take 5th Street north past the baseball diamond and a rusty old steam engine, toward a big cottonwood tree about a half-mile beyond where the pavement ends.

Rainbow Canyon, south of Caliente on Hwy-317, is one of Nevada's most scenic and least-known drives: colorful, high volcanic-tuff cliffs, railroad trestles, and idyllic farms and ranches line Meadow Wash. The pavement ends after 21 miles, but in dry weather you can continue 38 miles through Kane Springs Valley to connect back up with US-93.

Ash Springs and Alamo

From the Hwy-375 junction, US-93 turns due south again and enters some unexpectedly lush country, in the midst of which three large and faithful springs provide plentiful water for alfalfa farms and cattle ranches, as well as for the only bona fide lakes that US-93 encounters in more than 400 miles of its Nevada leg. Ash Springs—consisting of a single combination gas station, restaurant, and bar called

THE ALIEN HIGHWAY

West of US-93, stretching nearly to Death Valley and the California border, the 3.5-millon-acre expanse of Nellis Air Force Range has been turned by the U.S. government into its most top-secret testing ground. H-Bombs, U-2 spy planes, Stealth fighters, you name it—this is where projects no one is supposed to know about exist.

It's not surprising, then, that this lonely corner of the world has become a focus of an ongoing controversy pitting government secrecy against allegations that the Air Force has been using a corner of the base known as Area 51 to study UFOs and extraterrestrials. Fuelled in part by tabloid stories claiming an E.T.-like creature is being kept alive at Area 51 in a high-security compound underneath Groom Lake—and also by local businesspeople's realization that UFO tourism could mean big money—the hoopla has focused on the tiny village of **Rachel**, which has become to UFO-spotters what the grassy knoll is to JFK conspiracy theorists.

Rachel (pop. 99), the only community along the 100-mile stretch of Hwy. 375 (popularly known as the Alien Highway), is a block-long strip that holds the **Area 51 Research Center,** a mobile home that doubles as command post for UFO-spotters. The more lighthearted **Little A-Le-Inn,** is a typical bar and grill where you can munch on "Alien Burgers," down drinks like the "Beam Me Up, Scotty"(Jim Beam, 7UP, and Scotch) or peruse the range of UFO-related key chains, fridge magnets, and T-shirts. A-Le-Inn also rents motel rooms (702/729-2515) for around $30 a night.

"R Place"—is named after the nearby water source, which is believed to be part of a vast aquifer underlying much of eastern Nevada; earthquakes have thrust this particular water to the surface.

Twelve miles south of Ash Springs is Alamo, whose two motels, two truck stops, and 24-hour "Del Pueblo" Mexican restaurant are the only real services between Caliente and Las Vegas. Four miles south of town is Upper Pahranagat Lake; an old road runs along the eastern shore, with camping and picnic sites and big cottonwoods—one of the most idyllic spots on the whole Nevada portion of US-93. The water is close enough to the source at Ash Springs that it's relatively warm year-round. Lower Pahranagat Lake, a bit farther south, freezes in the winter.

Upper Lake is also home to the administration and maintenance facilities for the **Desert National Wildlife Refuge**, at one and a half million acres the largest refuge in the Lower 48. Elusive desert bighorn sheep enjoy protection within this huge habitat, alongside of which US-93 travels for the length of the aptly named Sheep Range. The road descends gradually into rocky and barren desert until finally, 70 miles from Alamo and 125 miles from Caliente, US-93 merges with the I-15 freeway for the high-speed haul into the Big Glow, Las Vegas.

If you time the drive into Las Vegas so you arrive around dusk, the western sky sports a purple sunset, while the horizon shines brightly from a billion amber street lights stretching from one end of the valley to the other. But wait: you're still more than 30 miles out! The downtown and Strip skylines are clearly discernible for a full half hour before you get to Ground Zero, but it's as if those 500 miles of two-lane byway are reluctant to give you up. Even though the road-way has widened to four-lane freeway, the halcyon trip down Nevada's nothingness lingers till the last possible moment, and then the transition is insanely abrupt: the deep desert, then wham bam, Sin City.

Radio station **KORK 920 AM** broadcasts all the hits of the 1940s and early 1950s, plus play-by-play of the Las Vegas Stars baseball games.

The wild sights and sounds of Las Vegas are described in the Las Vegas Survival Guide, on pages 694-695.

Henderson

Southeast of Las Vegas, US-93 joins courses with US-95 along Nevada's newest freeway, which recently connected Las Vegas with the rapidly growing industrial city of Henderson. Henderson itself is relatively young, even by Nevada standards. In 1941, the War Department selected this site, due to its proximity to unlimited electricity generated by six-year-old Hoover Dam, for a giant factory to process magnesium, needed for bombs and airplane components. Ten thousand workers arrived and within six months had built the plant and a town for 5,000 people. After the war ended, the factory was subdivided for private industry, and since then, Henderson has grown to be the third-largest city in Nevada, behind Las Vegas and Reno—the only three population centers in Nevada with more than 100,000 residents.

Though it doesn't even try to compete with the attractions of Las Vegas, Henderson does have two large and three small casinos (including the world's largest bingo parlor), and the very good **Clark County Heritage Museum** (daily 9 AM-4:30 PM; $1) located two miles south of town at 1830 S. Boulder Highway. For kids, take the tour of **Kidd's marshmallow factory** (call for directions; 702/564-5400).

South of Henderson, US-93/95 climbs up and over 2,367-foot Railroad Pass, and just beyond is the junction where US-95 cuts south, heading along the Colorado River to Laughlin, Nevada; Needles, California; and Yuma, Arizona. US-93 continues east, and a little north, to Boulder City.

Boulder City

Like Henderson, Boulder City (pop. 12,600) was founded and built by the federal government to house workers at Hoover Dam, what was then the largest construction project ever undertaken. Though the dam was completed in 1935, Boulder City continued under the feds' ownership and management for another 25 years; in 1960, an Act of Congress conferred independent municipal status on the town. Long-time residents purchased their houses and alcohol consumption was permitted for the first time in the town's history, though gambling remained forbidden. To this day, a full quarter century since "independence," Boulder City remains the only town in Nevada that expressly prohibits gambling, which may explain why it feels more like the Midwest than a suburb of Sin City.

If you're interested in the men and machines involved in building the dam, the **Boulder City/Hoover Dam Museum**, well signed at 441 Nevada Highway, is worth a look. The museum is hoping to move across the street into the historic (and newly restored) **Boulder Dam Hotel** (702/293-1808); the hotel also has a good dining room. There is a handful of motels and fast-food outlets in town, but the real draws are just below Boulder City—at the dam, of course, and the lake behind it.

Hoover Dam and Lake Mead

Approaching Hoover Dam from the Nevada side, in the eight miles from Boulder City you pass a Nevada Welcome Center, a National Park Service visitor center for Lake Mead National Recreation Area, the Gold Strike Casino, and a peculiar parade of electrical generators, transformers, and capacitors all secured by cyclone fencing topped by razor wire and barbs to keep out intruders.

Continuing along past the bronzed glass of the new **visitor center** (daily 8:30 AM-5:30 PM; 702/293-8906), which finally opened in 1995, 10 years behind schedule, US-93 rolls right over the top of the gargantuan wedge of Hoover Dam: nearly a quarter-mile across, 726 feet high, 660 feet thick at the base, all accomplished with a mere seven million tons (that's only 14 billion pounds) of concrete. Very popular 45-minute **tours** of the dam (daily 8 AM-6 PM in summer, 9 AM-3 PM rest of year; $5) leave from the small ticket office at the top, and food is available at the irresistible **Hoover Dam Snacketeria.**

*Hoover Dam marks the border between Nevada and Arizona, and between Pacific and mountain **time zones,** so set your clocks and watches an hour ahead if you're traveling east, an hour behind if you're heading west. Heading south, you'll pass no towns or services for some 75 miles, until you reach Kingman on old Route 66, so stock up and fill up before proceeding.*

Meanwhile, Lake Mead, the largest man-made lake in the western hemisphere, contains roughly 30 million acre-feet, or just over nine *trillion* gallons. It irrigates some 2.5 million acres of land in the U.S. and Mexico, and supplies electricity, from 17 electrical turbines inside the dam's base, to millions of people. The lake is a very popular recreation site, with thousands of water-skiers and fisherfolk flocking to its 500 miles of shoreline year-round.

ACROSS ARIZONA

Coming into Arizona across the top of Hoover Dam, US-93 cuts southeast across the length, and half the breadth, of the state, covering nearly 500 miles of desiccated desert. Starting at the Nevada border, US-93 makes a diagonal bee-line toward the old Route 66 town of Kingman, one of the few watering holes in Arizona's northwest quarter. From Kingman, the route follows the anodyne I-40 freeway east, then cuts south across another huge stretch of desert, passing through the dude-ranch resort town of Wickenburg before reaching the suburban outskirts of Phoenix, the state's capital and largest city. From this sprawling megalopolis, the route bends east into the mountains, following backroads past the controversial Biosphere II "space station" before hitting Tucson, another hugely horizontal city. South of here you'll enjoy the most feature-packed part of the trip, passing by the historic Spanish colonial communities of Tubac and Tumacacori before winding up at the enjoyable Mexican border town of Nogales.

Lake Mead Recreation Area

Most people visit Lake Mead, which covers some 160,000 acres and includes over 500 miles of shoreline, from the extensively developed Nevada side (see above for details). The only access on the Arizona side is from **Temple Bar**, 19 miles south of Hoover Dam, then another 27 miles northeast on a good

South of Hoover Dam, US-93 runs parallel to the older version of the highway, with numerous old bridges and sections of gravel roadway standing along the modern four-lane freeway.

From US-93 just north of Kingman, Hwy-68 runs due west to Bullhead City and **Laughlin,** Nevada, a booming gambling resort along the Colorado River. For information, contact the Laughlin Chamber of Commerce (702/298-2214 or 800/227-5245).

paved road; a small marina has boat rentals and a motel (520/767-3211 or 800/752-9669).

Stretching to both sides of Hoover Dam, the Lake Mead Recreation Area also incorporates the smaller Lake Mojave, clearly visible from US-93 and accessible at **Willow Beach** on the Colorado River, 14 miles south of Hoover Dam and four miles west of US-93.

Chloride

Marked by a big "C" inscribed in the hillside above it, the near-ghost town of Chloride (pop. 352), 53 miles south of Hoover Dam and 15 miles north of Kingman, then four miles east of US-93 on a paved, well-marked road, is the oldest and among the most evocative former mining camps in Arizona. Following the discovery of silver here in the 1860s, mining activities continued through the 1940s; the town is now preserved by its dedicated residents.

A couple of stores and cafes still cling to life, and occasional festivals and flea markets draw sizeable crowds of visitors. Mostly what there is to see are the odd bits of "folk art" so often found in the American desert: strange sculptures made of rusting metal and odd bits of junk, plus comical tributes to the mythology of the Wild West, like a fake "Boot Hill" cemetery with laconic epitaphs and hand-painted signs playing up the apocryphal legacy of the local "Hangin' Judge" Jim Beam.

Before the I-40 interstate bypassed it in the 1970s, Kingman was a vital desert oasis on the famous Route 66. For more, see the Route 66 chapter, beginning on page 628.

Kingman

Since its founding as a railroad town in 1880, Kingman, the only town for miles in any direction (pop. 12,750), has always depended upon passing travelers for its livelihood. Long a main stopping place on historic Route 66, and still providing the only services on US-93 between Hoover Dam and Wickenburg, or on I-40 between Flagstaff and Needles, Kingman is still more of a way station than a destination, though increasingly many people have relocated here in recent years, attracted by the open space and high desert air, and the low cost of living.

Everything that's ever happened in and around Kingman is documented to some degree at the **Mojave Museum,** 400 W. Beale Street (Mon.-Fri. 10 AM-5 PM , Saturday and Sunday 1-5 PM; $1), right on US-93 a block south of I-40. Besides the usual dioramas and displays on regional history, there's an extensive section devoted to local Hualapai culture and crafts, plus samples of turquoise mined nearby. There's also a display on the life of local boy Andy Devine, gravelly voiced character actor whose most famous role was as the driver in John Ford's *Stagecoach,* and a photograph of Clark Gable and Carole Lombard, who fled Hollywood to get married in Kingman's Methodist Church.

There are quite a few remnants of the old Route 66 cafes and motels along its route (now called Andy Devine Avenue) through Kingman, though most development has bordered the I-40 freeway. Among many places to eat are the very good **Mr. D's Route 66 Diner**, right downtown and impossible to miss thanks to its bank of neon, and the **House of Chan**, 960 W. Beale Street, on US-93 a block north of I-40, which serves a full menu of American food as well as Cantonese specialties. Besides the usual chain motels (two nice **Best Westerns**, two **Days Inns**, a **Holiday Inn**, and a **Travelodge**) accommodation options include the pleasant **Hill Top Motel**, 1901 E. Andy Devine Avenue (520/753-2198), where Timothy McVeigh stayed for a week before allegedly blowing up the federal building in Oklahoma City.

Andy Devine

Hualapai Mountain Park

To escape the summer heat, Kingmanites head south along a well-marked 14-mile road to Hualapai Mountain Park, where pines and firs cover the slopes of the 8,417-foot peak. Hiking trails wind through the wilderness, and there's a **campground** ($6) and a few rustic **cabins** ($25) built by the CCC during the New Deal 1930s; contact the **ranger station** (520/757-3859), near the park entrance, for detailed information or to make reservations.

Wickenburg

North of Wickenburg, US-93 is known as the **"Joshua Tree Parkway"** because it passes through many miles of cactus forest, the center of which is 30 miles from town.

In the middle of the Arizona desert, 60 miles northwest of Phoenix and 130 miles from Kingman, **Wickenburg** (pop. 4,500) grew up as a gold-mining camp in the 1860s and has survived as a low-key resort community. A few crusty prospectors still search for a strike, and cowboys are often seen riding through town, which makes Wickenburg a pleasant place to get a feel for the Old West, especially during the winter months when temperatures are mild and the sun shines nearly every day.

Wickenburg's reliably good winter weather accounts for the number of **dude ranches** dotting the surrounding desert, most of which are intended for long stays (a week at least) rather than passing travelers; for a complete list of properties, or further information, contact the **visitor center** (520/684-5479) in the old railroad depot on Frontier Street, a block west of US-93.

Two blocks south along Frontier Street and the railroad tracks, at the US-60/US-93 junction and Wickenburg's only stoplight, the **Desert Caballeros Western Mu-**

the Santa Fe Depot, Wickenburg

South of Wickenburg and the Hassayampa River Preserve, the highway crosses over the canal of the **Central Arizona Project,** which provides Colorado River water to Phoenix and Tucson.

At Wickenburg, US-93 officially comes to an end, replaced from here south to Phoenix by a joint US-60/89.

seum (Mon.-Sat. 10 AM-4 PM, Sun. 1-4 PM; $2.50) gives a broad overview of regional history, and contains a surprisingly good collection of Western art and sculpture.

Most of the places to eat are lined up along east-west US-60 (Wickenburg Way); try the **Gold Nugget** coffee shop at 222 E. Wickenburg Way, across from the **Best Western** (520/684-5445 or 800/528-1234).

Hassayampa River Preserve

One of Arizona's very few stretches of riverside ecology preserved in its natural state, the Hassayampa River Preserve, three miles southeast of Wickenburg on US-60/89, is a great place to break a journey. For most of its way, the Hassayampa River runs underground, but here it rises to irrigate a dense forest of willows and cottonwood trees, which in turn shelter an amazing variety of birds—over 200 species, from songbirds to raptors, are listed in the preserves' birders' guide.

The Nature Conservancy, which owns and operates the preserve, runs a small **visitor center** (Wed.-Sun. 8 AM-5 PM in winter, 6 AM-noon in summer; $5 donation) where you can pick up trail guides and maybe join a guided walk.

Phoenix sights and services are covered in a Survival Guide on pages 710-711.

The Apache Trail and the Superstition Mountains

East of Phoenix, US-60 runs as a four-lane freeway through the shopping-mall suburbs of Tempe and Mesa, but the sprawl ends suddenly around Apache Junction, which marks the beginning of the scenic Apache Trail. Winding along the Salt River, and named for the tribe that dominated the area a century ago, the Apache Trail was created in the early 1900s as a supply road during the construction of Theodore Roosevelt Dam; it now passes by a series of attractive state parks and odd little towns, while giving access to the beautiful Superstition Mountains.

cliff dwellings

From the US-60 freeway, take Idaho Road (exit 11) north onto the well-signed Hwy-88. After five miles the suburbs give way to the wild desert of **Lost Dutchman State Park** ($3 day-use fee), named for a legendary gold mine located nearby. Two miles farther is the overlook for the 4,535-foot phallus of Weaver's Needle, beyond which the road passes a series of reservoirs before reaching the entertaining tourist-trap hamlet of **Tortilla Flat** (pop. six), 18 miles from US-60 and named after the Steinbeck novella—which has nothing to do with Arizona, but who cares?

Beyond Tortilla Flat, which has a good cafe, a saloon with frequent live music, and a small motel, the road turns to dirt, and twists and turns through spectacular desert country for the next 27 miles to Roosevelt Dam, then heads southeast to join US-60 at Claypool.

For information on the Apache Trail, or on hiking and camping in the Superstition Mountains, contact the U.S. Forest Service **ranger station** in Mesa (602/ 835-1161).

While the route described here is far more scenic, the **I-10** freeway between Phoenix and Tucson is considerably faster.

South of Florence, Hwy-79 follows the **Pinal Pioneer Parkway,** the old main road between Phoenix and Tucson. The route is now lined by a series of signs pointing out palo verde trees, saguaros, and other desert flora.

Florence and Casa Grande Ruins National Monument

From Apache Junction, US-60 runs southeast for 15 miles to Florence Junction, where Hwy-79 (old US-89) cuts off to the south at **Florence**. One of Arizona's oldest towns, but now best known as the site of the state's largest prison, Florence has a pleasant, non-touristy Main Street of bars, general stores, and junk shops, parallel to and a half-mile west of the highway. The penal history is documented in gruesome detail at the **Pinal County Historical Museum** (Wed.-Sun. noon-4 PM; donations), 715 S. Main Street, where an actual hangman's noose and chairs from the retired gas chamber are displayed along with photos of people put to death.

Tom Mix monument

Cowboy actor **Tom Mix** died on October 12, 1940, when he crashed his 1937 Cord Phantom into a ditch along Hwy-79. The site is marked by a riderless horse, in a rest area 19 miles south of Florence.

The most popular destination around Florence is the **Casa Grande Ruins National Monument** (daily 7 AM-6 PM; $1), eight miles west of town off Hwy-287, which preserves some of the state's largest and most perplexing prehistoric remains. A small **visitor center** at the entrance gives some background on the Hohokam people who, approximately six centuries ago, built the four-story "big house" and the surrounding village, but no one knows what it was used for, or why it was abandoned.

copper bells

shell finger ring

BIO⬡² SPHERE

Biosphere II
One of the most ambitious, controversial, and just plain bizarre schemes to hatch in recent years, Biosphere II stands in the Arizona desert at the northern foot of Mount Lemmon. Developed by a new-age group called "Synergia Ranch," and funded by the Texas billionaire Ed Bass, Biosphere II was originally intended to simulate the earth's entire ecosystem, in order to test the possibility of building self-sustaining colonies on other planets. A crew of four "biospherians" spent two not entirely self-sustained years sealed inside, emerging in 1993, when another crew took their place.

Amidst allegations of corruption and deceit, the founders of Biosphere II were unceremoniously fired by Mr. Bass in 1994, and the project has since been redirected to focus on pure research—though the Biosphere II is still a sealed system, there are no longer any people locked inside, and scientists study the affects of "greenhouse gases" and other ecosystem changes. Media attention and tourist traffic have died down considerably, but you can still visit the very pretty site and take a self-guided tour (daily 9 AM-4 PM; $11.95).

The environmental activist and author **Edward Abbey,** who died in 1989, spent his last years living in the Arizona desert near Oracle Junction.

Located in a lovely desert canyon, the Biosphere facility (which was originally constructed in the 1970s as a corporate retreat for Motorola) also offers good meals in a small cafe and comfortable and inexpensive accommodations—rooms cost $50-80 a night depending upon the time of year, and there are tennis courts and a swimming pool. To reach Biosphere II, follow Hwy-79 to Oracle Junction, 25 miles north of Tucson, then turn east onto Hwy-77 for six miles; at the Biosphere II signs, turn south and follow the driveway for just over two more miles to the parking area, ticket booth, and gift shop.

For more information, call 520/825-6200 or 800/828-2462.

Tucson is covered in a Survival Guide on pages 724-725.

Mission San Xavier del Bac

Among the most strikingly memorable of all the Spanish colonial missions in the Southwest, Mission San Xavier del Bac was built over 200 years ago and still serves the native Tohono O'odham people. Known as the "White Dove of the Desert" because of the gleaming white plaster that covers its adobe walls, balustrades, and twin bell towers—one of which is domed, the other not—this landmark edifice was designed and built by Franciscan missionaries beginning in 1778; outbuildings date to the mid-1750s, and the mission was originally founded in 1700 by the Jesuit priest Eusebio Kino, who also established the mission farther south at Tumacacori.

Rising up from the flat desert plain, San Xavier presents an impressive silhouette, but what's most unforgettable is the Mexican folk-baroque interior, covered in intensely wrought sculptures and paintings of saints and religious imagery. Currently under restoration by a team brought in from Italy, these paintings and figurines are among the country's finest example of folk art, using painted mud to simulate marble, tiles, and crystal chandeliers.

In Amado, just west of I-19 at the Arivaca Road exit, a huge concrete cow's skull stands across from the popular **Cow Palace** restaurant, which is open daily 8 AM-9 PM.

The mission (daily 8 AM-6 PM; donations; 602/294-2624) is well signed and easy to reach, just 10 miles south of downtown Tucson off I-19 exit 92, then a half-mile west. Across the plaza from the church is a small Tohono-owned and -operated complex of very good crafts galleries plus a snack shop.

Titan Missile Museum

In just 15 miles south of San Xavier, you can travel from the colonial 1700s to the Cold War 1960s by stopping at the Titan Missile Museum, the only Intercontinental Ballistic Missile (ICBM) silo preserved intact and open to the public anywhere in the world. Near the sprawling retirement community of Green Valley (pop. 13,231), just west on Duval Mine Road from I-19 exit 69, the silo was in active use from 1963 until 1982, was declared a National Historic Landmark in 1994, and is now open for **tours** (daily 9 AM-5 PM; $5; 520/625-7736). The tours, which take around an hour, involve donning a hard hat and descending downstairs into the control room of the hardened silo, which still contains a 110-foot-tall Titan missile. Also on display are a partly dismantled rocket engine and a "re-entry vehicle," which would have held the nuclear-tipped warhead.

Between Tubac and Tumacacori, the Anza Trail follows a brief portion of the route taken in 1775 by explorer **Juan de Anza,** who led a group of colonists across the deserts to establish the city of San Francisco in 1776.

The I-19 freeway south of Tucson toward the Mexican border gives all distances in **metric** measures; speed limits, however, are still the same old 65 mph.

Tubac

Another good place to stop between Tucson and the Mexican border is Tubac, 45 miles from Tucson, just east of I-19 at exit 34. One of the first European outposts in what's now Arizona, Tubac was established as a Spanish presidio (fort) in 1751, and a century later boomed with the opening of gold mines nearby. The town's lively history is recounted at the **Tubac Presidio State Historic Park** (daily 8 AM-5 PM; $1) on the east side of town, from where you can walk a short (4.5-mile-long) portion of the **Anza Trail** south to Tumacacori and get a real sense of what it was like on the Spanish colonial frontier.

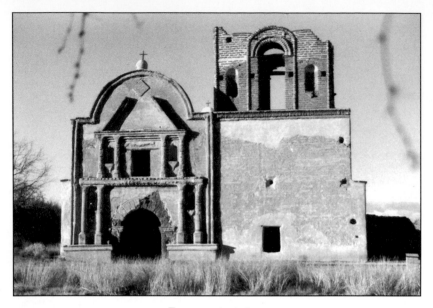

Tumacacori mission

Scattered around a dusty central plaza, just west of the presidio park, Tubac has developed into a small but diverting arts-and-crafts colony, with local artists frequently showcased in the **Tubac Center for the Arts** (Tues.-Sat. 10:30 AM-4:30 PM, Sunday 1-4:30 PM; free) on the north side of the plaza. A short walk south of the plaza, an excellent bookshop, **Tortuga Books**, and the popular **Cafe Fiesta**, which has very good salads and sandwiches, share space in the Mercado del Baca shopping complex at 19 Tubac Road.

Tortuga Books

Tumacacori National Historic Park

The preserved ruins of an impressive Spanish colonial mission stand at the center of Tumacacori National Historic Park (daily 8 AM-5 PM; $1), 19 miles north of Nogales, and just three miles south of Tubac, off I-19 exit 29. The site was used by missionaries as early as 1691, but it wasn't until 1800 that they set to work building the massive adobe church. Though never finished, thanks to Apache raids and the Mexican Revolution, Tumacacori stands as an impressive reminder of the religious passion of the friars and their efforts to convert local tribes.

Jazz bassist and composer **Charles Mingus** was born in Nogales on April 22, 1922, but soon after moved to L.A. with his father, a railroad worker.

Nogales

Arizona's largest border town, Nogales is also perhaps the most pleasant of all the "international" cities along the U.S./Mexico border. Promoted as *Ambos Nogales,* "Both Nogales," the twin cities are economically codependent, especially post-NAFTA; with the downturn in the Mexican economy, however, the influx of illegal immigrants caused a crackdown by the Border Patrol with as many as 500 arrests and deportations every day. The devalued peso has meant that few Mexicans can afford to come across and shop at Safeway, but Americans still while away evenings drinking cut-price beer in south-of-the-border cantinas. There are few real sights to see, but if you just want to spend an hour or two shopping for souvenirs and practicing your Spanish, Nogales is a painless place in which to do it. Drivers should park in the $4-a-day lots on the U.S. side and walk across; border formalities are minimal, and U.S. dollars are accepted on both sides. Though prices on the Mexican side aren't dirt cheap, they are lower than in the U.S.

For further information, or to find out more about traveling farther into Mexico, contact the **visitor center** (520/287-3685).

Mission San Xavier del Bac

US-83: THE ROAD TO NOWHERE

US 83: THE ROAD TO NOWHERE

What was once the only entirely paved route from Canada to "Old Mexico" (as postcards along the route still say), US-83 is still likely the shortest—from Swan River, Manitoba, dead south to Brownsville, Texas, and beyond to Matamoros, Mexico, seemingly without turning once. Its grim moniker, "The Road To Nowhere," is alternately unfair, and then again not severe enough, for the route navigates some of the widest and most aesthetically challenged landscapes in the country: the yawn-inducing rolling grasslands of the northern Great Plains, the beefy expanses of western Nebraska and Kansas, and the mesmerizing heat of the Texas/Oklahoma Panhandle, before following the lower Rio Grande south to the Gulf of Mexico. Yet on US-83 you'll also take in some phenomenal country: verdant farmland dotted with truly small towns, endlessly shifting prairie grassland, rufescent scrubby canyons, winding Missouri River roadways, and plain, isolated, where-the-hell-am-I agricultural expanses.

Following roughly along the 100th Meridian, US-83 marks the historic divide between the "civilized" eastern U.S. and the arid western deserts. Physiography aside, this route's cultural landscape centers around small but self-sufficient farm or cattle communities that date back to the last days of the Wild West, and are far enough off the tourist trail to retain an unselfconscious, aw-shucks quaintness. For endless miles in every direction, telephone and power poles provide some of the only signs of life between the highway and the distant horizon, though the towns—where average speeds drop suddenly from 70 mph to radar-enforced 25 mph or slower—are spaced just often enough along the highway to serve your food-and-fuel needs.

Perhaps best of all, US-83 manages to transnavigate this broad, odd nation, albeit north-to-south, without once grazing a conventional tourist attraction. Here in the nation's heartland, conversations over a daybreak breakfast, afternoons spent cooling off by municipal swimming pools, and twilight American Legion baseball games provide the stuff of truly memorable Road Trip diversions, and for that reason alone, US-83 remains a must-do long-distance byway.

For more information before setting out, contact the **National US-83 Headquarters,** Chamber of Commerce, Drawer 789, Perryton, TX 79070 (806/435-6575).

US-83 HIGHLIGHTS

ACROSS NORTH DAKOTA

Beginning at Canada's Manitoba border, US-83's route across North Dakota is a 285-mile-long rehash of childhood back-of-station-wagon dreamscapes: epic plains too green or golden-hued for your eyes to process rationally, and endless cultivated fields punctuated by umpteen farmers' cooperatives, storage bins, silos, and grain elevators. Hay bales of all shapes and sizes dry perilously close to the roadside, and Stetsoned figures in dusty pickups or mighty tractors amiably lift their index fingers off steering wheels in back-forty greetings.

US-83 doesn't really follow a straight plumb-line south—it just seems that way. After meandering from the border across the fertile residuals of ancient Lake Souris near lonely **Westhope**, the route seems to fall straight down the map while crossing the drift prairie south to **Minot**. Continuing south across the neck of giant **Lake Sakakawea**, US-83 winds across slightly more ambitious hills and plateaus along a historic and hardly changed stretch of the mighty Missouri River to **Bismarck**, the state capital and a better-than-expected place to spend some time. South of Bismarck US-83 cuts away from the riverfront through a pastry-rich pastoral landscape settled around the turn of the 20th century by German immigrants— including the parents of dance-*meister* Lawrence Welk—while a recommended detour follows the Missouri River across the huge, historic **Standing Rock Indian Reservation** that stretches into South Dakota.

A half-hour side trip east from US-83 along Hwy-5 brings you to the town of Bottineau, where a giant turtle named "Wee'l" has been constructed out of old tractor tires.

Westhope

US-83 begins winding its way from the Canadian border at the small U.S. entrance station (open 9 AM-10 PM only) six miles north of Westhope (pop. 575). Westhope, named by an optimistic Great Northern Railway official, is a good example of North Dakota's small agrarian towns. A few motels, cafes, and gas stations, a sparse two-block-long downtown, and that's about it. The **Gateway Inn** motel/lounge (701/245-6441) has tourist information on the area.

Six miles south of Westhope, US-83 zigzags west along Hwy-5 for five miles before sharply banking south. The next 37 miles to Minot are a straight shot south, passing nothing save two sweeping wildlife refuges and a solitary, nay, lonely **Domino's Pizza**, all by itself apart from occasional A-10s thundering overhead to and from Minot Air Force Base.

Minot

Snug in the Souris River Valley at the junction of US-2 and US-83, Minot (pop. 34,544; rhymes with "Why not?") evokes ambivalence from most travelers. Some loathe it outright for its apparent nothingness, but while it isn't exactly picturesque, there *are* worse aesthetic experiences on the Great Plains. At the very least, you'll find a fair range of cowboy hats to look at in the downtown stores.

Minot grew so rapidly after the Great Northern Railroad came through in 1887 that it was dubbed "Magic City," though perhaps "Event Capital" would be more apropos today, for despite the city's importance in other areas, most people visit during the huge State Fair (third week in July), and during October's burgeoning **Norsk Hostfest**, "North America's Largest Scandinavian Festival." The fairgrounds, along the grandly named Bur-

dick Expressway (Business US-2) a half-mile east of downtown, also hold the small **Pioneer Village and Museum** (daily 10 AM-6 PM, summer only), the usual assembly of turn-of-the-century buildings and artifacts gathered from all over the county.

In summer, when daytime highs hover in the humid mid-90's, Minot's most enticing attractions are the expansive gardens of **Roosevelt Park**, along the banks of the Souris River between the fairgrounds and downtown Minot. Named, liked everything else in North Dakota, for Teddy Roosevelt—there's a larger-than-life statue of him, astride a horse in full Rough Rider regalia—the shady green space also holds a large **swimming pool** (daily 1-10 PM in summer; $2) with a 350-foot-long water slide, a rideable miniature train ($2), and a 20-acre **zoo** (daily 10 AM-8 PM in summer, 8 AM-4 PM rest of the year; $3), with some obscure animals and a Northern Plains habitat.

What look like high-security parking lots all around Minot are actually underground missile silos, over 100 of which surround the town. They are still in use, under the command of Minot Air Force Base.

Minot marks the junction of US-83 and US-2, which runs across the country from Seattle via Canada to Bar Harbor, Maine. The latter route is covered in the "Great Northern" chapter, beginning on page 334.

Along with the usual crossroads barrage of franchised fast-food places, Minot supports a couple of breakfast and lunch-only cafes, including **Charlie's Main Street Cafe** at 113 S. Main Street, and **Gladys' Place** at 300 E. Central Avenue. Charlie's is right downtown, its fluorescent-lit pink vinyl booths full of gossiping Minot ladies, while Gladys' is three blocks east, near the train tracks and grain elevators, its fluorescent-lit brown vinyl booths full of gossiping Minot men; the food's good at both, and you get a pot of coffee when you order a cup.

After dark, choose from any of over a dozen haunts, from bingo parlors and low-stakes casinos to country-western honkytonks like **Tilly's**, housed in an old Standard Oil service station at 720 N. Broadway (US-83), or low-key beer bars like the **Blue Rider**, 118 1st Avenue SE, a smoke-free pub with what may be rural North Dakota's best selection of bottled brews—look for the "Grain Belt Beer" sign.

In the 1880s, Minot was one of the spots where scavenging "plains-combers" collected enormous piles of buffalo bones to be used in making fertilizer.

Motels are scattered along the congested arteries of both US-83 and US-2, so (except perhaps during the state fair) you shouldn't have trouble finding a place to sleep. The nicest place to stay is the **Best Western International Inn**, on US-83 at 1505

N. Broadway (701/852-3161 or 800/528-1234); less expensive local motels include the clean and quiet **Fairview Lodge**, across from the fairgrounds at 1900 E. Burdick Expressway (701/852-4488 or 800/836-2047).

In range for an hour or more in all directions, Minot's **KRRZ 1390 AM** broadcasts oldies from the 1950s and 1960s, along with Minnesota Twins baseball games.

The Minot **visitor center**, on US-83 south of downtown at 1040 S. Broadway (701/857-8206 or 800/264-2626), has more complete listings and detailed information on events and activities. Being so central to the state, Minot hosts everything from chili cook-offs to the state softball championships.

Lake Sakakawea and Garrison

Nearly 200 miles long and with 1,600 miles of shoreline along the dammed Missouri River, Lake Sakakawea is one of the largest man-made "lakes" in the U.S. There are countless things to do on the water, most of them involving fishing; in summer, a 24-hour fishing hotline (701/463-7376) has details of what's biting where.

East of Minot on US-2, the town of Rugby is nearly the **Geographical Center of North America.**

The pleasant town of Garrison (pop. 1,530), on the north shore of the lake and six miles west of US-83 on Hwy-37, serves as lake headquarters. Besides boasting a pair of red-roofed water towers labeled "Hot" and "Cold," Garrison has what may be the

country's only neon-signed City Hall. In the city park you'll find the **North Dakota Fishing Hall of Fame and Museum** (Friday 4-8 PM, Saturday noon-8 PM, and Sunday noon-4 PM, June-Sept. only), marked at the north end of Main Street by a photogenic fiberglass statue of "Wally-the-26-Foot-Walleye."

Garrison Dam

South of the extended bridge across Lake Sakakawea, and 12 miles west of US-83 via Hwy-200, the Missouri River backs up behind wide but low-slung Garrison Dam, the third-largest earth-filled dam in the U.S., which you can explore during hourly public **tours** (daily 7:30 AM-3:30 PM in summer; free). The powerhouse is enmeshed within a labyrinth of huge power stanchions, high-voltage lines, and transformers. You can also visit the adjacent **fish hatchery** (same hours as the dam) on the downstream side of the dam, where tanks hold hundreds and thousands of walleye, bass, and northern pike, plus rainbow and brown trout.

South of the turnoff to Garrison Dam, roadside interest along US-83 focuses on leviathan testimonials to engineering prowess. Huge tractors and bulldozers raise clouds of dust at the extensive **coal mining** operations around

Underwood—the whole area on both sides of US-83 has been strip-mined and restored, though current operations are hard to get a good look at—and most of the valuable black rock ends up at electricity generating plants like the **Coal Creek Station**, six miles north of Washburne and two miles off the roadway but *readily* apparent. This is the largest lignite-fired coal plant in the country, and one of the few that's open for **tours** (Mon.-Fri. 8 AM-3 PM; free; 701/442-3211, ext. 810); you can also get an up-close gawk at their **four-mile-long coal conveyor belt**, which passes over the highway in a tube.

However, unless you have an abiding interest in fossil fuels, a more interesting alternative to driving this stretch of US-83 is to follow the river's western bank south of Lake Sakakawea, where it reverts to its naturally broad and powerful self for the next 75 miles. Between Garrison Dam and Washburn, scenic Hwy-200 passes two of North Dakota's most significant historic sites, Fort Clark and the Knife River Indian Villages, both of which, though small, saw key scenes of the late 18th- and early 19th-century interactions between Native Americans and interloping European traders and explorers.

> Lake Sakakawea is one of many places in the northwestern U.S. named for the legendary Shoshone Indian woman, also known as **Sacagawea,** who accompanied the Lewis and Clark expedition across the Rocky Mountains.

Knife River Indian Village National Historic Site

Downstream from Garrison Dam along the west bank of the Missouri River, the Knife River Indian Village National Historic Site (daily 8 AM-6 PM in summer, daily 8 AM-4:30 PM in winter; free) is one of North Dakota's most fascinating historic places, and the only federally maintained site devoted to preservation of the Plains tribes' cultures. Standing above the Missouri floodplain, on the site of what was the largest and most sophisticated village of the interrelated Hidatsa, Mandan, and Arikara tribes, the park protects the remains of dozens of terraced fields, fortifications, and earthlodges, remnants of a culture that lived here for thousands of years before being devastated by disease within a few short decades of European contact.

Highlight of the park is an earthlodge, recently reconstructed using traditional materials, which gives a vivid sense of day-to-day Great Plains life. Measuring over 50 feet across, and 12 feet high at its central smoke hole, the earthlodge looks exactly as it would have when the likes of George Catlin and Karl Bodmer were welcomed by the villagers during the 1830s. Just north of the earthlodge spread circular depressions in the soil—which is all that remains of the Hidatsa community where in 1804 the Lewis and Clark Corps of Discovery was joined by the French fur trapper Charbonneau and his wife Sacagawea.

The modern **visitor center**, well signed off Hwy-200 at the south edge of the park, has high-quality reproductions of the drawings and paintings that Catlin, Bodmer, and others made of the Knife River Indian Villages, along with archaeological and anthropological summaries that help to bring to life these intriguing Native American peoples. The center also has **information** (701/745-3309) on

Knife River Indian Village

the many annual events, festivals, and powwows held at Knife River thoughout the year, including the Northern Plains Indian Culture Fest, late in July.

A half-mile south of the visitor center, the tiny town of **Stanton** (pop. 517) has two cafes, two bars, and two gas stations along its three-block main drag. The Mercer County Courthouse, at the center of Stanton, displays arrowheads and other Indian artifacts.

Fort Clark

Seven miles downstream from the Knife River site, well signed off Hwy-200, Fort Clark Historical Site (daily 8 AM-4:30 PM April-Oct.; free) is as eerily isolated as can be. One of three major fur-trading posts on the upper Missouri River, Fort Clark was founded by the American Fur Company circa 1831, primarily to trade with the

---

THE LEWIS AND CLARK EXPEDITION

Following the instructions of President Thomas Jefferson, Meriwether Lewis and William Clark set off across the continent in 1803 to explore the vast territory recently acquired from France in the Louisiana Purchase, in the hope of finding a viable trade route from the Mississippi River to the Pacific Ocean.

Sharing command of what was officially known as the Corps of Discovery, which included 33 soldiers and experienced "mountain men," plus the legendary Sacagawea, her husband Toussaint Charbonneau, and their infant Pomp, not to mention Lewis's Newfoundland dog, Seaman, Lewis and Clark blazed a route up the Missouri River, crossed the Rocky Mountains, and made their way west down the Columbia River, returning to St. Louis after two and a half years and over 8,000 miles of unprecedented travel.

Along with their copious journals, many good books have been written documenting the Lewis and Clark expedition and tracing their route, which has been declared the Lewis and Clark National Historic Trail. Much of the land they traversed has been altered beyond recognition, though numerous historic sights along the way have been preserved or protected as parks or museums; the best of these are described more fully elsewhere in this book.

Museum of Westward Expansion is an excellent museum underneath the Gateway Arch in St. Louis. See page 714.

Sergeant Floyd Monument is a stone obelisk marking the grave of the only expedition member to lose his life, from appendicitis. See page 437.

On-A-Slant Indian Village has been reconstructed atop the remains of a Mandan village. See page 135.

Fort Mandan, where the expedition spent the winter of 1804-05, has been reconstructed downstream from the original site. See page 132.

Knife River Indian Villages, along the banks of the Missouri, hold the remains of the Hidatsa village where Sacagawea lived before joining the Corps of Discovery. See page 129.

Lemhi Pass, on the Idaho/Montana border, is where the expedition first crossed the Continental Divide. See page 98.

Mandan Indians. The fort was visited by other tribes as well as the usual roll-call of adventurers, explorers, and frontier luminaries such as Prince Maximilian, George Catlin, and Karl Bodmer; unfortunately, the steamboats that plied the waters to bring supplies also brought smallpox, and in one tragic winter in 1837 the Mandan tribe's population was cut from 1,600 to 100. After the fur trade declined, Fort Clark was abandoned in 1860.

Today the tranquil site, approached on a narrow gravel-and-dirt road, is devoid of anything—a somber, quiet, unretouched piece of history stretching out on a grassy, flat-topped bluff overlooking the Missouri River. A walking trail has markers designating the locations of eight original buildings; depressions from an earthlodge village are still apparent.

The River of No Return is an impassable portion of the Salmon River. See page 97-98.

Traveler's Rest, in the Bitterroot Valley south of Missoula, was such an idyllic spot that the Corps of Discovery camped here on both the outbound and return legs of their journey. See page 95.

Fort Canby, overlooking the mouth of the Columbia River, has a small museum on the spot where the expedition first saw the Pacific Ocean. See page 28.

Fort Clatsop, a full-scale reconstruction of the wooden fort where the expedition spent a miserable winter in 1805-06, sits in lush forest along the Oregon coast. See page 30.

Tillamook Head, rising high above the Pacific Ocean, is the farthest point the expedition reached. See page 407.

THE LEWIS AND CLARK EXPEDITION
1804–1806

Fort Mandan

Back on the east bank of the Missouri River, north of Washburn and two miles west of US-83, Fort Mandan is a very rustic reconstruction of Lewis and Clark's winter quarters in 1804-05. Arriving here at the end of October after a tediously difficult six-month slog upstream from St. Louis, the expedition set up camp, which consisted of rough-hewn log cabins arranged to form a triangular palisade, surrounded by an 18-foot-high wall. Here the 44 men spent the winter, making friendly contact with nearby Indian tribes, most significantly those of the Knife River site—where Lewis and Clark hired the French fur trapper Charbonneau and his young wife, the legendary Sacagawea, who helped guide them across the Rockies.

As it flows across the south-central corner of North Dakota, the Missouri River also marks the dividing line between the central and mountain time zones.

The actual site of Lewis and Clark's encampment, some 10 miles upstream across the river from the site of Fort Clark, was long ago washed away by the ever-shifting Missouri River, but the full-scale, historically accurate replica fort, built in 1969 by local history buffs, is open all day and night with no admission charge, and gives a strong sense of the deprivations and discomforts suffered by the Corps of Discovery on their two-year expedition across the continent. The fort also has a basic **visitor center** (1-5 PM; free) and an adjacent park with outstanding though bare-bones camping ($5) right along the restless Missouri River. It's a great place to play Tom Sawyer, and on summer afternoons you'll see barefoot kids, shirtless in overalls, fishing and mucking along the banks.

Washburn: Cross Ranch State Park

Now a tranquil little highway town, Washburn (pop. 1,506) was once a frenetic Missouri River ferry crossing, served by steamboats from St. Louis. Besides Fort Mandan, two miles to the northwest, and nice riverside scenery, including some pleasant, dense spinneys, Washburn holds the **Cross Ranch State Park** ($2 per car), six miles southwest on Hwy-1806. The state's newest park, Cross Ranch consists of 560 acres of cottonwood-shaded Missouri River bottomland, and includes the remains of the ghost town of Sanger, numerous hiking trails, canoe rentals, and fine camping, with sites for RVs and for backpackers. There's also a fully furnished **log cabin**, in which you can stay for $35 a night; for details phone the **visitor center** (701/794-8741), which also has information on the annual Missouri River Bluegrass Festival, held Labor Day weekend.

In winter, the steps of the North Dakota state capitol are so treacherously icy that workers pile snow onto them to prevent people from walking up them.

Adjacent to the state park and owned by the Nature Conservancy, the **Cross Ranch Nature Preserve** (free) has one of the richest surviving native Missouri River valley ecosystems, including floodplain prairie and riparian forest, plus a resident herd of bison and some undisturbed Native American archaeological sites.

Thirty miles west of Bismarck, the "World's Largest Cow" stands along I-94 in New Salem.

From Washburn, a bridge across the Missouri River carries Hwy-200 northwest on a scenic loop past Fort Clark and the historic Knife River Indian Villages (see above for more).

Bismarck

Like many towns across the Great Plains, Bismarck (pop. 49,300) was named after a wealthy European, in this case the chancellor of the German Empire, in order to lure much-needed capital investment. The town grew exponentially following booms in the railroad industry, gold, and, most recently, oil and synthetic fuels; but it's still economically and culturally dependent upon its status as North Dakota's state capital. It's one of the smallest of the 50 in the U.S., but as state capitals go Bismarck rates quite highly for its size, with thousands of parkland acres, well-preserved historic districts, and an old-time boat ride along the Missouri River.

George Armstrong Custer

Bureaucratic Bismarck seems intent on glossing over its bawdy historical peccadilloes by building monuments to modernity like the capitol building, 19 stories of angular art deco nicknamed the "Skyscraper of the Prairies." The white limestone and classical symbolism seem out of place on the plains, but free **tours** (daily 8-11 AM and 1-4 PM) highlight the ornate interior's woodwork, stonecarving and metalsmithing.

On the grounds you'll find the usual memorial statues of noteworthy North Dakotans, starting with a large statue of **Sacagawea**, the guide of Lewis and Clark, carrying her newborn baby Baptiste and looking sternly forward; nearby is another popular subject, a **buffalo**, here rendered out of rusty steel reinforcing rod. A short walk away, the **North Dakota Heritage Center** (Mon.-Fri. 8 AM-5 PM, Saturday 9 AM-5 PM, Sunday 11 AM-5 PM; donations), has an informative array of historical and cultural exhibits, tracing the development of North Dakota from its geological underpinnings to its contemporary industries.

Though Bismark is the state capital, the selection of places to eat is on the meager side, with a few old buildings turned into ersatz but suddenly upscale pubs-*cum*-restaurants like **Peacock Alley**, 422 E. Main Street, serving predictable pasta and Cajun dishes. Across the street, a former train station has metamorphosed into a Mexican cantina called **Fiesta Village**, and a block away, off the corner of N. 3rd and E. Broadway, the **Green Earth Cafe/One World Coffeehouse** is a hip haunt which, as the name implies, is a hangout for the city's otherwise unobtrusive leftist fringe, sponsoring readings or performances of a disparate range of industrial, folk, and jazz music.

Along with the clusters of motels on the northern fringes of US-83 and along I-94, accommodation options include a **Best Western Fleck House Motel**, in downtown proper at 122 E. Thayer Street (701/255-1450), with cheaper-than-usual rooms from $35 a night.

For further information, contact the Bismarck **visitor center**, 523 N. 4th Street (701/222-4308 or 800/767-3555).

Between the two state capitals of Bismarck, North Dakota, and Pierre, South Dakota, the Missouri River has been dammed to form 200-mile-long **Lake Oahe.**

Follow US-83 south of Bismarck to visit Strasburg, North Dakota, birthplace of **Lawrence Welk,** whose childhood home still stands along the highway.

In his best-selling travelogue *Travels with Charley,* writer John Steinbeck wrote about Bismarck: "Here is where the map should fold. Here is the boundary between east and west. On the Bismarck side it is eastern landscape, eastern grass, with the look and smell of eastern America. Across the Missouri on the Mandan side it is pure west, with brown grass and water scorings and small outcrops. The two sides of the river might well be a thousand miles apart."

An outstanding alternative to US-83 between Bismarck and the South Dakota border is the narrow but well-maintained Hwy-1806, which meanders along the Missouri River taking in great hillocks and easy bluffs off to the left, or scintillating blue water ribboning beneath stark-white, standing-driftwood trees. Round a bend and you'll see a lagoon or a morass. Or admire a great panorama of 2,000-foot buttes to the west, all the way across the state line. Be sure to fill up on gas and supplies before you leave Bismarck since it's a 100-mile drive with few services along the way.

Mandan and Fort Abraham Lincoln State Park

A somewhat shabby cross-river sibling to the state capital, Mandan (pop. 15,177) is a shipping and warehousing center that grew up swiftly in the years after 1882, when the Northern Pacific railroad completed a bridge from Bismarck. Everything in Mandan, from cafes to beauty parlors, seems to be named after Lewis and Clark, but there's not a lot to see in town apart from two statues, one a 25-foot-tall Indian figure carved from a cottonwood tree standing at 601 6th Avenue, the other the requisite Teddy Roosevelt, in front of the train station on Main Street. These aside, the real reason to stop in Mandan is to enjoy a sandwich and a milk shake (or a rare cup of espresso!) at the lunch counter of the truly marvelous Americana-rich **Mandan Drug,** 316 W. Main Street.

Heading south along Hwy-1806 from Mandan along the west bank of the Missouri River, the first place you'll reach is sprawling Fort Abraham Lincoln State Park (daily 8 AM-dusk; $3), which was originally established by the Northwest Company as a fur-trading post in 1780. It eventually fell into the hands of the U.S. Army, which in 1872 changed the fort's name to the present one. Soon afterwards, General Custer arrived to take over the reins of command, and in 1876 the fort was placed squarely on the map and in the national press as the departure point for the doomed general and his 250 men, who met their demise at Little Big Horn. Abandoned in 1891, the fort was dismantled by settlers who salvaged the wood and bricks to build their own homes, and most everything here today is a reconstruction.

Theodore Roosevelt, Roughrider

The modern park covers nearly 1,000 acres, and contains a number of barracks, stables, and stores, plus a replica of Custer's house (daily 9 AM-5 PM; $4), where paid sycophants will lead you around, calling you "General" while conducting guided tours. Best of all is the **On-A-Slant Indian Village**, near the north end of the park, an excavated Mandan village dating from the mid-17th century, where you can explore four full-scale earthlodges re-created by the Civilian Conservation Corps in 1933-34. An adjacent **museum** (daily 9 AM-9 PM in summer, 9 AM-5 PM rest of the year; $3) gives an overall history of the region, from prehistoric times up through Custer's ill-fated adventure.

If you like the idea of *not* driving for a change, the **Fort Lincoln Trolley** (daily 1-5 PM in summer; $4) runs along the river between Mandan and Fort Abraham Lincoln, departing every hour or so for the 4.5-mile trip, leaving Mandan from a depot at 2000 S.E. 3rd Street.

US-83: Linton, Strasburg, and the Lawrence Welk Birthplace

While the scenery is superior along the Hwy-1806 detour, the trek south of Bismarck along US-83 is redeemed by one totally unique Road Trip destination: the **Ludwig Welk Farmstead** (daily 10 AM-6 PM in summer, by appointment rest of year; $3; 701/336-7519), boyhood home of Lawrence Welk. Located a mile north of the town of Strasburg, then 2.5 miles west from US-83 following well-signed dirt roads, this is the preserved homestead where the world-famous band leader and accordion player was born in 1903.

Though the Lawrence Welk connection is the main draw for most visitors, the farm is intended as memorial to his parents, who as part of an exodus of Bavarian-born Catholic farmers fled the Ukraine during the 1870s and 1880s when exemptions from military service were threatened. The promise of land brought the Welks in the 1890s. The clapboard house that stands today began as a sod house—the mud walls can still be seen in places—and is now full of odds and ends of furniture and memorabilia donated by the Welk family, who still own the land. Hand tools, a windmill, and farming implements are arranged around the yard, while in the hayloft a mannequin dressed as young Lawrence squeezes out polkas on the accordion—apparently, his early playing was so bad that he was banned from praticing in the house, though now his recordings are broadcast nonstop from a *M.A.S.H*-like speaker system strung around the grounds.

Much of southern North Dakota is still predominantly populated by descendants of the original wave of these immigrant "Germans from Russia" who homesteaded the region in the 1890s. Their influence is clearly apparent in the town of Linton (pop. 1,410), on US-83 18 miles north of the Welk homestead, where the **Model Bakery**, 117 N. Broadway, bakes up delicious, creamy custard *kuchen* and Germanic cakes and cookies Tues.-Fri., while in Strasburg (pop. 600), Welk's parents are buried in the cemetery behind the absolutely huge Catholic church that dwarfs the tiny town.

Both Linton and Strasburg also have the only-in-North-Dakota attractions of what must be the **world's smallest bowling alleys**: one is tucked away in back of the **Linton Cafe** on Broadway, while Strasburg's four-laner is behind the **Pin Palace Cafe** on Main Street.

The primary tourist attraction on the Standing Rock Indian Reservation is the **Prairie Knights** gambling casino, on Hwy-1806, 44 miles south of Mandan. To sample this little bit of Las Vegas-on-the-Plains, contact the resort (800/425-8277).

Standing Rock Indian Reservation: Fort Yates

Genuinely huge hills start to appear around the Standing Rock Indian Reservation, home to approximately 4,500 Sioux, spreading across the state line with a total of 880,000 acres. For outsiders, the main draw to the reservation, besides the fantastic roadside views and the glitzy Prairie Knights casino, is the original burial site of **Sitting Bull** in Fort Yates (pop. 183), the reservation headquarters. Though Sitting Bull was originally buried here, two miles west of Hwy-1806, the unimpressive site, marked by a boulder on the dusty road by a hand-lettered sign off on a side road, is certainly not what one would expect for the great warrior. He is now more suitably interred near Mobridge, South Dakota (see page 138).

The border between North and South Dakota is marked every half-mile by 720 stone monuments, each seven feet tall but half-buried in the ground. They were erected by the federal government in 1892; one stands right alongside Hwy-1804, on the eastern shore of Lake Oahe.

Across from the agency headquarters is another site sacred to the Sioux, the **Standing Rock** from which the reservation takes its name. In the correct angle of sunlight, the stone resembles a seated woman wearing a shawl. Legend holds that the woman, jealous of her husband's second wife, refused to move when the tribe decamped; a search party later found her, turned to stone.

South of Fort Yates the scenery is magnificent, particularly in the early morning and evening. Flawless blacktop winds through valleys and up ambitious, swooping hills of grazing land, and you won't even realize you're in South Dakota until you notice the gold border on the highway signs near Kenel, South Dakota.

ACROSS SOUTH DAKOTA

Two hundred and fifty-four miles of US-83 cut through eastern South Dakota's broad expanse, crossing mostly level but never slate-flat topography, and passing through what's known as the "Great Lakes" region of the state, most evident in and around Pierre. Instead of a multilane, transcontinental highway, US-83 across South Dakota resembles a country road, giving an up-close-and-personal look at farming and grazing lands, with an occasional jutting hill, ravine, or serpentine creekbed to break up the monotony. Classic South Dakota—no pretensions.

To either side of the North Dakota border, US-83 is little more than a beeline across the plains. Sadly, the Missouri River is well out of eyeshot, so we highly recommend following a scenic detour across the river through the huge Standing Rock Indian Reservation, linking up with US-83 again at Mobridge. After that you'll pass through small farm towns before reaching the state capital, Pierre, at the center of South Dakota.

Wild pheasants and other beautifully plumed game birds scurry about in the grassy verges along US-83 across the Dakotas.

Standing Rock Indian Reservation

Since US-83's route across northern South Dakota doesn't offer much stimulation for the senses, if you've got the time to spare, detour west along the Missouri River, leaving South Dakota via the "Lewis and Clark Highway," Hwy-1806. This scenic route brings you across the border in the middle of Standing Rock Indian Reservation, which falls mainly in South Dakota but stretches about 30 miles into North Dakota.

On Hwy-1806, at tiny Kenel, you veer a bit to the west, away from the muddy Missouri River and toward imposing 2,200-foot Rattlesnake Butte. You'll cross over huge bays on sweeping bridges, then roll into **Mobridge** (pop. 3,800), the biggest town between the North and South Dakota capitals. Mobridge, once a village of the Arikara tribe, is heavily dependent on the anglers who come to pluck the lunkers, walleye, and even 20-pound northern pike from Lake Oahe, here many miles wide.

In the way of food, Mobridge has nothing special. Try the traditional square meal at **Wrangler Motor Inn** (605/845-3641). Located a half-mile west on US-12 at 820 W. Grand Crossing, the Wrangler is the best stop on the stretch, with two dining rooms, a coffee shop, and rooms from $45 as well as a heated pool. The **Super 8**, also on US-12 West (605/845-7215), is cheaper.

*The town's name, **Mobridge,** stems from a hasty telegraph message transmitted in 1906 by an operator who needed a quick and clear reference to the area. He chose, at random, Mo for the Missouri River, and bridge, referring to the one then under construction by the Milwaukee Railroad.*

*On the walls inside the Scherr-Howe Arena, 212 Main Street in Mobridge, are bold 16- by 20-foot **murals** depicting Sioux history and culture. View them Mon.-Fri. 8 AM-12 PM and 1-5 PM; free.*

Sitting Bull Memorial

Driving six miles west of Mobridge on US-12 and then four miles south on a paved road, you'll find Sitting Bull's final resting place, after his body was disinterred in 1953 from Fort Yates in a controversial, surreptitious move. Whatever injustice or disrespect exhuming his body may have incurred, this magnificent view, high atop a palisade hilltop, is at least worthier than the previous site. The massive granite bust that serves as Sitting Bull's tombstone was carved by the late Korczak Ziolkowski, the sculptor who began the quixotic Crazy Horse Mountain carving near Mount Rushmore.

US-83: Selby, Agar, and Onida

Southeast of Mobridge you rejoin US-83 at diminutive Selby (pop. 707), the kind of sleepy, Middle American hamlet with children riding bikes home at dusk, teenagers rumbling down Main Street in their muscle cars, and a classic cafe on the main downtown drag serving cracked-mug coffee. On the northwest edge of town, near the US-12 and US-83 intersection, you'll find oasislike **Lake Hiddenwood State Park** ($3), with picturesque deep swales and oak and cedar trees surrounding a—as the name implies—secluded swimming hole. If you mentally transport yourself back a century and a half when explorers crossed these bone-dry parts and stumbled accidentally onto this lushness, the name's quite apt.

Between Selby and Pierre, there's nothing of dramatic importance. Highway hypnosis is kept at bay by the **Bangor Monument**, a roadside marker, five miles south of Selby, standing on the site of the vanished town of Bangor (a free book to the first reader who can tell us why Bangor merited a marker!); farther south, then 13 miles east of US-83, the **Cathedral on the Prairie** looms over the hamlet of Hoven (pop. 522). Neither are jaw-dropping in any way.

And then, finally, a town . . . or at least some grain elevators. Agar (pop. 82; "Home of the 1977 State B Track Champions") is a classic, single-sidewalk leg-stretch where the Pepsi machine is as large as the filling station it rests against. The same goes for little Onida (pop. 761), with a handsome onion-domed courthouse, a bright yellow, purple-capped water tower, and a cute city park complete with swimming pool and horseshoe courts. You'd hardly guess that this was once a thriving homesteader boomtown, full of transplanted New Yorkers who named it after Oneida, with no apparent reason for the spelling alteration; eat at **Niehoss's Cafe** downtown, or at the **Fireside Lounge**, a steakhouse and bar right on US-83.

Pierre

The second smallest and by far the sleepiest state capital in the country, Pierre (pop. 12,906; pronounced "Peer"), is an odd amalgam of South Dakota characteristics. Part farm town, part railroad town, and best of all, part river town, Pierre accurately embodies South Dakota's dominant activities. Located at nearly the geographic center of the state, quiet, easy Pierre is filled with natural attractions, totally lacking in the usual power-broker trappings of most state capitals.

The state **capitol** grounds, a verdant island of tranquility with an arboretum, features walking trails and the **Fountain Memorial** fed by natural gas. The fountain is dedicated to Korean and Vietnam War veterans and sits on the capitol's lake, home to thousands of migrating winter waterfowl. Nearby, the **South Dakota Cultural Heritage Center** (Mon.-Fri. 9 AM-4:30 PM, Saturday and Sunday 1-4:30 PM; free) has the usual interpretive historical displays, including the Verendrye lead plate, dating from 1743, which claimed the entire territory for France.

An odder museum is the **South Dakota National Guard Museum,** 303 E. Dakota (Mon.-Fri. 1-5 PM; free), which you can't miss because of the Sherman tank, the A-70 Corsair and the artillery pieces on the boulevard. You can also see General

Sioux Horse Effigy

Custer's dress sword here. For travel-weary roadhogs, the coolest museum is the hands-on **South Dakota Discovery Center and Aquarium** (Sun.-Fri. 1-5 PM, Saturday 10 AM-5 PM; $3), in the old Pierre Municipal Power & Light building at 805 W. Sioux Avenue, with loads of science exhibits.

With the lakes nearby, nature is really what draws folks to Pierre. Bordering the town to the south is long **La Framboise Isle Nature Area**, a perfect place to while away time, recuperating from the drive along the beautiful bay.

If you look under "Hotels" in the Pierre Yellow Pages, you'll find only one listing (and that's a Days Inn!), but there are the usual assorted places to stay on US-83 as it swoops in from the north and follows the wide landscaped boulevards beyond downtown. Along US-83, west of the state capitol building, lots of locally owned places offer single rooms from the bottom-barrel $20 range on up; the **Governor's Inn,** 700 W. Sioux Avenue (605/224-4200 or 800/341-8000), is at the top end of the price and comfort scale. Finally, this same can't-miss-it main drag holds that noteworthy **Days Inn**, 520 W. Sioux Avenue (605/224-0411) with single rooms from $30.

The downtown hole-in-the-wall **D&E Cafe**, seemingly lifted out of celluloid cliche into real life, includes original smoky floors and walls with forgotten wainscoting abused by multiple coats of coffee-brown paint. The food is classic short order with gum-cracking service on the side. Pierre's subtle upward spin has allowed the local **World of Donuts** (not bad doughnuts) to transform itself into a rather ambitious coffee shop at nightfall.

The gregarious staff at the **chamber of commerce** (800/962-2034), 108 E. Missouri Avenue, is chock-full of helpful information.

Houck's Buffalo Ranch, 25 miles northwest of Pierre on Hwy-1806, is a 53,000-acre spread supporting about 3,000 head of bison. The herd was used in the film *Dances with Wolves.*

Fort Pierre

South of Pierre, US-83 crosses the Missouri River, then takes you into Fort Pierre (pop. 1,900). It's not much now, but it has a rich history. As far back as 1817 it was known as Fort Pierre Chouteau, an American Fur Company trading post; and before that it was Ree and Arikara tribal lands. Located at the mouth of the Bad (Teton) River, Fort Pierre once was a thriving port. But it is better known as the site where Joseph La Framboise, a French fur trader, out of necessity stopped and erected a driftwood shelter, establishing the area's first white settlement.

Visit the old fort, now a National Park Service landmark spread out over 1.3 acres near town. At 115 N. Main Street in the center of town you'll find the **Verendrye Museum** (9 AM-6 PM May-Sept.), which has collections of South Dakota pioneer artifacts and a duplicate of the lead plate the Verendrye brothers, the first white men to enter South Dakota, planted here in 1743 to claim the land for France. The original plate is in the state Heritage Center in Pierre; the Verendrye brothers themselves are commemorated with a monument in small Centennial Park, off US-83 at the center of town.

It is legal year-round, and quite common, for locals to shoot the black-tailed prairie dog, considered an over-populated and overly gregarious varmint. For a five-buck general license, you can hunt all you want, though during the rainy season be careful not to get mired in the "gumbo-mud" on the area's unpaved roads.

Immediately south of Fort Pierre, typical South Dakota topography resumes: rolling black and green hills, and twisting creekbeds beneath sharp vertical drops of million-year-old geology. Barely out of the city are the **Gumbo Buttes** to the east, with shale deposits smacking more of northern Montana's scrape marks from open-pit mines.

Fort Pierre National Grasslands

Spreading across the plains south of Pierre along both sides of US-83, the 116,000 acres of the Fort Pierre National Grasslands are home to deer, pronghorn, jillions of waterfowl, and one of the most pervasive stretches of **prairie dog towns** in the region. The area doesn't offer developed campsites, but camping is possible, as is great fishing at some of the hundreds of small dams dotting the landscape.

Murdo

One of the duller stretches of US-83 is this 20-mile leg along the mind-numbing I-90 artery between the Fort Pierre grasslands and Murdo (pop. 700). Once a stop on the legendary Texas Cattle Trail and also used by stagecoaches, the town was named for cattle baron Murdo McKenzie, whose ranch pushed through some 20,000 head of cattle a year. The town of Murdo today still lives on the cattle industry. Stop by the unique **doll museum** (daily 9 AM-10 PM June-Aug., 1-10 PM in May and Aug.; $2), two blocks east of US-83 on US-16.

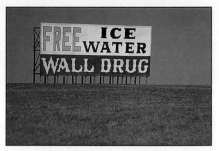

The one place that's definitely worth a stop is smack-dab at the diesel-blue polluted confluence of US-83 and I-90, where nostalgists will find the **Pioneer Auto Museum and Antique Town** (daily 7 AM-10 PM June-Aug., daily 8 AM-6 PM April-May and Sept.-Oct.; $5.25); pricey, maybe, but it's a 10-acre, 39-building collection of about 250 antique cars, with tons of other great items. Classic cars include a rare Tucker (the 1940s car with the central pivoting headlamp; George Lucas made a movie about it). There's also a nifty White Co. motor home from 1921, one of the earliest RVs, and, star of the show, Elvis Presley's 1976 Harley Davidson Electra Glide 1200 motorcycle. Pure Americana.

As you cruise along the I-90 freeway, keep an eye out for **Wall Drug** signs, advertising the world-famous site that is 100 miles to the west of US-83. If you go as far as Wall, you might as well continue on to Mount Rushmore, 50 miles farther along.

The public swimming pool across the street, and the TeePee Restaurant down the road ("We Will Sell No Coffee Over a Half-Hour Old") can round off your Murdo visit.

Rosebud Indian Reservation

Nothing much south of I-90 and Murdo until you come across a picturesque dale while crossing the White River, sheltering the first grove of trees in too long a time. South of White River, US-83 crosses the Rosebud Indian Reservation. After the signing of the Fort Laramie Treaty in 1868, the Sicangu Lakota, under the guide of Spotted Tail, were moved five times before finally being settled on this reservation. It's one of the smallest reservations on this route. The first town you'll encounter is **Mission**, the reservation's trading center. It's a strip of gas stations and a Rosebud/Sioux arts and crafts center. The heart of the reservation is the tribal headquarters (605/747-2381), five miles west on US-18, then 10 miles southwest on BIA Road in **Rosebud**. Most of the reservation's activities are centered here, including **rodeos** and **powwows**, often held on Saturdays and Sundays in the summer. The biggest powwow is the **Rosebud Sioux Tribal Fair and Powwow** in late August, where you can consume a traditional buffalo dinner.

Another eight miles southwest is tiny **St. Francis**, which has the **Buechel Memorial Lakota Museum** (daily June-Sept.; free), a museum dedicated to the Teton Sioux culture and begun by Fr. Eugene Buechel, a German Jesuit, avid botanist, and dedicated student of the culture.

Back on US-83, and another 23 miles south of Mission, is the tribe's most recent economic endeavor, the **Rosebud Casino**.

ACROSS NEBRASKA

The 257 miles from South Dakota to the Kansas border encompass two distinct regions: typical Midwestern wheat and cattle ranches, and the fascinating grass-coated sand dunes of central Nebraska's Sand Hills region. Contrary to popular belief, Nebraska isn't mostly corn; it's beef, lots and lots of it. US-83 passes by more cattle than it does people, with scant few communities along the way.

The powers that be don't neglect to mention your entrance into Nebraska, and it's a good thing, for the subtle changes in the topography (or the quality of the roadbed) won't necessarily be enough to clue you in. Your first stop south of the border is Valentine, then you cross the rolling Sand Hills region toward the railroad town of North Platte, former home of "Buffalo" Bill Cody. From North Platte it's a straight shot south across acres of corn to Kansas.

The **Sand Hills** of northwestern Nebraska form one of the largest areas of rolling dune geology in the world. They're also the largest tract of mid- to tall-grass prairie in North America, and, in the right light, they are absolutely beautiful.

Valentine

Just west of the 100th Meridian, the small town of Valentine (pop. 2,826) is a center of the extensive cattle ranching industry of the Sand Hills region, and the kind of tiny but prideful town that makes roadtripping fun. Seat of enormous Cherry County and situated at the northern edge of the 19,300-square-mile Sand Hills region, Valentine, which takes its name from a U.S. congressman, is a broad, well-maintained place that pays its bills with beef cattle fed to tenderness on the 800 species of grasses coating the region.

Considering the long stretches of road ahead, it's prudent to check out what the town's got, and there's quite a bit. Downtown—where the streetlights are hung with red and white banners emblazoned with the unsurprising town motto "Valentine, Heart of the Sand Hills"—the facade of the First National Bank holds the **largest brick mural** in Nebraska, with 1,200 square feet of images of longhorn cattle and the building of the transcontinental railroad built out of dark brown bricks. Of Valentine's **museums**, the most intriguing is **Sawyer's Sand Hills Museum** (daily 9 AM-6 PM in summer), on US-20 four blocks west of US-83. The museum offers a broad display, including some legitimately historical stuff, as well as a two-headed calf and a great collection of antique cars that still run. The **Cherry County Historical Society Museum**, next door to the pharmaceutically clean and well-stocked **visitor center** (800/658-4024) at the US-20/US-83 junction, is much more traditional.

Thanks to its cupidic name, Valentine is a popular place to send cards for delivery on February 14.

Nature lovers score well in this town. Seasoned canoeists and keen trout anglers, will want to tackle the rough **Snake River** some 15 miles southwest of town, near the short but powerful **Snake River Falls**. A 22-mile stretch of the more sedate **Niobrara River**, east of the Fort Niobrara Wildlife Refuge, offers top-notch canoeing and tubing and in fact is one of *Backpacker* magazine's best picks. The **Fort Niobrara Wildlife Refuge** is a residual of old Fort Niobrara, known for never fighting a battle during its 27 years on the prairie. Today elk, bison, and Texas longhorns roam its 19,122 acres of gorgeous, rolling dune prairie. There are many miles of hiking trails along the wild Niobrara River, which downstream tumbles over 60-foot **Smith Falls**, centerpiece of Nebraska's newest state park, off Hwy-12, 15 miles northeast of Valentine.

Valentine has the usual motels scattered along US-20 and US-83, including the **Trade Winds Lodge** (402/376-1600 or 800/341-8000), with doubles from $35. A few adequate **cafes** are sprinkled about, including the **Home Cafe** across from the **visitor center** at the US-82/US-20 junction, at the south end of town. The place most people go for an evening meal is the **Pepper Mill**, for steaks, seafood, and alfresco dining.

Valentine marks the junction of US-83 and US-20, one of our west-east routes across the country.

The Nebraska Sand Hills

South of Valentine are two fine natural areas, preserving and highlighting the unique ecosystems of the Nebraska Sand Hills. South along US-83 is the large **Valentine National Wildlife Refuge**, which, thanks to water seeped from the world's biggest aquifer, the Ogalala Aquifer, is home to both native rolling dune prairie and lowlands of lake, marsh, and sub-irrigated meadow. Lots of curlews, sandpipers, terns, and mule deer are found on the drives and hikes through the vaulted hills and long spiny grasses, and along the lakeshores.

Beyond this, the Sand Hills occasionally flatten out into simple, absolutely open range, with perhaps a ridge jutting out. The aspect of the land here shows itself as much more scabrous than the

Dakotas. Mauve, tan, and cream cows fleck the land, as do a few windmills: great, stark, American-Gothic windmills, not the Plasticine pseudo-efficient energy spinners seen elsewhere.

US-83 joins with Hwy-2 approximately 30 miles after leaving the Valentine Wildlife Refuge. Swinging east will take you to the one of the three huge **Nebraska National Forest** districts, among the largest man-made forest tracts in the world (20,000 acres total) and one of the oldest extant U.S. Forest Service nurseries. There's no visitor center per se, but ranger stations provide information. A smidgen to the east is classic, sleepy little **Thedford**, sunk low off the road in the reeds, weeds, and glens. The town isn't not much more than funky little houses, loud cicadas, and a combination gas station/cafe.

At the south edge of the Sand Hills, 100 miles west of US-83 via scenic Hwy-2, the totally unique **Carhenge**—the finest Detroit wheels, stacked on top of each other to form a steel Stonehenge—stands just outside the town of Alliance. For further details, see page 432.

Beyond that, the road jumps and descends for another 65 miles toward North Platte with very, very little to occupy your time other than scenic overlooks along the Dismal and South Loup Rivers.

North Platte

US-83 takes its time getting into North Platte proper. The drab outer fringes don't augur much better for the town itself. You approach the first fork of the Platte River, the North Platte, take a leisurely little swoop up and over it, pass scenic bluffs, then flash back to old Hell-on-Wheels ironhorse days. Old train tracks and brick facades lie off to the side, all blue-collar remnants of North Platte's railroad trade and transportation heydays.

Originally the site of a Union Pacific construction camp, North Platte nearly expired when the workers decamped for Colorado; but the 300 permanent residents were spared when the railroad chose it as a division point, securing the town's future. The city is still proud of its **Bailey Yard**, recently decreed by the *Guinness Book of World Records* as the largest railroad classification yard in the world. You

Buffalo Bill

can view it from a high platform four miles west of town on Front Street. Many of the city parks feature railroad displays, including 90-acre **Cody Park** along US-83. Within the park confines rests **Big Boy**, one of the world's largest steam locomotives.

But North Platte is more widely known as the home of Buffalo Bill Cody. The huge **Buffalo Bill Scout's Rest Ranch** (daily 10 AM-8 PM June-Sept., Mon.-Sat. 9 AM-5 PM and Sunday 1-5 PM April-May; $2), four miles northwest via US-30 and Buffalo Bill Avenue, is a state historical park with original dwellings. Cody's house, and some outbuildings, look much the way they did when Buffalo Bill lived here, from 1879 to 1913. This is where Buffalo Bill originated his rodeo with the "Old Glory Blowout" in 1882 and later housed his Wild West Show when not on the road. Tours are available, and the buffalo stew cookouts are popular. The town still whoops it up with the **Buffalo Bill Rodeo** in June.

Besides Buffalo Bill memorabilia, North Platte has an interesting WW II canteen mock-up, a great Railroad Town, and an eight-million-year-old, 200-pound, fossilized land tortoise, all on display at the **Lincoln County Museum** (daily 9 AM-8 PM in summer), 2403 Buffalo Bill Avenue, on the road to Scout's Rest Ranch.

Downtown North Platte is rather level, congested, and unimpressive. Here US-83 separates into two channels. In the heart of the city, on the median between the two, is the **Convention and Visitor's Bureau** (Mon.-Fri. 10 AM-5 PM; 308/532-4729) at 502 S. Dewey. Interstate 80 also whips through North Platte, so including the road you're on, there's no shortage of places to stay, including a **Motel 6** (308/534-6200) on the south side of town on US-83. There is a dearth of good, inexpensive restaurants with any sort of character; but 12 miles west of town **Butch's** reportedly serves the country's best prime rib and pork chops, so tender you can cut 'em with a fork.

As you continue south on US-83 to the power station, you'll run into a country road, going east and south, that leads to the **Sioux Lookouts**, one of the highest points above the Platte Valley. It's marked with a Sioux monument.

McCook

There's nothing much, community-wise, for the next 68 miles south from North Platte, but the road and landscape will hold your interest. You're privy to the few acres of genuine Nebraska corn, which eventually fold into encroaching knobby little rises, hollows full of oaks, or open range. Patches of corn grow in the fertile loam of the Republican River Valley north of McCook (pop. 8,100), originally called Fairview. With the arrival of the Burlington & Missouri Railroad, the town grew into a farm trade center. It's a sedate, content-enough place, with two good excuses for a brief stop. **The Museum of the High Plains** (Tues.-Sat. 1-5 PM, Sunday 1:30-5 PM; free), includes excellent fossil collections, some WW II prisoner-of-war artwork, a room dedicated to Sen. George Norris, and an old drugstore replicated in the very building where Kool-Aid was developed. The **George W. Norris Home** (Wed.-Sat. 10 AM-noon and 1-5 PM, Tuesday and Sunday 1:30-5 PM; $1), 706 Norris Avenue, is devoted to McCook's favorite son, the Nebraska senator who founded the Tennessee Valley Authority and promoted rural electrification during the New Deal 1930s.

South of McCook, the road turns grandly scenic (it's even marked as such on maps), and after 14 miles it crosses the Beaver River almost at the Kansas state line. The road is in excellent condition, passing over old brown trestles on a wide hard surface.

ACROSS KANSAS

Kansas is no mere geographical expression, but a "state of mind," a religion, and a philosophy in one.
—Carl Becker, *Kansas* (1910)

I like Kansas—that is, natural Kansas—better than I had expected to . . .
—Horace Greeley, *An Overland Journey* (1859)

The cliches have told you wrong: US-83 across much of Kansas—surprise, surprise—is actually a treat, not at all the interminable tedium of grainfield stretches you might expect. Yes, the physiography through most of the intrastate span is still dominantly flat, dry Northern High Plains, but it's compensated for, particularly in the north, with extensive irrigation that coaxes lusher patches of vegetation out of the dark rich soil.

US-83 ushers you along gaping, horizon-filled stretches broken by isolated lakes and occasional oases such as Oberlin or Oakley, home of the nearly famous Prairie Dog Town. Continuing south across the windblown plains and limestone hills, US-83 passes through the cow towns of Scott City and Garden City before crossing the Arkansas River into the baked-clay watercolor that stretches south into Oklahoma and Texas. One final Kansas stop is perhaps the best: Liberal, home of *Wizard of Oz* creator L. Frank Baum.

Oberlin

Cedar Bluffs, the first town, two miles after crossing the state line, is hardly noticeable, but funky little Oberlin, 10 miles later, is worth a stop. A picture-postcard town spread out along red-brick downtown streets, Oberlin was the site of the last Indian raid in Kansas on September 29, 1878; 19 settlers were killed. Two days earlier, a fierce skirmish had erupted between Chief Dull Knife's Northern Cheyenne, heading to regain their lands in the Dakotas, and an infantry contingent from Fort Dodge near what today is **Lake Scott State Park**. The Oberlin cemetery contains a memorial to the settlers who were killed, and the town has the late-September **Mini-Sapa Days**, a two-day festival commemorating the event. Downtown along S. Penn Avenue, the worthwhile **Decatur County/Last Indian Raid Museum** (Tues.-Sat. 10 AM-noon and 1-5 PM, Sunday 1:30-4 PM, April-Nov., opens one hour earlier in summer; $3), has eight preserved buildings, including a sod house.

Colby

Out of Oberlin, US-83 sweeps through beautiful farmlands, often paralleling railroad tracks, and passes through low, one-horse towns with high feed elevators. The road banks sharply west and then south after 15 miles. At that point you can either continue on until the road crosses I-70 near Oakley, or you can head west at the US-24 junction to ambitious Colby. The town itself is simply a service center for the wheat belt, but it does have the huge **Prairie Museum of Art and History** (Mon.-Fri. 9 AM-8 PM, plus Saturday 1-8 PM and Sunday 1-5 PM in summer only; $3) at 1905 S.

Franklin Street. The museum is a sprawling, 24-acre complex that includes rare porcelains, china dolls, assorted historical stuff, and the **Cooper Barn**, one of the largest barns in the state.

Oakley

Approximately five miles north of Oakley, a noxious olfactory insult alerts you to an upcoming interstate crossing. Here amid the gaseous assault of I-70 stands possibly the most bizarre tourist trap US-83 has to offer: **Prairie Dog Town** (daily 8 AM-8 PM, May-Oct.). This collection—"Home of the 8,000-lb. Prairie Dog"—is a combination petting zoo/freak show, with collections of the little dogs as well as dozens of birds, snakes, and other critters, many taken in as orphans, and even a six-legged calf.

Treeless Oakley (pop. 2,045) turns out to be an old, big-time railroad town, neither ugly nor picturesque, featuring lots of utilitarian bungalow architecture, massive diesel engines, and railroad tracks. It's unassuming but important, situated as it is at the junction of three major highways. The **Fick Fossil Museum** (Mon.-Sat. 9:30 AM-noon and 1-5 PM, Sunday 2-4 PM; free), at 700 W. 3rd Street, is housed just a few blocks east of US-83 in the public library. Well, it's definitely a museum, albeit featuring some unique exhibits: 11,000 shark teeth, a sod house, collections of pressed wildflowers, and some perfectly garish mosaics, including the Great Seal of the President of the United States, made entirely out of shark's teeth. It was created by—who else?—Mrs. Fick. The paleontological exhibits are quite good, too.

The I-70 Business Loop offers some anemic-looking motels and a couple of adequate cafes downtown; along the interstate, the usual 24-hour, truck-jockey hash is dished out at the **Mitten Cafe** or the **Jones Corner Cafe**.

Chalk Pyramids/Monument Rocks

South of Oakley, the road bolts straight for approximately 20 miles, and truck traffic can be incredibly heavy. The route cuts between an enormous sea of yellow flowers on one side and expanses of open range on the other. Later, the scenery peters out into a prickly dry, faint yellow, rocky desolation that signals the fringes of the Smoky Hills region.

The prime topographical feature of the Smoky Hills is the surreal Chalk Pyramids, also known as Monument Rocks, four miles east of US-83 via an unpaved county road. They're referred to in the old WPA *Guide to Kansas* as the "Kansas Pyramids." These highly eroded geological formations are composed of layers of ancient seabed from the Cretaceous period and were originally formed 80 million years ago. The impressive spires, karstlike formations, and shaley cliffs farther on have yielded thousands of excellent fossils of sharks, fish, and reptiles. The pyramids are on private land but access isn't difficult; however, there are no facilities.

Lake Scott State Park and Scott City

Midway across Kansas, 35 miles south of Oakley and the I-70 freeway, Lake Scott State Park is a true spring-fed oasis sheltering cottonwoods, ash, hackberry, and willow in vacuous, high-sky rangeland. Beyond offering a lovely and relaxing spot in which to unwind, Lake Scott includes Kansas's most intriguing historical site, **El Cuartelejo** ("The Old Barracks") pueblo, the only one in Kansas and the farthest north of any in the country. Originally settled in the 1660s by Taos Pueblo people fleeing the Spanish in New Mexico, the area became home to the Picuris about 30 years later. Both migrant groups joined with the local Plains Apache clan.

Neither group remained for long, and the deserted site became merely a spot for occasional nomadic squatting by the Pawnee, Spanish, and even French before eroding away. The site was discovered accidentally by Herbert Steele, the park founder, who stumbled onto the extensive irrigation ducts leading from spring areas to crop patches. Further excavation eventually revealed the pueblo sites, now considered the first permanent-walled structures in the state. The park has a few other historical points of interest, including a marker on the site of the fateful last battle between the U.S. Cavalry and escaping Cheyenne led by Chief Dull Knife. The battle set the stage for the massacre of settlers near Oberlin two days later. The park also has a private herd of elk and bison.

South of Lake Scott State Park, US-83 continues across the High Plains, with not a whole lot to disrupt the continuity until Garden City, another 45 miles south. The only town of any size is Scott City with its miles and miles of cattle fencing, feed yards, innumerable cattle companies, and big American flags greeting you (or waving goodbye) at the town limits. It's a hardy, industrious place, with everyone busy working. Hard.

South of Scott City are two mere blip-stop towns, both inappropriately named: Shallow Water and Friend.

Garden City

Though it has a classic red-brick downtown and a decent little zoo, Garden City is betther known for its huge public **swimming pool**: 337 feet by 218 feet, with over 2.5 million gallons of water. It's near the Arkansas River in Finnup Park, S. 4th

Street, and it's free! The classic Windsor Hotel downtown is a hotel no longer, but after its construction in 1886 this "Waldorf of the Prairies" drew lots of cowpoke-luminaries such as Buffalo Bill Cody. Garden City also supports the usual gas stations, motels, and fast-food but, best of all, a 4,000-acre **state buffalo preserve**, which may be viewed from US-83 south of town.

Garden City stands at the junction of US-83 and coast-to-coast **US-50;** that chapter begins on page 516.

Farther south, across the often dry-as-a-bone Arkansas River, oil pumps languidly dip their heads. This is where stereotypical Kansas landscape comes in: either stark desolation or—thanks to money and modernity—vast irrigation efforts. Prior to the advent of the reliable Ogalala Aquifer irrigation, overeager farmers almost ruined the region's fortunes plowing up the fragile buffalo grass for a one-season crop, before the wind blew the topsoil away. The hills that stood here prior to the Dust Bowl are gone completely now, and the landscape is endless, see-forever plains, marked by grain elevators a deceptive 10 miles away.

Liberal

First, the name. It's said that a munificent early settler came and dug a well, and whenever a dusty emigrant would offer money for a drink or the chance to wash his neck, the settler would say, "Water is always free here." One day the reply came, "That is mighty liberal."

Second, the adjectives: hot; dusty; treeless; flat. The inbound trip reveals the drab side of Liberal's oil, gas (the town lies on the eastern edge of an enormous natural gas field), and meatpacking industries, and the sights don't improve significantly beyond that. But that's the downside. Liberal, despite its paucity of aesthetic superlatives, isn't the worst place for a stop-off. Honest. There is one significant draw, the top-notch **Mid-America Air Museum** (Mon.-Fri. 8 AM-5 PM, Saturday 10 AM-5 PM, Sunday 1-5 PM; $3.50), 2000 W. 2nd Street. It's one of the largest air museums in the U.S. and has amassed an astonishingly diverse collection of aircraft covering the entire history of flight.

Otherwise, there's a lot of **Ozmania** in town, since Liberal was the home of *Wizard of Oz* author L. Frank Baum. An annual **Oztoberfest** blowout is held at **Dorothy's House** (Mon.-Sat. 9 AM-6 PM, Sunday 1-5 PM June-Aug., fewer hours rest of the year; $2), 567 E. Cedar Street, a combination historical museum and re-creation of the movie's Kansas sets. Also known as the **Coronado House**, the museum displays a horse bit from the expedition of Don Francisco Vasquez de Coronado and his troops, who passed through in 1541 searching for the fabled Seven Cities of Gold.

But the city's coolest event comes on Shrove Tuesday, with its annual, international, soon-to-be-famous **Liberal Pancake Race**, a competition between local housewives and their counterparts from Olney, England. They race a 415-yard, S-shaped course, each flipping a pancake along the way. The event purportedly dates from 1445 when a woman rushed to church with her pan still in her hand.

Outside of town is the majestic **Rock Island Line Railroad Bridge** across the Cimarron River. The "Mighty Sampson" is, at 1,200 feet long and 100 feet above the river, the largest of its kind.

US-54 and US-83 claim the majority of places to stay, including the $30-a-night **Travelers Lodge** (316/624-6203), on US-54 almost a mile northeast of the US-

THE DUST BOWL

Though it may not have been the biggest migration in U.S. history, it was certainly the most dramatic—entire families packing up their few belongings and fleeing the Dust Bowl of the Depression-era Great Plains. Beginning in 1933 and continuing year after year until 1940, a 400-mile-long, 300-mile-wide region roughly bisected by US-83—covering 100 million acres of western Kansas, eastern Colorado, and the "Panhandles" of Oklahoma and Texas—was rendered uninhabitable as ceaseless winds carried away swirling clouds of what had been agricultural land.

The "Dust Bowl," as it was dubbed by Associated Press reporter Robert Geiger in April 1935, was caused by a fatal combination of circumstances. This part of the plains was naturally grassland and had long been considered marginal at best, but the rise in agricultural prices during and after WW I made it profitable to till and plant. Farmers invested in expensive machinery, but when the worldwide economic depression cut crop and livestock prices by as much as 75%, many farmers fell deeply in debt. Then, year after year of drought hit the region, and springtime winds carried away the fragile topsoil, lifting hundreds of tons of dust from each square mile, and dropping it as far east as New York City.

By the mid-1930s, many of the farmers had been forced to abandon their land, and while some were able to rely upon a series of New Deal welfare programs, many more fled for California and the Sunbelt states. In this mass exodus, as recorded by photographers like Dorothea Lange, and most memorably in John Steinbeck's 1939 novel *Grapes of Wrath,* some 100,000 people each year packed up their few possessions and headed west, never to return.

Nowadays, thanks to high-powered pumps that can reach down to the Ogalala Aquifer, much of what was the Dust Bowl is once again fertile farmland, no longer as dependent on the vicissitudes of the weather. Much of the rest of the land was bought up by the U.S. government, and some four million acres are now protected within a series of National Grasslands that maintain the Great Plains in more or less their natural state.

54/83 junction. US-54 is also known as Pancake Boulevard doubtless because the strip lacks places to eat that aren't boisterous, family-style, and faux-western. The local chamber of commerce likes to describe it as "fast-food alley." Right downtown, though, on the west side of US-83 is a new cafe/caterer offering copious homemade lunch specials; look for the sandwich-board sign out front.

ACROSS OKLAHOMA

On its beeline to Texas, US-83 doesn't just cross Oklahoma; it forsakes it, merely nipping the panhandle for a 37-mile dash. You cross the border three miles south of Liberal, and the first things you see are a trailer park, a couple of bars, and a bingo hot-spot. They're inauspicious sights at best. And that's not even mentioning the slate-flat, wicked badlands, with heat bad enough in summer to occlude your vision of the blistering pavement, and preclude a drive at top speeds. After a while you're unable to conjure up synonyms for "endless," though there's plenty of time for it. Even the historical marker you think you eventually see winds up being in Texas.

The first town you come up to is diminutive **Turpin**, comprising a Phillips filling station now usurped by a Shamrock, also farm equipment places, and a motel or two sans signs.

And that's it. *Finito.* You keep stretching the atlas over the steering wheel (no danger in these parts), wondering where the hell **Gray** is, and why you care. It's supposed to be on this highway. You're sure of it. But for some reason it never appears. Before you know it, Texas looms outside the windshield, and damn if the aspect of the land doesn't change literally at the state line. Lots of trees, a historical marker, and hills.

ACROSS TEXAS

The old WPA *Guide to Texas* says that "no other route across Texas offers such differences in topography, produce, climate and people" as does US-83, which is still very true today. Starting at the Oklahoma border on the southern edge of the Great Plains, your route winds along the foot of the Cap Rock escarpment, then opens out onto the cattle country of Edwards Plateau where numerous river canyons provide respite from the mesquite scrub land, and finally ends up some 900 miles later at the Gulf of Mexico. Besides diverse landscapes, US-83 also passes through a virtual survey of Texas history: the prehistoric pictographs of Paint Rock; Mexican-American battlegrounds along the Rio Grande; 100-year-old frontier towns, built of red brick around their central courthouses; and the modern Gulf

In its 900-plus-mile crossing of Texas, US-83 is known as the Vietnam Veterans Memorial Highway, and forms the **longest stretch of highway** through any of the lower 48 states.

Many of the smaller, usually dirt, roads in Texas are labeled "FM," for farm-to-market, or "RM," for ranch-to-market, before their route numbers, i.e., "FM-1208." For simplicity's sake we have labeled them "Route."

Coast resort of South Padre Island. As you'll soon learn if you're perusing other Texas travel literature, this section of the state is, for the most part, ignored. Thus, you're definitely among an elite company, traveling along truly unbeaten paths.

Perryton

After passing by wheat fields and ranch lands, then negotiating a verdant alley of foliage occluding the highway signs, you arrive at medium-sized, agreeable Perryton (pop. 7,607), seven miles south of the Oklahoma border. The town was formed in 1919 when the Santa Fe Railroad came through; people in nearby towns simply picked up their stuff—buildings included—and shifted them here. Ochilton, eight miles south off US-83/Hwy-70, was one such town, before some 600 people moved the whole infrastructure. If you ignore the industrial oil-well litter on the outskirts, Perryton's not bad-looking, with spacious tree-lined streets. Self-styled "Wheatheart of the Nation," Perryton is the home of Mike Hargrove, former American League Rookie of the Year, and now manager of the Cleveland Indians; it's also the **US-83 Tourist Headquarters**; contact the tourism office at the Chamber of Commerce, Drawer 789, Perryton, TX 79070 (806/435-6575). This latter organization is also involved in trying to get US-83 named the official Central North American Trade Corridor, so their love and promotion of its historic two-lane charms is waning fast; still, they're the only central source of info on the highway.

A few miles north of Canadian, 10 miles east of the US-83/US-60 junction, and via a good paved road, you'll find the **Lake Marvin National Grassland,** which maintains one of the few surviving portions of the natural landscape that once covered the Great Plains—where the deer and the antelope once played and millions of buffalo roamed.

Visit the **Museum of the Plains** (Mon.-Fri. 10 AM-5:30 PM, Sat.-Sun. 1:30-5 PM) right on US-83 on the north side of town. The **Harvest Cafe** in town is about your only restaurant choice other than regional chains or steakhouses.

Canadian

South from Perryton, the landscape changes radically from the plains stretches, offering instead classic ranches with miles of fencing and great white gates à la *Dallas,* a few oil wells, small canyons with innumerable creekbeds, and craggy, fluted bluffs peppered with veldtlike vegetation.

Canadian (pop. 2,417) offers an auspicious view as you descend toward it. You plow through an imposing tunnel of trees and then cross the namesake river, once an important trail for early explorers; the crossing itself parallels anachronistic railroad trestles. Besides sustaining the only trees for miles, contemporary Canadian also has the interesting **River Valley Pioneer Museum** (Mon.-Fri. 9 AM-noon and 1-4 PM, Sat.-Sun. 2-4 PM) at 118 S. 2nd Street.

For food, within a block of the chamber of commerce you can choose between great doughnuts at **Ma Beasley's Donut Shop** (Mon.-Fri. 5:30 AM-noon), **Paula's Place,** and some lunch stands complete with the quintessential advertisement proclaiming "Good Eats." There are lots of seedy-looking motels on the north side of town, but east of the chamber of commerce a couple blocks is an alternative place to stay, the **Emerald House Bed and Breakfast.**

A couple of miles south of Canadian on suddenly four-lane US-83 stands a huge **brontosaurus** atop a high bluff; don't ask me why.

At Shamrock, US-83 crosses the legendary Route 66, whose full L.A.-to-Chicago odyssey is covered beginning on page 628.

Shamrock

Once a thumping, vesicant refining center built over one of the largest natural gas reservoirs in the state, Shamrock is a dusty, rusty old industrial town just south of I-40 at the junction of US-83 and historic Route 66, which survives as the "Business Loop" of I-40 through town. Though it's not a particularly lovely place, Shamrock at least ranges from grimly ugly and stifling near the highway to decompressively sedate in the town proper. Playing up the Irish connection, Elmore Park in town reportedly exhibits a sliver of the genuine **Blarney Stone**, encased in a hip-high concrete cylinder.

In between Canadian and Shamrock, **Wheeler** is a tiny town built around a square, full of signs advertising ostrich chicks for sale.

The old brown-brick Drummer's Hotel holds the **Pioneer West Museum** (Mon.-Fri. 9 AM-noon and 1-5 PM; free), with the usual stuff, but also an exhibit honoring astronaut Alan Bean. The town doesn't exactly enjoy an overabundance of cuisine, but it does have a couple of restaurants and cafes, including the **U Drop Inn**, a classic greasy spoon cafe (the building looks great, but the food doesn't always match) at the northeast corner of US-83 and old Route 66. Also along the highways you'll find gas stations and some of the cheapest sleep around, with fleabag motels advertising singles from $14.

South of Shamrock, US-83 passes over the Salt Fork of the Red River and through what are known as the **Rocking Chair Mountains**, named after a large cattle ranch established here in the 1880s by a group of British aristocrats, mainly younger sons of noble Scottish families. The only visible sign of their legacy survives as place-names like Aberdeen, Clarendon, and **Wellington** (pop. 2,450), 25 miles south of Shamrock. Wellington is now a major market town for the surrounding cotton plantations, and during harvest the gins run round the clock. However, you'd be hard-pressed to recognize the town; just off the highway, comprises a motel, a dilapidated Quonset-hut machine shop, another boarded-up structure, and a pile of small-town jetsam.

Childress

A vintage Texas town built around an old Spanish *zócalo*, Childress (pop. 5,055) is an important shipping and supply point for surrounding grain and cattle ranches, and serves as the market town for area cotton farmers. On the railroad at the junction of US-83 and US-287, and named after George Childress, the author of the Texas Declaration of Independence, Childress is also the hometown of eight-time world champion calf roper Roy Cooper.

An historical marker in Childress Park tells the story of the **Goodnight Trail**, the famed frontier cattle trail that passed through town.

The once picturesque downtown still houses the small but engaging **Childress County Heritage Museum** (Mon.-Fri. 9 AM-5 PM, Saturday 9 AM-1 PM; free) at 10 3rd Street NW (follow the signs), but the downtown is one short step from dry, depressed implosion—the result of every business relocating to the congested, annoying fringe highways. Depending on your time of arrival, the picturesque brick-cobbled streets and empty shells of formerly grand buildings smack more of a ghost town.

Virtually every local motel and restaurant lines US-287 (Avenue F) near the junction with US-83, and some sport disturbing signs such as "American-owned." Considering their location, all the motels suffer from a lack of quiet and privacy. The **Econo-lodge** (817/937-3695), right on US-287, offers doubles from $42; not the cheapest place, but it's likely to have better security. Most restaurants tend toward generic, motel coffee shops or glorified truck stops, but **Foster's Mesquite BBQ** on US-287 is unique and advertises special deals starting at $3.

Paducah

South of Childress, US-83 passes through a magnificent landscape of rich red and gold canyonlands covered with vast groves of trees. Paducah, 30 miles south of Childress at the junction of US-70, is a modest cotton town proudly arrayed around a central courthouse modeled after an Egyptian temple. The town offers little in the way of restaurants other than a doughnut shop and **Cracker's Steakhouse.** You can find a room at three motels west of US-83. These are the only options for more than an hour's drive south, so if it's quitting time, check out **The Town House,** the best of the lot.

West of Paducah along US-70 spreads the **Matador Ranch,** once one of the largest in Texas, with 450,000 acres of fenced pasture, and thirsty gullies amid semiarid canyons dotted with cedars and mesquite.

Hamlin and Swedona

Deep in the heart of Texas, surrounded by miles and miles of green grass, red earth, windmills, pump supplies, and peanut driers, the tidy town of Hamlin ("Home of the Pied Pipers"; pop. 3,248) is full of charming folks and streets lined by locust and mesquite trees. There's not much here, but the blue-roofed **Hatahoe Restaurant**, despite its ominous chain-like appearance, serves copious, cheap, and quite good meals. Standing next to the only stoplight in town, *this* is where to meet the area's characters over breakfast.

Seven miles west of Hamlin on Hwy-92 stood Swedona (swee-DOAN-ya), a farming community founded by Swedish immigrants in 1877 that held fast to the ways of the Old Country for over 50 years. All that remains today is a tranquil cemetery.

Anson

Eighteen miles southeast of Hamlin, at the junction of US-180, sits Anson, named in honor of Dr. Anson Jones, the last president of the Republic of Texas. Anson was also a stop on the legendary Butterfield Stage U.S. Mail route that ran between St. Louis and San Francisco from 1858 to 1861. In counterpoint to the grand courthouse standing in the central square, keep an eye out for the abandoned diner, made from what looks like an old Airstream trailer, along US-83 south of town.

Anson is a center for the local cotton industry, but the main event is the annual **Cowboy's Christmas Ball**, as described in the famous poem by **Larry Chittenden**.

It's four lanes all the way from Anson to Abilene, via I-20.

Abilene

At the junction of US-83 and I-20, Abilene sits approximately in the geographic center of Texas and has a population of over 100,000. Abilene's fundamentalist Christian seminaries and tame (for Texas) demeanor have earned it the much-used nickname, "Buckle of the Bible belt." Originally named after the raucous cowboy town

Anson marks the junction of US-83 and US-180, part of our cross-country Southern Pacific route, which is described more fully beginning on page 580.

The only real alternative to all-news, Tejano, or twangy C&W on your radio dial is Abilene's **102.7 FM,** which plays a mixed bag of 1970s hits—Jefferson Airplane, CCR, and the odd New Wave tune.

of Abilene, Kansas, Abilene, *Texas,* grew from nothing once the Texas and Pacific Railway came through in the 1870s. Then as now, cattle play a predominant economic role, though Abilene's economy has diversified into less classic Texas endeavors, such as the unavoidable military airbase and petroleum refinery. Abilene supports big-city amenities including a symphony, though the indigenous fundamentalism precludes more libertine nocturnal notions; in 1925, the town fathers made it a misdemeanor, in the eyes of the law, to "flirt in a public place"!

Abilene's downtown area, marked by a pair of 10-story towers, is not quite gentrified, but obviously galvanized for the attempt. The local **chamber of commerce** (915/676-2556) has relocated to a refurbished old train depot at 1101 N. 1st Street and dispenses loads of information on the area. Across the street, the grand old Grace Hotel, now refurbished and known as the **Museums of Abilene** (Tues.-Sat. 8 AM-5 PM and Thurs. 5 PM-8:30 PM; $2, but free on Thurs.; 915/673-4587), at 102 Cypress Street, houses an art museum, an engaging historical museum, and a children's museum. It's air-conditioned, and well worth a look.

If you choose to spend some time in Abilene, you won't want for excursions. The **Abilene Zoo** (daily 9 AM-5 PM, plus Sat.-Sun. 9 AM-7 PM in summer; $2) yields the **Discovery Center,** which features a great exhibit on Southwest habitats, comparing veldts and plains of places as diverse as Africa and the United States. West of town is the **Dyess Air Force Base** and its **Linear Air Park,** a collection of aircraft from WW II to Desert Storm; it's free and you paid for it, so you may as well check it out.

Abilene offers motels like **Motel 6** (915/672-8462) at 4951 W. Stamford, off I-20 at exit 282, not far from the junction with US-83; and the plusher **Kiva Inn** (915/695-2150) at 5403 S. 1st Street. The best place for food is the upscale **Cypress Street Station,** next to the museums in the heart of downtown Abilene; it's one of two espresso bars in town. Also worth searching out are **Mama Ruth's** at 1232 Grape Street, northwest of downtown in the Merchant Park Mall, open 24 hours for time-honored home cooking; and the classic Texan BBQ of **Joe Allen's,** on Treadway Boulevard (US-83 Business) at S. 13th Street, south of downtown in a unpromising industrial district. Open 11 AM-9 PM every day but Sunday, Joe Allen's smoky dark interior looks straight out of some beer commercial (though they don't serve beer here); the food is excellent, with mesquite-grilled staples such as chicken, sausage, or brisket, plus rib eye steaks by the pound.

Buffalo Gap

If you're passing through Abilene, don't miss the restored frontier town of Buffalo Gap (Mon.-Sat. 10 AM-6 PM, Sunday noon-6 PM; $4), 14 miles to the southwest via Hwy-89. It's not completely a tourist trap; cowpokes still reside here and a courthouse and jail are just two of 20-odd buildings dating from the late 1800s. Other buildings are done up as Wild West souvenir stands, and two hold good restaurants: **Judy's Gathering Place** for stylish Mexican food, and the **Perini Ranch** for steak and chicken.

South of Ballinger along US-83, keep an eye out for the massive stainless steel **cross,** set on a hill east of the highway.

Ballinger

The first large town you come to, 53 miles south of Abilene among the rolling sheepherding hills of the fantastic Edwards Plateau, is Ballinger (pop. 3,975). It's a lively little town with many of its brick and sandstone buildings dating from its inception in 1886 as Hutchins City, when the railroad came through. Standing along the banks of the Colorado River, the town now supports itself with agriculture. Catercorner to the **Coppini Cowboy Statue** on the courthouse square, Ballinger has the incredibly cheap and always packed **Texas Grill**, open 24 hours at the corner of US-83 and Hwy-67.

Paint Rock Pictographs

Fifteen miles south of Ballinger, a dirt road leads west to the Paint Rock Pictographs, the largest concentration of prehistoric drawings in Texas, with well over 1,500 brightly colored images covering a limestone bluff over the Concho River. These images, which are on private land, also explain the name of the tiny town of **Paint Rock**, a mile south where US-83 crosses the Concho River. In town, the first building you come to (there are only two or three all told) holds **Paint Rock Excursions** (Mon.-Sat. 9 AM-4 PM; 915/732-4418), which offers hour-long guided tours—sometimes by boat, when the river is high enough—of the pictographs, the only way to see them.

Menard

US-83 winds through another 40 miles of scrubby hills before reaching the fascinating old wool-products market town of Menard (pop. 1,775; pronounced "MAY-nurd"), standing in a lush valley along the San Saba River. A trading post and stop on the old cattle trails, Menard was originally founded by Franciscan missionaries in 1757, and many of its early structures survive or have been restored.

It's an eerily picturesque little town, with huge trees and a wide, wide bridge over the river. **Menardville Museum**, housed in the old Santa Fe railroad depot, contains a 150-year-old wooden bar from the now-defunct Legal Tender Saloon. A block south of the main drag, the **Historic Ditch Walk** follows the 10-mile Vaughn Agricultural and Mechanical Canal, a fancy name for an irrigation ditch that has served local farmers since 1876. The canal features remains of the old waterworks and colorful flower plantings, and the walk passes the 1899-vintage **Sacred Heart Catholic Church.**

Several historic limestone buildings in town date to the turn of the century. The Luckenbach Building (1903) contains the **Burnham Brothers Co.** (915/396-4572), the oldest U.S. retailer of game calls, from simple wooden instruments to state-of-the-art computerized devices that lure turkey, deer, elk, ducks, and other game.

Two miles east of town, off US-190 on the banks of the river, the cemetery and a few buildings are all that's left of the **San Saba Mission**, abandoned in 1758 after repeated Comanche attacks. Next to a golf course along Hwy-29, two miles west of town, the Spanish presidio that failed to protect the mission has been fully restored. The rebuilt chapel now houses a small museum, and portions of a later stone fort, named **Real Presidio de San Saba**, also survive intact. A simple inscription, "BOWIE," on the stone gate is thought to have been carved by Jim Bowie of Alamo fame. Bowie lived at the presidio ruins while searching for buried Spanish silver during the early 1800s.

Menard hasn't much in the way of places to eat, but **Decker's**, right on US-83, a small-town hole-in-the-wall store/cafe, sells great barbecued brisket plate lunches. The **Menard Country Store**, on US-83 at the south end of town, offers fresh pastries, cakes, breads, jams, and candies, as well as handicrafts marketed by the Menard Area Arts and Crafts Club.

During Menard's annual **Jim Bowie Days** in late June, visitors and residents gather for arts and crafts shows, mock gunfights, live music, and the outdoor production of *Song of Silver,* a musical patterned after Bowie's life story.

Fort McKavett State Historic Site

Twenty-three miles west of Menard via US-190 and Hwy-864, Fort McKavett (Wed.-Sun. 8 AM-5 PM from Labor Day to Memorial Day, daily 9 AM-6 PM rest of the year) was established in 1852 as the "Camp on the San Saba" by the 8th Infantry. It was soon renamed in honor of a U.S. Army colonel who was killed in the Battle of Monterrey during the war with Mexico. As with Fort Concho and other West Texas forts, Fort McKavett served as a first line of defense against Comanche raids along the Texas frontier and provided protection for travelers along the Upper San Antonio-El Paso Trail. Temporarily abandoned in 1859, the post was reestablished in 1868 by the 4th Cavalry after local residents lobbied for Army protection against renewed attacks. The cavalry was soon replaced by the 38th Infantry, a company of African-American troops. All four of the Army's black units, who came to be known as "Buffalo Soldiers" by the Indians, eventually served at McKavett, including the famous 9th and 10th cavalries. Fourteen of the original 40 buildings have been restored, including the officers' quarters, barracks, hospital, school, bakery, and post headquarters. Seven other buildings lie in ruins, and the rest are gone. The hospital ward serves as a visitor center and contains interpretive exhibits explaining the natural and military history of the area. A nature trail leads to the old fort kiln and the "Government Springs."

Junction

After passing through the attractively rugged but shallow canyonlands south of Menard—which make US-83 into a rollercoaster of a road, by Texas standards—the two-lane road crosses high-speed I-10 at the aptly named town of Junction. Once a major crossing where the east-west Chihuahua Trail met a branch of the north-south Chisholm Trail (now I-10 and US-83 respectively), Junction (pop. 2,799) sits at the edge of Texas's famed Hill Country, where the Edwards Plateau crumbles into limestone canyons and cliffs along the Balcones Escarpment. As in the areas to the immediate north, wool and mohair production are the main means of local livelihood, supplemented by pecan farming.

Places to eat line Main Street (US-83) through town—try the Milky Way, or Isaak's, which is open daily 6 AM-10 PM. Four motels just south of I-10 offer inexpensive to moderately priced rooms, including the well-maintained **Carousel Inn** at 1908 Main Street (915/446-3301).

To continue south along US-83, you can wind along Main Street or follow I-10 southeast for one exit, roughly two miles, to rejoin the old road.

Leakey and the Frio Canyon

Below Junction, US-83 continues southward through 55 beautiful miles of rolling ranches and native pecan orchards, entering a verdant, spring-filled region that was one of the last strongholds of the Lipan Apaches and Comanches. The rolling hills around Leakey (pop. 420; pronounced "LAY-key") hold limestone caves, some of which the Confederates mined for saltpeter—an essential ingredient of gunpowder—during the Civil War. At 1,600 feet above sea level, this is one of US-83's prettiest reaches through Texas, as the road follows the clear, cold Frio River through 17 miles of cypress, pecan, live oak, cedar, walnut, wild cherry, piñon, and mountain laurel. Some areas also have bigtooth maple and sycamore, a major tourist attraction in the late fall when the leaves change color.

Farther south along the eponymous river, the hamlet of Rio Frio (pop. 50) boasts the largest live oak tree in Texas. The centuries-old tree stands alongside Hwy-1120 on the east side of the Frio River.

You'll find a dozen or more camps and lodges between the highway and the river, which is popular for fishing and tubing. The tin-roofed, wooden-sided **Welcome Inn Motor Hotel** (210/232-5246) on US-83 in the center of town provides comfortable motel rooms and cabins; Leakey's best local eating is right across the road at the **Frio Canyon Cafe, Feed Store, and Exxon**.

About 10 miles south of Leakey along US-83 on the Frio River, the very pretty 1,420-acre **Garner State Park** (210/232-6132) offers campgrounds, cabins, hiking trails, canoe rentals, swimming, and a popular outdoor dance terrace.

Utopia

Fifteen miles east of Rio Frio via Hwy-1050, on the Sabinal River, the town of Utopia gained momentary fame when it appeared in television ads created by a national burger chain. Seven churches and a population of only 360 represent a legacy left by frontier circuit preachers who found this spot a heavenly place to hold camp meetings and save souls. The **Sabinal Canyon Museum** (Saturday 10 AM-4 PM, Sunday 1-4 PM) on Utopia's main street displays local arts and crafts, including antique handmade quilts, historic photos, farm implements, arrowheads, spurs, and other artifacts that outline Bandera County history.

Uvalde

Forty-one miles south of Leakey, US-83 crosses US-90 (the former San Antonio-El Paso Trail) at Uvalde, founded in 1855 and still centered around a broad square

US-377 traces a 22-mile scenic route along the Llano River southwest of Junction, bisecting typical Edwards Plateau tableaus of limestone arroyos studded with mesquite, oak, prickly pear, and yucca. **South Llano River State Park,** four miles southwest of Junction off US-377, protects 507 wooded acres and abundant wildlife (white-tailed deer, Rio Grande turkey, javelina), and offers facilities for picnicking, camping, hiking, canoeing, and swimming.

From Junction, I-10 continues southeast to San Antonio, passing through the Hill Country town of Kerrville, which hosts the very popular **Kerrville Folk Festival** around Memorial Day. For information, call 512/896-1155.

that originally served as a wagonyard for teamsters and travelers. Now a mostly Hispanic town of 15,000 residents, with a wide variety of buildings lining lushly verdant streets, Uvalde was the home of Billy the Kid's killer Pat Garrett during the 1890s; the corrupt lawman's house site is marked off US-90 a half-mile east of US-83. Another Western legend, celluloid cowgirl Dale Evans, hails from Uvalde.

The town's most famous native son, John Nance "Cactus Jack" Garner, served as Franklin Delano Roosevelt's first- and second-term vice president (1933-41); after retiring from politics, he returned to Uvalde and lived here until his death in 1967 at age 98. His home at 333 N. Park now contains the **Ettie R. Garner Museum** (Mon.-Sat. 9 AM-noon and 1-5 PM; 210/278-5018), a repository of memorabilia from Garner's political career. The 1891 **Grand Opera House** (Mon.-Fri. 9 AM-3 PM; free; 210/278-4184), on the square at 100 W. North Street, has been restored to a 390-seat live performance venue; it's open for free guided tours.

A number of motels line US-90 (Main Street) east of the town square, including the economic **Inn of Uvalde** (210/278-9173), a **Holiday Inn**, a **Best Western**, and the **Amber Sky Motel** (210/278-5602) at 2005 E. Main Street. Friendly **Jerry's Restaurant** (210/278-7556) at 539 W. Main Street features a classic, small-town South Texas menu of fajitas, *migas* (eggs scrambled with chiles, onions, and tortilla strips), catfish, steaks, and oysters. It's open Mon.-Sat. 6 AM-10 PM, Sunday 11 AM-2 PM.

Five miles west of Uvalde on US-90, a large roadhouse-style dance hall called **The Purple Sage** (210/278-1006) offers two floors of bars, live country-western swing bands, and dance floors. It's open weekends only; minors are admitted.

From Uvalde, US-90 runs 75 miles east to **San Antonio,** home of the Alamo and the prettiest city in Texas. For visitor information, contact the San Antonio visitors bureau (210/270-8748 or 800/447-3372).

South of Uvalde

As US-83 continues south from Uvalde, the highway descends farther onto the mostly flat Rio Grande Plain, entering a subtropical zone of seemingly endless chaparral. Amidst "brush country"—marked by a mixture of thorny cacti, mesquite, dwarf oak, black bush, and huisache—spread large irrigated farms known as the "Winter Garden of Texas" for the bounty of spinach and citrus crops they produce. Forty miles south of Uvalde sits **Crystal City** (pop. 8,245), the Zavala County seat and self-proclaimed "Spinach Capital of the World," where a **statue of Popeye** stands on the town square. Three miles south of Crystal City, the seasonal **Espantosa Lake** once served as an important water stop along the colonial mission trail between Mexico and Texas.

Ten miles farther south along US-83 is **Carrizo Springs** (pop. 5,745), another farming center and county seat of underpopulated Dimmit County. Twenty-five miles on, the flyspeck hamlet of **Catarina** (pop. 45) marks the end of the farmlands and the return to the range.

Laredo

Founded as the first nonmissionary, nonmilitary Spanish settlement in North America in 1755, Laredo is surrounded by the oldest ranch lands in the United States. With a population of over 155,000, about 90% of whom are Hispanic, the city is growing rapidly due to its position as the largest international trade center along the U.S.-Mexico border.

CRYSTAL CITY, TEXAS

POPEYE

Eighteen miles north of town, US-83 merges with I-35, then crosses the Rio Grande to meet Mexico 85 (the Pan-American Highway), forming a continuous road link between Laredo and the Panama Canal via Mexico and Central America.

At the heart of downtown Laredo, a block north of the Rio Grande, is the **Villa De San Agustín Historical District**, site of the original 1755 Spanish settlement of Villa de San Agustín. Numerous historic buildings surround the plaza, including a small stone building next to La Posada Hotel that served as the capitol of the short-lived Republic of the Rio Grande. It now houses a **museum** (Tues.-Sun. 10 AM-noon and 1-5 PM) containing a collection of memorabilia from the separatist movement of 1840.

To get a taste of South Texas culture, tune in to "Tejano 102," **KUVA 102.3,** for nonstop Tejano and traditional country-western tunes.

Nuevo Laredo, the quintessential Mexican border town, offers a well-developed downtown with everything from elegant dining to street vendors to cut-rate liquor stores, plus two leafy public plazas, all within walking distance of the International Bridge and downtown Laredo.

Southeast from Laredo

South of Laredo, US-83 follows a route parallel to the Rio Grande that was originally cut through the dry chaparral by Gen. Zachary Taylor's soldiers during the 1846-48 Mexican-American War. The 1953 construction of 87,000-acre **Falcon International Reservoir** submerged the town of **Zapata**, the new version of which lies 49 miles southeast of Laredo, followed by Roma (89 miles) and Rio Grande City (109 miles). Both the U.S. and Mexico use the dam and reservoir for hydroelectric power, flood control, and recreation along US-83. Camping is possible at **Falcon State Park** on the lake's southeast shore.

US-83 continues southeast along the Rio Grande, passing through several Texas border towns held together by a common historical and cultural thread: all were settled by Spanish colonists in the mid-18th century as part of the famous José de Escandón land grant.

The surviving 19th-century Spanish- and French Creole-style architecture in **Roma**, 40 miles southeast of Zapata, once the end of the line for steamboats sailing up the Rio Grande from the Gulf of Mexico, inspired director Elia Kazan to use the town as a film location for the 1952 movie *Viva Zapata!* starring Marlon Brando and Anthony Quinn. Across the river in the Mexican state of Tamaulipas, the narrow sandstone streets, old churches, and plazas of **Mier** haven't changed much since the Spanish era.

Farther along US-83 comes **Rio Grande City**, another former riverboat terminal. Among the historic buildings downtown is the renovated **LaBorde House**, 601 E. Main Street (210/487-5101), a Creole-style inn designed by Parisian architects in 1899. Rooms are moderately priced and meals at **Che's**, the hotel restaurant, are good. Other restaurants to look for in the area include the family-run **Caro's** (210/487-2255) at 205 N. Garcia, an inexpensive northern Mexican-style cafe.

CROSSING THE BORDER

At dozens of sleepy little towns across Southern California, Arizona, New Mexico, and Texas, the temptation to nip across the border and see something of our southern neighbor can be strong. It's only a hop and a skip away, and the crossing is usually simple and hassle free, but before you go it's good to know a few things about international customs—small "c" and big "C", as the U.S. Customs Service is not something to take lightly.

All that a U.S. citizen needs to cross the border for 72 hours or less (and be readmitted to the U.S. after your visit!) is proof of citizenship—a passport basically—and the burden of proof is on the traveler. Often, you can get by with just a driver's license, or simply an American-looking face, but this is risky business and you could well be turned back. To stay longer or to travel beyond the border areas, you need a *tarjeta de turistica* (tourist card), which is available free of charge from Mexican tourist offices, consulates or government offices at the ports of entry.

If you're thinking of heading south to stock up on Mexican beers or a rug or other handicraft, the much ballyhooed NAFTA treaty did nothing to change what you can bring back from Mexico: all merchandise is subject to a $400 duty-free limit, above which U.S. customs will charge a 10% duty based on fair retail value. Alcohol imports by individuals are limited to a whopping liter every 30 days—about two cans of beer—and it is illegal to import Mexican versions of trademarked items (perfumes, watches, even cans of Coke!) that are also sold in the Unitedv States. So don't risk having to leave something behind at the border—ask before you buy.

The most important advice I can offer is that, because of insurance and other legal concerns, it's best to leave your car on the U.S. side of the border and cross into Mexico on foot. If you do want to drive across, be sure you have a policy that specifically covers travel in Mexico—the AAA is a good source, since these policies must be written by Mexican companies, and they have reciprocal contacts. Insurance is important because if you are involved in any kind of collision, even a tiny fender bender, the police are required to impound the cars and hold the drivers in jail until the responsibilities are decided—not how you want to spend your time. Also, if you're tempted to cross the border simply to fill up on cheap Mexican gas, be aware that, because of a different rating method, the 92 octane unleaded ("Magna Sin" in Mexico) is the same as 87 octane gas in the U.S.

For more detailed information on traveling across the border, pick up a copy of Joe Cummings's excellent *Northern Mexico Handbook*.

Across the river from Rio Grande City is the small Mexican town of **Camargo** (established 1749), José de Escandón's first Nuevo Santander settlement. A Catholic **church** on the plaza dates to the early 1750s.

The Rio Grande Valley
Southeast of Rio Grande City the river and US-83 curve eastward toward the Gulf of Mexico through a broad delta region known as the Rio Grande Valley, despite the fact there are no nearby mountains to make it a true valley. Citrus orchards, interspersed with date palms planted as windbreaks, line the highway, while lush plantings of bougainvillea and poinsettias drape many of the houses in the string of towns that appear every few miles all the way to the Gulf. The population of the valley, which sits at the same latitude as the Florida Keys, swells with the arrival each winter of over 100,000 "Winter Texans" fleeing the colder midwestern states. This "snowbird" presence means there's a high concentration of RV and mobile home parks throughout the area, and some of the lowest daily, weekly, and monthly rates in the nation.

The westernmost, oldest, and largest of the valley towns, **McAllen** (pop. 90,000) started out as a terminus for a 1904 railway line parallel to the Mexican border. Eight miles from the center of McAllen across the Rio Grande is the Mexican city of **Reynosa** (pop. 375,000), a popular tourist destination for valley visitors. McAllen in return receives many Mexican visitors.

> Boosted by controlled watering and mild year-round temperatures, the rich alluvial soils of the Rio Grande Valley produce 56 varieties of fruits and vegetables, including citrus, sugarcane, onions, cucumbers, tomatoes, cabbage, and 99% of the aloe vera grown in the United States.

The McAllen area's unique attraction is **Los Ebanos ferry**, the last hand-pulled ferry across the Rio Grande. To get there, drive west from McAllen on US-83 to Hwy-886 (between Havana and Sullivan City), then turn left (south) and follow the mazelike road until you hit the river. In service daily 7 AM-3 PM, the ferry can carry three cars and a small number of pedestrians on each crossing. The fare is $1 per auto; pedestrians may ride for US 25 cents per person. On the Mexican side, it's two miles to **Díaz Ordaz**, a small cotton- and sorghum-farming center.

McAllen holds a large number of motels and restaurants on and off US-83, though the steady tourist trade makes it the valley's most expensive town to overnight in. At **La Casa del Taco**, 1100 Houston (210/631-8193), you make your own tacos from "the Sombrero," a stack of homemade tortillas under a straw hat. You can pile on fajitas (or *arracheras*), *frijoles a la charra*, grilled onions, and peppers. In nearby **Pharr**, **Armando's Taco Hut** at 106 N. Cage (210/781-1091) offers good, inexpensive Tex-Mex food, a great Tex-Mex jukebox, and occasional live *conjunto* music; open daily 7 AM-3 AM. Over in Reynosa, **Sam's** (2-00-34) at Allende and Ocampo is famous throughout the area for its inexpensive steak dinners, Mexican platters, and border specialties such as quail. It's open daily 11 AM-midnight.

About eight miles southwest of McAllen via Hwy-374 (west) and Hwy-2062 (south), **Bentsen-Rio Grande Valley State Park** (210/585-1107) preserves 588 acres of Rio Grande delta riparian woodlands and *matorral* (thorn scrub). Camping and picnicking facilities are available.

Harlingen
From McAllen, for the second time in its 2,000-mile journey from the Canadian border, US-83 continues as a full-fledged, multilaned freeway through San Juan,

Of the valley's 22 radio stations, 12 broadcast a portion or all of their programming in Spanish. Radio station **KIWW 96.1 FM** broadcasts Tejano music from nearby Harlingen. For country-western, tune in **KFRQ 94.5 FM.**

Raymondville, 23 miles north of Harlingen via US-77, has been a bootmaking center since at least the turn of the century. Family-run **Armando's Boot Co.** (169 N. 7th) and **Torres Custom Boots** (246 S. 7th) offer some of the best prices in the state for custom-made cowboy boots.

Alamo, and Weslaco, ending up 30 miles east in Harlingen. At the junction of US-83 and US-77 you'll find a **Texas Travel Information Center,** the best source of tourist information in this part of the state.

Harlingen's **Rio Grande Valley Historical Museum Complex** (Tues.-Fri. 9 AM-noon and 2-5 PM, Sunday 2-5 PM), at Boxwood and Raintree in the Harlingen Industrial Air Park three miles north of town, contains exhibits interpreting the history of the valley from the time of the Karankawa and Coahuiltecan peoples. At the nearby **Iwo Jima Memorial** stands the original sculpture from which the famous bronze statue of the flag-raising Marines (installed at the Marine Corps Memorial in Arlington, Virginia) was made.

A gaggle of chain motels and restaurants lines US-77 through Harlingen, including **Best Western, Ramada Inn, La Quinta, Rodeway Inn,** and **Motel 6. Vela's** at 613 W. Tyler serves inexpensive, authentic Valley-style Mexican food 24 hours a day. Rustic **Lone Star Restaurant** at 4210 W. Business 83 cooks mesquite-grilled steaks, barbecue, and Mexican dishes; it's open daily for lunch and dinner.

the original Iwo Jima Memorial sculpture

Brownsville

South of Harlingen, US-83 merges with US-77 for the final 26 miles to Brownsville, where you may well feel like you've unknowingly crossed the border into Mexico. One of the most historic cities in Texas, Brownsville retains its Spanish and Mexican heritage more than most places, particularly in the architecture of the downtown district around **Elizabeth Street,** which runs northwest from the 24-hour border crossing at **Matamoros, Mexico.** U.S.-Mexico trade supports the local economy via a Union Pacific rail terminus connected with Mexico's national railway over the Rio Grande; too, a 17-mile deep-sea channel in the river delta links the city with the U.S. Inland Waterway System and the Gulf of Mexico.

Besides the historic downtown, another must-see is the well-endowed **Gladys Porter Zoo** (daily 9 AM-5 PM; $6; 210/546-7187) at Ringgold and 6th Streets, named by zoo professionals as one of the country's 10 best zoological facilities.

Virtually every fast-food place in the city, even McDonald's and Dairy Queen, serves tacos of some kind. For Tex-Mex meals, one of the popular places in town is **Los Camperos Char Chicken** (1440 International Boulevard, open daily for lunch and dinner), where the house specialty is smoked, charbroiled chicken served with corn tortillas and red and green salsas. **Antonio's** (2921 Boca Chica Boulevard, Strawberry Square) and **Miguel's** (2474 Boca Chica Boulevard) make the best fajitas in the Rio Grande Valley. Both restaurants are open Mon.-Sat. for lunch and dinner, Sun. for dinner only. Across the border in Matamoros, dark and velvet-lined **The**

Drive Inn at Calle 6 and Hidalgo has been a border institution since 1916 for steak, continental, seafood, and Mexican.

Several modern hotels, from the **Motel 6** to the **Sheraton Plaza Royale**, representing all budgets, cluster along the highway just north of the city.

South Padre Island

Twenty-six miles northeast of Brownsville via Hwy-48 and the Queen Isabella Causeway, South Padre Island provides a strong contrast to the sleepy, historic towns of the Rio Grande Valley. Only the southernmost five miles of this 30-mile Gulf of Mexico barrier island are developed; sand dunes and tidal marshes dominate the remainder. Sportfishing in the Laguna Madre, the protected bay that lies between Padre Island and the mainland, is excellent.

In the developed zone, multistory hotels and condominiums line white-sand beaches on both the Gulf and Laguna Madre sides of the island. Rooms are easy to come by except during the annual Spring Break (March-April) when college kids from all over Texas and the Midwest fill the hotels and beaches with round-the-clock revelry.

Call the helpful **South Padre Visitor and Convention Bureau** (210/761-6433 or 800/343-2368) for a listing of hotel, condo, and beach home properties.

Sabal Palm Grove Sanctuary protects the last remaining grove of endangered Sabal palms in the Rio Grande delta (they are the only palm tree native to the continental U.S.). One of the first white-hunter-in-the-African-jungle movies, *Life Along the Delta,* was filmed here in 1930. From Brownsville, take Boca Chica Boulevard (Hwy-4) east, then turn right (south) on Hwy-3068. From the end of the road, turn right (west) on Hwy-1419 and follow the marked road to the sanctuary.

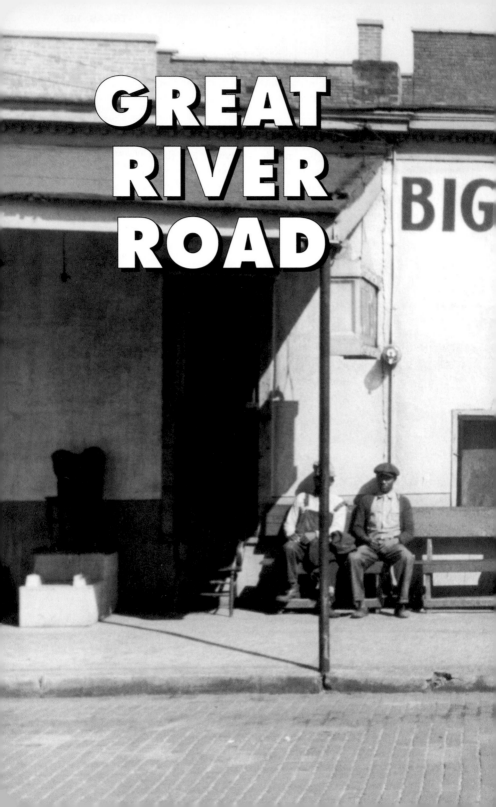

GREAT
RIVER
ROAD

BIG

GREAT RIVER ROAD

Old Man River, Father of Waters, "body of a nation," Big Muddy: by any name the mighty Mississippi River cuts a mythic figure across the American landscape. Who hasn't read Mark Twain or listened to *Showboat* and not dreamt of a trip down the Mississippi? If you're tired of waiting for somebody to buy you passage aboard the *Delta Queen* or to help you paddle among the 1,500-ton barges, then do what Huck Finn would have done if he'd had a driver's license: tag alongside the Mississippi on the Great River Road.

Created in 1938 from a network of federal, state, and local roads, the Great River Road—also known as the River Road, and commonly abbreviated to "GRR"—forms a single route along the Mississippi from head to toe. Designed to show off the 10 states bordering the Mississippi from its headwaters to its mouth, the GRR is nothing if not scenic, and anyone who equates the Midwest with the flat Kansas prairie will be pleasantly surprised. Sure, farms line the road, but so do upland meadows, cypress swamps, thick forests, steep bluffs, and dozens of parks and wildlife refuges.

Of course it isn't all pretty. There's enough industry along the Mississippi for you to navigate the river by the flashing marker lights on smokestacks, and a half-dozen major cities compete with their bigger cousins on the coasts for widest suburban sprawl and ugliest urban clutter. A pandemic of tacky strip malls has infected the region, too, but apart from the astounding growth in casinos (you'll never be more than 100 miles from a slot machine, from one end of the Mississippi to the other) the GRR resists the developers' bulldozers because its meanders are shunned by a century increasingly drawn to the straight, fast, and four-lane.

A full 50% longer than the comparable route along the interstates, the GRR changes direction often, crosses the river whenever it can, dallies in towns every other road has forgotten, and

The word Mississippi comes from the Algonquian *misezibi* meaning "water from land all over," or "great water."

If the rivers were being named today, the Mississippi River would flow into the Missouri River and not vice versa, since the Missouri is by far the longer of the two.

In general, roads along the GRR are good, though they vary from four-lane freeway to unpaved track, and Minnesota's unpaved roads are smoother than Louisiana's paved ones.

NAVIGATING THE GREAT RIVER ROAD

The GRR is identified by a green pilot's wheel with a steamboat pictured in the middle. Quality and quantity of route markers vary considerably from state to state: some states, like Minnesota and Illinois, are well marked, with advance warning of junctions, confirmation after turns, and reminders on remote backroads. Other states, like Louisiana and Mississippi, seem committed to hiding GRR signs miles from where they would serve any conceivable good. Missouri is terribly inconsistent, and Tennessee doesn't seem to have joined the program at all. Without a guide or a map, you simply cannot travel the length of the GRR just by following the signs.

There are variations—signposted as "Alternate" or "State Route"—and spurs, denoted by a brown pilot's wheel, which lead to various points of interest.

For a schematic map of the entire GRR and a guide to local happenings in each of the states along the route, send a dollar donation to the **Mississippi River Parkway Commission**, Pioneer Building, Suite 1513, 336 N. Robert Street, St. Paul, MN 55101.

altogether offers a perfect analog to floating downstream. If the road itself isn't your destination, *don't* take it. For those who do travel it, the GRR spares you the fleets of hurtling 40-ton trucks, creeping RVs, and that endless parade of interstate billboards, and rewards you with twice the local color, flavor, and wildlife (two and four-legged) found along any alternate route. Lest these tangibles be taken too much for granted, every so often the GRR will skip over to an interstate for a stretch to help you sort your preferences. Savor, and enjoy.

GREAT RIVER ROAD HIGHLIGHTS

ACROSS MINNESOTA

The Great River Road begins in Lake Itasca State Park and stairsteps along occasionally unpaved but well-graded backcountry roads through a mix of northern boreal forest, tree farms, and hayfields, all the while staying as close to its namesake as possible. By Grand Rapids, only 130 road miles from its source, the Mississippi has been transformed from a grassy brook barely deep enough to canoe to an industry-sustaining river fed by a half-dozen of the state's 10,000 lakes. Farther south, the red and white pines, paper birch, and big-tooth aspen give way to more farms while the route breaks from the surveyor's section lines to curve with the river across the glacially flattened state. By St. Cloud, the GRR enters an increasingly developed corridor that culminates in the hugely sprawling "Twin Cities" of St. Paul and Minneapolis, south of which the road slips into rural Wisconsin.

The Mississippi is the backbone of the North American Flyway: winter migration brings millions of Canada geese, snow geese, and canvasback ducks through its valley. Some 60% of all bird species in the U.S. are found along the GRR, including an ever-growing population of bald eagles.

Lake Itasca State Park

The GRR begins here among the cattails and tall pines, in the park that protects the headwaters of the mighty Mississippi River. The small, clear brook tumbling out of the north end of Lake Itasca will eventually carry runoff from nearly two-thirds of the United States and enough silt to make the muddy plume at the river's mouth visible from space. But at the headwaters, 2,550-odd meandering miles from the Gulf of Mexico, you can not only wade across the Mississippi, you can see the bottom. Here, drinking the river water won't cause cancer—an increasingly rare claim, unfortunately.

The Mississippi's humble beginnings were the object of chest-thumping adventurers and the subject of not-so-scholarly debate for decades before explorer Henry Rowe Schoolcraft, led by Ojibwa native Ozaawindib, determined this lake to be the true source of the nation's most legendary river in 1832. Schoolcraft's story, the tale of the battle to protect the park against logging, and lots of other Mississippi facts are found at the interpretive center just inside the park's north entrance (open year-round; $4 per car). Skeptics will also find out why professional geographers don't consider the two smaller lakes and the five creeks that feed Itasca competition for the headwaters title.

Explorer Henry Schoolcraft christened Lake Itasca with syllables from the Latin veritas caput, meaning "true head." The native Ojibwa called it "Omushkos," their word for elk, while the French trappers knew it as Lac La Biche, or Elk Lake.

The fact that the lakeshore has been "improved" from its naturally marshy state, the surrounding old-growth pine forest—the most extensive stand of virgin timber left in the state—and outdoorsy activities such as paved bike trails and boating all contribute to Itasca's popularity; rangers and bulletin boards at either entrance can explain what's going on when. Bike and boat rentals are available spring through fall opposite the park's headquarters. If you plan to camp (800/246-CAMP for site reservations, advised but not required), be sure to pack repellent for ticks and mosquitoes. Other accommodations include the grand turn-of-the-century **Douglas Lodge** and assorted lakeside cabins (all 800/246-CAMP), while just steps from the bike path and beach you'll find the immaculate, friendly, and bargain-priced **HI-AYH Mississippi Headwaters Hostel** (year-round; 218/266-3415), which has rooms for families and couples as well as single travelers. When not fishing or foraging for your meals, consider the Douglas Lodge dining room, where the menu includes regional blueberries, wild rice, and walleye pike.

Lake Itasca is near one of those special junctions of the Pie Belt and blueberry territory; come summer this is a marriage made in heaven. The town of **Lake George**, just east of the park, opens the pearly gates to their **Blueberry Festival** the last weekend of every July.

Walleye pike is a mild white fish sought by Midwest anglers from May through the cold of February. The walleye found in Minnesota restaurants all come from Red Lake, site of the only commercial walleye fishing allowed by law, and generally disappear from menus after October, when the lakes start freezing over.

Between Bemidji and Grand Rapids, the Great River Road follows a slower but more scenic parallel to transcontinental US-2, whose route across Minnesota is detailed on pages 365-371.

Bemidji to Grand Rapids: The Great River Road

Leaving downtown Bemidji along the edge of the lake, the GRR makes a series of backcountry loops through tree farms and the first national forest, crossing US-2 twice before snaking into Grand Rapids 100 miles later. As opposed to the busy and monotonous US-2, from which you see lots of scraggly jack pine and nary a body of water, the GRR hugs the red pine- and aspen-wooded shores of six lakes and crosses the ever-widening Mississippi eight times. Numerous signs point to unseen resorts, which in Minnesota don't offer luxury so much as proximity to good fishing. Fishing is serious business hereabouts, as is evident from the frequency of signs advertising Leeches-Minnows-Nightcrawlers.

Cass Lake was home to Ka-Be-Nah-Gwey-Wence, whose Anglicized name was John Smith, a Chippewa who lived to be 129 years old. It is said he never slept in a bed. It may be unrelated, but the lake enjoys a reputation for having some of the most beautiful and serene camping in the state.

Aitkin and Crosby

South of Grand Rapids the land rivals Kansas for flatness, yet the mix of farms and forest continues to lend visual interest to what could otherwise be achingly monotonous. The GRR alleviates boredom with its sinuous irregularity, the curves always hinting at the proximity of the Mississippi. For most of the way the river itself remains hidden, although regular signs for boat landings confirm its presence, and on occasion its broad channel and tree-lined banks roll into view.

For nearly 70 miles south of Grand Rapids you will have this rural road to yourself; then at the single stoplight in Aitkin the GRR joins busy Hwy-210, at the edge of the mid-state lakes region. Watch your compass needle for signs of deflection as you

Grand Rapids is near the heart of wild rice country: **Schoolcraft State Park,** alongside the GRR west of town, is a historic Indian wild-rice site, while presently most of the world's truly wild rice (as opposed to the paddy-grown variety) is hand-harvested late Aug.-Sept. in Deer Lake, less than 15 miles northwest of town off Hwy-38.

Given the extremely rural quality of most of Minnesota north of the Twin Cities, night drivers must be particularly careful of wildlife—fox, deer, raccoon, skunk—wandering onto the road.

proceed to the small but tidy town of Crosby, the center of Minnesota's "forgotten" iron range, the Cuyuna. The flood-prone mines have died out, but the surrounding landscape still bears evidence of mining's heyday, with lakes and hills created by strip and subsidence mining, and also by contemporary gravel quarrying. Crosby itself has a nice park fronting onto Serpent Lake, complete with a brightly colored Chinese dragon, while **Croft Mine Historical Park,** well posted on the edge of Crosby, profiles the iron-mining industry and an era, covering immigration and labor issues as well as the actual mining process. Machinery, period buildings, a gift shop, and a simulated underground tour round out the site's features (daily 10 AM-6 PM, Memorial Day-Labor Day; grounds and museum free, tour $3.50).

Between Grand Rapids and Brainerd, the official GRR takes a slow and somewhat scenic route along country lanes, though you'll save many hours (and not miss *that* much) by taking US-169 and Hwy-210.

Brainerd

South of Crosby, the GRR leaves the truck traffic and takes to the cornfields and sumac-laced forests again, passing as many barns as houses, the occasional lakeside hideaway, and some rural town halls; for a thumbnail overview of the area's settlement history, keep an eye peeled for the sundry historical markers along the way. After about 30 miles our route crosses the lake-sized Mississippi and rolls into the geographical center of the state: Brainerd.

That huge Potlatch paper mill along the banks of the river notwithstanding, the economy of this part of the state benefits greatly from recreation. In Minnesota this means lakes: over 400 within a 50-mile radius, with over 150 resorts or camp-

grounds on their shores. Brainerd, the commercial center of it all, began life in 1871 when the Northern Pacific Railroad chose to cross the Mississippi River here; the rail yards are still in the heart of town beneath the giant water tower, which resembles a Las Vegas-style medieval keep. Unfortunately the historic downtown has been badly "malled" by outlying shopping plazas, and the visual clutter of the strip along Hwy-210 (Washington Street) obscures the signs for the GRR, which winds along River Road on a grand tour of Brainerd's scenic backside.

Among the discount merchandisers, pawn shops, and empty storefronts of downtown there are still a few points of light, such as the area's first coffeehouse, the **Low Key Cafe**, on S. 7th Street; and **The Front Street Cafe**, across the tracks from that faux piece of Camelot. With free seconds on soups, mile-high meringue on the pies, and unbelievably low prices—plus a collection of commemorative plates to which words cannot do justice—the Front Street Cafe sets a hip standard for square meals.

Across from the water tower on the Hwy-210 side is the **Sawmill Inn**, a solid meat-and-spud place. The **Magic Skillet**, good for ribs and breakfasts, is also on Hwy-210, as are all the familiar names in fast food. The usual Midwestern restaurant rules still apply: eat dinner early, or do without.

Finally, don't be put off by the unprepossessing location of the **West Side Cafe**: the fact that it's in a gas station (the big Conoco on Hwy-210 a half-mile west of the Mississippi River) doesn't detract a whit from the fact that it serves some of the best pies for miles around, in a setting akin to an old Woolworth lunch counter. From seasonal rhubarb to tangy cherry to unusual carrot, none is too sweet, and the superb flaky crusts are baked to a full golden brown—for a dollar and change, it doesn't get much better than this. They're open daily 6 AM-10 PM and serve unlimited cups of coffee for 70 cents an hour—with weekly rates available on request.

Super 8, **Days Inn**, **Best Western**, and **AmericInn** motels are all clustered on Hwy-210 heading west out of Brainerd, while there's an **Econo Lodge** and a **Holiday Inn** right on the GRR (Hwy-371) on the town's southern outskirts. The cheapest decent sleep in town is the aging **Riverview Motel** (218/829-8871), smack dab in the tacky commercial stretch just west of Hwy-210's Mississippi crossing.

For a free vacation planner and complete guide to the area's family-oriented resort accommodations—or simply the latest local weather report—contact the Brainerd Lakes Area Chamber of Commerce's automated **information system** at 800/450-2838.

Crow Wing State Park and Little Falls
South of Brainerd the GRR speeds along Hwy-371, which yearns to be an interstate for the 30-odd straight miles it takes to reach Little Falls. Exceedingly flat and awash in a sea of corn, it gives

Brainerd also possesses a very large statue of Paul Bunyan's Big Blue Ox, Babe, standing in the parking lot of an amusement park at the junction of Hwy-210 and Hwy-371.

Throughout the upper Midwest, Friday night is the traditional night for a fish fry. Look for the backlit signboards or hand-lettered banners stuck out in front of the local VFW post or social club for a sample of the truly local variety.

In Minnesota and Wisconsin, the "On and Off" and "Off Sale" signs on many bars and roadhouse restaurants designate whether they can sell beer and wine for consumption on or off the premises.

Charles Lindbergh

no hint of the Mississippi except at Crow Wing State Park (open year-round; $4), with trails, picnic area, and camping beside the confluence of the Mississippi and Crow Wing Rivers. Native Americans, missionaries, fur trappers, and lumberjacks made this a thriving and mostly inebriated 19th-century townsite, but the forced removal of the Indians and the shift of trade to the rail crossing upstream turned Crow Wing into a ghost town; only cellar holes and old cemeteries remain.

At Little Falls the GRR neatly misses the fast food and gas claptrap that has sprung up on the Hwy-371 bypass, proceeding instead through the heart of town, which would probably still be recognizable to Charles Lindbergh, who spent his boyhood summers here. Running along the west bank of the river, the GRR passes by the **Charles A. Lindbergh House and History Center** (daily 10 AM-5 PM, May 1-Labor Day, weekends only rest of the year; $4) a mile south of town; the house, which sits on a beautiful stretch of the Mississippi, bears the unusual distinction of having been restored with the meticulous guidance of the aviator himself. Lindy wanted the site to honor his father, a five-term U.S. congressman, as well as himself, and so it does; exhibits also illustrate the junior Lindbergh's life and achievements after his historic solo flight across the Atlantic.

*South of Little Falls the GRR continues on its meandering way, but you can switch over to the uglier but much faster **US-10** or **I-94** freeways for the ride into the Twin Cities without missing anything significant.*

St. Cloud and Monticello

South of Little Falls the GRR again resorts to some unpaved rural sections, wide and well graded as always. Agriculture continues to dominate the landscape, but as our route approaches industrial St. Cloud (pop. 48,812), the loss of farms to suburban housing foreshadows what is to come downriver. Much of the development retains that raw look of Monopoly houses dropped on the land; if trees are in the way, it is apparently easier to bulldoze them than build around them.

St. Cloud was also home to the early automobile manufacturer, PAN Motor Company, which produced touring cars for a few years after WW I.

Bookended by a big paper mill at one end, and an ancient-looking prison and huge highway shopping malls at the other, St. Cloud is plainly a commercial and industrial center amid the cornfields. Our route nips across the Mississippi to pass **Sauk Rapids**, around whose hydropower the city grew; a small city park offers a closer view. Almost any view of the river from Sauk Rapids south to the Twin Cities will include something industrial, so it should come as no surprise that the Mississippi downstream from St. Cloud is contaminated by toxic metals and carcinogens like mercury, cadmium, lead, zinc, and polychlorinated biphenyls (PCBs). More surprising is the public disregard for these findings; despite muted cautionary pronouncements, people routinely fish for their dinners from downstream waters, and neither the EPA nor local governments seem willing to risk publicizing the real dangers with any sort of widespread ban.

The GRR follows 9th Avenue through St. Cloud before hitching along divided four-lane Hwy-75 at the city's southern perimeter, whizzing past acres of giant malls until crossing paths with our first interstate, I-94. Turning quickly away from the high-speed traffic, the GRR picks up a leisurely rural route again. While the interstate cuts a straight swath across the landscape, the GRR rolls through undulating farm-covered hills over which swallows perform their afternoon aerobatics, scooping insects out of the air.

When members of Lt. Zebulon Pike's 1804-05 expedition up the Mississippi first laid eyes on this land, it was covered in dense forest—try to imagine *that* as you drive the 30 miles to our fourth junction with I-94, Monticello. With the Twin Cities beltway only 25 miles away, this is a good opportunity to hop over to the interstate and simply make a beeline into or around Minneapolis and St. Paul, before the sudden sprouting of housing subdivisions and smokestack industries south of Monticello make the thought of virgin forest even more wildly improbable.

Cream of Wheat is one of the many cereals made in Minneapolis.

For information on visiting the Minneapolis/St. Paul metropolitan area, see the Survival Guide on pages 700-701.

ACROSS SOUTHWESTERN WISCONSIN

Heading out of St. Paul along the industrialized Mississippi riverbanks, the GRR crosses the St. Croix River at Prescott, Wisconsin, and wends south on Hwy-35 across a portion of the glacial plain whose rolling hills, sown in corn, account for an important part of the nation's breadbasket. The fertile soil here, as throughout the Midwestern grain belt, is a

Across the Mississippi from Monticello, 2.5 miles downstream from Elk River off US-10, the Oliver H. Kelley Farm preserves the 40 acres where the Patrons of Husbandry, an agricultural education and lobbying organization better known as "The Grange," was founded in 1867.

IF HARMONY

IS WHAT

YOU CRAVE

THEN GET

A TUBA

The Burma-Vita Company, based just west of Minneapolis, began erecting advertising signs along Hwy-61 near Red Wing and Hwy-65 near Albert Lea back in 1925. Over the next 38 years these signs and their witty rhymes appeared in nearly every state in the U.S. and made Burma-Shave one of the most recognized brand names in American business.

product of *drift:* pulverized soil left by mile-thick ice sheets scouring the ancient sediments of an inland sea for about two million years. Farther south, however, the GRR enters a very different landscape, known as the **Driftless Region**, a pocket of limestone bluffs and rocky uplands bypassed by all that rototilling glaciation. Stretching south into Illinois, this region affords dramatic views, a wildlife habitat, and a setting for one of the more painful episodes in Native American history: the devastating **Black Hawk War.**

The GRR follows two-lane Hwy-35 from Prescott south for nearly 100 miles, staying within closer view of the Mississippi for longer stretches than almost anywhere else on the route. The Corps of Engineers is a regular presence on the river from here south to the Gulf, most visibly with their locks and dams, but also with their dredges. It may not look shallow, but up here along Wisconsin's "west coast" the Mississippi doesn't naturally have the minimum nine-foot depth required by the "tows," those giant rafts of barges you'll see being pushed along the river.

Hwy-35: Main Street USA
At **Maiden Rock**, about 50 miles southeast of St. Paul and across the border into Wisconsin, Hwy-35 enters the heart of the **Driftless Region**, picking its way between steep bluffs and the wide Mississippi. Small towns, populations numbering only in the hundreds, cling to the margin, competing for the distinction of having the longest Main Street in the nation, if not the world; for some of these long hamlets the GRR is nearly the *only* street. These towns wear their age well, too busy with fishing or loading up barges to make themselves pretty for tourists, or to tear down every old building that no longer

seems useful. Most of these towns have at least a gas station, open late, and a road-house with Old Style or Pabst neon in the windows, open even later. Along with the riverside scenery, most also have a single tourist attraction: Amish crafts in Stock-holm; a replica of Laura "Little House on the Prairie" Ingalls Wilder's log cabin home near Pepin; a cheese factory in Nelson. Seven-mile-long Alma has an observation platform over Lock and Dam No. 4 where you can watch river traffic "lock through."

On an island near Red Wing, Minnesota, the **Prairie Island Nuclear Power Plant** is the northernmost of a half-dozen nuclear generating stations located along the Mississippi.

The river itself meanders little here, or what meanders used to exist have been flooded out by the staircase of Corps lakes and dams; instead of oxbows there are islands and sloughs, swampy backwater inlets and channels. As the valley widens—a product of the river's ancient restlessness—our narrow roller-coaster ride past tiny hamlets and scenic waysides (rest stops) begins to level out, but the bluffs continue to dominate the horizon on both sides of the Mississippi.

Between Minneapolis and La Crosse, Winona State University's **KQAL 89.5 FM** plays an excellent range of commercial-free pop music, including the Meat Puppets and early Hüsker Dü.

Trempealeau

At the sleepy hamlet of Trempealeau (pop. 1,039), the GRR would have you zigzag right through town, but detour a block down toward the river's edge to find the **Historic Trempealeau Hotel, Restaurant & Saloon** (608/534-6898), sole survivor of an 1888 downtown fire—maybe that's why the whole joint is smoke-free. The hotel dining room offers a surprisingly eclectic menu, from steak and seafood to Tex-Mex and vegetarian dishes; just head for the "Delicious Food" neon sign. The hotel also sponsors an excellent annual outdoor music series beginning with a Reggae Sunsplash the second weekend of May and featuring bands you've heard of throughout the summer (Steppenwolf and Asleep at the Wheel have appeared more than a few times). They rent canoes and bicycles to hardy souls desiring to try either the **Long Lake Canoe Trail** or the 100-mile network of **paved bikeways** that passes through town. Fi-nally, the hotel does rent rooms, too; all 12 share bathrooms and cost just $27 a night.

If you're practicing your Lake Wobegon language skills, be sure to say "You bet" in place of "You're welcome."

Shortly south of Trempealeau the GRR crosses US-53. Con-sider taking this interstate-wannabe into La Crosse to avoid the uninteresting 12 miles of stop-and-go traffic through Holman and Onalaska, La Crosse's northern abutters.

The first time you see the super grades of gas selling for less than the regular grade, you may think it's a mistake, but no: the high grades of gasoline are mixed with 10% ethanol, making them cheaper than the regular grade in this grain-rich state.

La Crosse

La Crosse (pop. 51,135) was named by fur traders who witnessed local Winnebago Indians playing a game strikingly similar to French lacrosse. It's an attractive place, but you wouldn't know that coming into town—mile after mile of food-gas-lodging establishments compete for attention. Successfully run the gauntlet and your reward will be finding the century-old downtown, the tidy residential neighborhoods, and the leafy University of Wisconsin-La Crosse campus.

Two miles east of downtown at the end of Main Street, **Grandad Bluff**, a lofty 590 feet over the city, gives a grand view of the Mississippi and the two states along its opposite shore. The view is a balm to any aesthete jangled by the commercial neon

carpet that welcomes travelers, too, for La Crosse actually looks rather attractive from above. Listen closely
and you might hear the University of Wisconsin
marching band practicing below.

La Crosse-based Heileman is widely recognized around
the upper Midwest for its Old Style brand beer. The **G.
Heileman Brewery**, right on the GRR at 1111 S. 3rd
Street (608/782-BEER or 800/433-BEER), has giant fer-
mentation tanks painted to look like the world's largest
six-pack. Free brewery tours are available daily 10 AM-3
PM, and a drinking fountain and tap in the parking lot
serve up fresh cold water straight from the source, 600
feet below the tarmac.

Slap *Spartacus* on the theater marquee and the heart
of downtown could easily be mistaken for a giant
Eisenhower-era time capsule. Within this classic commercial center a couple of coffeehouses have sprung
up. **Brew Note**, on Jay Street next to Deaf Ear Records, may be a little too polished,
but it does have the obligatory poetry nights, and good healthful food, too. **Painted
Alley**, around the corner at 129½ S. 4th Street, actually encourages brown-bagging
your food in to enjoy their coffees and desserts. Both stay open late.

Diners seeking less dainty fare should take the big blue Cass Street bridge (US-
61) over the Mississippi to Dr. J's Auto Clinic, just across the state line in La Crescent, Minnesota. Behind the good doctor (and almost invisible from the highway)
sits **Sabatino's 24-Hour Diner**, home of carbohydrates prepared to order, and well
deserving of its reputation for tasty Frisbee-sized omelets.

The Pearl, a polished-to-perfection confectionery at 207 Pearl Street, offers more
adult indulgences like fluorescent Blue Moon ice cream while the Andrews Sisters
harmonize in the background. If a double scoop of cookie dough isn't your idea of
lunch then try something wholesome, fresh, and filling from the deli of the **People's
Food Coop**, on 5th Avenue between Cass and King. Wash it down afterward with
one of the 200 bottled beers or 10 microbrews on draught at the **Bodega Brew Pub**,
on the corner of Pearl and S. 4th Streets, right downtown.

For accommodations, look to exits 2, 3, and 4 off I-90 for the budget national
chains. **Best Western, Holiday Inn, Radisson Hotel**, and **Courtyards By Marriott**
are also scattered around town, while local motels line South Avenue (the GRR),
such as the ranch-style **Redwood Motel**, 3305 South Avenue (608/788-0900).

Chat with anyone who spends time on the river from La Crosse south and you'll quickly learn about zebra mussels, an invasive species of freshwater clam from Europe that is becoming the kudzu of the Mississippi, carpeting boat hulls, intake pipes, native clams, and even live crawfish.

For a complete lodging and attractions guide, with map, call
the La Crosse Area Convention and Visitors Bureau (800/658-
9424) or visit their **information center** in leafy green Riverside
Park, where a 25-ton, 25-foot-tall statue of Hiawatha greets river
traffic with arms crossed and a politically incorrect plaque reading "Me Welcome You to Visitor Center."

Detour: Spring Green

Frank Lloyd Wright's famous country house and studio, **Taliesin**
(tally-ESS-en), is in Spring Green, 70 miles east of Prairie du Chien

BLACK HAWK WAR

Black Hawk was a leader of the Sac and Mesquakie Indians in northern Illinois during the feverish era of westward expansion into the newly opened Louisiana Purchase. As an ally of the British in the War of 1812, Black Hawk had done his best to force American settlers off the western frontier. By the time war hero Andrew Jackson rode his Indian-fighter reputation into the White House 16 years later, Black Hawk had been reduced to vain protests against the swindling and starvation of his tribes, forced to leave their rich cornfields for unfamiliar Iowa plains. Under Jackson, Native American genocide became a national obsession; amid such blind inhumanity an act as simple as searching for some empty land back in Illinois on which to plant corn became an "invasion" and act of war.

It was springtime on the upper Mississippi, in 1832, and while Sac-Mesquakie women and children tried to sow a crop, newspapers demanded the extermination of every Indian in the territory. Jackson sent in the army to round up the Sac-Mesquakie, but they botched the job: when Black Hawk tried to surrender he was fired upon; when he fought back, they ran. The war was on, and for the next three months Black Hawk's people were pushed north. Indians who surrendered were killed. Some of the Sac-Mesquakie followed Chief Keokuk, who was promised all that had once been promised to Black Hawk; Keokuk took the promises and ended up on a reservation in Iowa. The war ended at the Battle of Bad Ax, near present-day **Victory**, on August 1, 1832, but it wasn't a battle so much as a butchering. Caught by a gunboat and the army as he tried to cross the Mississippi, Black Hawk and his men came forward under a white flag. When the Indians identified themselves, the gunboat promptly opened fire. For the next eight hours the volunteer militias used axes, guns, cannon, and clubs to cut down the Indian warriors while women and children who succeeded in swimming the river were slaughtered on the other side. By various accounts some 90% of Black Hawk's people were killed. The Mississippi, survivors said, ran red with their blood. Black Hawk himself, captured and imprisoned, was paraded around the U.S. in chains; after he died his skeleton was displayed in the governor's mansion in Iowa, like a trophy.

If there is any doubt about the esteem 19th-century Americans had for Indian fighters, consider that among the officers sent against Black Hawk were these men: William Henry Harrison, Zachary Taylor, Abraham Lincoln, and Jefferson Davis.

via Hwy-60. Fully guided tours of the private residence and architecture school are offered daily May-Oct.; ticket prices range $7-35, depending on what's included in the tour (call 608/588-7900 for info and reservations). Spring Green is also home to the state's biggest tourist trap, the incredible **House on the Rock** (daily 9 AM-dusk; $14; 608/935-3639) with its "World's Largest" merry-go-round, kitschy collections of everything from dolls to replicas of the Crown Jewels, and the eponymous house, standing atop a 450-foot-high rock.

If it's summertime and you want an up-close look at the Mississippi, continue south with the GRR on the Wisconsin side about 30 miles to **Cassville,** a historic frontier town that holds one of the river's few surviving **car ferries** (daily 9 AM-9 PM, Memorial Day-Labor Day, weekends only in May and October; $5 per car; 608/725-5180 for 24-hour information).

Prairie du Chien

For most of the nearly 60 miles between La Crosse and Prairie du Chien, the GRR (Hwy-35) is again confined to the margin between the tall gray and yellow bluffs and the impressively wide, lakelike Mississippi. At times the roadway is so narrow that the few houses have to climb three stories up the irregular wooded slopes, while the railbed on your right is suspended over the water on viaducts. About halfway along there's a maze of small islands around the mouth of the Bad Ax River, with the occasional blue heron poised like a Giacometti sculpture in algae-covered sloughs. Dotting the curves alongside the road are a series of historical markers old enough to be artifacts themselves; most are related to the **Black Hawk War.**

Named by early 19th-century French voyageurs for the abundant native prairie dogs, Prairie du Chien could be rechristened Prairie du Kwik-Stop or Prairie du Pabst by the modern traveler cruising through downtown's W. Blackhawk Avenue. The town's main attraction is the posh **Villa Louis** (daily 9 AM-5 PM, May-Oct.; $5), which embodies the wealth that could be made in the fur trade back when every European dandy's head sported beaver-pelt hats. Built by the state's first millionaire, the house boasts one of the finest collections of domestic Victoriana in the country; signs point you to it from all over town.

ACROSS NORTHEASTERN IOWA

In its 140-mile course across Iowa, the GRR passes swiftly but unmistakably across the cultural and geographic North-South Divide. Separated by the Mississippi River from the rough topography of Wisconsin's Driftless Region, the southeastern corner of Iowa offers instead a taste of the state's trademark rolling plains covered with corn and soybeans. Menus are different, too: cattle here are raised for meat instead of milk, and Iowa is a leading producer of hogs (one of the state lottery games is called "Bring Home the Bacon," while radio ads encourage you to "eat more pork—the other white meat"). So say goodbye to walleye and hello to BBQ. Twangy country music, too, is no longer a novelty on the FM radio dial, and posters advertising local rodeos appear in store windows.

Running along the western bank of the Mississippi, our route tends to the tops of the bluffs, too, rather than to their base, which means the river is often spied from a distance and seems unrelated to the rolling landscape; fortunate-

Forty-six miles west of McGregor is the town of Spillville, where Antonin Dvorak was inspired to compose his symphony, *From the New World,* in 1893.

ly it continues to guide the curves of the road. Other than Dubuque, our route passes through towns so far from the beaten path they don't even rate a fast-food strip or Wal-Mart—appreciate this while it lasts.

McGregor and Guttenberg

Immediately across the pair of long bridges from Prairie du Chien, near the foot of the "original" Pike's Peak—Zebulon Pike came up the Mississippi before he went out to Colorado—McGregor is a river town whose enticing old saloons may tempt you to stop and watch boat traffic, if you manage to turn a blind eye to the garish Pink Elephant advertising the **Miss Marquette Riverboat Casino** complex. North of McGregor, right along the riverbank, the **Effigy Mounds National Monument** (daily 8 AM-5 PM; $2) preserves 1,500 acres of burial mounds shaped like birds and animals, traces of a native culture that lived along the Mississippi around 500 B.C.

McGregor was the hometown of the five children who grew up to found the **Ringling Brothers** circus.

Atop the bluffs, tidy frame farmhouses dot the landscape, with white barns, silos, and farmland aroma accompanying US-18 and US-52 as they loop inland south toward Guttenberg, another postcard-pretty old river town whose downtown lines the Mississippi. Entering the town, the GRR takes another look at the prairie's geological underpinnings as it cuts down to the river's edge. Guttenberg is indeed named in honor of Johannes Gutenberg, 15th-century inventor of printing from moveable type. Local legend has it that an official of French descent purposely added the extra "t" after German residents won a vote to change the town's name from the original Prairie la Porte.

South of Prairie du Chien, across from McGregor, Iowa, is the spot where **Louis Joliet** and his Jesuit companion **Jacques Marquette** caught their first sight of the Mississippi after coming down the Wisconsin River in 1673 while searching for a route to the Orient.

For a quick marine biology lesson, the **Upper Mississippi Fisheries Aquarium** at Lock and Dam No. 10 downtown displays live specimens of most of the river's fish species and includes a number of invertebrates (daily 8 AM-9 PM, May-Sept.; free; 319/252-1156).

You can take the Cassville ferry to the Iowa side some 10 well-signed miles southeast of Guttenberg, but of the Germanic eyeblink towns on the rolling uplands between Guttenberg and Dubuque, only **Balltown** is worth a stop to sample the food and decor at **Breitbach's**, a bar and restaurant that's so old Pres. Millard Fillmore issued the permit allowing it to open.

Dubuque marks the junction of the Great River Road and cross-country US-20, which is covered in full detail beginning on page 404.

Dubuque

After miles of Iowa prairie and river towns the GRR rolls into Dubuque (pop. 57,546), named for the 18th-century French voyageur, Julien Dubuque, who unsuccessfully mined for lead on land acquired from the Spanish. Finding lead wasn't the problem—Indians had dug lead by hand as early as 1680 for trade with the English—but getting it to market was. After the steamboat's invention and forced removal of native tribes in the late 1820s, mineral wealth became a major catalyst to settlement of the tri-state area around Dubuque, as town names like Potosi, Mineral Point, New Diggings, and Lead Mine attest. During the Civil War, just five counties around here supplied all the lead for the entire Union war effort.

The **Iowa Welcome Center** (800/79-VISIT), down on the waterfront, stands next to Dubuque's newest source of wealth, the **Casino Belle**, another of the long parade of riverboat casinos found all the way down to the Gulf of Mexico. Not able to wholly give in to sin, Iowa initially required gaming to be "low stakes," meaning that players were restricted to $200 per excursion aboard the boat. Once neighboring Illinois floated its own no-limit gameboats, Iowa had to amend its law to keep the golden goose from roosting somewhere else.

On the inland side of the compact downtown, a good view of the city and the Mississippi valley can be had at the top of the **Fenelon Place Elevator**, a small funicular cable car that proudly holds the title of "world's steepest, shortest scenic railway" (daily 8 AM-10 PM, April-Nov.; 75 cents one-way). If it's a tall lanky fellow at the controls of the 15hp motor up in the headhouse, and you're a base-ball fan, you might have fun trying to stump him with questions about the Minnesota Twins, his favorite team. He purports to know their starting lineups for every year back to 1961.

Dubuque is a very meat-and-potatoes place when it comes to food, and plan to dine early to catch restaurants before they close. Basic coffee shop breakfasts, lunches, and dinners are on the menu at **Dottie's Cafe**, downtown at 5th and Central, while the landmark **Bridge** steakhouse, on Main Street at the foot of the US-20 bridge (look for the neon "Good Food" sign) is a step or two up in price and quality. Near the Fenelon Place elevator, **Shot Tower Pizza** has an upstairs deck and beer by the pitcher. For entertainment, check out Main Street bars like **Loie** and **Admiral's High Hat Lounge**, which has live music most nights.

The ballfield created for the movie *Field of Dreams* has become a minor tourist mecca for rural **Dyersville,** 35 miles due west of Dubuque via US-20. For details see page 439.

A highly recommended 15-mile side trip is to **Galena,** southeast of Dubuque on US-20. Spawned by the early 19th-century lead rush, this was the early social and cultural capital of the Upper Mississippi and is now one of the best preserved historic towns in the country

The classic old hotel in town is the **Julien Inn**, 200 Main Street (319/556-4200 or 800/798-7098), providing rooms at $30-50, while the **Redstone Inn**, 504 Bluff Street (319/582-1894), offers comfortable B&B rooms in a stately downtown mansion. The usual chain motels line US-20 west of the river.

South of Dubuque, the GRR follows US-52 back up the bluffs past Julien Dubuque's original lead workings and across 45 miles of upland farms and wooded bottoms until the next Mississippi crossing at Sabula.

St. Donatus

Fifteen undulating agricultural miles south of Dubuque, the tiny hamlet of St. Donatus is widely advertised as a historic and picturesque Luxembourg village, but the only historic or picturesque feature is the handsome masonry of the Gehlen House and barn, opposite the Kalmes general store and restaurant. Upon much closer inspection (or guidance from the tourist informants in the Gehlen House) you could find some 80 other limestone structures built by immigrant Luxembourg masons before the middle 1800s, but their impressive handiwork is invisible to all but the most practiced eye, covered up by protective stucco. Most of the buildings are scattered around the countryside, too, but a few are found west of the Gehlen House; follow the signed turn to Lower Town.

Other eye-catching structures are the Catholic church and **Pieta Chapel** atop the adjacent Calvary Hill; if you wish to make a pilgrimage up the Way of the Cross, start behind the church burial ground, east of the Kalmes Store. The plain brick construction of the 14 stations belies the fact that this is the oldest outdoor Calvary in the United States. At the top of the hill is an 1885 reproduction of the du Bildchen chapel in Luxembourg, left unlocked for the devout. Appropriately, the hill is home to a flock of sheep awaiting the return of their shepherd; they do keep the brush down, but their habits mean you should be shod in something other than Birkenstocks or polished wingtips when making the trek up to the chapel. Nice view from the top—the other set of spires across the valley belongs to the German Lutheran St. John's Church.

The **Kalmes Restaurant and Tavern**, a focal point of the community since 1850, is so packed on weekend evenings you'll wonder if they're giving away food: but no, Iowans are just friendly and sociable as a rule. Belly up to the bar and see for yourself.

Bellevue and Sabula

The GRR (US-52) returns to the Mississippi valley at Bellevue, with its lengthy Main Street and Riverfront Park beside Lock and Dam No. 12, and stays in sparsely populated wooded lowlands until it reaches the junction of US-67, marked by the first stop sign south of Dubuque. Follow US-52 southeast into Sabula, an island of a town created by the Corps of Engineers when the pool above Lock and Dam No. 13, 16 miles downstream, flooded out the surrounding plains. Sabula's encompassing levees provide fine wetlands birdwatching.

From Sabula, cross the narrow causeways and Mississippi bridge into Illinois to be guided by the GRR's familiar pilot's wheel down to the Quad Cities.

Sabula takes its name from the Latin *sabulum*, meaning "sand."

From the end of November to the beginning of March, the American bald eagle nests along the middle and upper Mississippi. The best place to catch sight of one is below any of the dams, where turbulence keeps the river from icing over and fish injured or stunned by the dams make easy prey for the great bird.

ACROSS ILLINOIS AND MISSOURI

Our route along the middle Mississippi starts in northwestern Illinois, just below the Driftless Region, and proceeds through sandy floodplain and fertile prairie, nipping back and forth across the ever-locked and dammed Mississippi between Illinois and the generally more developed Missouri uplands. Here, small towns bypassed by much of the 20th century are more likely to be forlorn than quaint, a prelude to those southern states in which local ordinances appear to require the public display of rusty appliances. With a few exceptions—such as the historic Mormon town of Nauvoo, or Mark Twain's hometown Hannibal—

The names Black Hawk, Marquette, and Joliet continue to crop up, as this stretch of the Mississippi was their prime stomping grounds. South of the Quad Cities you'll see more of Abraham Lincoln, too, as the GRR shares the road with Illinois's Lincoln Heritage Trail.

The Illinois Bed & Breakfast Association offers a free guide to selected B&Bs around the state; request one directly from the IBBA at P.O. Box 295, Mossville, IL 61552.

our route now mostly runs through communities whose best years may have passed. This stretch of the GRR also includes one of the most dramatic sections of the entire route: the 25 miles around Grafton, Illinois, at the northern doorstep of St. Louis.

South of St. Louis, I-55 is the recommended route, as it bypasses an almost unbroken 50-mile string of auto dealerships, appliance stores, shopping centers, and other prefab conveniences lining US-61. Passing through the old river town of Sainte Genevieve, the GRR crosses the Mississippi once again by ferry, back to the corn, soybeans, and cicadas of Southern Illinois. Accents, "Bar-B-Q" signs, and Baptist churches leave no doubt that our route has entered the South; in summer the heat and humidity confirm this with a vengeance. Fortunately, after leaving the "American Bottom" the GRR skirts the edge of the Shawnee National Forest, whose shade brings up to 25° relief from the temperatures along the roadside fields on a sunny July day. Occasional levees, raised roadbeds, and brackish seasonal ponds are reminders that the mile-wide Mississippi is only temporarily out of sight of the GRR, which finally crosses into Kentucky beside the giant turbid confluence of the Mississippi and Ohio Rivers at Cairo.

Savanna

Across the Mississippi from Iowa, Savanna, Illinois, is an unlovely old railroad town that has grown into an unlovely antiques center, offering three antique minimalls along the main drag. There's a coffeehouse, too—the **Blue Moon**—to slake the thirst of all those shoppers who roll in from Chicago.

Savanna maintains a few pretty Victorian mansions up on the heights, but for a truly attractive vista take a detour in the opposite direction from Savanna, *north* from the end of the Iowa bridge to nearby **Mississippi Palisades State Park**, with its great eroded bluffs and fine river views.

THAT DIRTY WATER

If you're wondering how a major industrial corridor can coexist with critical wildlife habitat, the answer is that it can't, though most people are unaware of how serious the conflict is. The return of the bald eagle from the brink of extinction is undeniably good news; so is the enormous reductions in raw sewage and mercury releases over the last 20 years. But nearly 300 million pounds of toxic chemicals are still dumped into the Mississippi every year, and over a billion gallons of wastewater from cities and factories are discharged into the river *daily*.

Defenders of the status quo argue that the river does a fine job of dilution, as shown by how infrequently water quality standards are compromised. This conveniently ignores the fact that many toxins are bioaccumulators: whether you eat a single heavily contaminated fish during pregnancy or several years' worth of slightly contaminated fish prior to conceiving, the damage to your fetus can be the same. Pollutants also are very persistent, settling into river sediments only to be re-released through dredging or boat traffic. Such "sediment loading" isn't even considered by the states or the EPA when assessing water quality, nor has assessment criteria been updated to include over 1,000 compounds recognized in the last 20 years as toxic or hazardous to human health. Monitoring is also very haphazard, with half of the states bordering the Mississippi routinely failing to submit the data required to determine whether Maximum Contaminant Levels (MCLs) have been exceeded or not.

The river's health is reflected in its dependents. Filter-feeders like freshwater mussels are considered good barometers; of the 37 species found in the Mississippi, 22 are in decline and 11 are endangered or extinct on the upper portion of the river. Fish kills—die-offs caused by oxygen-depleted water or pollutants—number in the hundreds each year, and species such as largemouth bass, striped bass, and sturgeon are all in decline. Plenty of the surviving fish store an alphabet soup of toxins in their fatty tissue. DDT, banned in 1972, is *still* found in significant quantities in bottom-feeding species like catfish.

Meanwhile, millions of residents from the Twin Cities to New Orleans still obtain their drinking water from the Mississippi, and both commercial and recreational fishing are widely practiced.

Between Savanna and the interstate beltway around the Quad Cities are nearly 50 flat miles of river valley, dotted with small historic river and railroad towns vandalized by new commercial and residential construction. Agriculture is conspicuous, too, and the sandy soils between Savanna and Thomson are particularly known for their melon crops. While the Mississippi for the most part stays invisible from the GRR, the industry on its banks is clearly evident, especially at night. River access is at hand via a handful of **recreation areas** in the **Upper Mississippi National Fish and Wildlife Refuge**.

Hanover, Illinois, 20 miles north of Savanna on Hwy-84, is home to **Whistling Wings,** the world's largest mallard duck hatchery (Mon.-Fri. 9 AM-5 PM, Sat. 9 AM-noon; free; 815/591-3512). Over 200,000 mallards are raised annually for sale to refuges, restaurants, researchers, and individuals whose gardens lack that certain quack.

Le Claire, Iowa

On the northeastern edge of the Quad Cities, just off the I-80 freeway, lies the little town of Le Claire, famous once for its river pilots but now best remembered as William F. "Buffalo Bill" Cody's home. The **Buffalo Bill Museum**, on the waterfront, is dedicated to Cody's life (daily 9 AM-5 PM, May 15-Oct. 15, weekends only the rest of the year; $1). More interesting are the paddle wheelers that tie up alongside the small, gun-filled museum, one of which, the *Julia Belle Swain*, offers overnight cruises up to Galena, Illinois (800/ 331-1467 for info and reservations). **The Faithful Pilot**, on Le Claire's main street (US-67), is one of the best restaurants in the entire Quad City region, with creative, high-quality cuisine, a good wine list, and fine microbrews, all at prices you'd expect. The small bar at the back has views of the river, and the friendliest bartender along its banks.

The Quad Cities

Straddling the Mississippi at its confluence with the Rock River, the Quad Cities—Moline, Rock Island, Davenport, and Bettendorf—encompass an enormous sprawl of some 400,000 residents on what was once the home of the Sac-Mesquakie Indian nations, Saukenuk. While much of the cityscape is dominated by heavy industry, particularly on the Iowa side, points of interest are sprinkled throughout. Like a parking lot with flowers growing up through the cracks, look closely and you'll find a vital arts community, a gay/lesbian community, and even some excellent restaurants that break the typical Midwestern meat-and-potato mold.

If there's a must-see stop in the Quad Cities, it's the headquarters of tractor manufacturers **Deere & Company**, located on a rural stretch of John Deere Road (Hwy-5) in Moline. Architect Eero Saari-

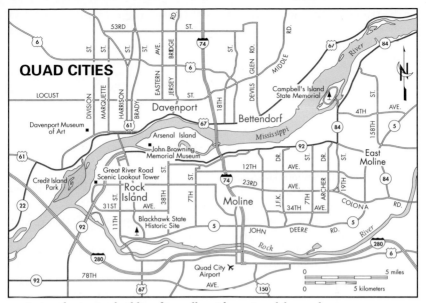

QUAD CITIES

nen's award-winning building fits well amid spacious lakes and landscaping, but the highlight is the product display floor's giant three-dimensional historical collage, **Reflections of an Era,** by Santa Fe artist Alexander Girard. Check out a new John Deere tractor, too, or take a free **tour** (Mon.-Fri. 10:30 AM and 1:30 AM, display floor open daily 9 AM-5:30 PM).

Along the river at the heart of the Quad Cities, adjacent to downtown Rock Island, is the former namesake of that city, now called Arsenal Island for the U.S. Army facility based there. Despite the look of the gatehouse at the southern entrance, the island is open to the public; besides an arsenal museum and Civil War cemeteries, there's a very good **Corps of Engineers visitor center** (daily 9 AM-9 PM in summer, till 5 PM rest of the year; free) on the island right next to Lock and Dam No. 15, where the operation of the locks can be seen from a penny-pitch away.

The first railroad bridge over the Mississippi linked Rock Island and Davenport in 1856. The railroad was promptly sued by a steamboat company whose craft was mortally attracted to the bridge piers. The plaintiffs argued that bridges violated their navigation rights; the defense lawyer's elegantly simple—and successful—rebuttal was to claim that a person has as much right to cross a river as to travel upon it. That lawyer was Abraham Lincoln. Today the railroad crosses the river on the upper deck of the old iron Government bridge, which swings open for the tows entering the locks; cars crossing between Rock Island and Davenport can ride the humming lower deck for free or take the modern concrete highway span below the dam for a 50-cent toll.

Thomson, 20 miles south of Savanna on Hwy-84, is the self-proclaimed **Watermelon Capital of the World,** and celebrates its "Melon Days" festival every Labor Day weekend. Country music, carnival rides, watermelon-eating contests, and free watermelon are the traditional highlights.

The Illinois side of Lock and Dam No. 13, accessible from the GRR just north of Fulton, is considered one of the best spots for bald eagle sightings.

The welcome sign for Le Claire alludes to a "famous green tree," a sight familiar in Mark Twain's day, but now long gone. The tree was the gathering point for the specialized "rapids pilots" who would guide boats through the 14-mile-long Moline Rapids that began below Le Claire.

The **Davenport Museum of Art**, 1737 W. 12th Street (open Tues.-Sun. till 4:30 PM; free, but donation suggested), has a good regional collection featuring Thomas Hart Benton and Grant Wood, along with parodies of Wood's most famous painting, *American Gothic*.

Quad Cities Practicalities

The average Quad City restaurant features steaks, burgers, fried catfish, and spaghetti (*not* pasta), or onion rings and chili dogs. If these selections tickle your palate, you'll have a surfeit of choices. Otherwise, except for Bettendorf, the downtown of each of the Quad Cities has a pocket of worthwhile restaurants and, yes, even coffeehouses.

In downtown Davenport, for example, look to Harrison and Brady Avenues within the first few blocks of both the casino landing and convention center to find several eateries, including the **Smile Coffeehouse** (313 Harrison), **Theo's Java Hut** (221 Brady) or, for more substantial fare, the **Thai House Restaurant** (Mon.-Fri. 11 AM-2 PM, 5-9 PM, Sat. 5-9 PM) on Harrison Avenue at W. 4th Street.

Downtown Moline is but a half-dozen blocks along 5th Avenue between I-74 and 14th Street; among its offerings are **Le Mekong** (Mon.-Fri. 11 AM-2 PM, 5-9 PM; Sat.-Sun. 5-9 PM) at 16th, the **Caffé Piccalo** on 14th, and for replenishing your backseat car buffet, **Heritage Natural Foods** up on 6th Avenue near 14th Street. Also in downtown Moline is the extraordinary **Lagomarcino's** (1422 5th Avenue), a soda fountain that still uses those conical paper cups in solid metal holders and serves drinks like "phosphates" in a setting virtually unchanged since it opened in 1908. Order a strawberry shake here and the flavor will come from scoops of real strawberries ladled over freshly made vanilla ice cream.

*Davenport celebrates the music legacy of native son and cornetist **Leon Beiderbecke** with the annual Bix Beiderbecke Memorial Jazz Festival, held at the end of July. A statue of Bix stands along the river, next to wonderful old (circa 1930) **John O'Donnell Stadium,** where the minor league Quad Cities River Bandits (tickets $3-6; 319/324-2032) play their home games.*

Rock Island's old downtown, 2nd Avenue, has experienced something of a revival with the appearance of a riverboat casino a block away; one pleasant result is "the District," centered around the 2nd Avenue pedestrian mall. At the 17th Street end is the **Quad City ArtsCenter Gallery** (Tues.-Sat. 10 AM-6 PM; free; 309/793-1213), where there's always something free and interesting happening on Friday evenings, Sept.-May. A block away at 1806 2nd Avenue is **All Kinds of People Espresso Bar & Bookshop**, serving fine yuppie sandwiches, soup, baked goods, and beverages (including microbrews), at not-so-yuppie prices; travelers may feel like they've found a magic doorway back to the Beat Generation when they see the book and journal selection in the back. Neighbors include Tony's Mexican American Restaurant, a.k.a. **Tony's Tacos**, with an authentic lineup of dishes right down to the *menudo*. **The General Store**, with its work-in-progress window gallery, is sort of like an open kitchen for artists, who follow their muse for all to see. Across the avenue on the corner of 18th Street is the **Blue Cat Brew Pub**, whose salads, seafood, and desserts go way beyond your average pub fare and whose beers, too, range from traditional to an esoteric orange coriander concoction. While the Blue Cat's kitchen is open until way past your proper bedtime, hungry night owls on weekends may also want to try nearby **Ruby's Creole & Cajun Restaurant** (1700 3rd Avenue), under the old "Dutch Inn" sign: between Friday 6 AM and Sunday 10 PM they never close.

For a truly regional diner experience, look in the phone book or ask directions to a **Maid-Rite Cafe** (there are seven in the area, three in Moline). A strictly upper Midwest phenomenon whose faded logo "Since 1926" can often be seen on old brick buildings or historic commercial storefronts up through Minnesota, the local Maid-Rites are unusually bright and polished, and come heartily recommended.

There are some 35 motels in the Quad Cities, including all the major chains, most with locations on both sides of the Mississippi. In Illinois the major clusters are both off I-74, one next to the airport and the other by John Deere Road; the same smorgasbord is replicated in Iowa off I-80's exit 295A (US-61 south) and at the Bettendorf/Davenport line off I-74's Kimberly Road (US-6 West) exit.

If you want extra printed information to orient yourself, there are two **Welcome Centers** nearby: one on I-80 eastbound, the other off I-80 westbound, across the Mississippi.

The Quad Cities visitors guide and B&B brochure are particularly recommended. To obtain info in advance call the Quad Cities Convention and Visitors' Bureau recorded **information line** (800/747-7800).

Through the Yellow Banks

For nearly 100 miles south of the Quad Cities, the GRR picks its way along a series of back roads through Illinois floodplain and prairie, most of which is under cultivation. Frequent small towns serve as reminders of the need for frequent stops by early stages, steamboats, and railroads. Most of the towns seem not to have changed much since the last steamboat or train whistle blew, although now there's neon in the bars, vinyl and aluminum siding on the houses, and farmers with high-powered four-by-fours on the roads. All the big towns sit on the opposite side of the Mississippi, a product of the enormous 19th-century expansion of the American frontier. On the west bank were all the embarkation points for settlers heading across the great prairie and Plains trails—the Oregon, the Mormon, the Santa Fe—so it was around those places that supply towns grew. Illinois could only sit and watch.

Nearly 45 miles south of the Quad City beltway, the GRR passes tiny **New Boston**, at the mouth of the Iowa River. The town is a historical footnote these days, having been surveyed by the young Abraham Lincoln after his stint in the army—a tour of duty during which his only combat was against mosquitoes, he later recalled.

Along the river farther south, near **Keithsburg** a sign welcomes travelers to Yel-

Beer aficionados should keep an eye out for a wheat beer called Millstream, brewed in Amana, Iowa. As it's not widely distributed, it's a rare find, well worth sampling. **Amana** itself is a long way fom the GRR, but is a neat place: a utopian agricultural community that later gave birth to the Radarange, the first commercial microwave oven.

For a complete rundown on arts and entertainment in Dubuque, Galena, and the Quad Cities, pick up a free copy of the monthly *River Cities' Reader*.

low Bank country, named for the deep layer of sand exposed in the river valley in this region. Because of this deposit, visitors can find sandburs and even cactus in the Big River State Forest south of town. Keithsburg used to be one of a number of button manufacturing centers located along the middle Mississippi: freshwater clams were dredged from the river bottom and their shells were used for making pearl buttons. Clamming is still the commercial occupation of a few hardy divers, although now the shells are almost exclusively used for "pearl seed," the sand-sized implant injected into commercial pearl oysters in the Pacific.

Burlington and Niota

Across the Mississippi River via an austere modern suspension bridge, Burlington was the frontier capital of Iowa, founded in 1808 and holding many Victorian homes and commercial buildings. It also has a riverboat casino, a Maid-Rite diner, and very busy downtown rail yards—home base of the Burlington Northern Railway.

At Niota, the ghost of a town that marks the next crossing south of Burlington, a nifty old double-decker swing bridge (trains below, cars on top) crosses the Mississippi, landing on the west bank next to a huge old state prison at the historic town of Fort Madison.

Nauvoo

Founded in 1839 by the Church of Jesus Christ of Latter-day Saints, the town of Nauvoo—a Hebrew word for "the beautiful location"—was named by Mormon leader Joseph Smith. Though the Mormons were forced to flee to Utah in 1846, today Nauvoo is a top destination for Mormon pilgrims, and the church has sponsored a massive historic preservation of old Nauvoo. Even if you're just passing through, you'll have plenty of opportunities to learn about Mormon history and religion, and the restored townscape is a noncommercial reminder of what frontier America looked like in the years before the Wild West was finally won.

A public park at the south end of the business district marks the site of the original Nauvoo temple, which when construction began in 1841 was the largest building west of Philadelphia. Now remembered by a scale model—which looks distinctly odd juxtaposed against the neighboring water tower—and a few exposed foundations, the temple had a remarkable series of stone capitals carved with sunburst motifs, one of which is displayed in a glass case. Other interesting historic Mormon-related sites include the store run by Joseph Smith and the home of Brigham Young. The home and workshop of Jonathon Browning, inventor of the repeating rifle, has been been restored along Main Street, south of the present downtown area.

For a map of the town and visitor information, stop by either the huge **LDS Visitors Center** (daily 9 AM-9 PM in summer, till 5 PM rest of the year; free; 217/453-2237 or 800/453-0022)—don't miss the archaeology exhibit on the second floor—or the more modest Reorganized Latter-day Saints-operated **Joseph Smith Historic Center**, down by the river at the corner of Hwy-96 and Water Street (daily 9 AM-5 PM; free; 217/453-2246). (The LDS is formed by Mormons who went to Utah, the RLDS by those who stayed behind.) At either, you'll learn Mormon interpretations of local history and find about crafts demonstrations and guided tours in restored 19th-century properties. The town operates its own info center, too.

The annual **Nauvoo Grape Festival,** held each Labor Day weekend, celebrates the wine business that arose after European immigrants moved onto farms abandoned by the Mormon exodus. As the town also acquired a blue cheese industry early this century after Prohibition shut down the beer-making trade, the centerpiece of the festival features "the Wedding of the Wine and Cheese," a medieval-style pageant borrowed from Roquefort, France.

Restaurants and lodging are all clustered along Mulholland Street (Hwy-96, a.k.a. the GRR) within a few blocks of the water tower. The **Hotel Nauvoo** is particularly well regarded for its belt-straining buffets. For picnic supplies, try the **Nauvoo Mill and Bakery** (Mon.-Sat. 8 AM-5 PM), near the Shell station.

For more complete practical information, contact the Nauvoo Chamber of Commerce (217/453-6648), uptown opposite the historic Hotel Nauvoo.

Warsaw

For a scenic dozen miles south of Nauvoo the GRR returns after long absence to the banks of the Mississippi, shaded by native hickory and oak, and then sidesteps yet another opportunity to enter Iowa, this time via US-136 west to Keokuk. Staying on the east bank, we follow a series of farm roads past gravel pits and fields for most of the 40-mile run down to Quincy.

First stop south of Nauvoo is what used to be the town of Warsaw. Patrons of the bars along the main drag probably think it still *is* Warsaw, but blocks of empty windows and shuttered doorways tell a different story. At the end of town the GRR threatens to turn amphibious as it rolls down past a towering grain elevator to the Mississippi's edge, bends south along the base of the bluffs past old house trailers, scruffy fields full of wildlife—including wild turkeys and river turtles waddling along the roadside—and old kilns visible in the limestone, and passes finally into cornfields planted in the fertile floodplain of the river.

Unfortunately, though the roads are good and the scenery fine, it is on this stretch that the first serious disappearance of the trusty GRR pilot's wheel occurs; a hint, perhaps, of what awaits farther south. You can't go far wrong, though: where the pavement dead-ends there's an opportunity to turn left, and all roads lead eventually to Hwy-96, which will bring you into Quincy on the (still unsigned) GRR.

Warsaw lends its name to a variety of geode found locally in profusion; inside, Warsaw geodes grow calcite crystals. Across the Mississippi, Keokuk geodes grow quartzite crystals inside their stony spheres.

Quincy

Midway between the Quad Cities and St. Louis, Quincy (pop. 39,681) is a modest-sized city, Germanic enough in its heritage to consider Pizza Hut an ethnic restaurant. A bastion of abolitionists before the Civil War, Quincy was also home to anti-abolitionist Stephen Douglas, the incumbent Illinois senator whose campaign debates with Abraham Lincoln put that tall country lawyer on the path to the White House.

The GRR follows the riverfront and again the pilot's wheel is missing, but the giant span of the Bayview bridge over the Mississippi will leave no doubt as to which way to turn to stay on track. However, most of the city perches on the tall bluffs above the GRR and is worth a drive-through if only to sample its textbook va-

---

MORMONS IN ILLINOIS

If you're passing through Nauvoo, you'll have plenty of opportunities to learn about Mormon history and religion. Nauvoo is Mecca for Mormons, or "Latter-day-Saints" (LDS) as members prefer to call themselves. In 1839, the Mormons purchased a large tract of swampy land along the Mississippi River, then set about draining swamps and building a city. Within a few years Nauvoo was not only the largest LDS settlement in America, but the 10th-largest city in the U.S. The emergence of such a powerful little theocracy generated resentment among outnumbered neighbors, and even some internal dissent. The friction escalated to violence on both sides, finally culminating in the 1844 arrest of Joseph Smith, Jr., church founder and president, for having sanctioned the destruction of printing presses used by some church members to question his leadership. While in the nearby Carthage jail, Smith was lynched by a mob and so became one of the Mormons' first martyrs. Amid ensuing disputes over church succession and renewed hostilities with non-Mormon neighbors, most residents followed Brigham Young across the Mississippi on the famous exodus to Salt Lake City.

Given Smith's martyrdom, the fact that he's buried here, and the Brigham Young migration's roots in the town, little wonder that Nauvoo attracts Mormon pilgrims by the busload. The Utah-based LDS faction has sponsored a massive restoration of old Nauvoo buildings, and the town now ranks as one of the capitals of historic preservation in the United States. Most of old Nauvoo is operated essentially as a big museum, totally free and open to the non-LDS public.

riety of residential architecture. Check out the **Gardner Museum of Architecture and Design** (Tues.-Sun. 1-5 PM; $2), in the old public library downtown on Maine and 4th, for an overview of both those topics. Then take a walk or drive through the East End, an area roughly bounded by Maine and State Streets between 16th and 24th. Filled with historic mansions along quiet tree-canopied streets, it's the perfect place to practice distinguishing Queen Anne from Tudor, prairie from gothic.

If you have thus far avoided the tried-and-true cooking of the **Maid-Rite** chain, Quincy gives you two chances to fix this oversight: the one that opens for breakfast is out on Broadway near 31st Street, near the strip of national fast-food chains, while the one with only lunch and early dinner hours is at 507 N. 12th Street. For something even more strictly local and downhome, slide back down to the waterfront under the bridge for some fried fresh fish at the **Sky Ride Inn** on Front Street, marked by a multicolored neon sign.

If you plan to spend the night, you'll find the **Holiday Inn, Travelodge,** and **Days Inn** downtown, while **Comfort, Fairfield,** and **Super 8** sit a few miles out on Broadway between the Quincy Mall and the local interstate-equivalent, Hwy-336. If you prefer antiques to HBO in your room, there are a couple of reasonable B&Bs; the **Kaufmann House,** in the heart of the historic mansions at 1641 Hampshire Street (217/223-2502), has doubles for $45-65.

For more information call the friendly and helpful **Convention and Visitors Bureau** (800/978-4748) or drop by their tourist information center in the **Villa Kathrine,** the you-won't-miss-it turn-of-the-20th-century Moorish residence on the bluffs overlooking the Mississippi, just beside the Gardner Expressway (Hwy-57).

Following Hwy-57 south through Quincy's industrial margin, the GRR merges into high-speed Hwy-336, then cuts west along US-36 across the mile-wide Mississippi into Hannibal.

Drop the top on your convertible and maybe you can land yourself a travel companion during the World Free Fall, an annual skydiving event that fills Quincy's skies with thousands of jumpers from all over the planet. Held at Baldwin Field between the first two weekends in August, the Free Fall is the legacy of one **Thomas Baldwin,** whose pioneering parachute jump from a balloon into a Quincy park in 1887 earned him two world exhibition tours.

Hannibal

It doesn't take a literature professor to figure out who Hannibal's most famous resident was: his name prefaces half the signs in town, and the names of his characters preface the other half. Cross the Mark Twain Memorial Bridge onto Mark Twain Avenue and if not bound for the Huck Finn Mall or Mark Twain Lake (or the Tom N' Huck Motel), turn onto 3rd Street (the GRR) near the Hotel Clemens and park yourself in the heart of historic old Hannibal. Visit the **Mark Twain Home** and newly relocated **Mark Twain Museum,** both at 208 Hill Street; take a very expensive ride on the almost miniature *Mark Twain* riverboat, docked at the Center Street Landing; browse through books by and about Twain at the Becky Thatcher Bookshop, 211 Hill Street; or eat Mark Twain Fried Chicken at the **Mark Twain Dinette,** 400 N. 3rd Street. Not to detract from the credit due him, but don't look for any modesty surrounding Mark Twain's achievements here.

Most of the Twainery is located downtown, within a few blocks of the river and pedestrianized Hill Street, and enjoyment requires at least a passing familiarity with (and fondness for) *Tom Sawyer,* Twain's fictionalized memoir of his boyhood here. Otherwise many of the enshrined places and allusions will mean little. South of

Mark Twain

Twain was a bit of an impractical investor, losing lots of money on lots of harebrained schemes while missing at least one spectacular opportunity, the telephone. Or so hindsight teaches us—but how much would *you* invest in a new invention by a guy who flies tetrahedral kites and makes devices to detect metal in the body? Twain said no, so Alexander Graham Bell took his invention to J.P. Morgan instead.

downtown along the GRR (Hwy-79), we pass Hannibal's most hyped attractions: the **Mark Twain Cave** (daily 8 AM-8 PM in summer, 9 AM-4 PM rest of year; $8) where costumed guides spin tales about Tom and Huck on an hour-long tour; and the family fun fair (and shopping mall) of **Sawyer's Creek**.

Hannibal being in the heart of the Midwest, its menus tend toward meat and starch, fried or charbroiled. Fancy fried chicken will be called "Cordon Blue"; fancy fried shrimp, "tempura." Vegetarians will have to nibble appetizers and side salads, or try **TJ's Supper Club** (daily 11 AM-2 PM, 5-10 PM) west of downtown on US-36, one of the only places with a meatless pasta dish. To immerse yourself fully in the Mark Twain experience, try the memorial chicken (or any of the other dishes) served all day at the Mark Twain Dinette on 3rd and Hill, adjacent to the Mark Twain Home in what looks suspiciously like a converted A&W.

Otherwise the **Riverview Cafe** (daily 11 AM-8 PM), in Sawyer's Landing along Hwy-79 south of town and atop the bluff, has possibly the best kitchen in town, with a view that may indeed be worth the slightly higher prices (some entrees are over $10). Don't let the surrounding kitsch of Sawyer's Creek arcades and gift shops keep you from venturing in. Meanwhile, dessert fans may wish to step into the **Ole Planters Restaurant** on Main Street downtown to sample the German chocolate pie, a specialty of the house. This species, like rhubarb, is predominantly found in pie cases along the middle Mississippi, so if you're planning a scientific sampling, start now.

Consistent with its status as a national tourist attraction, Hannibal has plenty of motels, B&Bs, and campgrounds. The **Hotel Clemens** at the base of the bridge is a Best Western; an **Econo Lodge** and **Travelodge** are a short distance away on Mark Twain Avenue (US-36). On US-61 southwest of town are **Days Inn**, **Super 8**, and **Holiday Inn**, along with some local motels.

For a complete list of lodgings, restaurants, and tourist traps, pick up a free guide from the **visitor center**, 320 Broadway (314/221-2477).

Since Missouri slacks off on maintaining GRR signs where they're needed, staying on course begins to require more effort for the next 75 miles, until we cross back into Illinois. As you leave Hannibal, for instance, the familiar pilot's wheel can be found on Main Street, but it won't point you to the right way out of town. So sidestep up to 3rd Street and follow scenic Hwy-79 south through Louisiana all the way to the town of Winfield.

Louisiana and Clarksville

For the first 20-odd miles south from Hannibal, the GRR ascends and descends the wooded tops of bluffs, pausing at scenic turnouts for views across the Mississippi

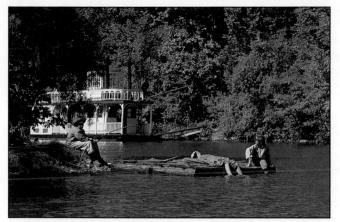

*Mark Twain
Outdoor Theatre*

Valley, here many miles wide. If you roll down the windows or stop to stretch your legs, listen for the omnipresent buzz of cicadas in the tangled undergrowth, sure signs of our ineluctable march south.

Another icon of the lower Mississippi, one that has extended its range north, like the fire ant, is the huge and pungent Hercules Chemical plant on the south side of the town of Louisiana (pop. 3,967). The town itself, like a Hannibal without Mark Twain, is full of 100-year-old brick cottages and warehouses, but looks like it has just about lost the battle against extinction—its Dairy Queen closed and up for sale, 15-year-old cars everywhere and thrift stores lining up downtown—just the kind of place *aching* to attract a glittering riverboat casino.

A short ways farther south, Clarksville (pop. 480) is another town with more of a past than a future, but some optimistic restorers of the riverfront historic block are counting on tourism to improve the town fortunes. Along 1st Street, down by the river and the railroad tracks, a pair of bars and cafes have been gussied up to tempt wayward travelers: the **Dug Out,** which serves beers and burgers, and **Mississippi Landing,** offering art and espresso.

Besides holding title to the **highest point along the Mississippi River,** 600-foot **Pinnacle Peak,** with a rusty old "Sky Ride" chairlift to the top ($5), Clarksville boasts what may be the largest concentration of **bald eagles** in the lower 48 states. In winter months they feed by the hundreds on fish below Lock and Dam No. 24 on the northern edge of town.

Winfield

Swinging away from the river south of Clarksville, the GRR re-enters the corn belt in great straight stretches of road over prairie still hilly enough that you can play peek-a-boo with approaching traffic over the miles of ups and downs, passing towns

The Twain mania is so overwhelming that little is made of Hannibal's other famous sons. Baseball lovers searching for some mention of **Joseph Jefferson "Shoeless Joe" Jackson** will look in vain; there is none. Neither is there any mention of **Ed Lear,** inventor of the eponymous jet, and also of eight-track tapes.

Missourians used to be nicknamed *pukes* back in the 19th century, which is what motivated an Iowan lawyer to actively campaign for the nickname *hawkeyes* for residents of his state, to forestall being designated something worse by regional slangmakers.

A caveat for vegetarians: while restaurants throughout the Midwest persistently equate iceberg lettuce with salad, as you progress south they also are seized by the belief that a salad is naked unless dressed with a pile of ham julienne and bacon dressing.

that often comprise little more than a few houses around a gas station and a grain elevator on a rarely used railroad siding.

Though it looks a lot like all the other riverside roadside towns along this stretch of the Mississippi, Winfield (pop. 592), 25 miles south of Clarksville, has the singular attraction of what's perhaps the best cafe in this neck of the woods: **Alice's Home Style Restaurant,** right on Hwy-79 at the center of town, next to the only stop sign. A classic "everybody knows everybody" cafe, Alice's serves up meals big enough to sink one of those barges, so beware: turkey and gravy with beans, mashed potatoes, big floury biscuits, and coffee or iced tea is a typical lunch, at a price that leaves enough out of a five-dollar bill to give a good tip. For an extra $1.50, tuck into one of the fresh-daily slabs of pie, with crust so short you'll find it in Webster's under "flaky."

At the north end of Winfield, 100 yards from Alice's, there's a clearly visible sign for the **ferry** (Mon.-Fri. 5 AM-8 PM, weekends 8 AM-9 PM, year-round; $3.50), which crosses the Mississippi about three miles east of town, just below Lock and Dam No. 25. There's no fixed departure times: the operator leaves when all the customers waiting are aboard, or when the ferry is full, and returns when he has a fare to bring back or when he spots you waiting—so drive right up to where you can be seen, and if it's after dark, keep your lights on.

If the ferry isn't running, St. Louis's suburban edge is 20 miles south along Hwy-79.

If you've been keeping track, you'll have noticed the lock and dam numbering skipped 23 between Hannibal and Clarksville. There are 29 Corps of Engineers-operated locks and dams on the Mississippi, from the unnumbered ones in the Twin Cities to No. 27 at St. Louis.

Calhoun County

Crossing the river from Winfield, Missouri, our route cuts across peninsular Calhoun County, one of Illinois's best-kept secrets. Cut off from the rest of the state by the Illinois River, connected to neighboring Missouri by ferry only, Calhoun is a world of its own. A third of the state's substantial peach crop is grown here on farms that have changed hands only a few times, if at all, since they were given out as land grants to veterans of the War of 1812; bypassing the summer farm stands, especially when the baseball-sized plumsweet tomatoes are in season, borders on criminal. Urban St. Louisans keep weekend getaways here, too, alongside shacks and trailers that accumulate debris like the Corps' dams accumulate Mississippi mud.

From the end of the ferry access road, detour north to **Batchtown** a couple miles away, stopping at **Friedel's Grocery** for a shake or malt as whim or muggy weather may demand. About three miles east of Batchtown you'll come to a junction with Hwy-1, which runs south to the state-run **Brussels Ferry** (frequent and free, 24 hours every day—flood or ice notwithstanding) across the mouth of the Illinois River. If the ferry is closed, there's a bridge at Hardin, 14 miles upstream; if the ferry is open, as is most likely the case, follow the clearly signposted route through the town of **Brussels,** whose public phone booth is possibly the town's sole civic improvement since the Coolidge administration. A handful of cafes and bars is evidence of the county's popularity with savvy weekenders from St. Louis; in summer, look for the small roadside trailer selling fresh fish, $2-3 a fillet, fried while you wait. The most popular haunt is the venerable **Wittmond Hotel** (618/883-2345) across from the water tower and post office at the heart of Brussels. The dining room here serves delicious, all-you-can-eat family-style meals (very popular on Sunday). They also rent rooms ($40 a night), have a timeless bar, and have an even more ancient-looking general store—complete with dusty old merchandise that looks like it dates back to when the enterprise opened in 1847.

The Illinois River

The Brussels ferry ride takes all of two or three minutes to cross this narrow reach of the Illinois River, along which Marquette and Joliet returned to Canada after their failure to find a westward-flowing river to the rich lands of Cathay and the Far East. René-Robert Cavelier, Sieur de La Salle, came down the Illinois eight years later in 1681, on the first expedition to specifically target the Mississippi. It was La Salle who claimed the Mississippi territory for his sponsor, King Louis XIV of France, and who went all the way down to the Gulf of Mexico (Marquette and Joliet turned back after the confluence of the Arkansas River). In more recent times the Illinois River was associated with the outbreak of typhoid fever in St. Louis, after engineers in typhoid-ridden Chicago took the sewage-laden Chicago River flowing through their city into Lake Michigan, reversed it, and made it flow backwards into the Illinois. This sort of give-it-to-the-next-guy attitude has prevailed along the Mississippi to this day. The Illinois River, for example, continues to add Chicago effluent to the Mississippi.

The familiar 12-spoke pilot's wheel waits at the end of the ferry off-ramp, ready to guide us the 50-odd miles south to St. Louis.

Besides the Brussels Ferry, the privately operated "Golden Eagle" paddle wheel ferry service runs across the Mississippi River between **Golden Eagle,** Illinois, and the Missouri shore, landing outside St. Charles. For current hours and fares, phone 618/883-2217.

Illinois recently ranked highest in the nation for industrial discharges of toxic materials into publicly owned sewage treatment facilities, and third highest in the nation for direct discharges of toxics into surface waters. Stretches of the Illinois River in particular are known for their very high levels of PCBs.

Pere Marquette State Park

If you're equipped for some hiking or biking, Pere Marquette State Park is a worthwhile three-mile detour from the ferry landing. The handsome **park lodge,** built by the Civilian Conservation Corps in the late 1930s, is noted for its 700-ton stone fireplace, massive tree-trunk roof supports, decorative ironwork, and outsized chess set in front of the ox-sized hearth that definitely can create a congenial chalet atmosphere, particularly if you time your arrival for evenings, midweek, or off-season to avoid the crowds. Cabins and lodge rooms are available for the same reasonable rates ($65-a-night doubles; 618/786-2331). Expect holiday and fall foliage weekends to be booked up to a year in advance; camping ($8; 618/786-3323) and tent rental are available.

The 20-mile **Sam Vadalabene Bike Trail** between Pere Marquette State Park and Alton is unquestionably the best venue for appreciating the scenery, even for a short walk, for here the GRR becomes a fast divided highway whose drivers don't appreciate slowpokes.

Grafton

Travelers coming from the north may have wondered why there has been so little evidence of the disastrous 1993 floods so far along our route; it's because the GRR has so far avoided all the upstream areas that were hit hard. That is about to change: resume following the GRR downstream from the Brussels Ferry and in just a few miles you'll pass through Grafton—or rather, what's left of it. Most of low-lying Grafton was flooded out by the Mississippi, forcing residents to relocate to higher ground. The few who have rebuilt according to new code requirements illustrate the river's mammoth rise as dramatically as their neighbors' mud-streaked walls, with new houses perched atop great concrete and steel stilts. Stop in any of the cafes, fish shacks, or galleries at the higher, southern end of town and you can pry stories about the "Flood of '93" from just about anyone. For unusual local flavor, stop by the **Chateau Ra-Ha Winery** at 230 E. Main Street to sample their specialty, mead, made with local honey.

Atop the bluffs over Elsah is the very Tudor campus of **Principia College,** the world's only Christian Science institution of higher education (public welcome Mon.-Sat. 9 AM-5 PM).

South of Grafton the GRR enters what is widely considered one of its most scenic stretches: towering limestone bluffs, their curving faces pocked with caves and overhangs, push the road to the edge of the lake above Lock and Dam No. 26.

Elsah

Speeding along, it's easy to miss the turnoff for Elsah, four miles south of Grafton, but even if you have to turn around and come back, it's worth it to check out this tiny hamlet tucked away in a cleft in the palisades. Listed in the National Register of Historic Places in its entirety, Elsah is an elegant architectural gem, with 19th-century cut stone and clapboard buildings and narrow lanes redolent of some idyllic English country village. Two small B&Bs and the **Green Tree Inn** (618/374-2821; $77-117 with tax) offer what most people would consider romantic getaways; the inn even has a tandem bike for guests. For meals there is only **Elsah's Landing Restaurant** (Tues.-Sun. 11:30 AM-7:30 PM), but the monopoly is well deserved: its made-from-scratch ethic pays off in all departments, with pies alone worth staying overnight for.

South of Elsah, before the bluffs give way to grain elevators at Alton, you'll catch a glimpse of the **Piasa Bird** (PIE-a-saw) high on the wall of an old roadside quarry. Marquette and other early explorers mention a pair of huge pictographs on the cliff face, representations of the Illini Indians' legendary "bird that devours men." Faded by the 1840s, the original site was destroyed by quarrying. The current 20-by-40-foot replica, based on various eyewitness descriptions, resembles something from the notebook of an adolescent Dungeons and Dragons fan.

Alton

At Alton, 20 miles northeast of St. Louis, the riverfront turns decidedly urban. The GRR races along the water, past tugboat docks, the tacky but hugely lucrative *Alton Belle* casino boat (the first in Illinois when riverboat gambling was made legal in 1991), sulphurous chemical plants, and spacious tank farms, all under the shadow of the great protective levee and a thicket of high-tension power lines.

Inland from the GRR, however, the town is surprisingly peaceful and quiet, its red-brick streets lined by mature trees and a range of modest but well-maintained 19th-century houses. Near 5th and Monument Streets at the south end of town, high on a hill above the riverfront, Alton's cemetery is dominated by a large column topped by a winged figure—a monument to one of Alton's most important individuals, the abolitionist newspaper editor **Elijah Lovejoy,** widely considered to be the nation's first martyr to freedom of the press and freedom of speech. Newspaper publisher, preacher, and political activist, Lovejoy—who coined the phrase "Freedom of the Press belongs to those that own one"—was lynched in Alton in 1837 by a mob of pro-slavery Missourians.

Around Alton, keep an eye out for the signs to the **Lewis & Clark Historical Site** to get a glimpse of the confluence of the Missouri and Mississippi Rivers rolling together in a muddy tide between swampy wooded banks. The merging of the rivers was violent enough to frighten early navigators, but dynamited rapids and upstream dams have changed all that. Despite considerable flood damage in recent years, the riprap-lined gully of what might once have been a pretty creek, and the rather forlorn condition of their memorial, the winter campsite of Meriwether Lewis and William Clark's Corps of Discovery is a peaceful place with simple tablets commemorating highlights of the journey that began here on May 14, 1804. For more on their epic trek, see pages 130-131.

Twelve miles south of Alton, the GRR briefly joins I-270 eastbound toward Effingham before exiting onto Hwy-111, a route illustrating the steady creep of suburban minimarts into the Illinois cornfields.

A life-sized statue of **Robert Pershing Wadlow,** the world's tallest human, stands on the campus of the Southern Illinois University Dental School, on College Avenue (Hwy-140), a mile or so east of the river. The Alton-born "gentle giant" was 8 feet 11$3/4$ inches when he died at age 22.

Cahokia Mounds State Historic Site

A couple of miles northeast of where the Great River Road hops onto the I-55 freeway for the final approach into St. Louis, a clearly marked "GRR Spur" leads to Cahokia Mounds State Historic Site (daily 8 AM-9 PM; free), the remains of the largest prehistoric American city north of Mexico. The park protects over 60 earthen mounds of various sizes built while Europe was in the Dark Ages by indigenous and enigmatic Mississippians. The largest hill covers 14 acres—more turf than the Great Pyramid of Cheops—but don't expect the works of the pharaohs: symmetrical grass-covered hills sitting in flat, lightly wooded bottomlands are what you'll find here, though the view of distant St. Louis, across the I-55 freeway from the 140-foot top of Monks' Mound, does lend some grandeur to the site. The sophisticated Interpretive Center (daily 9 AM-5 PM; $3 suggested donation), across US-40 from the Monk's Mound, is a recommended first stop for its displays, ranger talks, and a self-guiding recorded tour.

The St. Louis skyline with its landmark Gateway Arch comes into view shortly after the GRR joins I-55/70 westbound, about seven miles east of the Mississippi. Have some idea about where in the city you wish to end up, for the three interstates that converge on the Illinois doorstep fly off in different directions before you cross the Missouri threshold. It doesn't help that there are separate ramps for "St. Louis" (I-64/55) and "Downtown" (I-70) as you approach the bridge, either. If you find yourself hurtling for the wrong one, don't bother attempting an 80-mph swerve across four lanes: the ramps merge on the bridge itself before splitting into three at the Missouri end.

From Cahokia Mounds until our route returns to Illinois some 60 miles south of St. Louis, GRR signage will disappear; to stay on course and bypass the city, simply follow I-55.

Cahokia Mounds sit in the middle of the American Bottom, a floodplain whose gunpowder-black alluvial soils have long been considered among the richest and most productive in the world. However, Charles Dickens called it an "ill-favored Black Hollow" after enduring its mud, which had "no variety but in depth."

St. Louis is the junction of three of our routes: the GRR, transcontinental US-50 (beginning on page 516), and the legendary Route 66 (beginning on page 628). For coverage of St. Louis, see the Survival Guide on pages 714-715.

Sainte Genevieve

To avoid the worst of the suburban commercialization south of St. Louis, take I-55 as far as exit 162, where you can rejoin the GRR by picking up US-61 South; if you don't blink you may even catch sight of one of Missouri's rare pilot's wheel signs as the busy road ascends a ridge with a fine western panorama. About 55 miles south of St. Louis's I-270/255 beltway, the GRR comes to the modern commercial outskirts of Sainte Genevieve, one of several French trading posts established along the Mississippi in the wake of La Salle's 17th-century expedition. The town's new trade is tourism, as the B&Bs, "fine dining," and shops clearly illustrate. The beauty of Sainte Genevieve's restored 18th- to 19th-century remnants, including a brick belle of an old hotel, is marred only by the vinyl siding, AstroTurf front steps, and metal screen doors of their neighbors. **Sara's Ice Cream**, down by S. Main Street, provides more tasteful distractions.

> So many riverboats sank, collided, or blew up along the Mississippi between St. Louis and Cairo that this stretch was known to 19th-century boat pilots as "The Graveyard."

> If you were to camp under the protective overhangs of the Modoc limestone bluffs, you'd be continuing a long tradition: indigenous people began camping here roughly 10,000 years ago.

Since US-61 doesn't enter town, follow the small blue "Tourist Information" signs down to the old waterfront to find the area's historic places, and visit the **Great River Road Interpretive Center**, 66 S. Main Street (daily 9 AM-4 PM; free; 314/883-7097 or 800/373-7007), to get the skinny on the town's past and present.

The **Mississippi River-Modoc Ferry** (Mon.-Sat. 6 AM-6 PM, Sun. 9 AM-6 PM; $6; 314/883-7382) to Modoc, Illinois, is almost three miles out of town: follow Main Street north until it dead-ends at the ferry landing. Since the operator likes to knock off work early, plan on arriving before 5:30 PM. Twelve rural crop-lined miles from the Modoc Ferry we rejoin the GRR heading south on Hwy-3 to Chester; being Illinois, the (mostly) paved farm lanes have signs where necessary to keep you informed and on track.

Kaskaskia

Fifteen miles south of Sainte Genevieve, signposted off US-61, is old Kaskaskia, the first Illinois state capital and the only Illinois town now *west* of the Mississippi, thanks to an 1881 flood. "Town" is a generous overstatement: consisting of a church and a handful of farmhouses to begin with, the community has been all but washed away numerous times in its 250-year history, most recently in the 1993 Great Flood. Cut off from the Missouri shore by huge levees and a swampy river channel, Kaskaskia is a ghost with an illustrious past: it was here during the American Revolution that George Rogers Clark and his tiny force of Kentucky "Long Knives" launched their attack against British control of the huge, formerly French territory between the Mississippi and Ohio River valleys, a campaign so stunningly successful that it effectively doubled the size of the U.S. during the Revolution. After capturing Fort Kaskaskia (now across the river), the victorious Americans rang the 600-pound bell that hung in the French Catholic church; this bell, now in its own spartan iron-barred chapel, is called "the Liberty Bell of the West."

Chester

The GRR neatly skips around Chester, "Home of Popeye," via a pleasant riverbank detour, returning to Hwy-3 on the downstream side of town. Unless a doughnut stop is required at **Bill's**, a joint on Main Street frequented by Wimpy himself, this loop is preferable to town. A memorial to local boy Elzie Segar, creator of the spinach-guzzling scrapper, stands in a picnic area beside the bridge to Missouri; if you miss it, you'll have to turn around on the other side of the Mississippi. If you pass through on the second weekend of September, drop by Popeye's birthday party, with its big flea market of all the Popeye collectibles you never imagined existed.

Hwy-3: Shawnee National Forest

No town of any consequence impedes the GRR's 90-mile leg along the southern tip of Illinois. The roadside landscape continues to be cultivated, heat-loving corn and leafy soybean mixed now with milo, an animal feed crop whose Grape-Nuts clusters resemble grain sorghum. The bluffs of the Shawnee National Forest, whose recreational offerings are invitingly signposted with names like Oakwood Bottoms, Turkey Bayou, and Pine Hills, appear a couple of miles to the east, and follow the GRR through the old river valley. Much of the forested uplands are a botanical crossroads: glacier-borne northern species like the sumac and partridge berry; warmth-seeking southern species like the short-leaf pine; eastern species held back by the Mississippi, such as Virginia willow and silver bell; and western species with a toehold in the east, like Missouri primrose and Ozark coneflower; all count Southern Illinois as the edge of their natural ranges.

Shawnee National Forest contains some significant stands of old-growth forest which, like the spotted-owl habitat in the Pacific Northwest, were sold off in the 1980s to logging companies by the U.S. Department of Agriculture. Unfortunately for the trees, local loggers were spared much scrutiny since the national media never picked up the story.

Jonesboro

Just under 50 miles south of Chester, amid grainfields maintained by private duck-hunting clubs, the GRR is intersected by Hwy-146 at the village of Ware. Eight miles east of this junction is the small town of Jonesboro, whose **Dixie Bar-B-Q** (on the left before the courthouse rotary; closed Sunday) is definitely worth a side trip. Jonesboro's Forest Service **ranger station** is also worth a visit for a guide to the Shawnee's attractions, or request one in advance from the **Southern Illinois Tourist Council** (800/342-3100).

Keep a sharp lookout to spot the historic markers near Hwy-146 that give brief mention to the **Trail of Tears**, the 1838 winter death march of the Cherokee nation. Six years after wiping out Indians of the upper Mississippi in the Black Hawk War,

George Rogers Clark's fame as a war hero, Indian fighter, and explorer put him at the top of Thomas Jefferson's short list for leading an expedition into the Louisiana Purchase, but the aging Clark nominated his younger brother instead. Thus did **William Clark** join Meriwether Lewis for their historic journey to the Pacific.

Chester locals Frank "Rocky" Fiegel and William "Windy Bill" Schuchert were the inspiration for Popeye the Sailor and Wimpy the Hamburger Fiend. Popeye first appeared in print in 1929.

In September 1858 Jonesboro hosted the third of the seven senate campaign debates between challenger Abe Lincoln and incumbent Stephen Douglas, who tried to portray Lincoln as being out of touch with people over the issue of slavery. Although Illinois was a designated free state, this area had strong sympathies with the South.

From Hwy-3, follow Hwy-146 west toward the Mississippi River to reach a landmark lunch and dinner place, **Witz Restaurant** (618/661-1644), serving huge Sunday feasts and slabs of at least a half-dozen different pies. It's just east of the bridge to Cape Girardeau and is impossible to miss.

Cape Girardeau, on the Missouri side of the Mississippi River, was the boyhood hometown of radio talk-show host **Rush Limbaugh.**

Bible-packing 18th-century settlers of the uplands opposite St. Louis referred to their chosen homesteads as "Goshen" and to the flood-prone flats to their south as "Egypt." Comparisons between the Mississippi and Nile rivers were deliberately reinforced with place-names like Karnak, Joppa, Thebes, and Cairo; for generations now, all Southern Illinois has borne the nickname "Little Egypt."

The town of **Metropolis,** Illinois (pop. 6,700), along the Ohio River 25 miles northeast of Cairo but most easily accessible via Paducah, Kentucky, takes pride in its adopted super-hero son, Superman. A statue of him, and a quick-change telephone booth, stands near the offices of the *Daily Planet* newspaper, and every June a festival celebrates his crime-fighting efforts. For more information, contact the visitor center, 618/524-2714.

Pres. Andrew Jackson ordered the "Five Civilized Tribes" of the Cherokee removed to the arid plains of Oklahoma from their lands in the fertile Tennessee River valley. Five thousand people died along the thousand-mile journey, which passed through the state near here. On the Missouri side of the river, 10 miles north of Cape Girardeau, the 3,400-acre Trail of Tears State Park preserves the scene of this tragedy, with interpretive plaques marking the wooded bluffs.

Back on Hwy-3, just north of I-57 and the town of Cairo, the GRR passes **Horseshoe Lake Conservation Area,** an example of what happens when the river shifts to a new channel and leaves an oxbow lake behind. Now prime winter habitat for over a million migrating geese and ducks, its tupelo gum trees, bald cypress, and swamp cottonwoods foreshadow the scenery found downstream among the bayous of the Mississippi Delta.

Cairo

"A grave uncheered by any gleam of promise," was but one of Charles Dickens's unsympathetic descriptions of Cairo (CARE-oh), the town that presides over—and sometimes under—the meeting of the Mississippi and Ohio Rivers. Routinely submerged by floodwaters until the Corps of Engineers ringed the town with a massive stockade of levees and huge steel floodgates, Cairo's star shone briefly in the steamboat era and during the Civil War, when General Grant quartered his Army of the Tennessee here and Union ironclads were berthed along the waterfront. A few Victorian mansions built by boat captains remain, but otherwise the GRR's passage through town is best enjoyed with your eyes stuck firmly to the road.

What is worth seeing is the confluence of the two mighty rivers. Unless there's a flood in progress, do your watching from a small platform in **Fort Defiance State Park,** at the foot of the US-60 bridge to Missouri. Just don't expect the vista to be a pastoral one: as you stand on the spongy park lawn with a mighty river on either hand, the horizons are dominated by billowing smokestacks, the foreground by huge diesel-burning tows plowing up and down the brown tide. The unleaded you bought in Minnesota probably passed by here, and the bread flour you'll eat in Louisiana probably has, too.

There's a cluster of gas and food stores and a **Days Inn** at Cairo's northern edge, where I-57 crosses the GRR.

TRUTH – JUSTICE – THE AMERICAN WAY

ACROSS KENTUCKY AND TENNESSEE

With its crossing of the Ohio River from Cairo, the GRR enters the Lower Mississippi Basin, a long floodplain whose wetlands acted as a natural reservoir for floodwaters until the Corps of Engineers came along in the 1930s and hemmed it in with a thousand miles of levees, revetments, and wing dikes. Problem is, channeling and controlling the river has had exactly the opposite effect: flood crests are higher with two-thirds of the basin's carrying capacity cut off by the Corps, and people are sleeping closer to the restless giant now that wetlands have been drained and opened for development. But if it wasn't for the false security of the levees abutments along the river, the area would have no security at all.

Most of the GRR's 60-odd Kentucky miles are quite scenic, populated by only a handful of small towns, none of which has been overrun by tacky commercial strips. Upon crossing the Tennessee line the route promptly loses all trace of GRR signage, swallowed up, perhaps, by the nearby New Madrid Fault. Rising up off cultivated bottomlands around earthquake-created Reelfoot Lake, the GRR rejoins four-lane US-51 as it traverses the last 80 miles to downtown Memphis along devel-

In the south, drive like a Southerner: no matter what your speed, keep one arm dangling outside your rolled-down window, to be lifted up in lazy acknowledgment of passing vehicles and porch sitters. Single-handed driving won't be a problem: the arrow-straight roads are designed not to tax anybody's steering skills.

Assimilation through driving, Part II: Drive an American car, preferably a pickup, sport-utility, or huge sedan of any vintage in any condition. Driving a Honda, Saab, Volvo, or any foreign car with the stickshift on the floor will clearly identify you as someone from another planet, like Chicago.

If you need to do some of your own laundry in Mississippi or Louisiana, it isn't a laundromat you'll be searching for, but a washerette or washeteria.

oped uplands: southern short-leaf pine woods and cotton fields mixed with mobile homes, suburban ranch houses, and gas stations that double as the local video stores.

Wickliffe to Hickman

Skipping from the banks of the Ohio through small, thoroughly industrial Wickliffe, the GRR stays with US-51 southbound for about 16 miles, passing an "alternate" GRR turnoff that simply saves a visit to the center of staid old **Bardwell**, a town that grew up on the railroad rather than the river. Leaving the federal highway for a spell, our route takes an attractive 40-mile meander away from the river through wooded hill country, returning to the edge of the Mississippi at Hickman. If you're looking for a bite to eat, you might try the **Tickle Bone Bar-B-Q** in **Columbus**, midway along the meander; otherwise both Bardwell and Hickman have fast food.

West from Hickman, there's a small toll ferry to Missouri, if you desperately need to fetch something left behind. Heading south it's just another dozen rural miles to the Tennessee line.

Reelfoot Lake Area

Leaving Kentucky, the GRR enters a 40-mile stretch of low-lying bottoms, picking up Hwy-78 south. After passing the roadhouse bars and bait shops near Reelfoot Lake, a major recreation area and wildlife refuge created by the first New Madrid earthquake's sudden and massive landscaping, the route's dullness is broken only by a couple of one-horse towns and glimpses of smoke-

---

THE NEW MADRID EARTHQUAKE OF 1811

The strongest earthquake ever recorded in North America struck the Mississippi region on December 16, 1811. The Richter Scale wasn't around to measure it, but the New Madrid (MAD-rid) quake, named for the river town just across the Mississippi in Missouri, was felt in Boston, Detroit, and New Orleans. Fatalities are presumed to have stayed low because of the sparse frontier population, but there were sufficient witnesses to tell of geysers of mud and stone, great chasms splitting open and swallowing acres of fields and forest, tornado-like winds, and towns reduced to kindling. The Mississippi, it is said, ran backward. Louisville recorded some 1,800 aftershocks through the winter, before another massive quake on February 7, 1812, again caused fearful settlers to wonder if Judgment Day had come.

The **New Madrid Fault** that runs from Arkansas up the Ohio River valley is still active, minimally enough to generate predictions that California isn't the only place that should worry about The Big One. A strong sulphur odor is said to precede temblors.

IN SEARCH OF ELVIS

Scratch the surface of Memphis, and you'll always turn up a little Elvis, like pennies and pocket lint in an old sofa. That guy behind the counter? His mom used to give piano lessons to Elvis's step-brothers. That woman at the next table? Her after-school job was in the amusement park Elvis would rent out in its entirety just so he could ride the rollercoaster for hours on end. A frequent Graceland visitor during the Elvis years collected fuzz from the shag carpet to give to friends; maybe the woman paying for her coffee still has her piece. Even the owner of the greasiest old pizza joint will tell you how Elvis would come in with his band, "back when he was *nothin'*." Get used to it: Elvis is *everywhere*.

The font of all this meta-Elvisness is, of course, **Graceland,** on Elvis Presley Boulevard (US-51) about a mile south of I-55 (exit 5B) amid a clutter of burger joints and muffler shops. Seeing what happens when Elvis's questionable taste and Hollywood budget run amok with 1970s vogue is *almost* worth the $8-16 admission (higher prices include side attractions such as the King's private jet or his car collection). Where else, for example, can you wonder whether the man with the most gold and platinum albums on the planet vacuumed his own ceiling shag? Parking is an extra $2.

One place where you *won't* find Elvis is at the **Java Cabana,** 2170 Young Street, a block east of Cooper (except on a few overpriced postcards). As renowned headquarters of the First Church of the Elvis Impersonator, the J.C. would consider it *heretical* to mount any true likeness of Elvis himselvis on its walls—and dangerous, too, given the threat of legal action from Presley Enterprises if they did. The decor, of course, appropriately reflects the nature of the shrine, with a 24-hour coin-operated "blessed vista" in the front window and the Viva Memphis! Wedding Chapel in the back, presided over by a nondenominational Elvis impersonator. Naturally, the congregation is a gregarious mix of Medici and Kerouac improvising their own Eucharist with cappuccino, kosher pastries, Scrabble, and cigarettes. (Poetry night is Thursday.)

Serious pilgrims seeking to follow the King's path should, of course, consider obtaining professional help. Like the definitive *Placing Elvis, A Tour Guide to the Kingdom,* by Sharon Colette Urquhart. It's available from most Memphis bookshops, and from Paper Chase Press, 5721 Magazine Street, Suite 152, New Orleans, LA 70115, for $12.95 plus shipping.

Among the witnesses to the catastrophe of the first New Madrid quake were the crew of the *New Orleans,* the first steamboat on the Mississippi, making its maiden voyage from Pittsburgh to its namesake city. As it turned out, only the fact that the river was in flood made the voyage possible at all, for the paddle wheeler's draft was too deep to return upstream.

To Northerners, it was the Civil War. South of the line where most people start calling you "Ma'am" or "Sir" it becomes the "War Between the States." In the heart of Dixie it was and is the "War for Southern Independence." (In places Yankees fear to tread, it's the "War of Northern Aggression.")

Columbus, Kentucky (pop. 500), fancied itself a candidate for the new U.S. capital after Washington, D.C. was sacked and burned by the British in the War of 1812. At that time the town was very nearly the geographical center of the U.S.

In late September **Fulton,** Kentucky, hosts the International Banana Festival to celebrate its bygone days as "Banana Capital of the World," when 70% of all the bananas shipped to the U.S. used to be landed there. A highlight of the festival is the one-ton banana pudding.

Monday is traditionally red-beans-and-rice day at most true Southern home-style, barbecue, or soul-food restaurants, because Monday is traditionally wash day, and beans are a good dish to let sit and cook all day while you scrub your laundry.

stacks along the unseen Mississippi. A few miles before rejoining US-51 southbound at the gas-food-lodging fringe of **Dyersburg,** the GRR finally climbs out of the river valley and back onto more varied terrain. Unfortunately US-51 does its level best to mimic an interstate, cutting across contours rather than conforming to them and generally rendering the final 78 miles to downtown Memphis a forgettable blur.

For specifics on Memphis, consult the Survival Guide on pages 698-699.

ACROSS MISSISSIPPI

Between Chickasaw Bluff in Memphis and the Mississippi state line the GRR enters what's known as the Mississippi Delta. In one sense we've already been in it, for ecologically the delta is the vast alluvial plain between Cairo and the Gulf coast, but "The Delta" of popular myth is much more circumscribed, encompassing just 250 miles of King Cotton's realm between Memphis and Vicksburg; in his historical book *Where I was Born and Raised* writer David Cohn contends that the Mississippi Delta "begins in the lobby of the Peabody Hotel in Memphis and ends on Catfish Row in Vicksburg." As important as its proper boundaries is its dual legacy as a great Civil War battleground and cradle of nearly every American musical style from gospel, blues, and jazz to country and rock 'n' roll. The backbone of our route, US-61, is also legendary as the path of the Great Migration, the post-Depression exodus to the industrialized northern U.S. of some five million black sharecroppers displaced by the mechanized cotton harvester.

As the GRR—sans the familiar pilot's wheel—drops like a plumb line across the cotton fields, we recommend side trips to landmarks of this rich cultural heritage. Where the Delta ends at the foot of Vicksburg's bluffs our route begins mingling with ghosts from the South's plantation and Civil War past, briefly detouring along the pastoral Natchez Trace Parkway until reaching the antebellum confection of Natchez itself. The GRR finally rolls into Louisiana amid thick pine woods along US-61.

Northwest Mississippi: Casino Country

Leaving Memphis via US-61, the unsigned GRR enters De Soto and Tunica Counties, the place-names memorializing Hernando de Soto, the first European to see the Mississippi, and the combative

Tunica tribe who forced the Spanish conquistador's mosquito- and snake-bitten expedition to cross the river hereabouts in 1542. Outfitted with cannons, priests, slaves, pigs, war dogs, and 1,000 soldiers, De Soto spent years marching through southern swamps in quest of gold—but he was 450 years too early. Tunica County, one of the most destitute places in America for some 30 years, only became a gold mine in 1992 after the state legalized gambling. Several billion dollars of investment later, every big name in casinos lines the levee, glittering palaces plunked down amid the cotton bolls. Bugsy Siegel would be proud.

To aid the massive influx of people anxious to part with their money, US-61 is being turned into a high-volume, four-lane highway for some 50 miles from the Tennessee state line to the US-49 bridge from Arkansas. Motels, fast-food places, and gas stations are popping up like mushrooms after a spring rain, while the sorry-looking shacks that used to house the county's black sharecroppers are being torn down as quickly as possible, as if deleting the symbols will amend the history of peonage.

Turn off the GRR toward the Commerce Landing casinos to find the vestiges of **Robinsonville**, once home to blues guitarist **Robert Johnson**, whose skill is said to have come from the Devil. **The Hollywood** restaurant on Hwy-304 just opposite the post office has live blues some weekend nights, and gen-u-wine downhome good cookin' daily (lunch Mon.-Fri., dinner Thurs.-Sun.). Skeptics who doubt the ingenuity of Southern cuisine should come try the deep-fried dill pickle slices.

As "improvements" on behalf of the casinos strip the land of its relics, detour toward Hernando on Hwy-304 to visit what's being lost. About 10 miles east of the GRR, just past the junction with Hwy-301, is a small sign for

Country Charm, a weekends-only antique shop and museum whose collection includes a set of buildings the Delta is trying to forget: a shotgun shack, dog-trot house, pole barn, and slave cabin. Owner Beth Farnell will happily share her appreciation of these rough utilitarian structures, scavenged locally and restored with obvious dedication. Stand inside them, imagine life inside them, and soon, the birth of the blues in the Delta will start to make a whole lot of sense.

Following US-61 southbound, the GRR passes the edge of **Tunica,** with the classic grits-and-gravy, steak-and-potato **Blue & White Cafe,** before making a 35-mile beeline through the cotton fields and casino billboards to Clarksdale.

Moon Lake

Mississippi law doesn't require casinos to be riverboats, it merely requires them to float. All appearances to the contrary, the giant Las Vegas-style casinos in Tunica County are indeed floating, mostly in ponds dredged specifically to meet the letter of the law.

Twenty miles south of Tunica's casinos, just west of US-61, Moon Lake was home to one of the South's most famous Prohibition landmarks, the **Moon Lake Club.** Unlike speakeasies associated with thugs and tarts, this club was a family destination where parents could dance and gamble while the kids played by the lake. In a place and time when planes were still so rare the sound of their engines could interrupt work and empty classrooms, the club flew in fresh Maine lobster and Kansas City steak for its clientele of rich white Memphians.

Moon Lake has a literary history, too, appearing in a number of Tennessee Williams's dramas. Williams knew it well: not only was the club property owned by a cousin, but as a boy he had been a frequent guest, accompanying his grandfather, the Reverend Dakin, on parish calls throughout the county. The club was finally shut down by its own patrons after they learned the gambling franchise was tied to the Chicago mob, but the building still stands on Moon Lake Road, south of US-49. Now called **Uncle Henry's Place,** it's a casual gourmet seafood restaurant (by reservation only, 601/337-2757), characterful B&B, and annual host of the **Clarksdale Tennessee Williams Festival** opening night dinner (mid-October).

St. Louis likes to claim **Tennessee Williams** as a native son; while the family indeed moved there when Tom was in fourth grade, anybody who knew the Mississippi-born playwright will tell you he hated St. Louis "with a purple passion."

Another Moon Lake landmark, now gone, was country star Conway Twitty's roadhouse, the kind of place so rough that if you came in without a gun, they'd issue you one.

Thomas "The Silence of the Lambs" Harris hails from the tiny hamlet of Rich, just east of the junction of US-61 and US-49.

Helena, Arkansas

About a dozen miles west of the GRR and Moon Lake via US-49 is Helena, Arkansas, "the most deadly place on the river" to Union regiments in the Civil War stopped in their tracks by the festering malarial swamps that once surrounded the town. It began building a more sanguine reputation as the self-proclaimed "buckle on the Blues Belt" when a local station began broadcasting a flour company-sponsored live blues show back in the early 1940s. Now the second weekend of each October the **King Biscuit Blues Festival** (call 501/338-9144 for info) attracts fans by the tens of thousands to hear one of the best lineups of live gospel and blues in the nation. The **Delta Cultural Center** (daily till 5 PM; free) in the renovated rail depot downtown is an equally compelling reason to visit this small river town, with its fine historical displays on the lives of Delta inhabitants that neither deny nor ignore the shameful episodes. For the best burger in town—the "bluesburger," of course—look no further than **Casqui's**, across the street from the depot.

Clarksdale

The blues were born in the Delta, but they grew up in Clarksdale, 15 unswerving miles south along US-61 from the US-49 junction to Helena. The census rolls for this small town read like a musical hall of fame: Ma Rainey, W.C. Handy, Bessie Smith, Sam Cooke, Ike Turner, Muddy Waters, Wade Walton, John Lee Hooker, Big Jack Johnson,

and many others whose achievements are described—and may be heard—in the **Delta Blues Museum** (Mon.-Sat. 9 AM-5 PM; free; 601/624-4461 or 627-6820) next to the Carnegie Public Library at 114 Delta Avenue, on the corner of 1st Street. The museum offers maps of blues landmarks around town and around the state, and a calendar of blues events. The museum building underwent some major renovations and alterations in the winter of 1995-96, and may well be housed in additional spaces around Clarksdale; call to confirm hours and location.

According to blues legend, mediocre musician **Robert Johnson** traded his soul to Satan at "The Crossroads" of Highways 49 and 61 to become king of the blues guitar. Seventy years ago in Johnson's day, of course, *any* guitar-pickin' "musicianer" was thought to be in cahoots with the Devil.

Ever since W.C. Handy traded his steady gigs in Clarksdale for a career on Beale Street in Memphis, the Delta has exported its blues musicians to places where they receive wider recognition and a living wage, but come Friday or Saturday night and you'll see Clarksdale still cooks up some good hot blues. Try **Red's South End**, 395 Sunflower Avenue (601/627-3166), on the corner of Martin Luther King, Jr. Drive (4th Street); **Margaret's Blue Diamond Lounge**, 381 W. Tallahatchie Avenue near M.L. King (601/627-4060); or the **Rivermount Lounge**, 911 Sunflower (601/627-1971); all of which book live blues along with R&B, disco, and rap. If you're in town during the first weekend in August it would be a shame to miss the **Sunflower River Blues Festival**, staged at venues around town. Otherwise look for a compensatory memento at blues-rich **Stackhouse Records**, behind the steamboat facade at 232 Sunflower Avenue. This is also the home of the Rooster Blues record label, and a good place to find out about local goings-on.

The most famous shotgun house in Mississippi is the one in which **Elvis Aaron Presley** was born on January 8, 1935, in Tupelo, a half-hour east of Oxford. The name for these long and narrow three-room wooden boxes refers to the alignment of its doorways: a shot fired through the front door will pass clear through to the back without hitting a wall. Tupelo is also the birthplace of blues master **John Lee Hooker.**

Clarksdale has plenty of fast food, but the barbecue is better: try the **Ranchero**, on US-61 south of the first blinking traffic light, or **Abe's Bar-B-Q**, 616 State Street (US-61), at the center of town. For a surprising dose of Lebanese-Italian food amid the pork palaces, check out **Chamoun's Rest Haven** (closed Sunday), at 419 S. State Street, on US-61 just south of the Big Sunflower River.

US-61, a.k.a. State Street, is also where you'll find Clarksdale's motels, from a **Days Inn** across from the Ranchero to a **Comfort Inn** at the southern end of town. Least expensive is the **Plantation Inn** (601/624-6541), across from the Rest Haven, with doubles from $30. Popular with blues pilgrims is the old Afro-American Hospital, now the **Riverside Hotel**, 615 Sunflower Avenue (601/624-9163; $30-40), where in Room No. 2 vocalist Bessie Smith died in 1937 after a car accident out on US-61. The apocryphal version of this tragedy, dramatized by Edward Albee, suggests the singer might have survived if she hadn't been denied admission to white hospitals, but at least one doctor from the old Afro-American has disputed this.

For the most comprehensive motel listings and other Clarksdale **information**, contact the **Delta Blues Museum** (601/624-4461, a number shared with the library).

GETTING THE BLUES

If serious blueshounds sniff around enough, they will find the kind of swaggering, sweaty, Saturday-night juke joint that will always be synonymous with real Delta blues. You know the place: Budweiser on ice in a plastic cooler, clouds of cigarette smoke, some rough customers, hot dancing, and honest gut-wrenching blues played with an intensity that rattles your fillings. Yes, such places exist, but they don't run display ads in the local paper, or make the list of area attractions given out by local chambers of commerce. Given the state's deep racial divide you won't find many white chamber-of-commerce types in one of these predominantly black joints.

The really homegrown variety announces itself with hand-lettered signs on telephone poles and laundromat bulletin boards, if at all. They have no phone numbers, no advanced booking policy; you have to show up to find out who, if anyone, is playing. Ask around: the convenience store clerk, the men hanging around the commissary in one of the small towns off the main road, the person next to you at the barbecue counter. Keep in mind the blues are rooted in a condition of the Delta's black community that is no bed of roses; voyeurs slumming as tourists to hardship will be politely stonewalled at best. Even a juke-joint guide who trusts he or she is not being put inside a fishbowl for your entertainment may still hesitate to tell you where to go, since some places have a legitimate reputation as low-life dives. But with perseverance and the proper attitude, you'll get to where you want to go. And once you get there, don't worry about the reception: blues musicians welcome an appreciative audience, period.

Weekends, again mostly Saturday nights, are also about the only time you'll catch blues in the more commercial juke joints and clubs, simply because so many musicians have other jobs during the week. If you really want to be sure of hearing some blues, time your travels to coincide with one of the blues festivals happening throughout the summer months.

For a spine-tingling Delta experience of another order, it is still possible to find that private front-porch recital by a legendary bluesman too old or rooted on his farm to do tours, or that demonstration of a diddley-bo by a fellow who makes them, or that master lesson for an aspiring musician. These sessions carry their own ettiquette for tipping or gift-giving, so some familiarity with Southern protocol helps. Persistence pays off here, too, but the best ad-

Detour: Oxford

Do you need a break from the Delta yet? Has counting pickup trucks, propane tanks, and barbecued ribs induced a bad imitation drawl? How far would you detour for a well-stocked bookstore, a movie with subtitles, a restaurant that doesn't immerse everything in boiling oil? Sixty-two miles east of Clarksdale on Hwy-6 is the college town of Oxford, whose cultural amenities, though common to college towns from Amherst and Boulder to Madison and Santa Barbara, set it in a world apart from the rest of Mississippi. The college in question is "Ole Miss," otherwise

vice for would-be pilgrims and apprentices is to make the **Delta Blues Museum** (P.O. Box 280, Clarksdale, MS 38614; 601/624-4461, fax 601/627-7263) your first stop.

Recommended reading: *Living Blues* (301 Hill Hall, University of Mississippi, University, MS 38677; 601/232-5742; $18 per year), the bimonthly magazine of the music and the culture; *The Land Where Blues Began* by Alan Lomax (NYC: Pantheon Books, 1993); *Blues from the Delta* by William Ferris (NYC: Anchor Press, 1978); *Blues Fell This Morning* by Paul Oliver (NYC: Cambridge University Press, 2nd ed., 1990); *Rythm Oil* [sic] by Stanley Booth (NYC: Pantheon Books, 1991); and *Lost Highway* by Peter Guralnick (Boston: Godine, 1979). For invaluable advice on comprehending the incomprehensibilities of the South, look up the *Encyclopedia of Southern Culture,* edited by Charles Wilson and William Ferris (Chapel Hill: University of North Carolina Press, 1989). The entries under "manners" are particularly worth committing to memory.

The following is a partial list of annual Delta blues festivals, all in Mississippi unless otherwise noted.

Muddy Waters Day, Clarksdale (601/624-4461), first Saturday in April

Robert Johnson Day, Clarksdale (601/624-4461), first Saturday in May

Mississippi Crossroads Blues Festival, Greenwood (800/748-9064), last Saturday in May

B.B. King Homecoming, Indianola (601/887-4454), first Saturday in June

Eureka Blues Festival, Eureka Springs, AR (501/253-9344), first weekend in June

Bentonia Blues Festival, Bentonia (601/755-2278), first Saturday in July

Sunflower River Blues and Gospel Festival, Clarksdale (601/624-4461), first weekend in August

Northeast Mississippi Blues and Gospel Folk Festival, Holly Springs (601/252-4661), second Saturday in September

Mississippi Delta Blues Festival, Greenville (800/467-3582), mid-September

King Biscuit Blues Festival, Helena, AR (501/338-9144), second weekend of October known as the University of Mississippi, whose pleasant campus holds such treasures as B.B. King's entire personal collection of records, posters, photos, and more in the **U of M Blues Archive** (Mon.-Fri. 8:30 AM-5 PM; 601/232-7753; appointments required to listen to music), in Farley Hall across from Barnard Observatory. The renovated antebellum observatory actually houses the **Center For The Study of Southern Culture** (Mon.-Fri. 8:15 AM-4:45 PM; 601/232-5993), which sponsors exhibits, lectures, and screenings.

Holly Springs, 30 miles north of Oxford, is home to "the world's number one Elvis fan," Paul MacLeod, and his equally dedicated son, Elvis Aaron Presley MacLeod, who devote their lives to documenting every Elvis reference they find in newspapers, in magazines, or on TV. For a small donation you can visit their ever-vigilant 24-hour Elvis media monitoring station and artifact-filled shrine, **Graceland Too**, at 200 East Gholson Avenue.

One of the few GRR signs in the state of Mississippi stands along the 80-mile ride down the Delta from Clarksdale to Greenville; don't blink or you'll miss it.

Elsewhere under the leafy old oaks you'll find a large collection of primitive **Southern folk art** in the University Museums (closed Monday), and a collection of William Faulkner first editions in the J.D. Williams Library. Faulkner was a resident of Oxford for most of his life; readers of his novels will recognize in surrounding Lafayette County (luh-FAY-it) elements of Faulkner's fictional Yoknapatawpha. **Rowan Oak** (Tues.-Sat. 10 AM-noon and 2-4 PM, Sunday 2-4 PM; free), his house on Old Taylor Road off S. Lamar Avenue, remains as he left it when he died in 1962, with the bottle of whiskey by the old typewriter in his study almost, but not quite, empty. Squirrels do their acorn dance on the leafy property unmolested by the poachers who provoked Faulkner to print a sarcastic public advisory asking trespassing hunters to refrain from shooting his milk cow, too. Visit his gravesite by following the signs from the north side of the courthouse square; near the cemetery entrance lie other family members who didn't affect adding the "u" to their surname, including the brother whose untimely death Faulkner mourned in his first novel, *Soldier's Pay*.

When respects have been paid to Southern culture and it's time to eat, consider the **Cafe Olé** (parent to the one in Memphis) along the small neon strip at 1612 University Avenue for lively, generous, and inexpensive Tex-Mex food; or the **Harvest Moon** on the courthouse square for its deliciously eclectic California-style menu—meatless, by the way. At nearby Harrison Avenue, in what doubles as the lobby of a second-run/art-house cinema, **Hoka Theater & Cafe** serves vegetarian bar food for the undergraduate crowd at undergraduate prices amid a decor that is vividly political, playful, and about as subtle as MTV. They have Ben and Jerry's ice cream, too. If you've been hankering for a full Southern country breakfast or ham with red-eye gravy, then **Smitty's**, at 208 S. Lamar just south of the square, is for you. (That gravy gets its name from the coffee mixed in with the ham drippings.) Or take a 10-mile trip north on Hwy-7 to tiny **Abbeville** and sit down to fine fried catfish and other solid Southern dishes at the counter inside **Ruth & Jimmie's** nationally famous gas station-bait shop-grocery-and-cafe. You can't miss it.

Accommodations in Oxford include a **Holiday Inn** north of the courthouse, and other motels by the exits along Hwy-6.

The Oxford Tourism Council (601/234-4651) will happily provide more information and a calendar of cultural events; they also operate a **visitor center** in City Hall on the central square.

Highway 1

The official Great River Road actually bypasses Clarksdale along rural Hwy-1, which winds nearer to the river; to rejoin this riparian route, turn west on Hwy-322 toward **Sherard**, south of where the GRR races across one straight section after another, as if its engineers couldn't wait to get out of the Delta. The monotony of cotton is broken only by the occasional soybean, milo, and catfish farm; next to agriculture, "pond cat" is one of the Delta's hottest products.

The passing towns are mostly anonymous down-on-their-luck affairs filled with shotgun shacks, low-slung Creole-style bungalows, and old trailers that some people have nicknamed "doghouses" without any attempt at irony. What look like oil drums mounted on garden carts in the odd front yard are smokers, for doing barbecue just right; their presence sometimes implies the proximity of a social club or juke joint that may do only weekend business. Local stores, if they exist, are where men in overalls sit and stand in clusters, keeping an eye on the world. Some of these places are reputed to have backroom card games that would make any of the new casinos weep with envy. In autumn when the cotton is ready for harvest, huge truck-sized bales sit in the cleared muddy margins of the fields, and white fluff accumulates in drifts on the narrow loose shoulder, swirling in small eddies in your wake.

Meanwhile the Mississippi River does its snaky shuffle off to the Gulf of Mexico behind a continuous line of levees, a bayou here and cut-off lake there as proof of past indirections. Unlike the spreading deltas of the Orinoco or Nile, the Mississippi cuts a deeper channel as it rolls south, the deceptively unruffled surface hiding a flow four times greater than at the St. Louis Arch.

Greenville

Shortly after passing the 1,000-year-old Winterville Mounds and less-ancient Hub Cap City, two landmarks illustrating the range of human activity in the Delta from prehistory through the present, the GRR enters Greenville, one of the largest river ports in the state, its levees now lined by floating casinos. Hwy-1 through Greenville takes top honors for the least attractive strip of gas stations and minimarts yet encountered along the GRR, with a close second going to the intersecting Hwy-82 that enters town from the east.

Like Scripture verse quoted by a used-car salesperson, Greenville's covers don't do justice to its text, for the city has some fine cultural traditions, from the anti-Ku Klux Klan editorializing of Hodding Carter's *Delta-Democrat Times* during the 1950s and 1960s to the hot tamales at **Doe's Eat Place**. In the big

Before yielding to any temptation to simply drive down a dirt farm lane for a peek at the river that General Grant called "too damned muddy to drink, too wet to plow," keep in mind that Mississippi mud is as tenacious as it gets. If you've never had the pleasure of using gasoline to burn caked mud off your tires—after a tractor has pulled your car out—sink an axle into Alligator clay (named for a hamlet south of Clarksdale) and you might get a chance.

About 30 miles east of the GRR on Hwy-32 is **Parchman,** infamous home to the state prison farms, memorialized in songs like bluesman Bukka White's "Parchman Farm." The "Midnight Special," another oft-heard allusion in Delta blues lyrics, was the weekend train from New Orleans that brought visitors to the prison.

East of the GRR on Hwy-61 is small **Mound Bayou,** the oldest black town in the state. A man named Isaiah Montgomery, inspired by Booker T. Washington's prescriptions for black self-improvement, founded the all-black community in 1888 with support from his former employer, Jefferson Davis.

Across the Mississippi from Rosedale in a cotton field off Hwy-1 is **Rohwer, Arkansas,** where you can visit memorials to the 8,500 Japanese-Americans who were forced from their California homes and imprisoned here for the duration of WW II.

white building at 502 Nelson Street (follow N. Broadway to the brick churches, then turn toward the river), Doe's is known throughout the state for its good food and honest prices, and for the fact that you have to enter through the kitchen. The presence of tamales on menus all the way down to Natchez, and at roadside stands along US-61, is one of the more unusual Delta idioms, although this being the South the corn husks with their tasty corn meal and meat fillings are cooked in hot oil rather than steamed as they might be in East L.A. or El Salvador.

Second to Clarksdale in the Delta blues galaxy, Greenville's **blues clubs** (Boobah Barnes Playboy Club, for example) are all located around Thompson Avenue in a part of town that will make your mother's heart skip a beat; come in mid-September during the annual **Delta Blues Festival** and at least there will be the strength of overwhelming numbers to soothe her arrhythmia.

Late in the year when the pecan crop is in, you can buy pecans from vans or shacks beside the highway; look for the paper-shell variety or buy a nutcracker.

For **accommodations**, look along Hwy-82 near the junction with US-61, east of town: **Days Inn**, **Best Western**, **Ramada**, and **Hampton** are all there.

For more information contact the Greenville **visitor center** at 915 Washington Avenue (601/378-3141).

The town of Leland, eight miles east of Greenville on US-82, was the boyhood home of Muppet-master **Jim Henson.** About 30 miles east of Greenville, Moorhead is known in blues geography as the place "where the Southern crosses the Dog," an allusion to the Southern and Yazoo-Delta (a.k.a. "Yellow Dog") Railroads.

Highway 1 Revisited

Between Greenville and Vicksburg the GRR continues along Hwy-1 through the cotton-rich bottoms, the landscape as unvarying as the country music that dominates the radio dial. Before the Civil War this land was nearly uninhabitable hardwood forests and fever-riddled swamps, home to snakes, panthers, and mosquitoes. After Reconstruction the valuable oaks, sweetgum, and hickory were logged off, the swamps drained, and levees built; now just the snakes and mosquitoes remain.

At the junction with Hwy-14 the GRR turns abruptly west to mosey for 30 miles amid second-growth forest close to the Mississippi—across which stretches Louisiana—before rejoining

---

BIRTH OF THE TEDDY BEAR

The original Teddy Bear was inspired by a cub from the woods around Greenville: tied by a noose to a tree in the canebrakes, the cute fellow was found by Pres. Teddy Roosevelt while hunting here in 1902. His refusal to shoot the defenseless animal, publicized in a *Washington Post* editorial cartoon, garnered such popular approval that a New York firm requested the president's permission to name a stuffed toy after him. The only rub is, T.R. didn't actually refuse to shoot—because, in fact, he wasn't there. But neither was the cub! According to members of the hunting party, the president's guide, Holt Collier, a black veteran of the Confederate cavalry, was challenged to prove he could lasso a bear. So he did, when one came along through the swamp—an old and rather weak one, as it turned out, that splashed around in a slough before they cut him loose. T.R., however, having tired of waiting for game, had returned to camp and missed the whole episode.

US-61 again beside a Fina station in the hamlet of **Onward**. These woodlands are the edge of the lower Yazoo River basin, valuable wetlands habitat for the wood stork, bald eagle, and Louisiana black bear.

You won't notice many people lolling about on grassy lawns or parks in the southern Delta, for the simple reason that this has become the realm of the fire ant, whose stinging bite would shame a wasp into adopting some other line of work.

After the rigid flatness of the Delta, the final third of this leg rolls through low hills whose slopes seem downright dramatic, but don't let the novelty of a little scenery distract you from taking the US-61 Business turnoff, shortly after the highway grows to a fast four lanes.

Vicksburg

The "Red Carpet City of the South" didn't roll one out for the Union army during the Civil War; rather, the city so stubbornly opposed Union efforts to win control of the Mississippi River that Vicksburg became the target of one of the longest sieges in U.S. military history. The story of the campaign to split the Confederacy in half along the great river reached its dramatic conclusion in 1863 amid the strategic heights and ravines of the 1,800-acre **National Military Park** ($4 per car). Without a historical informant the old battlefield is merely an extensive collection of ornate monuments to the soldiers who died fighting over these grassy earthworks that spring. A visit becomes emotionally compelling after some accounting of the 47-day Siege of Vicksburg—the anecdotes of individual valor, of odd courtesies amid the bloodshed, of the tragedy and humanity that lies in such unequal measure behind the 16 winding miles of stone. Audiotape tours may be rented from the visitor center (daily except Christmas 8 AM-5 PM) for $4.50, with narration and sound effects, or you can hire a guide ($10 per hour, two-hour minimum, three hours recommended) to accompany you in your car and explain everything from battle strategies to the symbolism of the monuments. The advantage to a live guide is the opportunity to ask questions and to delve into whatever suits your curiosity, be it stories of the many women who fought incognito, or of the immigrants who enlisted to win citizenship, or of General Grant's legendary difficulties with drink. The **Vicksburg Convention and Visitors Bureau** (601/636-9421 or 800/221-3536) keeps a list of these very worthwhile guides.

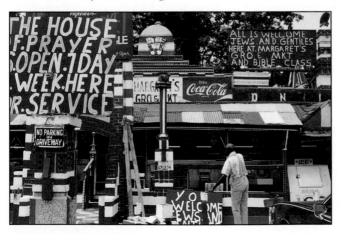

Margaret's Gro & Mkt

A few of the city's posh **antebellum houses** survived the Civil War intact, and during the post-war Reconstruction several additional mansions were added to the bluffs overlooking the river. Most of these homes are open to the public (average $5), and during the fortnight-long "Pilgrimages" in late March and mid-October, slightly discounted multiple-house tours are available. Begin at the cluster in Vicksburg's Garden District on Oak Street south of Harrah's Casino, where the old plantation division between the Big House and surrounding shacks has been unintentionally preserved; others are found in the pleasant cobblestoned residential area between 1st Street E and Clay. The architecturally varied mansions and their copious inventories of fine antiques are more fascinating to decorative arts aficionados than to history buffs, who may find tours illuminating more for what is omitted than included. Stories of deprivation and Union plundering, cannonballs in parlor walls, and other wartime relics are religiously enshrined, yet never a word is spoken about slavery.

To escape from the indoor onslaught of Louis XV marquetry or Chippendale claw feet, stop by **Margaret's Grocery** right on the GRR (old US-61) on the north side of town, at 4535 N. Washington Street (601/638-1163). At a glance, the assemblage of huge hand-lettered signs atop various red-and-white constructions resembles a fanatical Lego-Land, welcoming shoppers to the trailer-style convenience store. The Biblically-inspired injunctions to shop are worth at least a pause, but caveat visitor: the owner will talk your ear off if you aren't careful.

If you've ever tried to imagine a world without Coke, step into the **Biedenharn Museum of Coca-Cola Memorabilia**, smack downtown at 1107 Washington Street, and see where one man's ingenuity slew all hopes for such a world. Here in 1894 Joseph Biedenharn conceived of putting the strictly regional soda fountain drink into bottles, the better to reach new markets; the rest, as they say, is history. Toast worldwide domination with some of the classic stuff, straight up or over ice cream, or pay $1.87 to view galleries full of old promotional serving trays and the like.

For real food and drink check out the **New Orleans Cafe** across the street, basically a well-lit and spacious bar with decent Cajun dishes, imported beers, and a view of the Diversionary Canal. The canal was the city's response to the caprice of nature when in 1876 Vicksburg found itself facing a mudflat of flopping fish after the Mississippi River found itself a new streambed—overnight. Thanks to the diligence of engineers who redirected the Yazoo River, Vicksburg has its waterfront back, now complete with several sharks, whose slot machines and roulette wheels spin 24 hours for your entertainment.

For a traditional Southern feast, sit down to the communal round table at **Walnut Hills**, 1214 Adams Street at Clay (intersection 4; notice the numbers suspended from the traffic signals) and dig into the endless supply of classic regional dishes, from fried pork tenderloin to okra; given the fresh ingredients and depending on how much of a pig you can be, the moderate prices are a great value. An equally rib-stuffing meal at an even more amazing price is found weekdays at lunch in the friendly **Kitchen in the Garden,** a hole-in-the-wall tucked away at the end of 5th Street N, just off Main Street E. "Down-to-earth soul food" is the credo here, and it's no lie: try the fried chicken or fish for a real treat, and savor how pork fat makes greens so tasty. Many of the side vegetables come out of a can, but you can't expect Julia Child at these prices. The place is also open in the evening, when it attracts a rowdier crowd—which may explain why some of the seating is so rickety.

Reavey's Bar-B-Q at the corner of 1st Street N and Clay (intersection 6) serves some of the city's finest pork and beef ribs, while tamale addicts should seek out **Solly's Hot Tamales** on Washington Street south of the library (near intersection 26).

Vicksburg motels, found along I-20 between the Mississippi and the Military Park, include a wide selection of the national chains and their local imitators, the cheapest of which is the **Hillcrest Inn** (601/638-1491; $24-30). Or, for only $85-150, you can play Rhett and Scarlett for a night, pampering yourself with canopied beds and frocked shower curtains in one of the 10 camellia-draped tour homes that double as plush B&Bs. All have you whistling "Dixie," but true history buffs will want to request the Grant Room at **Cedar Grove** (800/862-1300), still furnished with the bed the general used after Union forces occupied Vicksburg. The staff claims ol' Sam was a bedridden drunk for his entire stay, but pay no attention—he was probably a poor tipper at the bar, and folks around here bear grudges over generations for things like that.

If your visit falls during Pilgrimage, don't expect easy pickings on rooms: most B&Bs are booked up to *two years* in advance for those weeks. For thorough and concise information on lodging and attractions, call the friendly **Vicksburg Convention and Visitors Bureau** (800/221-3536) or visit their **tourist information center** opposite the entrance to the National Military Park.

Port Gibson and the Natchez Trace

Neither the weather nor the road take any notice of the fact that you've left the low-lying Delta bottoms as the GRR heads south from Vicksburg along a wooded stretch of US-61. Trees or no trees, summer humidity will still glue your clothes to your car seat. Relief comes after 30 miles in Port Gibson, the town General Grant found "too beautiful to burn."

While the Union Army may have spared it, decades of economic doldrums haven't. Fine homes still grace the pleasantly shaded main drag, but most eye-catching is the giant Monty Python prop known as the Church of the Golden Hand. Actually it's the historic First Presbyterian Church, whose interior is lit by the gasoliers of the famous steamboat *Robert E. Lee,* the record-setting winner of the Great Steamboat Race of 1870. Newspapers of the day reckoned that millions of dollars were wagered on the outcome of the New Orleans-to-St. Louis race, which attracted international attention. The *Lee*'s three-day, 18-hour, and 14-minute victory was an upset for the favored titleholder, the *Natchez.*

Across the street from the Golden Hand stands an almost equally unusual building, **Temple Gemiluth Chessed**, an elaborate Moorish-arched temple built in 1891 by Port Gibson's then-prosperous Jewish community.

Vicksburg's street signs are small white croquet poles stuck into the grass at street corners, lettered vertically with a stencil; they must have cost a fortune to have escaped replacement by something useful. Rather than wonder at their illegibility, obtain a map from the visitor bureau folks.

The icon of Southern gentility and refreshment, the mint julep, was allegedly born in Vicksburg: water from fragrant Mint Springs in what is now the National Military Park was mixed with good Kentucky bourbon brought to town by riverboat captains. It almost goes without saying that Kentuckians and Tennesseans consider this to be pure fiction.

While Vicksburg's surrender allowed President Lincoln to declare that "the Father of Waters now flows unvexed to the sea," locals stayed vexed for over 80 years: because the surrender occurred on July 4, Independence Day wasn't celebrated in Vicksburg until the end of WW II.

Vicksburg has more engineers per capita than any other U.S. municipality: 3,500 of them, employees of the Mississippi River Commission, the Corps of Engineers, and the U.S. Army Waterways Experiment Station

Ruins of Windsor

A block south of the Golden Hand, take a right on Carrol Street to begin a quietly scenic 50-mile detour southwest to Natchez, first through the kudzu-draped woodlands along Bayou Pierre, and then along the serene Natchez Trace Parkway. The looping first part of this route follows Hwy-522 past nearly invisible old Indian mounds, abandoned homesteads, and picturesque old cemeteries rotting in the woods. Spot the giant stone columns poking through the treetops on the left near the old townsite of Bruinsburg and you'll have found the **Ruins of Windsor**: once the state's most lavish Greek revival mansion and landmark to river pilots, it was reduced by an 1890 fire to its bare Corinthian ribs.

Natchez Trace Parkway

Hwy-522 rejoins US-61 30 miles above Natchez, but we recommend the more relaxed Natchez Trace Parkway, which you'll cross about a mile before the US-61 junction. The parkway, which like the Blue Ridge Parkway is a scenic route operated by the National Park Service, follows the route of the old **Natchez Trace**, a Pre-Columbian Indian path that grew into the major overland route between the Gulf Coast and the upper Mississippi and Ohio River valleys in the years before steamboats provided a faster alternative. The Natchez Trace appeared on maps as early as 1733, and from the 1780s to the 1820s, when steamboats made it obsolete, the Natchez Trace was one of the nation's most traveled routes. Farmers and craftspeople in the Ohio River Valley would transport their products by raft downstream to Natchez or New Orleans, then return on foot, staying at the dozens of inns along the route while doing battle with swamps, mosquitoes, and bands of thieves.

The entire 430-mile length of the Parkway, which runs from Nashville south to the edge of Natchez, with a short break around Jackson (see pages 610-611), is well paved and makes a delightful driving route, with places of interest marked every few miles. Just north of Port Gibson at mile marker 41.5, the **Sunken Trace** preserves a deeply eroded, 200-yard-long section of the trail, the canopy of moss-laden cypress trees offering one of the most evocative five-minute walks you can imagine. Between Port Gibson and Natchez, sights along this short stretch range from the prehistoric **Emerald Mound**, with its commanding view of the woodlands, to **Mount Locust** at mile marker 15.5, a restored Trace roadhouse—possibly the oldest juke joint in the state, and the place to pick up parkway information.

The National Park Police keep the parkway under very thorough radar surveillance, by the way, so try to stay within the posted speed limit of 45 mph.

Natchez

Before the Civil War, Natchez (NATCH-iss) had the most millionaires per capita in the U.S., and it shows. If luxurious antebellum houses make your heart beat faster, this place might just put you in the local ICU with its innumerable white columns and rich smorgasbord of Italian marble, imported crystal, sterling silver, painted china, plush drapery, petit point, Hepplewhite, and ivory. That so much antebellum finery still exists is because Natchez, unlike Vicksburg, surrendered to Grant's army almost without a fight. Anti-Yankee sentiment may in fact run higher now than during the war, for Natchez was vehemently opposed to the Confederacy, and outspokenly against Mississippi's secession from the Union. For a town that was second only to New Orleans as social and cultural capital of a region with two-thirds of the richest people in America, most of whom owed their wealth to slave-picked cotton, you might call support of the Union a little incongruous. Of course, such apparent contradictions should come as no surprise from a community raised with genteel cotillions and the Mississippi's busiest red-light district side by side, although visitors won't find much evidence of the town's seedy past any more. Once-disreputable Natchez Under-the-Hill, eroded by Mississippi floods and community standards, is today but a single gentrified block of bars, restaurants, and shops. Gambling has been cleaned up and packaged aboard a permanently moored riverboat, and the most famous brothel in the South, Nellie's, finally closed after a 1992 fire killed the octogenarian owner.

Mamie Restaurant, Natchez

As befits the place that originated the concept, the biannual Natchez Pilgrimages (March and October) are twice as long as the typical 10-15 days done elsewhere. The number of **antebellum mansions** open to the public more than doubles, hoop skirts and brass-buttoned waistcoats abound, and musical diversions like the **Confederate Pageant** are held nightly. If you have patience for wistful recollections of the storied past, you can sample over a dozen of the architectural cupcakes year-round ($4-6 each, or selected multiple-house tickets from Natchez Pilgrimage Tours, at Canal and State Streets). Among the most fascinating is the one that didn't get finished: **Longwood**, the nation's largest octagonal house. Its grounds are fittingly gothic, too, with moss-dripping tree limbs, sunken driveway, and the family cemetery out in the woods.

Southern history doesn't merely comprise those Greek revival heaps and their *Gone With the Wind* stereotypes; for proof check out downtown's **Museum of Afro-American History and Culture**, at 307A Market Street across from the Courthouse parking (Wed.-Fri. 1-5 PM, Saturday 11 AM-4 PM; $1), also where you'll find interesting Black Heritage walking tour brochures. Large Jewish sections in the **City Cemetery** (follow signs for the National Cemetery, and the city's is along the way) also furnish evidence of the South's tapestried past. The marble statuary and decorative wrought iron offer a pleasant outdoor respite for weary mansion-goers, too.

Have you noticed how you usually have to pay a premium to avoid fried food in the South? Not so at **Pearl Street Pasta**, near the corner of Main Street, whose short dinner-only menu is eclectic, reasonably priced, and laced with vegetables that haven't been boiled to oblivion. **Magnolia's** in Natchez-Under-The-Hill is one of those rare Southern restaurants that doesn't even have a Fryolator; it's a surf 'n' turf kind of place with big-city prices. For big-city sophistication at moderate prices, head straight to **Liza's Contemporary Cuisine**, out on S. Canal Street next to the

Best Western. The seasonal menu adds a dash of California to the South, with flawless results. Veal with wild mushrooms and smoked garlic, grilled eggplant and shiitake, grilled quail with collard cornbread dressing, tuna with ginger wasabi . . . you get the picture. Unusually good wine list, too. While you wouldn't want to walk in wearing your baggy jeans and hooded sweatshirt, the emphasis is on food more than attitude, and the prices, though not cheap, are well worth it.

Natchez is almost the southern extremity of the Tamale Belt, and if this prospect gives you the DTs then sit down to a paperboard dish of them at **Fat Mama's** in the little log cabin on S. Canal Street at Biglane. Be warned, the delicious little things are greasy enough to wink back at you. The **Local Color Delicatessen** at 112 N. Commerce Street, almost across from the old Ritz marquee, offers good bargain-priced sandwiches, salads, gumbo, and the like, accompanied by occasional evening live music and the best jukebox in town. Rescued from Nellie's after the fatal fire, it'll still croon you some Elvis for a quarter while you peruse news clippings about the former madam's distinctive career or a copy of her will, all preserved under the glass tabletops. More local color can be found at either **The Corner Bar**, on Main and Canal, or **The Saloon**, in Natchez-Under-the-Hill, with its fine view of the Mississippi. Like New Orleans and Las Vegas, Natchez has no closing law, but in fact most bars do close when the last paying customers roll on home. If you prefer the company of chocolate shake drinkers, head over to **The Malt Shop**, on the corner of Homochitto and Martin Luther King Street.

Accommodations include a half-dozen familiar names from budget **Scottish Inn** (800/251-1962) to executive **Ramada Inn**, located along US-61 and US-84 both north and south of downtown. As could be expected from a major tourist destination with so many fine homes, Natchez is also brimming with B&Bs. By New England or California standards most put luxury within the realm of affordability, and even the tacky or tasteless bits thrown in with the genuinely historic elegance make a nice departure from pure Victorian pomp. Southern style, suffice it to say, is in a league of its own. As an example of local value, consider the **Highpoint** (800/283-4099): $80-125 fetches spacious rooms, a generous "plantation" breakfast, evening mint juleps, and friendly hosts whose political, Southern, and Confederate connections would make any storyteller green with envy. Reservations for the Highpoint and most of the other 30-odd B&Bs in town can be made through **Historic Inns of Natchez** (800/256-INNS) or **Natchez Pilgrimage Tours** (800/647-6742).

For an illustrated B&B guide and other useful information contact the **Natchez Convention and Visitors Bureau** (800/99-NATCHEZ). Keep in mind the enormous popularity of Pilgrimage requires seriously advanced bookings for either March or October travel.

Across the Mississippi from Natchez, the town of **Ferriday, Louisiana,** was where rocker Jerry Lee "Great Balls of Fire" Lewis and his cousin, evangelist Jimmy Swaggert, grew up.

There are no cotton fields around Natchez, because all the cotton that paid for these mansions was grown across the river in the Louisiana bottomlands.

Upon your departure from Natchez via US-61, a familiar pilot's wheel reminds you that indeed, the GRR exists, and you're on it. It's also one of the last GRR signs you'll see.

US-61 to the Louisiana Line

Rolling and curving past hay fields and woods, the distinctively red earth of southern Mississippi crowding the soft shoulders, the GRR passes quickly over the 45 miles to the state line, stopping just once for an intersection of gas stations on the edge of

Woodville. A few plantations may be seen, but the hand of humanity around here leans more toward the utilitarian, or plain ugly. Logging used to be a major industry hereabouts before WW I and again in the decade following WW II, when portable "woodpecker" sawmills buzzed through these hills and logged off whatever virgin pine and hardwoods had been left by earlier loggers. The local timber industry now runs toward pulpwood rather than saw timber, as that second- and third-growth forest alongside the road no longer supports much valuable but slow-growing ash, hickory, and oak. To get a better impression of what this land used to look like back in the days of the ivory-billed woodpeckers, turn west at that Woodville intersection and follow the Pinckneyville Road about 13 miles to the **Clark Creek Nature Area.** A short trail leads up to attractive **Tunica Falls** through woods that botanically have more common with the Ozarks and Appalachians than the rest of the lower Mississippi valley. The folks at old Duck Pond Grocery, a throwback to an era of small-town stores, can give directions to the trailhead if needed.

You won't see it from here, but just across the Mississippi is possibly the most significant piece of engineering anywhere along its length: the Old River Project. More than mere flood control, the project is designed to keep the Mississippi going down to Baton Rouge and New Orleans, rather than finding a new route to the Gulf via the Atchafalaya River. This actually happened during the 1948 flood, and there are hydrologists who predict it is only a matter of time before it will happen again—a potential catastrophe for downstream cities along both rivers.

ACROSS LOUISIANA

As the GRR approaches its southern end, land and river begin to merge. The Midwestern humidity pales next to Louisiana's semi-tropical climate (when was the last time your windshield fogged up driving with all your windows *open?*); bring a snorkel. Spanish moss drips from trees and snakes slither across the road. With giant levees on one side and standing water on the other, it's easy to imagine the land is sinking—and indeed, by the time you roll off elevated I-10 into New Orleans, you will be four to six feet *below* sea level.

From the St. Francisville ferry to the interstate bridge just west of New Orleans, we cross the Mississippi four times, threading along rough back roads between Acadiana's vast cane plantations and the notorious "Chemical Corridor" of industrial giants whose toxic discharges have produced another sobriquet: Cancer Alley. Here, too, you can see a series of fine antebellum plantation homes, some crowded so close to the petro-chemical plants that they have become gilded anachronisms in the pipefitter's forest. The road is not without its charms—a vividly painted church out in a field, or exquisitely gnarled and bent live oaks, festooned with epiphytes—but they are overshadowed by the specter of a land being poisoned for profit.

For free highway maps or other tourist information, stop at the **Louisiana Tourist Information Center** on US-61 south of the Mississippi state line.

St. Francisville

Louisiana is divided into parishes rather than counties, a subtle reminder of the French Catholic settlement of the state. Midway across West Feliciana Parish, turn west off US-61 at St. Francisville, an 18th-century settlement that grew up around the graveyard of an order of Capuchin monks in what was then Spanish West Florida. As you follow signs for Hwy-10 west to the ferry and pass houses whose contents spill out like the ragged stuffing of an old sofa and vintage cars in less-than-vintage condition, it takes a leap of faith to believe this place is a weekend resort for downstream urban dwellers, but in fact the surrounding mossy woods hide a number of "romantic getaways" and "executive retreats," some at prices that assume a dowry or expense account. Pick up an anecdotally rich walking tour brochure at the **West Feliciana Historical Society Museum** on Ferdinand Street (Hwy-10), and follow Royal Street, a block west of the museum, for a sample of the architectural charms that draw visitors to this curious little town. The **Magnolia Cafe**, in what looks like an old gas station at the corner of Ferdinand Street, is the best reasonably priced lunch stop (Mon.-Sat. 10 AM-4 PM).

Continue west on Hwy-10 until it dead-ends at the large car ferry ($1) to Pointe Coupee Parish. If you've just missed the boat, expect to wait about 30 minutes for it to complete the return journey, time easily spent admiring the belching chemical plants and rusting barges, or watching people catch crawfish along the muddy banks. Lest you consider skipping the ferry and proceeding to Baton Rouge via US-61, be advised that it is a sorry route: oil storage tanks, trailer parks, an auto-part-pawn-shop-minimart strip that defies all pejoratives, and finally, adding insult to injury, the once-but-never-again "Scenic Highway" with its grandstand view of the Exxon refinery.

According to the EPA, Louisiana is number one in the nation for reported toxic dumping. Yet it regularly fails to monitor or report on toxic and radiological contaminants in its public water supplies—meaning that companies report what they've dumped, but the state refuses to find out where it goes.

After disembarking on the west bank of the Mississippi, cross the steep revetment by the ferry landing and take the first left onto rough-paved Hwy-981 toward Port Allen.

Acadiana: Port Allen

In rural counterpoint to the tank farms on the east side of the river, the landscape in this corner of Acadiana is filled with sugarcane plantations and contentedly grazing cattle—at least for the first 32 miles. Stay within the shadow of the levee, turning as necessary, until you pass under the huge steel arches of the US-190 bridge and into residential Port Allen. A few miles of handsome Creole-influenced plantation homes and even a nice splash of art deco precede the junction with Hwy-1, a commercial strip distinguished only by the presence of that ubiquitous Acadian specialty, the daiquiri bar. Like a high-octane version of a Dairy Queen Slush, daiquiris come pre-mixed in a variety of sticky fruit flavors and sizes up to the quart that kicks: yes, an eye-crossing 32-ouncer. If that isn't enough, many of these bars have *drive-up windows*. In the eyes of the law, that piece of masking tape across the cup's lid makes it a "sealed container"; seems the law doesn't care about the straw.

Our route crosses back over the Mississippi on I-10, whose bridge looms on the horizon; as you take the approach ramp from Hwy-1 be sure to follow signs for the city, not the port, of Baton Rouge. If you want to bypass Baton Rouge altogether, follow Hwy-1 south from Port Allen to Plaquemine.

Baton Rouge

From the interstate bridge's lofty vantage point, Baton Rouge appears to be a largely industrial city, its skyline dominated by smokestacks, distilling columns, and the nation's tallest state capitol—essentially a 34-story monument to the populist demagoguery of Huey Long. Closer inspection yields little evidence of anything particularly attractive, with the sole exception of the **Old State Capitol** (Mon.-Sat. 10 AM-4 PM, Sunday noon-4 PM; $5), that clearly visible setpiece from *Ivanhoe*—the only thing missing is a moat. Inside the restored 1847 edifice are engaging computer-aided history exhibits, curated by the resident Center for Political and Governmental History. Practice your stump speeches from a podium whose TelePrompTer will cue you with famous soundbites from Louisiana politicians, or sit in a facsimile of a studio control room and search a digitized video database of newsreels and oral history clips. Study the unresolved 1935 Huey Long assassination: was the patronage-dealing, vote-buying potentate the target of premeditated murder, or was then-senator Long the victim of his five trigger-happy bodyguards' "friendly fire," aimed at a man who merely punched the boss? Review the evidence and draw your own conclusions.

The **Pastime**, a few blocks away on the corner of St. Louis and North Boulevard, almost under I-10, is one of those windowless smoky sports bars ideally suited for discussing political chicanery over po'-boys, fried fish, and beer. Best pizzas in town, too; try the one topped with crawfish tails for some local flavor.

The only other good dining prospects are clustered around the Highland Avenue entrance to Louisiana State University, a couple miles south of I-10. **Louie's Cafe**, on E. State across from the Super Fresh shopping plaza, is all-around exceptional: exceptional prices for exceptional portions of exceptionally good diner-style food.

A dozen miles west of St. Francisville and the Great River Road along Hwy-1, the small town of **Morganza, Louisiana,** was the place where the character played by Jack Nicholson was beaten to death in the classic 1960s road movie, *Easy Rider.*

About five miles southeast of St. Francisville on Hwy-965 is the **Oakley House,** where in 1821 John James Audubon came to work as a resident tutor while he completed the final 80 illustrations for his *Birds of America* series. His wife Lucy also tutored local women to help pay for the publication of his work.

The bridge that now carries US-190 over the Mississippi was built during the gubernatorial reign of the notorious "Kingfish," **Huey P. Long.** The structure was designed to be so low in order to prevent oceangoing freighters from passing, thus snuffing the chances of Vicksburg and other upstream cities competing with the port of Baton Rouge —now the nation's fifth busiest.

Since it's open 24 hours, there's no excuse to miss it. Facing the LSU gates is **The Chimes**, a restaurant and oyster bar (serving daily to midnight) with "100 beers from 24 countries" and frequent live music for the Lollapalooza crowd. Several other bars in the vicinity offer music with some regularity, but undergraduate projectile vomiting is a serious hazard (Louisiana's drinking age is still 18). Assess the sidewalk in front for a rough measure of how well a bar's patrons know their limits: if the volume of broken beer bottles and discarded "hurricane" cups is high, don a wetsuit or go elsewhere. Across the street from the Chimes is **Highland Coffees**, a genteel oasis amid the spilled beer, with the aroma of on-site roasting, *The New York Times,* and classical music to accompany that double tall mochaccino. Baton Rouge has an unusual number of Lebanese places, two of which bracket the gauntlet of bars on W. Chimes Street: the slightly upscale **Cafe Mediterranean** near Highland, and the more downscale **Arzi's**. Like every restaurant adjoining a campus teeming with hungry students, both are open daily, usually till 10 PM.

THE CHEMICAL CORRIDOR

Our 100-mile traverse of the Corridor begins on Nicholson Avenue (Hwy-30) southbound out of Baton Rouge. The LSU campus and stadium are quickly replaced by a rural landscape of cows, cricket oil wells, and high tension lines. Keep an eye peeled for the **Plaquemine Ferry/Burtville/Sunshine** turnoff (Hwy-327), about eight miles from I-10. It's about another eight miles to the small ferry itself (daily every 30 minutes, 5:15 AM-8:45 PM; $1), whose looping path across the Mississippi illustrates just how strong that current really is. On the western shore in dreary **Plaquemine** (PLACK-uh-minn), pick up divided Hwy-1 for a straight 25-mile shot through the cane fields to the foot of the Sunshine Bridge. En route, the white-walled enclosure surrounding **Nottoway** (daily 9 AM-5 PM; $8), the largest plantation home in the South, comes into view on the left, just before the sardonically named slice of poverty called **White Castle**. With 64 rooms totaling over an acre of floorspace, be glad you don't have to pay Nottoway's air-conditioning bills or do the dusting. A quick climb up the levee affords a panorama of both the gigantic house and the river, a view worth up to $200 for guests of the plantation inn (504/545-2730).

An even more dramatic perspective of the Mississippi, with its conga line of oceangoing freighters extending as far as the eye can see, comes from atop the **Sunshine Bridge**, named in honor of "Singing Governor" Jimmy Davis's most famous song, "You Are My Sunshine." If you haven't had your fill of Greek revival and wrought iron, cross the bridge (return toll $1) and turn briefly north to find Tezcuco and Houmas House, two more grandes dames now cheapened by the monstrous sprawl of a neighboring Dupont plant. Otherwise stay on the west bank and follow signs to Vacherie and Hwy-18, our last back road before meeting the interstate, 50 miles to the south.

River, levee, and road follow wide tacks across the humid sea of cane fields, tank farms, and towns frayed with stubborn neglect. With many houses now

While there's a Ramada Inn on Nicholson Drive near LSU, most of the conveniently located accommodations cluster around exit 151 on I-10, two miles west of the Mississippi in Port Allen. **Days Inn, Holiday Inn, Motel 6,** and a pair of local mid-range motels are all there, along with the local **visitor information center** for your glossy brochure needs.

Because the Mississippi in its natural, pre-Corps state created a raised channel for itself between embankments of silt, the river sits *higher* than a third of Louisiana. Which is why down here, the Mississippi cannot drain the surrounding land of its water.

Plantation Alley

To 19th-century passengers aboard the packet steamboats traveling the lower Mississippi, the great mansions adorning the river bends between Baton Rouge and New Orleans must have made an impressive sight. The houses are no less grand today but, sadly, their surroundings are. Petrochemical companies are the new masters of the stricken land and its neglected towns, and no amount of antebellum finery can hide it. People in the tourist business try to pretend it's still Plantation Alley, but to everyone else it's become the Chemical Corridor (see callout).

---

on stilts and all the cemeteries aboveground, you can almost feel the impounded water rising around you, and in fact, Hwy-18 would be fit only for ducks if the levees were breached. If you get caught in one of Louisiana's typical frog-strangling monsoons, you'll get a taste of what that would be like.

Moldering concrete mausoleums, houses with loud colors and louvered French doors, insouciant pedestrians along the levee, and potholes all may arrest your attention briefly, but **Oak Alley** (daily 9 AM-5 PM; $6.50; 504/265-2151), on Hwy-18 about 15 miles south of the Sunshine Bridge, will probably stop you in your tracks. This place is to antebellum plantations what Bora Bora is to islands, or the Golden Gate is to bridges: even if you've managed to avoid seeing its image on tourist brochures, it will look familiar—or rather, it will look exactly like it ought to. Plus, no cooling tower or gas flare mars the immediate horizon. For the full effect of the grand *alleé* of arching live oaks, all of which are nearly a century older than the current house, drive past the entrance a short ways. Besides the obligatory tour, there's lodging and a restaurant in buildings on the grounds in back of the main house.

If the meal you ate in Baton Rouge is but a doubtful memory, stop by the **Corner Drive-Inn** in Vacherie, a few miles past Oak Alley. It's a gas station-convenience-store-cafe offering authentic and cheap Vietnamese dishes, most of which aren't found on the menu, so ask. If you prefer standard American fried food, they have that, too.

Scattered housing begins to invade the sugarcane, and traffic starts to pick up as the route works its serpentine way past a pair of ferry landings, a nuclear power plant, and a huge Union Carbide factory with a cemetery felicitously occupying its front yard. By the time the GRR is within sight of the giant I-310 bridge, the tentacles of New Orleans's bustle are definitely apparent. This is it! The Great River Road is at its end. Hop on the interstate eastbound and inside of 25 miles you can be hunting for parking in New Orleans's Vieux Carré, or searching for a Sazerac to celebrate the end of your journey.

THE
APPALACHIAN
TRAIL

THE APPALACHIAN TRAIL

The longest and best-known hiking trail in the country, the Appalachian Trail winds from the north woods of Maine all the way south to Georgia. Dozens of guidebooks cover the hiking trail, but until now there has been no description of how to follow the route in a car. The following scenic roads come fairly close to paralleling the pedestrian route, taking in a number of fascinating cities, towns, and historic sites along with the—almost—continuous natural beauty. Best of all, with very few exceptions, the route follows magnificently scenic two-lane roads all the way from the top of New England to the heart of Dixie.

The Appalachian landscape, notorious for harboring an almost Third World level of economic deprivation, also holds some of the wealthiest areas in the entire country, the contrasting worlds often within a few miles of one another. Every resort and retirement community seems to have its alter-ego as former mill towns, now as dependent upon three-season tourism as they once were upon the land and its resouces.

The Appalachian Trail driving tour starts atop rugged Mount Washington in the heart of New Hampshire's Presidential Range of 6,000-foot peaks, the tallest mountains in New England and some of the hardest and most durable rocks on earth. From the mountains the route winds through the idyllic charms of rural New England, taking in the Connecticut River Valley with its summer homes and liberal-arts college communities.

On to the Berkshires, the summer destination of the Boston-New York culture vultures and intelligentsia for most of two centuries. As you approach within commuting distance of New York City, towns become even more prissy and pretty, as evidenced by the Litchfield Hills antique shops.

Skirting the Big Apple, our route ducks down through the Delaware Water Gap to enter the suddenly industrial Lehigh Valley, former land of coal and steel that's now struggling to find an economic replacement. South of here, you pass through the heart of the world-famous Pennsylvania Dutch Country, where the simple life is under the onslaught of package tourism. Then it's on to Gettysburg and Harpers Ferry, polar opposites of the Civil War, Gettysburg the beginning, and Harpers Ferry the beginning of the end.

Back in nature again, the route rides the crest of the mountains, through Shenandoah National Park and the Blue Ridge Parkway.

Driving north to south, you could follow the fall color in leisurely moves south; heading north, you'd be assured of catching the peak season at least somewhere.

APPALACHIAN TRAIL HIGHLIGHTS

ACROSS NEW HAMPSHIRE

"Live Free or Die" is the feisty motto of tiny New Hampshire, the state that hits the national limelight every four years when its political primaries launch the horse race for the White House. During the presidential campaign's opening stretch, locals have to turn into hermits to avoid having their votes solicited by every candidate running and their opinions polled by every reporter. Some of New Hampshire's million residents take the state's motto to heart, however, and when you see the ruggedness of the landscape you'll appreciate how easy it is to find isolation from the madding crowd.

Despite its apparent brevity, the route across New Hampshire provides a hearty sampling of the topographic spectrum from its start at New England's highest peak, Mount Washington, to neighboring Vermont amid the rolling farmland of the Connecticut River valley.

Mount Washington and Pinkham Notch

The star attraction of the White Mountains' Presidential Range, 6,288-foot Mount Washington stands head and shoulders above every other peak in New England. East of the Mississippi, only Mount Mitchell in North Carolina's Blue Ridge and Clingman's Dome in Tennessee's Great Smokies are taller. Despite its natural defenses—such as notoriously fierce storms that arise without warning—Mount Washington is accessible to an almost unfortunate degree. The **Mount Washington Auto Road** (weather permitting, mid-May to mid-Oct; $14 car and driver, $5 each additional adult; 603/466-3988) was first built for carriages over a century ago and switchbacks up the eastern side, while the **Mount Washington Cog Railway** climbs straight up from Bretton Woods at the mountain's western foot.

The best way to appreciate the mountain's granite cliffs, steep ravines, tumbling cataracts, and fragrant pines is on foot. Besides the **Appalachian Trail**, hikers will find a smorgasbord of routes to the summit, including the country's oldest continuously maintained hiking trail, the **Crawford Path**, in use for over 175 years. One-day ascents of Mount Washington are possible, most popularly by the relatively gentle **Tuckerman Ravine Trail** from the east. But don't be deceived by short trail lengths, as the elevation gain and frequent rough terrain can be quite taxing. The Tuckerman route mustn't be confused with the roughly parallel Huntington Ravine Trail, whose exposed ledges and steep pitches are strictly for vertigo-resistant hikers skilled at free climbing.

In New England, locals call their highways "routes," and we've followed suit, using Route as a generic term (Route 100 for example, rather than Hwy-100). The interstates (I-93) and federal highways (US-3) are abbreviated as usual.

Fall foliage is at its best when warm clear days are followed by cold nights that stop the essential pigment-producing sugars from circulating out of the leaves. Sugar production is low on cloudy days, while warm nights allow the sugars to disperse before the brightest colors are produced. For New Hampshire Fall Foliage Reports (Sept.-Oct. only), call 800/258-3608.

MOUNT WASHINGTON WEATHER

A mountain barely over 6,000 feet hardly deserves the same cautious respect as the 20,000-footers in the Patagonian Andes, yet people die from exposure on the flanks of Mount Washington every year. Easy access invites complacency, and a tendency to ignore trailside warnings advising retreat if you're unprepared for bad weather. But respect the facts of nature: simply put, the Presidential Range of the White Mountains experiences some of the worst weather in the world, rivaling both Antarctica and the Alaska-Yukon ranges for consistently raw and bone-numbing combinations of gale-force winds, freezing temperatures, and precipitation. Lashings by 100-mph winds occur year-round on Mount Washington, whose summit holds the title for highest recorded wind speed on the face of the planet (231 mph in April 1934). Cloudy days outnumber clear ones on the peak, where snowstorms can strike any month of the year. Even in the balmiest summer months the average high temperature at the summit hovers around 50° F. Compounding the weather's potential severity is its total unpredictability: a day-hike begun with sunblock and short sleeves can end up in driving rain and temperatures just 10° above freezing, or worse, in a total whiteout above tree line, even as a group of hikers a couple miles away on a neighboring peak enjoys lunch under blue skies and warm breezes.

The bottom line is, listen to what your mother always told you: be careful, and don't take chances. Learn to recognize and prevent hypothermia. Figure out your trail maps and compass *before* you get caught in pelting sleet above tree line. Better to feel foolish packing potentially unnecessary wool sweaters and rain gear for a hike in July than to have your name added to the body count.

Beset by tundra conditions more typical of terrain a thousand miles to the north, the Presidentials are noted for their alpine gardens and *krummholz,* wind-stunted trees that try to eke out a living among the boulders and ice-shattered rock above timberline. Hikers seeking these sorts of wilderness should consider ascending a neighboring peak rather than Washington's fully developed summit. Some of the alpine areas are off-limits to visitors, due to their fragility beneath too many hiking boots. As a general rule, be mindful of the stress plants constantly face from the weather, and try not to tread on the vegetation above tree line.

Without a doubt you can pick up the best **hiking information** for Mount Washington and the rest of the White Mountains at the **Pinkham Notch Camp**, on Route 16 south of the Auto Road. Operated by the venerable Appalachian Mountain Club (AMC), the year-round trailhead facility offers topographical maps, guidebooks, weather updates, and precautionary advice, as well as limited gear. The camp also offers snacks, a cafeteria, a 24-hour hikers' pack room with bathrooms and showers, scheduled shuttle van service, and the **Joe Dodge Lodge** ($30-35 bed only, $45-50 bed and board; 603/466-2727), a modern hostel with shared bunkrooms, a few private doubles, and great views from the library. For extended stays be sure to inquire about the significantly discounted package rates, or consider AMC membership ($40 yearly), which yields up to an additional $7 discount on all overnight stays—including package prices—at any AMC property.

Mount Washington Valley: Gorham and Jackson

North of 2,032-foot Pinkham Notch and the Auto Road, Route 16 descends gradually to intersect US-2 in the plain town of Gorham (pop. 3,173), whose main drag offers rather predictable, if unfranchised, fast food and family dining. If you're hungry for **information**, the **White Mountains National Forest Ranger Station** on Route 16 just south of town can provide recreation tips. For more basic needs like lodging referrals you can call the friendly **Northern White Mountains Chamber of Commerce** (800/992-7480) and get a list of motel phone numbers.

If you're serious about hiking in the region, you won't want to be without the *AMC White Mountains Guide,* the most trusted source of trail and campsite descriptions and site-specific hiking advice since 1907. It's available at the Pinkham Notch Camp, or you can order it in advance by phone (800/262-4455) or by writing to AMC Books, P.O. Box 298, Dept. BC, Gorham, NH 03581-0298.

Dropping sharply away to the south of the Notch is the Ellis River, along whose banks sits the northern gateway to the Mount Washington valley, resort-dominated Jackson (pop. 678). Given the number of lodgings among the attractive century-old clapboard homes, it seems the principal village occupation is innkeeper. The quantity of porches, gables, and chimneys hint at standard country B&B charms: lazy piazza breakfasts in summer, nooks and crannies brimming with cabbage roses and cotton voile, and crackling fires in your room at New Year's. A covered bridge beside Route 16, taverns filled with antiques, and winter sleigh rides complete the postcard image of Merry Olde New England. Reservations for Jackson's numerous B&Bs and country inns, which range in price $50-200, may be made by calling **Country Inns of the White Mountains** (800/562-1300), the **Jackson Resort Association** (800/866-3334), or the **Mount Washington Valley Visitors Bureau** (800/367-3364).

South of Jackson you leave Route 16 and pick up US-302, which heads west from **Glen**, a cluster of restaurants, a grocery store, and a bank ATM. If you're overdue for a little retail therapy you might consider continuing south on Route 16 to **North Conway**, one of the cornerstones of New England's factory-outlet circuit. City dwellers be warned: horrible flashbacks to your homeward commute may result if you venture into the shopping mall zone, where half-hour crawls along a five-mile stretch of highway are not unheard of on holidays, weekends, afternoons, summers, springs, and autumns.

Crawford Notch

US-302 between Glen and Twin Mountain passes through Crawford Notch, another of the White Mountains' high passes and centerpiece of an eponymous state park. After running a gauntlet of rental condos that crowd the base of the ski slopes near Glen, the road ascends the south side of the Notch and closely follows the Saco River through new-growth forest; the oaks and white pine of the lower valley give way to more birch and spruce as you gain elevation. Come autumn, the entire White Mountains National Forest is a riot of color: the northern oaks' dark reds, the birches' and aspens' golden yellows, purples from the white ashes and sumacs, and most brilliant of all, the blaze of orange from countless sugar maples, which set New England's fall foliage apart from the crowd. From mid-September through Columbus Day weekend, be prepared to slow down and take it easy on the roads as the so-called "leaf-peepers" drive like grandmothers. If you don't want to face a lot of No Vacancy signs, book your fall weekend accommodations as far in advance as possible, since throughout New England autumn ranks as the year's busiest season for motels and inns.

Crawford Notch offers good **day-hikes** to various waterfalls and vantage points such as **Frankenstein Cliff**, named for an artist whose work helped popularize the White Mountains, and 200-foot **Arethusa Falls**, the state's highest waterfall. During high spring runoff or after storms, Arethusa and nearby Ripley Falls on Avalanche Brook are among New Hampshire's most dramatic sights. **Camping** is available at the state-run **Dry River Campground** (mid-May to mid-Oct; $12), a primitive first-come-first-served, tent-only facility opposite the trailheads to both Frankenstein Cliff and Arethusa Falls, or along the Saco River at the private wilderness campground affiliated with the **Carter Notch General Store** (May-Oct.; 603/374-2779; $15-18). A modest step up from tents is the $15-a-night **AMC Crawford Hostel** (603/466-2727), whose large, spartan-but-heated bunkrooms, fee showers, and self-service kitchen are open year-round beside US-302. **Information** about trails in the area may be found at the hostel, along with some minor supplies, although **Pinkham Notch Camp** is still the overall best resource for hikers in the region.

North of Crawford Notch the highway joins the Ammonoosuc River headwaters as they flow toward the Connecticut River, passing **Bretton Woods** and the access road for the Mount Washington Cog Railway. The giant **Mount Washington Hotel** (800/258-0330) dominates the surrounding plain, its Vic-

Besides factory outlet stores, North Conway is also home to New Hampshire's most popular scenic **railroad,** running steam engines in summer and during the "Fall Color" season. Call 603/356-5251 or 800/232-5251 for schedules and fares.

Parking along New Hampshire highways is illegal, so don't be tempted to leave your car beside the road while you take a hike up that nearby hill—you may return to find it's been towed to some town 20 miles away.

Built in 1869, the **Mount Washington Cog Railway** has a maximum grade of 37.5%, surpassed by only one other nonfunicular railway in the world, in the Swiss Alps. Burning a ton of coal with each trip, the cinder-spewing engines take over an hour to ratchet up the three-mile track. Trips run from mid-May to mid-Oct. and cost $35; phone 603/846-5404 or 800/922-8825 for further information.

HIGH MOUNTAIN HUTS AND LODGES

From Mount Greylock, Massachusetts' highest peak, to Maine's Acadia National Park, the Appalachian Mountain Club maintains trails; operates a network of accommodations; sponsors educational programs; publishes maps and guides for hikers, canoeists, and kayakers; and in general has made itself synonymous with backcountry recreation in New England for well over a century. Many of their overnight properties are lean-tos and tent platforms, but some, like the High Mountain Huts, are complete mountaintop hostels. Eight staffed alpine cabins are strung out roughly a day's hike apart along the Appalachian Trail between Lonesome Lake, west of Franconia Notch, and Carter Notch, east of Hwy-16. Several are easily accessible, but others are a strenuous hike from the nearest trailhead; some are below tree line, while others lie well up in the clouds. All offer bunkrooms, cold-water bathrooms, and two hot meals a day during their full-service periods. None have heat or showers. Most are open only during the summer months, but two are open on a self-service basis year-round. Adult rates run from $15 (winter, self-serve) to $62 per person (Saturdays and August, including breakfast and dinner), although package stays and member discounts are available. Despite their price, the huts require reservations months in advance (603/466-2727).

For detailed descriptions of the huts and their access routes, consult either the *AMC White Mountain Guide* or *High Huts of the White Mountains*, available from AMC Books (800/262-4455).

torian luxury no longer standing in such grand isolation below the peaks of the Presidentials now that a ski resort sits across the highway, and motels and condos squat around its skirts. Built at the turn of the century by Pennsylvania Railroad tycoon Joseph Stickney, Mount Washington Hotel received its most lasting recognition as host of the 1944 United Nations International Monetary Conference, the historic meeting of financiers from 44 nations that established the World Bank and pegged the price of gold to the U.S. dollar. Since it recognized the U.S. as the strongest postwar economy and chose the dollar as the global standard for trade, the conference was perhaps even more influential than military victory in guaranteeing the longevity of U.S. dominion over the postwar world. Wander around the hotel's public areas and enjoy the grandeur (or a meal or a drink), but room rates are definitely in the "if you have to ask you can't afford it" category.

Franconia

Between the junction of US-302 and US-3 at **Twin Mountain** and the merging of US-3 with I-93 above Franconia Notch, you'll find the aging face of the area's long association with tourism: a variety of motel courts and "housekeeping cottages" at least as old as you are. Despite their outward dowdiness, several make a virtue of the rustic, but given their prime location most are hardly the bargains you might hope for, with rates running $40-80 a night. More interesting and historic lodging may be had on a 200-acre working farm in Franconia (pop. 811), where since 1899 the friendly Sherburn family's **Pinestead Farm Lodge** has offered simple rooms and warm hospitality at reasonable rates ($30-40 with shared bath and kitchen; 603/823-8121).

Dating back to the same era is **The Homestead** ($50-80 double; 800/823-5564), a country inn just west of Franconia on Route 117 in **Sugar Hill**. The township is aptly named: the "sugarbush" (groves of sugar maples) on Hildex Maple Sugar Farm, also on Route 117, contribute their unforgettable essence to breakfasts at **Polly's Pancake Parlor**, located in the farm's thrice-expanded 1830 carriage shed (open weekends only April through mid-May and late Oct., daily otherwise). Warning: after trying real maple syrup, you may never be able to go back to Aunt Jemima's or Mrs. Butterworth's again.

Possibly the most famous farm in the vicinity is **The Frost Place** (Sat.-Sun. 1-5 PM Memorial Day-June, Wed.-Mon. 1-5 PM July-Columbus Day; $3) on Route 116 south of the Franconia village intersection. Besides displays of Robert Frost memorabilia from his 11-year residency here and the property's 1.5-mile Poetry Trail, there's a regular program of readings by the current poet-in-residence, and occasional live music.

Franconia Notch

Franconia Notch is the tourist Grand Central of the White Mountains, in part because of the accessibility offered by I-93, which barrels through here, passing some of the most scenic country in the interstate system. "The Old Man in the Mountain," the state's mascot to judge from the tourist brochures, is found here in the granite cliffs of the Notch, along with a host of other tourist attractions—an aerial tram, the state's own "little Grand Canyon," covered bridges, a water park, and a trading post with trained bears. The combined admission fees to these attractions will sorely test budgetary restraint. Weaving under the interstate like the opposite strand of a DNA double helix is US-3, the old route through the Notch lined with stores and motels whose tackiness belongs to such a bygone era, it's almost historic. Of course, nature upstages all the gift shops and game rooms and requires no admission fee; for **trail information** consult with the AMC staffer on duty at the Franconia Notch State Park's tents-only **Lafayette Campground** (mid-May to mid-Oct.; $14) near exit 2 of the Parkway.

Lincoln and North Woodstock

Tiny North Woodstock (pop. 700) is a good example of what White Mountains towns used to look like before vacation condos popped up like prairie dog colonies; neighboring Lincoln (pop. 1,229) is the portrait of "after." The former is a handful of

Among the peaks of the southern Presidential Range overlooking Crawford Notch is Mount Jackson, named for neither the seventh U.S. president, Andrew, nor for the Confederate general, Thomas "Stonewall," but for a former state geologist, Charles.

North of Bretton Woods, a turnoff for the National Forest's tiny Zealand Campground leads to the trailhead for **Zealand Notch**. The trail passes through what's considered New England's finest example of forest regeneration, an area recovered from devastating turn-of-the-century fires.

For additional lodging and dining suggestions along the north side of White Mountains National Forest, see the description of US-2 between Lancaster and Gorham on pages 395-396.

Take those moose crossing signs seriously—dozens of collisions occur annually, and you can bet a car won't fare too well if it hits an animal that weighs well over half a ton.

Technically speaking, the six-mile stretch of I-93 that passes through the narrowest part of Franconia Notch isn't interstate at all, but the so-called Franconia Notch Parkway. Although divided and with limited access, it's only a single lane in each direction.

Cyclists who aren't ready to tackle 4,040-foot Cannon Mountain on fat tires will appreciate the nine-mile paved bike path through Franconia Notch, from just north of Cannon south to the Flume Visitor Center. Basically downhill all the way, the path is free of both pedestrians (a hiking trail is parallel but totally separate) and 'bladers (discouraged, as the grade has too many steep spots to be safe for most skaters). Check ahead for bike availability if staying at a local inn, or rent from the folks at Cannon's aerial tram ($8 and hour or $25-29 a day, depending on style rented; includes helmet and lock).

mostly unpretentious businesses at the junction of US-3 and Route 112, while the latter seems to be nothing but a strip of ski-clothing stores, malls, and motels at the base of the Loon Mountain ski resort. When Loon's condo-covered foothills fill to capacity during fall and winter holidays, the weekend population can mushroom more than tenfold to over 30,000.

As a rule, the Granite State isn't known for offering outstanding dining, certainly not like the Green Mountain State next door, which gives Northern California a run for its money in the small-town nouvelle-cafe department. The Lincoln area is typical, with its choice of aprés-ski pub grub, local pizza-and-grinder parlors (submarine sandwiches are called "grinders" in this state), and family dining on "Yankee soul food" like turkey, prime rib, and spaghetti with meatballs. New Orleans chefs aren't exactly quaking in their toques over the competition from the high-toned inns up here, either, but if you can set aside visions of Emeril's and K-Paul's, it's quite possible to enjoy satisfying home-style cooking in casual surroundings. Lincoln's **Country Mile** (closed Wednesday) opposite the Millfront Marketplace, for example, serves a fine breakfast, with from-scratch pancakes and breads. **Peg's Restaurant** on the main drag in North Woodstock also offers a decent breakfast and lunch (daily to 4 PM), while **Frannie's Place**, on US-3 seven miles south of Route 112, is worth a detour, particularly on nights when they feature the "All-U-Can-Eat" fish fry. Other dining options are easily found all along Route 112 from North Woodstock to the Loon Mountain base lodge.

Accommodations also line Route 112 in Lincoln and US-3 in North Woodstock, just south of exit 1 on the Franconia Notch Parkway. The rates remind you that, fast food aside, the area is first and foremost a resort destination: even the oldest, most rustic motel courts begin at $35, and during the busiest holidays rates typically double. The only year-round bargain—for singletons especially—is the nearest local equivalent to a home hostel: **The Cascade Lodge** (603/745-2722) in North Woodstock next to the handsomely restored Woodstock Inn. Resembling an old rooming house with its simple bedrooms and small shared baths down the hall, the Cascade becomes most like a hostel in summer when single "thru hikers" coming down off the Appalachian Trail stop for a hot shower and dry bed. During the summer they're "stacked like cordwood" in the doubles and triples of the old house by the cheerful, chatty, and chain-smoking owner, Bill Robinson. Rates are $18.50 a person B&B, or $15 a person lodging only.

The **information center** next to the I-93 overpass on the west side of Lincoln offers plenty of brochures for area motels and B&Bs, and the chamber of commerce operates a free phone reservation service (800/227-4191).

Down to the River
Between Lincoln and the Connecticut River, our route follows a succession of small state roads—Route 112 west, Route 118 south, and Route 25A west again—through

GO WITH THE FLOW

One of the first things first-time visitors to New England notice is its compact size: a crow flying 100 miles from almost any treetop outside of Maine will end up in the next state, if not Canada. But map distances bear absolutely no relation to travel time, thanks to the mountain ranges pitched up across northern New England.

So if you're sitting in your motel room in New Hampshire or Vermont wondering how far to drive for dinner, look to towns north or south. As a rule these will share the same valley since the Taconic, Green, and White Mountains are generally aligned like compass needles. In contrast, that next town to the east or west may as well be on the opposite side of the state so far as convenience is concerned. Whether winding along erratic streambeds or stitching their ways up the sides of passes between high peaks, east-west roads tend to be a slow grind in even the best weather, truly as tortuous as the wiggling lines on the map suggest. Heavy vehicles, cautious drivers, and foul weather make the going doubly difficult. Keep this in mind as you consider outings and side trips or you, too, will learn to say, "You can't get there from here."

some very characteristic New Hampshire landscape. Instead of "shoppes" and "pubs," you'll pass snowmobile dealers and mobile homes, old pickup trucks and shingles slung below mailboxes advertising homemade maple products, roofing contractors, mechanics. Houses nestled among the hardwoods spend nearly half the year wearing their insulation on the outside, the brunt of winter kept at bay with plastic swaddling and huge piles of split cordwood ready to stoke the stoves. Leaving the steep slopes of the national forest, the route starts to level off among small farms and hamlets composed of little more than a church, some houses, and a place to drop off the mail.

A few miles west of the clearly signposted Appalachian Trail crossing, Route 25A passes the **Sugar House** at Mount Cube Farm. When the maple sap begins to run in early spring, this rudimentary wooden shed is transformed by the heady aroma of boiling syrup—a bright event in what is otherwise known as Mud Season. This rite of spring depends entirely upon the weather: warm days and cold nights keep the sap flowing, while too much cold or warmth shuts it off. Generally the sugar season lasts from mid-March through April. If you spot the steam from the evaporator, stop by for a sample or, come summer, enjoy a full breakfast of fresh pancakes swimming in that New England elixir (Thurs.-Sat., 4th of July weekend to Columbus Day weekend; 603/353-4709).

About 35 miles from Lincoln our route hits the banks of the Connecticut River in small **Orford**, turning south on scenic Route 10 to Hanover, 15 miles downstream.

If you spot some beefy guys in skirts heaving telephone poles around at the base of Loon Mountain, you've probably stumbled across Lincoln's annual Highland Games, held the third weekend of September. Fortunately you don't have to toss a caber or know how to skirl to take part in the festivities. For info and advance tickets, call 800/227-4191.

For some reason (unmarried couples traveling Dutch? a ploy to fool the computationally illiterate comparison shopper?) most lodgings in the White Mountains advertise rates on a per-person rather than per-room basis, even though the minimum rates are almost always for two people.

Join the Army, take home a missile: that Titan rocket in the middle of wide-spot-in-the-road Warren, on Route 118/25, is a keepsake from a local gent's career in the Army's Missile Command down in Redstone, Alabama.

Hanover

Dartmouth College is the principal resident of attractive little Hanover (pop. 9,212), and it shows. Even people who attended schools cloned from office parks recognize Baker Library's tall clock tower and Georgian brick symmetry as the visual expression of all that's collegiate. When school is in session the cafes hum with undergraduate discourse, the downtown teems with students, and a varsity air envelops the historic campus and its sturdy neighbors. Between terms, however, the town's metabolism drops toward hibernation levels—which means there's no line for espresso.

That there *is* espresso at all is attributable to the Ivy League influence, just like the local architecture, dress, and cultural diversions. Concerning the last, Dartmouth's **Hood Museum of Art** (603/646-2900; free) and **Hopkins Center** (603/646-2422 for schedule and tickets), both facing the south side of expansive Dartmouth Green, remain the uncontested local hotspots for fine art, performing arts, and film.

Resources to consider when planning your trip: the White Mountains Attractions Association (800/FIND MTS outside New Hampshire, or 603-745-8720); Chambers of Commerce Statewide Reservation Service (800/ENJOY NH); and Weekly NH Events (April-Aug. only; 800/258-3608).

A predominantly undergraduate student body and a state drinking age of 21 means that double tall cappuccinos and lattes have replaced yards of beer for the majority of Hanover's young scholars. Which is why the **Dirt Cowboy Cafe** at the head of S. Main Street is usually a live wire until their 2 AM closing, tendrils of cigarette smoke and conversation weaving amid the earnest note-takers and book-readers seated beneath the latest local artist's showing. If you prefer French Press over Krups Drip, **Rosy & Jeke's** is the coffeehouse for you, at the corner of Lebanon and College Streets at the rear of the eponymous clothing store; their mocha in particular is more European (bitter chocolate, not semisweet) than those offered by cafes bowing to the American sweet tooth. On the subject of sweet, **Chez Francoise**, behind S. Main's Shawmut Bank building, features truly exceptional French pastries and croissants at doughnut-shop prices.

Espresso, yes, and sandwiches too: across S. Main from the bank, **Peter Christian's Tavern** (daily to 11:30 PM) offers decent soup-salad-sandwich fare in a mellow, fraternity-free setting. If you prefer thick-crust pizzas and calzones garnished with everything from kielbasa and sauerkraut to pesto chicken, try **Foodee's** at 45 Lyme Road, a

The
Hanover Inn

New Hampshire-based chain whose local outlet is just north of town on Route 10 in that modern building next to the Exxon station. When it comes to Italian, though, the last best word on the subject is the menu at **Café Buon Gustaio**, 72 S. Main Street, whose cuisine earns top honors and commands top dollar for both preparation and presentation (Tues.-Sat. dinner only).

For accommodations around Hanover, there's the stately, Dartmouth-run **Hanover Inn** facing onto the Green (603/643-4300); for affordable rooms, however, look under West Lebanon and White River Junction, below.

Lebanon and West Lebanon

Three miles south of patrician Hanover is the commercial busybody of West Lebanon, with its shopping plazas, traffic tie-ups, and familiar fast-*everything* clustered around I-89's two local exits. Sitting rather quietly a couple of miles east is the historic heart of the township, Lebanon (pop. 12,183), with a town green so spacious it seems less the center than the city park at the edge. Near the northwest corner is the main commercial block, or what's left since the malls arrived. It's kept alive in part by a pair of establishments well worth the detour from Hanover or West Lebanon: **Sweet Tomatoes**, facing Coburn Park (lunch weekdays till 2 PM, dinner nightly from 5 PM), the ever-popular trattoria whose gourmet pasta and wood-fired pizza pull in crowds from miles around; and **The Bean Gallery** just opposite, a very shiny, black, smoke-free temple to art and espresso, open from very early to very late every day but Sunday.

Back along the bonny banks of the Connecticut River in West Lebanon are more restaurants of note, such as the **Bangkok Garden** Thai restaurant in the Kmart Plaza on Route 12A (lunch daily to 3 PM, dinner Mon.-Sat. from 5 PM), or **The Seven Barrels**, on the other side of both Route 12A and the I-89 overpass. One of the brewpubs on the region's growing list, the Seven Bs has a good line of beers and a liberal sampling of English pub grub—bubble and squeak, toad-in-the-hole, fish 'n' chips—along with some concessions to modern American palates, such as veggie burgers, buffalo wings, and pasta specials. Usually very crowded.

Also well worth a visit is the **Four Aces Diner**, on Route 4 just uphill from the bridge to Vermont, with very good from-scratch diner fare at down-to-earth prices (Sun.-Mon. to 3 PM, Tues.-Wed. to 8 PM, Thurs.-Sat. to 9 PM). The classic 1950s **Worcester** diner, built into the side of a red clapboard mill, does all its own baking and has a soda fountain, too.

With I-89 passing through the town and I-91 just across the river in Vermont, there are several budget and chain **motels** on both sides of the Connecticut. Take your pick of **Radisson, Super 8, HoJo's, Comfort, Days,** and **Holiday Inn** between I-91's exit 11, just north of the I-89 interchange in Vermont, and I-89's exit 18 (Route 120) in Lebanon.

With the Dartmouth Outing Club responsible for maintaining hundreds of miles of trails, including over 75 miles of the Appalachian Trail, a part of which runs right through the campus, it's no surprise that Hanover is something of a hiking center, too. Various hiking maps and guides are available from the Outing Club's office in Robinson Hall (603/646-2428) and the Dartmouth Bookstore on S. Main Street.

A few years after New Hampshire and the other 12 American colonies began their revolt against mother England, Hanover and a handful of neighboring towns divorced themselves from the state to join Vermont, but the short-lived association fell apart in 1782, leaving the towns independent for four years before they reunited with New Hampshire.

In the basement of Baker Library is a set of frescoes by **José Clemente Orozco:** "An Epic of American Civilization," painted 1932-34. These dramatic murals are the Mexican artist's only commissioned work in the U.S.

ACROSS VERMONT

Vermont is quintessential New England: picturesque villages still served by cluttered country stores, small farms nestled among the granite ridges of the Green Mountains, and needle-sharp white church spires rising above forests ablaze with autumn colors. Precocious from birth—its constitution was the first in the U.S. to prohibit slavery and establish public schools—Vermont is known for such a strong liberal tradition that even the state's Republicans are moderates.

Before Vermont joined the U.S. in 1791 as the 14th state, it spent 14 years as the independent Republic of New Connecticut. Its name comes from the French verd mont, and appeared on maps as early as 1780.

Vermont is the only state currently represented by an Independent in Congress: Bernie Sanders, formerly the Socialist mayor of Burlington, Vermont's largest city.

From the Connecticut River, the route follows the contours of the land, keeping to the valleys between the steep surrounding ridges that carry the Appalachian Trail ever southward, or tagging along fast-running mountain streams that cut east-west. Besides the scenery, highlights include plenty of charming little towns, most of which support the casual restaurant and cafe whose inspired New American cuisine has made Vermont a realm in which Portobello mushrooms, balsamic vinegar, and tiramisu are, if not basic currency, at least fairly common coin.

White River Junction

Turn-of-the-century White River Junction (pop. 2,582) used to echo with the sounds of some 50 trains a day beating their metallic castanets over five separate rail lines. The

demise of the railroads and arrival of the interstate cloverleaf on the outskirts effectively mothballed the downtown area, but like good vintage clothing, the historic center has been rediscovered by an art-smart crowd that doesn't mind the holes and missing buttons. Exclusive galleries and expensive boutiques aren't invading the old brick storefronts around the tracks; on the contrary, the town looks like it's still expecting the New Deal to come pay a visit. However, **River City Arts** (802/296-2505) is able to keep the **Briggs Opera House** alive with music and theater, and the ever-changing menu of **Itas'ca** at the corner of North and South Main will typically include grilled fish, free-range chicken, soba noodles, and organic carrot juice (Tues.-Sat.,

---

FRESH BEER HERE

Living in the Upper Valley of the Connecticut River must be thirsty work. Or folks up here have a particularly well-developed appreciation for the finer beers in life. Whatever the reason, several microbreweries and brewpubs flourish within a very small radius of White River Junction.

The Seven Barrels lies on Hwy-12A beside the I-89 overpass in West Lebanon, New Hampshire. This brewpub offers a good line of beers—British bitter, I.P.A., oatmeal stout, various seasonals—a liberal sampling of English pub grub—bubble and squeak, toad-in-the-hole, fish 'n' chips—and some concessions to modern American palates—veggie burgers, buffalo wings, pasta specials. Usually very crowded.

Catamount Brewing Company offers tours and tastings of their English-style ales and seasonal brews at 58 S. Main Street, in White River Junction.

Mountain Brewers has a taproom (daily until 6 PM) at the junction of US-4 and Hwy-100A, west of Woodstock, Vermont, where you can try the state's most popular microbrew, Long Trail Ale. Their flagship ale is named after the route that inspired the Appalachian Trail: the 85-year-old Long Trail, a 255-mile footpath running along the spine of the Green Mountains from Massachusetts to Canada. They also have seasonals, stout, even a kölsch—a light, wheaty ale, perfect for quenching summer thirst.

---

closed 2:30-5 PM). Thirsty microbrew aficionados also generally admire the ales and lagers at the small **Catamount Brewing Company** at 58 S. Main Street.

If you're looking for lodging with more character than that of the chain motels along the interstates, consider downtown's **Hotel Coolidge** (800/622-1124; $34 double with shared shower, $55 private). Despite a passing resemblance to something from *Barton Fink*, it's a good value, and ripe with local lore. If you prefer luxurious country inns and B&Bs, continue to Woodstock for the largest selection in a small area.

Quechee and Woodstock

After White River Junction the route along US-4 enters the valley of the Ottauquechee River (auto-kwee-chee) in Quechee, a second-home community to country-clubbing executives from Connecticut and Boston. You'll cross **Quechee Gorge** almost without warning, but adjacent parking gives you a chance to take a second look at the dramatic little canyon or to stretch your legs along the rimside hiking trails before continuing the drive upstream.

"The good people of Woodstock have less incentive than others to yearn for heaven," said a 19th-century resident. It's a sentiment readily echoed today. Since its settlement in the 1760s, Woodstock (pop. 3,212) has become an exceedingly well-pre-

About 20 miles up the White River valley on Route 14 is the township of South Royalton, birthplace in 1805 of Mormon founder **Joseph Smith.** A huge solid granite monument and visitor center (daily 9 AM-5 PM) mark the spot, along with about 80,000 lights between Thanksgiving and Christmas.

Vermont has a statewide system of color-coded roadside commercial signage that makes it easy to find B&Bs and other services off the main roads, although the sign space is paid for and therefore shouldn't be mistaken for a comprehensive guide to what's out there.

served example of small-town New England, its classic village green, for example, still ringed with the tidy federal-style homes built by wealthy professionals of the newborn American republic. Now the historic village is home to wealthy retirees and inheritors, old money whose presence affords niceties like well-stocked wine racks at the general store, excellent performing arts at the Town Hall Theater, and the wherewithal to refuse any compromising commercial development. Having financially generous, conservation-minded residents like Laurance Rockefeller around hasn't hurt, either. To put it mildly, expansion of the tax base is *not* a pressing issue for this community.

Notice, as you approach Woodstock Village Green, that there are no overhead power lines on the two main downtown streets, Central and Elm. Laurance Rockefeller paid to have the lines buried back in 1973.

During summer and fall, walking tours are an excellent way to take stock of the town's history and architecture; call or visit the **Information Booth** (802/457-1042) on the Green for a schedule. Hiking trails lead up both the summits overlooking the town. A community blackboard at the corner of Central and Elm, a.k.a. the Town Crier, lists local events and activities all year.

For a long-distance "leaf-peepers" update on the progress of Vermont foliage, call the state's fall foliage hotline (24-hour recording, Sept.-Oct. only): 802/828-3239.

If you've admired the rolling fields and weathered wooden fences, savored the local apples and sharp cheddar, enjoyed the scent of mown hay or boiling maple sap, you'll appreciate an even closer look at New England's farms with a visit to the **Billings Farm & Museum**, on Route 12 north of the village (daily 10 AM-5 PM May-Oct., weekends 10 AM-4 PM Nov.-Dec. and Dec. 26-31; 802/457-2355; $6). Frederick Billings, better known as the builder of the Northern Pacific Railroad, began this working dairy farm in the late 19th century. Its restored farmhouse and huge barns illustrate the rural life in galleries, demonstrations, and hands-on activities; you can practice milking cows before entering that annual hand-milking contest held the second weekend of June.

If you prefer undomesticated nature, head up Church Hill Road on the west side of the Green to the **Vermont Institute of Natural Science** (daily 10 AM-4 PM except Sunday Nov.-April; 802/457-2779; $5). The institute devotes itself to environmental education and animal rehabilitation, but for casual visitors the highlight of the 77-acre nature preserve is the self-guiding trail through the **Raptor Center**, a set of 26 outdoor habitats for hawks, eagles, owls, and other birds of prey, all permanent convalescents from hunting or accidental injuries.

Windsor covered bridge

Hungry travelers will find plenty of choices around town, although some eateries assume you have a private endowment. The $8 burgers at downtown **Bentley's**, for example, are a tad high-priced, and garnishing a slab of grilled fish with a couple of carambola slices, a single steamed artichoke leaf, and a cold asparagus spear raises questions about whether there's a fashion photographer or chef in the kitchen. But consider the accompaniments: Vermont microbrews, Oriental carpets, Victorian sofas, and a casual, cheerful, talkative crowd. If you'd pay as much for good vibes as you tip for good service, it's worth a visit. East of the Green on Central Street is a rare alternative to the state's predominant American and continental fare: the **Star of India**, serving Northern Indian cuisine daily (closed 3-5 PM). For simple—or not-so-simple—deli items, try either **The Village Butcher**, across Elm from Bentley's, or Central Street's natural foods market **18 Carrots**, whose fresh, softball-sized muffins are tasty bargains. Several other cafes offer sweet treats and all the flavored cappuccino you could want, along with light meals; try the **Caffe Mill** on Central Street beside swift little Kedron Brook, and **Dunham Hill Bakery**, also on Central.

Accommodations run the gamut from $40 motels to $80 B&Bs to $200-a-night inns. Expect stiff increases during high season, which in Woodstock is most of summer and fall, along with the winter holidays. Budget lodgings are found outside the village or in neighboring towns: around the huge Killington ski area about 20 miles west on US-4, for example, summer is considered low season, so prices are set accordingly. Otherwise, the modest **Braeside Motel** (802/457-1366 or 800/303-1366 inside Vermont; $48-88 double) on the eastern outskirts of town is about as budget-friendly as you're going to get.

The local **chamber of commerce** (802/457-3555) can supply a directory of area lodgings in advance or in summer from their booth on the Green.

Bridgewater

Although the building still stands, the large woolen mill in Bridgewater (pop. 895) is long gone, the water-powered turbines and textile machines replaced by small shops selling a typically Vermont mix of antiques and ski apparel, new-age books, and gift-packaged Vermont foods. By the map, this tiny town stretched along the banks of the Ottauquechee seems well on the way to the middle of nowhere, but that's what lures visitors to most of the state: the fact that so much of it seems to have contentedly hung back with Rip Van Winkle and missed out on the neon competition for tackiest franchise mall. That said, Bridgewater *is* a gateway to one of the state's most important Somewheres: the ski resorts of central Vermont.

Upstream from the old mill lies another destination in its own right: the **Bridgewater Village Diner** (daily to 10 PM). Although not the prefab stainless steel variety, the BVD's a true diner in menu, price, and clientele. If pot roasts, chopped sirloin, piping-hot chowder, and breakfast anytime aren't reason enough to take a seat at the counter, any one of the half-dozen homemade pies should be. You won't find a better place in the state to listen to Vermont accents, either.

Vermont holds over a hundred **covered bridges,** several good examples of which are to be seen between Quechee and Bridgewater. Look for the 1836 Taftsville bridge west of Quechee, the Middle bridge in Woodstock, and the 1877 Lincoln bridge west of Woodstock. The nation's longest covered bridge crosses the Connecticut River at Windsor, about 15 miles southeast of Woodstock, with a 460-foot span built in 1866.

If you're in the area around mid-June, check out the **Quechee Hot Air Balloon Festival,** held over Father's Day weekend.

A jot west on US-4 at **Bridgewater Corners**, the route turns south on Route 100A toward Ludlow. The junction is just beside **Mountain Brewers**, whose taproom (open daily until 6 PM) is worth a visit if you haven't yet tried the state's most popular microbrew. Their flagship Long Trail Ale is named after the route that inspired the Appalachian Trail: the 85-year-old Long Trail, a 255-mile footpath running along the spine of the Green Mountains from Massachusetts to Canada.

Plymouth

Running a twisty seven miles south from Bridgewater, 100A passes through beautiful scenery and Plymouth Notch, birthplace of Calvin Coolidge, the only U.S. president born on the 4th of July. The small hilltop clutch of buildings is so little changed by this century, it's a wonder there aren't horses with carriages parked behind the visitor center instead of Subarus. Calvin's home (the "Coolidge Homestead"), his father's general store (named for a later owner, Florence Cilley), and his son's cheese factory are three of the 10 buildings open to the public (daily 9:30 AM-5:30 PM, Memorial Day to mid-Oct; $4; cheese factory open year-round, free), along with a mile-long meadow nature trail offering fine views of the Notch and its surroundings. The Coolidge Homestead is restored to its 1923 appearance when Col. John Coolidge administered the oath of office to his vacationing son, the vice-president, after President Harding died unexpectedly in San Francisco.

If you're looking for accommodations out where there are more stars than streetlights, try the **Salt Ash Inn** (doubles $75-150; 800/258-7258), an 1830s stagecoach stop at the junction of Routes 100A and 100 in Plymouth Union. Although Woodstock, Killington, and Ludlow are all within scenic 10- to 15-mile drives, surrounding mountains keep the twin notions of towns and business a world away. Alternatively, for a true night under the Milky Way, pitch your tent in Coolidge State Park (late May-early Oct.; $10) off Route 100A in Plymouth.

Route 100

Known as the "Skiers' Highway," serpentine Route 100 manages to pass the base of nearly every major ski resort in Vermont. Joining it midway through the state, our route follows a favorite stretch for cyclists, a mostly level dozen miles through the small farms (some of which sell maple syrup in spring) and posh-looking lakeside resorts of the Black River valley. Route 100 ends up in **Ludlow**, at the foot of Okemo (oh-KEY-mo) Mountain. Any doubts that skiing is the cash cow of the state's most lucrative industry—tourism—are quickly dispelled by just one look at the wall-to-wall inns, sportswear shops, vacation real estate offices, and restaurants along Ludlow's main drag. The town's star attraction is that 3,300-foot peak with its hundreds of acres of ski trails serviced by state-of-the-art *everything*, although seven other ski areas cluster like the Pleiades within a 25-mile radius.

During November and December hikers should be especially alert, as these months are hunting season throughout New England. Most hunters know to stay away from the most popular hiking areas, and are ready to head home by the time you finish breakfast, anyway, but it doesn't hurt to wear bright clothing and avoid practicing your bushwhacking during these months.

A handful of B&Bs in towns along Route 2 are represented by The American Country Collection reservation service (Mon.-Fri. 10 AM-5 PM; 518/439-7001; $10 reservation fee). Write to 4 Greenwood Lane, Delmar, NY 12054 for more information.

When garnished with Vermont-made Ben & Jerry's, apple pie à la mode is certainly nothing to sneer at, but if you really want to try apple pie the Vermont way, ask for a slab of sharp cheddar on the side instead of ice cream.

Between the end of ski season and the beginning of fall foliage, Ludlow's pulse nearly flatlines. Flocks of elderly, low-tipping Floridians migrate to the vast strings of condos around Okemo, if anything adding to the summer slowdown. In recent years mountain bikers and inn-to-inn cyclists have become a source of some life, but overall Ludlow, like many other Vermont ski towns, spends the warm months convalescing.

Fortunately yuppie recreation requires yuppie food, so when it comes time to do your pre-ride carbo-loading or aprés-ski whistle-wetting, you won't have to resort to a hamburger that's like the other billions and billions served. **Nikki's,** in the shopping plaza next to Okemo's access road, is your best bet for creative continental cuisine—from the pizza del mar appetizer to the no-holds-barred white chocolate mousse. Good wine list, too. If Momma Valenti's homemade lasagna or parmigiana is more your speed, continue south to the traffic light downtown and let her son welcome you into **Valenti's,** on the corner. Or if you're looking for a decent inexpensive breakfast, try **The Hatchery** across the street.

Proctorsville, five miles south of Ludlow on Routes 103 and 131, would be worth a detour if only to take a breath inside the **Baba á Louis Bakery** in the three-story frame building in the center of town. Of course you needn't settle for just the aroma: their loaves of long sourdough, anadama, fruit-nut, cheese-herb, whole wheat, and half-a-dozen other varieties are among the best fresh breads you'll find between Paris and San Francisco. Fine croissants, eclairs, cookies, and granola, too, all at exceptionally good prices. For a complete picnic, step into **Singleton's** market west of the bakery for deli meats and Vermont cheeses, or return to Route 103 and check out the high-quality **Black River Produce** store on the south side of the tracks.

Accommodations run mostly on the flashy side with either antique-filled Victorian inns or "modern rustic" motels and chalets, but there's also the very reasonable **HI-AYH Trojan Horse Hostel** (802/228-5244; $15-20 per person; closed April), with its shared or private rooms in a converted barn beside Route 100 less than a half-mile south of the main street. (They offer canoe rentals in season, too.) Otherwise, expect to shell out anywhere from a summertime low of around $50 (Best Western, 802/228-8188; The Mill Hotel, 800/335-MILL; or Whitney Brook B&B in Proctorsville, 802/226-7460) to a fall and winter weekend high of over $200 (The Andrie Rose Inn, 800/223-4846; or The Governor's Inn, 800/GOVERNOR).

Turning south out of Ludlow opposite the Black River Brewing Company (not a genuine brewpub, but it does offer many fine New England beers), Route 100 wanders along the eastern edge of the Green Mountains' high spine through one small town after another. With the exception of well-to-do **Weston,** a small place that makes a big business out of its country stores, skiing is clearly the name of the

President Coolidge recollected in his autobiography ". . . No doubt there have been kings who have participated in the induction of their sons into their office, but in republics where the succession comes by election I do not know of any other case in history where a father has administered to his son the qualifying oath of office. . . . It seemed a simple and natural thing to do at the time." His father, when later asked how he knew he could administer the oath, replied, "I didn't know I couldn't."

"Silent Cal" Coolidge was famous—perhaps unjustly—for being a man of few words. A White House dinner guest is said to have bet that she could make the president address her with at least three words; when confronted with this challenge, Coolidge replied, "You lost."

Okemo and its central Vermont sisters are best for intermediate skiers; while each has a few black diamond trails—Killington more than just a few, if you don't mind sharing them with the state of New Jersey on weekends—experts looking for more than a couple hours of challenging downhill terrain will get more for the price of their lift ticket among the half-dozen ski areas around Stowe and Waterbury, a couple hours farther north, where Route 100 crosses US-2 and I-89.

Buffalo Brook, which drains into Lake Echo north of Ludlow, was for almost 30 years the site of a gold-mining operation in the mid-19th century.

If your supply of driving music is getting stale, visit the gift shop at the **Weston Priory,** three miles north of town, and pick up a tape of something truly inspirational. To hear the resident Benedictine monks live, consult the bulletin board by the parking lot for a schedule of their public devotional services. From the Route 100/155 junction, take Route 155 north; the priory's driveway is the first left.

game for most of them: **Londonderry,** below Big Bromley; **Jamaica,** near Stratton Mountain; and **West Dover,** sandwiched between the impressive Mount Snow/Haystack complex. All the ski areas, of course, bubble with the usual superlatives about snowmaking, grooming, and fast chairlifts, while the towns boast colonial frame houses, snowboard shops, cafes, and country inns with discreet hand-carved wooden signs out front. Notice the details of the Vermont landscape: Saabs or pickups in the driveways, cupolas and weathervanes on the barn roofs, and expensive Kubota tractors for mowing the fields that, while no longer belonging to working farms, are groomed to postcard perfection.

Wilmington and Route 9

Route 100 leaves its panoramic view of Mount Snow as it descends into Wilmington (pop. 1,968), another picturesque village of 18th- and 19th-century shops and houses built along the Deerfield River. The chamber of commerce is named after the local ski resort rather than the town, so you know who pays the bills around here. Nevertheless, summers see a fair bit of activity in the galleries and antique shops, along with the occasional bus tour stopping by on its way to the North River Winery down in **Jacksonville,** seven miles farther south on Route 100. For classical music lovers, the **Marlboro Music Festival** marks summer's zenith at Marlboro College, Marlboro, a dozen miles east toward Brattleboro on Route 9. Between mid-July and mid-August several score of the world's finest classical musicians perform here in one of the nation's most distinguished annual chamber music series (for schedule and ticket info, call 802/254-2394).

Heading westward on Route 9 to Bennington, the route crosses the diffuse southern edge of the Green Mountains, which also means it crosses the path of the Appalachian Trail, the only place in Vermont where our route does so. Unlike the well-defined ridges in the northern part of the range, the southern Greens spread out over a fairly wide area, and roadless tracts between the Big Bromley ski area and the Massachusetts state line are quite visible as large blank spots on the map. **Woodford State Park** on Route 9 is a good base for hikes into these areas, either along the AT or tributary trails; besides camping at the park (late May-early Oct.; $12-16), there's a seasonal HI-AYH hostel at Prospect Ski Mountain's Greenwood Lodge (late May-late Oct.; 802/442-2547; $16 per person), about three miles farther west on Route 9. An excellent source of **hiking information** is the Green Mountain Club; their *Day Hiker's Guide to Vermont* and *Guide Book of the Long Trail* are both available direct from the GMC (RR 1 Box 650, Route 100, Waterbury Center, VT 05677; 802/244-7037) or from the local bookshops in Bennington and Wilmington.

Bennington

By far the largest town yet encountered on our route, Bennington (pop. 16,451) is a bustling little manufacturing and commercial center, named for a significant battlefield victory against the British-paid Hessians during the American Revolution, a sweet morale-booster that contributed to the defeat of Gen. "Gentleman Johnny" Burgoyne's army of Redcoats at Saratoga soon after. In the subsequent centuries Bennington's name has become synonymous with art: the decorative arts of the antebellum **United States Pottery Company**; the liberal arts of **Bennington College**, one of the nation's most expensive and exclusive private colleges; and the folk art of Mary Robertson "**Grandma**" **Moses**. The largest public collection of Moses's beguiling work is on display in **The Bennington Museum** (daily 9 AM-5 PM; $5), whose white-columned ivy-covered edifice is found on West Main Street in the graceful old part of town, near the 306-foot obelisk commemorating that 1777 victory (elevator to observation room, mid-April to Nov. 1).

If anyone starts erecting monuments to good dining instead of to old wars, this town would have another tower of stone beside the **Blue Benn Diner**, on US-7 north of downtown. The fact that it's a vintage 1940s Silk City certainly gives this cozy nonsmoking joint character, but what earns the seven-days-a-week loyalty of its patrons is the top-notch short-order cooking: from baked meatloaf and roast pork to broccoli stir-fry and multigrain pancakes, it's good, it's cheap, and it's served up so fast you'll barely have time to choose between Sinatra or Soundgarden on the wall-box juke at your table. The enchiladas are a match for any in San Antonio, although New Englanders still haven't gotten the hang of eating them for breakfast.

As an alternative to the Blue Benn's enamelled porcelain and dark varnished wood, try the **Brasserie**, in the Bennington Potters Yard. Excellent, creative, and healthful cuisine is accompanied by decent wines and fine desserts at reasonable prices.

Most of Bennington's **accommodations** are strung along Route 7A to the north and Route 7 to the south of downtown, all local names but for the Ramada and Best Western inns found on 7A. If you are in the market for a distinctive B&B, push on the dozen miles to Williamstown (covered under Massachusetts, below).

If you're fond of sharp cheddar, consider taking a particularly scenic loop south from Ludlow on Routes 103 and 35 or east from Londonderry via Routes 11 and 121 to historic little **Grafton,** arguably the prettiest town in Vermont. The **Covered Bridge Cheddar Cheese Factory** (gift shop, free tours) south of town makes some of the sharpest cheddar you'll ever taste. If you don't need tidy gift-wrapable blocks, ask in the Village Store for their "random cuts," irregular chunks sold for a steep discount.

Vermont has been synonymous with skiing since the beginning of the sport, with credit for both the first ski tow and first chairlift in the United States. Less well known is the state's love of tennis: there are more courts per capita here than anywhere else in the nation.

It ain't Texas, or even Cincinnati, but chili fans who find themselves near Mount Snow on the second Saturday of each August should be sure to drop in on the annual **Vermont State Chili Cookoff** (802/464-3333 for details).

Brigham Young, the man who led the Mormon exodus to Utah, was born in Whitingham, less than 10 miles south of Wilmington on Route 100. There's a small commemorative monument and picnic area on the Town Hall Common.

ACROSS MASSACHUSETTS

Hemmed in by the daunting topography of its surrounding mountains, Western Massachusetts is a world apart, blessed with an easygoing small-town character so dissimilar from that of the metropolitan seacoast that locals compare it to southern Vermont, or upstate New York, or anything, in fact, but Massachusetts. Given Boston's perennial neglect of the region, constituents often seem to wish it *were* another state.

Berkshire County might find the political clout so long sought if representation was based on culture and the social register rather than population.

By the early 19th century, farmland had replaced 75% of Berkshire County's forests. Now forests have reclaimed that 75% and more, but innumerable drystone walls serve as reminders of the once vast cultivated fields.

The region has been a magnet for performing arts and artists for over 150 years, and a playground for the rich and famous for over a century. To better sample this heritage and the associated culinary attractions, our route busies itself with the more populous valley floor. But remember, it never takes more than a few strategic turns to find splendidly rural backroads through woods as deep and undisturbed as those enjoyed by hikers along the Appalachian Trail.

Williamstown

To the visitor it appears as if stately Williamstown (pop. 8,220) is simply a nickname for the immaculate and graceful campus of Williams College—even the main commercial block is basically the corridor between dorms and gym. From their common 18th-century benefactor, Ephraim Williams, to the large number of alumni who return in their retirement, "Billsville" and its college are nearly inseparable. The town-gown symbiosis has spawned an enviable array of visual, performing, and edible arts, yet fresh contingents of ingenuous youth keep all the wealth and refinement from becoming too cloying.

Two of the town's crown jewels are the **Clark Art Institute** on South Street (Tues.-Sun. 10 AM-5 PM; free) and the **Williams College Museum of Art** (Tues.-Sat. 10 AM-5 PM, Sunday 1-5 PM; free) on Main Street opposite Memorial

Winslow Homer's Saco Bay is part of the collection at the Clark Art Institute.

Chapel, that Westminster Abbey knock-off. They make an outstanding pair: the Clark with its extraordinary collection of Impressionist paintings, including over 30 Renoirs; and the WCMA with its emphasis on changing exhibits of contemporary and non-Western art, set within gallery spaces that are themselves artfully conceived.

Another singular collection is stashed away on the second floor of Stetson Hall, the ivy-covered red brick building furthest behind Memorial Chapel's gothic bulk. If you can find it, the **Chapin Library of Rare Books** (Mon.-Fri. 9 AM-noon, 1-5 PM; free) will reward you with a display of all of our nation's important birth certificates: the Declaration of Independence, the Articles of Confederation, an annotated draft of the Constitution, George Washington's copy of the Federalist Papers, and two early versions of the Bill of Rights (with 17 and 12 amendments, respectively).

High-toned continental dining suitable for starched alumni banquets abounds in Williamstown, but if you're looking for truly fresh, interesting food, skip the inns and go to the **Cobble Cafe** on Spring Street (breakfast daily, lunch Mon.-Sat., dinner Tues.-Sat.), a place whose menu, ambience, and wine list will give San Franciscans déjà vu. A late-night dessert-and-drinks menu accommodates evening patrons of summer's annual **Williamstown Theatre Festival** (413/597-3399 for schedule) as well as anyone looking for some of the best not-too-sweet-or-gooey pecan pie money can buy. Next door, the **Clarksburg Bread Co.** (closed Sun.-Mon.) serves up soups, sandwiches, and a wealth of delicious baked goods until 4 PM. The hands-down best pizza joint is takeout-only **Hot Tomatoes** on Water Street, but in mild weather the nearby streamside park is well suited to lolling picnickers if you don't fancy perfuming your car with pesto or spicy sausage.

Wild Oats, the food co-op in the Colonial Shopping Center east of town on Hwy-2 (daily till 6 PM, Thursday till 8 PM), has a big selection of bulk items that will appeal to campers and hikers. Incidentally, the Appalachian Trail crosses Hwy-2 just 1.5 miles east of Wild Oats' front door.

A drive along Main Street (Hwy-2) will give you a view of most of Williamstown's accommodations, from the on-campus **Williams Inn** (413/458-9371) to the small motels out on the eastern edge of town. For a real treat consider **Field Farm** ($90 double, no credit cards; 413/298-3239) on Sloan Road in South Williamstown, five miles south along either Hwy-7 or scenic Water Street (Hwy-43). Occupying the 254-acre former estate of Pacific Northwest lumber tycoon

Singer sewing machine heir Robert Sterling Clark's huge art collection ended up in Williamstown in part because of the Cold War. In the late 1940s and early 1950s, the threat of a Russian nuclear attack seemed real enough that distance from likely bomb targets was a critical factor in choosing a permanent repository.

Lawrence Bloedel, the main house, designed in 1948, is a striking example of American modern architecture. If you have any love of Frank Lloyd Wright or Charles and Ray Eames, you'll be delighted by this live-in museum of contemporary design, with its huge picture windows, proto-Scandinavian furniture, and Lucite fixtures and walls adorned with selections from Bloedel's extensive 20th-century art collection, plus tennis courts, a swimming pool, nature trails, and breathtaking views of Mount Greylock across the valley.

Additional **information** is available from the Board of Trade's Information Booth at the center of town, or by picking up the latest copy of the free *Guide to Williamstown* from local shop and restaurant vestibules.

Mount Greylock

Massachusetts' tallest peak is the centerpiece of 12,500-acre **Mount Greylock State Reservation**, one of the state's largest and most popular possessions. Over 50 miles of trails, including some thigh-burning mountain-bike routes, wander along the re-

---

YE OLDE GENTRIFICATION

From central Vermont to northwest Connecticut you'll occasionally run across resentment toward second-home owners who, popular wisdom suggests, have invaded from out of state, buying up old farms or building expensive new houses on what was once pristine forest or prime grazing land, generally driving up property values and driving out the locals. These invading aliens—typically New Yorkers, or "212s" in the hip parlance of area codes, but Bostonians and Connecticut suburbanites, too—are mocked for their brazen self-importance, their stuffy contempt for small-town ways, their cravings for their hometown newspapers and foodstuffs. To hear waitresses and barflies kvetch about it, you'd think the problem is recent, but in fact it's almost as old as the hills. As far back as the 1850s, after the more arable Ohio Valley had been opened up to homesteading by improved transportation and Indian genocide, New Yorkers and Bostonians were buying up old country farmsteads abandoned by the westward migration. Like their modern successors, those early yuppies fixed up the old houses and embraced the restorative powers of nature. Perhaps some even raised a few local eyebrows with odd fad diets—eating Sylvester Graham's digestive crackers, for example, made from coarse-ground whole wheat—and unholy devotion to new lifestyle gurus like Henry David Thoreau.

The intervening years haven't diminished the importance of the development debate; they merely remind each wave of settlers that it's ingenuous to pretend they can enter the promised land and slam the gate behind themselves. Pressures to develop will continue, too, so long as it's more profitable to grow houses than food, or until self-interest succeeds in capturing all the rural peace and quiet within split-rail fences and picture-window frames.

forested slopes, most of which were heavily logged for fuel and pulp back in the 19th century. Rock ledges provide great views of the Hoosic River valley to the east and the Housatonic valley to the south, when the namesake mists aren't keeping the 3,491-foot summit wadded up in a damp ball of dingy cotton. During warm months access is a cinch: century-old Notch Road snakes its way up through the birch and spruce from Hwy-2 on the north side, while Rockwell Road ascends from Hwy-7 along the flanks of Greylock's southern neighbors. Combine these roads' 17 miles and you'll enjoy the most scenic driveable mountain ascent in New England, though keep in mind that both roads are narrow and steep, contoured with frost-heaves, enlivened by occasional hairpin turns, and—especially at dusk—prone to wandering wildlife. If you want to see over the forest and park without your car, climb the 105-foot **War Memorial Tower** on the summit. If the weather is good, you'll have a panorama from New Hampshire to Connecticut.

A stone's throw from the granite tower is the AMC's **Bascom Lodge** (mid-May to late Oct. only; 413/443-0011), a beautiful old stone and timber structure with shared bunkrooms and cold-water baths, overpriced at $30-50 but for the location, which is sublime despite the nearby TV relay mast.

Pittsfield

Once-thriving Pittsfield (pop. 48,622) is a classic example of a single-industry city on the skids: having first lost its commercial center to a giant mall in a neighboring town, Pittsfield then watched its major employer, General Electric, proceed to consolidate, cut back, downsize, and otherwise all but lock up and turn out the lights. Compared to the carefully preserved Norman Rockwell simplicity of many of the surrounding small towns, Pittsfield's aging industrial cityscape has made it the place most Berkshire weekenders strenuously try to avoid; despite the fact that its size, and the valley's topography, make this nearly impossible unless you have a resident's familiarity with the backroads, there are actually a few good reasons to pay the place a visit.

Baseball, for example. Catching a home game with the professional minor league **Pittsfield Mets** in Wahconah Park is widely regarded as exemplary of the American pastime as it used to be: gregarious fans, decent players, and cheap admission ($2.75 general, $3.75 grandstand, $6 box seats; 413/499-METS for schedule). Wahconah, built in 1919, has a charm of its own, with plastic owls hanging from the rafters for pigeon scarecrows, a mascot that looks like Mr. Potato-Head with baseball stitching, cheesy sing-alongs, and the famous Sun Delay, when play is suspended until the setting sun stops shining in the batter's and umpire's eyes.

Luxurious Cunard Lines used to serve their ocean-going passengers water exclusively from Williamstown, whose Sand Springs thermal mineral waters are as pure as any known on the planet. The 74° spring waters, still used by some hospitals and distributed by a small commercial bottler, have been enjoyed by bathers since at least 1762. The current bathhouse on the site is the Sand Springs Spa (Memorial Day to Labor Day; $7.50 single-day swim pass) on the north side of town, whose genial owners Fred and Helen George bought the place during their honeymoon visit back in 1950.

One of only two bicycle shops offering rentals along the route through Massachusetts is **Spoke Bicycle & Repair,** at 408 Main Street in Williamstown (413/458-3456), which also carries copies of the incomparable *Bike Rides in the Berkshire Hills* by Lewis Cuyler.

Possibly the most detailed and well-written guide to exploration of the Berkshires on foot is Lauren Stevens's *Hikes & Walks in the Berkshire Hills,* usually available in local bookstores and gift shops, or directly from Berkshire House Publishers, Box 915, Great Barrington, MA 01230.

For an up-to-the-day report on the spread of autumn color through the Berkshires during September and October, call for the local foliage report: 800/343-9072 from out of state, or 800/632-8038 within Massachusetts.

HANCOCK SHAKER VILLAGE

West of Pittsfield on US-20, Hancock Shaker Village is a well-preserved remnant of the religious sect known popularly as "Shakers" but formally as the United Society of Believers in Christ's Second Appearing, whose utopian communities flourished in the years before the Civil War. Shakers, as outsiders called them because of their occasional convulsions during worship, were dedicated to a communal life conspicuous in its equality between men and women, a natural corollary to their belief in parity between a male God and a female Holy Mother Wisdom.

The English-born leader of the group, Ann Lee, was in fact regarded by Shakers as the female, and second, incarnation of Christ. Though Puritan theocracy was ending, preaching this gospel did not endear her to many New Englanders in the decade following her arrival just prior to the American Revolution. During that war, Lee and her "children" sought their "Heaven on Earth," as seen in her visions. Mother Ann died near Albany, New York, of injuries sustained from repeated beatings, before any communities based on her precepts could be founded.

Hancock Shaker Village, third among the 24 settlements built in the U.S. by Lee's followers, survived 170 years, outlasting all but two others. It's now preserved as a living museum (daily 9:30 AM-5:30 PM April-Oct.; $10; 413/443-0188), with exhibits, tours, and working artisans interpreting the rural lifestyle and famous design skills of the Shakers. Appreciation of the efficiency, simplicity, and perfect workmanship consecrated within the "City of Peace" can quickly fill a couple of days if you let it. For a special treat secure a place at the candlelight Shaker dinners held on Saturday evenings; you can also sample Shaker cuisine in the Village Cafe.

HANCOCK SHAKER VILLAGE

Pittsfield is also a good place to remember the advice, "One-word: plastics" given to Dustin Hoffman in *The Graduate*, perhaps while taking a tour of General Electric's **Living Environments concept house**, located on New York Avenue across from parent GE Plastics. Primarily a laboratory for testing high-tech materials and technologies for home construction and consumer products, the "Plastics House" has attracted so much attention from folks wanting to window-shop the future that weekly reserved tours are offered to benefit the local chapter of the United Way (Thursday afternoons and some Saturday mornings; 413/442-6948 or 800/696-6948 for reservations; $6).

If associating plastics with Pittsfield seems novel, what about whales? Head out to Holmes Road, at the city's rural southern edge, and maybe you, too, will see the resemblance between the leviathan and the imposing outline of Mount Greylock, particularly if you view it from the study window of Herman Melville's **Arrowhead** (daily 10 AM-5 PM Memorial

Day to Labor Day, Fri.-Mon. remainder of the year; $4.50). That salty masterpiece of digression and most unloved of high-school reading assignments, *Moby-Dick,* was indeed written in this landlocked locale. While foremost a literary shrine, the spacious farm is also home to the Berkshire County Historical Society, whose well-curated exhibits are always interesting.

Arrowhead

As with its other attractions, when it comes to food Pittsfield has some real out-of-the-way gems. In the acute angle between East and Elm Streets, for example, is the semicircular facade of the **Pittsfield Rye Bakery,** a 1950s flying saucer of glass and blue tile with big bright cases of fresh muffins, bagels, and breads beckoning within. Farther along East Street, past the mammoth GE Polymer Plastics plant, you'll find a pair of Italian places around the corner from one another; both serve good food, sometimes great food, at unusually low prices. The one you won't miss is **elizabeth's borderland café,** in the shocking pink house on East Street, where all the pasta dishes are accompanied by fistfuls of crusty bread and wonderful salads, leaving little room for fine appetizers such as the *bagna caoda,* a must for anchovy lovers. For excellent pizza at a great small-town price, step around the corner to the **East Side Cafe** on Newell Street, a neighborhood bar whose comfort food and convivial atmosphere attract a family clientele.

Serious pilgrims on the path of Ishmael and the great white whale will want to visit the **Melville Memorial Room** on the upper level of the Berkshire Athenaeum—Pittsfield's public library.

Lenox

During the turn-of-the-century Gilded Age, the Berkshires were known as the "inland Newport" because of the opulent "cottages" that dot the South County landscape, principally around Lenox (pop. 5,100). Some 75 of these giant mansions still stand, built for an era in which "society" was a respectable, full-time occupation for folks with names like Carnegie and Westinghouse. Many of the houses have been converted to palatial inns, spas, or private schools; others are home to organizations whose presence makes Lenox a seasonal epicenter for professional performing arts. Besides **Tanglewood,** the local culture roster includes the **National Music Center** (800/USA-MUSIC), the **Berkshire Opera Company** (413/243-1343), and **Shakespeare & Company** (theatrical summer residents of novelist Edith Wharton's 1902 estate, **The Mount;** 413/637-1199). Add **Jacob's Pillow** dance festival in Becket (413/243-0745) and the **Berkshire Theatre Festival** in Stockbridge (413/298-5576), and you can understand why such a small town is such a big magnet for East Coast culture vultures.

Many an American industrialist's fortune came to rest among the Berkshire Hills, but the county's connection to the nation's wealth goes to the very fiber of the dollar. Crane & Co. of Dalton, just east of Pittsfield, has produced the paper for all U.S. currency since 1879.

Though local restaurant menus are obviously influenced by cosmopolitan tastes, don't be fooled into thinking their hours are, too: even in the height of summer, a search for a fine meal after 9 PM can lead to disappointment. And forget about Tuesday nights—you'll be stuck with bar food or pizza if you aren't careful.

The annual influx of cosmopolitan concertgoers affects everything in southwestern Massachusetts, most obviously the local restaurants, half of which cater to immigrants from Boston and New York. If you aren't counting nickels, try the eclectic American menu at the **Church Street Cafe,** where the tastes from the kitchen and accents from the diners are unmistakably reminiscent of some big city bistro. Other major contenders for the town's gourmet dining crowd lie within the same two-block area.

At the other end of the price spectrum is the mostly takeout **Salerno's Gourmet Pizza**, tucked off Franklin Street at no. 8, whose plain fast-food-style decor masks a practitioner of the delicious *abondonza* school of pizza. If you prefer food you can eat with a fork, take Main Street north of town to busy US-7/20, where even Italians will grudgingly admit that **Sweet Basil Grille** serves up good Italian fare—one of the few places in the region to make the passing grade. The prices are good when you read the menu, great after you see the portions. Just don't eat there alone if you like to linger over your food; with only 10 tables in the small dining room, singletons get the rush treatment.

Lenox brims with over 20 handsome B&B inns attractively situated amid wide lawns and gardens, including the **Birchwood Inn**, 7 Hubbard Street (800/524-1646), opposite The Church On The Hill; and the **Brook Farm Inn** on Hawthorne Street (413/637-3013), which offers over 700 volumes of poetry in the library, poets on tape, poetry readings on Saturday, and poems *du jour* for perusal before breakfast. Another popular option, right at the center of Lenox, is the **Village Inn**, 16 Church Street (413/637-0020), built in 1771 and featuring clean, comfortable

---

TANGLEWOOD

To cognoscenti, Tanglewood is the name of an expansive hilltop estate whose concert halls and sloping lawns are home to the Boston Symphony Orchestra and a plethora of visiting artists for 10 weeks each summer. To everyone else it's the one-word explanation for the long restaurant lines, flash flood of weekend South County traffic, and consensus of No Vacancy signs. From the end of June through to the beginning of September, anyone looking for a room will be guaranteed maximum frustration; if you want to be sure of a weekend room in and around Lenox during summer, reserve it in early spring, after which any place with the least bit of charm and comfort will have their weekends booked solid. The end of summer also is rather predictable, so there's no excuse for delaying your fall-foliage reservations.

While indoor tickets to Tanglewood performances are available in advance by fax, by mail, or through Ticketmaster (surcharge added), tickets for the lawns surrounding the Music Shed and Concert Hall are only available in person. For $10-15 you can buy an orchestral serenade beneath the stars—an exceptional value if the clouds don't burst (no rainchecks are given), especially when accompanied by gourmet victuals from a local deli or restaurant. Which is why you'll see most Tanglewood patrons sensibly outfitted with lawn chairs, blankets, and baskets instead of top hats and tails.

For complete program and ticket info, call 617/266-1492, or write the Boston Symphony Orchestra, Symphony Hall, Boston, MA 02115. From early June through Labor Day, you may also call the Tanglewood box office (413/637-5165). Once the season begins, weekly program updates are available (413/637-1666).

rooms and a very good restaurant at moderate prices—from $55 a night when Tanglewood is *not* in season.

Of course, if you prefer the anonymity of your favorite chain motels you'll find **Suisse Chalet, Quality Inn, Best Western,** and **Super 8** scattered along Hwy-20 between the Pittsfield-Lenox line and the I-90 interchange in neighboring Lee. For a complete list of these local accommodations, or for help with last-minute lodging referrals, call the **Lenox Chamber of Commerce** (800/25-LENOX) or visit their office in the Lenox Academy Building on Main Street across from the Post Office plaza.

Tanglewood occupies the former Dixey Estate, a Berkshire cottage whose grounds included the Red House, in which Nathaniel Hawthorne wrote *House of the Seven Gables* during his brief Berkshire residency.

Stockbridge

If the main street of Stockbridge looks vaguely familiar, perhaps it's because the town made its way onto Norman Rockwell canvases during the final decades of his career, when he lived and worked here. You may dismiss his illustrations as the epitome of contrived sentimentality, but the only people who don't find themselves grinning after a stroll through the unparalleled collection of **The Norman Rockwell Museum,** on Hwy-183 west of town, have hearts of solid flint (daily 10 AM-5 PM May-Oct. and weekends year-round, otherwise 11 AM-4 PM; $8). The town itself is worth a stroll, too, particularly past the grand houses along Main Street deliberately frozen in an idyllic past.

While most of the large estate homes are not open to the public, one of the county's more extravagant "cottages" is: **Naumkeag** (daily 10 AM-4:15 PM late May to Labor Day, weekends only through Columbus Day; $6, or $4 garden only), an 1885 mansion on Prospect Hill Road less than a mile north of downtown Stockbridge. The mansion amply illustrates why this region was regarded the state's Gold Coast a century ago; the impressively landscaped grounds, an attraction in their own right, are the site of an annual, summer-long exhibit of outdoor sculpture.

Sculpture is also the highlight of **Chesterwood** (daily 10 AM-5 PM May-Oct.; $6.50), off Hwy-183 just south of the Rockwell Museum. The residence was the summer home of **Daniel Chester French,** one of the most popular contributors to the *fin de siècle* American Renaissance, remembered best for his statue of the seated president in Washington, D.C.'s Lincoln Memorial. A tour of French's studio and house, now a property of the National Trust, or a walk around his 122 wooded acres graced with works of contemporary sculptors, quickly confirms why the sculptor once called his seasonal visits "six months . . . in heaven."

Edith Wharton, the first woman to win a Pulitzer Prize for her 1920 novel *The Age of Innocence,* drew upon local people and incidents in many of her works, including two of her most famous: *House of Mirth* and *Ethan Frome.* The house she designed and built for herself in 1902, called **The Mount** (Tues.-Sun. 10 AM-2 PM in summer only; $6; 413/637-1899), is just south of central Lenox, well signed off Plunkett Street.

The Stockbridge Indians, a band of Mahicans whose conversion to Christianity occupied some of the town's earliest settlers, were forced from this region in the 18th century. Their descendants now reside in central Wisconsin.

Stockbridge's Main Street hasn't always been the exclusive province of boutiques for coffee, curtains, and AARP members. Once upon a time it was also home to the eatery immortalized as the place where "you can get anything you want" by Arlo Guthrie in his song, "Alice's Restaurant Massacree." The building is now **Naji's,** 40 Main Street, somewhat pricey but serving the only Middle Eastern food for miles.

That Rockwell painting of the runaway kid with the policeman? The lunch counter setting was inspired by **Joe's Diner** in nearby Lee, a Central Street institution favored by everybody from local factory workers to New York celebrities.

Housatonic

The few miles of Hwy-183 between the museums in Stockbridge and the town line are a prime example of the Berkshires' back-road charms. Wrapping around an old mill dam on the Housatonic River, the road tags along beside the water as the rounded bulk of Monument Mountain rises to the east, followed quickly by the dark brick hulks of the old Monument Mills. "Entering Great Barrington," reads the sign, though the first glance suggests otherwise: if this place ever saw greatness, it was back in the era of steam locomotives. But looks deceive. Properly known as Housatonic, this village is becoming the funky country cousin of Manhattan's gentrified TriBeCa, with a cluster of working artists' studios among those old cotton mills along the river, and storefront galleries in the old commercial block beside the railroad trestle. Before you follow Hwy-183 south, park by the schoolyard or the lumber mill and stroll around. The **Front Street Gallery** and **Le Petit Musée** are typically open weekends (noon-5 PM), but serendipity is the operative concept in this town, so take a look anyway if you visit on a weekday in case somebody happens to be around. **Spazi Contemporary Art** and **RiCA**, on the east side of the river above the lumberyard and in the old trolley barn down the road respectively, keep somewhat longer hours (Thurs.-Sun. and Wed.-Sun. noon-5 PM), and can inform you of the open studio schedule for artists who work nearby.

When hunger pangs begin to diminish your art appreciation, step over to **Christina's Just Desserts** (daily to 6 PM) across from the schoolyard for tasty lunch fare and pastries. Or start a picnic basket with delicious, fresh, crusty sourdough from the **Berkshire Mountain Bakery** (Sun.-Thurs. to 10 PM) less than a mile south of the village on Hwy-183. To complete the basket, follow the highway another mile south to the **Taft Farms** roadside market. During apple-picking season Taft's wooden crates full of orchard-fresh fruit aren't to be missed.

Jutting up sharply north of the market parking lot, Devil's Pulpit on Monument Mountain is a good spot to enjoy your repast, which will be well earned by the half-hour climb to the rocky ledge with its unspoiled westward views (the eastern vista is scarred by gravel pits). Trailhead parking and picnic tables appear rather abruptly on the downhill side of US-7 north of the Hwy-183 junction; look for the discreet Monument Mountain Reservation signs (voluntary contribution suggested).

Great Barrington

While most South County towns have been spruced up like precious antiques, Great Barrington, with as many hardware stores as chic boutiques, is like grandma's comfortable old sofa, still too much in daily use to keep under velvet wraps. The town doesn't deplore the few tacky commercial lots around its fringes, perhaps because they can't detract from the handsome buildings at its core: the 1905 Mahaiwe Theater, all marble and gilt trim behind its marquee; the stone churches on wide

Main Street; and imposing Searles Castle, a former Berkshire cottage turned private academy.

The center of Great Barrington has a lot to offer hungry travelers. Fussy early risers seeking their cappuccino and muffins, or picnickers seeking the makings of a great spread, will want to check out **Daily Bread**, 17 Railroad Street, with its wholesome loaves and delicious baked goods. **The Berkshire Coffee Roasting Company**, nearby on Main Street, also serves up espresso drinks, teas, and bakery items, with the added benefit of the South County's best let's-hang-out atmosphere. **Bev's Homemade Ice Cream**, adjacent to Daily Bread on Railroad Street, is another source of caffeine, light lunch fare, and sugar, too, by the rich and creamy coneful.

Across from Bev's is **20 Railroad Street**, *the* place for burgers, sandwiches, and soups; its lively bar is the closest native example of a honky-tonk. On Castle Hill Street across the tracks from the town hall is the exceptional **Bronze Dog**, whose distinctive menu gives a starring role to organic and local meat and produce at quite palatable prices. Occasional freight trains rocket past, eliciting memories of the airy dining room's former life as the town depot.

South Egremont to the State Line

The more pastoral of the two roads into Connecticut follows Hwy-23/41 into South Egremont, another of those well-preserved villages entirely ensconced in the National Register of Historic Places—which is hardly a rare honor in Massachusetts. While the custom of baptizing property with cute monikers has seized altogether too many New Englanders, this is one place that genuinely deserves appellations such as Huckleberry Hollow, The Birches, and Wheelbarrow Hill Farm.

South Egremont is the northern gateway to the state's remotest corner, the town of **Mount Washington** (pop. 120). Within its wooded boundaries, Bash Bish Falls State Park, Mount Washington State Forest, and Mount Everett State Reservation all provide fine hikes on and off the Appalachian Trail. You can pick up a free trail map covering all three properties at State Forest Headquarters (413/528-0330). Take the signposted turn from Hwy-41 west of South Egremont Village, and follow the road past signs for Bish Bash Falls and Copake, New York, until you reach the end of the paving nine miles later.

You'll find good day-hikes beside the Connecticut state line off US-7A in Ashley Falls, at **Bartholomew's Cobble**, a designated National Natural Landmark ($3). Geology and weather have conspired to produce an outstanding diversity of flora, over 700 species, within a relatively small pocket of fern-covered boulder outcrops and broad meadows.

Monument Mountain was where Herman Melville and Nathaniel Hawthorne first met on an outing arranged by a New York publisher in 1850, the year the two writers took up residence in the area. Melville, who dedicated *Moby-Dick* to his friend, was disconsolate when Hawthorne later moved away without notice.

Looking for a distinctive, out-of-the-way B&B? Consider using a booking service such as the friendly and efficient Berkshire Bed and Breakfast Homes ($8 fee upon confirming reservation). Owner Eleanor Hebert represents unadvertised and reasonably priced properties all along our route through the Berkshires, from a working dairy farm in Williamstown to a circa 1815 colonial with pool in Sheffield, and plenty in between. Call 413/268-7244 (Mon.-Fri. 9 AM-5:30 PM) or write P.O. Box 211, Williamsburg, MA 01096 for more info.

When people think of electricity they think of Thomas Edison and light bulbs, but the roots of your local utility lie here in the nation's first commercial electrical system, created by transformer inventor **William Stanley** for Great Barrington's downtown in 1886.

If you're looking for a last-minute room at a local B&B or inn, save yourself a walk through the Yellow Pages with a single call to the Lodging Availability Hotline of the Southern Berkshire Chamber of Commerce (413/528-4006).

The last battle of Shay's Rebellion, an uprising of farmers demanding reforms to prevent foreclosures after the American Revolution dried up English credit, was fought in a field south of the village on Sheffield Road. A small stone obelisk marks the spot, coincidentally adjacent to the AT.

If you want to see for yourself how well suited the Housatonic River is for recreational canoeing, set up a rental with Gaffer's Outdoors on US-7 in Sheffield (413/229-0063; $25/weekdays, $35/weekends, or $35 for van shuttle and six hours of paddling time).

Watch out for deer on the roads at night!

Back in South Egremont, **Mom's Country Cafe** at the center of town is a friendly choice for a bite before or after a hike; you'll find country breakfasts, burgers, pasta, and soups. Inexpensive, too. **The Gaslight Cafe**, a few hundred yards farther east, is worth a stop for its pies alone, but you won't be disappointed with by omelets, sandwiches, and salads.

In a class by itself is **John Andrew's**, serving dinner and Sunday brunch at the corner of Hwy-23 and Blunt Road, almost at the New York line. The small, seasonally adjusted menu may be laced with the familiar—wild mushrooms, baby greens, balsamic this, wild thyme that—but the sum of the parts is without peer. For such an experience, even $30 a head will seem an absolute bargain; reservations are advised (413/528-3469; closed Wednesday off-season).

Besides South Egremont's pair of 200-year-old inns—**The Weathervane** (413/528-9580) and the **Egremont** (413/528-9580)—accommodations in the vicinity include several B&Bs, three of which lie along Hwy-41 in adjacent Sheffield, en route to Connecticut. If you want to linger over the excellent hiking without resorting to a tent, consider the **Race Brook Lodge** on Hwy-41, roughly six miles south of Hwy-23 (413/229-2916 or 800/645-3677). With a connecting path up to Mount Race right outside the front door, this cheerfully rustic "chintz-free zone" makes a perfect base for loop hikes along the AT. Sundays, a jazz combo jams in the dining room with a toe-tapping informality that matches the make-yourself-at-home milieu of the place.

ACROSS CONNECTICUT

Anyone who drives its interstates will appreciate why Connecticut enjoys a solid reputation among New Englanders as "the drive-through state," a dubious distinction it shares with New Jersey. The high-speed route between Boston and New York City, I-95, is something endured rather than enjoyed, but our route through the scenic northwest corner is as different from the grim coastal megalopolis as a tulip is from a truck tire. Like the neighboring Berkshires, Connecticut's Litchfield Hills are a traditional retreat for discerning city dwellers. The area is rich in forests, farms, and picturesque little towns laden with antiques. Fast food and discount shopping are as alien to this landscape as affordability, so if your purse strings are tight you'll want to keep moving; otherwise, linger a while and enjoy some of the rural charm so prized by those people you see on the cover of *Business Week*.

Salisbury and Norfolk

After extensive touring around New England, you risk taking white columns, wide porches, picket fences, and the obligatory Congregational steeple for granted. Prim little Salisbury, for example, at the junction of Hwy-41 and US-44, may elicit reveries about what small-town America would look like if strip malls ceased to exist. Spend an afternoon sipping cardamom-scented tea in tiny **Chaiwalla**, at the head of Main Street (US-44), or step over to Academy Street to nosh on a stylish lunch at the **Harvest Bakery** while regulars banter with the owner as they stock up on the delicious breads and desserts, and see if you don't conclude that franchising of fast food should be declared a misdemeanor.

Interestingly, Salisbury was once a heavily industrialized center of 18th-century iron mining and manufacture, with ore pits, forges, and blast furnaces nestled amid hills whose forests were chewed down to the rocky soil by the incessant appetite of the wood-burning smelters. That this Pittsburgh of the American colonies has become tidy and quaint 200 years later could suggest a moral about resilience and resurrection, but perhaps more germane is that Salisbury looks the way it does now because residents were willing to question whether land development is an inalienable right.

About 15 miles east of Salisbury on US-44 lies another pearl, Norfolk, even more manicured than Salisbury, which at least has an auto-body shop and lopsided old American sedans amid the imports on the roads. If any town has capitalized on being far removed from trading floors and board meetings, it's this one: with three public parks and the largest private forest in the state, Norfolk has considered its sheer scenic beauty a stock in trade for nearly a century. Between late June and early August, residents and their guests enjoy the Yale School of Music's **Norfolk Chamber Music Festival** on the Ellen Battell Stoeckel Estate opposite the village green; phone for schedule and ticket information (860/542-5537 during the festival season, or 203/432-1966 Sept.-May).

*Collin's Diner
in Cornwall*

Salisbury's Lakeville Furnace was the armorer of the American Revolution, supplying George Washington's troops with almost their entire arsenal of artillery and ammunition for the duration of the war.

One of the few Hutterite communities in the U.S. is located in Norfolk. The local Hutterian Anabaptist brethren are known in part for their handcrafted furniture and toys.

LIME ROCK PARK

On Hwy-112 a couple of miles west of US-7 you'll find **Lime Rock Park** (860/435-0896 or 800/RACE-LRP), a stock-car racetrack made famous in part by classic car rallies and the occasional appearance of celebrity drivers like Paul Newman and Tom Cruise. The sharp twisting descent from nearby Lakeville to the raceway is one of the prettiest back-road drives in the area.

If good beer is a stronger incentive than sonatas or waterfalls, you'll want to make a beeline for **The Pub**, in the handsome commercial brownstone at the center of town. With over 150 excellent brews from around the world, it almost wouldn't matter whether the grub's any good, but fortunately it is. The Cajun specials (Wed.-Thurs.) are a particularly good value.

As befits such an oasis as Norfolk, there's a handful of **B&Bs** in town costing $120 a night or more, and mostly catering to couples in search of the consummate we-deserve-it getaway. Bask in the rich Tudor woodwork and Tiffany windows of the **Manor House** (860/542-5690) while sipping tea by the fireplace—or between naps in your jacuzzi, if your credit can stand it. Don't feel up to masquerading as English gentry? Perhaps **Angel Hill** (860/542-5920) is the tonic you need, although if L-O-V-E sets your teeth on edge you may not appreciate how closely the place resembles Cupid's lair. A whimsical and flirtatious abundance of cherubs, angels, and hearts are accompanied by all the paraphernalia of romance: flowers, candy, liqueurs, cassettes of Enya, and books of famous love letters. If you prefer simplicity to a surfeit of down pillows, there's always the **Weaver's House** (800/283-1551), which resembles a small home hostel and has rooms from $50.

West Cornwall

Rivers are consistently some of the most attractive driving companions you could ask for, a fact proven once again as US-7 rejoins the Housatonic south of Lime Rock. The highway's scenic miles are further enhanced by the sudden appearance of a barn-red covered bridge, the one-lane gateway to idyllic West Cornwall. This is the kind of place that would tar and feather the first vinyl siding salesperson to walk into town, lest harm befall its small brookside bistro, antiquarian bookshop, or other clapboard buildings bearing signs from previous commercial lives (the meat market is now a video store).

South of town, **Housatonic Meadows State Park** offers riverside camping (mid-April to mid-Sept.; $10), perfectly situated for anyone considering a canoe or kayak rental from adjacent **Clarke Outdoors** (860/672-6365; $35-42 a day including transportation).

Kent

Like many of its Litchfield neighbors, 19th-century Kent (pop. 2,918) had a thriving iron industry until competition from larger Pennsylvania mines—with better access to post-Civil War markets—forced the local furnace to close. Now it's a bustling upscale market town, its main street (US-7) lined with antique shops, galleries, and boutiques. The "New York-Paris-Kent" art gallery in the old Pullman car behind the ice cream shop-née-depot, the gallery of African and Asian artifacts upstairs from the Foreign Cargo store, and the estate jewelry at Pauline's Place on the north side of town are examples of what's replaced blacksmith shops and wheelwrights.

But not every price tag around here ends in triple zeros. For proof, step into **The Villager** smack in the heart of town, where your scrambled eggs and burgers come as plain as you like or gussied up with Andouille sausage or avocado and salsa. "Reliable" is the word that comes to mind for an oasis like this: open daily, with prices that are rarely seen these days outside of the Midwest.

Camping is available for $10 a day all summer in state parks alongside Route 341 on either side of Kent: to the west in **Macedonia Brook State Park** (860/927-3238); and to the east in **Lake Waramaug State Park** (860/868-2592), whose campsites share the water's edge with a handful of posh inns and exclusive homes.

New Milford

The AT crosses the New York state line near Bull's Bridge south of Kent, and so should you—on Route 55 or Route 37—if you want
continues on page 264

Cyclists looking for itineraries among the Litchfield Hills—or anywhere else in the state, for that matter—should obtain a copy of The Connecticut Bicycle Book from The Coalition of Connecticut Bicyclists (P.O. Box 121, Middletown, CT 06457; 860/287-9903).

For further information on activities and services, or for a brochure of local auto tours, contact the helpful folks at the Litchfield Hills Travel Council (P.O. Box 968, Litchfield, CT 06759; 860/567-4506).

The only place to rent a bike in the Litchfield Hills is the friendly and knowledgeable **Cycle Loft**, located among the shops of the Litchfield Commons on Route 202 in Litchfield (860/567-1713; $6 an hour or $20 a day).

TO SEE, OR NOT TO SEE, NEW YORK CITY

In the northeastern U.S., all roads seem to converge upon—and become gridlocked in—New York City. However, there are a number of painless ways to deal with the city without driving miles out of the way, or driving yourself mad. Your primary resource is up-to-date information. Every Friday, the *New York Daily News* runs the "Gridlock Sam" column delineating all highway construction expected to cause delays. For minute-by-minute updates, tune in to one of the news radio stations such as WCBS (AM 880), which has traffic reports every 10 minutes on the eights (9:08, 12:38, etc.).

The best way to experience New York in passing is on I-95; this gives you a brief glimpse of the city's gritty glamor and a distant view of Manhattan's spires to the south. Unfortunately, the section that passes through the city, known as the Cross Bronx Expressway, is one of the worst stretches of road in the country. The many dangers include potholes, endless traffic jams, poor lighting, and frequent accidents caused by far too many cars and trucks. Nevertheless, the vast majority of vehicles pass through unscathed. For the smoothest, fastest trip, your best bet is to brave the Cross Bronx after midnight or before 11 AM on Sunday mornings.

If you want to see the Big Apple but would rather take public transportation than confront the city streets on your own, a number of outlying suburbs make good bases from which to see the city. From Connecticut and New York State, you can take the New Haven train line or the Harlem-Hudson line heading to Manhattan's Grand Central Station. For public transit from New Jersey, you must rely on numerous bus lines to the Port Authority bus terminal (8th Avenue and 42nd Street) or the PATH trains to Manhattan from Jersey City, Hoboken, or Newark.

Some of the more useful outlying towns are:

White Plains
Just over the border from the Bronx, heavily suburban Westchester County contains a number of small cities with good hotels, access to transportation, and a few tourist attractions of their own. White Plains, which lies along I-287 (running between I-95 and the Tappan Zee Bridge), is a corporate center filled with glass-walled office buildings. By train, it is about 45 minutes to Manhattan's Grand Central Station, and seven different highways lead from I-287 to various parts of the city. The New York State Thruway (I-87) will take you to FDR Drive on Manhattan's east side, while the Saw Mill River Parkway becomes the Henry Hudson Parkway running down the west side of Manhattan. Most hotels in the White Plains area cater to the expense account set and thus are not cheap. This includes the **Holiday Inn Crown Plaza** (914/682-0050) and the **Stouffer Westchester** (914/694-5400).

Tarrytown
On the bank of the Hudson River, Tarrytown offers good access by train and highway and a number of nearby tourist attractions. It lies on US-9 about a mile north of I-287; take the last exit before the Tappan Zee Bridge. During the 19th

century, many robber baron industrialists built their mansions in these green hills, and some of them are now museums open to the public. The most spectacular of these is **Kykuit**, a huge mansion surrounded by gardens on the Rockefeller Family Estate. You can tour the house June-Oct.; reservations are advised (914/631-8200). Tarrytown's most famous citizen was Washington Irving, author of the "Legend of Sleepy Hollow" (set in this area) and many other works. His estate, **Sunnyside**, stands on the river in Tarrytown and contains a large and fascinating collection of memorabilia (open year-round, 914/631-8200). Tarrytown lodgings include the **Courtyard by Marriott** (914/631-1122) and the **Hilton Inn** (914/631-5700).

Fort Lee, New Jersey
Across the Hudson, the state of New Jersey offers many lodging opportunities. I-95 crosses the river over the George Washington Bridge and passes through the city of Fort Lee, the beginning of New Jersey's vast suburbs. Downtown Fort Lee boasts a few office buildings and some moderately priced hotels, such as **Days Inn** (201/944-500) and **Holiday Inn** (201/461-3100). For public transit into Manhattan, take the New Jersey Transit bus to the Port Authority Bus Station. For the Cloisters medieval museum—the only tourist attraction in upper Manhattan—take the bus to the George Washington Bridge bus station.

Jersey City
Across the river from the tip of Manhattan, Jersey City is an industrial giant with excellent access to the Jersey Turnpike and to Manhattan via the Holland Tunnel. The **Quality Inn-Jersey City** (201/653-0300) stands right at the tunnel entrance and is about a block from the Newport Center Mall PATH station. PATH trains can take you either to the World Trade Center or to 33rd Street and 6th Avenue in Manhattan via Greenwich Village. Jersey City's main tourist attraction is **Liberty State Park**, just onshore from the Statue of Liberty, with a picnic area, a salt marsh nature walk, and the new, high-tech Liberty Science Center, filled with interactive displays popular with children. The park also offers ferry service to the Statue of Liberty and Ellis Island.

Newark
More lodgings can be found around Newark Airport, southeast of Jersey City. This area is more distant from New York but offers good public transportation by bus or PATH train from the Newark train station. Airport hotels include **Courtyard by Marriott** (201/643-8500), **Days Inn** (201/242-0900), and **Holiday Inn** (201/589-1000), all of which have rates around $75 a night. Few tourists visit Newark, a depressed industrial city. However, the **Newark Museum** at 49 Washington Street, a few blocks from the train station, is worth a visit, with small but excellent collections of American and European art and the largest display of Tibetan art outside Asia.

The I-84 freeway northeast of New York City is a real pain in the driver's seat, with lots of left exits, sudden shrinkings from three to two lanes, frequent construction, constant changes in speed limits, and too much traffic.

Wander amid the century-old ghosts of the region's iron industry at **Mine Hill Preserve,** the state's largest set of ore pit and furnace ruins, just off Route 67 between New Milford and Route 199. To get there, turn north on Mine Hill Road, immediately west of the Shepaug River bridge.

Hiking advice and trail guides are cheerfully dispensed from tiny Pathfinders, next to the Bank Street cinema in New Milford.

to enjoy a passing landscape that offers more fields and trees than guardrails and parking lots. Technically speaking there's still a large swath of New England between New York and New Milford, but most of this has more in common with the Indianapolis Beltway than with the Vermont countryside.

The infidels of prefab modular construction may be pounding at the gates, but aptly named Milford Green is still framed by a well-preserved backdrop of classic 19th-century architecture, from the church to the hardware store. New Milford also is a good place to grab a bite of Eastern European, Greek, or Tex-Mex food, on block-long Bank Street or around the corner on Railroad Street. Mellow **Bank Street Coffee House,** tucked below street level, can satisfy cravings for steaming latte or icy granitas. If you crave a memorable meal, check out **The Bistro Cafe** across from the black-glass white-tile art deco cinema, serving nori-wrapped tuna and oven-roasted duckling among the $15-and-up entrees of New American food. If you seek a feast for the senses, it doesn't get much better than this.

Town or country? is the question to ask yourself when selecting accommodations here: the **Homestead Inn** (860/354-4080) at the north end of the Green, for example, sits within walking distance of dinner or a movie; but for hayfields and starlight, consider **Barnes Hill Farm** (860/354-4404) on Route 37 in nearby Sherman, with its outdoor jacuzzi, access to local tennis courts, connections to the AT, and a pick-your-own berry farm across the road.

Between Danbury, Connecticut, and Port Jervis, New York, the Appalachian Trail runs parallel to our US-6 route, which is described on pages 490-493.

ACROSS PENNSYLVANIA

The hikers' Appalachian Trail runs across southern New York and western New Jersey, but our road route avoids the Garden State entirely, crossing instead the natural chasm of the Delaware Water Gap, whose forests, waterfalls, and wildlife are popular with city-dwellers escaping the New York City megalopolis. In its 150-mile length, the route pases through a succession of strikingly different places, starting with the densely populated industrial regions of the Lehigh Valley and the historic little town of Bethlehem, which plays up its Christmas connections more than its role as a formerly vital steelmaking center. Farther south, modern industry gives way to the traditional agriculture of Pennsylvania Dutch Country, world-famous for its anti-technology, Old Order Christian communities. Continuing southwest across the

Susquehanna River, you'll follow the route of the old Lincoln Highway through historic York, early capital of the United States, now home to a Harley-Davidson motorcycle plant. The last stop on the Pennsylvania leg of the route is the Civil War battlefields at Gettysburg, just shy of the Maryland border.

Delaware Water Gap National Recreation Area

Totaling some 30,000 acres of forest on both banks of the Delaware River, the Delaware Water Gap National Recreation Area stretches for 35 miles south of the I-84 freeway along two-lane US-209. Established in 1965, the park is still very much under development, though numerous hiking trails lead through hardwood forests to seasonal waterfalls, and the river itself offers abundant canoeing, swimming, and fishing. Though far from pristine, considering the park lies only 50 miles west of New York City, the natural beauty is surprisingly undisturbed.

The town of **Lackawaxan,** 15 miles northwest of I-84 on the New York/ Pennsylvania border, was long home to writer **Zane Grey,** and also holds an early prototype of the Brooklyn Bridge.

A few remnants of the area's historic agricultural villages have been preserved under the aegis of the park service, but the main attraction is the oddly named Delaware Water Gap itself, a deep cleft carved by the river into the solid rock of the Kittatinny Mountains. Artists, sightseers, and rock-climbers have admired this unique feat of geology for well over 100 years, but unfortunately the natural passageway is crisscrossed by all manner of road and railroad, including the six-lane I-80 freeway that runs right through it.

The tiny tourist town of **Delaware Water Gap**, south of I-80 at the far southern end of the park, provides the best views of the gap. A **visitor center** (908/841-9520 or 717/588-2435) sits along the river, just off I-80 at the first/last New Jersey exit, and offers exhibits on the geology and history of the region, as well as information on sundry recreational opportunities. **Pack Shack Adventures** (717/424-8533) rents canoes for $45 a day.

A 25-mile stretch of the Appalachian Trail cuts along a 1,200-foot-high ridge at the southeast corner of the park, crossing the Delaware River on an old bridge at the town of Delaware Water Gap.

There's not much in the way of developed accommodations in the park, though there is a handy **youth hostel** in Layton, New Jersey, four miles east of Dingman's Ferry via Hwy-560. At the southern edge of the Delaware Gap park, the most extensive tourist facilities cluster along the I-80 freeway in the towns of **Stroudsburg** (pop. 5,312) and **East Stroudsburg** (pop. 8,781), where you can choose between **Best Western** and **Super 8**; there's also a nice **Ramada Inn**, with two pools, off I-80 in Delaware Water Gap. Good food, however, is hard to come by.

The **Pocono Mountains,** which rise to the west of the Delaware River, hold Pennsylvania's odd version of the traditional honeymoon resort, featuring champagne glass-shaped jacuzzis in the rooms. Most of these are run by Caesar's World resorts (800/233-4141) and are outrageously priced—$350 a night on average.

Bethlehem

South of the Delaware Water Gap, Hwy-611 runs along the Delaware River until its confluence with the Lehigh River, five miles west of the remarkable small city of Bethlehem (pop. 71,400). Famous for its Christmas festivals, and as a fun place from which to mail Christmas cards, Bethlehem was originally established in 1741 by a group of Moravian missionaries. The missionaries' original circa 1803 chapel still stands at the heart of the compact, gas-lighted downtown district, its cemetery full of 200-year-old headstones laid flat so as not to offend God. Another engaging historic site is the **Sun Inn** (610/866-1758) at 564 Main Street, a well-preserved former tavern "where the leading figures of the Revolutionary era were entertained," says a plaque on the wall; it's now an expensive German restaurant but also offers guided tours ($2).

Across the Lehigh River from the tidy homes and shops of downtown Bethlehem stand the rusting remains of the **Bethlehem Steel Company**. Famous for fabricating engineering marvels such as the towers of the Golden Gate Bridge—cast here in sections, then shipped through the Panama Canal and assembled in San Francisco—the mill was mismanaged by incompetent executives and is now slated for demolition, despite the best efforts of local preservationists.

Every May, Bethlehem hosts a hugely popular Bach Festival rated as one of the best in country. For details, contact the visitor center (610/868-1513).

The Bethlehem **visitor center**, 509 Main Street (610/868-1513 or 800/360-TOUR) offers walking-tour maps of the historic sites and can also provide listings of restaurants and places to stay. Nearby, the sidewalk tables outside **Viennese Pastry**, 500 Main Street, are a great place to enjoy a wickedly rich piece of cake or a light lunch; for dinner, try the aforementioned **Sun Inn** at 564 Main Street. Near Lehigh University, on 4th Street across the river from downtown, **Godfrey Daniel's Coffee House** (610/ 867-2390) hosts a range of live folk and jazz music most nights.

The large **Hotel Bethlehem** (610/867-3711 or 800/545-5158), on Main Street overlooking the river, is centrally located, with doubles costing around $80 a night. There are also the usual national chains, including an Econo Lodge and a Comfort Inn off US-22, both with rooms for under $50 a night.

Allentown

Jim Thorpe

The town of **Jim Thorpe,** in the Lehigh Valley 30 miles northwest of Allentown off the Pennsylvania Turnpike (Hwy-9), 10 miles north of the Appalachian Trail, is a former coal-mining town with many 19th-century buildings. The town changed its name from Mauch Chunk in 1954 to honor the great Olympic athlete Jim Thorpe, whose remains lie in a granite mausoleum along Hwy-903 on the northeast side of town.

The seat of Lehigh County, Allentown (pop. 105,000) spreads west of Bethlehem, across a bend in the Lehigh River. The downtown area is large and lacks focus, though it does provide two very worthwhile stops, the bigger and better of which is the **Allentown Art Museum** (Tues.-Sat. 10 AM-5 PM, Sunday noon-3:30 PM; $3.50) at 5th and Court Streets. Here you'll find a good general collection of painting and photography as well as an entire room moved from the Frank Lloyd Wright-designed Little House. Allentown's other main attraction lies two blocks west at Church and Hamilton Streets: the **Liberty Bell Shrine** (Mon.-Sat. noon-4 PM; free), an old church that houses a replica of the famous bell that was hidden here for safekeeping during the Revolutionary War battles at Philadelphia.

Allentown boasts more all-American diners per capita than anywhere else in the country, with some two dozen spread around the metropolitan area. Streamlined **Tom Sawyer Diner** is open 24 hours every day on the south side of town, near where US-222 crosses the I-78 and Hwy-9 freeways; many more have been "modernized" and covered in charmless brick or plaster. Because it's the business center for the surrounding area, Allentown has lots of accommodation options, including **Comfort Inn, Days Inn, Econo Lodge**, and most other national chains.

Reading

Standing along the eastern banks of the Schuylkill River, Reading (pop. 78,380) is more interesting than its frightening title "Factory Outlet Shopping Capital of Southeastern Pennsylvania" would lead you to expect. Ornately turreted row houses line 5th Avenue (US-222 Business) through the residential districts, and downtown holds a number of well-maintained businesses and signs from the first half of the century, but there is very little for visitors to search out; perhaps the best place to stop is along US-222 on the north side of town, where **Schell's Hot Dogs, BBQ and Miniature Golf** offers almost everything a roadtripper could ask for. (Well, almost.)

For history buffs, however, two worthwhile places to visit sit southeast of Reading along the Schuylkill River. The closer of these is at Birdsboro, 10 miles from town and a mile north of US-422. The **Daniel Boone Homestead and Birthplace** marks the site where the great frontiersman was born in 1734. More interesting is the **Hopewell Furnace National Historic Site** (daily 9 AM-5 PM; $2), five miles south of Birdsboro via Hwy-345, which preserves intact an entire iron-making community that thrived here from the colonial era until the mid-1840s. Park rangers fire up the

Midway between Allentown and Reading, every June and July the weeklong Kutztown Folk Festival celebrates the arts, crafts, and culture of the local Pennsylvania Dutch communities, which are less austere than their Lancaster County counterparts.

TAKE A RIDE
ON THE READING
IF YOU PASS GO
COLLECT $200

The Monopoly "Chance" card "Take a Ride on the Reading—Collect $200," commemorates the railroad that formerly ran between Reading and Philadelphia.

ROADSIDE AMERICA

One of the quirkiest, kitschiest tourist attractions in the U.S., Roadside America (daily 10 AM-5 PM, 9 AM-6 PM in summer; $4; 610/488-6241) stands alongside the I-78 freeway, 20 miles northwest of Reading in the village of Shartlesville. Built by Reading native Laurence Gieringer over 60 years ago, Roadside America is a giant 3/8-to-the-inch scale model of bygone Americana, fleshed out with animated scenes that trace a typical day in the life of the country—circa 1941, when Roadside America first opened to the public. As you walk around the edges of the 8,000-square-foot exhibit, you can push buttons to make wheels spin, lights flash, and pumps pump, and you'll see a little of everything rural: an 1830s New England village featuring a church and choral music; a canyon and lake complete with waterfalls and resort cabins; a model of Henry Ford's workshop in Dearborn, Michigan, where he built one of the first "horseless carriages"; various turnpikes, canals, highways, and railroads; a coal mine; and a mock-up of the San Francisco Bay Bridge, the closest Roadside comes to a city scene.

Though it's definitely a fine example of kitsch, Roadside America is also an oddly compelling place, and only the hardest-hearted roadtripper will be able to hold back the tears when, every half-hour or so, the sun sets and Kate Smith bursts into "God Bless America."

furnace and demonstrate the primitive foundry, and exhibits trace the iron-making process—mining the ore, making charcoal, and fabricating the finished product, which here at Hopewell was primarily pig iron and stoves.

Ephrata Cloister

Ephrata and Lititz

South of Reading, US-222 runs along the western edge of the Amish and Mennonite-influenced Pennsylvania Dutch Country. The heart of this region is due east of Lancaster, but the area north of Lancaster also holds a number of related sites often missed by visitors. The most appealing of these is the **Ephrata Cloister** (Mon.-Sat. 9 AM-5 PM, Sunday noon-5 PM; $5), at 632 W. Main Street just west of the town of Ephrata. Founded in 1732 by a communal society of religiously celibate German Pietists, the Ephrata Cloister consists of a half-dozen well-preserved 250-year-old wooden buildings, which housed dormitories, bakeries, and a printing shop where the commune produced some of the finest illustrated books of the colonial era. Across Main Street from the entrance, the **Cloister Restaurant** serves very good home-style food for breakfast, lunch, and dinner in an overgrown 1940s diner.

West of Ephrata, eight miles north of Lancaster via Hwy-501, the tiny town of Lititz (pop. 8,280) is dominated by the huge **Wilbur Chocolate** candy factory at 48 N. Broad Street, which liberally perfumes the air with the smell of hot chocolate. Lititz also holds the nation's oldest operating pretzel factory, the **Sturgis Pretzel House** at 219 E. Main Street (Mon.-Sat. 9 AM-5 PM; $1.50), where you can twist your own; and the small but high-quality **Heritage Map Museum** (Mon.-Sat. 10 AM-5 PM; $3.50), which displays original maps from the 15th-20th centuries, and publishes and sells copies, too. Lititz is the final resting place of John Sutter, who owned huge chunks of pre-gold rush California and who

Two of the main tourist stops in the Dutch Country region are the towns of **Intercourse** (source of many snickeringly allusive postcards) and **Paradise** (the Paradise post office, just north of US-30 at the east end of town, is a popular place to mail from).

Midway between Lancaster and York, the town of Columbia holds what is arguably the country's best collection of timepieces in the **Watch and Clock Museum,** open daily at 514 Poplar Street. Also in Columbia is a beautiful bridge that used to carry the old Lincoln Highway (US-30) across the broad Susquehanna River.

died here in Pennsylvania while battling the Washington, D.C. bureaucracy to receive compensation for his confiscated land.

Back on US-222, two miles northeast of Lancaster, the state-run and well-posted **Landis Valley Museum** (Tues.-Sat. 9 AM-5 PM, Sunday noon-5 PM; $7) is a popular 40-acre "living history" park preserving and interpreting traditional rural lifeways of eastern Pennsylvania.

Lancaster

The only place approaching an urban scale in this part of Pennsylvania, Lancaster (pop. 55,600) is the region's commercial center, a former state capital that, for a single day during the Revolutionary War, served as capital of the country. Though most visitors view it as little more than a handy base for exploring nearby Pennsylvania Dutch Country, Lancaster does have a couple of attractions in its own

---

THE PENNSYLVANIA DUTCH COUNTRY

East of Lancaster, south of Lititz on Hwy-722, the old Lincoln Highway (US-30) runs through the heart of what has become internationally famous as the Pennsylvania Dutch Country. This is a very pretty, almost completely rural region, unremarkable apart from the presence here of various "Old Order" Anabaptist
(continues on next page)

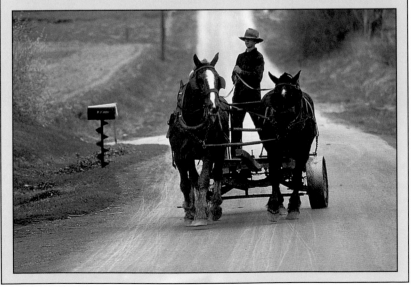

Christian sects, including Amish and Mennonites, who eschew most of the trappings and technological advances of the 20th century, including cars, electricity, and irrigation, and retain their simple ways. Long before the Peter Weir movie *Witness* gave their low-tech lifestyle the Hollywood treatment, visitors have been coming here to see these anachronistic descendants of German immigrants (Deutsche = Dutch) who settled here in the early 1700s, and to whom all outsiders are known simply as "English."

The best way to get a feel for the Amish and Mennonite ways of life is to follow back roads, by bike if possible, through the gently rolling countryside of Lancaster County, keeping an eye out for their horse-drawn buggies (Amish ones are gray, the Mennonites' are black). You can buy produce, breads, cakes, or "Shoo Fly Pie" from the many roadside stands marked by hand-lettered signs. For a thorough overview, stop at **The People's Place** (Mon.-Sat. 9 AM-5 PM; $3), 3513 Main Street in Intercourse (so named because it sits at the junction of two roads), which presents a multimedia show outlining the beliefs and culture of the Amish and Mennonite peoples along with displays of quilts and other handicrafts. More amusing is the restored one-room **Weavertown Schoolhouse**, populated by "authentic" audio-animatronic Amish school kids, along Hwy-340 a mile east of the town of Bird-in-Hand, 2.5 miles west of Intercourse.

Most of the many Amish-style restaurants in the region are huge and forbiddingly full of bus-tour hordes; one exception is **Stoltzfus Restaurant** (Mon.-Sat. 11 AM-8 PM, May-Nov. only; 717/768-8156) on Hwy-772 a mile southeast of Intercourse. A totally non-Amish but very good roadfood place is **Jennie's Diner**, open 24 hours every day on the north side of US-30, just east of the Hwy-896 intersection.

Though it won't give you any great insight into the Amish, one unique place to stay is the **Red Caboose Motel and Restaurant** (717/687-5000), a mile east of Strasburg on Paradise Lane. All the rooms are built inside old railroad cars, and the on-site restaurant simulates a train journey, with whistles blowing and a gentle rocking vibration to ease your digestion.

For complete listings of attractions, restaurants, and hotels, or to pick up handy maps or other information, stop by the helpful Pennsylvania Dutch **visitor center** (daily 9 AM-5 PM, longer hours in summer; 717/299-8901 or 800/735-2629), on US-30 between Dutch Country and Lancaster.

A word to the wise: in Dutch Country, remember that anything claiming to be "authentic Amish" definitely isn't. Also, please respect the Amish you see and refrain from taking photographs. Drive carefully, too.

right, such as the red-brick, pseudo-Romanesque **Central Market** at King and Queen Streets in the center of town. It hosts the nation's oldest publicly owned, continuously operating Farmer's Market, currently held all day Tuesday and Friday, as well as Saturday mornings. A block south on Queen Street, the ground-floor windows of the local newspaper trace local history through headlines, starting back in 1794 and continuing up through the present day.

York

Though it doesn't look like much from the highway, bypassed by both US-30 and the I-83 freeway, the medium-sized town of York (pop. 42,192) claims to be the first capital of the United States: late in 1777, the Articles of Confederation were adopted here by the 13 newly independent former colonies, and it's in that document that the name "United States of America" was first used. A significant number of historic buildings still stand in the quiet, low-rise downtown area, including the medieval-looking, circa 1740 **Golden Plough Tavern** and other colonial-era structures along Market Street at the west edge of the business district.

For all its historic importance, York is best known for its industrial prowess, which is saluted in a pair of unique attractions. The smaller of these is the oddly combined **Weightlifting and Softball Hall of Fame** (daily 9 AM-3 PM; free), 3300 Board Road off I-83 exit 11, basically a showcase for the sporting goods manufactured by the York Barbell Company. Much more compelling, and perhaps the best reason to visit York, is the

Harley Davidson assembly plant and museum, a mile east of town off US-30 on Eden Road. The popular guided tour (Mon.-Fri. 10 AM and 1:30 PM except July; free; 717/848-1177) takes about two hours. It begins with a brief history of the company, which is the only American producer of motorcycles still in business.

THE LINCOLN HIGHWAY

The main east-west route through Pennsylvania Dutch Country, US-30 is also one of the best-preserved stretches of the old Lincoln Highway, the nation's first transcontinental route. Planned and named in 1915, linking New York City's Times Square with the Panama Pacific International Exposition in San Francisco, the Lincoln Highway followed over 3,000 miles of country road across 12 states. A thousand miles of the original "highway" were little more than muddy tracks, scarcely more visible on the ground than they were on the still nonexistent road maps, but by the early 1930s the road was finally fully paved, following present-day US-30 as far as Wyoming, then bending south to follow what's now US-50, "The Loneliest Road in America," along the route of the Pony Express across Nevada and most of California.

Originally marked by telephone poles brightly painted with red, white, and blue stripes and a large letter "L," in 1928 the Lincoln Highway was blazed by more discreet concrete mileposts carrying a small bust of Lincoln—3,000 of these were placed, one every mile, by Boy Scout troops across the land, but only around a dozen still stand. As with the later Route 66, the Lincoln Highway was replaced by the interstates, but it does live on, in folk memory as well as the innumerable "Lincoln Cafes" and "Lincoln Motels" along its original route.

For a more thorough discussion of this old road's significance and legacy, read Drake Hokansen's excellent *Lincoln Highway: Main Street Across America* and contact the Lincoln Highway Association, P.O. Box 8117, St. Louis, MO 63156.

*Robert E. Lee,
Confederate commander
at Gettysburg*

*George Gordon Meade,
Union commander*

*Abraham Lincoln,
November 8, 1863*

The tour then takes you past a lineup of some 40 Harleys past and present, culled from the corporate collection of over 200 motorbikes. It proceeds onto the shop floor for a close-up look at the bikes being put together. A souvenir store is stocked with all manner of things with the Harley-Davidson logo, from T-shirts to leather jackets.

Gettysburg

Totally overwhelmed by the influx of tourists visiting its name-sake battleground, the town of Gettysburg (pop. 7,025) has survived both onslaughts remarkably unscathed. Despite the presence of sundry tourist attractions—wax museums, various multimedia reenactments of the battle and President Lincoln's Gettysburg Address, even a Lincoln Train Museum displaying over a thousand model trains that include a scale replica of the one Lincoln rode here in—once the day-tripping crowds have dispersed Gettysburg is actually a very pleasant place, with rows of brick-fronted buildings lining Baltimore and York Streets out from the circle at the center of town.

There are, not surprisingly, quite a few places to eat, including the atmospheric and inexpensive **Dobbin House**, south of town at 89 Steinwehr Avenue, serving above-average pub food in Gettysburg's oldest building. The same building doubles as the **Gettystown Inn** (717/334-2100), a moderately priced and pleasant B&B. The dozens of other places to stay include all the usual national chains.

Gettysburg National Military Park

Site of the most famous two-minute speech in U.S. history, and of the bloody Civil War battle that marked the high tide of Confederate fortunes, Gettysburg National Military Park surrounds the town of Gettysburg, protecting the scenes of the struggle as they were July 1-3, 1863, when 50,000 of the 165,000 combatants were killed or wounded. Over a thousand monuments mark the various historic sites around the 6,000 acres of rolling green pasture that form the park, and tape-recorded **tours** ($12) or park-approved **Battlefield Guides** ($20 per car) take you along a well-marked route past such places as Little Round Top, The Angle, and Cemetery Ridge, site of fabled Pickett's Charge.

A 230-acre farm on the southwest fringe of the Gettysburg battlefields was home to U.S. Army general and later president **Dwight D. Eisenhower** and his wife Mamie, and is now open for guided tours (daily 9 AM-4 PM; $3.60) that leave from the Gettysburg visitor center.

Most of the guided tours start and finish at the **visitor center** (daily 8 AM-5 PM; free) on Taneytown Road a mile south of town, in the shadow of a hideous Erector Set excrescence, the 310-foot-tall National Tower. In the visitor center, an extensive museum (free) puts the battle into context and displays a huge array of period weaponry. You can learn more by watching the battle unfold on the **Electric Map** ($2), which looks a lot like a boxing ring, or by studying the circular **Cyclorama** (free, $2 for sound and light show), a 26- by 356-foot painting that accurately portrays the events of the final day's battles. Across the road, the **Gettysburg National Cemetery** is the place where President Lincoln delivered his famous address on November 19, 1863.

ACROSS MARYLAND

Crossing the Mason-Dixon Line from Gettysburg into Maryland on US-15, our route veers west into the Appalachian foothills of Catoctin Mountain Park, site of the presidential retreat Camp David. The landscape here is quite rugged, and signs of life few and far between—an oasis of peace and quiet, under an hour by road from Baltimore or Washington, D.C. Winding south through the mountains of the Maryland Panhandle, the thin strip of land that stretches for some 75 miles between Pennsylvania and West Virginia, this route again meets the hikers' Appalachian Trail, then detours to visit the battlefield of Antietam, the well-preserved site of the worst carnage of the Civil War.

The Maryland state motto, *Fatti Maschi, Parole Femine,* is translated roughly as "Manly Deeds, Womanly Words"—*not* "Walk Like a Man, Talk Like a Woman."

The attractive and historic city of Frederick, 25 miles south of Thurmont at the junction of I-70 and US-15, holds the **Barbara Fritchie Candystick Restaurant,** a shocking pink 1950s diner on the old National Road (US-40), a mile east of I-70. Look for the giant candy cane out front.

Catoctin Mountain Park: Camp David
US-15 continues south from Gettysburg across the Maryland border, and there's little to stop for until **Thurmont** (pop. 3,500), "Gateway to the Mountains," where the route heads west on Hwy-77 into the green expanse of Catoctin Mountain Park. Fully recovered after centuries of logging activity, the park protects some 10,000 acres of hardwood forest, a handful of 1,500-foot peaks, and the presidential retreat at Camp David, hidden away in the woods and strictly off-limits to visitors; for security reasons it doesn't even appear on park maps. The park **visitor center** (Mon.-Fri. 10 AM-4:30 PM, Saturday and Sunday 9 AM-5 PM; 301/663-9388) along Hwy-77 two miles west of US-15 provides information on **camping** and maps of the many hiking trails, including a short trail from the visitor center to the preserved remains of the Blue Blazes whiskey still, where rangers demonstrate moonshine-making on summer weekends.

In Gathland State Park, on the Appalachian Trail east of Gapland off Hwy-67, the 50-foot terra-cotta arch of the **War Correspondents Memorial** was erected in the late 1880s in honor of journalists killed while covering the Civil War.

Spreading along the south side of Hwy-77, Maryland-run **Cunningham Falls State Park** offers more natural scenery and a very pleasant swimming area in Hunting Creek Lake. There's a snack bar and boats for rent.

Washington Monument State Park
From Catoctin Mountain Park, the route

the "original" Washington Monument

heads south on undivided Rte-6 and two-lane Hwy-17 along the hikers' Appalachian Trail, winding up at Washington Monument State Park between the I-70 freeway and the small town of **Boonsboro**. A 35-foot-tall, bottle-shaped mound dedicated to the memory of George Washington stands at the center of the park; Boonsboro citizens completed the monument in 1827, and thus it's the oldest memorial honoring the first U.S. president.

Atop a hill south of the park, across an old alignment of the National Road (US-40), the **South Mountain Inn** (301/432-6155) has operated as a tavern and inn since 1732, and now serves dinner nightly and lunch on weekends.

Antietam Battlefield

Between Boonsboro and the Potomac River, which forms Maryland's border with West Virginia, Antietam National Battlefield preserves the hallowed ground where over 23,000 men were killed or wounded on the bloodiest day of the Civil War—September 17, 1862. Atop a shallow hill at the middle of the park, a scant mile north of **Sharpsburg** off Hwy-65, the **visitor center** (daily 8:30 AM-5 PM; $2; 301/432-5124) offers films, museum exhibits, and interpretive programs that put the battle into military and political context. Though there was no clear winner, Antietam is said to have convinced Lincoln to issue the Emancipation Proclamation, officially freeing slaves in Confederate states and effectively putting an end to British support for the southern side.

Clara Barton, who tended the wounded during and after the Civil War's bloodiest battle at Antietam

ACROSS WEST VIRGINIA

In its short run across the eastern tip of West Virginia, US-340 passes through one of the most history-rich small towns in the U.S.: **Harpers Ferry**, located at the confluence of the Shenandoah and Potomac Rivers. Lovely mountain scenery surrounds Harpers Ferry, especially during early autumn when the hardwood forests rival Vermont's for vibrant color. South of Harpers Ferry, the hikers' Appalachian Trail runs directly along the Virginia/West Virginia border, east of the Shenandoah River atop the roadless crest of the Blue Ridge Mountains. The best route to follow by car, US-340 swings to the west through the historic mountain resort of **Charles Town** before entering Virginia.

Harpers Ferry is the national headquarters of the **Appalachian Trail Conference,** the nonprofit group that oversees the 2,144-mile footpath. For information, contact them at P.O. Box 807, Harpers Ferry, WV 25425 (304/535-6331).

Harpers Ferry

Climbing the steep slopes of the Blue Ridge Mountains, Harpers Ferry (pop. 300) embodies the industrial and political history of the early United States. Now protected as a national park, its many well-preserved wood, brick, and stone buildings are palpable reminders of early American enterprise: besides the country's first large factory, first canal, and first railroad, scenic Harpers Ferry saw John Brown's rebellion against slavery, and was later a strategic site during the Civil War.

Small museums, housed in separate buildings along Shenandoah and High Streets along the riverfront in the "Lower Town," trace the various strands of the town's past. From the Shenandoah River, the Appalachian Trail winds south down what the third president called "one of the most stupendous scenes in Nature," Jefferson's Rock. Crossing the Potomac River to the north, the AT climbs up to Maryland Heights for more spectacular vistas.

Especially in summer, when cars are banned from lower Harpers Ferry, the best first stop is the small **visitor center** (daily 9 AM-5 PM; $2; 304/535-6029) above the town along US-340. Park here and take one of the frequent free trams down to the historic area. Although most of Harpers Ferry is preserved as a historic site, the eastern portions along the Potomac riverfront are still in private hands, and here you can indulge your taste for fast food, wax museums, and schlocky souvenirs. There's also an **Amtrak** station, with trains serving Washington, D.C. on a very limited schedule. Near the visitor center, a **Comfort Inn** has comfortable rooms for around $50 a night.

Charles Town is the nation's only sanctuary for those once-trendy yuppie pets, Vietnamese pot-bellied pigs. If you want to scratch their stomachs or offer a donation for their upkeep, call 304/725-PIGS.

Charles Town

Founded in 1786, the former colonial resort of Charles Town (pop. 3,122) was named in honor of George Washington's younger brother Charles, who surveyed the site on behalf of Lord Fairfax. Many of the streets are named after other family members, over 75 of whom are buried in the cemetery alongside the **Zion Church**, on Congress Street on the east side of town. Charles Town, which shouldn't be confused with the West Virginia state capital, Charleston, later played a significant role in John Brown's failed raid on Harpers Ferry; after Brown was captured, he was tried and convicted of treason in the Jefferson County Courthouse at the corner of George and Washington Streets. A small **museum** (Mon.-Fri. 9 AM-5 PM; free) operates inside the old courtroom.

South of Charles Town, US-340 winds along the western slopes of the Appalachians for a dozen miles before entering Virginia east of Winchester.

East of Winchester, Virginia, this Appalachian Trail route crosses the transcontinental US-50 highway, which is covered beginning on page 516.

ACROSS VIRGINIA

The Appalachian Trail covers more ground in Virginia than it does in any other state, following the crest of the Blue Ridge Mountains from Harpers Ferry in West Virginia all the way south to the Tennessee and North Carolina borders. In the northern half of the state, the road route closely follows the hikers' route, and the two crisscross each other through the sylvan groves of Shenandoah National Park. Midway along the state the two routes diverge, and hikers turn west while the motor route follows the unsurpassed Blue Ridge Parkway along the top of the world.

Most of the time the route follows the mountain crests, though in many places you'll find fascinating towns and cities a short distance to the east or west. Best among these is Charlottesville, a history-rich Piedmont town that's best known as the home of Thomas Jefferson and the University of Virginia. Other suggested stops include the Shenandoah Valley town of Lexington, the "natural wonder" of Natural Bridge, and the engaging city of Roanoke.

Front Royal

The town takes its name, perhaps aprocryphally, from a Revolutionary War drill sergeant who, since his troops were unable to tell their left from their right, was forced to shout out "Front Royal Oak" to get them to face the same way. Front Royal (pop. 11,880) sits just south of I-66 at the entrance to Shenandoah National Park. Because of its key location, Front Royal has grown unwieldy in past decades but retains some semblance of its 19th-century self along Chester Street, a well-maintained historic district at the center of town, a block east of US-340.

Dinosaur Land, Front Royal

You'll find walking-tour maps and other information at the **visitor center,** 414 E. Main Street (703/635-3185 or 800/338-2576), which is housed in an old train depot. The usual battery of fast-food franchises line US-340 from the freeway south through town, as do motels like the **Twin Rivers,** 1801 Shenandoah Avenue (703/635-4101), a mile south of I-66.

At the foot of the Blue Ridge Mountains, 26 miles southeast of Front Royal via US-522, pristine colonial **Washington** (pop. 200) was surveyed by the future father of the U.S., George Washington, who named many of the streets after friends and family. The main attraction here is the **Inn at Little Washington** at Main and Middle Streets (703/675-3800), one of the only Mobil five-star resort hotels in the country, though with room rates starting at over $300 a night and dinners averaging $100 a head, it's definitely a special-occasion place to stay or eat.

Fall foliage in the Blue Ridge Mountains is stunning, though not as intense as in New England.

Shenandoah National Park

One of the most popular national parks in the east, especially during the fall foliage season when seemingly everyone in the world descends upon the place to "leaf-peep," Shenandoah National Park protects some 195,000 acres of hardwood forest along the northernmost crest of the Blue Ridge Mountains. Though the landscape looks natural now, it was in fact heavily cultivated until the 1920s, when the soils were depleted, farmers moved out, and the government began buying up all the land to return it to its original state.

Most people experience the park by driving spectacular **Skyline Drive** ($5 per car). A helpful brochure is handed out at booths along the route (one at either end and two mid-way). The drive opened in 1939 and runs (at 35 mph!) over 100 miles between the I-66 and I-64 freeways, giving grand vistas at every bend in the road. While such scenic driving is definitely memorable, by far the best way to really see the park is to get out of the car and walk along the many miles of trails that lead through the dense green forests to innumerable waterfalls and overlooks. If you have more time, the AT runs alongside Skyline Drive. It's accessible from dozens of different spots and feels miles away even when only a short walk from the roadway.

All of the Skyline's concession services—gas, food, and lodging—are operated by **ARA Virginia Skyline Inc.** (800/999-4714). Sites at the more popular **campgrounds** can be reserved in advance through MISTIX (800/365-CAMP). A few backcountry **cabins** are operated by the Potomac Appalachian Trail Club (703/242-0315), which also offers the best information on hiking in the park.

Mileposts (MM), arranged in mile-by-mile order from north to south, mark the best places to stop along Skyline Drive:

Halfway through Shenandoah National Park, US-211 runs west down to **Luray Caverns** (daily 9 AM–4 PM, till 6 PM in summer; $11), some of the largest and most impressive of the many caverns in the limestone Blue Ridge region—a single room measures 300 by 500 feet, and is over 140 feet high. It also boasts the "World's Only Stalacpipe Organ."

Pollution from metropolitan areas and from so many car-borne visitors has caused serious problems at Shenandoah National Park, both for the trees—many of which have been poisoned—and for the views people come to see. On an average summer day visibility is impaired and the surrounding valleys are often shrouded in smoggy haze.

Along with multicolored leaves, the autumn months bring hundreds of hawks, eagles, and other birds of prey to the mountains on their annual migration. You'll spot the greatest numbers of raptors in late September, when birdwatchers congregate for a "Hawk Watch" in the parking lot of the Holiday Inn, off I-64 along the crest.

Mile 0.6: Front Royal entrance station.

Mile 4.6: Climbing swiftly up from Front Royal in the north, the road reaches the main **visitor center** at Dickey Ridge, where you'll find a short nature trail.

Mile 21: On the shoulder of 3,474-foot **Hogback Mountain**, an overlook gives great views west over the meandering Shenandoah River. Access to the AT.

Mile 22.2: **Matthews Arm** campground.

Mile 24: Elkwallow **gas station** and store.

Mile 31.5: **Thornton Gap** entrance station; nearby Panorama restaurant deserves its name.

Mile 32.4: **Mary's Rock Tunnel**, a 13-foot bore cut through the granite in 1932; access to the AT.

Mile 41.7: **Skyland**, an early resort that preceded the establishment of the park, stands at 3,680 feet, the highest point on Skyline Drive. The lodge (703/999-2211 or 800/999-4714) has a dining room and other facilities, and offers horseback rides. Access to the AT.

Mile 50.7: Under a mile from the well-marked trailhead, **Dark Hollow Falls** drops over a 70-foot cliff.

Mile 51: **Byrd Visitor Center**, the other main visitor center in the park, marks the turnoff to **Big Meadows**, where there's a lodge (703/999-2221 or 800/999-4714), a campground, a **gas station**, and access to the AT.

Mile 56.4: A short steep hike scrambles up to the 3,300-foot-high summit of **Bearfence Mountain** for a 360-degree panorama.

Mile 65.7: **Swift Run Gap** entrance station.

Mile 79.5: **Loft Mountain** wayside area has a campground, showers (15 minutes of hot water for $1 in quarters), cabins, a store, a **gas station**, and access to the AT.

Mile 84.1: A parking area marks the trailhead for the rewarding two-mile hike to **Jones Run Falls**, tumbling over a mossy 45-foot cliff. Access to the AT.

Mile 98.9: Near the southern end of Skyline Drive, **Calf Mountain** provides a grand panorama over the Shenandoah Valley.

Mile 104.6: Rockfish Entrance Station. Skyline Drive ends at I-64, at mile 105.4.

Charlottesville

From the southern end of Shenandoah National Park, it's a quick 20 miles east on I-64 to Charlottesville (pop. 40,341), a richly historic college town that's one of the most enjoyable stops in the state. From the rolling green lawns of the University of Virginia campus to the neoclassical Monticello Monument on the hills above it, the legacy of Thomas Jefferson dominates Charlottesville. Jefferson lived and worked here for most of his life—when he wasn't out founding the country or serving as its president.

West of the compact downtown district, the **University of Virginia** campus was Jefferson's pride and joy. Not only did he found it and fund its early years, he planned the curriculum and designed the original buildings, a quadrangle of red brick Palladian villas that the American Institute of Architects declared the most perfect place in the country. Edgar Allan Poe lived and studied here briefly before dropping out in 1826. Poe's room, appropriately, is No. 13 in the West Range, and it's decorated to look like it did a century ago, with a few period belongings visible behind the glass door.

Charlottesville's other key site is Jefferson's home, **Monticello**—the domed building that fills the back of the nickel coin—well-signed off I-64 exit 121. Recently restored and open for tours (daily 9 AM–5 PM, from 8 AM in summer; $8), Monticello embodies the many different traits of this multifaceted man. The house was designed and built by Jefferson over a period of 40 years (1769-1809), and holds various gadgets he invented—including a double-pen device that made a copy of everything he wrote—and odd things he collected over the years, from elk antlers to recipes for home-brewed beer. The grounds, which in Jefferson's time included a plantation

To get a sense of life in the Shenandoah Valley, tune to **WSVA 550 AM** in Harrisonburg, which broadcasts updated farm and livestock prices every hour on the hour, and Rush Limbaugh for lunch.

worked by slaves, hold his mortal remains in a simple tomb beyond the vegetable gardens.

Down in the valley below Monticello, **Michie Tavern** (9 AM-5 PM; $6) is a touristy but interesting inn that opened in 1784 and was moved to the present site in the 1920s. Admission includes a tour of the parlors, bars, and upstairs rooms, as well as a dairy and a grist mill; it's also a restaurant serving "Olde Worlde foode" for the bus-tour hordes.

Like most college towns, Charlottesville provides a broad range of good places to eat, from bare-bones cafes like the **White Spot** at 1407 University Avenue, right across from campus, to more upscale places ranged along Elliewood Street around the corner. Among the nicest places to enjoy a meal is the lovely **Ivy Inn**, serving up New American food in a circa 1804 federal-style house at 2244 Old Ivy Road off US-250, west of the football stadium.

For more detailed information on visiting Charlottesville, contact the **visitor center** (804/293-6789), which is hard to miss on Hwy-20 off I-64 exit 121.

Staunton

West of the mountains from the south end of Shenandoah National Park on I-64, tidy Staunton (pop. 24,461, pronounced "STAN-ton") was founded in 1732 as one of the first towns on the far side of the Blue Ridge. Unlike much of the valley, Staunton was untouched during the Civil War, and now preserves its many 18th- and early 19th-cen-

---

THE BLUE RIDGE PARKWAY

Starting at the southern end of Shenandoah National Park, and winding along the crest of the Blue Ridge Mountains all the way to Great Smoky Mountains National Park, some 469 miles away, the Blue Ridge Parkway is one of the country's great scenic drives. This is especially true during autumn, when the dogwoods and gum trees turn deep red, and the hickories yellow, against an evergreen backdrop of pines, hemlocks, and firs. Spring is wildflower time, with abundant azaleas and rhododendrons blooming orange and pink throughout June, especially at the higher elevations.

First proposed in the 1920s, the Parkway was constructed 1935-67, when it grew from a network of local roads to the current route, along which billboards and commercial traffic are both banned. While the Parkway avoids towns and commercial areas to concentrate on the scenery, many interesting towns and other places along the way are well worth a detour.

For ease of use, the following description is divided into three main sections, starting with the drive south to Roanoke, described below. The Roanoke-to-North Carolina section is on page 284, and the final run south to the Great Smokies begins on page 287.

Mile 0: **Rockfish Gap**, at the southern end of Shenandoah National Park's Skyline Drive, marks the northern start of the Blue Ridge Parkway. I-64 and the AT cross here as well.

Mile 6.1: **Humpback Rocks** has a short trail leading through a reconstructed historic farmstead and a visitor center (703/943-4716). AT access.

tury buildings in a sizeable historic district around the boyhood home of Staunton's favorite son, Woodrow Wilson. Son of a Presbyterian minister, Wilson was born in 1856 in a stately Greek revival townhouse at 18-24 N. Coalter Street, now established as the **Woodrow Wilson Birthplace and Museum** (daily 10 AM-4 PM, 9 AM-5 PM in summer; $6), with galleries tracing his life as a scholar—he was president of Princeton University—and as U.S. president during WW I.

Woodrow Wilson

Staunton is also the home of the unique **Museum of American Frontier Culture** (daily 9 AM-5 PM; $7), right off I-81 on the east side of town. Oddly antiseptic, considering its rough and rural focus, this living history museum consists of four resurrected working farms, incorporating buildings brought over from Germany, England, and Ireland. The fourth farm, dating from antebellum Virginia, shows how various "Old World" traditions blended in America. The farms are inhabited by interpreters dressed in (very clean) period costumes busily husking corn, spinning wool, or working in the fields.

Staunton holds one of the best places to eat in the Shenandoah Valley, on US-250 just east of I-81 exit 222, near the frontier museum: the **Rowe Family Restaurant** (703/886-1833), which has been serving excellent, home-style cooking, from pork chops to banana cream pies, for the past 50 years.

Mile 29: **Whetstone Ridge** has a summer-only restaurant ($4 burger-and-fries), plus a gift shop and short nature trail.

Mile 34.4: **Yankee Horse** parking area has an exhibit on an old logging railroad, part of which has been restored, and a short trail to Wigwam Falls. AT access.

Mile 45.6: Junction with US-60, which runs west to the town of **Buena Vista** where there are motels and a great old general store, and to Lexington (see below).

Mile 63.6: Visitor center (804/299-5496), exhibits, and trails leading along the **James River and Kanawha Canal**. Lowest point on Parkway, 649 feet.

Mile 63.7: Junction with US-501, which runs west along the James River for 15 miles to Natural Bridge (see below).

Mile 76.5: Great views over both valleys from the **highest point** on Parkway in Virginia, 3,950 feet. AT access.

Mile 84-87: The most popular—and most developed—stretch of the Parkway, the 5,000 **Peaks of Otter** section includes a visitor center (703/586-4357), a gas station, a restaurant, and a very pleasant lodge (703/586-1081), which is open year-round. Three peaks rise above a small lake, and give great sunrise and sunset views; many good trails, including a two-mile loop to Fallingwater Cascades, let you escape the sometimes sizeable crowds.

Mile 100: **Curry Gap**, the last access to the AT, which cuts off west across the valley, then south into Tennessee.

Miles 106-121.4: The city of **Roanoke** (see below).

All the usual motels cluster around the I-64/I-81 junction, but you'll find the region's most pleasant accommodations at the rambling Victorian-era **Belle Grae Inn**, 515 W. Frederick Street (703/886-5151) in the center of Staunton, with B&B rooms from $65 a night.

Walter Russell

Mountain passes throughout the Blue Ridge are known as "gaps."

Swannanoa

High on a hilltop above the point where Skyline Drive runs into the Blue Ridge Parkway, Swannanoa (daily 9 AM-5 PM; $3) is a somewhat strange but beautifully sited shrine founded as a memorial to the painter, sculptor, and religious philosopher Walter Russell, "internationally known as the most versatile man in America," according to the promotional brochure. Terraced gardens dominated by a four-story statue "Christ of the Blue Ridge" surround a faux-Renaissance Italian palazzo, which houses the nonprofit educational foundation that since 1949 has been spreading Russell's message of brotherly love, art, and world peace.

At the entrance to Swannanoa, which rises above the south side of the I-64 freeway, a **Holiday Inn** shares the incredible views.

Lexington

Founded in 1778, and named for the then-recent Revolutionary War battleground, photogenic Lexington (pop. 6,959) is home to an estimable pair of Virginia institutions, the gender-embattled Virginia Military Institute, and Washington and Lee University, which meld into one another at the center of town. Numerous old brick buildings, including a typically southern lawyer's row around Courthouse Square, still stand around the town, which you can tour on foot or in one of the horse-drawn carriages that leave from the downtown visitor center.

Animated by an unusually crew-cut version of typical college-town energy, Lexington is redolent with, and proud of, its military heritage. Generals, in fact, have become the town's stock-in-trade: from 1859 until his death in 1863, Gen. **Thomas "Stonewall" Jackson** lived at 8 E. Washington Street, now a small museum (Mon.-Sat. 9 AM-5 PM, Sunday 1-5 PM; $4); he is buried in the small but well-tended cemetery a short distance west of downtown. General **Robert E. Lee** spent his post-Civil War years teaching at Washington and Lee, which was named after him (and his wife's ancestor George, yet another famous general). Lee is entombed in a crypt below the chapel, under a famous statue of his recumbent self, with his trusty horse Traveller buried just outside. Another influential old war-horse, Gen. **George C. Marshall**, is honored in a large eponymous museum (daily 9 AM-5 PM; $3) on the VMI campus; the museum traces General Marshall's role in WW II and salutes his Nobel Prize-winning "Marshall Plan" for postwar reconstruction.

If you've tired of fried food and meat, Lexington offers respite from the usual road fare: healthy soups and sandwiches at the **Blue Heron Cafe**, inside the Rockbridge Food Co-op at 110 W. Washington Street in the center of town. Another good reason to come to Lexington is to eat at the **Virginia House**, 722 S. Main Street, which has offered thick slabs of the house specialty, Virginia Ham, as well as mouthwatering pies—all prepared by the same ageless women who've run the place—for the past 30 years. However, business had slowed and quality dropped on my last visit; here's to hoping that things have returned to normal by the time you visit.

There are a number of comfortable and captivating places to stay in and around Lexington, such as the **Alexander Winthrow House**, 3 W. Washington Street (703/463-2044), or the **Llewellyn Lodge**, 603 S. Main Street (703/463-3235 or 800/882-1145), both friendly B&Bs within easy walking distance of the campuses and the historic town center.

For walking-tour maps, more general information, or further listings, contact the Lexington **visitor center**, 106 E. Washington Street (703/463-3777).

Natural Bridge

Held sacred by local Monacan Indians, and bought from King George in 1774 by Thomas Jefferson, the 215-foot-high notch of Natural Bridge is a remarkable piece of geologic acrobatics. Spanning some 90 feet, the thick stone arch bridges Cedar Creek at the bottom of a steeply walled canyon. To see the Natural Bridge, which is heralded as one of the "Seven Natural Wonders of the World" (others on the list include Niagara Falls, Yellowstone, and Giant's Causeway in Northern Ireland), you have to buy a ticket (daily 8 AM-dusk; $8; 800/533-1410)

from the unbelievably huge souvenir shop that fills the bottom of the old hotel. Natural Bridge is the focus of a once-plush resort complex that has definitely seen better times but still offers some 200 rooms in two hotels, also a wax museum ($7) of Virginia history in which you can watch the wax figures being made, dressed, and posed.

Not surprisingly, wonderfully tacky Roadside Americana surrounds Natural Bridge. Look out for an "Enchanted Castle" and a family of dinosaurs lining US-11 on the way in from I-81.

On Mill Mountain high above Roanoke, the 100-foot-tall **"World's Largest Man-Made Star"** shines nightly, lit by 2,000 feet of neon tubing.

Roanoke

Apart from Asheville at its southern end, Roanoke (pop. 96,397) is the only real city that can claim it's actually *on* the Blue Ridge Parkway. With block after block of brick-fronted business buildings, most of them adorned with neon, metal, and painted signs that seem unchanged since the 1940s, Roanoke makes a sudden contrast with the natural verdance of the rest of the

Parkway, but you may find it a welcome change after so many trees. Once a busy, belching, industrial goliath supported by the railroads, Roanoke has evolved into a sophisticated, high-tech city—the commercial, cultural, and medical center of southwest Virginia.

Roanoke's main visitor attractions lie right downtown in the **Center in the Square** complex, a restored warehouse that holds a wide variety of cultural offerings, including theaters, an art

Southeast of Roanoke, the **Booker T. Washington National Monument** (daily 9 AM-4:30 PM; free; 703/721-2094) preserves the plantation cabin where the influential black leader was born. The 225-acre site is 20 miles from Roanoke via Hwy-116 and Hwy-122.

For NPR news and non-commercial arts programming, tune to **WVTF 89.1 FM** in Roanoke.

The soft drink Dr. Pepper, which originated in Waco, Texas, was named for a pharmacist who worked in the town of Rural Retreat, Virginia, along I-81 near its intersection with the AT.

museum, a science museum, and a local history museum (Tues.-Sat. 10 AM-4 PM, Sunday 1-5 PM; $2). Also worth a look is the **Virginia Museum of Transportation**, 303 Norfolk Avenue (Mon.-Sat. 10 AM-5 PM, Sunday noon-5 PM; $4), which displays lots of old cars and trucks, steam and diesel locomotives, and horse-drawn carriages, plus a complete traveling circus—minus the performers, of course.

The town's best place to eat is **The Roanoker**, "The Home of Good Food since 1941," which serves traditional Virginia dishes and also does a tasty bowl of chili, a mile south of downtown off US-220 (Wonju Street exit) at 2522 Colonial Avenue. There are also a number of good cafes downtown, and if you're planning a picnic up in the mountains be sure to stop first at the historic **Farmer's Market** (Mon.-Sat. 8 AM-4 PM; free), downtown next to the Center in the Square, and active since 1874.

THE BLUE RIDGE PARKWAY, ROANOKE TO NORTH CAROLINA

South from Roanoke, the Blue Ridge Parkway winds another 100 miles before crossing the North Carolina border. This midsection of the Parkway runs at a lower elevation across a more settled and cultivated landscape than the rugged ridgetops followed elsewhere. In place of the spectacular vistas, along this stretch you'll see many more houses and small farms, a few pioneer cabins (preserved and not), and some picturesque cemeteries.

Miles 105-122: The city of **Roanoke** (see above).

Mile 129.6: **Roanoke Overlook** provides a grand view over the city.

Mile 154.5: A two-mile loop trail leads to a pioneer cabin overlooking the **Smart View** for which it's named. Blooming dogwoods abound in May.

Mile 165.2: At **Tuggles Gap**, the junction with Hwy-8 has a motel, a restaurant, and a gas station, also a small cemetery right along the Parkway.

Miles 167-174: The 4,800-acre **Rocky Knob** area contains a campground, a visitor center at Mile 169, and a 10-mile roundtrip trail at Mile 167.1 leading down through Rock Castle Gorge.

Mile 174: East of the Parkway along Greenwood Road, you'll find the summer-only **Rocky Knob Cabins** (703/593-3503).

Mile 176.1: A short trail leads to **Mabry Mill**, in use 1910-35. In summer, interpreters demonstrate blacksmithing and milling skills. A coffee shop (open May-Oct. only) sells old-fashioned pancakes made from stoneground flour, plus country hams and hamburgers.

Mile 177.7: Junction with **US-58**, marked by the clean and quiet **Blue Ridge Motel** (703/952-2244), which also has a good restaurant.

Mile 189: Near the midpoint of the Parkway, atop Groundhog Mountain, the **Doe Run Lodge** (703/398-2212) offers spacious, modern, chalet-style cabins (with a pool and tennis courts) and a "fine dining" restaurant.

Mile 216.9: Virginia/North Carolina border.

Places to stay range from the usual interstate motels to $80-a-night B&Bs like the **Mary Bladon House**, 381 Washington Avenue (703/344-5361). The handy **visitor center**, right downtown at 114 Market Street (703/345-8622 or 800/635-5535), offers lots more listings and information.

The border between Virginia and North Carolina was surveyed in 1749 by a team that included Thomas Jefferson's father, Peter.

ACROSS NORTH CAROLINA

Running along the crest of the Blue Ridge Mountains at the far western edge of the state, this route across North Carolina takes in some of the most beautiful scenery east or west of the Mississippi. Though not as immense as the Rockies or other western landscapes, this part of North Carolina abounds with rugged peaks and deep valleys, pastoral meadows, and ancient-looking mountain villages, some dating back to colonial times. It's all linked by the magnificent Blue Ridge Parkway, perhaps the country's greatest scenic drive.

The region's sole city, Asheville, is a proud old resort dominated by the ostentatious Biltmore Estate, "the world's largest private house," but everywhere else nature predominates—especially in the majestic Great Smoky Mountains National Park in the state's far southwestern corner.

Southeast of the Parkway along the Virginia/ North Carolina border, Mount Airy (pop. 7,156) was the boyhood home of **Andy Griffith,** who based much of his TV show *Mayberry RFD* on the region.

The Blue Ridge Parkway to
Great Smoky Mountains National Park

The highest and most memorable parts of the 469-mile Blue Ridge Parkway include the mountainous miles leading along the backbone of North Carolina. Following the southern Blue Ridge Mountains as they fade into the taller and more massive Black Mountains, the Parkway skirts three other mountain ranges before ending up at Great Smoky Mountains National Park on the Tennessee border. Spring flowers, fall colors, numerous waterfalls, and occasional eerie fogs that fill the valleys below make this an unforgettable trip no matter what the time of year; take your time and drive carefully, however hard it is to keep your eyes on the road.

The Virginia sections of the Blue Ridge Parkway are described above, on pages 280-281 and 284.

In the valley below Mount Mitchell, off I-40 northeast of Asheville, **Black Mountain College** was a lively intellectual and artistic nexus during the 1930s and 1940s, when the likes of Charles Olson hung out here.

The hikers' Appalachian Trail winds west of the Blue Ridge Parkway along the North Carolina/Tennessee border.

Blowing Rock

A quick two miles south of the Blue Ridge Parkway via US-221 from Milepost 291.9 lies the delightful little resort community of Blowing Rock (pop. 1,257)—the place to stop if you're only stopping once. The cool summer temperatures have been attracting visitors for centuries, and once you get past the hideous factory outlet mall that welcomes you to town, quaint old Main Street is a great place to stretch your legs while taking in the eclectic range of late Victorian buildings. Blowing Rock takes its name from a nearby cliff overlooking John's River Gorge, where updrafts can cause lightweight objects to be blown upwards rather than down; this effect, which earned Blowing Rock a mention in *Ripley's Believe It or Not!* as the only place "Where Snow Falls Upside Down," also inspired the Native American legend of a Cherokee brave who, rather than be forcibly separated from his Chickasaw lover, leapt off the cliff, only to be blown back into the arms of his sweetheart.

North Carolina's oldest tourist attraction, the **Blowing Rock** itself, two miles east of town via winding US-321 (daily 9 AM-5 PM, 8 AM-8 PM in summer; $4), is worth the admission, whether or not the "magic wind" is blowing. Check out the tremendous views from a platform suspended 3,000 feet above the valley below. Blowing Rock also offers a couple of enjoyable tourist traps, including an apparently gravity-defying "**Mystery Hill**" just off the Parkway, and the scenic, coal-fired steam trains of the **Tweetsie Railroad** four miles north of town on US-321.

Downtown Blowing Rock has a number of good places to eat. Try the ham-and-biscuit breakfasts at **Sunny's Grill**, or the family-oriented three square meals offered at **Buchanan's Restaurant**, across from the hardware store at the north end of town.

Across the highway from the Blowing Rock, the storybook **Green Park Inn** is a large historic resort hotel built in 1882. More modern conveniences are available at the **Cliff Dwellers Inn** (704/295-3121), right off the parkway on US-321. There are also a number of small local motels and a few B&Bs; for details, contact the visitor center (704/295-7851).

BLUE RIDGE PARKWAY: VIRGINIA TO THE GREAT SMOKIES

A couple of worthwhile detours—to the mountain hamlets of Blowing Rock and Little Switzerland and to the city of Asheville—are covered in greater detail below. From north to south, here are the mile-by-mile highlights along the Parkway:

Mile 216.9: Virginia/North Carolina border.

Mile 217.5: A very easy half-mile trail leads to the top of 2,885-foot **Cumberland Knob**.

Miles 238.5-244.7: **Doughton Park**, named for one of the politicians who made the Parkway possible, has a gas station, food, and the small **Bluffs Lodge** (910/372-4499) at Mile 241. Starting at the historic Brinegar Cabin (Mile 238.5), the four-mile Cedar Ridge trail is one of many rewarding dayhikes, all of which offer great views.

Mile 260.6: An easy mile-long trail leads to the top of **Jumpinoff Rocks** for a sweeping view.

Mile 285.1: **Boone's Trace**, a pioneer trail first blazed by Daniel Boone, crosses the mountains at this point.

Mile 291.9: Junction with US-221, which leads south to the lovely little mountain town of **Blowing Rock** (see above for more), two miles off the Parkway.

Miles 292-295: **Moses H. Cone Memorial Park** is a 3,600-acre former private estate, with many miles of mountaintop hiking trails centering upon the nonprofit Parkway Craft Center (daily 9 AM-5:30 PM, May-Oct. only; free).

Mile 304.6: The marvelous engineering feat of the **Linn Cove Viaduct** carries the Parkway around rugged Grandfather Mountain. Completed in 1987, this was the last part of the Parkway to be built. A small visitor center (open May-Oct. at Mile 304) has general information and exhibits on the viaduct's construction, which included pre-cast, post-stressed concrete box girders cantilevered in spans of 180 feet. Dense walls of rhododendrons border the Parkway south of the viaduct.

Mile 305.1: US-221, which used to carry the Parkway before the viaduct was built, leads a mile south to 5,837-foot **Grandfather Mountain**, the highest peak in Blue Ridge, now a private park (daily 8 AM-5 PM; $9) with trails and a zoo.

Mile 308.2: A half-mile, self-guided nature trail leads to 3,995-foot **Flat Rock** for a view of Grandfather Mountain.

Mile 316.4: Two miles northwest of the Parkway, **Linville Falls** crashes through a rugged gorge; trails lead to a series of overlooks. Visitor center and campground (704/259-0701).

Mile 331: At the junction of Hwy-226, the **Museum of North Carolina Minerals** (daily 9 AM-5 PM; free) displays all kinds and sizes of local gemstones, which you can watch being polished.

(continues on next page)

Mile 334: Junction with Hwy-226, which leads south to **Little Switzerland**, a resort community described more fully below.

Mile 339: **Crabtree Meadows** has rhododendrons, a gas station, and a nifty Flintstones-modern coffee shop (May-Oct. only).

Mile 355.4: West of the Parkway, the 1,650 acres of **Mount Mitchell State Park** include an observation tower, a campground, food service, and a visitor center (daily 8 AM-dusk; free; 704/675-4611). Trails lead above the tree line to the top of the 6,684-foot peak, the highest point east of the Mississippi River.

Mile 364.6: Best seen in late spring when the rhododendrons are in full bloom, the lush greenery of **Craggy Gardens** feels like an Appalachian Shangri-La. Nature trails lead from the visitor center (daily 9 AM-5 PM April-Oct.; free).

Mile 382: You can check out exhibits and demonstrations of Appalachian arts and crafts in the **Folk Art Center** (daily 9 AM-5 PM; free).

Miles 383-395: The historic mountain resort city of **Asheville** (see below) lies west of the Parkway.

Mile 407.8: Originally part of the 100,000-acre Biltmore Estate, the slopes of 5,721-foot **Mount Pisgah** were among the first places in the U.S. where sustainable forestry was practiced. A small "Cradle of Forestry in America" exhibit, focusing on the work of Gifford Pinchot, Biltmore gardener and founder of the U.S. Forest Service, is housed in a visitor center off the Parkway at Mile 412.

Mile 431: A self-guided nature trail leads through a first-growth spruce and fir forest, from the **highest point on the Parkway**, at 6,047 feet.

Mile 469: **Southern end** of Blue Ridge Parkway, at the junction with US-441 and the entrance to Smoky Mountains National Park.

A dozen miles west of the Blue Ridge Parkway via US-321 and Hwy-194, the village of Valle Crucis holds the circa 1883 **Mast General Store** (704/963-6511), a one-of-a-kind survivor that sells a little of everything, from gasoline to Gore-Tex parkas.

Little Switzerland

Another classic mountaintop vacation spot, located midway between Blowing Rock and Asheville, Little Switzerland was founded in 1910 around the **Switzerland Inn** (704/765-2153 or 800/654-4026), a stately old chalet-style resort that also operates a very popular restaurant right off the Blue Ridge Parkway at Milepost 334.

The inn stands on a crest, but the rest of Little Switzerland sits in the deep canyon to the east, spread out along Hwy-226 and a number of smaller side roads. The main stop is **Emerald Village** (daily 9 AM-6 PM April-Nov.; $4), on McKinney Mine Road 2.5 miles from the Parkway, where you can tour an old gemstone mine (above and below ground) and museums displaying everything from gemstones to mechanical music makers.

Asheville

What the English country town of Bath was to King George's London, the mountain resort of Asheville (pop. 61,607) was to the pre-jet set, pre-air-conditioned Deep South. When summer heat and humidity became unbearable, the gentry headed here to stay cool while enjoying the city's many grand hotels and elaborate summer homes.

The presence here of the world's biggest vacation house, the Vanderbilt family's **Biltmore Estate** (daily 9 AM-5 PM; $22.95; 704/255-1700 or 800/543-2961), is a testament to Asheville's primary position in the resort pantheon. The estate now covers 8,000 acres on the south side of town, though at one time it stretched up to the Blue Ridge Parkway. Surrounded by a series of flower gardens planned in part by Frederick Law Olmsted, the estate centers on a truly unbelievable French Renaissance-style mansion built in 1895. The 250-plus rooms hold everything from a palm court and a bowling alley to Napoleon's chess set to paintings by Renoir, Singer Sargent, Whistler, and others. Signs aplenty direct you to the estate, which stands just north of the I-40 exit 50 off Biltmore Avenue, across from the Historic Biltmore Village shopping mall that originally housed the estate's staff and workshops—a "model village" designed in gothic style by Richard Morris Hunt.

The rest of Asheville can't compete with the nouveau riche excess of the Biltmore Estate, and in fact it's a surprisingly homespun city, with a downtown commercial district filled with 1930s-era storefronts housing thrift stores and off-beat art galleries, as well as the welcoming pub-*cum*-performance space **Be Here Now**, 5 Biltmore Avenue (704/258-2071), where nationally known indie rock, jazz, and bluegrass bands stop on tour.

One truly worthwhile place to see in downtown Asheville is the nondescript old boardinghouse where author Thomas Wolfe grew up from 1900-20, preserved exactly as it was when Wolfe lived here—peeling paint, creaking floorboards, dodgy wiring, and all. The rambling house, officially the **Thomas Wolfe National Historic Site**, 48 Spruce Street (Mon.-Sat. 9 AM-5 PM, Sunday 1-5 PM; $1) across from the monstrous modern Radisson Hotel, is perhaps the most evocative of all American literary sites. In the details and, more importantly, in general ambience, it's identi-

Thomas Wolfe

cal to the vivid prose descriptions of the house he called "Dixieland," the primary setting of his first and greatest novel *Look Homeward, Angel.* After Wolfe's death from tuberculosis in 1938, the house was made into a shrine to Wolfe by his family, who arranged it to look as it did during their youth; one room contains his desk, typewriter, and other mementos of his life and work.

Two blocks south of the Wolfe memorial, where Broadway becomes Biltmore Avenue, **Pack Square** is the center of Asheville, surrounded by the county courthouse, the city hall, a small art museum, and the public library. This is where Thomas Wolfe's father ran a stonecutting shop, on whose porch stood the homeward-gazing angel, now recalled by a statue standing on the square's southwest corner.

The streets around Pack Square hold a few good places to eat, like the **Mountain Smokehouse BBQ** at 20 Spruce Street next to City Hall. There are more good places around the art deco-style Grove shopping arcade west of the square, including the **Laughing Seed Cafe**, serving heath-conscious food at 40 Wall Street.

Another of Asheville's literary lights was the short story writer **O. Henry,** who is buried in the Riverside Cemetery on Birch Street. Thomas Wolfe is buried here as well.

Asheville's long-standing relationship with visitors explains why the local minor league baseball team is called the Asheville Tourists. Call the ball club (704/258-0428) for tickets or further information.

You can spot the wild mountains southeast of Asheville in numerous movies including *Last of the Mohicans,* much of which was filmed around Chimney Rock near the oddly named town of Bat Cave.

If the Vanderbilts came to Asheville today, they'd probably stay at **Grove Park Inn Resort,** 290 Macon Avenue north of I-90 (704/252-2711 or 800/438-0050), a lovely rustic inn built in 1913 in the hills above downtown Asheville. Newer wings contain the most modern four-star conveniences, but the original lodge boasts rooms filled with authentic Roycroft furniture, the largest collection anywhere. Grove Park is like a live-in museum of arts-and-crafts style. If your taste and budget run more toward mainstream Americana, you may prefer the classic 1930s **Log Cabin Motor Court,** six miles north of Asheville off US-70 at 330 Weaverville Highway (704/645-6546). The usual chain hotels cluster along the interstates.

For further information on the Asheville area, contact the **visitor center,** 151 Haywood Street off I-240 exit 4C (704/258-6109 or 800/257-1300).

Cherokee

The Blue Ridge Parkway swings south from Asheville through Transylvania County on the approach to Great Smoky Mountains National Park, though you won't miss much by following the I-40 freeway to the junction with US-19, which links up with the end of the parkway at the park entrance. This stretch of US-19, winding over the foothills of the Great Smokies, is absolutely packed with roadside Americana—miniature golf courses, trout farms, souvenir shops, and lookout towers alongside pancake houses, BBQ shacks, and RV parks—but apart from this it's a very pretty drive, ending up 40 miles west of Asheville at touristy Cherokee (pop. 5,971).

The town is the Commercial center of the 56,000-acre **Cherokee Indian Reservation**, which was established here by a small band of Cherokee Indians in 1866, long after the rest of this once mighty tribe had been forcibly exiled to Oklahoma on the Trail of Tears. Cherokee is a last gasp of commercialism at the edge of the national park, a traffic-clogged gauntlet of places where you can See Live Bears, Eat Boiled Peanuts, or Pan For Gold.

Amidst the tourist-taunting sprawl, however, you'll find a couple of worthwhile stops, first of which is the **Qualla Arts and Crafts Shop** on US-441 a half-mile north of town, where you can buy or just admire the fine craftsmanship of Cherokee baskets or jewelry. Across the street, the **Museum of the Cherokee Indian** (daily 9 AM-5 PM, longer hours in summer; $4) traces tribal history, from the preconquest achievements—the Cherokee used a natural version of aspirin centuries before western chemists "discovered" it, for example—to their forced removal after gold was discovered here in the 1830s.

If you happen to like the flagstone-and-plate-glass "Flintstones modern" architecture of the early 1960s, you'll want to stop for a look, if not a meal, at the Sequoyah Cafeteria in the very center of town. Next door, the Cherokee Tribe's **visitor center** (704/497-9195 or 800/438-1601) provides lots of information on other places to eat and on the Cherokee area's many motels and campgrounds.

Great Smoky Mountains National Park

The most popular park in the U.S., Great Smoky Mountains National Park offers a taste of wilderness to some nine million visitors annually. Knoxville, Nashville, and Atlanta are all within a two-hour drive, and day-trippers visit mostly during late October for the annual display of fall color. The park covers 520,460 acres along the 6,000-foot-high crest of the Great Smoky Mountains, so-named for the fogs that fill the deep valleys. Before the park was established its lands were extensively logged—70% of the trees had been clear-cut by 1934, when the lands were protected as a national park. Fortunately, the forests have grown back to obscure any sign of past degradations, and the uncut portions form the most extensive stands of primeval forest in the eastern U.S.

The main route through the park is Newfound Gap Road (US-441), which runs northwest from Cherokee to the even more tourist-traveled Gatlinburg and Pigeon Forge in Tennessee. The

Novelist **F. Scott Fitzgerald** lived at Asheville's Grove Park Resort while visiting his wife Zelda, who had been committed to the Highland Hospital sanitarium, where she died in a fire in 1948.

For many years, Cherokee Chief Henry was known as **"The World's Most Photographed Indian,"** his image gracing countless postcards.

Just over the mountains on the Tennessee side of the Great Smokies, Dolly Parton owns, runs, and stars at **Dollywood** (800/DOLLY-WOOD), the country's biggest autobiographical theme park.

One of the nicest places to stay near the Great Smokies is the mountaintop **Snowbird Mountain Lodge,** 275 Santeetlah Road (704/479-3433), south of Cherokee between Robbinsville and the first-growth hardwoods of Joyce Kilmer Memorial Forest.

road winds steeply through dense forests packed with magnificent giant hardwoods, flowering poplar, dogwood, azalea, and rhododendron, and evergreen pines and firs at the highest elevations. Where the highway reaches the crest, a spur road runs parallel to the Appalachian Trail five miles west to 6,642-foot **Clingman's Dome**, the highest point in the park, where you can take a short but steep trail up to a lookout tower.

> Biologists estimate that some 500 native black bears live in the backcountry of Great Smoky Mountains National Park.

One of the most extensive "natural" areas—unlogged, old-growth forest, full of the park's oldest and tallest trees—lies at the very center of the park, off Newfound Gap Road on the north side of the crest. Starting at the popular Chimney Tops Picnic area, the well-marked, three-quarter-mile **Cove Hardwood nature trail** winds through a sampling of the park's most stately maples and other broad-leafed trees—the ones responsible for the best of the fall colors.

> The Appalachian Trail runs along the crest of the Great Smoky Mountains, crossing Newfound Gap Road at the center of the park.

Along Little River Road, west of the Sugarlands Visitor Center off US-441 at the park's northern entrance, stands another group of ancient trees. Midway along, trails lead to two marvelous waterfalls, Laurel Falls and Meigs Falls. Little River Road ends up at **Cades Cove**, where the preserved remnants of a mountain community that existed here from the early 1800s until the 1930s give a strong sense of Appalachian folkways. A church and a number of mills still stand, and interpretive staff offer guided walks and other programs explaining the history and culture of these mountain people—some 6,000 of whom used to live within the park boundaries. **Bike rentals** are available at the Cades Cove campground, and you'll find plenty of opportunities for rides along the old country lanes.

Another popular park destination is **Grotto Falls**, southeast of Gatlinburg via the Roaring Fork Road, where a short flat trail to the tumbling cascade leads through lush hemlock forest—an ideal environment for mushrooms, and for the 27 different species of salamanders that slither around underfoot; Great Smokies is the "Salamander Capital of the World."

The only beds available in the park are at **LeConte Lodge** (615/429-5704), atop 6,593-foot Mount LeConte, a six-mile hike from the nearest road. Ten fairly basic **campgrounds** (no showers or hookups) operate in the Great Smokies park, with

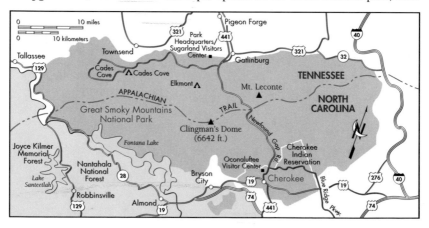

reservations taken only for the most popular ones at Cades Cove and Elkmont (800/365-CAMP); there are also bear-proofed backcountry shelters along the Appalachian Trail.

For more information, or to pick up the handy brochures (35 cents each) describing the park's array of flora, fauna, trails, and other features, stop by either of the two main visitor centers (both 8 AM-4:30 PM, longer hours in summer; 615/436-1200). North of Cherokee at the south entrance, the **Oconaluftee Visitor Center** stands alongside a restored pioneer farmstead, where crafts demonstrations are given in summer. From the **Sugarlands Visitor Center**, two miles south of Gatlinburg, Tennessee, you can take a short hike to Cataract Falls.

The many different salamanders native to the Great Smokies range from the tiny pygmy to the massive hellbender, which grows up to two feet long, head to tail.

Franklin's **1480 WVF AM** plays an entertaining combination of local news and contemporary Christian country music.

Between Franklin and Highlands, US-64 passes by several waterfalls and has been designated a **"Mountain Waters Scenic Byway."**

South to Georgia: Franklin

South from Cherokee and the Great Smoky Mountains, US-441 runs through the giant Nantahala National Forest, which stretches all the way to the Georgia border. It's a fast road, mostly divided four-lane freeway, passing through a fairly developed corridor of towns and small cities.

The biggest town in this part of North Carolina, Franklin (pop. 2,873) was founded in the mid-1800s on a shallow ridge overlooking the Little Tennessee River. Along with lumber milling, Franklin's main industry has long been the mining of gemstones—garnets, rubies, and sapphires—from the surrounding hills. Though mining is no longer commercially viable, many of these old mines have found new life catering to rockhound tourists, who for a small fee (around $1 per bucket, in addition to an entrance charge of around $5) can sift through gravelly ores searching for valuable finds. A half-dozen such places line Hwy-28 in the first five miles northwest of Franklin.

Franklin itself is a light industrial center, spread out around the intersection of US-441 and US-64, with a compact downtown area packed with gemstone and jewelry shops like **Ruby City**, at the north end of Main Street, which also has a small free museum. The **Hickory Ranch Restaurant**, at 126 Palmer Street a block off Main Street, is a popular place to eat fried chicken or BBQ while watching model trains rumble around the room; it also has an old-fashioned ice cream parlor. A block away, the **Franklin Motel**, 223 Palmer Street (704/524-4431 or 800/433-5507), has clean, comfortable rooms and a swimming pool for under $40 a night.

From Franklin, Hwy-28/US-64 heads southeast through the heart of Transylvania County, known as the "Land of Waterfalls" because of its many cascades. The biggest of these is 13 miles from Franklin and named, for some unknown reason, **Dry Falls**. From the well-signed parking area, follow a short trail that ends up underneath and behind the impressively raging torrent, a powerful white-noise generator you can hear long before you reach it. Another waterfall, known as **Bridal Veil Falls**, is a mile south from Dry Falls. Bridal Veil is much smaller than Dry Falls, but spills right along the road; the overhang is so deep that you can drive underneath it.

Two miles south from Bridal Veil Falls, US-64 enters the resort community of **Highlands** (pop. 900). Here Hwy-106 loops back to the southwest, giving grand panoramic views over the forested foothills before rejoining US-441 across the Georgia border in Dillard.

ACROSS GEORGIA

If Georgia brings to mind endless, flat cotton plantations, you'll be pleasantly surprised by the mountainous wilds of the state's northern tier. The great Appalachian ridge that runs along the East Coast has its southern foot here, high up in the forests of Rabun County, which packs natural wonders, outdoor adventures, and downhome Appalachian spirit into the state's small, isolated corner. Chattooga River whitewater—made famous by the movie *Deliverance,* and rated among the top 10 river runs in the U.S.—is the biggest draw, and sightseers can take in Chattooga's spectacular waterfalls. Christmas-tree farms, dairies, and car graveyards dot the old-time mountain towns, where rooted residents in homey cabins and old trailers grow corn in sideyards and advertise "Mountain Honey for Sale" on hand-painted wooden signs.

> The hikers' Appalachian Trail crosses the Georgia/North Carolina border roughly 10 miles west of Dillard, then veers southeast, coming to a finale at the 3,782-foot summit of Springer Mountain, where a photogenic sign marks the end (or the beginning) of the trail.

> The rocky crest of Black Rock Mountain marks the eastern **Continental Divide**—from here waters part to follow a path to either the Atlantic Ocean or the Gulf of Mexico.

Dillard

Just south of the North Carolina border, the highway hamlet of Dillard (pop. 199) is a mini-fiefdom of the Dillard family, whose name dates back to the 1700s in these parts. For generations, the Dillards have run a local hospitality empire based around the sprawling set of bungalows, lodges, and dining rooms all going by the name **Dillard House** (706/746-5348), on a hill above US-441 at the south edge of town. Heading up the complex is the Dillard House restaurant, famous for its all-you-can-eat country cooking: from its glass-walled patio, diners can enjoy plates of classic country ham, fried chicken, pan-fried trout, vegetables, cornbread, and assorted relishes and desserts. The legendary institution may today impress you as more institution than legend—bus tours dominate the clientele—but you never leave hungry. Rooms are around back—in low-slung lodges scattered near a swimming pool and tennis courts; prices hover around $60.

In addition to the rambling inn, the family oligarchy operates a row of roadside businesses off US-441, selling collectible and keepsake souvenirs.

Black Rock Mountain

At the wind-worn summit of 3,640-foot Black Rock Mountain, a flagstone terrace looks out over a grand Appalachian panorama: if there's no fog, you can see clear to the South Carolina piedmont 80 miles away and as far as the Great Smokies to the north. The highest state park in Georgia now occupies the slope's legendary mountain, offering hiking trails and accommodations in addition to the splendid vistas. Set off in a ring at the top of the mountain, 10 spacious cottages are removed from lowland civilization—no phones, no TVs, just fireplaces and porch rockers. The cottages cost $55-70 a night, sleep up to 10 people, and are rented all year—a nice snowy winter retreat. There's also a pair of $12-a-night campgrounds.

Black Rock Mountain State Park is three miles north of Clayton, well-signed to the west of US-441. For information, or for reservations for the cabins or the campgrounds, contact the park **visitor center** (706/746-2141) near the summit.

Foxfire Museum

Tucked away on the west side of US-441 just south of the turnoff to Black Mountain State Park, the modest Foxfire Museum (Mon.-Fri. 10 AM-4 PM; donations; 706/746-5318) displays a crowded collection of Appalachian arts and crafts. The museum is part of a radical (for rural Georgia) cultural and educational movement that began here in the mid-1960s when local schoolteacher Eliot Wigginton, frustrated in attempts to motivate his uninspired high-school students, assigned them the task of interviewing their elders about how things were in "the old days." The students, inspired with the newly discovered richness of their Appalachian heritage, assembled the written interviews into a magazine, which they named *Foxfire* after a luminescent local lichen.

The magazine expanded to a series of *Foxfire* books, and more than eight million copies sold worldwide. The collection exhaustively documented fading Appalachian folkways, and the program's twofold success—educational innovation and folklife preservation—further broadened as the then-emerging back-to-the-land movement seized upon these books as vital how-to manuals for subsistence farming, cookery, animal husbandry, and crafts making from found materials. The Foxfire organization still runs classes and summer programs around the country and on a 110-acre campus in the hills above the museum.

Mountain City

Passing through Mountain City (pop. 784) at the end of the day, drivers watch the monolith of Black Rock Mountain impose an early twilight on the broad valley to its east. Behind scruffy roadside cabins with their lean-to signs, the granite mountain's shadow slowly reaches past grazing black-and-white cows and tractors parked between haystacks.

The town itself stretches along US-441 for a few miles south from the Foxfire Museum, but the main attraction is the highway on York House Road, beyond the cows and hay and over the gully bridge, where you'll find trim white **York House** (706/746-2068) banked against the forest wall. This historic inn has been open for business since 1896, and not much has changed since then, except the addition of indoor plumbing in every room; rates run $64-69 for a comfortable room with a continental breakfast.

Chattooga River whitewater rafting

Slicing through the Appalachian wilderness at the junction of three states, the **Chattooga River** rates among the nation's top 10 whitewater river adventures, attracting some 100,000 visitors a year to Rabun County for rafting, canoeing, kayaking, tubing, swimming, fishing, and riverside hiking. The "Wild and Scenic" river was seen in the movie *Deliverance,* based on the book by Georgia poet and novelist **James Dickey;** ever since the movie was released, authorities have been pulling bodies out of the river—not toothless mountaineers but overconfident river-runners who underestimate the whitewater's power.

Clayton

The downhome mountain community of Clayton (pop. 1,613) is the largest town in Rabun County, and a good base of operations for excursions into the wild forest and Chattooga River areas to the east. Main Street, a three-block length of wooden storefronts on a sunny rise just west of US-411, still looks like you could hitch a horse at the curb to do your trading and salooning. The **Old Clayton Inn** (706/782-7722) at the center of town has been open for a century or so, though it's been tidied up considerably in the years since Burt Reynolds and crew stayed here while filming *Deliverance* on the raging Chattooga.

For roadtrippers, the best reason to plan a stop in Clayton is to sample the woodstove cookery at the **Green Shutters Restaurant**, just over a mile from town on S. Main Street (old US-441). Three family-style meals a day, accompanied by cinnamon rolls,

sweet potato bread, buttermilk biscuits, and corn muffins, are served in a small but cozy downstairs dining room looking out across a screened-in verandah at apple

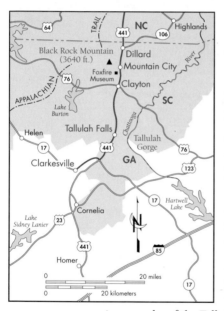

orchards and pasturelands. Unfortunately, the Green Shutters keeps limited hours (open daily except Tuesday 8-10 AM, 11 AM-2 PM, and 5-9 PM; 706/782-3342), so plan your trip accordingly. If the Green Shutters isn't serving, the **Clayton Cafe** on Main Street downtown slings downhome breakfasts, burgers, and other basic diner fare, while at the counter of the funky **Chick N' Coop** on US-441, locals enjoy a good-and-cheap Southern buffet.

The enthusiastic folks at the Rabun County Chamber of Commerce run a resourceful **visitor center** (706/782-4812) on US-441 north of town.

Tallulah Falls

Balanced precariously over the precipitous gorge that once held the thundering cascades of the Tallulah River, tiny Tallulah Falls (pop. 147) has an illustrious history. As word of the natural wonder spread, crowds were drawn to the breathtaking sight, and by the turn of the century Tallulah Falls was a fashionable resort, with several elite hotels and boardinghouses catering to lowland sightseers. But fortunes changed once the power company set its sights on harnessing water power for hydroelectricity. Over public objections, the completed dam (which sits at the north end of town, directly beneath the new bridge that carries US-441 over the river) slowed the water—and the crowds—to a

Following US-76 12 miles west from Clayton brings you to postage-stamp-sized **Moccasin Creek State Park,** Georgia's smallest state park. Nestled invitingly on the shores of Lake Burton off Hwy-197, it offers good fishing, a campground (706/947-3194), and family-style food at LaPrade's across the street.

trickle. Despite the still-impressive sight of the now-dry gorge, the resort ambience faded, and Tallulah Falls reverted to a rustic mountain community. Recently, after decades of talk about restoring the gorge's former glory, the power company agreed to test the waters and send the Tallulah River spilling through the gorge once again.

In the mountains northwest of Clarkesville, 15 miles along Hwy-17 and Hwy-75, the tiny town of **Helen** (pop. 355) turned itself into a tourist draw in 1969, remodeling all the buildings in mock-Bavarian decor and repaving the streets in cobblestones.

Tallulah Gorge

The dramatic, sheer walls of Tallulah Gorge have both haunted and attracted people for centuries. The wary Cherokee heeded legends that warriors who ventured in never returned, and many a curious settler had a waterfall or pool named in his honor—posthumously, after an untimely slip.

Tallulah Gorge is best seen from the mile-long scenic route (old US-441), which loops off east of the modern highway. Drivers can pull over at numerous parking areas and take one of several rough trails along the gorge's rim, though the best views are from the historic **Tallulah Point Overlook** (daily 9 AM-7 PM; free), a privately owned concession stand midway along the loop. You can stretch your legs or rent mountain bikes here ($25 a day; 706/754-4318; maps, water bottles, and helmets are included in the price).

Whether or not the waters are flowing, when you take in the sight of Tallulah Gorge, imagine walking a tightrope suspended 1,200 feet above the ground across its breadth. "Professor Leon" managed it (despite a stumble) in 1886; in 1970, the flying Karl Wallenda replicated the feat, walking across on a wire suspended from the Tallulah Point Overlook, where postcards and photos document his effort.

Clarkesville

The charming little town of Clarkesville (pop. 1,151) retains a sophistication dating back to its founding over 150 years ago by lowland Carolina and coastal Georgian plantation families seeking refuge from the oppressive summer heat. Best known as the home of the renowned country resort, Glen-Ella Springs Inn, Clarkesville sits at the lower slope of a river valley that stretches northwest to the faux-Bavarian town of Helen, and is surrounded by countryside perfect for a leisurely drive or bike tour past an old mill here, a covered bridge there, and old-time country stores in wooden cabins.

Clarkesville tucks urbane delights into its rustic country setting, with over 40 buildings, most of them former summer homes, listed on the National Register of Historic Houses. Downtown, three blocks of wooden storefronts, centering around a shaded plaza where numerous festivals take place, hold cafes and crafts shops.

The town square bistro, **Taylor's Trolley**, is set in a circa 1907 storefront with authentic turn-of-the-century decor and features daily specials such as mountain trout and prime rib; you can also slide up to the green marble-topped counter for a quick ice-cream soda or coffee and cobbler. From a long wooden cabin a mile south of town on Washington Street (old US-441), **Adam's Rib** serves a hearty breakfast of homemade biscuits and gravy, country ham, steak and eggs, and hotcakes. Come back at lunch for their buffet or specialty barbecued pork, beef ribs, and chicken.

The **Charm House** (706/754-9347) sits on a small knoll above US-441, and offers B&B lodging in a historic Greek revival mansion within a short walk of the square.

For further listings or more general **information**, contact the chamber of commerce (706/778-4654).

Hundred-year-old **Glen-Ella Springs Inn,** eight miles north of Clarkesville on Bear Gap Road off US-441 (706/754-7295 or 800/552-3479), is northern Georgia's premier country inn. Set on 17 lush acres, the historic two-story lodge holds 16 guest rooms, each of which opens to a porch with rocking chairs; rates run $75-135 a night.

Cornelia, the southernmost Appalachian town, is known for its **Giant Apple Monument** on Route 23 downtown, a tribute to the primary local industry.

On US-441 some six miles north of I-85, the tiny town of **Homer** hosts the "World's Largest Easter Egg Hunt." For dates and details, phone 706/677-2108.

Detour: Athens

If you've got the time and inclination, one of Georgia's most enjoyable destinations is just a slight veer to the east off our route: Athens, the coolest college town in the South. Famed in recent years for its lively music scene which gave the world the "alternative rock" bands B-52s and R.E.M., Athens is the home of the University of Georgia, whose Greek revival campus sits at the center of town, bordered on the north by a half-dozen blocks of cafes, bars, and book and record stores. Athens also holds a classic Road Trip destination: "**The Tree That Owns Itself,**" a second-generation mighty oak tree standing on a small circle of land at the corner of Finley and Dearing Streets west of campus, whose legal autonomy earned it a place in *Ripley's Believe or Not!*.

The main music venue is the R.E.M.-related **40 Watt Club**, 285 W. Washington Street (706/549-7871). Good cheap BBQ is available on the east side of town at **Weaver D's**, 1016 E. Broad Street, whose enigmatic slogan "Automatic for the People" was enshrined as an R.E.M. album title.

For listings of hotels or for more general **information**, contact the Athens **visitor center** (706/546-1805 or 800/653-0603).

From the foothills of northern Georgia, it's only an hour by freeway southwest to Atlanta; see the Survival Guide to this city on pages 680-681.

COASTAL EAST COAST

COASTAL EAST COAST

I f your impressions of the East Coast come from driving along the I-95 corridor through nearly nonstop urban and industrial sprawl, following our Coastal East Coast route will open your eyes to a whole other world. Alternating between wildly differing beach resort areas and lengthy stretches of pristine coastal wilderness, the route runs along nearly 900 miles of two-lane country roads, within earshot if not sight of the Atlantic Ocean almost the entire way. In place of the grimy concrete and soulless nether world of the interstate, this route passes through innumerable quirky seaside towns and timeless old fishing villages, interspersed with huge swathes of beaches, wetlands, and woodlands that have hardly changed since the first explorers laid eyes on them four centuries ago.

Starting in the north at the glitzy casino resorts of Atlantic City, and winding up in the south at the gracious old cities of Charleston and Savannah—two of the country's most beautiful places—this route truly offers something for everyone. Those searching for photogenic lighthouses or beachcombing solitude will love the undeveloped and usually deserted strands that stretch for miles along the low-lying islands that make up most of the coast, much of which, as at Assateague Island or Cape Hatteras, has been protected as national seashore parks. In contrast, the many beach resorts that dot the in-between areas vary from the grand Victorian charms of Cape May to the funky old Coney Island-style attractions of Ocean City and Myrtle Beach, with their boardwalks full of roller coasters, wax museums, and salt-water taffy stands.

Alongside the contemporary attractions are many evocative historic sites, including such unique places as Roanoke, where the first English-speaking colony in North America vanished without a trace in 1587. Lying south of the Mason-Dixon Line for almost all of its length, the route also visits many important Civil War sites, including Fort Sumter, where the first shots were fired, and the vital naval battlegrounds at Hampton Roads at the mouth of Chesapeake Bay. Midway along, we also pass one of the key sites of modern history, the windy sand dunes at Kitty Hawk where the Wright Brothers first proved that humans could fly.

Though this East Coast route will bring you to many well-known sights, its real attraction is the traveling, stopping off for fried chicken or barbecue at one of the hundreds of roadside stands, watching the shrimp boats pull into a sleepy dock and unload their day's catch, or simply chatting with locals at the general store or post office in a town that may not even be on the map.

ALONG THE NEW JERSEY SHORE

Since the New Jersey shore is so close to the major population centers of the East Coast, it's not surprising that New Jersey has among the busiest and most densely developed stretches of coastline in the country. What *is* surprising, however, is that beyond the boardwalk amusements and flashy gambling casinos of **Atlantic City**, the New Jersey shore offers a whole lot more. As is the case with most of the East Coast, the "shoreline" is actually a series of barrier islands separated from the mainland by wildlife-rich estuaries; these provide fishing and birdwatching opportunities, as well as a break from the ceaseless commercial and residential development along the ocean beaches. Bustling in summer, these beachfront communities—starting with **Margate** near Atlantic City, and running south through vibrant **Wildwood** before winding up at the dainty Victorian-era beach resort of **Cape May**—offer something for everyone, all within a 100-mile stretch of shoreline.

Heading south from Atlantic City, the 70-mph Garden State Turnpike (toll $1.50) runs inland while the slower but more engaging Ocean Drive follows local roads along the coastline over a series of five bridges, each charging a 50 cents toll.

Atlantic City

The world-famous beach resort of Atlantic City has ridden the ups and downs of history. Home of the world's oldest beachfront boardwalk and the first pleasure pier, Atlantic City also spawned the picture postcard. Perhaps most significant of all, the street names for Monopoly were coined after Atlantic City's, although the city's layout bears little resemblance to the board game (and there's no "Get Out of Jail Free" cards, either).

Atlantic City reached its peak at the turn of the 20th century, when thousands of city dwellers flocked there each weekend. Later on, as automobiles and airplanes brought better beaches within reach of New York and Philly vacationers, Atlantic City went into a half-century of decline until the 1970s, when **gambling** was legalized and millions of dollars flowed into the local economy from speculating real estate developers. First and foremost of these was Donald Trump, whose name is emblazoned on four of Atlantic City's five largest casino/hotels, including the massive **Taj Mahal**, which nearly cost him his fortune.

These days Atlantic City (pop. 38,000) has been transformed from a derelict relic into a glitzy gambling resort, attracting thousands of visitors and millions of dollars daily to its casinos. The clattering of slot machines and the buzz of the craps tables continues 24 hours a day year-round. The **Boardwalk**, backed by a wall of 25-story casino/hotels, is still the main focus, running along the beach for over two miles from **TropWorld** in the south to the **Showboat** (which has free parking). Few of the remaining piers offer much of interest. **Ocean One**, located opposite Caesar's casino at the foot of Arkansas Avenue, is an anodyne shopping mall on the site of the legendary Million Dollar Pier. Only the rebuilt Steel Pier holds the traditional seaside rides and arcade games. It's located opposite Trump's Taj Mahal at the foot of Pennsylvania Avenue. At the heart of Atlantic City, on the Boardwalk a block south of Park Place, stands the stalwart art deco **Convention Center**. The largest auditorium in the world when it was built, the convention center seats 22,000 and still houses a massive pipe organ; its console is on display in the lobby.

Besides representing Atlantic City's main attractions, the casinos hold almost all of the places to eat, apart from the dozens of fast-food stands along the Boardwalk. Two old favorites stand out from the crowd, both within blocks of the convention center: the chrome **White House Sub Shop** at 2301 Arctic Avenue, which is open until midnight every day, and publike **Dock's Oyster House** at 2405 Atlantic Avenue, a great seafood restaurant since 1871. Except for a number of seedy motels and $75-a-night national chains (**Comfort Inn, Days Inn, Holiday Inn**, etc.), the casinos also monopolize accommodation options—expect to pay around $100 a night, since bargains are hard to find even midweek, midwinter.

For complete listings and more detailed information, contact the Atlantic City **visitors center** (800/BOARDWALK).

> Considerable parts of Atlantic City—basically everything outside the casinos—are still derelict and more than a little dangerous. Be careful when exploring, and don't wander around after dark.
>
> To enjoy a day on the sands at many of New Jersey's beaches, you need to buy (and wear) a **beach tag,** which costs around $2 a day and is available at local tourist offices, shops, and fast-food stands.

Margate: Lucy the Elephant

Immediately south of Atlantic City, the tidy city of Margate (pop. 8,400) fans out along the shore, its solidly suburban streets lined by grand houses. Margate utterly lacks the reckless seaside qualities of its larger neighbor, but does include one classic remnant of the Jersey shore's glory days: Lucy the Elephant (daily open 10 AM-8 PM in summer, limited hours rest of the year; $2). The six-story wood-and-tin pachyderm, a curiosity built by real-estate speculators in the 1800s to draw customers to their newly laid out community, looms over the beach at 9200 Atlantic Avenue. The landmark architectural folly was used around the turn of the century as a tavern and a hotel, and now holds a small museum of local history. Visitors walk through the museum on the way up to an observation deck, disguised as a canopied seat on Lucy's back.

Lucy the Elephant

Ocean Drive: Ocean City and Wildwood

A series of local roads collectively known as Ocean Drive run along the south Jersey coast, passing through one after another family-oriented beach resorts, starting at Ocean City, "The Greatest Family Resort For a Vacation, or a Lifetime," 10 miles south of Atlantic City. Ocean City (pop. 15,500) was founded as a religious retreat in the late 1870s, and feels oddly suburban away from the beachfront boardwalk area. The boardwalk revolves around its old Music Pier, now known as **Gillian's Water Wonderland** amusement park, with water slides and a very large Ferris wheel.

Vacation homes, marinas, and miniature golf courses line the shore for the next 20 miles, reaching a peak at raucous Wildwood, which houses dozens of nightclubs and New Jersey's biggest beachfront amusement parks. Wildwood also boasts an extensive collection of 1950s roadside architecture. You can also stay the night in one of Wildwood's classic motels, or better yet, stop for a meal at the chrome-and-glass **Wildwood Diner** on Atlantic Avenue a block south of the main pier. For more detailed listings of places to stay and things to do, contact the Wildwood **visitor center** (800/WW-BY-SEA).

Cape May

A world away from the carnival atmosphere of the other shore resorts, Cape May, the oldest and most serene of the New Jersey beach towns, sits at the southern tip of the state. First settled in the early 1600s, Cape May's glory years ran from the 1850s to the 1890s as an upper-crust summer resort, when it rivaled Newport, Rhode Island, as the destination of choice for the power brokers of Philadelphia and New York City.

A few modern motels and mini-golf courses spread along Cape May's broad beaches, while the compact downtown district retains all its overwrought Victorian splendor. Century-old cottages now house cafes, boutiques, and art galleries, and it seems every other building has been converted into a quaint B&B. The town's ornate gingerbread mansions were constructed in the aftermath of a disastrous 1878 fire; among the better examples is the elaborate **Emlen Physick House**, eight blocks north of downtown at 1048 Washington Street, designed by noted Philadelphia architect Frank Furness.

To take the pulse of the Jersey shore's nightlife, tune to **WZML 100.7 FM,** which advertises nightly events and plays a proven mix of alternative rock hits, from Lou Reed to R.E.M.

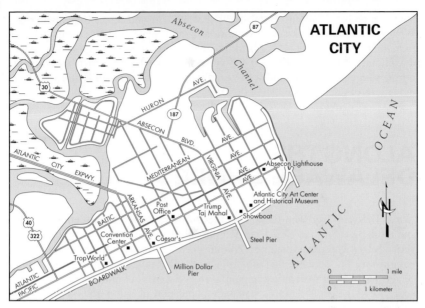

ATLANTIC CITY

It now houses the nonprofit, preservation-oriented **Mid-Atlantic Center for the Arts** and is open as a **museum** of late Victorian life (daily 10 AM-3 PM in summer, weekends only in winter; $5; 609/884-5404).

Pick up walking-tour maps of some of the town's 600 listed historic buildings at the **Cape May Welcome Center**, housed in an onion-domed former church right downtown at 405 Lafayette Street (609/884-9562). The center also carries brochures on Cape May's many fine **bed and breakfasts**, including the mansard-roofed **Queen Victoria** at 102 Ocean Street (609/884-8702), one of the few B&Bs that's open year-round. Cape May's oldest and most atmospheric place to stay is the

The **Wetlands Institute** (609/368-1211) five miles north of Wildwood, at 1075 Stone Harbor Boulevard, is one of the best places to experience the abundant natural life of the New Jersey shore. An observation tower looking over 6,000 acres of saltwater marshland provides excellent birdwatching opportunities, and there's also a museum with a touch-tank and aquarium.

CAPE MAY-LEWES FERRY

Running between the tip of the New Jersey shore and the heart of the Delaware coast, the Cape May-Lewes Ferry carries cars and passengers on a 70-minute ride across Delaware Bay. The trip costs $18 for a car and one passenger, plus $4.50 for each additional passenger. Schedules change seasonally, with boats leaving about every two hours in summer and every three hours in winter. For up-to-date times and other **information**, call 800/64-FERRY; **reservations** ($3; call 800/717-7245) are a very good idea but must be booked at least one day ahead of time.

FERRY
CAPE MAY-LEWES

Southern gothic **Chalfonte Hotel**, located at 301 Howard Street (609/884-8409). What the Chalfonte lacks in air-conditioning and other modern conveniences it more than makes up for with a bank of rocking chairs, full breakfasts, and huge, downhome dinners. Reservations for these and other B&Bs (which are essential during summer, and a good idea any time) can be made through **Historic Accommodations of Cape May** (609/884-0080).

ALONG THE DELAWARE SHORE

Across Delaware Bay from Cape May, the Delaware shore is considerably quieter and more peaceful than New Jersey's. Both shores, originally settled by Scandinavian whalers who established port colonies here in the early 1600s, share a common history. But because the Delaware shore is that much farther from the urban centers, it has been spared the rampant overdevelopment of much of the rest of the coast. Nevertheless, Delaware's statewide population of half a million doubles in summer as visitors from Baltimore and Washington, D.C. descend upon its coastal resorts, from historic **Lewes** to lively **Rehoboth Beach** to the untouched sands of **Delaware Seashore State Park**, stretching south to the Maryland border.

Lewes and Cape Henlopen
Sitting at the southern lip of Delaware Bay, Lewes is a sportfishing center that traces its roots back to 1631, when it was settled by the Dutch West India Company as a whaling port. Though this colony lasted only two years, Lewes calls itself the "First Town in the First State," commemorating its history in the false-gabled brick **Zwannendael Museum** at the center of town (Tues.-Sat. 10 AM-4:30 PM, Sunday 1:30-4:30 PM; free). Lewes also harbors huge sand dunes, a fine stretch of beach, and a **campground** with showers in 3,000-acre Cape Henlopen State Park, east of town at the mouth of Delaware Bay. Expect relative peace and quiet here, since most visitors, arriving off the Cape May ferry, simply rush through Lewes to the beach resorts farther south.

Rehoboth Beach
Fronting on the open Atlantic and just eight miles south of Lewes, Rehoboth Beach, whose biblical name means "room enough," was founded in the 1870s when church groups bought beachfront land, established the town, and extended a railroad line south from Lewes. With its small but lively boardwalk running along the broad beach, and only a short strip of T-shirt shops and arcades lining Rehoboth Avenue at the center of town, Rehoboth has retained a small-town feel despite the many thousands who descend upon the place during the summer. For years popular with bureaucrats escaping the sweltering summers of Washington, D.C., more recently Rehoboth has become a favorite holiday spot for Mid-Atlantic gays and lesbians.

The town's profusion of very good restaurants include the award-winning **Blue Moon** at 35 Baltimore Avenue, **LaLa Land** at 22 Wilmington Avenue, and elegant **Victoria's** in the Boardwalk Plaza Hotel at 2 Olive Avenue. There are also the more mainstream delights of **Thrashers French Fries** and sundry beer-and-burger stands along the Boardwalk.

For more detailed information, including listings of motels and beachfront B&Bs, stop in at the Rehoboth **visitor center**, 501 Rehoboth Avenue (302/227-2233 or 800/441-1329).

Delaware Seashore State Park

South from Rehoboth stretches one of the most pristine lengths of beach on the northern East Coast: Delaware Seashore State Park, which contains 10 miles of open beach with sparkling white sand, also acres of marshland estuary, thronged in season with migrating birds—and birdwatchers. The park is easily accessible from the beachfront Hwy-1. Beachfront resort towns are at either end of the park. **Dewey Beach** in the north draws a younger, collegiate crowd while **Bethany Beach** in the south attracts families. Approaching Maryland, towering condos line the shore near Fenwick Island, where an 1858 lighthouse marks the Mason-Dixon Line and state border.

ALONG MARYLAND'S EASTERN SHORE

Maryland, the most oddly shaped of the lower 48 states, shares the broad Eastern Shore peninsula with Delaware and a small piece of Virginia. The inland areas along the Chesapeake Bay with its many inlets and tributary rivers are filled with dozens of small colonial-era towns and fishing villages, while the Atlantic Coast is completely taken up by two very different beasts: the gloriously kitschy beach resort of **Ocean City**, and the untrammelled wilds of **Assateague Island National Seashore**. Heading inland around Assateague, the highway passes by a number of historic small towns, including captivating **Snow Hill**.

Running east from Annapolis to Ocean City across the Eastern Shore, **US-50**'s route across Maryland is covered on pages 574-578.

Ocean City

About the only place left on the entire East Coast that retains the carnival qualities of classic seaside resorts, Ocean City (pop. 5,146) has by far the best array of old-time fun-fair attractions. Stretching north from the main pier for over two miles along a broad, clean, white-sand beach, the wide wooden boardwalk is packed with enough water slides, merry-go-rounds, mini-golf courses, haunted houses, and bumper cars to entertain the hundreds of thousands of people who come here on summer weekends. There are also all the nearly forgotten old arcade games like skee-ball and pokerino, and midway contests (the kind where for $1 a try you can win stuffed animals and other prizes by shooting baskets or squirting water into clowns' mouths), while a ramshackle collection of fortune-tellers, T-shirt stands, and burger-and-beer bars completes the scene, forming a busy gauntlet along the lively promenade.

On a summer weekend Ocean City, which fills the narrow barrier island that stretches north from US-50 for over 10 miles, becomes Maryland's second-largest city, the population increasing from the resident 5,000 people to upwards of 400,000. Most of the fun is simply in getting caught up in the garish human spectacle of it all, but there are a couple of specific things worth searching out. For the price of a bumper car ride, you can enjoy the quirky collections of the **Life Saving Station Museum** (daily 11 AM-10 PM in summer, Sat.-Sun. noon-4 PM Nov.-March; $2) at the south end of the boardwalk, where alongside displays of shipwrecks and bathing suits you can compare and contrast bowls full of sand from 100 different beaches around the world. The museum also marks the starting point for the **trams** ($2) that run along the boardwalk for over two miles, north to where the modern 20-story condos and resort hotels line the rest of the island.

To go along with its great beaches, Ocean City has a radio station, excellent **WZBH 93.5 FM,** "The Beach," playing classic rock 'n' roll and broadcasting details of Ocean City's lively nightclub scene.

While much of Ocean City's charm is decidedly low-brow, the food is better than you might expect, with numerous places offering plates full of shrimp and pitchers of beer for under $10, and fresh-tasting fried chicken or crab cakes available from boardwalk stands like **Dayton Bros.**, across from the Life Saving Station. **Thrashers Fries** are available from a number of counters along the boardwalk, and you can top them off with a cone or shake from **Dumser's Ice Cream**, near the Wax Museum at the south end of the boardwalk. There are also many very good restaurants, including dozens of seafood places along Sinepuxent Bay on the western side of the island, like **The Angler** at the end of Talbot Street.

Places to stay are also abundant, but unfortunately far from cheap. Of the grand older hotels, only the **Commander** on 14th Street (410/289-6166 or 800/543-6986) is still open for business; modern motels like the **Comfort Inn**, at Boardwalk and 5th Street (410/289-5155 or 800/282-5155), charge $120 for a double that goes for $40 out of season, and upscale resort hotels like the **Sheraton Fontainbleau**, on Oceanfront at 101st Street (410/524-3535 or 800/638-2100) can cost upwards of $200 a night.

For more complete listings of motels, hotels, and restaurants, contact the Ocean City **visitor center**, in the Convention Center at 4001 Coastal Highway (410/289-2800 or 800/62-OCEAN).

Assateague Island National Seashore

At one time Assateague Island, the 10 mile-long barrier island on which Ocean City sits, stretched in an unbroken line all the way into Virginia. In 1933 a major storm created the broad inlet that now divides the bustling resort city from the near wilderness of Assateague Island National Seashore. One of the few areas of the Atlantic coast protected from commercial development, Assateague consists of some 10,000 acres covering over 20 miles. Recreational opportunities include hiking, swimming, camping, canoeing, clamming, and birdwatching; swarms of voracious mosquitoes, and a lack of water, keep the crowds to a minimum.

To reach the island from Ocean City, follow US-50 west for two miles and turn south on Hwy-611, which loops around Sinexpunt Bay before arriving at a small **visitor center** (daily 8:30 AM-5 PM; 301/641-3030). The center has a small aquarium as well as maps, guides, and up-to-date information about the national seashore.

Snow Hill and Pocomoke City

From Ocean City, the route turns inland around Assateague Island and Chincoteague Bay, following US-50 west for eight miles, then turning south on US-113 through the dark cypress swamps along the Pocomoke River. Twenty miles southwest of Ocean City, the tiny, 200-year-old town of Snow Hill (pop. 2,200) is worth a stop to take a look at the **Julia A. Purnell Museum**, 208 W. Market Street (Mon.-Fri. 10 AM-4 PM, Sat.-Sun. 1-4 PM, April-Nov. only; $2). The museum features a range of exhibits tracing Eastern Shore history and a unique Flea Circus consisting of dozens of fully dressed fleas. Pick up a walking-tour map of Snow Hill's many significant structures. Dating back to the 1790s, the **Snow Hill Inn** at 104 E. Market Street (410/632-2102) is a charming place to stay, with a small restaurant and three guest rooms.

Fifteen miles southwest of Snow Hill near the Virginia border on US-113, Pocomoke City, founded in 1780, is a prosperous market town with a few surviving historic homes on the Pocomoke River. At Pocomoke City, US-113 turns into US-13 for the final few miles south to Virginia.

Across the Virginia border, the southern half of Assateague Island includes the **Chincoteague National Wildlife Refuge,** noted for its long, wide beach and wild ponies. Access to this part of the island is through the small town of **Chincoteague** (see below for details).

Paddle a canoe through the wild Pocomoke Swamp with the Pocomoke River Canoe Company, 312 N. Washington Street (410/632-3971), next to the drawbridge in Snow Hill.

ALONG THE VIRGINIA COAST

Virginia's Eastern Shore is among the most isolated regions of the country, and its dozens of small towns and villages remain much as they have for centuries. Everything on the Eastern Shore is on a much smaller scale than on the mainland, and the many stands selling fresh corn and tomatoes along the roadside attest to the important role farming plays in the local economy. Although fast-food places, chicken-processing plants, and a couple of modern malls dot US-13, the main route through Virginia's Eastern Shore, the area is still mostly rural and undeveloped, with business loops turning off through the many well-preserved old towns. The numerous historic sites include colonial-era plantations and archaeological remnants of Native American tribes.

The highlight for most visitors is **Chincoteague**, a small commercial and sport-fishing port sitting at the entrance to massive **Chincoteague National Wildlife Refuge**, which faces the Atlantic Coast and offers the only ocean beaches in this part of the state. South of Chincoteague, US-13 runs down the center of the narrow Eastern Shore peninsula, giving access to the Chesapeake Bay waterfront at **Onancock**, then passing through numerous small towns like **Accomac** and **Eastville**, neither of which has changed much since Revolutionary times. Crossing the mouth of the Chesapeake Bay via a 23-mile-long bridge and tunnel brings you to maritime Norfolk and the state's main Atlantic resort, Virginia Beach, before the route turns inland and south into North Carolina.

Chincoteague

The Virginia **Welcome Center** at New Church, on US-13 at the northwest corner of the Eastern Shore, has maps and reams of visitor information.

The drive into Chincoteague (pop. 1,600, pronounced "CHINK-a-teeg"), a low-key fishing village, takes you across miles of glowing gold and blue marshlands, and through a gauntlet of quirky billboards advertising local motels, restaurants, and sportfishing charters. This mix of natural beauty and tacky tourism aptly reflects the character of the town, which is totally dependent upon summertime visitors but seems to wish that they'd all leave and let the locals go fishing. The main attractions, besides fishing, are the beaches and birdwatching opportunities offered by the nearby wildlife refuge (see below); however, one thing to do in town, besides eat tons of fresh clams, crabs, and other seafood, is visit the tiny **Oyster Museum** (daily 10 AM-5 PM in summer only; $2), a mile east of town on Maddox Boulevard. Its series of displays illustrate the history of oystering from the 1600s to the present.

A small bridge along Hwy-175, which runs 10 miles east from US-17, drops you at the heart of town, where casual seafood restaurants like the **Shucking House Cafe** and the **Landmark Crab House** line the small wharves that stretch along the bay. Among the many places to stay are several nice B&Bs, like the **Watson House** at 4240 N. Main Street (804/336-1564 or 800/336-6787). Recommended motels include the **Island Manor House** at 4160 Main Street (804/336-5436) and the **Waterside Motor Inn** at 3761 S. Main Street (804/336-3434).

Chincoteague National Wildlife Refuge
The Chincoteague National Wildlife Refuge is one of the largest refuges along the Atlantic flyway, attracting hundreds of species of birds, including egrets, herons, geese, and swans, and thousands of migrating ducks. A continuation of the Assateague Island National Seashore across the Maryland border (see above), the refuge contains hundreds of acres of marshland, excellent beaches, and a number of hiking and cycling trails. The refuge **visitor center** (daily 9 AM-4 PM; 804/336-6577) at Tom's Cove has detailed information on park activities as well as special exhibits on Chincoteague's famous **wild ponies**, which can usually be seen from the Woodland Trail that loops south from Beach Road.

Accomac
The first sizeable town on the Virginia section of the Eastern Shore, Accomac (pop. 525) is centered upon an ancient-looking red-brick courthouse, flanked by a series of wooden sheds converted into professional offices. The old library next door dates from the 1780s, and was used for years as a debtor's prison; the library, courthouse, and surrounding buildings make up one of the most extensive collections of colonial-era buildings in the country.

After wandering around the town, you may want to head to the comfortable, family-run **Owl Restaurant**, two miles north of Accomac on the east side of US-13. It's a great, inexpensive place, and you can choose from Southern standards like ham steaks or fried chicken, or local seafood specialties including Chincoteague clams and oysters. Sample one of their excellent pies for dessert. Conveniently, the owl is also a motel (804/665-5190).

Onancock and Tangier Island
The picturesque harbor town of Onancock (pop. 1,435, pronounced "o-NAN-cock"), on the Chesapeake Bay two miles west of US-13 via Hwy-179, is one of the nicest towns on the Eastern Shore. A short walking tour of over a dozen historical homes and churches begins at **Kerr Place** at 69 Market Street (Tues.-Sat. 10 AM-4 PM; $3), built in 1799 and now home to the Eastern Shore Historical Society. Another historic curiosity is the 150-year-old Hopkins and Bros. general store, on the wharf at 2 Market Street, which sells everything from sweet potatoes to postcards.

Stands selling fresh fruit and vegetables—particularly sweet corn and tomatoes—dot roadsides all over the Eastern Shore.

Midway along US-17, the town of Exmore holds the popular **Sally & Bob's Drive-In,** which serves homemade crab cakes and fresh roasted chicken.

Hopkins and Bros. is also the place to buy tickets for the ferry across the Chesapeake Bay to Tangier Island, an evocative old place where cars are banned and things have hardly changed since colonial times. The few hundred people who live here year-round earn their livelihoods catching crabs and the occasional oyster from Chesapeake Bay. Ferries for Tangier Island leave once a day from Onancock Harbor (804/891-2240). Travel time is one hour 15 minutes each way, and the roundtrip cost is $17.50. Visitors returning on the ferry have about two hours on the island, though the **Sunset Inn** (804/891-2535) makes an overnight stay possible, and good

The classic children's story *Misty of Chincoteague* is set in the area and tells how wild ponies—whose ancestors were sent here by English settlers in the late 1600s—are rounded up from the wildlife refuge on Assateague Island for a swim to Chincoteague. An annual auction in late July attracts thousands of spectators and benefits local firefighters.

Before the Chesapeake Bay Bridge/Tunnel was completed in 1964, ferries linking the Eastern Shore with the mainland docked at **Cape Charles,** west of US-13 eight miles south of Eastville. Barges still use the harbor, ferrying freight trains across the bay.

Norfolk's **WQWI 102.9 FM** plays classic 1970s soul and contemporary urban music.

seafood is available at the **Fisherman's Corner Restaurant** (804/891-2571).

Eastville

You can get a good idea of just how rural and quiet life is on Virginia's Eastern Shore by visiting Eastville (pop. 185), the seat of Northampton County. A mile west of US-17 on a well-marked business loop, Eastville centers on the red-brick courthouse and county jail—both still in use—and a handful of even older buildings dating back to the mid-1700s. Also on the square is the somewhat disheveled white clapboard **Eastville Inn**, which operated as a tavern for over 200 years; judging by the cobwebs and lack of furniture, they haven't done business for decades.

The Chesapeake Bay Bridge/Tunnel

One of the more impressive engineering feats on the East Coast is the Chesapeake Bay Bridge/Tunnel, which opened in 1964 at the mouth of the Chesapeake Bay. Almost 18 miles long, and charging a $10 toll, the structure consists of one high-level bridge, two deep tunnels, four islands, and many miles of raised causeway. Two miles from the southern end of the bridge, a fishing pier and restaurant operate on a man-made island.

Virginia Beach

From the toll plaza at the southern end of the Chesapeake Bay Bridge, US-60 heads east along Atlantic Avenue, passing through the woodland waterfront of **Seashore State Park** before winding up at the ocean and Virginia Beach (pop. 394,000), the state's most populous city and its one and only beach resort. Ten-story hotels—so tall they block the afternoon sun from reaching the sands—line the main drag, Atlantic Avenue, which is plastered with large signs banning cars from "cruising" the mile-long array of fun fairs, surf shops, and nightclubs.

Unlike many coastal towns, Virginia Beach also boasts a significant history. Virginia's first colonists landed at Virginia Beach on April 26, 1607, before settling upriver at Jamestown; the site is marked by a stone cross at Cape Henry, at the southern lip of Chesapeake Bay. The **visitors bureau**, on the west side of town at 2100 Parks Avenue (800/VA-BEACH), has walking and driving tour maps of Virginia Beach's many historic houses.

Dining options tend toward seafood restaurants hidden away in the resort hotels, though the **Pocahontas Pancake Shop**, on Atlantic Avenue at 35th Street, is worth a breakfast stop even without its irresistibly kitschy name. The **Jewish Mother Deli**, 3108 Pacific Avenue, serves up good sandwiches, doubling as a popular nightclub.

Perhaps the best reason to stop at Virginia Beach is that accommodations are much cheaper here than elsewhere in the area: beds at **Angie's Guest Cottage AYH Hostel** at 302 24th Street (804/428-4690) cost $12-50 a night; a double room at an oceanfront motel costs $35-85, depending upon the time of year. Choose from Best Western, Comfort Inn, Days Inn, Hilton, Holiday Inn, Howard Johnson, Sheraton, or dozens of local places.

Norfolk

During colonial times, Norfolk was the largest city in Virginia and one of the busiest ports in North America, though these days it's little more than an adjunct to the massive naval shipyards at Hampton Roads and Newport News. That said, it does hold a couple of worthwhile destinations, including the lovely **Chrysler Museum** (Tues.-Sat. 10 AM-4 PM, Sunday 1-5 PM; donations), on the north side of downtown off Olney Road and Duke Street. The personal art collection of the man who built New York's Chrysler Building is displayed inside a commodious Italianate building. Norfolk, a staunch Navy town, also holds the final resting place of controversial U.S. Army Gen. Douglas MacArthur, preserved alongside his personal papers (and his 1950 Chrysler Imperial limousine) at the MacArthur Memorial (Mon.-Sun. 10 AM-5 PM, free), inside Norfolk's old City Hall building at Bank and Plume Streets downtown.

DOUGLAS MacARTHUR

The Dismal Swamp

Across both sides of the Virginia/North Carolina border, for 30 miles down US-17, stretches a 750-square-mile wilderness known as the Dismal Swamp, low-lying wetland with rich growths of cypress, juniper, and hardwood trees. Though it once was three times as large as it is now, apart from some hidden lumber mills and a few small farms, most of the swamp seems unchanged since colonial times, when the loquacious William Byrd of Virginia described it as a "vast body of dirt and nastiness" where the "eternal shade that broods over this mighty bog, and hinders the sunbeams from blessing the ground, makes it an uncomfortable habitation for anything that has life. . . . Not even a Turkey Buzzard will venture to fly over it." Byrd's damning description is unfortunately more true now than ever. Because of industrial pollu-

The two deepwater harbors at the mouth of the Chesapeake Bay, **Newport News** and **Hampton Roads,** are the headquarters of the U.S. Navy's Atlantic Fleet and together form the world's largest naval base.

Virginia Beach is also the base of operations for Pat Robertson's Christian Broadcasting Network, which produces TV's fundamentalist *700 Club* and owns the cable Family Channel, reruns of *The Mary Tyler Moore Show* and $500 million in other entertainments. To tour the production facilities, call 804/523-7123.

The ubiquitous kudzu, an imported vine that can grow as much as a foot a day, has become a curse of the South. Shrouding the view in some places by draping itself over trees, shrubs, and abandoned buildings, kudzu sometimes seems to threaten even cars on the road.

tion and the inroads of development, the swamp no longer teems with the birds, bears, raccoons, and opossums that made their home here as recently as 30 years ago. Yet the swamp is eerily beautiful, the sense of decay and desolation counterbalanced by patches of honeysuckle that perfume the otherwise fetid summer air.

US-17 cuts south from Norfolk at the eastern edge of the swamp, running alongside the **Dismal Swamp Canal**, which was cut through in the 1790s as a private venture financed by George Washington and Patrick Henry, among others. The canal remained in active commercial use until the 1920s, though today traffic is limited to a few pleasure boaters and picnickers who stop for lunch in the many pull-outs along the highway.

From Norfolk, it's a 25-mile drive south to the North Carolina border, then another 20 miles before you reach Elizabeth City, the next place of any size.

ALONG THE NORTH CAROLINA COAST

Wild Atlantic beaches, a handful of tiny fishing villages, and some of the country's most significant historic sites make coastal North Carolina a great place to visit. A highlight for many vacationers is the miles of barrier islands that make up the **Outer Banks**, where busy resort towns like **Nags Head** con-

Linking Virginia and the Outer Banks, Hwy-168 is shorter than US-17, but has become a traffic nightmare in summer. The problem intensifies on Saturday, when rental properties "turn over," and 30,000 cars pack the single-lane highway.

If you're traveling along the Carolina coast in summer, be aware that the **hurricane** season begins in June and lasts through the end of September. These are deadly serious storms, so take heed of any warnings, and follow the evacuation instructions broadcast over radio and TV networks.

trast with the miles of pristine beaches protected on the **Cape Hatteras National Seashore**. Besides golden sands, the Outer Banks area includes two evocative historic sites: the dunes at **Kitty Hawk** where the Wright Brothers first took to the air, and **Roanoke Island**, site of the first ill-fated English effort to colonize the New World. Farther south, beyond the quirky small city of Wilmington, a moviemaking Mecca, the 300-mile coastal route turns inland around **Cape Fear**, heading toward the South Carolina border.

Elizabeth City

Facing an estuary that feeds the freshwater Albemarle Sound, 22 miles from the Virginia border, Elizabeth City (pop. 14,300) first earned its livelihood from trade on the Dismal Swamp Canal. Commercial traffic is negligible now, but that story, along with the history of Elizabeth City and the Dismal Swamp region, is recounted at the **Museum of the Albemarle** (Tues.-Sat. 9 AM-5 PM,

Sunday 2-5 PM; free), two miles west of town on US-17. Grab a bite at the **Waterstreet Cafe**, housed in a waterfront warehouse, or at the popular **Colonial Cafe** on McMorrine Street, a block from US-158, in the franchise-free downtown business district.

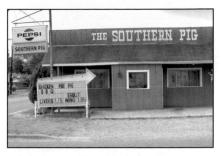

To reach the Cape Hatteras coast from Elizabeth City and US-17, cross the Pasquotank River drawbridge onto US-158. You'll pass through 30 miles of cotton fields and potato farmlands dotted with cattail-filled marshlands and sleepy rural hamlets before hitting the coast.

Kitty Hawk: The Wright Brothers National Memorial

Alternately known as Killy Hauk, Kitty Hock, and Killy Honk before its current name came into general use, Kitty Hawk to most people means one thing: the Wright Brothers' first powered airplane flight on December 17, 1903. Lured by the steady winds that blow in from the Atlantic and by the high sand dunes that cover the shore, Wilbur and Orville Wright first came to the Outer Banks in 1900, and returned every year thereafter with a series of prototype kites and gliders built out of

---

THE OUTER BANKS

The geography of the Outer Banks, a series of barrier islands stretching for over 200 miles along the entire coast of North Carolina, has changed dramatically over time, thanks to hurricanes and winter storms, not to mention human hands. Until lighthouses were built beginning in the late 18th century, the islands and the offshore shoals were so treacherous they became known as the "Graveyard of the Atlantic."

Nowadays the same places where pirates once ruled are given over to windsurfing, hang-gliding, sportfishing, and beachcombing, as the Outer Banks have become a tourist destination par excellence. The resident population of 25,000 caters to over six million annual visitors, but unlike its nearest comparison, Cape Cod, the Outer Banks area boasts only a few colonial towns. Unfortunately, substantial development during the 1980s building boom filled up much of the roadside landscape with ugly franchise sprawl. Most of the development has taken place in the north along the two parallel roads: US-158, usually called "The Bypass" but also known as "Croatian Highway," and oceanfront Hwy-12, a.k.a. "Virginia Dare Trail" and "Beach Road." Mileposts on both roads mark distances from north to south. There's plentiful lodging on Hwy-12, including chain motels and hotels such as **Best Western**, **Quality Inn**, **Days Inn Holiday Inn**, and dozens more; gas stations and fast-food restaurants line US-158.

Along the northern Outer Banks, bridges link Nags Head and Kitty Hawk with the mainland, though access to the less developed southern parts of the Outer Banks is limited to ferryboats.

Between Elizabeth City and the state's southern coast, you can wind inland around Albermarle Sound, or head east to the shore. If you're in any sort of hurry, be aware that the **inland route** along US-17 takes around three hours, while the **coastal route** around Cape Hatteras takes a full day or more to reach Jacksonville, where the two routes rejoin.

Hundreds of ancient ships and unfortunate sailors met their watery end in the shallow waters off Cape Hatteras. The remains of over 2,000 vessels lie along the entire Carolina coastline; a few are visible from shore at low tide.

bicycle parts that they fine-tuned to create the world's first airplane. Their tale is truly one of the great adventure and success stories of the modern age, and the site of their experiments has been preserved as the **Wright Brothers National Memorial.** First stop is the **visitor center** (daily 9 AM-5 PM; $2; 919/441-7430), which includes a number of exhibits tracing the history of human efforts to fly. Every hour rangers give engaging talks alongside a full-sized replica of the Wright Brothers' first plane.

The most affecting aspect of the memorial is the unchanged site where the brothers first flew. Each of the first four flights is marked by stones set on the grassy field. The first flight, with Orville at the controls flying into a 25 mph headwind, lasted 12 seconds and covered just 120 feet—barely more than a brisk walking pace. The 90-foot-high sand dune where Wilbur and Orville first took to the air has been planted over with grasses to keep it from blowing away. A series of paths climb to the top of the dune, where a 60-foot, wing-shaped granite pylon is inscribed with the words:

In commemoration of the conquest of the air by the brothers Wilbur and Orville Wright. Conceived by genius, achieved by dauntless resolution and unconquerable faith.

The park is well posted off US-158, on the inland side of the highway, two miles south of the Wright Memorial Bridge from the mainland. Though the memorial is definitely worth an extended visit, the towns around it are a bit disappointing—both Kitty Hawk and Kill Devil Hills are little more than narrow strips of commercial development.

Wright Brothers National Memorial

Jockey's Ridge State Park
The windswept 110-foot-high twin sand dunes of Jockey's Ridge State Park (daily 8 AM-sunset; free; 919/441-7132) tower over US-158 between Kitty Hawk and Nags Head. The highest sand dunes on the East Coast, Jockey's Ridge barely survived being bulldozed in the 1970s to form yet another Outer Banks resort; it's now one of the prime hang-gliding spots in the country—remember the Wright Brothers! Jockey's Ridge is also a nice place to wander the short boardwalk nature trail that points out the diverse plants and animals of the dune community. You may want to take your shoes off and scamper around the sands barefoot. If you feel especially daring, **Kitty Hawk Kites** across the highway gives **hang-gliding lessons** ($69; 919/441-4124 or 800/334-4777) and demos equipment to licensed pilots.

Orville and Wilbur Wright

Nags Head

The towns of the northern Outer Banks overlap each other and are so of a piece that only a sign tells you are in Nags Head, six miles south of Kitty Hawk, and one of the oldest and most popular resorts in the region. The few cottages and hotels dating from the late Victorian era face peaceful Roanoke Sound, while the more recent hotels, houses, and time-share condos perch—often on stilts to protect them from storm damage—directly on the broad Atlantic beaches.

roadside octopus, Nags Head

Nags Head is the most commercialized of the Outer Banks areas, and offers the widest range of visitor facilities. Accommodations are plentiful, but so are hordes of tourists. Good places to spend a night or two include the atmospheric but rather pricey **First Colony Inn** (919/441-2323 or 800/368-9390), in the middle of the island at 6720 S. Virginia Dare Trail/milepost 16, which offers a delicious breakfast and afternoon tea. The **Comfort Inn** (919/441-6315 or 800/221-2222), at the south end of Beach Road/milepost 17, has good-value rooms and is also the place to go for 1940s swing—the Big Band Preservation Society plays dance concerts here in the summer. Among the many motels is the classic 1950s-style **Viviana Motel** (919/441-7409) on Beach Road at milepost 16.4. Those fortunate enough to spend a week or more here can find a cottage rental through the **Outer Banks Ltd.** (800/624-7651).

The popular local hangout **Sam & Omie's**, near the east end of US-64 at 7228 S. Virginia Dare Trail/milepost 16.5, has featured inexpensive but well-prepared family fare for over 50 years. The upscale **Penguin Isle**, across the highway from the First Colony Inn, overlooks Roanoke Sound at 6708 US-158/milepost 16, with lovely sunset views and excellent seafood dinners.

Roanoke Island: Fort Raleigh National Historic Site

In an area known as Whalebone Junction at the south end of Nags Head, US-64 runs west over a causeway and bridge to Roanoke Island, site of the first English settlement in North America. The legendary "lost colony" was first established in 1585 by Sir Walter

Information on the **Cape Hatteras National Seashore** (see below) is available at the main National Park Service **visitor center** (daily 9 AM-5 PM; 919/261-4644), in the town of Kitty Hawk on US-158 at milepost 1.5.

The name **Nags Head** is derived from the practice of Outer Banks pirates, who tied lanterns around the heads of their horses to simulate boats bobbing at anchor. The lanterns lured passing ships onto shore, where they ran aground on the offshore sandbars.

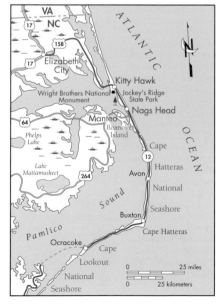

Raleigh, but the effort was not a success, and the survivors returned to England. In 1587, a larger expedition of 110 colonists arrived, including 17 women and nine children, but because of war with Spain there was no further contact with England until 1590. By that time the settlers had disappeared without a trace, which prompted numerous theories about their fate. Amidst an eerily dark and ugly forest, the original earthwork fortress is now excavated and reconstructed as the centerpiece of the small **Fort Raleigh National Historic Site.** Exhibits inside the visitor center (daily 9 AM-5 PM, longer hours in summer; free; 919/473-5772) include a few rusty artifacts and dry displays explaining the historical context of the colonial effort. There are also copies of the many beautiful watercolors and drawings of native plants, animals, and people produced by the original expedition's two immensely talented scientists, John White and Thomas Hariot.

Warmed by the Gulf Stream currents, the Outer Banks beaches are some of the best in the world, but the waters do not warm up appreciably until south of Oregon Inlet, and swimming in the northern stretches remains quite invigorating until July.

Manteo

The historic port of Manteo (pop. 950, pronounced "MAN-tee-o"), in the middle of Roanoke Island, between Fort Raleigh and the beach resorts of the Outer Banks, was named for the Native American who helped Sir Walter Raleigh and the Lost Colony. Manteo is the only county seat in North Carolina that's located on an island. You can still sense the town's proud seagoing history as you walk along the quiet streets near the tidied-up waterfront. Surrounded by pleasure boats, the main attraction here is the *Elizabeth II* (daily 10 AM-6 PM April-Oct., Tues.-Sun. 10 AM-4 PM rest of the year; $3), a full-sized, square-rigged replica of the type of ship that carried colonists here from England 400-odd years ago.

Manteo also has a couple of very good places to eat, including **Gabby's** on Budleigh Street across from the waterfront. This diner's previous incarnation as the Duchess of Dare was described in William Least Heat Moon's *Blue Highways.* Right on the water, **1587** is one of the coast's best restaurants, with a chef who has a deft hand with the region's unsurpassed seafood. The 1587 is located inside the aptly named **Tranquil House Inn** at 405 Queen Elizabeth Street (919/473-1404 or 800/458-7069), where you'll be lulled to sleep in a comfy bed to the sound of gently clanging halyards.

Raleigh's flag ship, Ark Raleigh

*For detailed listings of hotels and restaurants, and comprehensive information on visiting the Outer Banks, contact the **Dare County Tourist Bureau** (919/473-2138 or 800/446-6262), on US-64 and Budleigh Street in Manteo; or try the **Outer Banks Chamber of Commerce** (919/441-8144 or 800/446-6262).*

Throughout the summer, a waterfront theater adjacent to Fort Raleigh presents a popular production of **Lost Colony,** *which dramatizes the events of the ill-fated settlement. Call for details or tickets ($10; 919/473-3414 or 800/488-5012).*

*The section of Pamlico Sound known as **Canadian Hole,** near the town of Avon, is rated as one of the best windsurfing spots on the East Coast.*

Cape Hatteras National Seashore

The first piece of coastline to be protected as a national park, Cape Hatteras National Seashore stretches for 75 miles along the Atlantic Ocean. Starting in the north at Nags Head, and continuing south along slender Hatteras and Ocracoke Islands, the area preserved within Cape Hatteras National Seashore is the largest undeveloped section of the East Coast. It provides an increasingly rare glimpse of nature amidst ever-encroaching development. The few old fishing villages that stood here when the seashore was set aside in the 1930s are unfortunately exempt from anti-development prohibitions and have grown ugly and unwieldy, especially in the wake of the 1980s building boom. Nevertheless, the many miles in between remain almost entirely untouched.

South of Nags Head there's a **visitor center** (daily 9 AM-5 PM in summer only; 919/473-2111) and a nature trail winding along Pamlico Sound at the foot of **Bodie Island Lighthouse**, the first of three historic towers along the Hatteras coast. Continuing south across the Oregon Inlet, the midpoint of the Outer Banks, Hwy-12 runs south through the Pea Island National Wildlife Refuge, and a few short barrages of vacation condos and roadside sprawl, before reaching the heart of the park at Cape Hatteras itself. A turn south of Hwy-12 leads to the Cape Hatteras **visitor center** (daily 9 AM-5 PM in summer only; 919/995-4474), where a trail leads out to the famous **Cape Hatteras Lighthouse**. At 208 feet, the black-and-white striped lighthouse is the tallest brick lighthouse in the United States. Farther along this road is a summer-only **campground**, and the ocean beaches at the very tip of the cape are among the most spectacular anywhere.

Continuing south, Hwy-12 runs through **Buxton**, the seashore's main commercial center, an ugly gauntlet of fast-food restaurants, though **Bubba's BBQ** on Hwy-12, and **Billy's Fish House** farther south, are both better than average. Motels like the **Lighthouse View** (919/995-5680 or 800/225-7651) or the **Falcon** (919/995-5968 or 800/635-6911) are reasonably priced and clean.

Another collection of restaurants and motels awaits you in Hatteras, at the southern end of the island. Here, **ferries** run across to Ocracoke Island, another mostly unspoiled barrier island where you'll find great beaches and the pretty village of **Ocracoke**, at the island's southern tip. About the only Outer Banks town that hasn't lost its small-scale charm, Ocracoke is a great place to spend an afternoon walking or cycling along unpaved backstreets lined by overgrown gardens and weathered old homes. Enjoy a plateful of crab cakes at the **Island Inn**, on Hwy-12 at the center of town (919/928-7821).

The **ferry** between Hatteras and Ocracoke runs at least every hour on the hour 5 AM-midnight, year-round. It's free and takes about 40 minutes; call 800/BY FERRY for exact schedules and further information.

The village of Frisco, five miles north of the Hatteras ferry terminal, holds the small but surprisingly good **Native American Museum,** which boasts an extensive collection of artifacts from several tribes, including those from the Cape Hatteras area.

Cape Lookout National Seashore

If you liked the look of Cape Hatteras but want to avoid the crowds, plan a visit to the much wilder Cape Lookout National Seashore, another series of barrier islands stretching for 55 miles from Ocracoke to the south near Beaufort. It's accessible only by boat, and there are few roads or services once you're there, but it's a lovely place to hike or camp, collect seashells, or just wander along the peaceful shore. For more information, contact the park **headquarters** at 3601 Bridge Street in Morehead City (919/728-2250).

The pirate **Blackbeard,** a.k.a. Edward Teach, was killed near Ocracoke in 1718.

OCRACOKE-CEDAR ISLAND FERRY

Running between Ocracoke on Cape Hatteras, and Cedar Island on the Carolina mainland, the state-run ferry departs approximately every two hours (every three hours in winter) and takes close to two and a half hours each way. The cost is $10 per car. Call 800/BY-FERRY for current schedules and further information.

Not surprisingly, Beaufort, North Carolina is often confused with Beaufort, South Carolina. The former is pronounced "BO-fort;" the latter is pronounced "BYOO-furd," and is described on pages 330-331.

Beaufort and Morehead City

Known as Fishtown until it was renamed in 1722, the charming 18th-century town of Beaufort (pop. 3,800) has quiet streets lined with churches, cemeteries filled with weather-stained monuments, and whitewashed houses with narrow porches. The nautical-themed shops and restaurants along the busy Front Street waterfront, three blocks south of US-70, attract tourists and boaters traveling along the Intracoastal Waterway. The spacious **North Carolina Maritime Museum**, 315 Front Street (Mon.-Sat. 9 AM-5 PM, Sunday 2 PM-5 PM; free; 919/728-7317), features many informative exhibits on the region's nautical and natural history, as well as a truly impressive display of over 1,000 beautiful seashells. The museum offers daylong guided field trips to the dunes and marshes, but is perhaps best known for its annual **Wooden Boat Show** held the last weekend

in September, and for the **Strange Seafood Festival** in mid-August, when visitors can nibble on marinated octopus and squid, stingray casserole, and more traditional seafood.

Besides the handful of places to eat on the boardwalk, and the 24-hour **Mayflower Cafe** on US-70 at the east end of town, you'll find the best seafood three miles west of Beaufort, across the bridge in Morehead City, one of the state's three main industrial ports. Try the homemade seafood cocktail sauce and Tarheel hush puppies at the **Sanitary Fish Market & Restaurant**, 501 Evans Street; it's easy to find amidst the sportfishing boats a block south of US-70.

In Beaufort, B&B rooms are available in restored homes like the **Captain's Quarters**, 315 Ann Street (919/728-7711), or the larger **Beaufort Inn**, 101 Ann Street (919/728-2600). Morehead City holds motels like Best Western and Comfort Inn along US-70.

For more information, contact the Carteret County **visitor center** (800/786-6962).

Bogue Bank
Another string of barrier island beach resorts lines Bogue Bank, which runs south of Morehead City in a nearly east-west orientation for some 25 miles. None of the half-dozen family-oriented resort towns is particularly compelling, though all have freely accessible—but quite often crowded—beaches. The largest, **Atlantic Beach**, across a bridge from Morehead City, has a boardwalk backed by a go-cart track and small amusement arcade. A **State Aquarium** (Mon.-Sat. 9 AM-5 PM, Sunday 1-5 PM; $3) five miles west of town on Hwy-58, features extensive displays on the local loggerhead sea turtles.

At the northeast end of Bogue Bank stands **Fort Macon State Park** (daily 9 AM-5 PM; free), which centers on a well-preserved pre-Civil War fortress overlooking the harbor entrance. There's a nice dune-backed beach a mile to the west.

North Carolina's beaches are prime nesting grounds for the endangered loggerhead sea turtles. These huge turtles come ashore mid-May to late August by the light of the full moon. Each female lays over 100 eggs that hatch at the end of summer.

Jacksonville and Camp Lejeune
Midway between Beaufort and Wilmington, the coastline is taken over by the 100,000-acre U.S. Marine Corps base of Camp Lejeune. Established during WW II, and now home to the rapid deployment forces that saw action in Grenada and Beirut, Camp Lejeune is open to visitors interested in a nose-to-nose encounter with tanks, HumVees, and other lethal machines. Sentries will check you in and out at both ends of the surprisingly scenic 25-mile drive across the base (at an enforced maximum speed of 25 mph).

The characterless city of Jacksonville (pop. 30,000), on US-17 at the northwest corner of Camp Lejeune, is little more than a civilian adjunct to the base, with all the gas stations, fast-food franchises, and tattoo parlors you could want. On the south edge of town, just off Hwy-24 opposite a Sonic Drive-In, the 50-foot-long granite wall of the **Beirut Memorial** remembers the more than 250 Camp Lejeune Marines killed in Beirut in 1984 by a suicide bomber. Alongside a list of their names are the words "They Came in Peace."

Holly Ridge: "Venus's Flytrap Capital of the World"
US-17, the inland route across North Carolina, links up with the coastal route on the south side of Camp Lejeune, then continues south along the coast through the odd little community of Holly Ridge. The swamps around the town are an ideal environment for wild iris and azaleas, and for the thousands of insectivorous **Venus's flytrap** that grow wild here, many right along the highway. The flytraps, which Charles Darwin called "the most wonderful plant in the world," do not grow wild in any part of the world except the seacoast Carolinas; they're for sale (at about $3 for a small one) at a tiny store at the intersection of US-17 and Hwy-210, five miles south of town.

Also worth stopping for in Holly Ridge is the award-winning **Betty's Smokehouse Restaurant** barbecue, right on US-17.

Wrightsville Beach

It would be difficult and probably pointless to try to decide which of the hundreds of miles of beaches along the Atlantic Coast is the best, but if you're looking for clean strands and clear blue waters, Wrightsville Beach, 10 miles east of US-17 via US-74 or US-76, is a good bet. It's not all that different from dozens of other coastal resorts, but proximity to the lively city of Wilmington makes it a great place to stop. At the north end of the five-mile-long strand, look across the water at the palatial mansions of Figure 8 Island, where the stars stay when they're in Wilmington to make movies. Julia Roberts's million-dollar beach house in *Sleeping with the Enemy* was built here, though that house was torn down after filming to preserve the open sands.

Places to stay along the beach include a well-appointed **Holiday Inn,** and the comfortable **Blockade Runner Hotel** at 275 Waynick Boulevard (919/256-2251 or 800/541-1161) a half-mile south from the end of US-76, with a good restaurant, a nightclub, and bicycle rentals.

CarolCo Studios, makers of *Blue Velvet* and the "Terminator" movies, are based in Wilmington, and the town has become a busy center of film and TV productions.

Wilmington

Though it's surrounded by the usual miles of highway sprawl, the downtown business district of Wilmington (pop. 55,530) is unusually attractive and well preserved, its many blocks of historic buildings stepping up from the Cape Fear River waterfront. The largest city on the North Carolina coast, Wilmington was of vital importance to the Confederate cause during the Civil War, when it was the only southern port able to continue exporting income-earning cotton, mostly to England, in the face of the Union blockade. Wilmington also played an important role before and during the Revolution, first as a center of colonial resistance, and later as headquarters for the British troops.

Despite its lengthy and involved military history, Wilmington itself has survived relatively unscathed and now possesses one of the country's more engaging small-town streetscapes. Cobblestoned wharves and brick warehouses line the Cape Fear River, which also provides moorage for the massive 35,000-ton battleship USS *North Carolina* (daily 8 AM-dusk; $5). A couple of the warehouses, like the **Cotton Exchange** at the north end, have been converted to house boutiques and restau-

Wilmington waterfront

rants. A block inland, **Front Street** is the lively heart of town, a franchise-free stretch of book and record stores, cafes, and other businesses that's often used by film crews attempting to re-create a typically American "Main Street" scene.

Thanks in large part to its significant movie-making business, Wilmington has a number of excellent places to eat. **Elijah's**, a seafood grill at 2 Ann Street on Chandler's Wharf, overlooks the Cape Fear River, while the comfortable **Caffe Phoenix** at 99 S. Front Street is an excellent Italian bistro serving fresh pasta dishes and pizzas. Within stumbling distance are bars like the **Ice House** at 115 S. Water Street, which features jazz and blues bands, and the more rough-hewn **Barbary Coast**, 116 S. Front Street.

A convenient place to stay is the **Inn at St. Thomas Court**, downtown at Dock and 2nd Streets (919/343-1800 or 800/525-0909). Rates at the many chain motels and hotels are surprisingly low. The **Holiday Inn**, 4903 Market Street (919/799-1440), on US-17 three miles north of downtown, charges $45 a night, and there's also a **Howard Johnson's**, a **Hilton**, and the very nice **Best Western Carolinian** at 2916 Market Street (919/763-4653 or 800/528-1234).

For more information on visiting the Wilmington area, contact the **Cape Fear Convention & Visitor Bureau** in the 100-year-old courthouse at 24 N. 3rd Street (910/341-4030 or 800/222-4757). The free weekly tabloid, *Encore,* available at most shops and restaurants, lists events and entertainment options.

Between the east and west banks of the Cape Fear River, a **ferry** ($3) runs about once an hour between Fort Fisher and Southport. For current schedules and other information, call 800/BY-FERRY.

Cape Fear

There's not much worth stopping for along US-17 between Wilmington and the South Carolina border, and if you have time you might want to detour to the Cape Fear coast. Though it has lent its name to two of the most terrifying movies ever made, Cape Fear is not at all a scary place. The name was given to it by sailors who feared its shipwrecking shoals. Hundreds of vessels have been wrecked off the cape, including dozens of Confederate blockade-runners sunk during the Civil War embargo of Wilmington harbor.

South of Wilmington, US-421 runs along the east bank of the river through typical barrier island beach resort towns like Carolina Beach and Kure Beach. Near the south end of the island, **Fort Fisher State Historic Site** features the earthwork fortification that enabled Wilmington harbor to remain open to blockade-running ships throughout most of the Civil War. The fortress looks more like a series of primitive mounds than an elaborate military installation, but its simple sand piles proved more durable against Union artillery than the heavy masonry of Fort Sumter and other traditional fortresses. A **visitor center** (Mon.-Sat. 10 AM-4 PM, Sunday 1-4 PM, longer hours in summer; free) describes the fort's role, with details of the war's heaviest sea battle, when Union ships bombarded Fort Fisher in January 1865.

On the west bank of the Cape Fear River, Hwy-133 winds up at the pleasure-craft harbor of **Southport**, which is the halfway point between New York City and Miami, attracting sailors traveling the Intracoastal Waterway. It's also the site of the large Brunswick nuclear power plant.

Cape Fear itself is formed by **Bald Head Island**, at the mouth of the Cape Fear River, reachable only by boat from Southport. The **Old Baldy Lighthouse** on the island is the state's oldest, built in 1817.

ALONG THE SOUTH CAROLINA COAST

Just beyond the border into South Carolina, you suddenly hit the crass commercialism of the "Grand Strand," a 25-mile-long conglomeration of resort hotels, amusement arcades, and Coney Island-style Americana that centers on **Myrtle Beach**, the state's number one tourist destination. South of here things quiet down considerably, as coastal US-17 winds past the lush lowland marshes, passing through historic **Georgetown** and numerous preserved plantations before reaching **Charleston**, one of the most gracious and engaging cities in the southern U.S.

Along the coast near the South Carolina border, one place that's worth searching out is **Big Nell's Pit Stop,** which has attracted Myrtle Beach-bound travelers with huge breakfasts, tasty barbecue, and their Roadfood-rated Brunswick Stew. It's midway between Ocean Isle Beach and Sunset Beach, amidst the many fresh shrimp stands along Hwy-179.

Just south of the state border along US-17, the **South Carolina Welcome Center** in Little River (803/249-1111) has a large selection of maps, brochures, and visitor information.

Myrtle Beach boasts more golf courses, including a bewildering array of miniature golf courses, than anywhere else in the country.

Myrtle Beach: The Grand Strand

Standing at the center of the Grand Strand, Myrtle Beach (pop. 25,000) is one of the largest and most popular beach resorts in the country, attracting millions of visitors every summer. It's a huge, and in many ways hideous, place, with mile after mile of motels, Wal-Marts, and fast-food franchises lining all the main roads. The beaches, presumably the reason so many people come here, are backed by 20-story towers one after another of them forming an ugly "Costa del Concrete" for miles along the sands, which are surprisingly narrow and in some places completely submerged beneath the tides.

All of which isn't to say Myrtle Beach should be avoided; in fact, if you want to wallow in beachfront Americana, there are few better places to head. Myrtle Beach grew up around **The Pavilion** amusement park, at the east end of US-501 along Ocean Avenue and 9th Avenue N, which started in the 1920s as a dance hall (where the dance craze "The Shag" began). The park offers a classic array of roller coasters, Ferris wheels, merry-go-rounds, and midway arcade games. From Spring Break until the end of summer, the surrounding blocks are absolutely jammed with people showing off their well-formed bodies, though after school starts the resort gets suddenly quiet.

The best places to eat are in Murrells Inlet (see below), but there are also dozens of old-time burger stands like **Peach's** on Ocean Avenue across from The Pavilion. Accommodations in and around Myrtle Beach range from roadside motels to flashy resorts, and rates vary immensely depending upon time of year. A beachfront room at the centrally located **Holiday Inn** at 1200 N. Ocean Boulevard (803/448-1691 or 800/HOLIDAY), which costs $75 a night in August, may set you back only $30 in October; rates at plusher resorts like **The Breakers,** 2006 N. Ocean Boulevard (803/626-5000 or 800/845-0688), range $25-125 a night.

For complete listings and other information, contact the **visitor center**, 1301 N. King's Highway (803/626-7444 or 800/356-3016).

*The spring- and summer-blooming **crape myrtle** trees, with long branches of purple and red flowers, gave Myrtle Beach its name.*

Murrells Inlet

There are more picturesque inlets in the state, but the relatively unspoiled fishing village of Murrells Inlet, 12 miles south of Myrtle Beach, is worth a stop for the chance to sample its many excellent seafood restaurants. Lining a short Business Loop off US-17, these range from **Flo's Place** at the north end, to the waterfront **Anchor Inn** and **Dockside**, to the rustic **Oliver's Lodge** a mile south. If you've got the time and inclination to catch your own, sportfishing charter boats run from the marina, or you can put on some waders and head into the waters in search of clams, mussels, oysters, and crabs.

Brookgreen Gardens and Huntington Beach State Park

Carry insect repellent, keep car windows closed, and be prepared for mosquitoes, especially late in the afternoon, almost everywhere along the muggy South Carolina coast.

Well posted off US-17, four miles south of Murrells Inlet, Brookgreen Gardens (daily 9:30 AM-5 PM; $6.50) is a privately owned, 4,000-acre park on the well-maintained grounds of four colonial-era indigo and rice plantations. Oak trees laden with Spanish moss stand alongside palmettos, dogwoods, and azaleas as well as hundreds of sculptures, including many done by the owner, Anna Hyatt Huntington, who developed the site in the 1930s. Alligators and otters play in the simulated swamp and many species of birds fly around enclosed aviaries in a section of the gardens set aside as a wildlife park.

Across the highway is the 2,500-acre Huntington Beach State Park ($3 per car), which sits on land carved out of the Huntington estate and rented by the state. Besides a nice beach, it features the Moorish-style castle "Atalaya," Anna Huntington's studio.

*One of the more unusual radio stations in the country, **WLGI 90.9 FM,** is operated by the Ba'hai Faith and broadcasts a commercial-free mix of classic 1970s soul, contemporary jazz, and messages of peace, love, and understanding.*

Georgetown

Site of a short-lived Spanish settlement in 1526, the first European outpost in North America, Georgetown later became the rice plantation center of the colonial era. Bounded by the Sampit and Pee Dee rivers and the narrow inlet of Winyah Bay, Georgetown is one of the state's few deepwater harbors and is home to two huge steel and paper mills along US-17. Its downtown district along Front Street is compact and comfortable, with dozens of day-to-day businesses and a few cafes and art galleries filling the many old buildings.

Three blocks south of US-17, at the east end of Front Street, there's a pleasant waterfront promenade, where the clock-towered old town market now houses the **Rice Museum** (Mon.-Sat. 9:30 AM-4:30 PM; $2). Dioramas trace South Carolina's little-known history as the world's main rice and indigo producer, a past often overshadowed by the state's later tobacco and cotton trade. The rest of town holds many well-preserved colonial and antebellum houses, churches, and commercial buildings.

Across the Pee Dee River, a mile north of Georgetown on US-17, the **Bellefield Nature Center** (daily 10 AM-5 PM; $3; 803/546-4623)) was once the home of New

Deal-era statesman Bernard Baruch and his daughter Belle. The plantation buildings have been preserved in antebellum condition, complete with one of very few surviving slave streets. Despite their historic quarters, the nonprofit educational foundation that currently occupies the buildings is more involved with environmental concerns than with regional history.

A couple of good places to eat in Georgetown include the locals' favorite **Thomas Cafe** next to the Rice Museum at 6701 Front Street, and the **LaFayette Seafood Restaurant** on US-17 at 711 N. Church Street. If you're looking to stay at a good B&B, try the **King's Inn** at 230 Broad Street (803/527-6937). Chain motels line US-17, including the **Days Inn** at 210 N. Church Street (803/546-8441 or 800/850-0078).

For more information, or to pick up a self-guided tour map of town, contact the Georgetown County Chamber of Commerce, 102 Broad Street on the waterfront (803/546-8346 or 800/777-7705).

Hampton Plantation and McClellanville

The Santee Delta region along US-17 between Georgetown and Charleston once held dozens of large and hugely profitable plantations. One of the best preserved of these is now the Hampton Plantation State Park (Thurs.-Mon. 9 AM-6 PM; free), located 15 miles south of Georgetown, two miles west of US-17. Spreading out along the northern edge of Francis Marion National Forest, the 320-acre grounds feature a white wooden Greek revival manor house (tours Thurs.-Mon. 1-4 PM; $2) that once welcomed George Washington. The manor house was later home to Archibald Rutledge, poet laureate of South Carolina from 1934 until his death in 1973.

South from Hampton Plantation along US-17, a small sign and a flashing yellow light are all that mark the turnoff to the tiny, low country fishing village of McClellanville (pop. 383). It's the kind of place where neighbors drift in to sit on barrels and chat at **Graham's General Store**, and stop for a bite to eat at the charming **Village Creations Cafe** across the street—it's open every day but Monday for lunch and dinner and a traditional Sunday buffet. A short drive along Pinckney Street, the main road, brings you to the town hall (complete with a hurricane warning tower) and the town dock, where a substantial portion of South Carolina's shrimp and crab catch gets unloaded and shipped to market.

The original lyrics to Stephen Foster's song "The Old Folks at Home" began "Way down upon the Pee Dee River . . . " though he quickly changed it to the more sonorous "Suwanee."

Cape Romain National Wildlife Refuge

The unspoiled Cape Romain National Wildlife Refuge, south of McClellanville and five miles east of US-17, is one of the largest and most important sanctuaries for migratory birds in the Atlantic flyway. Thousands of great blue herons, pelicans, terns, and ducks join the resident population of wild turkeys, feral pigs, deer, and alligators, which have returned after Hurricane Hugo. The state has been thinking about building a visitor center here, but in the meantime, the refuge's few visitors park on a grassy lot and fish off the small pier, while a few boats take serious birdwatchers to the marshland's several small islands.

Along US-17 north of Charleston, sellers of African sweetgrass baskets line the highway outside Mount Pleasant, the only place in the U.S. where this traditional handicraft still flourishes. Women sit and weave at their individual roadside stands almost every day, but the weaving may soon be a lost art, as younger women are increasingly reluctant to take on this low-paid work; it takes four to five hours to weave a $20 basket.

Directly across from the refuge entrance on US-17 is the homey **SeeWee Cafe**, which has been open every day but Sunday for over 100 years. Some homemade specialties include a pineapple upside-down cake with pecans ($1.95) and a generous cup of she-crab with sherry on the side ($2.50).

Fort Moultrie National Monument

Sitting at the entrance to Charleston harbor, across from its better-known sibling Fort Sumter, Fort Moultrie (daily 9 AM-5 PM; free) overlooks the Atlantic with good views of passing ships and the city of Charleston. The location alone would make Moultrie well worth a visit, but most come because of its vital role in American military history. Originally built from palmetto logs during the Revolutionary War, and since rebuilt many times, the fort is a testament to the development of coastal defenses. Its well-preserved sections date from every major U.S. war between 1812 and WW II, when Fort Moultrie protected Charleston harbor from roving German U-boats. But the fort is most famous for its role in the events of April 1861, when Fort Moultrie touched off the Civil War by leading the bombardment of Fort Sumter.

Fort Moultrie is easy to reach from US-17: across the Cooper River north of Charleston, turn south onto Hwy-703 at Mount Pleasant, then follow signs along Middle Street to the fort.

African sweetgrass basket

Fort Sumter National Monument

Commanding an island at the mouth of Charleston harbor, Fort Sumter National Monument marks the site of the first military engagement of the Civil War. On April 12, 1861, a month after Abraham Lincoln's inauguration and four months after South Carolina had seceded from the United States, Confederate guns bombarded the fort for a day and a half before the federal forces withdrew. The structure was badly damaged, but no one was killed and the fort was held by the Confederates for the next four years, by which time it had been almost completely flattened. Later used as lighthouse station, and with a massive concrete battery inserted into its center in 1899, Fort Sumter has been partly restored, and is a key stop on any tour of Civil War sites.

The only way to visit Fort Sumter is by tour boat ($8.50; 803/722-1691), which leaves from the north side of Charleston at Patriot's Point, just off US-17 at the foot of the massive bridge across the Cooper River. Other boats to Fort Sumter dock at the City Marina, on the south side of Charleston, off US-17 at 17 Lockwood Drive.

Patriot's Point, where boats bound for Fort Sumter dock along the Cooper River, is also the anchorage of the aircraft carrier **USS Yorktown** (daily 9 AM-5 PM; $5), a floating museum complete with WW II-era fighter planes.

George Gershwin's opera *Porgy and Bess* was inspired by life in Charleston's Creole ghetto, specifically Cabbage Row, now a tidy brick-paved alley off 91 Church Street.

If you like the look of Charleston, you'll love Savannah, Georgia. It's just an hour's drive south via US-17 and I-95, and is covered on pages 720-721.

Charleston

Established in 1670 as the capital of South Carolina, Charleston more than any other Deep South city proudly maintains the aristocratic traditions established during the plantation era. Then the elite would flee the heat, humidity, and mosquitoes of their lowland fiefdoms and come here to cavort in ballrooms and theaters. Still ruled by old money, though no longer the state capital, Charleston is both pretentious—with more Gucci and Ralph Lauren-type boutiques than you'd expect in a city of 80,000—and provincial; locals like to say that Charleston is the place where the Ashley and Cooper Rivers meet to form the Atlantic Ocean. It's also surprisingly cosmopolitan, accommodating an historic ethnic mix of French Huguenots, Catholic Acadians, and African Americans from the Caribbean, who introduced the wrought-iron balconies and brightly colored cottages that give the city much of its charm.

Having suffered through a devastating earthquake, two wars, and innumerable hurricanes, Charleston has rebuilt and restored itself many times, yet it remains one of the South's most beautiful cities. Impressive neoclassical buildings line the streets, especially in the older, upmarket sections of town south of Broad Street and along the waterfront Battery. Charleston's many small, lush gardens and parks make it ideal for aimless exploring on foot rather than by car.

Many of the mansions and churches are open to visitors, but it's the overall fabric of Charleston, rather than specific sites, that is most memorable. Nevertheless, the 1828 Greek revival **Edmonston-Alston House** at 21 E. Battery (Tues.-Sat. 10 AM-5 PM, Sun.-Mon. 1:30-5 PM; $5) is definitely worth a look, as is the beautiful spire of **St. Michael's Episcopal Church,** 78 Meeting Street (daily 9 AM-5 PM; donations), which was modeled on the London churches of Sir Christopher Wren. A quarter-mile north, at Church and Market Streets, is the open-air **City Market,** known as the "Ellis Island of Black America," since over a third of all slaves arrived

A Grumman E-1B Tracer on the deck of the USS Yorktown, *at Patriot's Point.*

in the colonies here. Once the commercial center of Charleston, the market now houses a range of souvenir shops and touristy restaurants.

Outside the historic area a half-mile south of US-17, the **Charleston Visitor Center** at 375 Meeting Street (daily 9 AM-5 PM; 803/853-800) is a good first stop; watch the 21-projector multi-image slide show "**Forever Charleston**" (every 30 minutes; $2.50) and pick up a **day pass** ($1) to ride the DASH shuttle buses that loop around town. Across the street from the visitor center, the **Charleston Museum** (Mon.-Sat. 9 AM-5 PM, Sunday 1-5 PM; $5) has general exhibits on regional history and culture.

Thanks to its well-heeled populace and its considerable tourist trade, Charleston supports a number of excellent eateries. Around the City Market, choose from the very popular **Hyman's Seafood**, 215 Meeting Street, which has a variety of basic but good-value fresh fish entrees for around $10; the more sedate (and expensive) places nearby include the stylish, Mediterranean-inspired **Blossom Cafe**, 171 E. Bay Street, and the upscale and usually crowded **Magnolias** next door. Both are open until 11 PM or later. Bakeries and cafes line busy King Street, and there are some very formal places in the plush hotels.

Like its restaurants, Charleston's accommodation options tend toward the luxurious and expensive. Of the dozens of old fashioned but well-appointed B&Bs (all of which charge over $100 a night), the elegant **John Rutledge House**, 116 Broad Street (803/723-7999 or 800/476-9741) offers four-star comfort in a converted 1763 house. The romantic, Queen Anne-style **Two Meeting Street Inn** at 2 Meeting Street (803/723-7322) has been welcoming guests for over 50 years. Hotels in and around the historic district are similarly expensive, though you'll find chain motels, including a **Best Western**, an **Econo Lodge**, and a **Motel 6** along Savannah Highway (US-17) south of town, and more along the I-26 frontage north of town.

The Charleston accent is famous throughout the South. The word "garden" here is characteristically pronounced "gyarden," and "car" is "kyar," while the long "a" of Charleston (usually pronounced "Chaaahrleston") is as distinctive as JFK's "Harvard."

Charleston's **Spoleto Festival USA,** held late May to early June, is one of the top art and performance events in the country. For information, call 803/722-2764.

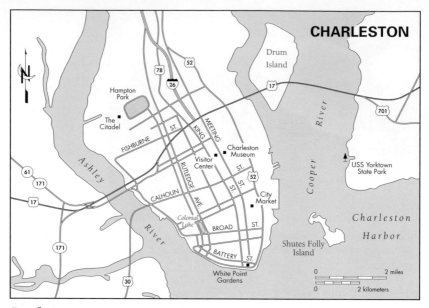

CHARLESTON

Beaufort

The second-oldest town in South Carolina, Beaufort (pop. 9,500, pronounced "BYOO-furd") is a well-preserved antebellum town stretching along a fine natural harbor, 18 miles south of US-17 via US-21. Established in 1710, Beaufort stands on the largest of some 75 islands dotting Port Royal Sound near the Georgia border. Beaufort was established in 1710, and dozens of colonial-era and antebellum homes line its quiet, small-town streets. Only two of these houses, the circa 1790 **Verdier House** and the Greek revival **Elliott House**, a block apart on Bay Street along the waterfront, are open to visitors, though you can pick up a walking-tour map of the others from the **visitor center** at 1006 Bay Street (803/524-3163).

Beaufort is perhaps best known as the home of the massive U.S. Marine Corps Recruit Depot at nearby **Parris Island** (803/525-3650), where you can watch drill sergeants bark at young men and women undergoing basic training. Near the southern tip of South Carolina, **Hilton Head Island** was founded in 1663, and since the 1960s has operated as a major destination resort. Information is available through the Hilton Head Island Chamber of Commerce (803/785-3673).

Though his house isn't on the visitor center map, and his story is seldom told, one of Beaufort's most noteworthy residents was Robert Smalls, who was born a slave but rose to become the first black captain in the U.S. Navy; Smalls later served five terms in the U.S. House of Representatives. After Jim Crow laws disenfranchised blacks, Smalls lost his seat and returned to Beaufort, living in his former master's house and taking care of his former master's widow, at 511 Prince Street. After his death in 1915, he was buried in **Beaufort's Baptist Tabernacle Church** at 907 Craven Street, where a small bust is all that marks his accomplishments.

The **Anchorage House**, housed in a circa 1765 building on the water at 1103 Bay Street, offers such low country specialties as a crabmeat casserole and she-crab soup with sherry. Places to stay include the waterfront **Best Western Sea Island Motel**, 1015 Bay Street (803/524-4121 or 800/528-1234); and the state's only four-star B&B, the lovely **Rhett House**, 1009 Craven Street (803/524-9030), where the film *Prince of Tides* was shot on location.

South to Savannah

From Beaufort, a confusing series of narrow and roadkill strewn two-lane highways—Hwy-170, Hwy-46, and US-17—run across the lowlands around Hilton Head Island toward the Georgia border. One place along here, the Savannah National Wildlife Refuge, is worth a stop for birdwatchers, but everyone will probably want to race along to that most gracious of historic southern cities, Savannah, which is described in the Survival Guide to Savannah on pages 720-721.

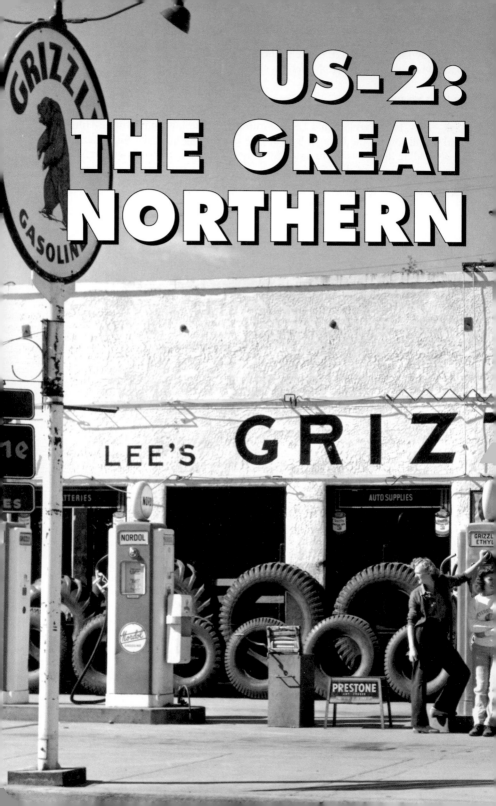

US-2: THE GREAT NORTHERN

US-2: THE GREAT NORTHERN

Though many come close, no other cross-country route takes in the variety and extremity of landscape that US-2 does. Dubbed the Great Northern in memory of the pioneer railroad that parallels the western half of the route, US-2 is truly the most stunning and unforgettable, not to mention longest, of all the great transcontinental road trips.

Starting in the west at the beautiful Pacific port city of Seattle, US-2 runs steeply up and over the volcanic Cascade Range, climbing from sea level to alpine splendor in around an hour. From the crest the road drops down onto the otherworldly Columbia Plateau, a naturally arid region reclaimed from sagebrush into fertile farmland by New Deal public works projects like the great Grand Coulee Dam, one of the largest pieces of civil engineering on the planet. From Washington, US-2 bends north toward the Canadian border, clipping across the top of the Idaho Panhandle before climbing up into the Rocky Mountain majesty of western Montana, a land of forests, rivers, and wildlife that culminates in the bold granite spectacle of Glacier National Park.

On the eastern flank of the Rockies the route drops suddenly to the windswept prairies of the northern Great Plains. Though empty to look at—especially when you're midway along the 1,000-mile beeline across Montana and North Dakota, wondering how long it will be until you see the next tree or peak—this is a land rich in history, where the buffalo once roamed freely, where Plains tribes like the Shoshone, Blackfeet, Sioux, and Cheyenne reigned supreme, and where the Lewis and Clark expedition followed the Missouri River upstream in search of a way west to the Pacific.

Midway across the continent, the Great Plains give way to the Great North Woods country of Minnesota—birthplace both of Paul Bunyan and Judy Garland—and then to the Great Lakes lumber and mining country of northern Wisconsin and Michigan's Upper Peninsula. Continuing due east, the route crosses the border into Ontario, Canada, through the capital city, Ottawa, and the francophile environs of Montreal before returning to the U.S. at lovely Lake Champlain in upstate New York.

From there US-2 passes through yet another mountainous landscape, the hardwood forests of the Green Mountains and the rugged granite peaks of New Hampshire's White Mountains, two very different ranges though only 50 miles apart. The route winds down to the coast of Maine, reaching the Atlantic Ocean at Bar Harbor and Acadia National Park.

Landscapes, rather than cities and towns, play the starring roles on this route. Between Seattle and Montreal, the biggest cities along the route are Spokane and Duluth. Still, after a few days spent following US-2 through small towns and wide-open spaces, you'll probably consider Duluth bustling and fast-paced; driving even a short stretch of the Great Northern highway is guaranteed to bring new meaning to the expression "getting away from it all."

US-2 HIGHLIGHTS

ACROSS WASHINGTON

The 350 miles of US-2 across Washington state contain enough contrasting landscapes to fill many states. West to east, the route begins at the industrial fringes of Seattle and the Puget Sound, passing through a couple of Victorian-era towns before climbing steeply up toward the towering peaks, dense forests, and pristine lakes of the Cascade Mountains. East of the Cascade crest, the rugged volcanic landscape suddenly becomes drier and much more sparse, the dense forests fading first into lush farmlands and orchards reclaimed from the natural desert, then continuing across increasingly barren sagebrush plains into Idaho.

Though it can be heavy on long summer weekends, and also in winter in the Cascades section, traffic along US-2 is usually light, since most of the 18-wheelers and other heavy vehicles follow the parallel I-90 freeway, which runs 25 miles to the south.

See pages 722-723 for the Survival Guide to Seattle.

Everett

At the west end of transcontinental US-2, 20 miles north of downtown Seattle via the I-5 freeway, busy Everett (pop. 69,961) is a heavy industrial center economically dependent upon two of the largest companies in the Pacific Northwest—the wood products conglomerate Weyerhauser and aircraft manufacturer Boeing. Apart from a few large turn-of-the-century mansions overlooking the extensive water-

front, it's a thoroughly blue-collar place with little to attract visitors. The one exception is the huge **Boeing assembly plant** on the southwest edge of town, well marked from I-5 exit 189, at the west end of Hwy-526. The factory, where they make 747s and 757s, is worth a look if only for the 11-story-high, quarter-mile-long building, which is said to be the largest in the world; first-come, first-served 90-minute tours (Mon.-Fri. 9 AM-3 PM; free) leave on the hour, but these fill up early in the day.

Snohomish

Though they're spreading fast, Seattle's suburbs haven't yet reached the tidy Victorian town of Snohomish (pop. 6,499), a 100-year-old former logging center that lines the north bank of the Snohomish River, 25 miles upstream from Puget Sound. Well-preserved warehouses and commercial buildings line 1st Street, a block from the river banks, while the hills above hold dozens of charming homes and quite a few impressively steepled churches. One of the old homes has been restored and now houses the **Blackman Museum** (daily noon-4 PM in summer, weekends only in

downtown Seattle

winter; $1). Located at 118 Avenue B, the museum features period-style furnishings and displays on the town's early history. The range of antique shops, taverns, and cafes, like the **Cabbage Patch** at 111 Avenue A, has made Snohomish a popular day-trip from Seattle, and it's well worth a short stop if you're passing by.

Gold Bar and Index
Much of the route traversed by US-2 on its way between the flatlands and Stevens Pass high up in the Cascades is given over to ski shops, bike shops, and espresso stands, all catering to Seattleites racing to and from the slopes. The one-time mining, logging, and railroad camp of Gold Bar stretches along US-2, halfway between Stevens Pass and Puget Sound. Besides all the gas stations and cafes you could want, Gold Bar also holds the well-posted trailhead (follow 1st Street north from the center of town) for the 3.5-mile hike to 250-foot **Wallace Falls**, one of the tallest in the North Cascades.

Farther west, Index, on a side road a mile north of US-2, sits at the western foot of the Cascade Mountains at the point where the scenery changes suddenly from pastoral to alpine. Besides two taverns, two general stores, and constant trains rumbling over the swimmably deep north fork of the Skykomish River, Index offers good food and comfortable lodging at the historic **Bush House Inn** (206/793-2312).

Skykomish
Lining the busy Burlington Northern railroad tracks, a block south of US-2, Skykomish is a quirky and engaging place that seems to belong somewhere else, some long time ago. The two-block town revolves around the rustic **Hotel Skykomish**, which has huge sunny balconies but few signs of life apart from **Flynn's Cafe** on the ground floor, where you can still get a good breakfast—so long as you're not in any hurry.

Deception Falls
Around eight miles east of Skykomish, a well-marked turnout along US-2 gives access to one of the region's prettiest and most historically significant sites. On the north side of the highway, the parking area's interpretive exhibits tell the story of

the Northern Pacific Railroad, the St.-Paul-to-Seattle route that was completed on this spot in 1883. A plaque displays a photograph showing the driving of the traditional golden spike, while other exhibits discuss the construction and importance of the railroad in the growth of Puget Sound.

If you're not interested in railroad lore, head along the 100-yard-long paved trail that loops back under the highway to the powerful cascade of Deception Falls. If you can stand the usually bone-chilling snowmelt, you'll be pleased to find a number of deep and clean swimming holes in the area.

Stevens Pass

At the crest of the Cascades, US-2 climbs over 4,061-foot Stevens Pass, the highest and northernmost Cascade pass that's kept open year-round. Stevens Pass was also a historically vital railroad crossing, though Amtrak and other trains now avoid the pass, detouring instead through an eight-mile-long tunnel cut through the mountains in 1929. In 1910, before the completion of the tunnel, which is the longest still in use in the western hemisphere, the pass was the site of the worst avalanche disaster in U.S. history: 96 passengers and railroad workers were killed by a mile-long snow slide.

Besides providing grand views of the nearby peaks and more distant valleys, Stevens Pass is also a popular **ski area**, with 10 chairlifts and a 1,800-foot vertical drop; for prices, ski conditions, and other information, call 206/973-2441.

Tumwater Canyon

Heading east through the Cascades toward Leavenworth, US-2 runs through the forests of Tumwater Canyon, a breathtaking place during the fall color sweeps, but quite scenic year-round. Much of the surrounding wilderness was badly burned during the summer of 1994, but the area along the highway survived pretty much unscathed; here the route follows along the Wenatchee River through aspen and evergreen forests.

Leavenworth

Sitting in the eastern foothills of the Cascades, Leavenworth has successfully transformed itself from an economically depressed railroad town into one of the most

Indian
eservation
Coleville
National
Forest
Newport
Creston
Spokane Indian
Reservation
Columbia
Davenport
Basin
Spokane
Spokane
WASHINGTON
IDAHO

popular day-trip destinations in the region. After the local lumber mills closed down in the mid-1960s, the town took advantage of its spectacular location and re-created itself as an ersatz Bavarian village, and it has been drawing huge crowds of tourists ever since. Check out the old photographs on the walls of **Der Markt Platz** shopping center, on the corner of 8th and Commercial Streets, for the whole story.

Over a dozen blocks of half-timbered pseudo-chalets and Tyrolean shopping malls house a range of low-budget crafts galleries and T-shirt stores, which you can escape by walking two blocks south to an attractively landscaped park along the Wenatchee River. Eat and drink at the elaborate mock-Bavarian McDonald's or any of a dozen sausage-and-beer gardens, the most bearable of which is **Gustav's Onion Dome Tavern**, on US-2 at the west end of town. The pleasant and moderately priced **Evergreen Inn** (509/548-5515), a block south of US-2 at 1117 Front Street, has quiet rooms and bike rentals.

Cashmere

At the heart of the Wenatchee Valley, surrounded by apple orchards and bare brown Cascade foothills, Cashmere (pop. 2,500) has an attractive downtown district, its unusual red-and-white striped metal awnings both shading the sidewalks and giving the town some visual identity. The main sight here is the

large **Chelan County Historical Museum** (Mon.-Sat. 10 AM-4:30 PM, Sunday 1-4:30 PM; $3), off US-2 at the east end of town, with an excellent collection of Native American artifacts and a free outdoor Pioneer Village made up of 18 different historic structures from around the county.

Cashmere is also the home of **Aplets and Cotlets** fruit-and-nut candy, started here in the 1920s by two Turkish brothers. The factory, across from the railroad depot at 117 Mission Street, is open daily for free tours and samples.

The block-long downtown district holds a handful of cafes and taverns including the popular **Coachman Inn**, 128 Cottage Avenue, which is open 6 AM-2 AM for breakfast, lunch, dinner, and occasional evening music. A block away at 229 Cottage Avenue, the quiet **Village Inn** (509/782-3522) has clean rooms from $40 a night.

Ohme Gardens County Park

Overlooking the confluence of the Wenatchee and Columbia Rivers high above US-2, Ohme Gardens County Park (daily 9 AM-5 PM, April 15-Oct. 15; $5) maintains

Leavenworth's reconstruction was inspired by Solvang, California (see pages 73-75), and by the commercial success of the **Squirrel House,** a tacky tourist trap on US-2, 15 miles west of town in the heart of Tumwater Canyon.

Two miles northwest of Cashmere, right along US-2, the sandstone slabs and spires of **Peshastin Pinnacles State Park** provide a popular rock-climbing spot.

nine acres of immaculate greenery that offers a cool contrast to eastern Washington's arid terrain. Created in 1929 by the Ohme family, the lush plantings of ferns and evergreens have transformed an otherwise rugged Cascade crest. Stone pathways wind past waterfalls and rocky pools, culminating in a rustic lookout that gives sweeping views of the Wenatchee and Columbia valleys.

Wenatchee

The largest city between Seattle and Spokane, Wenatchee (pop. 21,756) is the commercial center of the Wenatchee Valley, one of the world's most productive apple-growing regions—it's responsible for as much as half the nation's annual crop. The **Washington Apple Commission Visitor Center** (Mon.-Fri. 8 AM-5 PM, plus Sat.-Sun. 10 AM-4 PM in summer; free), a block north of US-2 below the Ohme Gardens, is the place to go to find out all about the state's apple industry, and to enjoy free apples and apple juice (not to mention potent air-conditioning).

Wenatchee's **Magic 900 AM**, KKRT, plays the hits of five decades, everything from Woody Herman to Stevie Wonder.

From Wenatchee, US-97 runs north along the west bank of the Columbia River to beautiful **Lake Chelan**, at the southern edge of the North Cascades National Park. For visitor information, call 800/4-CHELAN. US-2, which briefly shares the riverfront route with US-97, veers east at Orondo, some 15 miles north of Wenatchee.

Wenatchee stretches south from US-2, two miles of shopping malls, car dealerships, and anonymous highway sprawl before you reach the downtown business district. Many large fruit warehouses line the railroad tracks along the riverfront. One place worth stopping at is the excellent **North Central Washington Museum** (Mon.-Fri. 10 AM-4 PM, Sat.-Sun. 1-4 PM; $2), at 127 S. Mission Street, which contains extensive displays tracing the region's prehistoric and pioneer past, from native rock art to a working model of the railroad route over the Cascades. An adjacent building houses a large exhibit on Washington's apple industry, including an antique but fully functioning apple sorting and packing line.

Apart from every fast-food franchise known to humankind, Wenatchee doesn't offer many good places to eat. There are, however, lots of motels, ranging from the low-budget **Scotty's Motel**, 1004 N. Wenatchee (509/662-8165), where $30 doubles include use of the pool and sauna, to the upscale **West Coast Wenatchee Center Hotel**, 201 N. Wenatchee Avenue (509/662-1234).

Waterville

Standing at the center of fertile wheat fields 10 miles east of the Columbia River, the compact farming town of Waterville (pop. 1,000) was laid out in 1886 around the stately, whitewashed brick **Douglas County Courthouse**, which still stands at Birch and Rainier Streets, two blocks southeast of US-2. Most of downtown Waterville has been declared a National Historic District, and the four blocks of attractive brick buildings—still housing franchise-free banks, cafes, and grocery stores—make a pleasant place to pause on a journey across the state. Across from the historic but recently closed Hotel Waterville, the **Douglas County Historical Museum** (Wed.-Sun. 11 AM-5 PM in summer; donations), at 124 W. Walnut Street, has an intriguing display of objects tracing regional history, including Native American artifacts and a perfectly preserved pioneer post office.

Moses Coulee

One of the last vestiges of eastern Washington's unirrigated landscape, Moses Coulee is an 800-foot-deep gorge bounded by vertical walls of black volcanic basalt, brightened by splashes of green and orange lichen. From the rolling plains above, US-2 cuts down into the coulee, then back up the other side, passing through some of the Columbia River Basin's sole surviving sagebrush and giving a strong sense of how profoundly irrigation has changed the region.

Coulee City and Dry Falls

A shipping center for the wheat farms of eastern Washington, Coulee City (pop. 600) calls itself the "Friendliest Town in the West." Despite this claim, there's no more reason to stop now than there was during the pioneer days of the 1860s, when it was said that transfer times on stagecoaches and trains were arranged so that travelers were forced to spend the night in Coulee City, like it or not.

Northwest of town, the large Dry Falls dam impounds Columbia River water to form Banks Lake, and Hwy-155 runs along its sluggish shores between Coulee City and the Grand Coulee Dam. Though you can see the coulee's towering black basalt walls from this road, to get a sense of what the Grand Coulee looked like before the dams were built, follow Hwy-17 four miles south from Coulee City to where the 400-foot-high wall of Dry Falls stands out as the most impressive reminder of the region's tumultuous geology. Interpretive exhibits along the highway explain that during the last Ice Age, when the Columbia River flowed over the falls, this was the most powerful waterfall on the planet, twice as high as Niagara, and over three miles across.

Grand Coulee Dam

The centerpiece of the massive project of dams and canals that have "reclaimed" the Columbia Basin, the Grand Coulee Dam is one of the civil engineering wonders of the world. Built from 1933 to 1942 under the auspices of FDR's New Deal, at a cost of many millions of dollars and 77 lives, the dam is the largest concrete structure in the world: 550 feet high, 450 feet thick at its base, and nearly a mile across. Exhibits on the construction and impact of the dam fill the large, modern **Visitor Arrival Center** (daily 8:30 AM-10 PM in summer, 9 AM-5 PM rest of the year; free) just downstream, where you can listen to Woody Guthrie and Bonnie Raitt singing a continuous loop of "Roll On, Columbia." On summer evenings a very cheesy, half-hour laser light show (Memorial Day to September 30 nightly at 8 PM; free) is projected onto the

In Electric City, along Hwy-155 a mile southwest of Coulee Dam, take a look at the **Gehrke Windmill Garden,** a whimsical collection of whirligigs and windmills made by folk artist Emil Gehrke, who lived here until his death in 1979.

spillway of the dam. Take an elevator down into the powerhouses and inspect the massive turbines, which have a combined generating capacity of over six million kilowatts—half of which comes from the Third Powerplant, added in 1975.

There are three small towns around the dam, none of which is particularly enticing. You can see the light show from your room at the **Ponderosa Motel** (509/633-

2100) or the **Coulee House** (509/633-1101) in the town of **Coulee Dam**; eat and drink at the popular **Banks Lake Pub** on Hwy-155 in **Electric City.**

The Columbia Basin

The 150 miles of rolling farmland that lie to the east of the Cascades are a natural desert, receiving an average of 10 inches of annual rainfall. Though small-scale farming limped along here for over a century, the region underwent a wholesale change after WW II, when irrigation water from reclamation projects along the Columbia River and its many tributaries turned the sagebrush plains into the proverbial amber waves of grain.

US-2 runs directly across the heart of this sparsely populated, nearly treeless region, passing through a few very small towns. The blink-and-you'll-miss-it community of **Creston** is worth a stop for a bite to eat at cowboy-themed **Deb's Cafe,** right on US-2 in the center of town, serving good food for breakfast, lunch, and dinner and hosting country-western bands in the bar next door.

The agricultural flatlands around Spokane were the seat of power for Democratic Party leader and former Speaker of the House of Representatives **Tom Foley,** who was voted out of office in the Republican landslides of 1994.

Twenty miles east of Creston, **Davenport,** one of the oldest towns in eastern Washington, has a handful of quaint old houses as well as the small **Lincoln County Historical Museum,** a block south of US-2 at Park and 7th Streets, with a circa 1879 log cabin schoolhouse preserved next door.

Spokane

The only real city in eastern Washington, Spokane (pop. 173,000) feels even bigger than it is, thanks to its location amidst the agricultural hinterlands of the Columbia River Basin. First established as a fur-trading outpost around 1810, Spokane began to grow when railroads arrived in the 1870s, and has boomed since the advent of irrigation water in the 1940s. The second largest city in Washington, and the biggest between Seattle and Minneapolis, Spokane is economically dependent on warehousing and transportation, taking advantage of its busy railroads as well as its location at the junction of US-2, US-395, and the I-90 freeway.

One of Spokane's most popular roadside attractions is the giant-sized Radio Flyer wagon, standing two stories tall with a slide down the "handle." It's in Riverside Park, just off the I-90 freeway at the Division Street exit.

Though downtown Spokane boasts a number of grand buildings—one recent guidebook called Riverside Street between Jefferson and Lincoln "the loveliest three blocks in the Pacific Northwest"—Spokane really came of age when it hosted the 1974 World's Fair, for which much of the riverfront was cleared and converted to the attractive, 50-acre **Riverfront Park**. Designed by Frederick Law Olmsted a mere century earlier, the park gives good views of tumbling Spokane Falls. Besides an opera house and a convention center, other remnants of the fair include a **gondola ride** (daily 11 AM-dusk; $3) over the river, and a 1909 **carousel** ($1), complete with hand-carved wooden horses.

Northeast of downtown, across the Spokane River at 200 E. Cataldo Street, the five-story **Museum of Native Cultures** (Tues.-Sun. 9 AM-5 PM; $2) has one of the most extensive collections of prehistoric artifacts in the Northwest, including examples of native cultures from all over the New World. A short walk to the east, **Gonzaga University** is best known as the alma mater of Bing Crosby, who is fondly remembered in a small museum in the Crosby Library at the heart of the small campus. Spokane's other center of visitor interest is **Browne's Addition**, a turn-of-the-century residential district a mile or so west of downtown where, among many stately homes, the **Cheney Cowles Memorial Museum** (Tues.-Sat. 10 AM-5 PM, Sunday 1-5 PM; $3), at 2316 W. 1st Avenue, has an above-average range of exhibits tracing regional history.

There's no shortage of places to eat in Spokane, though only a couple are worth searching out. One of these is **Frank's Diner**, near downtown at 1500 W. 2nd Avenue, where very good and inexpensive meals are served in an elegant old railroad car, built in 1906 and moved here from Seattle in 1991. More upscale fare is served at **Patsy Clark's**, one of Spokane's finest restaurants, housed in an opulent old Browne's Addition mansion at 2208 W. 2nd Avenue. Spokane's most characterful place to stay, the **Fotheringham House B&B** (509/838-4363) is just across the street at 2128 W. 2nd Avenue. Motels line the main highways in and out of Spokane, especially along inaptly named Sunset Boulevard west of downtown from the end of 2nd Avenue; here you'll find a **Motel 6**, a **Holiday Inn**, a **Friendship Inn**, and many more.

For further information on visiting Spokane, contact the **visitor center**, 926 Sprague Avenue (509/624-1341).

Heading northeast from Spokane, US-2 crosses a few miles of suburban sprawl before winding through 35 miles of beautiful forested uplands toward Newport, on the Idaho border.

In summer, enjoy a Spokane Indians baseball game at Seafirst stadium. For details, call 509/535-2922.

Newport

Straddling the Idaho/Washington border, Newport (pop. 1,700) began as a small trading post on the Idaho side in 1889, then moved to Washington when the Great Northern Railroad arrived in 1892. The original townsite, overlooking the Pend Oreille (pronounced "PON-doo-ray") River, holds most of the modern shopping malls, while the railroad legacy still defines

To get a feel for local life, tune in to **KMJY 700 AM** in Newport, WA, which broadcasts country music, CNN news, and an hour-long "Swap and Shop" on-air flea market, daily 11 AM-noon.

much of the older part of town. Two depots face each other at the south end of three-block Main Street, one holding the offices of a lumber company, the other housing the small but enjoyable **Pend Oreille County Historical Museum** (daily 10 AM-4 PM; $1 donation).

Apart from the museum and the flag-bedecked businesses lining Main Street, there's not much reason to stop, though **Fry's Lounge Steak House** has very good food and overlooks the river on the northeast edge of town.

ACROSS IDAHO

Even though the route zigzags for some 75 miles along the Kootenai and Pend Oreille Rivers, it doesn't take long for US-2 to cross the narrow neck, known as the Panhandle, of northern Idaho. Following the Pend Oreille River east from Washington, the route passes through the resort community of **Sandpoint** before threading the deep gorge of the Kootenai River upstream toward Montana.

Priest River

Roughly five miles east of the Washington border, and taking its name from the renowned trout-fishing stream that flows into the Pend Oreille River nearby, Priest River (pop. 1,560) is both a supply center for hunters, anglers, and river-runners and a busy lumber town, with two huge Louisiana Pacific mills dominating the local economy.

Priest River may not look like much from the highway, but the three blocks of Main Street running south from US-2 hold an interesting mix of hardware and antique stores, taverns, and the popular **River Pigs** restaurant, at 114 Main Street.

Sandpoint

Located at the northern end of Lake Pend Oreille, Idaho's largest lake, Sandpoint (pop. 5,500) is a resort community with a relaxed, welcoming feel. As you might guess from the name, Sandpoint boasts a fine, quarter-mile-long beach just a few blocks' walk from town. The highly regarded **Schweitzer Mountain Resort** (208/263-9555 or 800/831-8810) north of Sandpoint attracts skiers in winter and mountain bikers in summer. The mix of Rocky Mountain scenery and abundant recreation has made Sandpoint a popular place to visit, and to live in, though it still feels like a small town.

The main business district, along 1st and 2nd Avenues between the lake and the US-2 frontage, fills a half-dozen blocks around the landmark Panida Theater. You'll find a number of good cafes here, like the **Whistle Stop** at 312 N. 1st Avenue, and the **Dancing Bear Juice Bar** at 109 Main Street, which doubles as a record store. A number of food stalls and crafts galleries fill the **Cedar Street Bridge**, an old bridge rebuilt as a shopping mall in the mid 1970s. Besides the rooms and condos at Sandpoint's resorts, there are many motels, including national names like **Super 8, Quality Inn,** and **Best Western,** as well as locals such as the **Best Spa Motel** (208/263-3532), two blocks west of US-2 at 521 N. 3rd Avenue.

For more information, or for details of Sandpoint's festivals, contact the chamber of commerce (208/263-2161 or 800/800-2106).

Bonners Ferry

Named after a ferry service across the Kootenai River that started here in 1864, Bonners Ferry (pop. 2,200) is a busy blue-collar town with a resource-based (read: logging and farming) economy. Though there's not a lot to see or do in town, beer drinkers may be interested to know that reclamation projects have turned the surrounding Kootenai valley into one of the country's prime hop-growing regions.

> Though it's a pretty languid place, Sandpoint has gained unwanted notoriety as the home of racist former Los Angeles Police Department detective Mark Fuhrman, whose presence compounded the infamy focused upon the neo-Nazi compound at Hayden Lake, 30 miles south of town.
>
> Bonners Ferry was the site of one of the last Indian Wars in the United States. In 1974, the local Kootenai tribe declared war on the U.S. government, to underscore their demands for better treatment. There was no violence, and the declaration won the tribe an 18-acre reservation.
>
> About 10 miles west of the Montana border, US-2 crosses the Moyie River on a 600-foot-high bridge, giving close-up views of the concrete dam standing over **Moyie Falls,** once one of Idaho's loveliest waterfalls, which the WPA *Guide to Idaho* described in 1938 as looking "not like water but tons of glass crystals."

ACROSS MONTANA

Crossing northern Montana roughly 40 miles south of the Canadian border, US-2 gives an up-close look at two very different parts of this huge state. The western corner on the slopes of the Rocky Mountains offers incredible scenic beauty and innumerable options for outdoor recreation. The resort towns of Kalispell and Whitefish sit at the western edge of magnificent Glacier National Park.

East of the park, which is by far the most popular portion of the route, two-lane US-2 (popularly known as the "Hi-Line") winds along the many tributaries of the broad Missouri River across flat, glaciated open range. A few low buttes and cylindrical grain silos rise up in sharp silhouettes, but the horizon is the dominant aspect, stretching for hundreds of miles in all directions. Apart from dozens of one-side-of-the-road blink-stops, the towns along US-2 in the eastern stretches of Montana—like **Culbertson, Wolf Point, Glasgow, Malta,** and **Havre**—are few and far between. It's here you realize what the "Big Sky Country" is all about: pacing a train at 70 mph and waving at the engineer, and never, repeat: *never,* passing a gas station with the tank less than half full.

Troy

On the banks of the broad Kootenai River, 14 miles east of the Idaho border, the mining and lumber-milling town of Troy (pop. 1,000) is at very nearly the state's lowest elevation—1,892 feet above sea level. There's not a lot to the place, apart from a short stretch of motels, gas stations, taverns, churches, and cafes—the best of which is the family-friendly **Silver Spur**, right on US-2—plus a small **historical museum** at the east end of town.

How big is Montana? It stretches for over 650 miles east to west, covers an area larger than New England and New York put together, but has a population less than that of San Jose, California.

Writer **Rick Bass** chronicled a season spent in the isolated Yaak River Valley in his award-winning novel, *Winter Notes*.

Most of the whitewater scenes from Meryl Streep's movie *The River Wild* were filmed along this stretch of the Kootenai River.

For most of the way between Troy and Libby, US-2 is bordered by marked turnouts where trails lead to the narrow twisting **old highway,** preserved as a hiking and cross-country skiing trail through the dense forest.

Kootenai Falls

Just off US-2, nine miles west of Libby and two miles east of Troy, the thundering cascade of Kootenai Falls drops down a half-mile-long series of terraces. A pair of hiking trails leave from the well-marked roadside parking area, one leading 400 yards upstream to the main falls, the other heading downstream to a rickety old swinging bridge that sways from cables suspended 50 feet above the green water.

Libby

Between Troy and the busy, semi-industrial Columbia Falls/Whitefish/Kalispell area, US-2 traverses 70 miles of Kootenai (pronounced "KOOT-nee") National Forest, much of which was badly charred by 1994 forest fires. The lumber town of Libby (pop. 2,750), 18 miles east of Troy on the banks of the Kootenai River, was first founded as a gold-mining camp but grew into its present, elongated form when the Great Northern railroad came through in 1892. Libby's lively history is told in displays inside the local **Heritage Museum** (Mon.-Sat. 10 AM-5 PM, Sunday 1-5 PM; free), housed in a 12-sided log cabin on US-2 at the east end of town.

Stretching parallel to the tracks, the US-2 frontage is lined by gas stations galore (the Conoco station offers **hot showers**) and a half dozen motels, including the **Sandman** (406/293-8831), which has a hot tub and doubles from $30, and a pricey **Super 8** (406/293-2771). The old business district is along Mineral Street between US-2 and the Amtrak station. Places to eat range from **Beck's Montana Cafe**, 2425 W. US-2 at the west end of town, to the upscale **Adam's Rib**, housed in an old church at 1207 Utah Avenue, three blocks south of US-2.

A number of pleasant **campgrounds** operate in and around Libby, including excellent spots in the nearby Cabinet Wilderness; for details contact the U.S. Forest Service ranger station (406/293-8861), which also handles reservations for Libby's unique accommodation option: spending a night or two in the **Baldy Mountain Fire Lookout Tower**, 20 miles north of town; it sleeps up to eight people, and costs $25 a night.

West of Glacier National Park, US-2 runs more or less parallel to US-93, which resumes its north-south axis through the towns of Whitefish and Kalispell. We've described both of these towns in the coverage of US-93, on pages 90-92.

Baldy Mountain is just one of dozens of retired **Fire Lookout Towers** available for rent across Montana and Idaho. Contact the U.S. Forest Service (406/293-8861) for further information.

If you're a fan of local newspapers, do what you have to do to get a copy of the excellent *Hungry Horse News* (50 cents), organ of record for stories of mountain lion maulings and other events in the Glacier National Park region.

Hungry Horse and Columbia Falls

Two intriguingly named but otherwise uninteresting towns line US-2 between Kalispell and Glacier National Park. The first, Hungry Horse, is mainly a service center for the large reservoir to the southeast, hence the billboards proclaiming the burg "The Friendliest Dam Town in the Whole World." Another collection of gas stations and industrial plants, including a massive Plum Creek lumber mill and an Anaconda Aluminum smelter, make up the much larger town of Columbia Falls (pop. 3,200) where, despite the name, there are no falls. There are, however, a couple of good places to eat, including the very popular **Pines Cafe**, on the highway at the southeast edge of town, and a totally intact **A&W Drive-in** farther east on US-2.

West Glacier

Like many tourist towns on the edges of our national parks, West Glacier has its share of tackiness, but here it's on a tolerably small scale. Amidst the billboards advertising scenic helicopter rides, taxidermy museums, and "The World's Greatest Maze," there are also cafes, taverns, gas stations, and a couple of comfortable, $55-a-night motels, including the **River Bend** (406/888-5662), right on the Flathead River, and the **Vista** (406/888-5311 or 800/831-7101), which is open all year.

GLACIER NATIONAL PARK

The wildest and most rugged of all the Rocky Mountain national parks, Glacier National Park protects some 1,500 square miles of high-altitude scenery, including the glaciers for which the park is named, more than 200 lakes, and countless rivers and streams. Knifelike ridges of colorful sedimentary rock rise to over 9,000 feet, looming high above elongated glacier-carved valleys. Grizzly bears, black bears, mountain lions, and wolves roam the park's wild backcountry, which is criss-crossed by some 700 miles of hiking and riding trails.

The park's main features are reached via 50-mile-long **Going-to-the-Sun Road**, a magnificent serpentine highway arguably the most scenic route on this planet. Climbing up from dense forests to the west or prairie grasslands to the east, this narrow road is the only route across the park's million acres; note that the road's middle section—everything east of Lake McDonald, basically—is usually closed by snow from late October until mid-June.

West of Logan Pass, lovely **Lake McDonald** is the park's largest lake, and also the most developed area, with an attractive lodge, two restaurants, a gas station, and a nice campground. A boat offers hour-long narrated cruises ($6) throughout the summer.

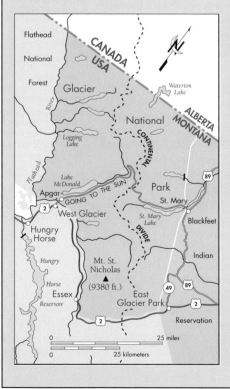

Between the lake and Logan Pass, five miles east of the Lake McDonald Lodge, **Avalanche Creek** is the most beautiful short hike in the park, winding through dense groves of cedar and fir alongside a creek that cascades noisily down a sharp cleft in the deep red rock. The two-mile trail ends up at Avalanche Lake, hemmed in by 1,500-foot-high cliffs.

The heart of the park is **Logan Pass**, a 6,680-foot saddle straddling the Continental Divide, which comes alive when the snow melts to reveal a rainbow of brightly colored wildflowers. Two very popular nature trails run from the large visitor center: the shorter but more strenuous one heads south on a wooden boardwalk across an alpine meadow to a viewpoint overlooking **Hidden Lake**; the High-line Trail runs north along a flat stretch across the foot of craggy Graden Wall to the Granite Park backcountry chalet (see below for details).

Along with the extensive facilities along US-2 at West and East Glacier, you'll find a couple of rustic lodges and motels within the park. The nicest of these is the intimate, comfortable—and inexpensive, with doubles starting at $60 a night—**Lake McDonald Lodge**, with a lovely lobby filled with comfy chairs arrayed around a fireplace, and lots of bearskin and buffalo rugs; it also serves the park's best food. Besides the grand lodges, a few other relics of Glacier Park's early days as a "Grand Tour" destination still survive: bright red, open-top vintage touring cars run along the Going-to-the-Sun Road, and two backcountry **chalets** built before WW I, and currently undergoing extensive renovations, allow visitors to overnight in the wilds without the hassles of hauling along tents and stoves.

For reservations or more detailed information, contact Glacier Park Inc., 406/226-5551 in summer, 602/207-6000 in winter.

For a more complete overview of the park, stop in at one of three main **visitor centers** in Glacier National Park, located at **Apgar** near the west entrance, at **Logan Pass** (summer only), and at the eastern entrance near the town of **St. Mary.** For more information, contact the park **headquarters** in West Glacier (406/888-5441).

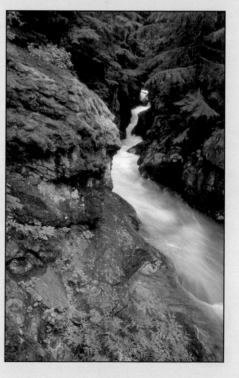

The many roadside crosses you'll see while driving through Montana each mark a traffic fatality. They were placed along the roads over the past 35 years by the American Legion; many are now elaborate shrines to lost loved ones.

The Flathead River and Essex

Avoiding the most extreme alpine scenery and the heavy winter snows, US-2 winds around the southern edge of Glacier National Park, climbing over the Continental Divide at 5,216-foot **Marias Pass**, the lowest of the Rocky Mountain passes, before dropping steeply down to the deep valley cut by the middle fork of the Flathead River. Though the road and the railroad are kept open year-round, there's very little visible development, but numerous trailheads access the southern reaches of the national park backcountry.

One place that's well worth a stop, or better yet an extended stay, is the **Isaak Walton Inn** (406/888-5700), a half-mile south of US-2 in the railroad village of Essex, midway between East and West Glacier. Especially in winter, when the inn overlooks miles of cross-country ski trails, this is one of the best (and least known) stops in the state. A more humble (and less expensive) version of the Glacier Park lodges, the inn was built to house railroad workers (which it still does) and is now a popular, year-round alternative to the often overbooked accommodations within the park. Rooms start at $75 a night. The inn also serves very good food for breakfast, lunch, and dinner.

Another place worth a stop in early summer is the so-called **Goat Lick** on US-2, near milepost 182 about five miles east of the Essex turnoff, where dozens of shaggy white mountain goats congregate around a mineral-rich spring.

East Glacier Park

Situated along US-2 at the southwest edge of the Blackfeet reservation, East Glacier Park is, as the name suggests, the eastern gateway to Glacier National Park. It's a tiny place, barely more than a wide spot in the road, with a couple of souvenir shops, Serrano's, a good Mexican restaurant, three fairly basic motels, and the small **Backpacker's Inn** (406/226-9392), which offers hostel bunks for $8 a night.

With the main park entrance over 30 miles to the northeast at St. Mary, East Glacier Park is not an especially convenient base, though it does have one compelling attraction: the **Glacier Park Lodge** (406/226-5551), the grandest of all the historic park lodges. Built by the Great Northern Railroad to attract visitors to the park (and to their trains), the lodge centers on a four-story lobby built of huge Douglas fir logs—each of which runs floor to ceiling, with the bark still on it. It's an impressively rustic space, and well worth a look, though the individual rooms are somewhat disappointing, especially at standard rates of over $100 a night.

North of US-2, just outside St. Mary's, **Johnson's Cafe**, well-posted atop a hill with great views of the nearby peaks, has been serving good food for over 40 years; the same family also operates a small **campground** and **motel** (406/732-4453).

The Blackfeet Indian Reservation

The 1.5-million-acre Blackfeet Indian Reservation, stretching north to the Canadian border along the eastern border of Glacier National Park, is a weather-beaten land home to 7,500 members of what was once the most powerful tribe on the Northern Plains. The Blackfeet, whose nomadic lives took them all over the plains in pursuit of buffalo, were feared and respected for

their fighting and hunting abilities, though contact with white traders brought smallpox, alcoholism, and other diseases that devastated the tribe. Their strength in battle won the Blackfeet concessions from the encroaching U.S. government, including a huge swath of land that in 1855 included everything north of the Yellowstone River between the Dakotas and the Continental Divide. Much of this land, including what's now the eastern half of Glacier National Park, was later bought back or simply taken away; the tribe now earns most of its income from ranching, and from oil and natural gas leases.

The Blackfeet's tribal headquarters and main commercial center is **Browning** (pop. 1,170), located on US-2 near the eastern entrance to Glacier National Park. Like many reservation towns, Browning has a desolate and depressing feel to it, but there are a couple of places worth stopping at, including the **Museum of the Plains Indian** (daily 9 AM-5 PM June-Sept., Mon.-Fri. 10 AM-4:30 PM rest of the year; free), near the west end of town at the junction of US-2 and US-89. Operated by the U.S. government's Bureau of Indian Affairs, the bland building contains a small collection of Plains Indian arts and crafts, mostly blankets and jewelry. Much more interesting, though harder to find, is the **Blackfoot Indian Writing Company**—maker of the finest Number 2s in the country, as well as Lindy pens— which you can tour informally (Mon.-Fri. 8 AM-2 PM; free; 406/338-2535 or 800/392-7326). The factory lies a mile off US-2 on the southeast edge of town, on the road to Heart Butte.

Blackfoot Indian Writing Company

Cut Bank

It's hard for travelers heading west along US-2 to believe that, despite having covered over 1,000 miles of undulating Great Plains, they have yet to reach the mountains. It isn't until Cut Bank (pop. 3,329) that the see-forever glaciation looks like it might be waning. You crest a hill and suddenly everything plateaus, despite wispy hints of the still-distant Rocky Mountains. Popularly known as the coldest city in the U.S., thanks to the presence of a U.S. weather-service monitoring station, Cut Bank is a friendly and pretty enough place, bisected neatly by US-2, a surgical line of tidy landscaped town to the south, and the gritty old Montana railroad town to the north.

The **Point Drive-In** is a classic roadster drive-up, while downtown, on US-2, the **Golden Harvest Cafe** is great for rubbing shoulders with the locals at breakfast, lunch, or dinner. At the east end of Cut Bank, a 27-foot-tall talking penguin stands next to the **Glacier Gateway Inn**, 1121 E. Railroad Avenue (406/873-5544 or 800/851-5541), the town's nicest motel.

Though the population is predominantly white, Cut Bank sits inside the eastern edge of the massive Blackfeet Indian Reservation, which stretches west to Glacier National Park.

The two-week-long **North American Indian Days** celebrations, held in mid-July on the Blackfeet Tribal Fairgrounds next to the Museum of the Plains Indian, attract native peoples from all over the USA and Canada. Call for information (406/338-7276).

Thirteen miles east of Browning, or 22 miles west of Cut Bank, a monument and picnic area along US-2 marks the most northerly point reached by **Lewis and Clark** on their cross-country expedition. On July 23, 1806, Meriwether Lewis, searching for the headwaters of the Marias River, made it this far, to a spot he called Camp Disappointment, before turning back because of bad weather.

Shelby

Despite what a quick map-read would indicate, or local tourist boosters would proclaim, Shelby is bustling mainly because the busy I-15 interstate crosses US-2 here, 25 miles south of Canada. Even then, Shelby's activity—typical truck-jockey, blue-smoke activity—is relegated to the town's sprawling west side. Otherwise, it's an oversized version of all the other Great Northern Railroad towns, one that extends farther than most along the tracks, with wide streets and an oddly steep hill flaring up to the south of downtown.

Shelby is not rowdy, nor does it necessarily roll up its sidewalks by 8 PM; the town's major claim to fame is that it hosted the 1923 world heavyweight fight between Jack Dempsey and Tommy Gibbons, a 15-round decision for Dempsey that was closer than it should have been. The match was produced as a publicity stunt to lure people to the oil boomtown, and Shelby built a 40,000-seat arena, but after Dempsey threatened to cancel the bout only 7,000 showed up. View a replica arena and many artifacts from the fight at the **Marias Museum of History and Art** (Mon.-Fri. 1-5 PM and 7-9 PM, Saturday 1-4 PM in summer; free) at the corner of 12th Avenue and 1st Street North.

For great shotgun-seat reading along the way, William Least Heat Moon's *Blue Highways* contains an honest, lyrical account of the highs, lows, and endless in-betweens along this stretch, including a brief account of a day in Shelby, MT.

Great food is standard at **Kathy's**, 156 Main Street, while the O'Haire Manor (406/434-5555) at 204 2nd Street S (look for the huge "Motel" sign on US-2) is one of Shelby's better half-dozen motels, with doubles from $35.

Located on the interstate, Shelby boasts the last good range of services for the next 100-plus miles from here to Havre, so be sure to fill up the tank before setting off. Heading east, US-2 crosses bare plains broken by cattle ranges, Cold War-era Minuteman silos, and occasional wheat farms but is otherwise pretty much devoid of interest. It's a thumb-on-wheel, greased-lightning, straight-shot road from here, miles and miles of your own thoughts. There is even, halfway along, a tauntingly blank historical marker, perhaps signifying the nothingness you're in.

Havre

The largest town along eastern US-2, Havre (pop. 10,200, pronounced "HAV-ver") was founded by the Great Northern Railroad and named, for no good reason, after the French port Le Havre, though you'd never tell by the pronunciation. Havre retains more than a little of its Wild West feel and has enough unusual attractions to merit an extended stop. North of town is a large area of eroded **badlands**, and just west of town behind the Holiday Village Shopping Center is one of the country's best preserved *pishgun*—a large cliff where herds of bison were driven to their deaths by Plains tribes. It's open late May-Sept. only and costs $3.50. Many of the

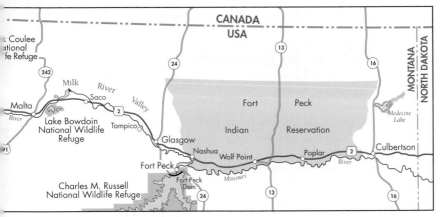

artifacts recovered from the *pishgun* are displayed inside nearby **H. Earl Clack Memorial Museum** (daily 9 AM-9 PM May-Sept.; donations). The museum also offers scheduled tours ($2) of the archaeological site as well as of **Fort Assiniboine**, eight miles southwest off US-87, the largest fort ever built in Montana—over 100 buildings, though only a couple remain. The fort was under the command of John J. Pershing.

The town itself is engaging and rowdy. Numerous poker clubs (everything has "casino" tacked onto it) and cowboy bars line the compact downtown area, underneath which is a defunct underground world of illicit bordellos and opium dens—all part of the whiskey trail that flourished a century ago and again during Prohibition, when bathtub gin—copious quantities from Canada a stone's throw north—was run through. Tours ($5) are available through **Havre Beneath The Streets** (406/265-8888) at 104 3rd Avenue.

About the only alternative to the local preponderance of twangy country or syrupy Christian radio stations is **CKRX 1090 AM**, broadcasting raucous rock 'n' roll out of Lethbridge, Alberta.

Along 1st Street (US-2) you'll find all the usual fast-food suspects, and good Italian food at **Navlikis** or Chinese at **Canton Chinese**, across the street at 439 W. 1st Street. There's also the smaller, fresher **Lunch Box** deli/cafe at 213 3rd Avenue. For a place to stay, the plush **Duck Inn** (406/265-9615) has a silly name but good rooms and a surprisingly nice restaurant. There are strings of others along US-2; for listings, contact the **chamber of commerce** (406/265-4383) right downtown at 518 1st Street.

Chinook and Chief Joseph

Chinook (pop. 1,500), which takes its name from the Northwest intertribal patois for the warm southerly winds that rip through the area in January and February, raising temperatures some 60-70° in a matter of hours, melting the winter snow, and allowing the cattle to forage. Now a small cattle ranching town, Chinook is best known for its proximity to the surrender site of Nez Percé Chief Joseph to the U.S. Army in 1877—which effectively marked the end of the Indian Wars of the Plains. The very good **Blaine County Museum** (Tues.-Sat. 8 AM-5 PM, Sunday 1-5 PM in summer, Mon.-Fri. 1-5 PM rest of the year; free), four blocks south of US-2 at 501 Indiana Street, includes an impressive collection of fossils and local pioneer artifacts, as well as an informative multimedia presentation on the events leading up to the final surrender of Chief Joseph.

Far more compelling, if the weather's fine and you can spare half a day, is the actual site where the Nez Percé were captured, now preserved (with an interpretive trail and a few plaques, but otherwise unchanged) as **Chief Joseph Bear's Paw Battlefield National Historic Park**, 16 miles south of Chinook via Hwy-240.

CHIEF JOSEPH AND THE NEZ PERCÉ

The odyssey of Chief Joseph and his 600 followers is perhaps the most familiar tale of the final days of freedom of the North American Indians. Having led his band over 1,600 miles throughout the summer from their lands in Idaho, from which they were forcibly removed by the U.S. government (which had "re-negotiated" an initial treaty, in effect reducing the Nez Percé's holdings by 90%), Joseph and the ragtag, exhausted Nez Percé, thinking the cavalry was farther south and Canada closer than either really was, chose to camp and rest here.

The U.S. Army, in hot pursuit, sent ahead a 400-man contingent, which reconnoitered the tribe and camped 12 miles to the southeast on September 28. The Nez Percé awoke to attack on September 30. The Army, expecting surprise, was fiercely resisted and a five-day siege ensued. After losing their herd of horses, 30 warriors, and three chiefs, and suffering high casualties among the women and children, the Nez Percé gave up. Chief Joseph's words upon surrendering were an eloquent and tragic encapsulation of the Native American experience:

Our chiefs are dead; the little children are freezing to death. My people have no blankets, no food . . . I want to have time to look for my children and see how many I can find . . . Hear me, my chiefs. I am tired. My heart is sick and sad. From where the sun now stands, I will fight no more forever.

Chief Joseph

After receiving promises from the US commanders that the Nez Percé would be allowed to return to Idaho, Chief Joseph instead suffered the government's forked-tongue duplicity. Most of the Nez Percé were dispersed to several reservations, eventually winding up in Oklahoma. In 1885, through the Herculean efforts of Chief Joseph and with help from his old nemesis Colonel Miles, some 120 Nez Percé were allowed to return to Idaho. Chief Joseph, however, was never allowed to see his homeland again, finishing out his days in exile on the Colville Reservation in Washington, where he is buried.

Fort Belknap Indian Reservation

Between Chinook and Malta, US-2 runs along the northern border of the Fort Belknap Indian Reservation, which covers some 650,000 acres stretching south to near the Missouri Breaks, a rock-and-sagebrush landscape that provided perfect hiding spots for outlaws like Kid Curry, Butch Cassidy, and the Hole-in-the-Wall Gang.

Butch Cassidy

The Fort Belknap reservation was established in 1887 to contain the surviving members of the once-feared Gros Ventre and Assiniboine Indians, who before siding with the U.S. Army against the Blackfeet were one of the major powers on the northern Plains. The tiny town of **Fort Belknap**, just south of US-2 about 25 miles east of Chinook, is the main reservation crossroads. The town hosts the annual **Milk River Indian Days** at the end of July, which features athletic contests as well as dances and country-fair festivities.

The larger town of **Harlem**, west of Fort Belknap and two miles north of US-2, is off the reservation but holds the tribal headquarters (406/353-2205); the 1939 WPA *Guide to Montana* described Harlem as "enlivened by the presence of Indians in bright and complicated mixtures of native and white dress. . . ."

As you approach Malta, the Milk River gives sly hints of lushness in the dust, showing a miragelike ribbon of verdancy south of the road, which itself is still rather bleak.

Malta

Twenty miles east of the Fort Belknap reservation is Malta, named for the Mediterranean island but otherwise just another ranching town that grew up along the Great Northern Railway. Besides the above-average **Philips County Historical Museum** (Tues.-Sat. 10 AM-noon and 1-5 PM, June-Sept. only; donation) in the old Carnegie Library at 133 S. 1st Street W, Malta holds the region's best place to eat, drink, and sleep: the landmark **GN Hotel** (406/654-2100) at 2 S. 1st Avenue E, which has a bar-*cum*-steak house, a cafe with good breakfast specials, and double rooms from $40 a night.

Roughly 20 miles north of US-2, the 15,500-acre **Black Coulee National Wildlife Reserve** (daily 8 AM-4:30 PM; free) shelters one of the few nesting areas of the white pelican in the northwestern U.S.

At the tiny farming town of **Saco**, 28 miles east of Malta, pride of place is given to the one-room schoolhouse where TV journalist Chet Huntley received his education.

Malta, where the eastbound and westbound trains of Amtrak's Empire Builder pass each other, is just one of dozens of flyspeck US-2 Montana towns with names borrowed at random by Great Northern Railway promoters from all over the globe. Heading along the highway, you pass near or through Dunkirk, Kremlin, Havre, Zurich, Harlem, and Tampico, all of which were founded by the railroad and settled in the main by Northern and Eastern European immigrants enticed here around the turn of the century by the railroad's offers of farmlands and homesteads.

Milk River Valley

East of Malta, the road and the railroad cross and recross the banks of the sluggish and narrow Milk River. Highway signs proclaim your entrance to "Beef Country"; just check out the menu options in the cafes and you'll know you've arrived. US-2 continues its jaunts over the Milk River tributaries, winding along the swampy **Lake Bowdoin National Wildlife Refuge**, once the state's best duck-hunting grounds and now warm-weather home to pheasants, grouse, and sage hens as well as pelicans, ibises, and herons.

Unless you're a keen birdwatcher, the only place worth stopping at along this stretch is 10 miles west of Saco, and four miles north of US-2. Here the large and enticing **Sleeping Buffalo Hot Springs** resort (406/654-2100) offers a huge (60 by 80 feet) naturally heated swimming pool as well as hot tubs (as hot as 106° F) and cabins from $30 a night.

Glasgow

Glasgow (pop. 3,600), on the north banks of the Milk River 50 miles west of Wolf Point, is one of the few Hi-Line towns that's more than a collection of grain elevators, though its own dominant visual aspects are spreads of combines and threshers. Founded as a railroad town by the Great Northern Railroad in 1889, Glasgow is now the largest town in northeastern Montana. Stop in for a look at the tremendously cluttered, diorama-filled **Valley County Historical Museum** (Mon.-Sat. 9 AM-9 PM, Sunday 1-9 PM, summer only; free) on US-2 at 8th Avenue, worth a look for its barroom exhibit.

In the premier issue of *Life* magazine (Nov. 23, 1936), documentary photographer Margaret Bourke-White profiled the town of Fort Peck as well as the other 18 boomtowns that sprang up in the surrounding area during construction of Fort Peck Dam.

Johnnie's Cafe at 433 1st Avenue S seves great roadfood but is closed on Sunday; the **Country Cafe** on the west side of town on US-2 features a Sunday buffet and 25-cent coffee, as well as the largest "EAT" sign this side of Texas.

Fort Peck and Fort Peck Dam

Fifteen miles south of Glasgow and US-2 via Hwy-24, the enormous Fort Peck Lake collects the waters of the Missouri River behind massive Fort Peck Dam, one of the largest construction projects of the New Deal era and still the world's second-largest earthen dam. From 1933 until 1940, a friendly invasion of ultimately 10,000 civilian workers, earning between 50 cents and $1.20 per hour, hacked, dug, poured, sweated, and wrested a sea out of High Plains desolation. As a result, 20-million acre-feet of water is impounded behind the nearly four-mile-long dam, corralled to a maximum depth of 220 feet and with a serpentine shoreline longer than California's—1,600 miles! Surrounding the whole sprawling lake are countless recreation areas, campsites, and other diversions; the reservoir is home to a huge array of wildlife, including elk, bighorn sheep, pronghorn, and migrating waterfowl, all protected within the **Charles M. Russell National Wildlife Refuge**.

Free tours of the old **powerhouse**, with a museum inside, are given hourly daily 9 AM-5 PM in summer.

Fort Peck Theater

The lake is most easiest approached via Hwy-117, 15 miles south from US-2 at the town of Nashua; you can also reach it from Glasgow via Hwy-24, along which there's an **information center** (406/526-3431 or 406/538-8706) whose chatty staff willingly supplies details on hiking, cycling, and camping in and around the refuge or other recreation areas.

Besides the dam and lake, the area's best surviving example of New Deal spirit is the snug town of Fort Peck (pop. 300), built from scratch to house the construction workers, though its current population is but a fraction of the 50,000 who once called it home. A few of the old buildings still stand, including the landmark **Fort Peck Theater** (406/228-9219) on Hwy-24, a huge draw in the area with its summertime plays and musicals. The **Fort Peck Cafe** has basic but good food, while one of the greatest places to stay near US-2 in Montana is the original **Fort Peck Hotel**, long dormant but recently taken over and touchingly (with nary an ounce of avarice) worked into a semblance of its classic old self. Rates start under $30 a night for a single or double with shared bath; the restaurant is by far the best in the area, as well.

Fort Peck Indian Reservation

The sprawling Fort Peck Indian Reservation, Montana's second-largest, stretches for nearly 100 miles along US-2, and for 50 miles north. Home to 6,800 Assiniboine and Yanktonai Sioux, but co-owned by non-Indians as a result of unscrupulous land dealings encouraged by the 1887 Dawes Act, the reservation offers few sights or services to outsiders. Travelers interested in tribal life have to make do with occasional events like the annual **Red Bottom Day** celebrations (held every June in Frazer, west of Wolf Point), the **Wadopana Pow Wow** (early August), or the **Wild Horse Stampede** rodeo in Wolf Point, the oldest rodeo in Montana.

The largest town, **Wolf Point**, is halfway across the reservation, 55 miles west of Culbertson. Wolf Point is certainly not frenetic with activity on a daily basis, and strewn corpses of some great antique vehicles rust on the outer fringes of town. Also in Wolf Point, on the lower level of the county library at 220 2nd Avenue, is the **Wolf Point Area Historical Society Museum** (Mon.-Fri. 10 AM-5 PM in summer only; donations), worth a look as much for the local artists' work as for exhibits detailing the region's fur-trapping and cattle ranching past, including a nice rifle collection. Also in Wolf Point you'll find some of the best cafes and motels for miles. The **Stockman's Cafe** at 220

Fort Peck Indian Reservation holds Native American celebrations an average of every other weekend. And the granddaddy of 'em all in Montana, July's **Wild Horse Stampede** in Wolf Point, is the oldest in the state; contact the tribe for more information (406/768-5155).

In winter, northeastern Montana suffers some of the worst weather in the lower 48 states, as arctic winds racing across the plains lower temperatures to average winter highs of 10° F.

Because trees are scarce on the eastern Montana plains, early settlers built homes by impaling slabs of sod over thin poles. A few of the museums in towns along US-2 display mock-ups of these **sod houses.**

Though it's hardly worth the 120-mile drive south along the Yellowstone River, the tiny town of Ismay (pop. 19) unofficially changed its name to **Joe, Montana,** in honor of the recently retired football superstar.

Main Street has low prices and downhome comfort food, while the **Sherman Motor Inn** (406/653-3600) at 200 Main Street includes a decent restaurant; room rates average $30 for a double. For more information on local draws, especially the prestigious rodeo, contact the **chamber of commerce** (406/653-2012) at 201 4th Street S.

Crossing between Montana and North Dakota, you switch between mountain and central time zones, so reset your timepieces.

Near the eastern edge of the reservation, **Poplar** is quickly crossed and forgotten, though its **Assiniboine/Sioux Tribal Museum** (Mon.-Fri. 8 AM-4:30 PM; free) exhibits some excellent relics from Custer's defeat at Wounded Knee, as well as artifacts relocated from the Chicago Historical Society.

Culbertson

Culbertson (pop. 850) is a quiet town with a disproportionate number of farm implement and feed dealers—the tourist brochures brag about the "ever-expanding SVO Oilseed processing plant." Located a mile east of town, the **Montana Visitor Center** (8 AM-8 PM in summer, 8 AM-5 PM May and Sept.; free) houses the outstanding **Culbertson Museum,** a huge, well-designed place. The guides can give you a lickety-split tour if necessary.

There are a couple cafes in town, including the classic breakfast-lunch-dinner **Wild West Cafe** right on US-2, immediately next to **M&Ms Place,** which is more of a lunch/dinner option. The **King's Inn,** 408 E. 6th Street (406/787-6277), is a clean, modern, $30-a-night motel.

Immediately west of Culbertson, keep your eyes peeled for a herd of local **bison** in a tiny valley, grazing peacefully alongside their calves.

ACROSS NORTH DAKOTA

Apart from the likeable small city of **Grand Forks**, at the state's eastern border, much of North Dakota's landscape lives up to those nondescript clichés from childhood family trips, and hems and rolls and yawns *forever.* Montana may be Big Sky Country, but North Dakota sure seems to be High Sky Country, the land where, if you tire of watching dancing golden wheat mirages, you can exercise your finger channel-surfing on the radio. It's a long, flat (and, dare we say it: dull) drive across the state, with little here but plains or pseudo-prairie, and even the most epic side trip offers minimal relief. The state has done what it can to help out bored travelers by eliminating roadside mowing for most of the trip across, opting for native prairie and a potential refuge for wildlife—and roadkill.

That said, the 300 miles across the state do hold a few points of interest, including Fort Union, an evocative outpost of the early frontier; popular Devil's Lake recreational areas; the agricultural centers of Minot and Williston; and the geographical center of North America, marked by a stone monument in the town of Rugby.

For an alternative to US-2 between the Montana border and Minot, if you have some time and the inclination to explore, swing south about 15 miles east of Culbertson, Montana, and join up with Hwy-1804, which follows the well-signed **Lewis and Clark Trail** along the Missouri River and sluggish Lake Sakakawea.

Fort Union National Historic Site
Astride the Montana/North Dakota border, standing proud atop the banks at the confluence of the Yellowstone and Missouri Rivers, the Fort Union Trading Post National Historic Site was once the largest and busiest outpost on the upper Missouri River. Despite the "fort" in its name, it was never a part of the U.S. military; it was, however, the most successful and longest-lived of all the frontier trading posts. In 1804, Lewis and Clark visited the site, which they called "a judicious position for the purpose of trade." Twenty-five years later, John Jacob Astor's American Fur Company proved them right, establishing an outpost here in a successful attempt to end the Hudson Bay company's monopoly on northwest trade. Linked by steamboat with St. Louis some 1,800 miles away, Fort Union reigned over the northern plains. Its bon vivant overseer, Kenneth McKenzie, the "King of the Missouri," kept the fine china polished and the wines cool in the cellar, offering a taste of displaced civilization to such luminary explorers as George Catlin, Prince Maximilian, and James Audubon.

The fort was abandoned as the fur trade declined in the 1850s, and portions of original buildings and walls were taken down by the U.S. Army in 1867 to construct Fort Buford, a mile to the east. In the late 1980s, the park service reconstructed the buildings atop the original foundations, giving a palpable if somewhat overly polished idea of how the old fort looked. McKenzie's old home and office, Bourgeois House, is now a **visitor center** (daily 8 AM-8 PM in summer, 9 AM-5:30 PM rest of the year; donations) with some surprising artifacts. The fort hosts occasional reenactments of boisterous frontier life: mid-June, for example, brings the annual **Fort Union Rendezvous**, a rollicking re-creation of fur-trapper gatherings to trade, talk, and compete in wilderness skills.

In the past, the historic sites of Fort Buford and neighboring Fort Union used to be more easily reached from Montana, though recent roadwork has made them accessible from either side of the border. Signs point the way south from US-2.

Fort Buford
Built in 1866 and now a state historic site, Fort Buford is eerily quiet, with only the stone powder magazine and a museum in an original soldiers' quarters open for viewing. Home to a company of "Buffalo Soldiers," as the Sioux called the black cavalrymen, the fort is best known for its sad contribution to the U.S. extermination campaign of Native Americans: it was here that Chief Sitting Bull surrendered to the U.S. Army in 1881, and here that Chief Joseph of the Nez Percé was brought after his "I will fight no more forever" surrender in Montana (see the special topic on page 354).

Across western North Dakota, tune to **KMHA 91.3 FM** for commercial-free country music and community news and features from the Fort Berthold Indian Reservation, home to descendants of native Mandan, Arikara, and Hidatsa tribes.

Sod Busters' Memorial

Roughly 65 miles southeast of Williston via US-85, the north unit of **Theodore Roosevelt National Park** preserves one of the largest intact areas of semi-natural Great Plains landscape.

Many places along the Missouri River are named for the intrepid and enigmatic Shoshone woman who guided explorers Lewis and Clark across the Plains in 1804. **Sacagawea** is alternately rendered as "Sakakawea" or "Sacajawea," and translated either as "Bird-Woman" or "Boat-Launcher."

Williston

The first settlement east of the Montana line, Williston (pop. 13,100) is a classic, just-big-enough, one-movie-theater town. Always a boom or bust kind of place, "Champion City" (no apparent reason for the self-proclamation) today has shed its turn-of-the-century roughshod image, turning away from wheat-growing and oil-pumping industries and staking a tenuous claim instead on tourism. Refineries and other heavy industry are still sorely prevalent in some areas of town, but the downtown area is basically overgrown, *Our Town* placid.

Apart from filling the tank before a trip to Fort Union or farther afield, there's not a lot to do in Williston except in May, when the **Roughrider Art Show** brings in a strong regional art collection. Responding to an impromptu breakfast poll, locals will likely recommend **Grandma Sharon's** as the eatery of choice; it's located right on US-2 on the east edge of town—attached to a Conoco station, as most good cafes in the northern Great Plains seem to be. At the junction of US-2 and Hwy-85 is a **Super 8** motel (701/572-8371), the best of many highway motels offering decent rooms from under $30 a night.

Epping

Like many other North Dakota rural communities, the old Great Northern railway town of Epping (pop. 55) has all but disappeared thanks to changes in farming practices, the railway's move to diesel instead of steam, and sundry other common complaints. Here, however, the fabric of the rapidly vanishing Great Plains lifeways have been partially preserved, thanks to the lifelong efforts of a (recently deceased) local preacher, who single-handedly preserved the abandoned buildings and artifacts as the **Buffalo Trails Museum** (Mon.-Sat. 9 AM-5 PM, Sunday 1-5 PM; $2; 701/859-4361), which grew to encompass almost the entire

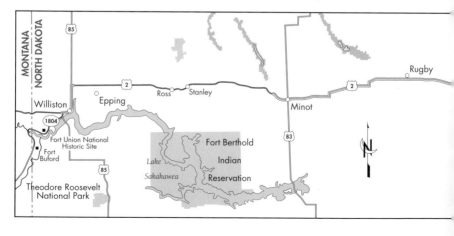

town. Main Street is still dusty dirt, and lined by a general store, a hardware store, a pool hall, and other essential services. Most of these old buildings have been converted to house an amazing array of animated dioramas (papier-mâché dummies dressed up like dentists and patients) and the usual old tools and other junk, but the best reason to stop may be the **Buffalo Inn Cafe** across from the museum entrance, serving good food daily but especially popular on Sunday, when farming families come from near and far to enjoy the $8 buffet lunch.

Ross and Stanley

East of Epping toward Minot, US-2 twists up and through a hundred miles of gentle chocolate-drop hillocks, residuals of the great Ice Age glaciers, with some beautiful, almost ski-slope rises and plateaus capped by an occasional abandoned squad of dwellings. Along the way, podunk villages whiz by: Ross (pop. 61), for example, is a typically funky old town with some dilapidated, boarded-up buildings and huge grain elevators that look more like spacecraft engines.

Just west of Minot, US-2 offers surprisingly fine views of the city and of a giant old railroad bridge spanning valley bluffs on the south side of the highway.

What look like high-security parking lots all around Minot are actually underground missile silos, over 100 of which surround the town. They are still in use, under the command of Minot Air Force Base.

The one sizeable place, Stanley (pop. 1,371), resting along the horizon-straight railroad tracks seven miles east of Ross and 47 miles west of Minot, is worth a stop for a whirl-a-whip at the old-fashioned soda fountain, inside the Rexall Drug Store on Main Street, north of US-2. There's also a free municipal campground at the north end of town.

Minot

Snug in the Souris River Valley at the junction of US-2 and US-83, Minot (pop. 34,544; rhymes with "Why not?") evokes ambivalence from most travelers. Some loathe it outright for its apparent nothingness, but while it isn't exactly picturesque, there *are* worse aesthetic experiences on the Great Plains. At the very least, you'll find a fair range of cowboy hats to look at in the downtown stores.

Minot grew so rapidly after the Great Northern Railroad came through in 1887 that it was dubbed "Magic City," though perhaps "Event Capital" would be more apropos today, for despite the city's importance in other areas, most people visit during the huge State Fair (third week in July) and October's burgeoning **Norsk Hostfest**, "North America's Largest Scandinavian Festival." The fairgrounds, along the grandly named Burdick Expressway (Business US-2) a half-mile east of downtown, also hold the small **Pioneer Village and Museum** (daily 10 AM-6 PM, summer only), the usual assembly of turn-of-the-century buildings and artifacts gathered here from all over the county.

In summer, when daytime highs hover in the mid-90's, Minot's most enticing attractions are the expansive gardens of **Roosevelt Park**, along the banks of the Souris River in between the fairgrounds and downtown Minot. Named, liked everything else in North Dakota, for Teddy Roosevelt—there's a larger-than-life statue of him, astride a horse in full Rough Rider regalia—the shady green space also holds a large **swimming pool** (daily 1-10 PM in summer; $2) with a 350-foot-long water slide, a rideable miniature train ($2), and a 20-acre **zoo** (daily 10 AM-8 PM in summer, 8 AM-4 PM rest of the year; $3), with some obscure animals and a Northern Plains habitat.

Along with the usual crossroads barrage of franchised fast-food places, Minot also supports a couple of breakfast and lunch-only cafes, including **Charlie's Main Street Cafe**, 113 S. Main Street, and **Gladys' Place**, at 300 E. Central Avenue. Charlie's is right downtown, its fluorescent-lit pink vinyl booths full of gossiping Minot ladies, while Gladys' is three blocks east, near the train tracks and grain elevators, its fluorescent-lit brown vinyl booths full of gossiping Minot men. The food's good at both, and you get a pot of coffee when you order a cup.

After dark, choose from any of over a dozen haunts, from bingo parlors and low-stakes casinos to country-western honky-tonks like **Tilly's**, housed in an old Standard Oil service station at 720 N. Broadway (US-83), or low-key beer bars like the **Blue Rider**, 118 1st Avenue SE, a smoke-free pub with interesting local art on the walls and what may be rural North Dakota's best selection of bottled brews—look for the "Grain Belt Beer" sign.

Motels are scattered along the congested arteries of both US-83 and US-2, so (except perhaps during the state fair) you shouldn't have trouble finding a place to sleep. The nicest place to stay is the **Best Western International Inn**, on US-83 at 1505 N. Broadway (701/852-3161 or 800/528-1234); less expensive local motels include the clean and quiet **Fairview Lodge**, across from the fairgrounds at 1900 E. Burdick Expressway (701/852-4488 or 800/836-2047).

The Minot **visitor center**, on US-83 south of downtown at 1040 S. Broadway (701/857-8206 or 800/264-2626), has more complete listings and detailed information on events and activities—being so central to the state, Minot hosts everything from chili cook-offs to the state softball championships.

Minot marks the junction of US-2 and US-83, which runs from Canada to Mexico. The latter route is covered in the "Road to Nowhere" chapter, beginning on page 124.

Rugby

Midway between Devil's Lake and Minot, Rugby (pop. 2,909) is an important agricultural hamlet, known to road wanderers as the town nearest to the **geographical center of North America**. The exact spot is marked with a two-story stone cairn along the south side of US-2, in front of the Conoco station. Not surprisingly, nearby is the **Pioneer Village Geographical Center Museum** (Mon.-Sat. 8 AM-7 PM, Sunday 1-7 PM in summer only; $3), featuring 27 restored buildings relocated here from around the county. The **Cornerstone Cafe**, inside the Conoco station, and the **Hub Motel** (701/776-5833) across US-2, complete the list of reasons to stop.

The landscape along this stretch of US-2 consists of immense stretches of hay fields typical of the Great Plains, and only occasional morasses of miniature cattails, goldenrod, and sunflower. The toponymy here is decidedly Anglocentric, with towns named Rugby or Leeds or York after the hometowns of English investors who, during the 1880s, pumped the fledgling towns full of cash. The populations, however, have always been decidedly Scandinavian.

In range for an hour or more in all directions, Minot's **KRRZ 1390 AM** broadcasts oldies from the 1950s and 1960s, along with Minnesota Twins baseball games.

Midway between Minot and Rugby, the tiny town of **Denbigh** is the burial site of **Sondre Norheim**, a Norwegian national hero who invented the telemark turn in XC skiing. Royalty have paid their respects here; you can too.

Devil's Lake and Fort Totten

The waters and wetlands south of the eponymous town of Devil's Lake (pop. 7,782) are one of the biggest natural draws in the state, with birdwatching, hunting, and fishing opportunities aplenty. The town itself, situated on the largest body of water in North Dakota, 58 miles east of Rugby and 85 miles west of Grand Forks, has clearly tried to remake itself into an upscale tourist trap, boasting lots of sandblasted "historic" buildings hung with spanking new signs. The whole community, cheery to a fault, seems done up in Sunday best, especially during the annual summer-long **North Dakota Chautauqua**, a reminder of the days when Devil's Lake was a major stop on the educational, recreational, and religious chautauquas that traveled across the country until the 1920s. The local **visitor center** (701/662-4903), on US-2 at the south edge of town, can provide information on the chautauqua and on area recreation.

Historic Fort Totten (daily 7:30 AM–dusk; free), 14 miles south of town on Hwy-57, is one of the country's best-preserved 19th-century military forts, with numerous restored buildings set around a spacious central square, as well as a museum and a theater (productions Thursday, Saturday, and Sunday in July and August). A rodeo and powwow, featuring highly competitive Native American dances, are held during **Fort Totten Days** the last weekend in July. Next to the fort is **Sully's Hill National Game Preserve**, a 1,600-acre refuge for bison, elk, deer, and other wildlife, which you may spot while hiking the nature trail.

Both the fort and the nature preserve are located on the 137,000-acre **Fort Totten Sioux Indian Reservation** (701/766-4221), centering around the mission village of **St. Michael's**, four miles east of the fort. The main attraction to visitors is the **Dakotah Sioux Casino** (800/WIN-UBET), one of North Dakota's largest, standing outside Tokio 18 miles southeast of downtown Devil's Lake.

Grand Forks

The oldest and second-largest community in North Dakota, Grand Forks (pop. 49,425), which boasts the tallest buildings between Spokane and Duluth, is a major city by northern Plains standards. (To put this into perspective, just think that the Grand Forks Air Force Base alone, with 12,500 residents, could be considered the state's sixth-largest city!) The local chamber of commerce brags that "our trees are taller than our buildings," and makes a lot of noise about the fact the city was recently judged one of the Top Ten most livable cities in the U.S.

ROADSIDE GIANTS OF NORTH DAKOTA

It may be the long cold winters, the endless flat landscape, or the incredible solitude of life on the northern Great Plains, but there's something about North Dakota that makes people do strange things. The most obvious signs of this odd behavior are the many giant sculptures that stand along the roadside all over the state. Bigger and better than their cousins elsewhere in the U.S., the Roadside Giants of North Dakota quite simply have to be seen to be believed.

The following are a few of the biggest and best:

World's Largest Turtle Nicknamed "Wee'l," this giant turtle was made out of old tractor tires, and stands along Hwy-5 near Bottineau, 45 miles northwest of Rugby.

World's Largest Buffalo This 60-ton giant looms over I-94 in Jamestown, 100 miles south of Devil's Lake.

World's Largest Cow "Salem Sue" stands along I-94 in New Salem, 30 miles west of Bismarck.

It may not be a cultural mecca, but Grand Forks can be a languid place to spend some time, its streets lined with gigantic mature shade trees and lovely homes, a welcome taste of suburban civility at the eastern edge of the interminable plains. From the junction with the I-29 freeway, US-2 bypasses the heart of town, so detour south along De Mers Avenue (Business US-2) for a more Americana-rich drive past rail lines, warehouses, wide business streets, and old steel-span bridges.

Owing to the large U.S. Air Force Base west of town, the University of North Dakota campus houses the **Center for Aerospace Studies**, which trains future pilots. The campus, which lines Grand Forks' massive railroad yards north of De Mers Avenue, also has a fine **museum of art** (Mon.-Fri. 9 AM-5 PM, Sat.-Sun. 1-5 PM; free) and the acoustically exquisite (Tony Bennett raved about it) **Chester Fritz Auditorium**, the local venue for touring national and international acts.

For weary roadtrippers, Grand Forks' best feature has to be the legendary **Whitey's Bar & Cafe**, 109 E. De Mers Avenue just east of the Red River bridge. Though legally in Minnesota, this is a true Grand Forks institution, a genuine speakeasy in its earliest incarnation but now much more a cafe than a bar. The interior is dominated by the fabulous art deco-styled "Wonderbar"— a horseshoe-shaped, stainless steel sculpture, surrounded by comfy booths with individual jukeboxes. Whitey's serves very good food all day long, seven days and nights a week, and a meal here (or at least a look-see) is worth planning your day around.

Another great place to stop is **Kegs Drive-In**, on old US-2 at 901 5th Street N (701/775-4993). Open since 1934, and the last of what was once a mini-empire of drive-in restaurants, Kegs is a basic burger bar with a key difference: the main shack is flanked by a pair of giant root beer kegs. There's car-hop service (which is why it's open during the day during summer only) and the food's good (Sloppy Joes are the house specialty), making Kegs a popular hangout for classic car collectors, who often fill the place on Saturday afternoons.

Grand Forks supports the usual groupings of places to stay, including a **Best Western**, a **Comfort Inn**, a **Days Inn**, an **Econo Lodge**, a **Holiday Inn**, and a **Motel 6** on the west side of town at 1112 N. 47th Street (701/775-0511), near the junction of US-2 and I-29.

Up until the oil crisis of 1974, when lawmakers enacted a national speed limit of 55 mph, Montana law stipulated only that drivers should travel at a reasonable and prudent speed, with no legal maximum, though speeds of over 100 mph were generally considered ticket-worthy. Despite studies showing that gas consumption and traffic fatalities would increase sharply, the national speed limit was raised to 65 in 1987; more recent legislation has returned speed-limit control to the states. You now can drive as fast as you want along Montana's interstates—though *not* US-2—during the day, so long as it's safe. This means Porsche and Ferrari owners no longer need to fly their cars to Germany to test how they drive in top gear.

ACROSS MINNESOTA

In its trek across northern Minnesota, US-2 offers nearly 250 miles of open road before winding up in the busy but surprisingly attractive lakefront city of **Duluth**. Midway across the state, after the endless wheat fields of the west, the scenery turns slightly turbid with the remnants of old iron mines and a series of still-busy lumber and paper mills. Opportunistic little cells of roadside community crop up to serve the beer-and-bait needs of those bound for the myriad "recreational opportunities" of Minnesota's "Lake Country" along the headwaters of the mighty Mississippi River. At either edge of this summertime playground, two largish towns, **Grand Rapids** and **Bemidji**, serve as gateways to the gaping spreads of Chippewa National Forest and many of Minnesota's 10,000 lakes.

The **Minnesota Welcome Center,** 11 miles east of the North Dakota border on US-2, has a full range of maps and information on both states.

Fisher

The only thing between Crookston and the North Dakota state line is little Fisher (pop. 413), nothing much now, but at one time a bustling frontier town due to its location at the navigational head of the Red River of the North. River traffic declined, however, and the railroad bypassed Fisher's Landing, thus dooming it. Not quite a ghost town, all it has today is a historical marker to the bygone days; At mealtimes, however, half the town can be found at the **Fisher Cafe**, across the street from the spindly water tower, three blocks south of US-2.

Near Fisher stretches the **Malmberg Prairie**, one of the few extant virgin prairies left, here protected by the Nature Conservancy.

Crookston

Crookston (pop. 8,119), 25 miles east of the North Dakota border, has a series of bridges over the meandering and tree-lined Red Lake River, which winds along the south side of the compact downtown business district. There's a statue of hardy pioneer Joe Roulette in front of the community center on US-2, and a small **Polk County Museum** (daily noon-5 PM late May to Sept.: donations), containing the usual slew of 19th-century stuff with the addition of the world's largest ox-cart, but that's about it as far as sights go.

There are also two rather big festivals in Crookston: August's Ox-Cart Days, and Red River Valley Winter Shows and Rodeo, which draws up to 40,000 visitors from the U.S. and Canada. Call 800/809-5997 for tourist info.

Erskine and Bagley

In the 100 miles east of the North Dakota border, US-2 spreads into a divided four-lane, climbing out of the fecund Red River Valley of the North (not to be confused with the *real* Red River Valley, down in Texas) onto the flat glaciated plains, while the roadside colors alternate between the dark reds and greens of sugar beets and the buff and leafy tones of the wheat, soy beans, and potatoes for which the area is known.

The tiny town of **Fosston,** midway between Erskine and Bagley, holds one of two stoplights on this 100-mile stretch of US-2. Fosston also marks the sudden switch between the Great Plains and the Great North Woods; the town motto is unusually appropriate: "Fosston, Where the Plains Meet the Pines."

Continuing east, US-2 passes occasional isolated pockets of trees, planted as windbreaks amidst the furrowed fields. In the tiny village of Erskine (pop. 422), a classic one-horse Midwest town, you'll find **Joe DiMaggio's Bar**, neither a misprint nor the genuine article. (The eponymous owner, Mr. D., is a Bronx native who used to get oodles of wrong numbers for the legendary Yankee Clipper. Not surprisingly, his bar is full of baseball memorabilia.) Erskine also has a municipal swimming beach on Lake Cameron, and takes civic pride in being the home of the "World's Largest Northern Pike."

Thirty miles east of Erskine, at the western turnoff to Lake Itasca, Bagley (pop. 1,388) features a large wildlife museum packed with stuffed polar and Kodiak bears, among 750-odd creatures, right on US-2 at the western edge of town.

Between Bemidji and Grand Rapids, US-2 runs parallel to the slower but more scenic Great River Road, which winds along the Mississippi River, from Lake Itasca all the way south to New Orleans. The entire route is detailed beginning on page 168.

Bemidji

Under a century ago, the northern forests of Minnesota were chock-full of lumber boom camps, with hundreds of mills and lumber works whining night and day, and dozens of saloons, brothels, and boardinghouses catering to the rough-and-tumble

THE LEGENDS OF PAUL BUNYAN

Like most other myths of the American frontier, the legend of Paul Bunyan is obscured in the mists of time. The source of the many legends describing Paul's life—such as that when he was born it took five storks to deliver him, and it took a whole herd of cows to keep him fed; that at just a week old he was big enough to wear his father's clothes; that he once bent a crowbar and used it as a safety pin to hold his pants together; that he was able to fell trees an acre at a time, and he used to whistle through a hollowed-out log—are impossible to trace, though their widespread popularity is due primarily to a public relations man at the Red River Lumber Company, William Laughead.

Beginning in 1914, and continuing for the next 20 years, Laughead and the lumber company, which was owned by the Walker family, founders of the Walker Art Center, published a series of illustrated booklets, recounting the stories already in general circulation around the logging camps. The booklets, bearing the full title, *"The Marvelous Exploits of Paul Bunyan as told in the Camps of the White Pine Lumberman for Generations, During Which Time the Loggers have Pioneered the Way through the North Woods from Maine to California, collected from various sources and embellished for Publication,* map the "Paul

Bunyan Belt" in towns that constructed statues of Paul and Babe, his big blue ox. The first large statue of Paul and Babe was built in 1937 in Bemidji, where they now stand along the lake; statues were later built in Klamath, California; Brainerd, Minnesota; Bangor, Maine; and many other logging towns.

logging trade. The ravenous cutting wiped out the stands—virtually nothing remains of Minnesota's primeval pine forests—and the camps disappeared as quickly as they sprang up, but the woods have repeatedly grown back, to be harvested on a more sustainable basis while still providing an eye-pleasing backdrop to the region's literally thousands of lakes.

From its boomtown roots, Bemidji (pop. 11,245) has long since settled down into a picturesque community—i.e., looking just as it did when Hubert Humphrey first ran for Congress—its compact and charismatic business district filling a half dozen blocks along the south shore of lovely Lake Bemidji. With three large mills still busily turning trees into wood products, Bemidji is a typically industrious lumber town, remarkable mainly for having assisted in the birth of that well-loved pair of legendary loggers, Paul Bunyan and his blue ox, Babe (see special topic above).

The main course of US-2 wraps around downtown Bemidji, so be sure to follow the Business Loop (old US-2), which passes up and over both the Mississippi River and Lake Bemidji while winding to downtown and a park where the town's big tourist draw, leviathan statues of **Paul Bunyan** and **Babe the Blue Ox**, have stood along the lakefront since their construction in 1937. Nearby there's a recently re-modeled **visitor center** (218/751-3541 or 800/458-2223), boasting a fireplace made with stones from every US state (apart from Alaska and Hawaii, which weren't states when the fireplace was first built) and sharing space with a small **museum** ($1.25) of taxidermied wildlife and odd historical items—including Paul Bunyan's axe and oversized underwear.

Along with Paul and Babe, Bemidji offers endless opportunities for water-skiing, canoeing, fishing, and autumnal leaf-peeping. It also has more than enough **cafes** to detain the most discerning roadtripping traveler. Top of the list is the **Maid Rite Diner**, across from the lake near the information center; a classic diner, it's open from 7:30 AM for hearty meals and homemade rhubarb pies. Other good places are **Griffey's Bakery** and the **Coachman's**, both of which are in the main business district, two blocks inland from the lake. The only cafe still open after 5 PM is **Clementine's Eatery** on 2nd Street, with regional specialties including *lefse,* a Norwegian *latke* or potato pancake, and (sometimes) fresh walleye pike. Dinner is a different story, and apart from the franchised chains lining US-2, your options are few. Best bet for dinner is **Union Station**, in the old railway building at 128 1st Street, a bar and restaurant serving pastas, steaks, the ever-present walleye, and the best wild rice salad around. **Tutto Bene** is a slightly upscale Italian place, with a pleasantly cool outdoor terrace; for late-night dining, **Dave's Pizza** at 15th and Irvine is open till 11 PM, till midnight on weekends.

Motels include the family-oriented **Edgewater**, appropriately situated on the lake at 1015 Paul Bunyan Drive (218/751-3600 or 800/776-3343), with its own beach and complimentary canoes available to guests; the national chains (**Best Western, Comfort Inn, Holiday Inn,** and **Super 8**) line US-2 west of downtown, away from the lake.

Chippewa National Forest

The scenery along US-2 between Bemidji and Grand Rapids turns on the color jets, the numbing agricultural morass giving way to the edges of the enormous—663,000 acres—Chippewa National Forest, a conglomeration of over 700 lakes, state parks and forests, recreation areas, U.S. Army Corps of Engineer dams—and

Big Fish Supper Club

some nifty driving highlights. It's also home to quite a few bald eagles.

Cass Lake, where the native Ojibwa tribe hosts summertime powwows, is on US-2 at the western end of the forest, and includes the U.S. Forest Service **headquarters** (218/335-8600) in addition to a bald eagle nesting site. **Deer River**, at the eastern edge of the forest, is handy mostly for cheap coffee and gas. In between, a 50-foot-long fish stands alongside the popular **Big Fish Supper Club** (218/665-2333) on US-2 at the hamlet of Bena, while most of the forest lands account for the **Leech Lake Indian Reservation.**

West of Grand Rapids, near **Cohasset,** a low ridge divides this area of Minnesota and distributes the rivers and streams into three watersheds: south to the Gulf of Mexico, north to the Hudson Bay, and east to the Great Lakes.

Grand Rapids

Navigational headwaters of the Mississippi River, Grand Rapids (pop. 7,976) is a small Frank Capra-esque kind of place, known for its four large in-town lakes (there are over 1,000 in this part of the state) and a great bridge over the river. The city can be a bit confusing in its layout, but its small size makes sightseeing manageable.

The city sits along the western edge of the famed Mesabi Iron Range and includes viewing sites at a handful of **open pit mines**. The iron mines are a thing of the past, but Grand Rapids is still a major lumber town, and you can tour the im-

possible-to-miss **Blandin Paper Mill** (Monday, Wednesday, and Friday, May-Sept. only; 218/327-6226; free). One of the country's largest mills, Blandin owns most of the surrounding forests and turns the trees into the stock onto which magazines like *Time* and *Sports Illustrated* are printed.

Three miles southwest of Grand Rapids, well signed along the Great River Road and equidistant via US-169 or US-2, the fine **Forest History Center** (Mon.-Sat. 10 AM-5 PM, Sunday noon-5 PM in summer; daily noon-4 PM rest of the year; $3) is a living-history replica of a 19th-century logging camp, complete with nature trails through the surrounding woods and energetic lumberjacks rolling logs and telling tall tales.

In the center of town, the **Central School Heritage and Arts Center** (Mon.-Sat. 9 AM-5 PM June-Sept.; rest of the year, 9:30 AM-5 PM; $3) is housed in a squat, three-story Victorian Romanesque-style grade-school building at the crossroads of US-2 and US-169. Here you'll find the county historical museum, with the usual "Main Street" of banks, stores, services, and pell-mell displays of farm equipment and logging gear.

Upstairs, however, is the real draw: the self-proclaimed "World's Largest Collection of Judy Garland Memorabilia," she of ruby-slipper fame having been born in Grand Rapids on June 10, 1922. Truly a cradle-to-grave biographical assembly, the collection displays everything from her first crib to photos of her early performances as part of the Gumm Sisters, a family vaudeville group, to fading images of the London house where she died of an overdose of sleeping pills on June 22, 1969, and a final shot of her tomb in Hartsdale, New York. There are also posters from most of her movies, and a copy of her costume from *The Wizard of Oz,* complete with ruby slippers. In front of the building, right along US-2, is a miniature "Yellow Brick Road" dedicated by some of the surviving "munchkins" who worked on the picture.

Grand Rapids is very proud of its most famous daughter, **Judy Garland,** and whoops it up every July with a festival in her honor.

The Central School also holds a unique place to eat: the school cafeteria, now a pleasant if somewhat frilly restaurant called the **First Grade**, specializing in homemade soups and sandwiches—and great pies.

The Grand Rapids **visitor center** (218/326-1251 or 800/472-6366), downtown at N.W. 3rd Street in the circa 1898 Great Northern Railroad depot, includes a 24-hour enclosed kiosk with information and a phone hookup to local **motels**.

Skyline Parkway and Hwy-61

One of the greatest loop trips in the country, Skyline Parkway is a 16-mile (30 with side trips) bucolic wind along the bluffs above Duluth. Accessed from West Duluth off I-35, the parkway takes in numerous historical sites, but it's mostly just jaw-drop scenery, especially **Hawk Ridge**, which offers perfect wind conditions for viewing up to 30,000 hawks, eagles, and falcons daily in fall; also along the ridge is a fantastic network of trails, boarding stations, and observation posts. The parkway, which was dedicated in 1939 by Norway's King Olav V, connects at its north end with famed Hwy-61, which, if you've got the time to spend, is an even more beautiful jaunt along Lake Superior's granite cliffs to Grand Portage and Canada, 150 miles to the northeast. Along the way are some of the country's best places to eat. Numerous **smokehouses** tout their smoked fish plucked from the frigid waters of the great lake.

Duluth

Though it doesn't get a lot of positive press, Duluth (pop. 85,493) has to be one of the most beautiful and underappreciated travel destinations in the Midwest, "a Lilliputian village in a mammoth rock garden," the old WPA *Guide to Minnesota* aptly noted. Gracefully etched into the side of tough, 800-foot granite slopes and gazing over the dark harbor hues, Duluth, from the attractively redone red-brick paving of gentrified Superior and Michigan Streets downtown to the grittier heights atop the bluff, quietly goes about its business, usually with foghorns belching in the background. It is a city of maritime and timber history, but it is a city of stunning, pervasive, pristine, *healthy* wilderness as well.

Tracts of forest, harbor preserves, shoreline, and parks flourish in the city, and there are dozens of interesting Great Lake or historical museums, mansions, lakefront walks, boat or foot tours, and festivals—from Native American powwows (mid-August) to midwinter sled-dog races. Many visitors start with the **Canal Park Maritime Museum** (daily 10 AM-9 PM in summer, 10 AM-4:30 PM rest of the year; free) on Canal Park Drive next to the Aerial Lift Bridge and the main **visitor center** (218/722-4011 or 800/4-DULUTH) at Endion Station, 100 Lake Place Drive. There's also a **ship watcher's hotline** (218/722-6489) if you want to head down to the harbor and check out the ore-boat traffic. Another good stop is **The Depot** (daily 10 AM-5 PM in summer, Sunday 1-5 PM in winter; $5), across I-35 but walkably close to the waterfront at 506 W. Michigan Avenue, an enormous, magnificently restored example of early city architecture as well as home to many of the city's artistic and cultural centers. Around it are historic locomotives and two dozen shops re-creating turn-of-the-century Duluth, right down to the old ice cream parlor.

Crossing the St. Louis River delta on the Bong Memorial Bridge (named after a famous WW II flying ace) between Superior, Wisconsin, and downtown Duluth travelers on US-2 are afforded a resplendent view of the harbor and Duluth's landmark, the **Aerial Lift Bridge**, a 385-foot-tall monster connecting the mainland to the mouth of the harbor.

The Aerial Lift Bridge over Duluth's harbor can be raised 138 feet in under a minute, to let ships pass underneath.

North Woods Public Radio broadcasts NPR news and other arts and cultural programming on a series of stations across northern Minnesota, including **KAXE 91.7 FM** in Grand Rapids.

On Hwy-33, 11 miles south of US-2 and 15 miles west of Duluth on the edge of the Fond Du Lac Indian Reservation, the town of **Cloquet** boasts the only gas station ever designed by famed architect Frank Lloyd Wright. Cloquet also has a large, Fond du Lac Indian-owned casino (800/321-0005).

Hwy-61 north of Duluth is the road that inspired the title of Bob Dylan's album *Highway 61 Revisited*. Dylan himself was born in the nearby iron-mining town of **Hibbing,** which is also where Greyhound Bus Lines got its start, shuttling between the mines and the town.

ACROSS WISCONSIN

The briefest stint US-2 spends in any state, in Wisconsin the route nevertheless navigates wisely, for it takes in the far, Lake Superior cap of Wisconsin's northern region, and includes a majestic 140-mile detour along the rough-and-tumble Lake Superior shoreline, home of rich history, gorgeous boreal forest, and pastoral and littoral scenery. All of these provide outstanding opportunities to stop and explore.

Northern Wisconsin is in the heart of big snow country, a promontory jutting into the maw of bad-tempered **Gitcheegumee,** where 35 inches of snow a month during the winter don't begin to crease a frown on a native Wisconsiner's face. So play it safe if you're traveling along Lake Superior then.

If you're here on a Friday evening, be sure to head to the Lake Superior hamlet of Cornucopia for the traditional Scandinavian Fish Boil, held at the Village Inn Restaurant (715/742-3941).

Superior

Both rival and best friend of bigger Duluth across the harbor, Superior (pop. 27,100) is sometimes the butt of jokes, usually regarding its comparatively lower geography, which means Superior catches all of Duluth's flotsam, its hardy, blue-collar mentality and mountains of coal, and an apparent lack of trees. It is also proud, along with Duluth, of being one of the busiest harbors in the nation, shipping millions of tons of ore a year from the nation's most inland port.

Superior's lack of pretense is perhaps its biggest attraction. The route on US-2 through the city is decidedly industrialized, featuring a seemingly endless amount—almost 30 miles—of bay shore crowded with trains, tracks, elevators, and spindly working piers jutting out into the lake almost to the horizon. The city itself is sedate but offers a few things of historical or Great Lake interest, including its biggest draw, **Fairlawn Mansion and Museum** (daily 9 AM-5 PM; $4), the sprawling 42-room ex-residence of a lumber baron. There are plenty of places to stay along the main strip through town, including a **Days Inn** a couple blocks north of the junction of US-2 and Hwy-53, which has rooms from $41. For more information, contact the **visitor center** (715/392-2773 or 800/942-5313), on US-2 at the point where it bears left into town, giving superior views both of the lake and town.

Hwy-13 Loop to the Apostle Islands

One of the best alternative routes on the Upper Midwest stretch of US-2 is Hwy-13's 100-mile loop along Lake Superior's western shores. The 45 miles, and at least four hours, that this loop adds to your journey across the state are without question worth it, taking in the superlative Apostle Islands, charming peninsula communities, and unbeatable road views.

Starting in the west at the blue-collar harbor town of Superior, Hwy-13 zigzags northeast to the lakeshore and follows it to picturesque Cornucopia. Each little hill you climb reveals a new view of mosaics of farmland, dispersed boats, and archaic farming equipment. East of Cornucopia, the road veers inland, emerging again onto the lakefront at the peninsula's main Ojibwa town, **Red Cliff**, which has a marina and boat slip, a lakeside campground within view of Basswood and Madeline islands, a casino, and an annual 4th of July **powwow**. The outskirts of Red Cliff include some lake views and some great views of open pastureland meshed with dense evergreen forests on what appears to be slight tableland. Boats and canoes are ever-present, scattered among rural jetsam, decades-old Chevys and Ford pickups, their classic rondure rusting mutely in the cattails. You whiz by tottering, one-eyed cabins hardly larger than hunting shacks, their grainy, weather-beaten shingled siding obscured by weeds.

The nerve center of the Apostle Islands region is the diminutive, laid-back resort village of **Bayfield** (pop. 775), the most touristy place in the area, though you'll hardly notice. Bayfield itself dates from 1856 and looks at first glance about as Lilliputian as you can get, with a curvy (10 mph on the corners) narrow road winding beside impeccably tailored cottages and modest local brownstone mansions. Virtually every hairpin turn offers an outstanding glimpse of the Apostle Islands and the boats plying the waters, especially on the far northern edge of town.

> The Apostle Islands harbored perhaps the only freshwater pirates in U.S. history. The "Twelve Apostles" buccaneers roamed the straits around Oak Island, plundering boats and hiding out in the island's good cover.

There are plenty of classy or quaint places to stay in Bayfield, from the ritzy **Old Rittenhouse Inn** (715/779-5111), which also serves good food, to cottages and motels; prices fall in direct proportion to your geographic distance out of town, of course. **Winnie's Hungry Mariner**, in the center of town, features breakfast all day, as well as lunch and dinner specials, and great pies. There are also plenty of **ferries** (or even windsleds over the ice) to Madeline Island or certain parts of the Apostles; prices vary greatly with the season. A unique draw is **Bayfield's Big Top Chautauqua** (715/373-5552), a revival of old traveling tent shows that offers great summertime concerts, plays, and musical revues; listen for it on public radio on Big Top Radio Network.

South of Bayfield, Washburn is a pleasant enough little community; it's also close to two **ski slopes**. Downtown parks offer great lake vistas and even a lakeshore walking trail. Approaching Ashland and US-2, Hwy-13 heads through classic Wisconsin agrarian stretches hacked from the wilderness, with occasional lake views, quick rises in wind, or foreboding dark thunderheads.

Ashland

As you enter Ashland on US-2, some 40 miles west of the Michigan border, Lake Superior finally pokes its great nose at you. Ashland (pop. 8,700), a big fish in sparsely populated north-woods Wisconsin, likes to call itself the "Garland City of the Inland Seas" but what it is really is a town full of trestles, all the roads dipping and drooping under the mud-brown wood framework or plain faded steel of Soo Line bridges. Built up on an ever-so-slight rise above the lake, the town has an attractive Main Street with many well-preserved old buildings—where else does Romanesque revival compete with neoclassical and art deco?—and a lakeshore lined with great parks, frigid-looking beaches, especially on the west side of town, and gritty pull-offs where you can gaze at the gargantuan **Ashland Soo Line Ore dock**, the largest of its kind in the world.

Registered on the National Register of Historic Places, **The Depot** at 400 W. 3rd Avenue is a luxurious restaurant inside a restored Soo Line depot, with great—but pricey—regional fare. Downstairs there's the very good **Northern Wisconsin Interpretive Center** (Thurs.-Mon. 10 AM-4:30 PM; $3) with displays on local history, especially railroads. The nicest hotel in town—with a fine restaurant to boot—is the grand **Hotel Chequamegon** (pronounced "shuh-WAH-muh-gun"; 715/682-9095), on the lakeshore at the junction of US-2 and Hwy-13. This was a century-old Victorian until a 1955 conflagration destroyed the original structure, but the reconstruction has sacrificed none of the decorative charm or taste; rates start at $75 in summer. There are plenty of other cheaper **motels** scattered throughout town; for listings contact the local **visitor center** (715/682-2500 or 800/284-9484), at 320 W. 4th Avenue.

In Northern Wisconsin, tune your radio to **WOJB 88.9 FM,** run by the Lac Court Oreille Ojibway Nation and featuring excellent, eclectic music as well as National Native and NPR news.

Along the border with Michigan, the first greeting Wisconsin proffers to westbound travelers is a giant liquor store's **corkscrew** statue, beckoning you to imbibe.

APOSTLE ISLANDS NATIONAL LAKESHORE

Deposited by retreating glaciers almost as an afterthought, the 22 micro- to mini-sized islands that represent the Apostle Islands National Lakeshore are among the best gems of the Great Lakes. These pristine, windswept sandstone islands, surrounded by the deep blue waters of Lake Superior, contain a fantastic array of bluffs, sea caves, beaches, rookeries, and forests, and offer memorable primitive camping, hiking, and unique kayaking. Information on courses and rentals is available in the town of Bayfield. One of the largest and most famous, historic **Madeline Island**, which technically isn't in the park since it's inhabited, has long been a popular Wisconsin escape spot, more for long-term vacationers than casual visitors, since services are limited.

The main National Park Service **visitor center** (715/779-3397) for the Apostle Islands is headquartered in the old county courthouse building on Washington Avenue in the center of Bayfield; a few contact stations are also scattered along the north shoreline or on the islands themselves.

The route to the Apostle Islands from US-2, looping along Hwy-13 between Ashland and Superior, is described above.

Bad River Indian Reservation

Home to one of Wisconsin's six Ojibwa communities, the Bad River Indian Reservation encompasses 56,697 acres owned by approximately 1,800 descendants of the original Ojibwa Loon Clan who settled near the delta confluence of the Bad and White Rivers; the reservation serves as the tribal **headquarters** (715/682-7111). The tribe holds its annual **Manonin powwow** in late August, and their local wood-products factory builds log-home kits.

From the eastern edge of the reservation, it's another 20 uneventful miles to the Michigan border.

ACROSS MICHIGAN'S UPPER PENINSULA

There are two alternatives across Michigan's Upper Peninsula (the "U. P."), which stretches for nearly 300 miles from Canada to Wisconsin between Lake Superior and Lake Michigan. Between Ironwood in the west, and Sault Ste. Marie on the Canadian border in the east, you can choose between **US-2** along the north shore of Lake Michigan, or the more direct option, **Hwy-28**, which runs near the south shore of Lake Superior near Pictured Rocks National Lakeshore; either way takes a full day, and this is not a place to try and make up time.

In either case, you're privy to one of the greater finds of the Midwest, the sparsely populated and thoroughly underappreciated (especially by the "trolls" of southern Michigan) land of the "Yoopers," as the proud residents have christened themselves, many still ensconced in the logging and mining enclaves their forebears founded. The U.P. boasts a surprisingly mountainous and larger-than-it-looks stretch of land dotted with boom-to-bust towns relying on summer tourism and one or more of the industrial triumvirate up here: timber, mining, and fishing.

Michigan's Upper Peninsula is almost always abbreviated "U.P." Residents often call themselves Yoopers.

All over the U.P. you'll see signs advertising **pasties.** The quintessential miner food, Cornish pasties (which rhymes with nasty, not tasty—hang onto the vowel a bit, like a true Yooper) were introduced to Copper Country 100-odd years ago by immigrant Cornish miners. These dense baked crust-pockets, stuffed with minced meat and vegetables, are ubiquitous in U.P. cafes and restaurants.

Ironwood

In the first 75 miles east of the Wisconsin border, you never really leave the forest, though you do pass dozens of decaying old mining towns built back when the U.P. made Michigan the country's biggest iron-ore producer. Approaching Ironwood, US-2 crests a rise that marks the edge of the roller-coaster hills of the Gogebic Range, which give great sunset views over the Wisconsin forests and distant Lake Superior.

The first U.P. town east of Wisconsin is Ironwood, the lead town of the Gogebic Range. This mountain town has grown into a big-time winter sports arena. The **Copper Peak Sky Flying Hill** (daily June-Sept.; weekends Sept.-Oct.) is North

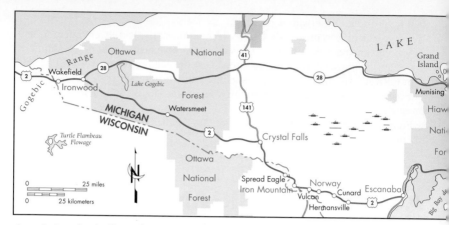

America's only ski-flying facility, and even sponsors international competitions; for a great view of much of three states and Canada, take a chairlift up.

Ironwood is worth a look for its absolutely huge, 52-foot-high fiberglass statue of **Hiawatha,** the fictional hero of Henry Wadsworth Longfellow's famous poem.

East of Ironwood, at the town of Wakefield, our route divides: US-2 runs south along Lake Michigan, while Hwy-28 veers north along Lake Superior.

The place to eat in Ironwood is **Mike's Cafe**, right on US-2 and serving huge breakfasts. Ironwood's also the only town along US-2 to keep the U.P. Finnish tradition of sauna alive; many of the $25-a-night motels strung along US-2, including the **Sandpiper Motel (906/932-2000)** right on the highway on the east side of town, boast real cedar saunas like the old country, alas without the birch twigs for self-flagellation in the snowbanks.

US-2: Ottawa National Forest

Just a dozen miles east of Ironwood, the immense verdant spread of the Ottawa National Forest begins. At 1.7 million acres, including subsumed state and county land, Michigan's largest national forest covers a vast amount of the western U.P. and contains some of the region's most diverse geology, flora and fauna, and simple isolated wilderness, including 35 waterfalls accessible from woodland trails. The road passes through epic tracts of trees obviously older and denser than anywhere else along the route. (North in the Porcupine Mountains stands one of the last remaining true wilderness areas in the Midwest.)

For information, the little town of **Watersmeet** has a U.S. Forest Service **ranger station (906/358-4724)** at the junction of US-2 and Hwy-45, and it serves as the access town to the grand **Cisco Chain of Lakes/Sylvania Wilderness**, a spattering of over 300 lakes offering fantastic recreation.

Crystal Falls

The first real town east of the Ottawa National Forest, Crystal Falls (pop. 1,950) is a charming, postcard kind of place built into a bluff near a rivulet waterfall on the Paint River. Time seems to stand still here, the town sporting original (read: *old*) street signs still pointing the way, and huge trees overhanging US-2 as it slowly hairpins through town. The only "sights" here are the local courthouse, won in a poker game in the 1880s, and a water-filled old pit mine outside of town.

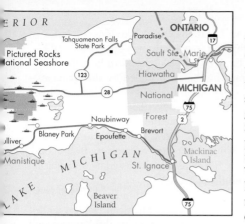

Southeast from Crystal Falls, US-2 passes something the western U.P. specializes in: numerous rock and ore formations jutting out of the hillsides, usually covered with graffiti. The road, still wide and black and smooth as glass, sweeps into the **Copper Country State Forest**, which gives every appearance of symmetrical reforestation, then flits through 15 miles of northern Wisconsin, zigzagging along a nice lake before passing through the oddly named town of **Spread Eagle**, just west of Iron Mountain.

Iron Mountain and Norway

Though separated by six blacktopped miles, the sister towns of Norway and Iron Mountain both grew up with the lumbering and iron-mining industry, producing over 300,000 tons annually from three big mines. Both are slightly somnolent but by no means decaying.

The larger of the two, Iron Mountain (pop. 8,525), backs up against the easy grade of its eponymous mountain, and seems casually strewn about in parts. The must-see here, everyone will tell you, is the local **Cornish Pump and Mining Museum** two blocks west of US-2 on Kent Street (Mon.-Sat. 9 AM-5 PM, Sunday noon-4 PM May-Oct.; $4), and it *is* great, with the most enormous steam-driven pump engine you could imagine. But the *real* must-see is the freebie, the **Majestic Pine/Roosevelt Mountain Ski Jump** (800/236-2447), most easily accessed west of town off US-2 onto Pine Mountain Road. This 90-meter jump hosts annual international competitions in February and is the site of the current U.S. distance record. The local gendarmes have given up trying to stop you from crab walking up it and getting the best view in the U.P., but it sure is creaky and intimidating.

> Rumor has it that the Majestic Pine/Roosevelt Mountain Ski Jump near Iron Mountain is where the "agony of defeat" ski-jump crash from the opening credits of ABC TV's *Wide World of Sports* was filmed.

There aren't many cafes to speak of in Iron Mountain—it specializes in supper clubs—but there is one unique lunch spot: **Bimbo's**, a bar on Main Street next to the Citgo gas station, north off US-2. Wednesday to Friday the place features lunches of its own "porketta" sandwiches, cut from a pig roast on Monday. They also have homemade Italian sausages.

The mines at Norway (pop. 2,910) were so close together and active that the village once caved in and they had to rebuild it down the hill. Gritty Norway—which once produced more shingles than anywhere else, as shown by the numerous houses still coated with gritty shingles—also boasts the area's best cafe, the **Country House Restaurant**, right downtown off US-2, where you can rub shoulders with virtually every local.

Another true find in Norway is **Piers Gorge**, a couple miles south off US-8, where the raging waters of the Menominee River scraped out this fascinating gorge on the border between Michigan and Wisconsin.

Escanaba

Fifteen miles west of Escanaba, at the eastern edge of the tiny Potawatomi Indian Reservation, you pass between the central and eastern time zones. Adjust your clocks and watches accordingly.

Between Norway and Escanaba, US-2 provides 45 miles of open, occasionally dipping, road with only sporadic breaks in the sameness of the birch or pine backdrops. In fact, it's so monotonous that you may not be at all miffed by the shamelessness that the powers that be in the town of **Vulcan** show by snowballing enormous billboards advertising—nay, hammering home—the **Iron Mine**, an obnoxious tourist trap where the heavy-handed self-promotion overwhelms the fact that it's a truly historic site. Continuing east, the hamlets are archetypally sleepy, like **Cunard**, which has a large aqua-colored warehouse that looks like a standing freezer-pack, or **Hermansville**, with sedate and spartan little dwellings up and off the road on a bluff.

Escanaba (pop. 13,659), with perfect geography at the mouth of the Escanaba River at the Little Bay de Noc, was born in typical Lake Michigan fashion, out of the country's insatiable need for timber and ore. At one time its three timber and ore docks contributed to the largest ore-shipping operation of its kind in the U.S., shipping that continues today. Yet it's difficult to get pumped up for Escanaba while you're negotitiating a seemingly endless switchback through strip mall/Kwiki Mart purgatory. Even trips to the **Delta County Museum** (daily 1-9 PM June-Sept.; free) or the renovated 1867 **Sandpoint Lighthouse** (same hours; $1) are disheartening, in view of the threadbare waterfront. The people, at least, are redeemingly friendly, and the annual **U.P. State Fair**, held here in August, is great. Escanaba also has the Hiawatha National Forest **ranger station** (906/786-4062) at 2727 N. Lincoln Road.

Hiawatha National Forest

Heading northeast from Escanaba, US-2 broadens into a fast four-lane along the Big and Little Bay de Noc, and you'll pass through a slew of little "resorts," some with their own beaches. As you head east toward Manistique, the landscape reverts to trees and more trees; you're in the chevroned conifers of the Hiawatha National Forest. There are two separate sections of this immense 879,000-acre forest, which has shoreline on three of the Great Lakes—Huron, Michigan, and Superior. The flyspeck communities here haven't changed much—ubiquitous flashing yellow lights, matchbox dwellings attached to bulbous propane gas tanks, and, in a few communities, forlorn old Soo Line railcars aging gracelessly on the tracks right off the highway. There might be a smoked-fish house or two, but more than likely it'll be a forgettable roadhouse offering greasy pasty at best.

The best turnoff comes in **Garden Corners**—don't blink—which spins you down Hwy-183 to the excellent **Fayette State Park** (May-Oct.; $3.50), an extant ghost community, original, not renovated. It's an impressive, perhaps eerie place, situated on a sheer limestone cliff peninsula.

Manistique

The only sizeable town between St. Ignace and Escanaba, Manistique (pop. 3,456) tends to underwhelm, apart from its Lake Michigan frontage. Mountains of gravel and mini-smokestacks line the road into town on the east side, and the sweetly pungent smell of paper permeates the air. Despite that, Manistique does have a sleepy tourist draw, with the lake right there and the bizarre **Kitch-Iti-Kipi** up the road in **Palms Book State Park,** where 16,000 gallons of water a minute bubble up, propelling tourists on rafts. Downtown is the **Imogene Herbert Museum** (daily 10 AM-4 PM in summer) with a nice century-old cabin and majestic brick water tower. Nearby, on Cedar Street off US-2, **Jax Bar & Restaurant** is a classic cafe with a single-sheet plastic menu and lots of newsprint scuffed into the original smoky Formica counter.

US-2: Along Lake Michigan

The route that US-2 follows along Lake Michigan between Escanaba and St. Ignace is one of the U.P.'s best autumn scenic drives. The true heart of U.P. lies here, with patches of pine or birch woodland followed by brief lakeshore, then a dormant ore-mine, a trailer park, or a long-abandoned fishing camp.

In Manistique, old US-2 (Hwy-94) crosses the **Siphon Bridge**—featured in Ripley's *Believe It or Not!* for being partially supported by water and having a roadway four feet below the water level.

The first hint of anything special comes in tiny **Blaney Park,** 22-odd miles east of Manistique, which boasts two grand B&Bs—the **Celibeth House B&B** (906/283-3409), an 1895 mansion with eight rooms from $50, and the posher **Blaney Lodge B&B** (906/283-3883), which June-Oct. maintains one of the best dining rooms in the U.P.—and even a private airstrip. The whole area was once a 22,000-acre company playground for the Wisconsin Land and Lumber Company and nowadays offers relief from the pervasive local architectural hybrid of ranch-style mashed with trailer home.

From the flyspeck town of **Gulliver,** 13 miles east of Manistique, a road leads southeast to Michigan's most picturesque lighthouse, at **Seul Choix Pointe.**

East of here, as you approach St. Ignace, the scenery becomes increasingly gorgeous: bay views give way only occasionally to pesky pockets of trees; then in one grand stretch, the lake breaks through fully, and you're literally skimming a beachside causeway. Bordering the road are huge dunes, real sand dunes with green tufts of mixed grass sprouting amidst the golden grains, and you hardly notice the little towns born as fishing villages—**Naubinway, Epoufette,** and **Brevort**—that line the highway.

St. Ignace

Coming into St. Ignace along US-2, travelers are tempted by a number of "scenic overlooks" west of town, all proffering a chance to stretch and view the often fog-shrouded Mackinac Bridge over blue Lake Michigan—not the deep steely blue of Lake Superior, which you'll see later; a gentler, more somber blue.

For concentrated kitsch, don't miss **Paul Bunyan Pasties** on US-2, eight miles west of the Mackinac Bridge; they're in the *Guinness Book of World Records* for having baked a 223-pound monster.

Picturesque St. Ignace (pop. 2,600) lies east of, and down a hill from, the concrete river of the I-75 freeway. This little town, at one time 70% French-Canadian, is more important than its obviously tourism-contrived loveliness would indicate, situated as it is at the crossroads of the upper and lower regions of Michigan, with Mackinac Island just across the bay. The town is busy and cheerful, in places gentrified and meticulously maintained; downtown you can stroll along a bright lake promenade lined with gift shops, tourist restaurants (every one of which has been renovated into overpriced hokum), and dozens of $35-a-night motels.

Straits State Park ($3 admission) outside St. Ignace off of US-2, not far from the junction with I-75, houses the **Father Jacques Marquette Memorial and Museum.**

Downtown is the fine **Marquette Mission Park and Museum of Ojibwa Culture** (daily 10 AM-8 PM May-Oct.; $2). The park is reportedly the burial site of Father Marquette.

The main attraction around St. Ignace, besides the landmark Mackinac Bridge, is the ferry ride to anachronistic **Mackinac Island**, one of the top draws in the Midwest. This flyspeck island has never had motor vehicles on it and is now billed as a sort of bygone-days living museum, actually a first-class tourist trap that's not embarrassing. Day-trips aboard ferries from St. Ignace cost around $11.

Running north to Sault Ste. Marie, I-75 passes through 50 miles of desiccated earth tones, broken by wide swaths of ersatz prairie and miniature stands of trees.

Goggle-eyed travelers come to St. Ignace just to stare at what locals like to call the "Eighth Wonder of the World," the **Mackinac Bridge,** one of the longest suspension bridges in the world at 7,400 feet (with approaches, the total length is over five miles). Lots of scenic views are found throughout the city and on US-2 west of town.

Sault Ste. Marie

Michigan's oldest community, and the third oldest in the U.S., Sault Ste. Marie (pop. 14,700, pronounced "soo saint ma-REE") is known historically for the tussles over the area between the French and British, and as the only land link between the U.S. and Canada for hundreds of miles. It is also the most populous but certainly not the most touristed of the Upper Peninsula towns—that title goes to St. Ignace—passed through on this route.

Beneath the steel-span International Bridge that links this Michigan town with Ontario's twin "Soo," the raging torrents that impelled French Fr. Jacques Marquette to dub the newly established mission *Le Sault de Sainte*

ROUTE-28: PICTURED ROCKS NATIONAL LAKESHORE AND TAHQUAMENON FALLS

There are two excellent reasons to bypass US-2 across the Upper Peninsula and to follow Hwy-28 instead. Pictured Rocks National Lakeshore, a lovely, undisturbed stretch of sand dunes, beaches, and colorful bluffs, lines Lake Superior in the middle of the U.P. It's best visited by boat, since there are no roads through it; in summer three-hour **cruises** ($17) leave about every two hours from the pier in **Munising**, right on Hwy-28 at the west edge of the park. In winter Pictured Rocks is a popular place to cross-country ski. For more information, contact the Pictured Rocks **visitor center** (906/387-3700).

Eventually, you come to a real gem, Hwy-123, a must-do road particularly during autumnal color sweeps. Head north past the outstanding—and popular—Tahquamenon Falls State Park. The 50-foot-high, 200-foot-wide Upper Falls here were mentioned in Longfellow's *Song of Hiawatha.*

Before winding back southward toward Hwy-28 and Sault Ste. Marie, take a jaunt through the vacation village of **Paradise** up to Whitefish Point for some of the best isolated beaches in the U.P.; the oldest lighthouse (circa 1849) on the Great Lakes; and the **Great Lakes Shipwreck Historical Museum** (daily 10 AM-6 PM, May-Oct.; $4), to learn about the wreck of the *Edmund Fitzgerald.* This legendary graveyard point is where the ship actually went down, with 29 crew members on board, in November 1975.

Marie, literally "falling waters of Saint Mary," are no longer readily apparent. The U.S. Army Corps of Engineers long ago corralled and tamed the rapids between 20-foot-higher Lake Superior and Lake Huron with four enormous locks, the largest and busiest in the world. During mining heydays the locks conveyed many times the tonnage of the Panama and Suez Canals combined—with no tolls paid. The locks are worthy of at least an hour's siesta; lush parks and a walkway line the locks, with observation points, Soo Lock boat **tours** ($12), the great but expensive **Museum Freighter** *Valley Camp* (daily 9 AM-9 PM; $6), and the landmark 21-story **Tower of History** at 326 E. Portage (daily 10 AM-6 PM May-Oct.; $3).

South of the water at 532 Ashmun Street is what may be the oldest operating restaurant in the U.P.: since 1902, the **American Cafe** has served up homey breakfasts, lunches, and Friday-night dinners (4-7 PM) in a warm atmosphere with just enough elbow room. If the American has character, then rollicking **Antler's** at 804 E. Portage, open daily at 11 AM, has attitude: voted the U.P.'s best restaurant by a couple of newspapers, it's always packed, usually with a waiting list.

The best place to stay, the **Water Street Inn B&B** (906/632-1900 or 800/236-1904), is near the locks at 140 E. Water Street. There are also dozens of motels.

For more information, the local **visitor center** (906/632-3301 or 800/MI-SAULT) is at 2581 Ashmun Street (Business US-75).

ACROSS CANADA

Between Sault Ste. Marie and the Canadian capital, Ottawa, Hwy-17 is the continuation of the Trans-Canada Highway; it is also the Voyageurs Trail, retracing the route taken by the early fur traders between their winter trapping grounds—the wilderness of forests, lakes, and streams to the north—and Montreal, the summer fur market. The scenery varies from rivers and forests to paper mills and coal mines, and most of the way Hwy-17 is a two-lane road with a 90 kph (55 mph) maximum and occasional passing lanes to help you get around the timber trucks.

East of Ottawa, it's a short run down Hwy-417/40 to French-speaking Montreal, Canada's second-largest city and one of the most European places in North America. Via Route 15 south of Montreal, travelers can reenter the U.S. near Vermont's Lake Champlain.

Sault Ste. Marie—The Soo

Crossing over the busy harbor from Michigan, the road enters Canadian Sault Ste. Marie (pop. 81,000), also known as The Soo, "Home of Canada's First Female Astronaut." Graffiti on a railway bridge proclaims: "This is Indian Land." Sault Ste. Marie was founded at the rapids—"sault" means "falls"—in St. Mary's River. Its original name was Bawating, "place of the rapids," where local tribes caught whitefish and tapped maple trees. French explorers arrived in 1622, and the Jesuits estab-

The double suspension bridge linking the Canadian and American Sault Ste. Maries gives memorable views of the Algoma Steel mill, the second largest in Canada, and the St. Mary's River rapids below. The Canadian and American locks here are among the busiest on the St. Lawrence seaway system. Flags in the middle mark the boundary between the two nations.

DRIVING IN CANADA

In Canada, the rules of the road change, as do the measurements. The speed limit on two-lane roads is 90 kilometers (55 miles) per hour, while on highways it is 100 kph (63 mph). Gas is generally more expensive than in the States and is sold by the liter for Canadian dollars. Most gas stations accept U.S. currency but give you a less-than-favorable rate of exchange. Cars are required to have their headlights illuminated night and day; to the unaccustomed, a daytime traffic jam can look like a massive funeral procession. Right on red is illegal in the Province of Quebec; in the rest of Canada, it is legal after stopping first. Another important difference is that proof of insurance is mandatory in Canada.

There is no checkpoint on the American side. The bilingual Canadian Customs officers usually do a cursory check, asking your address, reason for travel, and whether you are carrying firearms. For U.S. or Canadian citizens a passport is not necessary, though others should confirm their visa status before attempting to cross the border; it may be difficult (or impossible) to return.

lished a mission here later that century. Permanent settlement came with the fur trade in the 18th century; later lumber and transportation helped build the local economy. The Canadian locks were completed in 1895, allowing deep draft boats to pass from one lake to another. Today The Soo, and its sister city across the river, are mildly depressed industrial towns (though there is a big steel mill here). However, tourism is increasingly important to the local economy, and it may turn out to be the engine that leads to some revitalization.

To see downtown's sights, turn onto Bruce Street and drive two blocks, passing Queen Street, The Soo's depressed "Main Street," to Bay Street, which runs west to east. Here you'll find the Station Mall, the Art Gallery of Algoma (10 East Street), and an excellent view of the river and the International Bridge. A path near the bridge takes you down to **Roberta Bondar Park** (summer only), built around the original 1895 locks, which are no longer in operation; you'll also find an observation deck over the locks and an interpretation center.

At 129 Bay Street stands the Algoma Central Railway Terminal from which depart the **Agawa Canyon Wilderness Tours**, the area's main tourist attraction (705/946-7300). Throughout the summer, you can take daylong train trips north through a roadless wilderness featuring narrow river valleys and spectacular views. From January through March there is also a Snow Train for the hardy. Bay Street ends at Pim Street to the east; a left will take you by the **Ermatinger Old Stone House,** the oldest stone house in Canada west of Toronto (open daily in summer; Mon.-Fri. rest of the year). Built in 1814 by an early local fur magnate, the house has been restored with period furnishings. Demonstrations on preparing pioneer cuisine are given in the cookhouse.

Sault Ste. Marie lodgings include a couple of motels right on the river, such as the **Holiday Inn**, 208 St. Mary's River Drive (705/949-0611), and the **Bay Front-Quality Inn**, 108 Bay Street (705/945-9264). The cheaper motels are all found north of town on Hwy-17 (also known as the Great Northern Road) heading to

Thunder Bay. The Soo is something of a culinary wasteland; outside the riverfront motels, try **Arturo's** (705/949-0810) at 116 Spring Street downtown.

For entertainment, the hottest action is found at the Queen Street roller rink.

St. Joseph Island

East of Sault Ste. Marie, Hwy-17 winds along Lake Huron's North Channel waterfront for most the way to Sudbury. Roughly 30 miles (50 km) east, a turnoff heads south to St. Joseph's Island, part of the Manitoulin Island chain. The main sight here lies at the island's south end: **Fort St. Joseph National Historic Park.** When the fort was built by the British in 1796, it was the westernmost outpost of their Canadian empire. At first the fort protected the fur trade; it then served as a base for attacking the Americans during the War of 1812. The Americans burned the fort in 1814, and the park is built around its scenic remains.

At the island's north end is the tiny town of **Richards Landing**; the general store at the dock serves good burgers and soft ice cream.

Bruce Mines to Blind River

Twelve miles (20 km) east of the St. Joseph Island turnoff lies the town of Bruce Mines, founded in 1846 around some copper mines. The earliest settlers were miners from Cornwall in England. An old church south of Hwy-17 has been transformed into the **Bruce Mines Museum** relating the local history (summer only).

The road then runs slightly inland, returning to lakeside a dozen miles later at **Thessalon**, a lumber town just south of the road. Aside from a mini-mall and a supermarket, the main downtown attraction is Lakeside Park and its excellent beach. You can also find a beach at **Carolyn's Motel** (705/842-3330) just west of town. Carolyn's restaurant always has fresh fish on the menu. The island visible on the southern horizon, Drummond Island, belongs to the United States.

The next town is Blind River, so called because the mouth of the river of the same name is all but invisible from the lake. Blind River was originally a lumber town, but today it is home to a major uranium processing center, working ore from Elliot Lake a few miles to the north. The downtown **Village Museum**, besides its gift shop, art gallery, tourist information center, and great view of the lake, offers exhibits on local history, which is mainly logging and mining. The **Old Mill Motel** (705/356-2274) features a small beach.

Hwy-17 east toward Massey continues through flat land with occasional rocky outcrops. Just west of the settlements of Spanish and Serpent River, you have a great view across the North Channel, an arm of Lake Huron, to Manitoulin Island in the distance.

Massey and Manitoulin Island

As you continue east along Hwy-17, the next town, 45 miles (70 km) east of Blind River, is Massey, "The Home of Chutes Provincial Park and Lots of Friendly People," at the confluence of the Sauble and Spanish Rivers. The sole downtown tourist sight is the Massey Area Pioneer Museum, and the place to stay is the **Mohawk Motel** (705/865-2722), with "kozy rooms." East of town, just north of Hwy-17, Chutes Provincial Park offers swimming, camping, picknicking, and several scenic waterfalls along the Sauble River.

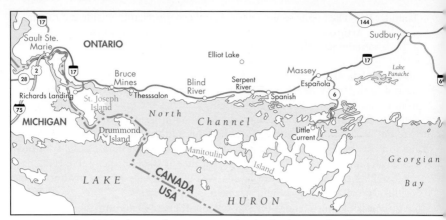

Twenty miles (32 km) east of Massey, 40 miles (64 km) west of Sudbury, Hwy-17 intersects with Hwy-6, which heads south to Espanola, home to the massive E.B. Eddy pulp paper mill, and then continues on to Manitoulin Island, the world's largest freshwater island, set in the northern end of Lake Huron. Manitoulin is a popular vacation spot, ringed with picturesque bays and excellent beaches; try Meldrum Bay, Providence Bay, and South Baymouth.

Approaching Sudbury, Hwy-17 continues over 30 miles (50 km) of rolling hills dotted with a few forests and many small dairy farms.

Sudbury

The clearest sign that you are nearing Sudbury (pop. 93,000) is that the pines disappear and the birches shrink into stunted dwarfs clinging to black rock outcroppings. Sudbury lies in the middle of a geological basin that contains one of the world's largest concentrations of nickel as well as numerous other precious metals. Originally an Ojibwa tribal settlement, the town began to develop after the 1883 arrival of the railway and boomed when nickel and copper were discovered here three years later. Uncontrolled development followed, and mines and processing plants sprang up all over the landscape.

INCO AND THE "BIG NICKEL"

To get an up-close look at the root of Sudbury's economy and ecology, follow Hwy-17 at the western edge of town. Along the busy highway rises the huge smokestack, one of the tallest in the world, that belongs to INCO, one of the world's largest nickel producers. A turn takes you up a denuded hilltop to the famous Big Nickel—exactly what it sounds like, a 30-foot-tall replica of a Canadian nickel—and the entrance to the mine of the same name, which has been turned into a museum (daily 9 AM-5 PM in summer only; $8). Here you can don a hard hat and descend 65 feet into this nonworking exploratory mine. You can also arrange guided tours of the INCO refinery here.

Soon the area was a classic industrial-era ecological disaster. No trees grew for miles around, and a haze of toxic smoke choked the inhabitants, who lived in narrow valleys below the mine heads. In 1950, Sudbury undertook a massive urban renewal and land reclamation project to return at least a vestige of the original beauty and unpolluted air to the area. For older residents, the city has changed dramatically for the better; the air is cleaner, and the city is dotted with trees. First-time visitors still may be shocked by the lack of vegetation and the huge industrial plants that circle the town. Today, Sudbury is Canada's most important mining community, producing 85% of the world's nickel and operating the country's largest copper mine.

As it passes through Sudbury, Hwy-17 turns into a crowded two-lane road with frequent traffic lights and a number of cheap motels. Turn south onto Paris Street to reach the heart of town, where you'll find the Downtown Mall and the Civic Square surrounded by government buildings. If you continue south on Paris Street, it becomes an expressway heading to Ramsey Lake and the attractive part of town. On the lakeshore stands the modern complex of **Science North**, a new science and technology museum featuring many hands-on displays for kids and a 3-D movie theater (daily 9 AM-5 PM; $8).

Among the better Sudbury hotels are the downtown **Best Western Peter Piper Inn**, 151 Larch Street (705/673-7801), and the **Travelodge Hotel Sudbury**, 1401 Paris Street (705/522-1100) south of town. **Pipers Dining Room** in the above-mentioned Best Western is one of the best local restaurants.

For more complete information, contact the Sudbury **visitor center**, 100 Elm Street (705/673-7133).

Sturgeon Falls

East of Sudbury, Hwy-17 enters the narrow Vueve River Valley lined with scraggly pines and picturesque rock outcroppings. Apart from a couple of very small towns—such as **Hagar**, with the **Manor** restaurant and a general store, and Verner, home to the grubby **Trans Canada Hotel**—it's mostly dairy farming country for the 80 miles (130 km) of Hwy-17 between Sudbury and North Bay.

In 1934, North Bay achieved worldwide fame with the birth of the **Dionne Quintuplets,** an event that kept the tabloid mills churning for decades.

The sole sizeable town between Sudbury and North Bay, Sturgeon Falls, 24 miles (38 km) west of North Bay boasts a few cheap motels, restaurants offering "Canadian and Chinese food," and the **Sturgeon River House Museum** for local history.

Approaching North Bay from Sturgeon Falls, 24 miles (38 km) to the west, Hwy-17 runs for a few miles along the north shore of Lake Nipissing, giving you a scenic view over the waters.

North Bay

The hills flatten out and birch trees replace pines as you enter the outskirts of North Bay ("Gateway to Opportunity"), its population of 55,000 making it the largest community between Sudbury and Ottawa. North Bay was originally a fur-trading post that boomed after the 1882 arrival of the railway. Today North Bay is a trade and transportation center, and its fur auctions are among the largest in the world. Many tourists use it as a jumping-off point for wilderness expeditions.

Just southeast of town, Hwy-17 joins Hwy-11, which runs south to Toronto. The road enters a zone of malls, fast-food places, and many motels, including a **Travelodge** (705/495-1133). At the last light there's a **visitor center** and the **Dionne Quintuplets Museum** (open daily, summer only) housed in the little cabin that was their 1934 birthplace (the house was moved from its original site).

The main attractions of downtown North Bay are a couple of malls and *Chief Commanda II Cruises* that leave from the Waterfront Park and follow the old voyageurs' route across Lake Nipissing (reservations required, 705/494-8167). Many of the motels are found on Lakeshore Drive, such as a **Comfort Inn** (705/494-8461) and the moderate **Lincoln Motel** (705/472-3231). The fancy restaurant in town is **Churchill's Prime Rib House** (705/476-7777) at 631 Lakeshore Drive.

The stretch of Hwy-17 between North Bay and Mattawa unreels a nondescript view of scrubby forests broken by the small community of Rutherglen.

Mattawa and the Ottawa River

Approaching Mattawa, Hwy-17 runs through scenic country largely empty of human habitation; the road hugs the river while rolling over steeper hills, through birch and pine forests and by many lakes and ponds. For the next 95 miles (150 km), the road is served by a couple of very small towns and a handful of gas stations and small motels and restaurants that are worth stopping at only from necessity.

The relatively large town of Mattawa ("There Is A Story Here Where Rivers Meet") lies at the confluence of the Ottawa and Mattawa Rivers. The town is home to two passable restaurants, **Draper's Bakery and Cafe** and **Mr. T's Family Restaurant**, as well as the **Mattawa District Museum** housed in a log cabin. Hwy-17 here hits the river downtown at a traffic light, then turns right; a left will take you to the museum, and beyond that the boondocks via Hwy-533. The Mattawa River is the focus of the Samuel de Champlain Provincial Park with campgrounds, canoeing, and hiking trails.

Just over 20 miles (30 km) east of Mattawa, the tiny town of **Deux Rivières** is an entrance to the enormous **Algonquin Provincial Park** lying a few miles to the south. This park encloses 3,000 square miles (7,600 square km) of untouched wilderness with a wide variety of wildlife, dozens of lakes, and hundreds of miles of hiking trails. The main entrance is southwest of Pembroke, via Hwy-60 through the south of the park.

The Ottawa River marks the border between Ontario and Quebec, whose bluffs may be seen across the water.

Except for a few moments when you can tune to CBC, you are largely out of radio range for much of this stretch.

Deep River and Chalk River

The first real town east of Mattawa is Deep River, Canada's first "Atomic Town," a planned community built for employees of the Chalk River labs. The **Diplomat Motor Hotel** (613/584-

1234) here dates to the Cold War era and would be equally at home in the former Soviet Union. The real attraction is the **Laurentian View Dairy Bar** a few blocks west, featuring downhome cooking and homemade ice cream.

Nine miles (14 km) farther east, you enter Chalk River. In 1945, this tiny logging center became the home of the first atomic reactor outside of the United States. Seven years later, Atomic Energy of Canada Ltd., a nuclear research organization, was founded here. At the **Chalk River Laboratories**, you can "tour the atomic age" and clamber around a research reactor (Mon.-Fri., summer only; 613/584-3311, ext. 4428).

Petawawa and Pembroke

Southeast of Chalk River, Hwy-17 crosses the namesake river of the town of Petawawa, home since 1905 to a Canadian Forces base. During WW II, the base was used as an internment camp, and it is now the home of the elite Airborne Unit of the Special Services Force. You can visit two small military museums on the base, but otherwise the area is strictly off limits, as the numerous signs along the road warn.

Wrapping around the eastern edge of Algonquin Provincial Park, Hwy-17 nears Pembroke, another timber town along the Ottawa River, north of the highway. The main sight here is the **Champlain Trail Museum**, with exhibits on local history, at the corner of Angus Campbell and Pembroke Streets. **Casey's Restaurant** at 100 Pembroke Street is the most popular downtown eatery.

Renfrew and Arnprior

Midway between Pembroke and Renfrew, you can see the Ottawa River loop north around Cobden, a little town on Muskrat Lake. Renfrew, another of Ontario's many Scots-founded towns, is now a center of high-tech industry.

Twenty seven miles (42 km) east of Renfrew, Hwy-17 approaches the banks of the Ottawa near Arnprior, another town on the route that began as a lumber center. Arnprior was founded in 1823 by Archibald McNab, a despotic Scottish lord who imported dozens of his countrypeople to the settlement and ruthlessly exploited them. This reign of terror ended when the townsfolk banded together and drove him away. Aside from the **museum** in the old stone post office building, downtown boasts three moderately priced motels.

Six miles (10 km) northwest of Renfrew, Hwy-17 passes **Storyland,** a summer-only amusement park that brings to life 40 different fairy tales.

Just west of the truck-stop town of Antrim, Hwy-17 crosses the Mississippi River, an ambitious stream that is not the "Father of the Waters" but a tributary of the Ottawa River.

Ottawa and Montreal are both covered in Survival Guides, on pages 708-709 and 702-703, respectively.

To Ottawa and Montreal

East of Arnprior, Hwy-17 continues its two-lane trek toward Ottawa with a 90 kph (55 mph) maximum speed posted; occasional passing lanes help you get around the timber trucks. The highway curves gradually southward, away from the Ottawa River through mostly flat woodlands and a few farms, then converts to four lanes for the run into Ottawa.

Hwy-17 is fairly boring between Ottawa and the Quebec border. You're better off taking Hwy-417, called the Queensway within the city, through which it slices. East of Ottawa the route curves south away from the river. Thirty miles (48 km) east of downtown, Hwy-417 loops north again for another 35 miles (56 km), reaching the river at the Quebec border. About a mile before that you'll spot a **tourist information booth**, open in the high season only.

Just across the border in Quebec, take Hwy-40 east toward Montreal. Twenty miles (32 km) later, the highway passes over the Lac de Deux Montagnes (Lake of Two Mountains) at the confluence of the Ottawa and St. Lawrence Rivers. It's another 20 miles (32 km) of industrial and office parks before you reach Montreal proper.

Travelers bound for Canada from the U.S. should be aware of the different rules of the road north of the border. See "Driving in Canada" on page 382 for more.

South to Vermont

From Hwy-10, head east for six miles (10 km), crossing the Pont Champlain and the St. Lawrence River, Canada's most important shipping artery, toward the intersection with Hwy-15. To the left of the road looms the lead-gray spire of La Prairie's Catholic church. Hwy-15 heads due south across a flat landscape whose black soil is dotted with corn and dairy farms. It's a little over 30 miles (48 km) to the Vermont border.

ACROSS VERMONT

Starting at the state's northwestern corner, US-2 crosses the heart of verdant Vermont. From the shores of Lake Champlain, our route winds south to the university town of Burlington, then east past Montpelier, the state capital, all the way to New Hampshire, some 150 miles in all. Paralleled for much of the way by the modern I-89 freeway, US-2 makes a slower but much more diverting alternative to the fast lane, passing through some of the state's most attractive small towns and giving an up-close look at its rural charms, not to mention Vermont's untrammelled mountains, forests, lakes, and rivers.

Between Vermont and the Canadian border, US-2 nips briefly and uneventfully across a corner of New York State, crossing the international border on the I-87 freeway between the U.S. and Quebec.

Lake Champlain Islands

After its brief jaunt across New York from the Canadian border, US-2 soars on a new concrete bridge over the northernmost point of Lake Champlain and enters Vermont on the Alburg Peninsula. Pancake flat and covered with cows, this is the least attractive part of the Lake Champlain region, which stretches south for over 25 miles and includes a series of islands. The islands themselves are very pretty to drive across, with the Adirondacks rising up to the west and the Green Mountains to the south and east, but there's not a lot to do; far more cows than people populate the route, and tractors clog the road, flinging clods of mud and manure (here pronounced "man-OO-ah") with abandon.

At the south tip of the peninsula sits the town of **South Alburg**, where **Cathy's Place** is an inexpensive local favorite restaurant (summer only). A turn west onto Hwy-129 leads to Isle La Motte, home of the 1666 first French settlement in Vermont. The site is now occupied by **Saint Ann's Shrine**, a popular pilgrimage destination featuring daily outdoor masses in summer and a granite statue of the explorer Samuel de Champlain.

Vermont has completely banned roadside advertising, replacing billboards with standardized signs symbolizing lodging, food, recreation, and other services available nearby.

Five miles and two bridges south of South Alburg, the town of **North Hero** (pop. 502) has a gas station, a stone courthouse, and a number of quietly luxurious vacation homes dating from the early decades of the 20th century. A mile south of town, **Shore Acres Resort** (802/372-8722) offers moderately priced lakeside rooms and a restaurant famed for its chocolate pie.

If it's dark or if you're in a hurry, the I-89 freeway is a much faster alternative to US-2 between Burlington and Montreal.

A mile north of the town of Grand Isle stands the **Hyde Log Cabin** (Wed.-Sun. 11 AM-5 PM in summer; $1), considered by many to be the country's oldest log cabin, dating from 1783. The interior contains period furnishings and exhibits on frontier life.

ETHAN ALLEN HOMESTEAD TRUST

Burlington was the home of **Dr. Nelson Jackson,** who in 1902 became the first person to cross the country by automobile.

In 1981, the people of Burlington elected one of America's few socialist mayors, **Bernie Sanders.** He was reelected three times and now is a Congressman from the "People's Republic" of Vermont.

Seven miles and another bridge to the south, the town of Grand Isle (pop. 1,642) ambitiously claims to be "The Beauty Spot of Vermont." A well-marked turn leads to tiny **Grand Isle State Park,** on the shores of the lake.

Winooski

From the Lake Champlain Islands, US-2 runs on a low-level causeway, rejoing the mainland at the entrance to **Sandbar State Park,** set in a forest with picnic tables and bathing areas and surrounded by sprawling marshes on either side. From here US-2 heads east through rolling hills, linking up with the I-89 freeway for the fast route into Burlington, 10 miles to the south.

If you have time, or an abiding interest in America's industrial heritage, consider making the detour just north of Burlington to Winooski, an old factory town now focusing on the totally restored Champlain Mill, downtown at 1 Main Street. This former woolen mill now houses over 30 specialty shops and restaurants, and the rest of town provides a blue-collar balance to Burlington's upscale airs.

Another reason to visit is to tour the restored farm of Vermont patriot Ethan Allen, preserved as the **Ethan Allen Homestead** (Mon.-Sat. 10 AM-5 PM, Sunday 1-5 PM in summer; $3.50) along Hwy-127 two miles northeast of Winooski.

Burlington

After the original French settlers were ejected from the Lake Champlain region in 1760 at the end of the French and Indian Wars, English settlers soon arrived, and Burlington was chartered in 1763. The area was abandoned during the Revolutionary War; afterward Ethan Allen, leader of the famous "Green Mountain Boys" band of guerrillas, and his brothers were granted huge tracts of land along the eastern shore of Lake Champlain.

The Allen brothers were ambitious: not only did they encourage settlement and industry in Burlington, but in 1791 they founded the University of Vermont here. The town boomed, aided by its strategic position on Lake Champlain, the quickest route between New York's Hudson River and Montreal. Burlington quickly became the center of Vermont industry, finance, education, and culture—a position it has held ever since.

US-2 passes right through the center of Burlington (pop. 39,100), first as Winooski Avenue in the north but later as Main Street, lined by motels and restaurants on the outskirts but eventually crossing the lively, sprawling campus of the **University of Vermont.** Downtown Burlington offers all the delights of a typical college town: bookstores, bars, ethnic food, and trendy but inexpensive shopping. At the center of town is **Church Street Marketplace,** a four-block pedestrian mall with two good bookstores, numerous cafes, and restaurants usually crammed with students. For food, the Chinese **Five Spice Cafe** (175 Church Street) and the **Daily**

Planet (on Center Street just east of the Marketplace), featuring pastas and Latin American dishes, are two local favorites.

Main Street continues four blocks west to Lake Champlain, where the **Burlington Waterfront Park** has a strollable boardwalk linking up with **Battery Park**, home to a collection of cannons pointing menacingly across the lake. In 1812, these cannons were used against British warships that bombarded the town.

On campus, the **Robert Hull Fleming Museum** (Tues.-Fri. 9 AM-4 PM, Saturday and Sunday 1-5 PM; donations) on Colchester Avenue on the north side of campus is the main visitor attraction, with a small but wide-ranging collection of fine and applied arts from ancient Egypt to the present.

Williston and Richmond

Between Burlington and Montpelier, US-2 follows the Winooski River valley, lined with dairy farms. For most of this journey, the road parallels the less-than-attractive concrete expanse of I-89. However, a few sights make the two-lane route preferable.

The first of these, Williston (pop. 4,887), sits roughly 10 miles east of Burlington, and less than a mile north of the freeway. Though on the large size by local standards, Williston is a classic northern New England town, its streets lined by towering maple trees and white clapboard houses.

A mile southeast of Williston, on the other side of the I-89 freeway, the country town of Richmond is home of the unique **Old Round Church**. Turn at the town's only stoplight and drive a half-mile south, where this 16-sided, two-story, white clapboard structure stands just east of the road. The church was built in 1813, the communal effort of five different Protestant denominations. They eventually feud-

---

THE SHELBURNE MUSEUM

Downtown Burlington's attractions are mainly mercantile; for more enlightening fare, head south on Union Street (US-7) five miles to the town of Shelburne. This is the home of the Shelburne Museum (daily 10 AM-5 PM, mid-May to mid-Oct. only; $15), an overwhelming agglomeration of historic buildings and artifacts hauled here from all over New England. Besides the 40-odd immaculately presented historic structures, the collection includes an original Lake Champlain paddle wheeler, a train, a full-sized model circus, gardens, and an enormous collection of European and American paintings and decorative arts. The core of the Shelburne collection was amassed by a rich and indefatigable collector, Electra Havemeyer Webb.

North of Waterbury Junction on Hwy-100, the ski resort of **Stowe** was built by the musical Von Trapp family, whose escape from the Nazis inspired *The Sound of Music.*

ed, of course, and the structure lapsed into civic use, becoming the town hall. Today it is used as a meetinghouse, and on summer weekends the local historical society gives guided tours.

Waterbury Junction: Ben & Jerry's

Though it's known for beautiful mountains and the brilliant fall color of its hardwood forests, Vermont's number one tourist attraction is none other than **Ben & Jerry's Ice Cream Factory,** a kind of hippie Disneyland in Waterbury Junction, on the hillside to the left of Hwy-100. Their brightly painted factory includes a number of large cartoonish artifacts strewn outside to play on—weird vehicles, whimsical picnic tables, and the like. Ben & Jerry began making its ultra-rich ice cream in 1978; today the company and its franchises sell its products across the country and abroad. The company is also famous for its activism, donating a percentage of its profits to philanthropies supporting "progressive social change."

Don't confuse Waterbury Junction, birthplace of Ben & Jerry's, with Waterbury, a satellite community of Montpelier with some large state government office buildings, located just *south* of the I-89 freeway. Waterbury Junction is about 1.5 miles north of Waterbury.

Running south from Waterbury, **Route 100** travels through the heart of the Green Mountains all the way south to Massachusetts, and is one of the state's most popular "leaf-peeping" routes. See the Appalachian Trail route on page 244 for more.

You can tour the factory (daily 9 AM-5 PM; $1; 802/244-TOUR for information), although production is halted on Sunday, holidays, and company celebration days—when you get a video presentation. The premises also feature a store selling gifts "with a socially responsible mission" and the less politically correct Scoop Shop featuring all 34 of Ben & Jerry's ice cream and frozen yogurt flavors. Outside are many picnic tables where you can enjoy the ice cream and a view over the valley.

Camp Meade

On US-2 just west of Middlesex stands Camp Meade, a Depression-era Civilian Conservation Corps camp that has been turned into a popular restaurant and motel (802/223-5537). It is also a shrine to the United States Armed Forces. A fighter plane, a tank, and military trucks adorn the grounds, a gift store sells army surplus, and the cabins are named after luminaries such as General Patton and Col. Oliver North. The restaurant sports camouflage tablecloths and a bomb suspended from the rafters. Local military enthusiasts pack the place for Sunday brunch.

Montpelier

The smallest capital in the country, Vermont's Montpelier (pop. 8,200) was settled in 1787 and named after a town in France. It was designated the state capital in 1805. Today Montpelier's economy is based around government, insurance, and tourism.

Your arrival in Montpelier is foretold by the gold dome of the capitol building hovering in the valley ahead. Constrained by the Winooski River on one side and the narrow valley on the other, Montpelier is so compact that you can park your car and find all the sights within a 10-minute walking distance. Road hogs beware: pedestrians rule in Montpelier; you must stop when they're traversing the designated crosswalks. A quick poll of Main Street shops reveals the cosmopolitan nature of the town. You'll find bookstores, coffee bars, bagel shops, and wine merchants, as well as multiple combinations of the same.

The north side of State Street opens up into a broad lawn fronting the **State Capitol,** the focal point of the People's Republic of Vermont (the state is one of the few with a thriving left-wing political movement). The original building was opened in 1808; it burned in 1859, whereupon the current, more heroic structure was erected from local granite. The statue on the dome represents Ceres, the goddess of agriculture; Doric columns hide a Revolutionary War cannon and a statue of Ethan Allen. The state legislature is only in session from January to April—being a Vermont politician is a part-time job; the rest of the year they go back to being farmers, businesswomen, and so on—but you can tour the building year-round (Mon.-Fri. 8 AM-4 PM; guided tours available). Atop the hill behind the capitol lies **Hubbard State Park,** a favorite rest and recreation spot for locals.

Near the courthouse is the **Vermont Historical Society Museum** (Tues.-Sat. 9 AM-4:30 PM, Sunday noon-4 PM) in a state office building. The museum's permanent displays illustrate Vermont's history, and you also find lots of 19th-century furniture and a small bookstore and gift shop.

Rising up a hill off State Street a few blocks west of the capitol, the **Green Mountain Cemetery** is filled with impressive granite monuments. Many of these were carved by the immigrant stonecutters of nearby Barre for their own family plots.

Montpelier residents take their eating seriously. Two of their favorite restaurants are the nouvelle American **Tubbs Restaurant,** housed in a converted jail, and its cheaper offshoot, the **Elm Street Cafe,** both found on Elm Street just off State Street. Montpelier fast food means bagels, Ben & Jerry's ice cream, and breads from **Manghis' Bakery** at 28 School Street. For upscale lodgings in period surroundings, the only place to go is **The Inn at Montpelier** (802/223-2727), two renovated 19th-century homes that have been joined into one hotel. The best moderate choice is the **Econo Lodge** (802/223-5258) on Hwy-12 south of the river.

North of Montpelier, watch sap being turned into delicious maple syrup at the **Morse Farm and Sugarhouse,** three miles from the capitol dome along Main Street and County Road.

Plainfield

Plainfield is where the 1960s live. This tiny town boasts a bookstore, a fly-fishing shop, and the **Maple Valley Country Store/Deli/Cafe/Pizzeria/Ice Cream Parlor,** the local hangout (tie-dye welcome). Just west of town is the campus of **Goddard College,** one of the nation's most renowned counter-cultural institutes of higher learning. Hitchhikers are common on US-2 between Montpelier and Plainfield.

Montpelier thrived off the granite quarries of the nearby town of Barre. The **Rock of Ages quarry** (daily 8:30 AM-5 PM in summer; free; 802/476-3119), four miles southeast of Barre off I-89 exit 6, is one of the world's largest. The quarries brought many skilled Scottish and Italian stonecutters to the area.

Danville

Ten miles east of Plainfield, US-2 finally turns north away from the **Winooski River,** a prime trout fishery, which it follows all the way from Lake Champlain. Leaving the Winooski River valley, US-2 hits **West Danville,** a summer community on the edge of Joe's Pond, a small lake ringed by vacation cabins. At the center of town, at the junction of US-2 and Hwy-15, you'll see a covered bridge and Hastings Store, the local emporium.

The next place you'll pass is Danville, yet another picture-postcard Vermont town, set on a hill surrounded by farms. The center of Danville is a classic New England village green, with a general store and the customary churches. Just off the green you'll find the headquarters of the **American Society of Dowsers** (Mon.-Fri. 9 AM-4:30 PM), whose members have refined their talents for finding water or mineral deposits using a wooden dowsing rod. The building houses a small exhibit on the history and practice of the art and a shop where you can buy dowsing books and dowsing rods.

The **Danville Creamery Restaurant**, right downtown (closed Sunday and Monday), is the place to eat.

St. Johnsbury

In the 19th century, the economy of St. Johnsbury (pop. 7,600) was based on maple products and the manufacture of platform scales—Fairbanks Scales, founded by the inventor of platform scales, still operates a plant east of town. Today it is northeast Vermont's commercial center, with four- and five-story brick buildings and a few 1960s frills. On the other side of the river, follow the signs for US-2. Turn right onto the main commercial street, passing **Northern Lights Bookstore and Cafe**, and then left on Eastern Avenue up to Main Street, where you take a left at the statue. This is the rich section of town, with large brick churches and stately 19th-century mansions.

Right at the intersection stands the **St. Johnsbury Athenaeum, Art Gallery and Public Library** (Mon.-Fri. 10 AM-5:30 PM) in a red-brick 1871 building. The building houses a surprisingly good collection of 19th-century paintings, the jewel of which is Albert Bierstadt's *Domes of Yosemite*. At the corner of Main and Prospect Streets, you'll find the 1890 **Fairbanks Museum and Planetarium** (Mon.-Sat. 10 AM-6 PM, Sunday 1-5 PM), a charming 19th-century-style center of knowledge. Two menacing stuffed bears greet visitors at the entrance. Under a vaulted wooden roof, the main two-story gallery exhibits a musty natural history collection in glass cases. The newer attractions include the Northern New England Weather Center and a planetarium.

St. Johnsbury's eating attractions include **Hilltopper Restaurant**, across the street from the Atheneum, and **Miss Vermont Diner** downtown. For motels, try the **Fairbanks Motor Inn** (802/748-5666) or **Aime's Motel** (802/748-3194), both on US-2 east of town.

Making a scenic alternative to the I-93 freeway, east from St. Johnsbury US-2 passes over the Memorial Bridge (1943) spanning the Passumpsic River. One mile east of the bridge you'll find the **Maple Grove Farms** complex based around an old mill building. Highlights include the maple museum and the "world's largest maple candy factory" (tours Mon.-Fri. 8 AM-4:30 PM, May-Oct.); the factory store is open year-round. Vermont is in the heart of maple sugaring territory, which runs all the way from Maine to Michigan.

Concord and Lunenburg

Approaching the New Hampshire border, US-2 heads across rolling rocky hills covered with forests, largely pine and birch, with a few scattered farms. This corner of the state, a recreational paradise of hills and lakes and few year-round residents, is known as the "Northeast Kingdom." The road drops down into the narrow, pastoral valley of the Moose River before reaching Concord, which features a country store and a small historical society. Concord was the home of the **First Normal School**, America's first teachers' academy, founded in 1823.

Fifteen miles east of Concord, along the banks of the broad Connecticut River, Lunenburg is a perfect New England village of white clapboard houses clustered around a church—Vermont specializes in this species of quaintness.

From Lunenburg, you can follow US-2 to the northeast, or take a highly recommended detour across the Connecticut River on a covered bridge, then proceed north along Hwy-135, rejoining US-2 at Lancaster.

ACROSS NEW HAMPSHIRE

Crossing the broad Connecticut River, which forms Vermont's 200-mile-long border with New Hampshire, US-2 makes a short but scenic run across the state. From the historic commercial center of Lancaster, just east of the state border, US-2 winds along the wide valley of the Israel River before reaching Jefferson, home to two of the state's biggest tourist traps. Continuing east, US-2 curves around the northern flank of towering Mount Washington and the rugged White Mountains, an area rich in outdoor recreation and scenic splendor. At Gorham, US-2 reaches the valley of the Androscoggin River, which it follows east into Maine.

Your welcome to New Hampshire is a sign—Brake for Moose—that announces that there have been over 200 car-moose collisions to date. Apparently moose are hard to see at night, because headlights shine through the legs, rather than on the body, of this towering beast.

Lancaster

Crossing over the Connecticut River from Vermont, you enter the outskirts of Lancaster (pop. 3,550), a market town that was first settled in 1764. US-2 becomes Main Street through Lancaster, lined with dozens of attractive old homes and churches, a cemetery on a knoll to the north, and, on the south side, a heroic red-brick courthouse that dates from 1887. At the junction of US-2 and US-3 at the west side of town stands the **Lancaster Historical Society.**

Two miles south of Lancaster via US-3, the mountaintop estate of the man who saved New Hampshire's forests from the lumber industry has been preserved as **John Wingate Weeks Historic Site** (Wed.-Sun. 10 AM-6 PM in summer only; $2.50), complete with a tourable mansion and an observation tower giving grand views of Mount Washington and Vermont's Green Mountains.

Just west of Lancaster, the broad **Connecticut River** flows south all the way to Long Island Sound. To the north of Lancaster it is a well-known trout stream; smallmouth bass and brown trout are abundant. If you weren't thrilled by the modern bridge that carries US-2 just upstream from Lancaster, head south of downtown on Hwy-135 five miles to an impressive old **covered bridge** that spans the Connecticut River and meets US-2 in the Vermont town of Lunenburg.

There are moderately priced motels on US-2 east of town, and downtown you'll find the **Lancaster Diner** and the **Lancaster Motor Inn** (603/788-4921).

Jefferson

High above the Israel River on the flanks of the White Mountains, the small resort town of Jefferson (pop. 965) is home to two big tourist draws. For the truly masochistic parent, about a mile west of Jefferson is **Santa's Village** (daily 9:30 AM-7 PM, summer only; $12, under age 4 free), with candy canes looming threateningly at the entrance, a Ferris wheel, a roller coaster, the Yule Log Flume, and, of course, Santa himself. Just east of town is **Six Gun City** (daily 9 AM-6 PM, summer only; $9.25), an erstaz Wild West town featuring cowboy skits ("Come on out, you varmints!"), frontier shows, a carriage museum, and a water slide.

Two accommodations in town deserve mention. The friendly **Applebrook B&B** (800/545-6504; $45-60 for a double or $20 per person in the seven-bed dorm) offers full Victorian splendor gilded with summer raspberries and a hot tub under the stars. **Jefferson Inn** (800/729-7908; $44-70 for a double, suites from $65) has a Dutch- and German-speaking innkeeper, panoramic views, and a swimming pond.

East of Jefferson the road ascends, the valley narrows, and the scenery becomes more spectacular with the Presidential Range looming to the south.

A roadside marker along US-2 just west of Jefferson commemorates the birth nearby of inventor **Thaddeus Lowe,** *who pioneered balloon aviation during the Civil War.*

Gorham

Gorham (pop. 3,173), incorporated in 1836, was another early tourist town; its boom began after the railroad came through in 1851. Tourism is still the main industry, from the summer tourists to the autumn "leaf-peepers" to the winter skiers. (Nobody visits much during the early spring mud season.) There is a **visitor center** on Main Street (US-2), and the **Gorham Historical Society** (Monday, Wednesday, and Friday 1-5 PM; donations) stands in an old depot at 25 Railroad Street, a half-block off Main Street.

For lunch and dinner try **Wilfred's**, specializing in bounteous and inexpensive turkey dinners; **Welch's Restaurant** serves the most popular breakfast. The **Royalty Inn** (603/466-3312), 130 Main Street, is a good full-service motel with a large health club next door.

Just east of Gorham, the road passes through a famous grove of birch trees. Here you find the pleasant **Town & Country Motor Inn** (603/466-3315) with some spa and resort facilities, such as saunas and a golf course. This is also where the **Appalachian Trail**, which runs from Maine's Mount Katahdin to northern Georgia, crosses US-2.

Mount Washington marks the start of this book's Appalachian Trail route, which follows along these landmark mountains all the way south to Atlanta. See page 228 for more.

ACROSS MAINE

Following the Androscoggin River across the New Hampshire border, US-2 enters Maine at the forested eastern flank of the White Mountains. Winding east along the river, the route passes through alternating mountain resorts and milltowns, starting at sedate Bethel and ending up 135 miles later at Bangor, once one of the wildest lumber towns in the country. From Bangor the route veers south toward the coast, hitting the Atlantic Ocean at beautiful Acadia National Park.

Bethel

At the far west end of its run across Maine, US-2 winds along the south bank of the Androscoggin River, through dense pine and birch forests of the White Mountain National Forest. Ten miles east of the border, along a placid stretch of the Androscoggin, Bethel (pop. 2,329) was first settled in 1774, and at the tail end of the Revolutionary War the town, then named Sudbury, suffered the last Indian raid inflicted on New England. In 1836, Gould Academy, one of Maine's oldest prep schools, was established here. Information on Bethel's many other well-preserved old buildings can be had from the circa 1813 **Moses Mason House**, 15 Broad Street, which doubles as a small museum (Mon.-Fri. 10 AM-4 PM; $2).

After the railroads came through, Bethel quickly became a center for White Mountain area tourism. The **Bethel Inn and Country Club** (207/824-2175 or 800/654-0125), founded in 1913, was one of New England's early health and fitness resorts and, surrounded by an 18-hole golf course, continues that tradition today. For upscale lodging and dining, this is the place to go. The **Red Top Restaurant** right downtown on US-2 is the polar opposite; try the hash. The **River View Motel** (207/824-2808), on the east side of Bethel at the junction of US-2 and Hwy-26, is the moderate lodging choice.

For outdoor enthusiasts, the **Sunday River Ski Area** (800/543-2SKI), six miles east of town, draws thousands of visitors to the area for skiing in winter and hiking and mountain biking in summer.

Just east of the Maine border, 10 miles west of Bethel, a sign marks a turn south from US-2 onto Hwy-113 toward **Evans Notch.** This narrow, mostly gravel road, which is posted Not Maintained For Winter Travel, runs along the Wild and Cold Rivers up to a stunningly scenic mountain pass.

From US-2 at Bethel, Hwy-26 runs southeast toward Portland and the coast, passing through the spa town of Poland Spring and the world's last remaining intact Shaker community at Sabbathday Lake, where a small museum gives tours (Mon.-Sat. 10 AM-4 PM in summer; $5).

the Shaker Museum at Sabbathday Lake

Rumford

US-2 continues along the north bank of the Androscoggin River for 20 miles—there is a nice picnic area with a covered bridge about 10 miles east of Bethel—before reaching Rumford (pop. 7,078), a grungy mill town with low brick buildings and a downscale downtown along the river. Somewhere beneath the heavy industry lie the Androscoggin Falls, which provided the hydropower that led to the original settlement of the town. Now, enormous steam-puffing smokestacks loom in the valley around the Boise Cascade Coated Paper Division—New England's largest paper mill—surrounded by huge piles of logs and wood residue. You may wish to leave town as quickly as possible, but the road winds around the valley—the Androscoggin makes an oxbow—passing some small malls and cheap motels before emerging into the countryside again.

Across the river a mile east of downtown Rumford, you enter Mexico, which is actually a gritty bedroom suburb for the mill workers. There is nothing Mexican about it except the name. The place to eat, if only for the atmosphere, is the Mexico Chicken Coop and Restaurant.

Rumford's main claim to fame is as the birthplace of **Edmund Muskie,** *governor, U.S. senator, and vice-presidential and presidential candidate in 1968 and 1972 respectively.*

Dixfield

Five miles east of Mexico, in the heart of the broad valley of the Androscoggin River, Dixfield (pop. 2,574) is a small town with a mild aura of the 1960s. The **Village Restaurant and Bakery** is the main meeting place, and you can also eat at the **Old Opera House Restaurant,** housed inside—what else—an old opera house.

At a junction in Dixfield, a single sign points the way toward Peru and Mexico. Paris, Leeds, Canton, Madrid, Belgrade, and Rome are also within 30 miles—only in America!

East of Dixfield toward Farmington, US-2 passes through wilder country, with excellent views of the tree-covered White Mountains rising to the west. A few scattered trailers and tar paper shacks mark the outskirts of northern Appalachia.

Midway between Dixfield and Farmington, the town of Wilton is home to famous shoemaker **G. H. Bass Company.**

Farmington

Like many other northern Maine towns, Farmington (pop. 4,200) was first settled by soldiers who fought in the Revolutionary War. The rolling hills that surround it still hold a few farms and orchards, but as elsewhere the economy revolves around trees—both as tourist fodder during the fall color sweeps, and as pulp for paper mills. There's not a lot worth stopping for, though the University of Maine at Farmington has an **art gallery** (Sun.-Thurs. noon-4 PM; free) at 102 Main Street downtown, showing local artists.

East of Farmington, US-2 runs through almost 20 miles of forests and farms alongside the Sandy River. At **Norridgewock**, first settled by French Jesuits in 1688, you reach the broad Kennebec River, which US-2 follows five miles east into Skowhegan.

Skowhegan

Crossing the Kennebec River on US-2, you enter Skowhegan (pop. 8,725). First settled in 1771 on an island in the Kennebec River, this mid-sized mill town was also the birthplace of the late Margaret Chase Smith, one of Maine's most renowned politicians and a 36-year veteran of the U.S. House and Senate. Her home is now the **Margaret Chase Smith Library Center** (Mon.-Fri. 10 AM-4 PM; donations) and includes a museum of her life and a conference center. The **Skowhegan History House** (Tues.-Fri. 1-5 PM in summer only; donations), 40 Elm Street, is a brick Greek revival structure with exhibits on town history. The **Old Mill Pub Restaurant** (closed Sunday) on Water Street serves inexpensive sandwiches and pasta dishes. The Skowhegan Art Colony outside of town is one of the nation's most renowned summer art schools.

East of Skowhegan, US-2 veers away from the river across low, rolling hills covered with pine and birch forests, the only signs of habitation a few trailers and scraggly farms.

Newport

Midway across the state, at the point where two-lane US-2 joins the high-speed I-95 freeway, Newport (pop. 3,036) is known as "The Hub of Maine." Like most other towns that play up their connections to the rest of the world, Newport is not really a place to linger, but it does have the **Collins Corner Family Restaurant** and the **Log Cabin Diner** on US-2, as well as a Wal-Mart and the usual array of fast food and cheap motels.

Between Newport and Bangor, 20 miles to the east, there's no good reason to follow old US-2; you may as well race across on I-95.

Bangor

Built on the banks of the Penobscot River, Bangor (pop. 33,200) is the largest town in northern Maine. This site was an important rendezvous for local tribes, who called it Kendusbeag, or "eel-catching place." In 1604 Samuel de Champlain sailed up the Penobscot River as far as Treats Falls here, but long-term settlement did not begin until 1769. Throughout the next century, Bangor was the most important lumber town of the eastern U.S.; it also developed into a ship-building center, and Bangor's lumber circled the globe. A large sector of the population was devoted to providing amusement for the loggers and sailors who would arrive in town with free time and fat wallets. In a riverside neighborhood called the Devil's Half Acre, dozens of bars, bordellos, and gambling dens competed to empty the men's pockets.

Nineteenth-century Bangor was as wide open as any town in the Wild West, but traces of rougher days have all but disappeared, though modern Bangor is still a center for the lumber industry: coming into town across the Penobscot River, you'll turn right onto Main Street and see a 31-foot statue of **Paul Bunyan**. The compact business center, mostly red-brick 19th-century buildings interspersed with church spires, lies a few blocks to the east of Paul Bunyan.

The **Bangor Historical Society** (Mon.-Fri. noon-4 PM; $2), in a circa 1836 Greek revival mansion at 159 Union Street, has the usual range of exhibits, furnishings, and paintings reflecting 19th-century life. Another place worth checking out is the **Cole Land Transportation Museum** (daily 9 AM-5 PM May-Nov.; $2), 405 Perry

---

In the town of Rangeley, an hour northwest of Farmington via Hwy-4, the **Wilhelm Reich Museum** (Tues.-Sun. 1-5 PM in July and August; $5; 207/864-3443) preserves the flat-roofed final home and tomb of the iconoclastic psychoanalyst, who died in 1957.

In 1976, the Kennebec River at Skowhegan was the site of the last log drive in Maine.

On Rte-201 just north of US-2 at Skowhegan, the **Skowhegan Indian,** a 62-foot statue billed as the "largest wooden Indian in the world," stands above the Kennebec River.

In August, Skowhegan is home to the **Maine State Fair.** Celebrated annually since 1818, it is one of the oldest in the country.

Road, which displays over 200 historic vehicles, from wooden wagons to modern 18-wheelers.

For a good quick bite to eat, try the **Bagel Shop**, a kosher restaurant in the heart of downtown Bangor at 1 Main Street. There are also a couple of inexpensive Indian places nearby. The pick of area lodgings is the **Phenix Inn** (207/947-3850), a restored 1873 hotel at 20 Westmarket Square downtown. The national chains have their motels out on US-2 just beyond the airport west of town, which is where the fast food is, too.

The area around Bangor is home to best-selling horror writer **Stephen King.**

Fifteen miles north of Ellsworth, the **Lucerne Inn** *is a 19th-century mansion converted into a hotel and restaurant surrounded by a golf course set on the slopes of a stunningly beautiful valley.*

Ellsworth

Ellsworth, chartered in 1763, began as a lumber town with its own opera house, but now is a thriving commercial center, located southeast of Bangor at the junction of Hwy-3 and busy old US-1. Downtown is lots of red brick and little excitement—all the action is out by the malls—but is worth a visit if only for a slice of pie at **Dick's**, a diner at 42 Main Street.

South of Ellsworth, Hwy-3 is the mainland's connection to **Mount Desert Island.** North of the bridge to the island, the land is flat and the roadside along Hwy-3 is heavily commercialized. Here the road enters mall country, with a Wal-Mart, numerous service stations, motels, and fast-food outlets. Following all that are a large **miniature golf** course and the private **Acadia Zoo.** The **Hancock County/Bar Harbor Airport** (car rentals and commercial flights) lies next to lobster pounds and cheap motels catching the Mount Desert overflow.

North of the cove, the road turns inland for seven miles, passing a miniature golf course, before emerging at the bridge to the mainland. This end of the island is relatively flat, forested, and covered with ponds and marshes. Just before the bridge,

MOUNT DESERT ISLAND

Mount Desert Island is an idyllic 11- by 14-mile chunk of forest-covered mountains and rocky inlets just off the coast of Maine. The island was first settled by the Penobscot people and was not explored by Europeans until 1609, when Samuel de Champlain named it Île de Monts Déserts and claimed it for France; the English razed the French settlement in 1613. In 1844, the Hudson River School's Thomas Cole painted a stunning series of scenes of Mount Desert. The island soon became a tourist attraction/summer playground for elite Eastern families, and many of the 19th-century elite built elegant "cottages" here, largely around Bar Harbor.

In 1916, the Mount Desert summer colony, led by the Pulitzer and Rockefeller families, donated most of the island's land to the federal government, to establish Acadia National Park. Unfortunately, a 1947 forest fire destroyed many of Bar Harbor's mansions.

you pass the entrance to the **Mount Desert Oceanarium** (daily 9 AM-5 PM, May 15-Oct. 15), where you can admire the harbor seals and visit the Maine Lobster Museum. Just beyond stands the **Island Information Center** and the turnoff to the left of Hwy-102 and Hwy-198, heading to Southwest and Northeast Harbors, respectively. Hwy-3 heads north over the short bridge and onto the mainland.

At 1,532 feet, **Cadillac Mountain** on Mount Desert Island is the highest point on the Eastern Seaboard of North America. It's also the namesake of the classy automobile marque.

Bar Harbor

Approaching Bar Harbor, Hwy-3 runs along Frenchman Bay, which borders the northeast corner of the island. Many of the national motel chains, including Holiday Inn and Marriott, have outposts along this stretch of Hwy-3. You also pass the terminus for the **ferry** to Yarmouth, Nova Scotia (800/341-7981), a six-hour cruise that will save you hours of driving time if you are continuing east. (The boats also turn into casinos when they reach international waters.) A half-mile out of Bar Harbor, you pass the College of the Atlantic, on the grounds of which you'll find the **Natural History Museum** (June-August). Housed in a granite summer "cottage," the museum offers exhibits and lectures on the region's flora, fauna, and geology.

The town of Bar Harbor (pop. 4,400), the largest on Mount Desert Island, has turned to catering to the less well-heeled visitor as the "Old Money" has retreated to more discreet settlements to the west, such as Northeast Harbor—a.k.a. "Philadelphia on the

Rocks." The town's principal thoroughfares, lined with gift shops, hotels, restaurants, and outfitters, are Main Street, Cottage Street, and West Street, which runs along the waterfront. The West Street pier is home to the **Lobster Hatchery** (daily 9 AM-5 PM in summer only), where you can see exhibits on the popular crustacean's life cycle. Lobsters occupy the center of the island's culinary life, and two places to sample them are **Fisherman's Landing** at 35 West Street, and the **Island Chowder House** at 38 Cottage Street.

If you are visiting during the summer high season, reserve your lodging well in advance; despite the dozens of motels and B&Bs here, the town is often booked solid. Rates vary widely depending on the season; lodgings in July and August may cost almost twice as much as in winter. Some of the more reasonable accommodations include the **Bar Harbor Motor Inn** (207/288-3351), next to the West Street pier, and the **Wonder View Motor Lodge** (207/288-3358) on Hwy-3 northwest of town. **The Colony** (207/288-3383), just beyond Hulls Cove, is an austerely classic bungalow resort.

Acadia National Park

Mount Desert Island's natural glories have been preserved by the establishment of Acadia National Park, occupying 41,634 acres of the island's most scenic areas. In

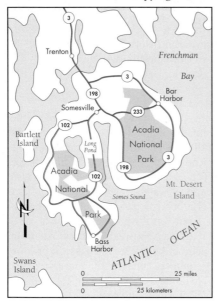

the summer, thousands flock to the park's hiking trails, which wind among the beautiful inland lakes and mountains. The narrow **Park Loop Road** (large campers and trailers prohibited) circles the eastern side of the park and passes the Thunder Hole tidal cavern and Sand Beach, one of the few sandy beaches in Maine.

Three miles north of Bar Harbor, on the edge of Hulls Cove, you'll see on the left the main **Acadia National Park Visitors Center** (daily 8 AM-4:30 April-Oct., till 6 PM July-Aug.; 207/288-3338), a good place to start a tour of the park. For information in advance, write P.O. Box 177, Bar Harbor, ME 04609. The visitor center marks the entrance to Park Loop Road.

US-20:
PORTLAND TO
PROVINCETOWN

US-20: PORTLAND TO PROVINCETOWN

From the wide-open spaces of the West to the dense urban jungles of the East, this route offers the longest and most involved road trip in the book. Connecting an exceedingly diverse range of places and totaling over 3,200 miles—many more if you count all the potential detours, side trips, and parallel routes—US-20 takes in a little of everything during its two-lane trek from Oregon's rugged coast to the glorious sea and sand of Cape Cod. Superlative sights include two wonders of the world, New York's Niagara Falls and Wyoming's Yellowstone National Park; the great cities of Boston and Chicago; and two halls of fame, one in Cleveland celebrating rock 'n' roll, the other in Cooperstown idolizing the American pastime, baseball. Odd museums, classic diners, idyllic towns, and post-industrial decay—you'll find it all along this great cross-country highway.

This route also offers unprecedented opportunities for following in the footsteps of pilgrims and pioneers. Starting in the West, the route parallels, and in places runs right on top of, the broad path that formed the Oregon Trail. The landscape across Oregon, Idaho, and Wyoming is still as lonesome as it was 150 years ago when pioneer families followed this one-way route to the promised lands of the Pacific coast. Midway across the country you can visit two notable monuments, Mount Rushmore and Carhenge; you also can test the wisdom of Walt Whitman, who wrote, "While I know the standard claim is that Yosemite, Niagara Falls, the upper Yellowstone and the like afford the greatest natural shows, I am not so sure but the Prairies and Plains last longer, fill the aesthetic sense fuller, precede all the rest and make North America's characteristic landscape." Drive across the Sand

Hills of northern Nebraska on your way past Iowa's "Field of Dreams," and see for yourself what's so great about the Great Plains.

Crossing the Mississippi River at Dubuque, which along with Galena on the Illinois side are two of the oldest settlements of what was once the nation's western frontier, US-20 stops off for a look at Chicago before winding east through the newly resurgent, former "Rust Belt" along the Great Lakes. Though scythed by freeways and malled very nearly to death, this region also holds some perfectly preserved historic sites, including Amish farmlands, the automobile plants responsible for the country's classiest cars, even the sleepy little town that inspired Sherwood Anderson's novel, *Winesburg, Ohio*.

In the East, there is so much to see that we've split the route into two alternates, both of which bypass the freeways and tourist traps in favor of more fascinating places, many you may never have heard about. The more traveled route follows US-20 along a historical middle ground between the slow boats of the Erie Canal and the high-speed toll road of the I-90/New York Thruway, winding along the north edge of the lovely Finger Lakes and detouring to the intriguing smaller cities of upstate New York before crossing the Hudson River into the Berkshires of western Massachusetts. The historic Mohawk Trail carries us past Lexington and Concord and into Boston, retracing Paul Revere's historic ride in reverse.

A southerly alternative is provided by little-known US-6, which twists across Allegheny hill country. Here "Pennsylvania Crude" oil was first discovered and coal mines fed the iron furnaces of Scranton. Here, too, Stephen Foster wrote folk songs, Zane Grey wrote his Wild West tales of the Riders of the Purple Sage, and Jack Kerouac first set off *On the Road*. Slipping around the backside of New York City's upper-crust suburbs, US-6 curves east across Connecticut and Rhode Island, among the picturesque villages and Industrial Revolution-era relics you just can't see from I-95, before winding up at the lively Cape Cod resort of Provincetown—the place where the Pilgrims *really* arrived in America, way back in 1620—weeks before setting foot on Plymouth Rock.

US-20 HIGHLIGHTS

Cannon Beach . . . . see pages 406-407
The Oregon Trail . . . . see pages 416-417
Craters of the Moon National Monument . . . . see page 420
Yellowstone National Park . . . . see pages 423-425
Carhenge . . . . see page 432
Mount Rushmore . . . . see page 432
Field of Dreams . . . . see page 439
Niagara Falls . . . . see pages 458-459
The Finger Lakes . . . . see pages 460-461
The Mohawk Trail. . . . . see page 472
Jack Kerouac's Lowell . . . . see page 475
Scranton . . . . see pages 485-488
Providence and Pawtucket. . . . . see pages 499–500
Lizzie Borden's Fall River . . . . see page 502
Herman Melville's New Bedford. . . . . see page 503

ACROSS OREGON

Starting at one of the state's most enjoyable small towns, the arts-and-craftsy Pacific Ocean resort community of Cannon Beach, this route traverses the heart of Oregon. From the salty cow pastures along the Pacific Ocean, over the evergreen mantle of the Coast Range to culturally vibrant Portland and the lush Willamette Valley, the route starts where history says we should end up—amid the bountiful land at the west end of the Oregon Trail. From Portland, the state's largest city, you'll climb into the Cascade Mountains alongside its signature peak, Mount Hood, whose volcanic cone can be seen for miles around. East of here the route drops from the forests down into the suddenly dry and desertlike landscape of the otherworldly Columbia Plateau, across which the highway rolls and rocks for 300 miles through old mining camps, fossil beds, and wide open desolation before crossing the Snake River into Idaho.

By state law, there is no self-service gasoline in Oregon; all stations have attendants who pump the gas for you. There's no sales tax, either.

Scenic US-101's winding route along the Oregon coast is covered more fully on the Coastal West Coast route; for more, see pages 29-41.

Cannon Beach marks the farthest point reached by the **Lewis and Clark** expedition to the West Coast. From here, they retreated back to their outpost at Fort Clatsop, near the mouth of the Columbia River, where they spent the winter of 1805-06.

Cannon Beach

Unlike most Oregon coast towns, Cannon Beach (pop. 1,221) is hidden from the highway, but it's one place you won't want to miss. Though it has long been known as an artist's colony, and has grown considerably in recent years thanks to its popularity as a weekend escape from Portland, Cannon Beach retains a rustic quality, a walkable size, and a coastline that rates second to none in the state.

In terms of traditional "tourist attractions" there's not a lot to do, but Cannon Beach is an unbeatable place to stop and unwind, or to go for long walks along the seven-mile strand and then retreat indoors to the many good galleries, cafes, and restaurants. For breakfast, fill up on eggs Benedict at the **Lazy Susan Cafe** (closed Tuesday and Wednesday. in winter), across from the Mariner Market at 126 N. Hemlock. Enjoy burgers and microbrews at **Bill's Tavern**, 188 N. Hemlock, or very good seafood dinners at the **Bistro**, 263 N. Hemlock. Both feature live music most weekends. Reasonably priced rooms near the beach and town can be found at the **Starfish Motel**, 9645 S. Hemlock (503/436-0639); **McBee Motel**, 888 S. Hemlock (503/436-2569); and smoke-free **Cannon Beach Hotel**, 1116 S. Hemlock (503/436-1392), a converted loggers' boardinghouse.

For details on the annual events and other general information, contact the Cannon Beach **visitor bureau**, 201 E. 2nd Street (503/436-2623).

Ecola State Park

North of Cannon Beach, a mile south of the junction between US-101 and US-26 from Portland, the rainforested access road through Ecola State Park leads you to one of the most photographed views on the coast: looking south you can see Haystack Rock and Cannon Beach with Neahkahnie Mountain looming above them. Out to sea to the northwest, the sight of **Tillamook Rock Lighthouse** to the northwest is also striking; operational from 1881 to 1957, the lighthouse is now used as a repository for cremated remains.

The rest of the park protects a series of rugged headlands stretching for nine miles along the coast, with many forested hiking trails. One trail leads to **Tillamook Head**, widely considered one of the most scenic portions of the Oregon Coast Trail System—the view from the top was memorialized by William Clark as "the grandest and most pleasing prospect" he had ever beheld. In 1806, Clark and a few other members of the Corps of Discovery expedition traversed the area in search of supplements to their diet of hardtack and dried salmon. They happily bought 300 pounds of tangy whale blubber from local Indians, but these days you'd better bring your own lunch to picnic atop bluffs with sweeping views of the rock-strewn Pacific.

At the end of May, Cannon Beach hosts the largest and most enjoyable sand castle competition on the Oregon coast, with some 10,000 spectators and as many as 1,000 participants turning out with their buckets and spades.

The word *"ecola"* means "whale" in the Chinookan tongue and was affixed to this region by the Lewis and Clark expedition, who found one of the leviathans washed up on a beach nearby.

North of Cannon Beach and Ecola State Park, at the junction where US-26 cuts inland from US-101, the **Crab Broiler** roadside diner (503/738-5313) serves crab and cheese dishes.

Sunset Highway

Running over the coastal mountains between Portland and the coast, US-26 is known to some as the Sunset Highway. Climb-

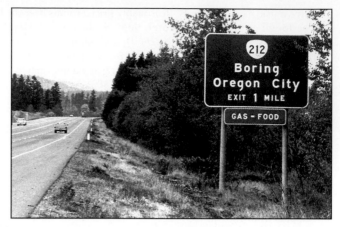

ing the edge of the coastal plain, the first stop is the old-growth spruce and fir forest preserved in **Klootchy Creek Park**, two miles east of US-101. Among the many huge firs and spruce trees is the "**World's Largest Sitka Spruce**," more than 215 feet high and almost 16 feet in diameter, marked by a sign along the north side of the highway.

Next, meander through dairy cattle country to Necanicum Junction. Here, turn northeast and head eight miles to **Saddle Mountain**. This off-road attraction has a very steep 2.5-mile hiking trail to the summit, with opportunities to view bleeding heart, Indian paintbrush, monkey flowers, and other rare plants and wild flowers. From the 3,283-foot top of the trail, you can usually see the mouth of the Columbia River and the spine of the Coast Range; on a clear day, the panorama includes 50 miles of Pacific coastline and Mounts Hood, St. Helens, and Rainier, with ugly acres of clearcuts in between. Primitive campsites are open mid-April to October; RVs and other wide bodies should avoid this narrow road.

Continuing east on US-26, about a mile before the hamlet of Elsie is the **Morris' Camp 18 Logging Museum** (503/755-2476). Visitors can examine logging equipment to get a feel for an era of misery whips, steam donkeys, and timberbeasts. If your visit conjures a logger's appetite, an on-site restaurant in a log building serves hearty roadfood.

Between here and Portland, US-26 winds through the verdant delights of the Coast Range, zipping through tunnels and sliding down slopes to the farm country of northwest Oregon. Before you hit the edges of suburbia, one more recreational opportunity is worth a gander: **Banks-Vernonia Linear State Park**, a 20-mile stretch of abandoned railroad that roughly parallels Hwy-47, from the town of Banks on US-26 to the tucked-away timbertown of Vernonia. Six well-marked trailheads along Hwy-47 provide access to this trail, Oregon's first linear recreational corridor.

Columbia Gorge

Portland is covered as a Survival Guide on pages 712-713.

The Mount Hood Highway

Starting out along Powell Boulevard east from Portland, US-26—now dubbed the Mount Hood Highway—follows, albeit in reverse, the final leg of the historic Oregon Trail. Passing first through the comically named photo-stop town of Boring, the road some 20 miles east of Portland reaches Sandy, a boisterous gateway to the mountains. Nestled in berry-farm country, Sandy is full of ski shops, pizza parlors, and other enterprises geared for outdoor enthusiasts, who fuel up at places like the **Kaffee Klatch**, a converted gas station serving decent java at 38871 Proctor Boulevard, or the **Elusive Trout** at 39333 Proctor Boulevard, a pub/restaurant serving gourmet hamburgers and homemade soup. After Sandy's lively commerce, the road ambles through pastureland and into the foothills of the Cascades.

Two more oddly named towns along US-26 hold good places to eat and drink before or after a day out in the mountains. The **Inn Between** (503/622-5400) in **Wemme**, one of the little wide spots clustered at the base of Mount Hood, has affordable eats varying from teriyaki chicken to macho nachos. After cruising Wemme, you'll come to another "W" town—**Welches Junction**, where the **Chalet Swiss** (503/622-3600) is famous for Northwest seafood or continental cuisine by chef Kurt Mezger.

The other suggested stop in Welches is the **Mount Hood Visitor Center** (daily 8 AM-4:30 PM; 503/622-4822) at 65000 E. US-26, operated by the U.S. Forest Service and loaded with maps, brochures, and other information on the mountain and surrounding recreational hotspots.

Government Camp and the Timberline Lodge

Just off US-26 at the southern foot of Mount Hood, Government Camp is but another wide spot in the road with a range of food and drink options. For espresso, microbrews, sandwiches, pizzas, and pastas, stop at the **Mount Hood Brewing Company** (503/272-3724), at the west end of town. Another good stop is the **Huckleberry Inn** (503/272-3325), open 24 hours a day, seven days a week, and famous for its wild huckleberry pies, huckleberry pancakes, and huckleberry shakes. If you're unable to move after a berry feast, the inn also offers low-priced rooms, and dorm beds from $12 a night per person.

Government Camp's main attraction is the **Mount Hood Ski Bowl** (503/272-3206), a year-round recreation center with skiing in winter and mountain biking in summer, plus guided horseback trips, go-carts, paintball games, and a 100-foot bungee jump.

An hour west of Portland, 20 miles from the coast, follow the Fishhawk Falls Highway north along the Necanicum River, then follow signs along Hwy-202 to the **Jewell Meadow Wildlife Area.** Here, particularly in the fall before hunting season starts, you can see rare Roosevelt elk and black-tailed deer; nearby is 100-foot Fishhawk Falls at Lee Wooden County Park.

South of US-26 on the western fringes of Portland, the mega-suburb of **Beaverton** is base camp for the high-tech companies of Silicon Forest and, most famously, corporate headquarters for Nike, the international sports apparel giant.

The fastest route east from Portland is I-84, which races through the Columbia Gorge and east along the Columbia River, rejoining US-26 at Ontario on the Idaho border.

East of the Mount Hood hamlet of **Zigzag,** US-26 drops to an old-fashioned, undivided two-lane road. Summer-only **Lolo Pass Loop** cuts off north on a scenic half-circle around Mount Hood to Hood River, a historic city on the Columbia River and I-84.

THE BARLOW ROAD

After long months of hardship and danger, pioneers nearing the end of the Oregon Trail had two choices when they reached the narrow gorge of the Columbia River: they could float their wagons down the perilous river to Fort Vancouver, or climb over the Cascades to the Willamette Valley via the Barlow Road, a route that parallels today's US-26. While much safer than the river route, the Barlow Road had its own precarious moments—emigrants struggled down muddy declines, hanging onto ropes hitched around trees to keep wagons from runaway destruction. Such moments assuredly gave the pioneers second thoughts about their choice of passage. At $5 per wagon and 10 cents a head for cattle, horses, and mules, following the privately owned Barlow Road was also expensive. Nonetheless, in 1845, the first year of operation, records report that 1,000 pioneers in 145 wagons traveled the route.

Heading east, you're going backwards along the Barlow Road, so bear that in mind as you take a few historical sites that record the struggles of pioneers on the last stretch of their 2,000-mile overland journey. At Tollgate Campground you'll find a reproduction of the **Barlow Road Tollgate**, where owner Sam Barlow stood with his hand out. The steepest section of the road was the **Laurel Hill "Chute,"** where wagons skidded down a treacherous grade; a sign and pull-out five miles east of Rhododendron mark the start of a short, steep hike up to the chute.

Look for other markers depicting Barlow Road history on Hwy-35, the loop road that traverses the eastern slope of Mount Hood north to Hood River. The first, **Pioneer Woman's Memorial**, is a quarter-mile north of the junction with US-26; a sign marks a right turn onto Forest Road 3530 and a grave site with a brass plaque commemorating the women who traveled the Oregon Trail. Two miles north of the junction is 4,157-foot **Barlow Pass**, where ruts grooved in the Barlow Road lead downhill from a parking area, mute testament to the perseverance of westward-driven settlers.

East of Government Camp, near the junction of US-26 and Hwy-35, which comes from Hood River and the Columbia Gorge, be sure to turnoff north toward Mount Hood to visit **Timberline Lodge** (503/231-5400 or 800/547-1406), an elegantly rustic national landmark built in 1937 by the Civilian Conservation Corps. The actual hotel seen in the creepy 1983 film, *The Shining*—in which Jack Nicholson plays a troubled writer who takes a job as winter caretaker in a snowbound mountaintop resort—Timberline Lodge is an unforgettable place, with a humongous fireplace, grand dining rooms, and an unbeatable setting. Rooms run $60-160. If you don't stay the night, check out the Cascade Dining Room's award-winning cuisine, the more casual pizza and sandwiches at the Blue Ox, and the Ram's Head Bar, which has locally brewed beers and ales.

Enticing though it is, snowcapped **Mount Hood** is also a difficult and dangerous peak to climb—there is no trail to the summit, and all routes require a high degree of technical ability and specialized equipment. There are lots of fine hikes around its base, however. For further details, contact the Mount Hood Visitor Center (503/622-4822) on US-26 in Welches.

Warm Springs Indian Reservation

East of the Cascades crest, US-26 becomes the Warm Springs Highway as it angles down out of the mountains across the sage and juniper country of eastern Oregon. Most of the land between here and Madras is part of the 600,000-acre Warm Springs Reservation, home to the Confederated Tribes of Warm Springs (Wasco, Paiute, and Warm Springs).

Near the eastern edge of the reservation, at the town of Warm Springs, hang a left on Agency Hot Springs Road, drive north for 11 miles, and you'll arrive at **Kah-Nee-Tah**, a resort complex that cheerfully blends modern and ancient lifestyles. You can soak in the famously soothing hot springs, play golf along the banks of the Warm Springs River, and savor salmon fillet cooked over an alderwood fire. Lodging at Kah-Nee-Tah, which means "Root Digger," ranges from tepees for $55 to one-bedroom cottages for $90; first-come, first-served primitive campsites are $15. Like the weather in central Oregon, rates are subject to change without notice; for further information, phone 800/831-0100.

Back on US-26, after passing through Warm Springs, you'll go down a little hill to the modern, 27,000-square foot **Museum at Warm Springs** (daily 10 AM-5 PM; $5; 503/553-3331). Check out exhibits of more than 20,000 artifacts, replicas of a Paiute mat lodge and a Wasco plank house, recordings of tribal languages, and a pushbutton-activated Wasco wedding scene. A quarter-mile east of the museum, where US-26 bridges the Deschutes River, the **Crossing Cafe** offers good food including Indian fry bread, usually followed by a slice of huckleberry pie.

Madras

After crossing the Deschutes River from the Warm Springs reservation, US-26 links up for a short while with US-97 through Madras, birthplace of the late actor River Phoenix. Contrary to its name, few in this hardworking town wear East Indian plaid, and the beatific followers of an Indian guru are red-clad memories: it's been over a decade since Bhagwan Shree Rajneesh and his disciples lived on their 175,000-acre commune, 30 miles to the northeast at the village of Antelope. There's not a lot to see or do in Madras, but there are a couple of handy places to stay. Named after the gnarly tree that happily grows where fir and pine would dry up and blow away, the **Juniper Motel** at 414 N. US-26 (503/475-6186) is easy to find and not too hard on your budget. Another choice, **Sonny's Motel and Restaurant**, 1539 S.W. US-97 (503/475-7217), has better amenities for a few dollars more.

One of Oregon's landmarks, and a celebrated challenge to rock-climbers, **Smith Rock** stands 17 miles south of Madras along US-97.

In every U.S. presidential election since Oregon became a state, the people of **Crook County** around Prineville voted for the winner; until, that is, they voted for George Bush in 1992, putting an end to their reputation as the national bellwether.

Prineville

From Madras, US-26 veers farther away from the Cascades, crossing the Crooked River National Grasslands, which mark the geographical center of Oregon. Strolling the streets of Prineville (pop. 5,355), a town with a vivid heritage of cattle and sheep ranching, you'll notice plenty of cowboy hats (or "gimme" caps, emblazoned with the logos of the wearer's favorite fertilizer or tractor company) atop the heads of dusty citizens piloting dusty pickup trucks. It's been a ripsnorter of a town since Barny Prine built his blacksmith and saloon here in 1868 following the discovery of gold in nearby hills; people of Prineville these days are ranchers, loggers, and miners, though tourism is slowly but surely taking its place as an economic force.

You can learn more about the region's history at the **A.R. Bowman Museum**, 246 N. Main Street (Mon.-Fri. 10 AM-5 PM, Saturday noon-5 PM; 503/447-3715). Two floors of exhibits include a campfire setup, a moonshine still, and a country store with a pound of Bull Durham tobacco. If you hanker after a sit-down meal, check out the **Ochoco Inn and Cinnabar Restaurant**, 123 E. 3rd Street, known for its generous and eclectic menu; **Barr's Cafe**, 887 N. Main Street, serves coffee-shop food 24 hours a day. Lodging choices include the **City Center Motel**, 509 E. 3rd Street (503/447-5522), in the middle of the city in the middle of the state, and eminently affordable. For a real treat, try the B&B at the **Historic Elliott House**, 305 W. 1st Street (503/447-7442), a Queen Anne-style Victorian built in 1908.

The drive along US-26 east of Prineville takes you up into the Ochocos, a low-slung gem of a mountain range once the heartland of the Paiutes. Seven miles from Prineville, US-26 borders **Ochoco Lake**, a popular recreational reservoir with fishing, boating, hiking, camping, and a picnic bench or two for travelers. There's not a lot of shade along the shore of this man-made lake, but it can serve as a quick lunch spot. The rest of the Ochoco range, which reaches heights of nearly 7,000 feet, holds acres and acres of lovely meadows, clear streams, and pristine pine forests.

Towns in eastern Oregon have taken to decorating their buildings with large and colorful murals, usually with historical or outdoorsy themes.

John Day Fossil Beds National Monument

East of the Ochocos, midway across Oregon, the John Day Fossil Beds National Monument documents many millions of years of prehistoric life, from thundering dinosaurs to delicate plants. Discovered in the 1860s by prominent geologist Thomas Condon, the beds contain one of the world's richest and most diverse concentrations of mammalian-dinosaur fossils. The eerie, empty moonscape can be easily toured from US-26. Start in the west with the **Painted Hills** section, two miles north of US-26, where trails and overlooks offer views of colorfully striated bluffs, volcanic rubble, and rock-solid evidence of the hardwood forests that covered the landscape a mere 30 million years ago. About 35 miles farther east, along US-26, the **Sheep Rock Unit** is the best place to see fossils in their natural state; the monument headquarters and a small museum are also here, housed inside the **Cant Ranch Visitor Center.**

There's also a more distant section of the fossil beds at Clarno, along the John Day River some 50 miles northwest of Painted Hills. The administrative offices for the John Day fossil beds are at 420 W. Main Street in the town of John Day (503/575-0271), 38 miles east of the Sheep Rock Unit.

The only noticeable human habitation near the fossil beds is **Mitchell**, two miles east of the turnoff for the Painted Hills section of the fossil beds, where the old-fashioned general store **Wheeler County Mercantile** captures the flavor of the 1870s. If you need sustenance more than gossip over the cracker barrel, stop by the **Blueberry Muffin Restaurant**, just past the turnoff to the Fossil Beds, for filling if not remarkable cuisine. You'll

ammonite fossil

find lodging with kitchens in Mitchell at the **Skyhook Motel** (503/462-3569).

John Day and Vicinity

After gazing at striped hillsides and fossilized bones, regain some perspective by strolling through any of the towns along US-26—Dayville, Mount Vernon, John Day, Canyon City, and Prairie City. Founded as miners' camps after gold was discovered in 1862, many now cater to the few visitors who brave a trip through this uninviting but unforgettable part of the world.

*The namesake of the fossil beds, **John Day,** was a fur trapper hunting along the Columbia River in 1810 when he was attacked by Indians. He turned up two years later at Astoria on the coast, but never again went anywhere near the river, the town, or the region that now bear his name.*

Starting in the west, the **Dayville Diggins** in Dayville will take care of your dust-choked palate. The **Fish House**, 110 Franklin (503/987-2124), a 1908 bungalow turned antique-bedecked B&B, will cater to both your appetite and road-weariness. Rates run $35-50, with tent camping for $5. Barbecue pits and horseshoe tossing are available to guests. Farther east, at the junction of US-26 and US-395, Mount Vernon is home to **The Wounded Buffalo**, a local landmark known for its Buffalo Bill Burger and juicy rib-eye steaks.

The town of John Day (pop. 1,836), the metropolis in this chain of gold towns, holds the area's one not-to-be-missed attraction: **Kam Wah Chung and Company Museum**, 250 N.W. Canton (Mon.-Thurs. 9 AM-noon and 1-5 PM, Saturday and Sunday 1-5 PM; $2; 503/575-0028), run by the city and located in a nice park just north of US-26 at the center of John Day. Built as a trading post in 1866-67, it became a general store for the Chinese workers who toiled in the mines. It continued to be the center of the local Chinese community until the early 1940s. In the 1880s, for example, more than half of the local population was Chinese. Included in a fascinating collection of actual items from the era are herbal remedies, canned goods, gambling paraphernalia, and a Taoist shrine. For more on the area's fascinating history, take a quick side trip south along US-395 to **Canyon City**, where the **Grant County Historical Museum** (Mon.-Sat. 9 AM-4:30 PM, Sunday 1-5 PM in summer only) stands at the center of this evocative, unrestored old mining town.

Back in John Day, the **Grubsteak Mining Company**, 149 E. Main Street (503/575-1970), has a sumptuous menu of rib eyes and other beef entrees. **The Dreamers Lodge Motel**, 144 N. Canyon Boulevard (503/575-1700), and **Little Mac's Motel**, 250 E. Main Street (503/575-1751), both have reasonable rates as well as intriguing names. Last but not least is the honestly named **Weary Traveler Laundromat**, 755 S. Canyon Boulevard (US 395).

*John Day's one and only radio station, **KJDY 1400 AM,** broadcasts country music and local news across eastern Oregon. Its newspaper, The Blue Eagle, comes out each Thursday.*

Prairie City

Back on US-26, the first town east of John Day is Prairie City, fast becoming a western false-front photo-op. A highlight is the **Dewitt Museum** (Thurs.-Sat. 10 AM-3 PM in summer only) on S. Main Street, housed in the restored western terminus of the Sumpter Valley Railroad, which operated between Baker and Prairie City 1909-47. The museum has 10 rooms of mining-era artifacts. A surprisingly hip hangout in Prairie City is **Ferdinand's**, 128 Front Street (503/820-9359). Once a butcher shop established in 1902, this restaurant/saloon has an impressive menu and a bounty of antiques. The most memorable images visitors take back to the road are a pair of beauties called "The Twin Virgins" surmounting a long bar that is an architectural marvel itself. The two sculptures were carved in Milan in 1879 and shipped around Cape Horn, up the Columbia by sternwheeler, and into the mining country via wagon.

Leaving the John Day watershed, US-26 ascends into the Blue Mountains, one of the last and most difficult obstacles on the Oregon Trail. The road then rambles through the Malheur National Forest, climbs over Dixie Pass (which is exactly one mile high—5,280 feet above sea level), and drops toward the Snake River plain. Apart from trees and the irrigated pastures of sprawling cattle ranches, there's little to see in the 120 miles between Prairie City and the Idaho border, though natural hot springs and hiking trails abound across the craggy volcanic landscape.

Halfway between Prairie City and Vale is the dividing line between Pacific and mountain time zones. Adjust clocks accordingly as you head over Eldorado Pass.

Vale

Vale (pop. 1,701), the seat of Malheur County, sits at the junction of US-20 and US-26, on the banks of the Malheur River where it's joined by smaller creeks and streams. The comparatively easy crossing and the presence of a natural hot spring made it a prime stopping place on the Oregon Trail. Markers around town point out the main sites of historical importance, including the **Malheur Crossing**, next to the bridge on the eastern edge of the town, where pioneers dunked their aching bods in the still-hot Malheur River springs; and **Keeney Pass**, just south of downtown Vale on Enterprise Avenue, where 150-year-old wagon ruts can still be seen along the roadside.

Oregon's biggest and most developed Oregon Trail historic site is at Flagstaff Hill, off I-84 near Baker City, where a set of well-preserved wagon ruts provide a focus for the extensive **National Historic Oregon Trail Interpretive Center** *(daily 9 AM-4 PM, till 6 PM in summer; free; 503/523-1843).*

Two more monuments are back in town. The **Stone House**, at the end of Main Street near Wadleigh Park, was built in 1872 to replace an Oregon Trail way station made of mud. Best of all is the simple Oregon Trail marker on the courthouse lawn, placed there by Ezra Meeker, who retraced the route in 1906 and started the groundswell of interest in the trail's history.

Taking a breather at Vale is an honored tradition—it was here that pioneers rested before climbing out of the Snake River Valley into the Blue Mountains—but if you're feeling tired and hungry after your own long treks through the dry gulches and sagebrush flats, these days there's not a lot to choose from. One entertaining option is a night at the **Bates Motel**, 1101 A Street W (503/473-3234); it has nothing to do with Hitchcock's *Psycho,* but has been run by the Bates family (no Normans among them) for over 30 years, offering clean showers and a good night's sleep.

For more information on Vale and the Oregon Trail, stop by the helpful **visitor center**, 275 N. Main Street (503/473-3800).

Ontario

At the Idaho border, along I-84 and the Snake River, Ontario (pop. 9,392) is the largest of many mid-sized farming and ranching communities in the surrounding area. A shipping point for spuds, onions, sugar beets, and beef, the town doesn't have a lot to offer visitors, though the **Cheyenne Social Club and**

Lounge, 11 S.W. 1st Street (503/889-3777), named after a 1970 western movie, offers affordable steak and seafood entrees in a nostalgic Wild West setting. The **Holiday Motel**, 615 E. Idaho Street (503/889-9188), is an alternative to the many franchised chain motels.

From Ontario, the quickest route east is the I-84 freeway, though US-20/26 follows a slow but scenic route along the Snake and Boise Rivers, much of it along the old Oregon Trail.

ACROSS IDAHO

US-20's route across Southern Idaho cuts through one of the most magnificently empty American spaces, an arid, volcanic region cut by life-giving rivers and isolating mountain ranges, with strange geological outcrops that encourage travelers to stop and explore the inhospitable land. Irrigation has altered the look of the land considerably, so much so that vineyards and lush fields now thrive in the otherwise barren gray-green sagebrush plains. But little else has changed since this region provided the greatest challenge to pioneers crossing the country along the Oregon Trail. Though visitor services have improved considerably in the intervening 150 years, southern Idaho is still a wild and demanding land. Like much of the West, it's also addictively satisfying.

The quickest route across Idaho is the I-84 freeway, though the historic Oregon Trail route, marked by large highway signs, follows a much more scenic route along the Snake River through sugar beet and potato farms and flyspeck towns.

Parma and Fort Boise

Just as US-20/26 does today, the historic Oregon Trail crosses between Idaho and Oregon at the confluence of the Boise and Snake Rivers, southwest of I-84 at the town of Parma. Sugar beets and onions fill the fields around the tiny town, which is dominated by a comically inaccurate replica of Fort Boise, one of the first European outposts in the Pacific Northwest.

THE OREGON TRAIL

In 1993, the 150th anniversary of the opening of the Oregon Trail renewed interest in this best known of emigrant trails across the Wild West. History buffs got together for summer-long reenactments of the arduous crossing, building authentic wagons and eating, dressing, and sleeping as the pioneers did—with the inestimable comfort of knowing that they, unlike their predecessors, could easily return home at any point.

From 1843 until the 1860s, some 400,000 men, women, and children followed this 2,000-mile trail, averaging four months to make the cross-country journey. Long followed by fur trappers and traders, and first charted by a series of U.S. Army expeditions led by Kit Carson and John C. Frémont in the early 1840s, the Oregon Trail followed the path of least resistance across the western half of the continent. Beginning at various points along the Missouri River, the trail followed the valley of the Platte River across the Great Plains, crossed the Rockies at Wyoming's gentle South Pass, then set off across the desert of southern Idaho. The most difficult parts were saved for the end, when emigrants had a choice of floating downstream on the turbulent Columbia River or struggling over the rugged Cascades to reach the Willamette Valley. Nearly half of the travelers who set off along the Oregon Trail from Missouri actually had other destinations in mind: more than 100,000 turned off south toward the California gold mines, and some 30,000 Mormons followed the route west to their new colony at Salt Lake City.

The Oregon Trail had many variants and shortcuts and was never a sharply defined track, but clear traces survive in a number of places along the route. Many evocative sites survive, often as reconstructions of pioneer forts, trading posts, and river crossings. There are also many fine museums along the way, not to mention the many good books on the subject, the best of which we've included in Road Trip Resources "Recommended Reading" on pages 739-743.

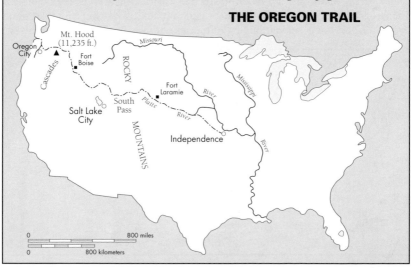

THE OREGON TRAIL

Many Oregon Trail sites are covered in more detail under our Road Trip routes. As shown on the map, some of the most interesting Oregon Trail sites are:

Oregon City. Western end of the Oregon Trail, 10 miles south of downtown Portland along the Willamette River.

The Barlow Road: To avoid the treacherous falls of the Columbia Gorge, many emigrants opted to follow this difficult toll road that cuts inland around Mount Hood. See page 410.

The National Oregon Trail Interpretive Center: A well-preserved set of wagon ruts and an array of historical artifacts are displayed here. See page 414.

Fort Boise: This fortress, a reconstruction of a fur trapping post built nearby in 1834, stands along the banks of the Snake River. See pages 415, 417.

Three Island Crossing State Park: One of the best places to get a feel for life as an Oregon Trail pioneer: Camp where they camped and swim where they swam, at one of the most important crossings of the Snake River. See page 419.

Fort Caspar: A credible reconstruction of a frontier fort houses a good museum and the remains of an early ferry and bridge over the Platte River. See page 428.

Fort Laramie: Located 40 miles southeast of Douglas, Wyoming, this restored fort is among the best stops on the contemporary trail. The most impressive set of preserved wagon ruts survive in an evocative state park outside Guernsey, upstream from the fort.

Santa Fe Trail Junction: For the first few miles, the Santa Fe and Oregon Trails coincided, and a sign here pointed the way: right to Oregon, left to Santa Fe.

Independence, Missouri: Where most travelers on the Oregon Trail began, this is also the site of one of the best museums on the subject of the westward migrations. See page 555.

Originally established in 1834 by the Hudson's Bay Company, the fort supplied travelers until the mid-1850s, when it was closed because of declines in demand and an increase in Indian hostilities. The less than authentic, steel-and-stucco reconstruction of the old fort stands along US-20 on the west side of town and is the site of annual "Old Fort Boise Days" in early May.

East of Parma, US-20/26 rejoins I-84 to cross the Boise River; from here, you won't miss much following the freeway into Boise.

Boise

Capital of Idaho and rated one of the most "liveable" cities in the U.S., Boise is a very pleasant medium-sized city of over 125,000 people. A lush green oasis in the middle of the barren lava lands of the Snake River plain, Boise was so named by *the Idanha Hotel*

fur-trappers for its dense groves of cottonwood trees ("bois" is French for "tree"), which made the area an especially welcome respite before irrigation turned the brown desert much greener than it naturally would be. The presence of the state government and the 12,000 students at Boise State University lend a degree of sophistication and vitality mixed in with the more usual Idaho trappings—more than anywhere else for miles, rollerblades and mountain bikes compete with pickup trucks as the main method of transportation here, and bookshops and espresso bars line the downtown streets.

Downtown Boise focuses on the **state capitol** (Mon.-Fri. 8 AM-6 PM, Saturday 9 AM-5 PM; free), on Jefferson Street between 6th and 8th Streets, a typically grand, neoclassical structure with a giant eagle atop its landmark dome. The usual exhibits of the state's produce fill display cases, and free guided tours are given upon request. South of the capitol, restaurants and cafes surround **The Grove**, Boise's convention center and main shopping complex featuring a large fountain through which daredevils like to skate and cycle. Don't miss **Taters**, which sells all manner of Idaho souvenirs, from postcards and fridge magnets to cookbooks describing 100 things you can do with potatoes.

Northeast from Boise, Hwy-21 makes a very scenic trip through the abandoned gold mines of the Sawtooth Mountains to Stanley, which is described more fully on page 99.

Boise's own **KBOI 670 AM** plays pop hits of the 1970s and Boise State Broncos football games.

East of downtown at 611 Grove Street, Boise's oldest building now houses the small but intriguing **Basque Museum** (Tues.-Fri. 10 AM-3 PM, Saturday 11 AM-2 PM; donations), documenting the culture of the Basque people who work in Idaho's ranching industries. Farther east, where Main Street turns into Warm Springs Road, the **Old Idaho Penitentiary** (daily noon-5 PM daily in summer, noon-4 PM rest of the year; $3; 208/368-6080) served as the main state prison for over 100 years from its construction in 1872. High sandstone walls, cut by prisoners, surround the complex, and the old cellblocks are now filled with displays on prison life—from collections of tattoos to the gallows where many prisoners met their end.

At Mountain Home, US-20 cuts off northeast from I-84, following a branch of the Oregon Trail known as **Goodale's Cut-off** across the harsh volcanic plains.

Boise doesn't offer a hugely exciting range of restaurants, though good places can be found around 8th and Main Streets in the downtown area. There are all the usual places to stay, plus the wonderful old **Idanha**, 928 Main Street (208/342-3611), built in 1901 and featuring ornate corner turrets, opulent public spaces, and Idaho's oldest public elevator. Rooms are good value at about $50 a night.

Mountain Home

Across southern Idaho, the I-84 freeway has effectively replaced the older highways, especially in the area southeast of Boise. The huge Mountain Home Air Force Base, 35 miles southeast of Boise, is the only thing for miles, which is no doubt by design: the base is a testing ground for the latest high-tech weapons systems and aircraft. One of the more contentious side effects of Mountain Home's presence is that the powers-that-be have decreed that much of the surrounding wilderness, including the wild Owyhee Mountains and almost the entire southwest corner of the state, should be closed to the public and turned into a bombing range—so pilots can gain experience firing missiles and dropping live munitions.

Eighteen miles south of Mountain Home and the I-84 freeway via Hwy-51, **Bruneau Dunes State Park** protects the highest free-standing sand dune in North America—rising over 400 feet above the Snake River plain. Since the temperatures can hit 100° throughout the summer months, mornings or sunsets are the best times to exercise your legs by climbing up and careening back down the white sands.

Although it's on the interstate, the town of Mountain Home has little more than the average, sparse services, including all the usual pizza places plus a few motels. **Best Western Foothills Motor Inn** is off I-84 exit 95 at 1080 US-20 (208/587-8477).

Glenns Ferry

The tiny town of Glenns Ferry, 28 miles southeast of Mountain Home on the Snake River and I-84, would hardly rate a mention were it not the site of one of the most important crossings on the old Oregon Trail. This site, now preserved as **Three Island Crossing State Park**, a mile southwest of town, gives one of the strongest impressions of the tough going for Oregon-bound pioneers. A very good **visitor center** (daily 9 AM-5 PM), with a Conestoga wagon out front, has displays of trail lore and history, and every August enthusiasts get together to reenact the river crossing. Go for a swim to cool off, and feel the powerful currents—more placid here than most anywhere else, which is why it was considered the best place to ford the river. This is also a fine place to camp; the usually clear night sky makes for excellent star-gazing and there's even a very docile herd of buffalo.

Bliss

Along with the chance to add to your collection of city limits signs, or to send a postcard saying you're in Bliss, this idyllically named town (pop. 186) is worth a stop to see the deep canyon of **Malad Gorge State Park** (daily dawn-dusk; free; 208/837-4505), well signed southeast of town, off I-84 exit 157. It doesn't look like much until you get out of the car and walk 100 feet down the trail, where you suddenly come upon a truly awesome sight: a 250-foot-deep gorge with a crashing waterfall. The freeway passes overhead, oblivious to the natural wonder directly below.

From Bliss, US-26 cuts due east from the I-84 freeway, running across hard-edged lava beds. Bliss also marks the turnoff onto US-30, which follows the old Oregon Trail along the south bank of the Snake River through the lovely, waterfall-rich region known as **Thousand Springs.**

Shoshone

The only town for miles in any direction, Shoshone (pop. 1,249) is a ranching and railroad center—with Amtrak service! Some of its buildings have been constructed from local volcanic rock. Though it's a fairly timeworn place, Shoshone looks great at sunset, when its steel water tower glows and places like the

Across the Snake River from Malad Gorge, **Hagerman Fossil Beds National Monument** contains what's been called "the richest known deposit of Pliocene Age terrestrial fossils," mainly horses *(Equus simplicidens)* that roamed the area some three million years ago. The undeveloped monument also preserves one of the longest sections of visible wagon ruts in the entire length of the Oregon Trail. The new **visitor center** is across the river in Hagerman (208/837-4793).

Frosty Isle Drive-In on the north side of town and the neon-signed **Manhattan Cafe** along the railroad tracks look especially appealing.

If you're hungry, thirsty, or low on gas, be sure to fill up here, as there are no services between Shoshone and Arco, 75 miles to the east.

Shoshone sits at the junction where US-20 crosses Hwy-75, which runs north to Sun Valley, and US-93, which runs south to Twin Falls. See page 102 for more.

Craters of the Moon National Monument

Described by writer Washington Irving as a place "where nothing meets the eye but a desolate and awful waste, where no grass grows nor water runs, and where nothing is to be seen but lava," the vast tracts of volcanic fields known as Craters of the Moon National Monument aren't totally devoid of life—they just look that way. Covering some 60,000 acres at an average altitude of 6,000 feet, the lava fields are but a small part of the extensive Snake River volcanic plain, which forms a 100-mile-wide swath across southern Idaho. The rounded cinder cones and acres of glassy black stone were formed between 2,000 and 15,000 years ago, and despite first impressions they do shelter a wide variety of plant and animal life, from pines and prickly pears to various raptors and a population of mule deer. May and June see abundant wildflowers, and temperatures stay cool, so it's altogether an ideal time to visit.

Easily accessible from a seven-mile loop road that runs south from US-20/26, the most striking remnants of the region's volcanic activity are the huge cones that rise above the generally flat plain. These huge knolls of lightweight cinder give great views of the overall area, but they're not volcanoes, and there's no crater to look down into. The closest Craters of the Moon comes to real craters are the **spatter cones** midway along the loop, where the deep openings are often filled with snow late into summer. The most interesting section of the monument is at the end of the loop, where—provided you have a flashlight—you can wander through subsurface **lava tubes** called Boy Scout Cave, Beauty Cave, and Indian Tunnel, which at 830 feet is the longest in the park.

For further information or to pick up the useful park brochures, stop by the small **visitor center** (daily 8 AM-6 PM in summer, 8·AM-4:30 PM rest of the year; 208/527-3257), where you ought to pay the $4 entry fee. A basic, 52-site **campground** offers water and restrooms but no showers, hookups, or dump station.

Arco

"The first city in the free world to be powered by nuclear-generated electricty," Arco (pop. 1,230) sits on the banks of the Big Lost River, so-called because it disappears a few miles downstream, vanishing into the volcanic labyrinth of the Snake River plain. Arco itself, a crossroads town straddling the junction of US-20 and US-93, doesn't have a lot to offer though it is a handy stop for gas or supplies. Signs and historic plaques point out its connections with the early days of nuclear power.

Northwest of Arco, the highest peak in Idaho, 12,662-foot **Mount Borah,** was lifted an additional two feet by a powerful 1983 earthquake that registered 7.3 on the Richter scale.

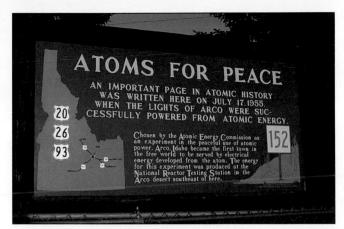

Atoms for Peace, Arco

If you have more than a passing interest in nuclear fission, you'll want to check out the anonymous-looking red brick structure 18 miles southeast of Arco on the south side of US-20, which holds the inoperative remains of **Experimental Breeder Reactor Number One.** Sitting at the edge of the massive Idaho National Engineering Lab, the deactivated reactor is open for self-guided **tours** (daily 8 AM-4 PM in summer only; free; 208/526-0050), on which you can get an up-close glimpse of the turbines and control room, even the fuel rods that produced the first nuclear power on December 20, 1951.

Idaho Falls

Taking its name from the wide but short waterfall completely tamed to form a pleasant green lake at the center of town, Idaho Falls (pop. 43, 929), at the junction of US-20 and I-15, is a busy big city with a very attractive, Middle American downtown set along the banks of the Snake River. Grain elevators and stockyards stand along the railroad tracks, train whistles blow throughout the night, and all manner of neon signs line the highways, offering a concentrated dose of rural Americana, while its hotels, supermarkets, and restaurants make Idaho Falls a handy last stop before heading on to the diverse wilderness areas that rise to the north, east, and west. Apart from the chance to wander around a business district that hasn't changed since 1956—if you have the time, nose around the Royal Shoe Shop at 321 Park Avenue, which reeks of leather and polish— you can stroll along the waterfront park, feeding the geese or just watching the waters tumble over the weirs.

Even if you're racing through, there's at least one classic roadfood haunt to check out: the **North Hi-Way Cafe** at 460 Northgate Mile (old US-20), marked by a huge flashing neon sign.

Rising to the east of Idaho Falls, the serrated crest of the **Grand Tetons** stands out along the Idaho/Wyoming border.

West of US-20, 15 miles north of Idaho Falls, the sleepy town of Rigby played a hugely important role in the development of contemporary culture: it was here that young **Philo T. Farnsworth,** the inventor of the cathode-ray television, grew up and went to school.

Rexburg's radio station **KRXK 98.1 FM,** plays oldies by request. Call in your favorite at 800/833-8211.

The border between Idaho and Montana, at 7,072-foot Targhee Pass, forms the **Continental Divide.**

For a place to stay, try the well-placed **Holiday Inn**, overlooking the falls at 475 River Parkway (208/523-800 or 800/432-1005); or the less expensive **Littletree Inn**, 888 N. Holmes Road (208/523-5993), with rooms from less than $40 a night.

In 1808, when fur trapper **John Colter** described the scenes he saw in what's now Yellowstone—gurgling, spouting steam vents, prismatic pools of sulfurous boiling water—nobody believed him, and many thought he was mad, calling the fantastic land "Colter's Hell."

Though the forests of Yellowstone are recovering, damage from the terrible fires of 1988 is still readily apparent around the western half of the park.

Rexburg

First settled in the 1880s, the town of Rexburg (pop. 14,302) is best known for the near-disaster of 1976, when the huge Teton Dam collapsed and unleashed eight billion gallons of floodwater onto the valley below. Fortunately, engineers noticed the warning signs and were able to evacuate the area beforehand; though damage was extensive, fatalities were few. Rexburg was initially established by Mormon homesteaders, and still has a pronounced Mormon feel; the **Teton Dam Museum**, 51 W. Center Street in the basement of the Mormon church across from city hall, has the usual displays of quilts and cattle brands tracing the history of the region, plus a large section devoted to the great flood of 1976. A short film shows the actual collapse of the dam. There's also an exhibit on the terrible forest fires that burned much of Yellowstone National Park in 1988.

From Rexburg, US-20 runs northeast through the Targhee National Forest, climbing from the Snake River plain along Henry's Fork River—one of the country's top fishing streams, loaded with cutthroat trout as big as 10 pounds—into the heart of the Rocky Mountains.

the first car at Yellowstone

West Yellowstone, Montana

Western gateway to Yellowstone National Park, the Montana town of West Yellowstone (pop. 913) sits just over the Idaho border, offering all the motels, gas stations, and cafes you could ever want, plus a lot more. The primary access point for early tourists visiting Yellowstone on the Union Pacific Railroad, West Yellowstone preserves a great deal of old-style tourist facilities—the old terminal is now the engaging if small **Museum of the Yellowstone** ($4), and the town's many roadside motels (there are more motel rooms than residents!) display a mouthwatering assembly of nifty neon signs while still serving the food-and-fuel needs of today's RVers. There's also a huge IMAX theater (daily 9 AM-9 PM; $6), in case you prefer the Memorex version to real-life Yellowstone.

West Yellowstone's main drag, Canyon Street (US-20), is lined by tacky souvenir shops. The excellent **Book Peddler**, 106 Canyon Street, boasts an espresso bar along with a wide array of fiction and nonfiction titles. The **Silver Spur** cafe, also on Canyon, serves a fine bowl of chili along with fluffy omelets. Motels abound on the backstreets, so drive around and take your pick, or call the **visitor center** hotline (406/646-7832 or 800/521-5241).

ACROSS WYOMING

Most visitors to Wyoming have one thing in mind: the unique sights of Yellowstone National Park. This amazing spectacle is deservedly the state's prime visitor attraction, but the rest of Wyoming holds a surprising variety of interesting places, from Wild West cow towns to the wide open spaces of the Great Plains. The least populated of the 50 states, Wyoming has more wide open space than just about anywhere else. If you like the idea of traveling for miles and miles without seeing anyone before coming upon a crossroads outpost where the post office shares space with the general store and gas station, you'll want to take the time to explore Wyoming.

Yellowstone National Park

Sitting astride the Continental Divide, high up in the northern Rockies at the northwest corner of Wyoming, Yellowstone National Park is one of the true wonders of the natural world. A veritable greatest hits of Mother Nature, the park is packed full of burbling geysers, magnificent canyons, raging waterfalls, and still-wild wildlife. The country's (and the world's) oldest national park, established in 1872, Yellowstone was first explored by frontiersman John Colter, who passed through in 1808; it's also one of the largest parts of the Lower 48 states never to be farmed or fenced.

You probably already know something about what Yellowstone has in store for you: the one essential Yellowstone sight is **Old Faithful Geyser**, in the southwest quarter of the park. One of the world's most famous natural features, Old Faithful is known for its clockwork eruptions, in which some 5,000 gallons of boiling water are sent 150 feet into the air, forming a solid, steamy column. Hundreds of people line up around the geyser waiting for it to blow, and rangers are able to predict it with good deal of accuracy—the visitor center will list the expected times of the day's eruptions, which occur roughly every 75 minutes and last for two to five. In between eruptions, take the chance to wander around to the dozens of other features in the Old Faithful basin, including a number of other geysers (the Old Faithful area has the greatest concentration in the world) as well as colorful pools and other geothermal features, all linked by well-marked boardwalks and trails along the Firehole River.

The other main sight is the **Grand Canyon of the Yellowstone River**, where a pair of powerful waterfalls cascade into a 20-mile-long, half-mile-wide, and 1,000-foot-deep canyon of eroded yellow stone. Parking areas line the north and south

One rarely mentioned aspect of life in Yellowstone is the profusion of bison droppings: everywhere you look—all around the geysers, hot springs, etc.—they've made their mark.

Note that the visitor season is very short—roads are usually blocked by snow from November until April, May, or June. To find out current road conditions, phone 307/344-7381.

In winter, the only road kept open is the one between Gardiner and Cooke City, Montana, at the northern edge of the park. The hardy can cross-country ski around the park or take a tour by Sno-Cat from Mammoth Hot Springs; for details, phone **T W Recreational Services Inc.** (307/344-7311).

At the Norris Geyser Basin, the small **Museum of the National Park Ranger** describes the evolution of the national parks; for instance, from 1886 to 1916 Yellowstone was under the protection of the U.S. Army!

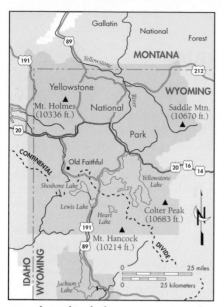

rims of the canyon, allowing access to trails along the edge of the gorge. A personal favorite is **Uncle Tom's Trail**, leaving from the south side of the falls. More a staircase than a trail, this route zigzags steeply down the walls of the canyon, bringing you face to face with the falls. Farther along the south rim is **Artist's Point**, which gives the classic view of the canyon. Also, two "**Brink of the Falls**" routes lead from the north side down to where the waters plunge.

Along with these two main attractions, there are many more sights to see, so take the time to visit the visitor centers, talk to the rangers, and find out what wonders await. Covering a roughly 100-by-100-mile square, Yellowstone is a big place, plenty big enough to absorb the many tourists who come here during the peak summer season. Whatever you do, don't try to see it all in one day; if time is tight, choose one or two places and spend all your time there. Get out of the car, hike a few trails, and enjoy.

Yellowstone Practicalities

Yellowstone's visitor facilities book up well in advance, so if you want the complete experience it's best to plan ahead as much as possible. **Accommodations** are the main thing you ought to sort out as soon as you can, as bed space is at a premium. The first choice is the wonderful **Old Faithful Inn**, next to the famous geyser. Built of split logs and huge boulders and exuding rough-hewn elegance, this delightful inn was completed in 1904 and maintains its original appearance. Rooms in the old lodge, without baths, cost about $40; a newer wing has larger rooms and modern conveniences for $100-250 a night. Another lodge at Yellowstone Lake is plusher but architecturally less distinctive. A half-dozen other inns, cabins, and motels are scattered around the park. All rooms are handled through the park concessioner, **T W Recreational Services Inc.** (307/344-7311), which also handles reservations for the park's campgrounds, most of which operate on a first-come, first-served basis and fill up by noon daily. **Backcountry camping** is another option, though be careful of bears and be sure to get a free overnight permit from the park rangers.

Places to eat include the usual cafeteria-type restaurants at all of the park's hotels and lodges, plus the truly remarkable dining

Though Buffalo Bill gets most of the publicists' ink, another famous Cody figure is the abstract impressionist "action painter" **Jackson Pollock,** who was born here.

Between Yellowstone and Cody, US-20 drops steeply through lovely **Wapiti Valley.** Teddy Roosevelt supposedly called this area "the most scenic 50 miles in America." It winds alongside the Shoshone River, which eventually flows into the Buffalo Bill Reservoir.

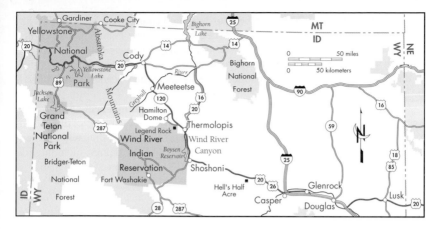

room at the classic Old Faithful Inn, with food that's as good as its gets in the national parks.

You'll find gas stations, gift shops, and general stores at just about every road junction in the park. There are **ranger stations** at most main features, and large **visitor centers** at Mammoth Hot Springs, Old Faithful, and the Canyon. For further information, contact **park headquarters** (307/344-7381).

The **Cody Nite Rodeo** (nightly at 8:30 PM; $8; 307/587-5155) at the huge rodeo grounds at the west end of town has been held June-Sept. since 1938, making it the nation's longest-running rodeo.

Cody

Eastern gateway to Yellowstone National Park, and an enjoyable overnight stop in its own right, Cody is a self-conscious frontier town and a busy center for local ranching and wood products industries. The outskirts along US-20 are lined by Wal-Marts, Kmarts, and all the fast-food franchises you could name, but the town center along Sheridan Avenue still looks like the Wild West town Cody was built to be.

Sitting on the Bighorn Basin plains at the foot of the mountains, Cody was founded in the late 1890s by Wild West showman "Buffalo Bill" Cody, whose name graces most everything in town, including the **Buffalo Bill Historical Center** (daily 7 AM-10 PM in summer, Tues.-Sun. 8 AM-5 PM rest of the year, closed December, January, and February; $7; 307/587-4771). One of the country's great museums—the center is divided into four main collections—and certainly the best in the Wild West, the Buffalo Bill Museum tells all you could want to know about the frontier showman. The Cody Firearms Museum displays more than 5,000 historic weapons. The Whitney Gallery of American Art, one of the country's most extensive collections of western art, displays important works by George Catlin, Thomas Moran, Albert Bierstadt, and

BUFFALO BILL'S WILD WEST·
CONGRESS, ROUGH RIDERS OF THE WORLD.

MISS ANNIE OAKLEY,
THE PEERLESS LADY WING-SHOT.

Remington. Saving the biggest and best for last, the Plains Indian Museum has an amazing collection of art and artifacts created by the diverse Plains Indian people, from beadwork dresses to a reconstructed Sioux village complete with full-sized te-pees. An array of leather moccasins adorn an entire wall, and pride of place is given to the extraordinary buffalo robe painted with scenes of the legendary Battle of Little Big Horn.

Also in Cody is **Trail Town** (daily 8 AM-8 PM mid-May to mid-Sept.; $3), a low-key but engaging collection of old buildings moved here from northwestern Wyoming and southern Montana. Wagons, buffalo robes, and other relics are on display. A memorial cemetery holds the remains of Wild West figures, including Jeremiah Johnson, whom Robert Redford played in the movie named for the man.

You'll find most of Cody's good places to eat on Sheridan Avenue. **Silver Dollar Bar and Grill**, 1313 Sheridan Avenue, serves great burgers and bottles of beer. A block away, the **Proud Cut Saloon**, 1227 Sheridan Avenue, has an interesting array of sandwiches at lunch and great steaks at dinner.

The historic **Irma Hotel** at 1192 Sheridan Avenue (307/587-4221; $40 in winter, $75 in summer), built by Buffalo Bill and named for his daughter, features a lovely cherrywood bar given by Queen Victoria, and an evening gunfight on the front porch. There are also lots of $30-a-night motels elsewhere along US-20; for complete listings, contact the **visitor center**, 836 Sheridan Avenue (307/587-2297).

Meeteetse

East of Cody, Hwy-120, a prettier alternative to US-20, angles south over the

Aviator **Amelia Earhart** was having a ranch home built for her near Meeteetse along the Greybull River in 1934, but construction stopped after she disappeared on her round-the-world flight.

rugged foothill badlands of the Absaroka (pronounced "ab-SOR-ka") Mountains, historic homeland of the Crow Indians but now equal parts cattle ranches and oil wells. Thirty miles along this lonely highway brings you to Meeteetse (pop. 375), one of the oldest settlements in central Wyoming and still much the same for the past 125 years. The broad Greybull River—and an occasional cattle drive—runs right through town, which still retains wooden boardwalks and hitching posts for cowboys' horses.

Besides being wonderfully evocative of an earlier era, Meeteetse also has a pair of good museums documenting diverse aspects of the region's past. Most unusual is the **Charles J. Belden Museum** (daily 9 AM-5 PM; free), which holds an extraordinary collection of cowboy photography that includes the first "Marlboro Man" ads, shot on the nearby Pitchfork Ranch by the eponymous rancher and photographer. Also worth a look is the **Meeteetse Archive**, in a turn-of-the-century bank building a block south along Main Street.

Along with an old but fully stocked general store, Meeteetse has a few restaurants (try **Lucille's** cafe or the **Broken Spoke** steakhouse) and the $30-a-night **Oasis Motel**, 1702 State Street (307/868-2551), with camping and a Conestoga wagon.

Legend Rock

One of Wyoming's most significant collections of petroglyphs, Legend Rock contains over 250 images dating back some 2,000 years, carved into sandstone cliffs in the oil-rich foothills of the Owl Creek Mountains. To get there, follow US-120 for 21 miles from Thermopolis, or 33 miles from Meeteetse, then turn south at the Hamilton Dome turnoff and follow the dirt road for eight miles to a locked gate. The petroglyphs are a quarter-mile beyond the gate. The Thermopolis Convention and Visitor's Bureau has detailed information.

Thermopolis

Despite the highfalutin' resonance of its classical-sounding name, Thermopolis (pop. 3,300) is a sleepy, dusty little retirement town surrounded by red rock canyons and centered among a remarkable set of natural hot springs. The land was bought in 1896 from local Shoshone chief Washakie on the understanding that the spring waters be kept open to the public, white and Indian alike. This spring, which flows at a rate of 20 million gallons of 135° F water daily, was the basis of Wyoming's first state park, which still covers the east bank of the Bighorn River. A state-run **bathhouse** (Mon.-Sat. 8 AM-6 PM, Sunday noon-6 PM; free) has showers and changing rooms—you can rent towels and bathing suits for a nominal charge. There are also a pair of commercial enterprises in the park—the **Hot Springs Water Park**, and **Star Plunge**—with water slides, saunas, and so on, charging $5 admission.

Across the river in the center of town, the enjoyable **Hot Springs Historical Museum** (daily 8 AM-5 PM; $2), at 700 Broadway, has a wide-ranging collection of historic photos, farming and oil-drilling implements, and even the cherrywood bar from the Hole-in-the-Wall Saloon where Butch and Sundance supposedly bellied up for a drink or two.

The Thermopolis **visitor center** (307/864-3192 or 800/786-6772), right at the entrance to the springs at 220 Park Street, has listings of motels and campgrounds and other information on the area.

Wind River Canyon

South of Thermopolis, US-20 winds through Wind River Canyon, one of the most memorable drives in a state of memorable drives. The 2,500-foot-deep canyon, with the highway on one side of the broad river and the railroad on the other, reveals millions of years of sedimentary rock. As you drive along heading south, you reach deeper and deeper into the earth; each layer is labeled with signs explaining its geological age and significance, with the oldest layers dating back to the Precambrian era, some 2.5 billion years ago.

Driving along US-20 between the Wind River Canyon and Shoshoni, keep an eye out for the many pronghorn antelope that play on the rolling rangeland.

Due in part to the visual effect of the uplifted sedimentary layers, the river at times gives the illusion of flowing uphill; this may explain why Indians and early explorers thought there were two distinct rivers, and called the canyon itself the "**Wedding of the Waters.**" The river still has two distinct names: upstream from Wind River Canyon, it is called the Wind River; downsteam from the canyon, it's called the Bighorn River.

At the south end of the river, Boysen Reservoir, a popular place for fishing and water-skiing, backs up behind Boysen Dam, which was completed in 1961. The land west of the reservoir forms the two-million acre Wind River Indian Reservation, home to descendants of the Eastern Shoshone and Northern Arapahoe tribes; a woman thought by some to be Sacajawea (the Shoshone guide of Lewis and Clark fame) is buried on the reservation, along the Wind River near Fort Washakie.

Shoshoni

Named for the Shoshone Indians who once held sway over this part of the Great Plains, the forlorn town of Shoshoni (pop. 497) sits at the junction of US-20 and US-26, at the southeast edge of the Boysen Reservoir. Since the oil boom went bust, most of the motels and cafes look like they're on the verge of drying up and blowing away, though recent plans for a massive toxic waste repository have brought a surge of new money.

There is, however, one excellent reason to stop: the **Yellowstone Drug Store**, at the center of Shoshoni's block-long business district. It sells the state's best milk shakes and ice cream floats at the ancient-looking soda fountain.

Between Shoshoni and Casper, the only attraction worth mentioning is the odd geology of **Hell's Half Acre**, a 300-acre concentration of grotesquely eroded stone south of US-20 amid the arid badlands landscape.

Casper

Casper was the heart of the oil fields that led to the notorious Teapot Dome scandal of 1924-27, in which members of President Harding's cabinet were indicted for taking bribes. Only one went to prison.

The Casper area's most popular radio station is **KTWO 1030 AM**, with country music, talk shows, and local news.

Like other towns in southern Wyoming, Casper began as a way station on the many trails that followed the North Platte River, first as a ferry crossing (log rafts were run by Salt Lake City-bound Mormons from 1847 to 1852; non-Mormons were charged $1.50) and later as toll bridges, culminating with the elaborate plank bridge built by Louis Guinard in 1859. The second-largest city in Wyoming, only slightly smaller than the capital, Cheyenne, Casper (pop. 46,742) is still dependent upon passing trade; its key location along the I-25 corridor has enabled Casper to survive the downturns in its other historic industry, oil.

The main places of interest in Casper (which was originally spelled Caspar) have to do with the westward migration. The Oregon Trail and the later Pony Express passed through on their way west. **Fort Caspar** (Mon.-Sat. 8 AM-7 PM, Sunday noon-4 PM; free), west of downtown off Hwy-220, is a New Deal-era replica of the original rough log fort and Pony Express station; there's also a reconstruction of the Mormon-operated ferry, and displays of pioneer artifacts in the small museum.

While the rest of the city has a definite blue-collar, roughneck feel, downtown Casper is also rich in 1930s Americana, with some great old movie theater marquees (tickets cost just $2), rusty neon signs, and deco storefronts, plus an above-par range of junk stores and secondhand bookshops. The one place you really ought to visit is the **Nicolaysen Art Museum** (Mon.-Sat. 10 AM-5 PM; $2; 307/235-5247), housed in an imaginatively converted old power plant at 400 E. Collins Street, next to the Chicago and Northwestern Railroad tracks, east of the town center. The finest contemporary art museum in Wyoming, with frequent shows of regional artists, the Nicolaysen also has a permanent collection of Plains Indian arts and crafts, plus a hands-on art center for children.

The **Red and White Cafe**, 1620 E. Yellowstone Highway (US-20/26), is a classic roadside greasy spoon, one of a handful along the old highway frontage. If you can't face fried food, there are a few "fine dining" places in and amongst the hotels along I-25, north of downtown. Also, the **Daily Grind**, 328 E. A Street, has good coffees, teas, and baked goods, and occasional evening poetry readings. Casper's accommodation prices are very low, with room rates at the many motels along US-20 starting under $20 a night; more modern places along the I-25 frontage include most of the national chains.

For detailed listings or other local information, contact the Casper **visitor center** (307/234-5311 or 800/852-1889) at 500 N. Center Street south of I-25.

Glenrock

Midway between Casper and Douglas along the south bank of the North Platte River, Glenrock (pop. 2,153) was a vital rest stop and supply station on the Oregon and other emigrant trails. Several downtown buildings have endured since its heyday, when Glenrock was known as Deer Creek Station. Some 20,000 migrants came through each year, many of them camping overnight at the "rock in the glen" on the west side of town, where a sandstone boulder still holds the names of passing pioneers.

Between Casper and Glenrock, US-26 winds along the river, but east of Glenrock the old road has been replaced by the I-25 freeway.

Douglas

Situated far enough off I-25 to retain its Wild West, ranch land character, the enjoyable town of Douglas (pop. 5,076) was founded in 1886 across the river from Fort Fetterman, which for the previous 25 years had protected traffic on the old Oregon and Bozeman trails along the North Platte River. The location of Owen Wister's genre-inventing novel *The Virginian*, and more recently birthplace of that

---

JACKALOPES 'R' US

Traveling around the Great Plains, you're bound to come across all sorts of oversized wildlife—giant fish, giant cows, giant bison—plus some more that defy anatomical description. Most of the latter— fur-bearing trout, in particular—are seen primarily on postcards, but at least one species can usually be found mounted on the wall of any self-respecting saloon or taxidermist's shop: the jackalope. So rare that one has never been seen in the wild, the jackalope has the body of a jackrabbit and the horns of an antelope; dozens of examples are dis-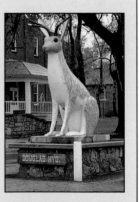
played around town, with the "world's largest" standing over eight feet head-to-tail in Jackalope Square at 3rd and Center Streets downtown. The enigmatic creature is also celebrated during Jackalope Days every June.

other Wild West icon, the **jackalope** (see sidebar), Douglas is a quietly picturesque small town with a wild history, and is a great place to break your long-distance road trip.

The Wyoming State Fairgrounds, along the river at the west end of Center Street, hosts a livestock-frenzied fair at the end of August, and also features the year-round **Pioneer Museum** (Mon.-Fri. 8 AM-5 PM, longer hours in summer; free; 307/358-9288), packed full of artifacts from the late 1800s—everything from rifles and a roulette table to fossils and farm implements. It also houses a Sioux-style hide tepee made for the movie *Dances with Wolves*. The wilder side of Douglas history is perhaps most vividly apparent in tombstones in the **cemetery** on the east edge of town at the end of Pine Street, where the legendary cattle rustler George Pike is interred beneath a marker that reads in part

> *Underneath this stone in eternal rest,*
> *Sleeps the wildest one of the wayward west.*

The best one-stop option for eating, drinking, and sleeping, in Douglas or most anywhere else for that matter, is the **Labonte Inn and Lounge**, 206 Walnut Street (307/358-9856), which offers a little of everything: bacon-and-eggs breakfasts, late-night beers, weekend country bands, and $35-a-night rooms. Another place to consider, **Through the Grapevine**, across the street from the giant jackalope, serves good coffee and lunchtime sandwiches. Other possibilities line the old US-20 alignment, on Richards Street in the east and the Yellowstone Highway on the west, forming a loop between exits off I-25.

For further information, contact the Douglas **visitor center**, 318 W. 1st Street (307/358-2950).

West of Douglas, five miles south of I-25, **Ayers Natural Bridge** arches 50 feet above La Prele Creek.

Douglas's own **KKTY 99.3 FM (1470 AM)** plays local news, country hits, and Colorado Rockies baseball games.

Lusk

A cattle-ranching and farming center, Lusk (pop. 1,500) is the largest town in the least populated county in the country's least populated state. It also boasts the only traffic light on US-20 between Douglas, Wyoming, and Chadron, Nebraska. And if those claims to fame don't make you want to stop, the **Stagecoach Museum** at 322 S. Main Street (daily 1-5 PM and 7-9 PM in summer, shorter hours rest of the year; $1) definitely will, if only to see the sole authentic 1880s Cheyenne-Deadwood Stagecoach—the one Doris Day sang about in *Calamity Jane*. (The only other stagecoach from this legendary route is now in the Smithsonian.) Behind the museum building is another frontier icon—a one-room schoolhouse—and along US-20 at the east edge of town a plaque points out a redwood water tower dating from 1886, when steam locomotives still chugged across the plains.

A marker on the south side of US-20, a mile east of Lusk, stands where US-20 intersects the **Texas Trail,** which in the 1870s and 1880s was a busy cattle train route between Fort Worth and the open ranges of Wyoming and Montana.

A worthwhile detour from Douglas or Lusk takes you 40-plus miles south to **Guernsey** on the North Platte River, where the best surviving set of Oregon Trail wagon ruts, cut shoulder deep in the soft sandstone, are preserved in a well-marked park.

Lusk also has a good range of motels, including the good value **Pioneer Court**, 731 S. Main Street (307/334-2640 or 800/528-1234). For food, try either of two diners: the **Coffee Cup** or **The Diner**, both on Main Street within a block of the stoplight. The Diner seems the more popular; the Coffee Cup has a better sign.

ACROSS NEBRASKA

In its 450-mile trek across Nebraska, US-20 passes through a surprising variety of landscapes. In the west, the highway skirts the edge of the huge and desolate Sand Hills, where North America's largest system of sand dunes underlies a grassy pastoral scene. Across the midsection the road runs parallel to the broad Niobrara River before reaching the bluffs above the Missouri River. It's one of the few in the Great Plains not blocked behind a dam.

One of the last reaches of the country to be settled and domesticated, northern Nebraska is still sparsely populated, and looks like the Great Plains are *supposed* to look. Towns are few and far between, and come and go in the proverbial blink of an eye; the rolling ranch lands are marked every mile or so by spinning Aeromotor windmills pumping up water for wandering cattle herds, while historical plaques point out the sites where, barely a century ago, cowboys rode and Indians did battle with the U.S. Cavalry. Besides being rich in Wild West history—and in prehistoric fossil beds—the region has a strong literary tradition, thanks to writers such as Mari Sandoz and John G. Neihardt. All in all, few corners of the country pay back time spent with as much interest as does northern Nebraska; hard to believe, perhaps, but true.

Harrison and Agate Fossil Beds National Monument

Just over the Wyoming border, the tiny town of Harrison is an attractive wide-spot-in-the-road, worth a stop to sample the huge burgers and silky milk shakes at **Sioux Sundries**, corner of Main and 2nd Streets. Twenty-three miles south of Harrison, on the banks of the Niobrara River, Agate Fossil Beds National Monument (daily 8:30 AM-5:30 PM; free; 308/436-4340) contains the 20-million-year-old remains of bison-sized pigs, twin-horned proto-rhinos, and other vanished creatures.

Nebraska publishes a handy free booklet about US-20's route across the state. Copies are available at most visitor centers, or through the Nebraska US-20 Association, R.R. 1, Box 218, Plainview, NE 68769 (402/582-3798).

The highway through Harrison was unpaved as recently as 1941.

Fort Robinson

Thirty miles from the Wyoming border, Fort Robinson was established in 1874 to control the 15,000 restless natives of the Red Cloud and Pine Ridge Sioux Indian agencies. Now a state park, and planted with groves of mature trees where 100 years ago all was grassland prairie, Fort Robinson has perhaps the most tragic and uncomfortable history of all the many old forts on the Wild West frontier: this is where the unarmed Sioux chief Crazy Horse was stabbed to death with bayonets while in the custody of the U.S. Army; it's where the controversial Red Cloud Treaty, in which the Sioux gave up the Black Hills, was signed; and it's where the last of the Cheyenne under Chief Dull

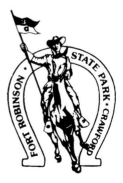

MOUNT RUSHMORE AND CARHENGE

Two of the nation's most distinctive outdoor sculptures stand along US-385 within a manageable drive from US-20. One is perhaps the best-known artwork in the U.S., the giant presidential memorial at Mount Rushmore. Roughly 100 miles north from Chadron, at the far eastern side of the beautiful Black Hills, Mount Rushmore is graced by the 60-foot heads of four U.S. Presidents—Washington, Jefferson, Lincoln, and Teddy Roosevelt—carved into a granite peak. It's equal parts impressive monument and kitschy Americana, and one of those places you really have to see to believe.

Another newer, less famous monument to America sits in a flat field along US-385 outside the town of Alliance, 62 miles south of Chadron. Built in 1987 as part of a local family reunion, Carhenge is a giant-sized replica of the famous Druidical ruin, Stonehenge; this one, however, is built entirely out of three dozen late-model American cars, stacked on top of one another to form a semi-circular temple.

For more information on Mount Rushmore, contact the Rapid City visitor center (800/487-3223). For more on Carhenge, call the Alliance Chamber of Commerce (308/762-1520).

Knife were killed in battle rather than transported south to a reservation in Oklahoma.

Knowing this history, it can be hard to take Fort Robinson as the hugely enjoyable respite it is today. The hundreds of hardwood trees make it an oasis on the generally treeless plains, and the whitewashed wooden barracks, many now converted to cultural centers and museums, give it the air of a college campus—especially on summer weekends, when the park turns into a living history museum complete with cookouts and evening melodramas.

Accommodations are offered in the officers' quarters, and there are many good camping spots; phone 308/665-2900 for details.

The only part of the park open year-round is the **Fort Robinson Museum** (Mon.-Fri. 8 AM-5 PM, longer hours in summer; $1) in the old headquarters building, with full displays on the fort's history, plus walking-tour maps of the entire post.

Crawford

Three miles east of Fort Robinson, and once one of the wilder boomtowns on the Wild West frontier, Crawford came to life in the mid-1880s after the U.S. Army rid the region of the warring Sioux, and has settled into a sedate life as a ranching and farming center. Pines and cottonwoods line the White River, making a pretty scene, though for visitors there's not much more than a gas station and a drive-in burger stand to detain you.

Oglala National Grasslands, 17 miles north of Crawford via Hwy-2, occupies nearly 100,000 acres along the Nebraska/Wyoming/South Dakota borders, highlighted by the eerie landscape of **Toadstool Geological Park**, where ancient fossils can be found amongst weirdly eroded figures. An archaeological site known as the **Hudson-Meng Bison Bone Bed** is a shallow arroyo holding the enigmatic remains of over 600 bison, plus stone tools and arrowheads, dating from approximately 10,000 years ago. For details on the grasslands, which offer good hiking and camping, contact the **ranger station** at 270 Pine Street (308/432-0300) in Chadron.

Chadron: The Museum of the Fur Trade

The largest town in northwest Nebraska, Chadron (pop. 5,588) sits at the northern edge of the Sand Hills region, bounded by pine forests to the south and the Pine Ridge Sioux Reservation to the north, across the South Dakota border. The highway frontage along US-20 isn't especially inviting, but the two-block town center preserves its turn-of-the-century character with sandstone and brick-fronted buildings along the south side of the still-used railroad tracks.

There's not a lot to do in Chadron, but it does make a handy base for trips north to the Pine Ridge lands and the Black Hills, or south to the marvelous Carhenge. Besides a couple of motels, including a Best Western and a Super 8, you can stay the night in the **Old Main Street Inn**, 115 Main Street (308/432-3380). Part old railroad hotel, part cozy B&B, the inn has a downstairs restaurant and saloon, and Chadron's only espresso machine. (The hotel is where in 1890 General Miles stayed before heading north to massacre helpless women and children at Wounded Knee.)

In 1893, Chadron's early boosters found a perfect way to get their town in the news: they sponsored a 1,000-mile horse race from Chadron to Chicago, which made front pages across the country. A plaque in front of the black-and-white Blaine Hotel, a block east of Main Street, marks the start of the race.

If you're anywhere nearby, don't miss the excellent **Museum of the Fur Trade** (8 AM-5 PM June-Sept., by appointment rest of the year; $1.50; 308/432-3843), on US-20 three miles east of downtown Chadron. One of the great small museums in the U.S., this privately run collection focuses on the material culture of the North American frontier. Its extensive displays bring to life the few first centuries of interaction between Native Americans and Europeans. Besides giving the overall historical context of the fur trade and its many related enterprises, the collection emphasizes the day-to-day realities of life on the Great Plains in the 18th and 19th centuries. Walls decked with weapons and bottles of whiskey (from the Americans), rum (from the English), and brandy (from the French) document the better-known aspects, but what captures your attention are the little things: packs of playing cards, a checkerboard—even a waterproof parka made out of seal intestines by the Inuit.

Behind the museum building is an in situ reconstruction of the fur trading post built in 1833 by the American Fur Company and home in the mid-1840s to French fur trapper James Bordeaux, who hosted such luminary "explorers" as John C. Frémont and Francis Parkman on their travels around the western U.S.

Museum membership is a good deal; for $6 a year, you get unlimited free admission and a subscription to the museum's quarterly journal.

In north-central Nebraska, an interesting radio alternative is the commercial-free country-western music broadcast from the Pine Ridge reservation on **KILI 90.1 FM.**

Gordon: Mari Sandoz Country

The tiny town of Gordon, midway between Merriman and Chadron, is a typical northwestern Nebraska ranching town with a strong connection to the "Storycatcher of the Plains," Mari Sandoz, whose many books document the lives and times of the surrounding Sand Hills region. Sandoz, who wrote about growing up on a nearby ranch in her first book, the haunting classic *Old Jules,* captured the spirit and history of the Great Plains in her many works of fiction and nonfiction, all of which are available in the **Mari Sandoz Room** (Mon.-Fri. 9 AM-5 PM, Saturday 9 AM-noon; free; 308/282-9972), 117 Main Street, north of US-20 beyond the grain elevators and railroad tracks at the center of town. The Sandoz museum, which shares space with the Ad-Pad stationery store, has extensive displays of her personal effects, and free pamphlets describing a driving tour of Sandoz-related sites in the area. For aficionados of her work, Mari Sandoz's sister, Caroline Sandoz Pifer, has a museum and research library at her home, 20 miles south of Gordon via Hwy-27, then six miles east on a gravel road; for details and hours, phone 308/282-1687.

Gas stations line the US-20 frontage, and the one-stop **Hacienda Motel** (308/282-1400), on US-20 west of US-83, has rooms and a popular restaurant and bar.

Merriman

East of Gordon, US-20 winds along the northern edge of the Sand Hills, coming within a few miles of the South Dakota border. The town of Merriman (pop. 151) may not look like much, but it does mark the turnoff north to the nearby **Arthur Bowring Sand Hills Ranch State Historical Park** (daily 9 AM-5 PM in summer; $2 per car), a working cattle ranch preserved pretty much as it was at the turn of the century. The site is lovely, with a sod house surrounded (in springtime, at least) by rolling green hills. A modern visitor center has displays on windmills and other facts of Sand Hills life, plus biographical displays on the politically powerful Bowring family, who lived and worked here from 1895 until 1985. To get there, head 1.3 miles north of town on Hwy-61, then two miles northeast following good signs.

Between Merriman and Valentine, US-20 passes through flyspeck former railroad towns including Kilgore (pop. 71), Crookston (pop. 99), and the Wild West false-fronts of bustling Cody (pop. 177), yet another "town too tough to die."

Valentine marks the junction with US-83, "The Road to Nowhere"; that chapter begins on page 124.

In Merriman, a block south of US-20, a roadside display shows the many different cattle brands used by Sand Hills ranches.

Johnstown

In the village of Johnstown just north of US-20, eight miles east of Ainsworth and 40 miles southeast of Valentine, a block of wooden storefronts and boardwalks were gussied up as a backdrop for a TV production of Willa Cather's *O Pioneers!* Behind the contrived facades you'll find a dusty old general store, and a beer bar and pool hall complete with backyard privy.

Kilgore marks the dividing line between central and mountain time zones; adjust your clocks and watches accordingly.

On Norden Road, 16 miles north of Johnstown, the Nature Conservancy protects the 50,000-acre Niobrara Valley Preserve, which has both Sand Hills and riparian ecosystems. Self-guided trails wind through the preserve past a small but expanding herd of bison.

Ainsworth

Roughly the midway point of US-20's long cruise across Nebraska, Ainsworth (pop. 1,800) calls itself the state's "country music capital" and hosts a popular concert and festival in early August. Ainsworth also hosts a Middle of Nowhere Festival in June, celebrated with a Wild-West-style trail ride and a black powder rendezvous. For details on either of these events, or on anything else to do with Ainsworth, contact the visitor center (402/387-2740).

Eat big burgers at **Big Jo's**, on US-20 on the east side of town, and stay the night at the **Remington Arms Motel** (402/387-2220).

O'Neill

East of Ainsworth, US-20 runs through an especially scenic section of the Sand Hills around the artsy hamlet of **Bassett** (home to Nebraska's only operating **drive-in movie theater**, the Pineview, right on US-20 west of town) before following the Elkhorn River to the town of O'Neill, 66 miles downstream. Nebraska's official "Irish Capital," O'Neill hosts a very popular St. Patrick's Day parade and celebration, but also has a fascinating history: the town was founded in 1874 by Irish settlers led by John O'Neill, who commanded a brigade of black infantrymen during the Civil War and afterwards became involved in the Fenian invasions of still-British Canada.

Another of O'Neill's many distinctions is that it has the only McDonald's along US-20 in Nebraska; this outlet is said to make O'Neill the "smallest town not on an interstate to have a McDonald's"—or something like that. A half-dozen motels line US-20 through town, including a Super 8 and the **Elms Motel** (402/336-3800), with rooms from $30 a night. Free camping, a large swimming pool, and a championship-class set of horseshoe-tossing courts are available in Carney Park.

Ashfall Fossil Beds State Park

Six miles north of US-20 via Hwy-59, from a well-signed junction two miles west of the tiny village of Royal, you can watch paleontologists at work uncovering giant fossils at Ashfall Fossil Beds State Park (Mon.-Sat. 10 AM-4 PM, Sunday 1-4 PM, longer hours in summer; $1; 402/893-2000). Unusual for a fossil bed, the skeletons here are preserved completely intact because the original residents—including prehistoric herds of rhinoceros, camels, and saber-toothed deer—got caught in a volcanic eruption some 10 million years ago. Since the bones haven't been disturbed, you can get a clear sense of the the creatures' size and the sheer numbers of their populations around a prehistoric watering hole.

If you want to learn more about the fascinating histories and cultures of the Great Plains, head south of US-20 to the the tiny town of Bancroft, where the **John G. Neihardt Center** (Mon.-Sat. 9 AM-5 PM; free; 402/648-3388) exhibits the personal collection of Nebraska's poet laureate and writer of the Native American classic *Black Elk Speaks*.

Eastern Nebraska

Because it's a fascinating part of the country, fairly detailed coverage has been directed at the places along US-20 across most of northern Nebraska. The same, however, cannot be said of Nebraska's far northeast quarter. To be honest, there's not a lot worth stopping for in the 90-odd miles west of the Missouri River (which marks the beginning of Iowa, where there's not a lot either). All of which is to say, if you're doing a long-distance haul along US-20, and time is tight, you can drive all night through northeast Nebraska and no one will ever point out anything you missed.

ACROSS IOWA

US-20 cuts straight across the midsection of Iowa between the
Missouri and the Mississippi Rivers, running along the invisible
border that divides the flat, agricultural tableland that distinguishes
the northern half of the state from the more heavily industrialized south. The first
industry here was lead mining in the 1840s, but the predominant activity these
days is livestock raising. Cows and pigs feed on the abundant corn that grows in
fields all along the highway. Popcorn is also a major crop.

> Over 95% of Iowa is cultivated farmland—the highest percentage of any U.S. state.

Sioux City

The honey-producing and hog-butchering center of Sioux City
(pop. 80,505) is not most people's idea of a vacation treat, but it
does offer a few diversions to the roadtripping traveler. Grain
elevators and huge brick warehouses fill the riverfront district;
and some interesting Victorian-era rooming houses stand on

> Sioux City's favorite daughters are the sisters and fellow advice columnists **Ann Landers** and **Abigail "Dear Abby" Van Buren.**

the surrounding hills, but otherwise the main attraction is the **Sioux City Public
Museum**, a mile north of downtown at 2901 Jackson Street (Mon.-Sat. 9 AM-5 PM,
Sunday 2-5 PM; free; 712/279-6174), with all the usual displays tracing the Native
American, pioneer, and agricultural histories of the area. There's another small mu-
seum, focusing on river history, in a drydocked riverboat that doubles as the Sioux
City **visitor center** (712/279-4840 or 800/593-2228), along the river near the Ar-
gosy riverboat casino.

Lewis and Clark buffs will also want to stop south of Sioux City at the **Floyd
Monument**, where a 100-foot stone obelisk marks the place where expedition
member Sgt. Charles Floyd—the Corps of Discovery's only fatality—died of appendicitis in August 1804, two months after they had set off from St. Louis. Besides the
historical homage, the site offers a great panorama of the Missouri River.

Sioux City doesn't offer a terribly enticing range of eating or accommodation options, though one long-standing local favorite, **Green Gables Restaurant,** a half-
mile north of downtown at 1800 Pierce Street (712/258-4246), has bountiful,
cheap food and very good desserts.

Sac City and Rockwell City

East of Sioux City, US-20 alternates between four-lane freeway and older two-lane
highway, passing acres of farmland and occasional towns. Sac City (pop. 2,492) is
one of the few places along this stretch of road that tries to preserve its past intact,
with a log cabin along US-20 and a small historical museum on Main Street. Twenty miles farther east, in Rockwell City (pop. 1,981), the **Leist Oil Company** has an
incredible collection of old neon and enamelled metal roadside signs advertising
cars, car parts, soda pop, and sundry other things.

Fort Dodge

Founded in the 1850s to protect settlers from roving bands of Sauk and Black Hawk Indians, Fort Dodge is today a sleepy Midwestern town, economically dependent upon local farms, gypsum wallboard plants, and a huge Friskies cat food factory. Amid many stately homes on the south side of downtown, one place really worth a look is the **Blanden Memorial Art Museum**, 920 3rd Avenue S (Tues.-Fri. 10 AM-5 PM, Saturday and Sunday 1-5 PM; free). Housed inside a grand neoclassi-

cal 1930s building, the collections include examples of pre-Columbian pottery, Renaissance sculpture, and Japanese prints. Modern paintings include works by people you wouldn't expect to find in the middle of Iowa—Max Beckmann, Marc Chagall, and Rufino Tamayo, to name three—along with works by Grant Wood and other Iowa artists.

The famous **Cardiff Giant,** a seven-foot tall skeleton supposedly unearthed in New York in 1869, was thought by experts to be the bones of a prehistoric man. However, the skeleton, which was kept on display by showman P.T. Barnum for the next 35 years, was later proven to be a hoax, carved from a slab of gypsum quarried at Fort Dodge.

Cedar Falls and Waterloo

US-20 turns to fast, four-lane freeway around Cedar Falls, a historic industrial town founded in the 1850s along the Cedar River. Now home to the University of Northern Iowa, Cedar Falls preserves the remnants of its manufacturing heritage with a half-dozen historical museums; for details, contact the **visitor center**, 10 Main Street (319/266-3593).

Waterloo is worth a look if you can be here on Memorial Day, when vintage car enthusiasts from around the Midwest participate in the Fourth Street Cruise.

Downstream from Cedar Falls, and similarly bypassed by the modern US-20 freeway, Waterloo (pop. 66,467) is a bigger and busier city, with an almost urban feel and yet more good museums, including the **Grout Museum** (which, despite the name, is a general science and history museum—not a collection of great tile-setting materials!). Waterloo is also home to the massive **John Deere Tractor** assembly plant on the outskirts of town at 3500 E. McDonald Street. The general tour (Mon.-Fri. at 9 AM and 1 PM; free) takes you through the main plant; upon request, they may arrange tours of the foundry and engine works. There's also a small shop where you can stock up on their trademark caps and souvenirs.

The Waterloo **visitor center**, 215 E. 4th Street (319/233-8350 or 800/728-8431), can help with practical information.

Quasqueton and Cedar Rock

Midway between Waterloo and Dyersville, the tiny town of Quasqueton (pop. 579) holds Cedar Rock, a wonderful riverside house completed in 1950 by architect Frank Lloyd Wright for local-boy-done-good businessman Lowell Walter, who got rich by developing and patenting a method of sealing highway surfaces. One of seven houses Wright built in Iowa, Cedar Rock is an excellent and complete example of his "Usonian" ideals, and everything in the house—from the soaring roof, the smooth flow of interior space, and the signature hearth, right down to designs of the carpets and cutlery—embodies Wright's idealized vision of middle-class American houses, designed for simple if stylish living in close accord with nature.

Carved into a limestone ridge overlooking a bend in the Wapsipinicon River, Cedar Rock is two miles northwest of Quasqueton, seven miles south of US-20, and surrounded by acres of rolling woodland. The house and grounds are now owned and managed by the state of Iowa and are open in summer only for guided **tours** (Tues.-Sun. 11 AM-5 PM; free; 319/934-3572).

Quasqueton itself is a great little place, worth a stop for a cup of coffee at the quaint **Big Q Cafe**, or dinner and a drink at the **Friendly Tavern**. The two face each other across Water Street at the center of the block-long town.

Dyersville: The Field of Dreams

"If you build it, he will come. . . ." Ever since the movie *Field of Dreams* came out in 1989, people have flocked to Dyersville (27 miles west of Dubuque) to reenact the fairy tale baseball movie, major scenes from which were filmed just outside of town.

Though Iowa's first white explorers were French, the earliest settlements in eastern Iowa were established by the English, which explains place-names like Epworth, Nottingham, and Manchester.

Acres of cornfield surround the rather municipal-looking diamond, and a small stand sells postcards, T-shirts, and other souvenirs. Though privately owned, the attraction is "open" daily 10 AM-6 PM April-Nov., and is free. To get there, take Hwy-136 north from US-20, then follow signs northeast along 3rd Avenue and Field of Dreams Road for about 3.5 miles from US-20.

Considering it's such a small town, Dyersville has a lot in store. Besides the Field of Dreams, the town boasts one of only 36 Catholic basilicas in the U.S. (St. Francis Xavier, that can't-miss gothic pile in the center of town). The **National Farm Toy Museum**, right off US-20 at 1110 16th Avenue (daily 8 AM-7 PM; $3), has over 30,000 miniature tractors and plows show-

You've kept up with the Joneses — You've been in Jones County!

casing 100 years of toys—from horse-drawn wooden ones to die-cast modern ones—many of them made by Dyersville's three model toy companies.

For details on any of the above attractions, or for suggested restaurants and accommodations, contact the Dyersville **visitor center,** just north of US-20 at 1424 9th Street (319/875-2311).

Dubuque

Between Dyersville and Dubuque, the old Chicago Great Western Railroad right-of-way has been converted into a very pleasant, 26-mile hiking and cycling trail.

The oldest city in Iowa, Dubuque (pop. 57,546) was founded in 1833 and named for French voyageur Julien Dubuque, who unsuccessfully mined for lead on land acquired from the Spanish (to whom France had ceded all territory west of the Mississippi, 40 years before they took it all back and sold it to Thomas Jefferson). Finding lead wasn't the problem—Indians dug lead by hand as early as 1680 for trade with the English—but getting it to market was. After the steamboat's arrival and the Indians' forced removal in the late 1820s, mineral wealth became a major catalyst to settlement of the tri-state area around Dubuque, as town names like Potosi, Mineral Point, New Diggings, and Lead Mine attest. During the Civil War, just five counties around here supplied all the lead for the entire Union war effort.

The Iowa Welcome Center down on the waterfront stands next to Dubuque's newest source of wealth, the Casino Belle, northernmost of the long parade of riverboat casinos found all the way down to the Gulf of Mexico. Not able to wholly give in to sin, Iowa initially required that gaming to "low stakes," meaning that players were restricted to $200 per excursion aboard the boat. Once neighboring Illinois floated its own no-limit gameboats, Iowa had to amend its law to keep the golden goose from roosting elsewhere. So much for the strength of conviction.

On the inland side of the compact downtown, a good view of the city and the Mississippi valley can be had at the top of the **Fenelon Place Elevator,** a small funicular cable car that proudly holds the title of "world's steepest, shortest scenic railway" (daily 8 AM-10 PM, April-Nov.; 75 cents one-way). If it's a tall lanky fellow at the controls of the 15-hp motor up in the headhouse, and you're a baseball fan, you might have fun trying to stump him with questions about the Minnesota Twins, his favorite team. He purports to know their starting lineups for every year back since 1961.

Dubuque is a very meat-and-potatoes place when it comes to food, and plan to dine early if you want to eat. Basic coffee-shop breakfasts, lunches, and dinners are on the menu at **Dottie's Cafe,** downtown at 5th and Central, while the landmark **Bridge** steakhouse, on Main Street at the foot of the US-20 bridge (look for the neon "Good Food" sign), is a step or two up in price and quality. Near the Fenelon Place Elevator, **Shot Tower Pizza** has an upstairs deck and beer by the pitcher. For entertainment, check out Main Street bars like **Loie and Admiral's High Hat Lounge,** which hosts live music most nights.

For a place to stay, the classic old hotel in town is the **Julien Inn,** 200 Main Street (319/556-4200 or 800/798-7098), with rooms for $30-50, while the **Redstone Inn,** 504 Bluff Street (319/582-1894), offers comfortable B&B rooms in a stately downtown mansion. The usual chain motels line US-20 west of the river.

ACROSS ILLINOIS

US-20 angles across northern Illinois from the Mississippi River to Lake Michigan, bringing you from the unglaciated scenery of the "Driftless Region" to the towering city of Chicago in less than 200 miles. The western stretches pass through hill-and-valley regions where water power and mineral deposits were harnessed by early industry. The old two-lane road is still in use, climbing onto stony ridges, then dropping into hardwood-forested valleys across the undulating region that stretches east from the Iowa border. This stretch of old road has as great a variety of barns and grain bins as anywhere in the country; however, there's considerable pressure to widen and "improve" it, so enjoy it while you can. In contrast, the rolling flatlands of the northeastern half is mostly Chicagoland suburbs mixed with occasional pastures and woodlands. Approaching Chicago, old US-20 all but disappears as a useful alternative, replaced by the busy I-90 freeway.

Northwestern Illinois was the site of many skirmishes between settlers and Indians during the Black Hawk War of the early 1830s.

Galena

Spawned by Wisconsin's mid-19th-century lead mining rush, Galena (pop. 3,647) became the social and cultural capital of the Upper Mississippi basin. In the 1840s, while Chicago was still a mean collection of tents in a swamp around Fort Dearborn, and the Twin Cities were but a trading post in the woods around Fort Snelling, Galena was producing upwards of 75% of the world's lead, and the town was filled with bankers, merchants, and speculators who built mansions, hotels, and emporiums stuffed with fine goods and furnishings from around the world. This part of the Driftless Region saw some of the greatest wealth and commerce of the upper Mississippi, with Galena alone higher in population—some 15,000 lived here during the Civil War—than the entire Minnesota Territory.

But the California gold rush, played-out lead mines, a river silting up from miner-induced erosion, and a national economic panic all drove Galena to become a handsome ghost town that nobody bothered to tear down. For 100 years it slumbered, but beginning in the 1960s Galena was resurrected as a quaint tourist town. The brick warehouses were converted into shops and galleries, and anything but the most subtle, hand-carved signage was banned: in Galena, preserving the historical complexion of the streetscape isn't just a good idea, it's the law. The outskirts, especially along the US-20 frontage, are fairly typical franchised sprawl, and there are still a few everyday businesses in the historic core (including a funeral parlor and a large and busy metal foundry), but the overall result is so complete that passing through the downtown levee floodgates is like entering Brigadoon. Even the innumerable galleries and shops selling "collectibles" (things you or your kids will wonder how to get rid of some day) can't spoil the remarkable effect of the place. One essential: park the car and *stroll.*

Besides the integrity of its mid-19th century buildings, Galena was the town that saw a local store clerk win both the Civil War and the presidency. The modest **Ulysses S. Grant Home** (daily 9 AM-5 PM except major holidays; $2 donation suggested; 815/777-0248), given to the general by a grateful group of local Republicans, sits up Bouthillier Street across the river from downtown. It is now a state historic site restored to the period immediately preceding Grant's move to the White House. A small museum behind the house traces Grant's life, from the Civil War to the presidency to his burial in Grant's Tomb.

Even if you're blind to Galena's manifold aesthetic and historical delights, you'll probably enjoy its culinary variety. Starting at 5:30 AM daily, the **Steakburger Diner**, on Main Street below the "Fresh Pies Daily" clock, dishes up your basic omelets and meatloaf at rock-bottom prices for a local clientele that drops in for a cuppa joe, smoke, and small talk. Only breakfast and lunch are served, until 2 PM. Within a block's walk, one of a handful of good local bakeries, **Jakel's Bäckerie**, offers white-flour-and-sugar salvation to all faithful dessert worshippers, and light lunch items, too. Heartier, less-refined baked goods, along with decent vegetarian fare, are found in the **Lost Art Cafe**, at the north end of Main near Franklin.

For a good, cheap dinner in a comfortable ambience, try the **Log Cabin**, 201 N. Main Street, Galena's oldest restaurant, with a great big green-and-red sign that predates the town's anti-neon ordinance; it's served industrial-strength Italian food, plus steaks and seafood, since 1937 and is well frequented by locals. Despite the supposed gentrification of the community and apparent sophistication of its residents, Galena restaurants serve up a lot of "continental" cuisine (a.k.a. dull). One of the best top-dollar exceptions is **Eldorado**, 219 N. Main Street, with a standout Southwestern-influenced menu and vegetarian choices way beyond the lettuce-and-tomato fare found elsewhere.

Thanks to the three large cheese plants along US-20 in the northwest corner of the state, Illinois is the top-ranked Swiss cheese producer in the U.S.

There are some 60-odd hotels, guest homes, and B&B inns here in "the B&B capital of the Midwest." The central **DeSoto House**, 230 S. Main Street (815/777-0090), was U.S. Grant's headquarters during his 1868 presidential campaign; rooms cost from

$80 a night. You'll find many other places to stay within walking distance of the historic area. The spacious and comfortable **Belle Aire Mansion** (815/777-0893) stands along US-20 west of town. If you're just passing through, the cheapest decent sleep in town is at the **Grant Hills Motel** along US-20 east of town, next to a small antique car museum.

The Galena/Jo Daviess County Convention and Visitors Bureau operates an excellent **visitor center** (815/777-0203 or 800/747-9377), across the river via a pedestrian-only bridge, in the old Illinois Central Railroad depot at the base of Bouthillier Street. Stacks of brochures cover everything from accommodations to bike tours. This is also the best place to **park** the car, as spaces are at a premium in the often crowded downtown area.

Mrs. Grant didn't like the fact that her late husband's statue in Galena's Grant Park showed the general with his hand in his pocket. Not that she wanted it changed. "Oh, no!" she told the sculptor, "leave it as it is, but dear me, I've told that man 20 times a day to take his hand out of his pocket."

Freeport

Midway between Galena and Rockford, the oddly named town of Freeport (pop. 25,840) is neither a port nor even near any body of water. According to the WPA *Guide to Illinois*, the name was bestowed by the wife of an early settler to satirize his fondness for providing free room and board to passersby.

Along US-20, 12 miles east of Galena, a 75-foot-tall lookout tower gives tourists a "Tri-State View" over the Driftless Area.

There's no free lunch here today, but Freeport does offer at least one good reason to stop: the **Union-Daily Ice Cream Parlour**, on Douglas Street two blocks north of the US-20 Business Loop. Enjoy a creamy, cool milk shake or sundae, then step next door to the small park, where an oddly distorted statue marks the site of the second **Lincoln-Douglas debate**, held here on August 27, 1858. A plaque quotes both men equally, with Lincoln's "This government cannot endure permanently half-slave and half-free" opposing Douglas saying, "I am not for the dissolution of the Union under any circumstance."

The multinational Kraft Foods got its start in **Stockton,** Illinois.

Jane Addams, founder of Chicago's reform-minded Hull House, was born in 1860 and is buried near the town of Cedarville, six miles north of Freeport.

Rockford

Spreading haphazardly along the leafy banks of the Rock River, Rockford (pop. 139,426) is a big, somewhat sprawling industrial city at the west end of the I-90 toll road from Chicago. US-20 bypasses the down-at-heel downtown area which, if the residents wore more hats, would look like a film set on "Main Street" of industrial America circa 1952. After exploring Rockford's nooks and crannies, including many nice parks and the quirky clocks collected inside the **Time Museum** (Tues.-Sun. 10 AM-5 PM; $3) in the Clock Tower complex at 7801 E. State Street off the US-20/I-90 junction, reward yourself with lunch or dinner at one of Illinois's great roadfood haunts, **The Rathskeller,** 1132 Auburn Street (815/963-2922), off Main Street a mile north of downtown Rockford. Since 1931, this Teutonic institution has been serving up skillets of sausage and potatoes, corned beef sandwiches, and very good desserts.

For more information, contact the Rockford **visitor center,** 211 N. Main Street (815/963-8111 or 800/521-0849).

If you have the time, Hwy-2 follows a lovely route from Rockford along the Rock River southwest to the quaint old town of Dixon, where the **Ronald Reagan Boyhood Home,** 816 S. Hennepin Avenue (815/288-3404) preserves the house where the Great Communicator spent his teenage years.

Union: Illinois Railway Museum

Between Rockford and Chicago, US-20 is a slow, winding, and poorly signposted alternative to the high-speed I-90 toll road. It's a leisurely route, with few identifiable attractions except for the road itself, which cruises through small towns surrounded by farmlands and lined by fruit-and-vegetable stands. The one real draw here is a mile east of the tiny town of Union, where the Illinois Railway Museum (daily 11 AM-4 PM, longer hours in summer; $7; 815/923-4000) displays a great range of track-based transportation: streetcars, trolleys, and railroad cars, with a working steam train running weekends throughout the year.

The great city of Chicago is covered as a Survival Guide on pages 684-685.

ACROSS INDIANA

So close and yet so far away from the excitement of Chicago, northern Indiana can't help but seem somewhat boring. In the northwest, the state is bounded by Lake Michigan, along whose shores Rust Belt hulks of derelict heavy industry stand side by side with the pristine sands of the fascinating and beautiful Indiana Dunes National Lakeshore. The northeastern corner, even in the estimation of the state tourist office, offers little more than a few lakes and the so-called "muck lands" around the Fighting Irish homeland of South Bend. In between stretch endless acres of rolling farmland, Amish homes, and other tourist-attractive agricultural communities.

Though its etymology sparks heated debates, the nickname "Hoosier" has come to connote all that is Middle American about Indianans—their independence, their practicality, and their thrift (or is it their cussedness, conservatism, and cheapness?).

Gary

Unless you have a particular interest in documenting Rust Belt decay, there's no real reason to turn off the I-90 or I-94 freeways southeast of Chicago.

If you ever watched and enjoyed the Hollywood musical *The Music Man*—in which the song "Gary Indiana" paints a picture of idyllic homespun Americana—you'll be surprised by the reality of the place. In contrast to the rural rest of the state, this far northwest corner of Indiana is among the most heavily industrialized and impoverished areas of the country. Massive factories and oil refineries are surrounded by decaying communities, and the streets are lined by strip malls, strip clubs, and stripped-down cars. During the region's heyday around the turn of the 20th century, the steel mills, foundries, and factories along the Calumet River pumped out millions of dollars' worth of products every day; nowadays, economic times are so hard that local authorities have to call in the National-Guard to police the streets.

Indiana Dunes National Lakeshore

Covering 15,000 acres along 15 miles of Lake Michigan shoreline, Indiana Dunes National Lakeshore is a striking and surprising collection of golden sand dunes, freshwater beaches, and dense forests, which poet Carl Sandburg said "are to the Midwest what the Grand Canyon is to Arizona." Formally established in 1972, the park includes a huge variety of plantlife—groves of maples and red oaks, pine tree and prickly pear cactus, grasslands and berry bushes—linked by many miles of hiking trails and highlighted by 125-foot Mount Baldy at the far northeast corner of the park.

Three huge steel mills and a number of small vacation home communities share space among the dunes. Also here, two miles northeast of the main visitor center, is the unusual **Beverly Shores,** a model community constructed for the "Century of Progress" World's Fair in Chicago in 1933 and reassembled here soon after in an attempt to attract buyers to a new resort community. Six of these then-futuristic structures survive along Lakefront Drive, including three steel-framed, enamel-paneled "Lustron" houses, designed to provide low-cost housing during the Great Depression. Next door is the "House of Tomorrow," an ordinary-looking house designed with an additional garage to hold the private plane every future family was sure to have.

Pick up maps, guides, and other information at the **visitor center** (daily 8 AM-5 PM, till 6 PM in summer; free; 219/926-7561) on Kemil Road between US-20 and US-12.

South Bend

With the great exception of the Indiana Dunes, there's not a lot worth stopping for east of Chicago until you reach South Bend. The largest city in Indiana's northern tier, South Bend (pop. 105,511) is best known as the home of the "Fighting Irish" of Notre Dame University, and home of the car- and carriage-making Studebaker Company. The Notre Dame campus is most visitors' destination, whether or not it's a Saturday during football season; the 1,250-acre campus, along Michigan Street a mile north of downtown, is worth a stroll to see its many Catholic icons, including a replica of the grotto of Lourdes and the famous "Touchdown Jesus." For more information, call the campus **visitor center** (219/239-7367).

On the south side of downtown, the **Studebaker National Museum,** 525 S. Main Street (Mon.-Sat. 9 AM-5 PM; $4; 219/235-9714), displays a comprehensive survey of carriages and motor vehicles produced by the South Bend-based company before it closed in 1963. Behind the museum, the 5,000-seat Coveleski Stadium hosts Midwest League baseball games of South Bend's Chicago White Sox affiliate; tickets costs $3-6 (219/284-9988).

One of South Bend's best restaurants, **Tippecanoe Place,** 620 W. Washington Street, is housed in the old Studebaker Mansion. Across the street is the **Book Inn,** a secondhand bookstore and B&B. For further information, contact the South Bend **visitor center,** 401 E. Colfax Avenue (219/234-0051 or 800/828-7881).

Elkhart

A light industrial center, once famous for producing over half the brass band instruments made in America, Elkhart now makes RVs and pharmaceutical products: drug giant Miles Laboratories was founded here in 1884 and still has a major presence. In many ways it's a sleepy little Midwest town, home to both the energetic little **Midwest Museum of American Art** (Tues.-Fri. 11 AM-5 PM, Saturday and Sunday 1-4 PM; $1; 219/293-6660), downtown at 429 S. Main Street in a restored bank building; and to the **S. Ray Miller Antique Car Collection** (Mon.-Fri. 1-4 PM; $3), 2130 Middlebury Street off US-20 on the east side of town, which has the Duesenberg convertible owned by Al Capone's barber among the 40 classic cars and automobile ephemera on display.

Elkhart was the boyhood home of writer **Ambrose Bierce,** whose family home stood five blocks west of downtown at 518 W. Franklin Street.

Indiana's Amish Country: Middlebury and Shipshewana

East of South Bend, US-20 again becomes a road worth traveling, especially through the quiet agricultural expanses around the towns of Middlebury and Shipshewana, heartland of Indiana's sizeable Amish populations. As in other Amish areas, it's the general look of the land, rather than specific attractions, that make it enjoyable to visit; as elsewhere, the few attractions that offer an "authentic Amish experience" leave a lot to be desired. One of the largest tourist traps, **Das Dutchman Essenhaus,** sits along US-20 at the west edge of Middlebury. Rather than fight your way through the bus-tour hordes, turn north here into the quiet town center, and stop by the **Village Inn,** 104 S. Main Street (219/825-2043). The country cafe is run by, and popular with, local Amish and Mennonites, who along with everyone else enjoy the hearty coffee-shop food—not to mention great homemade pies for $1 a slice.

Back on US-20, seven miles east of Middlebury, Hwy-5 runs north just short of a mile to the intriguing **Menno-Hof Mennonite-Amish Visitor Center** (Mon.-Sat. 10

AM-5 PM; $4 donation requested; 219/768-4117), outside the hamlet of Shipshewana. Operated by the local Amish and Mennonite communities, who built the large barn that houses the center during a six-day "barn-raising," the center gives an overall introduction to the Amish and Mennonite beliefs and lifeways. Surprisingly high-tech multimedia exhibits also tell of their resistance to modern technology, their long struggle for religious freedom, and their love of peace, which has helped them through centuries of torture and abuse—often at the hands of other Christians.

Auburn

Though it's a bit out of the way (20 miles south of US-20 via the I-69 freeway), lovers of vintage American cars will make the effort to visit the elegant **Auburn-Cord-Duesenberg Museum** (daily 9 AM-6 PM; $6; 219/925-1444), in a lovely art deco showroom at 1600 S. Wayne Street in the town of Auburn. Considered by most aficionados the finest, most innovative, and most all-around gorgeous automobiles ever produced in America, these instant classics were the brainchild of Auburn industrialist Erret Cord. During the 1920s and 1930s, Cord's company designed and produced the covetable cruisers right here in Indiana—Auburns and the front-wheel-drive Cords were produced in Auburn, while the "Dusies" were made in Indianapolis—and they're now on display inside the original showroom, built in 1930 and immaculately preserved.

The collection includes beautifully restored examples of all these classic makes, plus representatives of other classic roadsters—Packards, Cadillacs, even a Rolls-Royce or two—numbering around 150 altogether, and making this one of the top auto museums in the world. It also hosts an annual classic car festival every Labor Day weekend, attended by as many as 200,000 people.

Ten miles south of Shipshewana via Hwy-5, the tiny town of Topeka holds the **Yoder Popcorn Shop** (800/537-1194), one of many popcorn sellers whose signs you'll see all around this part of Indiana.

ACROSS OHIO

The many routes across Ohio along the Lake Erie shore have long been major thoroughfares. Traders and war parties of Iroquois and other Native American tribes regularly passed this way hundreds of years before European and American pioneers started coming through in Conestoga wagons. Nowadays, historical survivors, including a number of colonial-era taverns and other early roadside Americana, and a rapidly decreasing number of vegetable farms and greenhouses fill the flatlands, threatened by ever-expanding suburbia. All over northern Ohio you'll also see Rust Belt remnants of massive industrial activity that took place here from the 1880s to the 1950s, when the Great Lakes were the "Anvil of America," producing the bulk of the nation's—and the world's—iron, steel, and petroleum products.

Rather than try to follow one or another of the many old roads that crisscross the state, alternate between a variety of routes to either side of the part-tollway, part-freeway known as I-90. In the western half of the state, follow US-20 from Toledo through a rural landscape of gambrel-roofed, red-painted barns, daubed with "Chew Mail Pouch" signs and made immortal by Sherwood Anderson's classic portrait *Winesburg, Ohio*. Also, detour north to the lakeshore along US-6, which passes through idyllic summer home communities, gritty old ports, and one of the country's great old amusement parks, Cedar Point. East of the metropolitan Cleveland area, take US-20, which veers north along the Lake Erie shore, or US-6, which zigzags south through the fertile farming country of northeastern Ohio—a region described by the 1939 WPA *Guide to Ohio* as an "enchanting country of tumbling hills, valleys and forests."

One place worth a stop in the 50 miles of sandy scrub-oak country east of the Indiana border is the **Sauder Farm and Craft Village,** a living history museum on Hwy-2 outside the town of Archbold.

Toledo

One of Ohio's most important industrial centers, Toledo (pop. 332,900) is the third busiest Great Lakes port, with many miles of docks, bridges, warehouses, factories, refineries, and power plants lining the mouth of the Maumee River. That may not sound like a good reason to visit, but Toledo is a fascinating place, big enough to be impressive but small enough to get around and get a feel for. Downtown Toledo is a rather anonymous place that empties after 5 PM (that world renowned-expert on tedium, John Denver, went so far as to write a song saying, "Saturday night in Toledo, Ohio, is like being nowhere at all"), but the streets just south hold dozens of unrestored cast-iron warehouses and commercial buildings just waiting for the gentrifiers to arrive.

A mile west of the waterfront, Toledo's pride and joy is the very good **Museum of Art** (Tues.-Sat. 10 AM-4 PM, Sunday 1-5 PM; free), 2445 Monroe Street, where works by El Greco (who lived and worked in Toledo, Spain) highlight a survey of European painting. The real strength of the collection is its glassware, with dozens of beautiful goblets and vases dating back to Roman times.

Toledo's blue-collar multiethnicity has given rise to some good places to eat, starting with **Ansara's Board Room**, 233 N. Huron Street downtown, an only-in-Toledo combination of chop house and Middle Eastern restaurant housed in a dark, wood-panelled room. The one truly not-to-be-missed Toledo eatery is **Tony Packo's Cafe**, across the river at 1902 Front Street (419/691-6054); Packo's addictive chili dogs were made famous by Corporal Klinger (played by real-life Toledo native Jamie Farr) on the long-running TV series *M.A.S.H.,* and still pack the crowds into this East Toledo haunt—despite its location near a huge Toledo Edison coal-fired power plant.

For the full Toledo experience, chow down on Tony Packo's chili dogs before, during, or after a Toledo Mud Hens International League baseball game in nearby Maumee. For tickets and schedules, call 419/893-9483.

DETOUR TO DETROIT

Though Detroit (45 miles north of Toledo via I-75) is a ways off the route through Ohio, no guidebook as car-focused as this could feel complete without covering the "Motor City," heart of America's automotive industry. For detailed information, contact the visitors bureau (800/DET-ROIT). Here is a short list of things to see in and around Detroit:

Henry Ford Museum and Greenfield Village, 20900 Oakwood Boulevard, Dearborn (daily 9 AM-5 PM; $12; 313/371-1620). Just off US-12, 10 miles west of downtown Detroit, this 80-acre complex is a virtual microcosm of American history, holding everything from Abe Lincoln's law office to Thomas Edison's workshop, arranged to form an ideal village of American creativity.

Detroit Institute of the Arts, 5200 Woodward Avenue (Wed.-Sun. 11 AM-4 PM; $4). Along with its massive collection of art from around the world, this huge museum is worth a look for its powerful Diego Rivera mural, *Detroit Industry*, celebrating the workers who built Detroit's wheels.

Motown Historical Museum, 2468 W. Grand Boulevard (Mon.-Sat. 10 AM-5 PM, Sunday 2-5 PM; $4). Contained in the very house where Berry Gordy, Jr. produced the great hits of the 1960s, this museum documents the making of the Motown Sound by the likes of Smokey Robinson, Martha Reeves, Marvin Gaye, Stevie Wonder, the Temptations, and Diana Ross and the Supremes.

The Big Fist, middle of Woodward Avenue at Jefferson Avenue, downtown Detroit. In memory of the "Brown Bomber," Joe Louis, this 25-foot-high fist looms over Detroit's main thoroughfare, across from the landmark Renaissance Center.

Accommodation rates at the many motels around Toledo are lower than elsewhere, making it an even better place to break a journey. For more information, or for details on the lively **Rock, Rhythm and Blues Festival** held every Memorial Day, contact the Toledo **visitor center**, 218 Huron Street (419/243-8191 or 800/243-4667).

Maumee and Perrysburg

South of Toledo along the Maumee River, a pair of towns preserve important parts of western Ohio's early history. On the west bank of the river, Maumee (pop. 15,561; pronounced "Mommy") was founded in 1817 at the western edge of settled territory, and holds remnants of the Miami and Erie Canal as well as the Toledo Mud Hens baseball stadium.

Across the river, Perrysburg (pop. 12,251) is a pretty little town of white colonial-style houses, with a nice waterfront park and a short strip of restaurants and bars running east along Louisiana Street (US-20). A mile upstream from town, past the cemetery and a set of expensive-looking tract houses, **Fort Meigs** (Saturday and Sunday noon-5 PM, longer hours in summer; $4) is a full-scale 1950s reconstruction of the wooden fortress that played a key role in defending the frontier against British and Indian attack during the War of 1812.

Fremont

In Fremont (pop. 17,500), where in the 1700s native Wyandot Indians established a village along the main trail between Pittsburgh and Detroit, a small JCPenney and a movie theater provide a focus for the old-fashioned downtown along the Sandusky River, while strip malls and fast-food chains line the US-20 bypass and the access roads to and from the I-90 freeway.

Fremont's main attraction is the **Rutherford B. Hayes Presidential Center** (Mon.-Sat. 9 AM-5 PM, Sunday 1-5 PM; $4.50; 419/332-2081), south of US-20 at 1337 Hayes Avenue, which encompasses the 25-acre estate of Civil War general and former U.S. president Rutherford B. Hayes, who lived here 1873-93 and served as president 1877-81. The nation's first presidential library, the Hayes center includes the rather plain, red-brick family house and a large museum displaying his public and private papers, sundry mementos, and his daughter Fanny's doll house collection. Hayes is buried on a wooded knoll on the grounds, alongside his wife and their favorite horses.

In Clyde, the McPherson Cemetery along US-20 holds the remains of **Brigadier Gen. James "Birdseye" McPherson,** the highest-ranking Union officer killed in the Civil War.

Apart from the Hayes center, Fremont won't detain you for long. Eat breakfast or lunch with the locals at the **Po' Man's Cafe,** 108 S. Front Street, a block below State Street (US-20) in the old heart of town. Motels abound around town, including a Best Western, a Holiday Inn, a Travelodge, and the **Great Lakes Motel,** on US-20 at 1737 E. State Street (419/334-9797).

Clyde: Winesburg, Ohio

Five miles east of Fremont, the town of Clyde (pop. 5,776) is a perfect little place, still very much the typical farm town that the New Deal-era WPA *Guide to Ohio* said might well have served as a model for one of Thomas Hart Benton's murals of rural America: "Old Indian paths and sand ridges are now angular streets; cheek by jowl with an odd assortment of business houses is the railroad cutting across Main Street, gyved with station, elevator, and spur track; around the decorous houses are gardens, flower beds, and shrubbery tended by friendly and loquacious folk."

Clyde's brick-paved streets are still quiet, lined by mature trees and most of the same houses as when writer **Sherwood Anderson,** who was born in southern Ohio in 1876, grew up here in the 1880s and 1890s. Because the people of Clyde took offense at Anderson's sharply drawn and only slightly disguised portraits of them in his groundbreaking book *Winesburg, Ohio*—which was published in 1919, 20 years after Anderson left Clyde for Chicago—the town doesn't celebrate him in any obvious way. The only real sign of him is in the local library, 222 W. Buckeye Street, a block west of the town center, where visitors can check out a collection of his books and a short documentary video of his life and times. The library is also the best place to pick up the pamphlet that points out Anderson's home and the sites of many scenes from *Winesburg.*

Bellevue

The railroad and factory town of Bellevue, on US-20 seven miles east of Clyde, was the place where the psychopathic killer in the movie *Silence of the Lambs* held his victims hostage. As late as the 1940s, the town used the cavelike limestone sinkholes seen in the film for disposing of its wastewater; during heavy rains, underground pressure turned these into bubbling geysers spouting sewage all over town.

Needless to say, there's not a lot to tempt you to stop.

Sandusky: Cedar Point

Midway between Toledo and Cleveland, a fine natural harbor has enabled Sandusky to remain a busy port, albeit now more for recreational ferries to the offshore islands than for the coal and iron ore it once handled. The waterfront is good for a short stroll, and the town is rich in elaborate mid-1800s houses like the **Follett House Museum** (daily 1-4 PM; free), 404 Wayne Street, a well-preserved 1827 Greek revival house filled with period artifacts and a few displays on the area's history.

Another sort of history can be experienced at the old-time amusement park of Cedar Point (daily 10 AM-10 PM May-Sept., though hours vary; $25.95 adults, $4.95 for children four and younger; 419/626-0830), which has a dozen great roller coasters ranging from fragile-looking old wooden ones to high-speed modern monsters like the **Magnum,** a 15-story colossus that sends riders racing along at more than 70 mph, and the even more terrifying **Raptor,** in which riders swing on benches hanging upside down from the track—a complete inversion of the usual roller-coaster experience. Cedar Point is one of the most popular amusement parks in the Midwest, so expect crowds if you come on summer weekends. The 360-acre park sits on a peninsula across the water from downtown Sandusky, and has animal shows, a Lake Erie beach, and a water park called Soak City (which costs $5 extra), as well as restaurants and on-site camping and hotel accommodations.

Back in downtown Sandusky, stop for a bite to eat at **Markley's,** a classic little 1950s diner on the corner of Market and Wayne Streets, a block east of Columbus.

For more information on the Sandusky area, including Put-in-Bay and the offshore islands, contact the **visitor center**, 231 W. Washington Row (419/625-2984 or 800/255-ERIE).

Vermilion

One of the more attractive resorts on Ohio's Lake Erie frontage, Vermilion took its name from the rich red clay that colors the soil. Along with a fine beach backed by dozens of attractive summer homes, the town also holds the **Inland Seas Maritime Museum** (daily 10 AM-5 PM; $4), along the waterfront at 480 Main Street. The museum's usual array of scale models and paintings of ships is augmented with preserved timbers from Perry's ship *Niagara*, and a 62-foot-tall replica of a Lake Erie lighthouse.

A great old-fashioned ice cream and sandwich parlor, **Edna Mae's**, stands at 5598 Liberty Avenue at the center of town; for a more complete meal, try the comfortable **Old Prague Restaurant** next door.

On South Bass Island in Lake Erie, 15 miles by boat from Sandusky, a stone column commemorates the victory of **Adm. Oliver Perry,** who defeated a British fleet here on September 10, 1813, announcing his success with the laconic words, "We have met the enemy, and they are ours." The islands are popular summer resorts; contact the Sandusky visitor center for details.

The tiny town of Milan, two miles south of I-90 via US-250, was the birthplace in 1847 of the great inventor **Thomas Edison.** His childhood home at 9 Edison Drive is preserved as a museum.

Much of Oberlin's endowment comes from the bequest of Oberlin graduate **Charles Hall,** who in 1886, a year after graduating, discovered a viable process for refining aluminum and later founded Alcoa Corporation.

Oberlin

Away from the lakeshore, 25 miles west of Cleveland between I-90 and US-20, the attractive college town of Oberlin (pop. 8,191) serves up an idyllic slice of Middle Americana. Founded along with the surrounding town in 1833, Oberlin College has a history of being at the leading edge of American education, despite (or perhaps because of) its location far from the madding crowds. In 1937 Oberlin became the country's first coeducational college. It was also the first to embrace the education of African Americans; between 1835 and 1900, Oberlin awarded more degrees to black students than all other mainstream American colleges combined.

The Oberlin College campus spreads west of the town's green main square, which is also graced on the east side by the neoclassical facade of the **Allen Art Museum** (Tues.-Sat. 10 AM-5 PM, Sunday 1-5 PM; free), which displays an overall survey of world art—Japanese prints, Islamic carpets, and modern painting by the likes of Cezanne and Diebenkorn. Architecture fans should take note: the old gallery was designed by Cass Gilbert, who also planned a handful of Romanesque buildings on campus; a new wing was added in 1977 by Robert Venturi. The museum also offers guided **tours** ($5) of a nearby house designed in 1947 by Frank Lloyd Wright.

The town of Oberlin seems preserved in a time warp, totally devoid of the trend-swapping cafe culture of many college towns. Its few blocks are lined by an old five-and-dime, an Army surplus store, a hardware store, and the very good **Miranda Books** at 19 S. Main Street. There's also a classic **Dairy Twist** ice-cream and burger stand on US-20 just east of the Hwy-58 turnoff from Oberlin.

Cleveland is covered in the Survival Guide on pages 688-689.

Kirtland

The rolling farmlands of northeastern Ohio around Kirtland were, from 1831 to 1837, the center of the Mormon religion. Joseph Smith, Jr., along with 1,000 of his followers, settled here and built a large temple—the first Mormon temple anywhere—and developed industries and a bank (known as the "Kirtland anti-BANK-ing Company"). The bank failed in 1838 and Smith fled, first to Liberty, Missouri, and later to Nauvoo, Illinois, where in 1844 he was killed by a mob.

North of I-90 along US-20, a half-mile from the center of Mentor, a large white house is preserved much as it was when **James Garfield** lived here before assuming the presidency. Ten miles northeast, at 792 Mentor Avenue in Painesville, the **Rider Tavern** was built in 1818 along the stagecoach route between Buffalo and Cleveland.

The **Kirtland Temple** along Chillicothe Road (Hwy-306) is surrounded by pleasant gardens and open to the general public on guided **tours** (daily 1-6 PM, longer hours in summer; free; 216/256-3318). The stately Greek revival structure has a gleaming white interior built in part by Brigham Young, with elaborately crafted woodwork pulpits (one at each end) and an upstairs classroom with more of the unusual double pulpits. The temple and most of the town have been preserved under the auspices of the Reorganized Church of Jesus Christ of Latter Day Saints (RLDS), which was set up in 1852 by Joseph Smith, Jr.'s oldest son and those followers who didn't go west to Salt Lake City with Brigham Young.

A newer temple across the street is used for most services; adjacent to it is **Kokomo's**, a very good burger and milk shake stand.

Ashtabula

On the shores of Lake Erie, 18 miles from the Pennsylvania border, Ashtabula (pop. 21,633) is a large and busy pleasure-boating port, first dredged at the mouth of the Ashtabula River in 1826 and later home to some of the biggest shipyards on the Great Lakes. Now primarily recreation-oriented, Ashtabula still has a few signs of its industrial past, including the lakefront coal conveyor that forms an archway over the river, next to a squat lighthouse and a small local history **museum** (Fri.-Sun. 1-6 PM; donations) housed in the old lighthouse keeper's quarters.

A block south of the lakefront, pride of place goes to a burly bascule drawbridge and to the many turn-of-the-century industrial and business premises along Bridge Street that form a three-block parade of gift shops, bars, and restaurants, including the **Doxsie Deli and Ice Cream Parlour**, 1001 Bridge Street, open daily for sandwiches and sundaes.

Across Pennsylvania

US-20 takes little more than the proverbial blink of an eye to cross the 45 miles of northwestern Pennsylvania, which is part of Pennsylvania only because the country's founders thought it was unfair to deny the Keystone State a share of the Lake Erie shoreline. As there's not much worth stopping for here, I-90 is most travelers' route of choice.

Note: This part of Pennsylvania also marks the spot where two routes diverge: one continues along US-20 across upstate New York and on to Boston, while another follows US-6 from Meadville ("Birthplace of the Zipper") east across Pennsylvania, Connecticut, and Rhode Island, ending eventually at the tip of Cape Cod. The US-6 route is described beginning on page 477.

ACROSS NEW YORK

From inauspicious beginnings in the marshlands and vineyards of the Lake Erie "grape belt" at the state's far western tip, the portion of US-20 that runs across upstate New York cuts a wide, scenic swath through a diverse terrain of flatlands, rippling hills, and spring-fed lakes. This well-maintained, mostly four-lane road glides surreptitiously through four centuries of history, slicing through vast Dutch patroonships, serene Shaker colonies, blood-soaked Revolutionary War battlefields, Native American hunting grounds, the birthplace of the women's movement, Underground Railroad hideouts, and the long-calmed waters of the once-mighty Erie Canal. Sparkling baseball diamonds, dairy bars by the dozens, petrified creatures, stately longhouses, abandoned motor courts, prancing wooden horses, off-key nose whistles, and succulent, grill-toughened hot dogs are just a few of the countless other reasons to slow down and pull over early and often as you cross the Empire State.

The "Romance Road," as labeled by a 1940s travel writer, follows several old Iroquois Indian trails as it nudges its way through the western Niagara Frontier, then traces the 19th-century Great Western Turnpike through the Finger Lakes region before easing down into the historically rich Hudson Valley near Albany, where it begins a gradual ascent of the Taconic Mountains and Berkshire foothills that hug the Massachusetts border. All the way across the state, US-20 roughly parallels the crowded, rumbling I-90 New York Thruway toll road—a necessary evil that lures most of the diesel-spewing, view-obscuring 18-wheel traffic away from placid US-20 with a 65 mph speed limit and the promise of uneventful, predictable fast-food rest-stop dining experiences and fluorescent-lit motels.

While US-20 runs across the heart of New York State, US-6 crosses it farther south, after traversing the wilds of northern Pennsylvania. The New York portion of this route, which continues east through Connecticut and Rhode Island to Cape Cod, begins on page 490.

Westfield: New York's Wine Country

The salt-whitened, snowplow-scraped roadway and endless, slightly hilly expanse of shaggy, kudzu-like vineyards on the south side of the road continue for a dozen monotonous miles between the state line and proud, hardworking Westfield (pop. 3,500), known locally as Vine City because of its large Italian-American grape-growing community and its proximity to some of Chautauqua County's finest wineries. The **Johnson Estate Winery** (716/326-2191 or 800/DRINK-NY) and **Vetter Vineyards** (716/326-3100) are within a goblet's throw of Main Street (US-20), as are the waterfalls and hiking trails of nearby Chautauqua Gorge, seven sylvan miles long and 100 feet deep.

The tangy Concord grape was introduced to the region in 1859, but it wasn't until 1897 that Dr. Charles Welch and his father moved to Westfield and founded the factory that led to Westfield's long-standing nickname, "The Grape Juice Capital of the World." Though many of the canneries have since vanished, **Welch Foods** still maintains a large plant and its corporate offices on N. Portage Street, on the western edge of Westfield's compact downtown.

Across I-90 on waterfront Hwy-5, Lake Erie's Barcelona Harbor is home to the landmark **Barcelona Lighthouse**, which was the first lighthouse in the world to be lit by natural gas when constructed in 1830. Drop by **Jack's Barcelona Drive-In** for fast food or the **Barcelona Harbor House** for finer, sit-down fare with a lakeside view. The no-frills **Main Diner** back in downtown Westfield is a pleasant place to grab a cup of coffee and sandwich while watching the pickup trucks cruise up and down the several-block Main Street.

The **Sleepy Hollow Motel** at 7254 E. Main Road (716/326-3266) and the **Candlelight Lodge** at 143 E. Main Street (716/326-2830) are two low-priced lodging options. The what-you-see-is-what-you-get **Theater Motel and Restaurant** on the eastern edge of town lets you stare at an abandoned drive-in movie theater, grab a greasy bite to eat, and flop in a budget ranch motel room with a vineyard view without having to move your car.

Fredonia

US-20 trucks through the cherry orchards and vineyards of Portland and Brocton before ebbing into the center of neatly maintained Fredonia (pop. 10,400), the namesake of the Marx Brothers' beloved *Duck Soup* homeland. Site of the first natural gas well in the U.S. (1825), Fredonia was also the birthplace of the agricultural Grange (1868) and—ironically, for a town in the heart of the western New York Wine Belt—the Women's Christian Temperance Union (1873).

Downtown Fredonia boasts the gracefully shaded, New England-style Barker Commons town square, bordered by a restored opera house and a host of Greek revival, Italianate, Victorian, and gothic 19th-century commercial buildings. A stroll down tree-lined Central Avenue to the north of Main Street (US-20) reveals an equally diverse array of turn-of-the-century homes, which stand in marked contrast to the sterile modernity you encounter up the road in the several I.M. Pei-designed buildings that define the State University of New York (SUNY) Fredonia campus, site of the Buffalo Bills' summer training camp.

A **Days Inn** near I-90 and the restored, veranda-fronted **White Inn** at 52 E. Main Street near Barker Commons (716/672-2103) are two distinctly different answers to the proverbial lodging question. The White Inn's stately dining room may tempt you, as may the **Barker Brew Co.** at 34 W. Main Street, which offers slablike deli sandwiches and an alehouse full of great microbrews in a restored 1860 building fronting the commons.

East of Fredonia, the soot from the city's Red Wing shipping works seems to cast a drab pallor over the landscape, which deteriorates into an unkempt maze of vineyards and dilapidated barns bearing badly faded Mail Pouch tobacco billboards. The vineyards suddenly vanish east of dirty, downcast Silver Creek, replaced by the thick stands of scruffy pine trees and cigarette vendor stands that crowd the roadside along US-20's two-mile passage through the northeastern corner of the Cattaraugus Indian Reservation.

Eden: Original American Kazoo Company

US-20 bumps up north along the lakeshore through several miles of scraggly forest, and you won't miss a thing by taking the I-90/NY Thruway to exit 57A, which lands you on a two-lane backroad bound right for sleepy downtown Eden (pop. 3,088). Eden, a make-your-own-music lover's paradise that lays claim to an annual summer Corn Days festival, is home to the one-and-only Original American Kazoo Company museum, gift shop, and factory at 8703 S. Main Street. Established in 1916, the company boasts the world's only still-operating metal kazoo factory (most of the plastic ones are stamped out these days in China and Hong Kong). A restored, two-story clapboard house contains an all-too-country-store-cute gift shop and a tiny free museum offering an up-close-and-personal view of the factory's belt-and-pulley metal kazoo production line and the opportunity to sign a petition aimed at getting the kazoo declared America's national instrument.

After viewing a short, jumpy video extolling the virtues of one of the few musical instruments invented in the U.S., visitors can gaze at a cramped display of antique kazoos, ranging from an original wooden model to the bottle-shaped kazoos churned out to celebrate the repeal of Prohibition. A large sign chimes in with some fascinating kazoo-related trivia, finally putting to rest those long-vexing questions concerning the most requested tune played on the kazoo ("Far, Far Away"), the most popular kazoo (the slide trombone), the largest kazoo ever made (the 43-pound Kazoophony, replete with four mouth pieces, resonator, and cymbal), and the number of kazoo bands registered in the U.S. (15,000 and still counting). You can pick up an adenoid-popping nose flute, a trombone kazoo, and a variety of noisemakers in the gift shop on your way out, or grab some wax paper, rubber bands, and an empty toilet paper or paper towel roll and invent your own kazoo.

Orchard Park

A thick slice of suburban sprawl in the shadow of Rich Stadium (home of the Buffalo Bills football team), Orchard Park offers the culinary pleasures of the **Donuts and Cream** doughnut stand, 6494 E. Lake Avenue. In the heart of Orchard Park, dive into a salty, crusty sandwich full of a Buffalo specialty, beef on weck, or down a plate of fiery chicken wings (another local delicacy) at **Eckl's**, 4936 Ellicott Road, an area supper club institution since 1934; it's only open in the evening, so plan your route accordingly.

Detour: Buffalo

Founded as a Niagara frontier outpost in the early 1800s, Buffalo (pop. 328,100) exploded into a bustling shipping, manufacturing, and railroad center after the 1825 opening of the Erie Canal made the city the linchpin of trade between the Great Lakes, Canada, and the eastern seaboard. The departure of many factories and corporate headquarters to warmer, cheap-labor climes, has dented Buffaloans' self-confidence over the past several decades. Added to this are the legendarily difficult winters, which leave their mark in the many potholes and bumps pockmarking the city's concrete street grid; not to mention the Bills' seeming inability to win a Super Bowl. But the optimistic made-in-Buffalo spirit captured so eloquently in Verlyn Klinkenborg's 1990 magical portrait of Polish-American bartender Eddie Wen-

The south Buffalo suburb of Hamburg, "The Town That Friendship Built" and one of many supposed birthplaces of the hamburger, holds the retro **Uncle Joe's Diner,** open daily 6 AM-11 PM at 4869 S.W. Boulevard (US-20).

Another Buffalo suburb, East Aurora, was the home of **Roycroft Campus** (716/652-0571), a turn-of-the-century arts-and-crafts community whose furniture shops and studios still stand at the center of town.

Art Glass Window Pane, *by Frank Lloyd Wright*

zek, *The Last Fine Time,* lives on in the city's burly, passionate sports fans, spunky local music scene, spicy local eateries, and ample cultural resources.

A 10-minute drive from downtown up wide, tree-lined Delaware Avenue takes you past the **Albright-Knox Art Gallery**'s extensive collection of Picassos, de Koonings, and Pollocks, alongside the grassy expanses and ponds of **Delaware Park**, designed by Frederick Law Olmsted, the landscape architect for New York City's Central Park and Brooklyn's Prospect Park. You'll also see the marble neoclassical structure that has housed the Buffalo and Erie County Historical Society **museum** (Tues.-Sat. 10 AM-5 PM, Sunday noon-5 PM; $3.50) since its construction in 1901 for the historic Pan-American Exposition. The non-air-conditioned gallery can be a bit stifling on hot summer afternoons, but the wonderful "Made in Buffalo" and "Dividing the Land" local manufacturing and immigration exhibits should satisfy most of your local history thirsts.

Bookhounds will want to brave the leaning towers of tattered, bargain-priced old hardbacks leering from the dusty, grease-streaked windows of the dense, rewarding **Circular One Bookstore**, 799 Elmwood Avenue in the casually bohemian Elmwood Village neighborhood. A few blocks north, you can get the lowdown on the hottest local band or live music club at the venerable **Home of the Hits** record store at 1105 Elmwood Avenue—the place to pick up the city's biweekly *Arts Voice* for a listing of local clubs, films, and offbeat attractions, most of which are found in the funky, historic Allentown neighborhood along Allen Street.

The infamous **Anchor Bar**, "Birthplace of Buffalo Wings," is at 1047 Main Street on the southeastern edge of downtown. Skip the bland Italian entrees in favor of the bar's much-hyped specialty—the saucy, fiery, deep-fried chicken wings, now a great American fern bar cliche. Combine this required tourist activity with the more subtle pleasures of a AAA minor league baseball game at the Buffalo Bisons' beautiful 10,000-seat **Pilot Field** (716/852-4700), tucked away downtown at the corner of Swan and Washington Streets.

The quickest, least confusing way to zip right into the cast-iron heart of the Queen City is to take the dreaded I-90/NY Thruway to exit 53, from where I-190 races to the heart of the city's architecturally magnificent downtown, then north to Niagara Falls.

Most of the cheapest motels are clustered east of town around I-90 and the Buffalo airport. The in-town **Best Western**, 510 Delaware Avenue (716/886-8333), is a bit higher-priced, but its central Allentown location saves you hours of driving time and grounds you smack in the middle of the city's Allentown bar, restaurant, and club district.

Niagara Falls

If you have time for a quick upriver side trip, head up I-190 to that archetypal tourist trap, Niagara Falls. Everything costs on the U.S. side of the foaming falls—the famous *Maid of the Mist* boat ride costs $7.95, climbing the observation tower costs 50 cents, even the National Park Service charges $3 just for parking—but the very tackiest tourist attractions—Louis Tussaud's Waxworks, Movieland Wax Museum, and Marineland—are on the Canadian side. (It also costs 50 cents to walk back across Rainbow Bridge from the Canadian side, so take quarters if you go.)

Once you've seen the powerful falls, you might want to zoom northward on the Robert Moses freeway to the **Niagara Power Project Visitor Center** (716/285-3211) for a free view and technical lesson about how the surging Niagara River waters have been harnessed for local use. Heading back south to I-190, pull over at **Whirlpool State Park** for a shady picnic lunch and stunning vista below the free overlook of churning rapids doing battle in the river gorge below.

North Tonawanda
Between Buffalo and Niagara Falls, North Tonawanda is a tough-looking factory town concealing one of the Buffalo area's best-kept secrets, the **Herschell Carousel Factory Museum** (daily 11 AM-5 PM in summer, Wed.-Sun. 1-5 PM rest of the year; $3; 716/693-1885) at 180 Thompson Street a half-mile to the east of Hwy-265. The old, barnlike 1915 factory-shed houses a restored 1916 pulley-driven carousel and a stable of immaculately painted wooden steeds, zebras, roosters, ostriches, frogs, bears, and bulls hand-carved by the factory's immigrant artisans for the countless carousels and kiddie rides turned out by the factory in its 1920s, 1930s, and 1940s heyday for amusement parks from the Jersey Shore to Santa Monica. Check the factory log at the front desk or chat with one of the veteran carvers during one of the sporadic demonstrations to find out if your favorite hometown carousel was built at the Herschell factory. Chances are, it was.

Before this Coney Island state of mind has a chance to wear off, head back south along the Niagara River to two Tonawanda fast-food jewels, both specializing in foot-long red hots with "all that jazz" (sauerkraut, chili, onions, Cheese Whiz, peppers, relish, and mustard), long-cut cheese fries, and cold, sweet loganberry juice. The cleaner, brightly lit **Mississippi Mudd's**, 313 Niagara Street, also serves up some great butter-topped Louisiana sweet fries. **Ol' Man River**, 375 Niagara Street, makes up for this one-up-manship with its trademark Buffalo burgers, beef on weck sandwiches, and badly chipped plaster whale mascot, which flops over this grease joint's sagging roof like a bloated, roadfood-stuffed kidney bean.

Avon
East of Buffalo, US-20 widens to four lanes, making a rigidly straight run through the flat corn and hay fields that climb the gradually rising plateau toward the Finger Lakes district. This 40-mile stretch is virtually devoid of traffic, thanks to the faster-moving NY Thruway and serpentine Hwy-5, which links up with US-20 at Avon. Splash some cold homemade root beer down your throat to wake up and address the burning sensation left by the grilled, vinegar-doused, chili-drenched Texas Hot and Pork Hot Zweigle brand hot dogs that are family staples at **Tom Wahl's**, at the US-20/Hwy-5 junction. This rambling, log-beamed Avon institution has been a required tour-bus stopover since 1955 thanks to its soft ice cream, frosty mugs, and gut-busting Wahlburgers (ground steak on a six-inch bun, topped with a slice of grilled Virginia ham and Tom's special, mayonnaise-based sauce).

A 30-foot wooden Indian and white horse stand guard over opposite corners of the US-20/SR 5 and SR 15 intersection in nearby East Avon, where US-20 crosses I-390.

Detour: Rochester
There's plenty of culture in the sprawling Genesee River manufacturing center of Rochester (pop. 231,600), and the best of it is of the vernacular variety, making the 25-mile detour well worth your time and effort. Start your visit with the vast holdings of

the Americana-rich **Strong Museum** downtown (clearly marked off I-490), a 20,000-item collection of toys, appliances, dolls, perfume bottles, marbles, salt-and-pepper shakers, and classic board games that is a must-visit for closet pack rats and pop culture fanatics.

The **George Eastman House**, 900 East Avenue, is a 10-minute drive along Rochester's fashionable mansion-lined main boulevard. In addition to relaying the Horatio Alger-like story of workaholic Eastman's incredible success and philanthropy as the founder of the city's still-thriving Eastman Kodak Company, the 50-room Georgian mansion in which he lived before shooting himself in the head in 1932 also houses a fascinating exhibit ("Enhancing the Illusion") on the history of photography.

Before sampling one of western New York's thick Genesee Cream Ales, you should first stuff yourself with a "garbage plate" (two pork hots, baked beans, macaroni salad, home fries, and rolls on a sagging styrofoam plate) at **Nick Tahou's** industrial-strength downtown coffee shop, 320 W. Main Street at Broad Street, open 24 hours.

If you're in need of sleep, the usual chain motels line the I-390 freeway near the airport on the southwest side of town.

When the Rochester Red Wings AAA baseball team (716/467-3000) move into their new downtown Frontier Field home in spring 1996, they'll leave behind the oldest continually used stadium in the minors.

South of Rochester, the I-390 freeway runs alongside a still-intact section of the original Erie Canal waterway.

Canandaigua

East of the I-390 interchange, US-20 continues on its gentle, barely rolling course, gradually rising out of the flatlands to lap at the rim of the westernmost Finger Lake town, Canandaigua (pop. 10,700), an unassumingly pretty town that sits on a small hill to the north of the highway, overlooking the placid, 17-mile Canandaigua Lake. Iroquois legend has it that the 11 narrow

Niagara Falls

Finger Lakes (six of which—Cayuga, Onondaga, Oneida, Seneca, Tuscarora—bear the names of the Six Nations of the Iroquois Confederacy) were created by the handprint of God.

East of Canandaigua, **Calhoun's Books** at 1510 US-20 (315/789-8599) is a low-key but seemingly limitless treasure trove of dusty period postcards, old maps, prints, and books in various stages of neglect, collectibility, and historical importance. The information-hungry roadtripper will thrill to the store's casually organized storehouse of 1930s WPA/Federal Writers' Project state guidebooks, as well as the boxes upon boxes of early 20th-century "Greetings From . . . " hand-tinted postcard folios.

Geneva

Geneva (pop. 14,100) sits at the head of Seneca Lake, the largest of the Finger Lakes, but is cut off from this sailboat-flecked jewel by a sadly unimproved section of lakefront to the south of the US-20/SR 5 roadbed. A worthwhile detour off the busy four-lane highway is a quick pass through the busy downtown on Main Street, grabbing lunch or a cup of coffee at Leo's Diner before parking near Hobart and William Smith Colleges to take in a relaxing view of the lake.

Save your roadfood appetite for **Waterloo**, 10 miles east, where the sagging, peeling **Mac's Drive-In Curb Service Restaurant**, 1166 Waterloo-Geneva Road, dishes out creamy Richardson's root beer floats ($1.60), frosty 16-ounce mugs of Pabst Blue Ribbon ($1.45), butter-dipped sweet corn (50 cents per ear), and burgers-in-a-basket ($3, with french fries and cabbage salad) at an awning-covered counter or right at your car window.

Seneca Falls: Women's Rights National Historical Park

You'd never know it from the signs for "Peaches Sports Bar" and "Filthy McNasty's Saloon" that greet you as you roll through the diminutive red-brick town of Seneca Falls, but the American women's movement was born here when the first women's rights convention was spearheaded by Lucretia Mott and Elizabeth Cady Stanton in July 1848.

Picturesque, flag-draped downtown Waterloo has an all-American feel, befitting its contentious claim of holding the nation's first observance in 1866 of now-popular Flag Day.

The remains of the Wesleyan Chapel where the convention was held can still be viewed at the center of town, on a guided tour staffed by the well-informed National Park Service rangers who run the highly interactive visitor center of the **Women's Rights National Historical Park** (daily 9 AM-5 PM; free; 315/568-2991) at 136 Fall Street. A brief exhibit on the scandalous pants-like "bloomers" popularized in 1851 by local feminist Amelia Bloomer combines with displays on transcendentalism, abolitionism, and phrenology to place the rise of this revolutionary movement in historical context. A block away, the **National Women's Hall of Fame**, 76 Fall Street, is a reading-intensive monument to the likes of Georgia O'Keefe, Harriet Tubman, Emily Dickenson, Billie Jean King, and Jane Addams. You can listen to a saucy blues selection from Bessie Smith while dodging an endless stream of group tours.

Red's Place at 57 Fall Street, and the aforementioned **Filthy McNasty's** at 41 Fall Street, are dark, beer-soaked dens where you can scarf up chicken wings or sandwiches with a cold Genesee before wandering out back to gaze at the abandoned Seneca Knitting Mill. The falls in Seneca Falls disappeared in 1918 when the Cayuga and Seneca Canal flooded to form Van Cleef Lake. A five-minute drive east out of town along E. Bayard Street lands you at **Cayuga Lake State Park**, a shaded beach where you can sit by the lake, pitch some horseshoes or a tent, and ponder your rising cholesterol level.

Auburn

Along US-20 on the eastern outskirts of Auburn, keep your eyes peeled and your camera at the ready as you pass the beautifully maintained **Finger Lakes Drive-In Theater.**

Auburn (pop. 31,300) is a proud industrial city with a solid, hilly downtown and a rich stock of historical homes, including that of ex-slave and underground railroad heroine Harriet Tubman, hard to find but still standing at 180 South Street. You can also see the home of William H. Seward, the anti-slavery Whig governor of New York, founder of the Republican Party, and secretary of state under presidents Abraham Lincoln and Andrew Johnson, who single-handedly negotiated the purchase of Alaska in 1867. Seward's house at 33 South Street contains original furniture and historic exhibits, and is open for **tours** (Tues.-Sat. 1-4 PM; $3); he's buried in the town's Fort Hill cemetery.

Right downtown at 18 Genesee Street, the sparkling, streamlined **Hunter's Dinerant** offers 24-hour-a-day slices of thick lemon meringue pie and a panoramic view of the aging Genesee Beer sign that watches over the wide streets of the hill-hugging downtown.

Skaneateles

Roughly midway across New York State, Skaneateles (pop. 2,700) is a pristine, sun-dappled resort nestled on the crest of shimmering Skaneateles Lake. This popular summer family escape houses arts, crafts, and antique stores along its immaculate Genesee Street (US-20), which fronts the lakeside **Cliff and Thayer Parks**. A stroll up the main downtown north-south drag of Jordan Street leads you past the delightfully unadorned **Skaneateles Bakery** to the Skaneateles Historical Society's petite **Creamery Museum** and elm-lined side streets full of well-maintained Greek revival homes.

If you're hungry, the stuffy colonial **Kreb's Inn**, across from the lakefront at 53 W. Genesee Street, will empty your wallet with its pricey-but-hearty lobster, roast beef, and chicken specialties. Greasemonger roadfood-seekers will feel more at home at the high-quality but self-effacing **Doug's Fish Fry**, 8 Jordan Street, "not famous since 1962" for its beer, fried haddock, clams, and Coney Island hot dogs. West of downtown, the **Hilltop Restaurant** at 813 W. Genesee Street offers one-stop family dining—and bowling in the adjoining **Cedar House Bowling Center.**

A number of $40-a-night motels like the **Hi-Way Host**, 834 W. Genesee Street (315/685-7633), line US-20 east and west of Skaneateles.

Along US-20 just west of the I-81 interchange, the tiny crossroads of Cardiff is where the 10-foot, 2,700-pound "fossil" of the P.T. Barnum-hyped Cardiff Giant was "unearthed" as part of a sensational 1869 hoax.

Detour: Syracuse

A short, 25-minute side trip from US-20 north to Syracuse (pop. 163,900) via I-81 yields an informative tour of the fascinating **Erie Canal Museum** (daily 10 AM-5 PM; free) at 318 E. Erie Boulevard in the shadow of I-690. Housed in an 1850 weighlock building straddling the paved-over canal bed, the museum has a 65-foot restored 1850s canal boat, and offers guided walking tours (free) of the city that gave birth to the electric typewriter, the loafer, and the turn-of-the-century, arts-and-crafts-style furniture of Gustave Stickley. A short film describes the staggering impact of the canal's 1825 opening on the booming city, an impact also visible in the cast-iron commercial districts of the historic downtown, a short walk south.

Cazenovia and Madison

East of I-81, US-20 follows the route blazed by the old Great Western Turnpike over gradually steepening roller-coaster hills, past sweet-corn stands, dairy bars, and cabbage fields, and into the western reaches of picture-perfect Cherry Valley. After passing through the Syracuse suburb of Cazenovia, which offers a refreshing breeze from whitecapped Cazenovia Lake, US-20 rolls east for another 15 miles to Madison, where the roadhouse-like **Quack's Diner** harbors no delusions of grandeur, just a huge faded duck-adorned sign and a sprawling dining room where area families, Colgate University students, and antique hunters fresh from a weekend run gorge themselves on chicken dinners, milk shakes, and cling peaches in whipped cream. You can even buy T-shirts and coffee cups with the diner's trademark yellow duck mascot uttering such pun-ishing lines as, "It quacks me up to cook here."

Detour: Utica

Hilly downtown Utica (pop. 68,800) lies on I-90 about 30 minutes north of US-20 along the Mohawk River and New York state's Barge Canal, the sea-bound industrial water route that follows part of the pathway of the Erie Canal. Beer fans will want to make the trip to the **F.X. Matt Brewing Co.** at Court and Varick Streets west of downtown, where the old West End Brewery still pumps out gallons of Matt's trademark Utica Club and Matt's Premium regional beers alongside its more heavily promoted Saranac line of premium microbrews. In-depth tours of the compact, family-owned facilities take you through the entire production process—where you are apt to spy some contract-brewed Brooklyn Lager, New Amsterdam, Dock Street Ale, or Olde Heurich slipping out the door—and drop you off in a velvet-lined Victorian tavern for your complimentary two glasses of Saranac or frothy root beer.

Shake off your post-lager drowsiness with a thick, delicious cheeseburger, coffee, and slice of lemon meringue pie at the timeless **Triangle Coffee Shop**, 244 Genesee Street at Bank Place, which manages to cram four sit-down tables, seven counter stools, and a hungry crowd of professionals into its tiny, bright, triangular space. In the midst of even the most hectic lunch rush, the friendly waitresses still find the time to call every customer "Hon" and whip out a clean knife at a moment's notice to unjam a clogged ketchup bottle.

Northwest of Utica, the decidedly nonclassical city of **Rome** was the site of Fort Stanwix, which played a decisive role in the struggle for control of upstate New York during the Revolutionary War.

The Utica Blue Sox, a New York-Penn League baseball team, hold court June-Aug. a few miles south at cozy Donovan Park (315/738-0999 for game/schedule information), which serves up cold Matt's beers and stunning views of the summer sunset from the tiny stands running along the first-base line.

Richfield Springs: Petrified Creatures Museum

Back on US-20 east, refuel for the rolling road ahead at the ramshackle **Gatesdale Dairy Bar** in Bridgewater, which sports a cooler full of creamy, rich ice cream and a sagging neon sign featuring a dripping milk bottle under the portrait of a satisfied heifer in a floppy chef's hat. Continuing east, the road slows down and becomes a rural two-laner at Richfield Springs (pop. 1,565), a peaceful crossroads with a gazebo in the center of its grassy town square.

On the south side of US-20, at the crest of a large hill several miles east of Richfield Springs, sits the terminally tacky **Petrified Creatures Museum of Natural History** (Thurs.-Mon. 10 AM-5 PM; $7). The steep admission buys you an information-intensive (but entertainment-lacking) tour of outdoor chicken-wire Devonian fossil displays, narrated by a tape-recorded, nasal-voiced announcer. You also get a self-guided tour of the tiny wooded backyard site's collection of several garishly painted, life-sized dinosaur sculptures, and the option of using the proprietor's crusty old pickax to hack out a few fossilized keepsakes from the totally picked-over slate pit—where most of the "petrified creatures" came from.

Farther east, your time and money are probably better spent at Burger World, at the US-20/Hwy-80 junction, a cabin-styled family fast-food restaurant that lives up to its "We're more than just burgers" slogan with filling chicken cutlet, pork chop, and meatloaf dinner plates and tottering, five-scoop ice-cream cones. The takeout menu includes a 1927 map of the Cherry Valley Turnpike route now occupied by US-20.

Detour: Cooperstown

A dozen miles south of US-20 along Hwy-80, quietly bustling Cooperstown (pop. 2,200) has been known since 1939 as the home of the **National Baseball Hall of Fame** (daily 9 AM-5 PM, till 9 PM in summer; $9.50), where a beautifully organized timeline of dioramas and display cases walks you through the sport's greatest—and most embarassing—moments. You'll see a pair of cracked black

The combination admission ticket of $22 to the Baseball Hall of Fame also gains you entrance to the other two Cooperstown museums.

leather shoes worn by the ill-fated and latterly famous 1919 "Black Sox" player Shoeless Joe Jackson; the first plaster-covered batting helmet; and special exhibits on home run king Henry Aaron, amid a voluminous collection of uniforms, periodicals, programs, player records, scrapbooks, and film and audio holdings.

The neat, prosperous village of Cooperstown, founded in 1786 by the father of *Last of the Mohicans* novelist James Fenimore Cooper, has been transformed into a family tourist mecca, with the always-thronged Hall of Fame augmented by the subtler delights of the **Fenimore House Museum** (daily 10 AM-4 PM in summer, weekends only in winter; $9), which along with memorabilia of the writer has a massive new Native American artifacts collection and the equally engaging folk art and Hudson River School galleries. The Fenimore House is on Lake Street a mile north of town along the shores of Otsego Lake—the source of the Susquehanna River known locally as "Glimmerglass" for its spectacular, sparkling appearance.

Near the Fenimore House, the **Farmer's Museum** (daily 10 AM-4 PM in summer, weekends only in winter; $9) has illuminating exhibits on 19th-century rural life. Amid the dignified agricultural and local history exhibits that occupy most of the sturdy stone structures speckling this 1918 farm, the "remains" of the previously encountered Cardiff Giant lie in stony silence.

Avoid the in-town parking hassles and stash your car in one of the free lots near the Fenimore House. Then catch a city-operated trolley ($1.50 for an unlimited-ride day pass) down SR 80 toward downtown.

Surprisingly, the several-block central business district, where every other bookstore, restaurant, and variety store seems to be cashing in on their tourist customers' insatiable appetite for baseball-related camp and nostalgia, also holds **Black Bart's BBQ**, 64 Main Street, and the **Bold Dragon Bar and Restaurant**, 49 Pioneer Street, which serves up good 'n' greasy grub without a hint of major league interference.

There are literally dozens of motels from which to choose in the Cooperstown area, but remember to make your reservations far in advance to beat the summer rush. The **Glimmerglass Motor Inn** (315/858-2777) and **Bay Side Motor Inn** (607/547-2371) are among the countless lodging establishments crowding SR 80 between Cooperstown and US-20.

Three miles south of Cooperstown on Hwy-28, the **Corvette Americana Hall of Fame** ($8.50) is a must-see display of over 30 classic cars and every sort of Vette-related memorabilia.

Cherry Valley

East of the Cooperstown area, US-20 begins its roller-coaster ride through the patchwork of hillside cornfields and dairy farms that drape the bubbling landscape through the fertile Cherry Valley region. On the south side of US-20 near the crossroads of East Springfield, wander through a 1930s motor court and grab a filling stack of pancakes or slice of homemade pie at the **Otsego Diner and Motel**. Just south of the highway, attractive little Cherry Valley (pop. 600) contains a small local history museum that recalls this tiny crossroads' early 19th-century boom period as a rowdy turnpike stagecoach stop. A small obelisk in the village cemetery on S. Main Street pays homage to the residents killed in 1779 in the Cherry Valley Massacre, a British-backed Iroquois raid during the Revolutionary War.

East of Sharon Springs off US-20, **The TePee** is a 50-foot-tall, silvery, tepee-shaped attraction that has lured souvenir-starved travelers since 1950 with its array of Native American trinkets, famous TePee Taffy, and "Grand Panoramic View" telescope.

The **Tryon Inn** (607/264-3790) on N. Main Street (Hwy-166) serves up large, delicately prepared portions of pasta, seafood, steak, and poultry in an elegant 1927 dining room. The guest-house out back has a handful of rooms for rent at incredibly cheap rates that vary by season; you'll have to share a bathroom down the hall, but the peaceful, wooded setting and antique washbasins in each room make this a pleasant sleeping alternative.

Sharon Springs

The 19th-century spa and resort community of Sharon Springs (pop. 543) was once on a par with Saratoga Springs, but those days are long gone, and the silent streets are lined by the slowly crumbling remains of once-grand wooden Victorian-era hotels. It's not totally dead; in fact, Sharon Springs has seen something of a resurgence of its fortunes, thanks to its unlikely role as a seasonal escape for Hasidic Jews fleeing the heat of New York City summers.

The health-giving waters still flow in Sharon Springs, bubbling up into a small fountain in a gazebo in the small park at the center of town.

Cobleskill: Iroquois Indian Museum

Southeast of Sharon Springs, the road from tidy Cobleskill (pop. 5,268) to Howe's Cave bypasses the threatening new Wal-Mart and follows the brightly colored Howe Caverns and sly, psychedelic Secret Caverns signs up the hill to the Iroquois Indian Museum (daily 10 AM-5 PM; $5). The imposing, longhouse-shaped structure contains artifacts, arrowheads, and more recent works of art associated with the Native Americans descended from the Six Nations of the Iroquois Confederacy, as well as an interactive, hands-on children's museum. The museum's collection of contemporary Native American painting and sculpture also asks tough, probing questions about the one-dimensional casino culture that has recently come to dominate reservation life across the U.S.

Howe Caverns vs. Secret Caverns

All over this part of New York, massive roadside billboards blare out the competitive presence of Howe Caverns (marked by simple, yellow-and-black "Howe Caverns" directional signs) and Secret Caverns (on which a Deadhead-ish wizard beckons you onward with pesky lines like "If you haven't seen the underground waterfall, you ain't seen guano!"). Though located within two miles of each other, these two tourist attractions are about as far apart as Pat Boone and Jimi Hendrix.

The sanitized-for-your-protection **Howe Caverns** (daily 9 AM-6 PM; $11) boasts a well-lit, guided elevator and flat-bottomed boat tour of a 156-foot-deep underground cave. But you know you're in for something completely different the moment you enter the dark, foreboding **Secret Caverns**—through the mouth of a giant, leering bat. Don't let the "Abandon hope all ye who enter here" sign scare you off from taking the twisting (and twisted) one and a half hour guided trek down into the clammy 180-foot-deep innards along a narrow, randomly lit footpath, which terminates at a steaming, 100-foot waterfall. Sarcastic guides point out Frozen Niagara Falls, Grand Canyon, and Liberty Bell slices of stalactite/stalagmite Americana along the way, and the gift shop sells tie-dyed T-shirts, psychedelic bumper stickers, and coffee cups emblazoned with swirling designs and countless cavern-related barbs in the mold of "good to the last drop," "most of it's over your head," "the cavity dentists prefer," and "whole lotta hole."

Schoharie Valley

A nearly deserted US-20 climbs in and out of rippling extensions of the Cherry Valley and Susquehanna River watershed before cutting a dramatic path through the gorgeous Schoharie Valley around Esperance. An abandoned, sun-darkened set of Depression-era motor court cabins still stands in neat formation on the north side of the road, awaiting the waves of long-departed turnpike travelers whose unimaginative, fearful descendants now troll the lonesome, sterile NY Thruway. Dairy bars, hay bales, and yard sales proliferate nonetheless, as the wide, smooth four-lane road bestows limitless views of distant, farm-draped hills and hollows upon the patient traveler willing to pull off every now and then to take it in.

Outside of Duanesburg, the neat, geometric farmlands give way to a shaggier, flatter landscape, with creosote-soaked telephone poles and thick stands of weeping willows crowding the narrow two-lane roadway. The strip highway stretches about 10 miles west of the state capitol to McCormack Corners, where the **Corner Ice Cream** stand, 3914 Carman Road at US-20 and Hwy-146, is open daily 11 AM-10 PM for a last taste (subs, hot dogs, fish & chips, root beer floats, soft ice cream . . .) of the open road before US-20 sneaks into Albany along Western Avenue.

Albany

The New York state capital, Albany (pop. 101,100) was founded in 1609 when Dutch traders traveling up the Hudson River from New Amsterdam on Henry Hudson's ship *Half Moon* went ashore and established a fur trading post. As the gateway between upstate New York and the increasingly powerful New York City port, Albany remained a powerful trading center through the 1820s and 1830s, extending its reach with the opening of the Erie Canal and the city's growth as a central railroad terminus and manufacturing center. Nowadays, the legendary canal has long since vanished, and the glamorous New York Central railroad's French renaissance-style, turn-of-the century Union Station, at Broadway and Clinton Street, has been transformed into the sleepy corporate headquarters of the Fleet banking group—Amtrak passenger trains now stop at a lonely platform on the opposite side of the Hudson River.

As the seat of the New York state government, however, Albany still wields obvious political power. Its rich array of museums, parks, and tree-lined boulevards—plus a few barely preserved historical neighborhoods that survived the wrecker's balls in the early 1960s—confirm the fact that the Capital City is still very much alive and well. The towering granite slabs and flying-saucer-like structures that stick out at the heart of the 100-acre Empire State Plaza government center hold exhibition halls, theaters, a 44-story observation tower, and the excellent **New York State Museum** (daily 10 AM-5 PM; donations), which includes a sensitively organized exhibit on the state's Iroquois and Mohawk Native American cultures, replete with a reconstructed longhouse. A huge section devoted to the history of the metropolitan New York City area blows away anything in "The City That Never Sleeps," with a re-created Upper West Side Hispanic barber shop, a Horn and Hardart Automat food dispenser, and a restored 1940s car from the A-train IND subway line.

For a lengthier foray into Albany's local history, trek over to the **Albany Institute of History and Art**, 125 Washington Avenue (Tues.-Fri. 10 AM-5 PM, Sat.-Sun. noon-5 PM; donations), a 200-year-old gallery that houses an Albany oral history exhibit, a group of locally made cast-iron stoves, several rooms full of Hudson River School paintings from the likes of Thomas Cole and Asher Durand, and a crowded little Egyptian room with two minor league mummies.

A mile northeast of downtown, the rolling hills and meadows of the Olmsted-inspired **Washington Park** have a beautiful, art deco lakehouse that hosts outdoor concerts and theatrical productions in the summer months. In between downtown and the park, the blue-collar bohemian Lark Street neighborhood is Albany's answer to Greenwich Village, sporting several tattoo parlors and some good restaurants. **Margarita's**, 286 Lark Street, is open from lunch till late for low-priced Mexican food, while the roadhouse-style **Lark Tavern**, 453 Madison Avenue at Lark Street, serves big mugs of cheap beer in a cavernous, dark setting thronged with an eclectic mix of yuppies, old-timers, and artsy types. For late-night coffee and/or poetry, pop into **Lulu's**, 288 Lark Street, which doles out a potpourri of poetry readings, art exhibits, and open mike nights.

Back downtown, if all the high culture and power politics leave you hungry for a back-to-basics roadfood experience, head to **Jack's Diner**, 547 Central Avenue. This New Jersey-built 1930s chrome-plated diner car attracts a diverse batch of families, local crazies, and travelers with its hearty meatloaf and burgers, bottomless cups of coffee, and friendly, loquacious staff; it's open Mon.-Fri. 6 AM-7:30 PM, Saturday till 2:30 PM.

Your motel options are legion in the Albany area, but the **Motel 6** and **Quality Inn** off the I-90 Everett Road exit offer the best combination of value and central location. (They're also right next door to the **Albany Bowling Center** if you want to take out your pent-up carbound frustrations on any of your fellow travelers.) One very nice, centrally located place to stay is the **Mansion Hill Inn**, near the Governor's Mansion at 115 Philip Street (518/465-2038), which offers B&B rooms for around $100 and doubles as a fine restaurant.

For more detailed information, or to pick up walking-tour maps of Albany, contact the **visitor center**, 52 S. Pearl Street (518/434-1217 or 800/258-3582).

Some of downtown Troy's cast-iron buildings still bear the mark of the set designers who transformed them into backdrops for filmmaker Martin Scorsese's 1992 adaptation of Edith Wharton's *The Age of Innocence*.

Troy

The grave of Uncle Sam and the birthplace of the detachable shirt collar are both across the river in Troy (pop. 54,300), 10 minutes north via the I-787 freeway. A world removed from downtown Albany, this narrow riverfront city was strategically situated at the point where the Erie Canal headed west from the

TROY'S UNCLE SAM

Troy's prominent Uncle Sam monument, along the waterfront at River and Front Streets, memorializes bearded local meatpacker Samuel Wilson, who supplied beef to the soldiers quartered at the local Watervliet Arsenal during the War of 1812. Wilson's donations were quickly dubbed "Uncle Sam's beef," and the nickname and character have become the finger-pointing stuff of legend. Wilson himself is buried in the macabre, gothic hillside Oakwood Cemetery, at the head of 101st Street north of Troy via Oakwood Avenue. A vegan restaurant around the corner from the monument, Uncle Sam's Natural Foods at 77 4th Street, admonishes passersby with an "I want you . . . to enjoy good health" window poster.

Hudson River. It rose to national prominence as a manufacturing center in the 19th century, when its foundries and factories cranked out iron for stoves, stagecoaches, bells, and battleships.

Troy's factories have given way to a quietly picturesque college town, with Rensselaer Polytechnic rising on the steep hill to the east above the cast-iron business district downtown. In addition to its many impressive buildings, Troy's dense downtown has two great roadfood finds: **Manory's Restaurant**, Congress and 4th Streets, doles out stuffed combo sandwiches, home-cooked pasta, meat and seafood dinners, and really, really big breakfasts; **The Famous Lunch**, 111 Congress Street, is a delightfully worn-down greasy spoon with hand-lettered signs, tall wooden booths, and an eye-opening clientele of cops, winos, RPI students, and local businesspeople—nearly all of whom from noon to midnight every day but Sunday chow down on four-inch-long, chili-doused hot dogs served on Styrofoam plates with cold RC Colas on the side.

East to Massachusetts

If you want to cut some miles from your drive, the quickest route east from Troy is **Hwy-2**. This rural backroad takes you on a scenic but uneventful drive across the Taconics to Williamstown, Massachusetts. Alternately, you can follow old US-20 east through New Lebanon to Pittsfield, Massachusetts, then follow a short stretch of the Appalachian Trail route north to Williamstown.

For details on the Appalachian Trail route, see page 228

New Lebanon

Heading east from Albany across the Hudson River toward the Massachusetts state line, US-20 follows Columbia Avenue through the warehouse and factory town of Rensselaer, then climbs a long, retail-lined hill past innumerable liquor stores, minimarts, gas stations, and motels into the Taconic Mountains. After this 25-mile barrage of contemporary consumer culture, the tranquil hillside remains of **Mount Lebanon Shaker Village**, on the south side of US-20 a few hundred yards west of the Massachusetts border, come as a welcome relief.

Across the Massachusetts border, **Hancock Shaker Village** is a more visitor-oriented place to get a feel for the Shaker way of life.

Of the 20 Shaker communities once scattered over the eastern U.S., practicing a passionate but celibate form of Christianity, Mount Lebanon was the head ministry, founded here in 1785. The community endured until 1947, and some two dozen historic buildings still stand, including a 192-foot stone barn—the largest stone barn in the world when constructed in 1859—and a no-frills, but cleverly constructed, 1854 washhouse boasting hidden wall drawers and perfectly fitted floorboards. All of which is testimony to the Shaker edict, "Hands to work, hearts to God."

A small museum (daily 9:30 AM-5 PM in summer only; $4) gives background on the Shakers, sells some Shaker-style crafts, and has walking-tour maps of the former colony.

US-2: ACROSS MASSACHUSETTS

Across Massachusetts, follow the very scenic Route 2, also known as the "Mohawk Trail," across the state's northern tier, rather than US-20, which runs more or less underneath the Massachusetts Turnpike, I-90.

Passing across some of the least populous and most deeply forested acres in the whole Commonwealth of Massachusetts as you drive this route, you can imagine yourself in Vermont instead of the so-called Bay State. Picking its way over the flattened summits of the Hoosac Range foothills to the Green Mountains to the north, our route follows rock-strewn trout streams flecked with whitewater and shaded by boreal forests of hemlock, yellow birch, and red spruce—including some of the state's only remaining stands of old growth.

Midway across Massachusetts, Route 2 bridges the Connecticut River above Turners Falls, lopes into the trees, and emerges almost at Boston's back door, although pleasant diversions are not too far out of the way.

Pittsfield to Williamstown: The Appalachian Trail

The leafy amble up and over the ridge of the Taconics, which mark the border between New York and Massachusetts, brings you through a beautiful region dense with visitor appeal, including the ·Shaker communities along US-20 and the industrial and literary sites of Pittsfield, not to mention Williamstown, a New England poster town if ever there was one. This region is covered in detail in the Appalachian Trail chapter; for the full scoop on what to do in and around these broad green quads and red brick facades, see pages 248-253.

North Adams

NO
SASSING
YOUR
WAITRESS

Next-door neighbors could hardly be more dissimilar than Williamstown and North Adams, the working-class, former company town faltering just a few miles upstream of all that collegiate gentility. Nearly from its inception North Adams tied its fortunes to major manufacturing plants, churning out printed cotton until textiles went south, then rolling out capacitors for everything from the first atomic bomb to the television sets of the 1950s and 1960s. When electronics went solid-state and overseas, North Adams nearly died clinging to the belief that some new assembly line would come fill its sprawling 28-building 19th-century mill complex on the Hoosac River next to downtown. The long-awaited reprieve from welfare and unemployment finally seems to be taking shape, but folks who remember days of industrial wages on a union scale have a hard time envisioning their city being salvaged by . . . *art*. Conceived over a decade ago and then nearly aborted by statewide recession, the first 160,000 square feet of the Massachusetts Museum of Contemporary Art—**Mass MoCA**—are now under construction. If the master plan is ever fully implemented, the 13-acre "multidisciplinary cultural center" will become one of the world's largest art museums.

While the **Contemporary Artists Center and Gallery** in the historic Beaver Mill on north Route 8 may provide a hint of what may someday be the bread and butter of this town—or, rather, its wine and cheese—the region's first gravy train is faithfully recollected in the galleries of the **Western Gateway Heritage State Park** (daily 10 AM-5 PM late May to early Nov., closed Tues.-Wed. rest of the year; donations; 413/663-8059) on Route 8 just south of the Route 2 overpass. Occupying the renovated freight-yard buildings of the Boston and Maine Railroad, the park's visitor center highlights the landmark construction of the five-mile-long Hoosac Tunnel and North Adams's front-row seat on the Boston-to-Great Lakes rail connection it made possible.

In Massachusetts and the rest of New England, note the use of "Route" instead of "Hwy-," in keeping with regional practice.

Affluence gives Williamstown a decided edge over North Adams when it comes to good eating, but for local color detour down Route 8 about five miles to the spiffy little town of **Adams**, birthplace to suffragette Susan B. Anthony and present home to the incomparable **Miss Adams Diner** (breakfast and lunch daily). Sitting opposite the Congregational church on downtown Park Street, this handsome Worcester lunch car has all the steak and eggs, Blue Plate Specials, and tapioca pudding you'd expect from a place with a 1949 pedigree, but you'll also find good vegetarian specials, superb homemade pies (try the banana cream), and locally made Squeeze sodas. For a pleasant digestive, feed the meter with your extra pennies—yes, 12 minutes' parking costs but one cent—and stroll around the beautifully restored commercial district before returning to Route 2. Should the Miss Adams run out of **walking-tour** brochures from the local Historical Commission, the town hall just a couple doors down has a ready supply, accompanied by friendly suggestions.

It was during the blasting of the Hoosac Tunnel that nitroglycerin was first used as a construction explosive. A drunk assistant to the chief engineer discovered the dangerously unstable stuff could be handled safely when frozen.

Adams profited mightily from the protectionist trade policies of **Pres. William McKinley,** which is why his statue—by Augustus Lukeman, who also carved Atlanta's "Stone Mountain"—stands at the north end of Park Street. The work was commissioned by a local mill-owning friend after McKinley's 1901 assassination.

The Mohawk Trail

Taking its name from the warpath used for raids against Algonquian settlements along the upper Connecticut River Valley, the modern Mohawk Trail was the nation's first scenic highway, improved and paved as early as 1914 as part of a massive state effort to lure tourists into the cash-deprived farm belt of New England. If you're driving an overloaded or underpowered vehicle, you'll appreciate the thrill and radiator-popping risks that once attended the slow switchback grind up out of North Adams, around the attention-getting Hairpin Turn, and over the edge of the Western Summit, whose tidy **Wigwam Cottages** (May-Oct.; 800/223-4409; $60-70) have been taking in guests since Calvin Coolidge was still an unknown Northampton lawyer. Don't be fooled by the next short stretch of gentle ups and downs over the glacier-flattened mountain peaks of the Hoosac peneplain: the route's descent along the tortuous Cold River ravine quickens the pulse even in these days of power steering and anti-lock brakes, especially if you get sandwiched between a pair of 18-wheelers, whose burning brakepads sometimes scent the air all the way down the valley.

Scenic Loop Trips: Ashfield, Conway, and Colrain

Come fall, the sugar maples in the surrounding mixed hardwood forest add a blaze of brilliant orange to the landscape, making Route 2 a favorite of leaf-peepers between the end of September and Columbus Day weekend. If sharing the two-lane road with thousands of rubbernecking drivers becomes wearisome, consider taking a road less traveled. Almost any will do, but loops through Ashfield and Conway to the south of Route 2 or, for even greater isolation, Colrain and the Green River valley north of Route 2, are particularly nice, with glimpses of several historic covered bridges and enough pastoral beauty to more than compensate for the detours.

Shunning the main highway doesn't require skipping meals, either. For instance, there's thin-crust whole pizzas and slices at the **Country Pie Pizza Company** (open daily till 9 PM), across from Ashfield's rock-solid public library; given the fresh fancy toppings available, the prices are a real steal. Or coast down Route 116 to **Baker's Country Store**, just east of the old water tower, and sit down to a simple soup or sandwich amid the fishing tackle and canned goods. (If you like your pastry crusts short and white, be sure to sample the fresh pies, particularly in late summer during berry season.) A charming and whimsical find on the northern Route 112 loop is **The Green Emporium**, in Colrain's former Methodist church, where you can enjoy Mexican omelets and other made-to-order breakfast and lunch dishes in the company of creative, environmentally friendly merchandise and neon art.

To contemplate the landscape with the eye and tempo of a true country rambler it would be best to make a local **farm stay** or **B&B** the base for your perambulations. Friendly **Penfrydd Farm** in Colrain (413/624-5516) is a fine example of the former, with unpretentious $65-a-night rooms in an attractively renovated 19th-century farmhouse, a small herd of llamas, wonderful hilltop views across pastures and forest, and night skies thick with stars no city-dwellers will ever see from their roof decks. **The Farm at Ashfield** (413/628-4067) is another warm, hospitable, and reasonably priced retreat, far from just about anything you need to escape.

Shelburne Falls

Travelers who have stuck with Route 2 should take a turn at the signs for the lively, artsy little town of Shelburne Falls, which is actually two towns, Shelburne and Buckland, facing one another across the Deerfield River. Dining options include: espresso concoctions from Bridge Street's **Shelburne Falls Coffee Roasters**; vegetarian-friendly deli selections at the rear of **McCusker's Market,** facing the south end of the iron bridge; and richly sauced, red-meat-free entrees and salads at the **Copper Angel Cafe** across the street.

Next to the Copper Angel is one of the town's leading attractions, the **Bridge of Flowers**, a former electric trolley bridge converted to a linear display garden. The other oft-touted wonder is the sculptured riverbed below Salmon Falls, just east of Bridge Street: here, beside the spillway of diminutive Deerfield Dam and Powerhouse #3, the **Glacial Potholes** are popular for picnics, geological ruminations, hanging out with schoolmates, and boulder-hopping. Just don't fall asleep with your hearing aid turned down; the dam makes frequent releases of water, especially during the summer whitewater rafting season.

Greenfield

As Route 2 speeds down into the Connecticut River valley, it merges with north-south I-91 just long enough to skirt the county seat of Greenfield, a place once known for its cutlery,

You'll find excellent wooded streamside campsites in **Mohawk Trail State Forest** just above where the Cold River empties into the Deerfield. There are five year-round rustic cabins, too, but make reservations at least six months in advance (413/339-5504) if you have your heart set on staying in one.

Although early spring is aptly known as Mud Season throughout New England's back country, it's also when the sugar maple sap starts to flow. Boil away nearly 98% of the sap and you have genuine maple syrup delicious enough to make muddy, frost-heaved farm roads positively inviting. Call the Massachusetts Maple Phone (413/628-3912) to obtain a list of maple producers, or look for the "Hilltown Sugar Season" map at shops along this route.

tap-and-die, and other metals-related manufacturing. If you are looking for a bite to eat, follow Route 2A through town to the **Green River Cafe** at 24 Federal Street (Route 5/10 North). The menu might seem basic—soup, burgers, burritos, pasta stroganoff—but it's all outstandingly fresh, and the pies alone are worth a trip from almost anywhere in the county. It's closed Monday.

The proximity of the interstate has endowed Greenfield with some of the only **chain motels** in western Massachusetts. If you prefer a Howard Johnson's or Super 8 to a B&B, you'll find them beside the rotary at the junction of Route 2 and I-91; for one of the least expensive rooms in the state, take the interstate south two exits to the Motel 6 on Route 5.

Historic Deerfield

Just three miles south of Greenfield along Route 5, historic Deerfield is an immaculately preserved ensemble of houses dating from the early 1700s to 1850. Guides in each house discuss the lives, belongings, and historical contexts of the original inhabitants, often with such parental intimacy that you half expect these long-dead Ebenezers, Jonathans, and Marys to be napping upstairs. The whole town is recognized as one of the finest surviving colonial townscapes in America—in short, well worth a visit, no matter how brief—and is open daily (except Thanksgiving and Christmas; 413/774-5581; two-day admission $10) so there's no excuse for missing it.

East Franklin and North Worcester Counties

After crossing high over the Connecticut River atop the huge, art deco French King Bridge, the route passes through a few small communities along the banks of the Millers River before launching into a good stretch of almost nothing but forest, 40 miles of northern conifers and occasional stands of pale, peeling birch mixed with oaks typical of southern New England's central hardwoods. Bald eagles winter around the watershed for metropolitan Boston's drinking supply, Quabbin Reservoir, a few miles south of Route 2's exits 15 and 16. White-tailed deer sometimes bound across the periphery of vision and headlights, and rare is the journey unmarked by the hit-and-run death of a too-slow skunk, whose mortality is clearly broadcast over a half-mile radius. But as weekday traffic often demonstrates, beyond the trees and their wildlife lie a number of large towns that, while not bedroom communities for the state capital, do contribute significantly to the flow of commuters to Boston's outer ring of interstate office and technology parks.

Though nearly unimaginable today, some two-thirds of the landscape you see out your windows was totally deforested in the early 1800s. After some 150 years, that statistic has been easily reversed, although much of the forest along this stretch is relatively young, having grown up since a devastating hurricane in 1938 blew down nearly every pine tree in its path. An extraordinarily detailed set of handmade dioramas in the **Fisher Museum at Harvard Forest**, about a half-dozen miles south on Route 32 in Petersham (Mon.-Fri. 9 AM-5 PM, plus weekends May-Oct.; free), explain the history of modern human settlement in this part of the state, and plainly illustrate both natural forest succession and active forest management. After this introduction to silviculture, be sure to check out the town's classic village green with its ring of pristine white civic buildings, including the stately

LOWELL: JACK KEROUAC

At "five o'clock of a red-all-over suppertime" on March 12, 1922, Jack Kerouac—baptized John L. (Jean Louis) Kirouac by his French Canadian parents—was born in Lowell, a city sincerely regarded as one of the wonders of the world back when the Industrial Revolution was as fascinating as the Internet is now. Although this original Dharma Bum is more widely remembered for hanging out with Ferlinghetti in San Francisco or with Ginsberg in New York, or for pasting the Beat Generation firmly across the map of American culture, Kerouac also wrote five novels based on friends and familiar places in his native city, and his fictional work, from *On the Road* on, is that much more interesting when read in the context of his real life, here, along the Merrimack River.

Reciprocating Kerouac's lifelong love for Lowell, the National Park Service and the **Lowell National Historical Park**, keepers of the massive red-brick remains of America's first planned industrial city, publish a walking-tour brochure on Jack and his life in Lowell; they also help sponsor the annual **Lowell Celebrates Kerouac!** festival the first full weekend in October. Maps and guides to the man and the town are available from the **visitor center**, 246 Market Street (daily 8:30 AM-5 PM; free; 508/970-5000).

If you want to pay your respects to Kerouac, who died in Lowell in 1969, he is buried in Edsom Cemetery, two miles south of downtown Lowell via Gorham Street. Fans by the hundreds beat a path to his grave, which is on Lincoln Avenue between 7th and 8th Streets, marked by a pile of beer cans and other ritual offerings.

Even without the Kerouac connection, the town and historic park—with its working wate-powered looms, canal tours, and engaging interpretive tours—would deserve attention. Befitting its blue-collar past, Lowell is home to several classic diners— best of which is the excellent **Four Sisters' Owl Diner,** on Appleton Street near the Commuter Rail station.

Country Store, whose homemade fruit pies deserve as much attention as the Greek revival architecture.

As you approach the Tri-Town area of Leominster (LUH-min-ster), Fitchburg, and Lunenburg, rooftops begin to supplant treetops and Boston radio stations crowd the dial. Although "the Hub" is still some 30 miles away, its gravitational attraction seems to compel a majority of cars to exceed the speed limit. If you already know that you would rather walk barefoot over hot coals than be caught driving in Boston, you can start looking for accommodations now, as you are within the sphere of the **Commuter Rail** service to downtown (617/722-3200 or 800/392-6100). Purely by way of an example, the hour-long journey from the middle-of-nowhere Littleton stop to Boston's North Station, made 10 times daily on weekdays, five times daily on weekends, costs under $8 roundtrip—equivalent to a few hours' parking in most city lots.

Accommodations here, along I-495 on the 20-mile perimeter of the metropolitan area, are largely geared toward business travelers. The handful of B&Bs may be booked through the **Bed & Breakfast Folks** (617/275-9025), a private reservation service. There's also the aptly named **Friendly Crossways HI/AYH Hostel** on the Littleton/Harvard town line (508/456-3649; $15 for AYH members, $25 otherwise, private rooms for couples available)—just three miles, as it so happens, from the train station.

Concord

Fairly flying into the thick of metropolitan Boston, Route 2 runs along the outskirts of lovely little Concord, the destination of British Redcoats that fabled day in April 1775, when the war for American independence began. A reconstructed **Old North Bridge,** site of the "shot heard round the world," still arches o'er the placid Concord River next to open fields, drystone walls, and **The Old Manse** (daily except Tuesday, April-Oct.; $4.50), whose study window views are not so very different from when Ralph Waldo Emerson and Nathaniel Hawthorne lived here. The **Minute Man National Historical Park** maintains a free year-round visitor center on the hillside overlooking the famous battlefield; stop in and pick up a guide to the rest of the park's holdings along the "Battle Road" (Route 2A) between Concord and Lexington.

Although it often seems as if you can't toss a stick anywhere in eastern Massachusetts without hitting something of historic significance, this is especially true in Concord, where some of the most influential American writers either lived and worked. Visit a few of these literary lions—Emerson, Hawthorne, Henry David Thoreau, Louisa May Alcott, to name the most famous four—along "Author's Ridge" in **Sleepy Hollow Cemetery,** off Bedford Street northeast of the town center.

Visitors may be struck by the quantity of No Parking signs lining the streets of Concord, but the reason for this barrage of apparent inhospitality may be seen on any sun-drenched summer weekend, when long columns of cars bound for the beach at nearby **Walden Pond** jam the streets. Serious fans of Henry David Thoreau's little experiment in simple living may be able to overlook its overstressed condition, but more than likely you'll be taken aback by the erosion, the illegal kamikaze mountain bikers, the crowds, and the racket of passing commuter trains. Of course, there is still some magic to the place, although it usually takes a near-dawn in late spring or near-dusk in late fall to find any hint of transcendence along the pond's well-worn circumferential path.

A slightly different philosophy of simplicity may be found in the design of the nearby **Gropius House**, on Baker Bridge Road in Lincoln. Built in 1937-38 by and for Bauhaus founder Walter Gropius at the start of his tenure at Harvard University, this small showcase blends Bauhaus form-is-function precepts with traditional New England simplicity. Extremely knowledgeable guides give hourly **tours** (Fri.-Sun. noon-4 PM in summer; $5; 617/227-3956).

Perhaps you haven't got a week like Thoreau to row down the Concord River, but you can make your own abridged journey with a summer or fall canoe rental from South Bridge Boat House, 496-502 Main Street in Concord (508/369-9438).

For information about the Concord area, contact the historic Wright Tavern **visitor center**, 2 Main Street (508/369-3120), by the east end of the town common.

On to Boston

The remaining dozen miles to Boston are most quickly devoured along Route 2, although you can take slower Route 2A if you wish to follow the footsteps of those retreating British redcoats; either way will bring you to the same gateway for the metro area, Route 16 in north Cambridge. Whether or not you're staying outside the city, you would be well advised to leave your car in the Alewife "T" Station commuter parking garage ($4 a day) at the Route 2/Route 16 junction, and use the **MBTA subway** to get around the city.

For some helpful hints on visiting Boston, see the Survival Guide on pages 682-683.

US-6: ACROSS PENNSYLVANIA

Winding between the parallel I-90 and I-80 turnpikes, US-6 takes its time crossing the Keystone State, following the course of several ancient Indian trails and meandering rivers as the road wanders its way past a dizzying array of industrial wonders, hardscrabble factory towns, drive-in movie theaters, spit-polished diners, and farm-studded mountain valleys. In the west, the well-maintained two-lane roadway is clearly marked from the moment it crosses the Ohio border, with bright green signs labeling it the "Grand Army of the Republic Highway," a sobriquet US-6 has quietly borne since 1948.

Long before Pennsylvanians got turnpike and motor-touring fever, Native Americans carved twisting footpaths through the shady forests and narrow Allegheny Mountain valleys now navigated by US-6. In the western quarter of the state, the roadbed follows portions of the old Venango Trail, which provided a gateway to Lake Erie for the nomadic Senecas. Centuries before, Uncle Billy Smith and

Colonel Drake struck oil along the petroleum-rich beds of Titusville's Oil Creek, igniting a mad frenzy of speculation and boom-and-bust development that left its mark in the smoky refineries and gray, soot-stained towns that dot the craggy western Pennsylvania landscape.

As the rugged Allegheny landscape gives way to the tiny mountain farms and abandoned logging camps of the north-central portion of the state, the two-lane road winds through the bustling Allegheny River towns of Warren and Coudersport, and the New England tidiness of Wellsboro—the gateway to the deep Pine Creek Gorge region known as the Grand Canyon of Pennsylvania. Continuing east, US-6 suddenly transforms itself into a limited-access, concrete four-laner cutting a wide swath through the tough anthracite coal mining northeastern corner of the state. Here, the post-industrial and home-cooked charms of Scranton provide a welcome excuse for an extended stopover before tackling the monotonous stretch of dank, fetid swamps and wetlands that slope down to the damp, thickly forested Delaware Gap lowlands at the tri-state border of Pennsylvania, New York, and New Jersey.

When it was designated the "Grand Army of the Republic Highway" after WW II, US-6 begrudgingly parted with the Roosevelt Highway signposts it had proudly displayed since its construction as one of the state's original highways in 1923.

Meadville

The rigidly straight course cut by US-6 across Ohio's farm-dotted "Western Reserve" immediately gives way to a more casual, winding approach as you enter Pennsylvania, where you are greeted by a large blue sign bearing the state's geographically challenged tourism slogan, "Pennsylvania—America Starts Here," and a more discreet, rectangular, forest-green Grand Army of the Republic Highway marker. The narrow two-lane road, whitened by the ravages of winter storms and de-icing salts, is spattered with syrupy black tar drippings as it descends rolling, shaded hills studded with John Birch Society and gun show billboards near the campgrounds, and bait and tackle shops that service the vast Pymatuning Reservoir recreational area.

Gently twisting past a random mix of roadside hay bales, sweet corn vendors, ranch houses, deer crossing signs, and rusty trailer parks, US-6 becomes a four-lane divided highway with limited-access exit ramps before joining forces with US-322 and dumping you onto a featureless strip where Wal-Mart reigns supreme. This intense dose of highway sprawl marks the western edge of Meadville (pop. 14,300), the "Birthplace of the Zipper" (though invented as early as 1893, hookless slide fasteners did not become a commercial success until the Goodrich Company installed them in its popular galoshes in 1923). To get to the carefully hidden downtown, take Park Avenue past the motels (Super 8, Day's Inn, Holiday Inn) and minimarts that line US-6/322 outside of town.

The Talon zipper plant, which put this shady, peaceful college town on the map, has long since fled for cheap-labor climes. Rather than dwell on this departure, Meadville quietly goes about the business of maintaining its elm-shaded streets, parks, and ample stock of well-preserved 19th-century homes, and feeding off the profitable influx of college students who wander down the hill from Allegheny College's stately grounds to quench their collective thirst at the dark, smoky, working-class bars—like **Otter's Pub** and **Two's Company**—and restaurants that line North Street on the northern edge of the small but active downtown. Try the **Deerhead Inn**, 412 North Street, open 24 hours for cheap but filling spaghetti dinners in a cramped, windowless, and woodsy setting. Those with a ceaseless longing for reassuring dim lights, thick smoke, and loud, loud music will also want to head south of downtown to **Theodore's**, 964 Park Avenue, affectionately known locally as Teddy's, where a long, well-worn bar, a cooler full of Genesee beers, and a mixed bag of blue-collar locals and slumming collegians are the order of the night.

For a more salubrious educational experience, relax by the gazebo and grassy lawn of Diamond Park along shady Main and Chestnut Streets and take in the 1835 Greek revival architecture of the Unitarian church, before strolling over to view the Market House (continuously occupied since its construction in 1870 and now housing the Meadville Council on the Arts) on Market Street in the heart of the several-block downtown.

John Brown's Tannery

From Meadville, Hwy-77 runs northeast through a 10-mile, two-lane stretch of hardwood forest and rippling cornfields to the tiny crossroads of **New Richmond**, where Hwy-1033, a well-signed but bumpy dirt road, leads east past several modest homes and truck farms into a wooded clearing where the stone foundations of John Brown's Tannery rise from the grassy meadow floor.

Founded in 1815, **Allegheny College** is one of the oldest universities west of the Appalachians, and boasts a collection of beautiful historic Greek revival, Georgian, and federal-style buildings on its spacious campus on the north side of Meadville, at the crest of Park and Main Streets.

The future abolitionist operated a tannery here from 1825 to 1835—his longest period of continous residence in one place as an adult—after helping found the town of New Richmond with a band of settlers from Ohio's Western Reserve. Brown started the town's first post office and personally carried the mail to and from Meadville, where his outspoken nature almost got him lynched one night by an angry mob of Freemasons. The quick temper and passionate anti-slavery zeal that fired Brown's 1850s raids on Pottawatomie, Kansas, and Harper's Ferry, West Virginia (see page 275), seem like thunder from a distant storm in this quiet glen, where the graves of Brown's first wife and two of his infant sons attest to the hardships of the simple pioneer life he tried to forge from the rugged Pennsylvania wilderness.

Union City and Corry

US-6 is rejoined by its Lake Erie alternate, US-6N. The two roads run together past an Ethan Allen furniture company plant and a one-room local history museum as the highway slows to a tiny, snakelike main drag through sleepy Union City (pop. 3,537), where you are apt to spot several Amish farmers intently going about their in-town business. The peeling, weatherbeaten **Union City Dinor** at 48 N. Main Street is open Mon.-Sat. 6 AM-2 PM, staying open late for the usual Great Lakes Friday-night fish fry. On summer nights, the Dinor—which is how it's usually spelled here and in neighboring New York—makes a nice warm-up for an old-time drive-in movie up the road a few miles to the east at the **Corry Drive-In,** which charges just $5 per carload for first-run studio releases (weather permitting). Also in Corry, the **Day Lily Inn** (814/664-2894) offers affordable overnight accommodations in a modest B&B setting.

Between Corry and Warren, portions of the old US-6 roadway are undergoing major repairs, so be prepared for well-marked but time-consuming detours. The narrow, weed-strewn back roads take you past a tangle of unkempt overgrowth, junked cars, abandoned farmhouses, rust-coated farm machinery, and the occasional satellite dish and mobile home on cinder blocks—northern Pennsylvania's rural interpretation of the suburban ranch house ideal.

Titusville: Birthplace of the Oil Industry

Titusville celebrates its heritage with an annual "Drake Day" oil festival each August.

One place that roadtripping travelers through the wilds of western Pennsylvania really shouldn't miss is Titusville (pop. 6,400), the self-proclaimed "Birthplace of the Oil Industry." The fascinating **Drake Well Museum** (Tues.-Sat. 9 AM-5 PM, Sunday noon-5 PM; $4), a half-mile south of town off Hwy-8, relates the story of Col. Edwin Drake and driller Uncle Billy Smith's 1859 oil strike and the subsequent "black gold" rush it set off in the surrounding hills and creekbeds. A re-created model of the original well still pumps slippery, pure paraffin-based Pennsylvania crude, which you are encouraged to touch and smell by enthusiastic guides with an encyclopedic knowledge of local history and all things related to oil.

The museum also screens a humorously dated, but still entertaining, 1954 documentary film, *Born in Freedom,* starring a young, tentative Vincent Price as the pensive Drake (who, ironically, never reaped any financial rewards from his efforts and died in poverty in 1880 in Bethlehem, Pennsylvania) and tow-headed Alan Hale, Jr. (the Skipper in TV's *Gilligan's Island*) as a beefy, back-slapping drill hand.

The museum also boasts a rich library of oil-related and regional historical documents and early photographs detailing the incredible boom-and-bust cycle that gave birth to the nearby Oil Creek Valley town of Pithole, which saw its population shoot to 15,000 as speculators, con men, and prospectors poured into town to occupy the town's 57 hotels soon after another oil strike in 1865. Having the third-busiest post office in the state in its 1866 heyday, Pithole was virtually abandoned as soon as the oil ran dry in 1867. A free map and tour guide available at the museum direct you through Oil Creek State Park to the original town site, now an empty meadow of grasses and wildflowers.

Back in Titusville, stop at **Papa Carone's Restaurant**, 317 S. Franklin Street across the Oil Creek bridge (open daily from 11 AM), for a quick pizza slice, meatball sub, or soda.

Warren

Perched above the banks of a wide bend in the southward-flowing Allegheny River, downtown Warren (pop. 11,100) is a bustling jewel of Depression-era luncheonettes, dry goods stores, and a well-preserved commercial district in which sunfaded early 20th-century advertisements still adorn the dusty brick facades of many of the town's three- and four-story office buildings and warehouses. Park in the thriving central business district and wander along one of the shady side streets down to the river, taking in the old Liberty Theatre (on 3rd Avenue, now housing community arts productions), the neoclassical public library (on Market Street), and the tin-ceilinged, turn-of-the-century G.C. Murphy five-and-dime store on the corner of Liberty and Pennsylvania Streets.

Take a break with a meal or a cup of coffee at the timeless **Busy Bee Restaurant and Lounge**, open since 1936 for lunch and again for dinner at 229½ Pennsylvania Avenue. Across the street, **Roy's Texas Lunch** serves up a hearty, cholesterol-rich fare of red hots (hot dogs grilled in the tough western New York tradition), goulash, and macaroni and cheese in a more pedestrian, no-nonsense setting.

The all-purpose **Jefferson House Pub and Bed and Breakfast**, 119 Market Street (814/723-2268), features a wide array of sandwiches and mesquite-grilled main courses in the main dining room. The wide, wraparound porch that graces the exterior of this restored 1890 Victorian home is a powerful drawing card for those seeking to calm their road-jangled nerves. A **Holiday Inn**, a **Super 8**, and the locally owned and operated **Penn Laurel Inn** (814/723-8300), all on Pennsylvania Street on the western edge of town, offer reasonably priced lodging options.

Save your ticket stub from the Drake's Well Museum—it will earn you discounted admission to two dozen other historical sites operated throughout the state by the Pennsylvania Historical and Museum Commission. A free guide and map is available at the museum gift shop.

No matter how tempting its name may be, skip the 20-mile detour south to grimy Oil City (pop. 12,000), where mammoth Pennzoil refinery smokestacks blacken the skyline over the narrow, traffic-choked streets of this grimy, hardworking city still coming to grips with the recent flight of its lifeblood, the Quaker State corporation, to Texas.

Heading east from Warren on US-6, take note of the beautiful tile-roofed, hacienda-style building now serving as the main office for the United Refining Company. The twisted smokestacks and grease-streaked oil tanks loom behind this architectural oddity like a sinister urban industrial skyline.

Kane

Approaching Kane (pop. 4,590) from the west, the road rolls unassumingly through a series of farm-laden hills before zipping through a monotonous 20-mile slice of the pine-shaded Allegheny State Forest preserve. Sitting atop a high ridge, Kane's busy turn-of-the-century downtown sports the old **Temple Theatre** (now doing some prime business with the pre-pubescent crowd as Shirley Temple's Rollerskating Rink), an old **McCrory's** five-and-dime store, and the wonderful **Texas Hot Lunch** at 24 Field Street, an early-opening, late-closing bar and restaurant where chili-doused dogs are served hot off the grill with sweet relish, onions, and hot mustard at a price (90 cents each) bound to encourage multiple purchases.

The **Kane Motel** (814/837-6161) and **Kane View Motel** (814/837-8600) on the eastern edge of town are both within shouting distance of the turquoise-trimmed, first-run **Family Drive-In Theatre** on the north side of US-6, a few miles east of downtown Kane.

*Kane is proud of its favorite recent son, **Chuck Daly,** coach of the two-time NBA champion Detroit Pistons and the 1992 U.S. Olympic "Dream Team."*

Kinzua Bridge State Park

At the lonesome, nondescript crossroads of Mount Jewett (pop. 1,000), follow signs along a bumpy, narrow roller coaster of a road to Kinzua Bridge State Park, four miles north of US-6 amid dark pine *Deer Hunter*-like forest. The park straddles the steep Kinzua Creek Gorge, which was finally spanned in 1882 by the 301-foot-high, 2,053-foot-long Kinzua Viaduct, constructed by the Erie Railroad to extend its economic reach southward into the fertile McKean County coal, timber, and oil fields. At the time, it was the highest railroad bridge ever built, earning the structure its proudly worn badge as the "**Eighth Wonder of the World.**"

A short walk over the rough, tar-soaked railroad-tie crosswalk to the center of the bridge leads to an exhilarating view of the dense tree cover leading down the steep slopes to the narrow creekbed. Alternately, the **Knox and Kane excursion railroad** (814/837-8621 or 717/334-6932) offers a roundtrip package tour from nearby Kane or more distant Marienville for those who want to test the structural soundness of the steel-reinforced viaduct under the weight of a period passenger steam train.

Smethport

Back on US-6, dilapidated downtown Smethport (pop. 1,734) is home of **America's First Christmas Store** (800/841-2721), housed in a run-down brick building on the eastern edge of town along Main Street (US-6). If you lose out to your better judgment and find yourself overcome with that holly-jolly feeling, you might want to recuperate with a piece of homemade pie at the **Smethport Diner**, a modest, white stone structure that entrances weary roadtrippers with the romantic lure of electric candlelight dining.

East of Smethport, which marks the approximate boundary of western Pennsylvania's once-potent oil industry, an endless sea of junked cars, dense forests, and swampy lowland truck farms laps at the roadbed as US-6 passes through the historic Allegheny River ford of Port Alleghany.

*Every July, the Lumber Museum hosts the **Bark Peelers' Convention,** when wanna-be Paul Bunyans can try their hand at felling a tree or two amid bluegrass bands and country picnics.*

Coudersport: The Pennsylvania Lumber Museum

In tidy downtown Coudersport (pop. 2,800), a gazebo graces the pretty courthouse square across from the **Hotel Crittendon**, 133 N. Main Street (814/274-8320), where you can dine, drink, and crash for the night without ever setting foot outside. More reckless grub-guzzlers will want to check out **Mickey's Diner and Bakery** on E. 2nd Street for a cheap, filling meal, maybe following it up with a beer at the nearby King's Inn, which fronts rustic, damp-looking but photogenic motor court "cottages."

East of Coudersport, US-6 descends into thickly forested piney woods at the northern lip of the Susquehannock State Forest. A 10-mile-long, virtually retail-free stretch of road leads to the **Pennsylvania Lumber Museum** (daily 9 AM-4:30 PM; $3.50), which pays homage to the region's prosperous mid-19th-century lumber boom. A period logging camp, a two-story mill with circular saw upstairs and steam-powered engines below, and a chestnut log cabin from the Depression-era Civilian Conservation Corps (CCC) reforestation program are among the 3,000 lumber-related objects on display at this refreshingly self-effacing museum.

The **Nine-Mile Lakeside Cottage and Motel** (814/435-2394), on the north side of US-6 just east of the museum, features a set of redwood-stained motor court cabins for those who plan to make a weekend out of it.

Continuing east from the museum, US-6 wanders along the wooded Pine Creek Valley through **Galeton** (pop. 1,370) and the minuscule village of **Gaines**, approaching the western rim of the grandly named "Grand Canyon of Pennsylvania." A six-mile-long, pothole-strewn concrete road leads south from US-6 outside of Gaines to **Colton Point State Park**, built during the New Deal by the CCC to provide a dramatic alternate view of the gorge's shimmering waterfalls and craggy, tree-covered slopes. Check the weather before making this tough, bumpy detour, however, as even the slightest hint of fog will obscure the expansive vistas and transform the narrow park road into an eerie setting right out of David Lynch's dark, creepy *Twin Peaks*.

Wellsboro

The most popular jumping-off point for tourists who flock to the Grand Canyon of Pennsylvania for a weekend getaway, Wellsboro (pop. 3,400) has a gorgeous Main Street business district with a warm, comfortable feel created by the authentic gas-lit streetlights that line the lush, grassy median strip, and by the red neon glow of the flickering sign that fronts the historic, well-worn **Penn Wells Hotel**, built in 1869 and last remodeled in 1926.

A free walking-tour guide, available at the visitor center and most of the town's businesses, points the way to Wellsboro's main historic sight, the **Lincoln Door House** at 140 Main Street, which bears a red door donated in 1858 by then-Illinois governor Abraham Lincoln, whom the house's occupants had known before relocating to Wellsboro from Springfield, Illinois. A casual stroll along the shaded side streets to view some of Wellsboro's historic 19th-century homes is the town's main entertainment option, which otherwise consists of a movie at the one-screen **Arcadia Theatre** or a drink and a game of pool at the friendly **North Star Bar**, both on Main Street.

For food, the Penn-Wells Hotel's shabbily elegant **Mary Wells Dining Room**—which, sadly, bears no relation to the "My Guy" chanteuse—has hearty breakfasts and pricier pasta dinners, but the place to eat is the low-slung, green-roofed, porcelain-plated **Wellsboro Diner**, 19 Main Street, an immaculately restored Sterling diner car originally manufactured in 1939 by the J.B. Judkins Co. of Merrimac, Massachusetts. The diner closes its doors early, so make a point of grabbing an early dinner, or even earlier lunch or breakfast; if you are going to hang around town for a few hours, they will even custom-bake a pie of your choosing to tide you over for the rest of your trip.

The peeling yellow wallpaper, orange shag carpet, and grease-streaked curtains lining the hallways and rooms of the once-grand Penn-Wells Hotel arouse suspicions that the next wave of renovations are long overdue, and your overnight dollars are better spent at the adjacent **Penn Wells Lodge**, 4 Main Street (717/724-3463 or 800/545-2446), which has full facilities and rates from under $50 a night. The **Canyon Motel**, two blocks east at 18 East Avenue (717/724-1681 or 800/255-2718), has bargain-priced rooms from under $30. For something a bit more special, settle in at the cozy, Victorian-style **Four Winds Bed and Breakfast** (717/724-6141) on W. Main Street.

For more information, contact the Wellsboro **visitor center**, 114 Main Street (717/724-1926).

The Grand Canyon of Pennsylvania

The thickly forested mountain ravine known as the "Grand Canyon of Pennsylvania" bears little resemblance to the red rocks and more dramatic dropoffs associated with the eponymous Arizona landmark. That said, it's still an impressive sight—especially at sunset—with clouds hovering above its 1,000 feet of pine-covered walls.

To reach the Grand Canyon's eastern rim, take Main Street (SR 660) west out of Wellsboro, past beautiful Victorian homes and through a lush dairy farming district marked by cud-chewing cows and freshly painted barns and silos. The main "entrance" to the canyon is at Leonard Harrison State Park, which provides an easily accessed view of the gorge and a well-maintained trail dropping down to the river. The former Penn Central railroad right-of-way in the base of the canyon is being converted into a cycling and cross-country skiing trail. You can also see the canyon from Colton Point State Park on the west rim (see page 483 for more).

Towanda

US-6 rolls lazily through a 40-mile stretch of rich dairy farmland and gentle hills east of Wellsboro, through Mansfield and Troy and into Towanda (pop. 3,200), an odd mix of nicely maintained Victorian homes and a no-nonsense, telephone-pole-crowded downtown. Historical markers recite the achievements of Towanda's two most famous residents—19th-century politician David Wilmot, who authored the 1846 anti-slavery document known as the Wilmot Proviso; and composer Stephen Foster, who penned the now-ubiquitous "Camptown Races" while wandering the banks of the Susquehanna River as a student at the Towanda Academy in 1840-41.

You can get *just about* anything you want—in the way of breakfast or lunch—at **Alice's Restaurant**, 318 Main Street (6 AM-8 PM, Sunday 8 AM-1 PM). Or check out a movie at the still-operating **Keystone Theatre.**

French Azilum

From Towanda on down to Tunkhannock, US-6 runs a high ridge above the steep Susquehanna River bed, along the course of an ancient Seneca Indian trail. En route, the road passes within sight of the French Azilum, a short-lived agricultural colony of French aristocrats who fled here after the French Revolution in 1793 in the hope of providing safe harbor for Marie Antoinette and her son, the heir to the French throne. The colony more or less disintegrated in 1803 when most of the nobles were lured back to France by Napoleon's pardoning decree. The **Marie Antoinette Overlook,** on the south side of US-6 about six miles southeast of the Masonite mill town of Wysox, provides a sweeping view of the patchwork quilt of fertile flatlands on the south shore of the Susquehanna where the remains of Azilum still stand. The five log cabins and a model of the original village, which adjoin a large working dairy farm that extends to the river bank, are being restored by the Pennsylvania Historical and Museum Commission.

Though it's just across the river from US-6, extensive detours and road repairs make getting to the actual site a patience-trying endeavor that will eat up at least an hour of roundtrip driving time. The easiest way to get there from US-6 is to take Hwy-187 across the river from Wyalusing, continue for eight miles to Durell, then head west on Hwy-204, following the clearly marked signs to the site.

Tuckhannock and Factoryville

After passing through the false-fronted late-1890s banks and businesses lining the road through Wyalusing, US-6 continues its rapid downhill run to Scranton along a narrow ridge above the Susquehanna, pulling into the pleasant, flag-lined business district of aging lumber center Tunkhannock (pop. 2,251), where a Pampers disposable diaper factory now reigns supreme as the town's largest employer. The **Prince Hotel** (717/836-2292) in the center of town has a few old rooms upstairs at about $25 a night, within stumbling distance of the lively Red Lion Inn bar that occupies the first floor.

The dense evergreen groves crowding the two-lane road down the sharp, fast descent into the Scranton-Wilkes Barre area are broken by a sign at the outskirts of little Factoryville (pop. 1,310), advertising itself as the birthplace of turn-of-the-century New York Giants baseball hurler, Hall of Famer **Christy Mathewson**, who played for northern Pennsylvania factory and mill teams before establishing himself as the king of Upper Manhattan's Polo Grounds in the early 1900s.

Scranton is an easy place to get lost; from US-6, which skirts the northern lip of the city, take the Scranton Expressway (US-11) south into the downtown area.

A few miles south of Factoryville, along an abandoned Delaware, Lackawanna and Western Railroad right-of-way, US-6 suddenly widens into a four-lane, limited-access highway split by a steel guardrail median strip, whizzing past a crowded stretch of old motels, supermarkets, liquor stores, and mini-marts along the steep Moosic Mountain grade down into Scranton.

Scranton

The tough, sprawling coal town of Scranton (pop. 81,800) is in the midst of a remarkable revitalization that revolves largely around the successful, sensitively conceived promotion of its mighty industrial past as a regional tourist attraction. Aside from the diverse, engaging museums that celebrate Scranton's historical importance as a mining, manufacturing, and railroad hub, the city lays claim to a AAA minor league baseball team (the Philadelphia Phillies' affiliate, Scranton-Wilkes Barre Red

Barons), an architecturally rich downtown, and a savory set of greasy spoons, streamlined diners, dairy bars, and pizza joints.

The town was founded in the 1840s when brothers George and Seldon Scranton and their cousin, Joseph Scranton, started the Lackawanna Iron and Coal Company and built the Scranton Iron Furnaces, Lackawanna Avenue and Moosic Street, to produce iron rails for the construction of the Erie Railroad line. The brothers' need for a local rail spur led to the founding of the Delaware part of the Lackawanna and Western line in 1853, and firmly established the city as a major rail producer and railroad hub, a position that grew in importance in the 1890s when Scranton emerged as the center of the country's anthracite coal production.

The old 40-acre DL&W railroad yard and locomotive roundhouse on the west side of downtown Scranton have been exquisitely restored by the National Park Services as part of the **Steamtown National Historic Site** (for hours and prices call 717/961-2035), which finally opened its doors in July 1995. The sprawling rail yards contain steam-era locomotives, dining cars, and Pullman sleepers in the process of being restored, while a steam-powered passenger train makes short tourist excursions over to the nearby Iron Furnaces. Your time is best spent browsing the brightly lit roundhouse full of fascinating historical and technological exhibits that trace the development of steam railroading and the growth of the DL&W over its century-long reign as the mighty "Road of Anthracite" that, along with the Erie line, linked the key Atlantic and Great Lakes ports of New York and New Jersey to the lumber camps, coal mines, and oil fields of Pennsylvania. No details are spared, down to a glossary of colorful slang expressions from every walk of railroad life that explain why the caboose was known both as a "monkey house" and "brainboat," while "the pig's in the pen" was a downhome way of saying that a locomotive had just entered the roundhouse.

The **Anthracite Heritage Museum**, northwest of downtown in McDade Park via Scranton Expressway/US 11 to Keyser Street (daily 9 AM-5 PM; $3.50), celebrates the social and cultural history of the Welsh, Polish, Italian, Ukranian, and Lithuanian immigrant miners whose backbreaking labors allowed Scranton's mine owners and railroad barons to reap immense personal fortunes and build grand public buildings and private homes. In addition to detailing the dangerous working conditions and tragic history of the miners' labor movement, the museum tells the painful story of the breaker boys who picked out nonburnable slate from raw anthracite in massive, poorly ventilated coal breaker structures that dotted the Scranton skyline well into the mid-1900s.

THE FAMOUS HOUDINI MUSEUM

Long hours and hard-earned pay meant that Scranton's factory workers, railroad hands, and miners had to be selective when spending their minimal extra funds on family-minded social diversions like a traveling variety show, circus, or county fair. The Famous Houdini Museum, 1433 N. Main Avenue, commemorates the amazing showmanship of the Hungarian-born magician, Harry Houdini, one of countless traveling acts that passed through the area in the early 1900s. Scranton was then considered a proving ground for New York-based vaudeville performers eager to get the promotional backing needed to take their city-honed act on the road. The expression, "If you can make it in Scranton, you can make it anywhere," was coined by savvy promoters who viewed the demanding working-class immigrant audience as a litmus test that would gauge a particular act's ability to "play in Peoria" long before advertisers and film studios made focus groups and test markets a key part of all their market research efforts.

Owned and operated by two renowned magicians—Dorothy Dietrich and Jerry Bravo, who managed New York's Magic Towne House performance/dinner theater for 15 years—the cramped storefront Houdini Museum celebrates the mysterious life and achievements of Ehrich Weiss, who took the stage name of Harry Houdini when he decided to pursue a career as a magician after his family relocated from his boyhood home of Appleton, Wisconsin, to New York in the 1890s. Houdini's bewildering escapes from sausage skins, jail cells, coffins, and countless locks and straitjackets are recalled in a short video presentation, followed by a tour of the museum's vast collection of Houdini's favorite tricks, mechanisms, and scrapbooks. There's even a delightful live magic show.

For more free travel and local history information about northeastern Pennsylvania, log onto the independently maintained regional World Wide Web site at http://mtmis1.mis.semi.harris.com/pa.html.

In case you're wondering, the name of Scranton's neighbor, Wilkes-Barre, is pronounced "Wilkes Barry."

The Scranton/Wilkes-Barre Red Barons AAA baseball team play their home games at the 10,800-seat **Lackawanna County Stadium,** an AstroTurf arena cut into a hillside off I-81 west of town at the Davis Street exit in Moosic. Call 717/969-BALL for a schedule of home games and promotional events.

Next door to Anthracite Heritage Museum, the **Lackawanna Coal Mine Tour** (daily 11 AM-4:30 PM; $5) lets you experience the claustrophobia and terror of the miners' daily life firsthand with a railcar trip 300 feet deep into the bowels of a once-active anthracite mine.

Scranton Practicalities

All this history and museum-going is bound to make you mighty hungry—a condition Scranton can amply remedy. The Old Forge neighborhood extending west along Main Street a few miles from the Houdini Museum is home to a bevy of Italian family restaurants and bars that dish out the area's locally famous "Old Forge" white pizza—gobs of mozzarella and onions, no tomato sauce. This cheesy concoction cannot be ordered by the slice (the lack of sauce makes it dry out too quickly), and most of the neighborhood restaurants serve it—including **Talarico's,** 103 S. Main Street, and **Arcaro and Genell,** 443 S. Main Street—both of which are open only in the evenings. Downtown, **Coney Island Lunch** at 515 Lackawanna Avenue is the home of the Texas Wiener hot dog, while a five-minute drive on Moosic Street up the hill toward the University of Scranton lands you at the foot of red-trimmed, stainless-steel **Chick's Diner,** 1032 Moosic Street at Meadow Avenue, a classic all-night eatery with a loud, gregarious local clientele.

A place to appreciate even if you don't stay the night is the restored neoclassical 1908 train station, now the 145-room **Lackawanna Station** luxury hotel, 700 Lackawanna Avenue (800/347-6888). It summons the grandeur of the steam era with a revitalized Grand Lobby flanked by a set of rare Siena marble walls and mosaic murals. Most of the bargain-priced motel chains (Best Western, Hampton Inn, Days Inn, Red Roof Inn, Econo Lodge, etc.) cluster around Wilkes-Barre's I-81 exit 47. Smaller, locally owned motels line US-6 to the north of Scranton.

Along US-6 north of Scranton, the majestic **Circle Drive-In** movie theatre (717/489-5731) still shows first-run films high on a hilltop overlooking the Scranton Valley. A prime source of local nightlife and entertainment options is *The Weekender,* a free weekly newspaper published out of nearby Wilkes-Barre that can be picked up at bookstores, clubs, restaurants, and bars in the Scranton/Wilkes-Barre vicinity.

For more information, contact the Scranton/Wilkes Barre **visitor center,** 222 Mulberry Street (717/342-7711).

Honesdale

East of Scranton, US-6 veers away from the high-speed I-84 freeway, following a slow, twisting two-lane course through rugged anthracite fields and the fading remnants of the once-prosperous coal towns of Jermyn, Carbondale, and Steen. East of Steen, old road markers for US-6's original designation, The Roosevelt Highway, are still visible on the right side of the road, amid the damp undergrowth scuttling up from the creek coursing to the south of the roadway.

In downtown Honesdale (pop. 5,000), the **Wayne County Historical Society Museum**, 810 Main Street, houses a full-sized replica of the **Stourbridge Lion**, the locomotive that made the first commercial steam-engine run in the U.S. in 1829 in an effort to tow coal from the nearby mines to the Delaware and Hudson Canal. The **Maple City Restaurant** next door is a time-worn coffee shop where you can rest and fill your gills with coffee, a burger, and a slice of cherry pie before making the final run through the swampy, nondescript deer hunting area bordering the Delaware State Forest en route to Milford, Matamoras, Port Jervis, and Delaware Water Gap National Recreation Area.

Zane Grey

Milford

Just off I-84 at the northern end of Delaware Water Gap National Recreation Area, Milford (pop. 1,400) is a cutesy tourist town cashing in on the hordes of rafters, campers, and B&Bers who make the two-hour weekend journey here from New York and Philadelphia.

The **Blue Spruce Motel** motor court (717/491-4969) and **Milford Motel** (717/296-6411) on the northern outskirts of town off US-6 are the low-priced alternatives to the higher-brow **Tom Quick Inn** (717/296-6514) and **Demmick Inn** (717/296-9363) B&B resorts in the heart of overpriced downtown Milford.

Cool your heels in the air-conditioned comfort of the streamlined **Village Diner**, open daily 6 AM-9 PM at 620 W. Hartford Street a few miles north of Milford on US-6, which quickly joins with I-84 to cross the Delaware River into New York at Port Jervis.

The tiny town of **Lackawaxen,** along the Delaware River seven scenic miles north of US-6 along Hwy-590, holds two fascinating attractions: the preserved home of writer and trout-fisherman Zane Grey, and a unique suspension bridge built by Brooklyn Bridge designer John Roebling to carry a canal across the river.

Drive slowly when passing through Milford's deceptively peaceful central business district, because the local police maintain carefully concealed speed traps that result in heavy fines for even the most minor speed limit violation.

Milford marks the western junction of US-6 and the Appalachian Trail route, which runs south from here through Delaware Water Gap National Recreation Area. See page 265 for more.

US-6: ACROSS NEW YORK

According to the map, US-6's corner-cutting path across the southern edge of the state seems well outside New York City's sprawl, but there is no escape from the greater reality of the urban northeast: this part of the Atlantic seaboard is the original megalopolis. The map may not make it obvious that some tens of millions of people live within an hour's drive of this route, but the volume of traffic will. Despite a pleasant foray onto curvaceous and scenic parkways through Harriman and Bear Mountain State Parks, and a dramatic crossing of the Hudson River, US-6 is often immersed in long stretches of commercial roadside development, particularly east of the Hudson. Putnam County's seemingly endless strip malls will help anesthetize you against the urban landscape found all along the remainder of your journey. If you weary of studying the subtle regional differences in architectural and typographic vernacular, there are several chances to switch over to the bland but expeditious interstate.

Port Jervis

A curious mixture of small-town dereliction and commercial bustle, Port Jervis wears its empty storefronts like an elderly professor wears a fraying tweed jacket. Transportation has clearly been a major historical force here, with the influence of successive eras—the river, the railroad, and the federal highway—inscribed in the very layout of the town. For a glimpse of the long reign of the iron horse, check out the intriguing artifacts and photos in the restored waiting room of the old **Erie Lackawanna Depot** on Front Street. The arrival of the interstate provided the last major makeover, with the placement of I-84 on the outskirts of this everlasting pit stop sparing its center from the aluminum implants of modern prefabricators. Signs of the next shift—back to the sturdy brick commercial blocks beside the old depot—are visible in the "shoppe" signs sprouting among the old mom 'n' pop stores downtown.

The wary traveler seeking either the comfort and safety of a brand-name burger or the excitement of roast duck with plum-balsamic vinaigrette will have to hit the road, Jack, for this town still believes in the virtues of home cooking. **Homer's Coffee Shop**, unmissable at the corner of Orange and Main, is a prime example, with its democratic social club of elderly regulars, young tie-wearing businessmen, and tradespeople with company names stitched on their shirt pockets, all drawn to the bargain meals. Despite the acoustic tile and too-new counter and seating, it's a welcoming spot, with the added attraction of a soda fountain in case you need to wash down that turkey club or beef stroganoff with a Tin Roof Sundae.

With "soda bars" and confectionaries so plentiful in these parts, you may wonder if some local zoning law requires the vintage counters found in general merchandise stores, so residents can perpetually relive their collective youth.

Minisink Valley

Leaving Port Jervis and the Delaware River, the route gradually rises over a scenic dozen miles along the low flanks of the Shawangunk Mountains. Bright red leaves of late summer's sumac stand out amid the thick deciduous woods like the ripening apples in the many orchards whose roadside stands are always worth a stop as soon as autumn's crop is heralded by these hand-lettered declarations: "fresh-baked pies" and "fresh-pressed cider."

Shaking the country air off its shoulders, US-6 joins four-lane Rte-17M, chock full of fast drivers intent on cutting the corner between northward-tending I-84 and the big-city-bound New York Thruway, I-87. After a headlong dash eastward from one interstate to the next, US-6 peels itself from the rush and enters **Harriman State Park**. In utter contrast to the get-out-of-my-way style of later highway construction, the few parkway miles you'll sample here were intentionally designed to encourage the Sunday afternoon family outing in the motor car, the lazy meandering roadbed calculated to lengthen the journey and maximize exposure to the surrounding forests. Even the rustic Romanesque stone arch bridges attempt to harmonize with local rock outcroppings.

Hudson Valley: Hyde Park

Since the narrow toll bridge (75 cents) over the **Hudson River** affords only a quick glance for whomever is behind the wheel, pull into the parking lot on the west end before crossing to get a good vista of the spindly iron span between the steep palisades. Several state parks preserve this pretty stretch of the river: besides Harriman and the contiguous **Bear Mountain**, there's the sculptural park at **Storm King** to the north of this route, as well as the Georgia-to-Maine **Appalachian Trail**, which comes down out of the hills to cross this very bridge.

While there's no camping at Harriman State Park, there are hiking trails and even a swimming beach and a bathhouse at **Lake Welch;** take the Palisades Interstate Parkway south from the US-6 (Long Mount Parkway) rotary.

If you prefer a dash of history and decorative arts to a jog through the woods, take a detour upstream on Rte-9 about 35 miles to the small town of Hyde Park, just north of Poughkeepsie, for a peek into a pair of famous homes now preserved as National Historic Sites: the **home of Franklin D. Roosevelt** and the **Vanderbilt Mansion** (both houses Wed.-Sun. 9 AM-5 PM, grounds daily 7 AM-sunset; $5 for

West Point, the Army's famous military academy, is a few miles north of US-6— on the west bank of the Hudson, naturally.

FDR and $2 for Vanderbilt; 914/229-9115). Also on the grounds of FDR's home is the **National Archives' library and museum** (daily 9 AM-5 PM; admission free with Park Service fee; 800/337-8474). In the nearby village of Haviland, on parallel Rte-9G about two miles north of the presidential home, the **Eleanor Roosevelt Historic Site** (same Wed.-Sun. hours; free) will complete your ramble back to the era of the New Deal.

Westchester County

Soak up as much of that scenic Hudson valley as you can—it's the last commercial-free panorama you'll get until well into neighboring Connecticut. Once US-6 leaves the river it becomes a heavily developed corridor of suburban malls, muffler shops, quick-lube garages, office parks, and Park 'n' Ride lots for Manhattan commuters. Not that businesses don't try to sprinkle a dash of foliage around their parking lots—in fact, nearly everybody cultivates more than just token landscaping—but compared to the apple orchards you passed an hour ago and the quaint New England villages an hour ahead, these few dozen miles are hardly a sight for sore eyes.

If you want to make them go a little faster, the town of Brewster provides the first of three chances to hop onto I-84; if you stay on US-6—now a fast four lanes itself—you'll end up crossing the unmarked state line about 40 miles after you crossed the Hudson.

ACROSS CONNECTICUT

In nighttime satellite photos from space, Connecticut is that bright swath of light splayed between the major metropolitan hotspots of New York City and Boston. It may often seem to contain nothing more than suburbs and office parks, but in fact this third smallest state has some very pleasantly rural landscape tucked away in its northern corners. Expansive colonial farms and elegant frame houses are glimpsed briefly as you skirt their edges, but alas, the bulk of this route plainly parallels the dense mega-urban corridor along coastal I-95, 25 miles south. If the flux of traffic and strip malls becomes too overwhelming, escape north for a more circuitous but relaxing ride, or give up and join the jet stream on the adjacent (and occasionally contiguous) I-84/395 freeways.

Danbury marks the eastern junction of US-6 and the Appalachian Trail route, which winds north to Mount Washington and south all the way to Atlanta. For details, see pages 228-298.

Danbury

Since US-6 joins I-84 within a few miles of crossing the state line, it hardly matters which route you choose—and given the abutters vying for your business along every inch of the old road, you may actually find the interstate more scenic. US-6 skips off on its own for a few miles for a glimpse of upscale residential Newtown, only to merge again with the interstate on the far side of the town's huge flagpole.

Unless you can't hold out for the gourmet shops of Litchfield County, you may as well skip the diversion and stay aboard I-84 until exit 15, when the route gets out of its four-lane rut and gives you a good reason to slow down. For easy-to-find accommodations around Danbury, try the **Super 8** at the first I-84/US-6 junction in the state (exit 4), or the **Best Western** on US-6 at I-84 exit 9.

Southbury and Woodbury

Take some horse farms with lush green fields outlined by neat stone walls or zigzagging knit-pole fences, mix in big old clapboard colonials with wide lawns and wood split-shingle roofs, add a couple needle-spired churches and historic burial grounds beneath the tall maples and oaks, and you have all the trappings of a place that should live by the gentle stroke of a tall grandfather clock rather than the nervous second-splitting tick of a stopwatch. Alas, all of the Southbury and Woodbury residents who keep time by the old Seth Thomas wind-ups must be at home taking naps, while all the sprinters caught up in lives like 100-meter dashes are out taking turns trying to read the fine print on your rear license plate.

Since the rush of traffic on US-6 makes architectural appreciation impossible without suffering whiplash, stop by Woodbury's town office building on Main Street and pick up a free brochure detailing two local **walking tours** around the former sheep-raising capital of the American colonies, liberally endowed with fine 18th- and 19th-century structures. One colonial home open to the public is the restored **Glebe House** (Wed.-Sun. 1-4 PM, April-Nov.; 203/263-2855), on Hollow Road (Hwy-317) in southern Woodbury. The first Episcopalian bishop was elected by a secret meeting of clergy at this minister's farm in 1783 and consecrated by Scottish Anglicans a year later—an extraordinarily radical act in that age, because it required accepting two unorthodoxies: religious freedom (the Anglicans, after all, were the official church of the defeated enemy) and the separation of church and state. These liberties weren't enshrined in the Constitution, by the way, until three years later.

Long before bishops and the Bill of Rights, the land around here was farmed and hunted by Algonquian tribes like the Pootatucks, who finally sold it in 1659. **The Institute for American Indian Studies** (daily to 5 PM except Jan.-March, closed Mon.-Tues.; $4; 860/868-0518) off Hwy-199 in nearby Washington has extensive exhibits on exactly who these people were, what they did around here in the centuries prior to the "discovery" of their homeland, and how anthropology and archaeology have brought some of this information to light. The IAIS also reminds visitors that not all Indians are casino owners, and that traditional Native Americans continue to live and work here; crafts and technology demonstrations, performances, and workshops are offered. From Southbury take Hwy-67 north to Hwy-199, or from Woodbury take Hwy-47 to Hwy-199; the IAIS sign is about halfway between the Washington-Roxbury town line and the Hwy-47 junction.

Besides ecclesiastical history and colonial crafts, the Glebe House also possesses the only remaining garden in the U.S. designed by **Gertrude Jekyll,** the horticulturist who perfected what's known as the English country garden.

Waterbury: Holy Land

About 10 miles due east of Woodbury, the large old manufacturing town of Waterbury is home to Holy Land, above I-84 on the hill—look for the giant illuminated cross. Plaster, carpet remnants, reflective mailbox-style adhesive lettering, plastic dolls, and Biblical scripture are some of the basic ingredients in this folk art extravaganza built over a couple postwar decades by a very, very dedicated Christian. The fact that vandals had their way with the place for at least another decade or two doesn't deter devout pilgrims, and the utter ruin should certainly appeal to anyone with a dark, well-honed sense of irony and metaphor.

As long as you're in town, be sure to visit **Noujaim Middle Eastern Bakery and Grocery**, a plain-looking convenience store at 1650 E. Main Street near Hwy-69 (I-84 exit 23), for excellent Lebanese sweets and savories; if at a loss as to what to choose, start with the *kadaif* squares (shredded phyllo with pistachio paste).

Signs of Litchfield County: even the local IGA in Woodbury is called Le Bonne's Epicure Market. But don't let the name fool you—it's still an IGA at heart.

Litchfield County

From Woodbury to just past Plymouth, this route skirts the edge of Litchfield County, bucolic home to Manhattan-accented money, manners, and food (but mostly money), conspicuously framed by the white clapboard facades of some of New England's signature towns. Detour up Hwy-63, for example, and get an eyeful of the county seat of Litchfield, whose tidy green, stately old residences and photogenic churches epitomize the area's attractions.

Some exceptional meals are to be had in this place, but don't expect any early bird specials around here: local restaurateurs can and do charge exactly what they think the meals are worth, and given that their regulars include a fair number of big names from the mastheads of major Manhattan publishers to the credits of major Hollywood movies, you can bet self esteem is not in danger of any downswing in *these* kitchens.

West Street Grill, on the Litchfield Green, is widely considered one of the best restaurants in the state. If triple digits won't make you flinch at the end of your dinner, then lucky you won't have to worry whether to skip the appetizers or skimp on the wine simply to afford that fine crackly creme brulee or those tropical fruit sorbets for dessert. If you aren't so well-heeled, drop by for lunch and sample haute bistro cuisine and service as impeccable as the town is pretty, and maybe, just maybe, walk out with change for that $20. If you still want to be able to afford one of those lobsters by the time you reach Cape Cod, West Street's owners have a more *rustique* wood-fired brick-oven kind of place called **Grappa**, in the Litchfield Commons shops just west of the town center on Hwy-202; no one will question your expense report if you enjoy yourself here instead.

Topsmead

Just east of Litchfield off of Hwy-118 lies Topsmead, the former summer estate of Edith Morton Chase, daughter of a Waterbury brass magnate. Miss Chase bequeathed her hilltop Tudor mansion to the people of Connecticut after her death, along with over 500 acres of wooded and landscaped grounds; now **Topsmead State Forest** is one of the crown jewels of the state park system, ideal for rambles down to the bird blind in the woods, picnics upon the expansive lawns, or—if you packed your horse—afternoon canters along tree-lined farm lanes. Its status as a hidden treasure is due in no small part to the absence of good signage, but head east on Hwy-118 from Litchfield, take a right on East Litchfield Road, another right at Buell Road, and you won't miss the stone-gate entrance. Topsmead is open year-round until sunset, with house tours noon-5 PM on alternate weekends, June-Oct. (860/567-5694). By the way, that white residence opposite the parking lot is private property unrelated to the state forest; please don't confuse its inhabitants with park rangers.

Bristol

The influence of Litchfield County on US-6 may be seen in the dearth of billboards, the subdued signage, and the fact that national chain stores don't blanket the highway like tickertape at a parade. But even Litchfield's refinement and taste can't restrain the welter of "Petro Pantries" and other caterers to the convenience of the populous Connecticut River valley. For the 15 miles between busy Hwy-8 in Thomaston and the interstate on-ramp in Farmington, this route becomes the playground of paving contractors and outdoor lighting salespeople, and unless you're out shopping for mufflers, videos, hardware, sub sandwiches, or discount clothing, driving it becomes an act of penance.

Of course, behind the highway clutter are several attractions worthy of the name—two alone in the heart of Bristol, for example. A few blocks off US-6, the **American Clock and Watch Museum**, 100 Maple Street (daily 10 AM-5 PM March-Nov.; $3.50; 860/583-6070), has exactly what you'd expect—room after room of timepieces, over 3,000 in all—but expectation can't begin to detract from the ingenuity and craftsmanship on display. And yes, most of the collection keeps the correct time, as you'll find out at the top of the hour; stand in the newer wing of the

Litchfield must have something to recommend it: **Eugene Fodor,** well-traveled founder of the guidebook line that bears his name, calls it home.

Topsmead doesn't permit camping, but two nearby state parks do: **Black Rock S.P.** on US-6 east of Watertown, and **Burr Pond S.P.** just off Hwy-8 north of Torrington. For current fees and site reservations, call the State Parks Division at 860/566-2304.

You'll find the nation's largest collection of locks, keys, and Victorian hardware behind the plain brick facade of the **Lock Museum of America** (Tues.-Sun. 1:30-4:30 PM, May-Oct.; $3; 860/589-6359) in Terryville, opposite the Congregational church on Main Street (US-6).

Press on toward Hartford if you have a budget rather than a blank check for accommodations; otherwise, consider a stop at the all-suites **Centennial Inn,** on US-6 and Hwy-177 in Farmington (800/852-2052; $89-115 with full kitchen); or the friendly **Chimney Crest Manor B&B** on Federal Hill in Bristol (860/582-4219; $100-115, some suites with kitchens).

Mark Twain

building to catch the best cacophony of striking, chiming, and ringing. Not very far away, **The New England Carousel Museum,** 95 Riverside Avenue (Hwy-72), will charm any kid alive, even if the kid in question is old enough to remember Joni Mitchell's refrain about painted ponies going up and down. The beautiful collection of colorful antique jumpers and prancers is augmented by artisans doing restoration work or carving new carousel animals at one end of the long gallery (Mon.-Sat. 10 AM-5 PM, Sunday noon-5 PM; $4; 860/585-5411).

Hartford

If you're able to temper your first impressions of a city with an appreciation for its salad days—if you don't let generic modern covers obliterate the handsomely lettered pages from the past—then perhaps you'll be able to cultivate an instant liking for the state's capital, Hartford. A century ago it could have been said that this town was a pillar of the nation's civilizing forces: books and guns. Epitomizing the shift to a service economy, *Tom Sawyer* and Colt .45s have been superseded by actuarial tables and death benefits: Hartford is an insurance company town now, which may explain why the downtown sensibly rolls up its sidewalks and turns out the lights after the office towers empty out at 5 PM.

While mergers, downsizing, recession, defense conversion, and other euphemisms for bad times at the home office have bruised modern Hartford repeatedly in recent years, local history offers several excellent distractions, most famously in the form of the **Mark Twain House** (Monday and Wed.-Sat. 9:30 AM-4 PM, Sunday noon-4 PM; $6.50) at 351 Farmington Avenue, two right turns and under a mile from I-84 exit 46. Samuel Clemens (the pseudonymous Twain) built this grand Victorian mansion with Tiffany interiors and a shipload of fine furnishings in order to be close to his publisher. After 17 years of a lavish lifestyle—and the completion of some of his most famous novels—Clemens and his family gave up their Hartford life and moved to Europe to escape financial hardship. Besides guided tours, this restored National Historic Landmark hosts regular lectures, readings, "Conversations with American Humorists," and a summer "Twain at Twilight" concert series, which always includes some great gospel music—the author's favorite.

The distinction of being the oldest public art museum in the U.S. belongs to the **Wadsworth Atheneum,** an institution that hasn't rested on its 150-year-old laurels behind its prodigious stone facade at 600 Main Street in downtown Hartford (Tues.-Sun. 11 AM-5 PM; $7, free first Thursday of each month; 860/278-2670). Permanent collections ranging around the globe and across the ages are leavened with major traveling exhibitions, films, and gallery programs. The state's premiere showcase for contemporary artists is another of Hartford's crown jewels: **Real Art Ways** (Tues.-Sat. till 5 PM; galleries free; 860/232-1006), across from Pope Park on Arbor Street. Its recently expanded galleries and auditoriums host an eclectic Sept.-May film, video, music, and performance series (various admission fees), along with such annual special events as the January Gender Bender Ball, October Halloween party, and summer jazz festival.

Hartford Practicalities

Dining in downtown Hartford is a choice between your average convention hotel restaurant and the sort of watering hole that draws tie-loosening office workers more concerned with rinsing the taste of the office out of their mouths than with the complexity and freshness of the soup du jour. More interesting than either is a trip to the **Oasis Diner**, on Farmington Avenue walking distance east of the Twain House and open daily until midnight except Sunday, when it shuts earlier. It's an unusual double-wide stainless-sided 1949 Paramount diner, its excellent condition complemented by the retro-American menu, with new upscale touches like ricotta-stuffed French toast, veggie selections, Southwestern stylings, and Elm City Stout (from New Haven) on draft. While the Oasis fits the streamlined stereotype of the neon-reflecting jukebox-and-soda haven, neighboring West Hartford's **Quaker Diner,** 319 Park Road (off I-84 exit 43, then right), sheathed in boxy red brick, captures dinerdom's pre-Raymond Loewy roots right down to the Moxie soda and other staples as familiar to its first customers as Herbert Hoover's campaign promises. Prices are anachronisms, too, even on items like oat bran pancakes and spinach omelets; open for breakfast and lunch only.

If you plan upon spending the night around Hartford, you'll find a handful of familiar names in both Hartford proper (Sheraton, Holiday Inn, Super 8, Suisse Chalet) and on I-84 in adjacent East Hartford (Ramada, Holiday Inn), as well as a dozen miles north of the city near Bradley International Airport (Motel 6, Fairfield Inn, Holiday Inn).

Willimantic

US-6 separates from the interstate in East Hartford, following surface streets through a very nondescript urban landscape of housing from the 1940s and convenience stores from the 1980s. If idling at red lights staring at cigarette and liquor billboards fits your vacation plans, go ahead and keep tracking US-6; otherwise, we recommend picking up US-6 in Bolton after following I-84 and I-384 east out of the capital.

From Bolton it's a rapid 16 miles through the tree-lined Hop River valley, along a soon-to-be-bypassed stretch of highway notorious for its high accident rate. The 19th-century mill town of Willimantic (pop. 14,746) has been bypassed by a four-lane freeway, but if you have an abiding interest in the lives and labors of the people who worked in early American industry, stop by the small **Windham Textile**

Trinity College, on Summit Street near the center of Hartford, offers free Wednesday-evening concerts in June and August. Call 860/297-2139 for more info.

The best source of arts and entertainment listings in the region is the free weekly *Hartford Advocate,* available in newspaper boxes around town.

If you ever wondered where **Katharine Hepburn** acquired her accent, look no further than the affluent, liberal, old Connecticut Yankee enclave of West Hartford.

and History Museum (Thurs.-Sun. noon-5 PM; $3), 157 Union Street opposite the giant American Thread mill, which closed down in 1984 after doing business for 120 years.

East of Willimantic, US-6 quickly becomes more rural as it enters the state's most secluded quarter, picturesque Windham County.

Windham County: Pomfret and Vicinity

Although the major interstate I-395 cuts its way across eastern Connecticut from the coast, motorists rarely leave the passing lane long enough to take a peek behind the brow of the hills that border both the highway and the Quinebaug River, which are roughly parallel. If they did, they would find small valley towns raised around historic 19th-century milling operations and railroad depots, and rural hill towns with farmland cultivated with corn since before the arrival of the *Mayflower.*

Before crossing into Rhode Island, consider a detour through this historic landscape, either along Hwy-12, the mill town route, or Hwy-169, the old Norwich-Woodstock Turnpike. One of the most scenic highways in the northeast, if not the nation, Hwy-169 intersects US-6 in **Brooklyn**, hometown to Gen. Israel "Battle of Bunker Hill" Putnam, just five miles west of the I-395 freeway.

A century ago, wealthy New Yorkers spent their summers in the northeast corner of Connecticut, particularly in and around tiny Pomfret; now they own second homes here and send their kids to one of the two prep schools in town. Besides contributing to the community's graceful architectural treasury, the schools help support the year-round existence of the fine **Vanilla Bean Café** at the center of town, open till at least 8 PM most days, till 3 PM on Monday and Tuesday. If you aren't ashamed to park your rusting Pinto next to new Jaguars and BMWs owned by 17-year-olds, this casual counter-service eatery inside a restored old barn is worth a stop for excellent sandwiches, soups, and bakery goods, or for that eye-opening hit of espresso in the morning.

Predictably for such a lovely rural setting, there are plenty of **B&Bs** tucked into the Windham hills, as well as **camping** at the Wolf Den Campgrounds in **Mashamoquet Brook State Park** off Hwy-169/US-44.

For a complete up-to-date list of available lodgings here in what the tourism authorities call "The Quiet Corner," contact the **Northeast Connecticut Visitors District** (860/928-1228).

ACROSS RHODE ISLAND

In the half-hour it takes to cross Rhode Island, US-6 runs along the foot of the low hills that fill this coastal state's northern corners. It's a quiet, mostly rural region, and there's little to stop for until you reach the I-95 corridor at lively Providence, an entertaining, small city rich in history and college-town character.

Providence

Sitting at the north end of Naragansett Bay, Providence (pop. 160,728) was established in 1636 by Roger Williams, founder of the Baptist faith who had been exiled from neighboring Massachusetts for his religious views. A compact city climbing hills from the busy, partly industrial and partly recreational waterfront, Providence preserves its historic quarters intact, and boasts more colonial-era houses per square foot than any other American city. Along with the government bureaucracy of the nation's smallest state, Providence is also home to Rhode Island's two premier colleges, Ivy League Brown University and the Rhode Island School of Design.

The plush resort community of **Newport**, with its incredible collection of mansions, is 20 miles south of Providence. For information, contact the Newport visitor center, 23 America's Cup Avenue (401/849-8098 or 800/326-6030).

From the west, US-6 drops you at the center of town, where a confusing ganglia of roads, canals, and freeways intertwine at the base of the landmark **state capitol**, 82 Smith Street (daily 8:30 AM-4:30 PM; free), which was completed by McKim, Mead and White in 1904 and features a marble dome capped by a 12-foot-tall gilded bronze statue of the "Independent Man." Two hundred yards east of the capitol, across the railroad tracks and the narrow Moshassuck River, the **Roger Williams National Memorial**, 282 N. Main Street (daily 8 AM-4:30 PM; free), recounts his life in a three-minute slide show. The memorial stands at the heart of historic Providence, and the surrounding streets, especially Benefit Street a block farther east, contain some of the finest intact colonial and early federal-era houses in the country. Walking tours are offered by the Providence Preservation Society (401/831-7440).

At the south end of the historic center, the small **Museum of Art of the Rhode Island School of Design**, 224 Benefit Street (Wed.-Sat. noon-5 PM, Sunday 2-5 PM; $2), has an excellent survey of painting and sculpture from around the world. The marvelous **Providence Athenaeum**, 251 Benefit Street (Mon.-Fri. 8:30 AM-5 PM; free) exhibits selected items from its extensive collection of early American prints, maps, and books. Yet more culture is concentrated on College Hill above, where the grounds of Brown University mix with a leafy neighborhood of stately 200-year-old homes.

There are good restaurants in and around the historic center, but some of the best places to eat are in the predominantly Italian Federal Hill neighborhood, a half-mile west of the waterfront on the other side of the I-95 freeway. Try the very good **Grotta Azurra**, 210 Atwells Avenue, or any of a dozen other places packed along these few short blocks.

Walter Scott created history and inspired a new industry in 1872, when he started selling hot food from a converted horse-drawn freight wagon in Providence, thereby giving birth to the diner. The diner legacy will be explored in a new museum, to be housed in the former Narragansett Electric Co. building at 360 Eddy Street. For current information, contact museum director and diner expert Daniel Zilka (401/461-7932).

For the complete lowdown on who and what's playing in Providence's nightclubs and theaters, call the club report (401/455-8278) compiled by Brown University's alternative radio station, WBRU-FM.

In summer, complete your Pawtucket tour with a AAA-International League baseball game at McCoy Stadium, home of the Pawtucket Red Sox (401/724-7300).

Places to stay in Providence include the usual interstate hotels and motels, plus a few pleasant B&Bs in and around the historic core, like the **Old Court**, 144 Benefit Street (401/751-2002). For more complete listings and other information, contact the Providence **visitor center**, 30 Exchange Terrace (401/274-1636 or 800/233-1636).

Pawtucket

North and east of Providence, under a mile via the I-95 freeway or Main Street (old US-1), the blue-collar city of Pawtucket (pop. 72,644) has played a vital role in American history. Though it looks tiny compared to the massive factories of 19th-century New England, the plank walls of **Slater's Mill** (Tues.-Sat. 10 AM-5 PM, Sunday 1-5 PM in summer, weekends only March-May; $4; 401/725-8638), sitting in a pleasant waterfront park at the center of town, saw the start of America's Industrial Revolution.

Despite the export bans placed by England after the Revolutionary War, Derbyshire-born Samuel Slater succeeded in introducing the latest mechanized cotton spinning technology, which he had gleaned from an apprenticeship in Richard Arkwright's mills. Slater also brought with him significant management skills, and in partnership with others transformed American manufacturing from handicrafts to mass production.

Numerous exhibits trace the historical context of Slater's efforts, but the real reason to visit is to watch and listen as the eight-ton water wheel creaks and groans around and around, powering the many belts and pulleys that still turn the machines, much as they did in Slater's day.

Pawtucket's other significant historic site is also well worth a visit, though it can be more difficult to find: the **Modern Diner**, 364 East Avenue just east of I-95. A classic streamlined Sterling diner, the Modern was the first diner to be registered as an official historic landmark, but it's still open every day from 7 AM (8 AM on Sunday) for breakfast and lunch, with dinner available Tues.-Fri. until 8 PM. Check it out.

Old Slater's Mill

ACROSS MASSACHUSETTS

You won't find a pretty red carpet rolled out for US-6 in southeastern Massachusetts, where some of the Bay State's most economically depressed cities have paved over the coastal lowlands. The ivy-covered brick of Harvard Yard and the long weathered tobacco barns of the Pioneer Valley might as well belong to another state—or so it would seem as this route rolls by the gunmetal gray of retired naval vessels, acres of outlet malls, and hillsides carpeted with Victorian-era triple-decked, triple-family houses built for workers drawn to the great textile mills of the Industrial Revolution.

While there are comely seaside towns just to the south (along what the tourist brochures call the "Heritage Farm Coast"), the 30 miles of US-6 east of the Connecticut border are strictly for those with a romantic eye for commercial tack, or for anthropologists of urban decline; others are advised to stay on I-195 and make haste. Although US-6 is worth picking up again in Captain Ahab's home port of New Bedford, postcard views don't return in spades until after the Cape Cod Canal. Even here, you'll miss them if you stay on double-barreled US-6, so we recommend taking a spin along slow-but-scenic US-6A to catch the Cape's best face. The route finally comes to its conclusion in the lee of Cape Cod National Seashore's shifting dunes, on the narrow, cottage-lined streets of outermost Provincetown.

Fall River

Cotton mills put this town on the map, and their demise nearly wiped it off again. One of the nation's leading industrial cities at the turn of the century, Fall River (pop. 92,703) swiftly became one of the leading casualties of the Depression, propelled into a decade of bankruptcy by the triple whammy of mill flight to cheaper Southern labor, a devastating downtown fire, and the Wall Street Crash of 1929. Although receivership ended with WW II, the giant brick mills have only recently awakened from their decades of boarded-up slumber, reanimated by the factory stores that contribute to Fall River's new stature as southern New England's discount retailing center.

If 30% off assorted clothing and housewares doesn't lure you down the exit ramps, perhaps a fascination with warships will. A small armada awaits your exploration in **Battleship Cove** (daily 9 AM-sunset; $8), plainly visible from the interstate bridge over the broad, brackish Taunton River: the battleship *Massachusetts,* destroyer *Joseph P. Kennedy, Jr.,* submarine *Lionfish,* and a pair of P.T. boats from WW II.

Along the waterfront, adjacent to the anchored ships, the galleries of **Fall River Heritage State Park** (daily 10 AM-6 PM in summer, till 4 PM otherwise; free) tell the city's story with excellent archival photos and period artifacts, one of nine such innovative parks dedicated to the state's industrial, labor, and immigration history.

While numerous eateries in this city subscribe to the four major food groups—salt, grease, sugar, and carbonation—decent dining does exist if you're willing to hunt around for it. Excellent Italian can be had at **Puerini's Cafe/The Pasta Factory,** for example, in one of the former Border City mills at the end of Weaver Street, off N. Main Street (lunch Mon.-Sat., dinner Wed.-Sat.; 508/678-1030); or try hearty Eastern European stick-to-your-ribs soups and meats at the **Ukrainian Home** on Globe Street off Hwy-138 south—catercorner from Dunkin' Donuts. The latest immigration trends are reflected in the tasty, inexpensive Southeast Asian cuisine found at the **New Phnom Penh Restaurant** in the Angor Plaza (closed Monday; 508/324-4909) on Quequechan Street, next to the huge Wampanoag Mill factory outlet mall.

This being Massachusetts, there's also a fine 1950s diner, **Al Mac's,** at the base of President Hill on US-6 at the junction with the Rte-79/138 elevated highway. In great shape inside and out, this place not only serves coffee in pint-sized mugs, it

---

LIZZIE BORDEN

"Lizzie Borden took an ax/And gave her mother 40 whacks . . . ." If you've heard this couplet before, you're already acquainted with Fall River's most notorious citizen, a wealthy financier's daughter (and Sunday school teacher) accused of double murder in 1892. Lest children's rhymes prejudice your opinion of Ms. Borden, know that a jury of her peers returned a verdict of *not guilty.*

The **Fall River Historical Society** (Tues.-Fri. 9 AM-4:30 PM, weekends in summer only; $3.50) has a complete exhibit on the subject—including trial evidence and the alleged weapon—in its mansion headquarters at 451 Rock Street in the Highlands historic district.

stays open late: Sun.-Tues. till midnight (till 10 PM in winter), Wed.-Thurs. till 3 AM, and Fri.-Sat. till 4 AM (508/679-5851).

A small rash of chain names among local accommodations include a Howard Johnson, a Hampton Inn, a Holiday Inn, an Econo Lodge, and a Comfort Inn.

New Bedford

Predominantly Portuguese New Bedford is remembered as a capital of the whaling industry back in the days when sperma-ceti candles and whale oil lamps were necessities, not antiques. The city's harbor at the mile-wide mouth of the Acushnet River was home port for the East Coast's largest commercial fishing fleet until nearly two decades of flagrant overfishing brought the industry to collapse in 1995. Now the community hopes to sail out of its troubled economic waters with the launch of the state's first casino—and if you spot money growing on trees, you'll know the plan has lived up to its expectations.

That tall ship sometimes an-chored in summer near the mothball navy is the HMS *Bounty* (Fri.-Sun. 10 AM-6 PM, May-Oct.; $4; 508/673-3886)—or, rather, the movie version, built from the origi-nal naval blueprint for MGM's 1962 production starring Marlon Brando and Trevor Howard. A fully func-tioning sailing vessel used for education and training, the replica makes appear-ances at harbor and mari-time festivals around New England and Canada. Call ahead for the port schedule if you don't want to miss her.

Whether or not video poker brings pennies from heaven, the immutable charm of the downtown historic district will remain, with its cobblestone streets and brick facades virtually unaltered since Herman Melville shipped out of here in 1847 aboard a whaler bound for the Pacific. For a good orientation to the area, drop by the well-stocked **visitor center**, 47 N. 2nd Street (508/991-6200 or 800/508-5353), and join one of their free hour-long guided **walking tours**.

Before or after a stroll around town, head to the top of Johnny Cake Hill and visit the excellent **Whaling Museum** (daily 9 AM-5 PM; $3.50). Scrimshaw (carved whale ivory), tools of the whal-ing trade, historic photos, special maritime exhibits, and an 89-foot ship model are a few of the artifacts found in the not-to-be-missed museum collection maintained by the Old Dartmouth Historical Society. Across the street from the mu-seum, the gorgeous little **Seamen's Bethel**, built in 1832 and featuring a pulpit shaped like a ship's bow, was featured in a chapter of Herman Melville's classic *Moby Dick*.

New Bedford Practicalities

If the sounds of the seagulls' *scree*-ing around downtown whets your appetite for seafood, then drive down to **Davy's Locker**, way out on E. Rodney French Street at Billy Woods Wharf, where the ferry for Martha's Vineyard departs. There outside the rocky seawall you can watch the gulls wheel over the harbor as you dig into some of the freshest seafood in town. Given that you're in a city that's 60% Por-tuguese, you might consider acquainting yourself with this local cuisine, although if you're a light eater, bring along a pair of friends to finish your meal. For maxi-mum quality at a minimal (cash only) price, **Antonio's**, on Coggeshalle and N. Front Streets, slightly northeast of the I-195/Hwy-18 interchange (exit 15), is a good choice, as is **Vasco da Gama**, on the opposite end of town on Dartmouth at Washington, a block south of Metro Pizza (look for the 7UP sign over a plain brickfront barlike place). Kale soup, rabbit or shellfish swimming in spicy tomato-based sauces, and of course *bacalhau* (salt cod) are typical menu items, in portions designed to thoroughly satisfy a boat crew's most mutinous rumblings. On the other end of the dining spectrum are the sorts of places familiar with raspberry vinaigrette and romaine lettuce: **Phoebe's Restaurant**, for example, on S. 6th Street at Union (breakfast, lunch Tues.-Sun., dinner Fri.-Sat.), in a pleasantly airy 19th-century space behind a hefty granite facade; or **Freestone's**, at the corner of William and N. 2nd Streets, with its specialties of steak and seafood served daily until 11 PM.

Diner fans will appreciate New Bedford's offerings, too. The easiest diner to find is **Angelo's Orchid Diner**, a 1951 O'Mahoney stainless-sided model right on US-6 at Rockdale; its menu is solid short-order cookery enlivened by, you guessed it, a Portuguese influence. For a traditional Greek hand over the grill, check out the pristine **Shawmut Diner**, another 1950s O'Mahoney on Shawmut Avenue at Hathaway, near Rte-140

New Bedford isn't immune to the espresso craze, as proven by **Java Bean** on Water Street a block south of the Whaling Museum. Good biscotti, too.

For a good example of the kind of downhome folk music performance found in church and grange halls throughout New England, check out the **Tryworks Coffeehouse** (Saturday 8 PM, mid-Sept. to early May) in the First Unitarian Church on 8th and Union Streets.

A CAPE COD PRIMER

To avoid frustration visiting Cape Cod, it's best to understand its basic directions and seasons. The compass isn't your friend here, as you will discover when faced with highway signs stubbornly directing you *south* to Provincetown, when south would sooner bring you to Venezuela than to the Cape's northernmost town. Instead, the principal directions are up and down: *up-Cape* means westward, toward the rest of North America, while *down-Cape* is eastward, toward the Outer Cape, Provincetown, and the briny deep. Further distinctions are made between the three sides of the Cape's bended arm: *bay-side* is the entire convexity facing Cape Cod Bay; the *south shore* faces Nantucket Sound, between Buzzard's Bay and the Cape's "elbow" at Chatham; and the *backside* braves the open Atlantic from Chatham's elbow to Provincetown's "fist."

As it so happens, development of the Cape has also segregated itself fairly neatly between bayside US-6A, with its demure white-clapboard, gray-shingled neo-colonial villages, and the south shore's Hwy-28, a helter-skelter shock corridor of shopping plazas, motel courts, saltwater taffy shoppes, and eat-in-the-rough shacks that seem to consume more plastic dinnerware and frying oil than fresh fish.

But the most important aspect to Cape travel is timing: Between Memorial Day weekend in late May and Labor Day weekend in early September, several million tourists and "summer people" (seasonal residents) converge on this sandy spit, which is why traffic jams get measured in miles on good days, hours on bad. On the worst weekends—4th of July, for example—you could drive to Montreal in less time than it would take to cross the canal, drive 16 miles to Wood's Hole, find parking, and catch the next available ferry to Martha's Vineyard! Needless to say, pack your car as if you might have to live in it for a day or two.

(daily 5 AM-7 PM); the neon Indian alone makes it worth a visit.

Choices of accommodations are limited. The warmest welcome and greatest convenience to downtown attractions and restaurants is **Cynthia and Steven's B&B**, on 7th Street in the historic district (508/997-6433), where rooms with private baths go for $55-65. There's also a **Days Inn** on Hathaway Road by the airport, at I-195 exit 13B.

New Bedford's Acushnet Avenue has a significant place in the world of late 19th-century American art: **Albert Pinkham Ryder,** visionary "painter of dreams," was born here, across from the childhood home of **Albert Bierstadt,** Romantic painter of the American West.

Fairhaven

There was a time when families could signal their improving lot by moving out of New Bedford's hurly-burly mills and wharves and across the harbor to aptly named Fairhaven (stress the second syllable), which straddles US-6 within spyglass view of Johnny Cake Hill. Turn south on Main Street, at the intersection dominated by the palatial Italianate high school, and you'll discover a surprising amount of monumental gothic-spired civic architecture, most of it generously donated at the start of this century by Henry Huttleston Rogers, a native son and robber baron who made a mint as a direc-

---

If you *are* island-bound, know that a major turnover of cottage rentals occurs every fortnight, which is why the ferry landings are twice as hectic, with tickets and parking twice as scarce, on alternate Fridays. Factories in southern New England shut down for two weeks in July, flooding the Cape's south shore with workers and their families; August brings flocks of psychiatrists, lawyers, doctors, and other professionals to bayside towns, as well as to Chatham, at the Outer Cape's southern extremity. Meanwhile, campgrounds are often surprisingly full even midweek and in bad weather, in part because quadrupling and quintupling of rents during high season forces some of the Cape's more marginal residents to take summer sabbaticals in tents.

While high season may have its disadvantages, it's also when everybody is open for business, seven days a week, 16 hours a day. Out of season, businesses close up like flowers after a frost, not necessarily because the visitors have disappeared—fall and spring are quite popular with a discerning few hundred thousand people—but because the employees have. In high season, the Cape is in fact wholly operated by teenagers, students, and Irish on temporary work visas; after schools start in September, only the Irish remain as a skeleton crew—until their classes begin in October. (This employment phenomenon also explains why some places may be shuttered even as high season kicks in: they haven't lined up any help yet.) Sufficient workers or not, businesses that do stay open into the off season don't significantly lower prices until the dead of winter.

A final note: It is possible to escape the crowds, even in the height of summer. Parks and sanctuaries are notably free of ringing cash registers and sizzling deep-fryers, and even popular beaches can yield a mote of solitude if you keep in mind that about 90% of the Cape's visitors don't walk more than 20 minutes from their car.

The first Japanese resident of the U.S., **Manjiro Naka-hama,** lived in Fairhaven in the 1840s after returning with the whalers who res-cued him from shipwreck in the Pacific. Displays about "John" Manjiro and the town's sister city of Tosa-shimizu, Japan, are found in the Millicent Library.

Perhaps H.H. Rogers's finan-cial support for his home-town was compensation for the fact that his company's profits came at the expense of New Bedford's and Fair-haven's: the 1859 discovery of eastern Pennsylvania's oil fields dropped the bottom out of the market for whale oil and "coal oil" (coal-derived kerosene, a Fairhaven product).

A clam-eater's key: Steamers are usually soft-shell (longneck) clams, preferably caught on a muddy rather than sandy bottom (unless you like grit in your teeth), steamed and served with their salty "liquor" and drawn butter for dipping. Fuller-flavored hard-shell quahogs ("KO-hogs" or "K'WOGS") are a chef's favorite chowder clam, although some folks will bake and stuff them, too. Cherrystones and littlenecks are small quahogs served raw on the half shell, or sometimes steamed. Bon appetit!

"Mattapoisett" means "place of rest" in Algonquian—a name originally applied to a small neck about 25 miles west on Mount Hope Bay, in what's now the town of Swansea.

tor of John D. Rockefeller's Standard Oil Company. Stop by the marvelous Renaissance-style library on Center Street—described as "a heaven of light and grace and harmonious color and sump-tuous comfort" by Rogers's friend Mark Twain—for a **walking tour** brochure.

Besides Portuguese and Cape Verdeans, the local maritime trades have attracted a fair number of Norwegians—the Isaksen family, for example, whose waterfront restaurant down on Main Street, **Margaret's,** is one of the hands-down best places for seafood in the area. If deep-sea scallops are on the menu—probably fresh off the family's own boats—don't pass them by; as anyone around here will tell you, the tiny bay scallops from Mexico and China can't compare to the more flavorful and meaty Atlantic deep-sea variety.

Approaching Cape Cod: Buzzards Bay

Skirting the glacially formed coastline of Buzzards Bay—whose major shipping lane is especially visible at night, as vessels bound to and from the Cape Cod Canal blink like fireflies off-shore—US-6 passes through residential **Mattapoisett** and **Mari-on,** communities whose modest appearances belie both property values and average incomes, just as the sandy soil and brittle-looking trees belie the original swampy conditions that made this coast so ecologically rich for its native inhabitants, the Wampanoag Indians. A half-dozen small rivers still drain these coastal lowlands, but despite the occasional stands of tall reeds, it goes almost without saying that here, as in far too many places along the Atlantic seaboard, wetlands have been drastically reduced. Modern developers aren't exclusively to blame, however: settlers have been accelerating nature's designs ever since 17th- and 18th-century colonists stripped the land of its rot-resistant Atlantic white cedars—old-growth giants found here near the northern extent of their range—and thus con-tributed to the silting-up of fertile fish-feeding marshes and ponds.

This stretch of US-6 is still fertile territory for the fruits of the sea, especially if it's fried, broiled, or served up in creamy chow-der. The **Mattapoisett Chowder House** and **Oxford Creamery,** this latter in Marion, are two particularly good examples, the best you'll find between here and the Outer Cape. The Cream-ery—which, as the name implies, also specializes in ice cream—is the more low-key of the two, downright fast-food-like; it also is only open in summer, daily until 10 PM. If you prefer ham and brown gravy or spaghetti and meatballs to anything with shells or fins, the **Mattapoisett Diner** on US-6 is your dream come true.

US-6 becomes a sprawlmart as it joins Rte-25 and Rte-28 in **Wareham,** fast food and tire dealers greasing the approach to the WPA-era Sagamore Bridge over the

Cape Cod Canal. (US-6 eastbound crosses via the nearly identical Bourne Bridge, which feeds into I-195/495 if you aren't careful. Westbound travelers: stay awake in this stretch, or you could find yourself halfway to Boston.)

If you're looking for a place to park the ol' RV for the night before hitting the Cape, you might choose **Scusset Beach State Reservation** (508/888-0859) in Sagamore, on Cape Cod Bay; $8 gets you a full hookup near the beach, across the canal from the blinking hulk of a gas-fired electric generating station. More tent-friendly sites are found in Shawme-Crowell State Forest ($6; 508/888-0351), just over the bridge on Hwy-130 in Sandwich.

Bayside Cape Cod: Sandwich

Although it rides the ridge of the terminal glacial moraine that is body and backbone to the entire Cape, the forest-clad Mid-Cape Highway (US-6) affords few good vistas. Traffic willing, you'll sail clear ahead to the Outer Cape in about 30 minutes, surrounded by more green than blue. One preferred route is parallel US-6A: never more than a mile or two away, swimming steadily through towns otherwise invisible behind that protective march of pitch pine, this slower road is a good introduction to that part of the Cape that does its utmost to stay quaint without being too cute. Generally, it succeeds.

Take Sandwich, for example: its center, on Hwy-130 just south of US-6A, is composed of a small irregular green bordered by a tall white Christopher Wren-inspired church, a stately carriage-stop inn, and the Historical Society's **Sandwich Glass Museum** (daily 9:30 AM-4:30 PM April-Oct., Wed.-Sun. only Nov.-March; $3.50). Although the town's various glassworks could and did produce consummate artistic pieces, the bulk of their output was inexpensive mass-market stuff—such as 10-cent oil lamp chimneys—for household, rather than decorative, use. In other words, a collector's interest helps with the appreciation of the Glass Museum's rooms of lacy glass saucers, pressed plates, and molded jars, the vast majority of which are unmarked products of the Boston and Sandwich Glass Co., earliest and most famous of the region's 19th-century glass factories. Nearby on Pine and Grove Streets (follow signs from Hwy-130) is an even more diverse collection of Americana, the **Heritage Plantation of Sandwich** (daily 10 AM-5 PM mid-May to mid-Oct.; $8), where nearly 80 landscaped acres surround collections of Currier & Ives prints, military miniatures, antique autos, cigar store figures, American primitive portraiture—more unflattering likenesses of children have never been conceived—and even a working 1912 carousel.

Although not as attractive to mansion-building plutocrats as nearby Newport, 19th-century Marion was still among New England's most prominent seaside resorts, attracting such visitors as Pres. Grover Cleveland and novelist Henry James.

To learn more than you ever thought possible about thermometers, pay a visit to the world's largest thermometer collection proudly on display in the basement of Dick "Thermometer Man" Porter's home in Onset; call 508/295-5504 for directions.

Those low-lying square plots of land filled with short, dark-leaved shrubs and divided by narrow irrigation channels are some of Plymouth County's famous cranberry bogs. The cheeky red fruit is best seen during the October harvest, when it carpets the flooded fields.

If you're willing to pay a small price ($10-15) for the aid of a B&B reservation service, put yourself in the competent hands of either House Guests Cape Cod and the Islands (800/666-HOST) or Orleans Bed and Breakfast Associates (800/541-6226), the latter serving the Outer Cape only.

Massachusetts is one of two states that recognizes private property ownership down to the low tide line, which is why you should respect the No Trespassing signs you may encounter on some beaches. Fortunately, plenty are amended with "Walkers Welcome."

Sandy Neck

Continuing east on US-6A from Sandwich, keep an eye out for Sandy Neck Road (next to the Sandy Neck Motel), the turnoff to Sandy Neck and its namesake barrier beach ($8 summer parking fee). Here, six miles of windswept dunes provide a picturesque backdrop for contemplating the changing light upon the relatively calm waters of Cape Cod Bay. Depending on season and time of day, you may catch sight of passing white-tailed deer or such endangered shorebirds as the least tern and piping plover.

Between Sandy Neck and our reunion with US-6 in **Orleans**, there are some 18 beaches, most of which are found simply by turning north on whatever small residential or unimproved roads intersect the route. If you don't live here, expect to fork over a parking fee of $7 or $8 in season. Temporary residents and guests may obtain weekly or monthly permits; ask your hosts or the beach attendant to explain how. One way to skirt the parking fees for beach use is to spend the night locally and *walk* to the water.

Bayside Practicalities

Restaurants and motels tend to gravitate toward Cape Cod's south shore, and the few bayside establishments seem determined to make up in total billings what is lacking in total volume. If, on the other hand, you subscribe to the belief that a good meal is worth at least as much as a night's pampering at a little seaside inn, than treat yourself to sophisticated Italian cuisine at **Abbicci**, on US-6A in Dennis (reservations advised, 508/362-3501). Don't be fooled by the downhome yellow-clapboard exterior; the interior is as contemporary and artfully designed as the food.

You can always balance your budget the next day with a visit to **Jack's Out Back**, behind 161 Main (US-6A) in Yarmouth Port. The undisputed king of the Cape's white-bread cookery, Jack whips up basic breakfasts and lunches at rock-bottom prices—made possible in part by requiring that customers do everything but stand over the grill. Copious hand-lettered, phonetically spelled construction-paper signs combine menu items, warnings about selling unattended children into slavery, and instructions for writing up your own ticket and busing your own dirty dishes; follow these last to the letter or irascible ol' Jack will amuse his audience of regulars at your expense.

Between these two extremes, geographically and economically, is **Mattakeese Wharf** on Barnstable Harbor (turn at the traffic light east of Barnstable Village), a casual you-want-french-fries-with-that kind of place (open May-Oct. only) elevated from the pack by its quality seafood and great location. Enjoying bouillabaisse on the deck while looking out over the marina in that golden light of a late summer evening is the sort of experience liable to have you planning ahead to your next Cape vacation.

Take in excellent Cape Cod views from atop **Scargo Tower** in **Dennis**, on Scargo Hill Road; turn toward South Dennis at the Mobil station, then follow signs.

Not all the Cape's glass furnaces have been extinguished: the glass blowers of the **Pairpoint Crystal Company,** on US-6A in Sagamore (behind the Christmas Tree Shop), can be observed at work on weekdays.

One of many historic B&Bs along this stretch of the Cape is the **Isiah Hall B&B Inn**, 152 Whig Street in Dennis (508/385-9928 or 800/736-0160), within walking distance of the beach and costing less than a meal at Abbici's; doubles go from $60 a night.

For a full list of accommodation options, stop by a Cape Cod

Chamber of Commerce **information booth**—either at the Sagamore rotary just before crossing the canal, or mid-Cape at the junction of Rte-132 and US-6—to pick up an extensive directory to both south shore and bayside accommodations. Or call the Massachusetts Office of Travel and Tourism's **info line** (617/727-3201) and request a free copy of the latest *Massachusetts Getaway Guide.*

Dennis is the setting for the nation's oldest professional summer stock theater, the **Cape Playhouse** (box office 508/385-3911) on 6A just east of the Mobil station. If you prefer film over stage, the **Cape Cinema,** on the grounds behind the Playhouse, specializes in movies you won't find at the mall. If you arrive late, stick around until the lights go up after the credits or you'll miss one of the Cape's best public artworks, the mural of Prometheus on the cinema's ceiling.

Orleans and Eastham

The classic Cape Cod dwelling, a porchless, rectangular, peak-roofed shed not unlike an oversized shingle or clapboard Monopoly piece, should be a familiar feature of the landscape by the time you arrive at the Outer Cape towns of Brewster, Orleans, and Eastham, given the number of such houses along this part of route. US-6, 6A, and the south shore Rte-28 all come together here, just before the Cape narrows to its slender forearm.

Here, too, the **Cape Cod Rail Trail** (see below) mingles with this route, which is why in summer the streets crawl with cyclists in search of refreshment. If that's your goal, too, look no further than **The Brown Bag Restaurant and Bakery** (daily till 3 PM), on the corner of West Road and Old Colony Way, for decent omelets, soups, sandwiches, and quiche. For something to fill the cupholder on your dash, stop in at the **Orleans Whole Food Store** on Main Street a block south of the Rail Trail and 6A. For a taste of some of the best fried clams on the Cape, detour south about 10 miles to the **Kream 'n' Kone** (March-Nov.), opposite the A&P supermarket on Rte-28 between Chatham and Harwich.

Another of Cape Cod's many exquisite B&Bs is the **Whalewalk Inn**, 220 Bridge Road in Eastham (508/225-0617), where free bicycle rentals and delicious break-

---

CYCLING ON CAPE COD

After broiling yourself on the beach in a light marinade of SPF 45, enjoy one of the best Cape escapes astride a bike. The **Cape Cod Rail Trail**, a 25-mile, fully paved pedestrian and bicycle path between Dennis and South Wellfleet, is the foremost attraction for casual cyclists.

If you're driving to the trail, you'll find parking at either end or in Nickerson State Park, adjacent to where the trail crosses under US-6A in Brewster. Convenient bike rentals are available from **Rail Trail Bike Shop** on Underpass Road in Brewster; **Idle Times** on US-6A beside the trail at the main entrance to Nickerson State Park; **Orleans Cycle** in Chatham at the junction of the trail and Main Street, one block north of US-6A; and **Black Duck Bike Shop** in South Wellfleet, next to the tourist info booth. Rentals are also available in Provincetown and all over the Cape.

Three other paved bike paths are found in Cape Cod National Seashore, ranging from a one and a half-mile trail starting from the Salt Pond Visitor Center to the seven mile-plus, headwind-bucking meander through the dunes and kettlehole ponds behind Provincetown.

fasts make for an idyllic respite from the "real" world. Budget travelers will be pleased to find the well-situated and somewhat misnamed **Mid-Cape HI/AYH Hostel** on Goody Hallet Drive in Eastham (mid-May to mid-Sept.; $15, members $12; 508/255-2785).

Campers will want to check out **Nickerson State Park** on US-6A at the Brewster-Orleans line, one of the largest and most popular campgrounds in the state (year-round for RVs only, otherwise April 15 to Oct. 15; $6; reservations taken at 508/896-3491).

Cape Cod National Seashore

The remaining two dozen miles to Provincetown parallel Cape Cod National Seashore, a 40-mile-long National Park Service property encompassing the whole of the outermost coast: squat lighthouses, shrub-covered dunes, freshwater ponds, tidal flats, cedar swamps, and spectacular, often austere beaches whose boundaries are in constant flux. Pick up information detailing the various nature trails and interpretive programs at either the **Salt Pond Visitor Center** (daily 9 AM-4:30 PM, weekends only Jan.-Feb.; 508/255-3421), prominently signposted beside US-6 in **Eastham**, or the **Province Lands Visitor Center** on Race Point Road in Provincetown (see below).

Miles and miles of gorgeous beaches fill the seashore's Atlantic coast, but one of the park's highlights is a visit to **Sunset Hill** in Wellfleet, on Chequesset Neck Road heading toward Duck Harbor Beach. The late-afternoon views over Cape Cod Bay will reward the sedentary, while walkers will find a fine scenic escape along the Great Island Trail that begins from the hill's parking lot. Mind the tide tables if you do take a hike out to Jeremy Point, or you'll be wading on your return.

Wellfleet

The town of Wellfleet (pop. 2,493) is one of the Cape's most picturesque communities, favored for some reason by writers, psychiatrists, and oysters. Although home to a cluster of fine art galleries, crafts and clothing shops, and pricey restaurants, the place succeeds handsomely in finding a niche between self-conscious quaintness and residential seclusion. It's also blessed by two additional rarities: a public beach with year-round free parking (**Mayo Beach**, just west of the town pier) and a New American fusion-cuisine restaurant worth every dollar (**Painter's**, on Main Street beside the Duck Creeke Inn; dinner and Sunday brunch only; reservations 508/349-3003).

Alas, there are drawbacks: most of the town beaches are strictly for residents or local guests between late June and early September. Those that aren't off-limits charge $10. Painter's restaurant is only seasonal—winter food mavens seeking curried lamb with raita and arugula or snapping fresh tuna with gin-soaked juniper berries and lime tomato chutney will have to go elsewhere. If it *is* summer and you didn't intend to hang around till 5 PM to catch a bite to eat, drop in on the local sandwich-eaters at **Uncle Frank's** (a.k.a. Painter's Lunch), a friendly, inexpensive hangout next to Mayo Beach, in the same building as the Wellfleet Harbor Actors Theatre (W.H.A.T. box office, 508/349-6835).

While the Outer Cape has but one chain motel outside of Provincetown (a Sheraton on US-6 in Eastham), you'll still find plenty of characterful locally owned **accommodations**, from classic little prewar dune shacks sitting cheek-to-cheek along the beach, to B&Bs nestled among the pines. Save dinner money by staying at the **Little America HI/AYH Hostel**, beautifully situated between cranberry bogs and ocean beach in a former Coast Guard station on N. Pamet Road in nearby Truro (late June to early Sept. only; $15, members $12; 508/349-3889). It fills almost daily, so reservations are advised.

The Wellfleet Chamber of Commerce (508/349-2510) has an exceptionally comprehensive directory of lodgings, available by mail or from its information booth on US-6.

Provincetown

The end of your journey was almost the end of the line for another band of travelers, babes in the woods who came expecting warm weather—in November 1620. Had the *Mayflower* Pilgrims and their fortune-seeking shipmates been able to find sufficient fresh water, the cornerstone of American myth and clock-start of Anglo-American civilization might have been enshrined here in Provincetown rather than across the bay at Plymouth Rock. But no: The first landfall was eclipsed by the first Thanksgiving, and P'town (as natives and in-the-know locals call it) has had to butter its bread with something other than the national creation myth.

Where once the sea sustained P'town—as trading spot, whaling village, and fishing port—now the summer fun does. In 1901 Charles Hawthorne opened up an art school, christening the town with the art colony status that persists to this day. Bohemians followed, including the likes of John Reed, Eugene O'Neill, Susan Glaspell, and George Cram Cook, whose Provincetown Players made theater history. And on the heels of Greenwich Village's fashionable flock came the car-borne tourists, who have proven themselves as faithful as Capistrano swallows.

The summer trade prompts P'town to do its beach-boardwalk strut, as boatloads of day-trippers from Boston mob aptly named Commercial Street each afternoon, tanned couples mingle among the restaurants and outdoor cafes each evening, and fun-seeking Danceteria types fill up the bars and clubs each night. Out of season, however, the beach shuttle goes back to being a school bus, the wait for a table is negligible, and there's actually an off-chance that you'll find a place to park. Meanwhile, the sunsets are still worth a visit to **Herring Cove Beach**, even if they come at an earlier hour and require extra layers of clothing.

Whalewatching cruises aren't confined to the high-season crush, since the finback, minke, humpback, and right whales that feed offshore arrive in April and stay through October. Dolphin Fleet (800/826-9300), Provincetown Whale Watch (800/992-9333), and Portuguese Princess (800/442-3188) all offer daily trips out to the whales' feeding grounds in the Stellwagen Bank National Marine Sanctuary just offshore.

To at least vaguely disguise your off-Cape origins, you should know that Chatham is pronounced "CHAT-em," but Eastham is "EAST-ham."

If you've never watched a movie in the comfort of your own car, it's time you caught up with lost pleasures at the **Wellfleet Drive-In** on US-6 (in North Eastham, actually), a genuine throwback to the era of car-hops on roller skates and Mustang convertibles.

While portions of several Outer Cape beaches are traditional gathering spots for "naturists"—Herring Cove in P'town is probably the most well-known, drawing a largely gay, lesbian, and bisexual crowd—the national seashore beaches have a specific prohibition against nudity. If you see a park ranger, you should cover up to avoid a potential ticket.

The fury of the Atlantic constantly reworks Cape topography, borrowing up to 10 feet from the Outer Cape's cliffs each year for loan to Provincetown and Monomoy Island beaches, and stealing over 30 acres of ground through annual erosion and rising sea levels.

Pilgrim Monument

That 252-foot tower jutting up over the town is the **Pilgrim Monument and Museum** (9 AM-5 PM, but last admission at 4:15 PM, mid-March to Nov.; $5), with the best panorama on the Cape: in clear weather the entire peninsula can be seen, as well as the Massachusetts coast at Plymouth.

Sixteenth-century Europeans who regularly crossed the Atlantic to fish for cod along these shores saw a peninsula covered in beech and white oak, juniper and holly—mature forests consumed by the English colonial appetite for construction, firewood, turpentine, potash, and grazing land. Within a century after the *Mayflower* landing, tree and topsoil loss on the outer Cape was so severe, homes had to be built on stilts to avoid being buried by blowing sand. Today's beech forests around Provincetown are the product of a major campaign begun in 1893 to save the town from a sandy grave.

Provincetown Practicalities

After a day spent cycling amid dunes speckled with wild rose and beach plum, or admiring the handiwork of windowbox gardeners in P'town's cottage-lined lanes, you'll probably have an appetite for more than sugar-coated *trutas* (sweet potato fritters) from the **Portuguese Bakery** at 299 Commercial Street. If a harborside table is required, consider the moderately priced **Lobster Pot** at 321 Commercial just east of MacMillan Wharf (enter through the kitchen) for heaping portions of time-tested local favorites such as cioppino or *sopa do mar,* veggie pastas, and of course lobster every which way you want it. Open year-round, too—an exception in these parts. **Pucci's**, 539 Commercial Street (closed Thursday), commands such a first-row harborside seat that at high tide you're as good as in a boat. You don't need to compete for a table at sunset to savor the changing light on the harbor—it can also be enjoyed at the bar, or over lunch and breakfast.

For onshore dining, check out the multicultural menu—one of the few to please vegetarians—at **Napi's**, tucked away on Freeman Street at Standish, sort of opposite the **Iguana Grill**, the town's Dominican-Mexican contender. South-of-the-border spices also heat up the top-notch New American menu at **Lorraine's**, 229R Commercial Street (down the alley near the Pennsylvania Co. store), where you'll find some of P'town's best meals for the money. A burrito from **The Purple Cactus** in the Old Aquarium Building in the 200 block of Commercial Street will also leave your travel allowance intact. **Spiritus**, across the street at 190 Commercial, is another good low-cost savior, dishing up pizza, foccacia sandwiches, ice cream, and latte to a steady clientele of tattooed young smokers and slackers.

If you're more in the mood for a linen and crystal celebration, look no further than the **Martin House**, 157 Commercial Street (508/487-1327). Fine fireside dining in cozy 18th-century parlors won't come cheap, but if you have reason to splurge, this is the place to do it.

Somerset House

Cape Cod lodgings boarded up during the off-season

Planning to spend the night? If it's a summer weekend, make reservations or you may spend your time searching for a bed rather than basking on the beach. Friendly, efficient, and free, the **Provincetown Reservations System** (800/648-0364) can help find accommodations to match your budget and taste, or you can make the calls yourself with the aid of the chamber of commerce directory, available from its **information booth** (508/487-3424) at Lopes Square on MacMillan Wharf. The list of apartments, cottages, guesthouses, inns, motels, and B&Bs is extensive enough to invite speculation as to whether there is any house in all of town unavailable to visitors.

If you don't mind the occasional bout of late-night laughter from Commercial Street carousers, the **Somerset House**, 378 Commercial Street (508/487-0383), has comfortable rooms and a very central location in a bracketed old Cape Cod manse. Rounding out the lodging options are the national chains (two Best Westerns and a Holiday Inn); a pair of private campgrounds (Coastal Acres Camping Court, 508/487-1700; Dunes Edge Camp Ground, 508/487-9815); and the bargain-priced shared little cottages of the **Outermost Hostel** (May-Oct.; $14; 508/487-4378) on Winslow Street past the Pilgrim Monument parking lot.

US-50:
THE
LONELIEST
ROAD

U.S. GOVERNMENT
TEMPORARY QUARTERS

US-50: THE LONELIEST ROAD

The sole surviving non-interstate transcontinental highway, US-50 runs coast-to-coast through the heart of America. During its 3,200-mile odyssey from sea to shining sea, US-50 passes through a dozen different states and four state capitals, as well as the nation's capital, Washington, D.C. Along the route are some of the country's most magnificent landscapes: the Appalachian, Rocky, and Sierra Nevada mountains, the endless farmlands of the Great Plains, and the desiccated deserts of Utah and Nevada. It follows the footsteps of pioneers along the Santa Fe Trail and the route of the Pony Express, and gives an uncannily consistent timeline of national development. Heading west to east, you can travel back in history from the Wild West frontier of the mid-1800s, through lands the likes of Daniel Boone and countless others pioneered in the 1700s, before arriving at the Atlantic Ocean near some of the oldest and best-preserved colonial-era landscapes in the USA. All the way across the country, US-50 passes through literally hundreds of timeworn small towns, the great majority of which have survived untouched by the modern onslaught of Wal-Marts and fast-food franchises.

From its start at San Francisco, the route cuts across California's midsection, passing the state capital at Sacramento before following the route of the old Pony Express up into the Sierra Nevada to the shores of Lake Tahoe and into Nevada. The Nevada portion of the route, dubbed "The Loneliest Road in America" by travel writers and tourist boards, is one of the most compelling long-distance drives in the country—provided you find miles and miles of nothing more than mountains, sagebrush, and blue sky compelling. The Great Basin desert continues across half of Utah, but then the route climbs over the Wasatch Front and onto the national park-packed red-rock country of the Colorado Plateau.

Continuing east, you cross the Continental Divide atop the Rockies, then follow the Arkansas River along the historic Santa Fe Trail, passing many of the most significant sites of the Wild West frontier. For fans of vanishing Americana, the route really comes into its own here across the Great Plains, with its hypnotically repetitive landscape of water towers, windmills, railroad tracks, and grain elevators, and one small town after another, each featuring its variations on the archetypal lineup of cafe, post office, tavern, and general store.

Continuing across Missouri from Kansas City to St. Louis, US-50 crosses the Mississippi River into a much older and more settled landscape, through the agricultural heartlands of Illinois, Indiana, and Ohio. After climbing into the Appalachian backwoods of West Virginia, US-50 emerges suddenly into the wealth and power of downtown Washington, D.C., before passing through the still perfectly picturesque fishing and farming communities of Maryland's Eastern Shore. US-50 reaches the Atlantic at humongous Ocean City, one of the country's last great seaside resorts.

ACROSS CALIFORNIA

If you're interested in following the exact route of old US-50, which formed the original Lincoln Highway in the days before highways were numbered, from the foot of the Bay Bridge the old road wound southeast along the approximate route of today's I-580 freeway, up and over Altamont Pass (site of a huge wind farm and the Rolling Stones' notorious 1969 "Gimme Shelter" concert). From Tracy, old US-50 ran north to Sacramento, where it rejoins the current route.

Heading east from San Francisco across the heavy-duty Oakland Bay Bridge, the route across California starts off along the busy I-80 freeway through the urbanized San Francisco Bay Area. Passing diverse bayfront towns, including blue-collar Oakland and collegiate Berkeley, the busy and often congested eight-lane highway heads northeast across the historically important but increasingly suburbanized flatlands of the Sacramento Delta. Beyond Sacramento, the state capital of California, US-50 finally emerges, first as a freeway but later as a two-lane mountain road climbing through the heart of the Sierra Nevada foothills, where many of the small towns slumber in a gold rush dream of the 1850s. Continuing east, US-50 winds through endless tracts of pine forest before cresting the Sierra to reach alpine Lake Tahoe, a year-round resort lying astride the Nevada border.

For particulars on what to see and do in the City by the Bay, consult the Survival Guide to San Francisco on pages 718-719.

Oakland's native son Jack London worked in factories and along the waterfront near present-day Jack London Square before becoming the first writer to earn $1 million with his pen.

Oakland

Though many dismiss it as the West Coast equivalent of Newark, New Jersey, the hardworking and long-suffering city of Oakland (pop. 365,000) is actually a lively and intriguing place. The main attraction for visitors is its waterfront **Jack London Square** honoring the city's favorite prodigal son. Covering a few blocks at the foot of Broadway, the modern outdoor shopping complex contains a large bookstore, a couple of restaurants, an ancient log cabin supposedly lived in by Jack London in the Yukon Territory, and last but not least, the truly funky **Heinhold's First and Last Chance**, a rickety old saloon that's the only survivor from the waterfront's wild past, right on the water at 56 Jack London Square.

Oakland's other main draw is the excellent **Oakland Museum** (Wed.-Sat. 10 AM-5 PM, Sunday noon-7 PM; $4), housed in a landmark modernist ziggurat on the east edge of downtown, at 1000 Oak Street. Inside, exhibits cover everything from California's natural history to the photography of Dorothea Lange. An in-depth look at the state's popular culture is highlighted by a lively display of Hollywood movie posters, neon signs, jukeboxes, and classic cars and motorcycles.

Berkeley

The intellectual, literary, and political nexus of the San Francisco Bay Area, left-leaning Berkeley (pop. 120,000) enjoys an international reputation that overshadows its suburban character. The town grew up around the attractively landscaped University of California campus, which during the 1960s and early 1970s was the scene of ongoing battles between "The Establishment" and unwashed hordes of anti-war, sex-and-drugs-and-rock-and-roll-crazed youth. Today Berkeley maintains a typical college town mix of cafes and CD stores. Its site is superb, looking out across the bay to the Golden Gate and San Francisco.

The square-mile **University of California** Berkeley campus sits at the foot of eucalyptus-covered hills a mile east of the University Avenue exit off the I-80 freeway. Wander along Strawberry Creek, admiring the mix of neoclassical and postmodern buildings. Berkeley's cacophonous main drag, Telegraph Avenue, runs south from the heart of campus in a crazy array of tie-dye and tarot, lined by a half-dozen good cafes and some of the country's best bookstores.

There are dozens of good-value places to eat and drink in Berkeley, including one of the best breakfast joints on the planet, **Bette's Ocean View Diner**, 1807 4th Street, two blocks from the I-80 University Avenue exit, at the center of an artsy boutique-and-gallery district. There are also many top-rated restaurants, including world-renowned **Chez Panisse**, birthplace of California cuisine, located in the heart of Berkeley's gourmet ghetto at 1517 Shattuck Avenue (reservations essential; 510/548-5525).

Vallejo

Formerly an early capital of California, these days Vallejo is a blue-collar maritime town reeling from the closure of its huge and historic Mare Island naval shipyard, which from 1854 to 1994 built and maintained many of the country's fighting ships and submarines. Vallejo's bona fide attraction is the **Marine World/Africa USA** theme park (Wed.-Sun. 9:30 AM-5:30 PM, daily till 6:30 PM in summer; $24.95), on the north side of town just west of I-80, with 160 acres of elephants, tigers, sea lions, and killer whales, all trained to perform tricks on cue.

Vallejo effectively marks the edge of the San Francisco Bay Area. East of here the landscape turns suddenly flat and agricultural, with a few pockets of suburbia. Vallejo also marks the turnoff west to the Wine Country of the Napa and Sonoma valleys.

I-80 Towns

Between the San Francisco Bay Area and Sacramento, I-80 passes through an increasingly suburbanized corridor of towns like **Fairfield**, home of Travis Air Force Base and a large Anheuser-Busch beer refinery; **Vacaville**, site of the state's largest

In recent years Oakland has suffered one disaster after another. The 1989 earthquake did far more damage (and killed twice as many people) in Oakland than it did across the bay. In 1992 a terrible fire destroyed 3,000 hillside homes, killing 27 people.

San Francisco is easily accessible from both Berkeley and Oakland via the high-speed, trans-bay BART trains, which run between a half-dozen East Bay stations and downtown San Francisco.

The big "C" above the University of California campus is over 100 years old; it was the first of these giant letters, which have since been repeated on hillsides all over the country.

While Berkeley students were rioting in the streets in 1968, a Berkeley plumber was putting the finishing touches on the air-bubbling bath device that bears his name—Jacuzzi.

The town of Vallejo served as state capital of California on two different occasions in the gold rush years of the early 1850s.

psychiatric prison, where mass murderer Charles Manson is incarcerated; and **Davis**, where there's a University of California campus renowned for its wine-making school.

California's capitol as it appeared in the early 1900s. A 40-acre park surrounds the building; guided tours of both are offered in spring, summer, and fall. Call (916) 324-0333 for details.

Sacramento

Spreading for miles at the heart of California's 500-mile-long, agriculturally rich Central Valley, Sacramento is not what most would expect of the capital of the Golden State. Green and suburban, with only the state capitol and a few modern towers rising above the tops of the city's thousands of trees, Sacramento is a relatively quiet backwater that embodies the schizophrenic state, forming a sort of neutral ground between the major urban centers, which contain 90% of the state's population, and the rural rest, which covers 90% of the land.

Stretching along the banks of the Sacramento and American Rivers, which flow west into San Francisco Bay, the site was chosen as the state capital during the gold rush days of 1852, when Sacramento was the main jumping-off point for the Sierra Nevada mines. A number of buildings dating from that era have been restored to form **Old Sacramento**, a mildly diverting shopping complex and tourist trap along the riverfront, where ersatz paddle-wheel steamboats offer sightseeing cruises, and the excellent **California State Railroad Museum** (daily 10 AM-5 PM; $5) documents the history of western railroads. Three blocks east of Old Sacramento, across the busy I-5 freeway, stands the impressive **state capitol** (daily 9 AM-5 PM; free), completed in 1874 and recently restored.

Two other attractions are within a short drive of the capitol. **Sutter's Fort** (daily 10 AM-5 PM; $2), a replica of the frontier outpost constructed here in 1839 by Swiss settler Johannes Sutter, stands a half-mile north of the US-50/I-80 interchange, just west of the freeway at 27th and L Streets. The site also contains the very good **California State Indian Museum**, with exhibits tracing the history and cultures of the state's Native American tribes. For a change of pace, have a look at the **Towe Ford Museum** (daily 10 AM-6 PM; $5), next to the I-80/I-5 interchange at Front and V Streets along the river. The museum displays every Ford made from 1903 to 1952, from Model T's to massive Ford V-8s. During Memorial Day weekend, the **Sacramento Jazz Jubilee** (916/372-5277) draws an enormous crowd intent on hearing the 100 or so bands. Dixieland jazz features prominently, and in fact the festival represents the biggest Dixieland do outside of New Orleans.

Apart from the convenient collection of unremarkable "theme" restaurants in Old Sacramento, there's no one good part of town to head to for a meal—places to eat tend to be spread all over. **Jim Denny's Burger Stand**, right downtown at 12th and K Streets, is a classic 1940s-era lunch spot, while a half-mile east **Greta's Cafe**, 1831 Capitol Avenue, serves pizzas, salads, and sandwiches to the liberal-minded workers who staff the state government. Attached to a landmark 1920s movie theater, the **Tower Cafe**, 1518 Broadway a block south of I-80 at 16th Street, has healthy, multi-ethnic food and a world-beat attitude. (It's also where the Sacramento-based **Tower Records** CD and bookstore conglomerate got its start; both have stores across the street, open till midnight every night.)

Places to stay include a **Best Western**, a **Motel 6**, and a centrally located **Comfort Inn**, plus the friendly **AYH Gold Rush Home Hostel** (916/421-5954) off I-5 on the north side of town. Closer in, near Sutter's Fort, the **Bear Flag Inn**, 2814 I Street (916/448-5417), is a very nice B&B in the city's oldest residential neighborhood.

Sacramento also marks the official western end of US-50, as shown by the sign along the freeway: Ocean City, Maryland—3,173 Miles. Approaching from the west, take the downtown turnoff from I-80 and cross the river on landmark Tower Bridge, which drops you right at the center of Sacramento, on axis with the state capitol.

Between Sacramento and Placerville, US-50 is an eight lane freeway—and one of the California Highway Patrol's most lucrative speed traps, especially for westbound (downhill) travelers.

Placerville and Coloma

The main US-50 stop in the Sierra Nevada foothills, Placerville (pop. 8,400; elev. 1,860 feet) takes its name from the placer gold deposits recovered from the South Fork of the American River, which flows just north of town. Though the historic core of Placerville is well preserved, with a few cafes and bars paying homage to its rough-and-tumble past, the most authentic reminder of the town's gold-rush heritage is the **Gold Bug Mine** (daily 10 AM-4 PM in summer, weekends only rest of the year; $1), a mile north of US-50 off the Bedford Avenue exit. A stamp mill and other mining equipment stand outside the entrance to the mine tunnel, which you can explore on a self-guided tour.

The original site of the discovery of gold, Sutter's Mill, has been reconstructed as part of **Gold Discovery State Historic Park** in Coloma, now an idyllic place along

In 1849, quiet Sutter's Mill in Coloma became the focus of worldwide attention after gold was discovered there.

the banks of the American River, nine miles north of Placerville along Hwy-49.

If you want to explore the region's many evocative gold rush-era remnants, Placerville makes a good base, with its handful of motels (including a Best Western and a Days Inn) fronting the highway. For food, the agreeable **Bell Tower Cafe** serves classic Hangtown Fry and other diner-style dishes at 423 Main Street in the town center.

Two more interesting places to eat can be reached within a short drive of Placerville. The ancient and very popular **Poor Red's Barbecue**, housed in a gold rush-era stagecoach station in the hamlet of El Dorado, five miles south of Placerville on Hwy-49, has full lunches and dinners for very little money. East along US-50, take the Cedar Grove exit and pull into Camino, where the **Del Monte Express** serves a variety of gigantic burgers, all named after historic trains; the restaurant stands along an old logging railroad, and a model train runs continuously.

Throughout the gold-rush era, Placerville was known as Hangtown, with a reputation for stringing up petty thieves and other law-breakers.

Between Sacramento and Lake Tahoe, US-50 follows the route of the Pony Express, with highway markers and monuments pointing out historic sites along the road.

The American River and Lover's Leap

Some 20 miles east of Placerville, US-50 changes suddenly from a four-lane freeway into a twisting, narrow, two-lane road over the crest of the Sierra Nevada mountains. The usually busy highway runs alongside the steep banks of the American River, and the lushness of the western Sierra Nevada is immediately apparent as the road passes luxuriant groves of pine, fir, and cedar among which numerous old resorts and vacation cabins are tucked away.

About six miles west of the summit, the towering granite cliff of Lover's Leap stands out to the south of the highway, its 1,300-foot face attracting rock-climbers, while to the north the delicate cascade of **Horsetail Falls** offers a more serene pit stop. Climbing east up US-50's steepest set of hairpin turns, you'll reach 7,365-foot Echo Summit, which gives great views of the Lake Tahoe basin—the shining blue waters beckoning you along another steep stretch of US-50, downhill this time, if you're heading east, to the lakeshore itself.

South Lake Tahoe

One of the biggest (12 miles wide, 22 miles long, and 72 miles of coastline), deepest (over 1,000 feet in places), and cleanest lakes in the country, straddling the Nevada/California border at 6,220 feet above sea level, Lake Tahoe is a beautiful sight from any angle—from the crest of the alpine peaks surrounding it, from a car or bicycle as you cruise along the shoreline roads, or from a boat out on the lake itself.

Sitting, as the name suggests, at the southern end of Lake Tahoe, the ungainly resort community of South Lake Tahoe is a place of multiple personalities. On the

California side, low-rise motels line the US-50 frontage, and the atmosphere is that of a family-oriented summer resort, with bike-rental stands and T-shirt shops clogging the roadside. Across the Nevada border, glitzy 20-story casinos rise up in a sudden wall of concrete and glass, ignoring the surrounding beauty in favor of round-the-clock "adult fun"—gambling, racy nightclub revues, and more gambling. (For more on the attractions of Nevada's half of Lake Tahoe, see below.) A few strategically placed pine trees work hard to retain a semblance of the natural splendor, but in peak summer season it's basically a *very* busy stretch of road, on both sides of the state line.

To get away from it all, head along Hwy-89 around the west side of the lake to the magnificent state parks at **Emerald Bay**, or hike up into the mountains. For more detailed hints on hiking and cycling trails, stop by the U.S. Forest Service **ranger station** at 870 Emerald Bay Road (916/573-2600), near where US-50 cuts south from the lake. In winter, the Tahoe area turns into an extremely popular ski resort (Heavenly Valley on the south shore and Squaw Valley in the north are among the largest and busiest in the U.S., and there are dozens more all around the lake).

Despite the region's popularity, year-round prices for Tahoe accommodations are quite low; with two **Travelodges**, a **Motel 6**, and dozens of others to choose from, you shouldn't have trouble finding something suitable. Cross-country skiers or those in search of rest-and-relaxation should try **Sorenson's Resort** (916/694-2203 or 800/423-9949), 17 miles south of the lake via Hwy-89, where cozy cabins and a nice cafe sit in a peaceful valley right on the old Pony Express route across the Sierra.

Food, however, is not really a Tahoe strength, though for a carbo-loading breakfast head no further than the **Red Hut Waffle Shop** at 2723 US-50, west of the main motel strip. For a well-prepared and not overpriced dinner, try **Nephele's**, at 1169 Ski Run Boulevard at the foot of Heavenly Valley. The large casino hotels on the Nevada side all have reliably good if inherently dull restaurants.

For complete listings and year-round visitor information, contact the **Lake Tahoe Visitors Bureau** (800/AT-TAHOE).

ACROSS NEVADA

Between Lake Tahoe in the west and Great Basin National Park on the Utah border, US-50 crosses more than 400 miles of corrugated country, climbing up and over a dozen distinct mountain ranges while passing through four classic mining towns and the state capital, Carson City. Early explorers mapped this region, Pony Express riders raced across it, and the long-distance Lincoln Highway finally tamed it, but the US-50 byway has always played second fiddle to I-80, the more popular northern route across the state. Besides being a more scenic alternative to the mind-numbing, and therefore accident-prone, I-80 freeway, US-50 across Nevada has gained a measure of notoriety in its own right—it's known as the "Loneliest Road in America." As you travel along it you'll see road signs, T-shirts, bumper stickers, and even state-sponsored travel passports proclaiming it as such.

Stateline

Right where US-50 crosses from California into Nevada, the casino complex at Stateline forms, for a few short blocks, a mini-Las Vegas, with four 20-story resort hotels towering over the lakeshore. **Harvey's** (800/648-3361) started it all in the 1940s, with six nickel slot machines, still in use in a corner of the casino; it's now the largest, with over 650 lakeside rooms. **Harrah's** (800/648-3773), across US-50, is the most opulent, its luxurious 500-square-foot suites yours to enjoy for a mere $200 a night. Altogether, over 2,000 rooms are available, combined with at least that many more across the California border. The multitude of game-hungry visitors that converges here creates a definite charge in the rarefied atmosphere when the casino tables are turning at full speed.

Nevada Beach and Zephyr Cove

From the casino district at Stateline, US-50 winds along Lake Tahoe's southeastern shore for over 20 miles, passing by a pair of waterfront parks at Nevada Beach and Zephyr Cove (where you can ride the faux paddle wheeler MS *Dixie* on a two-hour cruise across the lake). Otherwise, lakeshore access is severely limited, since most of the waterfront is privately owned, though numerous roadside turnouts (most easily accessible to westbound, lakeside travelers) offer ample opportunities to take in unforgettable views.

Midway along the lake's eastern shore, US-50 turns sharply and begins climbing up and over the 7,140-foot crest of Spooner Pass, all the way giving great views (if only through the rear-view mirror) of the tantalizing blue gleam below. Dropping down swiftly into the Great Basin desert, US-50 links up with US-395 for the final few miles into Carson City.

Carson City

Nevada's state capital and third largest city, Carson City (pop. 40,443) was named in honor of Wild West explorer Kit Carson. Nestled at the base of the sheer eastern scarp of the Sierra Nevada, the city was founded in 1858—just a year before the discovery of the Comstock Lode riches, and six years before Nevada became a state.

Carson City is a hard place to characterize. Considering it's the capital, life is rather slow, with the main buzz being the few casinos like the **Carson Nugget** at 507 N. Carson Street on the main route (US-50/395) through town, which has a million-dollar collection of raw, unprocessed gold on display, along with roulette, craps, and blackjack tables and the usual army of old ladies feeding banks of slot machines.

Gambling aside, the one place to stop in Carson City is the excellent **Nevada State Museum** (daily 8:30 AM-4 PM; $3), which stands across the street from the stately capitol—and catercorner from the Nugget—at 600 N. Carson Street.

Housed inside the solid old U.S. Mint, built in 1870 to make coins from Comstock silver, are displays on mining (including a large, full-scale mock-up of a working mine), as well as on Nevada and Great Basin natural history. Also worth a look is the **Nevada State Railroad Museum** on US-50/395, on the south side of town.

Good Mexican meals are the order of the day at **El Charro Avitia**, south of town at 4389 S. Carson Street, and the specials at the **Carson Nugget** can be incredibly cheap ($2 steak sandwiches). However, the best and most expensive fare is served at **Adele's**, where power brokers broker their power at 1112 N. Carson Street (702/882-3353). Motels line Carson Street north and south of the capitol; try the classic 1950s-style **Frontier** at 1718 N. Carson (702/882-1377), the **Motel Orleans** at 2731 S. Carson (702/882-2007), or **Motel 6** at 2749 S. Carson (702/885-7710). Finally, if you're looking for something to do after dark besides gamble, Carson City also has what's possibly the country's cheapest movie theater, in the shopping mall a mile east of Carson Street on US-50: four screens show recent releases, and all seats cost $1.50, all the time.

For more complete visitor information, contact the **Carson City Convention and Visitors Bureau** (800/NEVADA1).

Virginia City

In 1859, prospectors following the gold deposits up the slopes of Mount Davidson discovered one of the richest strikes in world history: the **Comstock Lode**. Almost overnight, the bustling camp of Virginia City grew into the largest settlement between Chicago and San Francisco, and over the next 20 years nearly a billion dollars in gold and silver (in 19th-century money!) was grubbed from deep underground. Afterward the town very nearly dried up and blew away, but thanks in part to the 1960s TV show *Bonanza*, in which Hoss and company were always heading over to Virginia City for supplies or to fetch the sheriff, tourists discovered the town and gave it a new lease on life.

These days Virginia City is both a tacky tourist trap and one of the most satisfying destinations in the state. Reachable via a

In 1861, Orion Clemens was appointed secretary to the governor of Nevada Territory, and his younger brother Sam came with him to Nevada. Sam submitted dispatches of his mining and travel adventures around the territory to Virginia City's largest daily newspaper, the *Territorial Enterprise*. Sam eventually accepted a reporter's position on the newspaper and began perfecting his unique brand of Western frontier humor under the pen name **Mark Twain**.

The Castle, Virginia City's elegant 1868 mansion, was built by the superintendent of the Empire Mine.

very steep (grades in excess of 15%!) eight-mile drive up Hwy-341 from US-50, dozens of hokey but enjoyable attractions—like the amiable **Bucket of Blood Saloon**, which offers a panoramic view down the mountain—line the five-block-long main drag, C Street. The streets above and below—and I do mean above and below: the town clings to such a steep slope that C Street is a good three stories higher than neighboring D Street—hold some of the most authentic sites. B Street, for example, has the elegant **Castle**, Nevada's premier mansion, with all the original furnishings and fittings, a block south of the ornate Victorian **Storey County Courthouse** and the landmark **Piper's Opera House**. Down the hill on D Street was once a more raucous quarter, where brothels and opium dens shared space with railroad tracks, cemeteries, and the mines themselves: the Gold & Curry, the Ophir, and the Consolidated Virginia.

Before or after a wander around town, be sure to stop in to the excellent museum on the ground floor of the **Fourth Ward School** (daily 10 AM-5 PM May-Nov.; $2), the Victorian gothic landmark at the south end of C Street. Exhibits inside recount the lively history of Virginia City, from mining technology to Mark Twain, who made his start as a journalist with Virginia City's *Territorial Enterprise*. An intact classroom is preserved as it was in 1936 when the last class graduated. Another not-to-be-missed spot is the **Red Light Museum** (daily 11 AM-5 PM; $1), in the basement of the Julia C. Bulette Saloon on C and Union Streets, which displays an amazing barrage of antique condoms, pornographic postcards, opium pipes, and other sexually explicit oddities, impossible to describe.

Unless you're tempted by the many places to eat hot dogs and drink sarsaparilla along C Street, food options in Virginia City are very limited, though the **Brass Rail** and the **Delta Saloon** are both above par. For complete listings, contact the Virginia City **chamber of commerce** (702/847-0311).

Dayton

On the north side of US-50, just east of the turnoff for Virginia City, Dayton is one of the oldest settlements in Nevada. Gold was first discovered here in 1849, and later the town's massive stamp mills pounded the ore carried through the massive Sutro Tunnel from the fabulous Comstock Lode in the mountains above. The historic town center is little more than the two blocks of Main Street north from the traffic light on US-50, where you can choose from a couple of combination cafes-and-saloons, including the **Old Corner Bar**, a favorite hangout of John Huston, Arthur Miller, Marilyn Monroe, and company when they were in Dayton in 1960 to film *The Misfits*.

East of Dayton, around Lahontan Dam, irrigated fields of alfalfa quickly give way to 50 miles of sandy desert, tumbleweed, and scruffy grasses.

Fallon

Coming into Fallon, especially after crossing the Great Basin deserts of Utah and Nevada that stretch to the east, can be a shock to the system. First, relative to Nevada's other US-50 towns, Fallon is big: upwards of 7,000 residents, with all the attendant shopping malls, traffic lights, and fast-food franchises. Second, but perhaps more striking, Fallon is green: alfalfa, onions, garlic, and cantaloupe as far as the eye can see.

Though it had long existed as a crossroads for the surrounding mining camps, and was first laid out as a town around the turn of the century, Fallon didn't really begin to grow until the completion of La-hontan Dam west of town in 1915 brought irrigation water from the Carson River. Besides agriculture, Fallon's other main employer is the U.S. Navy, whose air base and target range is an important training center for carrier-based fighters and bombers—the "Top Guns" of Tom Cruise fame.

While it's not a particularly attractive place, Fallon does have what they accurately call "The Best Little Museum on the Loneliest Road in America," the eclectic and engaging **Churchill County Museum** (Mon.-Sat. 10 AM-5 PM, Sunday noon-5 PM; free) at 1050 S. Maine Street, less than a mile south of US-50. Otherwise, Fallon offers the ATMs, gas stations, and motels lining along US-50, as well as the usual Pizza Huts and Subways, and a handy 24-hour Safeway.

> About the only radio station along this stretch of US-50 is Fallon's **KBLB 980 AM**, which plays a standard array of country hits.

Sand Mountain and Grimes Point

The 110 miles of US-50 between Fallon and Austin, the next town to the east, look pretty empty on most maps, but there's more to see than you might think. In the midst of a U.S. Navy target range, where supersonic fighters play electronic war games across the alkali flats, there are historical plaques marking Pony Express and Butterfield Stage way stations, a solitary brothel, and two unique attractions—a singing sand dune and an extensive petroglyph site.

Ten miles east of Fallon, the extraordinary grouping of petroglyphs at Grimes Point is not to be missed. Just 100 yards north of US-50, a self-guided trail leads past hundreds of images etched into the lichen-covered, espresso-brown basalt boulders. Some 8,000 years ago, when the carvings were made, Grimes Point was on the shores of now-vanished Lake Lahontan, a prime hunting and fishing ground for prehistoric Great Basin peoples. These days fast and fierce lizards, and the occasional antelope, share the arid setting with the shiny rocks, into which a huge array of abstract and figurative images have been pecked and chiseled. If you're intrigued and want to know more, stop by the excellent Churchill County Museum in Fallon, which runs guided tours of nearby **Hidden Cave** where significant archaeological remains have been uncovered.

Sand Mountain, 15 miles east of Grimes Point, 84 miles west of Austin, and just a half-mile north of US-50, is a giant sword-edged sand dune that makes a deep booming sound when the cascading crystals oscillate at the proper frequency—somewhere between 50 and 100 hertz. On weekends you're more likely to hear the sound of unmuffled dirt bikes and dune buggies, but at other times the half-hour trudge to the top is well worth making, to watch the swirls of sand dance along the ridges.

> At the turnoff to Sand Mountain, a sign marks the official **"Loneliest Phone on the Loneliest Road in America."**

> Forty-five miles east of Fallon, Hwy-361 heads south to the magnesium-mining company town of Gabbs. East of it lies fascinating **Berlin-Ichthyosaur State Park,** which holds an only-in-Nevada combination of a 100-year-old ghost town and 200-million-year-old marine fossil quarry.

Austin

Some 110 miles east of Fallon and 70 miles west of Eureka, tiny Austin (pop. 300) huddles well above 6,000 feet on the north slope of the mighty Toiyabe Mountains. The steep incline of Main Street (US-50) as it passes through town attests to the precariousness with which Austin has clung to life since its 10-year mining boom ended—in 1873. Unlike Fallon or Eureka, which wear their prosperity on their sleeves, Austin hangs onto the rustic, steadfastly unwhitewashed nature that was once—and in some places, remains—central

THE PONY EXPRESS

Of all the larger-than-life legends that animate the annals of the Wild West, none looms larger than that of the Pony Express. As is typical of frontier adventures, accounts of the Pony Express are often laced with considerable exaggeration, but in this case the facts are unusually impressive. Beginning in April 1860, running twice a week between St. Joseph, Missouri, and Sacramento, California, where it was linked with San Francisco by steamship, the Pony Express halved the time it took to carry news to and from the West Coast, making the 1,966-mile trek in just 10 days. Eighty riders (including 14-year-old William "Buffalo Bill" Cody, who made the record single run of 322 miles) were employed to race between the 190 stations en route, switching horses every 10-15 miles and averaging 75 miles per run—day or night, in all kinds of weather, across 120° deserts or snowbound Sierra passes.

Covering nearly 2,000 miles of the wildest and ruggedest land on the frontier, the Pony Express established the first high-speed link between the two coasts. At a time when the nation was divided against itself, with the Civil War looming on the horizon, the Pony Express connection played a key role in keeping the valuable mines of California and Nevada in Union hands. A private enterprise that lasted just 18 months and lost considerable amounts of money before being put of out business for good, the Pony Express proved that overground connections across the still-wild western U.S. were both necessary and possible.

The completion on October 28, 1861 of the transcontinental telegraph made the Pony Express obsolete overnight, and not so much as a saddle survives from this legendary endeavor. Apart from a few postmarked letters, and various statues and plaques marking the Pony Express route, there are very few tangible signs of it today. The most evocative sites survive in the dry Nevada desert, within easy access of the US-50 highway.

East of Fallon, for example, the highway runs right on top of the old Pony Express route, and the remains of two relay stations can still be seen. One is at **Sand Springs**, at the foot of Sand Mountain. More substantial remains survive at **Cold Springs**, 32 miles east, where plaques recount the history and where a mile-long trail brings you to what was once among the most isolated and dangerous of the Pony Express stations.

to Nevada's character. Austin takes its central assignment seriously, since the state's exact geographical center is a mere 12 miles to the south.

According to local legend, a Pony Express rider accidentally discovered silver ore here in 1862, and the rush was on. Prospectors fanned out from Austin, which was named after the Texas hometown of one of its founders, to establish Belmont, Berlin, Grantsville, Ione, and dozens of other boomtowns-turned-ghost towns; roughly $50 million in gold and silver was shipped out over the next 10 years. Since then Austin has experienced a long, melancholy decline, though recent efforts to mine the abundant turquoise and barium in the region have met with some success.

A two-minute drive (at 10 mph) along Main Street takes you past all there is to see in Austin today. The impressive steeples of the Catholic, Methodist, and Baptist churches dominate the townscape, while at the west (downhill) end of town you can glimpse **Stoke's Castle**, a three-story stone sentinel built in 1897 and lived in for all of a month. It looks best from a distance, looming over the cemeteries at the west end of town, but if you want to get closer, follow Castle Road for about a half-mile south from US-50.

For its 300 residents, Austin has three gas stations (it's a very long way to the next town, so fill up here), three motels, and three cafes: the ancient **International**, moved here board by board from Virginia City in 1863, opens first at around 6 AM, followed by **Carol's Country Kitchen** at 7 AM, then the **Toiyabe Drive-in**. All three are right on Main Street and close around 9 PM.

Hickison Petroglyph Recreation Area

Bookended by 7,000-foot mountain ranges at either end, the route between Austin and Eureka is perhaps the longest, flattest, straightest stretch of the entire trans-Nevada length of US-50, over 70 miles of Great Basin nothingness. Cattle ranches fill the plains, which were crisscrossed by early explorers like John C. Frémont, who passed through in 1845, as well as by the Pony Express and the Butterfield Stage. Such recent history, however, pales in comparison to the relics from the region's prehistoric past, particularly the fine petroglyphs carved into the rocks on the eastern side of 6,594-foot Hickison Summit, 25 miles east of Austin and 45 miles west of Eureka.

Now protected as part of the BLM-operated Hickison Petroglyph Recreation Area, the petroglyphs stand in a shallow sandstone draw on the north side of the highway. A half-mile trail loops through sagebrush, junipers, and piñon pines from the parking area-*cum*-campground past dozens of these enigmatic figures, some of which are thought to date back as far as 10,000 B.C. Somewhat surprisingly, so far they are graffiti-free.

Across Nevada, US-50 follows the route of the Lincoln Highway, the nation's first transcontinental route.

Eureka

Right in the middle of a 100-mile stretch of spectacular Great Basin scenery, Eureka is one of the most engaging and enjoyable stops in the state. Unlike a lot of places along the Loneliest Road, Eureka is fairly thriving, thanks to numerous gold mines still in operation in Eureka County, including the largest and most productive in the U.S., the Newmont Mine near Carlin.

The four blocks of 100-year-old buildings lining the steeply sloping, franchise-free Main Street (US-50) are a mix of well-restored brick and wood storefronts alongside less fortunate ruins, some merely sets of cast-iron pilasters holding up false fronts.

The focal point is the grand 1879 **Eureka County Courthouse**, still in use. Behind it stands the **Eureka Sentinel Museum** (Mon.-Fri. 11 AM-5 PM, shorter hours weekends), with displays tracing the lively local history as well as typesetting equipment and printing presses of the newspaper published here from 1870 to 1960.

Besides an intriguing place to stroll around (walking-tour booklets are available from the Sentinel Museum and many local shops), Eureka is also a good place to break a journey. Two comfortable places to stay are the recently reopened **Jackson House** hotel and bar (702/237-5577) on Main Street, and the deluxe **Parsonage House B&B** (702/237-5756) on Spring Street, both evocative and historic. Good food is served at both the **Owl Club** cafe and the casino, right on Main Street. There's also a Chevron station and an E-Z Stop convenience store, neither of which is open past 10 PM.

The state-run Nevada Commission on Tourism sponsors a tongue-in-cheek promotion in which travelers along US-50 can earn themselves a certificate saying **"I Survived the Loneliest Road in America"** by getting their official US-50 travel passports stamped at locations along the highway. For details, phone 800/237-0774 or contact the commission at Capitol Complex, Carson City, NV 89710

Ely marks the junction of US-50 and our US-93 route, and is covered on pages 106-107.

Connors Pass and Major's Place

East of Ely, US-50, spliced together with US-6 and US-93 into a single two-lane highway, continues for 25 miles before crossing the narrow waist of the Schell Creek Range at 7,722-foot Connors Pass. As you ascend toward the pass, the air cools and freshens, the single-leaf piñon and Utah juniper appear and increase and, cresting the summit, the mighty Snake Range, including 13,061-foot Wheeler Peak, comes into view.

East of the pass, at Major's Place (no services), US-93 cuts due south, heading 80 long, solitary miles to the next contact with humans at Pioche, while US-50 heads east toward Great Basin National Park.

The route east out of Ely toward Great Basin National Park is an official "scenic route," rolling across sagebrush plains and climbing over the Schell Creek and Snake mountain ranges through dense groves of pine and juniper.

The world's oldest known bristlecone pine, dubbed **Prometheus,** was cut down on Wheeler Peak by the U.S. Forest Service in 1964, which discovered too late that, at 4,900 years old, the tree had been the oldest living thing on earth. A cross-section of the trunk is displayed at the Bristlecone Convention Center, 150 6th Street in Ely.

Ely's lively **KELY 1230 AM** plays "the best of everything": oldies from the 1950s and 1960s, plus Rush Limbaugh at lunchtime.

Great Basin National Park

Approaching Nevada from the east, travelers are greeted by the towering silhouette of **Wheeler Peak**, at 13,063 feet the second highest and most impressive mountain in the state; from the west, similarly sheer escarpments tower over lush green open range for miles and miles along US-50. In 1987 the 77,000 acres around Wheeler Peak were designated Great Basin National Park, but its remote location has made it one of the least-visited national parks in the United States. Hikers and campers will have no trouble finding solitude amidst the alpine forests, ancient bristlecone pines, glacial lakes, and small ice field.

Thanks to the well-maintained road climbing to over 10,000 feet, the wilderness areas are easily accessible to people willing to take a short hike, though many visitors go no farther than the park's centerpiece, **Lehman Caves**. Geological forces have been sculpting Lehman Caves for roughly 70 million years, but they weren't noticed until homesteader Absalom Lehman stumbled upon the small entrance to the caves in

1885. They were declared a national monument in 1922, and since then only minor improvements have been made, leaving the mind-bending limestone formations alone—no flashy light-and-sound show, just hundreds of delicate stalagmites, stalactites, helictites, aragonites, and the like. Hour-long guided tours ($4) are conducted at intervals throughout the day; on summer evenings at 6 PM there's a memorable candlelight tour. Tours leave from the small **visitor center** (daily 8 AM-5 PM, longer in summer; 702/234-7331), which has details of hiking and camping as well as exhibits on Great Basin wildlife—from birds and bats to mountain lions. There's even a small summer-only cafe.

If you're not camping and self-relying, or if you are and want a break, the nearest food and drink are at the foot of the park in tiny **Baker** (pop. 55), which boasts one gas station, the seven-room **Silver Jack Motel** (702/234-7323), and the friendly, homey **Outlaw Bar and Grill**, which serves breakfast, burritos, and beer from early till late.

Back on US-50, just west of the Utah/Nevada border stands the **Border Inn** cafe/gas station/motel, open 24 hours a day. Apart from Baker, the only other reliable services are in Ely, 70 miles west, or in Delta, 85 miles to the east, so pass by at your peril.

ACROSS UTAH

For most of the way across Utah, the high-speed I-70 freeway has replaced US-50, but if you have time to take a couple of detours you'll be rewarded with some of the most incredible scenery in the world. Most of this is concentrated in the southeastern corner of the state, where a number of national parks, including Canyonlands and Arches, preserve the sandstone "Canyon Country" of the Colorado Plateau. In the west a few old mining towns stand amidst the arid desert of the Great Basin. Distances are huge and services few and far between, but if you have the time and plan ahead, this is one of the most satisfying and memorable corners of the country.

Delta
About 85 miles east of the Nevada border, the landscape changes suddenly from barren desert to lush pastures around the town of Delta, which is irrigated by the green Sevier River. Delta bills itself the "Gateway to Great Basin National Park,"

and it does have a **Best Western** and other motels, gas stations, and a large super-market—but very little else to attract visitors. One place worth a stop is the small **Great Basin Museum** (Tues.-Sat. 10 AM-4 PM; free), a block north of Main Street at 328 W. 100 North Street. The museum features local history exhibits, including a small display of artifacts relating to **Topaz Camp**, an internment camp set up in the desert west of Delta by the U.S. government to imprison Americans of Japanese descent during WW II.

Little Sahara Recreation Area

From Delta, US-50 officially cuts southeast across I-15, linking up with I-70 at Salina. Our route, however, follows US-6 (old US-50) toward the Salt Lake area, then east over the Wasatch Front, rejoining official US-50 at Green River.

From Delta, the route follows the Sevier River northwest, racing across the featureless desert for 32 miles before reaching the well-posted turnoff north to the Little Sahara Recreation Area. Visible from the highway four miles north of US-6, the Little Sahara Recreation Area holds 60,000 acres of sand dunes and sagebrush flats, the prettiest parts of which are preserved for hikers and campers, though motorcyclists and ATVers can overwhelm any sense of peace and tranquility, turning it into a campground from hell.

Eureka

Fifty miles east of Delta, 20 miles west of the I-15 freeway, the weather-beaten town of Eureka (pop. 750) climbs steeply up surrounding mountainsides at the heart of the once-thriving Tintic Mining District, where as recently as the 1930s thousands of miners dug millions of dollars' worth of gold, silver, copper, and lead out of the ground every year. Now the massive wooden head frames of long-closed mine shafts stand high above the houses and prefab trailers that cling to the slopes, while fading signs advertise the **Golddiggers Restaurant** and the **Silver Club Bar**, both of which are still open—for now at least—along Main Street.

Though diehard residents still speak of plans to reopen one or more of the mines, prosperity seems a distant dream in Eureka, and while it's not quite a ghost town, it is well on its way there. The glory days are recounted in the small **Tintic Mining Museum**, next to city hall on Main Street, and at the west edge of town a historical plaque stands alongside the heavy timber head frame of the Bullion-Beck Mine, one of the area's most productive.

Santaquin and Springville

Heading east from Eureka, our route bends across rock-strewn sagebrush hills around the southern shore of Utah Lake toward the I-15 freeway. Utah Lake, which is freshwater in contrast to the briny expanse of the Great Salt Lake to the north, used to be much larger than it is now, before so much of it was diverted to water the apple, peach, and cherry orchards that line US-6 around Santaquin—whose three gas stations are the last reliable source of fuel for westbound travelers until Delta, 70 miles to the southwest.

From Springville, the **Salt Lake City** megalopolis stretches north along I-15 for nearly 100 miles, from Provo to Ogden. For more information or help with accommodations, call the Salt Lake City **visitor center** (801/521-2868).

From Santaquin, follow the I-15 freeway north to Springville, where you'll find one of the cleanest and most comfortable truck stops in the U.S.A., the **Mountain Springs Motel** (801/489-3641), which besides good food, cheap gas, and $35-a-night rooms, offers free showers with every fill-up.

Soldier Summit

Heading east from the Greater Salt Lake City area, the drive along US-6 (old US-50) up and over 7,477-foot Soldier Summit is truly beautiful, as the two-lane highway passes through bright red sandstone canyons along the stark eastern side of towering Wasatch Front, then twists alongside pines and cottonwoods to the crest.

BUTCH CASSIDY AND THE HOLE-IN-THE-WALL GANG

Long before Paul Newman played him alongside Robert Redford's Sundance Kid, Butch Cassidy was one of the great outlaw legends of the Wild West. Thanks to his habit of sharing the proceeds from his crimes with the widows and children of men killed or ruined by bankers and cattle barons, Butch Cassidy earned a reputation as the "Robin Hood of the Wild West." That, plus the fact he never killed anyone while committing his crimes, gained him popular admiration from the cowboys, miners, and homesteading pioneers among whom he worked his trade.

Born Robert Leroy Parker to a family of Mormon farmers in Beaver, Utah, on Friday the 13th of April, 1866, the man who came to be known as Butch Cassidy spent his youth as a ranch hand in Utah, Colorado, and southern Wyoming. The first major crime attributed to Butch Cassidy is the robbery of a bank in Telluride in 1889, which netted him and his three accomplices some $20,000. From 1894 to 1896 he was imprisoned in Wyoming for cattle theft, and following this he joined up with Harry Longabaugh (a.k.a "The Sundance Kid") and the rest of the Wild Bunch gang. Together they robbed over a dozen banks, trains, and stagecoaches throughout the West, netting an estimated $350,000 in five years. One of their many daring heists was the daylight robbery of a coal-mining company in Castlegate, Utah, in April 1897; while the payroll was being taken from a train, Butch simply grabbed the satchel and rode off in a cloud of dust, $9,000 richer.

The summit itself, where there's a handy gas station-*cum*-general store (their motto: "Radiators Filled, Bladders Emptied"), marks the boundary between the Colorado River drainage and the Great Basin.

victims of the 1900 Scofield mine disaster

Castlegate and Helper

Dropping down from Soldier Summit, US-6/191 winds along the Price River through Castlegate, a steeply walled sandstone canyon lined with working coal mines, many of which you see from the highway. While most now rely on heavy machinery to do the dirty work of digging out the coal, the Castlegate area has been the site of the two worst mining disasters in Utah history: 173 men and boys killed in a 1924 explosion, and another 200 killed at nearby Scofield on May Day, 1900.

Tiny Helper (pop. 2,148), at the downstream edge of Castlegate, six miles northwest of Price, is a classic railroad town preserved almost unchanged for nearly a century. The six-block downtown area, fronting onto the tracks, includes so many turn-of-the-century brick- and stone-fronted buildings that it's been declared a National Historic District—though the sad truth is that most of these have stood abandoned since the railroad switched to diesel power in the 1950s. Before that, Helper was a buzzing boomtown; it earned its name in 1892 when the Denver and Rio Grande Railroad built a depot and roundhouse here to hold the "helper" engines that were added to trains to help push them over Soldier Summit, 25 miles to the west.

Though the line of boarded-up hotels, bars, and pool halls along Main Street may not encourage you to linger, the excellent **Western Mining and Railroad Museum** (Mon.-Sat. 9 AM-5 PM in summer; donations) at 296 S. Main Street contains enough raw material on railroading and coal mining, not to mention the region's diverse immigrant cultures, to keep you occupied for an hour or more. There's also a brief display recounting the exploits of Butch Cassidy and his Robber's Roost gang, who raided banks and rustled cattle throughout the region in the late 1890s, hiding out in surrounding hills. Behind the museum, an outdoor lot displays some of the giant machines used in the coal mines, which unlike the railroad still employ a large number of local people.

Price

The largest city in eastern Utah, Price (pop. 8,712) is located roughly midway between the I-15 and I-70 freeways, 65 miles northwest of Green River. Coal is so prevalent in the area that roadcuts reveal solid black seams, but the town itself is lush and green, thanks to irrigation provided by the Price River, which flows south from town into the Green and Colorado Rivers.

Coal mining, and to a lesser extent agriculture, still power Price, and you won't miss much by following the bypass around the town center. That said, the small **Prehistoric Museum** at 155 E. Main Street (daily 9 AM-6 PM in summer; donations) is worth a look for its extensive displays on the Native American cultures of the region, and for its range of full-sized dinosaur skeletons, including a stegosaurus and a mammoth. Many of these were reassembled from fossils collected from the **Cleveland-Lloyd Dinosaur Quarry**, 30 miles south of town.

Price also has all the highway services travelers might need: numerous gas stations, places to eat, and six motels, including a **Days Inn.**

Southwest from Price, bound for Green River and the I-70 freeway, US-6/191 runs alongside the busy Denver and Rio Grande mainline railroad through a region of arid plateaus highlighted every few miles by brilliantly colorful, weirdly sculpted sandstone mesas. Though barren and empty at first glance, the region is particularly rich in two things: coal mines and, more unusually, dinosaur bones. (Why do you think they call them fossil fuels?)

Green River

Straddling the eponymous river on the north side of the I-70 freeway, Green River (pop. 744) makes a handy base for exploring southeastern Utah, but it offers very little in and of itself. The town holds numerous 24-hour gas stations, a couple of good places to eat (try the **Tamarisk**, overlooking the Green River at 870 E. Main Street), and a handful of motels, including a nice **Best Western**, a **Motel 6**, and the small **Mancos Rose Motel** at 20 W. Main Street (801/564-9660), which has the cheapest rooms.

Even if you don't need fuel, food, or a place to sleep, Green River offers one very compelling reason to stop: the spacious modern **John Wesley Powell River History Museum** (daily 8 AM-8 PM in summer; 9 AM-5 PM rest of the year; $1).

In 1869 Powell and his crew were the first to travel the length of the Colorado River through the Grand Canyon; though the legendary explorers started their epic adventure in Green River, Wyoming, not here in Utah, the spacious modern museum, on old US-50 along the east bank of the Green River, is the best single repository of artifacts relating to their feat. The collection concentrates on Powell in particular and on waterborne transport in general, but there are also displays chronicling the adventures of other early explorers (including Juan de Oñate in 1605 and the Domínguez and Escalante expedition of 1776), and of fur-trappers, miners, and Mormons—all of whom contributed to the exploration and mapping of the American West.

Canyonlands National Park

Green River also makes a good base for exploring the remote wilderness of the **San Rafael Swell,** a massive fold and uplift of the earth's crust that spreads west of town to both sides of the I-70 freeway.

Uranium mined from Temple Mountain, west of Canyonlands, was used to make the first atomic bombs.

The largest and least-visited park in the Southwest, Canyonlands National Park is both breathtakingly beautiful and totally inhospitable, an arid wilderness of high plateaus and deep canyon carved by the mighty Green and Colorado Rivers. The park is divided into three very different areas, each of which is at least a 100-mile drive from the others, so it pays to plan ahead. The most popular section, the Island-in-the-Sky, stands high above the confluence of the rivers and gives the most sweeping panoramas—100 miles in every direction from over 6,000 feet above sea level. South of the rivers, **The Needles** district holds 50 square miles of spires, arches, and canyons and is the best place to undertake lengthy hikes. One trail leads from the end of the road, where there's a primitive campground, down to the mouth of Cataract Canyon on the Colorado River. The third and final area of Canyonlands, **The Maze**, is west of the rivers and virtually inaccessible.

There's a **visitor center** near the entrances to Island-in-the-Sky and The Needles. The Canyonlands headquarters in Moab, 125 W. 200 S (801/259-7164), also has extensive information. Adjacent to Canyonlands are two state parks, **Dead Horse Point** in the north and **Newspaper Rock** in the south, both of which are well worth a look.

Arches National Park

A word of warning: Even if you're not planning to venture from your car, it's a good idea to carry at least a gallon of water per person when traveling in the desert.

The annual **Fat Tire Festival,** held the week before Halloween, brings mountain bikers to Moab from all over the world. Phone 801/259-5333 for details.

Taking its name from the hundreds of naturally formed sandstone arches scattered here, Arches National Park is the most feature-packed of southeast Utah's national parks. Ranging in size from around three feet to nearly 300 feet in span, the arches are the result of erosion over millions of years, the same agent that formed the thousands of brilliantly colored spires, pinnacles, and canyons that cover southeast Utah. Piñon pines and junipers add a splash of green to the red and brown backdrop, but mostly what you see are red stone and blue sky—lots and lots of both.

The park's highlights can be easily reached from the 20-mile paved road that runs through the center of the park. A **visitor center** (daily 9 AM-5 PM; 801/259-8161) at the entrance, east of US-191 and five miles north of Moab, has maps, pamphlets, and displays on the geology and natural history of Arches. Beyond here the road switchbacks uphill past the sandstone skyline of **Park Avenue** before reaching a turnoff east to **The Windows**, whose dense concentration of arches and spires is required viewing, no matter how little time you have. Four miles beyond The Windows, a dirt road leads east to **Wolfe Ranch**, trailhead for **Delicate Arch**, the park's most postcard-worthy feature, a three-mile roundtrip hike. Three miles farther along the main road, **Fiery Furnace** is an otherwordly collection of narrow canyons, which despite the name is quite cool and shady; park rangers give guided walks here throughout the summer. At the far end of the road there's a first-come, first-served **campground** ($10) and a two-mile trail leading to **Devil's Garden**, where you can see **Landscape Arch**, the park's largest (and second largest in the world, by about a foot)—291 feet across and 105 feet high.

JOHN WESLEY POWELL AND THE CANYONS OF THE COLORADO RIVER

Of the many chronicles of the exploration of America's western frontier, few have stood the test of time better than those written by John Wesley Powell, who led the first expedition down the Colorado River through the canyons of Utah and Arizona. Until Powell's journey, the entire Colorado Plateau region, roughly 200 miles wide and some 500 miles long, was a large blank space on the map, simply labeled "Unexplored."

Powell's life story reads like something out of Horatio Alger. Born in upstate New York in 1834, "Wes" Powell grew up in the Midwest and attended various frontier colleges where he taught himself the fundamentals of geography, geology, and other natural sciences. Volunteering for service in the Civil War, he rose to the rank of major despite losing the lower part of his right arm at the Battle of Shilo. After the war he took up a position as professor of geology in Illinois, and led summer research trips to the Rocky Mountains in search of fossils.

In 1869, thanks to his wartime friendship with then-President Grant, he secured a small measure of federal funding for an ambitious survey of the Colorado River and its as-yet unexplored canyons. Powell organized a party of 10 men, who set off in four boats from the newly completed Union Pacific railroad at Green River, Wyoming, on May 24, 1869. Three months, 900 miles, one mutiny, and many near-disasters later, Powell and party emerged at the mouth of the Grand Canyon, the first people to pass through the canyon by river. To this day, Powell's enthusiastic and painstakingly accurate accounts of these magnificent red-rock canyons are the most readable and evocative descriptions of the region—required reading for any interested traveler.

Moab

Driving across southern Utah, you have two main options: race along I-70 and get somewhere else in a hurry, or slow down and search out the truly unforgettable scenery the state has to offer. One of the best places to base yourself for an exploration of the region is Moab (pop. 3,971), an old uranium mining town that's located 30 miles south of the freeway, surrounded by two national parks (Arches and Canyonlands) and hundreds of thousands of acres of desert wilderness.

Thanks to *Outside* magazine and the recent mania for outdoor athleticism, in the past five years Moab has experienced a massive tourist boom—Edward Abbey, cantankerous poet of the Southwest who wrote his first book, *Desert Solitaire,* about a season spent at nearby Arches National Park, would probably turn in his grave if he saw the gangs of Lycra-clad mountain bikers milling around Moab's Main Street T-shirt stores and brewpubs. But despite the addition of fast-food franchises and hundreds of new motel rooms, Moab is still a dusty little back-of-beyond hamlet, albeit one that gives easy access to the wilds nearby.

If you're not prepared to camp out in the backcountry (if you are, see Arches and Canyonlands for details), Moab has the usual franchised motels, including a **Days Inn**, a **Travelodge**, a **Ramada**, and a **Super 8**, plus local ones like the **Apache**, 166 South 400 E (801/259-5727 or 800/228-6882), where John Wayne slept while filming *Rio Bravo* here in 1950. Budget travelers will appreciate the **Lazy Lizard Hostel,**

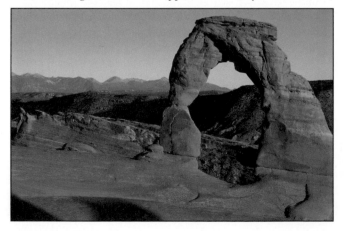

Delicate Arch at Arches National Park

1213 S. Hwy-191 (801/259-6057), which costs $7 for a bed but lacks air conditioning; showers for nonguests cost just $2.

Eat healthy veggie fare on the patio of **Honest Ozzie's,** open daily 7 AM-10 PM in summer at 60 N. 100 West Street, or enjoy a gourmet dinner at the upscale **Center Cafe** at 92 E. Center Street. **Cattleman's Restaurant,** a mile south of town at 1991 S. Main Street (US-191), is a 24-hour coffee shop.

For westbound travelers, there's a helpful Utah state **Welcome Center** (daily 8 AM-8 PM in summer, 9 AM-5 PM in winter) on I-70 at Thompsons Springs, 39 miles west of the Colorado border.

For more information on visiting the Moab area, contact the **Grand County Travel Council** (800/635-6622), or stop by the very helpful **Moab Information Center** (daily 8 AM-9 PM; 801/259-8825) at Main and Center in the middle of town. There you can pick up a free copy of *Moab Happenings,* which lists accommodations, restaurants, local events, and recreation opportunities—from mountain-bike trails to river-rafting expeditions.

The prettiest route east from Moab, Hwy-128, winds along the broad and brown Colorado River past 25 miles of swimming, kayaking, and camping spots. Hwy-128 links up with I-70 23 miles west of the Colorado border at junction 212, near the former sheep-ranching center of **Cisco,** a ghostly old US-50 crossroads abandoned after completion of the interstate—the decaying old buildings forming a perfect backdrop for some post-apocalyptic MTV video.

ACROSS COLORADO

Driving across southern Colorado on US-50 takes you through almost every landscape landlocked North America has to offer. From the geological wonderland of the Colorado River plateau, which stretches west into Utah, the route climbs up and over the 13,000-foot Rocky Mountains, which form a formidable wall down the center of the state. Continuing east, the alpine meadows, deeply etched river canyons, and snow-covered peaks of the southern Rockies fade away into the flat, agricultural prairies that stretch east across the middle of the country. While there is considerable ranching and farming, outdoor recreation—fishing, hiking, skiing, and mountain biking—is the basis for the economy, and the region is well provided with tourist facilities, especially in the mountainous middle.

Grand Junction

Thirty miles east of the Utah border, US-50 diverges from the high-speed I-70 freeway at the city of Grand Junction (pop. 29,034) on the Colorado River. After all the desert that surrounds it, Grand Junction feels much bigger than you'd expect, with its thriving old downtown, complete with cobblestoned streets, odd bits of outdoor sculpture—and tons of free parking. Catering to passing traffic, Grand Junction's I-70 frontage has all the motels and places to eat you could want. Downtown holds one really nice older place, the **Hotel Melrose** at 337 Colorado Avenue (970/242-9636), which has clean and comfortable rooms from $20, $25 with private bathroom—just look for the red neon sign. More complete listings are available from the **visitor center** off I-70 at exit 31 (970/244-1480).

Like the rest of western Colorado and eastern Utah, the Grand Junction area is rich in two things: the scenic splendor of rivers and red-rock canyons, and fossilized dinosaurs, a fine array of which are on display in the **Museum of Western Colorado** (Tues.-Sat. 10 AM-5 PM; $2), downtown at 248 S. 4th Street and in their "Dinosaur Valley" faux fossil beds, two blocks away at 362 Main Street.

Colorado National Monument

Rising nearly 2,000 feet above the Colorado River, southwest of Grand Junction, the brilliantly colored cliffs of Colorado National Monument are simply impossible to miss. Deep canyons, alive with piñon pines and cottonwood trees, nestle at the foot of sheer rock walls, at the top of which you get panoramic views over miles and miles of the Colorado Plateau. The 23-mile-long **Rim Rock Drive** winds along the tops of the cliffs, giving quick access to numerous trails for up-close looks at the various layers and hues of sandstone and shale, which have eroded over the eons into masses of sculpted stone.

To reach the monument from US-50 in downtown Grand Junction, follow Grand Avenue west to Broadway (Hwy-340) across the river; the monument's main entrance is four miles southeast of town, and there's another, off I-70 exit 19, at the northern end of the park. Both are very well signed, and an entry fee of $5 per car is charged, though cyclists foolhardy enough to tackle the steep climb are usually waved through for free.

There's a large **visitor center** (daily 9 AM-5 PM; 970/858-3617) at the main entrance, and a basic **campground** ($10) four miles from the northern entrance to the monument, near the top of the Book Cliffs.

Delta

From Grand Junction, US-50 briefly becomes a four-lane freeway, then reverts to two lanes following the Gunnison River as far as Delta (pop. 3,789). The half-dozen building-sized murals of elk and local agricultural products support Delta's claim that it is "The City of Murals," but the biggest attraction to travelers is the reconstructed **Fort Uncompaghre** (10 AM-4 PM Wed.-Sun.; $3), at the confluence of the Gunnison and Uncompaghre Rivers on the northwest side of town. One of the best and most authentic "living history" museums in the country, the city-sponsored fort re-creates the lifestyles of trappers and traders who first settled in the western Rocky Mountains in the early 1820s. Ed Maddox, the fort's well-versed live-in guide, takes you around the small palisaded compound, discussing the historical context of the fur trade while demonstrating (and encouraging visitors to take part in) the arts and crafts necessary for frontier life: metalworking, tanning, and tomahawk-throwing, not to mention hunting, shooting, and fishing.

The New Deal-era documentary photography project, which included Walker Evans and Dorothea Lange and which provides most of the frontispieces to the chapters in this book, was directed by **Roy Stryker**, who spent his youth on a ranch outside Montrose.

Delta has its fair share of motels (including a **Best Western**) and fast-food places. It's also home to a classic piece of roadside Americana: the solid-stone cabins of the **Westways Court Motel**, on US-50 in the center of town.

Southeast of Delta, US-50 runs along the banks of the Uncompaghre River, passing lots of farms and one very large Louisiana-Pacific lumber mill at Olathe, midway to Montrose.

Montrose

With the San Juan Mountains standing out to the south, and Black Canyon just up the road, Montrose, a farming community of some 9,000 souls that spreads from the heart of the fertile Uncompaghre (pronounced "un-com-PA-gray") Valley, makes a good base for exploring the region.

Though the town itself is less charming than many others in the region (it's roughly twice as big but only half as interesting as Delta, for example), it does have plenty of motels and places to eat, especially along US-50 east of downtown.

Eight miles east of Montrose, Hwy-347 turns off north toward the Black Canyon of the Gunnison National Monument.

Black Canyon of the Gunnison National Monument

Some of the hardest and oldest rocks on earth form the sheer walls of 2,000-foot-deep Black Canyon of the Gunnison, the deepest and most impressive gorge in the state. The river cutting through the canyon falls faster than any other in North America—dropping 2,150 feet in under 50 miles—and the canyon bottom is so rugged that there are no trails along it. Unless you're a serious mountaineer, you'll have to content yourself with looking down into it from the rim, which is accessible on the north side via Hwy-92, and from US-50 on the south via Hwy-347. The **visitor center** on the south rim provides details on hiking trails and camping, and can tell you more than you ever wanted to know about the canyon's unique geology: for instance, unlike the Grand Canyon with its layers of exposed rock, the Black Canyon is basically one solid hunk of stone.

Gunnison and Crested Butte

Upstream from the Black Canyon turnoff, US-50 parallels the Gunnison River, renowned for its excellent trout fishing and kayaking, though sadly the once-raging waters have been backed up behind a series of dams to form an ugly, 15 mile-long reservoir. Midway along, the highway crosses Blue Mesa Dam. At the dam, a scenic detour, Hwy-92, cuts off north around the Black Canyon of the Gunnison National Monument, while US-50 continues climbing toward Gunnison (pop. 4,636). A crossroads town with the only airport for miles, Gunnison is made livelier than many Colorado towns by the presence of Western State College, whose students were responsible for the huge "W" that fills a mountainside north of town. To get a feel for Gunnison, stop by the lively **Steaming Bean** coffeehouse, downtown off US-50 at the Hwy-135 junction.

If you're taken with the scenery around Gunnison and want to see more, head north along Hwy-135 and the Gunnison River to the area's skiing and mountain-biking center, Crested Butte (pop. 898), 25 miles away. As in Telluride and Aspen, this 100-year-old gold-mining camp won a second lease on life thanks to tourism, though compared to other Colorado places Crested Butte is low-key and somewhat cheaper; it also has some of the best restaurants in the state, ac-

The first explorers to pass through this part of the Rockies were the Spanish missionaries **Domínguez and Escalante,** in 1776.

cording to the Denver *Post* and others. For details, contact the **chamber of commerce** (970/349-6438 or 800/545-4505) on the south side of town.

Heading east up Monarch Pass, US-50 passes through a gorgeous alpine landscape of meadows and cattle ranches.

Monarch Pass

East of Gunnison, the landscape changes swiftly as US-50, and a few masochistic cyclists, climb steeply toward 11,312-foot Monarch Pass. The pass marks the highest point on US-50 and straddles the Continental Divide; the 30 feet of annual snowfall on the east side of the pass end up in the Atlantic, while (in theory, at least) moisture falling farther west makes its way to the Pacific. There's a ski area here in winter, and in summer you can ride a **tram** (daily 8 AM-6 PM; $5) or hike to a nearby summit for a 360-degree view over the Rocky and Sangre de Cristo Mountains.

Salida

Sitting alongside the Arkansas River at the eastern foot of Monarch Pass, Salida (pop. 4,737; elev. 7038) is an old railroad town gradually switching over to the tourist trade. Close your eyes to the sprawl of Wal-Marts and McDonald's along US-50, and follow 1st Street along the river to the historic downtown. Here, a half-dozen brick buildings house a slightly hippyish range of cafes—the **Laughing Ladies** and the **First Street Cafe** are both good bets—and outdoor supply shops, including **Headwaters**, 228 N. F Street (719/539-4506) right along the river, which rents and sells mountain bikes and kayaks and is the best source of information on the area's wealth of recreational opportunities. The comfortable **Manhattan Hotel** (719/539-3138), a B&B, shares the historic building. A new **Days Inn** and a slew of other places to sleep line US-50.

East of Salida, river rafters can be seen riding the rapids of the Arkansas River for most of the next 45 miles. Steeply walled sandstone gorges alternate with broad meadows and sagebrush plains all the way to Royal Gorge.

Royal Gorge

It would be easy to object to the rampant commercialism of Royal Gorge (daily 7 AM-6 PM; $10), but if you don't mind seeing impressive works of humankind amidst a stupendous show of nature's prowess, I heartily recommend a visit. The gorge itself is unforgettable, its sheer red granite cliffs dropping over 1,000 feet straight down to the Arkansas River, and the experience is enhanced by a barrage of civil engineering feats, including aerial trams, incline railways, and an impossibly delicate suspension bridge, all enabling visitors to experience the area in diverse ways. You can look down from the rim, dangle from a gondola across to the other side, and from there follow a short nature trail that offers good views of Pike's Peak.

Walk back across the wooden planks of the bridge—which is the highest in the world, but feels like a rickety old seaside pier—then drop down on a funicular to the gorge's bottom, where you can stand alongside the raging river, listening to the roar or admiring the famous Denver and Rio Grande Railroad line that passes through the gorge, in places suspended out over the river from the solid rock walls.

The main problem with Royal Gorge, apart from the steep admission fee, is that to get there you have to run a gauntlet of some of the tackiest tourist traps in creation, worst of which is the self-proclaimed "Real Historic Buckskin Joe—Gunfights and Hangings Daily." Similarly hyped outfits line the well-marked, two mile-long road to Royal Gorge, which cuts south from US-50 eight miles west of Cañon City.

From US-50, one of the West's most scenic (unpaved but easily passable) drives, Phantom Canyon Road, 25 miles west of Pueblo and seven miles east of Cañon City, winds north to the old mining camp, now prosperous gambling town, of **Cripple Creek.** Looping back to US-50 on similarly scenic Shelf Road, the 60-mile roundtrip takes at least three hours.

Cañon City

One of the last remaining Wild West towns in the lower 48 states, Cañon City (pop. 12,687) is carved out of the eastern flank of the Rocky Mountains. Over a mile high and surrounded by a ring of 14,000-foot peaks, Cañon City's short Main Street, a block north of US-50, is lined by workaday saddle shops, gun shops, book

Cripple Creek's first newspaper office, 1892

shops, and saloons (eight in four blocks!). But the local economy prospers not so much from tourism as from prisons: 14 in all, including Colorado's newest maximum-security penitentiary, and its oldest, the **Territorial Prison** (daily 9 AM-5 PM; $3) at the west end of Main Street, in which 32 cells have been preserved as a somewhat gruesome but compelling museum.

Cañon City's main attraction is the surrounding scenery, particularly the views along **Skyline Drive**, accessible from just west of town. It's a three-mile, one-way drive across the top of an 800-foot hill, as close to riding a roller coaster as you're ever likely to get while inside a passenger car. Royal Gorge to the west (which the city owns and operates; see above) makes a good base, with a few moderately priced motels like the **Pioneer**, 201 Main Street (719/269-1745) next to the old prison, a **Days Inn**, and a **Best Western**. Breakfast at the **Waffle Wagon**, tucked away at 315 Royal Gorge Boulevard (US-50), and enjoy a burger and milk shake at the **Burger Baron** farther east.

According to the WPA *Guide to Colorado,* the poet **Joaquin Miller,** who served as mayor, judge, and minister in Cañon City's early days, wanted to change its name to Oreodelphia, to highlight the region's many gold mines. Local miners, however, protested, insisting that "the place is a canyon, and it's goin' to be called Cañon City."

Pueblo

At the foot of the mountains, 38 miles east of Cañon City and 150 miles west of the Kansas border, the heavily industrialized city of Pueblo (pop. 98,640) spreads to both sides of the Arkansas River. Colorado's third-largest city, Pueblo was founded by legendary black fur-trapper **Jim Beckwourth** in 1842, but the town really grew in the 1870s following the arrival of the railroad and the discovery nearby of vast amounts of coal. Steel mills, including some of the largest west of the Mississippi, still stand around the fringes of the pleasant, tree-lined city center, but with the mountains so close there's little here worth stopping for. US-50 bypasses the north edge of town, crossing the I-25 freeway with its usual phalanx of motels, including a **Motel 6**, a **Holiday Inn**, and a **Super 8**, and fast-food franchises.

For the next 50 miles east of Pueblo, an impressive backdrop of snowcapped Rocky Mountains rises to the west, while two-lane US-50 itself is lined by roadside stands selling fruits, flowers, and vegetables. US-50 becomes a divided four-lane freeway at **Rocky Ford**, a small and quiet farming community that comes alive every August during a celebration of its nationally known cash crop, cantaloupes.

La Junta

For eastbound travelers La Junta (pop. 7,637), a busy railroad town on the banks of the Arkansas River, is where we begin tracing the historic Santa Fe Trail. The name La Junta, which means "the junction," is apt, since the town has long been a key crossroads, first on the Santa Fe Trail and now as the division between the main line and the Denver branch of the Santa Fe Railroad, and as the junction of US-50 and US-350. Besides gas stations and a good range of places to eat (Mexican restaurants are a particular strength), La Junta also offers the excellent **Koshare Indian Museum** (Tues.-Sun. 9 AM-5 PM; $2), on the campus of Otero Junior College on the south side of town.

Unfortunately for westbound US-50 travelers, La Junta also marks the spot where the "Mountain Branch" of the Santa Fe Trail finally cuts away to the south, following what's now US-350 through the Comanche National Grassland and con-

SANTA FE TRAIL

For over half a century, beginning in the 1820s and lasting until the railroads were completed in the 1880s, the Santa Fe Trail was the primary link between the U.S. and the Spanish and Mexican Southwest. Running from the Missouri River ports around present-day Kansas City, the trail angled along the banks of the Arkansas River, splitting west of what's now Dodge City into two routes: the Mountain Branch, which US-50 follows, and the quicker but more danger-ous Cimarron Cut-off, across the arid plains of the Jornado del Muerto. The two branches rejoined before climbing the Sangre de Cristo Mountains into what was then, as it is now, the capital of the Southwest, Santa Fe.

Unlike many of the routes across the Wild West frontier, the Santa Fe Trail was established by commercial traders rather than emigrant pioneers, and travel along it was active in both directions: merchants from the U.S. brought manufactured goods by the wagonload, which they exchanged for Mexican silver. First blazed by trader William Becknell in 1821, the year the newly in-dependent Republic of Mexico opened the border (which Spain had kept closed), the 750-mile-long trail was surveyed by the U.S. government in 1826, and traffic increased slowly until the Mexican-American War brought Santa Fe, and all the land in between, under U.S. control. Military forts were estab-lished to protect traders from the marauding Comanche and other native tribes; at the time of the Civil War commerce along the trail reached at peak, with over 5,000 wagons making the trek to Santa Fe, carrying over $50 mil-lion worth of trade goods. The extension of the railroads across the Great Plains in the 1870s diminished the importance of the trail, and by 1880, when the Santa Fe railroad reached Santa Fe itself, the trail became a part of history.

(continues on next page)

THE SANTA FE TRAIL

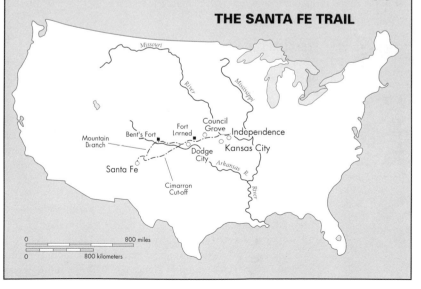

Though US-50 follows the Santa Fe Trail almost exactly, from Las Animas east to Kansas City, very little remains apart from outposts like Bent's Fort and Fort Larned and a few all-but-invisible stretches of old wagon ruts. Numerous plaques mark historic sites, and it's still possible to get a powerful sense of what the trail might have been like—provided you take the time to park the car and walk even a few hundred yards in the footsteps that crossed here a century ago.

The following are some of the most evocative sites along the Santa Fe Trail, west to east.

Santa Fe: The oldest city in North America, preserving a vivid taste of its Spanish, Mexican, and American past.

Bent's Fort: A reconstructed adobe trading post along the banks of the Arkansas River in the Rocky Mountain foothills. See below for more.

Fort Larned: A well-preserved U.S. Army fortress, intact since the 1850s and protecting a fine set of wagon ruts. See page 550 for more.

Council Grove: The last American town on the trail west, hardly changed since the heyday of the trail. See pages 552-553 for more.

Westport: Now surrounded by suburban Kansas City, this was the real start of the trail from the 1840s on.

Independence: The original start of the Santa Fe and the Oregon Trails, with a fine museum detailing the westward movements. See page 555 for more.

tinuing over Raton Pass into New Mexico and on to Santa Fe. We don't cover the rest of the route, though for Santa Fe itself contact the visitor center (505/984-6760 or 800/777-2489).

William Bent ran Bent's Fort on the Arkansas River from 1833 to 1848. Besides minding the store, Bent served as an unofficial ambassador to area tribes.

Bent's Old Fort

From La Junta, an interesting quick detour off US-50, Hwy-194 runs along the north bank of the Arkansas River to one of Colorado's most evocative historic sites, Bent's Old Fort (daily 8 AM-6 PM in summer, 9 AM-4 PM in winter; $2). It lies eight miles east of La Junta, or 15 miles west of Las Animas. From 1833, when it was built by the fur traders William and Charles Bent, until 1848, when war with Mexico and increasing unrest among the local Arapahoe, Apache, and Cheyenne tribes put an end to their business, Bent's Fort was the Southwest's most important outpost of white civilization and a stopping place for travelers, trappers, and explorers, including John C. Frémont, Francis Parkman, and just about every other Wild West luminary.

Though it was abandoned and left to decay for over 100 years, the large adobe fort has been authentically rebuilt by the National Park Service, and now stands as a palpable reminder of the early years of the frontier era. Thick adobe walls, 15 feet tall with circular bastions at the corners, protect a roughly 100-square-foot compound. Rangers dressed in period clothing work as wheelsmiths, coopers, and carpenters, or process the many buffalo robes and beaver pelts piled up in storerooms.

Las Animas

The farming community of Las Animas (pop. 2,481) takes its name from the Arkansas River tributary originally known as Río de las Ánimas Perdidas en Purgatorio—the River of Lost Souls. Las Animas is also the place where, on November 15, 1806, Lt. Zebulon Pike first laid eyes on the Rocky Mountains peak that now bears his name—Pike's Peak, 120 miles to the northwest.

Beyond Las Animas, US-50 continues its gradual descent across the Rocky Mountains foothills. The area was first known as Big Timbers for the tall cottonwoods that grew here along the Arkansas River, though most of these trees were cut down soon after the arrival of white settlers. In the 1840s and 1850s, local Cheyenne, Arapaho, Kiowa, and Apache tribes bartered bison hides at William Bent's trading post, and Wild West explorer **Kit Carson** died here on May 23, 1868, in his family home at what was then the U.S. Army's Fort Lyon, south of present-day US-50. Carson's remains were later moved to Taos, New Mexico, and his lands were flooded after the Arkansas River was dammed to form the large John Martin Reservoir, which stretches most of the way downstream to Lamar.

Lamar

Following the Arkansas River downstream toward the Kansas border, US-50 runs along what was known as the "Mountain Branch" of the Santa Fe Trail, a longer but safer alternative to the main route along the Cimarron Cut-off. There's little to see here apart from acres and acres of irrigated farmlands, though the region's main town, Lamar (pop. 8,343), is worth a quick stop. Very good Mexican-American food is available all day long at the **Main Street Cafe** in the center of town. A block away, the handy state-run **Welcome Center** (719/336-3483) in the old Santa Fe depot on the east side of Main Street (US-50) has reams of information on the area and the rest of Colorado.

Lamar's **KCC 93.3 FM** plays good country music and broadcasts Colorado Rockies and Broncos games.

ACROSS KANSAS

In its nearly 500 miles across Kansas, US-50 and its selected variants pass across the agricultural heartland of America, winding through dozens of small farming towns that dot the generally level landscape. (Locals definitely seem to prefer the word "level" to the equally accurate "flat," if only because it sounds less boring.) This is the heart of the "Wheat Belt," where most of the country's grain is grown—as much as half the bread baked in America is made from Kansas wheat—and it's also prime cattle country, with towns like Dodge City and many less famous ones maintaining their historic dependence on cows and cowboys.

All the way across Kansas, we follow almost exactly in the footsteps of the trappers and traders who braved the Santa Fe Trail along the western frontier, stopping at preserved old outposts like Fort Larned and Council Grove while tracking the few more evocative remnants of this pioneer Wild West corridor.

The dividing line between central and mountain time zones is 15 miles west of Garden City. Set your clocks accordingly.

Garden City and Holcomb

Apart from numerous feedlots fattening cattle for slaughter, and a few wheat, corn, and beet farms fed by water diverted from the Arkansas River, there's not much to see in the 120 miles of barren plains that stretch east from the Colorado border. Garden City, the region's biggest town, is at about the halfway point and has the attraction of a 4,000-acre **Buffalo Preserve**, southwest of town off US-83. There are also gas stations, motels, and fast-food places, and best of all, a truly huge public **swimming pool**: 337 by 218 feet filled with over 2.5 million gallons of water. The pool is near the Arkansas River in Finnup Park, on S. 4th Street, and it's free!

On the western outskirts of Garden City, US-50 runs through the meatpacking town of Holcomb, notori-

Garden City was founded in 1879 by C.J. "Buffalo" Jones, one of many larger-than-life characters who populated the Wild West frontier. One of his many achievements was the capture and preservation of a small herd of buffalo, the descendents of which populate the Buffalo Preserve on the south side of town.

ous as the site of the *In Cold Blood* murders documented by Truman Capote. In 1959, Perry Smith and Richard Hickock ruthlessly and without provocation killed the entire Clutter family during a robbery attempt; both of them were eventually captured, convicted, and executed.

Dodge City

One of the most notorious places on the Wild West frontier, Dodge City (pop. 21,129) can be something of a disappointment if you come here looking for a rip-roaring frontier town. In its heyday, which lasted roughly from 1872, when the railroad arrived, to 1884, when the cattle drives were effectively banned, Dodge City was the undisputed capital of the buffalo-hunting, cattle-driving Wild West, with as many as 100 million bison hides and seven million head of cattle shipped out from here in that decade alone. At the same time, Dodge City was known as "Hell on the Plains," famous for its gunfights and general lawlessness, despite marshals like **Bat Masterson** and **Wyatt Earp** keeping order and planting bad guys in the Boot Hill cemetery above town.

However, almost nothing in Dodge City survives from that era. Boot Hill, for example, was bought by the city and is now the site of a small office building. Most of what you see dates from the 1920s at the earliest. Dodge City is still a busy farming and cattle-ranching community, with extensive stockyards and slaughterhouses surrounding the small downtown area, but for travelers there's little here apart from one of the Midwest's tackier tourist traps, the fake but fun **Boot Hill Museum** (daily 8 AM-8 PM in summer, shorter hours rest of the year; $6) and its re-created Front Street, where actors stage gunfights and "medicine shows" throughout the day; there's also an evening burlesque show, featuring "Miss Kitty and her Can Can Girls." Not surprisingly, Boot Hill is hard to miss, well marked on the west side of town, just north of the railroad tracks off Wyatt Earp Boulevard (US-50/56), the main route through town.

At Garden City, 50 miles west of Dodge City, US-50 crosses US-83, the "Road to Nowhere," which follows the 100th Meridian from Canada to Mexico. That chapter begins on page 124.

Near Cimarron, 32 miles east of Garden City and 16 miles west of Dodge City, the main track of the Santa Fe Trail crossed the Arkansas River and headed southwest across the waterless plain of the Jornada del Muerto on what was known as the **Cimarron Cut-off.** This desolate region is also where, in 1831 during the earliest days of the trail, legendary mountain man **Jedediah Strong Smith** was killed by a band of Comanche warriors.

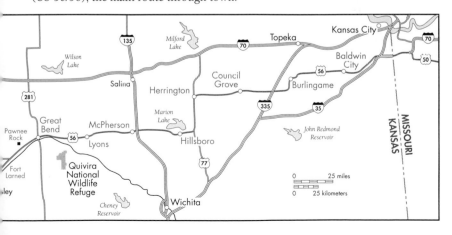

Dodge City sits atop the 100th Meridian, long considered the dividing line between East and West. It's also the approximate midpoint of the coast-to-coast journey.

Across the street from Boot Hill stands the **Kansas Teachers' Hall of Fame** (Sunday 11 AM-3 PM; free), with plaques and a wax museum remembering contributions to education in the state. (Yes, it is the first and only such place in the U.S.) Wyatt Earp Boulevard (US-50) also holds most of Dodge City's eating options, as well as large and popular **Econo Lodge** and **Super 8** motels.

West of Dodge City, the highway runs right on top of the historic Santa Fe Trail. One of the best-preserved sections of **trail ruts** is nine miles west of Dodge City, just past the Howell grain elevator. Marked by a large sign, the ruts lie in a rolling field 100 yards north of the parking area and are basically a broad depression in the soil, approximately 800 yards wide and two miles long.

Paralleling the mainline Santa Fe Railroad across the flattest, emptiest 50 miles of Kansas cornfields, east of Dodge City we follow US-50 as far as Kinsley, where we switch onto US-56 (old US-50) to follow the Santa Fe Trail.

Fort Larned

One of the best-preserved vestiges of the Santa Fe Trail, Fort Larned (daily 9 AM-5 PM; $1; 316/285-6911), now six miles west of US-56 via Hwy-156, was established in 1859, and for the next 20 years troops stationed here protected travelers on the Santa Fe Trail from the threat of attack by local Arapahoe and Cheyenne tribes. The fort also served a vital role in the many Indian Wars of 1860s, but by 1878, when the trail was no longer in active use, the fort was deactivated. It was sold and used as a ranch until 1960, but has survived the intervening years in excellent condition. Careful restoration by the National Park Service has made Fort Larned an excellent place to experience what the frontier really looked like, albeit from the military perspective.

Sandstone buildings, which replaced the original adobe after the end of the Civil War, surround a 400-square-foot parade ground, and interior rooms have been filled with accurate reproductions of original fixtures and fittings, ranging from barracks to blacksmith's shops to a large storehouse. A nearby farm preserves a set of ruts surviving from the Santa Fe Trail days, though you really need to have an active imagination to get much from them.

In between Fort Larned and US-56, the **Santa Fe Trail Museum and Cultural Center** (daily 9 AM-5 PM; $3; 316/285-2054) is a private, nonprofit museum focusing on the overall history of the Santa Fe Trail region. Diorama-like exhibits feature full-scale mock-ups of wagons and frontier trading posts, and behind the main building are a sod house and a one-room schoolhouse.

Back on US-56, the town of **Larned** has a typical crossroads collection of motels and McDonald's. There's also the unique **Central States Scout Museum**, 815 Broadway (Saturday and Sunday 9 AM-5 PM; $1), full of exhibits telling the story of Kansas Boy Scouts through the years.

Pawnee Rock

Just eight miles northeast of Larned, a half-mile north of US-56 and the Arkansas River, Pawnee Rock was once one of the most important landmarks on the Santa Fe Trail. However, so much of the original 60-foot-high tower of Dakota sandstone has been quarried—to build houses as well as the roadbed of the Santa Fe railroad—that it's little more than a stubby hump. But you can still get a grand view of the surrounding countryside from the easy trail that leads to the rock's much-diminished summit.

Great Bend

Spreading along the northern bank of the Arkansas River at the northernmost point on its sweep across central Kansas, Great Bend (pop. 15,427) was originally established as a fort along the Santa Fe Trail, but really began to grow after the railroad came through. As with Dodge City to the southwest, the arrival of the railroad in 1872 attracted cattle drovers from the Chisholm Trail, who turned Great Bend into a raucous Wild West town. It's now a quiet rural city, earning its livelihood from wheat farms and, since the 1930s, oil.

There's not a lot to see or do in Great Bend, though the outskirts of town are more promising, starting with the engaging **Barton County Historical Society Museum** (Tues.-Sun. 1-4 PM; $1; 316/793-5125), just south of the railroad tracks and the river along US-281. Farther afield, the Great Bend area holds two of the largest wildlife refuges in Kansas, **Cheyenne Bottoms** to the northeast and **Quivira** to the southeast, both of which offer excellent birdwatching opportunities.

Great Bend does have a fairly good range of places to eat, with franchise fast food supplemented by a handful of Mexican restaurants like **La Mexicana**, **La Estrella**, and the **Kiowa Kitchen**, all along 10th Street (US-56). The **Black Angus Steak Ranch**, 2920 10th Street serves excellent steaks as well as family-friendly breakfast and lunch. Along with a **Holiday Inn**, a **Best Western**, and a **Super 8**, another reliable place to stay in Great Bend is the **Traveler's Budget Inn**, 4200 W. 10th Street (316/793-5448), with double rooms for under $30.

Lyons

The farming, oil-drilling, and salt-mining town of Lyons (pop. 3,688), 30 miles due east of Great Bend, doesn't look much different from most other Kansas towns, but it has an unusually impressive history. There's a 150-foot-long intaglio serpent carved into the prairie eight miles northeast of town, and some Santa Fe Trail ruts, but the most compelling remains are those left behind by Coronado's expedition through the region in 1541, in search of the fabled golden city of Quivira. Exhibits on all of these, as well as Indian and pioneer American cultures, are displayed inside the modern, purpose-built **Rice County Historical Museum** (Mon.-Sat. 9 AM-5 PM, Sunday 1-5 PM; $1.50) at 105 W. Lyon Street, two blocks south of the landmark county courthouse off US-56.

From Great Bend, Hwy-96 and US-183 run 35 miles northwest to the town of Lacrosse, home to the **Kansas Barbed Wire Museum** at 202 W. 1st Street (913/222-2607).

Two miles west of Lyons along US-56, a large cross marks the site where Father Padilla, who accompanied Coronado on his expedition and returned the following year to convert the natives, was killed by unreceptive Indians, thereby becoming the first "Christian martyr" in the present-day USA.

McPherson

From a distance across the flat plains, the towering grain elevators make McPherson (pop. 12,422) look more impressive than it really is. Thirty-five miles east of

Lyons, it marks the junction of US-56 and the I-135 freeway between Salina and Wichita. You can fill the gas tank or get a bite to eat (all the usual franchise food places and gas stations are here).

The small **McPherson Museum**, well-marked in a residential district at 1130 Euclid Street (Tues.-Sun. 1-5 PM; donations; 316/241-5977), displays rooms furnished in typical turn-of-the-century Kansas style. It also holds the world's first man-made diamond, produced by Willard Hershey, a local chemistry teacher. More entertaining, if you happen upon one, are the many, irregularly scheduled public **auctions** held around town; fast-talking auctioneers take bids on various lots, ranging from real antiques to boxes of junk and cast-off clothes.

The gold medal-winning 1936 U.S. Olympic basketball team was formed by a company team at a McPherson oil refinery.

*The central Kansas farmlands around **Goessel** are home to the largest Mennonite community in the United States.*

Herrington and Hillsboro: Mennonite Country

One of the centers of the local Mennonite community, Hillsboro (pop. 2,704), 13 miles west of US-77, serves as market center for the area's highly productive farmlands. Tabor College, on the east side of town, is the most visible sign of the Mennonite presence; though it's a coed nondenominational college about half the students are local Mennonites.

The tidy town of Goessel (population 506), 15 miles southwest of Hillsboro, was also founded by Mennonite farmers, and now holds the worthwhile **Mennonite Heritage Center**, 200 N. Poplar Street (Tues.-Sat. 10 AM-5 PM, Sunday 1-5 PM; $3; 316/367-8200), where numerous buildings, including two schools, a barn, and a bank, have been moved for preservation. The flat black earth around Goessel is among the world's greatest producers of wheat, in particular the hearty hybrids able to withstand the Midwest winter. The original seed, known as "Turkey Red," was brought to Kansas in the early 1870s by Russian Mennonites who immigrated here after their 100-year exclusion from military service was rescinded.

Zigzagging east from Hillsboro and then north along US-77/US-56, after another 37 "level" miles US-56 reaches the town of Herrington, whose central square holds a monument to Father Padilla, part of Coronado's expedition that passed through southern Kansas in search of the mythical Golden City of Gran Quivira.

Council Grove

Just 75 miles southwest of the suburban sprawl of Kansas City, 25 miles west of the I-335 Kansas Turnpike, Council Grove (pop. 2,228) still looks much as it did over a century ago when, from the 1830s to the 1860s, it was the most important of all way stations on the Santa Fe Trail. Council Grove's lush maples and oaks were the last hardwoods available on the long route west across the treeless plain, which meant traders and travelers could make final repairs and stock up on spare axles and other essentials. It was also the western extent of "safe territory"; beyond here travelers were subject to frequent attacks by hostile Indians.

Nowadays the town proudly preserves its many historic sites, and in many ways serves as the most not-to-be-missed stop for modern travelers heading along the Santa Fe Trail. The sites of two of the most important trail icons, the **Council Oak** under which in 1825 the native Kansa and Osage Indians agreed to allow Americans to cross their territory, and the **Post Office Oak** that served as a natural mes-

BLUE HIGHWAYS TO PRAIRYERTH

After traveling 13,000 miles of back road through the nooks and crannies of 38 states to write his first book, the author of road trip classic *Blue Highways,* William Least Heat Moon, began work on a very different study. Straying no farther than the 744 square miles of Chase County, Kansas, Moon embarked upon what he termed a "deep map" of the area that sits atop the lush rolling Flint Hills, the nation's last remaining grand expanse of tall grass prairie, split by US-50 and the Santa Fe Railroad.

The result was the 1991 book *PrairyErth,* a 600-plus-page evocation of history and contemporary life in this otherwise unremarkable corner of the country, which Moon describes as being "five hours by interstates from home, eight hours if I follow a route of good cafe food." Combining folk history and contemporary anecdotes with captivating quotes from sundry novels, Native American legends, travel guides, essays, and old newspaper clippings, this unique project—which has been described as the nonfiction equivalent of the Great American Novel—manages to capture the rhythms of ranching life in the middle of the great American nowhere.

In order to follow the Santa Fe Trail, our US-50 route bypasses the whole of Chase County, but readers of either of William Least Heat Moon's books may want to make a short pilgrimage by following the I-35 Kansas Turnpike from Kansas City or Hwy-177 south from Council Grove.

sage center for early travelers, are marked along Main Street (US-56), east of the bridge over the small Neosho River. Four blocks west, the **Last Chance Store** at Main and Chautauqua Streets has served as a bank and a post office in the years since it was built in 1857.

In between, the banks, cafes, and stores along Main Street, which the Santa Fe Trail followed through town, make little obvious effort to cater to tourists, and the town basically goes about its day-to-day business without forgetting its extraordinary past. The **Hays House**, in the center of town at 112 W. Main Street (316/767-5911), lays fair claim to being the oldest restaurant west of the Mississippi; originally built as a frontier home, and later serving as a saloon, supply post, courthouse, and hotel, it has stood on this site since 1847. Now modernized, it is still the focus of the town's social and political life and is open all day—with excellent fried chicken. Across Main, the soda fountain inside the **Aldrich Apothecary** has good milk shakes. The best place to stay is the comfortable **Cottage House Hotel** at 25 N. Neosho (316/767-6828 or 800/727-7903).

Further information is available from the Council Grove **visitor center**, 313 W. Main Street (316/767-5882 or 800/732-9211).

Writing about US-50, *Blue Highways* author **William Least Heat Moon** has said that "for the unhurried, this little-known highway is the best national road across the middle of the United States."

Kinsley, Kansas, calls itself Midway, USA. It lies equidistant from New York to San Francisco.

Burlingame and Baldwin City

Between Council Grove and Kansas City, US-56 passes through the lovely cattle-ranching grasslands of the northern Flint Hills, zigzagging at 90-degree angles through one-time coal-mining towns like Worden, Overbrook, and Scranton. Burlingame (pop. 2,735), the largest of this bunch, is noteworthy for its very broad, brick-paved 20-mph Main Street (US-56), lined by diverse 100-year-old buildings painted with a barrage of signs advertising player pianos as well as the usual liquor, food, and auto parts.

The **Kaw Mission State Historic Site,** in Council Grove five blocks north of Main on Mission Street, was built by Methodist missionaries in 1851 as a school for local Indian children. Students included Charles Curtis, who served as U.S. vice president from 1929 to 1933.

At the northeast edge of the Flint Hills, 13 miles west of the I-35 freeway from Kansas City, US-56 skirts the leafy, brick-paved streets of Baldwin City (pop. 2,961), a small town that was once a main rest-and-repair stop on the Santa Fe Trail—four days' travel west of Independence. In 1858, the first college on the western frontier was founded here in a three-story sandstone building now preserved as "The Castle," alongside a combination general store and post office on the east side of the pleasant campus of Methodist-run **Baker University.** The library (Mon.-Fri. 8 AM-5 PM; free) three blocks west displays the **Quayle Collection** of rare religious texts, including clay tablets dating from Old Testament times, and a range of hand-bound bibles, arranged to trace the development of printing techniques and typography styles.

For the rest of the way east to Kansas City, US-56 parallels the I-35 freeway across lush rolling grassland pastures and farms, marked in places by signs reading "Old US-50." Along this route, two miles west of Gardner, an historical marker stands on the site where the westbound Santa Fe and Oregon Trails once divided: For many years, a crude wooden sign pointed travelers in the proper direction: left to Santa Fe, right to Oregon.

ACROSS MISSOURI

From Kansas City, and its noteworthy neighboring towns of Independence and Liberty, US-50 makes a lazy trek across Missouri's rolling prairie farmlands, stopping at the historic railroad town of Sedalia before reaching the state capital, Jefferson City, roughly midway across. Continuing east, climbing through second-growth hardwood forests of the Ozark uplands, US-50 is a slow and not particularly scenic road; we suggest following a similarly slow but more interesting detour, Hwy-100, which winds through a number of historic towns along the banks of the Missouri River before approaching St. Louis via the I-44 freeway.

More than anywhere else on this cross-country trek, to be honest if you're in any sort of a hurry you won't miss much by taking the 70-mph I-70 freeway straight across Missouri from Kansas City to St. Louis, 250 miles away.

For details on visiting Kansas City, see the Survival Guide on pages 692-693.

Independence

A quiet suburb lying on the northeast fringe of greater Kansas City, Independence (pop. 112,301) doesn't look like a special place, but it is. One of the country's most history-rich small cities, Independence came to life during the early years of the westward expansion, serving as the jumping-off point for the Santa Fe and later Oregon and California Trails.

A century later, Independence again gained prominence as the hometown of U.S. Pres. Harry Truman, who lived here from boyhood until his death in 1972.

Harry S. Truman

The city-run **National Frontier Trails Center** (Mon.-Sat. 9 AM-4:30 PM, Sunday 12:30-4:30 PM; $3), four blocks south of the town square at 318 W. Pacific Street, is one of the best museums dedicated to America's pioneers. Beginning with a brief account of Lewis and Clark, the exhibits explore the heyday of the Santa Fe Trail, which throughout the 1820s and 1830s made Independence the leading town on the western frontier. The later Oregon Trail, on which some 300,000 people left Independence for the West Coast, is recounted through an engagingly displayed series of diary entries and drawings made by pioneers.

While very little remains from the pioneer days, Independence has hardly changed since Harry Truman grew up here around the turn of the 20th century. The soda fountain where he held his first job, and the courtroom where he presided as judge, still stand in the town square. His home, northwest of the square at 219 N. Delaware Street, is open for **tours** (daily 9 AM-4 PM; $2), and the large **Harry S. Truman Library** (daily 9 AM-5 PM; $2) four blocks north contains his presidential papers, a replica of his White House office, and the gravesites of Truman and his wife Bess.

Clinton's Soda Fountain, at 100 W. Maple Street ("Where Harry Had His First Job"), still serves milk shakes and sandwiches. For chicken dinners and apple fritters, head 10 miles south of Independence to **Stephenson's Apple Farm Restaurant**, 16401 E. US-40 at Lee's Summit Road.

The antique-packed **House of Hoyt**, halfway between the Truman House and the Truman Library at 626 N. Delaware Street (816/461-7226), is a lovely place to stay, with the best B&B breakfasts (and the most comfortable front porch) in the Midwest. The **Serendipity B&B**, 116 S. Pleasant Street (816/833-47190), is more all-American, straight out of a century-old Sears, Roebuck and Co. catalog.

Liberty

Another ideally named small town on the fringes of Kansas City, Liberty (pop. 20,459) is worth a visit for rather different reasons. This is where, on February 13, 1866, **Jesse James** and his brother Frank staged the first-ever daylight bank holdup, getting away with over $60,000. The bank building itself, at 103 N. Water Street on the northwest corner of the preserved-in-amber town square, is pretty much as it was, complete with the vault, safe, and banknotes; it's now a small **museum** (Mon.-Sat. 9 AM-4 PM, Sunday noon-4 PM; $2).

Outlaw Jesse James grew up near Liberty.

A block north of the square stands another historic site, the oxymoronic **Liberty Jail** (daily 9 AM-9 PM; free) at 216 N. Main Street, where Mormon prophet Joseph Smith and his followers were imprisoned during the winter of 1838-39. It's a significant site for Mormons, and has been faithfully reconstructed.

Liberty also has a good place to eat: the **Fork and Spoon Cafe**, west of the square at 12 W. Kansas Street.

Sedalia

East of Kansas City the roadside along fast, four-lane US-50 is endless open, rolling prairie, most of it planted in wheat and corn. As with most of the West, early development here occurred along the railroad lines, which were constructed beginning in the 1850s; the region wasn't substantially settled until the Civil War years. Towns boomed when the trains arrived, but most went bust as the tracks were extended westward to Kansas City and beyond.

In 1867, the militant prohibitionist **Carry Nation** moved to the village of Holden, nine miles south of US-50 via Hwy-131, with her alcoholic first husband Dr. William Gloyd, who died the following year.

Sedalia hosts a **Scott Joplin Ragtime Festival** every June, and the annual **Missouri State Fair,** which attracts thousands of people here every August. For details, call the Sedalia visitor center (816/826-2222).

Sedalia (pop. 19,808), 75 miles east of Kansas City, was one of the few that survived, growing into a small city thanks to its position straddling the main line between St. Louis and Kansas City. Sedalia reached its peak of prosperity around 1900, when both the Missouri-Pacific and the Missouri-Texas railroads had their maintenance shops here. The empty storefronts downtown surrounded by secondhand farm equipment are perhaps misleading, since the town offers three worthwhile places to stop for food. **Eddie's** on Hwy-50 just west of Ohio (the main downtown street that the courthouse is on), a Sedalia establishment since 1937, serves steak burgers, with the steak ground fresh each day. The best homemade pie in Sedalia is at the **tea room** (open 11 AM-1:30 PM approximately, or until they run out of food) at the Maple Leaf Antique Mall. Go early for the best pie selection. **Le Maire's Cajun Seafood**, on S. 65 Hiway just south of 32nd Street, has great fried catfish, boiled shrimp, crablegs, frog legs, crayfish, and other swamp, creek, and seafood fare.

Sedalia's boisterous heyday is perhaps best recalled by the ragtime songs of composer **Scott Joplin**, who lived and worked here.

Jefferson City

Roughly at the center of the state, 130 miles west of St. Louis and 140 miles east of Kansas City on the south bank of the Missouri River, Jefferson City (pop. 35,481) is a strangely small and somnolent place. The handsome neo-classical **state capitol** (daily 8 AM-5 PM; free), modeled on the U.S. Capitol and completed in 1918, is the central landmark, rising from the river at the heart of town. Inside, the rotunda and ground floor area is packed with informative exhibits tracing the state's political and natural history, while hourly **guided tours** take in the entire building, including a famous mural by Thomas Hart Benton on the walls of the third-floor House Lounge.

Below the capitol, along the river and the railroad tracks, a trio of brick buildings from the mid-1800s, including one that still serves as the city's Amtrak station, are preserved in a parklike setting. On a knoll just east of here stands the Governor's Mansion, but otherwise there's precious little to see or do.

If you find yourself in Jefferson City, good salads, soups, and pasta dishes are available at **Madison's**, 216 Madison Street. The **Big Dipper** on High Street has ice cream and sandwiches. Both places are within a block of the capitol.

The great frontiersman **Daniel Boone** settled along the northern banks of the Missouri River in 1799, and lived near what's now the town of Defiance for the next 20 years until his death in 1820.

Hwy-100: Hermann and Washington

Turning off US-50 at Linn, 20 miles east of Jefferson City, Hwy-100 offers a more interesting and not much longer alternative to the uneventful US-50 route east to St. Louis. Following the Missouri River downstream, you eventually fetch up at the town of Hermann (pop. 2,754), founded by German immigrants in 1837. Surrounded by small wineries and standing right on the riverfront, Hermann reminds some visitors of a Rhine Valley village, its German heritage kept alive at the **Historic Hermann Museum** (daily 10 AM-5 PM; $1), housed in the old Deutsche Schule at 4th and Schiller Streets downtown.

East from Washington, Hwy-100 merges into the high-speed I-44 freeway, which runs roughly on top of historic Route 66. For more on Route 66, see the chapter beginning on page 626.

Another 30 miles downstream, or roughly 50 miles from the Gateway Arch at downtown St. Louis, the timeless town of Washington (pop. 10,704) rises on narrow streets above the broad Missouri River. Now packed with upscale restaurants and B&B inns—the **visitor center**, 323 W. Main Street (314/239-2715), has extensive listings—many of the town's balconied brick buildings date from the mid-1800s, when large numbers of Germans settled the region.

SCOTT JOPLIN: THE KING OF RAGTIME

Music is among the most mobile of the arts, equally affecting anywhere and anytime, but many forms are strongly identified with a given place and era. New Orleans means jazz, the Delta has the blues, Detroit will always be equated with the Motown sound, and if credit were given where credit is due, Sedalia, Missouri, would join the above places as the source of another classic African-American music—**ragtime.** The first ragtime tunes, so-called because of their ragged, syncopated rhythms, were played in the early 1890s, but later came into full flower out of the musical mind of Scott Joplin, the universally acclaimed king of ragtime.

Born in 1868 near Texarkana, Texas, to a former slave and freeborn mother, Scott Joplin was one of six children in a musical family. After moving around the Midwest throughout his youth, in the late 1890s Joplin settled in Sedalia, which was then a raucous railroad town, where he studied music theory at Sedalia's small black college. To pay his way, Joplin played piano at many of the clubs that lined Main Street in Sedalia, which had a reputation both for multiracial harmony and as an adult playground of bars and brothels catering to the many itinerant men passing through; as late as 1940, *Life* magazine said Sedalia still had one of the "most notorious red-light districts" in the Midwest.

One of these nightclubs gave its name to the *Maple Leaf Rag,* the composition that made Joplin's reputation and which, at a penny-per-sheet royalty, earned around $500 a year—enough to support him, but far from a fortune. Joplin later lived in St. Louis, where the home in which he wrote *The Entertainer* (the piece used as theme song in the movie *The Sting*) is preserved as a museum. Eventually Joplin ended up in New York, where he sought but failed to find support for his increasingly complex orchestral and operatic compositions. Scott Joplin died, poor and all-but-forgotten, on April 1, 1917.

The small **Washington Historical Society Museum**, 314 W. Main Street (Saturday and Sunday 10 AM-5 PM; free), has exhibits on early settlers and the town's current main industry (after tourism, that is): manufacturing **corn-cob pipes.**

For details on visiting St. Louis, see the Survival Guide on pages 714-715.

ACROSS ILLINOIS

US-50 runs straight across over 150 miles of Southern Illinois's pancake-flat farmlands—acres of wheat, corn, and soybeans as far as the eye can see. For much of the way, US-50 follows the "Trace Road," a slightly raised causeway originally traced across the swampy marshlands by the same prehistoric people who built the enigmatic mounds at Cahokia, which still stand in the eastern suburbs of St. Louis. Midway across Illinois, US-50 passes through the quirkily historic town of Salem (birthplace of two American icons: William Jennings Bryan and Miracle Whip), then crosses over the Wabash River into Indiana.

Cahokia Mounds, a massive prehistoric ruin marooned in the suburbs of northeast St. Louis, is described more fully in the Great River Road chapter on page 199.

Lebanon

From the dangerous and decrepit industrial districts of East St. Louis, US-50 follows the I-64 freeway east from St. Louis across the flat prairie, whose fertile alluvial soil has earned it the nickname "Little Egypt." The highway parallels the Illinois Central Railroad through a dozen small towns, the most significant of which is Lebanon (pop. 3,688), 20 miles east of the Mississippi River. An attractive town, with a number of stately mansard-roofed Victorian-era commercial buildings now housing antique shops along Main Street and St. Louis Street (US-50), Lebanon grew up around the bucolic campus of McKendree College, founded here in 1828 and one of the oldest in Illinois.

East of Carlyle, 22 miles west of Salem, a very delicate suspension bridge built in 1860 still stands just north of the more modern US-50 highway crossing the Kaskaskia River.

The best reason to stop, however, is the small **Mermaid House Hotel**, on US-50 at 114 E. St. Louis Street. Charles Dickens, who visited the area to see the rich but muddy prairie east of town, stayed here for a night in 1842, and described it in *American Notes* as comparing "favorably with any village ale house of a homely kind in England." After spending most of the past 150 years as a private home, the building is now undergoing restoration, but is open for tours (Saturday and Sunday 10 AM-4 PM; donations).

Salem

Halfway across Illinois, just east of the busy I-57 freeway, US-50 cuts through the center of Salem (pop. 7,470), a historically fascinating if visually less-than-thrilling city best known as the birthplace and boyhood home of William Jennings Bryan. The turn-of-the-century politician and orator, who served as leader of the Democratic Party for 15 years, prosecuted the so-called "Monkey Trial" of 1925 and led the successful attack on Tennessee schoolteacher John Scopes (who, coincidentally, was also born and raised in Salem) for breaking a local ban on teaching evolution. Bryan was born in 1860 in the small frame house at 408 S. Broadway, four blocks south of Main Street (US-50). It has been preserved as a small **museum** (daily except Thursday 1-5 PM; free). There's a small statue of Bryan, crafted by Mount Rushmore sculptor Gutzon Borglum, on Broadway a half-mile north of Main Street, in front of the Roller-Rama skating rink.

Besides William Jennings Bryan, Salem has given America two very important things. The **G.I. Bill of Rights**, also known as the G.I. Bill, which entitled military veterans to subsidized education and other services, was first proposed by the local American Legion branch before being signed into law in 1944. **Miracle Whip** was created at Max Crosset's Cafe on Main Street before being sold to Kraft Foods (for $300) in 1931.

The birthplace of Miracle Whip, Max Crossett's Cafe, is now a parking lot at the center of Salem.

Salem has a good place to eat, **Austin's Restaurant** on US-50 just west of town, and two good inexpensive motels, the **Lakewood** (618/548-2785) and the **Continental** (618/548-3090), next to each other on US-50 just east of town.

Olney and Lawrenceville

The flat farmlands of southeast Illinois are dotted with occasional oil wells and signs painted on barn sides encouraging travelers to "Chew Mail Pouch Tobacco," but towns are few and far between. The first of these is the attractive town of Olney (pop. 8,664). Besides boasting a large number of grand old mansions set behind broad green lawns along quiet, leafy streets, Olney has the singular attraction of **albino squirrels**, which were set loose in town around the turn of the century. By 1940, the *WPA Guide to Illinois* noted that "thousands of the little animals now scamper about the parks and courthouse square, and frisk over lawns, trees, and rooftops," though these days you're most likely to see them if you head to the small **animal sanctuary** and arboretum (618/392-2241) south of the courthouse square.

Perhaps the best reason to detour through Olney is to sample the incredibly good, inexpensive burgers and milk shakes at **Hovey's**, on old US-50 at 410 E. Main Street—look for the Mike's Ice Cream sign.

East of Olney, US-50 reverts to two-lane highway, running for 23 miles before passing by Lawrenceville (pop. 4,897), which stakes its claims to fame on two very different fronts. It was named for U.S. Navy Capt. James Lawrence, best remembered for his dying words, "Don't give up the ship," during the War of 1812. Later, in 1845, Lawrenceville gained notoriety as the first place in Illinois to execute a woman by hanging.

East of Lawrenceville, follow the old road south of the modern freeway, crossing the Wabash River into Indiana at historic Vincennes.

ACROSS INDIANA

From the Wabash River at its western end, to the Ohio River in the east, the 170 miles of southern Indiana that lie in between presents an immensely varied landscape. The hilly eastern sections are surprisingly rugged, though the central and western reaches are comparatively flat and largely agricultural. Besides numerous well-preserved historic Ohio River towns like Madison and Aurora, there are a number of unlovely industrial sections, especially around Bedford and the famous limestone quarries in the central parts of the state.

Vincennes

First settled by the French in 1732, and fought over during the Revolutionary War, Vincennes (pop. 19,859) remained a lawless frontier until 1803, when it was named the territorial capital. A handful of early buildings, including a bank, a church, and a newspaper office, have been restored as the **Indiana Territory State Historic Site** (Wed.-Sat. 9 AM-5 PM, Sunday 1-5 PM; free) at 1st and Harrison Streets in the historic downtown area. The **George Rogers Clark National Historical Park** is a classical, pillared memorial building honoring Revolutionary War general Clark (brother of William Clark, of Lewis and Clark fame). It wouldn't look out of place in D.C.

The Wabash River between Indiana and Illinois marks the boundary between the central and eastern time zones. Subtract an hour heading east, add an hour heading west.

The area around Vincennes is very flat farming country, notable for its large Amish communities (and numerous roadside "Amish Kountry Korner" stores and cafes), especially around **Logootee**, 30 miles east of Vincennes.

French Lick and Mitchell

Between Vincennes and Bedford, US-50 races uneventfully through the hilly groves of the Hoosier National Forest, but a worthwhile detour winds south through the hometowns of two of Indiana's best-known sons. The first of these, on Hwy-56 just south of US-150, is French Lick (pop. 2,087), where Boston Celtics star Larry Bird, "The Hick from French Lick," learned his game. The town itself is little more than a two-block-long business district—pick up souvenirs at the **French Lick Five and Dime** at 111 Maple Street. During the mid-1800s, the surrounding area was a popular resort, and thousands of Midwesterners came here to stay at posh hotels and take the mineral-rich waters that still flow from local artesian springs.

The other famous hometown, Mitchell, is about six miles south of Bedford, and was the boyhood home of astronaut Virgil "Gus" Grissom, who captained Mercury and Gemini space flights before dying in the Apollo 1 disaster. There's an impressive memorial—a 30-foot-high limestone statue of a Titan rocket—to Grissom at the entrance to Spring Mill State Park a few miles east of Mitchell; the memorial has exhibits about Grissom's career as a test pilot and in the space program. The state park also contains a reconstructed pioneer village with a working water-powered grist mill and demonstrations of pioneer crafts. The town's other memorable sight has vanished: the acres and acres of yellow school buses, in varying stages of completeness, which used to fill huge yards around the Carpenter School Bus factory before it closed in 1995.

Bedford

Nicknamed "Stone City" because it holds some of the largest and most famous limestone quarries in the country, Bedford (pop. 13,817) is a busy, industrial-looking city, the largest on the Indiana stretch of US-50. The quarries that earned Bedford's reputation are still in use, producing the durable stone that has clad many high-profile structures, including the Empire State Building. Though you can see the limestone in situ at many road cuts along US-50, perhaps the most prominent examples in Bedford are the monuments and gravestones in the cemeteries lining the highway through town.

Bedford's main hard-rock attraction is **Bluesprings Caverns** (daily 9 AM-5 PM May-Oct.; $7), five miles west of downtown on US-50, where you can descend into a cave and take an hour-long boat tour along the largest underground river in the U.S.

*Blue-collar Seymour is the birthplace of rock star **John** "Don't Call Me Cougar" **Mellencamp,** whose songs fill the jukeboxes of local bars and cafes.*

Brownstown, Seymour, and North Vernon

Roughly 27 miles east of Bedford and 10 miles west of the I-65 freeway, Brownstown (pop. 2,872) is an unusually pretty Indiana town set around a large central square shaded by 100-year-old maple trees. An old-fashioned general store and a couple of downhome restaurants make it worth a brief stop, particularly during the annual Watermelon Festival in late August.

East of Brownstown, it's a scenic 10 miles to Seymour (pop. 15,576), with its many motels (including a Holiday Inn and an Econo Lodge), fast-food franchises, and 24-hour gas stations marking the junction with the I-65 freeway.

Twelve miles east of Seymour, turn south from US-50 at **North Vernon** onto Hwy-7, which runs toward the Ohio River town of Madison across miles of rolling farmland, closely paralleling the route of Morgan's Raid, when Gen. John Morgan and 2,000 Confederate soldiers invaded Indiana during the Civil War.

Madison

Madison and the Ohio River Towns

A long but very worthwhile detour from US-50, **Hwy-56** loops south along the Ohio River. The riverside here is rich in history, and the

60-mile drive along Hwy-56 passes by modest tobacco farms and timeless small towns, the pastoral scene marred only by occasional power plants, most of them across the water on the Kentucky side.

Though the drive is nice enough in itself, it's most worthwhile because it brings you to **Madison** (pop. 12,006), one of the best-preserved historic Ohio River towns. Now a popular vacation destination, especially during the **Chautauqua Arts Festival** in late September and the rowdier **Madison Regatta** during the 4th of July, when 200-mph hydroplanes race along the river, Madison has managed to stay alive economically without sacrificing its small-town charms. Wandering around a few blocks of the franchise-free Main Street—one of the first in the country protected by the National Trust for Historic Preservation—you can enjoy a milk shake at the soda fountain in the back of **Rogers Drug Store**, listen to the town gossip while getting a haircut at the chrome and red-leather barber shop, or tour the many **historic homes**. The best of these is the impressive Greek revival mansion of Civil War financier James Lanier, now a state **museum** (Tues.-Sat. 9 AM-5 PM, Sunday 1-5 PM; free) near the river at 511 W. 1st Street. Also worth a look is the perfectly preserved **doctor's office** at 120 W. 3rd Street, which served as the only hospital between Cincinnati and Louisville from 1882 to 1903, when it was closed and preserved intact; it's now open for tours (Mon.-Sat. 10 AM-4:30 PM, Sunday 1-4:30 PM; $2).

Besides the wealth of Americana, Madison has a number of good places to eat along Main Street, including **Our Place** and **Lacey's**. Places to stay range from the 1847 federal-style **Schusser House B&B** at 514 Jefferson Street (812/273-2068 or 800/392-1931) to the motel-type rooms at the **Clifty Inn** (812/265-4135) in wooded Clifty Falls State Park, a mile west of town. For complete information on Madison, contact the **visitor center** at 301 E. Main Street (812/265-2956 or 800/559-2956), across from the landmark Jefferson County Courthouse.

A couple of other towns are worth a stop on the way upriver from Madison toward Cincinnati. Twenty miles east of Madison, the town of Vevay, the birthplace of Edward Eggleston, author of *The Hoosier Schoolmaster*, is marked at the west end of a short parade of shops along Main Street. Farther along, nine miles

Hwy-56 along the Ohio River is marked the "George Rogers Clark Trail" in honor of the 25-year-old soldier and explorer who, during the Revolutionary War, defeated British forces in what was then the Northwest Territory. His younger brother William was the Clark of Lewis and Clark.

south of US-50, the village of **Rising Sun** holds a handful of frontier-era structures as well as one of the state's better collections inside its museum (Sunday 1-4 PM only) at 212 S. Walnut Street.

Aurora and Lawrenceburg

Our Ohio River detour along Hwy-56 rejoins US-50 at Aurora (pop. 9,192), a small riverside town that's well worth at least a brief stop. The highlight here is the handsome **Hillforest Mansion** (Tues.-Sun. 1-5 PM; $4), an exuberant survivor from the steamboat era whose colonnaded facade is topped by a circular lookout tower from which residents could gaze out at river traffic up and down the Ohio. Built in 1852 and preserved in fine condition, the hillside mansion gives a strong sense of how comfortable and sophisticated life was for the wealthy, even on the so-called frontier.

East from Aurora, approaching the Ohio state line, US-50 forms a seedy gauntlet of roadside motels, diners, cut-rate liquor stores, and fireworks stands, all competing with giant billboards for the tri-state trade. Lawrenceburg (pop. 4,375), along the I-275 freeway three miles west of the Indiana/Ohio/Kentucky border, seems to revolve around the sale of cheap booze, perhaps because the main employer is the massive red-brick **Seagram's** distillery at the north end of Main Street—one of the oldest and largest in the USA.

Aurora, Indiana, is home to Aurora Casket Company, a leading producer of caskets in the USA.

The view of Lawrenceburg from US-50 is unpromising, and railroad tracks and a huge levee now cut off the town from the waterfront; however, the historic town center, south of the highway along Walnut Street, holds a number of interesting old buildings dating from the steamboat era of the early 1800s, when Lawrenceburg was a favorite Ohio River port of call. Among the many church spires competing for preeminence is that of the Presbyterian church, where in 1837 orator Henry Ward Beecher (father of Harriet Beecher Stowe, she of *Uncle Tom's Cabin* fame) held his first pastorate.

ACROSS OHIO

Winding along the Ohio River from Indiana, US-50 cuts east from Cincinnati across the hill-and-valley country of southern Ohio before finally crossing the Ohio River into West Virginia. The 220 miles US-50 takes to cross the state are a fairly constant mix of upland forest and bottomland farms, with a single industrial district in the middle, around Chillicothe, and a refreshing small college town, Athens, farther east.

North Bend

East from the Indiana line, US-50 winds along the partly industrial, partly rural Ohio River waterfront, without much to detain you before Cincinnati. The one place really worth a stop is the hamlet of North Bend (pop. 541), five miles east of the state border. A tall sandstone obelisk, overlooking the river and US-50 amidst a 14-acre park, marks the final resting place of William Henry Harrison (1773-1841), the ninth president of the United States, who lived here for many years when North Bend was a thriving frontier port. Born in Virginia, Harrison came to fame fighting Shawnee tribes in and around the Ohio Valley, and served in Congress for many years before he was elected president; he died of pneumonia after only a month in office. His grandson Benjamin Harrison, who became president in 1889, was born in the nearby family home in 1833.

Continuing along US-50, five miles west of downtown Cincinnati, the tiny **Anderson Ferry** ($2.50 per car, 25 cents for foot passengers) has been chugging back and forth since 1817, though the broad river is nothing like the busy river it was back then. But as recently as 1940, the WPA *Guide to Ohio* wrote that "fleets of barges pushed by snub-nosed towboats crawl along the motionless water; and now and then appears one of the Greene Line packets, all white and triple-decked."

For details on visiting Cincinnati, see the Survival Guide on pages 686-687.

Mariemont

From Cincinnati, US-50 follows surface streets through the warehouse and residential districts along the Ohio River, before becoming a freeway for the quick drive east to Mariemont (pop. 3,118). Built in the mid-1920s as one of the nation's first planned communities, Mariemont's mock-Tudor downtown centers around the very comfortable **Best Western Mariemont Inn**, right on US-50 at 6880 Wooster Pike (513/271-2100). Across the street there's a branch of the excellent local ice-cream chain, **Graeter's**, and the sole surviving neighborhood of Mariemont's original 1920s half-timbered homes is an easily walkable block to the southeast.

East of Mariemont, US-50 crosses the Little Miami River at the scenic town of **Milford** before racing east across 40 miles of flat and sparsely settled farming country to Hillsboro.

In the past 30 years much of Ohio has been turned from farmland to suburbia, a development that inspired Pretenders singer and Ohio native Chrissie Hynde to write "My City is Gone"—which coincidentally is the theme song for Rush Limbaugh's radio program.

I went back to Ohio / but my pretty countryside
Had been paved down the middle / by a government that had no pride
The farms of Ohio / had been replaced by shopping malls
And Muzak filled the air / from Seneca to Cuyahoga Falls

Hillsboro

Hillsboro (pop. 6,235), 60 miles east of Cincinnati and 40 miles west of Chillicothe, is the biggest and busiest town along the way. Besides the gas stations and good cafes like **Maggie's Snack Shop**, Hillsboro has a unique, alcohol-related history. During Christmas 1873, the town's 13 saloons were closed down by one of the country's earliest temperance movements, and more recently, country singer **Johnny** "Take This Job and Shove It" **Paycheck** did time in prison for shooting a man in Hillsboro's North High Saloon.

East from Hillsboro toward Chillicothe, US-50 winds past whitewashed farmhouses and broad cornfields flanked by low hills. The region also holds two remnants of the "mound builder" culture that once lived here. Just west of the sleepy village of Bainbridge, turning south onto Hwy-41 brings you to the more impressive **Serpent Mound**, which stretches alongside a creek for almost 1,500 feet. The **Seip Mound**, 16 miles west of Chillicothe, is another of the region's many archaeological sites.

Chillicothe and Mound City

In the middle of the state, Chillicothe (pop. 21,923; pronounced "chill-a-COTH-ee") comes as a sudden surprise after the pastoral landscape that surrounds it. It is one of the state's oldest industrial centers; since 1812 Chillicothe's economy has revolved around the massive Mead Paper mill on the south side of town, whose red-and-white striped smokestack belches a pungent white cloud around the clock.

Heavy industry aside, Chillicothe has done an admirable job of preserving its history, most notably in the recently spruced-up "First Capital" district along Main Street (US-50) downtown. Dozens of elaborate late Victorian commercial buildings and Greek revival-style mansions, mostly dating from the mid-1850s, surround the overwrought Ross County Courthouse, which has a different entrance for each government department.

While the downtown area is worth a quick stroll, specific sites are few, and the area's real attraction is three miles north of town via Hwy-104. Officially known as the Hopewell Culture National Historical Park, but usually called **Mound City**, this complex of prehistoric burial sites sits on the west bank of the Scioto River, just beyond a huge prison complex. Two dozen distinct, grass-covered mounds, the largest of which is about 15 feet high, are reachable on a mile-long trail that starts at the **visitor center** (daily 8 AM-5 PM; $2), where films and exhibits explore aspects of this 2,000-year-old culture.

> Midway between Chillicothe and Hillsboro, Bainbridge was the site of the first dental school in the U.S., now a **dental museum** at 208 W. Main Street (US-50).

> Chillicothe served as capital of the Northwest Territory from 1800 to 1802, and later as the first capital of Ohio.

Chillicothe makes a good place to break a journey. **Johnny's Famous Fried Chicken**, on US-50 next to McDonald's a mile west of downtown, serves very good food but closes at 8 PM. The $30-a-night **Chillicothe Inn** lies a half-block north of US-50 at 24 N. Bridge Street (614/774-2512); there's also a Holiday Inn and a Travelodge.

Chillicothe is known throughout Ohio as the site of **Tecumseh**, an outdoor pageant dramatizing the life of the eponymous Shawnee Indian warrior. Shows are at 8 PM nightly in summer ($13; 614/775-0700). More fun, and cheaper, are the baseball games played by the Frontier League **Chillicothe Paints** (bleacher seats $2; 614/ 773-TEAM), who play from June through August near Mound City.

Athens

East of Chillicothe, US-50 passes through Vinton County, one of the state's poorest and least developed regions. Hidden amidst forested hills, the remains of coal mines and overgrown, rail-fenced cornfields line the next 50 miles, and little has changed (for the better, at least) since the WPA *Guide* described the scene in 1939: "Abruptly the road sweeps into a rock-bound gorge dotted with the rickety houses of hill-folk . . . who make a living by seasonal mining, moonshining, trapping, or on Government relief projects."

After all this rural poverty, US-50 finally arrives at Athens (pop. 21,265), one of the most attractive small towns in Ohio. Set, like its classical namesake, on a series of hills, Athens is an idyllic little town that has grown up around the leafy campus of Ohio University, which opened here in 1809. Brick-paved streets lined by bookstores, copy shops, and clothing stores, mostly catering to the college's 18,000 well-groomed twenty-somethings, fill the eight-block "Uptown" neighborhood along College and Court Streets on the north side of the neoclassical College Green, a National Historic Landmark dating from 1816.

US-50 follows the Hocking River and bypasses the heart of town, so follow Stimson Avenue or State Street from the highway, past the town's best cafe and nightspot, **Another Fool's Cafe** at 24½ E. State Street, two blocks from campus. Accommodations include a **Days Inn** and other motels along Columbus Road (US-33) on the north side; further information is available from the **visitor center** (614/592-1819 or 800/878-9767) in the city park on US-50 east of town.

East of Athens, US-50 passes through 40 miles of scrubby second-growth forests and the abandoned but enticingly named coal-mining towns of Guysville and Coolville, before reaching the West Virginia border at the Ohio River and Parkersburg.

Southeastern Ohio has one of the country's greatest concentrations of barns painted with "Chew Mail Pouch Tobacco" signs.

ACROSS WEST VIRGINIA

The longest and slowest 220 miles in US-50's transcontinental crossing, the section across West Virginia twists, turns, and climbs its way over the rugged Allegheny Mountains. Starting along the Ohio River in the western, more developed half of the state, US-50 runs as a fairly fast freeway before beginning its climb into the rugged hill country, one of the country's most economically depressed corners, where everything seems straight out of a Depression-era Walker Evans photograph.

Though there are many fine hardwood forests and whitewater rivers, the lingering impression West Virginia leaves behind is of all-but-abandoned old railroad towns and poverty-stricken former coal-mining country, with rusting appliances and broken-down cars filling the front and back yards of the shanties, shacks, and trailer parks alongside the highway.

Parkersburg

Northern West Virginia's largest and most heavily industrialized city, Parkersburg (pop. 33,862) is located strategically at the junction of the Ohio and Little Kanawha Rivers. The town's economy is based around an unusual pair of employers: the federal Bureau of the Public Debt, which redeems U.S. Savings Bonds, and a massive DuPont Teflon factory. Though the first impression can be fairly bleak—the approach into town is lined by porno shops and strip clubs—Parkersburg does merit a closer look.

The **Blennerhasset Museum** (Tues.-Sun. 9:30 AM-5 PM; $1), housed in a turn-of-the-century brick warehouse at 2nd and Juliana Streets, traces regional history, with a focus on the escapades of the Irish aristocrat Harman Blennerhasset, who in 1806 conspired with Aaron Burr to establish an independent fiefdom in Texas and the Southwest. If you're interested, you can ride a paddle wheeler to and from the Ohio River island on which Blennerhasset built the palatial home where the plot was hatched. The house has been restored as a state park, and **boats** ($4) leave hourly from Point Park, which is two blocks west of the museum, under the railroad bridges and on the far side of the 25-foot concrete flood walls at the confluence of the rivers.

Fort New Salem

Between Parkersburg and Clarksburg, US-50 winds along as a fast, four-lane freeway through a one-time oil- and gas-producing region dotted with tiny, all-but-forgotten towns. The small farms are cultivated by descendants of Scotch-Irish immigrants who settled here in the late 18th century. One place that's well worth a stop is Fort New Salem (Wed.-Fri. 10 AM-5 PM, Saturday and Sunday 1-5 PM; $2), 14 miles west of Clarksburg. Just south of US-50, on the campus of half-Japanese Salem-Teikyo University, the fort is a credible reconstruction of the frontier outpost of palisaded log cabins, erected near here in 1795.

Clarksburg

Birthplace of Confederate Civil War hero Thomas "Stonewall" Jackson, Clarksburg (pop. 18,059) is a tidy railroad town sitting on a branch of the Monongahela River. The downtown area is a sampler of turn-of-the-century commercial buildings, great for taking pictures of old signs and brick walls, but with no particular sights to see. The town's large Italian population supports numerous good restaurants like **Minard's Spaghetti Inn**, 813 E. Pike Street on old US-50, at the Joyce Street exit off the freeway.

On the east side of Clarksburg, US-50 climbs a steep hill before becoming suddenly urban and ugly at **Bridgeport**, which straddles the I-79 freeway, around which the highway is lined by a two-mile sprawl of Wal-Marts, Kmarts, franchised fast-food chains, and **motels**, including a Holiday Inn, a Comfort Inn, and a Days Inn.

Grafton

Grafton (pop. 5,524), the first large town west of Winchester, Virginia, grew up as a bustling railroad town beginning in 1852 but is now among the most economically and socially depressed places in this economically and socially depressed state. Run-down houses and abandoned churches on brick-paved streets drop down the steep hills to the Tygart River and the railroad tracks, where a monumental station and a couple of grand but boarded-up hotels are grim reminders of Grafton's formerly busy self.

Besides its impressive physical setting, Grafton's main claim to fame is as the birthplace of Mother's Day, first celebrated here in 1908 in a Methodist church that's been converted into the **International Mother's Day Shrine** (Mon.-Fri. 9:30 AM-3:30 PM; donations), on Main Street across from the old train station.

East of Grafton, the landscape becomes more mountainous, and isolated villages replace the small towns that line the western half of the route.

Arthurdale

Northeast of Grafton, a half-hour north of US-50 via Hwy-92, the homestead community of Arthurdale was the first and perhaps the most important of the many anti-poverty rural resettlement projects initiated during the Depression-era New Deal. Though not the largest, Arthurdale was prominent because of the personal involvement of then-First Lady Eleanor Roosevelt, who not only helped plan the project but also visited many times, handing out diplomas at school graduations.

Beginning in 1934 with the construction of some 165 homes, plus schools and factories, a cooperative farm, a health center, and a small hotel, Arthurdale was an ideal community set up to relieve the dire living conditions of unemployed Morgantown coal miners. Most of the houses are still intact and still inhabited by the original homesteaders or their descendants. The old community center is being restored and now holds a small **museum** (daily by appointment; 304/864-3959) that chronicles the whole story.

South of Grafton, US-119 passes through the town of **Phillipi,** where the largest covered bridge in the state spans the Tygart River. Originally constructed in 1852, the 285-foot-long red-and-white bridge was badly burned in 1989 but has been totally restored.

The village of **Aurora,** at the west edge of Cathedral State Park, has gained a measure of fame for its fight to "Retire the Penny." At the local Dairy Queen, for example, all prices are rounded up or down to the nearest 5 cents.

Midway across western Maryland's short stretch of US-50, around a mile east of Redhouse, the **US-50 Quilt House** has hundreds of high-quality handmade quilts.

Across West Virginia, US-50 follows the route of the colonial-era Northwest Turnpike, which was surveyed in 1748 by a 16-year-old George Washington.

Cathedral State Park

Four miles west of the Maryland border, US-50 runs right through Cathedral State Park, where over 130 acres of stately hemlocks constitute one of the few first-growth stands left in this lumber-hungry state. Beyond here, US-50 makes a quick seven-mile jaunt across a corner of Maryland before crossing the north branch of the Potomac River back into West Virginia.

From the bridge, US-50 climbs steeply up the densely wooded Alleghenies, twisting over 3,000-foot-high ridges with turns so tight the posted speed limit is 15 mph—the going is very slow, and not much fun if you're prone to car sickness.

Romney and the Eastern Gateway

The oddly shaped arm of eastern West Virginia, which juts between Maryland and Virginia at the headwaters of the Potomac River, is promoted as the "Eastern Gateway" and offers quick access to the mountainous wilderness of Monongahela National Forest that stretches south of US-50, and to the raging whitewater of the Cheat and Gauley Rivers. Originally inhabited by Shawnee Indians, the region was settled during colonial times as part of the six million-acre Virginia estate of Lord Fairfax. The B&O railroad came through in the 1850s, which made the region strategically important during the Civil War, nowhere more so than around Romney (pop. 1,966), the Eastern Gateway's largest town, which changed hands over 50 times in four years of fighting.

Heading east toward Winchester, US-50 passes through mountain hamlets like Capon Bridge (on the West Virginia side) and Gore (on the Virginia side), which consist of little more than a gas station, a tavern, and a post office, plus one or two antique stores selling everything from colonial-era furniture to old highway signs. It's hard to help feeling light years from the modern world, even though Washington, D.C. is only 90 miles away.

ACROSS VIRGINIA

Dropping from the Allegheny and Appalachian Mountains of West Virginia, US-50 enters Virginia at the northern tip of the Shenandoah Valley, passing through the center of the quietly attractive small city of Winchester. Continuing east, in short order the road climbs the foothills of the Blue Ridge Mountains and crosses the Shenandoah River, delighting John Denver fans and carrying travelers through the heart of the ultra-wealthy "Hunt Country" of northern Virginia, a rural and unspoiled landscape of small towns, horse farms, and vineyards that's home to more well-connected millionaires than just about anywhere in the USA.

Patsy Cline, September 8, 1932-March 5, 1963

Approaching the outer suburbs of the nation's capital, however, US-50 swiftly loses its luster, and while you *can* follow it through miles of suburban sprawl on both sides of the I-495 Beltway, you might prefer to follow the misleadingly numbered I-66 freeway—which has nothing at all to do with the *real* Route 66—into the city. In any event there's little worth stopping for in the 22 miles between Dulles Airport and D.C. itself, though US-50's final approach takes you past the startling Iwo Jima Memorial statue, arriving in D.C. at the Lincoln Memorial.

Winchester

Northern Virginia's largest city, Winchester (pop. 21,947) is a surprisingly quiet and very pleasant small city, best known for the extensive apple orchards that fill the surrounding countryside. The I-81 freeway, complete with the usual sprawl of shopping malls and fast-food franchises, cuts across US-50 along the east side of Winchester, but the downtown district is eminently strollable, especially the pedestrianized Old Town area of Loudon Street, between Piccadilly (US-50) and Cork Street.

After apples, Winchester is probably most famous as the hometown of **Patsy Cline**, the inimitable country singer who died in a plane crash on March 5, 1963, at age 30. Patsy Cline, whose greatest hits include "Crazy," "Sweet Dreams," and "Walking After Midnight," lived in Winchester from age 3 to age 16 in a small house at 608 S. Kent Street near downtown, and dropped out of high school to earn money making milk shakes at **Gaunt's Drug Store**, south of downtown at Loudon Street and Valley Avenue. She's buried in **Shenandoah Memorial Park**, a mile southeast of town.

Other sites associated with Patsy Cline are included in the handy brochure "Celebrating Patsy," available free at the **Kurtz Cultural Center**, in Old Town Winchester at 2 N. Cameron Street (Mon.-Sat. 10 AM-5 PM, Sunday noon-5 PM; free; 540/722-6367), which also has extensive displays on local and Civil War-era history and culture. For listings of eating and accommodation options, contact the Winchester **visitor center** (540/662-4135 or 800/662-1360).

US-50 crosses the Appalachian Mountains at 1,100 foot-high Ashby Gap, 15 miles east of Winchester. The scenically sited and magnificently preserved town of **Harpers Ferry,** West Virginia, 26 miles north of US-50 via US-340, is the center of the **Appalachian Trail,** and is covered in detail on pages 275-276.

One place worth stopping at in the D.C. suburbs is the **Tastee 29 Diner,** 10536 Lee Highway (US-50) in Fairfax, a classic chrome and blue enamel diner that's open 24 hours every day.

Middleburg

Located at the heart of northern Virginia's "Hunt Country," where senators, ambassadors, and aristocrats mix at multimillion-dollar country estates, Middleburg (pop. 549) is a small but immaculate town with a four-block business district packed with antique shops, art galleries, real estate agencies—and a lone Safeway supermarket, just west of the only traffic light.

Many of Middleburg's brick- and stone-fronted buildings date from colonial times, including the **Red Fox Inn**, 2 E. Washington Street (540/687-6301 or 800/277-0844), on US-50 at the center of town. Originally built in 1728 as a coach inn and tavern, it's now a comfortable and upscale B&B and restaurant.

There's a couple of other places to eat, including the affordable **Magpie Cafe** and **Huckleberry's** ice cream and sandwich shop, both at the west end of Washington Street.

East of Middleburg, US-50 winds through gently rolling farmlands for a dozen miles before hitting the outlying suburbs of Washington, D.C.

John Brown 1800-1859

Manassas National Battlefield Park

Site of the first major land battle of the Civil War, Manassas National Battlefield Park has been preserved intact despite the suburbanizing pressures of the surrounding towns, and despite the aborted efforts of the Walt Disney Company to build a massive American history-themed amusement park nearby. The prospect of battle-view tract houses still looms in the future, but for now Manassas (which in the North was also known as Bull Run) is among the most evocative of all the Civil War sites, its five square miles of rolling hills and woodlands kept as they were, with few intrusions of modern life.

Manassas, which controlled transportation links between Washington, D.C., and the Shenandoah Valley, was the site of two major battles. The first battle, fought here on July 21, 1861, was strategically inconclusive, though the fact that the Confederate "rebels" forced the overconfident Union army into a panicked retreat surprised the many onlookers who had traveled out from Washington to watch the fighting, and foreshadowed the next four years of war. The second battle, fought August 28-30, 1862, followed the instatement of Robert E. Lee as commander of the Confederate forces. That conflict marked the beginning of the bloodiest year of fighting, culminating in the battle of Gettysburg the following July.

Confederate hero Thomas "Stonewall" Jackson earned his nickname at the first battle of Manassas, where his steadfastness under fire helped rally rebel troops.

Hundreds of monuments and memorials, along with rows of artillery set up along battle lines, dot the grassy hills and point out the many key moments of the battles. A loosely structured 1.4-mile walking tour begins at the small **visitor center**, where audiovisual displays and collections of military artifacts give a sense of what the war was like.

To reach Manassas Battlefield, follow the I-66 freeway from Washington, D.C., or the Lee Highway (US-29) west from Fairfax. From US-50, follow US-15 or the smaller Hwy-659 south.

For details on visiting Washington, D.C., see the Survival Guide on pages 726-727.

ACROSS MARYLAND

Racing out of Washington, D.C., on a high-speed multilane freeway, US-50 accesses one of the state's most popular destinations, the colonial Chesapeake Bay port town of Annapolis. From Annapolis, heading toward the Atlantic coast and the massively popular beach resort of Ocean City, the final leg of US-50's 3,200-mile transcontinental trek is a mad dash across 100 miles of Maryland's Eastern Shore. This is one of the more captivating areas in the northeastern U.S., but the four-lane US-50 freeway doesn't encourage sightseeing, so if you want to get a feel for the *real* Eastern Shore of piney woods, cornfields, and fishing fleets, you'll have to follow the many back roads and search out the many historic towns and villages—many of which we point out as worthwhile detours, including some that are among the oldest and most carefully preserved in the nation.

In Annapolis, **WRNR 103.1 FM** is an anarchic modern rock station, playing everything from The Animals to Frank Zappa.

Annapolis

State capital of Maryland, and one of the most attractive and well-preserved historic cities in the U.S., Annapolis (pop. 33,187) is one place you won't want to miss. First settled in 1649 and chartered in 1708, Annapolis makes fair claim to being the oldest city in the country. Its historic importance was as the nation's first capital, though it's now best known for its maritime heritage, both as a yachting center and as home of the U.S. Naval Academy, which stands guard along the Chesapeake Bay waterfront.

The historic center of Annapolis is just south of US-50 via Hwy-70, which leads straight to the **State House** (daily 9 AM-5 PM; free), where the U.S. Congress met in 1783-84 and ratified the Treaty of Paris, thus ending the Revolutionary War. From the State House, Main Street drops downhill to the City Dock waterfront, where a

*skipjacks on
Chesapeake Bay*

visitor center has walking-tour maps and guides to the wealth of historic buildings, including the beautiful colonial-era **Hammond Harwood House** (Mon.-Sat. 10 AM-4 PM; $4) at 19 Maryland Avenue, two blocks north.

Annapolis has a number of good places to eat, including the venerable **Chick & Ruth's Delly**, 165 Main Street, and the waterfront **Middleton Tavern**, 2 Market Space, with fine fish and chips. Apart from the historic **Maryland Inn**, 16 Church Circle (410/263-2641), most of the places to stay are anodyne motels along US-50 west of town; the visitor center (410/280-0445) has complete lists of options.

West of St. Michaels, at the far end of Hwy-33, **Tilghman Island** is home port for Chesapeake Bay's sole surviving fleet of skipjacks, the unique sail-powered vessels used to harvest oysters from the bay.

The Eastern Shore is excellent bicycling country, with generally flat, quiet roads winding through farmlands, forests, and waterfront fishing villages. The State of Maryland publishes a useful free guide; see Road Trip Resources for the phone number.

Chesapeake Bay Bridge

Before the five-mile long Chesapeake Bay Bridge was completed in the early 1950s, Maryland's Eastern Shore was physically and spiritually an island, protected by the broad Chesapeake Bay from the sprawling modern cities of Washington and Baltimore, and cut off at its neck by the Chesapeake and Delaware Canal. Now thousands of travelers cross the bridge each summer, many of whom race right through on US-50, headed for the coastal resorts like Rehoboth Beach ("The Beltway by the Bay") and Ocean City. The bridge itself has a toll of $3, charged to eastbound travelers only.

At the west end of the bridge, US-50 lands at **Sandy Point State Park**, where you can swim, hike, or launch a boat. At the eastern end, US-50 is joined by US-301, and together the two roads race along as a four-lane freeway as far as **Queenstown**, a busy port in the early 1800s but now little more than an upscale suburb of the greater Baltimore/Washington urban area.

Easton

Midway across Maryland, 20 miles southeast of the Chesapeake Bay Bridge, US-50 bypasses the well-preserved heart of Easton (pop. 9,372), where the stately Talbot County Courthouse overlooks a compact business district that could easily pass as an English country High Street. Besides the many 18th-century structures, including a federal-style townhouse at 25 S. Washington Street that's been converted into the Talbot County historical society **museum** (Tues.-Sat. 10 AM-4 PM, Sunday 1-4 PM; $2), the most interesting place to stop is the white wood-frame **Third Haven Meeting House**, on the edge of town on South Washington Street, built in 1684 and still in use by a Quaker congregation.

The classic place to stay in Easton is the stately **Tidewater Inn,** a recently restored landmark in the center of town at 101 E. Dover Street (410/822-1300 or 800/237-8775), which offers guests free carriage rides around town and the option of a 4:30 AM breakfast—designed for early-rising duck-hunters. Easton also holds the comfortable **Bishop's House** B&B, at 214 Goldsborough Street (301/820-7290), and the usual range of motels and fast-food places along the US-50 frontage.

St. Michaels and Oxford

The pride and joy of the Eastern Shore is the Chesapeake Bay village of St. Michaels, a colonial-era shipbuilding center turned yachting haven that's home to the excellent **Chesapeake Bay Maritime Museum** (daily 10 AM-4 PM, longer hours in summer; $6). Located right on the waterfront at the center of town, the museum has extensive displays of skipjacks and other historic sailing vessels—which you can watch being restored in the museum workshops. There are also diverse pieces of fishing and hunting gear, plus a working lighthouse, all displayed to conjure up traditional Eastern Shore maritime life.

Though full of lovingly maintained old houses and commercial buildings as well as working wharves, chandlers, and sail lofts, St. Michaels, it has to be said, is definitely a major tourist trap, with the usual array of souvenir shops, overpriced restaurants, and overquaint B&Bs.

After seeing the museum and wandering around the town, if you want to get a feel for the unspoiled Chesapeake follow the signs southeast from St. Michaels to the **Tred-Avon Ferry** (daily 7 AM-sunset; $4.50 a car, 75 cents pedestrian each way), which shuttles across the Tred Avon River every half-hour or so to Oxford (pop. 700), a sleepy little village that has hardly changed since the 1760s, when it was one of two authorized ports-of-entry into colonial-era Maryland. Wander along the waterfront or south along Morris Street to the village center, through what may be the best-preserved colonial town left in America. There are no museums or displays proclaiming Oxford a special place, though no less an authority than James Michener (who lived in St. Michaels for many years) did go so far as to say that the crab cakes served inside the circa 1710 **Robert Morris Inn** (410/226-5111) opposite the ferry dock were among the best he'd ever tasted; at $20 a plate they're a bit rich, but the inn is an evocative old place, with rooms at $70-220 a night.

From Oxford, you can ride the ferry back by way of St. Michaels, or return directly to US-50 via Hwy-333.

Cambridge

Founded in 1684 on the south bank of the broad Choptank River, unlike sleepy Oxford, busy Cambridge (pop. 11,514) is a market town for the surrounding farmlands. Still somewhat industrial in feel, thanks to its now-closed canning and packing plants, Cambridge does have some attractive corners, though its one apt but unique sight is the decaying old **Cape Charles ferry**, which once sailed south to Norfolk but is now moored on the northwest side of the US-50 bridge over the Choptank River.

Cambridge is also home to the Eastern Shore's most bizarre range of annual festivals, from the winter National Muskrat Skinning Championship to powerboat and antique airplane fairs held throughout the summer; for details, contact the **visitor center** (410/228-3575).

Salisbury

Though largely modern and commercial, Salisbury (pop. 20,059) has preserved part of its older townscape in a pedestrianized downtown shopping district and in the Newton Historic District, a collection of dainty Victorian-era houses along Elizabeth Street. The one place to stop is the **Ward Museum of Wildfowl Art** (daily 10 AM-5 PM; $4), which has a comprehensive collection of carved decoys and other hunting-related arts and crafts.

Though not an especially attractive place to stop, Salisbury does have one of the Eastern Shore's better diners, **Phippin's North 13** on US-13 a mile north of US-50, serving standard breakfast fare (from 6 AM) and a range of local fish and seafood platters for dinner (daily until 9 PM).

Crossing the coastal wetlands and estuaries, US-50 races east from Salisbury, bypassing a few small towns like Willards and Whaleyville, which are best seen by following the Hwy-346 frontage road. The two routes run parallel, joining each other 30 miles east in the old-time beach resort of Ocean City.

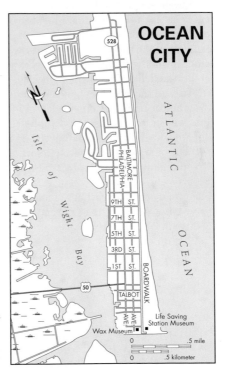

Ocean City

About the only place left on the entire East Coast that retains the carnival qualities of classic seaside resorts, Ocean City (pop. 5,146) has by far the best array of old-time fun-fair attractions. Stretching north from the main pier for over two miles along a broad, clean, white-sand beach, the wide wooden boardwalk is packed with enough water slides, merry-go-rounds, mini-golf courses, haunted houses, and bumper cars to entertain the hundreds of thousands of people who come here on summer weekends. There are also all the nearly forgotten old arcade games like skee-ball and pokerino, and midway contests (the kind where for $1 a try you can win stuffed animals and other prizes by

To go along with its great beaches, Ocean City has the excellent **WZBH 93.5 FM,** "The Beach," playing the world's greatest rock 'n' roll (from the Rolling Stones to the Sex Pistols to Pearl Jam), and broadcasting details of Ocean City's lively nightclub scene.

The rest of the Atlantic Coast, north and south from Ocean City, is covered in the Coastal East Coast chapter beginning on page 300.

shooting baskets or squirting water into clowns' mouths), while a ramshackle collection of fortune-tellers, T-shirt stands, and burger-and-beer bars completes the scene, forming a busy gauntlet along the lively promenade.

On a summer weekend Ocean City, which fills the narrow barrier island that stretches north from US-50 for over 10 miles, becomes Maryland's second-largest city, the population increasing from the resident 5,000 people to upwards of 400,000. Most of the fun is simply in getting caught up in the garish human spectacle of it all, but there are a couple of specific things worth searching out. For the price of a bumper car ride, you can enjoy the quirky collections of the **Life Saving Station Museum** (daily 11 AM-10 PM in summer, Sat-Sun. noon-4 PM Nov.-March; $2) at the south end of the boardwalk, where alongside displays of shipwrecks and bathing suits you can compare and contrast bowls full of sand from 100 different beaches around the world. The museum also marks the starting point for the **trams** ($2) that run along the boardwalk for over two miles, north to where the modern 20-story condos and resort hotels line the rest of the island.

While much of Ocean City's charm is decidedly low-brow, the food is better than you might expect, with numerous places offering platefuls of shrimp and pitchers of beer for under $10. Fresh-tasting fried chicken or crab cakes are available from boardwalk stands like **Dayton Bros.**, across from the Live Saving Station. **Thrashers Fries** are available from a number of counters along the boardwalk, and you can top them off with a cone or shake from **Dumser's Ice Cream**, near the Wax Museum at the south end of the boardwalk. There are also many very good restaurants, including dozens of seafood places along Sinepuxent Bay on the western side of the island, like **The Angler** at the end of Talbot Street.

Places to stay are also abundant, but unfortunately far from cheap. Of the grand older hotels, only the **Commander** on 14th Street (410/289-6166 or 800/543-6986) is still open for business. Modern motels like the **Comfort Inn**, at Boardwalk and 5th Street (410/289-5155 or 800/282-5155), charge $120 for a double that goes for $40 out of season, and upscale resort hotels like the **Sheraton Fontainbleau**, on Oceanfront at 101st Street (410/524-3535 or 800/638-2100), can cost upwards of $200 a night.

For more complete listings of motels, hotels, and restaurants, contact the Ocean City **visitor center** in the Convention Center at 4001 Coastal Highway (410/289-2800 or 800/62-OCEAN).

US-80:
SOUTHERN PACIFIC

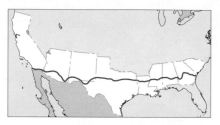

Following old US-80 and its contemporary equivalents across the nation's southern tier takes you through more varied cultural and physical landscapes than you'll find along any other cross-country route. Throughout this 3,000-mile journey you can shift from one world to another in the time it takes to watch a football game. Heading east from the golden sands of San Diego, within 100 miles you reach the harshly beautiful Southwest deserts, their trademark saguaro cacti creating a backdrop straight out of a Roadrunner cartoon. The route's central segment crosses the thousand-mile, "you can see for two days" plains of New Mexico and Texas, where pumpjacks jig for oil and cattle graze beneath a limitless sky. To the east spreads another land, starting at the cotton-rich Mississippi Delta and continuing along the foot of the Appalachians to the bayous and sea islands surrounding the country's most beautiful city, Savannah.

Especially memorable is the diversity of people and of prevailing customs along the route, all highlighted by a range of accents and lingos. For travelers, this cultural diversity is perhaps most accessible in the food. Many regional American cuisines—Tex-Mex, Cajun, Creole, BBQ, to name a few—were originally developed somewhere along this route, and roadside restaurants continue to serve up local specialties that lend new meaning to the word "authentic." Along the open borders between Texas and New and old Mexico, in unselfconscious adobe sheds with corrugated metal roofs, chile-powered salsa accompanies roast steak fajitas; in Louisiana, entrees featuring catfish fillets or bright red boiled shrimp grace most menus; and everywhere you turn, roadside stands dish out reputedly the best BBQ in the universe. We've noted favorite places along the route, but all you really need do is follow your nose, or look for a line of pickup trucks, and you'll find yourself in culinary heaven.

On an equal footing with the fine food is the incredible variety of music you'll hear, whether it's in a Texas honky-tonk or in the juke joints and gospel-spreading churches of Mississippi and Alabama. Along the Mexican border, from San Diego well past El Paso, radio stations blast out an anarchic mix of multilingual music, part country-western, part traditional Mexican, with accordions and guitars and lyrics flowing seamlessly from one language to the other and back—often in a single line of a song. Along the way, you can visit the hometowns of Buddy Holly, Little Richard, and Otis Redding, or pay your respects at the final resting places of Hank Williams, Jimmie Rodgers, and Duane Allman. After dark, listen to the current and next generation making music in roadside bars and clubs.

A wealth of distinctive literature has grown out of these regions, and you can visit dozens of characteristic literary scenes, live and in the flesh: Carson Mc-Cullers's "Ballad of the Sad Cafe" and other tales, which capture 1920s life in Columbus, Georgia; Cormac McCarthy's wide-open tales of the Texas frontier; the diner from *Fried Green Tomatoes;* and the original God's Little Acre and Tobacco Road. But there's also sober history, from Wild West Tombstone and Bonnie and Clyde's death site, to the Dallas intersection where JFK was assassinated, to the streets of Selma, where the Civil Rights Movement burst forth onto the nation's front pages. Best of all, many of the most fascinating places along the way remain refreshingly free of the slick promotion that greets you in more established tourist destinations. The relatively low profile of tourism, and the fact that only a few regional cities lie in wait to swallow your vacation dollars, help make this particular trip a relatively inexpensive one—but even at twice the price, it would be well worth experiencing.

ACROSS CALIFORNIA

From the Pacific bays and golden beaches of San Diego, you can choose between two routes as you head east across Southern California: the high-speed I-8 freeway up and over pine-forested mountains, or a winding drive along the Mexican border.

We've covered the slower, more southerly route that follows the remnants of old US-80 through sleepy border towns. Leaving San Diego, old US-80 followed El Cajon Boulevard, which is full of some great roadside Americana, circa 1930-1950, though unfortunately it's all in generally poor, and in places dangerous, condition. A pair of unique roadside attractions have survived the ravages of time—the funky old Desert View Tower, and the oddly endearing "Official Center of the World" at tiny Felicity. Included is a quick side trip south of the border to Tecate. But no matter which way you choose, eventually you'll have to cross 75 monotonous miles of the Mojave Desert, a barren, dry, and inhospitable land.

The fastest and prettiest route from the coast to Tecate lies on the Mexican side of the border, where a high-speed modern highway runs through the rugged mountains east of Tijuana.

Campo marks the southern end of the **Pacific Crest Trail,** which winds for 2,638 miles between Canada and Mexico.

The diverse attractions of San Diego are covered in a Survival Guide on pages 716-717.

Tecate

Leaving San Diego, old US-80 followed El Cajon Boulevard, which is lined by a dozen miles of unsightly but surviving motels, cafes, and gas stations before it reaches the foothill town of La Mesa, where old US-80 and the high-speed I-8 freeway turn onto the two-lane blacktop of Hwy-94. Twisting to the southeast around the 4,000-foot peaks of the Cleveland National Forest, the road traverses classic Southern California landscape: rolling, chaparral-covered hillsides rising above grassy ranch lands and stately valley oaks.

After passing through **Jamul** and **Dulzura,** two quiet ranching towns that appear on the verge of extinction as San Diego rapidly approaches, some 40 miles east of downtown you'll spot a sign marking the turnoff south to the Mexican border town of Tecate (pop. 45,000). Known around the world as the source of tangy Tecate beer—by most accounts, the brew that started people drinking beer with a squeeze of fresh lime—Tecate is in the top tier of enjoyable border towns, if only by virtue of being cleaner and quieter than Tijuana. Stops include the usual restaurants and souvenir shops; the main stop is the **Tecate Brewery** itself, the biggest building in town, located on Avenida Hidalgo a half-dozen blocks from the border. Free **tours** (Saturday 10 AM-4 PM) include samples.

Because of insurance concerns, it's a good idea to leave your car on the U.S. side of the border and cross into Mexico on foot. For more on traveling in Mexico, by car or other means, see page 162. East of Tecate, Hwy-94 runs along the U.S. side of the border for 41 miles before joining the I-8 freeway.

Campo

Set in a broad valley midway between Tecate and the I-8 freeway, tiny Campo (pop. 1,102) has one main attraction, the **San
Diego Railroad Museum** (Saturday, Sunday, and holidays 9 AM-
5 PM; free), well-posted at the west end of town on Forest Gate
Road. Along with an extensive outdoor collection of old locomotives and carriages, the museum offers rides (noon and 2:30
PM; $10) on restored trains, a 16-mile roundtrip through the
surrounding countryside.

Jacumba

South of the I-8 freeway on a surviving stretch of the old US-80
highway, Jacumba is a former spa and resort town where Clark
Gable, Marlene Dietrich, and countless others soaked themselves silly in the free-flowing natural hot springs. Established
in 1852 as a station on the stagecoach mail route across the
desert, Jacumba had its heyday during the 1920s, and while little remains apart
from the water, it makes a great offbeat place to stop. The mineral-rich hot springs
still flow into outdoor pools and private jacuzzis at **Jacumba Hot Springs Spa**,
44500 Old US-80 (619/766-4333), which includes motel rooms for around $40,
and a good on-site restaurant and bar.

> | DON'T TAKE |
> | A CURVE |
> | AT 60 PER |
> | WE'D HATE |
> | TO LOSE A CUSTOMER |
> | **Burma-Shave** |

For more information on
visiting **Anza-Borrego
State Park,** contact the
ranger station in Borrego
Springs (619/767-4684).

Ocotillo: The Desert View Tower

Southern gateway to the splendid, 600,000-acre Anza-Borrego
State Park, the largest and wildest desert park in the country,
Ocotillo lies north of the I-8 freeway on the old US-80 highway (designated S2 on
maps). Ocotillo itself is little more than a gas station-*cum*-grocery store, bar, and
volunteer fire station, but five miles east of town on old US-80, the **Desert View
Tower** (daily 9 AM-5 PM; $3; 619/766-4612) is worth searching out. The four-story,
cut-stone structure was built by Burt Vaughn in 1922 to commemorate the pioneers who struggled across the arid desert. Inside the tower, a small but interesting
museum displays a haphazard collection of desert Americana such as Navajo blankets and Native American artifacts, with similar items on sale in the gift shop. At
the top of the tower, an observation platform offers views across 100 miles of desert
landscape, broken only by the I-8 freeway. Around the base of the tower lie a number of bizarre boulders and small caves, all carved during the Depression by an out-
of-work engineer named W.T. Ratliffe—another, more vivid memorial to the
pioneers. The tower stands six miles east of the Jacumba turnoff from I-8, on In-
Ko-Pah Road; billboards point the way.

East of the tower, old US-80 is designated as S80 and runs
parallel to I-8 all the way east to El Centro, passing through
ghostly old industrial towns like Plaster City and Seeley.

From 1858 to 1861 the
original Butterfield Stage,
which carried mail and
passengers from St. Louis to
San Francisco, followed the
approximate route of I-8
across Southern California.
The route was originally
blazed by Spanish explorer
Juan de Anza, on his way to
found San Francisco in 1775.

El Centro

Located some 50 feet below sea level, midway across California
at the heart of the agricultural Coachella Valley, El Centro (pop.
31, 384) was founded in 1905 and has since bloomed into a

bustling small city, thanks to irrigation water diverted from the Colorado River. Melons, grapefruit, and dates are the region's prime agricultural products, along with alfalfa grown to feed the many dairy cows. There's not a lot here that doesn't depend upon farming.

Though not much of a destination, El Centro is still the best place to break a journey between San Diego and the Arizona border, so fill your gas tank if nothing else. Places to eat include **Millie's Kitchen**, a popular truck-stop cafe on 4th Street south of I-8, and the usual franchise fast-food places. All the national motel chains are here as well, along with neon-signed local ones along the I-8 Business Loop, advertising rooms for as little as $18 a night.

El Centro is the winter home of the aerial acrobats of the U.S. Navy's **Blue Angels**, who can sometimes be spotted practicing their loops and rolls in the skies around the city. It is also the birthplace of **Cher.**

From El Centro, it's a quick 10 miles south across the Mexican border to **Mexicali,** capital of Baja California and a busy big city focused more on commerce than on catering to tourists.

When driving in the desert, always keep the gas tank as full as possible, and always carry at least one gallon of drinking water per person. In case of trouble, stay with your car. Don't walk off in search of help; let it find you.

The Algodones Dunes

In the middle of the southern Mojave Desert, 42 miles east of El Centro, a rest area south of the I-8 freeway at the Grays Well Road exit gives access to the enticing sands of the Algodones Dunes, which stretch to both sides of the freeway for over 50 miles. The slender dunes, which measure at most 10 miles across and reach heights of 200 feet, often cover the highway in blowing sandstorms. Though you can amble around on foot, be aware that the dunes themselves are under constant abuse from hordes of motorcycles and dune buggies.

According the WPA *Guide to California* (and postcards on sale in Yuma), the remains of a **wooden plank road**, built across the sands in 1914 and later used as part of the original US-80 highway, still parallel the south side of the freeway. I never found any sign of it, however. The All-American Canal, which waters the Coachella Valley, runs alongside I-8 on the north side of the freeway.

Felicity: "The Center of the World Pyramid"

One of the odder sites in the Southwestern deserts—and competition for this title is pretty fierce—sits just north of the I-8 freeway in the tiny but happily named town of Felicity (pop. four). Local resident Jacques-Andres Istel—author of a children's fairy tale concerning a scholarly, fire-breathing dragon named Coe who lives at the center of the world reading fireproof books and eating the nearby Chocolate Mountains—convinced France, China, and Imperial County that Felicity is, legally and officially, the center of the world.

A 25-foot-high pink terrazzo pyramid stands above the exact spot, which you can visit on regular guided **tours** (daily 10 AM-5 PM, late November to mid-April only; $1; 619/572-5000); the fee also buys a certificate saying you've stood at "The Official Center of the World." You can climb a set of stairs that used to belong to the Eiffel Tower, and sift through sundry souvenirs in the gift shop.

The **Colorado River** forms the border between California and Arizona, and marks the line between the Pacific and mountain time zones.

Winterhaven

The last California town before the Colorado River, Winterhaven is the modest center of the Quechan community on 44,000-acre Fort Yuma Indian Reservation. A few reminders of its pre- and post-colonial past are displayed inside the small **Fort Yuma Indian Museum** (Mon.-Fri. 7 AM-noon, 1-4 PM; $1) alongside the white-walled St. Thomas missionary church. Both structures overlook the Colorado River from atop Indian Hill off the end of 1st Street.

ACROSS ARIZONA

Between the Colorado River, which divides Arizona from California, and the Phoenix-Tucson megalopolis in the middle of the state, there is not very much to attract the traveler off the freeway. However, the rather complete absence of interesting places in southwestern Arizona is more than made up for by the wealth of fascinating things to see in the state's southeast corner. Here you'll find such legendary sites as Tombstone—home of the OK Corral—and other finely presented reminders of the state's Wild West heritage, along with some of Arizona's most beautiful natural scenery.

Along with dozens of Spanish-language stations north and south of the Mexican border, Yuma's **KBLU 560 AM** plays oldies and local news.

Yuma

Among the hottest and driest towns in the country, Yuma (pop. 54,900) was first settled in 1779 at the site of one of the few good crossings along the Colorado River. Dozens of decaying old adobe buildings around town testify to Yuma's lengthy history, and a select few places are preserved as historic parks. The **Yuma Quartermaster Depot**, along the river at the north end of 4th Street (daily 10 AM-5 PM; $2), has been restored to its appearance prior to the arrival of the railroad in 1876, when supplies for U.S. troops throughout the Southwest arrived here by steamboat from the Gulf of California.

Around the time the railroad arrived, a full century after its founding by Spanish missionaries, Yuma was the site of Arizona Territory's main prison. Built out of stone and adobe by convicts struggling in the 120° heat, over the next 33 years until it was closed in 1909, the prison earned a reputation as the "Hellhole of Arizona," due in large part to the summer heat and the brutality of its regime, though park rangers emphasize the fact that prisoners had access to a library and other facilities unusual at the time. Now preserved as the state-run **Yuma Territorial Prison** (daily 8 AM-5 PM; $3), well-posted along the north side of I-8 at the 4th Street exit, the site consists of a few of the cells and the main gate, as well as a small museum.

From the prison, a rickety pedestrians-only steel bridge leads across the Colorado River to California and the **St. Thomas mission church** on the Quechan Indian Fort Yuma Reservation. The entire riverfront area, much of it under the I-8 bridge, is being restored as the Yuma Crossing Park.

Along with the usual national franchises, Yuma has a number of decent places to eat, ranging from the big breakfasts and afternoon BBQ at **Brownie's Cafe**, open daily 6 AM-9 PM at 1147 S. 4th Avenue (old US-80), to the pool tables, burgers, and sandwiches at ancient **Lutes Casino**, 211 Main Street in the desolate old downtown area. Voted the "Best Place to Stop in Yuma" by the *Arizona Republic* newspaper, Lutes is a barnlike hall full of old photos, political posters, street signs, and all manner of junk, well worth a look at least for its passionately played domino games.

Along with the national chains (two Motel 6's and a Travelodge), places to sleep in Yuma include the pleasant **Yuma Cabana**, 2151 S. 4th Avenue (520/783-8311 or 800/874-0811), with palm trees and a nice pool.

Yuma to Gila Bend: I-8

Spanning 110 miles of barren desert east of Yuma, between the U.S. Air Force's 14 million-acre Barry M. Goldwater Bombing Range and a U.S. Army Proving Ground, the I-8 freeway follows the route of early Spanish explorers and settlers on the flat but forbidding Camino del Diablo, along the banks of the usually dry Gila River.

East of 767-foot-high Telegraph Pass, 20 miles outside Yuma, the old US-80 highway reappears along the north side of the freeway, running through old-time desert outposts. If you're hungry, the flyspeck ranching community of **Tacna** has a great place to eat: **Basque Etchea**. Take I-8 exit 42, then head north across the railroad tracks. It's open every day but Monday 11 AM-10 PM for great lamb chops and a full menu of other dishes. **Dateland**, 25 miles farther east along I-8, has a cafe and gift shop selling dates in all possible forms, but otherwise there is really nothing to stop for between Yuma and Gila Bend.

Gila Bend

The only place approaching a town between Yuma and Phoenix or Tucson, Gila Bend (pop. 1,747) is regularly the "Hottest Spot in the Country"—a title of which it is so proud that, more than once, it's been caught inflating the numbers. First settled as a main stop on the Butterfield Stage route, Gila Bend doesn't offer much relief for the senses, though it does have all the gas stations, rest

rooms, restaurants, and motels you could reasonably expect to find in the middle of the Arizona desert.

One particularly fun place to eat is the **Space Age Coffee Shop,** open 24 hours at 401 E. Pima Avenue, downtown off exit 115. It's part of the Best Western Space Age Lodge motel (520/683-2273 or 800/528-1234). Both are essential stops for any Jetsons-aged traveler.

Twenty-two miles west of Gila Bend, off I-8 at exit 102, a road leads 11 miles north to **Painted Rocks State Historic Park,** where an array of petroglyphs, carved into the boulders by the Hohokam people around A.D. 1400, cover the rocks.

Phoenix is covered in a Survival Guide on pages 710-711.

Casa Grande Ruins National Monument

Just as there is almost nothing to see in the 110-mile stretch of I-8 between Yuma and Gila Bend, there is nothing much to stop for in the 120-odd miles between Gila Bend and Phoenix or Tucson. From the I-8/I-10 junction and the cotton-farming town of Casa Grande (pop. 19,082), a worthwhile detour runs east to the well-posted Casa Grande Ruins National Monument, which preserves some of the state's largest and most perplexing prehistoric remains. A small **visitor center** (daily 7 AM-6 PM; $1) at the entrance gives some background on the Hohokam people who, approximately six centuries ago, built the four-story Big House and the surrounding village, but no one knows what Casa Grande was used for, or why it was abandoned.

North and south of the Casa Grande area, the I-10 freeway parallels our US-93 route, which passes a few enticing desert oddities such as the famous Biosphere II earthbound space station.

From Gila Bend, Hwy-85 runs south to the beautiful and totally deserted **Organ Pipe Cactus National Monument,** before linking up with Hwy-86 to loop east to Tucson.

Tucson is covered as a Survival Guide on pages 724-725.

Saguaro National Monument-Rincon Mountains

A dozen miles east of Tucson, on the slopes of the Tanque Verde and Rincon Mountains, the eastern half of the fabulous Saguaro National Monument covers 57,000 acres of rolling desert landscape. Named in honor of the anthropomorphic saguaro (SWA-row) cactus, which here reach heights upwards of 40 feet and live as long as 200 years, the monument is best seen by following eight-mile Cactus Forest Drive, along which numerous trails give close-up looks at the multilimbed succulents. For more information and

The saguaro cactus blooms in May, and its creamy white blossoms are the Arizona state flower.

details of hiking opportunities, stop at the **visitor center** (daily 8 AM-5 PM; 520/296-8576), where the $4-per-car entry fee is collected.

On the road to the Rincon Mountains section of the monument, **Colossal Cave** (daily 9 AM-5 PM, longer hours in summer; $6.50) is a huge old limestone cavern which offers, if nothing else, a cool escape from the sweltering summer heat. One of the state's most enduring tourist attractions, Colossal Cave was used in Wild West times by train robbers who escaped here with $62,000; the money bags were recovered, but not the money.

Benson's radio station **KAVV 97.7 FM** plays lots of good Waylon-and-Willie-type country hits, plus captivating accounts of local news and activities.

Advertised by signs all along the freeway, one of the country's odder roadside attractions stands atop 4,975-foot Texas Summit, along I-10 at exit 322: **The Thing** (hours vary; 75 cents admission). A gas station, a gift shop, and a Dairy Queen stand in front of a prefab shed full of stuff ranging from a Rolls Royce once used by Adolf Hitler to The Thing itself, a mummified corpse whose "secret identity" has yet to be revealed. "What is it?" the signs ask . . . .

Benson and the Amerind Foundation

On the banks of the San Pedro River, Benson (pop. 3,824), already home to a large and stable population, was founded as a Santa Fe railroad connection to booming Tombstone and the Mexican harbor town of Guaymas. Trains still rumble through town, but there's not much to see apart from fading roadside signs. The **Horse Shoe Cafe**, 121 4th Street across from the railroad tracks, is where locals go to eat.

From Benson, our route cuts south on old US-80 (now Hwy-80), while I-10 races east over the mountains that 100-plus years ago were a stronghold of Apache warriors under Geronimo and Cochise. If you're following the interstate, a couple of sights are worth looking for. The more satisfying of these, the Amerind Foundation Museum (daily 10 AM-4 PM, closed Monday and Tuesday in summer; $3; 602/586-3666), lies 12 miles east of Benson, off Dragoon Road a mile southeast of I-10 exit 318. Started in 1937, the private, nonprofit museum is devoted to the study of local Native American cultures, with everything from ancient arrowheads to contemporary Pueblo pottery on display in the spacious mission-style buildings. Not surprisingly, the best collections are of Hopi, Navajo, and Apache artifacts, with well-presented exhibits of ceremonial and domestic objects—kachina dolls, rugs, and ritual costumes.

Tombstone

While I-10 races east over the mountains, our more scenic route, promoted by tourism authorities as the "Cochise Trail," winds south on old US-80 through the Wild West town of Tombstone, "The Town too Tough to Die." The route loops along the Mexican border before rejoining I-10 across the New Mexico border.

Though it's just 22 miles south of the freeway, and regularly inundated by busloads of tourists, the rough-and-ready mining town of Tombstone (pop. 1,220) has kept itself looking pretty much as it did back in the 1880s, when 10,000 miners called it home and one of the more mythic events of the Wild West took place here: the shoot-out at the OK Corral. Historians, and everyone in Tombstone, still debate the chain of events of October 26, 1881.

Every Sunday at 2 PM, historic gunfights are reenacted on the Tombstone streets. In October, Tombstone comes alive with a weekend of shoot-outs and parades during Helldorado Days. For details, contact the **visitor center,** 4th and Allen Streets (602/457-2211).

Was Wyatt Earp a sharpshooting savior, out to make Tombstone safe for decent society? Or was he really a grandstanding cowboy whom history has romanticized? Decide for yourself after hearing all sides of the story. The **OK Corral** (daily 8 AM-5 PM; $2) is still there, a block south of Fremont Street (old US-80), off Allen Street between 3rd and 4th Streets, with life-sized, black-leather-clad figures taking the places of Virgil and Wyatt Earp facing down the Clanton brothers. Next door to the OK Corral, the entertaining **Historama** (daily 9 AM-4 PM; $2) re-creates the events at the OK Corral through movies and animatronic figures.

The dead men, and many hundreds of others, ended up at **Boot Hill Cemetery** (daily 8 AM-6 PM; free), along the highway at the northern edge of town, where you can wander among the wooden grave markers inscribed with all manner of rhyming epitaphs.

Considering the huge numbers of people who descend upon Tombstone every day, and the gauntlet of T-shirt shops catering to them, the town is still an appealing place to visit. Eat breakfast, lunch, or dinner at **Nellie Cashman's,** 5th and Toughnut Streets, Tombstone's oldest eatery. Enjoy a cool drink at the **Crystal Palace Saloon,** 5th and Allen Streets, or at the local biker hangout **Legends of the West,** two doors down at 414 Allen Street. Places to stay are not extensive, nor very expensive: try the centrally located, $40-a-night **Tombstone Motel,** on the main road at 502 E. Fremont Street (520/457-3478).

Divide Monument

About 20 miles southeast of Tombstone, three miles west of Bisbee at the 6,030-foot Mule Pass summit of old US-80, the much-abused stone obelisk of the Divide Monument commemorates the convict-laborers who first constructed the road in 1913. The monument stands in a somewhat scruffy parking area directly above the modern tunnel, and from it you get a great panorama view of the surrounding Mule Mountains, certainly among the most beautiful in Arizona.

FLY'S PHOTOS

Wild West photographer Camilius S. Fly, whose work forms one of the primary records of life in frontier Arizona, had his main studio in Tombstone, now restored as part of the OK Corral. His images, displayed in the small gallery, include some of the earliest photos taken of Chiricahua Apache warrior Geronimo, as well as shots of Wyatt Earp, "Doc" Holliday, and many others. What Matthew Brady was to the Civil War, Fly was to Tombstone in its 1880s heyday.

Bisbee

A classic boom-and-bust mining town, Bisbee (pop. 6,288) is one of the most satisfying offbeat destinations in Arizona, combining scenic beauty, palpable history and a good range of places to eat, drink, and enjoy yourself. Climbing up winding streets lined by 100-year-old structures—Victorian cottages, board shacks, and stately brick churches—Bisbee has attracted a diverse population of desert rats, bikers, working artists, and new age apostles, all of whom mix amiably in the town's cafes and bars.

The heart of Bisbee lies north of old US-80 along Main Street, stretching west from the **Bisbee Mining and Historical Museum** (daily 10 AM-4 PM; $3), which displays dioramas, old photos, and sundry artifacts inside the old Phelps Dodge company headquarters. Main Street has many cafes, antique shops, art galleries, and restaurants.

The main event in Bisbee is the **Copper Queen Mine.** Put on a hard hat and a miner's lamp, and descend into the mine shafts, which were in operation until WW II. Hour-long **tours** (daily 9 AM-3:30 PM; $8) leave every 90 minutes from the Queen Mine building, just south of downtown along old US-80.

One of Arizona's most unforgettable sights, the massive **Lavender Open Pit** forms a gigantic polychrome crater along Hwy-80, just south of the Queen Mine. Named not for its color—which is more rusty red than purple—but for a mine superintendent, Harry Lavender, this was a true glory hole with ore deposits that provided the bulk of Bisbee's eight billion pounds of copper before they ran out in 1974.

At the center of Bisbee, the **Copper Queen Hotel,** looming over downtown along Howell Street (520/432-2216), has been the best place to stay since it opened in 1902. Most of the rooms have been upgraded to include modern conveniences without losing the old-fashioned charms, and rates start at $65. Another nice place to stay is the **Bisbee Inn,** 450 K Street (520/432-5131), overlooking Brewery Gulch and offering B&B rooms (shared bathrooms) from about $45 for two.

The Copper Queen Hotel has a good restaurant and popular bar; other good bets include breakfast or lunch at **Cafe Cornucopia** and dinner at the gourmet **Cafe Roka**, across from each other along Main Street. Brewery Gulch, which runs north from Main Street at the east side of downtown Bisbee, once held over 50 different saloons and gambling parlors; it's considerably quieter now, but still home to such fun haunts as the **Stock Exchange** bar, inside the old Bisbee Stock Exchange, and **St. Elmo's**, which has live music most nights. Bisbee also has a couple of espresso bars, like **Cafe Renaissance** at the foot of Brewery Gulch.

For further information, walking-tour maps, or details of special events, contact the Bisbee **visitor center**, 7 Main Street (520/432-5421).

The Border: Douglas and Agua Prieta

Like Bisbee, the border town of Douglas (pop. 12,822) grew up on copper mining, which here lasted until fairly recently: the huge smokestack of the Phelps-Dodge smelter a mile west of town was in operation until 1987, processing ores from mines in Mexico. Now most of the economy revolves around cross-border trade with *maquiladora* plants in its much larger Mexican neighbor, Agua Prieta (pop. 80,000), which in the past decades has quadrupled in size.

There's not a lot to see in either Douglas or Agua Prieta, though Douglas does boast one fabulous attraction: the landmark **Gadsden Hotel**, 1046 G Avenue (520/364-4481). Rebuilt in 1928 after a fire destroyed the 1907 original, the spacious gold-leafed lobby—one of the grandest public spaces in the state—has a pretty Tiffany-style stained-glass mural decorating its mezzanine. The small and basic rooms start at a bargain $35, and there's also a good Mexican-American restaurant and a very popular bar, the Saddle and Spur, its walls decorated with over 200 cattle brands from area ranches.

Cave Creek and Chiricahua National Monument

For the 50-odd miles between Douglas and the New Mexico state line, old US-80 cuts diagonally across the southeast corner of Arizona, a rugged country of mountains, canyons, and volcanic outcrops rising above sagebrush plains. There's not much to see along the highway, but to the northwest rise the enticing Pendregosa Mountains, whose forested peaks, now protected as part of the Coronado National Forest, long served as sanctuary to Chiricahua Apaches and sundry outlaws and wanted men.

While you can also reach them from the north off I-10, the best access to the mountains from the south is via the aptly named hamlet of **Portal**, west of old US-80 from the New Mexico border, where the **Portal Peak Lodge, Store and Cafe** (520/558-2223) is a welcoming oasis, offering fresh food and comfortable rooms.

La Vuelta de Bisbee, a highly competitive professional cycling race held every April, sees hundreds of world-class riders racing up and down Bisbee's steep streets.

One of the famous events in Bisbee's busy history occurred in July 1917, when over 1,000 miners on strike for better pay and conditions were forcibly deported—literally railroaded out of town and dumped in the desert outside Columbus, New Mexico.

Travel along the Mexican border is enlivened immeasurably by the many radio stations, varying from the country twang of Douglas's KDAP 96.5 FM to the many south-of-the-border stations that play a part-English, part-Spanish Tejano mélange typified by songs like "Mama, No Deje Que Sus Hijos Grow Up To Be Vaqueros."

Agua Prieta was the site of skirmishes between revolutionary **Pancho Villa** and the Mexican army.

A monument along the highway, a half-mile east of the tiny town of Apache, points out the nearby site where Apache warrior **Geronimo** finally surrendered to the U.S. Army in 1886.

Much of southeastern Arizona is still open range, so keep an eye out for livestock on the highway.

Above Portal rise the sheer cliffs of Cave Creek Canyon, which writer William Least Heat Moon described in *Blue Highways* as "one of the strangest pieces of topography I've ever seen," its pale sandstone walls looking like a sun-bleached twin of Utah's Zion National Park. A narrow but passable (except in winter) 20-mile dirt road from Cave Creek climbs over the mountains' pine-covered, 7,600-foot-high crest, ending up in the west at the foot of intriguing **Chiricahua National Monument,** a veritable "Wonderland of Rocks" whose contorted shapes were formed out of soft volcanic stone by eons of erosion.

The **visitor center** (daily 8 AM-5 PM; 520/824-3560) near the monument entrance has information on hiking, camping, and wildlife-watching opportunities in the Chiricahuas. Be aware that there are no services—gas, food, or lodging—near the park.

ACROSS NEW MEXICO

Between Arizona and Texas, the I-10 freeway crosses the part of New Mexico known as the Bootheel, for the way it steps down toward Old Mexico. Until the Gadsden Purchase of 1853, all this was part of Mexico, and the Hispanic influence still dominates the Anglo-American. The few towns here, like Lordsburg and Deming, were founded and remain primarily based on the railroad, and offer little for the passing traveler. However, at least one place is definitely worth a stop: the historic village of Mesilla, set around a dusty plaza just south of the region's one big city, Las Cruces.

Lordsburg and Shakespeare
Coming in from southeastern Arizona, old US-80 rejoins the I-10 freeway at a crossroads community aptly called Road Forks, and 15 miles farther east the free-

way swerves south to bypass the town of Lordsburg (pop. 2,951). Named not from any religious conviction but in honor of the Southern Pacific railroad engineer who plotted it in 1880, Lordsburg has little to offer other than its 17 gas stations, 11 cafes (try the **Holiday** at the center of town, or 24-hour **El Charro** next to the train station), and 10 motels, which line "Motel Drive," the three-mile-long I-10 Business Route (old US-80).

Like something out of *The Andromeda Strain*, Lordsburg feels oddly abandoned, as if everyone has just packed up and left town. However, one good reason to stop is New Mexico's best preserved ghost town, Shakespeare, three miles south of Lordsburg on a well-marked dirt road. Briefly home to some 3,000 silver miners during the early 1870s, Shakespeare was abandoned when the mines dried up, only to be reborn during another brief mining boom in the 1880s. By the 1930s it was turned into a ranch by the Hill family, whose descendants still live here, care for the buildings, and conduct irregularly scheduled guided **tours** (weekends 10 AM and 2 PM; $3; 505/542-9034) of the Grant House saloon, the general store (where you can buy books and postcards), and the Stratford Hotel, where Billy the Kid washed dishes as a young boy.

After delving into Texas at El Paso, you'll enter New Mexico again near Carlsbad Caverns National Park, which is described on page 598.

Across New Mexico, towns along the interstate post road signs that total up their tourist services. Deming, for example, has 27 gas stations, 21 restaurants, and 13 motels.

Deming

Some 60 miles east of Lordsburg, halfway to Las Cruces, the dusty ranching and farming community of Deming (pop. 10,970) advertises itself as "Deming—Home of Pure Water and Fast Ducks." This motto, which is repeated on billboard after billboard along I-10, makes more sense than it may at first: Deming's water comes from the underground Mimbres River, and every year at the end of August the town hosts duck races (for living ones, not the rubber kind) with prizes of some $10,000 going to the winners.

All this is little more than a cheap ploy to get hapless (or bored stiff, or both) travelers to turn off tedious I-10 and visit their city. Fortunately, it's not a bad place, boasting the excellent **Deming-Luna-Mimbres Museum**, 301 S. Silver Street (Mon.-Sat. 9 AM-4 PM, Sunday 1-4 PM; donations), three blocks south of Pine Street (old US-80), Deming's main drag. Besides the usual range of old pottery, sparkling rocks, and pioneer artifacts, the museum displays an endearing collection of old toys, dolls, quilts, and dental equipment—well worth a quick look at the very least.

If you're hungry, avoid the usual franchised fast-food places and head to the **Hot Creek Saloon** downtown, which is a fun place for burgers, beers, and a game of pool or two. For Mexican food, including excellent *chiles rellenos*, check out the **Cactus Cafe**, along the freeway at 218 W. Cedar Street.

Rooms range from local places like the **Butterfield Stage Motel**, at 200 W. Pine Street (505/544-0011), to a **Best Western**, a **Holiday Inn**, and a **Motel 6** (off I-10 at exit 85). Best

Silver City, an evocative old mining town high in the mountains 45 miles northeast of Lordsburg, was another early stomping ground of Wild West outlaw **Billy the Kid** and makes an excellent sidetrip between Lordsburg and Deming.

Midway between Lordsburg and Deming, where I-10 imperceptibly crosses the 4,585-foot **Continental Divide,** Bowlin's Trading Post sells fireworks, rattlesnake eggs, and sundry other road trip essentials, as advertised by dozens of billboards along the highway.

Deming's own **KNFT 102.9 FM** plays Top 40 country hits of the past 25 years.

In southwestern New Mexico, the I-10 freeway roughly parallels the route followed in the 1850s by the Butterfield Stage, the 2,800-mile-long main overland link between St. Louis and San Francisco.

Along US-70 some 50 miles northeast of Las Cruces, **White Sands National Monument** protects over 60,000 acres of gleaming white gypsum dunes.

Mesilla was founded across the Rio Grande on the Mexican side of the border in 1848, after the agreement of the Mexican-American War gave everything to the north to the Americans. Four years later, Mesilla became (legally at least) American again, after the Gadsden Purchase bought the entire "Bootheel" region for $10 million.

place to camp is southeast of town in **Rockhound State Park** ($8; 505/546-1212), where besides finding nice sites with hot showers you can collect up to 15 pounds of geodes, agates, or quartz crystals—something the rangers urge you to do.

Las Cruces and Mesilla

Spreading along the eastern banks of the Rio Grande, at the foot of the angular Organ Mountains, Las Cruces (pop. 62,126) is the commercial center of a prosperous agricultural and recreational region. Named for a concentration of pioneer grave markers, Las Cruces was first settled by Spanish missionaries but is now a thoroughly modern, American-looking place, with all the gas stations you could want, plus 130 restaurants and 31 motels (from a **Motel 6** to an upscale **Hilton**), but nothing really worth searching out.

The best thing about Las Cruces is its nearness to a truly neat little place, the historic village of Mesilla, three miles southwest of Las Cruces via Hwy-28. Low-slung adobe buildings set around a shady central plaza hold a couple of historic sites—including an old jail from which Billy the Kid escaped in 1880—and a pair of excellent cantina-type restaurants, including very popular **La Posta** and less pricey but equally good **El Patio**. Also in Mesilla, on Barker Road across Hwy-28 from the plaza, the **Gadsden Museum** (daily 9-11 AM, 1-5 PM; $2) traces local history from pre-conquest to current times.

Southeast from Las Cruces and Mesilla, our route dips south across the Texas border to El Paso, then continues on US-180 some 60 miles east before reentering New Mexico to take in Carlsbad Caverns National Park. For the run to El Paso you have your choice between I-10 or slower and more scenic Hwy-28, which parallels the freeway through dusty small towns along the banks of the Rio Grande.

ACROSS TEXAS

Mileage-wise the haul across Texas is the longest part of this coast-to-coast route, but as far as things to see, the state doesn't offer a very high quotient per gallon. In the far-western stretches near **El Paso**, to maximize scenic interest, follow the slower but significantly more attractive route along US-180 past the beautiful **Guadalupe Mountains**, and veer into New Mexico to see the remarkable **Carlsbad Caverns**.

From Carlsbad it's a straight shot across the painfully flat Llano Estacado, which stretches to both sides of the New Mexico/Texas border; this section of the route is one of the least action-packed in the country—there's literally nothing for miles, apart from oil derricks, cattle ranches, and cotton plantations. Only a few of the sporadic towns here have any historic claim or aesthetic interest; it's basically a

A TORTILLA BY ANY OTHER NAME

Carne adovada, calabacitas, posole, sopaipillas . . . . Menu items like these put you squarely in the lower left-hand quadrant of any U.S. map. But how do you know whether you're eating traditional New Mexican cooking, Southwestern Cuisine, or the popular hybrid known as Tex-Mex? Truth is, they're all hybrids, launched nearly five centuries ago when the Spanish brought European spices and domestic animals to combine with indigenous ingredients. As Spanish and Mexican settlers followed El Camino Real north from Chihuahua to Santa Fe, culinary distinctions grew out of regional variations in locally grown products along the way.

What's new is the categories: a generation ago, folks just helped themselves to "Mexican food." Still, certain characteristics distinguish each cuisine. In New Mexico, the chiles set the dishes apart—and set your taste buds afire. New Mexico's Mesilla Valley is to chiles what California's Napa Valley is to wine production. When you order a local specialty, the server may ask, "Red or green?"—referring to red or green chile. You can ask which is hotter and order accordingly, or try a little of each one.

Tex-Mex, as its name implies, draws from both sides of the international border, from grazing lands where *vaqueros* roast meat over mesquite fires. Hearty foods like *carne asada* (grilled meat) are accompanied by refried beans, guacamole, flour tortillas, and *pico de gallo*—an essential tomato and chile salsa. Fajitas, too, once signaled Tex-Mex territory, but that was before the rest of the country discovered the tasty strips of skirt steak.

When the food fusion goes farther afield than Mexico and the American Southwest, as in, say, Southwestern roasted chile bruschetta or spring rolls with green chile, you know you've entered the nebulous realm of contemporary Southwestern Cuisine, and all bets are off. The world-class chefs of Santa Fe recognize no limits, creative or otherwise. The world is their blue-corn fried oyster.

long day's drive across the open plains. If you're in a hurry, you won't miss much by following the I-20 freeway between El Paso and the Dallas/Fort Worth metropolitan area.

In eastern Texas, the landscape gradually evolves into that of the Deep South, the dense pine woods doing their best to disguise the historic dependence on the oil industry—with profits far more apparent in the towers of Dallas than here at the poverty-stricken source. Again, the interstates offer a faster way across, and you can turn off where you want to visit the few sites of interest, like tiny **Kilgore**, home of the "World's Richest Acre" and the captivating East Texas Oil Museum.

A tip for tender palates: if the chile's heat has you reaching for your Dos Equis, don't. Like water on gasoline, beer, soda pop, and even ice water only spread the fire. Try milk or, failing that, chew on a tortilla.

El Paso

Part of the largest international community in North America, El Paso (pop. 515,342) was originally settled because of its site at the easiest crossing of the Rio

Grande. It later grew into a vital way-station on the transcontinental Butterfield Stage and Southern Pacific Railroad. As its name suggests, for most people El Paso is a place to pass through, but there are many things here for visitors to enjoy.

One of the most interesting aspects of El Paso is the border itself, which for years followed the Rio Grande (known as the Río Bravo in Mexico), whose frequent changes in course caused innumerable problems for the two governments. Finally, in 1963, the river was run through a concrete channel so it could not change course. The border is now the location of the **Chamizal National Memorial**, on San Marical Street off Paisano Drive, where a small museum (daily 8 AM-5 PM; free) tells the border story and is surrounded by a pleasant green park. The Bridge of the Americas leads across to Ciudad Juárez (pop. 1.5 million) on the Mexican side.

Q. Why do they call it Texas?
A. Because it "Texas" so long to drive across.

El Paso has two claims to fame: it's the home of **Tony Lama** boots, which are available at significant discounts at four showrooms around town; and the **UTEP** campus, along I-10 west of town, has the only buildings in North America designed to look like Tibetan monasteries.

Another unique attraction hidden away amidst El Paso's horizontal sprawl is the Spanish colonial missions that still stand southeast of downtown. The oldest missions in what is now the United States, this trio of churches—Ysleta, Socorro, and San Elizario—stand along the well-signed "Mission Trail," between the Rio Grande and I-10, roughly 15 miles from the center of town.

Along with the missions, all of which are still in use, El Paso holds a number of small special-interest museums, including ones dedicated to such diverse subjects as the U.S. Border Patrol, Napoléon Bonaparte, and frontier medicine. Four more—the U.S. Army Air Defense Artillery Museum, the Third Cavalry Museum, the Museum of the Non-Commissioned Officer, and the Fort Bliss Museum—are located at Fort Bliss, tracing El Paso's significant military history. All four are free and open daily 9 AM-4:30 PM.

Places to eat in and around El Paso tend, not surprisingly, to specialize in Tex-Mex food. Peruse the menus at **JJ's Drive-In**, 5326

Socorro Mission

Doniphan, off I-10 exit 11; at classic old **Forti's Mexican Elder**, 321 Chelsea Street east of downtown near the Paisano Avenue exit off I-10; and at **Grigg's**, east of town near Fort Bliss at 9007 Montana Avenue (US-180), which has been serving classic New Mexican food since 1939.

El Paso's finest place to stay is the grand old **Camino Real Paso Del Norte Hotel**, 101 S. El Paso Street (915/534-3000), one of the classiest hotels anywhere, with a beautiful bar off the lobby and rates (starting around $85) lower than you might think. All the usual mid-range chains are here too, plus a handy AYH-approved youth hostel at the historic Gardner Hotel, 311 E. Franklin Street (915/532-3661).

For maps or more information on El Paso or neighboring Juárez, contact the **visitors bureau** downtown at 1 Civic Center Plaza (915/534-0653 or 800/351-6024).

> El Paso's hard-to-find Concordia Cemetery (it's just northwest of the I-10/US-54 junction) is the final resting place of **John Wesley Harding,** the "Fastest Gun in the West" before he got killed in 1895.

Hueco Tanks State Historic Park

In the 100 miles of arid West Texas desert between El Paso and the Guadalupe Mountains, look forward to precious little but the tiny Hueco Tanks State Historic Park (daily 8 AM-dusk; $2) on the fringes of Fort Bliss, some 30 miles east of El Paso, then eight miles north on Hwy-2775. Established to preserve the approximately 5,000 pictographs painted on the basalt boulders, the 850-acre park also protects the remains of a stagecoach station and an old ranch house. The "tanks" of the title are naturally formed rock basins, which collect rainwater and have made the site a natural stop for passing travelers, from prehistoric natives to the Butterfield Stage.

> For the first 35 miles east of El Paso, US-180 runs along the southern edge of gigantic Fort Bliss, which stretches north for 50 miles into New Mexico and is home to about 20,000 U.S. troops.

Some 35 miles east of the Hueco Tanks turnoff, the tiny highway town of **Cornudas** has a nice cafe—"Home of the World Famous Cornudas Burger"—and a row of false-fronted Wild West buildings.

Guadalupe Mountains National Park

The only national park in the whole of Texas, Guadalupe Mountains National Park covers the rugged peaks that rise along the New Mexico border, 110 miles east of El Paso. Formed as part of the same Capitan Reef of limestone that caused the great caverns of Carlsbad, the Guadalupes, a cool contrast to the surrounding desert, rise in sheer faces about 2,000 feet above the desert floor and offer the chance to experience many different and contrasting eco-systems side by side, within easy reach of the highway.

Unless you're prepared to do some serious mountaineering—which is really the only way to experience the grandeur of the park or to see signs of the abundant wildlife (including mountain lions)—the best way to get a feel for the Guadalupes is

Climb **Guadalupe Peak**, the highest point in Texas at 8,749 feet, via a very steep three-mile-long trail from the main visitor center along US-180.

to walk through **McKittrick Canyon**, in the northeast corner of the park. From the **visitor center** (daily 8 AM-4:30 PM; free; 915/828-3251) at the end of the road, a well-marked, well-maintained, and generally flat 3.5-mile trail winds along a stream, through a green landscape that changes gradually from the cactus of the Chihuahuan Desert to the oaks, walnuts, and maples of the inner canyon. It's best in spring, when the desert wildflowers bloom, or in autumn, when the hardwoods turn color.

The Guadalupe Mountains area is a corner of the central time zone; everything to the north and west, including El Paso and Carlsbad, is on mountain time.

Carlsbad Caverns National Park

Carved out of the solid limestone of Capital Reef by eons of dripping water, the Carlsbad Caverns contain over 30 miles of underground caves, some over 1,000 feet across. A two-mile trail (daily 8 AM-3:30 PM; $5) drops steeply from the large visitor center; or you can board an elevator and ride 750 feet straight down to the "Big Room," where after wandering among the countless stalactites, stalagmites, and other formations, you can chow down on cheeseburgers at a classic 1950s-style cafeteria. Everyone has to ride the elevator back to the surface.

The trail down to the caverns closes early in the afternoon, so that visitors don't interrupt the increasingly popular spectacle of the "**Bat Flight**," in which hundreds of thousands of Mexican freetail bats swirl out of the caverns at sunset. Every evening (usually around 7 PM, except in winter when the bats have migrated to Mexico), rangers give a brief free talk about bats—proselytizing about how really great and harmless they are—waiting for them to set off into the night.

The nearest places to stay and eat are in **Whites City**, along Hwy-180 at the turnoff to the park. Built by and named after James White, who first promoted the caverns as a tourist destination, this is basically a giant complex of motels, restaurants, and souvenir shops. Rooms at the two **Best Westerns** (505/785-2291 or 800/CAVERNS) cost about $60 a night.

North of Carlsbad Caverns, state-run radio station 530 AM broadcasts Ricardo Montalban continuously recounting the story of the famous **Goodnight-Loving cattle trail**, which ran along the nearby Pecos River.

Carlsbad

Twenty miles northeast of the Carlsbad Caverns, the town of Carlsbad (pop. 25,000) makes its living from the 750,000 tourists who visit the caves every year, and has the motels to prove it: lining Canal Street (US-180), the main road through town, you'll find national chains like Best Western, Holiday Inn, Motel 6, and Travelodge, and funkier local counterparts like the **Stagecoach Inn**, 1819 S. Canal Street (505/887-1148). There's also one very good Mexican restaurant, the **Casa de Cortez** at 506 S. Canal Street, a plain brown brick building where locals come for heaping helpings of *frijoles refritos* and *chiles rellenos*; no booze, no credit cards, but great fresh *sopaipillas*.

Apart from the caverns, the one other thing to see in the Carlsbad area is the **Living Desert State Park** (8 AM-sunset; $3), four miles northwest off US-285, which shows off the plant and animal life of the arid Chihuahuan Desert region.

LUBBOCK: PANHANDLE MUSIC MECCA

The largest city in northwest Texas, Lubbock (pop. 186,206) is a busy and unattractive agricultural center, best known for having given the world Buddy Holly, whose songs ("Peggy Sue," "That'll Be The Day," "Rave On") paved the way for rock 'n' roll. For music fans, the trip downtown to pay homage at the statue of Buddy at the corner of 8th Street and Avenue Q is well worthwhile. He's surrounded by plaques honoring other Lubbock boys and girls made good, including Roy Orbison, Waylon Jennings, Tanya Tucker, and Joe Ely. Buddy, who died in a 1959 plane crash at age 22, is buried near the entrance of Lubbock Cemetery, at the east end of 31st Street.

Another main attraction of Lubbock is Prairie Dog Town, in Mackenzie State Park at the northeast edge of downtown, somewhat hard to find off Avenue A.

For more information, contact the tourist office at Avenue K and 14th Street (806/763-4666 or 800/692-4035).

US-180: The Llano Estacado

From Carlsbad, US-180 crosses the Pecos River, then snakes across the barren Llano Estacado, the "Staked Plain," which covers most of eastern New Mexico and the Texas Panhandle. Supposedly named by early explorers who drove wooden stakes into the ground to mark their way, the Llano Estacado area is pretty much the same on both sides of the border—flat, dry, and mostly devoid of settlement. For eastbound travelers, this is the place where oil first becomes noticeably important—pumpjacks can be seen pumping away along US-180, from here all the way to Alabama.

This is also cowboy country, thanks to the extensive pastures irrigated by water pumped up from aquifers deep underground. For travelers, however, the dominant image is of land stretching out far and wide: mile after mile after mile of endless flat cotton fields, interrupted every now and then by brilliant green alfalfa fields and a few surprisingly large towns like **Hobbs**, New Mexico (pop. 29,115), right on the border, its street lined by various "Drilling Supply" companies and huge piles of old pipe. Texas towns like **Seminole** (pop. 6,342), **Lamesa** (pop. 10,809)—which is pronounced "Lameesa" and does have an intact old Dairy Queen Drive-in right on US-180—and **Snyder** (pop. 12,195)—which has a life-sized statue of an albino buffalo on its courthouse square—give few good reasons to stop and, to be honest, there's not much in the 325-odd miles between the state border and the fringes of Fort Worth.

As part of a federal program known as WIPP—the Waste Isolation Pilot Plant—the underground salt mines east of Carlsbad are in the process of being adapted into a contentious disposal site for the nation's nuclear waste.

Lamesa's radio station **KYMI 107.9 FM** plays everything from *norteños* to Hank Williams (Sr. and Jr.), plus intriguing announcements of local news and events.

Gail

Midway between Lamesa and Snyder, the tiny town of Gail (pop. 189)—which the *Texas State Travel Guide* describes as a "cow town without bank, theater, railroad, hotel, doctor, or lawyer"—was the site of violent feuds during the land rush of 1902, the history of which is recounted in the tiny **Borden County Museum** (Thurs.-Sun. noon-4 PM; $1). The town, and the county, are named in memory of pioneer surveyor and newspaper editor **Gail Borden**, who is perhaps best known as the inventor of condensed milk and founder of Borden Foods.

Sweetwater

If you've decided to take the high-speed route along I-20, midway across Texas you'll pass Sweetwater, where every March, during the **Rattlesnake Round-Up**, townspeople get together and collect hundreds of rattlers from the surrounding ranch lands, winning prizes for the biggest, shortest, and most snakes handed in.

The town also sells all manner of rattlesnake-related souvenirs, and any time of year, Sweetwater—which was first settled in the 1850s and now earns its livelihood mining gypsum for use in wallboard—is worth a stop for a meal at one of the best restaurants in West Texas, **Allen's Family-Style Meals**, 1301 E. Broadway (915/235-2060) on old US-80.

At the town of Anson, US-180 crosses US-83, the original "Road to Nowhere," which is described beginning on page 122.

Albany

Albany, one of the more interesting towns in this part of Texas, was first settled as a stage stop on the route of the Butterfield Overland Mail in 1854. It's still a tiny place, with no more than 2,000 residents, but it has a lively feel and, more surprisingly, a small but intriguing art museum (Tues.-Sat. 9 AM-5 PM, Sunday 2-5 PM; free) in the Old City Jail at 211 S. 2nd Street. A big surprise in the middle of the ranch lands, the museum contains an outstanding permanent collection of art by Modigliani, Picasso, and others, and also displays Chinese ceramics from the Tang and Ming dynasties.

The nearby courthouse is the oldest in Texas, in use since 1883. Fifteen miles north of Albany on US-283, **Fort Griffin State Historical Park** (daily 8 AM-10 PM; $3 per car) preserves the remains of the main base of U.S. Cavalry sorties against the Comanche raiders during the late 1860s.

The I-20 town of **Cisco,** 45 miles east of Abilene, is where **Conrad Hilton** bought and ran his first hotel, the Mobley, in 1919. East of Cisco the town of Eastland has two world-class oddities. The middle entrance to the county courthouse displays the embalmed body of "Old Rip" the Toad, who survived 29 years embedded in the cornerstone of the old courthouse before being discovered, alive, when it was being torn down. A few blocks away at 411 W. Main St., the post office contains a huge stamp-themed mural made entirely of 11,217 postage stamps, created over a seven-year period by former postmistress Marene Johnson (a postcard of the mural is available).

For information about Dallas/Fort Worth consult the Survival Guide on pages 690-691.

Terrell

East from Dallas, US-80 is, except during rush hour, a fast four-lane freeway across the suburbs. A dozen miles east of downtown, a huge number of antique shops fill prefab industrial sheds along the highway, just before the freeway merges into I-20.

The old road parallels the freeway through Terrell (pop. 12,490), the birthplace of the U.S. Department of Agriculture Cooperative Extension Service program, which first brought modern science and technology to traditional family farms in the 1930s. Terrell's small airport is home to the unique **Silent Wings Museum** (Tues.-Sat. 10 AM-5 PM, Sunday noon-5 PM; free), which has one of the only fully restored CG-4A gliders in existence, along with lots of exhibits recounting the exploits of glider planes during WW II.

Grand Saline

East of Terrell, US-80 winds over rolling hills, where small farms grow fruits and berries in the sandy loam. Halfway between Dallas and Longview spreads Grand

602 US-80: SOUTHERN PACIFIC

The salt deposits under Grand Saline are estimated to be over 16,000 feet thick and nearly 10,000 feet across, enough to supply the world's needs for the next 20,000 years.

South of I-20, the town of **Tyler** grows thousands and thousands of roses, including the famous yellow ones, the "National Rose of Texas." For roadtrippers, Tyler is also worth a stop for the fine food at **Bodacious Bar-B-Q,** hard to miss on the north side of I-20 at the Hwy-14 exit and open daily 10 AM-9 PM.

Saline, so named because of the massive mines of salt used as a spice and preservative since at least the early 1800s, when displaced Cherokee Indians discovered the deposits here. At first the salt was reclaimed from the broad salt flats that spread out from the town, but mine shafts were later dug to reach the hard-rock salt hundreds of feet beneath the ground. Morton Salt now owns and operates the mines. Hot water is pumped underground, the resulting brine is evaporated and crystallized, and the salt is packaged for home and industrial uses.

Longview and Kilgore: Oil!

The pine-covered, red earth hills around the busy industrial center of Longview (70,311) are covered with creaking old pumpjacks, still pumping up the East Texas oil that has kept the region economically afloat since the 1930s. Longview itself has a neat and usually deserted old downtown area with brick-paved streets, but the one real attraction is the famously good Creole food at **Johnny Cace's Seafood and Steak House,** on US-80 east of downtown at 1501 E. Marshall Road.

The East Texas oil business has gone through numerous booms and busts since it gushed into existence in December 1930 at a well outside Kilgore (pop. 11,066), on the south side of I-20. Ten miles southwest of Longview via US-259, this smaller and quieter oil town is a much more satisfying place to visit, with street lamps disguised as oil rigs and a set of 100-foot-tall derricks standing along the railroad tracks in memory of the **"World's Richest Acre,"** a plot of downtown land that produced over 2.5 million barrels of oil through the 1960s. The site was so productive and so valuable that one of the wells was drilled through the terrazzo floor of a local bank, and over a thousand derricks once loomed over the downtown area.

The history of the local petroleum industry is recounted in entertaining detail at the **East Texas Oil Museum,** (Tues.-Sat. 9 AM-4 PM, Sunday 2-5 PM; $3.50) on the campus of Kilgore College, on Ross Street off US-259. The museum includes displays of drilling equipment and old gas stations, plus a simulated "elevator ride" a mile deep into the earth to show off the oil-bearing geology. Also on the Kilgore College campus is a small museum devoted to the **Kilgore Rangerettes,** a college-trained precision drill and dance team that performs at college and professional football games.

Kilgore is decidedly not a typical tourist destination, with only minimal motels and restaurants available, though there is at least one good place to eat: **Lupe's,** serving up traditional Tex-Mex food on US-259 north of downtown.

Marshall and Jefferson

North of I-20 some 25 miles west of the Louisiana state line, Marshall (pop. 23,682) is one of the older, and once among the wealthiest, towns in Texas. Now a fairly quiet place, in its early years Marshall was the commercial capital of the East Texas cotton country, and during the Civil War two local residences served as the Confederate capital—of Missouri. This anomaly, along with general regional history, is chronicled in the **Harrison County Historical Society Museum** (Tues.-Sat. 9 AM-5 PM, Sunday 1:30-5 PM; $2), housed in the supremely ornate, yellow brick courthouse on the town square. Nearby, have a look at the magnificently restored circa 1896 **Ginocchio Hotel,** on Washington Street across from the train station.

If you have the time and inclination to get a more palpable sense of the varied culture and history of East Texas, take US-59 15 miles north of Marshall to Jefferson (pop. 2,199), an almost perfectly preserved bayou town that looks much as it did during the 1870s when, with a population of nearly 30,000, it was the busiest inland port west of the Mississippi. Most prominent of the hundreds of historic structures here is the 1858 **Excelsior House,** 211 W. Austin Street (903/665-2513), which offers free tours daily and has rooms from around $50 a night. Nearby, you can tour Jay Gould's private railroad car, the *Atalanta,* or simply explore the many good antique shops, cafes, and restaurants, like the Creole-flavored **Black Swan,** 210 Austin Street. For more information, contact the Jefferson **tourist office** at 115 W. Austin Street (903/665-2672).

ACROSS LOUISIANA

Northern Louisiana, which covers some 200 miles of forested, rolling hills between Texas and Mississippi, is a far cry from the Cajun fun of the southern half of the state. A Baptist-dominated "Bible Belt" heartland, it's also a very diverse place, part heavily industrial, part poor rural backwater, with a mix of people and products that encapsulates its transitional position between the agricultural Deep South and the petrochemical plants of Texas.

The main city here is the oil town of Shreveport, which has recently become a prime place for gamblers, with flashy casinos lining the riverfront. However, you'll mostly find small towns ranging from Gibsland (where Bonnie and Clyde met their doom) to the college town of Ruston (home to Louisiana Tech and Grambling Universities).

Shreveport

A King Cotton town that thrived in the antebellum years and survived the war physically, though not economically, unscathed, Shreveport (pop. 198,525) is now a busy industrial city rising on the west bank of the Red River. Along with its industrialized ugly stepbrother, Bossier City (pronounced "BO-zyur") across the river, Shreveport is a center of the Louisiana oil business—which is small only when compared to that of Texas, and still hugely important despite slumps in supplies and prices. Also, the cities emerged in recent years as two of the hotspots of Louisiana's nascent gambling industry, with four major casinos—including the lively **Horseshoe,** a four-story faux riverboat floating in a shallow pond on the Bossier City side—along the riverfront attracting people from all over the tri-state "Ark-La-Tex" region.

Downtown Shreveport is the usual mix of turn-of-the-century brick buildings and boarded-up shopfronts, loomed over by

North of Shreveport on Hwy-1, **Oil City** has one of the region's better history museums, housed inside the old railroad depot and displaying a wonderful collection of old postcards.

Shreveport is named in honor of **Capt. Henry Shreve,** who in the 1830s cleared the Red River of a 165-mile-long logjam that had blocked navigation. He then "bought" the land from native Caddo Indians.

a solitary 10-story glass office tower, with a handful of interesting structures surviving near the riverfront; walking-tour maps of the area are available from the **visitor center,** a block west of the river at 629 Spring Street (318/222-9391 or 800/551-8682).

The nicest part of town is the leafy Highland district, stretching south from the end of Market Street, south of I-20 between the river and the new I-49 freeway. This is where you'll find the grand old houses of the landed gentry, many of which look like they belong in *Gone With The Wind,* despite the fact that almost all of them date from the 20th century. The Highland district also holds two of Shreveport's better places to eat: the **Centenary Grill,** 1309 Centenary Boulevard, and **Don's Seafood House,** 3100 Highland Avenue, both serving moderately priced Cajun-spiced specialties. All the usual hotel and motel chains line I-20.

GIBSLAND, LOUISIANA

"AUTHENTIC BONNIE & CLYDE FESTIVAL"

See Where The Outlaws Were Killed 59 Years Ago

FESTIVAL
MAY 22, 1993

Gibsland: Bonnie and Clyde

East of Shreveport, the old US-80 highway winds through dozens of somnolent little towns, following the rolling land while crisscrossing back and forth under the high-speed I-20 freeway. After passing the pawn shops and girlie bars outside Barksdale Air Force Base, the route parallels railroad tracks along the remains of an historic log turnpike, built in the 1870s to provide all-weather passage across the muddy bogs and bayous.

Apart from the usual barrage of roadside businesses, there's not a lot to stop for until you reach the tiny town of Gibsland (pop. 1,224), just south of I-20, 45 miles east of Shreveport. This pleasantly unremarkable little hamlet has one unique claim to fame: it was here, in 1934, that the notorious Depression-era gangsters Clyde Barrow and Bonnie Parker (a.k.a **Bonnie and Clyde**) were ambushed and killed. A small town-run museum tells their story, and sells gruesome postcards of their bullet-riddled bodies, while every May locals dress up and stage gun battles and car chases—more for cops-and-robbers fun than out of any real dedication to historical accuracy.

A battered stone marker, eight miles south of Gibsland along Hwy-154, stands on the site where the desperate duo—who in "real life" were nasty cold-blooded murderers, nothing like the romantic pair played by Warren Beatty and Faye Dunaway in the Hollywood movie—were shot by state troopers.

At Grambling University's **KGRM 91.5 FM,** student DJs play a wide range of classic soul, reggae, and R 'n' B, plus contemporary rap and hip-hop.

One of the most significant concentrations of archaeological remains in Louisiana is known as **Poverty Point,** 18 miles north of I-20 off Hwy-17, where 3,000-year-old burial mounds have been protected as a 400-acre state park.

Ruston

Roughly halfway across the state, Ruston (pop. 20,027) calls itself the "Peach Capital" but is best known for its two major colleges: Louisiana Tech, which is right in town but lacks the expected collegiate ambience; and smaller Grambling University, one of the nation's top black schools, three miles west of town, just south of I-20.

There's not a lot to look out for, but a number of local and franchised fast-food places line California Street (US-80) on the south side of town.

Monroe

Considering that it is one of the largest towns in northern Louisiana, Monroe (pop. 54,909) feels strangely abandoned, even though the downtown area has a number of classic commercial buildings dating from the period between the two World Wars, and even though Victorian-era warehouses and hundreds of ancient-looking "shotgun" shacks line the railroad tracks and US-80.

Apart from its photogenic architecture and fading roadside signs, Monroe doesn't really offer much reason to stop, though the gorgeous greenery of the **Louisiana Purchase Gardens and Zoo** (daily 10 AM-5 PM; $3.50), south of I-20 off US-165, makes it a great place to stretch your legs (or take a steam train or boat ride) among the moss-draped oaks and cypress trees.

East of Monroe, it's an hour's drive across the bayous before you reach the fascinating city of Vicksburg, across the Mississippi River.

stone marker where Bonnie and Clyde were killed

ACROSS MISSISSIPPI

US-80, which for much of the way has been replaced by the I-20 freeway, cuts across the middle of Mississippi, passing through its three largest cities—Meridian, Jackson, and Vicksburg—whose small sizes show how rural and diffuse the state still is. Only Jackson, the capital, is anything like an urban center, with a couple of "skyscrapers" and nearly 200,000 people. Mostly what you see along this stretch is small farms and Civil War battlefields, the most extensive and important of which rises above the Mississippi River in Vicksburg.

All across Mississippi, you'll see highway signs emblazoned with the insipid slogan "Only Positive Mississippi Spoken Here."

Vicksburg makes contentious claim to being the birthplace of both jazz (which authorities such as Duke Ellington have said is named after local musician Charles "Chaz" Washington) and of the mint julep (supposedly invented here and taken upstream by riverboat gamblers to Tennessee and Kentucky).

Vicksburg

The "Red Carpet City of the South" didn't roll one out for the Union army during the Civil War. Instead, Vicksburg (pop. 20,908) so stubbornly opposed Union efforts to win control of the Mississippi River that it became the target of one of the longest sieges in U.S. military history. The campaign to split the Confederacy in half along the great river reached its dramatic conclusion in 1863 amid the strategic heights of the now 1,800-acre **National Military Park** ($4 per car). Without an informant the old battlefield is merely an extensive collection of ornate monuments to the soldiers who died fighting, but a visit becomes emotionally compelling after you hear the anecdotes of individual valor and odd courtesies that took place amid the 47 days of bloodshed; audiotape tours may be rented from the **visitor center** (daily 8 AM-5 PM except Christmas) for $4.50, with narration and sound effects, or you can hire a guide ($10 an hour, two-hour minimum, three hours recommended) to accompany you in your car and explain everything from battle strategies to General Grant's legendary difficulties with drink. Along with providing the usual tourist brochures, the **Vicksburg Convention and Visitors Bureau** (601/636-9421 or 800/221-3536) keeps a list of these very worthwhile guides, of whom one of the best is Betty England.

A few of the city's posh **antebellum houses** survived the Civil War intact, and during the post-war Reconstruction several mansions were added to the bluffs overlooking the river. Most of these homes are open to the public (average $5), and during the fortnight-long "Pilgrimages" in late March and mid-October, slightly discounted multiple-house tours are available. Begin at the cluster in Vicksburg's so-called "Garden District, on Oak Street (south of Harrah's Casino), where the old plantation division between the Big House and surrounding shacks has been unintentionally preserved; others are found in the pleasant cobblestoned residential area between 1st Street E and Clay. The architecturally varied mansions and their copious inventories of fine antiques are more fascinating to decorative arts afi-

DEEP SOUTH ROADSIDE SHRINES

Among the many pleasures of traveling around the southern states is the likelihood of coming upon a striking monument in the middle of nowhere. Rural back roads that for miles and miles have run quietly through woodlands or along cotton fields will be suddenly marked by giant crosses or a pylon of hand-lettered signs. In the Midwest, you'll often see a fiberglass dinosaur or other giant creature constructed by some well-intentioned civic organization and intended to draw highway traffic to local businesses. In the South, however, what you see are intensely personal creations, built by eccentric and often outcast individuals (99% of them men), and instead of acting as an advertising gimmick they usually spout chapter and verse of Scripture, warning about the impending Apocalypse or the inevitable coming of Judgment Day.

Among the Deep South roadside shrines, don't miss the one that stands outside Margaret's Grocery on the north side of Vicksburg, Mississippi (see next page), where an assemblage of huge hand-lettered signs preach Biblically inspired injunctions at passersby. Another one within a short drive of US-80 is in Prattville northwest of Montgomery, Alabama, where W.C. Rice has constructed an intense garden of white crosses that resembles a military cemetery. Rice himself, who lives on-site, always wears a large wooden cross around his neck and is said to be friendly to visitors.

The best known of these "Gardens of Revelation," as scholar John Beardsley has called them in his excellent book of the same name, is Howard Finster's Paradise Garden, near Summerville in the Appalachian foothills of northwest Georgia. Recently famous for his primitivist paintings, which have appeared on album covers by R.E.M. and Talking Heads, Finster has created a series of Gaudi-esque shrines, embedding seashells, bits of tile and old car parts into concrete forms. Pictures of Henry Ford, Hubert Humphrey, and Hank Williams are arrayed alongside dozens of signs quoting Scripture, but the spirit of the place is best summed up by Finster's own verse: " I built this park of broken pieces to try to mend a broken world of people who are traveling their last road."

Only an hour from Atlanta, the Paradise Garden is now one of the more popular attractions in the area, and is open daily 9 AM-5 PM, with no admission charged (donations are welcome). To get there, head north from Summerville on US-27 for three miles to Pennville, and turn right at Jim's Auto Supply.

These shrines are by no means limited to states south of the 35th Parallel; northern states have their share as well, including two of the most intense: the Garden of Eden in Lucas, Kansas, and Holy Land outside Waterbury, Connecticut (see page 494).

cionados than to history buffs, who may find tours illuminating for what is omitted rather than included. Stories of deprivation and Union plundering, cannonballs in parlor walls, and other wartime relics are religiously enshrined, yet never a word is spoken about slavery.

To escape from the indoor onslaught of Louis Quinze marquetry or Chippendale claw feet, stop by **Margaret's Grocery**, on the Great River Road (US-61-Business) on the north side of town. At a glance resembling a fanatical Lego-Land, the assemblage of huge hand-lettered signs atop red-and-white constructions, welcoming shoppers to the trailer-style convenience store with Biblically inspired injunctions, is worth at least a pause. Caveat visitor: the owner will talk your ear off if you aren't careful.

If you've ever tried to imagine a world without Coke, step into the **Biedenharn Museum of Coca-Cola Memorabilia**, smack downtown on Washington Street, and see where one man's ingenuity slew all hopes for such a world. Here in 1894 Joseph Biedenharn conceived of putting the strictly regional soda fountain drink into bottles, the better to reach new markets; the rest, as they say, is history. Toast worldwide domination with some of the classic stuff, straight up or over ice cream, or pay $1.87 to view galleries full of old promotional serving trays and the like.

For real food and drink check out the **New Orleans Cafe**, across the street from the Biedenharn Museum, basically a well-lit and spacious bar with decent Cajun dishes and imported beers. For a traditional Southern feast, sit down to the communal round table at **Walnut Hills** east of downtown on Adams Street at Clay (intersection 4; notice the numbers suspended from the traffic signals) and dig into the endless supply of classic regional dishes, from fried pork tenderloin to okra; given the fresh ingredients and how much of a pig you can make of yourself, the moderate prices (all you can eat for $8!) are a great value. An equally rib-stuffing meal at an even more amazing price is found weekdays at lunch in the friendly **Kitchen in the Garden,** a hole-in-the-wall at the end of 5th Street N, just off Main Street E. "Down-to-earth soul food" is the credo here, and it's no lie: try the fried chicken or fish for a real treat, and savor how pork fat makes greens so tasty. Many of the side vegetables are out of a can, but you can't expect Julia Child at these prices. **Reavey's Bar-B-Q** at the corner of 1st Street N and Clay (intersection 6) serves some of the city's finest pork and beef ribs. Tamale addicts should seek out **Solly's Hot Tamales** on Washington Street south of the library (near intersection 26).

Vicksburg motels, found along I-20 between the Mississippi and the Military Park, include a wide selection of the national chains and their local imitators, the cheapest of which is the **Hillcrest Inn,** just off I-20 exit 5 at 40 US-80 (601/638-1491; $24-30). Or, for $85-150, you can play Rhett and Scarlett for a night, pampering yourself with canopied beds and frocked shower curtains in one of the 10 camellia-draped tour homes that double as plush **B&Bs.** All have you whistling "Dixie," but true history buffs will want the **Grant Room at Cedar Grove,** 2300 Washington Street (601/636-1000 or 800/862-1300), still furnished with the bed the general used after Union forces occupied Vicksburg. (The staff, of course, claims ol' Sam was a bedridden drunk for his entire stay, but pay no attention—he was probably a poor tipper at the bar, and folks around here bear grudges over generations for things like that.)

If your visit falls during Pilgrimage, don't expect easy pickings on rooms: for those weeks, most B&Bs are booked up to *two years* in advance. For thorough and concise information on lodging and attractions, call the friendly **Vicksburg Convention and Visitors Bureau** (800/221-3536) or visit their Tourist Information Center, opposite the entrance to the National Military Park, off I-20 exit 4B.

Vicksburg's street signs are small white croquet poles stuck into the grass at street corners, lettered vertically with a stencil borrowed from some government bulk food warehouse. They must have cost a fortune to have escaped being replaced by something useful. Rather than wonder at their illegibility, obtain a map from the visitors bureau folks.

While Vicksburg's surrender allowed President Lincoln to declare that "the Father of Waters now flows unvexed to the sea," locals stayed vexed for over 80 years: because the surrender occurred on July 4, Independence Day wasn't celebrated here until the end of WW II.

Vicksburg's **Diversionary Canal** was the city's response to the caprice of nature when in 1876 Vicksburg found itself facing a mudflat of flopping fish after the Mississippi River found itself a new streambed—overnight. Thanks to the diligence of engineers who redirected the Yazoo River in 1902, Vicksburg has its waterfront back, now complete with several sharks, the kind whose slot machines and roulette wheels spin 24 hours for your "entertainment."

Vicksburg has more engineers per capita than any other U.S. municipality: 3,500 of them, employees of the Mississippi River Commission, the Corps of Engineers, and the U.S. Army Waterways Experiment Station.

The tiny town of **Vaughn,** 30 miles north of Jackson via the I-55 freeway, was the site of the crash that killed legendary train engineer **Luther "Casey" Jones.** A small museum, a mile east of I-55 exit 133, has exhibits on Casey and the history of railroading in the South.

After burning Jackson to the ground during the Civil War, Gen. Ulysses S. Grant is said to have coined the expression "War is Hell."

Clinton and the Natchez Trace

The one-time Choctaw Indian agency of Clinton, north of I-20 10 miles west of Jackson, was renamed in 1828 in honor of New York Gov. DeWitt Clinton, who oversaw construction of the Erie Canal. Now a small cotton-growing and shipping center, in its early years the town sat on the notorious Natchez Trace, now followed by the blissfully pleasant Natchez Trace Parkway, which runs southwest from Clinton to Port Gibson (see page 218 for more).

Though it survived the Civil War relatively unscathed, Clinton later saw some of the worst Reconstruction-era race riots in the state, with an estimated 50 unarmed blacks killed during a single rampage in 1875.

Jackson

Spreading west from the banks of the Pearl River, Jackson (pop. 196,637) was established as state capital in 1822. Named for Andrew Jackson, hero of the Battle of New Orleans during the War of 1812 and later president of the U.S., it was destroyed during the Civil War but is now a properous city, Mississippi's political and commercial heart and biggest city—though you wouldn't know it by the somnolent look of the place.

The very attractive Greek revival **Old State Capitol**, built in 1838 and used until 1903, rises at the center of town at State and Capitol Streets, and is open for free self-guided **tours** (Mon.-Fri. 8 AM-5 PM, Saturday 9:30 AM-4:30 PM, Sunday noon-4:30 PM) of the building and the well-presented historical exhibits that fill it. The few other fine old antebellum buildings—under a dozen altogether—that survive around Jackson were used by Union forces and were thus spared destruction. These include the art-filled **Governor's Mansion,** a short walk east of the old capitol, at 300 E. Capitol Street (Mon.-Fri. 9:30-11 AM; free), and **The Oaks,** 823 N. Jefferson Street (Tues.-Sat. 10 AM-3 PM; $3), in which General Sherman lived. Restored to prewar splendor, The Oaks is furnished with period antiques and, surprisingly for the South, the sofa from Abraham Lincoln's law office.

The main attraction is the **Mississippi Agriculture and Forestry Museum** (Mon.-Sat. 9 AM-5 PM, Sunday 1-5 PM; $3; 601/354-6113), a 40-acre complex on Lakeland Drive northeast of downtown, off I-55 exit 98B. Despite the dull name, it's a hugely engaging and entertaining place, with a composite "Crossroads Town" made up of authentic buildings, including a general store, filling station, and sawmill brought here from all over Mississippi. Nearby is a fully restored working farm, and museum exhibits trace state history with an emphasis on transportation and agriculture. The whole complex is well worth a look—if only so you can say you've visited the **National Agricultural Aviation Hall of Fame,** which displays historical and contemporary crop-dusting equipment along with sundry devices used in the days before pesticides to catch cotton-eating boll weevils.

The museum complex stands next to the very popular **Jackson Generals** minor league baseball stadium (tickets $3-5; 601/981-4664). On the stadium grounds, the must-see **Dizzy Dean Museum** (Tues.-Sat. 11 AM-6 PM, Sunday 1-5 PM during baseball season only; $1) details the life and times of characterful baseball player and announcer Jay Hanna "Dizzy" Dean.

A high proportion of Jackson's best places to eat are hidden away in shopping malls, such as the Northpark Mall off I-55 exit 103, at 1200 E. County Line Road. There you can choose from a **Morrison's Cafeteria** (the true taste of the South, from the country's biggest chain of cafeterias) and other familiar franchises. Downtown, the best bet is upscale **Iron Horse Grill**, 320 W. Pearl Street, serving "New American" food for lunch and dinner in a building that's on the National Register of Historic Places.

For a one-of-a-kind Mississippi eating experience, take a trip 20 miles southeast of Jackson via US-49 to the hamlet of Mendenhall (pop. 2,463), where the **Mendenhall Hotel Revolving Tables**, right on Main Street (601/847-3113), serves all-you-can-eat, family-style portions of absolutely great food— biscuits and cornbread, fried chicken, juicy ham steaks, barbecued beef, and at least a half-dozen vegetables, all to be washed down with pitchers of sweet iced tea—in the dining room of a very comfortable old railroad hotel. Lunch (only) is served 11 AM-2 PM every day; worth planning your trip around—don't miss it!

Places to stay in Jackson tend to be either anodyne highway motels or anodyne chain hotels. Among the nicest is the **Best Western Metro Inn**, 1520 Ellis Avenue off I-20 exit 42B (601/355-7483 or 800/528-1234). For a more complete list or for any other information, contact the Jackson **visitors bureau**, 921 N. President Street (601/960-1891 or 800/354-7695).

Meridian

The last city before the Alabama border, modern Meridian (pop. 41,036) is a medium-sized industrial center that started from rubble in the aftermath of the Civil War. Now perhaps best known as the junction of I-20 and I-59 south to New Orleans, Meridian owes its existence to strategic geography: after the native Choctaw Indians were removed in 1831, Meridian became a railroad junction and served as a Confederate stronghold until Sherman destroyed it in February 1864, saying afterwards, "Meridian no longer exists." Despite this, the town recovered with a vengeance, and from the 1890s until the 1930s Meridian was the largest and most prosperous city in this very poor state, as shown by the many fine Edwardian and art deco buildings that still stand (in varying stages of repair) around the downtown area.

The **Dentzel Carousel** (daily 1-5 PM; 25 cents), in Highland Park on 41st Ave at State Boulevard, is a cheerful and historic wooden merry-go-round dating from the 1890s preserved in its original condition. Another offbeat but interesting Meridian "attraction" is the gravesite of the **"King and Queen of the Gypsies,"** Emil and Kelly Mitchell, whose circa 1914 plot in Rosehill Cemetery (west of downtown on 40th Avenue between 7th

Between Jackson and Meridian, US-80 runs parallel to I-20 across the pine forests of **Bienville National Forest,** replanted in the 1930s after lumber companies clearcut the original pine groves. The town of Forest is just one of a series of quirkily named communities along this route; others include Hickory and Chunky, 13 miles west of Meridian.

The incidents recounted in the film *Mississippi Burning* (the murders of civil rights workers by Ku Klux Klan members in June 1964), took place in the small town of Philadelphia, 30 miles northwest of Meridian.

Continuing its musical traditions, Meridian is also the birthplace and corporate headquarters of the **Peavey Electronics** company, amplifier and instrument makers to Eddie Van Halen and others at $500 million per year.

SLEEP, BABY, SLEEP

The collision of Mississippi's rural past with the early stages of industrial development was embodied in the life and work of Meridian's favorite son, Jimmie Rodgers, whose original mixing of black Delta blues and white Appalachian folk songs earned him the title "Father of Country Music." What Elvis Presley was to the 1950s, Rodgers was to the previous generation. Born in Meridian on September 8, 1897, Rodgers worked briefly on the railroad, lost his job after coming down with tuberculosis, then became the original overnight success. After he was discovered by an RCA talent scout in 1927, Rodgers' first record, "Sleep, Baby, Sleep," sold over a million copies. For the next five years he called himself the "Singing Brakeman" and was the world's bestselling recording artist. Rodgers's life and legend are honored in the small **Jimmie Rodgers Museum** (Mon.-Sat. 10 AM-4 PM, Sunday 1-5 PM; $2; 601/485-1808) at 41st Avenue and 19th Street in Highland Park, well signed two miles northwest of downtown. It contains all manner of odd Rodgers-related memorabilia, plus his boots and his custom Martin guitar. Jimmie Rodgers died of tuberculosis in May 1933, and is buried alongside his wife in Oak Grove Cemetery, two miles south of Meridian.

and 8th Streets) is a place of pilgrimage for Gypsies from all over America. Marked by a set of wrought-iron patio furniture and traditional headstones, the grave is often piled high with fruit and other offerings.

Meridian has one classic place to eat: **Weidman's Restaurant**, downtown at 208 22nd Avenue (601/693-1751), where you can choose from the greatly varied menu of traditional Southern dishes—and great pies—in a wood-paneled, brass-railed dining room that's packed with moose-heads, mounted fish, and photos of everyone famous who's ever eaten there. Family-owned and -operated for 125 years, Weidman's is open 6 AM-9 PM every day; pass by at your peril.

Places to stay in Meridian lie along the I-20 and I-59 junction; for listings or other information contact the **visitor center**, 721 Front Street (601/693-1306 or 800/748-9970).

ACROSS ALABAMA

Our route across the midsection of Alabama cuts through the rural Black Belt—a name that comes from the richly fertile but often swampy lowland soil, but which also reflects its predominantly African American population. Prime cotton-growing country, central Alabama was feverishly supportive of slavery and secession—Montgomery, the state capital, was also the first capital of the Confederacy—and later became a crucible in the civil rights battles of the 1950s and 1960s.

Events of both of these historical moments provide most of what there is to see and do in the state, but the intimate scale of things—even the biggest city, Montgomery, feels like a sleepy, small town—makes for an enjoyable tour, as does the fact that for most of its 230-odd miles, US-80 alternately becomes an old-style two- and four-lane highway, far away from the anodyne interstates, passing through some of the South's most interesting places.

For soothing soul or Sunday Gospel in west-central Alabama, tune to **WNPT 102.9 FM.**

Demopolis

Standing just north of US-80 on a bluff above the east bank of the Tombigbee River, Demopolis (pop. 7,512) has an interesting history to explain its unusual name—which means "City of the People" in Greek. In 1817, a band of French aristocrats in exile for their allegiance to Napoléon arrived here after the U.S. Congress granted them the land to found a colony based on growing grapes and olives. Not surprisingly, the colonists, a group of soldiers and courtiers whom the WPA *Guide to Alabama* described as "cultured people . . . from the glittering drawing rooms of the French aristocracy . . . none of whom had ever set foot in a plowed field," failed miserably, and survived thanks only to the local Choctaw Indians, who gave them food and taught them to grow viable crops.

By the 1820s the last of the French had quit, and the lands were swiftly taken over by slave-owning American cotton planters, whose mansions still stand in and around town. The biggest and best of these is **Gaineswood**, 805 Whitfield Street E (Mon.-Sat. 9 AM-5 PM, Sunday noon-5 PM; $3), just north of US-80 off Cedar Street next to the high school. The finest antebellum mansion in Alabama, and one of the top three in the country according to the *Smithsonian Guide to Historic America,* Gaineswood began as a rough cabin in 1821 and over the next 40 years grew into a classic Greek-revival manor, built by slaves according to pattern-book designs. Most unusually, it is still decorated with the original furniture, fixtures, and fittings.

The other well-maintained plantation home still standing in Demopolis is **Bluff Hall**, 405 Commissioners Avenue (Tues.-Sat. 10 AM-5 PM, Sunday 2-5 PM; $3), overlooking the river at the west edge of town. Smaller than Gaineswood, but more attractively situated, Bluff Hall contains a wider array of furniture, with pieces dating from throughout the 19th century; the kitchen in particular is packed with Victorian-era gadgets.

Demopolis's franchise-free downtown fills four blocks of Washington Street east from Bluff Hall and the river. It's centered upon one of the South's oldest public squares, with a cast-iron fountain and many comfy benches.

Apart from the family-oriented **Riverview Landing** north of town on US-43, the standard places to eat (**Hardee's, McDonald's,** and a 24-hour **Mr. Waffle**) line US-80, as does a **Days Inn** (205/289-2500 or 800/325-2525), the only accommodation option.

> The **Tombigbee River** at Demopolis comes to life the first weekend of December for Christmas on the River, when lighted, animated "floats that really float" parade downstream.

> Though little more than a speck on the map, tiny **Faunsdale** (pop. 175), on the south side of US-80 about 15 miles east of Demopolis, is worth a stop to enjoy the gorgeous home-cooked food and live music at the **Faunsdale Bar and Grill** (Wed.-Sun. 5-9 PM only) in the brick-built, block-long center of town.

> Alabama's original state capital, **Cahawba** was founded along the Alabama River in 1820 but was totally abandoned by the 1860s. Its few buildings and other remains are preserved as a state historic park (daily 8 AM-5 PM; free), 13 miles southwest of Selma via Hwy-22 and Hwy-9.

Selma

A full century before it played a seminal role in the Civil Rights Movement of the 1960s, Selma (pop. 23,755) was second only to Richmond as an industrial arsenal for Confederate forces—Selma's foundries and forges produced weapons, ammunition, and ironclad warships, including the legendary CSS *Tennessee*—and altogether accounted for nearly half of Confederate-made munitions. As in Richmond, the factories were destroyed by Union forces toward the end of the war in April 1865, but a few blocks of downtown's Water Avenue were spared and now form one of the few intact antebellum business districts left in the South. Hundreds of Civil War-era houses line Selma's streets, marked by blue shields and forming one of the largest collections of historic houses in the country.

Along the north bank of the broad Alabama River, Water Avenue's five blocks of well-maintained commercial structures, many now housing antique shops, include the former St. James Hotel, 1200 Water Avenue, the oldest hotel still standing in the South, built in 1837 but now housing Meadows Tires store. At the west end of Water Avenue, the humpbacked landmark **Edmund Pettis Bridge** still carries old US-80 over the river, and at the foot of the bridge the small but significant **National Voting Rights Museum**, 1012 Water Avenue (Tues.-Sat. 1-5 PM; donations) uses photographs and handbills to tell the story of the civil rights struggles of the 1950s and 1960s.

Five blocks east, at the other end of the Water Avenue historic district, on the site of Selma's largest Civil War foundry, the **Old Depot Museum** (Mon.-Sat. 10 AM-4 PM, Sunday 2-5 PM; $4) traces regional history from before the Civil War up through the Civil Rights Movement, and features a large selection of Confederate currency, much of which was printed in Selma. The depot also marks the juncture of Selma's Civil War history with the more recent battles for civil rights: north along Martin Luther King (formerly Sylvan) Street, markers point out the unchanged sites of key moments in the Civil Rights Movement up to the 1965 March to Montgomery led by Dr. King. Twenty different displays explain the significance of Selma and point out the historic importance of such sites as the Brown Chapel AME church, where marchers set off toward Montgomery before being violently turned back at the Edmund Pettus Bridge; and the simple brick social housing of the George Washington Carver Homes, where most of the original activists lived.

Responding to the civil rights marches of 1965, Pres. Lyndon Johnson said, "At times, history and fate meet at a single time, in a single place to shape a turning point in man's unending search for freedom. So it was at Lexington and Concord. So it was a century ago at Appomattox. So it was last week in Selma, Alabama."

While Selma offers more vivid history per square foot than just about anywhere else in the South, it unfortunately doesn't have much in the way of good places to eat. Two exceptions to this are **Ed's Pancake House**, 1617 Broad Street (US-80), and **Major Grumbles**, off Water Avenue at 1 Grumbles Alley, which serves up fried chicken and steaks in a converted cotton warehouse overlooking the river. Stay the night at **Grace Hall**, 506 Lauderdale Street (205/875-5744), a green-shuttered circa 1857 Italianate cottage converted into a nice $75-a-night B&B. Motels along US-80 include a **Best Western**, 1915 W. Highland Avenue (205/872-1900), and a **Holiday Inn**.

Dozens of sites in Selma and Montgomery, and many more along US-80 between them, are being preserved and protected as part of the **Civil Rights Movement National Historic Trail.** US-80 is also marked as the "DeSoto Trail," in memory of the Spanish explorer who passed this way in 1540.

For further information, including details of the Alabama Tale Tellin' Festival held in Selma each October, contact the **visitors bureau**, 513 Lauderdale Street (205/875-7241).

Montgomery's "Y102," **WHHY 102 FM,** plays nonstop MTV hits.

Montgomery

Original capital of the Confederate States of America, and now the state capital of Alabama, Montgomery (pop. 187,106) is among the more engaging destinations in the Deep South. Not surprisingly, much of what there is to see has to do with the Civil War, which officially started here when Jefferson Davis gave the order to fire on Fort Sumter. Montgomery survived the war more or less unscathed and is now a very pleasant little city with lovely houses lining leafy streets and an above-average range of restaurants, thanks to the presence of politicos and the 6,000 students at Alabama State College.

Montgomery's landmark is the circa 1851 **state capitol** (Mon.-Sat. 9 AM-4 PM, Sunday noon-4 PM; free), which served as the Confederate capitol for four months in 1861 and is still in use. A bronze star on the west portico marks the spot where Jefferson Davis took the oath of office on February 18, 1861, and a spiral staircase surrounded by historical murals climbs the three-story domed rotunda. Moved to a site across the street from the capitol in 1921, the **White House of the Confederacy** is where Jeff Davis and family lived before moving to Richmond. Yet more Confederate memorabilia is on display next door at the **State Archives and History Museum** (Mon.-Sat. 9 AM-5 PM; free), which has displays tracing Alabama history from Creek Indian and pioneer times up through today.

A single block west of the state capitol complex stands the **Dexter Avenue Baptist Church**, a simple brick building where Martin Luther King served as pastor from 1954 to 1960. One of the key landmarks of the Civil Rights Movement, it was here that supporters rallied around Rosa Parks in the Montgomery bus boycott of 1955-56, which caused an end to official segregation. Downstairs from the church a large mural depicts Dr. King's leading role in the civil rights struggles.

Around the corner from the Dexter Avenue Church, Montgomery's most powerful site is the **Civil Rights Memorial**, two blocks west of the state capitol at the entrance to the Southern Poverty Law Center, 400 Washington Avenue. Designed by Vietnam Memorial architect Maya Lin, the monument consists of a circular black granite table inscribed with the names of 40 people killed in the struggle for civil rights, with a brief description of how and when they died radiating like the hands of a clock from a central water source, which flows gently over the edges of the stone. Behind the table, a waterfall tumbles over a marble wall inscribed with Martin Luther King's favorite Biblical passage, which says that we will not be satisfied "until Justice rolls down like water, and righteousness like a mighty stream." The new **Rosa Parks/Bus Boycott Historical Monument**—installed 40 years after event; Ms. Parks attended the ceremonial "opening" in 1995—is outside the Eureka Theater.

Montgomery also has sites to see that have nothing at all to do with the Civil War or the Civil Rights Movement. The first of these is the **Hank Williams Memorial**, marking his final resting place on the northeast side of downtown in Oakwood Cemetery, 1304 Upper Wetumptka Road. Hank Williams was an Alabama native and singer and writer of such enduring classics as "Your Cheating Heart," "Jambalaya," "Hey, Good Lookin'," "I'm So Lonesome I Could Cry," and "Lost Highway." Williams's last concert in Montgomery took place on December 28, 1952, three days before his death; he died in the back of his Cadillac while en route from Knoxville, Tennessee, to a scheduled New Year's Day concert in Canton, Ohio. His song, "I'll Never Get Out of This World Alive," was rising up the charts at the time of his demise. His grave is on the east side of the central circle, with a marker alongside it on which his son Hank, Jr. asks people not to vandalize. A life-sized statue of Hank (Sr.) stands downtown on Perry Street, across from City Hall.

Another notable local was **Zelda Fitzgerald**, who was born and raised in Montgomery and later lived here with her husband F. Scott while he wrote *Tender is the Night* during the winter of 1931-32. The house, south of downtown at 919 Felder Avenue, has been converted into apartments, one of which (Apt. B) is now a small museum (Wed.-Fri. 10 AM-2 PM, Saturday and Sunday 1-5 PM; 205/264-4222) that details their lives through videos and memorabilia. It's the only museum dedicated to either of them, anywhere.

Montgomery, which has one of the largest livestock industries in the South, boasts at least one good steakhouse, the **Conestoga**, 3903 Atlanta Highway (US-80), northeast from downtown. For breakfast or lunch, try

Hank Williams' grave site

the country-style **Farmers Market Cafe**, downtown at 315 N. McDonough Street.

Places to stay include the usual national chains, plus the pleasant **Riverfront Inn** at 200 Coosa Street (205/834-4300), in the historic riverfront district west of downtown; and the very comfortable, turn-of-the-century **Lattis Inn B&B**, 1414 S. Hull Street (205/832-9931), in a residential neighborhood a half-mile south of I-85.

Montgomery's **Maxwell Air Force Base,** established by the Wright Brothers in 1910, is now home to the Air University and War College, national finishing school for fighter pilots and military tacticians.

For more information, contact the **Montgomery Visitor Center**, 401 Madison Avenue (205/262-0013) north of the capitol, next to the restored buildings of Old Alabama Town.

Tuskegee

Midway between Montgomery and the Georgia border, Tuskegee (pop. 12,257) is a medium-sized town that has grown up around the **Tuskegee Institute**, founded in 1881 by the industrious former slave, Booker T. Washington, in order to help black Americans rise up the economic ladder. Now a National Historic Site, many of the early buildings built by student laborers still stand around the 1,500-acre campus, but the main points of interest are close to the entrance off Old Montgomery Road. Here you'll find the **Carver Museum** (daily 9 AM-5 PM; free), which traces the career of Tuskegee teacher George Washington Carver, with displays of the various products Carver developed during his life-long tenure at Tuskegee.

Facing the Carver Museum across the lawn is the strikingly modern Tuskegee Chapel, designed by noted architect Paul Rudolph in 1969 but unfortunately rarely open to visitors because of budgetary concerns. The graves of both Booker T. Washington and George Washington Carver are next to the chapel.

East of Tuskegee, the I-85 freeway races up to Atlanta while US-80 continues due east to the engaging old industrial city of Columbus, across the Georgia border.

Phenix City

Across the Chattahoochee River from Georgia, Phenix City, apart from being oddly spelled, is interesting only for being the site of Fort Mitchell National Cemetery— the "Arlington of the South," holding the graves of soldiers from the Civil War to Operation Desert Storm. Before the cemetery was established, this is where thousands of native Creek Indians were rounded up in 1836 before being sent west on the notorious Trail of Tears to Indian Territory in Oklahoma.

ACROSS GEORGIA

Running across the middle of Georgia, US-80 follows the "fall line," a geological divide where rivers drop in a series of rapids from the higher Piedmont Plateau to the lower coastal plain. Because the fall line marked the limits of navigation in from the sea, settlements naturally sprung up along it: **Columbus** was founded on the banks of the falling Chattahoochee, while in the middle of the state **Macon** was built along the Ocmulgee River.

These, the second- and third-biggest cities, respectively, in this still-rural state, are the only real cities our route passes through, and both are fascinating places in very different ways. Apart from these exceptions, however, in its trip across Georgia US-80 takes in more than 300 miles of rolling countryside covered with dozens of dozens of small towns; runs along ancient-looking two-lane blacktop winding through thick hardwood-and-pine forests; and passes stately white columned farmhouses with wide lawns and run-down tin-roofed shacks with yards full of rusting refrigerators and old bangers-on-blocks.

In the west, you can detour to explore the surprisingly simple homes of two U.S. presidents, Franklin Delano Roosevelt at **Warm Springs**, and Jimmy Carter at **Plains**. Or wander through the unsung collection of Elvis Presley memorabilia at **Buena Vista**—the biggest assembly outside Graceland. East of Macon toward Savannah and the Atlantic Coast, US-80 has been replaced by the much faster I-16 freeway, bypassing numerous small towns across an agricultural region that was devastated during General Sherman's Civil War "March to the Sea." Fortunately, Sherman spared the colonial capital **Savannah**, a lushly verdant gem generally considered to be the most beautiful city in North America.

Especially in the western half of the state, US-80 runs across rolling Piedmont countryside past extensive orchards at the heart of "Georgia Peach" country. Follow You-Pick-'Em signs in early summer for a field-fresh selection or stop at roadside stands along the route selling this Georgia specialty along with other local fruits and vegetables.

The Chattahoochee River between Alabama and Georgia officially marks the line between the central and eastern standard time zones, though Phenix City, Alabama, also observes Georgia time.

Information about Savannah can be found in the Survival Guide on pages 720-721.

Columbus

Crossing the Chattahoochee River from Alabama to Georgia, look north to see the rushing waterfalls around which the city of Columbus (pop. 179,278) grew. Built on the site of a Creek Indian village, Columbus is now Georgia's second largest city, home of the brutal Army Ranger training school at Fort Benning and also host of the 1996 Olympic Games softball competitions. During the Civil War, its iron foundries and water-powered factories converted to munitions production, but Columbus was untouched until Union Gen. James H. Wilson stormed across the Chattahoochee in 1865; unaware that the treaty of Appomattox had already ended the war, "Wilson's Raiders" destroyed much of the city. The huge brick textile mills now lining the river's eastern bank date from the post-Reconstruction years up through the turn of the century, when Columbus emerged as an industrial giant, an era captured in the stories of Columbus author Carson McCullers.

Most city sights are conveniently located in a compact riverside district. Stroll along the new Riverwalk promenade for a close-up look at the river, or rumble down the cobblestone lanes of Broadway and Front Street past block after block of graceful old homes and fountain-studded parks. Stop by the Italianate mansion that houses the **Columbus Historical Society** at 700 Broadway (Mon.-Fri. 9 AM-5 PM) for maps and guided tours ($2) of several neighborhood homes, including the former residence of J.S. Pemberton, the inventor of **Coca-Cola**. The elegant little Springer Opera House, 103 10th Street, is the highlight of the adjacent commercial district, where beautifully renovated buildings mix with funky shops selling wigs and voodoo trinkets.

On a hill east of downtown, a half-mile from the river, the **Columbus Museum**, 1251 Wynnton Road (Tues.-Sat. 10 AM-5 PM, Sunday 1-5 PM; free), is the major cultural center for the region, with engaging displays tracing the history of the river valley from the time of the Creek Indians—don't miss the 20-minute movie "Chattahoochee Legacy," which screens frequently throughout the day. A wide-ranging collection of fine and folk art is on display in the spacious galleries. Overall, this is one of the state's more captivating small museums, well worth an hour at least.

South of downtown at the foot of 4th Street, the modest **Confederate Naval Museum** (Tues.-Fri. 10 AM-5 PM, weekends 1-5 PM; free), next to the stadium constructed for the 1996 Olympic women's softball competition, contains the charred remnants of two ironclads and other naval memorabilia. Southeast from the museum, Victory Road winds toward Fort Benning, holding most of Columbus's budget accommodations amidst a gauntlet of strip clubs and pawn shops catering to the young soldiers.

The nicest place to stay is the **Hilton Hotel**, 800 Front Avenue (706/324-1800 or 800/HILTONS), impressively carved out of a foundry started here in 1853. The Ironworks next door has been converted into a convention center and performance space and is the site of the city's major festival, the RiverFest, in April.

At either end of historic downtown, restaurants span the range from downhome to upper-crust. **Country's on Broad**, 1329 Broadway, serves up classic country cookin' and barbecue in a spruced-up 1940s bus depot. Historic **Goetchius House** (pronounced "GET-chezz"), overlooking the river at 405 Broadway, serves upscale dinners Mon.-Sat.—if the chateaubriand is too rich for your blood, stop for a mint julep at their speakeasy downstairs. The adventurous might try the lunch counter of the **Dinglewood Pharmacy**, out past the museum at 1939 Wynnton Road, for an unusual local specialty, the Scrambled Dog, a hot dog buried under chili, onions, and oysterettes.

For more information on Columbus, contact the **visitor center**, 801 Front Avenue (706/322-1613 or 800/999-1613).

Knoxville, 25 miles west of Macon and just north of US-80, is built around a typical southern courthouse square, which holds a monument to the local girl, Joanna Troutman, who designed the Lone Star flag of Texas. She gave the flag, which featured a blue star on a white background but which was otherwise identical to the current one, to a battalion of Macon volunteers heading to fight for the Texas Republic.

In 1975, then-governor of Georgia **Jimmy Carter** announced his bid for the presidency at FDR's Warm Springs cottage.

Warm Springs:
FDR's Little White House

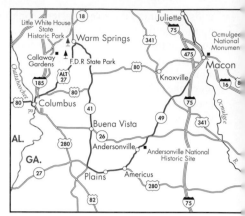

About 15 miles north of Columbus, the rising, forested flanks of Pine Mountain attract flatlanders in search of cooler temperatures and an overlook of the surrounding countryside. In 1924, the therapeutic natural hot springs here also drew the future Pres. Franklin Delano Roosevelt who, in between losing the election for vice-president in 1920 and winning the governorship of New York in 1928, was struck with polio and left unable to walk. FDR loved the area so much he built a wooded, three-bedroom retreat called the Little White House (daily 9:30 AM-4 PM; $4) and established a treatment center nearby for himself and fellow polio sufferers, funded by a charity that grew

into today's March of Dimes. He returned regularly over the next two decades and as president formulated much of the "New Deal" and managed the conduct of WW II while staying here. On the afternoon of April 12, 1945, FDR died, leaving an unfinished portrait propped on an easel.

The house and grounds are very much like they were when Roosevelt died, with a small museum displaying various artifacts, including a wall of crafts items made under the auspices of various WPA programs. Also here are the heavy leg braces FDR wore during public appearances, and the dark blue Ford V-8 convertible with hand controls he drove around the Warm Springs countryside.

FDR's characteristic pose

At nearby **FDR State Park** (on land donated by Roosevelt) you can take in the terrific views, swim at the pool, hike a portion of the 26-mile Pine Mountain Trail, or stay the night in one of the many state park cabins (706/663-4858 for reservations). In the little town of Warm Springs (pop. 400), a half-mile north of the Little White House park, **Mac's Bar-B-Q**, a block east of US-41, has hickory-smoked ribs and chicken; and the historic **Hotel Warm Springs**, 17 Broad Street (706/655-2114), offers B&B accommodations. There's also plenty of crafts, gift, and antique stores to browse through.

West of Warm Springs off US-27, **Callaway Gardens** has 14,000 lushly landscaped acres (daily 7 AM-7 PM; $7.50 adults, $1 children) covered in topiary gardens, a lakeside swimming beach, and dazzling displays of colorful flowers, plus the Day Butterfly Center, a 7,000-square-foot atrium with exotic varieties of free-flying butterflies. Resort accommodations are available (706/663-2281 or 800/282-8181).

Buena Vista: The Elvis Presley Collection Museum
and the National Country Music Museum

It's not in many guidebooks, and there aren't any billboards to help you find your way, but one of the more intriguing places in west-central Georgia has to be Buena

Vista (pop. 1,472), a half-hour's drive southeast of Columbus, 20 miles south of US-80 on Hwy-41. It looks a lot like many other Deep South towns, with a tidy array of auto parts stores and other businesses lining a central courthouse square, but this square has two attractions you won't find anywhere else, thanks to the dreams of local-boy-made-good Mike Moon, who's trying to turn Buena Vista into the Branson of the South.

Buena Vista's main event is the **Elvis Presley Collection Museum** (daily 10 AM-6 PM; $6), a multimillion-dollar assembly of records, posters, guitars, photographs, jumpsuits, scarves, rings, and sunglasses made, played, or worn by The King. It's the largest collection of Elvisania outside Graceland and includes such unforgettable oddities as the clothes hamper from his Hollywood home, his 1965 World Book encyclopedia, and the 1967 Cadillac he drove on his honeymoon, along with enough bedroom and bathroom suites to satisfy even the most hard-core admirer of 1960s and 1970s interior design.

A more music-centered collection fills an old cotton warehouse catercorner across the square at the **National Country Music Museum** (same hours and prices as the Elvis Museum). Also owned by Mr. Moon and formerly housed in Pigeon Forge, Tennessee, this is at least as entertaining and a lot more "educational" than its sibling, showing off everything from Conway Twitty's limousine to the mangled wreck that almost killed Barbara Mandrell. Lots of other cars (including Jerry Lee Lewis's 1954 Cadillac Coupe de Ville) stand alongside a series of display cases filled with such intriguing items as Bill Monroe's mandolin, Merle Haggard's guitar, Linda Ronstadt's satin shorts, Johnny Cash's .44 Magnum (and his bright red bedroom suite), and the first dollar Elvis ever earned.

Buena Vista is also a main stop for country music performers like Mickey Gilley and George Jones, who play throughout the year at the **Silver Moon Music Barn** (800/531-0677), two miles south of town.

Plains: Jimmy Carter

Beyond Buena Vista, around 45 miles southeast of Columbus via US-280, Jimmy Carter's hometown of Plains (pop. 116) stands as a living monument to small town America. Here, in a town that's small and remote even by South Georgia standards, the 39th president of the United States was raised, mounted his presidential campaign, and now officiates on matters of international diplomacy—that is, when he isn't teaching Sunday School at the Maranatha Baptist Church. Though the Carter family compound is off-limits, visitors can see Carter's high school, stop by Brother Billy's old gas station (the only one in town), and buy signature peanuts at the general store.

Much of Plains has been proclaimed the "Jimmy Carter National Historic Site," and self-guided touring maps are available at the **visitor center** (daily 9 AM-5 PM; 912/824-3413) in the old train depot, which served as Carter's campaign headquarters in 1976 and again in 1980.

Ten miles northeast of Plains, in the market town of Americus (pop. 16,512), the wealth generated by the region's cotton plantations is embodied in the towering brick **Windsor Hotel**, 125 W. Lamar Street (912/924-1555 or 800/678-8946). A truly elegant Victorian-era hotel with a three-story atrium lobby, one of the grandest interior spaces in the state, the Windsor is worth a look, and makes a great base for exploring central Georgia.

Andersonville Prison

Ten miles north of Americus, the Andersonville National Historic Site (daily 8 AM-5 PM; free) stands on the site of the largest and most notorious Confederate military prison. During the final 18 months of the Civil War, as many as 30,000 Union soldiers were imprisoned here in overcrowded conditions, and 13,000 died as a result of disease, poor sanitation, and exposure. Once this was uncovered after the war, public outrage was so great that the camp's commandant, Capt. Henry Wirz, was convicted of murder and hanged in Washington, D.C., though historians generally agree that there was little he could have done to alleviate the suffering.

Only a few parts of the prison have been reconstructed, but the prisoners' harrowing stories are told in a small museum (which also recounts the stories of American POWs during wars up through Vietnam) and most affectingly through the thousands of gravestones in the Andersonville National Cemetery, a half-mile north of the prison site.

In early spring, Macon's 200,000 cherry trees come into bloom.

The low-lying areas north and south of Macon along the Ocmulgee River suffered severe flooding in 1994, but have fully recovered.

Macon

Near the geographic center of the state, the city of Macon (pop. 106,612) was founded along the Ocmulgee (oak-MUL-gee) River in 1825, and flourished with the cotton trade. The downtown area holds dozens of well-preserved, historically significant public buildings, including a 110-year-old **Opera House** at 651 Mulberry Street and the turn-of-the-century **Douglass Theater** on Broadway west of Mulberry Street, where such Macon-born music legends as Lena Horne, Otis Redding, Little Richard, and the Allman Brothers got their start.

Following the completion in September 1995 of the long-awaited **Georgia Music Hall of Fame**, a $6 million project going up across Martin Luther King Boulevard, the theater is slated for renovation and re-opening. Until then, the best place to get a sense for Macon's multicultural heritage is the small but eye-opening **Harriett**

Tubman Museum (Mon.-Fri. 10 AM-5 PM, weekends 2-6 PM; $1) a block away at 340 Walnut Street (912/743-8544), which features a mural of the city's famous African-American natives along with African-oriented arts and crafts.

Macon's antebellum mansions stand on a low hill at the north end of downtown, having survived the Civil War unscathed apart from one brief battle: while most of Sherman's troops skirted by to the north, a band of Union soldiers engaged young Confederate soldiers at the city limits and fired a cannonball that landed in the foyer of a stately residence, now known as the **Cannonball House**, 865 Mulberry Street. A small museum (Tues.-Fri. 10 AM-4 PM, weekends 2-4 PM; $3) behind the house displays the usual barrage of Confederate memorabilia, and inside the house you can see the dented floor and original cannonball.

A block back toward downtown Macon from the Cannonball House, stunning **Hay House**, 934 Georgia Avenue (Mon.-Sat. 10:30 AM-4:30 PM, Sunday 2-4 PM; $6), is among the most beautiful antebellum houses in the state. You can see these two and other restorations on a guided walk led by an ersatz tour guide posing as Sidney Lanier, the city's famous 19th-century poet; call Sidney's Old South Tours ($9 adults, $4.50 children; 912/743-3401).

Besides the wealth of history, Macon also has a number of good places to eat. Among the very best, and a Macon institution, is **Len Berg's**, downtown off Broadway and Walnut in Old Post Office Alley. Since 1908 the restaurant has been serving up heaping helpings of fried chicken and other Southern treats, plus platefuls of sweet Vidalia onion rings and fresh-baked pies for dessert (lunch only, every day but Sunday 11 AM-2:30 PM). Among the mansions north of downtown Macon, you may recognize the white columns of **Beall's 1860 Restaurant**, 315 College Avenue, from an early Allman Brothers Band album cover. If the upscale American fare is beyond your budget, try the bare-bones **H&H Restaurant** downtown at 807 Forsyth Street, where the huge portions of downhome fare are still prepared by "Mama" Louise Hudson, who cooked for the band on their roadtrips. Another reliable option is **Morrison's Cafeteria**, in the Macon Mall a mile east of I-475, one of a chain of restaurants serving reasonably priced Southern specials such as fried catfish, red beans and rice, and peach cobbler.

One of Macon's antebellum Greek revival mansions has been converted into the very comfortable **1842 Inn**, 353 College Street (912/741-1842), with tons of historical ambience for as little as $65 a night. Otherwise, choose from the many chain motels lining the interstates around town.

For more information on visiting Macon, contact the **visitors bureau**, 200 Cherry Street (912/743-3401 or 800/768-3401) inside the massive old Terminal Station.

> The Allman Brothers' "Ramblin' Man" was "born in the back seat of a Greyhound Bus, rolling down Highway 41," but most of today's traffic follows its modern replacement, I-75.

Ocmulgee National Monument

Across the Ocmulgee River, well-signed from I-16 exit 4, two miles east of Macon along the Emory Highway (US-80), the settlement now preserved as the Ocmulgee National Monument was a center of pre-conquest Native American culture. By the time the first colonists arrived, it had been inhabited for over 800 years, with remains dating from A.D. 900.

From the small, WPA-era **visitor center** (daily 9 AM-5 PM; free; 912/752-8257), where you can watch a short film and admire pieces of elaborate pottery found on the site, a short trail leads you to a restored earthlodge (complete with thinly disguised air-conditioning ducts!), where you walk through a narrow tunnel to the center of the circular, kiva-like interior. The trail continues past the excavated remains of a Creek Indian trading post, then crosses a set of railroad tracks before climbing a 45-foot-high "Great Temple Mound," where you can see downtown Macon across the rumbling I-16 freeway—two thousand years of "culture" in one very pleasant half-mile walk.

Juliette: Fried Green Tomatoes at the Whistle Stop Cafe

Tucked away upriver on the Ocmulgee, in the heart of the Piedmont forests of middle Georgia, sits the town of Juliette, recently somewhat revived after a long slumber because of its Whistle Stop Cafe. The cafe, town, and river were the backdrop for the 1991 film *Fried Green Tomatoes*, based on Fannie Flagg's novel.

A landmark pit stop for locals and savvy travelers since 1966, the misnamed **Surf 'n' Turf** serves up killer barbecue in a concrete-block restaurant, a quarter-mile south of I-16 at the Hwy-29/Soperton exit.

You can get its famous barbecue, along with a plate of fried green tomatoes, Mon.-Sat. 8 AM-2 PM, Sunday noon-7 PM. Juliette lies due north of Macon along US-23, or 10 miles east of the I-75 town of Forsyth via Juliette Road.

Off I-16: Dublin, Vidalia, and Lyons

According to travel writer Kap Stann, author of *Georgia Handbook*, a local preacher with a loyal following claims that Vidalia has been visited by several UFOs in the past few years.

Named by its Irish founders in 1812, Dublin (pop. 16,312) continues to celebrate its Irish heritage at an all-out St. Patrick's Day festival that lasts two weeks. The historic district is centered along Bellevue Avenue, where you can glimpse the town's graceful old homes and look inside the local historical museum (Tues.-Fri. 1-4:30 PM; free) at Bellevue and Academy Streets.

Chappell's Mill, on US-441 a dozen miles north of town, continues to grind corn by the old dry-mill process. Call first to see the mill in operation and pick up a small bag of stone-ground grain for around four bits. Eat at **Ma Hawkins Cafe**, 124 W. Jackson Street near the downtown courthouse, which has grits and greens and other Southern specialties.

East of Dublin, around 15 miles south of I-16, Vidalia (pop. 11,078) is known to food lovers around the world as the home of the delectable Vidalia onion, so sweet it can be eaten raw, like an apple. To the locals, this single crop represents a $30-million industry. In late April and early May, follow the scent to the Vidalia Onion Festival for taste treats. The **Vidalia Welcome Center**, 2805 Lyons Highway, can hook you up with tours of local onion farms and processing plants in spring; they also offer cotton and tobacco tours in the fall.

Five miles east of Vidalia on US-280, find the **Robert Toombs Inn** at 101 S. State Street (912/526-4489) in downtown Lyons (pop. 4,502) to enjoy a meal at its refined restaurant, a drink at its full bar (a rare find in South Georgia), and an overnight stay in its period-furnished B&B rooms.

Statesboro

Directly on old US-80, 12 miles north of I-16, Statesboro (pop. 15,854) was also one of Sherman's stops. Here in 1864 his troops torched the courthouse; today's historic courthouse dates from the late 19th century. Georgia Southern University, with an enrollment of 10,000, dominates the town and has a small museum on campus displaying a 26-foot Monasaur skeleton.

If you're feeling hungry, generous Southern buffets are served boardinghouse-style (bring your plate to the kitchen when you're through) at the **Beaver House Restaurant**, in a large white columned mansion at 121 S. Main Street. For one reasonable price, you receive serving dishes full of meats, vegetables, cornbread, and biscuits.

Fort Pulaski

The drive east from Savannah to the Atlantic Ocean passes through picturesque fishing villages standing out from serene marshlands, where a maze of riverlets and creeks weaves through the tall green reeds, and fishing boats bob along the tidal waters as they head off to harvest shrimp and oysters.

Amid the calm stands Fort Pulaski National Monument (daily 8:30 AM-sunset; $1; 912/786-5787), 15 miles east of Savannah on US-80, a well-preserved stone-and-brick fortress completed in 1848 at a commanding site at the mouth of the Savannah River. Its prominent island site originally held colonial-era Fort Greene, which was demolished by a hurricane in 1804 and replaced by the architecturally impressive, pentagon-shaped bulwark that survives in its battered and breached state today, surrounded by a moat and many acres of grassy lawn.

Near Fort Pulaski, just west of the Bull River Bridge along US-80, **Williams Sea Food Restaurant** is a popular place to sample local cuisine. Harder to find, but worth the effort to reach, is the **Crab Shack**, on Estill Hammock Road (912/786-9857), where "The Elite Dine in Their Bare Feet" on plates of shrimp-and-sausage, "Low Country Boil," and Key Lime Pie raved about by such dignified aficionados as the *New York Times*.

Tybee Island

You made it! The Atlantic Ocean at last! One of many islands filling the delta at the mouth of the Savannah River, the town of Tybee Island (pop. 2,842) is a funky old family-oriented resort, with four blocks of corn-dog stands and miniature golf courses lining Butler Avenue, the eastern end of 3,000-mile US-80, just 18 miles east of central Savannah.

Locally famous for the annual Beach Bum's Parade in the middle of June, Tybee Island's main attraction is its endless and usually uncrowded white sand beaches. Another magnet is the wacky, slightly ersatz, diner-style **Breakfast Club**, right at the center of things at 1500 Butler Avenue, open daily 6 AM-1 PM.

At the north end of Tybee Island, whence the Union forces bombarded Fort Pulaski during the Civil War, a centuries-old lighthouse stands next to the WW II-era concrete bunkers that house the **Tybee Museum** (daily 10 AM-6 PM in summer, shorter hours rest of the year; $2; 912/786-5801), which includes the old lighthouse keeper's cottage among its collections tracing the island's history.

Between Macon and Savannah, Swainsboro's **KISS 98.1 FM** airs CCR, R.E.M., and all the latest NASCAR news.

North of US-80 via US-1, the town of Wrens (pop. 2,414) was the boyhood home of **Erskine Caldwell,** author of the classic novels *Tobacco Road* and *God's Little Acre*, both of which were set in this part of rural Georgia.

Ten miles south of I-16 at the intersection of US-280 and US-301, the town of Claxton bills itself as the **Fruitcake Capital of the World.** In the fall fruitcake-making season, the Claxton Bakery in the center of town offers free samples of the 3,000 tons of fruitcake they pound out each year.

Beginning in 1829, construction of Fort Pulaski, proclaimed "as strong as the Rocky Mountains," took 18 years, used 25 million bricks, and cost just over a million dollars. During the Civil War, its seven-foot-thick walls withstood bombardment by the Union forces' new rifled cannon for only 30 hours, which prompted the fort's surrender in April 1862.

ROUTE 66:
THE
MOTHER
ROAD

BAR-B-Q 15   STEW BEEF 15

HAMBURGER   HOT DOG   CHILE   H

L & L EAT SHOP

DRINK

Coca-Cola

ROUTE 66: THE MOTHER ROAD

Route 66's mystique continues to captivate people around the world. Running between Chicago and Los Angeles, "over two thousand miles all the way" in the words of the popular R&B anthem, this legendary old road passes through the heart of the U.S. on a diagonal trip that takes in some of the country's most archetypal roadside scenes. If you're looking for great displays of neon signs, rusty middle-of-nowhere truck stops, or kitschy Americana, do as the song says and "get your kicks on Route 66."

But perhaps the most compelling reason to follow Route 66 is to experience the road's ingrained timeline of contemporary America. Before it was called Route 66, and long before it was even paved in 1926, this corridor was traversed by the Old Trails Highway, one of the country's first transcontinental roads. For three decades before and after WW II, Route 66 earned the title "Main Street of America" because it wound through small towns across the Midwest and Southwest, lined by hundreds of cafes, motels, gas stations, and tourist attractions. During the Great Depression, hundreds of thousands of farm families, displaced from the Dust Bowl, made their way west along Route 66 to California, following what John Steinbeck called "The Mother Road" in his vivid portrait, *The Grapes of Wrath*. After WW II, many thousands more expressed their upward mobility by leaving the industrial East bound for good jobs in the suburban idyll of Southern California—again, following Route 66, which came to embody the demographic shift from the Rust Belt to the Sun Belt.

Beginning in the late 1950s and continuing gradually over the next 25 years, old Route 66 was bypassed section by section as the high-speed interstate highways were completed. Finally, in 1984, when the last stretch of freeway was finished, Route 66 was officially decommissioned;. the old route is now designated "Historic Route 66."

Though it is no longer a main route across the country, Route 66 has retained its mystique in part due to the very same effective hype, hucksterism, and boosterism that animated it through its half-century heyday. It was a Route 66 sight, the marvelous Meramec Caverns, that gave the world the bumper sticker, and it was here that the American art of vacation as driving tour first flourished. Billboards and giant statues along the highway still hawk a baffling array of roadside attractions, tempting passing travelers to swim alongside giant blue whales, to see live rattlesnakes, mountain lions, and other creatures on display in roadside menageries, or to stay at "Tucumcari Tonight—2,000 Rooms."

The same commercial know-how and shameless self-promotion has helped the towns along the old route stay alive. Diners and motels play up their Route 66 connections, however tenuous they may be, and thanks to the numerous guidebooks and magazine articles that proclaim the charms of the old road, many bona fide Route 66 landmarks are kept in business by nostalgic travelers intent on experiencing a taste of this endangered American experience. That said, along many stretches of Route 66, the contrast between characterful old-road landscape and contemporary franchised freeway culture is painfully sharp. Many quirky old motels and cafes hang on by a thread of hope, sit vacant, or survive in memory only—all for want of an interstate exit. In fact, of all the routes covered in this book, Route 66 is the closest to the freeways; for many stretches you'll be forced to leave the old two-lane and follow the super slabs that have been built right on top of the old road.

Route 66 passes through a marvelous cross-section of American scenes, from the golden sands and sunshine of Los Angeles, past the Grand Canyon and the Native American communities of the desert Southwest, to the gritty streets of St. Louis and Chicago. Whether you are motivated by an interest in its history, feel a nostalgic yearning for the good old days the route has come to represent, or simply want to experience firsthand the amazing diversity of people and landscapes that line its path, Route 66 offers an unforgettable journey into America, then and now.

ROUTE 66 HIGHLIGHTS

ACROSS CALIFORNIA

From the beautiful beaches of Santa Monica, through the citrus-rich inland valleys, over mountains and across the demanding Mojave Desert, Route 66 passes through every type of Southern California landscape. The old road, which survives intact almost all the way across the state, is marked for most of its 315 miles by signs declaring it "Historic Route 66"; in the Mojave desert the route is also marked as "National Old Trails Highway," its title before the national numbering system was put into effect in the late 1920s.

The sights and sounds of Los Angeles are covered in a Survival Guide on pages 696-697.

Route 66 across Los Angeles

For diehard purists, Route 66 across Los Angeles still exists intact. Old Route 66 had its western terminus at the edge of the Pacific Ocean in Santa Monica, on a palm-lined bluff a block north of the city's landmark pier. Where Santa Monica Boulevard dead-ends at Ocean Boulevard, a brass plaque marks the end of Route 66, the "Main Street of America," also remembered as the "Will Rogers Highway," one of many names the old road earned in its half-century of existence.

For travelers along old Route 66, the soaring **Colorado Boulevard Bridge** at the western edge of Pasadena marked the symbolic entrance to Los Angeles. Recently restored, the bridge arches across Arroyo Seco along the south side of the Ventura Freeway. Pasadena also holds some of Southern California's most significant art and architecture; for information, contact the visitors bureau (818/795-9311).

Two blocks east of the ocean, stretch your legs at Santa Monica Place, an indoor/outdoor shopping mall and icon of Southern California urban culture. This portion of the route still holds reminders of the damage inflicted by the 1994 Northridge earthquake. Continuing east, old Route 66 followed Santa Monica Boulevard through Beverly Hills and West Hollywood, eventually merging into Sunset Boulevard for the long winding drive to downtown L.A. The route ends up at the historic core of the city, Olvera Street and the Plaza de Los Angeles State Historic Park.

From downtown L.A., hop onto the Pasadena Freeway for a trip back to freeways past: opened in 1939, when it was called the Arroyo Seco Parkway, this was California's first freeway and featured such novel concepts as stop signs at the entrances.

The San Gabriel Valley

East of Los Angeles, though effectively swallowed up long ago, the San Gabriel Valley was many westbound travelers' first taste of Southern California. After crossing the Mojave Desert and the high mountains, Route 66 dropped down into what

WIGWAM MOTEL, RIALTO, CALIFORNIA —
A CLASSIC "PROP-MOTEL" DESIGN, THE WIGWAM VILLAGES WERE THE BRAINSTORM OF FRANK REDFORD, WHO WAS INSPIRED BY A TEE-PEE-SHAPED DRIVE-IN RESTAURANT IN LONG BEACH, CAL., IN THE 1930'S. REDFORD PATENTED HIS WIGWAM MOTIF, & BUILT SEVEN OF THEM. THE FIRST, IN HORSE CAVE, KENTUCKY, WAS DESTROYED RECENTLY. #2 IS IN NEARBY CAVE CITY, KENT. ONE OF THE ORIGINAL 7, IS STILL OPERATING IN HOLBROOK, ARIZONA. #7 WAS IN RIALTO (ABOVE), ON THE FAMOUS FOOTHILL BOULEVARD — OLD RT 66... THESE 14 UNITS CURVE AROUND THE FRONT OFFICE, WHICH ADJOINS A TEE-PEE IN THE CENTER OF THE COMPLEX IS A COURTYARD & TINY, KIDNEY-SHAPED SWIMMING POOL. by R Waldmire

At the western edge of San Bernadino, a remnant of old Route 66 road culture still survives: the 19 plaster tepees that form the **Wigwam Motel,** at 2728 W. Foothill Boulevard.

might have seemed like paradise: orange groves as far as the eye could see, a few tidy towns linked by streetcars, and houses draped in rose vines and bougainvillea. The San Gabriel Valley embodied this suburban ideal until the mid-1950s, when Route 66 gave way to high-speed freeways, and the orange groves were replaced by endless grids of tract houses.

If you're willing to search and to close your eyes to the mini-malled sprawl, Route 66 still offers a window onto this golden age. Winding between Pasadena and San Bernardino, along the foothills of the sometimes snowcapped San Gabriel Mountains, the old road links a number of once distinct communities.

From Pasadena, old Route 66 runs along Colorado Boulevard, turning into Foothill Boulevard around the landmark ractrack at Santa Anita. (The Marx Brothers filmed *A Day at the Races* here.) Foothill Boulevard, which is signed as "Historic Route 66," jogs along the foothills through **Azusa**, home of the classic Foothill Drive-In and one of the country's oldest McDonald's restaurants— complete with red-tiled arches. In **Upland**, the old road features a grass median strip, and runs right past a statue of the pioneer "Madonna of the Trail," which officially marked the western end of the National Old Trails Highway, the immediate precursor to Route 66.

In the 1950s, San Bernardino was where **Maurice and Richard McDonald** perfected the burger-making restaurant chain that bears their name. In 1961, the McDonald brothers sold their company to Ray Kroc; the rest is fast-food history.

At **Rancho Cucamonga**, Foothill Boulevard crosses the I-15 freeway, which is the quickest route over Cajon Pass. The old Route 66 alignment continued east for another 15 miles, passing through Fontana, birthplace of the Hell's Angels' Motorcycle Club, before bending north at San Bernardino to join I-15 at the summit.

Cajon Pass
Very picturesque stretches of the old road go over Cajon Pass, though it is not a through route; the main road is now I-15. At the top, turn off the freeway and stop for a burger and fries at the **Summit Inn,** one of the few survivors of the old road along this stretch of highway.

Victorville

It takes about two hours to get here from the end of the I-15 freeway up at Cajon Pass, but it's not until you reach Victorville, the distant extent of Los Angeles's sprawl, that old Route 66 begins to seem real—as real as Hollywood cowboys, anyway. Victorville, a rapidly growing desert community of over 50,000 residents, is home to the **Roy Rogers and Dale Evans Museum** (daily 9 AM-5 PM; $4; 619/243-4547), a living memorial to America's favorite cowboy and cowgirl, west of I-15 at

the Roy Rogers Drive exit. Along with an encyclopedic collection of old movie stills and posters stand the stuffed remains of Roy and Dale's favorite animals: Roy's horse Trigger (a larger-than-life concrete copy of Trigger stands in front of the museum as well); Dale's horse Buttermilk; their dog Bullet; plus hundreds of trophy heads of other less-loved creatures. Roy himself is often on hand to welcome visitors, yet the homespun charm he and Dale have created here may get lost amidst the large-scale renovation and expansion the museum is currently undergoing.

Hula Ville, formerly California State Landmark No. 939, has gone through hard times since the 100-year-old creator and caretaker, "Fry Pan" Miles Mahan, was forced to retire in 1995, but the hundreds of beer bottles and hand-lettered memorials to sundry bums, hobos, and other travelers he called his friends have been moved to the California Route 66 museum in Victorville.

San Bernardino County is the largest in the United States.

Victorville is also home to a small new **California Route 66 Museum,** on the old road at 16849 D Street (Thurs.-Sun. 10 AM-4 PM; donations; 619/261-US66), with a small but growing collection of road signs, photographs, and reminiscences.

Old Route 66 follows 7th Street through town, past a few neon-signed old motels like the **New Corral,** 14643 7th Street (619/245-9378) with its animated bucking bronco, and the large **Green Tree Inn** restaurant, 14173 Green Tree Boulevard.

For more information, contact the **Victorville Chamber of Commerce** (619/245-6506).

Old Route 66 Loop: Oro Grande, Helendale, and Lenwood

Between Victorville and Barstow, old Route 66 survives as an "old roads" trek across the Mojave Desert. The 36-mile route, called the

Old National Trail Highway, parallels the railroad tracks and the usually parched Mojave River, passing through odd little towns like Oro Grande—still home to a huge cement plant and lots of good junk shops—and Helendale, where you can find the nearly famous stripper's "museum," Exotic World. Outside Barstow at the west end of Main Street, keep an eye out for the Christian Motorcycle club sign welcoming you to Lenwood, a crossroads near where the old road reconnects with I-15.

Barstow

Though by population it's under half the size of Victorville, the burly railroad and transportation center of Barstow (pop. 21,495) seems a much bigger place. Located midway between Los Angeles and Las Vegas, at the point where I-15 veers north and I-40 takes the place of old east-west Route 66, Barstow was the first large watering hole west of the Arizona border, a role it still plays judging by the numerous truck depots arrayed around town. It's scruffy and a little scary in the way railroad towns can be, and along Main Street, the old Route 66 corridor, many of the old cafes and motels are now closed and boarded up. The most visible exception is the landmark old **El Rancho Motel** at 112 E. Main Street—the one whose 100-foot neon sign is supported by a pair of massive pylons visible from all over town—which now serves as a homemade Route 66 museum and souvenir store.

The **Mojave Desert** is one of the driest places on the planet; parts of it receive an average of under three inches of rainfall annually, sometimes going for more than two years without getting a drop.

Daggett and Newberry Springs: *The Bagdad Cafe*

East of Barstow all the way to the Arizona border, old Route 66 survives in a series of different stretches alongside the I-40 freeway. The first place of interest, Daggett, is a rusty old mining and railroad town six miles east of Barstow along the north side of the freeway. A couple of abandoned old hotels keep company with one still-functioning restaurant, the **Daggett Restaurant**, serving bowls of chili and ice-cold beers along the south side of the tracks. Old Route 66 runs due east from Daggett, past the region's current claim to fame: the acres of shiny mirrors of the **Solar One power plant**, an experimental electricity generating station three miles from Daggett and north of the old road.

Fifteen miles east of Daggett come the next I-40 junction and the next small town, Newberry Springs, where the popular Percy Adlon movie *Bagdad Cafe* was shot at the **Sidewinder Cafe**, open daily 6 AM-8 PM for the best food on this stretch of old Route 66. The old road continues along the south side of I-40 for another

Almost the entire area between I-40 and I-15 has been set aside as the **East Mojave National Scenic Area,** but left in limbo by a lack of federal funds. One of many places here worth the trip is Mitchell Caverns at the center of Providence Mountains State Park. For more information, contact the ranger station (619/326-3896) on old Route 66 in Essex. The 28-mile stretch of old Route 66 from Essex to Kelbaker is closed, perhaps permanently, because a bridge is out.

Amboy Crater has been the focus of a contentious plan which would turn the entire area into a massive trash dump, eventually forming a mountain 400 feet high, a mile wide, and three miles long, growing by up to 21,000 tons a day.

According to Route 66 historian Tom Teague, author of the book *Searching for 66,* Santa Fe Railroad supply points across the Mojave Desert were named in alphabetical order: Amboy, Bristol, Cadiz, Danby, Essex, Fenner, Goffs, Home, Ibex, Java, and Klinefelter.

Huge chunks of the Mojave Desert have been used as military training grounds since WW II, when **Gen. George Patton** prepared his tank battalions for battle in the North African desert. As many as 90,000 soldiers were based here during the war years; the remains of the camp can still be seen in the desert along Crucero Road, just north of the I-40 Ludlow exit.

25 miles, passing the lava flows of Pisgah Crater before crossing over to the north of the freeway for the final 10 miles into Ludlow, where old Route 66 rejoins the freeway.

Old Route 66 Loop: Ludlow, Amboy, and Chambless

If you want a quick and convincing taste of what traveling across the Mojave Desert was like in the days before air-conditioning and cellular phones, turn south off I-40 at Ludlow, 50 miles east of Barstow, and follow the well-signed "National Old Trails Highway," one of the many monikers Route 66 has carried over the years, on a 75-mile loop along the old road. At Ludlow, where two gas stations, a coffee shop, and a motel represent civilization between Barstow and Needles, the old road wends slightly southeast, passing first through Bagdad, a turn-of-the-century gold mining town now defunct. Continuing east, old Route 66 cuts across another lava flow, this one part of the Amboy Crater, beyond which another road heads south to Twentynine Palms and Joshua Tree National Monument.

Midway along the old road loop, Amboy (pop. 2) is a museum-worthy assembly of roadside architecture that has survived solely due to the willpower of its lord, master, and owner since 1938, Buster Burris. Since traffic dropped with the building of I-40, the whole town—complete with a classic late-1940s roadside cafe called Roy's, a motel, and a set of gas pumps—has been for sale, and only the cafe is still open, at irregular regular hours.

From Amboy, it's another 48 miles back to I-40 at the town of Fenner. The 28-mile stretch of the old route from Essex to Kelbaker is closed because a bridge is out. From Essex, detour up to I-40. If you're keen on traveling as much of the old road as possible, another stretch of Route 66 runs east from Fenner on a roller coaster of undulating two-lane blacktop, parallel to the railroad track through the desert hamlet of **Goffs**; stop for a burger or a cold drink at the Goffs General Store. Fifteen miles east of Goffs, old Route 66 joins up with US-95, which continues north to Las Vegas, 90-odd miles away, and south to I-40, linking up with the freeway 10 miles west of Needles.

Needles

Founded soon after the Santa Fe Railroad came through in 1883, and named for the group of sharp stone spires that stand near where I-40 crosses the Colorado River from Arizona, Needles (pop. 5,191) is one of the hottest places in the country, with summertime highs hovering between 100 and 120° for months on end. Though unbearable in summer, Needles is a popular place with winter snowbirds escaping colder climes; it also has a very rich Route 66 heritage. Besides magnificent El Garces Hotel, which is undergoing long-term renovation into a historical museum, the stretch of old Route 66 through Needles—along Broadway, alternating along both sides of the freeway—holds the Route 66 Motel, with its great arrow-shaped sign, and the more inviting Old Trails Inn, 304 Broadway (619/326-3523). Across the street from the "Welcome to Needles" wagon, and known as the "Palm Motel" during its Route 66 heyday, the Old Trails Inn has been brought back to life as a nostalgic B&B thanks to the Wilde family, who run the place and have lived in Needles for over 40 years. Bed and board cost around $50 a night for two people, worth double that for the chance to hear Hank Wilde's vivid tales of the *real* old Route 66.

Needles is a friendly town and well worth getting to know. Drive around a while to get your bearings, and stop by the chamber of commerce office (619/326-2050), at Front and G Streets across from El Garces, for a free map or other useful information.

ACROSS ARIZONA

Even if you're not a die-hard Route 66 fan, traveling the old route across Arizona is bound to convert you. The high-speed I-40 freeway gives quick access to some of the best surviving stretches of the old road. Starting at the Colorado River, the route runs from the arid Mojave Desert past remarkable old highway towns along two of the oldest, still-driveable stretches of the Mother Road.

Midway across the state, the route climbs onto the forested (and often snowy) Kaibab Plateau for a look at the mighty Grand Canyon. East of Flagstaff, the old road is effectively submerged beneath the freeway, which drops down to cross desolate desert, passing through dessicated towns and the Petrified Forest National Park. Remnants of numerous old roadside attractions—Indian trading posts, wild animal menageries, "Sleep in a Teepee" motel courts—all survive in varying degrees of preservation along Arizona's section of Route 66.

Lake Havasu City and London Bridge
The first stop east of the Colorado River, nine miles from the border and 23 miles south of I-40, Lake Havasu City is a thoroughly modern vacation town built around a thoroughly odd centerpiece: London Bridge, brought here stone by stone between 1967 and 1971. Terribly tacky souvenir shops and faux London pubs congregate around the foot of the bridge, which spans a man-made channel to a large island, but the bridge itself is an impressive sight.

The Amtrak station in Needles stands next to what was formerly El Garces Hotel, one of many palatial railroad hotels run by **Fred Harvey.**

Needles was the boyhood home of Snoopy and Charlie Brown cartoonist **Charles Schulz,** and is featured in the comics strips as the desert home of Snoopy's raffish sibling Spike.

From Needles, it's a quick 25-mile drive north along the river into Nevada to visit the gambling center of **Laughlin.** From here you can loop back onto old Route 66 at Oatman. Since the mid-1980s Laughlin has boomed into a sparkling city with huge casinos and over 10,000 cheap rooms. Try the Circus Circus-run Colorado Belle (702/298-4000 or 800/458-9500) if you want to stay in a fake paddle wheel riverboat for as little as $25 a night.

Crossing the Colorado River from California, look downstream from the I-40 freeway to see the arching silver steel bridge that carried Route 66 up until 1966. It's still in use, supporting a natural gas pipeline; beyond it, the red-rock spires for which Needles is named rise sharply out of the desert plains.

Unless you plan to retire here—or simply relax on a boat on the river—there's not a lot to do at Lake Havasu. Have an English muffin and a cup of tea, pay your respects and take a photograph or two, then hit the road again.

Old Route 66: Oatman

One of the most demanding, desolate, and awesomely satisfying stretches of the old road climbs from I-40 along the Colorado River, beginning just east of the California border and rejoining the freeway at Kingman. Following at first along the water before cutting across a stretch of desert that brings new meaning to the word "harsh," the resurfaced roadway passes no signs of life on this 50-mile loop. Be sure you and your car are prepared for the rigors of desert driving.

LONDON BRIDGE

It may not have stood out as the finest of engineering art when it spanned the Thames, but London Bridge is a marvelous sight in the middle of the Arizona desert. A replacement for a series of bridges that date back to medieval times, inspiring the children's rhyme, "London Bridge is Falling Down," this version of London Bridge was constructed in the 1830s. When it was no longer able to handle the demands of London traffic, the old bridge was replaced by a modern concrete span and its stones were put up for sale in 1967.

Bought by property developer Robert McCulloch for $2.4 million, the 10,246 blocks of stone were shipped here and reassembled at a cost of another $3 million. After a channel was cut under the bridge to bring water from the Colorado River, the Lord Mayor of London flew in to attend the rededication ceremonies in October 1971; the bridge now stands as centerpiece of a retirement community that's home to some 25,000 residents. There's no admission charge to see this oddly compelling sight, its finely carved stonework standing in permanent rebuke to the tacky stucco, mock Tudor souvenir shops lining the base of the bridge.

From I-40 and the California border, take the Park Moabi exit and follow Hwy-95, then Hwy-66, due north; you can also reach Hwy-95 directly from Needles or from Laughlin, Nevada. (Westbound drivers have it the easiest—simply follow the well-signed "Historic Route 66" west from Kingman, exit 44 off I-40.) Whichever way you go, you can't avoid the steep hills that bring you to Oatman (elev. 2,700 feet), an odd mix of ghost town and tourist draw that's one of the top stops along Route

The crossing over the Colorado River at the California/Arizona border was the site of illegal but effective roadblocks during the Dust Bowl, when vigilante mobs turned back migrant Okies if they didn't have much money.

66. A gold mining town whose glory days had long faded by the time I-40 passed it by way back in 1952, Oatman looks like a Wild West stage set, but it's the real thing—awnings over the plank sidewalks, bearded roughnecks (and a few burros) wandering the streets, lots of rust and slumping old buildings. The gold mines here produced some two million ounces from their start in 1904 until they panned out in the mid-1930s; at its peak, Oatman had a population of over 10,000, with 20 saloons and a half-dozen hotels lining the three-block Main Street. One of these, the old **Oatman Hotel** (520/768-4408), was where Clark Gable and Carole Lombard spent their first night after getting married in Kingman in 1939; you can sample Oatman's highly recommended Navajo tacos, have a beer in the downstairs bar, peer through a plexiglass door at their "Honeymoon Suite," or spend the night in one of the other $35 rooms, unchanged for half a century.

Saloons and rock shops line the rest of Main Street, where on weekends and holidays Wild West enthusiasts act out the shoot-outs that took place here only in the movies. Oatman does get a considerable tourist trade, but after dark and out of season the town reverts to its rough-and-tumble ways, and the conservative, libertarian bent of most of the local population ensures that nothing is likely to change Oatman's crusty charms.

For more information, contact the small but helpful **chamber of commerce** (520/768-8070).

East from Oatman the road climbs up and over the angular Black Mountains before dropping down past the recently reactivated gold workings at **Goldroad**. Steep switchbacks make the 2,100-foot change in elevation over a very short eight miles of blacktop, and the route then continues across comparatively level plains for an-

At **Yucca,** Arizona, just south of I-40 exit 26, and 18 miles west of Kingman, the Ford Motor Company maintains an automobile "proving ground" where they run cars for countless miles around an oval track in the hottest summer heat.

For the hits of the 1960s, tune to "Radio Crazy," **KRCY 105.9 FM.**

other 20 miles into Kingman, which seems like a bustling metropolis after this hour-plus roller coaster of a drive.

Kingman

The only town for miles in any direction since its founding as a railroad center in 1880, Kingman (pop. 12,750) has always depended upon passing travelers for its livelihood. Long a main stopping place on Route 66, and still providing the only all-night services on I-40 between Flagstaff and Needles, the town remains more a way station than a destination despite the increasing number of people who have relocated here in recent years, attracted by the open space, high desert air, and low cost of living.

Everything that's ever happened in and around Kingman is documented to some degree at the **Mojave Museum,** 400 W. Beale Street (Mon.-Fri. 10 AM-5 PM, Saturday and Sunday 1-5 PM; $1), right on US-93 a block south of I-40. Besides the usual dioramas and displays on regional history, there's an extensive section devoted to local Hualapai culture and crafts, as well as samples of turquoise mined nearby. There's also a display on the life of local boy Andy Devine and a photograph of Clark Gable and Carole Lombard, who fled Hollywood to get married in Kingman's Methodist church.

The stretch of Route 66 through Kingman was renamed in memory of favorite son **Andy Devine,** who was born in Flagstaff in 1905 but grew up here, where his parents ran the Beale Hotel. One of the best-known character actors of Hollywood's classic era, the raspy-voiced Devine usually played a devoted sidekick, the sort of role taken by Gabby Hayes, whom Devine replaced in the later Roy Rogers movies. Devine's most famous role was as the wagon driver in the classic 1939 John Ford western *Stagecoach.* He remained active in films and TV until his death in 1977.

Quite a few of the old Route 66 cafes and motels still flourish alongside the old road, now called Andy Devine Avenue through town; modern development borders the I-40 freeway. Among many places to eat are the very good **Mr. D's Route 66 Diner,** right downtown and impossible to miss thanks to its bank of neon; and the **House of Chan,** 960 W. Beale Street, on US-93 a block north of I-40, which serves a full menu of American food as well as Cantonese specialties. Besides the usual chain motels—two nice Best Westerns, two Days Inns, a Holiday Inn, and a TraveLodge—accommodation options include the pleasant **Hill Top Motel,** 1901 E. Andy Devine Avenue (520/753-2198), lately infamous as the place where Timothy McVeigh stayed for a week before allegedly blowing up the federal building in Oklahoma City.

For more information, or to pick up a copy of the town's very good Route 66 brochure, contact the Kingman **visitor center,** 333 W. Andy Devine Boulevard (520/753-6106).

Kingman marks the intersection of Route 66 and north-south **US-93,** which heads north to Las Vegas and southeast to Phoenix and the Mexican border. For more, see page 86.

Hualapai Mountain Park

To escape the summer heat, Kingmanites head south along a well-marked 14-mile road to Hualapai Mountain Park, where pines and firs cover the slopes of the 8,417-foot peak. Hiking trails wind through the wilderness, where there's a campground ($6) and a few rustic cabins ($25) built by the CCC during the New Deal 1930s. Contact the ranger station (602/757-3859) near the park entrance for detailed information or to make reservations.

Old Route 66 Loop: Hackberry, Valentine, and the Hualapai Reservation

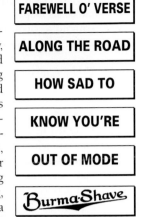

FAREWELL O' VERSE

ALONG THE ROAD

HOW SAD TO

KNOW YOU'RE

OUT OF MODE

Burma-Shave

Probably the most evocative stretch of old Route 66 runs northeast from Kingman through the high desert Hualapai Valley, along the Santa Fe Railroad tracks through all-but-abandoned towns bypassed by the "modern" interstate world. Leaving Kingman on a 20-mile-long straightaway, the road (now named Hwy-66) bends back south around the Peacock Mountains through the old railroad town of Hackberry, home to the ever-evolving **International Bioregional Old Route 66 Visitor Center and Preservation Foundation.** A marvelous establishment, created by renowned Route 66 artist Bob Waldmire, the center serves multiple purposes: the 22-acre site includes everything from cactus gardens to a solar oven, while the main building, built in 1934 as the Hackberry General Store, now houses a museum and gift shop, and a library with books on Route 66 and the complete works of Thomas Paine, Thomas Jefferson, and other free thinkers. Future plans include the development of a hostel and B&B, but for now, whenever Bob's around, you can be assured of a warm welcome and a hot cup of coffee. For more information, call or write: P.O. Box 46, Hackberry, AZ 86411 (520/769-2605).

Downhill from the Route 66 center, the old town of Hackberry grew up along the original alignment of Route 66, which continues east across a small section of the Hualapai Indian Reservation, centered around the village of Valentine. Another 10 miles east brings you to the town of Truxton, where the **Frontier Cafe** on the south side of the highway is the one reliable place to eat in this sparsely populated region—good pie and great chat, open weekdays 7 AM-7 PM, weekends 9 AM-5 PM. **Grandma's Bar** across the highway gives you another chance to sample local lore and lifeways.

Another mile east is the boundary of the main Hualapai (pronounced "WALL-ah-pie") reservation lands. The 700-strong tribe has its community center at the

Old Hackberry Store, HACKBERRY, ARIZONA (ALT. 3,500 FT.)

town of **Peach Springs** which, although marking the halfway point of this 90-mile, old-roads loop, offers little reason to stop. It's mostly a prefab BIA housing project with no services. There is a great old filling station, but it has been on the verge of collapse for many years.

Grand Canyon Caverns

A dozen miles east of Peach Springs, 26 miles from I-40, a large green sign marks the entrance to Grand Canyon Caverns (daily 10 AM-5 PM, 8 AM-6 PM in summer; $7.50; 520/422-3223), which has somehow mangaged to survive despite being bypassed by the I-40 superslab. Once one of the prime tourist draws on the Arizona stretch of Route 66, the Grand Canyon Caverns were discovered and developed in the late 1920s and still have the feel of an old-time roadside attraction. Start your tour at the gift shop, buy a ticket, and hop on the elevator, which drops you 300 feet to underground chambers, including the 18,000-square-foot Chapel of the Ages. Tours last around 45 minutes. There's also a motel (doubles $22 in winter, $45 in summer) and a restaurant on the site.

Midway between Peach Springs and the caverns, Hwy-18 cuts off 65 miles to the northeast toward the Havasupai Indian Reservation, which includes one of the most beautiful and untrammelled corners of the Grand Canyon. For further details, contact the tribally owned and operated **Havasupai Lodge** at 520/448-2111.

Seligman

At the east end of the long loop of old Route 66, the sleepy little town of Seligman (pop. 510; pronounced "SLIG-man") is a perfect place to take a break before or after rejoining the interstate hordes. The town retains a lot of its historic character— old sidewalk awnings, and even a few hitching rails—and offers lots of reasons to stop, but two of the biggest are the brothers Angel and Juan Delgadillo, ringleaders of local Route 66 preservation efforts. Angel is the town barber, and his shop is a pilgrimage point for old roads fans; Juan, the practical joker of the pair, runs the wacky **Snow Cap Drive-In** a block to the east. The burgers, fries, and milk shakes are plenty good, but Juan's sense of humor is more than a little strange: he has handles on doors that don't open, a sign that says "Sorry, We're Open," and a menu advertising "Hamburgers without Ham." Behind the restaurant, in snow, rain, or shine, sits a roofless old

Delgadillo's Snow Car

Chevy decorated with fake flowers and an artificial Christmas tree. Go ahead, ask him why.

Apart from the Delgadillo brothers, Seligman also has a very good cafe, the **Copper Cart**, at the center of town; a neat old mock-Tudor railroad station that once doubled as a Harvey House hotel and restaurant; a half-dozen motels including the **Historic Route 66**, 500 W. Route 66 (520/422-3204); and the **Black Cat** saloon, where actor Nicholas Cage has been known to stop in for a drink or two.

Between Seligman and Ash Fork, a nice section of the old Route 66 two-lane runs just north of, and parallel to, the I-40 freeway.

Between Ash Fork and Flagstaff, a long but beautiful scenic loop winds along US-89 and US-89A through Prescott, Jerome, Sedona, and wonderful Oak Creek Canyon.

Williams

The last Route 66 town to be bypassed by the I-40 freeway, Williams (pop. 2,532; elev. 6,780 feet) held out until the bitter end, waging court battle after court battle before finally surrendering on October 13, 1984. Despite the town's long opposition, in the end Williams gave in gracefully, going so far as to hold a celebration-*cum*-wake for the old road, highlighted by a performance atop the new freeway overpass by none other than Mr. Route 66 himself, Bobby "Get Your Kicks" Troup.

Williams today is primarily a gateway to the Grand Canyon, but it also takes full tourist advantage of its Route 66 heritage. The downtown streets sport old-fashioned street lamps, and every other store sells "authentic" Route 66 souvenirs, but the town is nonetheless a charming place, especially in the off-season, when Williams is little more than a bedroom community for Grand Canyon-bound travelers.

Apart from the Route 66 connections, Williams's pride and joy is the vintage **Grand Canyon Railway**, which whistles and steams its way north to the canyon every morning March-Dec., taking roughly two hours each way and allowing a three-hour layover—or longer, if you go up on one train and come back another day. Call for current schedules and fares (roundtrip tickets cost $50; 800/THE-TRAIN), or stop by the historic depot, a former Harvey House hotel restored in 1990.

As any good road trip destination must, Williams has at least one decent place to eat breakfast, **Old Smokey's Pancake House**, 624 W. Bill Williams Avenue at the west end of town. The restaurant is also home to a landmark old Route 66 restaurant, **Rod's Steak House**, 301 E. Bill Williams Avenue, in business since 1946.

For a place to stay, try any of the town's many motels, such as the **Westerner Motel**, 530 W. Bill Williams Avenue (520/635-4312 or 800/385-9313); or the British-run **Norris Motel** (520/635-2202), at the far west end of town, offering clean rooms from under $30 a night, rising to $55 a night in summer.

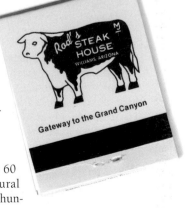

For more information, contact the **chamber of commerce**, 200 W. Railroad Avenue (520/635-4061).

Detour: Grand Canyon National Park

From the east end of Williams, Hwy-64 continues 60 miles due north to one of the wonders of the natural world, the Grand Canyon of the Colorado River. Two hundred miles long, a mile deep, and anywhere from five to 15 miles across, the Grand Canyon defies description, and if you're anywhere nearby you owe it to yourself to stop for a look. This book can do little more than hint at all there is to see and do there, but if you have time for nothing else, hike down into the canyon to get a real sense of its awesome scale.

Most of what you need to know to enjoy a visit is contained in the brochure you're given at the entrance, where you pay the $10-per-car fee, or can be found out at the very good **visitor center** (daily 8 AM-5 PM; 520/638-7888). Here you can pick up information about the park's many hiking trails, the canyon's geology, the burro rides that take you down and back up again, and splendid Phantom Ranch, a rustic complex of cabins and dormitories halfway down the canyon.

To make advance reservations for acommodations, a good idea at any time of year but essential in the peak summer months, phone the park concessionaire, the **AMFAC Corporation** (303/297-2757). This is the new name for the company started by Fred Harvey way back in 1876. The most characterful and best-value place to stay is the **Bright Angel Lodge**, which overlooks the canyon; there are also many other motels and swanky **El Tovar Hotel**, where rooms cost from $200 a night. If all these are full, accommodations are available outside the park's southern boundary at **Tusayan**, including a Best Western and a Quality Inn.

> In his 1945 guide to Route 66, Jack Rittenhouse wrote, "Cowboys and Indians can be seen in their picturesque dress on Flagstaff streets year 'round. . . ."

Flagstaff

An old railroad and lumber-mill town given a new lease on life by an influx of students at Northern Arizona University, and by the usual array of ski-bums and mountain bikers attracted by the surrounding high mountain wilderness, Flagstaff (pop. 45,857) is an enjoyable, energetic town high up on the Coconino Plateau. The natural beauty of its forested location has meant that, compared to other Route 66 towns, Flagstaff was less affected by the demise of the old road. That said, it still takes pride in the past, notably in the form of the **Museum Club**, 3404 E. Route 66 (520/526-9434), an old roadhouse brought back to life as a country-western nightclub and ad-hoc nostalgia museum. There are also dozens of vintage neon signs along the old Route 66 alignment: check out the Western Hills Motel and the Grand Canyon Cafe downtown, and the Flamingo Motel five blocks west.

SONGS OF ROUTE 66

Get your Kicks on Route 66

If you ever plan to motor west,
Travel my way, that's the highway that's the best,
Get your kicks on Route 66.

It winds from Chicago to L.A.,
More than 2,000 miles all the way
Get your kicks on Route 66.

Now you go through St. Looey, Joplin, Missouri
And Oklahoma City is mighty pretty.
You'll see Amarillo, Gallup, New Mexico,
Flagstaff, Arizona, don't forget Winona,
Kingman, Barstow, San Bernardino.

Won't you get hip to this timely tip:
When you make that California trip
Get your kicks on Route 66.
Get your kicks on Route 66.

—Bobby Troup

One of the most popular road songs ever written, and a prime force behind the international popularity of Route 66, "Get Your Kicks on Route 66" was penned by jazz musician Bobby Troup in 1946 while he was driving west to seek fame and fortune in Los Angeles. Troup consistently credits his former wife Cynthia, with whom he was traveling, for the half-dozen words of the refrain. The rest of the song simply rattled off the rhyming place-names along the way, but despite its apparent simplicity, it caught the ear of Nat King Cole, who made it into a hit record and also established the pronunciation as "root" rather than "rout," as repeated in later renditions by everyone from Bob Willis to the Rolling Stones.

If you haven't heard the song for a while, there's a jazzy version by Bobby Troup along with some lively Route 66-related songs, including a world-weary "What's Left of 66" by traveling troubadour Jason Ecklund, on the 1995 compilation tape and CD, *The Songs of the Route 66—Music from the All American Highway,* available at souvenir stores en route and from Lazy SOB Records, P.O. Box 49884, Austin, TX 78765.

Flagstaff also has a pair of non-Route 66 related attractions. First and foremost of these stands on a hill at the west end of Flagstaff, reachable from the west end of Santa Fe Avenue (old Route 66): the **Lowell Observatory**, established in 1894 by Percival Lowell and best known as the place where, in 1930, the planet Pluto was discovered. A visitor center (daily 9 AM-5 PM in summer, shorter hours rest of the year; $3) has descriptions of the science behind what goes on here—spectroscopy, red shifts, and expanding universes, for example—and the old telescope, a 24-inch refractor, is open for viewings 8-10 PM most nights in summer. For more detailed information, call the observatory at 520/774-2096. The other main draw, the **Museum of Northern Arizona** (daily 9 AM-5 PM; $4), perches at the edge of a pine-forested canyon three miles northwest of downtown via US-180, the main road to the Grand Canyon; extensive exhibits detail the vibrant cultures of northern Arizona, from prehistoric Anasazi to contemporary Hopi, Navajo, and Zuni.

Downtown Flagstaff has more than enough espresso bars—probably a dozen within a two-block radius of the train station—to satisfy its many multiply pierced, twentysomething residents. There are also ethnic restaurants specializing in Greek, Thai, German, or Indian, so finding suitable places to eat and drink will not be a problem. For breakfast and lunch, it's hard to beat **Kathie's**, a cozy cafe at 7 N. San Francisco Street.

Accommodations, too, are plentiful, and you can pick either the motel with the most appealing sign, or step back into an earlier time and stay at the classy old **Hotel Monte Vista,** right on old Route 66 at 100 N. San Francisco Street (520/779-6971 or 800/545-3068). It was good enough for Gary Cooper, and has been restored to its Roaring Twenties splendor.

Flagstaff's San Francisco Street was named not for the California city but for the nearby volcanic peaks, so called by early Spanish missionaries and still held sacred by the native Hopi Indians.

For more complete listings or other information, contact the visitor center, right downtown at 101 W. Route 66 (520/774-9541 or 800/842-7293).

Flagstaff very nearly became an early movie center, when young **Cecil B. DeMille** stopped here briefly while scouting locations to shoot the world's first feature-length film, a Western called The Squaw Man. It was snowing in Flagstaff that day, so he moved on to L.A.

Walnut Canyon National Monument

The most easily accessible of the hundreds of different prehistoric settlements all over the southwestern U.S., Walnut Canyon National Monument (daily 8 AM-4 PM, 7 AM-5 PM in summer; $4; 520/526-3367) is also one of the prettiest places imaginable, with piñon pines and junipers clinging to the canyon walls, and walnut trees filling the canyon floor. On the edge of the canyon, a small visitor center gives the historical background, but the real interest lies below, on a short but very steep path that winds through cliff dwellings tucked into overhangs and ledges 400 feet above the canyon floor.

The entrance to the monument, which contains some 300 identified archaeological sites, lies seven miles east of Flagstaff, accessible from I-40 exit 204.

Don't Forget: Winona

East of Flagstaff, following old Route 66 can be a frustrating task, since much of the roadway is blocked or torn up or both. Unlike the long stretches found in the western half of the state, here the old road exists only as short segments running through towns, and most of the way you're forced to follow the freeway, stopping at exit after exit. Among the places worth considering is the one town mentioned out of sequence in the Route 66 song: "Flagstaff, Arizona, don't forget Winona," which, alas, is now little more than a name on the sign at I-40 exit 211.

East of Winona, the route drops swiftly from the cool pines onto the hot red desert, but old-road fanatics will want to take the time to explore what remains of two old-time tourist traps lining the next 20 miles of highway.

First of these is **Twin Arrows**, where if you're lucky a pair of red arrows will point you toward a small but thriving cafe, right off the freeway at exit 219. Continuing east, approaching exit 230, the freeway crosses deep Diablo Canyon, where an old Route 66 bridge still spans the dry wash, and the walls of a half-dozen bleached buildings are all that's left of the **Two Guns Trading Post**, just south of exit 230. A roadside attraction par excellence, Two Guns had a zoo full of roadrunners, gila monsters, and coyotes, and one building still has a sign saying Mountain Lions—all for the entertainment of passing travelers. According to various reports down the Route 66 grapevine, Two Guns has been on the verge of reopening in recent years, but most of the time the old road is blocked by a sign reading No Trespassing by Order of Two Guns Sheriff Department. Probably a good thing, since the old buildings are all dangerously close to collapse. It's an evocative site, nonetheless, and photogenic in the right light.

Meteor Crater

Three miles east of Two Guns, Arizona's second most distinctive hole in the ground, Meteor Crater, sits six miles south of I-40 exit 233. Measuring 570 feet deep and nearly a mile across, the crater is a privately owned tourist attraction, offering an "Astronauts Hall of Fame" as well as a chance to look down into the huge hole; you can't climb down into it, however.

Meteor Crater is open daily 8 AM–5 PM, longer hours in summer, and costs $7.

Winslow and Holbrook are the nearest towns to the Navajo Indian Reservation, home of radio station **KTNN 660 AM**, which broadcasts a fascinating mélange of Navajo chants and Jimi Hendrix riffs. It's the only station in the U.S. that broadcasts *all* of the Dallas Cowboy football games—in Navajo.

Winslow

Winslow, Arizona, didn't make it into Bobby Troup's original Route 66 hit list, but the town more than made it a generation later with the Eagles tune "Take It Easy," which begins, "Standin' on a corner in Winslow, Arizona," a line that has caused more people to turn off in search of the place than anything else. What you may find in Winslow is not a lot, actually. Chain motels and fast-food franchises stand at either end of town around the I-40 exits, and in between, a couple of cafes and cheap motels are the only signs of life along the old Route 66 frontage, which followed 2nd Street eastbound and 3rd Street westbound.

In between the I-40 and Route 66 is the funky **Old Trails Museum**, 212 Kinsley Street (hours vary; 520/289-5861), which sells a range of "Standin' on the Corner" T-shirts, and displays a few reminders of Winslow in its heyday. Down the block, on 2nd and Kinsley, a little sign stakes a claim to being *the* corner the Eagles sang about; in 1994, Eagles songwriter Don Henley donated $2,500 to help develop the spot into an appropriate monument.

At the west end of Joseph City, right off I-40 exit 274, stop at the **Jackrabbit Trading Post,** the one whose signs you've probably noticed over the past hundred miles, and take a picture or buy a postcard of the giant jackrabbit, one of a long line of creatures who have stood here since 1949.

snow kachina doll

Kiowa beaded cradle board, circa 1890-1907

Navajo jewelry

Holbrook

Holding a concentrated dose of old Route 66 character, Holbrook (pop. 4,686) is definitely worth a quick detour off the I-40 freeway. More than the other Route 66 towns in eastern half of Arizona, it still feels like a real place, with lively cafes and some endearing roadside attractions. Be sure to stop at **Joe and Aggie's**

Hopi coiled basket, circa 1920s

Cafe at the center of town, and check out the dinosaur collection outside the **Rainbow Rock Shop** a block away on Navajo Boulevard near the railroad tracks. Best of all, stop for the night at the marvelous **Wigwam Village**, 811 W. Hopi Drive (520/524-3048) at the western edge of town, and sleep in a concrete tepee. One of around a dozen built across the country, this one opened in 1950 and was fully modernized in 1988. Rooms cost around $35 a night, so you really should stay here at least once in your life.

Another worthwhile place to stop is the **Navajo County Museum** (Mon.-Fri. 8 AM-5 PM, plus Saturday in summer; free) in the old Navajo County Courthouse, four blocks south of I-40 at the corner of Navajo Boulevard (old Route 66) and Arizona Street. The collections are wide-ranging and include a walk downstairs to the old county jail, in use from 1899 until 1976. The museum is next door to the **Holbrook Chamber of Commerce** (520/524-6558), which has walking and driving tour maps and general information on the town.

Painted Desert and Petrified Forest National Park

The easternmost 60 miles of I-40 across Arizona are little more than one long speedway, since any sign of the old road has been lost beneath the four-lane interstate. One place worth a stop is Petrified Forest National Park. The polished petrified wood on display in the visitor center is gorgeous to look at, but seeing the stuff in its raw natural state is not particularly thrilling. The story of how the wood got petrified is interesting, though: about 225 million years ago, a forest was buried in volcanic ash, then slowly embalmed with silica and effectively turned to stone. You can take a look at 93,000 acres of the stuff outside the visitor center.

While the park contains a vast array of prehistoric fossils and pictographs as well as the petrified wood, one of the more interesting sights is the old **Painted Desert Inn**, a Route 66 landmark during the 1920s and 1930s that was converted into a museum and bookstore after the park service took it over in the 1960s. There are no services here, or anywhere else in the park, but the desert views, especially at sunrise or sunset, are worth lingering for.

East of the park, along the New Mexico border, Arizona welcomes westbound travelers with an overwhelming display of trading-post tackiness—huge concrete tepees stand at the foot of brilliant red-rock mesas, while gift shops named everything from "F Troop" to "Dances With Wolves" hawk their souvenirs to passing travelers.

Thirty-eight miles north of I-40 from exit 333, a mile west of the town of Ganado, the **Hubbell Trading Post National Historic Site** is a frontier store preserved as it was in the 1870s, when trader John Hubbell began buying the beautiful rugs made by local Navajo weavers.

ACROSS NEW MEXICO

Following old Route 66 across New Mexico gives you a great taste of the Land of Enchantment, as the state calls itself on its license plates. There is less of the actual "old road" here than in other places, but the many towns and ghost towns along I-40, built more or less on top of Route 66, still stand. In Albuquerque, Route 66 runs through the center of this sprawling Sun Belt city, while in other places finding the old road and bypassed towns can take some time, though the effort is usually well rewarded.

Western New Mexico has the most to see and the most interesting topography, with sandstone mesas looming in the foreground and high, pine-forested peaks rising in the distance. Paralleling the Santa Fe Railroad, the route passes through the heart of this region, and numerous detours—to Inscription Rock and Chaco Canyon, among others—make unforgettable stops along the way. In the east, the land is flatter and the landscape drier as the road approaches the Great Plains.

Stretching for over a dozen miles across the border between the two states, Hwy-118 runs north of the I-40 freeway, following old Route 66 between exit 357 in Arizona and exit 8 in New Mexico.

Gallup

Despite the obvious poverty and other signs of genuine despair, Gallup (pop. 19,154) is a fascinating town. Founded in 1881 when the Santa Fe Railroad first rumbled through, and calling itself "The Gateway to Indian Country" because it's the largest town near the huge Navajo and other Native American reservations, Gallup has some of the Southwest's largest trading posts offering great deals, and one of the best strips of neon signs you'll see anywhere on old 66. Gallup also hosts the annual "Inter Tribal Ceremonial," perhaps the largest Native American gathering in the country, held every August in Red Rock State Park eight miles east of Gallup, and culminating in a Sunday parade that brings 30,000 people out to line old Route 66 through town.

For travelers intent on experiencing a little of the charms of old Route 66, Gallup also has **El Rancho**, 1000 E. Route 66 (505/863-9311), a delightful old hotel lovingly restored to its 1930s glory. Built by a brother of movie director D.W. Griffiths, El Rancho is like a national park lodge at the heart of which is a large two-story lobby with a huge stone fireplace. All the rooms in the old wing are named for the movie stars who have stayed here over the years—the W.C. Fields Room, the John Wayne Room, the Marx Brothers Room (sleeps six), even the Ronald Reagan Room—and signed glossies of these and many more actors and actresses adorn the halls. Rooms cost $40-65 a night for two people, depending upon the individual room and the time of year. El Rancho also has a good restaurant serving regional food daily 6 AM-10 PM, and a gift shop selling souvenirs and fine jewelry, pottery, and rugs made by Native American craftspeople. The shop's owner, Armand Ortega, is one of Gallup's most respected dealers.

For further listings or more information, contact the Gallup **visitors bureau** on the north side of I-40 exit 22, at 701 Montoya Boulevard (505/863-3841 or 800/242-4282), which will no doubt try to direct you away from the many classic motels lining Route 66, like the **Log Cabin Inn** in the middle of town, offering rooms for as little as $15-20 a night, $85 a week. Many of these are scary-looking enough to give your mother sleepless nights; for peace of mind there are all the usual chains as well—nearly 2,000 rooms altogether—if El Rancho is fully booked.

Detour: Inscription Rock and El Malpais

Western New Mexico is among the most beautiful places on the planet. One of the best drives through it, Hwy-53, loops south of I-40 between Gallup and Grants across the Zuni and Navajo Indian Reservations. Skirting the southern foothills of the 9,000-foot Zuni Mountains, the route follows ancient Indian trails that Coronado used on his ill-fated 1540 explorations, winding past piñon-covered hills, open grasslands, and the fascinating graffiti collection of El Morro National Monument.

Every bit as impressive and memorable as the cliff dwelling of Mesa Verde, the extensive archaeological remains protected inside **Chaco Culture National Historical Park** are well worth your time. Though it's an hour's drive from I-40 via unpaved roads, the park is one of the wonders of the Southwest desert; for details, call 505/786-7014.

Better known as Inscription Rock, the 200-foot-high sandstone cliffs of El Morro have been inscribed by travelers like Juan de Oñate, who wrote his name with a flourish in 1605, after he discovered the Gulf of California.

Atop the cliffs are the partially excavated remains of a small Anasazi pueblo dating from around A.D. 1200. A two-mile loop trail to the inscriptions and the ruins starts from a small **visitor center** (daily 8 AM-5 PM; till 7 PM in summer; $4 per car; 505/783-4226), where exhibits outline the history of the site. The trails are closed an hour before sunset, so get here early enough in the day to enjoy the beautiful scenery. There is also a small campground (no showers, pit toilets) amidst the junipers.

East of Inscription Rock, after crossing the Continental Divide where there's a roadside rest stop, Hwy-53 winds along the edge of the massive El Malpais lava flow—thousands of acres of pitch-black, concrete-hard, glassy sharp rock—before rejoining I-40 and old Route 66 at Grants.

Grants

Along with the usual Route 66 range of funky motels and rusty neon signs, the former mining boomtown of Grants has the unique attraction of the **New Mexico Museum of Mining** (Mon.-Sat. 9 AM-6 PM, Sunday noon-6 PM; $2), right downtown on old Route 66 (Santa Fe Avenue) at the corner of Iron Avenue. Most of the exhibits trace the short history of local uranium mining, which began in 1950 when a local Navajo rancher, Paddy Martinez, discovered an odd yellow rock that turned out to be high-grade uranium ore. Mines here once produced half the ore mined in the U.S., but production has now ceased. From the main gallery, ride the elevator down to the highlight of the mining museum: a credible re-creation of a uranium mine, complete with an underground lunch room emblazoned with all manner of warning signs.

Midway between Grants and Gallup, I-40 crosses the 7,250-foot Continental Divide, where the "Top O' the World" dance hall used to tempt travelers off old Route 66. From here (exit 47), it's possible to follow the old road for 30 miles, running east along I-40 as far as Grants.

Across the street from the Mining Museum, the **Uranium Cafe** is still in business (we hope), serving up breakfast and lunch every day and dinner on Friday and Saturday. Just look for the atomic neon sign, a Route 66 landmark.

Broadcasting on 530 AM around the Acoma area, actor Ricardo Montalban narrates the story of the pueblo's conquest by the Spanish, and the story of the building of San Esteban church high atop the mesa.

Acoma Pueblo: Sky City and Enchanted Mesa

A dozen miles east of Grants and 50 miles west of Albuquerque, one of the Southwest's most intriguing sites, Acoma Pueblo, stands atop a 357-foot-high sandstone mesa. Long known as "Sky City," Acoma is one of the very oldest communities in North America, inhabited since A.D. 1150. The views out across the plains are unforgettable, especially the Enchanted Mesa on the horizon to the northeast.

Few people live on the mesa today, though the many adobe houses are used by Pueblo craftspeople, who live down below but come up to the mesa-top to sell their pottery to tourists. To visit, stop at the visitor center at the base of the mesa, and join a guided tour (daily 8 AM-4 PM, till 7 PM in summer; $6; 505/252-1139 or 800/747-0181). Tours begin with a bus ride to the mesa-top and end with a visit to **San Esteban del Rey Mission**, the largest Spanish colonial church in the state. Built in 1629, the church features a roof constructed of huge timbers that were carried from the top of Mount Taylor on the backs of neophyte Indians—a distance of more than 30 miles.

Acoma Pueblo is 15 miles south of I-40, from exit 96 (eastbound) or exit 108 (westbound). Between these two exits, another stretch of old Route 66 survives, passing crumbling tourist courts and service stations across the Laguna and Acoma Indian Reservations.

If you're here in summer, check out an Albuquerque Dukes home game, at the stadium on the corner of University and Stadium, off I-25 and south of Route 66. For schedules and prices, call 505/243-1791.

Albuquerque

Roughly located at the center of New Mexico, the sprawling city of Albuquerque (pop. 463,300) spreads north and south along the banks of the Rio Grande and east to the foothills of 10,000-foot Sandia Crest. By far the state's biggest city, Albuquerque is a young, energetic, and vibrantly multicultural community, which among many features boasts a great stretch of old Route 66 along Central Avenue through the heart of city— eight miles of diners, motels, and neon.

Albuquerque was also the home of the great travel writer and war correspondent **Ernie Pyle.** His old house, at 900 Girard Avenue a half-mile south of Central Avenue, later became the city's first public library, which includes his collected works and a few personal items on display.

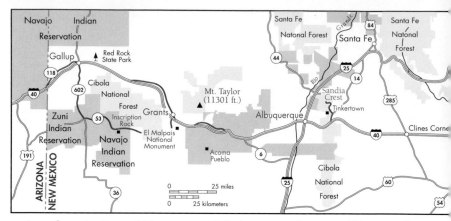

Apart from the Route 66 legacy, one of the best parts of town is **Old Town**, the historic heart of Albuquerque. Located a block north of Central Avenue, at the west end of the route's cruise through the city, Old Town offers a quick taste of New Mexico's Spanish colonial past, with a lovely old church, the circa 1706 San Felipe de Neri, as well as shops and restaurants set around a leafy green park. An information booth in the park has walking-tour maps of Old Town and other information about the city. Another Old Town attraction, one that carries on the Route 66 tradition of reptile farms and private zoos, is the **Rattlesnake Museum** (daily 10 AM-6 PM; $2), 202 San Felipe Street, where you can see a range of rattlers from tiny babies to full-sized diamondbacks, about 50 altogether.

A very different look into New Mexico's varied cultural makeup is offered at the **Indian Pueblo Cultural Center** (daily 9 AM-5:30 PM; $3; 505/843-7270 or 800/766-4405), a block north of I-40, exit 158 at 2401 12th Street. The center is owned and operated by the state's 19 different Pueblo communities; its highlight is a fine museum tracing the history of the region's Native American cultures, from Anasazi times up to the Pueblo Revolt of 1680, with the contemporary era illustrated by video presentations and a mock-up of a typical tourist—camera, shorts, and all. There's also a small cafeteria where you can sample food like fry bread and Navajo tacos. On most weekends ceremonial dances are held in the central courtyard, free and open to the general public.

The best range of places to eat lies within walking distance of Old Town. It includes the very good Mexican food at **La Hacienda**, 302 San Felipe Street, with a front porch overlooking the park; and the mix of Mexican and American diner food at **Garcia's**, 1736 W. Central Avenue beneath a glorious neon sign. The excellent **Route 66 Diner**, housed in an old Phillips 66 station at 1405 E. Central Avenue near the University of New Mexico campus, burned down in 1995 and reopened in February 1996, serving top-quality burgers, malts, and shakes, and regional specialties like blue corn pancakes, 8 AM-midnight, Sunday till 10 PM. Another old Route 66 landmark, **Mac's La Sierra**, serves up "Steak in the Rough" and other beefy specialties in a cozy, dark wood dining room west of town at 6217 W. Central Avenue.

Like most of New Mexico, Albuquerque has a ton of inexpensive accommodations, with all the usual chain motels represented along the interstate frontage roads.

For the total Route 66 experience, stay the night at lovely **El Vado**, 2500 W. Central Avenue (505/243-4594), a well-maintained 1930s motel between Old Town and the Rio Grande. The nicest old hotel has got to be the grand **La Posada**, a block off old Route 66 at 125 2nd Street (505/242-9090 or 800/777-5732), one of the first inns built by New Mexico-born hotel magnate Conrad Hilton; doubles here start at $85 a night.

For more information, contact the Albuquerque **visitor center**, 121 Tijeras Road (505/842-9918).

Tinkertown and the Sandia Crest

Not that there's any shortage of wacky roadside Americana along what's left of Route 66, but one of the most endearing of them all, Tinkertown (daily 9 AM-6 PM April-Oct.; $3; 505/281-5233), is a quick 10-minute drive north of the old road. Like an old-fashioned penny arcade run riot, Tinkertown is a marvelous assembly of over a thousand delicately carved miniature wooden figures, arranged in tiny stage sets to act out animated scenes—a circus Big Top complete with side show, a Wild West town with dancehall girls and a squawking vulture—all housed in a ramshackle building made in part out of glass bottles and bicycle wheels, created over the past 45 years by Ross and Carla Ward and family. It's impossible to describe the many odds and ends on show here—one display case holds over 100 plastic figures taken from the tops of wedding cakes, for example—especially since the whole thing is always being improved and "tinkered" with, but the spirit of the place is aptly summed up in the Tinkertown motto: "We Did All This While You Were Watching TV." The Dalai Lama loved it, and so will you.

To get to Tinkertown, turn off I-40 at exit 175, six miles east of Albuquerque, and follow signs for Sandia Crest; Tinkertown is on Hwy-536, 1.5 miles west of the Hwy-14 junction, hidden off the highway among the juniper trees.

Sandia Crest itself is another 12 miles uphill at the end of Hwy-536, National Scenic Byway; the ridge offers a phenomenal panorama from an elevation of 10,678 feet. Some 80 miles of hiking trails wind through the surrounding Cibola National Forest. Back on Hwy-14, four miles north of I-40, the **Sandia Mountain Hostel** (12234 N. Hwy-14 in Tijeras; 505/281-4117) offers clean bunks in a bike-friendly environment.

Santa Rosa

The I-40 freeway has bisected the town of Santa Rosa (pop. 2,263) and cut its old Route 66 frontage in two, but for over 65 years, travelers crossing New Mexico

Albuquerque's "Coyote Radio," **KIOT 102.5 FM,** plays a lively range of alternative popular music, from Hank Williams and John Lee Hooker to Talking Heads and the Grateful Dead.

True completists of the Route 66 tour, and anyone interested in the art and architecture (and food!) of the American Southwest, will want to make the detour to the state capital, Santa Fe. The original Route 66 alignment ran north from Albuquerque along the I-25 corridor, then curved back south from Santa Fe, along what's now US-84, to rejoin I-40 west of Santa Rosa. For further information on the city, contact the **Santa Fe visitor center** (505/984-6760 or 800/777-2489).

Clines Corners, midway between Albuquerque and Santa Rosa off I-40 exit 218, is a truck stop cafe that dates back to 1934 and is, as the signs say, Worth Waiting For—for the huge gift shop if not for the unexciting food.

East of Santa Rosa, along the south side of I-40 as far as Cuervo, you can trace one of the older stretches of Route 66, only partly paved, and best done in a 4WD or on a mountain bike. Here you get an indelible sense of what travel was like in the very early days, when less than half the route's 2,400-odd miles were paved. Another stretch of old Route 66 now serves as the runway for Santa Rosa's small airport.

Along I-40 near Cuervo, Ricardo Montalban broadcasts a brief, State of New Mexico-sponsored history of Route 66 on **530 AM.**

Along the Pecos River via US-84, some 50 miles southwest of Santa Rosa, the grave site of Wild West legend **Billy the Kid** is outside the town of Fort Sumner. The grave is part of a private museum (daily 9 AM-5 PM; $2) adjacent to the eponymous fort where 7,000 Navajo people were imprisoned from 1864 to 1869.

along Route 66 and I-40 made a point of stopping here for a meal at **Club Cafe,** "The Original Route 66 Restaurant Since 1935." Thanks to signs lining the road for miles in both directions, emblazoned with the smiling face of the "Fat Man," the Club Cafe became nationally famous for its always-fresh food. Despite its "EZ-OFF, EZ-ON" location right along the interstate, the restaurant closed in 1992 but has been on the verge of re-opening many times since. If you're lucky, it will be open when you pass through. If not, try **Joseph's,** on old Route 66 a half-mile southwest of I-40 exit 275, which has very good food at reasonable prices.

Santa Rosa's other main attraction is unique: the **Blue Hole,** a 60-foot wide, 80-foot-deep artesian well filled with water so crystal-clear that it draws scuba-divers from all over the western states to practice their underwater techniques here. The water of the Blue Hole, at around 61°, is too cold for casual swimming, but in the summer heat it's a great place to cool your heels. The Blue Hole is well signed at the end of Blue Hole Road, a half-mile south of old Route 66.

Tucumcari

Subject of one of the most successful advertising campaigns in Route 66's long history of roadside hype, Tucumcari (pop. 6,831) looks and sounds like a much bigger place than it is. Also known as "the town that's two blocks wide and two miles long" (though Tucumcari Boulevard, which follows the route blazed by old Route 66 through town, stretches for closer to seven miles between interstate exits), Tucumcari does have a little of everything, including a great range of neon, but it can be hard to explain the attraction of the town that hundreds of signs along the highways once trumpeted as Tucumcari Tonight— 2,000 Motel Rooms.

Hype or no hype, Tucumcari is a handy place to break a journey, and even if you think you can make it to the next town east or west, you will never regret stopping here for a night if you stay at the **Blue Swallow Motel,** 815 E. Tucumcari Boulevard (505/461-9849).

No less an authority than *Smithsonian* magazine called the Blue Swallow "the last, best, and friendliest of the old-time motels," and thanks to the endless hospitality of owner Lillian Redman, few who stay here disagree.

Across Route 66 from the Blue Swallow stands another survivor, the old **Tee Pee Trading Post,** worth a look to add to your collection of Southwest or Route 66 souvenirs. For a place to eat, try the Mexican food at **La Cita,** under the turquoise and pink sombrero on the corner of 1st Street and old 66.

The line between Texas and New Mexico marks the boundary between central and mountain time zones. Set your clocks and watches accordingly.

ACROSS TEXAS

Known as the Panhandle because of the way it juts north from the rest of Texas, this part of the route is a nearly 200-mile stretch of pancake-flat plains. Almost devoid of trees or other features, the western half, stretching into New Mexico, is also known as the Llano Estacado or "Staked Plains," possibly because early travelers marked their route by driving stakes into the earth. The Texas Panhandle was the southern extent of the buffalo-rich grasslands of the Great Plains, populated by roving bands of Kiowa and Comanche Indians as recently as 100 years ago. Now oil, gas, and helium production, as well as trucking and Route 66 tourism, have joined ranching as the region's economic basis.

Even more so than in New Mexico or Oklahoma, old Route 66 has been replaced by I-40 most of the way across Texas, though in many of the ghostly towns like McLean, Shamrock, or Vega, and the sole city, Amarillo, old US-66 survives as the main business strip, lined by the remains of roadside businesses. A select few are still open for a cup of coffee and a sharp taste of the living past.

Vega and Old Tascosa

Between Amarillo and the New Mexico border, the landscape is identical to what lies east of the city: endless flat plains dotted with occasional oil derricks and Aeromotor windmills. Vega, midway between the border and Amarillo, is a sprawling cowtown that marks the turnoff onto US-385, which heads north to the remains of Old Tascosa. During the 1870s the town was one of the wildest on the Texas frontier. Twenty-two miles north of I-40, just east of US-385 on the north bank of the Canadian River, a few buildings, a barbed-wire museum, and the old Boot Hill cemetery have been preserved; the entire townsite is part of **Cal Farley's Boys Ranch** (daily 8 AM-5 PM; free; 806/372-2341), a working 10,000-acre cattle ranch that doubles as a foster home for some 400 troubled teenagers.

Most of the Panhandle's 20 inches of annual rain falls during summer thunderstorms that sweep across the plains between May and August.

In Amarillo, radio station **KIXE 940 AM**—"Kicks," as in Get Yours—plays a lively variety of 1940s swing and earlier jazz, as well as crooners like Bing and Perry, to help get you in the Route 66 mood. The best alternative is on the other dial, where the local Amarillo College station, 89.9 FM, prides itself on playing "less music from dead guys."

Amarillo

At the heart of the Llano Estacado, midway across the Texas Panhandle, Amarillo (pop. 157,615—and yes, you pronounce the "l"s) is a busy big city that retains its cowboy roots. Center of the local ranching industry that raises some two million head of cattle each year, Amarillo is also one of the few places on earth where helium is produced; an estimated 90% of the world's supply comes from here.

Old Route 66 followed 6th Street through Amarillo, past the brick-paved streets of the Old San Jacinto district around Western Avenue, where you can wander amongst ancient-looking gun and saddle shops and numerous Wild West-themed clothing shops. East of downtown, follow East Amarillo Boulevard past a line of authentic honky-tonks around the 20-acre **Western Stockyards**, at Grand Avenue and 3rd Street. Livestock auctions are held here most weekday mornings; Tuesday is the biggest day. Visitors are welcome and there's no entry fee. Phone for details (806/373-7464).

On US-60 west of the town of Panhandle, 11 miles northeast of Amarillo, a wire fence on the south side of the road protects the **First Tree in Texas,** planted here on the desolate plains in 1888 by settler Thomas Cree. The trees growing here today are seedlings taken from the orginal "Bois D'Arc" tree, which was killed by pesticides in 1969.

Along with the one and only health-food place, the **OHMS Cafe,** downtown at 619 S. Tyler Street, Amarillo is known for its many good steakhouses, including the **Iron Horse Cafe,** 401 S. Grant Street, housed in the old train depot near the stockyards. The most famous has to be the **Big Texan Steak Ranch,** which started along Route 66 and now stands on the east side of Amarillo off I-40 exit 74, marked by a false-front Wild West town and a giant cowboy atop a billboard. This is the place where they offer free 72-ounce steaks, provided you eat it all, plus a few extras, in under an hour. If you don't make it, the cost is around $35.

There's a $50-a-night motel featuring a Texas-shaped swimming pool at the **Big Texan** (806/372-5000), and dozens of inexpensive chain motels (two Travelodges, two Comfort Inns) stand along the I-40 and I-27 frontages, so rooms shouldn't be hard to find. For more complete listings or other information, contact the **visitor center** (806/373-7800 or 800/692-1330).

Palo Duro Canyon State Park

Lovely Palo Duro Canyon, one of the most beautiful places in all Texas, is just 25 miles southeast of Amarillo, east of the town of Canyon via the I-27 freeway. Cut into the Texas plain by the Prairie Dog Fork of the Red River, Palo Duro streches for over 100 miles, with canyon walls climbing to over 1,200 feet. Coronado and company were the first Europeans to lay eyes on the area, and numerous Plains tribes, including Apache, Kiowa, and Comanche, later took refuge here.

From the end of Hwy-217, a well-paved road winds past the park **visitor center**, from where a short trail leads to a canyon overlook. Beyond here the road drops down into the canyon and follows the river on a 15-mile loop trip through the Canyon's heart. It's prettiest in spring and fall, and fairly popular year-round; for more information, or for camping reservations, contact the **visitor center** (daily 8 AM-5 PM; 806/488-2227).

CADILLAC RANCH

No, you're not seeing things—there really *are* nearly a dozen Cadillacs upended in the Texas plain west of Amarillo. Two hundred yards south of I-40 at the Hope Road exit some five miles west of Amarillo, where old US-66 rejoins the interstate, the rusting hulks of 10 classic Caddies are buried nose-down in the dirt, their upended tail fins tracing design changes from 1949 to 1964.

A popular shrine to America's love of the open road, Cadillac Ranch was created by the San Francisco-based Ant Farm artists' and architects' collective in May 1974, under the patronage of the eccentric Amarillo helium millionaire Stanley Marsh III, on whose "Toad Hall" ranch they sit. The cars were all bought, some running, some not, from local junkyards and used car lots at an average cost of $200 each. Before the Cadillacs were planted, all the hubcaps and wheels were welded on, a good idea since most of the time the cars are in a badly vandalized state. Every once in a while advertising agencies and rock bands tidy them up for use as backdrops during photo shoots.

There's a well-worn path from the frontage road if you want a closer look, and visitors are allowed anytime, day or night.

Canyon: Tex the Giant Cowboy

On your way to or from Palo Duro Canyon, be sure to stop by the Cowboy Cafe, on US-60 west of Canyon, marked by the towering statue of Tex, the giant cowboy. Not that you need one, but another great reason to visit Canyon is the excellent **Panhandle-Plains Historical Museum** (Mon.-Sat. 9 AM-5 PM, Sunday 1-5 PM; donations), one of the state's great museums, with extensive exhibits on the cultural and economic life of the Panhandle region and its relations with Mexico, the Texas Republic, and the United States. The museum, which is housed in a WPA-era building, has a special section on pioneer rancher Charles Goodnight, who once owned a half-million acres and was also an early pioneer in saving the bison from extinction. His cabin is preserved in the Pioneer Town behind the museum.

McLean

Founded around the turn of 20th century by an English rancher, Alfred Rowe, who later lost his life on the *Titanic* in 1912, McLean is now the most evocative town along the Texas stretch of Route 66. Bypassed only in the early 1980s, the old main drag is eerily silent, with only a few businesses—a barber shop, a boot shop, and some motels, including one with a fine Texas-shaped neon sign—holding on despite the drop in passing trade.

Since McLean is now headquarters of the state's "Historic Route 66 Association," efforts are being made to preserve the town in prime condition, which explains the lovingly restored Phillips 66 station and the other odds and ends on display around town.

Shamrock

Once a thumping refining center built over one of the largest natural gas reservoirs in the state, Shamrock (pop. 2,286) is a dusty, rusty old industrial town just south of I-40 at the junction of US-83 and historic Route 66, which survives as the "Business Loop" of I-40 through town. Though it's not a particularly lovely place, Shamrock's sedate style in the town proper will help you decompress.

In keeping with its name, Shamrock hosts a large parade and celebration every St. Patrick's Day—but with no green beer, since it's in a dry county. Further playing up the Irish connection, Elmore Park in town reportedly exhibits a sliver of the genuine Blarney Stone, encased in a hip-high concrete cylinder.

The old, two-story, brown-brick Drummer's Hotel holds the **Pioneer West Museum** (Mon.-Fri. 9 AM-noon and 1-5 PM; free), with two floors of the usual cast-off oddities giving many strange looks into the past 200 years of life on the Texas Panhandle. Along with a wall covered in barbed wire, a room replicating a pioneer dentist's office, hundreds of old photos, and many fine musical instruments, an exhibit honors astronaut Alan Bean. The town doesn't exactly suffer an overabundance of cuisine, but it does have a couple of restaurants and cafes (the Route 66 landmark **U Drop Inn,** a classic greasy spoon cafe in the art deco building, looks great but has closed) south of I-40 at the northeast corner of US-83 and old Route 66. Also along the highways you'll find gas stations and some of the cheapest sleep around, with fleabag motels advertising singles from $14.

The town of **Groom,** 40 miles east of Amarillo on the north side of I-40 at exit 113, holds one of the more eye-catching sights along old Route 66: a water tower that leans like the Tower of Pisa.

East of McLean along the old Route 66 frontage, north of the freeway near exit 148, a skeletal sign still spells out the command: Rattlesnakes Exit Here.

US-83, which runs from Canada to Mexico across the heart of the Midwest, crosses Route 66 at Shamrock. The entire route is covered in "The Road to Nowhere" chapter, beginning on page 124.

ACROSS OKLAHOMA

Apart from occasional college football teams, Oklahoma doesn't often get to crow about being the best in the country, but as far as Route 66 is concerned, the state is definitely number one. Containing more miles of the old highway than any other state, and in far better condition, this is definitely Mecca for old roads fans.

Underneath the promotional hoopla that Route 66 generates everywhere it ever went, all over Oklahoma, signs declare that barely a century ago this was Indian Territory, last refuge of Kiowa, Apache, Comanche, and other tribes before the U.S. government took even this land away from them during "land rushes" in the 1890s. A few years later oil was discovered and the state started on one of a series of boom-and-bust cycles. The Dust Bowl exodus of the 1930s was the greatest downturn, as thousands of Oklahoman families headed west on Route 66. Many of the towns along the road take bittersweet pride in *The Grapes of Wrath* connections.

Texola and Erick

The first town over the Texas border, Texola has dried up and all but blown away since it was bypassed by I-40, but a few remnants still stand, awaiting nostalgic photographers. The only signs of life hereabouts are the shouts and swears emanating from the combination pool hall and beer bar housed in the large metal shed on the south side of the old highway, where you're welcome to watch the most passionate domino games this side of Yuma, Arizona.

East from this borderline ghost town, a mile south of the I-40 freeway, a nice stretch of late-model Route 66 continues as a four-lane divided highway, passing through the great little town of Erick (pop. 1,083) six miles east of Texola. Route 66 through town has been renamed Roger Miller Boulevard in memory of the late favorite son. Erick has another unique draw, the **100th Meridian Museum** (Friday and Saturday 9 AM-4 PM, except during severe weather; donations), on Route 66 at the only stoplight in town. Displays inside trace life on what used to be considered the edge of the habitable world—everything west of the 100th Meridian was officially thought to be the "Great American Desert—and also explain that Erick used to be on the Texas border, until the border was realigned.

In Jack D. Rittenhouse's original Route 66 guidebook, published in 1946 and now widely available in reprinted versions, he described Erick as "the first town you encounter, going west, which has any of the true 'western' look, with its wide, sun-baked street, frequent horsemen, occasional sidewalk awnings, and similar touches."

The museum, and the other three buildings at the crossroads, all have chamfered corners and form an oblong X-shaped intersection rather than the usual 90-degree square. North of Route 66, next to the Texaco station along the I-40 frontage at exit 7, make time and save room in your stomach for a stop at **Cal's Diner**, a marvelous old place with creaky wood floors, fresh-baked bread, short-order home-style food, and a generous dose of Midwest hospitality from the hosts, former navy cook Cal Rogers and his family. The diner is open all day, every day, 6 AM-9 PM, till 10 PM in summer. As the sign says, You'll Be Glad You Did.

Erick was the hometown of singer and songwriter **Roger Miller,** the original "King of the Road."

Sayre

If you want a quick flashback to the dark days of Steinbeck's *The Grapes of Wrath*, turn north off the I-40 freeway into sleepy Sayre (pop. 2,881). The landmark Beckham County Courthouse, which looms over the east end of Main Street, was prominently featured in the movie version as Henry Fonda and the rest of the Joads rattled down Route 66 toward California. While on Main Street, stop in for a milk shake at the friendly fountain in the **Owl Drug Store** on the corner of 4th Street. Take a look in the ever-expanding **Shortgrass Country Museum** (hours vary; free), housed in the old Rock Island Line railroad depot at 106 E. Poplar Street, with changing displays documenting regional history from Cheyenne times to the arrival of homesteading settlers during the great Land Rush of 1892. East of the museum stands a giant grain elevator that has rusted into a gorgeous orange glow.

Elk City

The first—or last, depending on your direction—sizeable town east of the Texas border, Elk City (pop. 10,450) was a popular stopover on Route 66, as evidenced by the many old motels along the various alignments of the old highway through town. Unfortunately, the mom-and-pop operations along 3rd Street (Business I-40) and brick-paved Broadway have closed and been replaced by national chains, all of which are here.

Long before Elk City had its Route 66 heyday, it was a wild frontier town along the cattle trails from Texas to Dodge City, Kansas. The area's cowboy and pioneer history is recounted in the **Old Town Museum** (Tues.-Sat. 10 AM-5 PM, Sunday 2-5 PM; $3), a re-created Wild West town complete with doctor's office, schoolhouse, and rodeo museum. During the 1940s oil was discovered underground, and the town experienced another short boom; this aspect of Elk City's past is the focus of the small **Anadarko Basin Museum,** housed in the lobby of the old Casa Grande Hotel at 107 E. 3rd Street. Most impressive is towering Rig 114, a record-breaking, 180-foot-tall drilling rig installed in the park next to the museum in 1990.

Clinton

Named for Judge Clinton Irwin and not for President Bill, Clinton (pop. 9,268) started life as a trading post for local Cheyenne Arapahoe people, and is now in the spotlight as home of the official **Oklahoma Route 66 Museum,** near the west end of town at 2229 Gary Boulevard (405/323-RT66). Unlike many other "museums" along the route, this one is a true showcase and not just another souvenir stand. Funded by a variety of state and local sources, the museum reopened in late 1995 after undergoing a massive, million-dollar expansion and improvement, and is definitely the best museum of the old road along the old road. Collectors from all over the country donated signs, artifacts, and memorabilia, which have been organized into a com-

BOOKS ON ROUTE 66

Considering the old road's great fame, it's hardly surprising that over a dozen different books in print deal with the Route 66 experience. Some are travel guides, some folk histories, others nostalgic rambles down what was and what's left along the Mother Road. Photographic essays document the rapidly disappearing architecture and signage, and at least one cookbook catalogs recipes of dishes served in cafes along the route. The following is a sampling of favorite titles, most of which can be found in stores along the route if not in your local bookstore.

The Grapes of Wrath, John Steinbeck (Viking, 1937). The first and foremost Route 66-related story, this compelling tale traces the traumatic travels of the Joad family from Dust Bowl Oklahoma to the illusive Promised Land of California. Brutally vivid, *The Grapes of Wrath* was an instant bestseller at the tail end of the Depression and was the source of Route 66's appellation, "The Mother Road."

A Guide Book to Highway 66, Jack Rittenhouse (University of New Mexico, 1989). A facsimile reprinting of the self-published 1946 book that the late author sold door-to-door at truck stops, motor courts, and cafes along the route.

Route 66: A Guidebook to the Mother Road, Bob Moore and Patrick Grauwels. The most detailed driver's guide to old Route 66, packed with mile-by-mile instructions and information as well as photographs and illustrations.

Route 66: The Mother Road, Michael Wallis (St. Martin's Press, 1987). Richly illustrated, thoroughly researched, and engagingly written guide to the old road. This is more armchair companion than practical aid, but the book captures the spirit of Route 66, and the writer has been a key force behind its preservation and rediscovery.

Route 66 Traveler's Guide, Tom Snyder (St. Martin's Press, 1990). State-by-state description of Route 66, with an emphasis on the stories behind the sights you see. Illustrated with 1930s-era Auto Club maps adapted to show the path of modern freeways but still evoking the spirit of the old road.

Searching for 66, Tom Teague (Samizdat House, 1991). More personal than other titles on Route 66, this book of vignettes describes the author's interactions with the many people along Route 66 who have made it what it is. As a bonus, the book is illustrated with the fine pen-and-ink drawings of Route 66 artist Bob Waldmire, some of which are reproduced in *Road Trip USA* as well.

prehensive exhibition of Mother Road history and culture not to be missed by any Route 66 aficionado.

Clinton also has the very nice McLain Rogers public park, with a swimming pool and water slides, at the center of town along 10th Street (old Route 66), next to the Route 66 Miniature Golf Course.

For food, the **Tradewinds** restaurant across from the Route 66 museum is reliable and good value, but the best place to eat in Clinton is **Pop Hick's Restaurant**, on the east side of town at 223 Gary Boulevard, a traditional roadie rest stop that's open 24 hours for great food and low prices. West of town along the I-40 frontage at exit 62, **Jiggs Smoke House** is a tiny cabin selling BBQ sandwiches but specializing in beef jerky.

Elvis himself stayed at the **Tradewinds Best Western**, adjoining the restaurant at 2128 Gary Boulevard (405/323-2610), with doubles from $35 a night. If that's full, there are at least 10 other motels from which to choose.

For more on Clinton's Route 66 connections, contact the helpful **visitor center**, 400 Gary Boulevard (405/323-2222 or 800/759-1397).

For westbound travelers, El Reno marks the first appearance of one of the longest-running ad campaigns along Route 66: dozens of billboards advertising "Tucumcari Tonight," 350 miles from its New Mexican subject.

Hydro: Lucille's

There's no clearer contrast between the charms of the old road and the anonymity of the interstate than tiny Hydro, midway between Clinton and Oklahoma City on the west bank of the Canadian River. A wonderful length of old Route 66 runs along the north side of I-40 exit 89, right past the ancient service station and souvenir stand operated by Lucille Hamons since 1941. Though it's just 50 yards from the fast-lane of the freeway, visiting Lucille's place to buy a soda or a postcard and have a quick hello with the energetic proprietor is a Route 66 rite of passage, and offers a rare chance to sit and talk with someone who has lived the history of the road. Unfortunately, environmental restrictions mean Lucille can no longer sell you a tank of gas, but otherwise her little outpost is unchanged since the glory days of the road.

West of Lucille's, a surviving, six-mile stretch of old Route 66 follows the lay of the land up and down, offering a better sense of the landscape than does the new road, completed in 1966, which has cut and filled and bridged the route to death. East of Lucille's, the old road turns north briefly through the somnolent center of Hydro.

El Reno and Yukon

Despite its recent notoriety as the site of the federal prison where alleged Oklahoma City bomber Timothy McVeigh was kept while awaiting trial, El Reno (pop. 15,414) has a long history. First established as Fort El Reno in 1874, as part of U.S. Army efforts to subdue the Cheyenne, the town later saw duty as a P.O.W. camp during WW II; more recently it earned a measure of fame as the site of a motel seen in the off-beat road movie *Rain Man*. In the movie, the motel was in Amarillo, but the "real" one, called the Big Eight, still sits along old Route 66 at the east edge of town; just look for the sign, a leftover from the movie, which says "Amarillo's Finest" and continues to baffle passersby. For hungry roadtrippers, another place not to pass by is **Robert's Grill**, 101 W. Wade Street, open daily 6 AM-9 PM, Sunday 11 AM-6 PM, and famed since 1926 for its Fried Onion Burger. Every Memorial Day, Robert's cooks up the "World's Largest Hamburger," a 500-pound behemoth.

East of El Reno, all the way into Oklahoma City, old Route 66 runs along the north side of the I-40 freeway; in places it's a three-lane road, with a dangerous passing lane in the center. The last real town beyond the OKC suburbs is Yukon, home of country crooner Garth Brooks and of a giant "Yukon's Best Flour" grain mill, whose huge sign lights up the night sky and draws shutterbugs off the highway. Also worth a stop in Yukon are the Chisholm Trail mural, the town's huge roller rink, and **Johnnie's Cafe**, all on old Route 66 along Yukon's short Main Street.

Oklahoma City

The cruel bombing of the federal building in 1995 shattered the peace and quiet of Oklahoma City, the state's capital and largest city. There are no outward signs, apart from a vacant lot where the building once stood, and as yet no memorial to the men, women, and children killed in the blast, but the impact of that day will be felt for years.

On the western outskirts of Oklahoma City, commonly abbreviated "OKC," Bethany is the home of the **Route 66 Trading Post**, 6229 39th Expressway, which sells a great selection of memorabilia and just about every Route 66 guide ever published.

Following old Route 66 across Oklahoma City can be confusing, but if you're heading west to east, keep an eye peeled for the Route 66 Bowl on 39th Street; a bottle-shaped building on Classen Boulevard; and a retro McDonald's featuring a "Speedie" sign and carhop service, on the corner of 23rd Street and Pennsylvania Avenue.

It's hard to go about your nostalgic Route 66 tour in the aftermath of such a tragedy, but Oklahoma City was one of the primary stops along the Mother Road: in the song, it was the only place along the route singled out for praise, no doubt more for the easy rhyme ("Oklahoma City is mighty pretty") than for its special charms. The city was the biggest boomtown of the 1889 Land Rush, when Oklahoma was opened for white settlement after being set aside "for eternity" as Indian Territory. Between noon and sundown on April 22, over 10,000 people flocked here to claim the new lands—many of them having illegally camped out beforehand, earning the nickname "Sooner," which is still applied to the state's university football teams. A second boom took place during the Depression years, when oil was struck; there are still producing wells in the center of the city on the grounds of the state capitol, one of the few in the country without a dome.

Across from the capitol along a late stretch of Route 66 at 2100 Lincoln Boulevard, the **Oklahoma State Museum of History** (Mon.-Sat. 8 AM-5 PM; free) has exhibits tracing the state's history, with special collections on the Native American presence, on pioneers, and on the oil industry. There's also a sizeable oral history of the Mother Road.

Oklahoma City boasts a number of non-Route 66 related attractions, best of which is the **National Cowboy Hall of Fame** (daily 9 AM-5 PM; $6), a huge complex at 1700 N.E. 63rd Street, a half-mile west of I-44 off I-35. Spacious modern galleries, and a comprehensive display of everything from Charley Russell paintings to John Wayne's kachina dolls, make this one of the nation's top Western art collections—after the Gilcrease in Tulsa (see page 665), the Buffalo Bill Center in Cody (see page 425), and the Amon Carter Museum in Fort Worth.

Ten miles north of the cowboy museum, on the campus of Oklahoma Christian University at 2501 E. Memorial Road, at the far edge of OKC's nearly endless sprawl, **Enterprise Square** (Tues.-Sat. 9 AM-4 PM, Sunday 1-4 PM; $5) is a very odd place, a high-tech Horatio Alger story designed to instruct busloads of schoolkids about how America was built by hard work and free enterprise. Oklahoma City is also the home of the **National Softball Hall of Fame** (Mon.-Fri. 9 AM-4:30 PM; $1, teams in uniform free), off I-35 at 2801 N.E. 50th Street, which includes a quirky museum and souvenir shop; it also hosts the national championships on a complex of diamonds.

Oklahoma City has more BBQ stands and steakhouses than just about anywhere else in the country, and the overall range of restaurants is very good. One old Route 66 landmark, the Kentucky Club speakeasy and roadhouse once frequented by Pretty Boy Floyd, still survives in a new guise, gussied up as the **Oklahoma County Line**, an upscale BBQ restaurant on the northeast edge of town, near the Cowboy Hall of Fame at 1226 N.E. 63rd Street. Other places to check out are the friendly and cholesterol-conscious **Classen Grill**, off old Route 66, next to the I-44 freeway at 5124 Classen Boulevard; and popular **Ann's Chicken Fry House** along the 39th Street Expressway (old Route 66) west of downtown—look for the police cars in the parking lot. For a quiet respite from the highway life, stop by **Sleepy Hollow**, 1101 N.E. 50th Street near the Softball Hall of Fame, for a family-style dinner of steaks or fried chicken accompanied by fresh veggies and great desserts.

The usual interstate chain motels include a **Super 8**, 1117 N.E. 17th Street (405/232-0404) across from the capitol; and a handy **Comfort Inn**, 4445 N. Lincoln Boulevard (405/528-6511 or 800/221-2222), in a modern building on old Route 66 north of downtown.

For more complete information on visiting Oklahoma City, contact the **visitor center**, 123 Park Avenue (405/297-8912 or 800/225-5652).

North of OKC, Route 66 continued through the town of **Edmond,** the place where aviator Wiley Post is buried (he was the pilot killed in the same crash as Will Rogers), and notorious for the fact that a disgruntled postal employee killed 14 of his co-workers here in 1986.

Old Route 66: Arcadia, Chandler, and Stroud

Between OKC and Tulsa, the I-44 Turnpike carries 99% of the traffic, but the old road is still here, paralleling the freeway all the way but hard to reach because there are so few access points—exits are spaced 15 to 30 miles apart. Lots of towns along here vanished after being bypassed, but the fortunate few that were given freeway exits have stayed alive and now thrive on nostalgic Route 66 trade.

Northeast of Oklahoma City, one of the state's best surviving stretches of Route 66 runs for over 30 miles along the north side of the turnpike, accessible at the east end from I-35 at exit 141. East of the interstate, the first stop is the old highway town of Arcadia (pop. 320), which holds a recently restored red round barn built in 1898. If you're hungry, stop at the old motel converted to house **Bob's Bar-B-Que** and enjoy a plate of ribs, briskets, or hot links.

The old road runs east from Arcadia along the north side of I-44, crossing under the freeway, but with no legal access to it, west of Chandler. Three miles west of Chandler stands a metal barn emblazoned with a photogenic Meramec Caverns—Stanton MO sign, and Chandler (pop. 2,596) itself is one of the most idyllic old Route 66 towns in Oklahoma. The town stands out for a number of good reasons, not least of which is the restored Phillips 66 station at the center of town. For a place to stay, the classic **Lincoln Motel**, 740 E. 1st Street (405/258-0200), along old

Route 66 at the east edge of town is still as neat and tidy as it was the day it opened in 1939—two dozen cabins, each with an American flag and a pair of yellow lawn chairs for watching the world whizz by. For food, choose from a handful of good cafes in town.

Continuing east, old-roads fanatics will probably want to follow the winding alignment of Route 66, which continues along the south side of the turnpike for over 40 miles. On the west side of Stroud (pop. 2,666), at the next I-44 exit, check out the **Rock Cafe**, a Route 66 relic built in 1939 out of paving stones from the original highway, and still churning out better-than-average roadside fare.

East of Stroud, old Route 66 runs past the tidy little town of **Depew** before crossing I-44 again at exit 196. From here east, it zigzags back and forth along the freeway for the next 25 miles, all the way into Tulsa.

Tulsa is also the home of **Oral Roberts University,** marked by a futuristic, 15-story tower and an 80-foot-high pair of praying hands along Lewis Avenue, six miles south of downtown.

Tulsa was the home of **Cyrus Avery,** the gas-station owner whose grass-roots organizing and lobbying efforts eventually resulted in Route 66 acquiring its official designation during the 1920s.

Tulsa

Though it has some fine art deco buildings built during the boom years of the Oklahoma oil industry, and though it boasts the Thomas Gilcrease Institute, one of the country's top art museums, Tulsa is not many people's idea of a good time. Route 66 used to wind into town along Southwest Boulevard, then cut across the city along 11th Street, but now high-speed freeways scythe through the city and very little remains of the old roadside landscape. As Michael Wallis writes in his Route 66 bible, *The Mother Road,* Tulsa has "turned its back on the old road and the businesses that made a living from the highway traffic . . . and sold out for the fast lanes of the Interstate. "

That said, and if your time is limited, spend it at the **Thomas Gilcrease Institute** (Mon.-Fri. 9 AM-5 PM, Sunday 1-5 PM; donations), on the northwest edge of Tulsa. Bought with the fortune Gilcrease made when oil was discovered on his land, the collection includes some of the most important works of Western American art and sculpture, with major works by Thomas Moran, George Catlin, and others, plus Native American artifacts and early maps that put the frontier region into its historical contexts. Also on the grounds is Gilcrease's old house, now home to the Tulsa Historical Society and displaying photographs and objects related to the evolution of the city.

One of Tulsa's premier Route 66 attractions was the giant Blue Whale, in the suburb of Catoosa, northeast of Tulsa along the stretch of the old road that runs from I-44 exit 240. In its heyday, traveling families would stop here to play in the pool, slide down the slides, and have a picnic on the grass, but the park closed down long ago and was left to crumble. As with so many other long-suffering Route 66 landmarks, the Blue Whale now benefits from fund-raising efforts toward restoration.

For dinner or a drink, the liveliest part of Tulsa is the Brookside district, south of downtown around 34th Street and Peoria Avenue, where there's a handful of trendy cafes, nightclubs, and restaurants. For a taste of old Route 66, stop at the retro **Metro Diner**, 3001 E. 11th Street, which isn't a *real* diner but still serves decent diner food.

The usual chain hotel and motels line all the freeways, and there's a reasonably inexpensive **Howard Johnson's** downtown at 17 W. 7th Street (918/585-5898), with doubles from under $40 a night.

For more complete information, contact the Tulsa **visitor center**, 616 S. Boston Street (918/585-1201).

One of the country's grand old country-western radio stations, **KVOO 1170 AM**, "The Voice of Oklahoma," can be heard for miles around Tulsa.

Claremore

Twenty miles northeast of Tulsa, Claremore (pop. 13,300) is a bigger-than-average Route 66 town, one that will be forever connected with its favorite son, Will Rogers. Rogers was born nearby in a rough log cabin "half-way between Claremore and Oologah before there was a town at either place," on November 4, 1879. He rose from a vaudeville career as a side-show rope-tricks artist to become one of the most popular figures in America, thanks to his folksy humor.

Before he could retire back home to Claremore, Rogers was killed in a plane crash in 1935; his land was later turned into the **Will Rogers Memorial** (daily 8 AM-5 PM; donations), a mile west of downtown Claremore on a hill overlooking the town. A statue of Rogers greets visitors at the front door, and his tomb is here, along with a small archive and museum that recount his life story.

Foyil

Between Claremore and Vinita, old Route 66 survives in regular use, alternating between two-lane and divided four-lane. The most interesting wide spot along this stretch of hallowed road is Foyil, which maintains one of the last surviving stretches of the pink-hued concrete once used to pave Route 66. But the real attraction

Foyil was the hometown of **Andy Payne,** the Cherokee youth who in 1928 won the "Bunion Derby," a coast-to-coast footrace that followed Route 66 from Los Angeles to Chicago, then headed east to New York City—equivalent to running a marathon and a half every day for the 86 days it took him to finish.

Northeast of Foyil, midway to Vinita and the next I-44 connection, the town of **Chelsea** holds a little prefabricated house, at 10021 S. Olive Street, which was bought through the Sears Roebuck mail-order catalog and shipped here from Chicago by train in 1913.

hereabouts is four miles east of town via Hwy-28, where in the 1940s and 1950s folk artist Ed Galloway sculpted an outdoor garden of giant totem poles—the tallest is over 90 feet—and other Native American-inspired objects out of concrete. After fading and weathering for many years, the poles were restored in 1993-94, and now are a fascinating place to stop for a picnic or to simply admire the effort that went into these "Watts Towers of the Plains."

Vinita

Old Route 66 crosses the Interstate again at Vinita, where the region's Native American heritage is brought into focus at the **Eastern Trails Museum** (Mon.-Sat. 1-4 PM; free), next to the public library at 215 W. Illinois Street. The exhibits center on the Cherokee "Trail of Tears," which brought the tribe here after a forced march from North Carolina in the 1830s, but the museum also covers general history of the surrounding area.

Vinita is home to the Will Rogers Memorial Rodeo, held here each August since 1935, the year he died; Rogers had attended secondary school in Vinita after growing up near Claremore.

The "Largest McDonald's in the Free World," as it used to be called, bridges the I-44 freeway at Vinita. It doesn't serve all that much food, but counting cubic feet it's the biggest outside Bejing.

South of Miami, one of the oldest paved stretches of Route 66 was constructed only one lane wide, because in 1926 the state did not have enough money to build a full-width version. Not surprisingly, this length of the road became known as the "Sidewalk Highway."

Miami, Commerce, and Quapaw

In the far northeastern corner of Oklahoma, a fine stretch of old Route 66 leaves I-44 exit 313 from the town of Miami, zigzagging to the Kansas border. Passing through a former mining region, this stretch of old Route 66 is fascinating but more than a little disturbing because of the obvious poverty of this leftover region; the corner of Kansas it crosses is also not among the highlights of a Route 66 tour.

However, the town of Miami holds the magnificent Spanish revival-style Coleman Theater, built in 1929 and luxuriating in the riches that came out of the surrounding lead and zinc mines. The mines shut long ago, leaving huge piles of tailings to mar the roadside. The next town along, Commerce (pop. 2,426), was another old mining town, noteworthy as the boyhood home of the late great Yankee player Mickey Mantle, in whose honor the old Route 66 alignment down Main Street has been renamed.

Quapaw, the first or last Oklahoma town you visit, depending upon your direction, is another fading old mining town, worth a look for the many murals painted on the walls of downtown businesses. The Kansas border is another three miles farther along.

ACROSS KANSAS

The shortest and least scenic stretch of Route 66's eight-state run is its 14-mile slice across the southeast corner of Kansas. Be careful not to blink your eyes, or you'll be saying, as Dorothy did in *The Wizard of Oz*: "We're not in Kansas anymore."

If you're coming from Oklahoma, Baxter Springs is the first town you reach. **Murphy's Restaurant**, on the corner of 11th Street, is open daily 6 AM-2 PM. In a previous incarnation, the same building housed a bank robbed by Jesse James in 1876. East of Baxter Springs are a couple of old bridges and a few other Route 66 relics. In Riverton, the next town along, the **Eisler Brothers Store** is headquarters of the small but active Kansas Route 66 Association and an essential stop for fans of the old road—and of fine old-fashioned milk shakes whipped up there.

During the Civil War, Baxter Springs saw one of the worst massacres in the country's history, when 87 Union soldiers, held prisoner by William Quantrill's rebel Confederate forces, were killed by gunshots to the back of the head. A monument to the soldiers stands in **Baxter Springs National Cemetery,** the second oldest military cemetery in the nation, off US-166 two miles west of town.

The last town in Kansas is Galena, a rough-looking place where the only businesses still open are a convenience store and a cocktail bar. Main Street gives off an air of less-than-benign neglect, but if you're feeling brave, search for the funky **Galena Mining and Historical Museum**, just off the main drag and marked by a big Old 66 sign. Inside the restored railroad depot, old newspaper clippings give a glimpse of town life during its Depression-era mining heyday, and various rusting tools and machines testify to the work that once went on here.

ACROSS MISSOURI

The Ozark Highlands of southern Missouri, which Route 66 crosses in its 300-odd-mile journey between Illinois and Kansas, are about the only significant hills the road crosses east of Arizona. This plateau region, though not by any means alpine or breathtaking, is visually dynamic in a way the broad flatlands of Illinois and the Great Plains rarely are. Though the I-44 freeway has replaced the old road all the way across the state, many signs of the old highway line the surviving stretches of the original route, and every exit drops you within a moment's drive of the Mother Road. Missouri also holds one of the greatest of the old Route 66 tourist attractions—Meramec Caverns, an extensive set of limestone caves offering the most over-the-top underground tour you can take.

On the Kansas/Missouri border, tune to **KRPS 89.9 FM** for classical music and NPR news.

Carthage was the boyhood home of naturalist Marlin Perkins, host of Mutual of Omaha's "Wild Kingdom" TV show. A life-sized statue of him stands in Central Park, three blocks southwest of the courthouse square. Carthage was also the girlhood home of Wild West outlaw **Belle Starr**.

If you have a soft spot for hyberbolic sentimentality, one not-to-be-missed monument is the **Precious Moments Chapel** (daily 9 AM-7 PM in summer, 10 AM-7 PM rest of the year; $1), featuring the wide-eyed characters from the greeting card series. The chapel is well signed, west of US-71 on the southwest edge of Carthage.

A great stretch of old Route 66, renumbered Hwy-96, runs for 50 miles along the north side of I-44 between Carthage and Springfield, passing rolling pastures and little towns like Avilla and Halltown, with antique shops and abandoned cafes lining the old highway frontage.

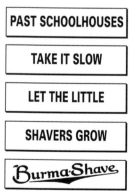

Joplin

If you travel the old Route 66 alignment across Kansas, you'll also pass through Joplin (pop. 40,961), a Missouri border town that's the industrial center of the tri-state region. Formerly a lead- and zinc-mining town, Joplin is not an especially pretty place, better known for its high-quality limestone than for its cultural offerings. Though many of its businesses have fled to the fringes, Joplin's downtown area does hold one unlikely attraction, a vibrant mural by artist Thomas Hart Benton depicting life in Joplin at the turn of the century. The mural, which turned out to be the artist's final complete work, is in the lobby of the banal 1960s-era Municipal Building, east of Main Street at 303 E. 3rd Street.

The well-signed Route 66 alignment through Joplin still holds many old signs and other survivors from the glory days of the old road, including the popular **R&M Restaurant**, 2331 E. 7th Street, which opens daily at 5:30 AM.

Carthage

Six miles north of the I-44 freeway, right on old Route 66, Carthage (pop. 10,747) is a perfect little town, looking for all the world like the model for the idyllic though fictional town of Hill Valley from the *Back to the Future* movies. The center of Carthage is dominated by the outrageously ornate limestone Jasper County Courthouse, which features a local history mural and an open-cage elevator in the lobby. The rest of the town is fairly franchise-free, away from the interstate at least, and the residential areas hold well-maintained Victorian houses. The downtown area also holds at least one good cafe, **Our Place** on Main Street, and within a short walk is an elegant B&B, the **Leggett House**, 1106 Grand Avenue (417/358-0683).

Red Oak II

On the northeast edge of Carthage, off Hwy-96 three miles from the town center, an entire pioneer Missouri town has been moved from its original site 25 miles away and reassembled as Red Oak II (daily 10 AM-6 PM, closed January and February; free; 417/358-9018). Heralded by roadside Burma-Shave signs, the buildings here have been preserved as a credible replica of a crossroads town, circa 1929, and include an antique Phillips 66 gas station, a fully functioning general store, a blacksmith's shop incongruously filled with penny arcade games, and a small cafe. A small museum tells the life story of Belle Starr, the Carthage woman who became a Confederate spy and Wild West gunslinger.

Because it's off the main road, Red Oak can be hard to find; look for the propane gas tank along Hwy-96 (old Route 66), and drive north for a mile from there.

Springfield

The largest city in southern Missouri, Springfield (pop. 140,000) doesn't feel nearly as big as it is, though it does sprawl for many miles in all directions. It was here in 1926 that plans for Route 66 were made, and the city preserves much of the old highway frontage along St. Louis Street east of downtown, as well as the grandly named "Chestnut Expressway" west of downtown. The 20-mph speed limit on downtown streets—and tons of free parking—enable Route 66 pilgrims to pay homage to the town's Arabesque landmark Shrine Theater, 601 E. 1st Street (405/258-0200), which still hosts occasional shows.

Springfield is also celebrated as the place where "Wild" Bill Hickok killed fellow gambler Dave Tutt, apparently because Tutt wore the watch he'd won from Hickok playing cards. A plaque in the central square tells one of many variations on the tale.

One place you have to see to believe—though the bass angler in your family will already know about it, for sure—is "The World's Greatest Sporting Goods Store," **BASS Pro Shops Outdoor World**, 1935 S. Campbell Street. Along with acres of floor space, the store has a 140,000-gallon fish tank, a 40-foot waterfall, and even its own McDonald's.

Springfield has a couple of the earliest and most stylish models of the Steak and Shake burger chain, and all the franchise restaurants and motels you could want, lined up around the I-44 exits.

For more detailed information, contact the **visitor center**, 3315 E. Battlefield Road (417/881-5300 or 800/678-8767).

Detour: Branson

A Middle-American Las Vegas with all the tackiness and none of the style, Branson is a century-old Ozark resort that hit the big time in the 1980s through clever promotion and cunning repackaging of country-and-western music and god-fearing recreation. There are over 30 major performance venues in Branson, and looking down the list of people who make a living playing here all summer—the Osmond Brothers, Tony Orlando, Andy Williams, and Jim *"I Don't Like Spiders and Snakes"* Stafford—you'd think that anyone who had a hit record or a TV show, or who can sing in a twang and impersonate a country-western star, can have their own showcase theater. Most offer two shows a day plus optional breakfast shows at 10 AM— imagine Hank Williams doing one of those—for the hordes of bus tours transported here every summer.

However cruel this assessment sounds, once you visit you'll see it is, if anything, not biting enough. Branson simply embodies everything that's annoying and disappointing about mass-merchandising of "culture"—a Disney version of American music without the slightest sense of humor or moment of sincere feeling.

But go see it and judge for yourself. Branson is south of Springfield on US-65. The Ozark Mountain area around Branson is still a lovely place to explore. For visitor information, contact the Branson **visitor center** (417/334-4136).

Lebanon and Rolla

Between Springfield and St. Louis, the I-44 freeway has been built right on top of the old Route 66 corridor, and dozens of ruins of old motels, motor courts, gas stations, and other highway-dependent businesses line the remains of the old road, which serves as a frontage road for most of the way. There are plenty of antique shops and cafes to make the journey interesting, but unless you have all the time in the world you may want to stick to the interstate, which offers a scenic drive through the upland forests of the Ozark plateau.

Along I-44 east of Rolla, the roadside is lined by ramshackle wooden stands which, at the end of summer, sell grapes from local vineyards. The stands are located along the frontage roads, but people stop along the freeway and walk to them.

The two biggest towns along the way, Lebanon and Rolla, grew up along the railroad in the late 1850s, and both now boast essential stops for old-roads fans. Lebanon has one of the best known junk shops along the entire old road (and there *are* hundreds): **Hall-Moore Stuff Company**, a huge old stone barn crammed with, well, stuff; it's on old Route 66, north of I-44 between exits 130 and 135. In Rolla, **Route 66 Motors**, on old Route 66 on the north side of I-44 between exits 189 and 195, is a classic-car dealership that doubles as a source of Route 66 and general automobile-related nostalgia. Housed in a converted gas station, the dealership has all the books, porcelain signs, and posters you've ever wanted to see or buy.

Among its many other claims to fame, Meramec Caverns is known as the "Birthplace of the Bumper Sticker."

Meramec Caverns

The best stop along old Route 66's trek across Missouri, and one of the most enjoyable and charming roadside attractions along the entire Mother Road, Meramec Caverns (daily 10 AM-4 PM, longer hours in summer; $9.50; 314/468-CAVE) is a set of limestone caves advertised by signs on barns and buildings all along the route, and all over the Midwest. First developed during the Civil War, when the natural saltpeter was mined for use in manufacturing gunpowder, the caves were later popularized as a place for local farmers to get together for dances; the largest room in the caves is still used for Easter Sunrise services and occasional crafts shows and chamber of commerce meetings. Meramec Caverns opened as a tourist attraction in 1935 by Lester Dill, who guided visitors through the elaborate chambers.

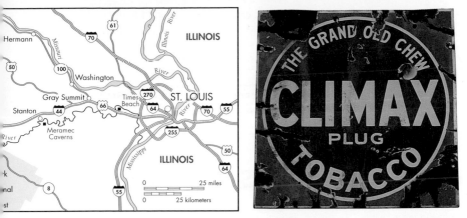

Jesse James used these caverns as a hideout, and at least once took advantage of the underground river to escape through the secret "back door." The natural formations are among the most sculptural and delicate of any cave you can visit, and the man-made additions are all low-tech enough to be charming: the hand-operated light show ends with a grand finale of Kate Smith singing "God Bless America" while Old Glory is projected onto a limestone curtain.

Meramec Caverns is near the town of **Stanton**, 55 miles west of St. Louis, three miles south of I-44 exit 230. There's a small cafe and a motel on the grounds, which spread along the banks of the Meramec River. At the I-44 exit, the odd little **Jesse James Museum** (daily 9 AM-5 PM; $3) insists despite all evidence to the contrary that a 100-year-old man who turned up in Stanton in 1948 was in fact Jesse James.

From Gray Summit at I-44 exit 251, Hwy-100 runs northwest along the Missouri River to the historic towns of Washington and Hermann, which are covered in our US-50 trip. See page 557 for more.

The best of many Route 66 survivors along the I-44 frontage roads is the **Red Cedar Inn,** on the south side of the freeway along the banks of the Meramec River a mile east of Pacific. Open since 1934, the Red Cedar serves dinner every day but Tuesday.

Times Beach

There's no plaque or notice marking the spot, but the story of Times Beach (pop. 0) deserves mention. Founded in the 1920s as a mountain getaway along the Meramec River, thanks to Route 66 the town grew into a working-class commuter suburb, with no paved streets except for the highway, which passed through the center of town. Times Beach remained a quiet hamlet until 1982, when the federal gov-ernement discovered that the industrial oil sprayed on streets to keep down dust had in fact been contaminated with toxic dioxins. The toxic waste, combined with a flood that buried the town for over a week, made Times Beach uninhabitable, and in 1984 the government paid $33 million to buy Times Beach and tear it down.

You can see what's left of Times Beach from the freeway—large fences surround the site, which looks like it was hit by a bomb blast—

One of St. Louis's last remnants of fabled Route 66 is an art deco clock now inside a shopping arcade on Delmar Avenue's 6600 block, rescued from the demolished Route 66 Drive-In.

It can be maddening to follow old Route 66 across St. Louis, but many of the key spots—Ted Drewes Frozen Custard Stand, and the location of the Coral Court Motel—can be reached by heading south from I-44 to Hwy-366, which follows Watson Road and Chippewa Avenue into and out of the city.

but the closest you can get to it is the old Route 66 bridge over the river, where 24-hour guards will turn you back to the freeway. Work is still in progress to remove the last traces of dioxin, and once that's done no one knows what will happen.

St. Louis, which marks the junction of old Route 66, cross-country US-50, and the Great River Road along the Mississippi, is covered as a Survival Guide on pages 714-715.

ACROSS ILLINOIS

Heading diagonally across the state between St. Louis and Chicago, what remains of Route 66 is a surprisingly rural cruise through endless fields of corn. Despite the urban conglomerations at both ends, for most of its nearly 300-mile trek here, Route 66 and its modern usurper, I-55, pass along flat prairies with nary a smokestack or skyscraper as far as the eye can see.

Old Route 66 used to cross the Mississippi River on the **Chain of Rocks Bridge,** which still stands, complete with its unique 45-degree bend at the midway point.

Another reason to veer off the path of old Route 66 is to pay a visit to a more contemporary landmark, the quirky **Brooks Catsup Bottle** in the town of Collinsville.

The heavy industrial and poverty-stricken suburbs of East St. Louis aren't terribly rewarding for travelers in search of the Mother Road, but a couple of intriguing attractions—one a prehistoric city, the other a water tower shaped like a catsup bottle—are worth searching out. The only real city along the route and the state capital, Springfield, has preserved its sections of Route 66, as have most of the small towns en route. All of them play up their Route 66 connections, and most boast at least one true old-road landmark.

Cahokia Mounds State Historic Site

Old Route 66 followed today's I-270 from the north side of the city, but one of southern Illinois's biggest attractions sits directly east of the Gateway Arch, off the I-55/70 freeway at exit 6. Clearly visible to the south side of the interstate, the enigmatic humps of Cahokia Mounds State Historic Site (daily 8 AM-9 PM) are the remains of the largest prehistoric Indian city north of Mexico. Over 60 earthen mounds of various sizes were built here by the indigenous Mississippian culture while Europe was in the Dark Ages; the largest covers 14 acres—more turf than the Great Pyramid of Cheops.

But don't expect the works of the pharaohs: symmetrical, grass-covered hills sitting in flat, lightly wooded bottomlands are what you'll find here. The view of distant St. Louis from the 140-foot-top of

Monks' Mound lends an odd sense of grandeur to the site, and a sophisticated Interpretive Center (daily 9 AM-5 PM; $3 suggested donation) is a recommended first stop for its displays, ranger talks, and self-guiding recorded tour.

On the stretch of old Route 66 that forms the frontage road at I-55 exit 63, near the town of **Raymond,** a marble statue of the Virgin Mary forms a shrine that has become known as "Our Lady of the Highways."

Mount Olive and Litchfield

East of St. Louis, the first really interesting stretch of old Route 66 begins at I-55 exit 41, and runs along the east side of the freeway for over a dozen miles. First stop is the hamlet of Mount Olive (pop. 2,126), which in the early 20th century was a bustling coal-mining center. It's now a sleepy little community where the only signs of its mining past are in the cemetery, along old Route 66 at the northwest edge of town. Near the entrance is a granite shaft rising from an elaborate pedestal, which serves as a memorial to "Mother" Jones, the celebrated union activist who died in 1930 at age 100. Her grave is nearby, marked by a simple headstone.

North of Mount Olive, the old road continues for seven miles to Litchfield, another old mining center that is home to one of the best of the many good Route 66 restaurants, the **Ariston Cafe,** right in the heart of town. The food is a step or two up from the usual roadside fare, and the white linen and refined decor have earned it a spot in the Route 66 Hall of Fame; it's open daily 11 AM-11 PM. The rest of Litchfield reeks of the old road, with cafes, motor courts, and old billboards aplenty.

Parts of the old road survive between Litchfield and Springfield, but the route is incomplete and confusing; I-55 makes much shorter work of the 25-mile drive.

Springfield

As the Illinois state capital, Springfield (pop. 105,277) embodies the rural small-town character of most the state and feels much farther away from Chicago than the two-hour drive it actually is, traffic willing. Springfield also takes the "Land of Lincoln" state's obsession with Abraham Lincoln to its height, for it was here that Honest Abe worked and lived from 1837 to 1861. He left Springfield after being elected president and was buried here after his assassination at the end of the Civil War.

The only home Lincoln ever owned, now a National Historic Site at 8th and Jackson Streets (daily 8:30 AM-5 PM in winter, 8 AM-8 PM in summer; free), is the focus of Springfield's extensive memorial to him. Other nearby sites include the law offices where he practiced, at 209 S. 6th Street; the train depot at 10th and Monroe Streets where he left Springfield for Washington, D.C.; even the family pew in the First Presbyterian Church, 321 S. 7th Street. Lincoln's Tomb, an impressive monument that includes the remains of his wife and three of his four children, is two miles north in Oak Ridge Cemetery.

GO COZY FOR DOGS
LOCATED ON HISTORIC ROUTE 66 SINCE 1949, SPRINGFIELD, ILLINOIS

Though quite sincere and understated, the Lincoln homage can overwhelm. Even the tried-and-truest Lincoln admirers may pass on the chance to look at his bank account book, on display in the Bank One branch at 6th and Washington Streets. One place that lets you escape from Lincoln Land is the beautiful **Dana-Thomas House** (Wed.-Sun. 9 AM-4 PM; $3; 217/782-6776) at 301 E. Lawrence Avenue, a half-mile south of the state capitol. Designed by Frank Lloyd Wright in 1902, it is the best preserved and most fully furnished of his houses and is open for hour-long guided tours. Another worthwhile place is the **Oliver Parks Telephone Museum**, near the Lincoln Home at 529 S. 7th Street (Mon.-Fri. 8 AM-5 PM; free), where you can see a fascinating collection of antique telephones—over 100 on display—assembled by a longtime Ma Bell employee.

Springfield also has a favorite Route 66 watering hole, the **Cozy Dog Drive-In**, on the old road south of downtown at 2935 6th Street. The birthplace of the corn dog, which here goes by the nicer name "Cozy," this Hall of Fame haunt was founded in 1949 by Ed Waldmire and has been run since his death by son Buzz, the self-declared "smart and good-looking brother" of Route 66 artist Bob Waldmire, who runs the Route 66 center in Hackberry, Arizona (see page 639). Check out the small Route 66 museum; pick up a few postcards or your favorite libertarian, gun-loving, and nose-thumbing bumper stickers; or simply sit and chow down on a Cozy Dog or two—four dogs and a big basket of french fries cost around $4.39.

The **A. Lincoln Motel**, next to Cozy Dog at 2929 S. 6th Street (217/525-6670), comes complete with a photogenic neon version of the familiar face from the penny coin. Almost all the national chain hotel and motels have operations here, so you shouldn't have trouble finding a room.

For more information, contact the Springfield **visitor center**, 109 N. 7th Street (217/789-2360 or 800/545-7300).

Lincoln

The only town named for Abe in his lifetime, Lincoln (pop. 15,418) took his name before he became a famous figure. As a young lawyer, Abraham Lincoln drew up the legal documents for founding the town but warned developers that he "never knew of anything named Lincoln that amounted to much." At the dedication ceremonies, Lincoln supposedly "baptized" the place by spitting out a mouthful of watermelon seeds—hence the plaster watermelon and historical plaque remembering the great event, next to the train station at Broadway and Chicago Streets in the center of town.

Nearby, the **Mill Restaurant** at 738 Washington has been in business since 1931, serving up a famous veal cutlet and good coffee to go—they are Dutch, after all.

On the south side of Lincoln, along a section of Route 66 that's now the frontage road of I-55 exit 123, the landmark Pig Hip restaurant stood from 1937 until 1991, when it closed down. The Pig Hip, and the motel next door, are vivid ghosts of the good life along the old road.

McLean and Shirley

Westbound drivers will encounter this pair of places in the more sonorous order of Shirley and McLean, but wordplay aside, the stretch of Illinois farmland between Bloomington and Springfield is rich in Route 66-related heritage. In McLean, 47 miles from Springfield and 15 miles from Bloomington, old Route 66 emerges from the shadow of I-55 at the **Dixie Truckers Home**, the oldest and best truck stop in Illinois and home of the Route 66 Hall of Fame. Besides getting a very good burger and fries, you can have a look at the plaques and artifacts that line the corridors and tell the stories of the many people along Route 66 who made it such a special place to get your kicks.

From the Dixie, follow old Route 66 along the west side of I-55 for just over four miles north to another stop, **Funks Grove**, where the friendly Funk family has been tapping trees and making delicious maple sirup (that's how they spell it) since 1891. If you're here in the spring you can watch them tap the trees and hammer in the spouts; each tree can produce four gallons of sap a day, but it takes 50 gallons for each gallon of the final product. Free tastings are available, and a full range of bottles is on sale.

From Funks Grove, the old road continues north, rejoining I-55 after four miles near the town of Shirley, for the run into (or through) Bloomington-Normal.

Bloomington-Normal

Hometown of Adlai Stevenson (and Col. Henry Blake of TV's *M.A.S.H.*), Bloomington sits at the junction of five different interstate freeways surrounded by miles of cornfields. Its one claim to fame is that it shares a main street, Franklin Avenue, with neighboring Normal; it's also the only place in the world where that

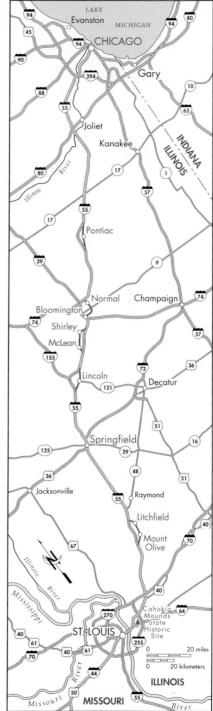

classic bar snack, Beer Nuts, is made. For tours and tastings, stop by the Shirk Products factory at 103 N. Robinson Street (309/827-8580).

For more hearty sustenance you can visit the **Steak and Shake** at 1219 Main Street, the first of many for this Midwest-based chain of quality fast-food restaurants.

Pontiac

Some 90 miles southeast of Lake Michigan, the former coal-mining town of Pontiac (pop. 11,428) surrounds the stately circa 1875 Livingston County Courthouse. The courthouse's green lawns hold the usual battery of monuments, including one to the namesake Ottawa chief whose visage also graces the General Motors marquee. According to the WPA *Guide to Illinois,* another of these monuments, the Soldier and Sailors Monument, received the shortest presidential dedication in history when, in 1902, it was "dedicated with a few hasty words by President Theodore Roosevelt, before an audience of less than a dozen people, who congregated briefly under a terrific downpour."

Pontiac is also home to a long-lived Route 66 landmark, the **Old Log Cabin Inn** on Pontiac Road on the north edge of town. When the road was rerouted behind the original location, the inn was jacked up and flipped around; the old road, which dates from 1918, is still there, behind the cafe along the railroad tracks.

From the Log Cabin, you can follow old Route 66 northeast through small towns, though the route is obscure and not all that rich in history or aesthetic delights. The final alignment of the old road is now Hwy-53, which runs along the east side of I-55 through Odell, Dwight, Wilmington, and Joliet.

Across Chicagoland

Following the first or last leg of Route 66 across Chicago and its hinterlands is really not worth the effort for anyone except the most die-hard end-to-ender—even

Jack Rittenhouse, in his original 1946 guide to Route 66, didn't bother to describe the route until it reached Plainfield, 35 miles southwest of the Loop. For a symbolic end point, you can use the grand old Art Institute of Chicago in Grant Park along the lakeshore, since the last US-66 shield used to hang from a streetlight just south of the gallery. If Chicago is your "end of the road," you'll probably prefer to avoid the final few miles of surface streets and make your way to town as quickly as possible via I-55; starting from Chicago, as the song says you should, you may be more willing to take the time to see what's left of the Mother Road.

*At the outer edge of the Chicagoland suburbs, the old Route 66 town of **Wilmington** holds the much-loved Rocketman statue, outside the Launching Pad cafe on Hwy-53.*

From Lake Michigan, the old road ran west via Adams Street (take Jackson Boulevard eastbound; both are one-way) before angling southwest along Ogden Avenue—a long, diagonal exception to the city's main grid of streets. In **Cicero**, which prides itself on having been a haven to Al Capone and other mobsters during the Prohibition era, one oddity worth checking out is "The Spindle," a tower of ruined cars impaled on a 50-foot steel spike standing in the parking lot of a shopping mall at the corner of Cernak and Harlem Avenues, two miles north of old Route 66.

Farther southeast, you have to follow the I-55 freeway, which was built right on top of old Route 66 through suburban **Plainfield**, where Route 66 crossed the old Lincoln Highway. The old road then follows the Des Plaines River and the Chicago Ship and Sanitary Canal as far as **Joliet**, where Route 66 resurfaces again, here as Chicago Street (Hwy-53). The route then continues as a four-lane frontage road along the east side of I-55 through Pontiac, a good place to join it.

The sights and sounds of Chicago are covered in a Survival Guide on pages 684-685.

AUDIO VIDEO COMPUTERS

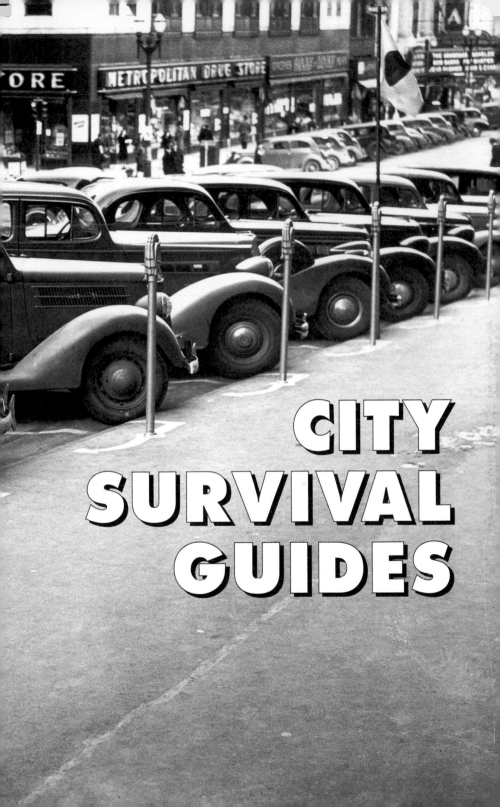

CITY
SURVIVAL
GUIDES

ATLANTA

Metropolis of the South, with a youthful and energetic population rapidly approaching three million in the metropolitan region, Atlanta has emerged as one of the most dynamic communities in the country. State capital of Georgia and world headquarters of those dual flagships of American culture, Coca-Cola and CNN, Atlanta is the financial and cultural heart of the "New South." In general people here are gracious and welcoming, so much so they could seem like walking parodies of Southern hospitality if they weren't so genuinely sincere. A lot is riding on the success of the 1996 Olympics, but win or lose, Atlanta is here to stay.

Arrival and Getting Around

Atlanta's **Hartsfield International Airport**, one of the five busiest in the country, is a dozen miles south of downtown Atlanta, at the junction of the I-85 and I-285 freeways. All the usual car rental companies operate branches here, and the Atlanta Airport Shuttle **vans** ($9 each way; 404/766-5312) supplement the MARTA **trains**, which take around 15 minutes and costing a flat $1.25. **Taxis** cost about $15.

The I-75/I-85 freeway cuts through the center of Atlanta, while the I-20 freeway skirts its southern edge. The downtown area is compact and manageable, but if it's too hot for a lengthy stroll, ride the well-organized rail and bus system operated by **MARTA**, the Metro Atlanta Rapid Transit Authority (404/848-4711). Note also that seemingly every other thoroughfare includes the word "Peachtree" in its name, so check twice before getting completely lost.

Where to Go

Underground Atlanta: Atlanta began as a railroad junction (its original name was simply "Terminus"), and the early streetscape has been preserved and restored in this warren of shopfronts underneath the center of the modern city on Alabama Street between Peachtree and Central.

Martin Luther King, Jr. National Historic Site: The visitor center is at 522 Auburn Avenue (daily 9 AM-5 PM; free; 404/331-3920). A mile east of downtown, in the heart of the "Sweet Auburn" neighborhood, this four-block area holds many important landmarks in the life of Dr. King, including his tomb emblazoned with the words "Free at Last, Free at Last" on the grounds of the **Center for Non-Violent Social Change**, 449 Auburn Avenue.

Atlanta History Museum, 130 W. Paces Ferry Road (Mon.-Sat. 10 AM-5:30 PM, Sunday noon-5:30 PM; $7; 404/814-4000). Amidst the gracious mansions of the Buckhead neighborhood, three miles north of downtown, this large modern complex contains 80,000 square feet of displays tracing Atlanta history and culture. Two tourable old houses on the property complete the collection.

Where to Stay

Days Inn—Downtown, 300 Spring Street (404/523-1144 or 800/325-2525). Clean, comfortable rooms at downtown's best rates. Doubles from $60.

Woodruff Inn, 223 Ponce de Leon (404/875-9449). Well-maintained circa 1915 Midtown house offers $65-a-night B&B rooms. Across the street from Mary Mac's Tea Room, it doubles as the **Atlanta International AYH Hostel,** where dorm beds cost around $14—an ideal combination for hungry budget travelers.

Westin Peachtree Plaza, 210 Peachtree Street (404/659-1400 or 800/228-3000). The world's tallest hotel, rising 73 stories above downtown, is packed with all the expected facilities, including a revolving rooftop restaurant. Doubles range $175-275.

Where to Eat

Beautiful Restaurant, 397 Auburn Avenue (404/233-0080). Real good soul food, especially in conjunction with a visit to the adjacent Ebenezer Baptist Church.

Mary Mac's Tea Room, 224 Ponce de Leon Avenue NE (404/876-1800). Known throughout the South for its large portions of downhome fare such as jambalaya, catfish, and fried chicken.

The Varsity, 61 North Avenue (404/881-1706). Near Georgia Tech, right downtown off I-75, this claims to be the world's largest drive-in, serving up very good chili dogs, onion rings, and more Coca-Cola than anywhere else on this earth.

Information

Check out the usual barrage of tourist information at the **Atlanta Convention and Visitors Bureau,** 233 Peachtree Street (404/521-6600). Daily newspapers are the morning *Constitution* and the evening *Journal*.

The telephone **area code** for Atlanta is **404.**

BOSTON

Three and a half centuries of headline-making have given Boston a superabundance of historical significance, all within a city that's surprisingly compact. Besides being the stomping grounds for high-profile celebs including Paul Revere, Mother Goose, and the Kennedy clan, "the Hub" is also home to Harvard, MIT, Wellesley, and some 60 other mostly private institutions of higher learning. Puritan ghosts still linger, though, so while the club scene is vibrant, the coffee shops legion, and bookstores and copy shops nearly outnumber video stores, don't expect to shop for wine on Sunday or eat out for dinner after 10 PM.

Arrival and Getting Around

Boston sits spiderlike at the center of a web of major highways and interstates, including I-90, I-93, and I-95. Convenient for air travelers, **Logan International Airport** is just a seven-minute ride across Boston Harbor from downtown—if you take the **Water Shuttle** to or from Rowes Wharf (every 15 minutes weekdays, 30 minutes on weekends; $8). Logan is also connected to the city by scheduled and on-demand vans, the Blue Line subway, and taxis. Amtrak **trains** and various **bus companies** also count Boston among their top destinations.

All the hotels, restaurants, and attractions you might want lie within walking distance of "**The T,**" the generic name for the Massachusetts Bay Transportation Authority's network of subways, buses, trolleys, ferries, and commuter trains. Buy "passports" for unlimited one-, three-, or seven-day travel ($5-18) at any commuter rail or Amtrak terminal, the Alewife subway terminal in Cambridge, the Airport subway station, or the visitor center on Boston Common.

Where to Go

John Hancock Observatory, 200 Clarendon Street at Copley Square (Mon.-Sat. 9 AM-10 PM, Sunday 10 AM-10 PM; $3.75; 617/247-1977). Take the Orange Line from the Back Bay Station or the Green Line from Copley. It's the tallest building in New England and its 60th floor is simply the best place to get an overview of Boston.

The Old North Church, 193 Salem Street (daily 9 AM-5 PM, services Sunday at 9 AM, 11 AM, and 4 PM; free; 617/523-6676). Take the Green or Orange Line to Haymarket Station. The two lanterns displayed on the steeple sent Paul Revere on his midnight ride. Paul's house, the oldest in Boston, is a block away at 19 North Square.

Boston Harbor Islands State Park (617/727-5290): From late May through early October, Bay State Cruise Lines ($7 roundtrip; 617/723-7800) departs daily to

Georges Island from beside the New England Aquarium. Georges is the base for free water taxis that circle five more islands offering hiking, beachcombing, exploration of old stone forts, and even camping (June-Sept.; permit required, 617/727-7676).

Where to Stay

Boston HI/AYH Hostel, 12 Hemenway Street, near the Green Line's Hynes/ICA station (617/536-9455 or 800/444-6111). Book private rooms ($40) a month in advance. Dorm beds $16 AYH/HI members, $19 nonmembers (membership required May-Oct.), parking $10 per day.

John Jeffries House, 14 Embankment Road, near the Red Line's Charles station (617/367-1866). At the foot of historic Beacon Hill, across from the Charles River Esplanade, this Victorian inn provides comfort and convenience. Doubles from $85, parking $12 per day.

Where to Eat

Biba, 272 Boylston Street, next to the Green Line's Arlington station (617/426-7878). With a chef who has long defined the experimental edge of Boston cuisine, this is arguably one of the best restaurants in the city. Expensive, so dress the part.

Cafe Liberty, 497b Massachusetts Avenue, Cambridge, two blocks from the Red Line's Central Square station (617/492-9900). Swig coffee at this spacious smoke-free basement with Macintosh terminals, sofas, old college texts, and a trippy Middle Earth decor.

Information

Drop by the **Boston Common Visitor Center** on Tremont Street near the Park Street T station for all your fan-folded flyer needs. **The Greater Boston Convention and Visitors Bureau** (617/536-4100 or 800/888-5515) and the **Massachusetts Office of Travel and Tourism** (800/477-MASS) offer lists of attractions and accommodations. Once in town, pick up a thick Thursday edition of *The Boston Globe*.

The telephone **area code** for all of Boston is 617.

CHICAGO

New York may have bigger and better museums, shops, and restaurants, and Los Angeles more people, but Chicago is still the most all-American city, and one of the most exciting and enjoyable places to visit in the world. Commercial capital of Middle America, Chicago's location between the settled East and the wide-open West helped it give birth to many new things we now take for granted: the skyscraper, the blues, and the atomic bomb.

Apart from **The Loop**, the skyscraper-spiked lakefront business district that holds the world's tallest and most impressive collection of modern architecture, much of Chicago is surprisingly low-rise and residential. Also surprising, considering its inland location, is that Chicago has the highest percentage of immigrants of any American city. Whatever their origin, however, residents take particular pride in identifying themselves as Chicagoans, and despite the city's rusting infrastructure and perenially losing baseball teams, their good-natured enthusiasm for the place can be contagious.

Arrival and Getting Around

Chicago is home to America's busiest and most infuriating airport, **O'Hare** (ORD), 17 miles northwest of the Loop and well served by CTA subway trains, shuttle services, and taxis. The airport has all the usual car rental firms as well. Chicago is also the hub of the national Amtrak system, with **trains** pulling into Union Station from all over the country. Interstate 55 from St. Louis follows the old Route 66 (see page 628); other primary highways are east-west I-80 and I-90, which replace the US-20 route, and a half-dozen north-south freeways. Traffic can be horrendous, so you'll really be better off leaving the car behind and riding the CTA elevated ("El") subway and bus system (312/836-7000), which serves the entire city around the clock.

Where to Go

Chicago River by Boat, North Pier, 455 E. Illinois Street (daily May-Oct. only; $15; 312/922-3432). Operated by the Chicago Architecture Foundation, these informative and enjoyable tours give an unusual look up at the city's magnificent towers from a boat on the Chicago River.

The Magnificent Mile, N. Michigan Avenue. North of the Loop, across the Chicago River, this mile-long shopping strip holds many of the city's top shops, restaurants, and hotels. Starting with the gothic-style **Tribune Tower**, the "Mag Mile" ends in the north with two blocks of very posh shops next to the 95-story **John Hancock Center**.

Frank Lloyd Wright Home and Studio, 951 Chicago Avenue, Oak Park (daily 11 AM-4 PM; $6; 312/848-1976). For a fascinating look into the life and work of the great architect, take a guided tour of the house he designed and lived in and worked in from 1890 to 1910. This turn-of-the-century suburb, just 10 miles west of the Loop at the end of the Lake-Dan Ryan CTA "El" line, was also the boyhood home of Ernest Hemingway.

Wrigley Field, 1060 W. Addison Street (312/404-2827). The Cubs playing at Wrigley Field is more than just another baseball game. Watching is a rite of passage into the deepest meanings of the national pastime.

Where to Stay

Arlington House International Hostel, 616 W. Arlington Place (312/929-5380). Dorm beds near Wrigley Field are central Chicago's only real budget accommodation.

Best Western River North, 125 W. Ohio Street (312/467-0800). Great location in the trendy River North gallery district, within walking distance of the Loop and Mag Mile. Doubles from $85.

Where to Eat

The Berghoff, 17 W. Adams Street (312/427-3170). Picture-perfect turn-of-the-century saloon and steakhouse serving up excellent food in luscious, wood-paneled room. Cash only, sometimes crowded.

Billy Goat Tavern, 430 N. Michigan Avenue (312/222-1525). Underground beer-and-burger bar made famous by John Belushi's "cheeseboiga, cheeseboiga . . . no Coke, Pepsi" routine on *Saturday Night Live*.

Information

The best source of information is the Chicago Office of Tourism, 78 E. Washington Street (312/744-2400), which has maps and all the usual ad-packed promotional brochures. The two daily papers are the *Sun-Times* and the *Tribune*.

The telephone area code for Chicago is 312.

CINCINNATI

Spreading along the north bank of the Ohio River, Cincinnati was once the largest and busiest city on the western frontier. But as the railroads converged on Chicago, Cincinnati was eclipsed as the prime gateway to the western United States. Cincinnati has won accolades from a broad range of notables, including Winston Churchill, who called it "the most beautiful of America's inland cities." Mark Twain, however, said that he wanted to be in Cincinnati when the world came to an end—since it's always 20 years behind the times.

Cincinnati's population of some 400,000 ranks it just ahead of Toledo as Ohio's third largest city. Even if you're racing through, no roadtripper in his or her right mind should pass Cincinnati without sampling its excellent food—mounds of chili, stacks of melt-in-your-mouth ribs, and scoops of Graeter's ice cream await.

Arrival and Getting Around
Cincinnati lies along the north bank of the Ohio River, very near the Kentucky border just across the river, and Indiana. US-50 is the main east-west route, with I-74 providing a link from Indianapolis, and I-71 running to Louisville. I-75 runs north-south through Cincinnati between Detroit and Atlanta.

Train service is all but nonexistent, though most major airlines fly into the **Greater Cincinnati International Airport,** which actually lies southwest of downtown in Kentucky. Getting around town is best done by car.

Where to Go
Museum Center, Union Terminal, Ezzard Charles Drive off I-75 exit 1 (Mon.-Sat. 9 AM-5 PM, Sunday 11 AM-6 PM; 513/287-7000 or 800/733-2077). On the northwest edge of downtown you'll find this 1930s art deco railroad station, converted into one of the best museum complexes in the country. Check out the **Cincinnati Historical Society** ($5), the **Museum of Natural History** ($5), and the **Omnimax** theater ($3).

Mount Adams: Once connected to downtown by an incline railway, this 300-foot-high hilltop neighborhood has emerged from years of neglect as an artsy district of crafts shops and cafes like the **Cafe Vienna** at 1141 St. Gregory Street.

Nearby **Eden Park** holds the respected **Cincinnati Art Museum** (Tues.-Sun. 10 AM-5 PM; $5).

Covington, Kentucky: Most of Cincinnati's once vibrant waterfront area, known as "The Basin," has been torn down in the name of urban renewal. You can find the sole survivors of old Cincinnati across the river in Covington, Kentucky, close enough to walk to across the **Roebling Bridge**, built in 1865 as a precursor to the Brooklyn Bridge.

Covington Landing, a huge barge moored at the foot of the Roebling Bridge, is one of Cincinnati's best nightlife spots, with over a dozen places to eat, drink, and be merry.

Where to Stay

Hundreds of rooms are available in national chain motels along the I-71 and I-75 freeways, including a **Travelodge** and a **Days Inn** on Central Parkway (US-127), three miles northwest of downtown. Families will like the **Embassy Suites** (606/261-8400) overlooking the Ohio River from the Kentucky side of Roebling Bridge.

Where to Eat

Camp Washington Chili, corner of Hopple and Colerain, three miles north of downtown, right off I-75 exit 3. This place is known for its chili, poured over spaghetti and served either "3-Way" (spaghetti, chili, and grated cheese), "4-Way" (add onions), or "5-Way" (add beans). It's open around the clock (except Sunday).

Montgomery Inn at the Boathouse, 925 Eastern Avenue (513/721-RIBS). According to Bob Hope and the late Billy Carter, the best barbecued ribs in America are served here, in a modern riverfront building on old US-50. In tandem with the original **Montgomery Inn**, 9440 Montgomery Road (513/791-3482), the restaurant manages to get through more than 200 tons of ribs annually—more than anywhere else in the country.

Information

Head to the **Greater Cincinnati Visitors Bureau**, 300 W. 6th Street (513/621-2142 or 800/344-3445), or its branch on the main concourse of the Museum Center (see above). Daily newspapers are the morning *Enquirer* and the afternoon *Post*.

The telephone **area code** for Cincinnati is **513**.

CLEVELAND

Poor Cleveland. Just when it seemed on the verge of recovering some semblance of civic pride thanks to the success of the Rock and Roll Hall of Fame and the Cleveland Indians making it to the World Series, everything went black when pro football's much-loved Browns abandoned the city for new pastures—in Baltimore, as if to add insult to injury.

For decades, Cleveland was one of the biggest of all the Great Lakes industrial giants, with John D. Rockefeller's Standard Oil leading the way. Despite spending much of the past 50 years reeling from Rust Belt decay, the city seems to be on the verge of coming back to life, energized by Jacob's Field, the always sold-out downtown baseball stadium that opened in 1994. The Rock and Roll Hall of Fame opened with a splash at the end of 1995, and anchors the ongoing effort to resurrect the unsightly waterfront known as "The Flats."

Arrival and Getting Around

The main airport, **Hopkins International**, is 12 miles southwest of downtown, linked by I-71 freeway and RTA subway to central Cleveland. The **RTA** subway ($1.50; 216/621-9500) also serves the Cleveland Museum of Art (Red Line/University Station) and the southern suburbs, but getting around by car is probably easiest.

In the downtown area, finding your way around the Cuyahoga River waterfront takes patience, as many roads dead-end and some of the old bridges are closed to traffic. Explore on foot or take the "Downtown Loop" shuttle bus service (50 cents).

Where to Go

Rock and Roll Hall of Fame, North Coast Harbor (daily 10 AM-5:30 PM; $10.90; 216/781-ROCK or 800/493-ROLL). This striking modern building houses a barrage of multimedia exhibits, 50,000 square feet of galleries, and a 165-foot tower.

Cleveland Museum of Art, 11150 East Boulevard (Tues.-Fri. 10 AM-6 PM, Saturday 9 AM-5 PM, Sunday 1-6 PM; $4; 216/421-7340). Surrounded by the green and leafy campus of Case Western Reserve University, five miles east of downtown, this is one of the country's great art collections, presenting a broad survey of western art. Surrounding areas hold **Rockefeller Park, Lakeview Cemetery, and Murray Hill**.

Jacob's Field, Carnegie Avenue at Ontario Avenue (tickets $6-15; 216/241-8888 or 216/420-4240). This is the place that made Cleveland a winner—inspiring not just the Indians baseball team, but a general renaissance of civic pride. Packed full with 42,000 fans every game, so reserve tickets as far in advance as possible.

The Flats: Cleveland's old heavyweight industrial district, lining the Erie lakefront and the twisting Cuyahoga River, is known as "The Flats." Despite wholesale demolition, enough of these gigantic old mills, factories, and warehouses still stand, overlaid by a network of bridges to form a feast for the eyes of any post-industrial amateur archaeologist.

Where to Stay

Cross-Country Inn, 25200 Sperry Drive (216/871-3993). Ten miles west of downtown Cleveland, off I-90 exit 156 in the town of Westlake, but offering clean, low-priced rooms. Doubles from $45.

Stouffer Renaissance Cleveland Hotel, 24 Public Square (216/696-5600). Formerly known as the Tower City Plaza, this beautiful old hotel has been immaculately updated into the city's nicest place to stay. Doubles range $100-200.

Where to Eat

Great Lakes Brewing Company, 2516 Market Avenue, Ohio City (216/771-4404). West of the Cuyahoga River, in an artsy low-rent district, with good food, great beer, and generally convivial crowd.

Miller's Dining Room, 16707 Detroit Avenue (old US-20), Lakewood (216/221-5811). Old-fashioned Middle American home cooking, served up nonstop since 1950: roast beef, roast birds, creamy whipped potatoes, fresh baked rolls, and classic fruit pies.

Slyman's, 3106 St. Clair Avenue (216/621-3760). Best corned beef in Cleveland bar none, in a light industrial and warehousing district east of I-90, a half-mile from downtown.

Information

For more details, contact the Cleveland Convention and Visitors Bureau, 3100 Terminal Tower, 50 Public Square (216/621-4110 or 800/321-1004). The morning *Cleveland Plain Dealer* is the main daily newspaper.

The telephone area code for Cleveland is 216.

DALLAS/FORT WORTH

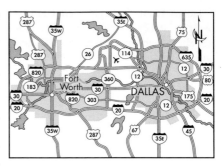

Like warring branches of an extended family, Dallas and Fort Worth are inseparable arch-rivals. Both towns lay fair claim to being capitals of their respective industries: the older of the two, Fort Worth, calls itself "Cowtown" but has a surprisingly sophisticated range of cultural centers while retaining much of its Wild West past. Upstart Dallas, which grew from nothing after the discovery of oil in east Texas during the 1930s, plays the role of nouveau riche to the nth degree as home to Neiman Marcus and TV's eponymous soap opera.

Arrival and Getting Around
Linked (or is it divided?) by a trio of fast freeways (I-20, I-30, and Hwy-183), Dallas and Fort Worth lie some 25 miles apart across the plains of northeast Texas. Each city is circled by its own ring road, and two north-south freeways (I-35W through Fort Worth, and I-35E through downtown Dallas) complete the high-speed network.

    Dallas/Fort Worth International Airport (DFW), midway between the two cities, is the region's main airport and one of the largest and busiest in the world. **SuperShuttle** vans (817/329-2000) will carry you to either town from the airport for about $10. All the usual **car rental** firms operate at the airport.

Where to Go
Kimbell Art Museum, 3333 Camp Bowie Boulevard, Fort Worth (Tues.-Sat. 10 AM-5 PM, Sunday noon-5 PM; free; 817/332-8451). One of the most perfectly beautiful modern buildings on the planet, this small museum stands across the street from the Amon Carter Museum.

    The Stockyards, on Main and Exchange Streets, two miles north of downtown Fort Worth. For a taste of how Texas used to be, spend some time wandering around these two short blocks of turn-of-the-century buildings, stretching west from the still-busy Fort Worth Stockyards. One of the city's most popular places to eat, drink, and be merry; after dark, check out **Billy Bob's** (817/624-7177), the world's largest honky-tonk.

    Texas School Book Depository, "**The Sixth Floor**," 411 Elm Street, Dallas (daily 9 AM-6 PM; $6; 214/653-6666). Offering the gruesome novelty of looking out from the very same place where Lee Harvey Oswald shot (or didn't shoot) President John F. Kennedy on November 22, 1963, this extensive museum describes the historical context and discusses the myriad of conspiracy theories. Oddly, the entire museum is copyrighted, so No Photography signs abound.

Where to Stay

Benbrook Lake, six miles southwest of Fort Worth off US-377 (817/292-2400). A half-dozen campgrounds ring this very large reservoir. Sites cost $10.

Stockyards Hotel, 109 E. Exchange Avenue, Fort Worth (817/625-6427). Bonnie and Clyde (both of whom are buried in Dallas) stayed in this turn-of-the-century hotel, which has been restored and redecorated according to various themes. Doubles are $75.

Adolphus Hotel, 1321 Commerce Street, Dallas (214/742-8200). Historic four-star downtown hotel, built in 1912 by beer magnate Adolphus Busch and worth a look for the plush interior even if you can't afford the $200-a-night rates.

Where to Eat

Cattlemen's Steak House, 2458 N. Main Street, Fort Worth (817/624-3945). If it's meat you want to eat, this is the place: steaks of all cuts and sizes, plus barbecue and some seafood. Dinner every day, lunch weekdays only.

Joe T. Garcia's, 2201 N. Commerce Street, Fort Worth (817/626-4356). This may or may not be the World's Biggest Tex-Mex restaurant, but it sure can feel like it. Food is top-notch, and served on a family-style menu.

Prince of Hamburgers, 5200 Lemmon Avenue, Dallas (214/526-9081). A northwest Dallas institution, this drive-in has been serving burgers, fries, and milk shakes since 1927.

Information

For maps and more extensive information, contact the Dallas **Visitors Bureau** in Union Station (daily 9 AM-5 PM; 214/746-6677). Fort Worth has three visitor centers, including one in the Stockyards at 130 E. Exchange Avenue (817/624-4741). If you want help making hotel reservations, call **Hotel Accommodations of Texas** (800/428-4464). The *Dallas Morning News* is the main daily paper.

The telephone **area code** for Dallas is **214**; for Fort Worth it is **817**.

KANSAS CITY

Though it covers a huge area, stretching for some 20 miles on both sides of the Missouri/Kansas border, and nearly 30 miles north to south, Kansas City (pop. 450,000) never really feels like a big city. It's more like a conglomeration of small towns, once separate from each other but now joined together by tract house sprawl and surrounded by the 100-mile-long I-435 Beltway. The historic center of Kansas City lines the south bank of the Missouri River, where 30-story skyscrapers stand above hefty brick warehouses, huge stockyards, railroad tracks, and banks of grain elevators all testifying to Kansas City's role as the main distribution point for Midwestern farm products.

All of this isn't meant to imply the city is ugly, just that it sometimes seems to go on forever, and that places of interest can be hard to find. Besides the ones described below, another place definitely worth a visit is the historic town of **Independence**, on the northwest outskirts of Kansas City (see page 555).

Arrival and Getting Around

Kansas City spreads to the north of transcontinental US-50 highway, at the junction of the I-29, I-35, and I-70 interstate freeways. Small but efficient **Kansas City International Airport** (KCI) sits 15 miles northwest of downtown.

To get around Kansas City, drive. As in Los Angeles, which Kansas City resembles more than residents of either city are likely to admit, cars rule the roads. Distances are huge and public transportation is basically nonexistent.

Where to Go

Negro Baseball Leagues Museum, 1601 E. 18th Street, Suite 201 (Mon.-Sat. 10 AM-4:30 PM, Sunday noon-4:30 PM; $2; 816/221-1920). Very new small museum dedicated to documenting the black professional baseball leagues that existed side by side with the majors before the color barriers began to break down in the late 1940s. The museum is located a mile east of downtown KC, in the 18th and Vine neighborhood, heartland of Kansas City's postwar jazz scene.

Hallmark Visitors Center, Main and 25th Streets, on the top floor of the Crown Center shopping mall (Mon.-Fri. 9 AM-5 PM, Saturday 9:30 AM-4:30 PM; free; 816/274-5672). Midway between downtown and Westport, Kansas City's one unique attraction is less nauseatingly saccharine than you might expect. Fourteen galleries trace the history of the Hallmark company (which started here in 1910); most of the exhibits focus on the design and production processes behind the 50,000 different types of greeting cards ($3.8 billion worth!) they sell each year.

Where to Stay
All the usual chain motels line the I-435 beltway. There's a good-value **Red Roof Inn** on I-435/US-50 in Overland Park (exit 80), and another near Independence. In downtown Kansas City, the anonymously named **Historic Suites of America**, two blocks from the City Market at 612 Central Avenue (816/842-6544), offers spacious accommodations in a well-converted 100-year-old warehouse.

Places to Eat
Arthur Bryant's, 1727 Brooklyn Avenue (816/231-1123). Meat-eaters drive for miles to eat at this classic no-frills rib shack. Located near the Negro Leagues Baseball Museum.

    Stroud's, 1015 E. 85th Street (816/333-2132). Away from downtown, but not far from US-50 in a photogenic roadhouse on the south side of the city (take the Holmes Road exit off I-435), Stroud's simply perfect fried chicken is rated by *Roadfood* writers Jane and Michael Stern as the very best in the country. With huge portions of mashed potatoes, peppery gravy, and sweet cinnamon buns, it's certainly hard to beat.

Information
Contact the Kansas City **visitor center** (816/221-5242 or 800/767-7700) at 1100 Main Street, or stop by the state-run **Missouri Information Center** (daily 9 AM-5 PM; 816/861-8800), near I-435 east of downtown on I-70 at exit 9.

    The city's main daily newspaper is the *Kansas City Star.* For other listings of events and activities, consult the free weekly *NewTimes* or *Pitch,* or phone the Jazz Hotline (816/763-1052).

    The telephone **area code** for Kansas City is **816**.

LAS VEGAS

Las Vegas is the biggest, brightest, and most brazen boomtown in the history of the world, and its prosperity is at an all-time high. In the past seven years, five megaresorts and another dozen resorts have opened in Las Vegas, which now claims nine of the 10 largest hotels in the world. By the end of 1996, Las Vegas will top the 100,000-room mark, almost more than New York and Chicago *combined.*

Thirty million visitors already lose six billion dollars in the casinos here every year, and there's no end in sight: another four properties, all with more than 2,500 rooms, are planned along "the Strip" (a.k.a. Las Vegas Boulevard South), and at least a dozen more are rumored to be on the horizon.

Arrival and Getting Around

If you'd like to pretend the whole thing is a hallucination, a mere mirage in the Mojave Desert, you can barrel straight through Las Vegas on the freeway. But don't turn your head! It's an illusion only if you see it with one eye.

If you're going to brave a tour through the belly of the beast, your exits all stem from I-15: take Main Street for downtown; or Sahara, Flamingo, and Tropicana (these are names of streets as well as casinos) for the Strip.

McCarran International Airport (LAS), one of the 10 busiest in the country, is only a couple of miles east of the Tropicana/Strip intersection. The local bus is $1, low in cost but high in adventure. Limos and shuttles will take you to your hotel or motel for less than $5. Taxis from the airport are about $10-12 for Strip destinations, $15-18 for downtown.

Where to Go: Casinos

Hard Rock Hotel/Casino, 4555 Paradise Road (702/693-5000 or 800/473-7625). The coolest and among the newest places in town. Off the Strip and small by Vegas standards, but where else can you play Jimi Hendrix slot machines (a line of "Purple Haze" pays $200) while listening to nonstop classic rock 'n' roll?

Luxor, 3900 Las Vegas Boulevard S (702/262-4444 or 800/288-1000). It's the most distinctive, housed inside a mammoth (29 million cubic feet) glass pyramid at the southern end of the Strip. On the second level are the high-tech attractions: motion simulators, 3-D and IMAX movies, and state-of-the-art arcade games.

Where to Stay

Circus Circus, 2880 Las Vegas Boulevard S (702/734-0410 or 800/634-3450). Cheap rooms (doubles from $25 a night) at the center of the Strip, with a carnival midway, circus acts, and low-stakes table games.

Excalibur, 3850 Las Vegas Boulevard S (702/597-7777 or 800/937-7777). Over-the-top Vegas kitsch, in the form of a turreted castle dwarfed by one of the world's largest hotels—4,032 rooms, usually around $50 a night.

Where to Eat

For great cheap food, try the snack bars downtown, especially at the Horseshoe, Golden Gate, and El Cortez; on the Strip, try the Holiday Inn Boardwalk, Westward Ho, and Slots A Fun. You'll find fast-food courts at the Riviera, Caesars, and MGM; the Flamingo Hilton has a good quick cafeteria, the Food Fantasy, and there's a neon McDonald's on the Strip.

The best all-you-can-eat buffet is at the Rio Suite Hotel Casino, off the Strip at 3700 W. Flamingo Road, west of I-15 (702/252-7777 or 800/888-1808). Palace Station, Bally's, Golden Nugget, and Fremont (in that order) also feature good buffets.

Information

Perhaps the most telltale sign that Las Vegas has become one of the world's premier destinations is the proliferation of guidebooks about the place. In 1988, Las Vegas had two farcical travel guides; as of 1996, there were 12. To become even superficially familiar with this blinding desert oasis, read *The Unofficial Guide to Las Vegas* by Bob Sehlinger, Compass American Guides' *Las Vegas* by Deke Castleman (who provided most of the above information), and the current issue of the *Las Vegas Advisor* newsletter (800/244-2224).

The *Las Vegas Review-Journal* is the big morning daily; the *Las Vegas Sun* is the smaller afternoon paper.

The telephone **area code** for Las Vegas is **702.**

LOS ANGELES

Love it or hate it, one thing you can't do about L.A. is ignore it. Thanks to Hollywood in all its many guises (movies, television, the music industry), and a recent spate of natural and unnatural disasters (earthquakes, fires, floods, high-profile murder trials), the city is always rearing its head.

A guide as brief as this can only point you in the right direction. In keeping with its car-centered culture, this suggested tour focuses on five different recommended drives.

Arrival and Getting Around
Most flights into Los Angeles arrive at LAX, on the coast southwest of downtown, where you'll find all the usual shuttles and car rental agencies.

Avoid "rush hour" traffic (7 AM-10 AM, and 3-8 PM), pave your own way on the surface streets, or take advantage of the **L.A. Department of Transportation's** (213/626-4455) network of buses, Metrorail trains, and handy DASH minibuses.

Where to Drive
Mulholland Drive: This classic L.A. cruise starts in the east within sight of the Hollywood sign, passes by the city's most valuable real estate, and ends at the northern tip of Malibu on Pacific Coast Highway (PCH).

Sunset Boulevard: The 27-mile course starts at Olvera Street, then winds west past Gower Gulch. In West Hollywood's nightclub district it's dubbed the "Sunset Strip." Through Beverly Hills, Brentwood, and Bel-Air, Sunset is lined by colossal mansions. It finally hits the beach just south of the **J. Paul Getty Museum** (Tues.-Sun. 10 AM-5 PM; free; call for parking reservations, 310/458-2003).

Santa Monica Boulevard, Route 66: Turning off Sunset Boulevard at the eastern edge of Hollywood, Santa Monica Boulevard runs past **Hollywood Memorial Cemetery** (daily 9 AM-5 PM; free; 213/469-1181), where various luminaries are entombed. Old Route 66 runs through trendy West Hollywood, Beverly Hills, and Century City, finally reaching the Pacific at Ocean Boulevard and the Santa Monica Pier.

Wilshire Boulevard: L.A.'s main commercial artery starts at the heart of downtown, cuts through MacArthur Park, and runs west to the "Miracle Mile" (don't miss the **Petersen Automotive Museum**, 6060 Wilshire Boulevard; Tues.-Sun. 10 AM-6 PM; $7; 213/930-CARS). After passing the foot of Rodeo Drive, the route crosses the "World's Busiest Intersection" where Wilshire passes beneath the San Diego Freeway before winding up at the bluffs above Santa Monica Bay.

Pasadena Freeway: "The World's First Freeway," started in 1934 as the Arroyo Seco Parkway, is a traffic-clogged time warp. Despite its archaic design, it's a fun drive, especially late at night, when the gleaming towers of downtown rise seemingly inches away from your windshield.

Where to Stay

Leo Carrillo State Beach Park, Pacific Coast Highway at Mulholland Drive, Malibu (805/986-8591 or 800/444-7275). Camp in this sycamore-filled canyon across Pacific Coast Highway from a beautiful little beach for $15 a night.

Santa Monica International Hostel, 1436 2nd Street, Santa Monica (310/392-0325). Clean, low-cost accommodations just two blocks from the beach across from Santa Monica's lively 3rd Street Promenade.

Beverly Hills Hotel, 9641 Sunset Boulevard, Beverly Hills (310/276-2251 or 800/283-8885). Stop by this grande dame of L.A. hotels for breakfast or a late-night drink at the legendary Polo Lounge if you can't manage the $350-a-night (and up) room rates.

Where to Eat

Barney's Beanery, 8447 W. Santa Monica Boulevard (213/654-2287). Crusty old West Hollywood roadhouse with famous chili, lots of good inexpensive food, a range of beers, and plenty of pool tables.

Kate Mantellini, 9109 Wilshire Boulevard (310/278-3699). Upscale mid-1980s version of traditional dark wood supper club, with great food served till 2 AM.

Apple Pan, 10801 W. Pico Boulevard (310/475-3585). An ancient landmark on the West L.A. landscape, serving the best hamburgers on the planet. Take a seat at the counter and dive in to a pile of chunky fresh-fried French fries, but be sure to save room for a slice of their wonderful fruit pies.

Information

Stop by the **Los Angeles Convention and Visitors Bureau,** 695 S. Figueroa Street (213/689-8822 or 800/228-2452) for the usual array of information. To find out about current events and issues, read the mammoth *Los Angeles Times* or the free *L.A. Weekly.*

L.A.'s metropolitan area has a half-dozen different **area codes,** so to minimize confusion, the appropriate prefix has been included in all the phone numbers given.

MEMPHIS

Memphistan gifts to American culture include the supermarket, the drive-in restaurant, the chain motel, Elvis, and FedEx. This is not to say "The City of Good Abode" lacks character—just the opposite—but its charms are like homebrew or overripe cheese: musty, sharp, and lingering, with unpredictable side-effects.

In the 1870s the city was nearly wiped out by yellow fever. This century the fever has been racism, with white flight abandoning the city to pawn shops, loan and check-cashing outfits, and thrift stores. Sprawling county development and a valid fear of violent crime keep suburbanites inside their malls. However, although you wouldn't guess it from the Graceland tour prices, Memphis offers lots of affordable food and fun.

Arrival and Getting Around

Memphis International Airport is across I-55 from Graceland, about seven miles south of downtown. Take a shuttle van ($10) or taxi ($20) to downtown or rent a car. The Great River Road is augmented by north-south I-55 and east-west I-40. Greyhound arrives downtown, while the Amtrak station is at 545 S. Main Street.

Getting around Memphis is best done in a car, not least because parts of town can suddenly switch from very safe to potentially dangerous in between the main tourist areas.

Where to Go

Beale Street, downtown between 2nd and 4th Streets, has been honky-tonk central ever since native son W.C. Handy set up shop in the early 1900s with the blues he'd learned in Mississippi. Sanitized for your protection, it's now a new! and improved! version of its old self. At night, stroll with the tour bus crowd along the block of clubs (including B.B. King's at 143 Beale), curbside bars, and T-shirt mongers. By day, check out the voodoo potions in the justly famous **A. Schwab's Dry Goods Store**, 163 Beale Street.

Sun Records: The original studios (daily 10 AM-5:30 PM; $5), where Elvis recorded his first tracks, are a short walk east at 706 Union Avenue.

National Civil Rights Museum, 450 Mulberry Street (Monday and Wed.-Sat. 10 AM-5 PM, Sunday 1-5 PM; $5; 901/521-9699). One place you shouldn't miss is this eloquent memorial, south of Beale Street behind the restored facade of the Lorraine Motel, where Dr. Martin Luther King, Jr., was assassinated in 1968.

Graceland, 3765 Elvis Presley Boulevard (US-51), take exit 5B about a mile south of I-55 (daily 9 AM-5 PM, 8 AM-7 PM in summer; $9-17; 901/332-3322 or 800/238-2000). A visit says little about his music, but speaks volumes about his mystique (where else can you see a living room with shag carpet on the ceiling?). Tours take at least two hours. Reservations are suggested, and parking is an extra $2.

Where to Stay

Lowenstein-Long House, 217 N. Waldron Boulevard (901/527-7174). Nice B&B inn ($70 single or double) with a dorm-style hostel on the side ($10 per person, $30 for a private room).

The Peabody, 149 Union Avenue (901/529-4000 or 800/PEABODY). Twice daily the red carpet is rolled out so the Peabody Ducks can scuttle to and from their sparkling fountain office, to the delight of kids and flashbulb manufacturers. Doubles $160 and up.

The major chain hotels line the I-240 beltway. To learn more about Memphis accommodations, call the free booking service, **Pennywise Marketing** (Mon.-Fri. 9 AM-5 PM; 800/206-5829).

Where to Eat

Buntyn Restaurant, 3070 Southern Avenue, east of the Mid-South Coliseum (901/458-8776). Head here for cheap, authentic Southern cookery: excellent batter-fried chicken, heaps of mashed potatoes with thick gravy, and sweet pies. Open Mon.-Fri. 11 AM-8 PM.

La Montagne, 3550 Park Avenue at Highland (901/458-1060). Come to this cozy cottage for fresh, lean, and from-scratch cuisine at reasonable prices. Closed Sunday and 2-5 PM.

Information

Contact the **Memphis Convention and Visitors Bureau** (901/543-5333 or 800/873-6282) or drop by their Beale Street information booth.

For entertainment listings pick up *The Memphis Flyer,* or buy a copy of the *Lowlife Guide to Memphis* ($2.50 from Shangri-La Records, 1916 Madison Avenue).

The telephone **area code** for Memphis is **901.**

MINNEAPOLIS/ST. PAUL

The Twin Cities share an area code, the Mississippi River, and an old rivalry that's stoked by sports fans, high schools, and barflies who give advice to out-of-towners. In general, Minneapolis boasts more fashion, culture, and reflective glass, while St. Paul has a greater small-town feel, fewer tourist attractions, and better baseball. Together, the Twin Cities are a typically sprawling American metropolis with

an atypically wholesome reputation: safe, liberal-minded, welcoming of strangers, and inclined to go to bed early. Such sensibility might be boring—unless you're looking for somewhere to raise kids—but don't fret, there's enough to keep the visitor fully entertained.

Arrival and Getting Around

The Twin Cities sit at the crossing of I-35 and I-94. Located seven miles south of downtown, the **Minneapolis-St. Paul International Airport** is served by 10 major airlines, with Northwest Airlines exercising the home-field advantage. **Amtrak** serves the Twin Cities from its station diplomatically located between the two city centers.

A wide-reaching network of public **buses** operated by the MTCO, a.k.a. the "T," favors commuters and mall shoppers, but if you have the time or plan a day downtown, they beat feeding the meters.

Where to Go

Minneapolis Sculpture Garden, Lyndale Ave. S near I-94 (daily 6 AM-midnight; 612/375-7577; free). Dominated by Claes Oldenburg and Coosje van Bruggen's giant *Spoonbridge and Cherry,* this is one of the city's finer urban oases, with 40-some works of art spanning Henry Moore to Jenny Holzer. Next door to the garden is the **Walker Art Center** (Tues.-Sat. 10 AM-8 PM, Sunday 11 AM-5 PM; free on Thursday, otherwise $4; 612/375-7622), rightfully renowned as one of the nation's finest contemporary art museums.

Museum of Questionable Medical Devices, St. Anthony Main, North Minneapolis (Mon.-Fri. 5-9 PM, Saturday 11 AM-10 PM, Sunday 12-5 PM; free; 612/379-4046). Here you can learn about phrenology (the study of the skull's conformation based on the belief that it is indicative of mental facilities and character), see devices to cure baldness or the ravages of age, and read about the promises of quacks and manufacturers through the ages.

Where to Stay

Regency Plaza Best Western, 41 N. 10th Street, downtown Minneapolis (612/339-9311 or 800/423-4100). One of the least expensive of the downtown hotels and there's free parking, too. Doubles range $66-72.

Kaz's Home Hostel, South Minneapolis (call 612/822-8286 for reservations and directions). Staying with the friendly Kaszynski clan is like visiting your great aunt or going home for a visit a decade after your parents cleaned out your room. At least they left your Hardy Boys collection intact. The rate is $10 per person.

Where to Eat

Nye's Polonaise Room, 112 E. Hennepin Avenue, North Minneapolis (612/379-2021). Dimly lit plush-boothed 1950s power-broker restaurant that could have witnessed the birth of the three-martini lunch. Surf and turf solid, with sing-along piano entertainment nightly. Just over the bridge from downtown. Serves nightly until 10:30 PM.

New Riverside Cafe, Riverside at Cedar, Minneapolis (612/333-4814). Cafeteria-style service and prices belie the quality and flavor of the food dished up in this employee-owned vegetarian place. Great desserts, and nice gallery-like setting. Open daily except Sunday (brunch only) to 11 PM or later.

Mickey's Dining Car, 36 7th Street opposite the bus station, downtown St. Paul (612/222-5633). Haute cuisine it ain't, and half the regulars treat it as a social service agency, but this 1937 O'Mahoney is a fine example of what has become an endangered species since the proliferation of golden arches. Try the mulligan stew, if you dare. Open 24 hours.

Information

The Greater Minneapolis Convention and Visitors Association (612/661-4700) can provide information on hotels, restaurants, public transit, and attractions; write 4000 Multifoods Tower, 33 S. 6th Street, Minneapolis, MN 55402, or visit their **information center** in the Skyway at Minneapolis City Center, 40 S. 7th Street. Both the *Minneapolis Star Tribune* (the largest circulation daily newspaper) and *City Pages* (one of two local free weeklies) provide entertainment listings.

Guides to the Skyway, downtown Minneapolis's seemingly infinite indoor mall, are in every copy of *Skyway News,* free for the taking at each entrance. ATMs, mailboxes, and phone booths have all generally migrated off the city streets and into this four-mile-long climate-controlled corridor.

The telephone **area code** for Minneapolis and St. Paul is **612.**

MONTREAL

Located on an island in the St. Lawrence River, Montreal is Canada's second-largest city, with the largest French-speaking population outside La France. Hotbed of the separatist movement, Montreal tolerates the polyglot federalism of Canada, but the accent here is definitely on the "French" in French-Canadian. Cultural identity remains volatile here, but pragmatism rules: Quebecois never lose sight of the importance of tourism to the local economy. You—and your money—will be welcomed everywhere. (Note: All prices listed below are in Canadian dollars.)

Arrival and Getting Around

Two international airports serve Montreal. The closer, **Dorval**, lies 22 km (13 miles) west of downtown and is used for domestic and U.S. flights. International flights land at **Mirabel**, 55 km (33 miles) north of town on Hwy-15.

From the U.S., the main highway routes are 20, 15, and 10, respectively entering from the west, south, and east. The main bus station is the **Terminus Voyageur** atop the Berri-UQAM Metro station, while inter-city trains arrive at the **Gare Centrale** under the Queen Elizabeth Hotel on Belmont between University and Mansfield.

The **Metro**'s orange and green lines connect downtown with most tourist destinations. Metro fares vary depending on length of trip; you can also buy multitrip tickets. City bus service is ubiquitous. Taxis are moderately priced compared to those in major U.S. cities.

Note that most street addresses are in French; we've written them in English.

Where to Go

Mount Royal Park (daily sunrise-sunset; 514/872-1415). The city takes its name from this 700-foot-high hill, now a tree-covered park just north of downtown. Planned by Frederick Law Olmsted and opened in 1876, the park offers roads, stairs, and paths leading to a belvedere, from which you have a sweeping view of the city and the St. Lawrence River.

Basilique Notre-Dame, Place d'Armes (daily 7 AM-6 PM, till 8 PM in summer). The twin towers of this neo-gothic church, completed in 1870, are the prime landmarks of Montreal's modern skyline. The sumptuous interior, which seats 3,800, is closer in spirit to Victorian-era theaters than to the gothic cathedrals on which it is modeled. The organ is one of the largest in North America.

Place Jacques Cartier: Just off the riverfront, this two-block, cobblestoned square is the heart of Old Montreal. The surrounding buildings are mainly 19th century—the mansard-roofed Hotel de Ville (circa 1878) at the top of the hill is Montreal's city hall—but a number of earlier structures still stand nearby. In the summer the square is transformed into an open-air market, but you can sample area restaurants year-round.

Where to Stay

Chateau Versailles, 1659 Sherbrooke Street W (514/933-3611). Four Victorian townhouses have been converted into one charming hotel filled with antiques. Doubles $99.

Queen Elizabeth Hotel, 900 Rene Levesque Boulevard W (514/861-3511). This battleship-shaped structure in the heart of the downtown features comfortable rooms for moderate rates, an excellent restaurant (the Beaver Club), and a location right on top of the train station. Doubles are $109.

YMCA, 1450 Stanley Street (514/849-8393). This modern Y is centrally located downtown right next to the Peel Metro stop. Doubles are $37.

Where to Eat

Les Halles, 2105 rue de la Montagne (514/842-2482). The grande dame of Montreal restaurants, Les Halles was recently renovated. Expect less stuffy decor and cuisine a little more nouvelle.

Milos, 5357 Park Avenue (514/272-3522). This excellent Greek seafood restaurant imports absolutely fresh fish from around the world grilled before your eyes and served with a squeeze of fresh lemon.

Information

Before you arrive, contact the **Greater Montreal Convention and Tourism Bureau** at 1555 Peel Street, Suite 600, Montreal, PQ, Canada H3A 1X6 (514/873-2015 or 800/363-7777). If you are already in the city, the main tourism offices are the **Centres Infotouristes** at 1001 Dorchester between Peel and Metcalfe and at the Place Jacques-Cartier, 174 Notre Dame Street E. The English-language daily is the *Montreal Gazette.* Two good free weeklies, particularly the alternative-minded *Mirror,* feature entertainment listings and current events.

The telephone **area code** for Montreal is **514.**

NEW ORLEANS

World-famous party town—with great music, great food, and all-night bars (unique for America, you can drink on the streets here)—New Orleans really needs no introduction. With deep roots going back to the earliest days of European settlement in North America, New Orleans is proud of its multicultural heritage. Its people, its buildings, and especially its food reflect a uniquely diverse and tolerant culture; after New Orleans, anywhere else in the country can suddenly seem deeply WASPish and puritanical.

Arrival and Getting Around

New Orleans International Airport is in Kenner, a dozen miles northwest of town via US-61 or I-10. **Airport Shuttle** buses (504/465-9780) run into town for about $10; taxis cost twice that much. Greyhound and Amtrak both arrive in dodgy-after-dark downtown areas.

By road, the I-10 freeway loops south around Lake Ponchartrain through the heart of New Orleans, absorbing north-south traffic off I-55. To reach the French Quarter, follow I-10 and get off between exits 234 and 236; park the car (lots charge $5-8 a day) and stroll.

The famous "Streetcar named Desire" is now on display in the courtyard of the old U.S. Mint in the French Quarter, but the rattling St. Charles Avenue streetcars still trundle around the clock to the Garden District ($1 each way). Historic red-and-gold trolleys carry tourists along a two-mile riverfront route from the French Market ($1.25 each way).

New Orleans is an ideal walker's town, with picturesque buildings lining narrow alleys and side streets. If you tend to get lost, remember that traditional directions (north, south, east, west) are usually replaced by lakeside, riverside, downriver, and upriver, respectively.

Where to Go

French Quarter: Centered upon Bourbon Street, now lined with tacky souvenir stalls and strip clubs, this square mile brims with wrought-iron balconies on picturesque brick buildings.

Walking tours of the French Quarter leave from Jackson Square.

U.S. Mint, 400 Esplanade (Tues.-Sun. 10 AM-5 PM; $3). The mint holds excellent collections tracing the history of two New Orleans institutions: jazz music and Mardi Gras.

Preservation Hall: For redolent ambience and live traditional Dixieland jazz, drop by 726 St. Peter Street (nightly from 8 PM; $3; 504/522-2841).

Garden District: Ride the St. Charles Avenue streetcar west to the city's oldest suburb, where antebellum mansions and gnarled oak trees fill the blocks along St. Charles. Along the Mississippi River at the west edge of the Garden District lies **Audubon Park,** which now holds a large zoo (daily 9 AM-5 PM; $8) and the campus of Tulane University.

St. Louis Cemetery Number 1, 400 Basin Street at St. Louis Street. This is the final resting place of voodoo priestess Marie Lavaeu. The small cemetery is also the perfect place to picnic with an Anne Rice novel. Don't go alone—muggers are even more of a threat than vampires.

Where to Stay

YMCA, 920 St. Charles Avenue (504/568-9622). Private rooms with shared bathrooms, plus use of pool and gym. Men, women, and couples welcome. Doubles are $40.

Dauphine Orleans Hotel, 415 Dauphine Street (504/586-1800 or 800/521-7111). Medium-sized modern hotel just a block off Bourbon Street at the heart of the French Quarter, with pool, free newspapers, and continental breakfast. Doubles range $75-175.

Where to Eat

Antone's, 713 St. Louis Street (504/581-4422). One of the world's oldest, Antone's serves classic French-Creole cuisine to a who's who of New Orleans society. Expensive, formal, and popular—come for a late lunch or prepare to wait for a table. Great wine list.

K-Paul's Louisiana Kitchen, 416 Chartres Street (504/524-7394). Chef Paul Prudhomme popularized Cajun-style "blackened" food all over the country, but saves the very best examples for his own very popular French Quarter place.

Information

Drop by the **New Orleans Metropolitan Convention and Visitors Bureau** at 1520 Sugar Bowl Drive (504/566-5011), or in the French Quarter at 529 St. Ann Street (504/566-5031). The main daily paper is the *Times-Picayune*, with a Friday tabloid listing entertainment and events.

The telephone **area code** for New Orleans is **504**.

NEW YORK CITY

New York City is either the Big Apple or the Great Satan. Some people avoid it like the plague, denying themselves the incredible variety of food and culture; others can't bear to leave the glorious buzzing mosaic that makes New York unique in the world. Love it or hate it, New York *is* New York, and this great metropolis is undeniably the capital of the capitalist world, with the best museums, the best shops, the best sights, and the best restaurants in the world.

Arrival and Getting Around

There are three major airports in the area, LaGuardia and John F. Kennedy in Queens, and Newark across the Hudson in New Jersey. Amtrak and local New Jersey trains arrive at Penn Station (7th Avenue and 32nd Street), while the local Connecticut and New York State lines terminate at Grand Central Station (Park Avenue and 42nd Street). Intercity buses depart from the Port Authority terminal at 8th Avenue and 41st Street.

By road, the main routes are I-95 entering from the southwest and northeast, and I-87, the New York State Thruway, from the north. From the west, you can also reach the city on I-80 and I-78. The island of Manhattan is connected to the mainland by toll bridges and tunnels, including the Triborough Bridge to New England and the George Washington Bridge and Lincoln and Holland Tunnels to New Jersey.

If you want to see the city but would rather not deal with its traffic, hassles, and high hotel rates, see our "To See, or Not To See, New York City" feature on pages 262-263.

Where to Go

The Statue of Liberty/Ellis Island: Rising 22 stories from an island in New York Harbor, the Statue of Liberty is probably the most famous sculpture in the United States. Its sculptor, Frederic Bartholdi, conceived of it as a gift to the republic by the admiring French people. The statue's original theme was "Liberty Enlightening the World," but it later came to represent America's welcome to new immigrants, a perspective that sadly seems to have dwindled in recent years. Just to the north of Liberty Island lies Ellis Island, site of the United States Immigration Station, renovated as the **Immigration Museum**, that processed over 12 million immigrants in the early decades of this century.

The Empire State Building: King Kong climbed this quintessential New York building (which was completed in 1931), and so can you. High-speed elevators whiz you to the 102nd-floor observation deck (open 9:30 AM-11:30 PM) where, 1,250 feet above the street, you can see 80 miles on a clear day.

Where to Stay

Carlton Arms Hotel, 160 E. 25th Street (212/679-0680). In the early 1980s, a squad of cutting-edge artists, including Keith Haring, were given carte blanche to redecorate the rooms of this inexpensive hotel. You will not be bored. Doubles cost $69.

Washington Square Hotel, 103 Waverly Place (212/777-9515). Tweedy bohemians like this small hotel right off the fabled square at Greenwich Village's heart. Doubles are $110.

Where to Eat

Japonica, 100 University Place (212/243-7752). Sushi fever swept over New York about 15 years ago and never left. This Greenwich Village favorite is known for its inventive and scrupulously fresh sushi. Reservations suggested.

Ratner's, 138 Delancey Street (212/677-5588). A couple of years ago, Ratner's huge interior was destroyed in a fire. Somewhere they found the same tacky chandeliers and marbled mirrors—it looks unchanged. Ever-suffering waiters serve excellent dairy food with a thick slice of old-time Jewish Lower East Side atmosphere.

Information

The **New York Convention and Visitors Bureau** (212/397-8222) will overwhelm you with suggestions. There are also tourist information booths at Grand Central Station and on 42nd Street between 7th and 8th Avenues. The *New York Times* is the newspaper of record, but the *Daily News,* followed by *Newsday* and the *New York Post,* generally have better local coverage. In addition to the *Village Voice, New York Magazine* and *The New Yorker* magazines, try some of the free weeklies, such as the *New York Press,* for listings of events.

The telephone **area code** for Manhattan is **212.** The Outer Boroughs (Brooklyn, Queens, the Bronx) are in the **718** area code, but are still a local call from Manhattan.

OTTAWA

Canada's capital, Ottawa (pop. 307,000) is one of the most peaceable and pleasant of the world's great cities. Even though winters are freezing cold, tourism is now the city's number two industry, and there are enough excellent museums, parks, and other sights to comfortably fill a couple of days or more. Along with Francophone Hull across the river, Ottawa offers a wide variety of restaurants and cuisines; allow yourself time to savor them, because between here and Seattle our route crosses a vast culinary wasteland. (Note: All prices listed below are in Canadian dollars.)

Arrival and Getting Around
Ottawa's airport is 20 minutes south of the city, but handles very few flights; shuttles from there into town cost $10, $15 roundtrip. The major east-west access is via Hwy-17, the Trans-Canada Highway, described in our US-2 "Great Northern" trek; within town, this becomes the Hwy-417 freeway. From the south, Hwy-31 links up with Hwy-401, the interstate freeway along the north shore of Lake Ontario.

Getting around Ottawa is easy, since most of the sights are gathered around Parliament Hill, which holds the most prominent buildings. Outlying areas are well served by buses operated by OC Transpo (613/741-4390), which has a high-tech info system at every stop. Fares are $1.60 in exact change.

Where to Go
National Gallery of Canada, 380 Sussex Drive (daily 10 AM-6 PM, May-Oct.; Wed.-Sun. 10 AM-5 PM, Oct.-April; free; 613/990-1985). Spend some time at this imposing, glass-walled museum, which contains large European (Rembrandt to the post-impressionists) and American collections, as well as the world's most extensive display of Canadian art.

Next door, in the former National Archives building, "Hitler's Car" and mock-ups of WW I trenches are the popular centerpieces of the **Canadian War Museum** (daily 9:30 AM-5 PM, closed Monday in winter; $2.50; 613/776-8600).

Byward Market, north of Rideau Street between York and George Streets. An open-air relic dating from the 1830s, the market features dozens of fruit, vegetable, and meat vendors as well as a few gift stores for tourists. The blocks just to the north of the market are lined with inexpensive bars, cafes, and ethnic restaurants attracting crowds on weekend evenings.

Where to Stay

Albert House, 478 Albert Street (613/236-4479). Large mansion converted into one of Ottawa's nicest B&B inns. Doubles from $65. If they're full, you can call the **Ottawa Bed and Breakfast Association** (613/663-0161) for a referral.

Holiday Inn-Market Square, 350 Dalhousie Street (613/241-1000). One of Ottawa's better values, located right next to bustling Byward Market. Doubles from $95.

Ottawa International Hostel, 75 Nicholas Street (613/235-2595). Reason enough to stay overnight in Ottawa: this well-run hostel is housed in the old jail, and guests sleep in bunks in the cells—the solitary confinement cells are now the laundry. Very central, 10 minutes' walk from Parliament Hill. Beds $19 a night, $15 for HI/AYH members.

Radisson Hotel Ottawa Centre, 100 Kent Street (613/238-1122 or 800/333-3333). In the heart of downtown, catering to business and political interests—with Ottawa's only revolving rooftop restaurant, "LaRonde." Doubles from $90.

Where to Eat

Blue Cactus Bar and Grill, 2 Byward Market (613/241-7061). One of many good restaurants in the historic Byward Market, featuring Tex-Mex food in a cheery setting.

Cafe Henry Burger, 69 Rue Laurier (819/777-5646). One of many fine French restaurants across the river in Hull, Quebec, this stylish haunt is across the street from the Canadian Museum of Civilization. Unusually for French places, this one offers an extensive vegetarian menu.

Information

Visitor information is available from the **Ottawa Convention Authority**, 111 Lisgar Street (613/237-5150), who publish a handy free guide to the city. Also try the **Ontario Ministry of Tourism** (800/905-2746), and the **Canadian Automobile Association-Ottawa**, 2525 Carling Avenue (613/820-1890).

Daily newspapers include the *Citizen*, and *Sun*, and Francophone *Le Droit*.

The telephone **area code** for Ottawa is **613**; for Hull it is **819**.

PHOENIX

The million-plus people who have settled in the "Valley of the Sun" in and
around this capital city have nearly
succeeded in obliterating any sense
that the land here ever was, and still is,
a desert. Golf courses, swimming
pools, lakes, and waterfalls are everywhere, with only a few carefully
coiffed cacti remaining to testify to the
natural state of things.

Phoenix really is a sprawling mess,
expanding by many acres every day, but there is something oddly charming about
the place—an anything-goes, Wild West spirit manifest in the city's ongoing ability
to grow and thrive despite the lack of natural advantages.

Arrival and Getting Around

Phoenix sits at the junction of the I-10 freeway and I-17 from Flagstaff and the
Grand Canyon, with other local freeways, the "Hwy-202 Loop," Hwy-51, and the
US-60 "Superstition Freeway," completing the high-speed overlay. Note that
Phoenix proper is surrounded by a half-dozen legally independent communities—
Scottsdale, Mesa, Tempe—differentiated only by the design of their street signs.

Phoenix's busy **Sky Harbor International Airport** is about a mile southeast of
downtown, with all the usual shuttle services and car rental companies.

Though there is a skeletal bus service, trying to get around town without a car is
hazardous to your health. In a word, *drive*.

Where to Go

Heard Museum, 22 E. Monte Vista Road (Mon.-Sat. 9:30 AM-5 PM, Wednesday till 9
PM, Sunday noon-5 PM; $5, free Wednesday evenings; 602/252-8840). Explore this
marvelous museum devoted to the native cultures of the Southwestern United
States. The permanent galleries trace the history and diversity of prehistoric peoples
and contemporary tribes. Don't miss the amazing collection of Hopi kachina dolls.

Taliesin West, 108th Street at the east end of Cactus Road (daily 9 AM-4 PM; $10;
602/860-2700). Frank Lloyd Wright lived, worked, and taught here in the Arizona
desert, handcrafting the complex of studios, theaters, and living quarters that survives as an architecture school. The guided tours will tell you all you want to know
about the architect and his grand plans.

Hall of Flame, 6101 E. Van Buren Street (Mon.-Sat. 9 AM-5 PM, Sunday noon-4
PM; $4; 602/275-3473). It's altogether appropriate that a city named for mythologi-
cal rebirth from the ashes should be home to this museum, which displays one of
the world's largest collections of fire-fighting equipment in air-conditioned industrial sheds in Papago Park.

Mystery Castle, E. Mineral Road (Tues.-Sun. 11 AM-4 PM; $3; 602/268-1581). A populist parallel to Frank Lloyd Wright's high-style Taliesin West, this "Watts Towers of the Desert" was built out of rubble and scrap material by Boyce Gulley, whose daughter Mary Lou gives brief tours of the ramshackle mansion, telling the tale of its construction. Take 7th Street seven miles south till it dead-ends at South Mountain Park, then follow signs east.

Where to Stay

Biltmore Hotel, 24th and Missouri Streets (602/955-6600 or 800/528-3696). Beautiful resort tucked away on spacious grounds on the far north side of Phoenix. Stop by for a look if you can't manage the $200-a-night rates.

San Carlos Travelodge Hotel, 202 N. Central Avenue (602/253-4121 or 800/528-5446). Well-maintained older hotel in the heart of downtown. Rooms cost $40-60.

Lost Dutchman State Park, off Hwy-88 east of town (602/982-4485). Simple campsites, with showers, in the foothills of the lovely Superstition Mountains. Sites are $8.

Where to Eat

El Bravo, 8338 N. 7th Street (602/943-9753). Nondescript but excellent little hole-in-the-wall Mexican place, with some of the city's best food.

Majerle's, 24 N. 2nd Street (602/253-9004). Popular sports-oriented bar-and-grill, across from Phoenix Suns' home court and owned by hot-shot player Dan Majerle.

Information

The Phoenix area **visitors bureau** puts out the usual range of practical information for travelers; the office is downtown at 400 E. Van Buren Street (602/254-6500). The main newspaper is the *Arizona Republic.* Check the free weekly *New Times* for alternative coverage of current issues.

The telephone **area code** for Phoenix is **602.**

PORTLAND

Oregon's largest city with 450,000 residents (1.5 million in the metro area), Portland lies 110 miles inland from the Pacific Ocean on the Columbia River. Due to its strategic location, the pioneer municipality grew so fast it was nicknamed Stumptown for the hundreds of fir stumps left by early loggers. Portland's riverfront park and numerous winding greenways attest to the fact that this minimetropolis is not a smokestack town but a community that values art and nature as highly as commerce. Along with the largest (5,000-acre Forest Park) and the smallest (24 inches-in-diameter Mill Ends Park) urban parks in the nation, Portland holds more movie theaters, restaurants, microbreweries and bookstores per capita than any other U.S. city.

Arrival and Getting Around
Portland is served by **Portland International Airport** (PDX), a recently completed Greyhound bus station north of downtown at 550 N.W. 6th Avenue, and a nearby Amtrak station at 800 N.W. 6th Avenue. The main highways passing through Portland are north-south I-5 and, from the east through the Columbia Gorge, I-84.

Getting around Portland and the surrounding three-county metro area is a breeze thanks to efficient and timely Tri-Met buses and a light rail called MAX, which circle the downtown area around Pioneer Courthouse Square. There's no charge for rides within the "fareless square," which covers much of downtown; for further information, call 503/238-RIDE.

Where to Go
South Park Blocks: The shady 25-block area is southeast of downtown, between Park and Ninth Avenues. Trees, statues, and street furniture line the series of small parks bounded by two of Portland's prime museums: the Portland Art Museum, 1219 S.W. Park Avenue ($5), which displays both European paintings and Northwest Indian artifacts; and the Oregon Historical Society at 1200 S.W. Park Avenue ($4).

Powell's Books, 1005 W. Burnside Street (503/228-4651). One of Portland's most famous haunts, located at 10th Avenue and Burnside Street across from the Blitz Weinhard Brewery, Powell's is reportedly the largest (and certainly among the best) new-and-used book shop in the world. Powell's also rents out worthwhile audiotape tours of downtown, and operates a very good travel store at 6th and Yamhill, on Pioneer Courthouse Square.

Where to Stay
Clinkerbrick House, 2311 N.E. Schuyler Street (503/281-2533). Nicely decorated turn-of-the-century house in residential East Portland, offering B&B rooms for around $75 a night.

Portland International Youth Hostel, 3031 S.E. Hawthorne Boulevard (503/236-3380). This big old bungalow is comfortable, clean, and close to East Portland's "Hip Strip" of cafes, bars, and restaurants. At just $11 a night, it's best to make reservations during the busy summer season.

Where to Eat
Esparza's Tex-Mex, 2725 S.E. Ankeny Street (503/234-7909). Hidden away behind a hole-in-the-wall facade off Burnside Street, this hot spot is famous for its corn-meal pancakes with chicken and cactus sauce, smoked pork tacos, and other authentic Tex-Mex dishes.

Jake's Famous Crawfish, 401 S.W. 12th Street (503/226-1419). For nearly a century Jake's has been the place to go in Portland for the finest, freshest seafood. Warm woodsy decor, a marvelous wine list, and great desserts make this a Road Trip standout.

Ringside, 2165 W. Burnside Street (503/255-0750). The Ringside is famous for its great steaks, monster onion rings, and Hemingwayesque ambience—hunting trophies and boxing photos adorn the walls, and many diners choose to eat at the glaring red bar.

Information
The best source of visitor information on Portland is the **Portland Visitors Association,** 26 S.W. Salmon Street (503/222-2223 or 800/962-3700). Free maps are available at Powell's Travel Books on Pioneer Courthouse Square, which also stocks the best range of local guidebooks. The daily newspaper is *The Oregonian*, which operates the Inside Line (503/225-5555), a free 24-hour news and information service. The free *Willamette Week* has the best take on entertainment and current local political issues. A local events hotline (503/233-4444) supplements the media sources listed above.

The telephone **area code** for metropolitan Portland is **503**.

ST. LOUIS

Founded by French fur trappers in 1764, during the following century St. Louis served as a prosperous outpost of "civilization" at the frontier. The city was the starting point for the Lewis and Clark expedition. Much later, Charles Lindbergh, in his *Spirit of St. Louis,* was the first man to fly across the Atlantic.

St. Louis is at heart a city of small neighborhoods such as blues-oriented Soulard south of downtown, or the collegiate West End district near Forest Park. But all are united in mutual appreciation of the city's flagship product, Budweiser.

Arrival and Getting Around

St. Louis sits amid a fat web of major interstates (I-55, I-70, I-64, I-44), federal highways (US-40, US-50, US-61, US-67), and the **Great River Road.** You'll find plenty of parking downtown.

Nine major airlines serve **Lambert-St. Louis International Airport,** 14 miles west of downtown. A light-rail system ($1) connects the main terminal to downtown, as do numerous shuttles ($8), taxis ($18-20), and car rental facilities. **Amtrak** connects the city to points east and west from a small station near downtown.

Cab fares run high. Within the confines of a narrow corridor from the airport to the Illinois waterfront, the light-rail **MetroLink** (314/231-2345) is an excellent way to hit the major tourist attractions; travel downtown on weekday afternoons is free, and one- and three-day passes are available from vending machines.

Where to Go

Gateway Arch, on the riverfront at the foot of Market Street (daily 9 AM-6 PM, longer hours in summer; 314/982-1410). Rising from the west bank of the Mississippi River, Eero Saarinen's 630-foot stainless steel monument still dominates the city skyline. Under the legs of the Arch, officially called the Jefferson National Expansion Memorial, the **Museum of Westward Expansion** chronicles the human wave that swept west; a small **tram** ($5) carries visitors to an observation chamber at the top of the arch.

Anheuser-Busch Brewery, 1127 Pestalozzi Street (Mon.-Sat. 9 AM-4 PM; free; 314/577-2626). The world's largest brewery, and home of those famous Clydesdales, is open for free tours every day but Sunday.

Soulard (soo-LARD) spreads north of the brewery, a pocket of red-brick rowhouses with a thriving outdoor market at its north end and a concentration of good blues clubs around Geyer Avenue in its center.

Scott Joplin House, 2658 Delmar Boulevard west of Jefferson (Mon.-Sat. 10 AM-4 PM, Sunday noon-5 PM; free, tours $2; 314/533-1003). You don't have to be a rag-time fan to appreciate this isolated survivor of old St. Louis, which served as Joplin's home for three years at the turn of the century, when the composer was at the height of his career. Tour includes a player piano recital, some of the piano rolls created by Joplin himself.

Where to Stay
Days Inn at the Arch, 333 Washington Avenue (314/621-7900 or 800/325-2525). Least expensive downtown motel; doubles are $50-90.

Huckleberry Finn Youth Hostel, 1904-08 S. 12th Street at Tucker (314/241-0076). This edge of Soulard isn't attractive yet, but it's safe enough and convenient to food, nightlife, and downtown. Rate is $12 a person; inquire about private rooms.

Where to Eat
Ted Drewes Frozen Custard, 6726 Chippewa Street (314/481-2652). A city insti-tution, right on old Route 66 in South St. Louis. Sample Ted's "concrete," a frozen dairy-and-egg concoction so thick you can turn it upside down and not lose a drop. Closed for the winter Dec.-March.

McDonald's: "The Only Floating McDonald's in the World," styled like a Missis-sippi riverboat and moored just south of the Gateway Arch. Put aside any anti-fran-chise sentiments and soak up the kitsch.

Information
The **St. Louis Convention and Visitors Commission** (314/421-1023 or 800/247-9791) operates a well-stocked information center downtown at the foot of Wash-ington Avenue beside I-70. The city's daily newspaper, the *Post-Dispatch,* features entertainment and events ideas, while the free alternative weekly, *The Riverfront Times,* includes the most comprehensive club and event listings.

The telephone **area code** for all St. Louis is 314.

SAN DIEGO

Set along a huge Pacific Ocean harbor at the south-western corner of the country, just a few miles from the Mexican border, San Diego embodies the Southern California ideal. The city's economy has long been based around the U.S. Navy, and until the 1960s, extensive tuna-fishing fleets filled the rest of the busy harbor, which more recently hosted the America's Cup yachting races.

Despite a metropolitan population of 2.5 million people, San Diego still feels very small and anything but urban. For visitors and residents alike, the city's main attractions are its usually sunny climate and miles of clean and uncrowded beaches.

Arrival and Getting Around
The city of San Diego bends diagonally around its natural harbor, which makes orientation occasionally confusing. The main **airport**, Lindbergh Field, is on the waterfront, while Amtrak **trains** and Greyhound **buses** arrive downtown on Broadway. By road, the I-5 freeway runs directly through downtown San Diego, between Mission Bay and the Mexican border, while the I-8 freeway comes in from the east via Mission Valley.

Downtown is walkable, and with a bike you could see most everything in a day. Or take advantage of San Diego Transit buses ($5 day-use pass; 619/234-1060), which fan out from downtown.

Where to Go
Cabrillo National Monument (daily 9 AM-5 PM, longer hours in summer; $4 per car; 619/557-5450) is a memorial to the exploits of Juan Cabrillo, who discovered the bay at Point Loma in 1542. Trails run past fortifications, a lighthouse, and tide-pools, offering unforgettable views.

La Jolla: The name, which translates roughly as "The Jewel," is appropriate to this coastal, upscale neighborhood near U.C. San Diego. The recently renovated Museum of Contemporary Art (619/454-3541) overlooks the ocean at 700 Prospect Avenue. Enjoy surfing, beachcombing, and skin diving, not to mention tons of good cafes, restaurants, and galleries.

Balboa Park: This lushly landscaped 1,150-acre spread on downtown's northwest edge was laid out as part of the 1915 International Exposition celebrating the completion of the Panama Canal. The gorgeous, Spanish-revival-style buildings have been preserved in marvelous condition, and now house sundry museums. A passport ($18), available from the **visitor center** (619/239-0512), allows entrance to any eight of the park's dozen museums.

Balboa Park is also home of the **San Diego Zoo** (daily 9 AM-4 PM; $15; 619/234-3153), one of the largest and most popular zoos in the world.

Tijuana, Baja California: Head "south of the border" for a taste of another culture—one that's surprisingly not all that foreign. Take the "Tijuana Trolley" from downtown ($2), or park in one of the $8-a-day lots along the border and walk.

Where to Stay

Armed Services YMCA, 500 W. Broadway (619/232-1133). Not just for military personnel, with dorm beds at $14 a night.

Hotel Del Coronado, 1500 Orange Avenue (619/522-8000). This fabulously grand Victorian-era resort hotel still caters to the four-star trade with rooms from $150.

Old Town Travelodge, 2380 Moore Street (619/291-9100). Reliably comfortable and clean motel in the middle of the Old Town district. Swimming pool, and doubles from around $40.

Where to Eat

Hamburger Mary's, 308 University (619/491-0400). Like other branches of the San Francisco-based chain, this is a lively, often wild bar and restaurant serving burgers, pastas, and grilled meat to a gay and lesbian-friendly clientele.

Hob Nob Hill, 2271 1st Avenue (619/239-8176). Classic old coffee shop with a menu (and a clientele) that's hardly changed for two generations. Great for breakfast—the pecan waffles are worth driving all night for—as well as home-style lunch and dinner daily.

The Spot, 1005 Prospect Avenue, La Jolla (619/459-0800). Longtime locals' favorite, two blocks from La Jolla cove, serving hefty portions of burgers, barbecue ribs and chicken, and pizzas.

Information

The best variety of information is available from the **San Diego International Visitors Center,** 11 Horton Plaza (619/236-1212), downtown at 1st and F Streets. The main daily paper is the *San Diego Union-Tribune.*

The telephone **area code** for San Diego is **619.**

SAN FRANCISCO

San Francisco is easily the most enjoyable city in the United States. Its undulating topography turns every other corner into a scenic vista, while its many engaging neighborhoods are perfect for aimless wandering. Check out the exotic shops of Chinatown, the corridors of power of the Financial District, the Italian cafes of North Beach, the hippie holdouts of Haight-Ashbury, or the brilliant murals of the latino Mission District. Museums document everything from gold rush history to cutting edge modern art, while a stellar collection of restaurants offers the chance to sample gourmet food from around the world—all in an easily manageable, densely compact small city.

Arrival and Getting Around
The main routes into San Francisco by road are **US-101**, which runs from San Jose in the south and across the Golden Gate Bridge from the north, and **I-80**, which heads in from the east via the Bay Bridge. **San Francisco International Airport** (SFO) lies 15 miles south of the city, and handles the great majority of domestic and almost all international flights.

San Francisco is one of the few American cities, at least on the West Coast, where you really don't need a car, since distances are short and public transportation quite extensive; the gridded street plan makes it easy to find your way around. San Francisco public transit is operated by the S.F. Municipal Railway ("Muni"; 415/673-6864), whose buses, trams, and cable cars will take you all over the city.

Where to Go
Hyde Street Pier. Most of San Francisco's northern waterfront is consumed by the tacky tourist traps of Fisherman's Wharf, apart from the western end at the foot of Hyde Street, where a half-dozen historic ships are moored as part of the San Francisco National Maritime Historic Park. Cable cars drop down from Russian Hill, a nice pedestrian promenade runs along the waterfront west to the military relics and dynamic arts complex at Fort Mason, and Ghirardelli Square is just a block away.

Golden Gate Park. One of the country's finest parks, Golden Gate Park stretches for over three miles across the city's midsection, from Haight-Ashbury to the Pacific Ocean. Reclaimed from the natural sand dunes that covered the area until the 1890s, the park is mostly open green space, with the exception of its eastern end, where you'll find the **M.H. de Young Memorial Museum** (415/750-3600), one of the city's major visual arts venues; and the **Asian Art Museum** (415/668-8921), which displays Asian masterpieces from China, Japan, India, Nepal, Tibet, Korea, Iran, and other Eastern cultures.

Adjacent to the Asian Art Museum is the lovely **Japanese Tea Garden** (415/558-4268), and across the music concourse stands the **California Academy of Sciences** (415/221-5100), the city's natural history museum.

Where to Stay

Holiday Lodge, 1901 Van Ness Avenue (415/776-4469 or 800/367-8504). Classic 1950s motel at the far end of the California Street cable car line. Doubles are $85.

San Francisco International Youth Hostel, Building 240, Fort Mason (415/771-7277). Bunk beds in unbeatable bay-view locale. Free parking; beds $14 per person.

San Remo Hotel, 2337 Mason Street (415/776-8688). Friendly, family-owned hotel between North Beach and Fisherman's Wharf. Shared bath; doubles $60.

Where to Eat

Cha Cha Cha, 1801 Haight Street (415/386-5758). Escape the Haight-Ashbury hippie scene at this reasonably priced cafe, serving excellent tapas and Caribbean delicacies.

Zuni Cafe, 1658 Market Street (415/552-2522). Great food—salads, pizzas, and a roast chicken so good it's been featured on NPR's *All Things Considered*—served in stylish Civic Center hangout. Open early till late (midnight most nights), with a great oyster bar, too.

Information

The **San Francisco Convention and Visitors Bureau** publishes a good free street map and offers extensive listings of attractions, accommodations, and restaurants. Contact them in advance at 201 3rd Street, Suite 900, San Francisco, CA 94103; or stop by the **visitor center** (415/974-6900) at Hallidie Plaza, next to the Muni station and cable car turntable at Powell and Market Streets downtown. San Francisco's daily newspapers, the morning *Chronicle* and the afternoon *Examiner,* both run events listings. Pick up free papers, like the *Bay Guardian* and the *SF Weekly,* at cafes and bookstores throughout the Bay Area.

The telephone **area code** for San Francisco is **415**.

SAVANNAH

Founded in 1733 as the first settlement in Georgia, Savannah today preserves its original neoclassical,
colonial, and antebellum self in a welcoming, unselfconscious way. Before
and after the Civil War, Savannah was
Georgia's main port, but as commercial
shipping tailed off, the harbor became
primarily recreational—the 1996
Olympic yachting competitions will
race offshore. Savannah has resisted

turning itself into an "Old South" theme park and, Olympics aside, you'll have to
search hard to find souvenir shops, overpriced knickknack galleries, or snooty
boutiques.

Arrival and Getting Around
Savannah's main airport, a dozen miles west of town, is served by short-hop flights
from Atlanta; many hotels run free shuttles. From Macon, I-16 is the main route
from the west, while I-95 races past, 20 miles west of downtown, on its high-speed
jaunt up and down the eastern seaboard. East from Savannah, US-80 runs to the
coast at Tybee Island, completing its 3,000-mile "Southern Pacific" road trip (see
page580 for more).

Getting around is blissfully easy, as Savannah is the country's preeminent walker's town, with cobblestone lanes, a wealth of architecture, and a checkerboard of
small squares packed within a mile-square center.

Where to Go
Factor's Walk: This promontory along the Savannah River holds the Cotton Exchange and other historic buildings. River Street, linked from the top of the bluffs
by a network of stone stairways and cast-iron walkways, is lined with restaurants
and nightclubs. At the east end of River Street, you'll find the **Ships of the Sea Museum** (daily 10 AM-5 PM; $3).

Historic Savannah: Savannah has over 1,000 registered historic landmarks in its
downtown area. Maps for self-guided walking tours are available from the visitor
center, but don't miss the Owens-Thomas House, 124 Abercorn Street, overlooking
Oglethorpe Square (Tues.-Sat. 10 AM-5 PM, Sunday and Monday 2-5 PM; $5;
912/233-9743), with its fine furniture and lovely garden.

Savannah's 20 main squares are filled with historical plaques and monuments:
Chippewa Square, at the center of town, was the site of Forrest Gump's bus bench;
Reynolds Square, near the waterfront, has a statue of John Wesley, who established
the world's first Sunday School here; and **Forsyth Park**, at the south edge of the
district, is modeled after Paris's Place de la Concorde.

King-Tisdell Cottage, 514 E. Huntingdon Street (Mon.-Fri. noon-4 PM, Saturday and Sunday 1-4:30 PM; $3; 912/234-8000). South of central Savannah in the Victorian district, this well-restored circa 1896 cottage holds a fine museum of African-American culture and history.

Telfair Academy of Arts, 121 Barnard Street on Telfair Square (Tues.-Sat. 10 AM-5 PM, Sunday 2-5 PM; $3; 912/232-1177), is one of the finest galleries in the South.

Where to Eat

Chimney Creek Crab Shack, 10 miles east of Savannah, off US-80 on Estill Hammock Road (912/786-9857). Plates of shrimp and sausage and Key Lime Pie get rave reviews from such dignified aficionados as the *New York Times*.

Johnny Harris, 1651 E. Victory Drive (912/354-7810). On old US-80 on the way to the coast, this is Savannah's oldest restaurant (circa 1942) and one of the fanciest barbecue places in the world.

Mrs. Wilkes Boarding House, 107 W. Jones Street (912/232-5997). For an unforgettable Southern family-style breakfast or lunch, stop at this central Savannah home. Don't leave Savannah without eating here.

Where to Stay

Savannah International Hostel, 304 E. Hall Street (912/236-7744). Spartan accommodations in a turn-of-the-century Victorian home. Dorm beds are $14, private doubles $30.

Bed and Breakfast Inn, 117 W. Gordon Street (912/238-0518). Nice rooms in circa 1853 townhouse off Monterey Square. Doubles are $60-75

Information

Obtain details from the Savannah Convention and Visitors Bureau, 222 W. Oglethorpe Avenue (912/944-0456 or 800/444-2427). Once in town, go to the Savannah Visitors Center, 301 W. Broad Street (Mon.-Fri. 8:30 AM-5 PM; weekends and holidays 9 AM-5 PM; 912/944-0455), in the old Georgia Central railroad terminal just west of the historic center.

The telephone area code for Savannah is 912.

SEATTLE

An engaging combination of scenic beauty, blue-collar grit, and high-tech panache has made Seattle one of the most popular cities in the United States. A young city, historically and demographically, Seattle has managed to preserve much of its heavy industrial heritage while cultivating a strong, high-wage economy: two of America's most colossal companies, Boeing and Microsoft, are based here. Eco-conscious, civic-minded Seattle has also given birth to such diverse phenomena as grunge music, Starbuck's McCoffee chain, and mountain bike-mounted police patrols. Surrounded by the waters of the Puget Sound and numerous lakes, with a backdrop of the snowcapped Cascade and Olympic Mountains, evergreen Seattle can be an entrancing city—at least when the sun comes out.

Arrival and Getting Around
Seattle's main airport is **Seattle-Tacoma International** ("Sea-Tac"), midway between the two cities, a half-hour drive south of downtown Seattle via the I-5 freeway. The usual array of rent-a-car companies operate there, as do **shuttle** services; Amtrak and Greyhound serve the fringes of downtown. By road, the main route from the north and south is the I-5 freeway; from the east, I-90 and US-2 cross the Cascades. Ferryboats run across the Puget Sound from the Olympic Peninsula and western Washington.

Seattle's freeways are usually packed. Fortunately, you can park your car and rely on the city's first-rate public transportation system; **metro buses** operate daily 6 AM-1 AM ($1; 206/447-4800 or 800/542-7876), and a **fare-free zone** covers much of the downtown area.

Where to Go
Pike Place Market: The heart of tourist Seattle, Pike Place Market is a raucous farmers, fish, and crafts market with hundreds of stalls filling a hilly site between downtown and the waterfront. For a respite, head two blocks south to the Robert Venturi-designed **Seattle Art Museum,** 100 University Street (Tues.-Sun 10 AM-5 PM; $6; 206/654-3100), and enjoy the amazing collection of regional Native American art and artifacts on display.

Pioneer Square: At the south edge of downtown, a half-mile from Pike Place Market, this 30-block historic district preserves the city's original core. A small museum (daily 9 AM-5 PM; free) at 117 S. Main Street recounts the Klondike gold rush era, and next door, the endlessly browsable **Elliott Bay Book Company** (206/624-6600) has a good cafe in its basement.

Seattle Center, Broad Street and 5th Avenue N (206/684-7200). Built for the 1962 World's Fair, this 75-acre park is a little bit of Disneyland on the north side of downtown Seattle. Ride a **monorail** (80 cents), take the elevator to the top of the landmark **Space Needle** ($6.50), learn something at the **Pacific Science Center** ($6.50, $8 includes IMAX show), or ride the bumper cars at the summer-only **Fun Forest** (85 cents a ride). Seattle Center also holds the city's opera, symphony, and ballet.

Where to Stay
Alexis Hotel, 1007 1st Avenue (206/624-4844). A high-style hotel in a handy downtown location, midway between Pike Place and Pioneer Square. Doubles are $150.

College Inn, 4000 University Way NE (206/633-4441). Out near the University of Washington, this B&B is popular with youthful and budget-conscious travelers. Doubles are $60-75.

Where to Eat
Chinook's, 1735 W. Thurman Street, at the Fishermen's Terminal (206/283-4665). Located in a huge, modern, warehouse-like space in the home port of Seattle's salmon fishing fleet, this industrial-scale restaurant features an extensive menu of fish, plus burgers and pasta dishes.

The Trolleyman Pub, 3400 Phinney Avenue N, on the Lake Washington Ship Canal (206/548-8000). More than an adjunct to the excellent Red Hook Brewery, this popular pub is a very good restaurant in its own right, with rich soups and hearty pastas that just happen to go well with a pint or two of beer.

Information
Contact the **Seattle-King County Convention and Visitors Bureau**, 520 Pike Street, Suite 1300 (206/461-5840). The *Seattle Weekly* (75 cents) keeps up on entertainment and events.

The telephone **area code** for Seattle is **206**.

TUCSON

Though it's half the size of Phoenix, Tucson is at least twice as nice a place to visit. With more palpable history than anywhere in the Southwest outside New Mexico, a lively university community, and some of the most beautiful deserts anywhere on earth, Tucson is worth taking the time to get to know.

With daytime temperatures averaging over 100°, Tucson is scorching during the summer months (early May to late September), so try to visit during the rest of the year.

Arrival and Getting Around

The main I-10 freeway runs northwest to southeast along usually dry Santa Rita River at the western edge of town. From here, Tucson stretches east for more than 10 miles, and north toward the foothills of the Santa Catalina Mountains. The main east-west route across town is Speedway Boulevard.

Tucson's very small **airport** is south of I-10, eight miles from downtown, with all the usual shuttle and car rental companies. It's all but impossible to get around town without a car, though Gray Line (520/622-8811) and others offer bus trips to popular tourist attractions.

Where to Go

Arizona Sonora Desert Museum (daily 8:30 AM-5 PM, longer hours in summer; $7.95; 520/883-2702). Get a sense of the Sonora Desert's abundant flora and fauna at this creatively presented zoological park. It's 14 miles west of town in Tucson Mountain Park, near the "Old Tucson" movie studio-theme park.

Mission San Xavier del Bac (daily 8 AM-6 PM; donations; 520/294-2624). Among the most memorable of all the Spanish colonial missions in the U.S., this landmark edifice was built more than 200 years ago and still serves the native Tohono O'odham people. See pages 118-119 for more.

Sabino Canyon (daily 8:30 AM-dusk; 520/749-3223). Climbing the foothills of the Santa Catalina Mountains, this popular park offers seasonal waterfalls, a (nearly) year-round creek, and good trails all the way up to the 9,157-foot summit of Mount Lemmon. Sabino Canyon is 17 miles east of town, well signed off Tanque Verde Road.

Davis-Monthan Air Force Base (Monday and Wednesday only, 9 AM; free; 520/750-4570). Check out the rows and rows of surplus military aircraft lined up for what seems like miles. Peek at them from the highway (follow Kolb Avenue north of I-10, on the east side of town) or sign up for one of the popular tours.

Colossal Cave (daily 9 AM-5 PM; $6.50; 520/647-7275). Come summer, this is the coolest place in town: a huge limestone cavern at a refreshingly crisp 50°. It's 20 miles southeast of Tucson near Saguaro National Monument. See page 588 for further details.

Where to Stay

Catalina State Park, 12 miles north of Tucson off US-89 (520/628-5798). Best camping in the Tucson area, on the slopes of the Santa Catalinas. Sites (with showers) cost $8, first-come, first-served.

Congress Hotel, 311 E. Congress Street (520/622-8848 or 800/722-8848). Lively, youth-oriented hotel, hostel, cafe, and nightclub, at the heart of downtown. Dorm beds cost $15, rooms $45.

Arizona Inn, 2200 E. Elm Street (520/325-1541 or 800/933-1093). This classic Arizona resort has changed little since the 1920s, when it was a favorite winter haunt of the Rockefellers and other elites. Rooms are $80-180.

Where to Eat

Big A Restaurant, 2033 E. Speedway Boulevard (520/326-1818). Collegiate burger bar next to the University of Arizona. The place to drink beer and watch sports on TV.

Jack's Original BBQ, 5250 E. 22nd Street (520/750-1280). Zero-atmosphere, bare-bones barbecue place serving great food, including the best beans west of Texas, since 1950.

Janos, 150 N. Main Street (520/884-9426). Possibly the best restaurant in the state, serving delicious (and very expensive) nouvelle cuisine in a landmark adobe home.

Information

Head to the **Metropolitan Tucson Visitors Bureau,** 130 S. Scott Street (520/624-1817 or 800/638-8350), or pick up the morning *Daily Star,* the afternoon *Tucson Citizen,* or the free *Tucson Weekly.*

The telephone **area code** for Tucson is 520.

WASHINGTON, D.C.

Washington, D.C., is an unforgettable experience. The monuments and monoliths that line the city's many grand avenues embody nearly two centuries of American political history, and the city's world-class museums offer everything from ancient art to the first flying machines. Best of all, almost everything is free.

Assuming most visitors will find their way to the White House, the presidential monuments, and the museums along the Mall, this guide focuses on lesser-known sights, ones you rarely have to wait in line to see.

Arrival and Getting Around

Washington National (DCA) is D.C.'s main airport, very near downtown and easily accessible on the Metro subway system. **Dulles** (IAD), out in the western suburbs, handles most international flights. Both airports offer the standard car rental chains and good ground transportation into the city center.

D.C. lies on the busy north-south I-95 corridor, encircled by the I-495 Beltway. US-50, supplemented in the west by I-66, is the main east-west artery.

The city's basic layout is fairly simple. The jagged diamond of D.C. is divided into four quadrants—NE, NW, SE, SW—with the Capitol at the center. East-west streets begin alphabetically from the Mall; north-south running streets are numbered from the Capitol; and diagonal avenues are named for states.

Parking is difficult. The few on-street spaces around the Mall are the only alternative to expensive lots downtown. Avail yourself of the handy Metrorail "Metro" subway (202/637-7000), which serves most of the places you'll want to go. Fares vary depending upon distance; all-day passes cost $5. Metro also runs a network of buses servicing Georgetown, downtown, and the suburbs.

Cab fares are quite low in Washington. Fares are not metered, but charged at a flat rate based on a city zone system. They generally run between $2.60 and $10.20.

Where to Go

The National Museum of American History, on Constitution Avenue between 12th and 14th Streets (daily 10 AM-5:30 PM; free; 202/357-2700), is a huge and endearingly quirky museum displaying a little of everything. Also worth a visit are the **National Museum of American Art** and the **National Portrait Gallery**, which jointly occupy the two-block old Patent Office Building at 8th and G Streets.

The **Frederick Douglass National Historic Site**, 1441 W. Street SE (daily 9 AM-4

PM; free; 202/426-5961) is a simple Victorian house dubbed Cedar Hill, home to the pioneer civil rights activist Frederick Douglass from 1877 until his death in 1895.

At 100 Raoul Wallenberg Place, the **U.S. Holocaust Memorial Museum** (daily 10 AM-5 PM; free; 202/488-0400) offers a sobering, disturbing, unforgettable experience. Three floors of exhibits display photographs, films, and other documentary evidence of the Holocaust, including a boxcar used to transport Jews to concentration camps, and a pile of shoes taken from murdered victims.

Where to Stay

The **Hay Adams Hotel**, 1 LaFayette Square NW (202/638-6600), is a lovely old hotel directly across from the White House. Lushly appointed, with a grand lobby full of expense-account lobbyists. Doubles are $200.

Howard Johnson Lodge, 2601 Virginia Avenue NW (202/965-2700), is a good value, family-oriented hotel located across from the Watergate complex. Rooftop pool, free parking. Doubles are $80.

Washington International AYH Hostel, 1009 11th Street NW (202/737-2333), offers clean, air-conditioned rooms near the Metro Center within walking distance of the White House. Dorm beds cost $15.

Where to Eat

At the **Calvert Cafe**, 1967 Calvert Street NW (202/232-5431), you can slump down in the dark leather booths and enjoy some of D.C.'s best Mediterranean food.

In the **Senate Dining Room**, U.S. Capitol Building (202/224-4870), rub elbows with your elected officials while sampling the famous bean soup. Open to the public Mon.-Fri. 8 AM-9 PM.

Entertainment

When **Congress** is in session, the best show in town is watching your elected officials in action. More traditional entertainment includes the vast array of high-culture offerings at the **Kennedy Center** (202/467-4600) and movies at the **Biograph**, 2819 M Street NW (202/333-2696). Check the *CityPaper* for listings.

Information

A helpful **visitor center** near the White House at 1445 Pennsylvania Avenue (202/789-7000) offers maps and listings. The Committee to Promote D.C. (202/724-4091) provides similar information as well as extensive discount accommodation listings.

D.C.'s daily newspapers are the *Washington Post* and the *Washington Times*; the free weekly *CityPaper* contains entertainment and event listings. For Smithsonian details call the automated information line (202/357-2700).

The telephone **area code** for D.C. is **202**.

ROAD TRIP
RESOURCES

ROAD TRIP RESOURCES

SERVICES

HOTELS AND MOTELS

Best Western 800/528-1234
Budgetel Inns 800/428-3438
Comfort Inns 800/228-5150
Courtyard by Marriott 800/321-2211
Days Inn 800/325-2525
Econo Lodge 800/553-2666
Friendship Inns 800/453-4511
Hilton Hotels 800/445-8667
Howard Johnson Lodges 800/654-2000
Hyatt Hotels 800/233-1234
ITT Sheraton Hotels 800/325-3535
Marriott Hotels & Resorts 800/228-9290
Motel 6 . . . . 800/466-8356
Quality Inns 800/228-5151
Ramada Inns 800/228-2828
Red Lion Inns 800/547-8010
Rodeway Inns International 800/228-2000
Super 8 Motels 800/800-8000
TraveLodge Hotels 800/578-7878

CAR RENTAL COMPANIES

Advantage Rent-A-Car 800/777-5500
Alamo Rent A Car 800/462-5266
Avis Rent A Car 800/331-1212
Budget Rent a Car 800/527-0700
Dollar Rent A Car 800/800-4000
Enterprise Rent a Car 800/325-8007
Freedom Rent a Car 800/331-0777
Hertz Rent-A-Car 800/654-3131
National Interrent 800/227-7368
Payless Car Rental 800/729-5377
Rent-A-Wreck 800/421-7253

Thrifty Car Rental............................800/367-2277
Ugly Duckling Rent a Car 800/843-3825
U-Save Auto Rental 800/272-8728
Value Rent a Car 800/468-2583

CAMPERS AND RV RENTALS

Cruise America-Motorhome Rentals 800/327-7778
Recreational Vehicle Rental Association......800/336-0355

Driveaways

One attractive, inexpensive option for a long-distance road trip is to take a driveaway car—like Sal and Dean did in *On the Road*. It's not a perfect solution, since there are a number of conditions to which you must agree, but a driveaway car saves rental charges or wear and tear on your own machine and can add an element of adventure to any trip.

Basically, you agree to transport someone else's car from A to B. You generally have to average 400 miles a day and follow the most direct route; additional miles over a certain total will cost you extra. Also, you usually can't get a car that needs to go exactly where and when you want to go, so flexibility is a key. Delivering the car at the other end can also be a problem, since the person whose car you drive may live far away from public transportation and is under no obligation to help you get on your way.

Sometimes you can arrange a driveaway by scanning the classified ads in newspapers, but the most common way is to call up a company like *Auto Driveaway*, whose local offices are listed under "Automobile Transporters" in the Yellow Pages. Ask them what they have available, and once you've convinced them you're a responsible person (and a safe driver—they'll want to see a copy of your driving record), you'll need to leave a small deposit to cover the insurance deductible. Check the car for defects or damage before you sign for it, and think about the likely gas mileage, as they only buy the first tank.

INFORMATION

ROAD CONDITIONS HOTLINES

Note: Some of these hotlines require the use of touch-tone phones. Also, toll-free lines usually are valid only within each state.

Keys:
weekdays = normal business hours
24 hours = a person answers 24 hours/7 days per week
recording = available at all times unless otherwise noted

Alabama	conditions	334/242-4378 (24 hours)
Arizona	conditions	602/252-1010, ext. 7623
	construction	602/255-6588
Arkansas	conditions	501/569-2374
	construction	501/569-2227 (weekdays)
California	conditions	916/445-7623 or 800/427-7623
Colorado	conditions	303/639-1234
	construction	303/757-9228 (weekdays) or 303/573-7623
Connecticut	conditions and construction	800/443-6817 (CT only)
	construction	203/594-2650 (weekdays)
Delaware	conditions	800/652-5600 (DE only)
	construction	302/739-6677
District of Columbia	conditions	202/936-1111
Florida	no central source	
Georgia	conditions	404/656-5267 (weekdays) or 404/624-7890 (24 hours)
Idaho	conditions	208/336-6600
	construction	208/334-8888
	county roads	208/345-7680
	state highways	208/334-8005
Illinois	conditions	312/368-4636 or 217/782-5730 (in winter)
	construction	800/452-4368 (May-Oct.)
Indiana	conditions	317/232-8300 or 317/232-8298
	construction	317/232-5115 (weekdays)

Iowa................conditions......................515/288-1047
................................construction...................515/239-1471 (weekdays)
Kansas..............conditions and construction ...812/941-7422,
................................812/291-3000, or 800/585-7623
Kentucky ....conditions and construction ...800/459-7623
Louisiana...........conditions......................504/379-1541 (weekdays)
Maine...............conditions......................207/287-3427 (Nov.-April 24
................................hours, May-Oct. weekdays)
................................construction...................207/287-2672 (weekdays)
Maryland...........conditions......................800/543-2515 (MD only)
................................construction...................800/323-6742 (MD only)
Massachusetts .....conditions......................617/374-1234 (weekdays)
Michigan ....no central source
Minnesota..........conditions......................800/542-0220 or 612/296-3076
Mississippi.........conditions......................601/987-1212 (24 hours)
Missouri............no central source
Montana............conditions......................800/332-6171 or 406/444-6339
Nebraska ....conditions and construction ...402/479-4512 (weekdays)
................................conditions (winter)............402/471-4533 or
................................800/906-9069 (NE only)
Nevada.............conditions and construction recordings for:
................................South—Las Vegas...............702/486-3116
................................Northwest—Reno 702/793-1313
................................Northeast—Elko................702/738-8888
New Hampshire ...conditions......................800/918-9993 (NH only) or
................................603/271-6900
New Jersey ....conditions and construction
................................for the Turnpike.................908/247-0900, ext. 2 (24 hours)
................................conditions and construction
................................for the Garden State Parkway ..908/727-5929

New Mexico........conditions......................505/827-5594
................................construction...................800/432-4269 (NM only)
New York...........conditions for the
................................New York Thruway.............800/847-8929
North Carolina.....conditions and construction ...919/549-5100, category 7623
North Dakota ......conditions......................701/328-7623 (ND only) or
................................800/472-2686
Ohio ....conditions......................614/466-7170 (weekdays)
Oklahoma ....conditions......................405/425-2385
................................construction...................405/521-2554 (weekdays)

Oregon..............conditions......................800/976-7277 (OR only) or
                                                    503/889-3999
Pennsylvania.......conditions and construction
                    for the Turnpike.................800/331-3414 (PA only);
                                                    717/939-9551, ext. 7
                    conditions for the Interstate ...814/355-6044 or 814/355-6049
Rhode Island.......conditions......................401/738-1211
                    construction....................401/277-2468 (weekdays)
South Carolina.....conditions and construction ...803/737-1030 (24 hours)
South Dakota ......conditions and construction ...605/367-5707
Tennessee ....no central source
Texas...............conditions......................800/452-9292 (weekdays)
Utah................conditions and construction ...801/964-6000
Vermont ....conditions......................802/828-2468 (weekdays)
Virginia.............conditions and construction ...800/367-7623 (VA only)
Washington ....conditions...........................800/695-7623 (WA only)
                    for Puget Sound area 206/368-4499
                    Mountain Pass Report (Nov.-April) ..206/434-7277
West Virginia ......conditions......................304/558-2889 (recording)
Wisconsin ....conditions (winter) and
                    construction (summer).........800/762-3947 (WI only)
Wyoming............conditions......................307/635-9966
                    construction....................307/777-4437 (weekdays,
                                                    summer)

ROAD CONDITIONS IN CANADA

Alberta...403/246-5853

British Columbia ....900/451-4997 (fee)

Manitoba 204/945-3704

New Brunswick....................................800/561-4063 (Canada only)

Ontario 800/668-2746

Quebec...514/873-4121

Saskatchewan 306/787-7623

TOURISM INFORMATION

Alabama Bureau of Tourism and Travel ....334/242-4169 or 800/252-2262

Arizona Office of Tourism ....602/542-8687 or 800/842-8257

Arkansas Dept. of Parks and Tourism ....501/682-7777 or 800/628-8725

California Division of Tourism....................916/322-2881 or 800/862-2543

Colorado...no central source

Connecticut Tourism Office ....203/258-4355 or 800/282-6863

Delaware Tourism Office ....302/739-4271 or 800/441-8846

Florida Division of Tourism 904/487-1462

Georgia Department of Tourism ....404/656-3545 or 800/847-4842

Idaho Department of Commerce....................208/334-2470 or 800/635-7820

Illinois Bureau of Tourism.........................217/782-7500, 800/822-0292,
or 800/223-0121

Indiana Division of Tourism.......................317/232-8860 or 800/759-9191

Iowa Division of Tourism..........................515/242-4705 or 800/345-4692

Kansas Travel and Tourism Department ....913/296-2009 or 800/252-6727

Kentucky Dept. of Travel Development............502/564-4930 or 800/225-8747

Louisiana Office of Tourism.......................504/342-8119 or 800/633-6970

Maine Publicity Bureau ....207/623-0363 or 800/533-9595

Maryland Office of Tourism ....410/767-3400 or 800/719-5900

Massachusetts Office of Tourism ....617/727-3201 or 800/447-6277

Michigan Travel Bureau............................517/373-0670 or 800/543-2937

Minnesota Office of Tourism ....612/296-5029 or 800/657-3700

Mississippi Tourism Division ....601/359-3297 or 800/927-6378

Missouri Division of Tourism ....314/751-4133 or 800/877-1234

Travel Montana 406/444-2654, 800/847-4868,
or 800/548-3390

Nebraska Division of Travel and Tourism ....402/471-3791 or 800/228-4307

Nevada Commission on Tourism ....702/687-4322 or 800/638-2328

New Hampshire Office of Travel and Tourism ....603/271-2666 or 800/386-4664

New Jersey Division of Travel and Tourism ....609/292-2470 or 800/537-7397

New Mexico Department of Tourism...............505/827-0291 or 800/545-2040

New York State Division of Tourism...............518/474-4116 or 800/225-5697

North Carolina Travel and Tourism Division......919/733-4171 or 800/847-4862

North Dakota Tourism ....701/224-2525 or 800/435-5663

Ohio Division of Travel and Tourism...............614/466-8844 or 800/282-5393

Oklahoma Tourism and Recreation Department ..405/521-2406 or 800/652-6552

Oregon Tourism Division ....503/986-0000 or 800/547-7842

Pennsylvania Office of Travel Marketing...........717/787-5453 or 800/847-4872

Rhode Island Tourism Division ....401/277-2601 or 800/556-2484
South Carolina Division of Tourism 803/734-0122
South Dakota Tourism ....605/773-3301 or 800/732-5682
Tennessee Tourist Development 615/741-2158
Texas Tourism Division ....512/462-9191 or 800/452-9292
Utah Travel Council ....801/538-1030 or 800/200-1160
Vermont Travel Division ....802/828-3236 or 800/837-6668
Virginia Division of Tourism ....804/786-4484 or 800/932-5827
Washington Tourism Development ....360/586-2088 or 800/544-1800
West Virginia Division of Tourism and Parks .....304/558-2286 or 800/225-5982
Wisconsin Division of Tourism ....608/266-2161 or 800/432-8747
Wyoming Division of Tourism ....307/777-7777 or 800/225-5996

CANADIAN TOURISM INFORMATION

Alberta ....403/427-4321 or 800/661-8888
British Columbia.....................800/663-6000
Manitoba............................204/945-3777 or 800/665-0040
New Brunswick 800/561-0123
Ontario...............................416/314-0944 or 800/668-2746
Quebec...............................514/873-2015 or 800/363-7777
Saskatchewan ....306/787-2300 or 800/667-7191

NATIONAL PARKS AND FORESTS

National Park Service
Camping information: 800/365-2267

Mid-Atlantic Region
143 S. 3rd Street
Philadelphia, PA 19106
215/597-3679

Midwest Region
1709 Jackson Street
Omaha, NE 68102
402/221-3448

North Atlantic Region
15 State Street
Boston, MA 02109
617/223-5199

Pacific Northwest Region
909 1st Avenue
Seattle, WA 98104-1060
206/220-4013

Rocky Mountain Region
P.O. Box 25287
Denver, CO 80225
303/969-2503

Southeast Region
75 Spring Street SW
Atlanta, GA 30303
404/331-4996

Southwest Region
P.O. Box 728
Santa Fe, NM 87501
505/988-6012

Western Region
600 Harrison Street
Suite 600
San Francisco, CA 94107
415/744-3929

U.S. FOREST SERVICE

Camping information 800/280-2267

National Headquarters
12th St. and Independence Avenue SW
P.O. Box 96090
Washington, D.C. 20090
202/447-3957

Eastern Region
310 W. Wisconsin Avenue
Milwaukee, WI 53203
414/297-3693

Intermountain Region
324 25th Street
Ogden, UT 84401-2310
801/625-5354

Northern Region
200 E. Broadway
P.O. Box 7669
Missoula, MT 59807
406/329-3511

Pacific Northwest Region
333 S.W. 1st Avenue
P.O. Box 3623
Portland, OR 97208-3623
503/221-2877

Pacific Southwest Region
630 Sansome Street
San Francisco, CA 94111
415/705-2874

Rocky Mountain Region
740 Simms Street
Golden, CO 80401
303/275-5050

Southern Region
1720 Peachtree Road NW, Suite 850S
Atlanta, GA 30309-2417
404/347-4191

Southwestern Region
517 Gold Avenue SW
Albuquerque, NM 87102
505/842-3292

ORGANIZATIONS

American Automobile Association is an indispensable resource, and no traveler in his or her right mind should hit the road without a membership card. Besides the free roadside assistance, 24 hours a day across the country, they also offer free maps, useful guidebooks, and tons of related information. Look in the Yellow Pages for a local office, or contact the national headquarters.

> 1000 AAA Drive
> Heathrow, FL 32746
> 800/922-8228

Lewis and Clark Heritage Foundation is a remarkable organization that aims to preserve places related to and promote interest in the epic journey of the Corps of Discovery. Their newsletter, *We Proceeded On*, keeps members up to date on scholarship and current events.

> P.O. Box 3434
> Great Falls, MT 59403

Lincoln Highway Association is a group of old-roads aficionados who work to preserve remnants of the nation's first coast-to-coast highway and to promote its memory. They also get together for annual meetings to retrace the route.

> P.O. Box 8117
> St. Louis, MO 63156

National Route 66 Federation is the only nationwide, nonprofit organization committed to revitalizing Route 66, and to promoting awareness of its historic role as the Main Street of America. Members receive a high-quality quarterly magazine, and all dues go directly toward lobbying governments to preserve what's left of Route 66.

> P.O. Box 423
> Tujunga, CA 91043-0423
> 818/352-7232

Oregon-California Trails Association is dedicated to the preservation, appreciation, and enjoyment of all the trans-Mississippi migration trails to the West —the trails that made the United States an ocean-to-ocean nation.

> 524 S. Osage Street
> P.O. Box 1019
> Independence, MO 64051-0519
> 816/252-2276

Santa Fe Trail Association works to promote public awareness of and appreciation for this historic trail between Kansas City and Santa Fe, which connected the young United States with Mexico.

> Santa Fe Trail Center
> R.R. 3
> Larned, KS 67550

Anyone interested in the cultural landscape lining America's highways and byways will want to join the **Society for Commercial Archaeology**, an all-volunteer organization working to preserve and interpret roadside culture. Studies cover everything from diners to giant roadside dinosaurs, and the enterprise is geared toward appreciation and enjoyment of quirks and crannies of the highway environment. Dues are $25 a year, and members receive a magazine and a quarterly newsletter, which details preservation efforts as well as get-togethers for annual tours of different regions.

> Society for Commercial Archaeology
> National Museum of American History, Room 5010
> Washington, D.C. 20560
> phone: 202/882-5424

RECOMMENDED READING

ROADSIDE AMERICA

American Diner: Then and Now, by Richard J.S. Gutman (HarperPerennial, 1993). Lushly illustrated, encyclopedic history of that great American roadside institution, from its humble beginnings in the lunch wagons of the late 1880s to the streamlined stainless-steel models so beloved of art directors everywhere.

American Quest, by Jack Barth (Fireside Books, 1990). The subtitle, "He went looking for America and found it all over the country" sums up what this book is about. An anarchic tour of roadside culture, in which the author takes a job in the "Largest McDonald's in the Free World," visits Babe Ruth's grave, and traces the route of *Easy Rider* in a rented Cadillac.

Americans on the Road: From Autocamp to Motel, 1910-1945, by Warren James Belasco (M.I.T. Press, 1979). The best book there is about the early evolution of automobile-based tourism. Engagingly written, with clever analysis and an eye for the telling detail. Well worth searching for, but it can be hard to find.

Autoamerica: A Trip Down U.S. Highways from World War II to the Future, by Ant Farm (E.P. Dutton, 1976). An anarchic, cheerful look at America's love/hate relationship with the automobile, by the boys who brought you the Cadillac Ranch.

Documenting America 1935-1943, edited by Carl Fleishauer and Beverly W. Brannan (University of California Press, 1988). The most complete collection of New Deal photography yet published, this book traces the work of Dorothea Lange, Walker Evans, Marion Post Wol-cott and the many others who documented the facts of life in Depression-era America. Large format, with many revealing essays and over 300 images.

Flattened Fauna: A Field Guide to Common Animals of Roads, Street and Highways, by Roger M. Knutson (Ten Speed Press, 1987). Lighthearted look at that under-studied ecosystem, the highway. Besides being a helpful guide to identifying the sundry dead objects along the roadside, the book also details the natural life and habitats of the unfortunate road-killed creatures.

Gardens of Revelation: Environments by Visionary Artists, by John Beardsley (Abbeville Press, 1995). Lushly illustrated, intelligently written guidebook celebrating the "idiosyncratic genius, tenacious faith and unalienated labor" that has gone into the creation of hundreds of different sculptural environments across the country, from L.A.'s Watts Towers to Georgia's Paradise Garden.

The Highway as Habitat, by Ulrich Keller (UCSB Art Museum, 1986). Vivid photography of the American roadside, circa 1943-55, produced under the auspices of the Standard Oil Company by Roy Stryker, who led the New Deal documentary programs of the Farm Security Administration.

100 Years on the Road : The Travelling Salesman in American Culture, by Timothy B. Spears (Yale University Press, 1995). An oddly compelling little book, captivating and entertaining despite the academic tone.

The Lincoln Highway: Main Street Across America, by Drake Hokansen (University of Iowa Press, 1987). The bible of Lincoln Highway history, tracing America's first transcontinental highway from its beginnings in 1915 to its gradual fadeout in the post-interstate world.

Open Road: A Celebration of the American Highway, by Phil Patton (Simon and Schuster, 1986). An energetic account of how the American roadside landscape came to look the way it does today, masterfully blending a discussion of the economic and political forces behind the nation's highway network with a contagious enthusiasm for the inherent democracy the automobile embodies.

Orange Roofs, Golden Arches: The Architecture of American Chain Restaurants, by Philip Langdon (Knopf, 1986). Fascinating study of the story behind the look of franchised restaurants, from Fred Harvey's turn-of-the-century railroad whistle-stops, through the rise and demise of drive-ins in the postwar era, to today's mass-market fast-food emporia.

Pump and Circumstance: Glory Days of the Gas Station, by John Margolies (Little, Brown, 1993). Profusely illustrated coffee-table book that uses photographs, advertising, enamel signs, road maps, and brief but revealing text to track the development of the essential feature of the American highway landscape, the gas station.

Roadside America, by Jack Barth et al. (Fireside Books, 1986 and 1993). The first and still the best guidebook to the wackiest and weirdest attractions along the Great American Roadside. Organized by theme rather than by location, but still an entertaining and agreeable travel companion.

Roadside Empires: How the Chains Franchised America, by Stan Luxemburg (Viking Books, 1985). Business-oriented history of franchised fast-food industry, treating the major chains as financial successes without dimishing their usually negative impact on local businesses —and palates. No illustrations, unfortunately.

Where the Road and the Sky Collide: America Through the Eyes of its Drivers, by K.T. Berger (Henry Holt, 1993). A folk history of America's automotive obsession, this is the second of a pair of informal studies of cars and their drivers, written by two brothers, Kevin and Todd Berger, a psychologist and a journalist. Their earlier book is *Zen Driving: Be A Buddha Behind the Wheel of Your Automobile.*

TRAVELOGUES

American Guide Series: Federal Writers Project Guides to the States. Invaluable documents of the state of the nation during the 1930s and 1940s, these state-by-state, somewhat socialist-minded guidebooks were compiled during the Depression and later by teams of writers put to work under the auspices of the New Deal Works Project Administration (W.P.A.). Many great writers, including John Steinbeck and Jim Thompson, contributed to the series, selected volumes of which have been brought back into print by small presses.

Blue Highways: A Journey Into America, by William Least Heat Moon (Little, Brown and Company, 1982). One of the best-selling travel books ever written, this intensely personal yet openhearted tale traces the path of a part-Indian, part-time English teacher who travels the back roads "in search of places where change did not mean ruin and where time and men and deeds connected."

Drive, They Said: Poems About Americans and Their Cars, edited by Kurt Brown (Milkweed Editions, 1994). If you like to drive, and like to read or write poetry, you'll love this thick volume of contemporary verse, which samples the work of over 100 poets. See Stephen Dunn's offering in these pages.

Elvis Presley Boulevard: From Sea to Shining Sea, Almost, by Mark Winegardner (Atlantic Monthly Press, 1987). An energetic mix of road trip journal and coming-of-age autobiography, this short book recounts a summer-long tour around the southern and central United States. The Elvis obsession hinted at by the title is only a small part of the book, which looks at many of the odder corners of America.

Great Plains, by Ian Frazier (Farrar, Straus and Giroux, 1989). In-depth, top-to-bottom study of the wide-open land where the buffalo roamed, tracing historical themes like water, cowboys, and Indians, while capturing the contemporary scene.

Highway 50: Ain't That America, by Jim Lilliefors (Fulcrum Publishing, 1994). A cranky journalist heads west from Ocean City, Maryland, following the longest and loneliest road across the continent to California. Working his way along, and spending more time in dingy bars than in the great outdoors, the writer has packed the book with vivid portraits of the downside of rural America.

The Journey Home: Some Words in Defense of the American West, by Edward Abbey (Plume, 1991). A posthumous collection of essays, anecdotes, and vituperative epistles relating the self-described "agrarian anarchist" writer's lifelong love of the open spaces of the intermountain West.

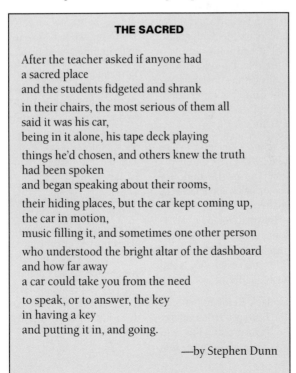

THE SACRED

After the teacher asked if anyone had
a sacred place
and the students fidgeted and shrank

in their chairs, the most serious of them all
said it was his car,
being in it alone, his tape deck playing

things he'd chosen, and others knew the truth
had been spoken
and began speaking about their rooms,

their hiding places, but the car kept coming up,
the car in motion,
music filling it, and sometimes one other person

who understood the bright altar of the dashboard
and how far away
a car could take you from the need

to speak, or to answer, the key
in having a key
and putting it in, and going.

—by Stephen Dunn

Let Us Now Praise Famous Men, by James Agee, photographs by Walker Evans (Houghton Mifflin, 1941). The talented collaborators spent the summer of 1936 living with three families of poor white cotton sharecroppers in the Appalachian foothills of northwest Alabama, and together created a vivid and compassionate portrait of rural America during the depths of the Great Depression.

The Lost Continent: Travels in Small Town America, by Bill Bryson (Secker and Warburg, 1989). Iowa-born British transplant returns to America in search of material for his sarcastic commentary on contemporary life. Hilariously funny in parts, meanspirited in others, and packed with trivial truths about life in the land of liberty.

Mad Monks on the Road, by Michael Lane and Jim Crotty (Simon & Schuster, 1993). Two left-of-center, postmodern pilgrims set off from Paradise and spend the next eight years on the road, graduating from a 1972 Econoline van to a queen-sized Fleetwood Bounder mobile home and generally getting up to no good while putting the camp back into camping and producing their notorious mobile magazine, *Monk.*

Making Hay, by Verlyn Klinkenborg (Vintage Departures, 1986). The enigmatic title is truer than you might think, for this is a book about alfalfa, about farming, and about the patterns of life in two very different places: the plains of Iowa, where the writer grew up on farms now worked by high-tech machines; and the mountain valleys of Montana, where hay is still made the old-fashioned way.

On the Road, by Jack Kerouac (Viking, 1957). What the Beatles were to music, the Beat were to literature, and this wild ramble of a road story was Kerouac's first Number One hit, inspiring a generation or two to hightail it along America's highways in the tracks of Sal Paradise and Dean Moriarty.

Out West: American Journey Along the Lewis and Clark Trail, by Dayton Duncan (Viking Penguin, 1987). The best travel book since *Blue Highways,* this marvelous tale retraces the route blazed by the Corps of Discovery on their epic adventure. With a combination of concise history lessons, captivating storytelling, and wry humor, Duncan vividly points out what has and hasn't changed in the 200-odd years since the captains first trekked across the country and back.

Road Scholar: Coast to Coast Late in the Century, by Andrei Codrescu (Hyperion, 1993). Taken from a PBS TV series, this series of vignettes tracks the progress of the Romanian-born poet and commentator as he travels from New Orleans to San Francisco via New York, Las Vegas, and a hundred other places along the way.

Spirit of Place: The Making of an American Literary Landscape, by Frederick Turner (Sierra Club Books, 1989). A multilayered tapestry of biography, travel writing, and literary criticism, this wonderful book explores how different locales have inspired and defined many of America's greatest writers.

Travels with Charley: In Search of America, by John Steinbeck (Viking, 1962). Rambling around "this monster of a land" in his camper Rocinante, accompanied only by his eponymous French poodle, Steinbeck returns to his California haunts from self-imposed exile in New York to find that, even if you can't go home again, there are many intriguing things along the way.

Zen and the Art of Motorcycle Maintenance: An Inquiry into Values, by Robert M. Pirsig (William Morrow and Company, 1974). The subtitle points out this big book's more ponderous aspects, but at its best this is a captivating, full-throttle ride down America's back roads in search of meaning in the modern age.

PERIODICALS

Out West: The Newspaper That Roams. For nearly 10 years, writer Chuck Woodbury has been traveling the back roads of the western U.S., documenting in a 32-page quarterly tabloid the many wild and wonderful things he finds there. Chuck, wife Rodica, daughter Emily, and a team of contributors cover the people they meet and the places they eat, photograph funny signs and roadside dinosaurs, and generally bring the open road alive, straight to your mailbox. They also run a very good mail-order bookstore.

Out West
408 Broad Street, Suite 11
Nevada City, CA 95959
916/478-9080 or 800/274-9378

Roadside Magazine. Doing for the northeastern U.S. what *Out West* does out west, *Roadside* covers the back roads and small-town Main Streets, with a particular focus on diners, those uniquely American institutions that are a traveler's best friend. Along with articles aimed at "getting America out of the franchises, the malls, the Interstates," and back into the real things that foster community and make

this country interesting, each issue includes a "Diner Finder," which lists, locates, and describes the make and models of all the surviving diners in a certain area. For more information, contact:

Coffee Cup Productions
P.O. Box 652
West Side Station
Worcester, MA 01602
508/791-1838

Route 66 Magazine. An impressive full-color quarterly, entirely dedicated to the Mother Road and to the people and places, past and present, that have made it such an icon of restless America. Strong graphics, lively writing, and not *too* many ads make it a great resource for armchair or front-seat readers. For subscription information, contact:

Route 66 Magazine
P.O. Box 66
Laughlin, NV 89028-0066
702/298-5703

Yesterday's Highways: Exploring the U.S. Off the Interstates. This homespun newsletter has the expressed aim of inspiring "persons of all ages, whether by armchair or actual experience, to travel and explore the back roads and history of America." *Yesterday's Highways* comes out every two months and features a very handy, mile-by-mile guide to various old roads, describing their histories and characters as well as listing practical information for travelers.

Yesterday's Highways
49 Church Street
Weaverville, NC 28787

ROAD TRIP TIME LINE

???..........................The wheel is invented

30,000 B.C.-A.D. 1500....Native American trails criss-cross North America.

600 B.C....................Babylonians use tar to pave streets.

A.D. 500 ....Mississippian culture builds great mound city at Cahokia, opposite St. Louis.

A.D. 1150.................Pueblo villages of Acoma and Moenkopi established.

1539-42....................Hernando de Soto explores southeastern United States. On June 18, 1541, his party crosses the Mississippi River, and he dies a year later near present-day Vicksburg.

1540-42....................Arriving overland from Mexico, Coronado explores southwestern deserts in search of the fabled Seven Cities of Cíbola.

1542........................Juan Cabrillo explores the coast of California.

1579........................Sailing from the Hawaiian Islands, Sir Francis Drake explores the coasts of Oregon, Washington, and northern California.

1585.................................Sir Walter Raleigh establishes ill-fated colony at Roanoke, North Carolina.

1607........................First successful British colony established at Jamestown, Virginia.

1609........................Spanish colony at Santa Fe, New Mexico established.

Nov.-Dec. 1620............Pilgrims arrive in Massachusetts on the *Mayflower.*

1682........................Starting from near Lake Michigan, La Salle descends the Illinois and Mississippi Rivers to the Gulf of Mexico.

1742-43....................Coming from French Canada, the de la Verendrye brothers explore North and South Dakota, claiming the land for France.

1770........................Spain establishes first Franciscan missions in California.

1781........................Cornwallis surrenders at Yorktown at end of Revolutionary War.

1791........................Bill of Rights ratified as first 10 amendments to the Constitution.

1803........................Louisiana Purchase.

1804-06....................Lewis and Clark lead Corps of Discovery across continent, from St. Louis to mouth of the Columbia River and back.

1805-06....................Zebulon Pike explores southern Great Plains and Rockies.

1808......................Importation of slaves into the U.S. prohibited by Congress.

1821......................Santa Fe Trail first opened by businessman William Becknell.

1825......................Erie Canal opens, between Albany and Buffalo, New York.

1826......................Jedediah Strong Smith becomes first white man to cross from Rockies to southern California overland. He repeats the feat the following year.

1838......................Cherokee Indians forced west along "Trail of Tears."

1843......................Oregon Trail opened.

1848......................California gold rush, and migration of Mormons from Nauvoo to Utah.

1853......................Gadsden Purchase completes present-day outline of lower 48 United States.

1858-61...................Butterfield Overland Mail links St. Louis and Los Angeles via El Paso.

1859......................Nation's first successful oil well drilled in Pennsylvania.

1860-61...................Pony Express links Missouri and California.

April 12, 1861............Confederate forces fire on Fort Sumter, South Carolina.

April 9, 1865 ....Lee surrenders at Appomattox.

May 10, 1869..............Transcontinental railroad completed at Promontory Point, Utah.

1870......................Boardwalk resorts open at Atlantic City, New Jersey.

June 25, 1876.............Battle of Little Big Horn—"Custer's Last Stand."

1877......................Amzi Lorenzo Barber establishes Trinidad Asphalt Company, and gives Washington, D.C., the nation's first asphalt-paved streets.

1884......................Santa Fe Railroad links Los Angeles, Santa Fe, and Kansas City.

1883......................Northern Pacific Railroad links Seattle and St. Paul, Minnesota.

1886......................Karl Benz creates the first car by adding a motor to a tricycle. Coca-Cola invented by Atlanta pharmacist John Pemberton. Geronimo surrenders to General Miles.

1893......................Southern Pacific Railroad links Los Angeles and New Orleans; Great Northern links Seattle and St. Paul. "Rural Free Delivery" of mail introduced. Frank and Charles Duryea build first American motor car in Springfield, Massachusetts on September 21, 1893.

1895........................First gasoline-powered cars sold in U.S., made by Duryea Motor Wagon Company of Springfield, Massachusetts. Duryeas also win first automobile race in U.S., covering a 50-mile course around Chicago at an average speed of five mph.

1896........................Buffalo, New York, becomes first major city to pave all its streets.

1898........................"Stanley Steamers" introduced. Pepsi-Cola invented.

1899........................A "Stanley Steamer" climbs Mount Washington, New Hampshire.

1900........................Steering wheel replaces the tiller for first time, on a Packard "Ohio." Electric cars outnumber gasoline-powered cars 2 to 1.

1901........................Oil discovered at Spindletop field in eastern Texas. Speedometers introduced by Oldsmobile.

1903........................Henry Ford founds Ford Motor Company. Wright Brothers make first powered flight. To win a $50 bet, Dr. Horatio Jackson, along with his chauffeur and dog, becomes first person to drive across the country, taking 65 days.

1904........................Only 40,000 out of a total of over two million miles of U.S. roads are fully paved. Bicyclist organizations lead charge for better public roads. Henry Ford sets world land speed record of 91 mph.

1905........................Total number of cars on roads: 75,000.

1907........................Nation's first "gas station" opens in St. Louis.

1908........................General Motors incorporates. Ford Motor Company introduces the Model T.

1909........................Nation's first mile of rural highway is paved. Alice Ramsey becomes first woman to drive across the country—the trip took 41 days.

1911........................First Indianapolis 500-mile race held.

1912........................Nation's first lane markings are painted onto the streets of Redlands, California.

1915........................Total number of cars on roads: 2.3 million. The Lincoln Highway, the country's first coast-to-coast route, is marked from New York to San Francisco.

1916........................General Pershing leads U.S. Army into Mexico in pursuit of Pancho Villa. Federal Aid Road Act establishes first federal funding for road-building.

1918........................Wisconsin introduces the concept of numbering roads and highways. First three-color traffic signal is installed.

1919......................First A&W Root Beer stand opens, in Lodi, California. Dwight Eisenhower leads a military convoy across the country, which takes two months and points out the need for well-paved transcontinental roads.

1920......................Beginning of Prohibition. Total number of cars on roads: 6.5 million.

1921......................Original White Castle hamburger stand built in Wichita, Kansas, foreshadowing the arrival of fast food. First Pig Stand drive-in opens, between Dallas and Fort Worth.

1922......................Balloon tires and gas gauges introduced. Ford Motor Company produces nearly half of nation's four million new cars and trucks.

1925......................System of numbering federal highways is introduced, to replace route names. The "shield" symbol is designed by Michigan engineer Frank Rogers. First "Burma-Shave" signs installed along Minnesota highways. World's first motel opens, in San Luis Obispo, California.

1926......................Route 66 established, winding between Chicago and Los Angeles.

1927......................Ford ceases production of Model T, having sold 27 million of them. Lincoln Highway, the first coast-to-coast highway, is paved all the way from New York to California.

1933......................End of Prohibition.

1934......................First Steak and Shake opens, in Normal, Illinois.

1935......................Howard Johnson pioneers franchising restaurants. First parking meters installed.

1939......................Norman Bel Geddes popularizes freeways with his Futurama display at the New York World's Fair.

1940......................Total number of cars on roads: 20 million. Pennsylvania Turnpike opens. Arroyo Seco Parkway, now the Pasadena Freeway, opens. First Dairy Queen opens.

1941......................Mount Rushmore dedicated.

1944......................National System of Interstate and Defense Highways authorized by Congress. Basic wartime gasoline ration is two gallons per week. National speed limit is 35 mph.

1946......................Bobby Troup composes "Get Your Kicks on Route 66," which becomes a hit record for Nat King Cole.

1947......................Henry Ford dies.

1949......................VW Beetle introduced in the United States. Tastee-Freez founded in Chicago. Richard and Maurice McDonald perfect cheap fast food: 15-cent hamburgers, 10-cent French fries.

1952......................First Holiday Inn opens, in Memphis, Tennessee. The New Jersey Turnpike opens.

1953......................McDonald's open first restaurant featuring the "Golden Arches" in Phoenix, Arizona, followed soon after by one in Downey, California, that still stands—under threat of imminent demolition by corporate headquarters.

1954......................Dwight Eisenhower adds phrase "under God" to the Pledge of Allegiance.

1955-56...................Boycott ends racial segregation on public buses in Montgomery, Alabama.

1956......................Interstate Highway system inaugurated, planning 42,500 miles of freeways with federal funds paying 90% of the estimated $27 billion. (The cost so far has been over $125 billion.)

1957......................Ford launches the Edsel—the first car designed by market research polls.

1958......................First Pizza Hut opens, in Wichita, Kansas.

1959......................Ford cancels the Edsel—after losing $350 million.

1960......................First Hardee's established, in Greenville, North Carolina

1961......................Roy Kroc buys McDonald's for $2.7 million.

1962......................First Chart House opens, in Aspen, Colorado.

1963......................Last set of Burma-Shave signs taken down. California is the first state to require emission controls on cars.

1964......................Pontiac's GTO, with its triple-carbed, 350 horsepower V-8 engine, ushers in the era of the "muscle car." First Arby's opens, in Youngstown, Ohio.

1965......................First TGI Fridays opens, in midtown Manhattan.

1969......................First Wendy's opens, in Columbus, Ohio.

1972......................McDonald's installs first "McDonaldland" children's playground.

1974......................"Arab oil crisis" causes federal government to set a national speed limit of 55 mph. Cadillac Ranch is constructed outside Amarillo.

1975......................Bruce Springsteen releases *Born to Run*.

1977......................First Chuck E. Cheese Pizza opens, in San Jose, California.

1984......................Chrysler introduces the original minivan. Last stretch of old Route 66 still in use, at Williams, Arizona, is bypassed by the I-40 freeway.

1992......................Lyn St. James becomes first woman to complete the Indy 500, finishing 11th.

Currently, there are over 175 million licensed drivers in the U.S., driving 200 million registered vehicles along four million miles of paved roads and highways.

MAPS

INDEX

AFRICAN-AMERICAN HERITAGE AND PEOPLE

MINOR LEAGUE BASEBALL TEAMS

Buffalo Bisons (NY): 458
Chillicothe Paints (OH): 566
Jackson Generals (MS): 610
Pawtucket Red Sox (RI): 500
Pittsfield Mets (MA): 251
River City Bandits (IA): 188
Rochester Red Wings (NY): 460
Scranton/Wilkes-Barre Red Barons (PA): 488
South Bend White Sox (IN): 446
Spokane Indians (WA): 343
Toledo Mud Hens (OH): 449
Utica Blue Sox (NY): 464

COOL COLLEGE TOWNS

COURTHOUSE SQUARES

ELVIS

FESTIVALS AND EVENTS

GARDENS OF REVELATION

Bottle Village—Simi Valley, CA: 78
Gehrke Windmill Garden—Coulee Dam, WA: 341
Holy Land—Waterbury, CT: 494
Margaret's Grocery—Vicksburg, MS: 216, 607, 608
Paradise Garden—Summerville, GA: 607
Tinkertown—Tijeras, NM: 651
Totem Poles—Foyil, OK: 666

GREAT ROADS

Blue Ridge Parkway: 280-281, 284, 285, 287-288
Going-to-the-Sun Road: 348-349
Hwy-1—Big Sur, CA: 67
Mohawk Trail: 472
Natchez Trace Parkway: 218
Route 66: 626-677
Skyline Parkway: 370
US-50—Nevada and Utah ("The Loneliest Road"): 523-539
US-93—The Real "Loneliest Road": 86-121
US-6A—Cape Cod, MA: 507-509

MUSICIANS

NEW DEAL PROJECTS

Arthurdale, WV: 569
Fort Peck Dam, MT: 356-357
Grand Coulee Dam, WA: 341-342
Hoover Dam, NV: 112
Mission La Purisima, CA: 73, 74
Pfeiffer-Big Sur State Park, CA: 68

PRESIDENTS

ROADSIDE STATUES

Brooks Catsup Bottle—Collinsville, IL: 672
Cadillac Ranch—Amarillo, TX: 655
Carhenge—Alliance, NE: 144, 432
Giant Prairie Dog—Oakley, KS: 147
Hiawatha—Ironwood, MI: 376
Hiawatha—La Crosse, WI: 178
Iwo Jima Memorial—Harlingen, TX: 164
Iwo Jima Memorial—Arlington, VA: 572
Marlin Perkins—Carthage, MO: 668
Paul Bunyan—Bangor, ME: 399
Paul Bunyan—Bemidji, MN: 367-368
Paul Bunyan—Brainerd, ME: 173
Paul Bunyan—Klamath, CA: 44
Popeye—Crystal Springs, TX: 160
Sitting Bull—Mobridge, SD: 138
Statue of Liberty—Newark, NJ: 706
Steve Prefontaine—Coos Bay, OR: 37
Superman—Metropolis, IL: 202
Tex the Giant Cowboy—Canyon, TX: 656
Wally the Walleye—Garrison, ND: 128
World's Largest Buffalo—Jamestown, ND: 364
World's Largest Cow—New Salem, ND: 364
World's Largest Frying Pan—Long Beach, WA: 28
World's Largest Six Pack—La Crosse, WI: 178
World's Largest Man-Made Star—Roanoke, VA: 283
World's Largest Turtle—Bottineau, ND: 364
World's Largest Wooden Indian—Skowhegan, ME: 399
World's Tallest Man—Alton, IL: 199

PHOTO AND ILLUSTRATION CREDITS

Arizona Office of Tourism 121, 589; Mike Booher 316, 331; Karl Bremer 219; Michael Bruner 41, 85; Buffalo Bill Historical Center, Cody, Wyoming 425, 533; Buffalo Fine Arts Academy, 457; California Department of Parks and Recreation 52, 54, 56, 58, 59, 66, 70(2), 518, 520, 522; Todd Clark 105; Colorado Historical Society 543; Ekstrom Library 86-87, 122-123, 332-333; Festival of Arts of Laguna Beach 82(2); Louise Foote 535; Mike Gassmann 672; Shellee Graham 645; Philip Greenspun (philg@mir.edu) 302, 316, 329, 349, 400, 513, 538; Hannibal Convention and Visitor's Bureau 194; Heard Museum, Phoenix, AZ 646(4); Henry Ford Museum 449; Houdini Museum 487; Illinois State Tourism 674; Jamie Jensen 42, 65, 83, 102, 112, 117, 119, 127, 135, 157, 178, 367, 421, 432, 443, 450, 528, 587, 588, 605, 633, 640, 654-655, 659, 664, 670, 671(2); Marjorie Jensen 319; Jimmie Rodgers Museum 612; Mike LeMasters 548, 551, 553; Library of Congress 3, 14-15, 150, 160, 166-167, 226-227, 299, 403, 514-515, 579, 626-627, 678-679, 728-729; Maryland Office of Tourism 575; Memphis Convention and Visitor's Bureau 205; Metropolis Convention and Visitor's Bureau 202; Mississippi State Division of Tourism, 218; Missouri Division of Tourism 195; Montana Historical Society, Helena 93, 356; Monterey Visitor and Convention Bureau/Martin Brown 65; Michael Murphy 164; National Archives 266, 354, 537, 590(2); North Carolina Travel and Tourism/William Russ 322; North Dakota Tourism Department/Dawn Charging 360, 364(3); Oklahoma Tourism and Recreation Department/Fred Marvel 662, 663; Oregon Tourism Department/Rick Schafer 30; Oregon Tourism Department/Dan Sherwood 39; Oregon Tourism Department/Steve Terrill 34; Out West Newspaper/Chuck Woodbury 408, 621 (bottom), 636; Doug Pappas 209, 242, 277, 304, 369; Pasadena Convention and Visitor's Bureau 630; Pennsylvania Dutch Convention and Visitor's Bureau 269; Jeff Perk 23, 494; Bob Race 37, 38, 40, 46; Redwood Empire Association 54; Kevin Roe 438, 439, 466, 467, 677; San Luis Obispo Convention and Visitor's Bureau 72; Santa Cruz Parks and Recreation Department 59; Frank Schmidt 652; South Dakota Tourism 141, 432; State Historical Society of North Dakota 133; State of Nevada 109; State of Washington Tourism Division 18, 28, 337, 342; Sterling and Francine Clark Art Institute 249; Sun Valley Co. 101; Bill Swislow 215; Tacoma Public Library 23; Texas Department of Commerce/Elizabeth Grivas 156; Texas Department of Commerce/Richard Reynolds 596; Texas Department of Commerce/Tourism Division 599, 655; Texas Tourist Agency/R. Reynolds 165; Ben Thompson 260, 541, 562; Turner Entertainment 370; Craig Tuttle 39; Utah State Historical Society 534; Virginia Division of Tourism 312; Bob Waldmire 631, 639, 656, 661, 673, 676; Bill Weir 120, 182; Painting of Andy Devine by Mildred Wheeler 115; Wickenburg Chamber of Commerce 115; Stephen Wolf 303, 317; Wyoming Division of Cultural Resources 144, 355, 426

Cadillac Ranch is © Copyright 1974, by Ant Farm (Chip Lord, Hudson Marquez, Doug Michaels)

The wonderful black-and-white images used as frontispieces to the various chapters in this book were created in the 1930s and 1940s by some of the country's finest photographers, working under the direction of Roy Stryker. From 1935 to 1943, Roy Stryker headed the federally funded, New Deal-era documentary projects known as the Resettlement Administration and the Farm Security Administration. After the war, he hired many of the same artists when he worked in the advertising department of Standard Oil of New Jersey. The photographs made under federal auspices are collected at the Library of Congress; the Standard Oil photographs are collected at the Ekstrom Library at the University of Louisville.

Half-title page: Early motorist at the Grand Canyon. Photographer unknown. (Library of Congress number 607262, 262-7119)

Coastal West Coast: Marion Post Wolcott (Library of Congress number LC-USF-34-56924-E)

US-93: Edwin Rosskam (Standard Oil of New Jersey)

US-83: John Vachon (Standard Oil of New Jersey)

Great River Road: (Cairo, Il, 1940) John Vachon (Library of Congress number LC-USF-33-1883-M3)

The Appalachian Trail: Walker Evans (Library of Congress number LC-USF-342-8274A)

Coastal East Coast: Russell Lee (Library of Congress number 11392-M4)

US-2: Edwin Rosskam (Standard Oil of New Jersey)

US-20: Arthur Rothstein (Library of Congress number LC-USF-34-26922-D)

US-50: John Vachon (Library of Congress number 1631-M4)

US-80: Russell Lee (Library of Congress number LC-USF-34-35601)

Route 66: Russell Lee (Library of Congress number LC-USF-33-5184-M4)

City Survival Guides: John Vachon (Library of Congress number LC-USF-34T01-8964-D)

Road Trip Resources: Marion Post Wolcott (Library of Congress number LC-USF-34-56932-E)

ACKNOWLEDGMENTS   A proverbial cast of thousands—in ranger stations, visitor centers, and cafes across the country—have helped shape this book, and I hope that someday I get the chance to show each of them how it turned out. For making it happen, I am grateful for the support and enthusiasm of the entire team at Moon Publications, especially Bill Newlin, without whom I never would have spent half my recent life on the road, and Taran March, without whom those many miles would never have added up to anything more than the endless stream of run-on thoughts and tangential digressions I first presented, 300,000 words ago.

For sage advice at every turn, I am grateful to Deke Castleman and Barry Parr. To all my other road-tripping cohorts and contributors, thanks for seeing the humor in impossible deadlines, and for doing such fine work for so little money, particularly Jeff Perk, who added his keen sense of quality pie to the mix; Andy Coe, who suggested "The Road to Nowhere" route; and Kevin "Roots" Roe, for 11th-hour guidance, encouragement, and musical accompaniment. I am also deeply indebted to Doug Pappas for sharing his love and knowledge of the old roads, his library of photos, and his complete set of WPA travel guides; to the Fairy Queen of St. Louis, Sandy LaRouche, who got arrested for trespassing while we paid our last respects to the Coral Court Motel (R.I.P. 1995); and to Chuck Woodbury, Michael Wallis, Dayton Duncan, Phil Patton, Ian Frazier, Tom Teague, and all the other writers on whom I have relied for insight, information, and inspiration. Finally, to all (well, most) of the people who live and work in the places I've passed through and written about—thanks for being there.

I am also sincerely grateful for, and still amazed by, the quantity and quality of input we've received about these old roads via the Information Superhighway, from our hundreds of "virtual" readers prior to the print publication of this first edition. I want to express my absolute thanks for the generosity and positive spirit of our collective correspondence. It has been a huge motivation for me just to know you're out there.

(To the makers of my Apple PowerBook, and my trusty, made-in-California Toyota Corolla—and the car rental companies who have let me take the words "free unlimited mileage" to outrageous lengths—if you happen to be looking for a corporate spokesman, I'm open to any reasonable offers.)

Since my personal life has been inseparable from this book for a long time, I owe my friends and extended family a long thank you—for listening to me babble about all the wondrous unknown things out there on the Great American Highway, and for not minding when I've dropped in out of the blue, or been away whenever they came to visit. I would also like to dedicate this book to Brando Jensen, the coolest cat that ever lived, and finally to express my devotion and gratitude to my dear wife Catherine Robson, for 10 years (and counting) of seeing the bright side, meeting me in the middle, and making everything turn out right.

—Jamie Jensen

ABOUT THE AUTHOR   Jamie Jensen has been immersed in road trip culture from an early age, thanks to a childhood spent drinking drive-in milk shakes and riding roller coasters in Los Angeles—before they tore everything down. After a three-year stint hitchiking around the country, making hay in Kansas and Oklahoma, sailing boats on the Chesapeake Bay, painting houses in Boston, and living in the storeroom of a Manhattan music studio, he returned to California and earned a degree in Architecture from UC Berkeley, then moved to England, where he began writing about America. He has since written an authorized biography of the Grateful Dead, and contributed to travel books from Rough Guides, Dorling Kindersley, and Michelin Travel Publications.

He now lives in Northern California.

Road to Nowhere Contest

Moon Publications wants to send you on a road trip across the USA. We're looking for stories about road trips you've taken or always dreamed of taking: trips of glory or disaster, personal epiphanies or roadside rendezvous.

How to Enter

In 500 words or less tell us about your most interesting road trip experience. All entries must be typed and written in English. Entries will be judged by a panel of Moon Travel Handbook authors, and the top-ten stories will be published in a special *Road Trip USA* issue of *Travel Matters,* Moon Publications' newsletter.

Entries can be transmitted via e-mail to travel@moon.com or via regular postal mail to: Road to Nowhere Contest, PO Box 3040, Chico, CA 95927-3040 USA. Entries must include the author's full name, mailing address, and phone number. All entries must be received by January 15, 1997.

Winners Will Receive:

First Prize: One lucky winner will receive a 14-day road trip. Moon will provide 14 nights' accommodations and $25 a day gasoline allowance.

Second Prize: One second prize winner will receive a seven-day road trip including seven nights' accommodations and $25 a day gasoline allowance.

Third Prizes: Eight third prize winners will receive a free copy of a Moon Travel Handbook to the US state of their choice, a *Road Trip USA* car sunshade, and a *Road Trip USA* bumper sticker.

Experience the spontaneity and culture of the old US highways and share your cross-country driving adventures.

Enter Today!

MOON TRAVEL HANDBOOKS
THE IDEAL TRAVELING COMPANIONS

Moon Travel Handbooks provide focused, comprehensive coverage of distinct destinations all over the world. Our goal is to give travelers all the background and practical information they'll need for an extraordinary travel experience.

Every Handbook begins with an in-depth essay about the land, the people, their history, art, politics, and social concerns—an entire bookcase of cultural insight and introductory information in one portable volume. We also provide accurate, up-to-date coverage of all the practicalities: language, currency, transportation, accommodations, food, and entertainment. And Moon's maps are legendary, covering not only cities and highways, but parks and trails that are often difficult to find in other sources.

Below are highlights of Moon's North America and Hawaii Travel Handbook series. Our complete list of Handbooks covering North America and Hawaii, Mexico, Central America and the Caribbean, and Asia and the Pacific, are listed on the order form on the accompanying pages. To purchase Moon Travel Handbooks, please check your local bookstore or order by phone: (800) 345-5473 Monday-Friday 8 a.m.-5 p.m. PST.

THE NORTH AMERICA AND HAWAII TRAVEL HANDBOOK SERIES

"Moon's greatest achievements may be the individual state books they offer. . . . Moon not only digs up little-discovered attractions, but also offers thumbnail sketches of the culture and state politics of regions that rarely make national headlines."

—*The Millennium Whole Earth Catalog*

ALASKA-YUKON HANDBOOK
by Deke Castleman and Don Pitcher, 460 pages, **$14.95**
"Exceptionally rich in local culture, history, and reviews of natural attractions. . . One of the most extensive pocket references. . . . An essential guide!"
— *The Midwest Book Review*

ALBERTA AND THE NORTHWEST TERRITORIES
by Nadina Purdon and Andrew Hempstead, 466 pages, **$17.95**
"*Alberta and the Northwest Territories Handbook* provides strong coverage of one of the most rugged territories in Canada."
—*The Bookwatch*

ARIZONA TRAVELER'S HANDBOOK
by Bill Weir and Robert Blake, 448 pages, **$17.95**
"If you don't own this book already, buy it immediately"
—*Arizona Republic*

ATLANTIC CANADA HANDBOOK
by Nan Drosdick and Mark Morris, 436 pages, **$17.95**
Like a corner of Europe, Canada's eastern seacoast provinces boast Irish brogue, Scottish kilts, Highland flings, and a rich heritage of British influence. *Atlantic Canada Handbook* provides extensive coverage of this region, including New Brunswick, Nova Scotia, Newfoundland, and Prince Edward Island. While there are many guides to Canada, none offers the detailed regional coverage of this comprehensive handbook.

BIG ISLAND OF HAWAII HANDBOOK
by J.D. Bisignani, 349 pages, **$13.95**
"The best general guidebooks available"   —*Hawaii Magazine*

BRITISH COLUMBIA HANDBOOK
by Jane King, 375 pages, **$15.95**
"Deftly balances the conventional and the unconventional, for both city lovers and nature lovers."
                                   —*Reference and Research Book News*

COLORADO HANDBOOK
by Stephen Metzger, 470 pages, **$18.95**
"Hotel rooms in the Aspen area, in the height of winter sports season, for $20-$30? . . . who but a relentless researcher from Moon could find it?"   —*The New York Daily News*

GEORGIA HANDBOOK
by Kap Stann, 350 pages, **$17.95**
". . . everything you need to know to enjoy a journey through Georgia."   —*Southern Book Trade*

HAWAII HANDBOOK
by J.D. Bisignani, 1004 pages, **$19.95**
Winner: Grand Excellence and Best Guidebook Awards, Hawaii Visitors' Bureau "No one since Michener has told us so much about our 50th state."   —*Playboy*

HONOLULU-WAIKIKI HANDBOOK
by J.D. Bisignani,
365 pages, **$14.95**
"The best general guidebooks available."   —*Hawaii Magazine*

IDAHO HANDBOOK
by Bill Loftus, 282 pages, **$14.95**
"Well-organized, engagingly written, tightly edited, and chock-full of interesting facts about localities, backcountry destinations, traveler accommodations, and cultural and natural history."
                                   —*Sierra Magazine*

KAUAI HANDBOOK
by J.D. Bisignani, 274 pages, **$13.95**
"This slender guide is tightly crammed. . . . The information provided is staggering."
                                   —*Hawaii Magazine*

MAUI HANDBOOK
by J.D. Bisignani, 393 pages, **$14.95**
Winner: Best Guidebook Award, Hawaii Visitors' Bureau
"*Maui Handbook* should be in every couple's suitcase. It intelligently discusses Maui's history and culture, and you can trust the author's recommendations for best beaches, restaurants, and excursions."
                                   —*Bride's Magazine*

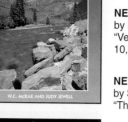

MONTANA HANDBOOK
by W.C. McRae and Judy Jewell, 450 pages, **$17.95**
"Well-organized, engagingly written, tightly edited, and chock-full of interesting facts about localities, backcountry destinations, traveler accommodations, and cultural and natural history."
—*Sierra Magazine*

NEVADA HANDBOOK
by Deke Castleman, 473 pages, **$16.95**
"Veteran travel writer Deke Castleman says he covered more than 10,000 miles in his research for this book and it shows."
—*Nevada Magazine*

NEW MEXICO HANDBOOK
by Stephen Metzger, 322 pages, **$14.95**
"The best current guide and travel book to all of New Mexico"
—*New Mexico Book League*

NORTHERN CALIFORNIA HANDBOOK
by Kim Weir, 779 pages, **$19.95**
"That rarest of travel books–both a practical guide to the region and a map of its soul."
—*San Francisco Chronicle*

OREGON HANDBOOK
by Stuart Warren and Ted Long Ishikawa, 520 pages, **$16.95**
". . . perhaps the most definitive tourist guide to the state ever published."
—*The Oregonian*

TEXAS HANDBOOK
by Joe Cummings, 598 pages, **$17.95**
"Reveals a Texas with a diversity of people and culture that is as breathtaking as that of the land itself."
—*Planet Newspaper,* Australia

"I've read a bunch of Texas guidebooks, and this is the best one."
–Joe Bob Briggs

UTAH HANDBOOK
by Bill Weir and Robert Blake, 458 pages, **$16.95**
"What Moon Publications has given us—at long last—is a one-volume, easy to digest, up-to-date, practical, factual guide to all things Utahan. . . . This is the best handbook of its kind I've yet encountered."
—*The Salt Lake Tribune*

WASHINGTON HANDBOOK
by Don Pitcher, 630 pages, **$18.95**
"Departs from the general guidebook format by offering information on how to cope with the rainy days and where to take the children . . . . This is a great little book, informational, fun to read, and a good one to keep."
—*Travel Publishing News*

WYOMING HANDBOOK
by Don Pitcher, 495 pages, **$14.95**
"Wanna know the real dirt on Calamity Jane, white Indians, and the tacky Cheyenne gunslingers? All here. And all fun."
—*The New York Daily News*

Hit The Road With Moon Travel Handbooks

ROAD TRIP USA
Cross-Country Adventures on America's Two-Lane Highways

by Jamie Jensen, 800 pages, $22.50
This 800-page Handbook covers the entire United States with 11 intersecting routes, allowing travelers to create their own cross-country driving adventures. Of the featured routes, six run west to east from coast to coast, and five run north to south from Canada to Mexico.

Packed with both practical information and entertaining sidebars, *Road Trip USA* celebrates the spontaneity and culture of the American highway without sacrificing the essential comforts of bed and bread. In addition to engaging commentary on literally thousands of sights and diversions, readers will find such essential information as the locations of diners with the best apple pie and the call letters of good radio stations on lonely stretches of road.

The World Wide Web edition of *Road Trip USA* has been generating excitement on the Internet for over a year. The *Road Trip* exhibit includes a map with hundreds of original entries and links to local Internet sites. WWW explorers are encouraged to participate in the exhibit by contributing their own travel tips on small towns, roadside attractions, regional foods, and interesting places to stay. Visit *Road Trip USA* online at: **http://www.moon.com/rdtrip.html**

MOONBELT

A new concept in moneybelts. Made of heavy-duty Cordura nylon, the Moonbelt offers maximum protection for your money and important papers. This pouch, designed for all-weather comfort, slips under your shirt or waistband, rendering it virtually undetectable and inaccessible to pickpockets. It features a one-inch high-test quick-release buckle so there's no more fumbling around for the strap or repeated adjustments. This handy plastic buckle opens and closes with a touch, but won't come undone until you want it to. Moonbelts accommodate traveler's checks, passports, cash, photos, etc. Size 5 x 9 inches. Available in black only. **$8.95**

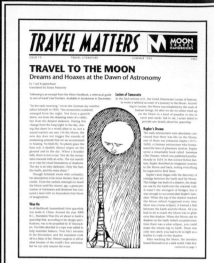

TRAVEL MATTERS

ISSUE 13 · TRAVEL LITERATURE · SUMMER 1995 · FREE

TRAVEL TO THE MOON
Dreams and Hoaxes at the Dawn of Astronomy
by Carl Koppeschaar
translated by Susan Massotty

Travel Matters

Travel Matters is Moon Publications' free newsletter, loaded with specially commissioned travel articles and essays that get at the heart of the travel experience. Every issue includes:

Feature Stories covering a wide array of travel and cultural topics about destinations on and off the beaten path. Past feature stories in *Travel Matters* include Mexican professional wrestling, traveling to the Moon, and why Germans get six weeks off and Americans don't.

Transportation tips covering all forms of transportation by land, sea, and air. Transportation topics covered recently have included driving through Baja California, new Eurail passes, trekking in Tibet, and biking through Asia.

Health Matters, by Dirk Schroeder, author of *Staying Healthy in Asia, Africa, and Latin America,* focusing on the most recent medical findings that affect travelers. Learn about Hepatitis A and B, critical travel supplies, and how to avoid common ailments.

Book and Multimedia Reviews providing informed assessments of the latest travel titles, series, and support materials. Recent reviews include The Rough Guide to *World Music, Passage to Vietnam* CD-ROM, and *I Should Have Stayed Home: The Worst Trips of Great Writers.*

The Internet page, which provides updates on Moon's WWW site , online discussions, and other travel resources available in cyberspace. A wide range of topics have been covered in this column including how to go online without going crazy, the Great Burma Debate, and details on Moon's *Road Trip USA* project.

Fellow Traveler, a reader question and answer column for travelers written by an international travel agent and world traveler.

To receive a free subscription to *Travel Matters,* call (800) 345-5473, e-mail us at travel@moon.com, or write to us at:

Moon Publications

P.O. Box 3040

Chico, CA 95927-3040

Please note: subscribers who live outside of the United States will be charged $7 per year for shipping and handling.

WWW.moon.com

MOON TRAVEL HANDBOOKS

NORTH AMERICA AND HAWAII

Alaska-Yukon Handbook (0161) $14.95
Alberta and the Northwest Territories Handbook (0676) $17.95
Arizona Traveler's Handbook (0714). $17.95
Atlantic Canada Handbook (0072) $17.95
Big Island of Hawaii Handbook (0064). $13.95
British Columbia Handbook (0145). $15.95
Colorado Handbook (0447) $18.95
Georgia Handbook (0390) $17.95
Hawaii Handbook (0005). $19.95
Honolulu-Waikiki Handbook (0587) $14.95
Idaho Handbook (0617). $14.95
Kauai Handbook (0013) $13.95
Maui Handbook (0579) $14.95
Montana Handbook (0498). $17.95
Nevada Handbook (0641) $16.95
New Mexico Handbook (0153). $14.95
Northern California Handbook (3840) $19.95
Oregon Handbook (0102) $16.95
Road Trip USA (0366). $22.50
Texas Handbook (0633) $17.95
Utah Handbook (0684) $16.95
Washington Handbook (0455). $18.95
Wyoming Handbook (3980) $14.95

ASIA AND THE PACIFIC

Australia Handbook (0722) $21.95
Bali Handbook (0730). $19.95
Bangkok Handbook (0595) $13.95
Fiji Islands Handbook (0382) $13.95
Hong Kong Handbook (0560) $15.95
Indonesia Handbook (0625). $25.00
Japan Handbook (3700) $22.50
Micronesia Handbook (0773) $13.95
Nepal Handbook (0412) $18.95
New Zealand Handbook (0331) $19.95
Outback Australia Handbook (0471). $18.95
Pakistan Handbook (0692). $22.50
Philippines Handbook (0048). $17.95
Southeast Asia Handbook (0021). $21.95
South Korea Handbook (3204) $14.95
South Pacific Handbook (0404). $22.95
Tahiti-Polynesia Handbook (0374) $13.95

Thailand Handbook (0420). $19.95
Tibet Handbook (3905) $30.00
Vietnam, Cambodia & Laos Handbook (0293) $18.95

MEXICO

Baja Handbook (0528) $15.95
Cabo Handbook (0285). $14.95
Cancún Handbook (0501) $13.95
Central Mexico Handbook (0234). $15.95
Mexico Handbook (0315). $21.95
Northern Mexico Handbook (0226). $16.95
Pacific Mexico Handbook (0323) $16.95
Puerto Vallarta Handbook (0250). $14.95
Yucatán Peninsula Handbook (0242) $15.95

CENTRAL AMERICA AND THE CARIBBEAN

Belize Handbook (0307) $15.95
Caribbean Handbook (0277). $16.95
Costa Rica Handbook (0358) $18.95
Jamaica Handbook (0706). $15.95

INTERNATIONAL

Egypt Handbook (3891) $18.95
Moon Handbook (0668). $10.00
Moscow-St. Petersburg Handbook (3913) $13.95
Staying Healthy in Asia, Africa, and Latin America (0269) $11.95
The Practical Nomad (0765). $13.95

PERIPLUS TRAVEL MAPS
All maps $7.95 each

Bali	Jakarta	Phuket/S. Thailand
Bandung/W. Java	E. Java	Sabah
Bangkok/C. Thailand	Java	Sarawak
Batam/Bintan	Kuala Lumpur	Singapore
Cambodia	Ko Samui/S. Thailand	Vietnam
Chiangmai/N. Thailand	Lombok	Yogyakarta/C. Java
Hong Kong	N. Sumatra	
Indonesia	Penang	

WHERE TO BUY MOON TRAVEL HANDBOOKS

BOOKSTORES AND LIBRARIES: Moon Travel Handbooks are sold worldwide. Please write to our sales manager for a list of wholesalers and distributors in your area.

TRAVELERS: We would like to have Moon Travel Handbooks available throughout the world. Please ask your bookstore to write or call us for ordering information. If your bookstore will not order our guides for you, please contact us for a free title listing.

Moon Publications, Inc.
P.O. Box 3040
Chico, CA 95927-3040 U.S.A.
Tel: (800) 345-5473
Fax: (916) 345-6751
E-mail: travel@moon.com

IMPORTANT ORDERING INFORMATION

PRICES: All prices are subject to change. We always ship the most current edition. We will let you know if there is a price increase on the book you order.

SHIPPING AND HANDLING OPTIONS: Domestic UPS or USPS first class (allow 10 working days for delivery): $3.50 for the first item, 50 cents for each additional item.

EXCEPTIONS:

Tibet Handbook and *Indonesia Handbook* shipping $4.50; $1.00 for each additional *Tibet Handbook* or *Indonesia Handbook.*

Moonbelt shipping is $1.50 for one, 50 cents for each additional belt.

Add $2.00 for same-day handling.

UPS 2nd Day Air or Printed Airmail requires a special quote.

International Surface Bookrate 8-12 weeks delivery: $3.00 for the first item, $1.00 for each additional item. Note: Moon Publications cannot guarantee international surface bookrate shipping. Moon recommends sending international orders via air mail, which requires a special quote.

FOREIGN ORDERS: Orders that originate outside the U.S.A. must be paid for with either an international money order or a check in U.S. currency drawn on a major U.S. bank based in the U.S.A.

TELEPHONE ORDERS: We accept Visa or MasterCard payments. Minimum order is US$15. Call in your order: (800) 345-5473, 8 a.m.-5 p.m. Pacific standard time.

ORDER FORM

Be sure to call (800) 345-5473 for current prices and editions or for the name of the book store nearest you that carries Moon Travel Handbooks • 8 a.m.–5 p.m. PST.
(See important ordering information on preceding page.)

Name: _____ Date: _____

Street: _____

City: _____ Daytime Phone: _____

State or Country: _____ Zip Code: _____

QUANTITY	TITLE	PRICE

Taxable Total_____

Sales Tax (7.25%) for California Residents_____

Shipping & Handling_____

TOTAL_____

Ship: ☐ UPS (no P.O. Boxes)   ☐ 1st class   ☐ International surface mail

Ship to: ☐ address above   ☐ other _____

Make checks payable to: **MOON PUBLICATIONS, INC**. P.O. Box 3040, Chico, CA 95927-3040 U.S.A. We accept Visa and MasterCard. **To Order**: Call in your Visa or MasterCard number, or send a written order with your Visa or MasterCard number and expiration date clearly written.

Card Number: ☐ **Visa**   ☐ **MasterCard**

☐ ☐ ☐ ☐   ☐ ☐ ☐ ☐   ☐ ☐ ☐ ☐   ☐ ☐ ☐ ☐

Exact Name on Card:_____

Expiration date: _____

Signature: _____

THE METRIC SYSTEM

1 inch = 2.54 centimeters (cm)
1 foot = .304 meters (m)
1 mile = 1.6093 kilometers (km)
1 km = .6124 miles
1 fathom = 1.8288 m
1 chain = 20.1168 m
1 furlong = 201.168 m
1 acre = .4047 hectares
1 sq km = 100 hectares
1 sq mile = 2.59 square km
1 ounce = 28.35 grams
1 pound = .4536 kilograms
1 short ton = .90718 metric ton
1 short ton = 2000 pounds
1 long ton = 1.016 metric tons
1 long ton = 2240 pounds
1 metric ton = 1000 kilograms
1 quart = .94635 liters
1 US gallon = 3.7854 liters
1 Imperial gallon = 4.5459 liters
1 nautical mile = 1.852 km

To compute celsius temperatures, subtract 32 from Fahrenheit and divide by 1.8. To go the other way, multiply celsius by 1.8 and add 32.